THE
SLAVE
TRADE

THE
SLAVE
TRADE

*The History of the
Atlantic Slave Trade:
1440–1870*

HUGH THOMAS

PICADOR

First published 1997 by Simon & Schuster Inc., New York

First published in Great Britain 1997 by Picador
an imprint of Macmillan Publishers Ltd
25 Eccleston Place, London SW1W 9NF
and Basingstoke

Associated companies throughout the world

ISBN 0 330 35437 X

3 5 7 9 8 6 4

A CIP catalogue record for this book is available
from the British Library.

Typeset by Florencetype Ltd, Stoodleigh, Devon
Printed and bound in Great Britain by
Mackays of Chatham plc, Chatham, Kent

CONTENTS

INTRODUCTION

I REMEMBER AS IF IT WERE YESTERDAY the day when I began to be interested in the slave trade: it was thirty years ago. I was dining in London. At the table, among others, there was the Prime Minister of Trinidad, the historian Dr Eric Williams. Hearing that I was making a study of the causes of the Cuban Revolution, he expressed astonishment that I should contemplate writing such a book without reading his own works, such as *A History of Trinidad and Tobago* (completed, he spiritedly explained, in ten days while his people were celebrating carnival) and, above all, *Capitalism and Slavery*, a copy of which came to my house next day, by messenger, from the Trinidad High Commission.

A swift perusal of the latter showed me the fascination of the eighteenth-century Caribbean, and I devoted much attention, in what became a history of Cuba, to slavery and the slave trade on that island.

I became particularly interested in a Basque, Julián Zulueta, the last great slave trader of Cuba (if you will permit the adjective) and, therefore, of the Americas, a man who started quite humbly, as a trader in all sorts of goods, in Havana in the 1830s but who by the late 1840s was a byword for evil-doing in the minds (and logs) of the British naval patrol trying to prevent the slave trade; for Zulueta had his own large sugar plantations in Cuba to which he would bring, in fast clippers often built in Baltimore, 500 or 600 slaves direct from Cabinda, just to the north of the River Congo.

Being a modern man, Zulueta would usually have his slaves vaccinated before they set off across the Atlantic, and by the 1850s he began to use for the passage steamboats capable of carrying over 1,000 captives; being a Catholic, he had his slaves baptized before they left Africa. What sort of man could he have been, I asked myself, who was carrying on the slave trade in a Christian colony four centuries after a pope, Pius II, had condemned the practice of enslaving baptized Africans? And how did Zulueta justify his insatiable demands for slaves almost a century after Adam Smith had dryly insisted that they were less efficient than free men? Why was he subsequently made a marquis by the Spanish government; and when he styled himself Marquis of Alava was he thinking as much of the name of his sugar plantation as of his home province? And what happened to his great fortune? And to his papers?

At the time I did not follow up these questions very far, but I did write an article on the subject in 1967 for the *Observer*, on the invitation of

Anthony Sampson, to mark what appeared to be the centenary of the end of the slave trade. The subject continued thereafter to lurk in my mind, as did an interest in other slave traders, on other countries, other men who made money from 'ebony' or 'black cargoes', such as the Irish-Frenchman Antoine Walsh of Nantes who also carried Bonnie Prince Charlie to Scotland by boat, the *Du Teillay*, or James de Wolf, of Bristol, Rhode Island – he became a United States senator; or other merchants who built beautiful houses, like so many slavers of Liverpool; or of Lisbon; or of Seville; or of Middleburg, the Roosevelts' home in Holland – home, too, after that family had left for New Holland, of the largest Dutch slave-trading company of the eighteenth century. In the 1980s I even wrote a novel, *Havana*, about John Kennion, a Liverpool Unitarian who had a commission to import slaves to Cuba in 1762, after the British capture of that island during the Seven Years War.

I once walked round the still-elegant streets of Walsh's Nantes, many of which survived the Allied bombardment of 1944, and recalled how the onetime slave-trading residents of the mansions on the Île Feydeau, in the 1780s, sent their dirty linen to be laundered in Saint-Domingue (Haiti) where the mountain streams were said to wash whiter than any in Brittany. David Hancock, in a fine recent book, named his central figure, Richard Oswald, 'a citizen of the world' – as well he might be called, for he had property in Scotland, London, Florida, Jamaica, and Virginia, as well as a share in Bence Island, off Sierra Leone, which he used as a depot for slaves (he and his partners built a golf course there for the benefit of waiting captains and others, on which the caddies were slaves in kilts). Because of his knowledge of America, Oswald was one of the negotiators at the Peace of Paris in 1783, along with, on the United States side, old business associates such as Benjamin Franklin and above all Henry Laurens, of Charleston, South Carolina, the latter also, in his early life, a large-scale slave trader to whom Oswald had often carried black slaves. How curious it is to imagine the two of them there in Paris, in the Rue Jacob, by the corner of the Rue des Saints Pères, rich men by virtue – among other things, to be sure – of innumerable slave transactions linking Europe, Africa, and the Americas, and negotiating the liberty of North America.

In my idle reading, I found, too, as good a candidate of my own to rival Hancock's 'citizen of the world': Bartolommeo Marchionni, a Florentine merchant and banker in Lisbon who had sugar plantations in Madeira in the 1480s; who financed the journeys of the great Portuguese travellers to Ethiopia in 1487; who had a ship in da Gama's expedition to India in 1498, as also in Cabral's expedition which discovered Brazil – probably by mistake – in 1500; who suggested to the King of Portugal that he should use his, Marchionni's, compatriot Vespucci for a journey to Brazil in 1501; and who was a monopoly trader in slaves from the Benin River in the 1490s, carrying captives not only to Portugal and Madeira but also to Elmina, on the Gold Coast, where he sold them to African merchants for gold, finding a better price from them than he would have achieved in Lisbon.

As a result of this interest, stretching back half of a lifetime, I decided, a few years ago, to write my own history of the slave trade. It may be said that that is now such well-ploughed ground that there is no room for any new cultivation; that Philip Curtin and his successors have counted the statistics of the slave trade as well they can ever be; that every harbour and people concerned have their own historians, many of whom have been meeting at productive conferences all over the world for years. David Brion Davis has transformed the history of abolition by his wonderfully erudite volumes. The history of the cowrie shell (so much used a currency in Africa for so long) has been written, as has the history of the Birmingham gun, much used as barter for so many slaves.

But any commercial undertaking involving the carriage of millions of people, stretching over several hundred years, involving every maritime European nation, every Atlantic-facing people (and some others), and every country of the Americas, is a planet of its own, always with room for new observations, reflections, evidence, and judgements. Further, it was the slave merchants themselves, sitting in their fine counting houses in London or Lisbon, men who often never saw slaves but profited from their sale, who interested me; and those had been rather ignored in the controversies over the exact number of slaves carried, and the percentage profit.

The slave trade was, of course, an iniquity. All the same, every historian must recall Hugh Trevor-Roper's warning: 'every age has its own social context, its own climate, and takes it for granted. . . . To neglect it – to use terms like "rational", "superstitious", "progressive", "reactionary", as if only that was rational which obeyed our rules of reason, only that progressive which pointed to us – is worse than wrong: it is vulgar.'[1]

Further, the study of this commerce can offer something to almost everyone. If one is interested in international morality, one can ask how it was that in the seventeenth century several Northern European countries hesitated so little before abetting a revival on a large scale of an institution which had nearly been abandoned in the region by the year 1100, and sometimes, as in England, with something like abolitionist tones in the archbishops' statements against the practice. 'We were a people who did not trade in any such commodities,' proudly said Richard Jobson, an English trader, when offered slaves by an Arab trader in the River Sénégal in 1618[2] – but at much the same time Sir Robert Rich, whose portrait by Van Dyck hangs in the Metropolitan Museum in New York, was securing a licence to take such captives to his new plantation in Virginia. If one is concerned about economic history, one can ask whether there is anything in the idea of Dr Eric Williams that the industrial revolution in England was financed by profits from Liverpool slave traders. If Church history is

one's speciality, one can wonder why the condemnations of Pope Pius II
and three other popes were ignored in Catholic countries, and how
Jesuits managed to be as deeply implicated as anyone. It might be interesting, too, to explore the precise terms in which Pope Pius condemned
the traffic in slaves, and perhaps speculate why Catholic philanthropists
of the sixteenth century, such as Bartolomé de las Casas, did not at first
extend the generous sympathies which they so warmly offered American
Indians to the black Africans.

If the history of popular movements is a preoccupation, the abolitionist movement, so well organized by the Quakers in England and in
the United States, must surely seem the first example of such a thing. If
commerce with undeveloped countries concerns one, one can dwell on
the role of the slave trade in Africa, and calculate, or at least speculate
about, what lasting effect it had on the local economies, and also wonder
(with a historian of Sierra Leone) whether there could have been any
gains from the four hundred years of contact with Europeans on these
terms: income, organization of trade, new crops, knowledge of new technology. Then one might put the question whether Britain's substantial
participation in the slave trade during the eighteenth century – the
country's slave captains were carrying about 35,000 captives across
the Atlantic every year in the 1780s, in about ninety ships – was compensated for by the lead which British statesmen later gave in abolishing the
commerce and, turning gamekeeper to the world after having been its
poacher-in-chief, dedicated diplomacy, naval power, guile, and financial
subsidies to bring the trade to a conclusion? In this connection, one can
ask whether that British policy was the decisive element in concluding
Brazilian slave trading in the 1850s or Cuban in the 1860s. While considering this ambivalent British position, perhaps one should examines why
it is that John Hawkins remains a national hero, although his three voyages to the Caribbean in the 1560s, one of them with Francis Drake on
board, were primarily slaving voyages. If one is interested in Jewish
history, one can also explore Mr Farrakhan's accusations that Jews dominated the traffic in African slaves. But one would be hard put to find more
than one or two Jewish slave traders in the Anglo-Saxon traffic (Aaron
Lopez and his father-in-law, Jacobo Rodrigues Ribera, of Newport, Rhode
Island, are the only ones known to me). It is true that much of the slave
trade in the sixteenth and seventeenth centuries in Lisbon was financed
by converted Jews, New Christians, or *conversos*; though whether such a
person is to be seen as a Jew is not something on which I should wish to
pronounce: several of the traders concerned proclaimed their or their
forefathers' Christian conversion as genuine to the very last torture
afforded by the Inquisition, even if the Holy Office caused to be burned to
death in Mexico and in Lima several prominent slave merchants, whom
they denounced not for trading slaves but for the greater crime of 'judaizing'. If one is as critical of Islam as Mr Farrakhan is of Jewry, one can

explore how far the medieval trans-Saharan trade in black Africans, from the coast of Guinea, was managed by Arab mullah-merchants in the first centuries after the Muslim penetration of Africa, long before Prince Henry the Navigator's ships were seen in West Africa. One can ask, too, whether there is truth in the oft-repeated claim that the Portuguese treated their slaves better in 'the Middle Passage' from Angola to Brazil than the Anglo-Saxons who carried similar cargoes to the Caribbean or to the southern colonies of North America.

If one is interested in the history of the British monarchy (and who, it often seems, is not?), one could do worse than explore the role of James, Duke of York (after whom New York is, so inappropriately, named), as President of the Royal African Company, whose mission was partly to trade in slaves. Or one could wonder if it is true, as Wilberforce's most recent biographer, the late Robin Furneaux, suggested, that that tantalizing comment in Thomas Clarkson's *History* of the abolition of the African slave trade (that there was something, he could not say what, about Pitt's inability to make the end of the slave trade a government issue) is to be explained by King George III's hatred of the abolitionists – as strong as that of his son, the future William IV, who as Duke of Clarence led the House of Lords' opposition to Wilberforce, Pitt, Burke, Fox, Sheridan, and Canning, and all the others of 'the brightest and the best' of the 1790s.

If one is looking for villains in this matter, and some are, one should certainly indeed look at royal families more severely than at Jewish ones: I am partly thinking of the rulers of Benin, the kings of Ashanti, Congo, and Dahomey, and the Vili rulers of Loango, who sold great numbers of slaves over many generations, but also of monarchs in Europe, such as one of my own heroes, Ferdinand the Catholic, King of Aragon. 'Athlete of Christ', as he was named by the Pope, he gave the first licence to carry slaves on a large scale to the New World, since he wished them to extract gold from the mines of Santo Domingo. But then perhaps Ferdinand cannot be blamed specially for agreeing to the transfer of slaves from one part of his dominion to another, for his agents seem to have bought the Africans concerned in Seville, they having been carried there by merchants of Lisbon such as Bartolommeo Marchionni. Like everyone in his age, Ferdinand would have supposed that, unpleasant though it might be to be a slave, to be owned by a Christian master was infinitely better than being a subject of an infidel. One could find King John III of Portugal responsible for an even more dangerous innovation, for he, in 1530, agreed that slaves from Africa might be taken direct to the Americas. And how can we exclude the Sun King himself, Louis XIV, from our selective castigation, for his ministers agreed to pay a bounty for every slave delivered to the New World – a bounty that was still being paid in 1790, the year when Thomas Clarkson, in Paris to publicize the cause of abolition, was told by the Minister, Necker, recently recalled to power, that he dared not show the diagram of how slaves were stowed on the ship *Brookes* of Liverpool to the Sun King's successor-but-one, Louis XVI, because it would distress him too much?

Still, historians must not look for villains. I would hate to be reproached for reading *Alice in Wonderland* because the author was a great-grandson of the slave trader Lutwidge of Whitehaven; or Chateaubriand because the writer's father, at Saint-Malo, was both a slave merchant and, once, a slave captain; or Gibbon because the ease which enabled him to write his great work without other occupation derived from a fortune accumulated by his grandfather, a director of the South Sea Company, whose chief preoccupation was to carry African slaves in British ships to the Spanish empire. I should not like to have to boycott the plays of Beaumarchais since that author once sought to obtain the same monopoly from the Spanish Crown. Who would refuse to visit Brown University, that fine foundation in Providence, Rhode Island, because it owes so much to John Brown, who was happily trading in slaves in that city in the 1770s? No one, surely, would refuse to take seriously John Locke, even as a philosopher of liberty, because he was a shareholder in the Royal African Company, whose initials, RAC, would be branded on so many black breasts in Africa during the last quarter of the seventeenth century.

I have a personal reason for hoping that the sins of no collateral ancestors can be visited on the present generation: in the Archivo de Indias in Seville (that best and greatest of imperial archives, to which the American scholar Irene Wright dedicated a sonnet), where I have, in researching the conquest of Mexico, spent some of the most fruitful days of my life, I discovered that a ship bringing twenty slaves to Havana Bay in 1792 was captained by someone from Liverpool by the name of Hugo Tomás.

I have tried in this book to say what happened. In seeking the truth, I have not thought it necessary to speak of outrage on every page. But all the same the question is, how was the business tolerated for so long? In my chapters on abolition I have touched on that; but, at the end of some years spent writing this book, I now cannot think of the traders in slaves, or the captains of the slave ships, as 'worse' than the slave owners, who after all constituted the market. There were brutal owners of slaves, such as Frederick Douglass's putative father, and reasonably kind slave captains, such as John Newton. A few African rulers tried to escape from participation in the transatlantic trade. Mostly they failed. All were caught up in a vast scheme of things which seemed normal at least until 1780.

For only a few parts of this book have I done archival research (for example, Ferdinand the Catholic's decision to send black slaves to the New World in 1510; the career of Bartolommeo Marchionni; of the licence to carry slaves granted by the former Emperor Charles V; of various moments of the Spanish slave trade; and of some aspects of the end of the trade to both Cuba and Brazil). But I have tried to look at original sources, where available. In this respect, I wish to pay special thanks to: the late Elizabeth Donnan, whose *Documents Illustrative of the Slave Trade to America* was a great assistance; and also to Philip Curtin, whose *The Slave Trade: A Census* was a wonderful guide and whose figures I have only modestly revised. Enriqueta Vila Vilar's remarkable studies on the sixteenth and seventeenth century Spanish trade, especially *Hispanoamerica y el comercio de esclavos*, were the best introduction to that theme. The marvellous long essay by David Brion Davis, *The Problem of Slavery in Western Culture*, was my stepping stone to the moral questions, while Charles Verlinden's *L'Esclavage dans l'Europe médiévale* opened my eyes to the persistence of the institution of slavery during the ages of faith.

I am most grateful to the directors of the libraries and archives where I have been able to study: in particular, those of the Archivo de Indias in Seville; the Biblioteca Nacional in Madrid; the Archivo Histórico Nacional in Madrid; the Real Academia de la Historia in Madrid; the Palazzo Ricardi in Florence; the Bibliothèque Nationale in Paris; the New York Public Library; Widener Library, Harvard; the Murger Memorial Library of Boston University; the London Library; the library of the House of Lords, in particular the librarian, David Jones, and his assistants; Cambridge University Library; the Public Record Office, Kew; and the British Library. This will be the last time that I shall express my gratitude to those who work as assistants in the last named's inspiring Round Reading Room, the most beautiful library in Europe, about to be destroyed by the ignorant philistines who have recently directed British cultural life. I am also grateful to a number of people who read chapters of the book at an early stage – for example, Sir Hugh Lloyd-Jones, and Dr Felipe Fernández Armesto – as to Oliver Knox and my wife, Vanessa, who kindly read the proofs and made many invaluable suggestions. My gratitude to Michael Korda, at Simon & Schuster, is profound; he was a constant encouragement. I am also grateful to Tanya Stobbs and Mary Mount of Macmillan, for their care and assiduity, as to Nicholas Blake, who ensured that, though the book was originally set in the United States, there are no Americanisms. He saved me from other howlers. Gillon Aitken and Andrew Wylie, my agents, were admirable. An immense amount of hard work on this book was done by Gypsy da Silva, also at Simon & Schuster; I must thank her and her copy editor Terry Zaroff-Evans for their patience and meticulous attention to the details of the production.

HUGH THOMAS

London, March 1997

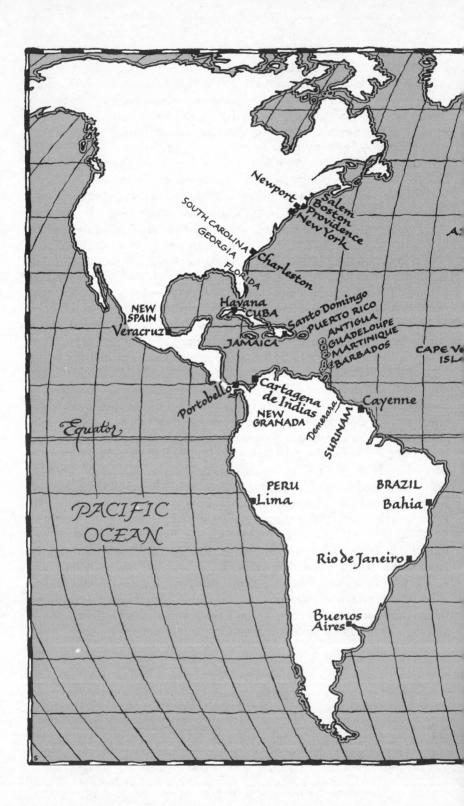

Liverpool
London
Bristol
Amsterdam
Nantes
Le Havre
La Rochelle
Bordeaux
Oporto
Seville
Sanlúcar
DEIRA
RY ISLES

quin

gal
bia
Sierra
Leone
Elmina
Whydah
Benin
Calabar
PRÍNCIPE
SÃO TOMÉ
congo
Loango
Cabinda
Luanda
Benguela
Mozambique

MALDIVES

LANTIC
CEAN

MADAGASCAR

The Atlantic Slave Trade

Book One

GREEN SEA
OF DARKNESS

*'Green Sea of Darkness' was the
medieval Arab description for
the Atlantic Ocean, used to
indicate the terrors of the waters
beyond Cape Bojador, which the
Portuguese rounded in 1434*

1

WHAT HEART
COULD BE SO HARD?

'What heart could be so hard as not to
be pierced by piteous feeling to see that
company?'

Zurara, Chronicle of the Discovery
and Conquest of Guinea

'VERY EARLY in the morning, because of the heat', a few Portuguese
seamen on the decks of half a dozen hundred-ton caravels, the new
sailing ships, were preparing, on 8 August 1444, to land their African
cargo near Lagos, on the south-west point of the Algarve, in Portugal.

This cargo consisted of 235 slaves. On arriving on the mainland,
these people were placed in a field. They seemed, as a contemporary put
it, 'a marvellous sight, for, amongst them, were some white enough, fair
enough, and well-proportioned; others were less white, like mulattos;
others again were as black as Ethiops, and so ugly, both in features and in
body, as almost to appear . . . the images of a lower hemisphere.

'What heart could be so hard', this contemporary chronicler, Gomes
Eannes de Zurara, a courtier attached to the brother of the King of
Portugal, the inventive Prince Henry, asked himself, 'as not to be pierced
with piteous feeling to see that company? For some kept their heads low,
and their faces bathed in tears, looking one upon another. Others stood
groaning very dolorously, looking up to the height of heaven, fixing their
eyes upon it, crying out loudly, as if asking help from the Father of nature;
others struck their faces with the palms of their hands, throwing themselves at full length upon the ground; while others made lamentations in
the manner of a dirge, after the custom of their country. . . .

'But to increase their sufferings still more', the writer continued,
'there now arrived those who had charge of the division of the captives,

and ... then was it needful to part fathers from sons, husbands from wives, brothers from brothers. No respect was shown to either friends or relations, but each fell where his lot took him.'

Zurara then permitted himself a prayer to the fashionable goddess Fortune: 'O mighty Fortune, who with thy wheel doest and undoest, compassing the matters of the world as it pleaseth thee, do thou at least put before the eyes of that miserable race some understanding of matters to come, that the captives may receive some consolation in the midst of their great sorrow. . . .'[1]

The arrival of this collection of Africans was a novelty which many came to observe, among them Prince Henry, the chronicler Zurara's hero. He watched, impassive, from his horse, and himself received forty-six of those slaves present, the 'royal fifth'. He gave thanks that he was saving so many new souls for God.

Most of the captives who were on this day the cynosure of all eyes were Azanaghi (now usually known by their Berber name of Sanhajah or Idzagen), from what is today the southern part of the modern state of Sahara, or the northern part of Mauritania. These people later seemed to a Venetian adventurer, Alvise Ca'da Mosto, who would visit them in their own land, 'tawny, squat and miserable': in comparison with the blacks from farther south, who for him were 'well-built, noble-looking men'.[2] Yet the Azanaghi were one of the most important families of the veiled Tuaregs, a tribe who had, for generations, been traditional raiders of cities such as Timbuktu and other settled places on the Middle Niger. Arab geographers placed them as living near 'the Gleaming Mountain' and 'the City of Brass', separated from the unknown land of the blacks to the south by a 'Sea of Sand ... very soft to tread, in which man and camel may sink'.[3] They had adopted Islam in the eleventh century, but had known remarkably little about that faith till an inflammatory teacher, Ibn-Yasin, a Muslim Berber from the University of Qayrawan (Tunisia), preached to them and captured their imaginations with an austere 'fundamentalist' message, which promised, through barbarity and sectarianism, an eventual end to all fighting and disunion. So began the ruthless Almoravid movement – which, in the beginning, caused widespread destruction.

For in the service of unimpeachable ideals the ancestors, or at least collateral ancestors, of the humble captives in Portugal in 1444 had – zealots all, dressed in skins and riding camels – swept through first Morocco and then the Iberian peninsula and, for a time, ruled an empire which stretched from the Rivers Niger and Sénégal in Africa to the Ebro in Spain. Ibn-Yasin's hermitage, or ribat (the Almoravids were 'people of the ribat'), in his years of struggle, was not far from that same Arguin whence the slaves of 1444 were stolen. It is thus possible that some of the Portuguese concerned to guard the new arrivals were, as a result of rape or seduction 300 years before, their distant relations.

Zurara described how, even in the fifteenth century, the Azanaghi often made 'war on the blacks, using more ruse than force, because they are not as vigorous as their captives'. The remark shows why the slaves brought to the Algarve were of so many colours: those captured by the Portuguese raiders included men and women who had already been enslaved by the Azanaghi. If the chronicler's comment about white and black slaves is accurate, the captives would have also included some who were bought in markets from the ubiquitous Muslim salesmen.

Most of the captives of 1444 had been taken by the Portuguese in a village where: '. . . they [the Portuguese], shouting out, "St James, St George, and Portugal," at once attacked them, killing and taking all they could. Then might you see mothers forsaking their children, and husbands their wives, each striving to escape as best they could. Some drowned themselves in the water, others thought to escape by hiding under their huts, others stowed their children among the seaweed, where our men found them afterwards. . . .'[4]

The leader of the Portuguese in this expedition was Lançarote de Freitas, a successful young official previously engaged in collecting taxes, but now captain of a newly formed company for trade to Africa, established at Lagos (the town where de Freitas had been an official), for 'the service of God and the Infante Henry'.[5] De Freitas was known as a 'man of great good sense', who had been brought up in the large and interesting household of Prince Henry.

The seizure of slaves, rather than their purchase, was then a far from unusual practice in both Europe and Africa. These 'razzias', as the odious practice of man-stealing was known, were carried out throughout the Middle Ages in Spain and Africa by Muslim merchants, and their Christian equivalents had done the same. Muslims were justified by the Koran in seizing Christians and enslaving them; the Christians, in their long drawn out reconquest of Muslim Spain, had conducted themselves similarly.

This voyage of de Freitas's was the first serious commercial venture to West Africa by the Portuguese, whose business leaders, as a result, became as convinced of the benefits of such expeditions as they had previously been sceptical. The merchants of Lisbon had been hoping for gold from West Africa. They had found some, but slaves were in more ample supply. Prince Henry was not displeased: the money which he obtained by selling his share of the slaves could be used to finance further endeavours, including journeys of pure discovery.

The chronicler Zurara probably thought that the captives owed their fate to the sins of their supposed ancestor Ham, cursed by his father, Noah, after seeing him naked and drunk. It was both a Christian and a Muslim tradition to suppose that the descendants of Ham had been turned black. Zurara may also have been influenced by the work two centuries before of Egidio Colonna, who had written that if people did not have laws, and if they did not live peacefully under a government, they were more beasts than human, and therefore could legally be enslaved.[6] No doubt Zurara would have considered that the Africans brought back to Portugal in 1444, whatever their origins, were just such people.

2

HUMANITY IS DIVIDED
INTO TWO

*'Humanity is divided into two: the masters
and the slaves.'*

Aristotle, Politics

IN HIS DESCRIPTION of the sale of slaves at Lagos in 1444, Zurara, the court chronicler, was writing of what has since seemed a turning point in history. Yet few occurrences thus named remain so after scrutiny; and the Portuguese, along with all Southern Europeans of that time, were accustomed both to slaves and to slavery.

Most settled societies at one time or another have employed forced labour; and most peoples, even the proud French, the effective Germans, the noble English, the dauntless Spaniards, and, perhaps above all, the poetical Russians, have experienced years of servitude.

Slavery was a major institution in antiquity. Prehistoric graves in Lower Egypt suggest that a Libyan people of about 8000 BC enslaved a Bushman or 'Negrito' tribe. The Egyptians later made frequent raids on principalities to their south and, during the Eighteenth Dynasty, also launched attacks by sea, to steal slaves from what is now Somaliland. Slaves built, or at least helped to build, the innovations of the world's first agricultural revolution: the hydraulic system of China and the pyramids of Egypt. The first Code of Laws, that of Hammurabi, silent on many matters now considered interesting, included clear provisions about slavery. For example, death was prescribed for anyone who helped a slave to escape, as well as for anyone who sheltered a fugitive – a foretaste of 2,000 years during which slaves figured in most such compilations.

In the golden years of both Greece and Rome, slaves worked as domestic servants, in mines and in public works, in gangs, and individually, on farms, as well as in commerce and in cottage industries. They both managed and served in brothels, trading organizations, and workshops. There were slaves in Mycenae, and Ulysses had fifty female slaves in his palace. The Greeks were appreciative employers of them: Athens had in her heyday about 60,000 slaves. Her police force was a body of 300 Scythian archer slaves; her famous silver mines at Laurium employed over 10,000 slaves until a rebellion in 103 BC; and twenty slaves – perhaps a quarter of those so employed – helped to build the Parthenon. The Athenians used slaves to fight for them at Marathon, even though they freed them first.

The Romans made use of slaves in all the categories employed by the Greeks, though they had many more domestic ones: a prefect in the days of the Emperor Nero might have 400 in his house alone. There may have been 2,000,000 slaves in Italy at the end of the republic. From the first century BC to the early third century AD, the use of these captives was the customary way in which prosperity was created. That did not mean all these were equal: rural and urban domestic slaves lived different lives; a man working in a gang in the fields had a different life from one in a workshop in the city; some slaves practised as doctors or lawyers, and others acted as major-domos to noblemen, or as shepherds in the hills. Cicero's slave Tiro was his confidential secretary and was well educated: he even invented a shorthand called after himself.

Half a million captives seem to have been required every year in Rome during its most self-confident age – say, 50 BC to AD 150. The Roman state itself possessed innumerable slaves: 700, for example, were responsible for maintaining the imperial city's aqueducts. Perhaps one out of three members of the population was a slave during the early empire. One rich lady, Melania, is said to have liberated 8,000 slaves in the early fifth century AD, when she decided to become a Christian ascetic.[1]

In both Greece and Rome slaves were in origin captives taken in war, or obtained by a razzia on an unsuspecting island or city. Fifty-five thousand captives are said to have been taken after the Third Carthaginian War, and Caesar, it will be recalled, brought 'many captives home to Rome' from the Gallic Wars. Many Germans were enslaved in later centuries. Then Septimius Severus brought 100,000 captives home after defeating the Parthians at Ctesiphon. Fifteen thousand Gallic slaves a year were exchanged for Italian wine in the first century BC. Piracy and brigandage also played their parts in providing Rome with the labour which she desired.

Markets specifically for slaves, such as those at Chios, Rhodes, and Delos, were developed early during the golden age of Greece. Ephesus was the largest market of the classical world for hundreds of years, though the evidence as to the numbers sold there is unsatisfactory. These markets were popular places of resort for all patricians. The majority of captives sold there would have come from the East. The sale of slaves born within the Roman empire was also a thriving enterprise. Some were probably bred deliberately for markets.

Many slaves of old Rome were fair Celts or Germans, including Saxons: 'The beautiful faces of the young slaves', wrote Gibbon, 'were covered with a medicated crust or ointment which secured them against the effects of the sun and frost.'[2] They must have been from Northern Europe, perhaps from the historian's own land.

Black slaves also existed in antiquity. Egypt had always sought to secure her southern frontier with Nubia militarily, but commerce crossed it in both directions. Herodotus spoke of an Egyptian trade in black slaves; during the most fortunate times of the pharaohs the Nubians regularly dispatched down the Nile tributes including Ethiopian captives as well as gold and cattle. Blacks, surely slaves from Ethiopia, fought in Xerxes' army, as they did in that of Gelon, Tyrant of Syracuse. Ethiopians are recorded in many parts of the Mediterranean in those days: as dancers and boxers, acrobats and charioteers, gladiators and cooks, prostitutes and personal servants. Black heads are to be observed on Greek vases, as on Alexandrian terracottas, and a first-century mosaic at Pompeii shows a black slave serving at a banquet. Seneca spoke of 'one of our dandies with outriders and Numidians'.[3] The Roman playwright Terence had been a slave in Carthage and, according to Suetonius, may have been a mulatto. A useful guide to navigation in the second century AD, of the Red Sea, by Periplus, talks of a maritime slave trade from the East African coast to Egypt. For black Africans seemed attractive. Seneca is supposed to have remarked that Roman men believed black women were more sensual than white, and Roman women had a similar voluptuous admiration for black men: the poet Martial praised a lady 'blacker than night, than an ant, pitch, a jackdaw, a cicada'.[4] In the Bible, the Queen of Sheba was always described as beautiful as well as black; and the Song of Solomon in the Vulgate included the firm declaration: 'I am black and beautiful, O daughters of Jerusalem, like the tents of Kedar, like the curtains of Solomon.'[5] Herodotus, who travelled as far up the Nile as Elephantine, the frontier city with Nubia, called the Ethiopians 'the most handsome of peoples'.[6]

Not all the black Africans in the classical Mediterranean were slaves. Eurybatus, a black herald who accompanied Odysseus to talk to Achilles, was, presumably (the recollection of him was one of the ways by which Penelope recognized her husband); and a certain Aethiops, perhaps a black African freeman (or was it just a nickname?), was present at the founding of Corinth.

At least from the time of Xenophanes (the first European to write of the physical differences between blacks and whites), in the sixth century BC, the Greeks and the Romans were unprejudiced on grounds of race: they were quite insensible as to whether someone with black skin was superior to someone with white, or vice versa. So it is scarcely surprising that miscegenation was neither repugnant nor unexpected. No laws mentioned the matter. Many Ethiopians married Greeks or Egyptians. In the eighth century BC, Ethiopians, who had provided soldiers and slaves to Memphis, even conquered Egypt and gave it its Twenty-fifth Dynasty.

Nearly all the black Africans of the ancient world came from Ethiopia through Egypt. Several expeditions were sent in that direction, and Pliny the Elder records more than one; all the same, in the second century AD, a caravan route seemed also to open at Lepcis Magna, in what is now Libya, linking the Roman empire with Guinea.

Wild suggestions have been made that the ancient civilization in Greece had both an Egyptian and a black origin. That imaginative view, which, if true, might affect any history of the Atlantic slave trade, derives from a story reported by a Greek historian, Diodorus of Sicily, in the first century BC. But there is no evidence for the claim; it is no more likely that the mythological first King of Athens, Cecrops, was black than that the lower part of his body was that of a fish. Socrates may have been black, but the odds are heavily against it; Cleopatra may have had black blood, but it is most improbable.

The Athenians were the first to seek a reason for discussing, as well as explaining, the institution of slavery (as of most other matters). For example, Aristotle, in the first book of his *Politics*, firmly said: 'Humanity is divided into two: the masters and the slaves; or, if one prefers it, the Greeks and the Barbarians, those who have the right to command; and those who are born to obey.' That seemed to imply that, to an Athenian, everyone who was not Greek could be captured and enslaved – even should be. Aristotle also said: 'A slave is property with a soul.' Thus he accepted slavery as an institution. He declared that 'the use of domestic animals and slaves is about the same; they both lend us their physical efforts to satisfy the needs of existence'. But he also noted that some had argued that 'the rule of a master over slaves is contrary to nature, and that the distinction between master and slave exists only by law . . . and, being an interference with nature, is thus unjust'. These ambiguous propositions would have importance in the sixteenth century, when Aristotle was looked upon as the guide to almost everything.[7]

Plato, for his part, compared the slave to the body, the master to the soul. He took for granted the enslavement of foreigners, though he desired to end that of Greeks.[8]

Yet Euripides, the playwright, realized that there was more to the matter than the philosophers thought; for example, he caused Polyxena in *Hecuba*, born to marry kings, to declare that she preferred death to being enslaved. His contemporaries, the Sophists, took that reflection to its logical conclusion: they even argued that slavery had no basis in the law of nature, since it derived from custom. The rhetorician Alcidamas, when demanding that the Spartans free the Messenians, thought that distinctions between a freeman and a slave were unknown to nature. The

Cynics thought that a slave maintained a free soul, even if he was the instrument of his master's will; and Diogenes observed that the man who relied on captive labour was the true slave. Such sophisticated reflections had no effect on practice.

The Romans established the status of a slave (*servus*) by law and distinguished him from a serf (*colonus*). A slave in Rome was an object, *res*, unable to make a will, bear witness in civil cases, or make criminal charges – even if (by a law of Hadrian) he was also theoretically protected against murder and from physical harm at the hands of his master. Yet the mere fact that a Roman slave could also be punished for crimes suggests that the law envisaged the idea of a slave as a person, not just as a thing.

The criticisms of slavery by great Latin writers denounced the idea of cruelty to slaves rather than questioned the institution. Thus Cicero and Seneca hoped that slaves could be treated humanely, but they never contemplated an end of slavery. Cicero, who thought that all inequality (hence slavery) could be explained by degeneration, wrote in *De Republica* that the reduction of conquered peoples to slavery was legitimate if the people concerned were unable to govern themselves; Seneca developed the idea that slavery was a bodily affair: the spirit would remain a thing apart. The latter also thought that (Zurara's) goddess of Fortune exercised her rights over freemen and slaves alike; in Rome, as in Greece, manumission was, after all, not uncommon.

In the last years of the Roman republic, and again under the Antonine emperors in the second century AD, some humane improvements were introduced in servile legislation. The changes did not alter the fundamental definition that a slave was someone's property. But they did indicate that a master's rights over his slaves, like his rights over other property, were restricted in specific ways. The Emperor Antonius Pius, for example, in the second century AD, sought to reduce the arbitrary character of the institution of slavery; but he also declared that the power of masters over slaves should remain unquestioned. He justified his humanitarian laws by saying that they were in the interests of the masters.

These innovations were partly the product of two influences: that of later Stoic philosophy, and of Christianity; the first of these was the most subversive. Henceforth, at all events, if a master were to treat a slave badly, he would have to sell him. If he were to abandon an infirm slave, that slave could be enfranchised. All the same, neither Stoic nor Christian questioned the institution of slavery. The condition was assumed to be from eternity. If a master did not exercise all his rights over his slaves, that concession was never binding, always revocable. The Stoic Epictetus, himself born a slave and freed by his master, even wondered whether enfranchisement would benefit *every* slave, though he was also concerned about the evil effects of slavery on masters.

Christ's teaching that 'all things whatsoever ye would that men should do unto you, do ye even so unto them', along with the idea of St Paul that 'God hath made of one blood all men and all nations of men', played a part in the history of abolition in the United States in the nineteenth century; but, in the early days of Christianity, Christ's failure to talk specially of slaves was taken to imply that they were excluded from divine generosity.[9]

St Paul, like Seneca, thought that slavery was something external. So he recommended that slaves serve their masters 'with fear and trembling'. He thought that every man should abide 'in the same calling wherein he was called. Art thou called being a slave? Care not for it: but if thou mayest be made free, use it rather' (the English Authorized Version curiously translates *servus* as 'servant', not 'slave').[10] The apostle believed, it is true, that the slave who receives the call to be a Christian is 'the Lord's freeman'. But the implication was that that liberty could only be expected in the next world. The Epistle to Philemon the Greek described how the apostle returned a fugitive slave, Onesimus, to his master, though he did recommend indulgence. That action was later used by churches to reject the idea that escaping slaves had the right to sanctuary in their church, as common criminals did; and the eighteenth-century French Huguenot trader Jean Barbot thought that the Epistle gave evidence that, though slavery was lawful, slaves should be well treated. An early Christian bishop, and a medieval one, could comfort himself with the reflection that Christ had, after all, come not to change social conditions but to change minds – *non venit mutare conditiones sed mentes*. What, the 'bondsman was inwardly free, and spiritually the equal of his master'? No matter: in external matters, he was a mere chattel. Slaves could of course look forward to freedom in the next world. In the meantime, they should endure their terrestrial condition for the glory of God, whose ways were inscrutable.[11]

Several centuries after St Paul, the austere Father of the Church St John Chrysostom advised the slave to prefer the security of captivity to the uncertainties of freedom. St Augustine agreed. He thought that the first cause of slavery was the sin 'which has subjected man to man'. But that 'had not been done without the will of God, who knows no injustice'. Augustine, born at Hippo in North Africa, believed in the equality of races: 'Whoever is born anywhere as a human being, that is, as a rational mortal creature, however strange he may appear to our senses in bodily form, or colour, or motion, or utterance, or in any faculty, part, or quality of his nature whatsoever, let no true believer have any doubt that such an individual is descended from the one man who first existed.' All the same, sin made many men slaves; and Augustine remembered the Curse of Ham in Genesis.[12] Then St Ambrose, commenting on St Paul's Epistle to the Colossians, believed that masters had duties to slaves. He also suspected that God had intended all men to be free, but that the tragic conditions of human life meant that some who were naturally free might, as a result of war, be reduced to slavery. The General Council of the Christian Church (c. 345) at Gangra, in Paphlagonia (that is, northern Turkey), condemned all who under pretext of religion taught slaves to despise their masters; one of the Councils of Carthage (419) refused the right even of enfranchised slaves to bear witness in court. Pope Leo the Great proclaimed in 443 that no slave could become a priest. The Emperor Justinian later sought to change that provision, and to arrange for the entry of slaves into the priesthood if their masters did not oppose the matter; but, though a slave's collar has been found bearing the inscription 'Felix the Archdeacon', the tolerance implicit in the designation had little effect during the late Western empire.

In one of his last speeches, in a debate in the House of Commons in 1806, that passionate friend of liberty Charles James Fox would declare that it was 'one of the glories of Christianity to have gradually extinguished the slave trade, and even slavery, wherever its influence was felt'.[13] That effulgence was, however, hidden for many centuries.

All the same, even if the Church did not question the institution of slavery, it did encourage manumission: the actions of the saintly Melania have been recalled; and a certain Hermes, converted to Christianity in the days of Hadrian, is said to have freed 1,250 slaves one Easter. A decree *Manumissio in ecclesia* was also approved by the Emperor Constantine the Great in 321.

It was only in the case of Jews that later Roman law was in any way less than helpful to masters. Constantine, however, declared that no Jew could own a Christian slave. If a Jew bought a slave who was not Jewish, and forced him to be circumcised, the Code of Theodosius gave that slave a right to liberty. A law of 417 refined the matter: no Jew could buy Christian slaves. Even if he were to inherit one, he could only keep him on the condition that he not try to convert him to Judaism. Thus, very early in history, the problem of Jews and slaves was posed, though not quite in the way that has seemed appropriate to polemicists of the twentieth century.

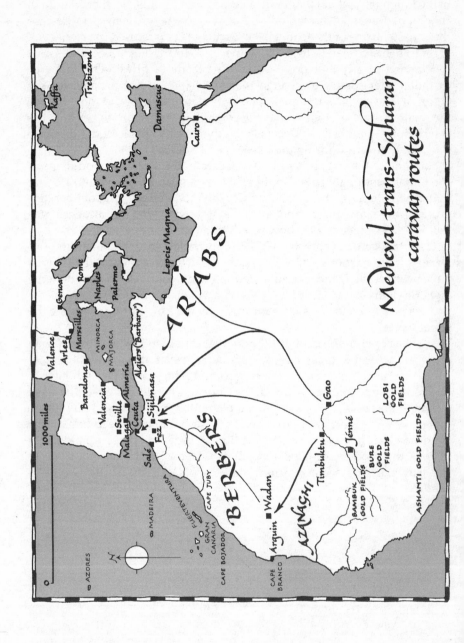

Medieval trans-Saharan caravan routes

Kaffa
Trebizond
Damascus
Cairo
Lepcis Magna
ARABS
Rome
Genoa
Naples
Palermo
Marseilles
MINORCA
MAJORCA
Valence
Arles
Barcelona
Valencia
Seville
Almería
Málaga
Algiers (Barbary)
Ceuta
Sijilmasa
Fez
Salé
FUERTEVENTURA
CAPE JUBY
MADEIRA
GRAN CANARIA
CAPE BOJADOR
AZORES
CAPE BRANCO
BERBERS
AZ NAGHI
Arguin
Wadan
Timbuktu
Jénné
Gao
BAMBUK GOLD FIELDS
BURE GOLD FIELDS
LOBI GOLD FIELDS
ASHANTI GOLD FIELDS

1000 miles

3

THE SLAVES
WHO FIND THE GOLD
ARE ALL BLACK

*'The slaves who find the gold are all black
but if, by a miracle, they manage to escape
from them, they become white.'*

Valentim Fernandes, c. 1500

AT THE END of the Roman empire, most ancient institutions collapsed. So did most families, gods, and traditions. But slavery survived. In the worst years of the Dark Ages, Scythian slaves could still be bought in Antioch, and Gothic ones could be found in Rome. Slaves too played a part in the overthrow of the empire. Thus Alaric's army of 40,000 included many fugitive slaves, many of them Goths in origin. The partisans of the Emperor Honorius in Spain even armed slaves to fight the Franks. In 423, the usurper John seized power in Ravenna and, having no troops, he enfranchised and armed the slaves of the nearby *villae*. In Gaul, runaway slaves were frequent in the Franks' invading armies.

The 'barbarians' swiftly drew close to the peoples whom they had conquered. It was not their purpose to break up the old social order. Rather, they wanted to capture it. They needed no convincing that their new estates needed slave labour, for they had always used slaves whenever they could, even when they had been nomadic, and they had often suffered from Roman slaving raids in the past.

The new masters of the old Roman world obtained most of their slaves by capture in war; and war was then incessant. There was not only continual fighting between the different Anglo-Saxon monarchies, but by them against the Celts in the west of Britain: wars that often seemed mere manhunts for Celtic slaves. The Franks, too, were always fighting – against Bretons, or Aquitainian Goths – and usually bringing back slaves as booty. In the new post-imperial culture, slaves were also made as a result of punishments (a criminal who could not pay a fine allocated to the victim might be reduced to slavery). Most slaves in Visigothic Spain seem to have derived from that source; or from debts; or from simple poverty, for men and women deliberately sold themselves, or their children, into bondage for the sake of a better life. Gregory of Tours, the sixth-century historian, recalled that in Gaul of his day, 'merchants reduced the poor to slavery in return for a morsel of food'.[1]

Slave markets maintained their rhythm, if at a slower beat than in the past; and in Visigothic Spain Jewish merchants were prominent among those providing slaves for sale – Celts or Suevi, no doubt – until the rising tide of anti-Semitism in the seventh century restricted their activities.

The laws of most of these successor states to Rome reflected Roman practice, though they adapted them to the new age: a Burgundian decree, for example, declared that a slave was worth five and a half oxen, or five hogs. There are many references to slavery in Anglo-Saxon, Lombard, and Frankish codes: innumerable provisions related to punishments for slaves who tried to cross the borderline between bondage and liberty; and, in some ways, the rules read as if they were harsher than those of Rome. Out of nearly 500 Visigothic laws which survive (their kings were great lawyers), almost half refer to some aspect of slavery. St Isidore of Seville, who at a bleak time established a philosophical entente between Christian and Gothic customs, had, meantime, no doubts about the divine origin of slavery: 'Because of the sin of the first man, the penalty of servitude was inflicted by God on the human race; to those unsuitable for liberty, he has mercifully accorded servitude.'[2] It will be remembered that in *Tristan and Isolde* Tristan's first mission was to kill Morold, a knight from Ireland who came regularly to Cornwall to obtain slaves.

So throughout the early Middle Ages slaves constituted a highly prized section of the population of Europe, including Northern Europe. How large a proportion of the population of Charlemagne's empire constituted slaves is a matter for speculation. But certainly, during the Carolingian 'Renaissance', slave markets, like learning, prospered. Saxons, Angles, Wends, and Avars could all be bought at Verdun, Arles, and Lyons, at whose 'great fairs' *slavs* soon became also a prime commodity. Verdun prided herself on her production of eunuchs, most of them being sold to the Moors in Spain. Louis the Debonair, Charlemagne's heir, unlike his father, followed a defensive policy. So slaves as prisoners of war were less easy to come by. He sold licences to trade slaves to the powerful merchants whom he knew, who were concerned to buy and sell abroad as well as in France.

Still, there remains doubt as to whether all these *servi*, to use the Latin word for them, were slaves proper – chattel slaves, that is – rather than serfs, persons with some rights of property. The words are confusing, for soon after 'slavery' vanished in Northern Europe. The reasons are disputed. Was it because feudal lords found that they could not feed a labour force all the year round and decided to employ them only during the harvest? Was the eclipse of the old institution the consequence of the use of 'new technology' – especially on smallholdings (or associations of smallholdings) – which made slave labour inappropriate: for example, large carthorses, with frontal collars; frontal yokes for oxen; the new flail, or the wheeled plough with a mould-board; iron tools; or, above all, the diffusion of watermills (such a wonderful release from the old hand mill, which had given such exhausting work to slaves for so long)? Or were all the feudal lords too poor to be able to afford new slaves? Were there too few foreign wars which could bring home captives in the early Middle Ages (especially in competition with the Muslim markets of the Mediterranean)? Did new lords find it to their economic advantage to free their slaves in return for rent, becoming landlords rather than masters? Did the descendants of slaves rise in the world to merge with a mass of once-independent farmers who were in decline, to form a new class of serfs? Or were slave revolts (such as that against King Aurelius in Asturias in 770) and the mass slave escapes of the time too much for masters to endure? (In Visigothic Spain, King Egica in 702 tried to persuade the entire free population to help him seek runaway slaves.)

The idea that some element of morality introduced by a more penitent Church played a part should not be entirely ignored. Balthilde, an Anglo-Saxon slave of Erchinoald, the *maire du palais*, married King Clovis II (the first *roi fainéant*) in 649, and she became known for her efforts both to stop the slave trade and to redeem those already enslaved (she is now very properly St Balthilde). Slaves were beginning to be allowed, in however humble a posture, to enter churches; and there was some intermarriage between freemen and slave girls. The mere act of baptism proved that slaves were men, or women, with souls. Then in AD 960 the Bishops of Venice sought to win divine forgiveness for what they admitted to have been their past sins in selling slaves by seeking to prohibit Venetians from engaging in the trade. In England, manumission became increasingly frequent before 1066, especially by bishops in their wills, and the practice seems to have become almost a commandment. William the Conqueror gave his support to ecclesiastical rules forbidding the enslavement of Christians, as did Henry I. Archbishop Anselm, at the London Council of 1102, denounced the practice of selling Englishmen as 'brute beasts'; his pious contemporary Bishop Wulfstan preached against the practice of selling English slaves from Bristol to Ireland.[3] But it is unclear whether they would have minded selling Frenchmen – or Welshmen, come to that – and the Church remained a slave owner. Much earlier, the goldsmith St Eligius was found enfranchising 'only' a hundred of the slaves whom he offered to the new Monastery of Solignac, near Limoges.

The truth seems to be that many causes for the fall of the ancient institution came together during the eleventh century in Northern Europe. There seem to have been no slaves to speak of by then in central Italy, nor in Catalonia, nor in central France. In Spain the old slave system was on the verge of collapse at the time of the Moorish conquest. Thereafter, the grandsons of many who had been slaves began to be converted into serfs, men with obligations to masters (who provided their houses, as in the *mezzadria*, the sharecropping arrangement of Italy) but who also worked on their own to gain some part of their living. In northern France it became evident that serfs not only produced more than slaves did, but they required no permanent guards. All the same, there seems to have been what a modern French historian has called '*un moment privilégié*', a 'discontinuity', when slavery was dying, and before serfdom had been properly established.[4]

England carried through these changes a little later than did her Continental neighbours. But after the Norman Conquest the new lords freed many of the slaves whom they found on the estates which they seized, and these then joined the ranks of the lower peasantry. 'Domesday Book' records only 25,000 *servi*, or about a tenth of the labour force (many were ploughmen, living completely at the lord's disposal, and in his house). But the Norman Conquest was the first such invasion of England which did not increase the number of slaves in the country. Thereafter the feudal system was introduced, in a more coherent way than anywhere on the Continent, by the King and his tenants, the new lords. By 1200 slavery had disappeared in England, even if William Wilberforce, in a famous speech 600 years later, introducing in the English House of Commons a discussion of the slave trade, talked of child slaves from Bristol being sold to Ireland as late as the reign of Henry VII – an aspect of the troubles of the latter island which has not otherwise received attention.[5]

The state of slavery was, however, quite different in Southern Europe. In all the countries which bordered the Mediterranean the institution prospered in the Middle Ages. The reasons were, first, that that sea, and its shore, constituted a permanent war zone between Christians and Muslims; and, second, that slaves continued to be a priority in Islam. Christians and Muslims alike in the Mediterranean still considered that the institution of slavery had a firm basis in Roman and canon law, in the Bible, and also in the Koran – though the latter specifically, and often, proclaimed that to free a slave was one of the most praiseworthy of acts. The third Caliph Othman had done so: he was said to have bought over 2,000 captives simply for the purpose of liberating them.

Just as the entire population of Carthage had been enslaved after its capture by Rome, so, in the early eighth century, the swift conquest of Visigothic Spain by the Moors was followed by mass enslavements of Christians. Thirty thousand Christian slaves are said to have been sent to Damascus, as the prescribed fifth of the booty due to the Caliph after the fall of the Visigoths. These slaves were fortunate, since the Koran allowed the killing of all males in cities which resisted, and merely the enslavement of their wives and children. Years later, Willibald, a Kentish pilgrim to the Holy Land, was helped by a Spanish 'Chamberlain to the King of the Saracens', who may have been a survivor of these. In Medina it was for a long time easy to meet Christian slaves of Spanish origin. Abd ar-Rahman III, the most gifted of the caliphs in Córdoba, in Spain itself, employed nearly 4,000 Christian slaves in his palace of Madinat az-Zahra, outside that city. The great al-Mansur, Grand Vizier of that caliphate in the late tenth century, launched over fifty attacks on Christian territories, from all of which he brought back slaves: 30,000, it is said, after his conquest of León. When he died, at Medinaceli in 1002, his friends lamented that 'our provider of slaves is no more'.[6] As late as 1311 Aragonese ambassadors at the General Council of the Church at Vienne claimed that there were still 30,000 Christian slaves in the kingdom of Granada.

Islam in fact accepted slavery as an unquestionable part of human organization. Indeed, Mahomet took over the system of slavery upon which ancient society was based, without question. The greatest of Arab historians, Ibn-Khaldun, believed that it was through slavery that some of the strongest Muslims, such as the Turks, learned 'the glory and the blessing and [had become] exposed to divine providence'. By Islamic law, if a people were to convert to Islam before a battle against a Muslim army, their lives, goods, and liberty had to be respected. There were also some tolerant rules, such as that 'it is essential that a captured polytheist [the Koran's euphemism for a Christian] receives his nourishment and good treatment up till the time that his fate is decided'.[7] Slave children were not to be separated from their mothers till they had attained the age of seven. Thus the laws of Islam were in some ways more benign in respect of slavery even than those of Rome. Slaves were not to be treated as if they were animals. Slaves and freemen were equal from the point of view of God. The master did not have power of life and death over his slave property.

Not all Christians in Moorish Spain were enslaved after their subjection. Some Christian princes to begin with could even keep their own slaves. But they were not permitted to have Muslim ones, or black ones: the latter were especially coveted by Muslim noblemen, since they were in short supply.

The Muslims of Spain carried on their pursuit of slaves beyond the borders of the old Visigothic realm. For example, they raided France for captives from a base in the Camargue, and they made razzias to Arles in 842, to Marseilles in 838, and to Valence in 869. Throughout the High Middle Ages there were also innumerable acts of Mediterranean piracy in which Christians were seized by Muslims (or Muslims by Christians), the captures being followed by long negotiations for ransoms. Entire religious orders, such as the Mercedarians, were founded in Christian Spain to deal with the matter. How often did innocuous-seeming little ships set off from the northern coasts of Africa in order to seize Christians from the shores of the North! And how often, too, did similar ships leave from Barcelona or Majorca with a similar goal.

The Muslims of Spain also bought slaves, and on a large scale. One important source, after the revival of prosperity under the Carolingians, was the still largely pagan Slav territories (the people lent their name to the institution, and the word 'Slav' later became a synonym in Arabic for 'eunuch'). Merchants in the eastern marches of Germany would drive captives to markets in the Mediterranean – sometimes via Walenstad in Austria – or Venice – sometimes via Koblenz, on the Rhine, or Verdun. These prisoners might also travel south, down the Saône and the Rhône, and be embarked at Arles. Thence, crossing the Mediterranean in a middle passage as disagreeable as, if shorter than, that of the Atlantic in later days, they would be landed at Almería, the main port of Muslim Spain. They might be shipped thence to any Muslim port, even to Baghdad or Trebizond, Cairo or Algiers.

There grew up, too, a thriving two-way commerce in slaves between Christian merchants of Europe, such as Normans (the Vikings often carried away slaves), and the Muslims of the Mediterranean and of the Atlantic coast. Christian representatives in Arab ports sought to obtain treaties, and consuls, to protect themselves. Sometimes they were successful. But they were prevented from penetrating the African interior by the Arab merchants who controlled the trade there. Those middlemen offered sought-after African products as well as slaves – gold, ivory, ebony, dyed goatskins, chillies, or malaguetta peppers (the 'grains of paradise') in return for European treasures such as glass beads, weapons, and woollen goods. Sometimes black slaves from Guinea might be exchanged for blond ones from Poland.

Thus in the early Middle Ages, at all the Muslim Mediterranean courts and especially those of al-Andalus, there were gathered together, as in an international brigade of servitude, Greek, Slav, German, Russian, Sudanese, and black slaves. These latter, the sought-after black men and women from Guinea, would have been brought across the Sahara from Timbuktu to Sijilmasa, an important market town in southern Morocco.*

---

* The name 'Guinea' appears to be a corruption of 'Jenné' (Djenné), a trading town on the River Bani, a tributary of the Upper Niger; or, of the Berber word for 'black', namely, aguinaou.

With them came ivory which was used by the famous Islamic school of ivory carving at Cuenca. One historian of al-Andalus writes of the 'vast hordes of slaves' brought in during the tenth century. Among the merchants who dealt in these slaves from Guinea was the father of the Andalusian historian Ahmad ar-Razi, who was not the last such writer to have financed his research by a fortune accumulated by a slaving forebear.

The Umayyad rulers of Córdoba, acting in imitation of the Abbasid caliphs in Baghdad, began to employ slaves as soldiers, and by the middle of the ninth century the Caliph there had a slave army of 60,000 'silent ones', so named because being German, English, or Slav they spoke no Arabic. Yusef Ibn-Tashufun the Almoravid favoured the use of these Christian slaves against Christian rulers: they fought well. Even though Muslim power was in decay by the end of the fourteenth century, Christian slaves also worked on the Alhambra in Granada.

Slaves could prosper in Muslim courts, and the son of one such, the Slav Badr, became Governor of Córdoba. Many caliphs had children by slave mistresses, and so it was that Abd ar-Rahman III was the son of a Christian slave girl. Some of the rulers of the *Taifas*, the tiny principalities which sprang up in Spain after the collapse of the caliphate of Córdoba in the eleventh century, were slaves in origin: for example, Sabur, the slave King in Badajoz, was probably born Sapor, a Persian; and the ruler of Denia, near Valencia, may once have been a Sardinian slave.

Perhaps some black slaves were included in the largely Berber army of Gebel el-Tarik which crossed to Spain in 711. Abd ar-Rahman I, the founder of the Umayyad caliphate in Córdoba, employed a black slave to manage his harem. Al-Hakam I, in the ninth century, surrounded himself with 'mamelukes [Egyptians] and blacks'. Al-Hakam II, a hundred years later, had a black slave bodyguard, as did the most powerful King of Granada, Muhammad V, in the mid-fourteenth century.

The Christians in Spain emulated Muslim behaviour. True, they began their reconquest of the peninsula by killing the Muslim populations of the towns which they seized. But by the end of the eighth century captured women and children were made into slaves, as were some men. Execution began to seem a waste of a resource. A prime purpose of Christian adventurers and municipal councils in penetrating Muslim territory indeed soon became to find slaves. In 1143 a Castilian king, Alfonso VII, made an expedition to Andalusia, and brought back Muslim slaves from Carmona, near Seville, as from Almería. Slaves (principally from Eastern Europe) also began to be given as presents, along with gold, to Christian kings of Spain by Muslim tributaries. Muslim slaves were at work on the rebuilding of the Cathedral of Santiago de Compostela about 1150, just as Christian slaves were working on the Mosque of Kutubiyya at Marrakesh.

Castilian razzias, copying Muslim ones, increased in the thirteenth century. The recovery of the great cities of al-Andalus led to the enslavement of thousands who were received with enthusiasm by the conquerors and their followers. Many of the Muslims' slaves from all over the Mediterranean and beyond also passed directly into Castilian hands. King Alfonso III of Aragon is also said to have sold 40,000 Moors after his capture of Minorca (in 1287); and the best historian of this subject has suggested that it might be enough merely to halve that figure in order to establish the truth.[8] It must have been easy for Ramon Llull, the Majorcan mystic and agitator, to buy a Muslim slave about that time, who would teach him Arabic. The extraordinary Arab traveller Ibn-Battuta described a Christian raid in 1352 for slaves on the coast of al-Andalus between Marbella and Málaga, perhaps at the fishing port of Torremolinos. The raid must have been similar to that of the Portuguese a hundred years later in West Africa, which brought the Azanaghi back to Prince Henry and the Algarve.

Thus it is no surprise that slavery, though apparently in decline about AD 1000, as it was north of the Pyrenees, received detailed attention two hundred and fifty years later in the major Spanish legal code, the 'Siete Partidas' of King Alfonso the Wise. That famous document specified that a man became a slave by being captured in war, by being born the child of a slave, or by letting himself be sold. The code, compiled in the 1260s, confirmed Roman definitions of slavery, though in some respects it was more tolerant (certainly it was more so than the rough Visigothic laws), for example, allowing that a slave might marry against his master's will, and that, once married, couples could not be separated. If marriages occurred between slaves with different masters, an effort had to be made to let them work in the same place. If a compromise could not be achieved, the Church had to buy both slaves. Children would take the status of their mothers, so that, if the latter were free, the children could be also. A slave who was badly treated could complain to a judge, and a master who killed a slave could be tried for murder. Castration was forbidden as a punishment. Slaves were to be allowed to inherit property. There was no suggestion in the code that slavery might be an evil in itself. But manumission was possible, and slaves who could afford it could buy their liberty. King Alfonso also provided, bearing in mind that medieval Spain was a country of several cultures, that neither Jews, Moors, nor heretics could legally own Christian slaves.[9]

These provisions in theory governed Spanish-owned slaves not just for the remainder of the Middle Ages but, however inadequately applied, or explicitly amended, in one way or another until the nineteenth century.

By 1100 there were in Christian Spain (or Portugal) few slaves who had the same faith as their masters but many Muslim ones, living alongside a small class of free Muslims. Most of the captives were in one way or another servants in noble households, though some worked in workshops or on farms. Many of them were sold, often outside Spain. Thus in the thirteenth century, Arles, Montpellier, Narbonne, Antibes, and Nice were important markets for slaves obtained from Africa. Venetian, Genoese, or Florentine merchants often did the selling. Barcelona was important too, its traders busily selling 'sarrasines' or 'Moors' to buyers in Sicily and Genoa. Palma de Mallorca ran Barcelona close as a slaving port in the fifteenth century. Thus we hear how Thomas Vincentius of Tarragona, settled in Genoa, bought there, in the course of the summer of 1318, two white slaves (probably Moors), two olive-skinned ones, one slave from the Crimea, two Turks, and a Greek. Greek slaves were then fashionable in Barcelona, being easily obtained in the Catalan Duchy of Athens; and slaves from the Crimea were as easily acquired thanks to the Genoese colony at Kaffa (the modern Feodosiya). Other important sources for slaves were Sardinia and Russia: thus, we read how on '24 April 1409, Johannes Vilahut, notary of the royal chancellery and bourgeois of Barcelona, was sold to Narciso Jutglat, bourgeois of Palma, a Russian neophyte, aged 27, named Helen'. There were Circassian, Armenian, and Turkish slaves as well as Balkans of all sorts and particularly Albanians (in 1450, 'Jacobus d'Alois, coral fisherman of Barcelona, sold to the widow of a merchant of the same city an Albanian named Erma, aged 25'). The ethnic diversity was nearly as remarkable as it was in al-Andalus.[10]

Ports in Aragon's southern Italian dominions were also slave ports in the fifteenth century, above all Naples and Palermo. Sales there by Spanish merchants were frequent.

In Aragon and Valencia, though Christian razzias and kidnappings, especially at sea, continued, commerce played a more important part in providing slaves for Europe. No doubt that should be seen as a step towards civilization.

After the fall of Constantinople in 1453 slaves imported from Russia or the Black Sea became more rare. The conquest of Crimea by the Ottomans brought an end to the Genoese trading post at Kaffa. The shortage was compensated for in Spain by imports of slaves from the recently discovered (or rediscovered) Canary Islands. For example, after the 'revolt' of Tenerife, a single merchant of Valencia brought back eighty-seven *guanches* (Canary Island natives) on one ship.

Black African slaves were also becoming quite numerous, on the Mediterranean coast of Spain and elsewhere. In the 1250s, already, Moorish traders were to be found offering black slaves from Guinea at fairs in Guimarães, in northern Portugal; and blacks bought in North Africa were being sold in Cádiz at the end of that century. In 1306, two inhabitants of Cerbère, on the Spanish-French border, sold 'to Bernard Gispert, of Santa Coloma de Queralt, in Catalonia, a "black Saracen", called Alibez, for 335 sous'. At the end of the fourteenth century, in 1395, King Juan I of Aragon reclaimed two 'Ethiopians' (a generic word still used for all Africans) who had hidden in the Monastery of Santa María de Besalú – one of them claiming that he was the son of the King of Ethiopia. Then in 1416 Jaume Gil, hotelier of Igualada, no distance from Santa Coloma, bought 'an Ethiopian negress', Marguerite, known as Axa before she was baptized, from Elisenda, the widow of an apothecary, for 139 Aragonese gold florins. The records of the markets of those days indeed seem to contain increasing mention of 'black Tartars', of Algerians, even of black Christians from Tunis, and some from Sudan or Cyrenaica. The Africans of Barcelona were numerous enough, in the mid-fifteenth century, to form there a black *cofradia*, a black Christian brotherhood, such as existed already in both Seville and Valencia – though the direction of these must always have been in the hands of freemen.[11]

There were more slaves in Seville – the 'needle's eye', in a later judge's phrase – in the fifteenth century than anywhere else in Spain.[12] They were to be found in the Arenal, where ships for trading were loaded, even selling goods in public squares and in market places. Moors and Moriscos (white slaves, *esclavos blancos*), had usually been captives in war (either from Granada or captured in Mediterranean wars) and were often disliked; but blacks (*esclavos negros*), who often became Christians and accepted Spanish culture, were easily absorbed.

Slaves were also to be found in Italy: not just in commercially adventurous cities such as Genoa, Venice, and Florence, but also in Rome. A law of 1441 in Genoa showed how seriously the slave trade was taken then: a slave ship with one deck could henceforth only carry thirty slaves; with two it could carry forty-five; and one with three, sixty. (These were regulations of a kind which Northern Europe, after it had re-entered the slave traffic in the seventeenth century, would not repeat till 1790 on the occasion of Sir William Dolben's bill in England.) It was laid down in Florence in 1364 that all kinds of slaves might be imported, provided they were not Catholics. Most of those brought in were Tartars from Kaffa; at least one Florentine firm, that of the family of Marchionni, had a foothold there in a prominently Genoese-dominated city. Between 1366 and 1397 nearly 400 slaves were sold in Florence (mostly women). Many Greek slaves were also sold in Italy, along with Albanians, Russians, Turks, and 'Moors'. In the late fifteenth century Venetians probably enjoyed the services of about 3,000 slaves from North Africa or Tartary. Anxiety was sometimes expressed because there were too few slaves (for example, in a debate in the Senate in Venice in 1459); but there was also fear lest slaves might become so numerous as to constitute a danger to the city: a familiar cry in later slave societies in the Americas.

The southern shore of the Mediterranean afforded an even larger market for slaves in the late Middle Ages than the northern one. No doubt Christian captives dominated the field, mostly kidnapped on the high seas or in maritime raids on Spanish or Italian ports or villages. All the same for hundreds of years black slaves, especially girls and young men, had also been sought after by Arab merchants for use in Muslim courts, from Córdoba to Baghdad, as servants, concubines, or warriors. The slave girls of Awdaghost, on the Upper Niger, were prized as cooks, particularly skilled, reported the traveller al-Bakri, at making exquisite pastries out of a mixture of nuts and honey. In the fourteenth century, another traveller, al-Umari, described the empire of Mali, the largest West African monarchy of the time, also on the Upper Niger, as deriving great profit from 'its merchandise and its seizures by razzias in the land of the infidel'. The successors of the Mali, the emperors of the Songhai, would customarily give presents of slaves to their guests. In Fez, in the early sixteenth century, the Emperor gave Leo the African, a Moor born in Granada who later lived at the brilliant court of Pope Leo X in Rome, 'fifty male slaves and fifty female slaves brought out of the land of the blacks, ten eunuchs, twelve camels, one giraffe, twenty civet-cats.... Twenty of the male slaves', he added, 'cost twenty ducats apiece, and so did fifteen of the female slaves.' The eunuchs were worth forty ducats, the camels fifty, and the civet-cats 200 – the high cost of the last item being due to their use in making scent.[13]

Egypt had a taste for black eunuchs in the tenth century. Admittedly, they were largely able to satisfy this caprice by trading with the territories to their immediate south. A treaty of AD 651 obliged the Nubians to deliver 360 slaves a year to Egypt, and there were Muslim conventions with other conquered peoples in North Africa. Then many of those who set off northwards from the sub-Saharan Sudan would take with them black slaves, whom they would customarily sell when they arrived at their destination.

The enthusiasm for blacks was, to be sure, nothing like a private interest of the Muslims: they were also popular as slaves in Java and India in the Middle Ages; even the Chinese seem to have liked East African slaves, a desire presumably satisfied by Muslim merchants in Canton.

The numbers involved in trans-Saharan trading are difficult to estimate. Could there have been 7,000 black eunuchs in Baghdad in the tenth century? Was it the sheer number of black slaves in the fields of Mesopotamia which inspired there the great rebellion of slaves led by Ali Ibn-Muhammed at the end of the ninth century? Princes in Bahrain in the eleventh century are credited with holding 30,000 black slaves, mostly employed in gardening or at least domestic agriculture. In 1275 10,000 natives of the region of the Upper Niger are said to have been sold in Egypt 'after a military campaign'.[14] The chief buyers would have been the slave soldiers the Mamelukes, who seized power in Egypt in 1250 and in the fourteenth century dominated the Near East. An Egyptian claimed that Mansa Musa, the most remarkable Sultan of the Niger empire of

Mali, sold, during his pilgrimage to Mecca of 1324, 14,000 female slaves in Cairo in order to meet his travelling costs. The exaggeration in statistics in all societies before the twentieth century, from the size of armies to deaths in action, is notorious. Still, anything between 5,000 and 20,000 slaves may have been carried north annually from the region of the Niger to the harems, the barracks, the kitchens, or the farms of the Muslim Mediterranean and Near East during the late Middle Ages; and not just to North Africa, since Sicily, Sardinia, Genoa, Venice, and even parts of Christian Spain had, as has been suggested, their black slaves in the fifteenth century. The enslavement of black Africans recently converted to Islam might be forbidden to Muslims. All the same, the caliphs and emirs turned a blind eye to it. Thus the black King of Bornu, in what is now Nigeria, complained bitterly to the Sultan of Egypt in the 1390s that Arab tribesmen were always seizing 'our people as merchandise'.[15]

This trans-Saharan trade, between West and North Africa, probably began in one form or another as early as 1000 BC, when the desert was sometimes crossed by oxen and carts drawn by horses. The commerce was encouraged by both the Carthaginians and the Romans. After the introduction of the camel, the essential element in communications in Africa till the advent of motor vehicles in the 1920s, it prospered even more. The most important route in Roman days was that which led to Muzuk, the capital of Fezzan, in what is now southern Libya. That linked Tripolitania and Egypt with the cities on the central bend of the Niger. There were, however, even in antiquity, other roads to the Mediterranean. With the fall of Rome, this trade, such as it was, evaporated. But it revived when in 533–5 Byzantium reconquered North Africa. Probably a few slaves were always brought along these routes, including in classical times.

The Arab conquests of North Africa in the seventh century, though at first destructive, eventually contributed to the restoration and expansion of the trans-Saharan trade.

Leo the African, who travelled in this region, spoke of twenty cities between Morocco and Tripoli which enjoyed 'great traffic into the land of the blacks'.[16] The most important of these places – Fez, Sijilmasa, and Ghadames – were inland towns, whose merchants never traded directly with the Christian Catalans, Italians, and Majorcans who were established on the coast. Christian traders were allowed to settle in Marrakesh but nowhere else. The medieval European monarchies in consequence knew little of the details of this flourishing trade between the Maghreb and the people of Guinea.

The main medieval Arab route across the Sahara to Morocco was that from Timbuktu to Sijilmasa. Though Muslim merchants were the most important traders, a few Jewish, Berber, and black ones also played a part.

This commerce was limited, first, by the length of the journey – seventy to ninety days or longer – and, second, by the requirement that all goods (other than slaves) had a high value in relation to their weight. The crossing was dangerous, and could not be made at certain times of the year: there were sandstorms in the summer, as well as sharp changes in the temperature from day to night. Water was always short, and marauders were frequent. It was easy to become lost. It may easily be that as many as a quarter of the slaves died en route.

Of the other goods carried, gold was significant, at least from AD 800. It became more and more important (in the eleventh and twelfth centuries) after first the Muslim countries of the Mediterranean, and then several European ones, adopted that metal as their currency. West Africa was Europe's main source of gold in the late Middle Ages, although the place itself was quite unknown to Europe.

The racial mixture in West Africa was interesting. Before the Arab invasions, the land was principally inhabited by two peoples: in the north-west, the Hamites – called Libyans or *Barbari* by the Romans, and Berbers by the Arabs, a word actually deriving from *Barbari* – and black people to the south of the desert. The arrival of the Arabs brought a most troubling extra element. All the same, the Berbers retained most of their individual characteristics, as highland tillers of the soil and lovers of freedom. They were rarely moved by religious enthusiasm, and were able, on the whole, to preserve their purity of race. But in the south there was much mixture. Thus the people of Timbuktu had black skin but much Berber blood. They thought of the black Songhai, in the Middle Niger Valley, as savages, though the powerful ruling dynasty of that monarchy was Berber in origin. In the desert the Hamitic Tuaregs were the dominant people at the time of the coming of the Arabs, who named them 'the veiled people', though in truth they adopted the use of veils only after the year 600. They may have had a time as Christians, for even after they adopted Islam their favourite emblem was a cross, and they continued to be monogamous. In the fifteenth century they controlled, and maintained, the desert's oases and pastures, and they levied tolls on the caravan routes crossing the Sahara. In the confusion which attended the collapse of the Roman empire they also acquired the large herds of camels which were the basis of their strength.

The distinguishing feature of West Africa was that it was a territory in which the peoples from the desert, such as these Tuaregs, were in the habit of making constant raids on settled communities in the well-watered and prosperous peripheries – on the Mandingos, for example, or the Songhai, from whom, among other things, they stole slaves. The desert peoples hated agriculture and needed slaves to tend the oases. The Tuaregs and the Arabs liked to employ blacks in this capacity, even though they despised them: a tenth-century traveller from Baghdad, Ibn-Hawkal, wrote that he had 'not described the country of the African blacks . . . of the torrid zone . . . because, naturally loving wisdom, inge-nuity, religion, justice and regular government, how could I notice such people as these . . . ?'[17] Ibn-Battuta, who has been mentioned before, was also horrified to find that the blacks, whom he had in the past known as slaves, were the masters in their own country. He complained of the food he found there, and thought that this bad food showed that 'there was no good to be hoped for from these people'. But he comforted himself all the same by travelling back to Fez with a caravan of 600 black slaves.[18]

Raiding in what the Arabs named 'the Country of the Blacks', the Beled es-Sudan, the tropical rainforest of the Guinea coast, also became a traditional occcupation of Muslims of the plains, especially during dry weather.

Arab power expanded the trade in slaves. By the fifteenth century Muslim merchants, usually mullahs, dominated the marketing of them, as of most other things. These holy men constituted an international brotherhood, for they were not attached to any kingdom. They obtained their captives much as the Muslims had done in Spain and elsewhere: by razzias into nearby towns, whose inhabitants they stole without bothering about a pretext. But they also bought slaves, which meant little more than that they let others do the stealing for them.

Medieval West Africa, after all, constituted a part of the civilization of Islam, if only a frontier zone. That Muslim connection had many positive sides. Indeed, the coming of Islam explains why, by the fifteenth century, the region had mostly advanced beyond a subsistence economy to one using production for exchange. The architect Es-Sahili had come there from Moorish Spain to introduce the idea of stone buildings into the land of Guinea. Craftsmen and hunters as well as fishermen and farmers by then sustained a vigorous commercial life extending over long distances, not just to the Mediterranean. Markets existed, often arranged according to an elaborate plan by which sellers met in rotation, large commercial exchanges being held once a fortnight, smaller ones once a week. Iron of different sizes, copper bars, copper wristlets, manillas (rings of metal used as necklaces or bracelets), and even cowries from the Maldive Islands in the Indian Ocean, all items which would play a part in the Atlantic slave trade, were widely used as currency. The slave dimension of West Africa was stimulated also by the extension of Islam into the region.

West Africa itself had known slavery on a small scale before the coming of Islam, and had done so since the establishment there of settled agricultural societies. African kings who collected and sold slaves for lucrative export to the north usually kept a few for their own use. But the Islamic monarchs, such as the emperors of Mali or their successors to great power on the Middle Niger, the Songhai, ushered in a new stage: these rulers were powerful men, with large armies at their disposal, and considerable territories to exploit. Many of their monarchs employed slaves as a kind of Praetorian Guard, on the assumption that if they were foreigners they must be reliable.

In the early sixteenth century Leo the African found that at Bornu, just beyond the Songhai empire, on the southern end of the easternmost, Garamantian road to the Mediterranean, slaves were usually exchanged for horses: fifteen or twenty slaves for a single Arab horse. The low cost was because the Songhai had an almost limitless stock of captives: they had only to raid their weaker neighbours to the south in order to obtain all that they needed. Slaves were used for all kinds of purposes: for example, the commerce in gum on the River Sénégal was made possible by the use of slaves in the harvest from March till July. Slaves were also used in mines: the Lisbon typographer and translator Valentim Fernandes, a traveller of Moravian origin who would go to Benin in the 1490s, described how seven kings, possessors of seven mines of gold, 'have slaves which they put into the mines, and they are given wives; and they engender and raise children in the mines. . . .' He added mysteriously, 'The slaves who find the gold are all black but if, by a miracle, they manage to escape from them, they become white because colour is modified in the mines.'[19]

When in what is now western Nigeria the Oyo kingdom of the Yorubas came into being (perhaps during the early fifteenth century), there were several thousand palace slaves. Many slaves worked in agriculture: in the 1450s the Venetian Alvise Ca'da Mosto found that kings on the River Sénégal, tributaries of the Songhai, and before them of the Mali, had numerous slaves, obtained by pillage, 'which they make use of in various ways, above all to cultivate their lands. . . .'[20]

In West Africa, slaves seem to have been the only form of private property recognized by African custom. They also represented the most striking manifestation of personal wealth.

This was the world touched at the periphery by de Freitas's expedition in 1444, which, the ships aside, must have seemed to the Africans a conventional, not a revolutionary, event.

Some of the slaves seen by Zurara on that day at Lagos in the Algarve became 'good and true Christians': the Azanaghi wore their Mohammedanism lightly, and were more easy to convert to other religions than those living further inland in Africa. Some were freed. Some were put to work on the sugar estates founded further south in Portugal, often by Genoese investors. Four of those present on that day in Lagos in 1444 were given to monasteries or churches. Of these, one was merely resold by the church to which he had been presented, for it needed money with which to buy decorations. One other, sent to the Monastery of São Vicente do Cabo, became a Franciscan friar.

The expressions of regret and pity by Zurara, though they may now seem modest, were among the few to be recorded not just at that time but for several centuries. Perhaps the goddess Fortune, to whom the chronicler prayed, was a greater friend of man than more sophisticated deities.

4

THE PORTUGUESE SERVED
FOR SETTING DOGS
TO SPRING THE GAME

*'The Portuguese served for setting dogs to
spring the game, which as soon as they had
done was seized by others.'*

Willem Bosman, 1704

THE EVENTS OF THAT early summer morning in 1444 in the Algarve when
over 200 slaves were first offered to the Portuguese had their beginnings
centuries before, during the earliest attempts of European peoples to
explore Africa.

In the sixth century BC, the Pharaoh Necho sent down the Red Sea
an expedition which returned, two years later, through the Strait of
Gibraltar. Herodotus tells the story. But there is little other evidence
of such an early circumnavigation.

The Carthaginians attempted a similar expedition a hundred years
later, but down the West Coast. They sent out a large party under Hanno,
one of the two magistrates of the state. He may have founded some
colonies and, passing the River Sénégal, perhaps reached Sierra Leone,
where he discovered an island full of apes, mostly females. He returned
to say that he had founded a port and named it Cerne. The story was
recorded in the Temple of Moloch in Carthage, but the exploit was soon
forgotten.

Later the Persian Sataspes sailed down the coast of West Africa with
another fleet and found, he reported, small black people with clothes
made of palm leaves.

No further such adventure seems to have been mounted until the
fifteenth century AD. For these incurious generations, the assumption was
that Africa was impossible to circumnavigate, since the Indian Ocean
was believed to be landlocked. Some Arab journeys undoubtedly were
made, but it is quite unclear where they went.

It was for many generations supposed that Cape Bojador, to the south of Cape Juby in what is now the Rio de Oro, was the *ne plus ultra* of wise seamen. Beyond it, white sailors were supposed to turn black, and a Green Sea of Darkness was believed to open up. One might expect to meet sea monsters, and rocks which could turn into serpents. The sun would send down sheets of liquid flame, the mist would be impenetrable, and the currents and reefs unnavigable. But, then, no one quite knew the whereabouts of Cape Bojador; it was even confused with Cape Juby.

A new era of discoveries was begun by Italians, in the late Middle Ages the most enlightened of European peoples. In 1291 Ugolino and Vadino Vivaldi and probably Teodosio Doria, from Genoa, set out with a flotilla of galleys to reach India by way of West Africa. Their declared aim was to outmanoeuvre the Venetians, who had secured control over trade through Egypt from the east. They thus established the agenda, so to say, of nautical ambition for the next 200 years. Their ships were lost, but the memory of their attempt remained – though it has been suggested that in truth they set out west, for the New World rather than south for the Old. Then, about 1320, another Genoese, Lanzarotto Malocello, an adventurous captain who had had dealings with Cherbourg, in the remote English Channel, and the Low Countries, as also with the closer Ceuta, in Morocco, went to look for the Vivaldis and planted a Spanish flag in the Canary Isles (known to antiquity as the Fortunate Isles, or the Garden of the Hesperides, and never quite forgotten). Malocello gave his Christian name to one island of that archipelago, which it retains to this day. Other Mediterranean cities were soon interested. The Florentine Boccaccio tells how a journey was made about 1340 to West Africa by a group of adventurers which included Portuguese, Spaniards, Genoese, and Florentines (the commander was Angiolino del Teggia, of Florence), who communicated as they sailed by whistling. They brought back four inhabitants of Tenerife – *guanches*, who presumably ended their days as slaves – as well as redwood, sheepskins, and tallow.

In those days, Jewish merchants in Majorca had many dealings with their co-religionary trading partners in the ports of North Africa. Those Jews, it will be remembered, had more freedom to move about in the Arab world than their Christian counterparts. They were goldsmiths in Fez, and some Jewish colonies were established still further south, even in the oases of the Sahara, their members sometimes marrying local Berbers or blacks, such as the Fulani in Senegambia. There were, too, some Catalan merchants in the sultanate of Tlemcen, forty miles inland from the Mediterranean, near Oran.

Much information, therefore, became available in Spain, and the famous cartographers of Majorca put it to good use. So Angelino Dulcert, probably of Palma, was in 1339 able to design a sea chart which gave accurate pride of place to an African monarch, Mansa Musa of Mali, known for his wealth and for that extravagant hadj of 1324 of which mention has been made. Dulcert also depicted a 'road to the land of the blacks', as well as a 'Saracen King' beyond the Atlas Mountains who owned mines 'abounding in gold'.[1] The idea was intoxicating! So it was scarcely surprising that Jaume Ferrer, also from Majorca, should set off in 1346 to look for a much talked of River of Gold (the territory now known as Rio de Oro); but he, too, vanished, as the Vivaldis and Doria had done.

Across the Mediterranean, in Aragon, an anonymous Franciscan wrote a book which described an imaginary voyage down the West African coast to that River of Gold, which seemed to lead to the presumed land of Prester John, a legendary Christian emperor cut off from Europe by infidel Muslims: that land was Ethiopia, whose monarchs had indeed joined the Christian Church in its early days (St Augustine had written, '*Aethiopia credit Deo.*') The author, like many others, confused Ethiopia, for long a synonym for Africa, with Mali, but much in his book was correct. Not long after, about 1400, Abraham Cresques, also a Majorcan, in a remarkably accurate map (the 'Catalan Map', as it has become known) drew attention to a gap in the Atlas Mountains and wrote, 'Through here pass the merchants who come from the lands of the blacks of Guinea.'[2]

The expeditions to the Canary Isles were not concerned exclusively with gold. Thus in the fourteenth century occasional cargoes of islanders were carried as slaves to both Portuguese and Andalusian ports. In 1402 Jean de Béthencourt and some French friends, also on their way to the River of Gold, brought back to Seville some indigenous slaves after their conquest of the larger Canary Islands in the name of Castile. They were sold in Cádiz and seem to have been taken to Aragon and some ended their days in Genoa.

The turning point for European journeys to West Africa came in 1415 when the Portuguese mounted a military expedition and took Ceuta, then one of the greatest commercial entrepôts on the south coast of the Mediterranean, and the northern terminus of several caravan routes in Africa. The Genoese had recorded commerce with Ceuta for 250 years, and the conquest may have been suggested by them, though there were many motives behind the decision to attack – the political ambitions of the Portuguese princes, and a highly developed sense of destiny inspired among them by chivalrous literature. These half-English *infantes*, the future King Duarte and his brother Henry the Navigator, who with their father, King João I, had earned their spurs as knights in this enterprise, are said to have heard from some Moorish prisoners of the details of the passage of trains of merchants and camels, carrying beads made in Ceuta, among other things, for exchange with gold and slaves, to Timbuktu on the Niger and to Cantor on the Gambia, news that inspired Henry 'to seek the lands by the way of the sea'.[3]

If he did not know of them before, Henry also learned at Ceuta of the black slaves available from Guinea, for he observed in the battle, as many

Portuguese did, the special prowess in the fighting of a tall African, one of the innumerable slave soldiers in whom Muslim monarchs placed so much faith.

Henry the Navigator is an important pioneer in the history of the transatlantic slave trade. He might be said to be a representative European of his day, since he had both English ancestors – through his maternal grandfather, John of Gaunt – and much Spanish and French blood. He is, though, a curiously elusive hero, a gregarious bachelor who liked neither wine nor women, a patriot, yet more a businessman than a typical prince. But he was persistent and energetic, as well as charming and open-minded. He had both curiosity and religious zeal. He was austere, but combined the pride of a nobleman with the determination of an entrepreneur. Henry, despite his swarthy complexion, probably never shook off the lowering influence of his dominating English mother who, it was said, found the court in Lisbon a sewer, and left it a nunnery.

As the Portuguese should have anticipated, the principal centre of trade in North Africa was moved by the Muslims from Ceuta, after its fall to the Christians, to other places, so the routes across the Sahara did not pass under Portuguese control. But Prince Henry decided for himself that the source of African gold, the coast of Guinea, might be reached by sea (he may have been influenced, as was Columbus later, by Florentine cosmographers). There might be other commercial benefits which in the long run would make an effort at exploration worthwhile: the hope of obtaining slaves may have loomed in his calculations, and the peppers – 'grains of paradise', or malaguetta – from the future Grain Coast (approximately the modern Liberia) were already known in European markets, because of the trans-Saharan trade.

The 'gold of Guinea' was in truth produced in remote zones: near the upper waters of the Sénégal; at Bambuk, between the Rivers Sénégal and Falémé; and 200 miles away, at Bure, near the junction of the Niger and its tributary, the Tinkisso. Other gold fields were in the forests of what later became known as Ashanti, and Lobi, on the higher waters of the Black Volta. But the Portuguese assumed that they could reach those magic sites by sea.

The idea of a land campaign to find the sources of the gold of Guinea did not occur to Prince Henry – fortunately, since no doubt it would have been doomed to failure, just as Arab and Moorish expeditions south from Sijilmasa along the ancient caravan road had been, when mounted in, respectively, the eighth and the eleventh centuries.

Prince Henry eventually established his headquarters on Cape St Vincent in the extreme south-west of Portugal, at Sagres, and built a palace, a chapel, an observatory, and a village for workers. The notion that he gathered around him a school of cosmographers and astronomers is a legend, but he did have the services of experts such as Jacome or

Jaime Ribas, a Catalan cartographer of distinction. He also ordered the expansion of the port of Lagos, twenty miles away to the east of Sagres, and there were built 'the best sailing ships afloat', as the Venetian Ca'da Mosto would put it later.[4]

Prince Henry's doings were partly financed by his own clever investments in, for instance, the monopoly of fishing for tuna along the coast of the Algarve, and in a fishery on the Tagus; and partly from subsidies from the Order of Christ, a knightly association founded in Portugal concerned to carry on the war against Islam in their own territory with money obtained from the Templars, when that undertaking had been dissolved a century before. Prince Henry was grand master of the order, a post which carried the added benefit that he gained the profits from its fairs, held at Tomar, as well as from leasing houses and shops round the fairground.

The first ventures of the Prince were the seizure of the deserted islands of Madeira, and the Azores. Madeira may have been occupied partly to prevent the Spaniards from doing the same: a motive for imperial expansion which would be often repeated in the history of Europe. Prince Henry became the Governor (*in absentia*), and managed the place thereafter. Both Madeira and the Azores were lightly colonized by Portuguese from the Algarve, along with some Flemings: the Azores were even known as the Flemish Islands for a time, when Jacome de Bruges was the first Governor there. Both yielded dye material: 'dragon's blood', a resin, and orchil, obtained from lichen. Madeira (so called from the Portuguese for 'wood' because of its timber-bearing forest) could also offer wax and honey, as well as wood. Like the Azores ('the Hawks'), it had no men to seize, for it had been uninhabited before. The settlers there were conscious of the innovation; the first children to be born on the main island were duly named Adam and Eve.

Prince Henry was always as interested in these Atlantic islands as he was in Africa: they were certain moneymakers, and the African adventures were more speculative. All the same, he continued to send probing voyages along the African coast, as far as Cape Juby, where Béthencourt had anchored for a few days after his conquest of the Canaries (Cape Juby is visible from the Canary island of Fuerteventura). In 1434, Gil Eannes, a native of the Algarve and one of the best sailors in Portugal, was charged to go and look for gold from beyond Cape Bojador: in 'seas none had sailed before', in the phrase of Camoëns, though possibly some Genoese had done so, as of course had Hanno and his sailors. Gil Eannes probably sailed in a simple square-rigged single-masted *barca*, partly decked if decked at all, of only about thirty tons, flat-bottomed, with a shallow draft, and with a crew of about fifteen, who would have expected to row much of the time – the same kind of ship as had been used often before in unsuccessful attempts to round the promontory (wherever indeed it was).

Eannes rounded what he took to be the evil cape, to find that his white sailors did not turn black, the Green Sea of Darkness was on that day 'as easy to sail in as the waters at home', the sun did not set down sheets of liquid flame, and even the currents and reefs seemed navigable, provided that one did not sail too close to the shore. Eannes brought back to Portugal a sprig of rosemary gathered on the shore south of the landmark.[5]

Rosemary promised little in the way of trade. Nevertheless, a year later, Eannes set off again, this time accompanied by Afonso Gonçalves Baldaia, the royal cupbearer, and reached a spot about 150 miles south of the cape. Here they saw with satisfaction the footprints of both men and camels, at a point which they named Angra dos Ruivos (Creek of Red-Haired Men, now Garnet Bay). In 1436 Gonçalves Baldaia sailed again and, after two of his men engaged in a pointless fight with some inhabitants, at last reached the long sought-after Rio do Ouro, which turned out to be a bay and not a river, nor to be the centre of any trade in gold. Gonçalves Baldaia went further on, halting only at a rock which he called Galha Point, Point of the Galley (now Piedra de Gala), a little short of a promontory soon to be known as Cabo Branco (Blanco).

For several years after 1436 Prince Henry was occupied with matters nearer to home, such as the disastrous siege of Tangier. But in 1441, two new Portuguese captains, Antão Gonçalves and Nuno Tristão, set out, separately, to Cabo Branco, a designation which they gave the place because of the white of the sand before it. (It is in the extreme north of the modern state of Mauritania.) Here some hills began to rise for the first time out of the desert, but at first sight there was still nothing but sand to be seen. Yet on the south side of the cape they found a market run by Muslim traders, and a halt for the camels and caravans of the interior. The people were black but, being Muslim, were dressed in Moorish style, in white robes and turbans. Here the Portuguese received a small quantity of gold dust, as well as some ostrich eggs; and, as Gonçalves had always desired, his men also seized some black Africans, twelve in number, to take back to Portugal ('What a beautiful thing it would be', this commander had told his men, 'if we could capture some of the natives to lay before the face of our Prince').[6]

These people were nearly all Azanaghi, as would be most of those sold in Lagos in 1444. They seem not to have been carried off to serve as slaves – though one of them, a woman, was a black slave, presumably from somewhere in the region of Guinea. They were taken as exhibits to show Prince Henry, much as Columbus would bring back some Indians, fifty years later, from his first journey to the Caribbean.[*]

[*] *The Azanaghi had remained in touch with Europe through trade with the Muslim kingdom of Granada; thence, thanks to Genoese merchants in Málaga, they imported so many white china cups made in Venice that these became almost a currency.*

The Portuguese at home showed no special interest. Black slaves were known, as has been amply shown; already in 1425 a Portuguese vessel had seized a Moroccan slave ship off Larache, with fifty-three black men and three black women, all from Guinea, who had been profitably disposed of in Portugal. But Prince Henry, according to the sycophantic chronicler Zurara, was very pleased: 'How great his joy must have been ... not for the number of those captives, but for the hope, O sainted Prince, you had for others in the future.'[7]

These new captives included a local chief, Adahu, who spoke Arabic. He negotiated his own release, and that of a boy from his own family, on the understanding that if he were taken back to where he had been found he would deliver some black slaves in exchange.

So the next year, 1442, Antão Gonçalves sailed back to Cabo Branco and from there, or from just below it to the south in the Bay of Arguin, brought not only some gold dust from West Africa, some fine salt, and a few ostrich eggs, but about ten black Africans, 'from various countries' (that is, presumably, some from a long way away), who were presented to him, apparently, by an Arab mounted on a white camel. It became evident to the Europeans that Cabo Branco and the Bay of Arguin to the south of it were, with their islands, important trading places.

This news fired the interest of Prince Henry, for whom any slave, black or white, obtained from an African was a slave saved from a fate worse than death; and so the next year, 1443, Nuno returned to anchor off an island in the Bay of Arguin. Here he found an 'infinite number of herons, of which he and his crew made good cheer', presumably in a stewpot; and they captured fourteen men, off canoes which they were rowing using their feet as oars. Tristão and his men made these men into slaves without feeling any need to negotiate their purchase. They later gathered another fifteen captives, the crew regretting that 'their boat was so small that they were not able to take such a cargo as they desired'.[8]

Then a year later, in 1444, Lançarote de Freitas's company for trade to Africa was formed at Lagos. Trade with Africa remained a royal monopoly; so de Freitas, like hundreds of others after him, had first to seek a licence to travel. He was accompanied by Gil Eannes, the first captain to have passed Cape Bojador.

There are several reasons why the Portuguese should have been the first Europeans to embark on these interesting journeys. Theirs, in a sense, were the seas in which the first discoveries were made, even if they shared them with Castile; and Castile, in the fifteenth century, was a country turned in on itself, always on the brink of civil war. The same was true of England, busy fighting in the early fifteenth century to preserve her possessions in France, and in the second half divided by a fratricidal conflict between Prince Henry's cousins. Portugal was generally maritime; her coasts were dotted with little fishing villages; her Jewish and Genoese visitors had endowed Portuguese merchants and captains with a respect for maps, as for magnetic compasses, apparently an Italian invention of the twelfth century.

Meantime, since 1317 the Portuguese fleet had always been managed by the Pessagno family from Genoa, whose contract with the King in Lisbon specified that he should always have available twenty experienced Genoese captains (one of them, indeed, was for a time that Lanzarotto Malocello who rediscovered the Canaries).

The Portuguese were also good shipbuilders. The lateen-rigged caravel was their modification of the Moorish vessel that had long been sailing off North-west Africa; it could sail closer to the wind than any others, though it was less useful in a following wind than a ship with square sails. Portuguese fishermen, too, had been busy off Moroccan coasts for generations. The country had a confident middle class, whose influence had increased at the end of the fourteenth century, when the old nobility had been destroyed in civil wars. The monarchs of the Aviz family, with their bastard blood, had favoured merchants by a series of fiscal concessions, and the curious royal capitalism which then developed meant that Portuguese merchants abroad were really royal consuls. Portugal was far from isolated: there were so many merchants trading in Seville in the early fourteenth century that there was a street named 'Calle de los Portugueses'. The whole country seemed a 'wharf between two seas', for it was in Lisbon or Oporto that Northern Europe could obtain Mediterranean produce such as dried cod, olive oil, salt, wine, and almonds. There were, too, English, Flemish, and Florentine merchants in Lisbon as well as Genoese ones: and as early as 1338 the Bardi of Florence had special privileges as corsairs – to seize captives at sea for ransoms from North Africa.

From 1444 onwards Zurara's history mentions in every chapter kidnappings of more and more Africans by Portuguese captains in ever more southern latitudes. 'How they returned to the shore and of the Moors that they took' and 'How they took ten Moors' are typical chapter headings in the work. Zurara describes the events as if the Portuguese were carrying out a great feat: winning new souls for God. Ca'da Mosto, the Venetian adventurer who travelled with the Portuguese, wrote, a little later: 'The Portuguese caravels, sometimes four, sometimes more, used to come to the Gulf of Arguin, well armed, and, landing by night, surprised some fishermen's villages. . . .'[9]

The technique of these captures was inherited from attacks on Moors in Portugal or in Spain: there was little innovative about it. For this side of the African adventure had not been foreseen by those who began it. After all, it had been assumed that to the south of the desert there was a great Christian monarchy. Yet the early history of the Western discoveries on the African coast went hand in hand with that of a new Atlantic slave trade. This brought money to Prince Henry and other promoters of the expeditions. Sometimes the captures were easy but sometimes, Zurara said, 'our men had very great toil in the capture of those who were swimming, for they dived like cormorants, so that they could not get hold of them; and the capture of the second man caused them to lose all the others. For he was so valiant that two men, strong as they were, could not drag him into the boat until they took a boathook and caught him above one eye, and the pain of this made him abate his courage, and allow himself to be put inside the boat. . . .'[10]

These ventures continued to be private ones, for which the merchant had to obtain a licence from the Crown – that is, from Prince Henry. Most of the new entrepreneurs were businessmen from Lisbon, though in 1446 the Bishop of the Algarve fitted out a caravel for the slave trade (it sailed as one ship among nine). Always these vessels were accompanied by a notary sent by Prince Henry to ensure that he received his fifth of the booty.

The seizure of these desirable African slaves did not delay scientific discovery, for it made exploration financially worthwhile. Thus in 1444 Dinis Dias, a new captain with imagination, discovered the Sénégal, the first great tropical river to be found by Europeans as yet, and by far the biggest which the Portuguese had encountered since leaving the Mediterranean. It was a waterway leading to (for it flowed directly from) the richest of the West African gold fields, whence the 'silent trade in gold' was carried. With the impetuous currents which it caused at sea, the Portuguese supposed the Sénégal somehow to be a branch of the Nile, as did most others at that time, because of its alluvial behaviour in summer. It had been on an island in the lower reaches of the River Sénégal that five centuries before the Tuareg Ibn-Yasin conceived the popular austerity of the Almoravid movement, from which had derived their formidable conquests in Spain and Portugal during the early twelfth century.

The north bank of the river was a territory of Azanaghi; and the south bank, at least near the mouth, was in the 1440s inhabited by two peoples, the Wolofs and the Serers, both with reasonably large populations. The Portuguese thereafter saw the Sénégal, identified by two palm trees on the southern bank, as the dividing line in West Africa, separating the Moors from the 'fertile land of the blacks', in Ca'da Mosto's words. 'It appears to me', that Venetian went on, 'a very marvellous thing that, beyond the river, all men are very black, tall and big, their bodies well formed; and the whole country green, full of trees, and fertile; while, on this side, the men are brownish, small, lean, ill-nourished, and small in stature.'[11]

The whole territory was a pleasure to the Portuguese, who found there something of the promised land which they had been expecting:

cultivated fields, and a tropical savannah, natives very different from those whom they knew in the Mediterranean, offering the travellers the flesh of elephants to eat and ivory to take home. Ca'da Mosto said that the King of the Wolofs was poor, a youth of about his own age, who supported himself largely by raiding neighbours and selling the captives to Moorish or even Azanaghi merchants.

Further on, Dias came upon a green and beautiful headland covered with trees, running far out into the ocean; there the desert came to an end, and the lusher tropics began. He named it Cabo Verde. That is where the equinox also begins, for here the days and nights always have equal length. When, a few miles to the south, Dias reached the island of Gorée (he called it Ilha da Palma), off what is now Dakar, he realized that thereafter the coast of Africa began to turn east.

By this time the Africans were beginning to learn how to defend themselves against the Europeans, using their wooden longboats, made from tree trunks, with considerable intelligence. Being powered by paddles, they did not depend on the winds. One of Prince Henry's protégés, Gonçalo de Sintra, 'who had been his stirrup boy', lost his life looking for slaves on one of these expeditions, as did one of the pioneers of earlier days, Nuno Tristão. A Danish nobleman, Vallarte, the first Northern European to sail to West Africa, who had joined Prince Henry's court, was also captured and killed, off Gorée, in 1448. Thus the promised land was shown to have many snares. Nor was every expedition a financial success: one armada of twenty-seven ships, which had been assembled from several Portuguese ports – Madeira and Lisbon, as well as Lagos – and was captained again by Lançarote de Freitas, spent a long time off the coast in 1445, and brought back only about sixty slaves.

The Portuguese soon began to buy rather than kidnap slaves. A captain named João Fernandes apparently initiated this change, on the explicit orders of Prince Henry. He offered to stay behind on the coast of the Bay of Arguin in 1445 in order to gather information, in temporary exchange for an old leader of the region. Fernandes did remain in Africa for a year, won over the local people, and learned of markets where both slaves and gold might be exchanged for quite modest European goods. A year later he told Antão Gonçalves, who relieved him, that he had met Ahude Meymam, a Muslim merchant, who owned some black slaves whom he wished to sell. Gonçalves bought nine of these blacks, as well as some gold dust, in return for 'some things which pleased the chief . . . (though they were small and of little value)'. Arguin was the centre of this transaction, the first of hundreds of thousands of such carried out by Europeans over the next 400 years.[12]

These events on the West African coast introduced the Portuguese to that interesting phenomenon, the Muslim merchant who was also a holy man. Free, austere in style of life, and as a rule the only literate persons in the region, these merchants were endogamous, self-sufficient, and well informed. Although they were described as Moorish by the Portuguese, many of them were black. They usually lived as a state within the state (whatever state it was), practising strict Islam, and trading black pagans as slaves, rarely Berber Muslims. Belief in Islam implied a useful communion with the other long-range operators. Nothing shows better the cosmopolitan nature of Islam than the discovery by the fourteenth-century traveller (or romancer) Ibn-Battuta in Sijilmasa, in southern Morocco, that his host was the brother of a man whom he had met a few years before in China.

The slaves whom these merchants had to offer the Portuguese were no doubt usually – as most slaves were, in that region as elsewhere, as they had been in antiquity and in medieval Spain – captives in war, or in raids. The Tuaregs had been used for so long to raid the black principalities to their south for slaves that at first sight (even in the nineteenth century) freemen seemed to be 'white', or Berber, and slaves black. But there were always a few 'white' slaves, some of whom would have lost their liberty as a result of punishment for crimes or who had been sold by their parents into slavery. Had the Portuguese not bought the captives offered by the mullahs, these would have been sold to merchants operating the Sahara trade; and one or two of them just could have ended up in Spain or Portugal by that route, as a few slaves from Africa had already done.

The attitude of the Africans to transactions of this kind with the Europeans can only be guessed. The sale by any ruler of a person of his own people would have been looked on as a severe punishment; when African kings or others sold prisoners of war, they regarded the persons concerned as aliens, about whose destiny they did not care, and whom they might hate. For there was no sense of kinship between different African peoples. Such prisoners, however obtained, were the lowest people in society and even in Africa would have been used to do heavy work, for example in gold mines.

By 1448 about 1,000 slaves had been carried back by sea to Portugal or to the Portuguese islands (the Azores, Madeira). Most had been procured by privately financed expeditions, one or two by Genoese, such as Luca Cassano – the earliest example of a non-Portuguese in the Atlantic slave trade, who set himself up on the island of Terceira, in the Azores. To serve the traffic a castle as well as a trading post was being built on the biggest island in the Bay of Arguin (it was finished in 1461). It was a dour place, lying between the limitless ocean (as it then seemed) and the sands of the Sahara, but it had good water and, for a century, it was the most important European gateway into the western Sahara. Arguin was both a revival of the Phoenician model of a fortified trading post, and the forerunner of a whole chain of similar establishments along the African coast. Its construction enabled the Portuguese, in a regular fashion, to lay their hands on at least some of the gold of Bambuk, on the River Falémé, which had in the past been carried across the Sahara to the North African coast. Elsewhere the trade in slaves, as in gold and other things, was carried on, as it would be in many places off Africa for many centuries, from ship to shore.

The indigenous people of these territories, to the south of the Sénégal, the Wolofs and the Serers, were no doubt astonished at some manifestations of Portuguese enterprise: at the boats, for example, some thinking them at first to be fish, others birds, or perhaps just phantoms. But, in the end, the Portuguese wanted to trade – slaves, gold dust, or whatever else might be of interest – and these demands represented continuity rather than innovation. Had not the Arabs been accustomed to exchange Berber horses for slaves? The Portuguese did the same. In the 1450s the Venetian Ca'da Mosto reported, in the first realistic account of West Africa by an explorer, how he received ten or fifteen slaves in Guinea in return for one horse: a price that may have seemed good to anyone who recalled a Salic Law that had laid down that a single male slave had the equivalent value of a stallion, a female one a mare. (But slaves were exchanged in the Oyo empire for Arab horses at an even better price.) No wonder Ca'da Mosto later wrote that he went to trade in 'Guinea' because of the profit that could be made 'among these new people, turning one *soldo* into seven or ten' (his family had ruined itself in Venice).

These exchanges naturally led to an increase in the number of horses in the region so that, by the end of the century, the King of the Wolofs, in his capital 200 miles inland (he was overlord of five coastal peoples), would be able to mount a substantial force of cavalry, even though by then prices had fallen and the Portuguese had often to accept an exchange of six or seven slaves for a horse.

By the mid-1450s other arrangements for this extension of the African trade had been settled satisfactorily, with European goods from numerous countries (woollen and linen cloth, silver, tapestries, and grain) being regularly bartered for slaves. Ca'da Mosto thought that in this decade 1,000 slaves were exported annually to Europe from the African coast.

The Venetian spent a day or two with a Wolof king, the Damel Budomel of Cayor, on the Sénégal, who treated his subjects with arrogance, they being obliged to approach him naked, prostrate themselves, and throw dirt over their shoulders. This monarch always had with him about 200 followers and appeared to have 'good powers of reasoning and deep understanding of men'. In his realm, slavery was often a punishment for even moderate offences.[13]

In a local market men and women crowded round the Venetian, rubbing him with spit to see if the white of his skin 'was dye or flesh'.

Budomel also asked Ca'da Mosto whether he knew 'the means whereby he could satisfy many women, for which information he offered me a great reward'.

Later the Venetian traveller reached the mouth of the River Gambia. This second great navigable waterway of Africa discovered by Europeans allowed traders to penetrate the interior of the continent, for it was deep enough for a ship drawing fifteen feet of water to sail over 150 miles inland. In most ways it is more manageable than the Sénégal, its sister river to the north. The tidal reaches on the estuary were known for their salt, so desired in the interior; while the river flows a long time through a flat land with pasture for both wild and domestic animals. Near its source, also, there were the mountains at Bure, on the headwaters of the Niger, which really did produce gold. The metal could be obtained at the market town of Cantor on the Gambia.

The following year, 1456, Ca'da Mosto returned, and on that occasion sailed up the Gambia sixty miles, his intention being to reach the land of the Songhai. He did reach a town ruled by one of the vassals of that empire, a certain Battimaussa, where the river was still a mile in breadth, and where its lively commercial atmosphere and trading recalled to the Venetian 'the Rhône near Lyons'. He did a good deal of trading, including for slaves, and also accompanied a leader of the Nomi on a hunt for elephants near the mouth of the river. He observed horses in use, even if there were 'very few' of them.

Returning to the open sea, Ca'da Mosto again turned south, and saw further rivers. He did not turn back till he reached one he called the Rio Grande, now known as the Jeba; from there he could see the Bissagos Islands, a major source of slaves for Europeans for many generations.

This intelligent traveller requested permission from Sonni Ali, the ruthless Emperor of the Songhai, to send a mission to Timbuktu, but nothing came of the idea. What interest had that 'master-tyrant, libertine and scoundrel', as he was described by Es-Sadi, the historian of the western Sudan, in trading with white Europeans? His main trading partners were the Arabs in the Maghreb, with whom he could exchange more beneficially his eunuchs and other slaves in much greater numbers than he could sell to the Portuguese in their pretty boats.[14]

At that time, south of the River Gambia, and south too of the Wolof kingdoms, the coastal polities of Africa were small, often only about 1,000–2,000 square miles, rarely consisting of more than one entity, though perhaps with several semi-dependent autonomous settlements. That was especially so in the territory between the Rivers Gambia and Sierra Leone, where the towns of small ethnic groups such as the Baga, the Pepel, the Diola, and the Balante were really overgrown villages, kraals, of about forty houses. There were some towns where Portuguese could without embarrassment talk of the leader as the king. The most usual form of government seems, however, to have been what Ca'da Mosto called a despotism of the richest and most powerful caste.

Always the Portuguese would enter into negotiation with the local rulers, either small-scale or grand, and these became as it were allies with the newcomers, jointly concerned to make profits from trade. These peoples of the region south of the Sahara with whom the Portuguese were in touch were far from unsophisticated: they wove and used cotton and linen, they fished from well-built light canoes (an essential element in economic life), pottery had been practised for centuries, they had recognizable chiefs, and of course they traded. Cotton goods had long been an object of commerce in inland Senegambia: 'Every house had its cotton bush', an observer of 1068 had written, in regard to Mali, and 'cloths of fine cotton' were exchanged, often for salt, the most sought-after product of the coast, in the view of the empires of the savannahs of the interior, where there was none of it.[15] Millet, fish, butter, and meat were also traded, as were dyes from indigo. On the upper River Sénégal, gum from acacia trees was well established in the markets. The fact that the banana, which seems to derive from Asia, had reached West Africa before the Europeans suggests an international interconnection of great range.

In the far interior, there were, and had been for many generations, much more formidable states: above all, the empire of the Songhai, who on the ruins of the swiftly vanishing Mali with her 10,000 horsemen, had by now established an empire that dominated most of the western Sudan. This was one of the most sumptuous political enterprises ever to be established by black people. The capital at Gao, on the Middle Niger, was a vast unwalled city with rich markets where slaves, obtained by razzias from neighbouring peoples, as well as horses, scarlet Venetian cloth, spurs, saddles, bridles, and gold, were all sold – and had been long before the Portuguese had begun to trade on the coast. Like the Mali, and indeed the Ghanaian, empire which had preceded it, the Songhai controlled trade between West and North Africa. As far as slaves were concerned, they obtained them from the land of the 'pagans' – that is, the non-Muslims. There was a boast that within a single day a prince could bring back 1,000 by raiding the south. The Songhai used them on royal farms when they were not selling them to the Arabs of the Maghreb.

The establishment by the Portuguese of a small trading post, *feitoria*, at Arguin, and the export thence of a few thousand slaves, seemed neither significant nor outrageous.

As befitted an imperial people, the Songhai used gold for money, though without any inscriptions; elsewhere, cloth (in Timbuktu, the turquidi cloth of the Hausa city of Kano), bars of salt, cattle, dates, and millet were employed as substitutes. Horses had been bred for hundreds of years; they were to be seen in West Africa as early as the tenth century AD. Cities on the Niger, such as Segu, Kankan, Timbuktu, and Djenné, as well as Gao, numbered over 10,000 people in 1440, some being perhaps as large as 30,000. The Hausa cities of Katsina and Kano, on its high rock, had perhaps 100,000 each. Other settlements had been established along the edge of the forest in the south, such as Bono-Mansu and Kong. All had substantial markets, even if the houses and mosques were mud-built.

The smelting of iron and steel in West Africa was similar to that in Europe in the thirteenth century, before the advent of power driven by the waterwheel. Senegambia* had iron and copper industries, and the quality of African steel approached that of Toledo before the fifteenth century. These metals equipped most African households with knives, spears, axes, and hoes. Goldsmithery was of a high quality: 'The thread and texture of their hatbands and chainings is so fine that ... our ablest European artists would find it difficult to imitate them', a Dutch captain wrote in 1700.[16] It is true that the West Africans did not have wheeled vehicles, but those were still rare in Europe. Nor did they use horses for carrying goods long distances, since they were vulnerable to the tsetse fly in the forests near the coast. But it would be false to depict West Africa, at the moment of its contact with Portugal, and Europe, as lived in by primitive peoples. In many respects, they were at a higher level than those whom the Spaniards and Portuguese would soon meet in the New World.

A new character to Portuguese exploration was given by the early settling in West Africa of traders from Lisbon, including some exiled criminals, who set themselves up on the estuaries of rivers, sometimes making homes for themselves in the interior. A few settled in villages where they took black girls as wives, and they and their mulatto descendants often joined African society fully, taking part in the appropriate celebrations, abandoning Western clothes, tattooing their bodies, and becoming every year less European. These so-called lançados (lançados em tierra, men who had thrown themselves onshore), or tango-mãos (a European trader who had had his body tattooed), were resented by the Portuguese authorities, principally since they were able to escape all the regulations which the Crown imposed on overseas trade, including taxes. But the lançados were in general well received by the Africans, who went out of their way to make them happy: in return they were naturally expected to conform to their hosts' customs. They played an essential part in cementing commercial relations between the Europeans and the Africans

Casual sexual relations seem to have begun early between the Portuguese and the Africans: Valentim Fernandes wrote in 1510, 'If one of our white people arrives at the house of a black, even if it is the King, and asks for a woman or a girl to sleep with, the man there gives him several to choose from, and the whole thing is done in friendship and not by force.'[17]

* The region between the two rivers Sénégal and Gambia.

The slaves imported from Guinea were received, with all other goods from Africa, by the Casa da Guiné in Lagos. An elaborate ritual for reception was formulated, including inspections and paying of duty before sale. It was at that time supposed that the country suffered from a shortage of labourers. So African slaves were soon being bought by bishops and noblemen, artisans and court officials, and sometimes even by working men. By 1460 the holding of black slaves had become a mark of distinction for Portuguese households, as it had been in the past for Muslim ones; and Africans were from the beginning preferred to the 'good for nothing, rebellious and fugitive' white slaves (Muslims)[18] – unless they were black Muslims, as were many Wolofs. Africans, after all, were usually potential Christians. Had not one of the Three Kings, Balthasar, been black?

African slaves began to perform many functions in Portugal: they became ferrymen in Lisbon and other cities, or were hired out for heavy physical labour, as stevedores or as builders, in hospitals or in monasteries. Some slaves were to be found in sugar plantations, though these were not very successful in Portugal: the cane took too much richness from the soil, and plantings could not be repeated. Slaves were sometimes also employed as interpreters in Lisbon and on ships going to Africa; in theory at least, when one of these slaves secured four slaves for his owner, he would be given his freedom.

When it was realized that the Africans liked music, African bands of drummers and flute players were encouraged in Lisbon. These slaves brought to Portugal a little of their music and some of their dances, and many maintained their own language, adapting it to create a pidgin Portuguese, *fala da Guiné* or *fala dos negros*. Some soon adapted to a purer Portuguese – especially, of course, those born in Portugal. Slaves were from now on to be seen at Portuguese ceremonies. In 1451 black dancers performed at the wedding by proxy of the Infanta Leonora, Prince Henry's niece, to the Holy Roman Emperor Frederick III. A slave posing as a black monarch from Senegambia sang in African-Portuguese at the wedding of the Infanta Joana in 1455 to King Enrique IV of Spain (an ill-fated wedding, as it turned out). Some Portuguese masters freed their slaves at their death. Others seduced them (though that was illegal) and freed any subsequent children, sometimes obtaining legitimization for them. Every variety of sexual relationship was practised with black slaves; and a few white women took them as lovers.

Portugal secured approval from three popes for these activities. First, in 1442, the Venetian Pope Eugenius IV approved Prince Henry's expeditions to Africa (in the bull *Illius Qui*). Since other European monarchs had shown themselves unenthusiastic about joining in such an adventure, and since the Portuguese were incurring many expenses, as Prince Henry's representatives in Rome insisted, Pope Eugenius did not hesitate to grant to Portugal exclusive rights over her African discoveries. Then in the 1450s Popes Nicholas V and Calixtus III gave an even warmer approval for the undertakings in three further bulls.

No two popes were more different in manners than these. The first was a great humanist, the second was austere; the first was a patron of the arts, the second was concerned to assist his relations. One was a Genoese, the other a Valencian. But their policy towards Portugal in Africa was much the same – possibly since neither gave much time to the question.

Nicholas V – Tommaso Parentucelli, a native of Sarzana, on the riviera in the Genoese republic – was the son of an impoverished doctor. He had been librarian to the Bishop of Bologna, Niccolò Albergati, whom he had succeeded. No pope since the Carolingian era built as much as Nicholas. He conceived the idea of building a new Cathedral of St Peter, inspired the translation of innumerable Greek texts into Latin, and founded the Vatican Library: an institution that lasted even longer than the Portuguese slave trade.

Calixtus III was a septuagenarian Spaniard, born Alfonso de Borgia, from Játiva near Valencia, a professor of canon law, a royal counsellor, and for many years Archbishop of Valencia, a city which then had an important market for slaves. Borgia had been a severe bishop, but though in no way a humanist he was also known as generous and kind, especially, admittedly, to his nephew, the future Pope Alexander VI, to whom he gave the purple at the age of twenty-five.

Nicholas tried to enlist Christendom to unite against the threat of Islam. When this attempt failed, he issued the bull *Dum Diversas* in 1452, which allowed the King of Portugal to subdue Saracens, pagans, and other unbelievers – even to reduce them to perpetual slavery. This clause was obviously intended to include the natives of West Africa. Nicholas followed that bull with *Romanus Pontifex* of 8 January 1454, which approved what Prince Henry and the Portuguese had done up till then, hoped that native populations might soon be converted to Christianity, and gave formal support for a Portuguese monopoly of trading with Africa – not just the region of Ceuta but all the territory south of Cape Bojador. The conquests in the latter lands were to be perpetually Portuguese, as well as 'all the coast of Guinea and including the Indies' – the last word then indicating, more or less, everywhere supposed to be on the way to China. The bull approved of the conversion of the men from Guinea. It also supported Henry's desire to circumnavigate Africa and find a new way to India, and spoke of the benign consequences to be expected from enslaving pagans.[19]

This bull was solemnly proclaimed in the Cathedral of Lisbon, in Portuguese as well as in Latin.

Between the emission of the first and second of the bulls Constantinople had fallen to the Turks, leaving the Pope the uncontested first prince of Christendom (a Russian cardinal, Isidore, had been captured and sold as a slave after that catastrophe, though he had reached Rome within six months). The fall of Constantinople had one unexpected consequence: it stimulated the Genoese, whose trade in the Black and Aegean Seas was seriously interrupted if not destroyed, to intensify their interest in the West and the Atlantic (Venetian business was less affected, since it had concentrated on Egypt). So the Genoese now financed the development of alum deposits at Tolfa, near Rome, to make up for the loss of those at Phocaea, near Smyrna; they invested in new plantations of sugar cane in the Algarve, in Andalusia, and then in Madeira. Nothing suggests a direct connection between the merchants of Genoa and the Genoese Pope. All the same, the family of that Prince of the Church was in commerce, and Nicholas must have been aware of the interests of his fellow citizens.

His successor, Calixtus III, issued the bull *Inter Caetera* in March 1456. That agreed that the administration of the new Portuguese dominions and interests should be directed by the Order of Christ, the knightly association of which Prince Henry the Navigator was the leader.

These bulls represented a triumph for Portuguese diplomacy: Prince Henry had been alarmed at Spanish interference in what he looked on as his, or Portuguese, waters. The King of Castile had in 1449 given a licence to the Duke of Medina Sidonia, the lord of the port of Sanlúcar de Barrameda, where the River Guadalquivir reaches the Atlantic, to exploit the land facing the Canary Islands as far south as Cape Bojador. In 1454 a Castilian ship bound for Guinea was seized by the Portuguese. The Castilian King Juan II protested. The Portuguese replied that Pope Eugenius had agreed that Guinea was theirs. Prince Henry's diplomats in Rome prevailed on the Pope to say that he knew that Portugal had conquered Africa as far as Guinea: a wildly imaginative concept. They also spread the rumour that it was impossible for any ordinary boat to beat its way out of the Gulf of Guinea and return to Europe. They sought too to reserve all the charts for their own use, and seized ships without a licence and hanged the crews. A Spanish captain named de Prado whom the Portuguese found selling arms to the Africans was burned alive in order to discourage others. Such actions did not entirely prevent Genoese and Spanish interlopers; and Diogo Gomes, sent to West Africa by Prince Henry to establish good relations with the rulers, reported in 1460 that these foreign merchants were damaging Portuguese trade a great deal: 'For the natives used to give twelve Negroes for one horse, now they gave only six.'[20]

All these famous bulls underwriting the Portuguese endeavours were decided upon because of the perceived need to act forcefully against Islam, seen, after the fall of Constantinople, as now menacing Italy itself, as well as Central Europe. Calixtus III bound himself by a solemn vow to recover Constantinople and restore the Christian position in the eastern Mediterranean. He did his best to organize a last crusade to achieve that aim. The schemes of Prince Henry fitted into that plan. All the same, it will always seem surprising that it should have been a pope from Spain, Calixtus III, who confirmed the grand destiny of that country's despised neighbour, in Africa and beyond.

5

I Herded Them As If They Had Been Cattle

'Twenty-two people ... were sleeping, I herded them as if they had been cattle towards the boats.'

Diogo Gomes, c. 1460, on the
River Gambia

THE PORTUGUESE SEARCH for new lands, and the discovery of new peoples and crops, continued during the 1450s, even though Prince Henry's practical mind was increasingly on his business interests in Madeira and in the Azores. Thus an uninhabited volcanic archipelago some 300 miles to the west off Cape Verde was glimpsed in 1456 by the Venetian Alvise Ca'da Mosto on his second voyage, sailing under Portuguese protection.

These Cape Verde Islands became, after 1462, an essential part of the Portuguese enterprise in Africa. The largest of the islands, given the name of Santiago, was soon colonized and cultivated. The beneficiaries of the discovery were an experienced captain, Diogo Afonso, a squire of the household of Prince Henry's brother Fernão, who discovered most of the islands; and a Genoese, Antonio di Noli, Governor of the islands until his death in 1496.

Within a generation cotton was planted. But the main value of these settlements was to hold slaves from the African coast facing them, and the islands established a protectorate over the region for that purpose. They were soon inhabited by mulatto *lançados*.

In 1458, meantime, Prince Henry had dispatched Diogo Gomes, with three caravels, to negotiate treaties with the Africans. His mission was to assure the rulers that the Portuguese would henceforth not steal slaves nor anything else on a regular basis, but would barter for them, like honest men. He was also to arrange for visits from Africans to Portugal. Gomes made his way even further up the Gambia than his predecessors had done, as far as the then legendary market city of Cantor, 200 miles from the sea, completely under Songhai rule. When the news came that 'the Christians' had arrived, many neighbouring peoples sent curious observers, and Gomes was given a vivid indication of the quality of the gold which might become available there. He also received a great many presents, including ivory. He had some curious religious conversations, in the course of which one king, Nomimansa, who ruled the headland by the mouth of the river, boldly declared himself a Christian, without more ado. Gomes, of course, also took back some black slaves. He seems to have gone beyond his own self-denying ordinance not to kidnap: he recalled that he took 'twenty-two people who were sleeping, I herded them as if they had been cattle towards the boats. And we all did the same, and we captured on that day . . . nearly 650 people, and we went back to Portugal, to Lagos in the Algarve, where the Prince was, and he rejoiced with us.'[1]

A new expedition of discovery in 1460, the last mounted during the lifetime of Prince Henry, and led by Pedro de Sintra, discovered a point 500 miles beyond the Gambia, which was named Sierra Leone, apparently because of the shape of the mountain there. Henry was dead before he could hear of this.

As well as slaves, the Portuguese were still interested in gold, ivory, and the peppery 'Guinea grains' which came from the stretch of territory to be known in consequence as the Grain Coast, covering modern Liberia. Portuguese captains negotiated for these on the River Gambia, and Genoese merchants of Lisbon marketed them as a substitute in Europe for the peppers obtained through Venice from the East Indies. As for gold, it could be bartered for easily enough at Cantor, on the Gambia.

The goods exchanged with African leaders were European and Mediterranean, not only Portuguese. Cloth taken to Africa by the Portuguese came from Flanders, France, even England. Damask delighted the Africans. Some wheat was carried from Northern Europe. Brass goods came from Germany – especially 'armilles', bracelets, which began to be made in Bavaria specially for this trade, and there was also a demand for monstrous ornaments of solid brass, and brass pots and basins, often later melted down and recast according to indigenous tastes. Glass came from Venice in the form of beads. Spiced wine from the Canaries, or Jerez in Spain, was also popular, as were knives, hatchets, Spanish swords, iron bars, conch shells from the Canaries, and especially copper rods, for which the appetite of some African communities was insatiable. Candles were as interesting to Africans as they later were to the Mexicans, and many African monarchs became fond of trumpets. Finally, one of the great favourites in many harbours of West Africa in the early days of the slave trade were 'lambens', striped woollen shawls made in Tunis or Oran, which had long been known to the West Africans, thanks to the Sahara caravans. All these goods were easily obtained in Lisbon or, if not, in Antwerp, and carried to Portugal by the ubiquitous Genoese traders.

After the journey of Pedro de Sintra to Sierra Leone, and the death of

Prince Henry in 1460 (he left only eleven slaves), exploration was discontinued for ten years. The Portuguese settled down to the commercial exploitation of the territories which they had already discovered. King Afonso V seemed more interested in regulating the trade which Prince Henry had made possible than in expanding it. He was also concerned with the conquest of Morocco. At the same time, some of the slaves in Portugal seemed for a time to be giving trouble. In 1461, for instance, the representatives to the Cortes (the Portuguese parliament) of the city of Santarém, forty miles up the Tagus from Lisbon, complained that to serve the feasts which the slaves of the town organized to celebrate Sunday and other religious festivals some chickens, ducks, and even lambs had been stolen, and plans for escape had been hatched. So the Cortes forbade the slaves to hold such parties. Preventing black Africans from assembling in groups would be an obsession in Portugal for generations.

All the same, the black slaves of Portugal continued to take part in religious ceremonies, fitting in with the customs of the country – dancing in churches being one of them. There was a brotherhood of the Virgin of the Rosary, a specifically black community, in Lisbon by 1460.

The most interesting economic development was the growing prosperity of Madeira. Sugar cane had been planted successfully there in 1452, by Diogo de Teive, on the initiative of Prince Henry, to whom de Teive was an equerry. The cane was brought from Valencia, which had grown sugar while it was still under Muslim rule. Several merchants belonging to the best commercial families of Genoa – Luis Doria, Antonio Spinola, Urbano and Bautista Lomellino, Luis Centurione – came from Seville to establish plantations. The Islamic advance in the eastern Mediterranean, after all, was threatening the Venetian sugar plantations in Crete and Cyprus; the Crusaders' plantations in Palestine had long been lost to Islam; and Sicily, a producer of sugar from cane for several generations, was also menaced. Portuguese sugar plantations had never fulfilled their promise. Now Madeira seemed the best alternative. Well-watered terraces were therefore built, some by *guanche* slaves, from Tenerife; and African slaves were introduced there at much the same time as cane – the famous marriage between sugar and slaves, which has played such a tragic part in history, being celebrated for the first time in this Atlantic island. As would happen in Barbados and elsewhere in the Caribbean 200 years later, the earlier-established farmers of other crops were driven into bankruptcy.

The sugar mills of Madeira used a modern system of two rollers, powered either by water, men, oxen, or horses, cogged to one another so that the cane could be squeezed between them. That method had been devised in Sicily.

By 1460 sugar was already being exported from Madeira to Flanders and to England; by 1500 the island would have about eighty sugar mills (and over 200 growers of cane) and be the biggest exporter of sugar in the world, producing annually 100,000 *arrobas* of white sugar.* Most planters by then were Portuguese, but there remained a few Florentines, Flemings, and Genoese, while the Lomellino family of Genoa were responsible for the marketing of the product.

Another crop carried by the Genoese to Madeira was the Cretan Malvoisie grape, which led to the production of the great wine of that name – Malmsey wine, to the English – which has never lost its charm, and was sometimes carried to Africa as another export for exchange with slaves.

Yet one more economically promising island under Portuguese rule was soon Santiago in the Cape Verde Islands, whose settlers had gained for themselves the right to collect slaves from the coast of Africa facing the archipelago. They shortly extended their range to include the Wolofs on the River Sénégal. Because of its good security, Santiago would become the biggest slave depot ('factory') of the sixteenth century, and the various tiny Portuguese bases on the coast – on, for example, the River Cacheu – became in effect colonies of that island. But efforts to turn one or another of the Cape Verde Islands into centres of sugar cultivation, on the model of Madeira, were unsuccessful. Rainfall was unreliable, and even the well-protected Santiago seemed at risk to Spanish attack. The little sugar grown on there came to be used exclusively for making rum, which thus began its great history as a commercial product traded on the African coast.

A modest consideration of the philosophy of capturing and holding these new African slaves began too. There was, for example, *A Garden of Noble Maidens*, a guide for young ladies, written about 1460 by Fray Martín Alfonso de Córdoba, an Augustinian friar (who, judging from his name, was probably a converted Jew, a *converso*). This collection of pious precepts was commissioned by Isabella, the Portuguese Queen of Castile, niece of Prince Henry, and mother of Queen Isabella the Catholic, who read it as a girl. On the subject of slavery, Córdoba argued that 'the barbarians are those who live without the law; the Latins, those who have law; for it is the law of nations that men who live and are ruled by law shall be lords of those who have none. Wherefore they may seize and enslave them, because they are by nature the slaves of the wise.'[2] The argument would later be rejected by Queen Isabella when considering her American indigenous subjects. But it seems to have governed her attitude to black and Moorish slaves.

There was one somewhat ambiguous condemnation of the new trade in slaves in these years, this time from papal authority. The intelligent, far-sighted, and cultivated Pius II, Aeneas Sylvius (Piccolomini), wrote on 7 October 1462 to a titular Bishop of Ruvo in Italy (who had assumed responsibility for Portuguese Christians in West Africa) in which he

---

* *An* arroba *was equivalent to about 12 kilos (26½ pounds).*

criticized the slave trade in terms which obviously applied to the Portuguese in Guinea. Taking a position somewhat different from that of his predecessors, Nicholas V and Calixtus III, Pius threatened severe punishments to all who should take new converts into slavery.* But the Pope did not condemn the slave trade as such; he only criticized the enslaving of those who had been converted, who of course were a tiny minority of those brought back to Portugal;† and other evidence about Pius's acceptance of slavery in Italy shows that the Pontiff was not censorious about the institution in general. He was, after all, a great Renaissance prince; the Renaissance implied the recovery of the practices and traditions of 'the Golden Age', of antiquity; and antiquity, as has been amply shown, never questioned slavery, nor the slave trade, on humanitarian grounds. Indeed, it relied on it. Thus painters of the Renaissance would depict slavery as a normal part of modern, as of classical, life. Carpaccio in 1496 seems to have painted a black slave rowing a gondola in his *Healing of a Possessed Man*. The revival of the slave trade was to be an integral part of the recovery of the ideas of antiquity.

On the death of Prince Henry responsibility for Africa and the Cape Verde Islands was given to the Infante Fernão, his nephew; but he was uninterested, as was his brother King Afonso V. The latter eventually handed over the opportunity, and the responsibility, for Africa to a well-known entrepreneur of Lisbon, Fernão Gomes, for an annual payment of 200,000 réis, on the interesting condition that every year he explore another 300 miles (100 leagues) of new coastline. This unusual scheme was remarkably successful. Starting from Sierra Leone, captains sailing under Gomes's direction swiftly found the Grain Coast (southern Sierra Leone and what is now Liberia), and then, sailing directly east, the Ivory Coast (Cape Palmas to Cape Three Points, the modern Côte d'Ivoire); and the coast that the Portuguese at first called El Mina,‡ where they were at last close to gold mines, those of the Akan forest, which had been developed by the Dyula (Mandingo) traders in the fourteenth century; most of their product had hitherto been carried north to Europe by those same Dyulas across the Sahara. The territory eventually became known as the Gold Coast (running about 200 miles east from Cape Three Points to Cape St Paul).

Fernão Gomes, father of a new generation of explorers – and slave traders – was already a rich merchant of Lisbon when he was offered this great opening. He had served in the Ceuta campaign as a boy, as later in

---

* *His phrase was* 'Tum ad Christianos nefarios, qui neophytos in servitutem abstrahebant, coercendos, tantum scelus ausuros censuris ecclesiasticis perculit.'
† *So the* New Catholic Encyclopedia *(1967, vol. 13, p. 264) is misleading when it claims, 'The slave trade continued for four centuries, in spite of its condemnation by the Papacy, beginning with Pius II on October 7, 1462.'*
‡ *'El Mina' may be a corruption of 'A Mina,' 'the mine' in Portuguese, but more likely it comes from 'el-Minnah,' Arabic for 'the port'.*

that of Tangier, had travelled to Africa, and even came to dance well that sad African dance the mangana. When he was later granted a coat of arms he took the device of three heads of Africans on a silver background, each with golden rings in the ears and nose, and a collar of gold round the neck; his descendants were known as the Gomes da Mina.

Further east, beyond the Gold Coast lay the so-called Slave Coast (Dahomey and Togoland, between Cape St Paul and Lagos), though no slaves were taken from there till the sixteenth century. The people had no tradition of maritime activity, because of the heavy surf and the long sandbar that runs parallel to the coast for some 200 miles. Further still to the east, where the land begins to turn southward, lay the dangerous Bight of Benin, into which five rivers ran: the so-called Rio Primeiro (the First River), the Rio Fermoso (the Beautiful, or the Benin, River), the Rio dos Escravos (the Slave River), the Rio dos Forcados (the Swallowtail River), and the Rio dos Ramos (the Creek River).

By 1475 the Portuguese were to be found not only buying slaves in the estuaries of these waterways, for transport back to Portugal or Madeira, but also taking them to be sold to Africans at Elmina, where they were traded for gold – usually gold ornaments, for 'the gold merchants gave twice the value for them obtained' in Portugal[3] – and the African merchants preferred, or insisted on, receiving part of the price for the gold in slaves.

This trading in the Gulf of Benin was managed on the African side by two peoples of the coastal region, the Ijo and the Itsekiri, who bought their slaves at inland auctions or sold criminals of their own community. For a time the leaders of the powerful state of Benin itself stayed apart from, and may even have been unaware of, this Portuguese coastal activity, for their merchants mostly traded with the interior, not with their poorer cousins on the sea.

In 1471 one of Gomes's lieutenants, Fernão do Po, discovered, in addition, the delta of the Niger, and a little beyond it eastwards an island which he called Fermoso, the Beautiful, though it was subsequently called after him (Fernando Po, as it has become known in Spanish), inhabited by a people called the Bubis. Other captains, João de Santarém and Pero de Escobar, discovered uninhabited islands which they christened O Principe (17 January 1472), Ano Bom (1 January 1472) and São Tomé (21 December 1471, first called San Antonio), to the south. They then crossed the equator. Either in 1475 or 1476, the year when Gomes's contract ran out, one of his captains, Rui de Sequeira, reached a cape which he named for Saint Catherine, well south of the River Gabon. By now the verb 'to discover', descobrir, was coming to be used for the first time in connection with these remarkable explorations.

All these journeys were difficult, with currents which assisted the captain during the outward, south and eastward passage, but made the return dangerous; the pole star disappeared near the equator, and near the shores there were mists and many dangerous shallows. The achievements of the Portuguese in these years were therefore all the more remarkable. Still, Gomes, however far his men had gone, would not have been able to fight off Spanish and other interlopers; so it was no doubt as well, for Portugal at least, that the heir to the throne, Prince João, in 1474 asked for, and gained, the African proprietorship. This revived a much needed royal interest in Africa.

The Spaniards were indeed still exploring Africa. Despite the papal reservation of the entire coast to Portugal in the 1450s, Diego de Herrera from Seville, successor to the Medina Sidonias as controller of the three eastward-facing islands of the Canaries, with his son Sancho, had begun to make systematic raids on the neighbouring coast of Africa. From there, they seem to have repeatedly kidnapped Berbers. Perhaps this adventurer made forty-six African landings in all, sometimes, as in 1476, carrying back in a single ship 158 'Moors'.

The demand for African slaves was growing in Spain. In 1462, for instance, a Portuguese merchant, Diogo Valarinho, was given permission to sell slaves from Lisbon in Seville. (Most were originally from the coast between the River Sénégal and Sierra Leone, probably Wolofs.) By 1475 there were enough black slaves in Spain to demand a special judge for blacks and mulattos (*loros*). This magistrate, Juan de Valladolid, himself a black, had previously been attached to the court.

But this trading with Spain was not popular in Portugal: the parliament of the country, fearful of losing control over the new labour force, complained to the King of the practice of selling black slaves abroad. They were speaking in what they conceived to be the interests of Portuguese agriculture. A special use, for example, had been found for Africans in draining marshes. A few black slaves were still working on Portuguese sugar plantations established in the Algarve by Genoese merchants, such as Giovanni di Palma, to whom a property had been given as long ago as 1401, on condition that he plant sugar. But the Portuguese King benefited from the trade to Spain, and sales of slaves continued. A Czech traveller, Václav Sasek, noticed in 1466 that the King of Portugal was making more money selling slaves to foreigners 'than from all the taxes levied on the entire kingdom'.[*4]

The commercial interest in slaves made it understandable that when the monarchs of Castile and Portugal went to war with one another, in the 1470s, the former was even more free with licences to Spanish captains to break into Guinea. Numerous journeys were made there from Seville and the ports of the Rio Tinto, bringing back slaves as well as gold and ivory. 'Everybody was scheming to go to that country', wrote the Castilian

---

* *The names of some of the Spanish merchants concerned in buying these slaves and reselling them (Hernán de Córdoba, Alfonso de Córdoba, Johan de Ceja, perhaps really Écija, and Manuel de Jaén) suggest that they were* conversos.

chronicler Hernando del Pulgar, a friend of the court.[5] On one such occasion, a Spanish captain from Palos, the port whence eventually Columbus would sail to the Caribbean, set off to Senegambia and traded some slaves for a cargo of brass rings, small daggers, and coloured cloths. The Spanish captain invited the African ruler concerned in these negotiations to dine aboard his ship; the African accepted, with his chief advisers and some of his brothers. As happened on several other occasions in the long history of the traffic in slaves from West Africa by Europeans, the guests were captured and carried off to Spain. There the African ruler insisted on his eminent position and talked so persuasively to Gonzalo de Stúñiga, the commander of the fort of Palos, that he was sent home to Africa, and some of his relations were also later exchanged. (But the remainder of these slaves were marched to Seville, a long enough journey, and sold there.) Another Castilian, Carlos de Valera, set out in 1476 with a fleet of twenty to thirty caravels and brought back 400 slaves; he also captured Antonio di Noli, the Genoese Governor of Santiago, in the Cape Verde Islands – for whom his friends paid a ransom. Both the Duke of Alba and the Count of Benavente sent forty-five-ton ships to Elmina the same year; how many slaves they brought back is unknown, but Benavente's captain brought back an elephant, much admired in Medina del Río Seco for many years. A Catalan, Berenguer Granell, and a Florentine, Francesco Buonaguisi, were also conceded licences by the Queen of Castile to trade in Guinea in 1477; while the Catholic Kings themselves sent an armada of twenty caravels in early 1479, under Pedro de Covides. To show the seriousness of the interest, Fray Alfonso de Bolaños was named as special nuncio to convert the infidels 'in the Canaries and in Africa and in all the Ocean Sea'.[6]

These Spanish adventures did not all prosper. Thus, in 1475, one Castilian vessel, crewed by Flemings, set off for Guinea to look for slaves, but the whole ship's company was captured by Africans and, apparently, eaten. The royal fleet, with all its stores provided by the merchants Granell and Buonaguisi, was seized by the Portuguese. In 1479 Eustache de la Fosse of Tournai set off for Guinea on the *Mondanina*, a Castilian ship. He recalled from Mina: 'They led us many women and children which we bought, and then we resold them there' (an early testimony of slaves' being sold, as well as bought, in Africa). The exchange was that two slaves – a mother and her son – were bought in Sierra Leone for a barber's basin and three or four large bronze bracelets; and they were sold for twelve or fourteen weights of gold at Shama, at the mouth of the modern Ghanaian River Pra.[7]

But in January 1480 four Portuguese ships commanded by Diogo Cão, subsequently one of the greatest Portuguese explorers, surrounded the *Mondanina*, and captured de la Fosse and his merchandise. The Fleming was condemned to death in Portugal for going to Guinea without permission, but he escaped and made his way home to Bruges.

All the same, three or four Spanish expeditions a year were

successful in the late 1470s and brought back black Africans for the Spanish domestic market.

Nor were Spaniards the only interlopers: English merchants wanted to enter the African trade in 1481, and were only excluded after a special Portuguese embassy to King Edward IV in London which thereby must be seen as having delayed the beginning of the English slave trade several generations.

The difficult relations between Spain and Portugal were regularized in 1480 when, at a treaty of peace signed at Alcáçovas, near Évora, in the Alentejo, in return for Portugal's surrender of all claims to the throne of Spain, the Queen of Castile recognized the Portuguese monopoly in Africa: indeed, the Spaniards also accepted Portuguese control of commerce in Fez, Madeira, the Azores, and the Cape Verde Islands. Spanish ships would thenceforth not venture without permission into 'the islands or lands of Guinea'. In return, Portugal would leave the Canary Islands, as well as a stretch of African coast facing it between Cape de Aguer and Cape Bojador, to be exploited by Castile.

This was more of a Portuguese triumph than it seemed at the time, and it permanently affected the history of Africa and the slave trade.

Spain saw the treaty both as a licence to fish for her much-desired hake off the coast of Africa, and as an approval to continue Herrera's slaving expeditions in the same territory. There, opposite Fuerteventura, they built a small fortress, Santa Cruz de la Mar Pequeña, which acted as a centre for much small-scale slave-trading in the last quarter of the fifteenth century. Las Palmas became an important slave market. When Diego García de Herrera died in 1485, his sons and his son-in-law continued his work. They did generally keep, though, to the zones where Castile was legally entitled to trade. Only a few ventured to the south to Sénégal. Sometimes, too, thenceforward, Portuguese captains would stop at the Canary Islands on the way home, despite their Spanish administration; and a few black slaves previously taken to those islands entered the Portuguese dominions in that way. After the establishment of the Cape Verde Islands as a major centre for Portuguese trade, both Canary Islanders and Spanish traders from Seville would often go there to buy black slaves (the brothers Fernando and Juan de Covarrubias, from Burgos, for example, would soon have their own factor there). Another source of slaves for Andalusia was the raids which the Christian knights of Castile, especially from Jerez, made on the coast of the Maghreb. Similar raids were made by the Portuguese, operating from Ceuta.

One consequence of importing these slaves was to inspire the Canary Islands to grow sugar much as Madeira had done, especially in Tenerife, capital being contributed not only by Genoese and Portuguese but also by German bankers, such as the Welsers of Augsburg. The first sugar mill was set up in 1484, the islands began to produce as much sugar as

Madeira in the early sixteenth century, and African slaves were soon used there too on a large scale.

One or two Italians sought to enter this tempting Guinea trade by overland journeys. For example, Antonio Malfante, a determined merchant from Genoa, reached Tuat, a group of oases of which Tamentit is capital, acting for the Centurione bank; and a Florentine, Benedetto Dei, who worked for the rival bankers Portinari, set himself up for a time in the 1470s in Timbuktu, selling Tuscan and Lombard fabrics.

The Portuguese, meantime, were establishing themselves ever more firmly on the coast of Africa. Prince João became King João II in 1481, and, henceforth, Portuguese adventure was part of an interesting innovation: monarchical capitalism. João was called 'the perfect prince', and he almost deserves that title, being not only a modern ruler in the school of his contemporaries Louis XI of France and Henry VII of England, but he was also the great-nephew and spiritual heir of Henry the Navigator. In African developments his policies were consistent and far-reaching, returning to the exploratory tradition of Prince Henry, without, however, having to think of the implications for his own properties.

This monarch's first move in Africa was spectacular. In 1481, the first year of his reign, Diogo da Azambuja, an experienced official who had long served the royal family, was dispatched to build a fortress at Elmina on the Gold Coast (São Jorge da Mina), the first substantial European building in the tropics. Azambuja appeared off shore with a hundred masons and carpenters, as well as quantities of timber, bricks, and lime, and above all stone. The purpose was primarily to check European interlopers, but the place was also close to the auriferous River Ankobra, and to a road leading to the gold supplies in the Akan forests. It was on the border of two small local principalities, those of Komenda and Fetu.

King João took the decision to go ahead with this investment against the advice of his chief advisory council, whose members thought the place too precarious. Azambuja had, however, investigated the coast before he chose the site, a promontory at the mouth of the bay. A beach to the east provided an excellent landing place for ships of up to 300 tons; careenage could be carried out to the north-west, on the river. The castle much increased the safety of Portuguese fleets, for ships no longer had to lie offshore for weeks while the African traders bartered slowly; at least on this coast, henceforth, goods brought from Portugal could quickly be carried into the castle, and the cargo for the return journey – including slaves – could be held in store rooms. The stay of a merchant ship could be much shorter. That reduced both costs and the risk of disease. Being on the sea, Elmina had few mosquitoes and thus (though the interconnection was not understood) little malaria. Fresh water was maintained in a brick-built reservoir, with pipes contrived to lead directly to ships' barrels.

The corner towers were solid, built on Italian designs to resist bombardment from, say, heavy artillery. New salients in the form of

Italian-style bastions were added in the next few years. Portugal soon maintained a governor, a factor, and a garrison of fifty troops.

A local prince, Caramança 'King Ansa' – it is unclear if he was a king of Komenda or a nobleman – had been reluctant to allow this establishment, as might have been expected, but Azambuja secured his grudging agreement – a foretaste of many subsequent arrangements between Europeans and Africans over the centuries. Elmina was self-consciously a royal establishment: private merchants were not allowed near it.

A few other, smaller, Portuguese trading posts were soon established nearby, at Shama, Accra, and, seventy miles west of Elmina, Axim, of which the last named was built as a fort in 1503–8 (Shama was given a fort in 1560). Though the justification for these fortresses was the pursuit of gold and the defeat of Spanish pretensions, they were all soon being used as depots for captives, many of whom were held there for long periods. Some slaves continued to be bought from people in the delta of the Niger and sold to local African merchants. Others were held for work at the fortresses: in the smithies, in the carpenters' shops, and in the kitchens.

At home, Lagos on the Algarve was now abandoned as Portugal's main African port, and matters were regularized in Lisbon for the reception of African goods, including slaves. In 1473 a law had been introduced providing that all slaves brought from Africa were to be taken first to Portugal, not sold elsewhere first. The requirement for such a law suggests that many Portuguese captains were really selling elsewhere – perhaps in Seville, perhaps in Valencia. After 1481 all ships setting off for Africa were asked to register in Lisbon, in the Casa da Mina, a converted warehouse on the ground floor of the Royal Palace, on the waterfront. A subsection of this, the House of Slaves (Casa dos Escravos), was founded in 1486 in the Praça da Tanoaria, also on the Tagus, with João do Porto as its first Director. This royal official was named the 'receiver of all Moors and Mooresses and whatever other things which, God willing, may come to us from our trade in Guinea'.[8]

These institutions, influenced by Genoese precedents (and themselves influencing Spain after 1500), were responsible for ensuring that the slaves reached the markets, that duty was paid, and that permits to trade were issued. About 1,000 slaves a year were probably still being shipped to Portugal, though, since the imports were irregular, the figures could have been higher; no records seem to have survived the famous and destructive earthquake of 1755.

The likelihood is that many of the slaves continued to be sold in Castile, even if they were first registered in Lisbon; and in 1489 a

---

* Slave duties were substantial. There was first a vintena, a 5 per cent duty on all goods including slaves; but there was also a quarto, or 25 per cent, always taken in kind. When shippers of slaves began to be charged these duties in the Cape Verde Islands or São Tomé, other duties were charged in Lisbon – for example, the dízima and sisa.

Portuguese merchant, Pedro Dias, established himself in Barcelona, actively selling slaves from Guinea. (One buyer explained that he had bought from Dias a black woman and her daughter, who had been captured in a 'just war'.)[9]

The explorations continued. Gomes's captains had been dismayed to find that after the delta of the Niger the African coast ran south for as far as anyone could see, so that the route to India was still none too close.

In 1486 the Portuguese sent João Afonso Aveiro to explore further the five 'slave rivers' of the Benin coast which seemed to the previous voyagers at once so full of menace as well as of commercial promise. By that time the explorers had learned something of the Kingdom of Benin itself, probably through buying slaves who had the information. The requirements of the slave trade at Elmina also dictated a greater need for knowledge of where the slaves which the Portuguese captains had been buying came from. Ozulua, the *Oba* (King) of Benin, had also learned something of the pretensions of the remote Portuguese monarch who was claiming a monopoly of trade from Europe to West Africa, who seemed to be so indefatigably interested in finding the whereabouts of a certain Prester John (who was of the same Christian religion), and who had recently had the impudence to name himself 'Lord of Guinea' – though the title would have meant nothing to the ruler of Benin.

Aveiro found the 'great city of Benin' a revelation, almost as Cortés, thirty-five years later, was astounded by Mexico-Tenochtitlán. He was interested in the 'tailed peppers' of Benin, which he rightly thought would be a better competitor of Indian pepper than malaguetta. Aveiro was glad to hear of a king in the east, the *oghene*, who concealed himself behind silk curtains and apparently held the cross in veneration, to whom even the *obas* of Benin customarily paid reverence: surely that must at last be Prester John? *Oba* Ozulua, after a talk with the explorers, agreed to send 'a man of good speech and wisdom', the Chief of Ughoton – the port of Benin, as it were – to Lisbon to become acquainted with the Christian way of life.

This Chief of Ughoton did go to Lisbon and returned, bringing to his king an (alas now unknown) 'rich present of such things as he would greatly prize', having agreed, on behalf of the *Oba*, that a trading centre should be established at Benin. Aveiro returned with him to set up this outpost.[10]

A contract to trade on the Benin River between 1486 and 1495 was leased by the Crown to a Florentine banker long resident in Lisbon, Bartolommeo Marchionni. Probably he carried slaves back from the Slave River directly to his plantations in Madeira as well as to Lisbon, and then sold some in Seville, where he also had many commercial operations.

There was one other Portuguese political intervention on the African coast in these days, but far to the north, on the River Sénégal. There in 1486 a dispute occurred in the succession to one of the Wolof monarchies.

King Bemoin asked for help, and 'the Perfect Prince' João agreed to give it, on the condition that Bemoin convert to Christianity. The Portuguese sent missionaries, but Bemoin vacillated. The emissaries were ordered home. Bemoin then panicked, and sending King João 100 slaves begged his European friends to continue their help. Before that could be forthcoming, Bemoin was forced to flee from his throne, and took refuge in Arguin, whence he was carried to Portugal. There he was baptized with the name of João II and awarded a coat of arms. He returned to Sénégal, accompanied by Pero Vaz da Cunha, an intemperate courtier, with the support needed to establish a fortress for himself. But no sooner had they reached the territory of the Wolofs than Cunha accused Bemoin of treachery and had him executed. The former returned to Portugal without more ado. The affair had no immediate sequel.

In 1486 the Portuguese began the settlement of São Tomé, the 'large and magnificent' island, always with 'the benefit of a fine fresh breeze', on the equator, in the Gulf of Guinea, facing the River Gabon. This island had been discovered fifteen years before, by Santarém and Escobar, but it now received a formal letter naming it a captaincy. There were no indigenous African inhabitants. The first settlers were apparently deported Portuguese criminals, but Alvaro de Caminha, the third Governor, took with him 2,000 'young Jews' – that is, children separated from their parents. These were the children of Jews expelled from Spain and enslaved by the King of Portugal since their parents had not paid enough to ensure their residence in his territory. Caminha was also given a licence to import 1,080 slaves over five years to serve the plantations which the Court hoped would be established. Most of these came from Benin or one or other of the five 'slave rivers' nearby. He also brought a few sugar specialists from Madeira.

From the earliest years, these plantations grew sugar cane, making use of the many streams to provide power for watermills. As had once occurred in Crete and Cyprus under Venetian direction, and on Madeira and the Canaries more recently, all used slave labour. São Tomé thus constituted one more stepping stone between Mediterranean and American sugar development: a real harbinger of the Caribbean. In 1500, to encourage further Portuguese settlement, a monopoly of trading slaves and other goods with coastal Africans from the mainland opposite was granted to the colonists of São Tomé; and in the early sixteenth century slaves would also be assembled at the island, to be taken up the coast of West Africa on a journey of thirty days or so to be sold at Elmina (for a time, a slave ship with 100 to 120 captives on board would leave São Tomé for Elmina every fifty days).

Long before these developments – indeed, just after the building of Elmina, in 1482–3 – Diogo Cão, an old associate of Prince Henry, from an old family of the northern province of Tras-os-Montes, the captain who had captured the *Mondanina* in the war with Spain in 1480, set off to continue the voyages of exploration. Sailing south from Santa Catarina, which had been reached by Rui de Sequeira seven years before, he anchored first off the beautiful Bay of Loango, then the trading port of the powerful kingdom run by the people known as the Vili; and next, to the south, he found the colossal River Congo, which he called first the Rio Poderoso, then Rio do Padrão – for he left behind on the estuary at Mpinda a stone or wooden column, a *padrão*, which he had specially brought for the purpose.[11]

After a few months of local exploration, which included some journeys upriver, and some ineffective conversations with the Sonyo people, Cão set off again south for what is now known as Angola.

Leaving another column at Cabo de Santa María, south of Benguela, he returned to Portugal with slaves from there, along with other presents, not to speak of some Mwissikongo hostages, whom he had seized as a guarantee of the safety of his own expedition. He had failed, however, to carry out his purpose of circumnavigating Africa, though it was supposed, on his return to Lisbon, that he had been 'close to the Arabian Gulf'.

In 1485 Cão went back to Angola and sailed still further to the south, this time leaving other columns at a point which he named Montenegro, near Cabo de Santa María, and at Cabo Cruz, in Damaraland. He also returned the hostages whom he had taken on his earlier voyage, and ascended the main stream of the Congo for nearly one hundred miles, navigating the whirlpool known as Hell's Cauldron. After some time, he entered into a complicated relationship with Nzinga, the King of Congo (Kongo), a more substantial ruler than any whom he or his countrymen had hitherto found in Africa. That monarch's capital was Mbanza Kongo, fifty miles east of Hell's Cauldron and about thirty miles south of it. Congo was a Bantu state which had been established in the fourteenth century. The King lived in a palace in the centre of a maze and was attended by drummers and trumpeters using ivory instruments; if he ate with his fingers, he ate well, as did, separately, his Queen, who was customarily surrounded by slaves; when she travelled, they clicked their fingers as if they were castanets. The provincial subdivisions of Congo were sophisticated, and there was a currency consisting of *nzimbu* shells found on the island of Luanda, though sometimes raffia-palm cloth was used as well. The monarchy, a relatively recent establishment (in that way comparable to the empires of the Mexica and the Inca in America), subsisted on a complex system of tribute. The Congo used both copper and iron, and the women made salt by boiling sea water. Slaves were well established as one of several kinds of tribute, but the monarchy had not been tempted to trade them on the large scale which the trans-Saharan route made possible for the rulers of Guinea.

Cão (he may have made three journeys, not just two) returned to Portugal with more slaves, as well as an emissary of the Congolese named Caçuta who, baptized in Lisbon as João da Silva, soon learned

Portuguese and returned with an ambassador of Portugal, Gonçalo de Sousa. The Portuguese formally recognized the Congolese monarch as a brother-in-arms and an ally. They tried to convert the people by sending missionaries and sought to educate some Congolese young men in the fundamentals of Christianity at the Monastery of São Eloi in Lisbon. Craftsmen, agricultural labourers, masons, and even housewives were sent from Portugal to Congo to give lessons in carpentry, building, and housekeeping while in the 1490s two printers from Nuremberg travelled to São Tomé, probably intending to work for the Congolese. Finally, King Nzinga was baptized as King João I on 3 May 1491, along with six chiefs who took the name of Portuguese noblemen.

This conversion represented a triumph of Portuguese endeavour, but did not fulfil its promise. Congolese Christianity was marked by a merger of African with European saints and images, not the conquest of the former by the latter. Another consequence was the development of a new source of slaves for Portugal.

Cão died after his voyages to Congo and so, in the end, it was not he but Bartolomeu Dias who set off in 1487 on the famous journey from Lisbon to find India. Some of the royal counsellors thought that the voyage would be too expensive and that Portugal would do better to continue to trade slaves and seek gold in the kingdoms bordering the Atlantic than to venture into the unknown of the Indian Ocean – if indeed that sea existed. But, benefiting from the achievements of his predecessors, especially those of Cão, Dias sailed straight to Congo, steering clear of the Gulf of Guinea, and left a column at Cabo da Volta (the modern Lüderitz, in Namibia). His fleet was blown round the Cape of Good Hope, and he then sailed north along the coast of East Africa as far as Cabo Padrone (where he left another column) before his crew insisted on returning. Only on his way back did they see that 'for so many ages unknown promontory', the southern cone of Africa.

The main sources for the African slave trade to the Americas for 350 years, from the Bay of Arguin to beyond the Cape of Good Hope, were thus discovered by Europeans five years before the Genoese Columbus set off on his famous voyage. The Portuguese also knew by 1492 how the Rivers Gambia and Sénégal served as connections with a rich empire far inland, and how the River Congo was a colossal waterway. Five years after Columbus's first voyage, the often underestimated East African sources of slaves were also found, when Vasco da Gama, en route for India, stopped at such important future slaving ports as Quilimane, Kilwa, Malindi, and Mozambique Island – indeed to observe that in these 'very large and beautiful' cities a flourishing trade in black slaves was already carried on. Mombasa, for instance, employed 500 archer slaves, much as Athens had once done – except that these were black.

All the same, the Portuguese knowledge of Africa was confined to the coast. The interior was still, and would continue to be for many generations, barred to them by malarial mangrove swamps and impenetrable rainforests.

As far as the home country was concerned, a routine had been established which would be emulated in respect of journeys to America: the right to carry slaves was given to a succession of privileged merchants, who were obliged to pay an annual tax established by the Crown, which was thereby committed to the enterprise.

Part of the reason for the Portuguese success in these early dealings was that they were prepared to act as middlemen carrying all kinds of goods along the coast in their excellent caravels. The Portuguese could thus be seen in some ways as intruding effectively, if brusquely, into an already established commercial network. Leo the African would later describe, in his geography, written in Rome for the Renaissance Pope Leo X, how the kings in West Africa particularly liked rosaries made from a bright-blue stone which the Portuguese took them from the Congo.

All the black slaves traded in Portugal, Spain, and Africa were regarded then as just one more form of commodity, and though prized, not as an especially unusual one. Treaties had by then been established with most of the kings or other leaders on the West African littoral, to whom a succession of Portuguese monarchs would regularly send presents. Portuguese merchants made substantial profits from the slave trade; and though the details are missing, in 1488 King João told Pope Innocent VIII, the Genoese Giovanni Cibo, that the profits from the slave trade were helping to finance the wars against Islam in North Africa. Meantime, numerous African aristocrats or princes were to be found in Portugal at the end of the fifteenth century – probably more so than at any time later.

In Spain itself the institution of slavery was given an impetus by the last wars between Spain and the Muslim monarchy of Granada. Thus, in 1481, the successful Moorish attack on Zahara, in the foothills of the Sierra de Ronda, led to the enslavement of several thousand Christians; in reply, King Ferdinand enslaved the whole population of the nearby rebellious city of Benemaquez. He did the same when he conquered Málaga in 1487: a third of the captives were sent to Africa, in exchange for Christian prisoners held there; a third (over 4,000) were sold by the Spanish Crown to help to pay for the cost of the war; and a third were distributed throughout Christendom as presents – a hundred went to Pope Innocent VIII, fifty girls were sent to Isabella, the Queen of Naples, and thirty to Leonora, the Queen of Portugal. There is a record of a consistory held outside Rome in February 1488, at which Pope Innocent distributed his share of captives as presents to the assembled clergy.*

---

* The fall of Málaga also meant that the well-established Genoese merchants there, such as the Centurioni and the Spinolas, used to selling European goods to Muslim traders (English woollen goods as well as paper from Genoa), had to adapt. Most left for Seville.

After the end of the war in Granada, in 1492, Queen Isabella had several female Muslim slaves in her service; and a traveller would note that the Marquis of Cádiz, one of the heroes of that conflict, had the same on his estates. It was, therefore, perhaps appropriate that the decisive division within the Moorish kingdom of Granada, which led to the Christian triumph, should have derived from the affection of the penultimate monarch there, Abdul Hassan, for a beautiful Greek slave, Zoraya.

The trade in slaves from the Canary Islands was also prospering. Although in the 1470s Queen Isabella had declared the natives to be under her protection and free from enslavement, the inhabitants of the island of Gomera were in 1488 reduced to slavery after what was seen as a rebellion; and the same occurred in Gran Canaria in 1493, when Alonso de Lugo conquered that island and made at least 1,200 slaves of the inhabitants. He probably enslaved even more in Tenerife. The rebellions were scarcely serious affairs, and the punishments were quite out of proportion to the protest. Genoese merchants living in Seville or Sanlúcar de Barrameda seem to have sold these Canary Islanders.

But the slave trade in Seville, in blacks and Muslims as well as in Canary Islanders, was now dominated by Florentines: for example, Bartolommeo Marchionni and the Berardi brothers, friends of Columbus (though there were even a few English: Robert Thorne, Thomas Mallart). In 1496, the Berardis concluded a contract with Lugo after the conquest and colonization of the smallest island of the Canaries, La Palma: slaves, cattle, and other goods were to be shared half-and-half between them and the conquerer.

The dominant personality in this traffic in slaves at the end of the fifteenth century was undoubtedly Bartolommeo Marchionni, of Florence. A member of the Marchionnis who had traded extensively in Kaffa, in the Crimea – a great source of Tartar slaves in the early fifteenth century – he had slave trading in his blood. He had gone to Portugal in 1470 as *garzone*, office boy, to the Cambini family, merchant bankers of his home city, which had many connections with Lisbon, as with the Medici bank: one of the fathers of the firm, Niccolò di Francesco Cambini, for example, had been the Medicis' representative in Naples in the early years of the century. The Cambinis in Lisbon dealt in leather from Ireland, sugar from Madeira, silk from Spain, not to speak of grain from Sintra and Olivenza (then part of Portugal), and no doubt some of their goods were supplied to captains sailing for Africa to barter for slaves. Marchionni, fitting in easily among the other Florentines in the great city on the Tagus, such as Girolamo Sernighi and Giovanni Guidetti, made money in the late 1470s, when Spain and Portugal were at war. Perhaps he was inspired to move into slaving by Antoniotto Uso di Mare, a Genoese who had served Henry the Navigator in the 1450s by buying Africans on the River Gambia; he died in 1462 – while an agent for the Marchionni family in Kaffa. At all events, Bartolommeo Marchionni helped to finance some of the 'Perfect Prince' João's expeditions to Africa. So did his fellow Florentine Tommaso Portinari, much to the disgust of the latter's master, Lorenzo de' Medici, the Magnificent, for Portinari left him many debts. Marchionni then established sugar plantations in Madeira. In 1480 the King of Portugal allowed him and Girolamo Sernighi to be listed as citizens of Portugal, a rare concession at that time. The same year the King sold to Marchionni the right to trade slaves from Guinea and spices for the sum of 40,000 cruzados. Thus began the slaving career of one of the most protean of merchants, the range of whose activity would scarcely be equalled in the four centuries during which the traffic lasted. Marchionni's licence, which included the right to trade elephant tusks, was repeated in 1486, this time covering the Slave River in the Gulf of Benin, and it was later extended to 1495, in return for further large payments.*

Marchionni had agents in Seville, João and Juanotto Berardi, as early as 1480, with privileges guaranteed by the Catholic Kings. These Florentines were friends of Columbus and were later also agents in that city of Lorenzo di Pierfrancesco de' Medici of Cafaggiolo, the head of the younger (and subsequently the dominating) branch of the Medicis. Marchionni had too a representative in Florence (Guidetti), especially concerned with the sale there of 'teste nere', 'black heads'.

In the late fifteenth century the average import of black slaves to the market of Valencia alone was 250 a year. As usual, Marchionni had Florentine agents acting for him in that prosperous city, in this case the brothers Costantino and Cesare de' Barchi. The former sold over 2,000 African slaves between 1489 and 1497, apparently all Wolofs. (They came via Santiago, in the Cape Verde Islands, where the Barchis had a concession.) Some continued to reach Valencia direct in Portuguese ships which, illegally, evaded contact with Lisbon.

Occasionally there were acts of piracy against these slave vessels, and the Catholic Kings even once had to pronounce against some Basque marauders ('Biscayans or Guipuzcoans') who seized a ship belonging to 'our dear' Marchionni, with 127 slaves on board. (The expression suggests that Marchionni's relations with the Catholic Kings were almost as good as those he had with the monarch of Portugal.)

After 1497 the slave market slumped in Valencia, fewer than ten slaves a year being sold by Cesare Barchi. But, all the same, Barchi had successors in the city, who also worked for Marchionni, such as the Portuguese João de Brandis and the Spaniard Antonio Jacobo de Ancona, with slaves from Benin figuring among their cargoes. There were also substantial sales of Africans in Valladolid, Toledo, and Medina del Campo, as well as in Barcelona and Seville.

---

* *Marchionni paid 6,300,000 réis for each year that he held a contract, 1493–5, a 1,000 per cent increase on the previous term.*

The German traveller Thomas Münzer, briefly in Lisbon in the 1490s, reported that all slaves sold in Portugal for export 'passed through Marchionni's hands, being afterwards sold on all the southern coasts of Spain or Italy'.[12] Münzer exaggerated: between 1493 and 1495, about 3,600 new slaves were registered with the Casa dos Escravos in Lisbon, while the number that can be attributed definitely to Marchionni reached only 1,648. Still, he was by then the largest entrepreneur in the field. Marchionni was thought to be 'the richest banker in Lisbon', an intimate of the King, in 'the best position to know all his secrets'. Assuredly, his properties in Madeira used slaves from the Canary Islands as well as from Africa.

Marchionni was interested in everything. He provided a letter of credit to King João which enabled the intrepid Afonso de Paiva and Pero da Covilhã to go to Ethiopia in 1487; he owned the *Santiago*, one of the ships taken by Vasco da Gama to India in 1498; in 1500 he provided another ship, the *Anunciada*, which sailed with Cabral on the second Portuguese journey to India, discovering Brazil on the way (the *Anunciada* was later used in the Valencian slave trade). Marchionni invested heavily also in subsequent voyages to India, and in 1501 the fleet of João da Nova not only included ships partly owned by Marchionni but carried his first representative, Leonardo Nardi, to the East; and it was also apparently Marchionni who suggested to King Manuel of Portugal that his fellow Florentine, already known as a great cartographer and explorer, Amerigo Vespucci, who had been living in Seville as another correspondent of Lorenzo di Pierfrancesco de' Medici, and who had already been once to the New World, should go back there, this time on Portugal's behalf in 1501. This he did; and Marchionni probably financed that great expedition which discovered so much of Brazil and convinced Vespucci, and soon the world, that the Europeans had encountered a new continent, not an outlying cape of India or China. The career of this extraordinary individual is a reminder that Max Weber and R. H. Tawney were mistaken in thinking that international capitalists were the product of Protestant Northern Europe. Yet his personality is elusive. No portrait of him survives, nor does any anecdote which illuminates his character. All the same, it will not seem surprising that, in the next century, it should have been this same Florentine Marchionni who would provide the first substantial supplies of slaves that the King of Spain would allow to be sent to the New World, which had by then been discovered by a Genoese.[13]

AZORES 1427

MADEIRA 1418-19

CANARIES 1424

CAPE NUN

CAPE BOJADOR 1434 Gil Eannes

ANGRA DOS RUIVOS 1435 Gil Eannes and Afonso Gonçalves Baldaia

CAPE BLANCO 1441 Nuno Tristão and Antão Gonçalves
ARGUIN 1445 Nuno Tristão

CAPE VERDE ISLANDS
1456
Ca'da Mosto
1462
Diogo Afonso

Senegal

Niger

CAPE VERDE 1444 Dinis Dias

Gambia

BISSAGOS
ISLANDS

CAPE PALMAS 1460-61 de Sintra

FERNANDO PO 1471 Fernão do Po

João de Santarém
and
Pero Escobar
1471-72

O PRINCIPE O
SÃO TOMÉ

ANO BOM

CAPE LOPEZ 1473 Lopes

CAPE CATARINA 1475/6
Rui de Sequeira

CONGO RIVER 1483

N

Portuguese discoveries
in the late 15th century

CABO CRUZ 1484
Diogo Cão

0   2000 miles

CAPE OF GOOD HOPE 1488 Bartolomeu Dias

6

THE BEST AND STRONGEST
SLAVES AVAILABLE

King Ferdinand the Catholic ordering that
200 Africans be sent to the New World,
1510

THE GREAT DREAMER Christopher Columbus lived for a time on Portugal's plantation island of Madeira, with its then ample population of slaves. He married the daughter of Bartolomé Perestrello – an elderly fellow Genoese who had been a protégé of Prince Henry and was the Governor of the second-largest island of the archipelago, Porto Santo. Columbus had also worked as a sugar buyer for the Genoese banking family of the Centuriones; and he had visited the Portuguese fort of Elmina, on the coast of Guinea, probably in 1482, soon after its foundation – ten years before he made his first crossing of the 'Green Sea of Darkness'. Columbus must have seen slaves in the Canary Islands, working on the sugar plantations which he himself knew well, as also in Seville and Lisbon.

Columbus, therefore, was a product of the new Atlantic slave-powered society, and made evident his knowledge of the trade in Africans in a letter to the Catholic Kings in 1496, in which he pointed out that when he was in the Cape Verde Islands slaves had sold at 8,000 maravedís a head. So it would not have been surprising if he had carried a few black slaves to the Caribbean on his first or second voyage. But there is no indication that he did so, though Alonso Pietro, the pilot of his favourite ship, *Niña*, on which he returned from the first voyage, is said to have been a mulatto; and a free black African is sometimes said to have accompanied Columbus on his second voyage, in 1493. On his third voyage to the Caribbean Columbus sailed via the Cape Verde Islands, and he might easily have picked up an African or two from that entrepôt. Some unrecorded black slaves are supposed to have reached the New World before the end of the fifteenth century, but, again, there is no evidence of it.

Meantime, in 1493, Pope Alexander VI, a nephew of the first Borgia pope, Calixtus III, drew a line across the world to indicate the zone of influence of Spain as opposed to that of Portugal. So what one Borgia began, another completed. The subsequent Treaty of Tordesillas divided the world in a way which influenced it for ever, though the division, setting a line 270 leagues west of the Cape Verde Islands, was disputed till 1777.

Determined to show some reason for his discoveries, and with gold in short supply in the Caribbean, Columbus sent back from Santo Domingo to his Florentine friend in Seville, Juanotto Berardi, associate of Marchionni, the first known cargo of slaves to cross the Atlantic: Taino Indians, and in a west–east direction. These men and women were not natives of Hispaniola, but captives from other islands whom Columbus considered, merely because they resisted him, to be cannibals, though they ate the flesh of their captives merely in order to appropriate their valour to themselves, as they believed. Of this consignment, carried to Spain by Antonio de Torres,* nothing more seems to be known, but Torres returned to the Caribbean and, the following year, brought back another, larger, consignment, of 400 slaves. Half of these died when the ships entered Spanish waters: 'The cause I believe to be the unaccustomed cold,' wrote Michele Cuneo, a Genoese on board. The rest were received by Amerigo Vespucci, then still working for Berardi. The King ordered these slaves to be sold in Seville on 12 April 1495, but next day the sale was annulled, because of doubts about the legality of the scheme. Cuneo thought, 'They are not people suited to hard work, they suffer from the cold, and they do not have a long life.'[1]

In 1496 Columbus himself returned to Spain with thirty Indians whom he hoped to dispose of as slaves. They were sold at 1,500 maravedís each, but the Queen ordered Juan Rodríguez de Fonseca, a young deacon of good family in Seville, already her chief adviser on matters relating to the Indies, to delay the sale once more till the legal implications could be settled. All the same, a few slaves from these boat-loads were dispatched to row in the royal galleys. In the late 1490s Columbus was thinking of sending back to Spain 4,000 slaves a year, which would bring in 20,000,000 maravedís, he thought, with an outlay of only 3,000,000. That Columbus thought that Hispaniola could continue to produce so many slaves regularly suggests that the Indian population had not yet begun anything in the way of a vertiginous decline.

The trade in the Indians never reached the dimensions promised by Columbus, but all the same 300 disappointed Spanish immigrants to Hispaniola returned to Seville in 1499, each with an Indian slave as a

---

* Torres was a brother of Pedro de Torres, cupbearer to Prince Juan, and son of Juan Velázquez, cupbearer to the King: one of the many prominent members of the Velázquez family active at the court of Spain. Another was Diego Velázquez, first Governor of Cuba.

leaving present from Columbus. The Queen was annoyed: 'What power from me has the Admiral to give anyone my vassals?' she is supposed to have asked in anger.[2] In 1500 the survivors were released and sent home, on the Queen's order.

Three years later, Isabella, though repeating that no Indians under her dominion were to be hurt or captured, decreed nevertheless that 'a certain people called "cannibals"' might be fairly fought and, if captured, enslaved, 'as punishment for crimes committed against my subjects'.[3] This was not the first nor the last time a ruler would seem to be influenced by two separate sets of advisers. The Queen obviously had been told a series of tales about the evil of cannibals, who were said not only to eat her subjects but to resist their Christian teaching. That designation 'cannibals' must have covered the slaves whom Alonso de Hojeda and Amerigo Vespucci brought back from the Bahamas after their journeys of discovery along the north coast of South America in 1499. ('We agreed to seize shiploads of the inhabitants as slaves, and to load the ships with them and turn toward Spain. We went to certain islands and took by force 232 persons and set course for Castile.'[4] Two hundred survived the journey, to be sold in Cádiz.) Cristóbal Guerra also 'took and killed certain Indian men and women in the island of Bonaire ... and sold many of them in the cities of Seville and Cádiz and Jerez and Córdoba and other places'.[5] Vespucci returned with slaves from his voyage along the coast of Brazil, and these Cristóbal Guerra also sold in Cádiz, Jerez, and Córdoba.

Among those who remembered these 'Indians' in Seville was the future apostle of the Indies, Bartolomé de Las Casas, whose father had been to Hispaniola on Columbus's second voyage, and who came home at this time.

Very slowly, black slaves also began to be seen in the new Spanish imperial possessions. But this occurred without fanfare, and with false starts. Thus a decree of 1501 forbade imports to the Indies of slaves born in Spain, as well as Jews, Moors, and New Christians – that is, converted Jews. The purpose of this, the first of many Castilian prohibitions on the subject in the Indies which were not fulfilled, was to prevent the contamination of the natives by people who already knew the language of empire. All the same, some merchants and captains privately gained permission to carry to the Indies occasional black slaves, from the large stock of them available in Seville or elsewhere in southern Spain. The first such trader seems to have been a rich *converso*, a silversmith, Juan de Córdoba, a friend of Columbus, and later of Cortés, who in 1502 sent a black slave with some other agents to sell goods on his behalf – clothes, no doubt – in Hispaniola. With Luis Fernández de Alfaro, a former captain of merchant ships, Córdoba would found the Yucatán company which traded to the newly discovered Spanish dominion of New Spain (Mexico). Both were friends and allies of the conquistador Hernán Cortés.

Other merchants who secured licences for slaves in 1502 included Juan Sánchez and Alonso Bravo, also of Seville, apparently both old Christians.

That same year, an efficient and far-sighted, if ruthless and hard-hearted governor-general, Nicolás de Ovando, was sent to the Caribbean. He was ordered to compel the natives of the islands to work: 'Because of excessive liberty', his royal instructions curiously said, 'the Indians flee from the Christians and do not work. They are, therefore, to be compelled to work . . . to be paid a daily wage, and well treated, as the free persons such as they are, rather than as slaves.'[6] Ovando was also allowed to carry with him black slaves born in the power of Christians – that is, those born in Spain or Portugal; and we must presume that some of them arrived because a few months later the new Governor, already in Santo Domingo, changed his mind about them. He asked that their import be suspended, since they not only seemed to be taking every opportunity to run away but were encouraging the Indians to rebellion; and when, in 1504, the Spanish Crown allowed ten years' free commerce with Hispaniola the trade in slaves was excepted, along with gold, silver, arms, and horses – all presumably because they were needed in Europe.

The issue of whether or not to allow African slaves to the Indies dogged the governorship-general of Ovando, and there were several more changes of policy. In 1504, for example, Alonso de Hojeda was permitted to take across five white slaves (that is, Muslims). In 1505 seventeen black slaves were permitted to be sent to Hispaniola, with a promise of more; yet the next year Ovando was ordered to expel 'Berber and pagan slaves'.[7] In 1509 the example of Juan de Córdoba was followed by Dr Diego Álvarez Chanca, an erudite royal physician from Seville who had accompanied Columbus on his second voyage: he, too, commissioned a black slave, Juan de Zafra, to sell goods in the New World on his behalf. Ponce de León, meantime, took some Africans with him in the conquest of Puerto Rico in 1508; and, two years later, Gerónimo de Bruselas, presumably a Fleming, who worked as a founder of precious metals on that island, was given authority to import two black slaves there to assist his labours.

Sugar cane seems to have been already brought, incidentally, in a very modest way, to the Caribbean: perhaps even by Columbus on his second voyage, in 1493. A colonist named Aguilón was anyway growing cane in Concepción de la Vega, Santo Domingo, by 1505; he is said by Las Casas to have ground the cane with 'certain wooden instruments which obtained juice'.[8] No doubt these were brought from Madeira or the Canary Islands.

A decisive change of strategy occurred in respect of slaves in the New World soon after Ovando left his governorship in 1509. Diego Colón, Columbus's son, amiable and intelligent but weak and improvident, succeeded him in command of the 'empire', an enterprise which still consisted only of Hispaniola and Puerto Rico, even if it already had pretensions to the north coast of South America. The native Indians were by then in rapid decline, less from the diseases brought by the Europeans (the first epidemic was that of smallpox in 1518) than from loss of faith in the future and from the overwork to which they were submitted in the mines and fields. Whatever the original population of Hispaniola in 1492, there were in 1510 only about 25,000 people able to work. These Indians had already shown themselves to be nothing like such good workers as black Africans, many of whom were accustomed to domestic animals and who also resisted diseases well. Africans, too, were better able to work with horses than were indigenous Indians, for the Mandingo, the Fula, and the Wolof peoples, at least, had an equestrian tradition. A 1511 report to the King would declare that the work of one black slave was equal to that of four Indians. The gold mines, especially those in the Sierra Cibao and San Cristóbal, both in the centre of the island, preoccupied the Spanish Crown. Diego Colón wrote to King Ferdinand about the shortage of labour at the end of 1509, explaining that the Indians found it very hard work 'to break the rocks in which the gold was found'.[9] The King was annoyed. Only in May, he had given carte blanche to Colón to import all the natives from the neighbouring islands that he wanted: they could be kidnapped in, say, the Bahamas, 'in the manner [in] which they have been brought on other occasions, so that those needed will be placed in our enterprises, and the others be given in allotment, in Hispaniola, in the manner that has been used until now'.[10] A commercial partnership in Concepción fitted out ships for the kidnappings. But Indian slaves did not constitute the answer to the problem of labour in Santo Domingo, even if their price went up from 50 to 150 gold pesos. Many Lucayans, as the natives of the Bahamas were then called, died on the journey to Hispaniola. Other Spanish kidnappings in the still unconquered island of Cuba were no more profitable. The only part of the newly discovered territories where the Spaniards restrained themselves from stealing slaves was the island of Margarita, where they wanted the indigenous people to continue diving for pearls.

So it was not surprising that in Valladolid, on 22 January 1510, King Ferdinand should have given authority for fifty slaves to go to Hispaniola for the benefit of the mines – they had 'to be the best and strongest available'.[11] Then three weeks later, on 14 February, in Madrid, the King asked the Casa de Contratación – the new bureaucracy in Seville which managed Spanish maritime activities – to send another 200 slaves as soon as possible, to be sold in Santo Domingo 'little by little' to whomsoever desired to buy them. The documents signed by the King do not specify that these slaves should be Africans, so in theory they could have been Moorish or even Canary Islanders, but there is no doubt that Africans, though Africans already in Europe, were intended. Henceforth the sale of all such captives would be regulated, as was the payment of taxes (two ducats per head to the Crown) for a licence. Regulation, as always, led to contraband. But the requirement to buy this permit would become an important source of income for the Crown.

This was the beginning of slave traffic to the Americas. Gold in Hispaniola was the lure.

King Ferdinand was not a man to hesitate over the fate of slaves or the slave trade. Despite his grand titles of 'Athlete of Christ' and 'Catholic King', awarded him by Pope Alexander VI, he was a practical politician, not an idealist. As such, he was as much admired by Machiavelli, his contemporary, who saw him as having risen to 'being for fame and glory the first king of Christendom', as he would be by Spanish Carlists in the twentieth century, one of whose polemicists, Victor Pradera, would end a description of what he hoped for from a 'new state' with the hollow expectation that it would resemble the Spain of the Catholic Kings.[12] In regard to human beings, Ferdinand had already deported substantial sections of the Jewish and Moorish populations of his realm, and enslaved many of the latter. He had approved slaving expeditions in the Caribbean for 'Carib' or 'cannibal' Indians. His treatment of his unfortunate daughter, Juana, who was too sensitive to be a princess of that era, was cold-hearted. He would have remembered the participation of Castilians in the trade to Guinea during the war with Portugal in the 1470s and, probably, he had employed some of the slaves then made.

In 1510 Ferdinand was in truth concerned less with the New World than with the conquest of Tripoli, on which he had embarked in order to remove the threat of piracy from the western Mediterranean. He mentioned that engagement in his first letter to Diego Colón about the slaves. He was also disturbed that his unpopular if attractive second wife, Germaine de Foix, had not produced a male heir for him. Ferdinand would have spent little time considering the fate of a few hundred black slaves being moved, as he probably thought would be the case, from one part of his dominions to another. Being surrounded by slaves in Spain, he would have seen no reason why such captives should not be sent to the Americas. Three hundred and eighty-two Muslim slaves had been sold in Valencia the previous year, most of them deriving from Cardinal Cisneros's conquest of Oran; indeed, the capture of that city had even produced for Spanish masters a number of Jewish slaves. 'Indian' slaves were also still to be found in Spain, including in these days some from Brazil, and Canary Islanders were also available.

The chief influence with the King, virtually the Minister for the Indies, was that perplexing bishop and bureaucrat, Juan Rodríguez de Fonseca. Fonseca, then Bishop of Palencia, was empowered to act almost independently in matters concerning the new empire. A protégé of Queen Isabella but an enemy of Columbus as of Cortés, he was a man who put every obstacle in the way of imaginative ventures in the New World, yet who sought to get as much money for the Crown from it as he could. He was cultivated and intelligent, for he had been a student of the great humanist Lebrija at Salamanca, and he encouraged many Flemish artists to Spain. A master of detail, with a remarkable memory, Fonseca would have recalled how in 1496 Queen Isabella had asked him to arrange for some of the Tainos brought back from the Caribbean by Columbus after his second voyage to row in the royal galleys; and how few had survived. He must have known from personal experience in Seville – he had been Archdeacon there at the beginning of his swift rise to preferment – that black slaves were different.

It would be foolish to make this dedicated public servant into a villain, to blame for all that went wrong in the Spanish Indies during the first years after Columbus's voyage; all the same, while he was a power in Spain, the instruction of the late Queen, his patroness, that only cannibal Indians should be enslaved was interpreted very broadly: one had only to declare such-and-such an island as 'Carib' to ensure that the slave trade there was approved.

There were others concerned in these fateful decisions. For example, an Aragonese secretary of Ferdinand's, Lope Conchillos (his signature is on both the documents approving the dispatch of slaves, along with that of the King), a *converso*, worked closely with Fonseca, and he probably saw that the slave trade might be a method of increasing royal revenue; perhaps his own, too. After all, the King of Portugal had made 2,000,000 réis in 1506 from the slave trade, from taxes and duties; and that news must have been known at the Spanish court.

Both Fonseca and Conchillos, as well as the King, incidentally, had a direct interest in the dispatch of these slaves, since they would two years later have groups of Indians personally allocated to them in a new division carried out in Hispaniola which meant – in effect if not in law – a grant of land and mines, since the properties concerned were in the main districts where gold had been found.

The senior official of the Casa de Contratación, the Chief Pilot, was now the imaginative and much-travelled Florentine Amerigo Vespucci. He would also have given his advice on all these matters, for he knew the shortcomings of the indigenous Indians of the Caribbean at first hand. Just a year before, Vespucci had advised Archbishop Ximénez de Cisneros on the question of taxation of commerce with the New World: should goods shipped to the Indies be managed exclusively by a single individual? Or should there be unrestricted trade, in which case how would the taxes be collected? The argument would later affect slaves as much as cloth.

One man who would have been pleased at the King's decision and was concerned in the execution of the policy was the present representative in Seville of Bartolommeo Marchionni, Piero Rondinelli, another Florentine, who had succeeded Juanotto Berardi as the most influential merchant in Seville. Rondinelli by now had interests in sugar in the Canary Islands, in silk, in velvet, and English cloth, as well as in supplying the Indies with dried beef, clothing, and slaves. He probably obtained most of the slaves made possible by Ferdinand's licence from Marchionni in Lisbon: a document in the Archivo de Indias shows that to carry out the King's plans, a hundred black slaves were bought in Lisbon and sent to Diego Colón in Santo Domingo, for he was to organize the sale there. Another hundred were sent direct from Seville in the *Trinidad*, as part of an expedition led by Diego Nicuesa, a conquistador who was lost at sea off Panama – though not before he had delivered his slaves.

After this decision by Ferdinand, a few black Africans were sent every year to the Americas – perhaps fifty annually, and usually in ones and twos. For example, a permit was given to a certain Gaspar de Villadiego for ten slaves, to a colonist named Alonso de Rueda for three, to Juan Ponce de León for another six. There were obviously some remaining doubts about the desirability of this innovation: in July 1510 the King asked Luis de Lizarazo, a conquistador who already held a property with fifty Indians, to explain 'what point there was in carrying more slaves to the New World'.[13] Surely those first 400 granted in 1510 were enough. The King also wondered why the blacks whom he had had sent had died so fast: 'Look after them well,' he added.[14] One or two more white (Muslim) slaves were also sent, as requested by a conquistador, Hernando de Peralta, in 1512.

The advent of black slaves did not mean an end to the local Indian slave trade. Thus King Ferdinand gave approval in a new ordinance of June 1510 to more seizures from other islands of Indians, who were to be brought to work in Santo Domingo; and indeed a steady flow of these unfortunates continued to Hispaniola, Cuba, and Puerto Rico. The Governor of Cuba, Diego Velázquez, sent an expedition to the Bay Islands off Central America in 1516, and after some setbacks onshore brought back 400 slaves. One such enterprise went badly wrong, however: while their boat was lying off what is now Havana the Indians rebelled, killed the Spanish crew, and sailed themselves home – an early example of a successful slave rebellion. The island of Barbados probably got its name from these slave-raiding activities, since the slaves found there, and sometimes sent to Madeira, were unlike the other Tainos bearded.

A few of the first generation of black slaves in the Americas played a part in the next wave of conquests. Diego Velázquez had had a few African slaves with him in 1511–12 in his occupation of Cuba, an island which would eventually develop a black culture more profound than anywhere else in the Spanish empire. Vasco Núñez de Balboa had a black slave, Nuflo de Olano, with him (as well as a dog) when he first saw the Pacific, and he soon had thirty of them building boats on that ocean. Pedrarias probably had Africans with him when he established the first European colony on the American mainland, in Panama. Cortés was accompanied by two or three slaves in his conquest of Mexico, as a picture of him in Fray Diego Durán's book suggests. Survivors of ancient Mexico living in the 1550s later assured Fray Bernardino de Sahagún that there were indeed a number of 'curly-haired' black men among the first 500 conquistadores who came with 'Don Hernando'.[15] African slaves also went to 'New Spain' with Pánfilo de Narváez, the conquistador who sought unsuccessfully to supplant Cortés, and one of them, Francisco de Eguía, seems to have been the first to carry smallpox to that country, in 1519. The most famous black African in Cortés's expedition was, however, a free man, Juan Garrido, who was later known as the first 'European' to plant wheat in Mexico, on his farm at Coyoacán. Later a 'black Moor' from Morocco, Esteban, accompanied Cabeza de Vaca on his heroic walk from Florida to Mexico between 1528 and 1536 – the first serious exploration of North America. Pedro de Heredia also had a substantial body of slaves from Africa when he founded Cartagena de Indias in the early 1530s. So did Diego García, Sebastian Cabot, and Domingo Martínez de Urala in the first Spanish approaches to Buenos Aires.

During these years, following a denunciation of the colonists of Hispaniola from the pulpit by the Dominican Fray Antonio de Montesinos in 1511, a complicated controversy was beginning about the treatment of the indigenous peoples of America. The arguments lasted forty years, and it is much to the credit of Spain that there was such a debate. What other empire can boast such a discussion, and at so high a level? During the years 1511–13 the most searching questions that any imperial nation can ask of itself were at least posed. But the discussion as to whether the Indians were men, and whether it was permissible to enslave them, completely ignored the status of black African slaves, with their greater experience of agriculture, their greater endurance, and their longer connection with Europe.

In Spain, meantime, licences to carry African slaves to the Americas continued to be granted. One was given in 1517 to Jorge de Portugal, son of Álvaro de Portugal, the Portuguese Ambassador to Spain (an illegitimate son of the Portuguese royal Duke of Braganza), and a close friend of the late Queen Isabella, to import 400 black slaves to the Indies. No taxes were to be paid. But it does not seem that this nobleman did much about the matter: Jorge de Portugal was at the time the commander of the castle of Triana in Seville, and was preoccupied with local politics there. His father, incidentally, had been a business associate of Marchionni, so perhaps the idea of his son's entering the slave trade derived from him.

Soon the complete collapse of the population of the Caribbean changed the African slave trade to the Americas into a major enterprise. The great efforts made to substitute the labour of the population of the islands by enslaving people on the mainland, in the Bahamas, and else-where was proving unsuccessful, though some slaving expeditions of the conquistadores in these years continued: Juan Bono, a Basque shipmaster, one of the hardest men in the Spanish Indies, who afterwards took part in Pánfilo de Narváez's expedition against Cortés, mounted a particularly scandalous raid in Trinidad in 1517; and the first Spanish expedition to Mexico, that of Hernández de Córdoba the same year, was sent at least partly to find slaves, perhaps from the Bay Islands. A substantial trade in Indian slaves from the mainland, from what is now Nicaragua, would do something to make up for the shortages of labour in the Spanish Caribbean in the 1530s; but that terrible chapter in the history of America was only just beginning.

At all events, early in the reign of the new King Charles, soon to be the Holy Roman Emperor Charles V, in 1518, the Spaniards in the islands requested their government to permit the dispatch of more black slaves, to compensate for the loss of the indigenous population. These requests came both from the hard-bitten leaders of the deeply distressed colony on the main Spanish island, Hispaniola, and from those who might at first sight have seemed to be among the most liberal of Spaniards. For example, in January 1518 Judge Alonso Zuazo, who was seriously concerned about the fall in the Indian population, wrote to Charles V about ways to increase the workers of the New World. He said that the land there was the best in the world, 'where there is neither cold nor too much heat nor anything to complain of. Everything is green, and everything grows, just as when Christ, in the great Augustan peace, came to redeem the old world.' Now, the judge went on unctuously to say, there was something similar in the arrival of Charles, who could redeem the New World. Zuazo's recommendation was that a general licence should be given for the 'import of *negros*, ideal people for the work here, in contrast to the natives, who are so feeble that they are only suitable for light work'. It was foolish, Zuazo added, to suppose that, if brought there, 'these blacks would rebel: after all, there is a widow in the isles belonging to Portugal [Madeira, no doubt] who has 800 slaves. Everything depends on how they are governed. I found on coming here that there were some robber blacks, others having fled to the mountains. I whipped some, cut the ears off others and, in consequence, there are no more complaints.' Zuazo added that already there were excellent plantations of sugar cane. Some grew cane as thick as a man's wrist. How wonderful it would be if large factories for making sugar could also be built![16]

A similar request for black slaves was made by the four Jeronymite priors who were, most surprisingly, the Crown's governors in the islands at that time. One of these holy men, Fray Manzanedo, wrote to Charles V that 'all the citizens of Hispaniola demand Your Majesty to give them a licence to be able to import blacks, because the Indians are insufficient to sustain them in the island'.[17] He argued that as many women should be sent as men, and they had to be *bozales* – that is, slaves straight from Africa – for slaves bred in Castile might turn out rebellious. They had to come from 'the best territories' in Africa, by which he meant anywhere south of the River Sénégal, in order to avoid any Muslim taint.

These requests were strongly supported by Fray Bartolomé de las Casas, already the self-constituted advocate of the interests of the indigenous population. His desire to protect the Indians from ill-treatment blinded him for many years to the need to guard against similar mistreatment of Africans. Like all enlightened men of his time, he believed that an African enslaved by Christians was more fortunate than an African in domestic circumstances.

At first, Las Casas was concerned to send a few – twenty only – of the slaves who were already in Seville to the Americas, rather than pursue new ones in Africa, as recommended by his colleagues. Later, however, he would suggest larger numbers: thus in 1535 he sent a letter to the King saying that 'the remedy of the Christians is this, that His Majesty should think it right to send to each one of the islands 500 or 600 blacks or whatever other number seems appropriate'.[18] Only later still, in the 1550s, when writing his *Historia de las Indias*, did he explain that he had realized that it was wrong to seek to replace one form of slavery with another – though the book was not published for another 350 years.[19]

King Charles accepted the recommendations of Zuazo, Las Casas, and the priors. The court was then at Saragossa, the King being eager to placate the Aragonese. Subsequently the most conscientious of Holy Roman Emperors, Charles was at that time only eighteen years old. So far as policy in the Americas was concerned, he was in the hands of his advisers. Of these, the closest with regard to the Indies was still the implacable, ubiquitous, meticulous, and indefatigable Rodríguez de Fonseca, who had by now become Bishop of Burgos.

The consequence was that on 18 August 1518 permission to import black slaves into the New World was granted to a friend of the King's, one of those clever Flemish courtiers who inspired such suspicion among Spaniards, Lorenzo de Gorrevod (Laurent de Gouvenot, or Garrebod), Governor of Bresse in Burgundy, and the Emperor's major-domo.[20] He was born a Savoyard, having been brought, with other counsellors of the Crown, to the Low Countries by the Emperor's aunt, the Regent Margaret, who had previously been married to Count Philibert of that Alpine territory. 'The second most avaricious of the Flemings', as he was considered by the Spaniards, he had wanted to receive, as a perpetual fief for himself, the whole of the new territory of New Spain, Mexico, which Cortés was about to offer to the Emperor. But, as a compensation for not receiving that grant he was now to be allowed to import no fewer than 4,000 blacks, direct from Africa, if need be, into the new territories of the Spanish empire. A subsequent document (signed by the King, Fonseca, and secretaries Cobos and García de Padilla) told the royal officials not to collect taxes on the import of these slaves.

The background of this decision, like that of King Ferdinand in 1510 to allow a mere 400 slaves to be taken to the New World, is difficult to reconstruct. No surviving document describes any discussion, no chronicler dwells on the matter, nothing suggests that any courtier or adviser, nobleman or merchant, disagreed.* There was certainly some opposition among Spaniards such as Las Casas to the grant of such a licence to a foreigner; but not about the principle of the policy. The King signed the document approving Gorrevod's contract, but if he thought twice about the matter he would have considered that he was acting to save the lives of American Indians by agreeing to the petitions of the eloquent Las Casas and of the Jeronymite priors.

Gorrevod was interested in the money to be made from his licence, not in the actual consequences, good or evil. He immediately sold his privilege to Juan López de Recalde, the Treasurer of the Casa de Contratación in Seville. That official resold it in turn to others, using Alonso Gutiérrez, Treasurer of Madrid, as an intermediary. The final buyers were, predictably, a group of Genoese merchants established in Seville, by now so experienced in Spanish commerce. They bought the rights for 25,000 ducats – that is, six ducats a slave. These Genoese were Domingo de Forne (Fornes), who acquired the right to carry 1,000 slaves, Agustín de Ribaldo (Vivaldo), a nephew of the rich Cypriot Ribaldos, and Fernando Vázquez, who were jointly able to carry 3,000 slaves. These merchants named as their agents Juan de la Torre, of Medina del Campo, the greatest of Castilian internal markets; Gaspar Centurione (another Genoese, though a Castilianized one); and Juan Fernández de Castro, of Seville.

This first major consignment of slaves for the Americas was thus in every sense a European enterprise: the grant of the Flemish-born Emperor was to a Savoyard, who sold his rights, through a Castilian, to Genoese merchants – who, in turn, would of course have to arrange for the Portuguese to deliver the slaves. For no Spanish ship could legally go to Guinea, the monarchs of the two countries were then allies; and anyway only the Portuguese could supply slaves in that quantity.

This grant was not for an absolute monopoly: many minor licences to carry slaves to the Indies continued to be given; for example, Álvaro Pérez Osorio, Marquis of Astorga, also obtained a licence in 1518 to send 400 black slaves to the New World – which permission he too sold to Genoese bankers.

Some of these slaves were destined for the new sugar farms. The planter Aguilón, who already had such a farm on Santo Domingo in 1505, had been by now joined by others, assisted by sugar masters from the Canary Islands; the historian Gonzalo Fernández de Oviedo brought back some sugar to show to King Ferdinand in 1515, on his deathbed; for it was beginning to be found that sugar cane could be grown in

---

* In addition to the signatures indicated in the text, there is a note following the Yo el Rey: 'Señaladas [signed by] de obispo y de Don García de Padilla . . .' The obispo (bishop) must be Fonseca, and in similar documents that is made explicit.

the Caribbean as easily as the indigenous crops of the country. Cristóbal de Tapia (Cortés's enemy in 1522) applied from Santo Domingo to import fifteen slaves to work on his new sugar mill there – a vertical three-roller mill, powered by oxen.* By the 1530s Santo Domingo would have the luxury of thirty-four such mills, all worked primarily by Africans and three owned by Genoese (Vivaldo Fornes, Jacome de Castellón, and Esteban Justiniani), all of whom had been concerned in trading slaves also.

Later grants allowed the sugar industry to start up in Puerto Rico: the first mill was built there in 1523 by Tomás de Castellón, a brother of the pioneer in Santo Domingo, in what was then called the plains of San Germán, now Añasco, which was from the beginning worked by slaves. (By 1530 there were nearly 3,000 slaves on that island, and only 327 whites.) There was at least one sugar mill in Jamaica by 1527, founded by the second governor, Francisco de Garay, while the first mill in Mexico seems to have been established by Hernán Cortés in 1524. Again, Genoese were concerned in both furnishing the slaves for this property and in selling the sugar produced.

Mines also demanded slaves. In 1524 permission was granted to import 300 African slaves into Cuba to work in the gold mines at Jagua. That the Church of Rome was as interested in importing Africans as any conquistador can be seen from a petition of the Bishop of Puerto Rico and Inquisitor-General of the Indies, Alonso Manzo, for permission to bring in twenty blacks. This was granted. Their task was to dig for gold, required to finance the projected Cathedral of San Juan (which they would also help to build). Franciscans and priests also often had black slaves as servants. So did simple conquistadores. Time and again we hear how this or that adventurer arrived with 'his horses and slaves', ready for some unexpected homeric contest.

Another important colonial enterprise which involved the use of black slaves was a fantastic scheme of Las Casas for the north coast of South America. The plan was that forty Spanish colonists should set off with ten black slaves each, to avoid any temptation of misusing Indians. The idea was approved, but most of the settlers were dispersed in the Caribbean before they reached the intended site of the colony. Those who did go were all slaughtered, with their slaves, by Indians who had not yet learned to distinguish between good and bad Spaniards.

Gorrevod's grant for the transport of slaves ran out in 1526. The Spanish Crown's preference was still to give licences to specific merchants, along with, sometimes, the benefit of not paying the usual taxes. So Charles V granted his new secretary, Francisco de los Cobos, a licence to send to the Indies, including to New Spain, 200 black slaves, exempt from all import charges. Of course, no one expected that that

---

* *It seems probable that this three-roller mill was invented by Pietro Speciale in Sicily.*

permission would be taken advantage of by Cobos in person. Sure enough, he sold it to two German merchants then in Seville, Jerónimo Sayles (Hieronymous Seyler, or Seiler) and Enrique Guesler (Heinrich Ehinger), both of Constance, who were the representatives of the famous bankers of Augsburg, the Welsers; and to three more Genoese (Leonardo Cataño, Batista Justiniani, and Pedro Benito de Bastiniano). The two Germans were also the beneficiaries of a new, larger licence granted by the Emperor in February 1528, to import 4,000 further slaves over the next four years to be sold at forty ducats each. That was the year when the Welsers also received a commission to govern the territory known as New Andalusia, now Venezuela, as a partial repayment of the Emperor's debts to them.

Sayles and Guesler paid 20,000 ducats for this second privilege, but the usual Portuguese middlemen (the principal being a factor in Santo Domingo, Andrea Ferrer) delivered Africans whom the Spaniards thought inferior, and there were not enough of them. Licenciado Serrano wrote in 1530: 'The Germans bring in very bad blacks, so much so that, despite the great necessity that we have for them, no one buys.'[21]

This setback was followed by a monopoly contract granted to one only of the two Germans, Guesler, though he was soon associated with a citizen of the mercantile city of Medina del Campo, Rodrigo de Dueñas. But his deliveries still did not satisfy the settlers of Santo Domingo. The Bishop of the colony wrote in 1530 to the King in Castile that the survival not just of his island but that of Puerto Rico and Cuba depended on the availability of African slaves; he suggested that the colonies be allowed to import them without licences.

For a time there was no attempt to limit the market. Already in 1527, Alfonso Núñez, a merchant of Seville, in the name of Comendador Alonso de Torres of Lisbon, undertook to sell to Luis Fernández de Alfaro, a friend of Hernán Cortés, one hundred black slaves, of whom four-fifths had to be men, the rest women. They would be procured in Santiago, in the Cape Verde Islands, and, after being taken to Spain, sold in Santo Domingo. Two years later Fernández de Alfaro himself sent to buy slaves in the Cape Verde Islands, for he had a contract with Juan Gutiérrez of San Salvador, Triana, to supply another hundred blacks for Santo Domingo. Actually, a Portuguese decree of 1512 had ordered that all slaves procured in the Cape Verde Islands or elsewhere had to be sent direct to Lisbon, but that rule, like so many emanating from that capital, was often ignored, as innumerable licences issued at the Casa de Contratación in Seville suggest. Then in 1530 a well-known lawyer from Seville, himself experienced in the Caribbean, Alonso de Parada, proposed to the King a new policy: that he should regularly arrange to buy from his brother monarch in Portugal all the slaves who were needed in the Spanish empire (to begin with, about 4,000 slaves) and ship half of them to Hispaniola, 1,500 or 1,600 to Cuba, and the remainder to Jamaica. Half of the total should be women, so that the men should feel at home and perpetuate themselves in the New World.

Nothing was decided, and so the way was open for a series of slave merchants based in Seville. The first of these was Juan de la Barrera, who, returning from the Indies to Seville about 1530, already wealthy from the sale of cloth and food, became after the collapse of the German monopoly one of the richest men in his home city, with factories (that is, deposits) for slaves as well as other goods, in Cartagena de Indias, Peru, Honduras, Cuba, and New Spain. Unlike nearly all other slave merchants, he himself made the regular Seville–Cape Verde–Veracruz journey in one of his own boats.

De la Barrera's itineraries point to an important change. Up till now, most African slaves were taken from Europe to the Americas. But one ship, *Nuestra Señora de Begoña*, belonging to the Genoese Polo de Espindola of Málaga, left São Tomé in 1530 with 300 slaves direct for Hispaniola, and there were no doubt others. Characteristically for a significant innovation relating to the slave trade, there was a lawsuit about details of the matter: Espindola sued Esteban Justiniani, the local representative of the Genoese Agustín de Vivaldo, one of the residuary buyers of Gorrevod's licence, who took the matter to the Council of the Indies.[22] This case concerned rich men: Vivaldo was by then the Crown banker in Seville; and Justiniani was a pioneer of sugar in Santo Domingo.

From then on the slaves taken to the Spanish empire usually came direct from Africa. King João III of Portugal gave explicit permission to captains to ship slaves both from the Cape Verde Islands and from São Tomé to the Americas. He does not seem to have hesitated a moment before agreeing to this, any more than Ferdinand had vacillated in 1510 about arranging for slaves to be sent to Hispaniola. In 1533 nearly 500 slaves were so taken, direct from São Tomé to the Spanish Indies, and in 1534 about 650 travelled thus, even though at that time the royal factor at São Tomé was still sending over 500 slaves a year to Elmina and 200 or 300 a year to Lisbon. These voyages were carried through, even though rules had been written against the shipment of slaves born in Europe to the Spanish Indies, since those slaves were now supposed to be potentially a liability.

Thereafter black slaves, linked to their masters, would play an even more decisive part in European ventures in the Americas. Diego de Ordaz, before his journey to the River Orinoco, received formal permission to carry slaves with him; his one-time comrade in Mexico, Francisco de Montejo, obtained a licence for a hundred slaves for use in his conquest of Yucatán. When Francisco Pizarro received royal backing for his expedition to Peru he had a licence to take two African slaves for his personal use, and to carry with him fifty African slaves (a third to be women). One of these was Juan Valiente, who rose to become a commander in the conquest; and an African assistant master of artillery was allowed the title of captain. Titu Cusi, son of the Inca Manco, thought that in the Incas' determined effort to set fire to the thatched roof of their palace of Suntur Huasi in Cuzco during the siege of 1536, African slaves stationed on the roof extinguished the flames, even if others thought that the Virgin Mary herself was responsible, with the help of the Archangel Michael.

Between 1529 and 1537 the Crown gave over 360 licences to carry slaves to Peru from Africa, most of them to Pizarro and his immediate family. When Pedro de Alvarado went down to Peru from Guatemala in 1534 to try to share in the plunder of the new zone of opportunity he took with him 200 Africans, and probably most of them stayed there after he had been bought out of the adventure by Diego de Almagro. In 1536 400 new slaves from Africa were reported to have embarked for Peru in the previous six months; 150 Africans accompanied Diego de Almagro to Chile in 1535; and one or two at least were with Pedro de Valdivia on his later journey there. In 1536, when the President of the Audiencia (Supreme Court) in Hispaniola was prevailed on to send help to the Pizarros, who were besieged by the Inca Manco, '200 Spanish-speakirg blacks' who were 'very good at fighting' were sent.[23] The same year we find the ex-Vicereine María de Toledo receiving a licence for 200 slaves, of whom a third were to be women: that seems to have been the largest single consignment until then though the next year two bankers, Cristobal Franquesini (born in Lucca) and Diego Martínez (a Portuguese), secured licences for 1,000 slaves and 1,500 respectively.[24]

Another Peruvian conquistador, Hernando de Soto, received a licence to take fifty slaves on his doomed journey to Florida in 1537. (Menéndez de Avilés would take 500 in 1565, on his successful one.) Coronado also had African slaves with him on his journey to the 'seven cities of Cibola' in 1540.

The provision of slaves for the New World was now becoming what it was to be, in ever-increasing dimensions, for the next 350 years: a source of profit for the merchant as well as for the Crown. One could buy slaves in Europe or Africa for forty-five or fifty pesos, and sell them in America for at least double that. Prices were increased in the New World because of the taxes; but despite denunciations of frauds by the Court in Spain, merchants and local officials turned a blind eye to the regulations, making the numbers of slaves imported as difficult to establish for the Crown as, later, for the historian. In consequence, Hispaniola seemed 'a new Guinea' to Fernández de Oviedo in the 1530s: there were more people of African blood there than Spanish.[25]

Friendships of a kind were sometimes formed, in these early days of the history of European America, between the Spaniards and their African slaves. For in Peru, as in Mexico, the blacks sometimes identified themselves with their Spanish masters, who came to rely on them in many battles against the Indians. The slave of Almagro, Margarita, was wonder-fully loyal to her master, who freed her on his death. When Francisco Hernández Girón rebelled against the Viceroy in Peru in 1553, his first re-cruits were also African slaves. In the Caribbean an understanding of a sort was created between black and white in consequence of the fierce attacks made, particularly in Puerto Rico, by Caribs from the Lesser Antilles. Raids by French 'pirates', on towns and farms near the coasts, in Cuba as in Santo Domingo, also inspired good relations between masters and slaves.

There were, however, several dangerous signs. The first major slave rebellion of black Africans in the New World took place in Hispaniola in 1522. The slaves were then seeking to escape rather than to overthrow the Spanish community. More radical motives were to be found among the black slaves who sought to inspire the Zapotecs in Mexico to fight the Spaniards in 1523. These rebels were justly celebrated by romantically minded Spaniards, such as the poet Juan de Castellanos, as excellent fighters:

> Clever are these Wolofs and brave,
> With the vain hope of becoming knights

There was another rebellion in Santo Domingo in 1533, when the few surviving local Indians rose against the Spaniards under a chief known as Henríquez, and many Africans joined them. The subsequent guerrilla war lasted ten years. There was a similar revolt in Puerto Rico in 1527. In 1529 the new city of Santa Marta, founded by Rodrigo de Bastidas on what is now the coast of Colombia, was destroyed in a revolt of African slaves. A conspiracy of blacks in New Spain in 1537 led the Viceroy Mendoza to demand a suspension of the dispatch of the new slaves whom he had earlier requested. Smaller revolts were reported at Carta-gena in 1545, Santo Domingo again in 1548, and Panama in 1552. All these rebellions were in the end crushed, brutally, but in all these instances a few Africans escaped into the forests of America, eventually to mix, or fight, with the indigenous people. By 1550, in Mexico, a well-known group of escaped slaves lived as robbers in forests near the mines of Tornacustla, thus beginning a long history of banditry in Mexico.

The indigenous people of the New World did not find the concept of slavery an innovation: slaves, with something close to the European defi-nition of the term, were well known in Mexico, Peru, and most of the other major societies. It was one of the many, to the conquistadores, comforting similarities between the two systems of living. Slaves in old Mexico, for example, may have constituted a tenth of the population, almost all obtained by capture in war. These captives were primarily required for human sacrifice. They also played a part in agriculture in the coastal regions rather than in the valley of Mexico. True, there were no slaves on the large islands of the Caribbean. But the Caribs, in the Lesser

Antilles, employed their captives as slaves; and when some of them began after 1530 to attack the Spanish settlements in, for example, Puerto Rico, they often carried off black slaves and used them in their own communities. Perhaps there were in consequence as many as 2,000 African slaves in Carib hands in 1612.

Some of the peoples in Brazil and Central America, such as the Tupi or the Cueva Indians, had slaves, too, always secured as captives in war.

Still, and despite the use of slaves for human sacrifices, the conquistadores knew perfectly well that there was a difference between the way the Indians and they themselves thought of slaves: the first judges in the Audiencia of New Spain in 1530 pointed this out in a letter to Charles V when they wrote that servitude in ancient America was very different from what it was in Europe: for 'they treat slaves as relations, while the Christians treat them as dogs'.[26]

The shortage of available slaves in the Americas meant that despite the regulations, and the preference for Africans, a few 'white slaves', Moors, were also shipped. Licences to import females of this people were indeed granted in the 1530s: to Rodrigo Contreras, Governor of Nicaragua, in 1534; to a certain Rodrigo Zimbrón in Mexico; to the widowed sister-in-law of Bartolomé de Las Casas; and to Hernando, brother of the conquistador Pizarro.

As for Portugal in America, Pedro Álvares Cabral had in 1500 discovered Brazil on the second Portuguese voyage to India; Marchionni, who owned one of the ships in the fleet, even wrote that Cabral had 'discovered a new world'.[27]

Brazil was at first not much appreciated, for it was considered unimportant in Portugal, offering nothing but slaves and redwood. Still, the first were perfectly acceptable: thus the ship *Bretoa*, returning to Portugal from Brazil in 1511, listed thirty-five indigenous slaves along with the parrots, jaguar skins, and brazilwood. Naturally, Marchionni was a partner, with a New Christian, Fernão de Noronha, in the ship's outfitting. Eighty-five Brazilian slaves were sold in Valencia in 1515–16 by a specialist in such men, Juan Miguel Dabues, as well as a few slaves from the real India, not the Indies, brought back from round the Cape of Good Hope by Portuguese shippers. Sebastian Cabot, then sailing on behalf of the King of Spain, also kidnapped the four sons of a chief of the Carijó Indians in the region of the River Plate and maintained them as slaves in his house in Seville in the late 1520s.

Still, the pattern of the future of the great dominion was being established, for a little sugar was grown in Brazil before 1520, the first sugar technician had been ordered for Brazil by 1516, and there may even have been two or three small mills there by then.

Only after 1530, however, did the Portuguese begin to contemplate conquering Brazil. King João III might well have taken no initiative to promote settlements there, based on captaincies allocated to individual leaders, had he not been afraid of French involvement, much as the British established Nigeria in the late nineteenth century in order to avoid French colonization. In Brazil, France did tenuously establish herself at Rio de Janeiro during the 1540s, in a colony which she curiously named 'La France Antarctique'. French traders in redwood, such as captains serving the Viscount of Dieppe, the remarkable shipbuilder Jean Ango, were as common a sight on these coasts for a time as their Portuguese colleagues, for the red dye obtained from brazilwood was fashionable at the cultivated court of François I. But in 1530 King João, by one of those extraordinarily impudent actions of which Europeans were capable in the sixteenth century, divided the 3,000 miles of coast in Brazil to which he thought he was entitled under the Treaty of Tordesillas between fourteen grantees, who would establish there their captaincies; as indeed they did.

The import of Africans into the 'Land of the True Cross', as Brazil was first known, was in the early days small-scale: the Portuguese had at their disposal during this period native Indians, who cut the logs for the commerce in redwood with great energy, entranced by the contact with metal tools. There was a flourishing 'factory', where Indian slaves were sold; these were mostly reserved for use in Brazil, however, and after 1530 a decree forbade any of the new grantees to send back to Europe more than twenty-four slaves a year – an indication that higher numbers had probably been sent.

The continuing 'Old World trade' in slaves from Africa remained more important than the Atlantic one in Africans or Indians during the first quarter of the sixteenth century. It seems possible that over 12,000 slaves may have been exported by the Portuguese in these years to Europe and 5,000 to the North Atlantic islands such as Madeira, the Azores, and the Canaries. Portuguese coastal trading in Africa also continued: slaves taken from, say, Arguin or Benin to Elmina were exchanged for gold. The advantage was considerable: the African gold merchants still paid higher prices for slaves than they fetched in Lisbon. The stealing of captives direct from the coast of Africa by Spaniards based in the Canary Islands also went on: every year in the early sixteenth century two or three journeys seem to have been made. In 1499 Alonso Fernández de Lugo, the Spanish Captain-General of the Canary Islands, even went so far as to speak of Las Palmas as 'the most important market for human beings'.[28] The new Treaty of Sintra of 1509 gave over the stretch of the African coast between Cape de Aguer and Cape Bojador to Portugal which had for the previous thirty years been reserved to Spain, but allowed Spaniards to continue trading there. Canary Islanders and *sevillanos* alike went to buy slaves from the Portuguese in the Cape Verde Islands and a few others, more intrepid, went further south, illegally, and bought slaves in Guinea, or from the settlers of São Tomé. Alongside this the Portuguese maintained a small export of Moorish slaves from Agadir, an Atlantic Moroccan port which they held for much of the early sixteenth century.

The Portuguese tried to meet the Spanish demands for slaves for their empire. But there were difficulties. Thus the trading post at Benin, or its port Ughoton, on the Benin River failed to work well, for the death rate was high among the Portuguese, and the conventional trade there (in pepper, ivory beads, and muslin) did not prosper. The people of Benin had not become Christians, and the magical king Prester John remained elusive. Still, all kinds of Portuguese slave buyers, and some Genoese or Florentines – with licences, of course – were still regularly putting into one or another of the 'five rivers', and carrying off slaves, though the three annual galleons bound for Elmina were now surpassed in importance by those of São Tomé, whose Governor in the early 1500s, Fernão de Melo, arranged with Lisbon that in return for a monopoly of buying slaves in the 'slave rivers' his island should also supply Elmina with all the slaves whom they needed. Perhaps a hundred a year would be a reasonable estimate. Usually these slaves of Benin would be paid for in copper or brass manillas: twelve to twenty-five a slave in the 1490s, fifty-seven by 1517. The metal would often be melted down and turned into something more beautiful.

The *Oba* of Benin responded slowly to these requests, and arranged that male and female slaves should be bought in different parts of the market, and – exceptionally in the history of the African slave trade – he sought to restrict the sale of males, eventually banning their export.

The island next door to São Tomé, Príncipe, was settled by Portugal soon after 1500. The Governor there in 1515 was Antonio Carneiro, who had been secretary to the King, and who eventually won for himself Governor Melo's monopoly of slave exports from the 'five rivers' to Elmina. He probably traded 1,000 slaves a year between 1515 and 1520, of whom half went to Elmina, though his rivals in São Tomé, Melo's heirs, sought to outmanoeuvre him.

Carneiro abandoned his contract in 1518 and the settlers of São Tomé recovered it. By then the place had become a plantation island of its own: there were probably about 5,000 or 6,000 slaves concentrated there, working on sixty or so sugar mills. But the settlers consistently failed to deliver the necessary number of slaves to Elmina, and there was a consequent falling off in deliveries of gold to Portugal – which had reached a peak of nearly 600 kilograms a year in the 1490s. So, though São Tomé was still the base for its arrangements, the Portuguese Crown began to engage directly in the trade in slaves. A royal official in São Tomé henceforward gathered the slaves from all over West and Central Africa, including some from the Congo. Though he was also charged to buy camwood (a hard red wood, ideal for making the cabinets which the nouveau riche in Lisbon needed to house their new possessions), ivory,

Benin cloth, muslin, and beads, his instructions show that his main concern was to find slaves (for each of whom he was not to pay more than forty manillas): the document was indeed entitled 'Our slave trade in the Isle of São Tomé'.

Yet the King was to be as much outmanoeuvred as Carneiro had been, in this case by interlopers from São Tomé.

Elmina did not, however, depend uniquely on the region of Benin for its slaves, for shipments from there were often too slow and too few. Thus in 1518 a Portuguese wrote from that castle to Arguin asking for the delivery of forty or fifty slaves, preferably all men, and the best young ones available, for use as porters in the mines in the forests of Akan. Yet by 1535 such demands were beginning to be unnecessary, since 'great caravans of blacks' would usually arrive at any port frequented by the Portuguese, 'bringing gold and slaves for sale. Some of the slaves have been captured in battle, others are sent by their parents, who think they are doing their children the best service in the world by sending them to be sold in this way to other lands where there is an abundance of provisions.'[29]

By then the always uneasy friendship between the King of Portugal and the *Oba* of Benin was waning. In 1514 the *Oba* sent two courtiers to Lisbon in order on the one hand to request cannon; and at the same time to offer to become a Christian. To finance this journey he gave the emissaries twelve slaves to live on by selling them as and when they needed money.

After many disagreeable adventures, these men reached Lisbon. There King Manuel I of Portugal ('the Fortunate') undertook to send missionaries and other clergy to Benin; 'and, when we see that you have embraced the teachings of Christianity', he said, 'there will be nothing in our realm with which we will not be glad to favour you, whether it be arms, or cannon, and all other weapons of war for use against your enemies. . . . These things we are not sending you now . . . because the law of God forbids it.' Manuel also asked the *Oba* to open his markets in order to allow trade to be carried on freely.[30]

Though some priests and monks did go to Benin the negotiations came to nothing, for the *Oba* died, being killed by his own soldiers during a war with neighbours. By then, though the slave trade from São Tomé was expanding, that from Benin was in decline: slaves reaching the former colony were coming from other parts of the African coast. High prices in Benin made those other sources more attractive; and the rigid determination of the next *Oba* to refuse to export male slaves, except in unusual circumstances, was having an effect, since the Portuguese, their Spanish clients, and the gold miners in Elmina all wanted 'prime male slaves', not women.

The beneficiaries of the change (if the matter can be so stated) were the Congolese. In 1512 King Manuel of Portugal sent an embassy under

Simão da Silva to his 'brother' the Christian King Afonso of Congo, who had succeeded to the throne after a battle with his brother in 1506 – in which, it was said, Santiago miraculously appeared on his side: the first appearance of that legendary inspiration on African soil. Da Silva's embassy was charged to bring back information, copper, ivory, and slaves – the last item being the most important.

King Afonso was a convinced but eccentric Christian, and in his capital, now rechristened São Salvador, 150 miles up the Congo, he was busy reading volumes of theology as well as Portuguese law. Afonso had given his councillors the titles of dukes, marquises, and counts; and many of them had also taken Portuguese surnames (Vasconcelos, Castro, Meneses, even Cortes). Schools were open for the teaching of both Portuguese and the Christian religion. A son of Afonso, Enrique, had also become Bishop of Utica (that is, Carthage), but was permitted to live in Funchal, Madeira; the diocese included Congo.

That appointment led Pope Leo X, in his declaration *Exponi Nobis*, to enable other Christian 'Ethiopians' (by the word he intended to include West Africans) to become priests or monks, assuming that they exercised their functions in their own homelands. During the middle of the sixteenth century several blacks and mulattos availed themselves of these opportunities. All were, of course, freemen; and some were ex-slaves.

Under King Afonso's direction the Congolese were inspired to adopt a Western style of life, and the Portuguese set up a trading post at Mpindi, at the mouth of the River Congo, which became their main port in the region, and where they also expected to draw on the Congo's copper. At first Afonso was delighted by the new openings for trade. The copper under his control was of a high quality, and he exported about 5,000 manillas between 1506 and 1511, comparable in quality to those made by the Bavarians; many of these were used in the slave trade in the Gulf of Guinea.

This monarch soon saw that he, too, could make money from the slave trade, provided that he controlled it himself; and he therefore appointed a special factor charged to supply the Portuguese, and gave him *nzimbu* shells with which to buy the slaves. But the Portuguese demand for these captives after the decline of their source in Benin soon began to seem excessive. Afonso had only a few slaves available, those being obtained in wars with the neighbouring Tio state of Makoko, higher up the River Congo, near Malembo Pool. So the Congolese began to raid their neighbours, the Mbundu. Yet Portuguese demand, because of the insatiable desires of the settlers of São Tomé, and because some local Portuguese insisted on being paid their wages in slaves, still outran supply. After a while, Afonso was persuaded to abandon his royal monopoly and henceforth, as if he had been a European monarch, sought merely to tax the exports of slaves, not to control them. Other African peoples apart from the Congolese began to adapt to the new conditions of trade. Thus the Pangu a Lungu, a people who had seized a stretch of the north coast of the River Congo, were beginning to raid its south bank specifically to obtain slaves. By 1526 King Afonso was complaining that the slave dealers, whom, of course, he initially had encouraged, were leaving his realm depopulated: 'There are many traders in all parts of the country. They bring ruin. . . . Every day people are kidnapped and enslaved, even members of the King's family'[31] – the kidnapping being done by Congolese, not Portuguese, who only constituted the market.

Eventually this problem was resolved by the establishment of regular slave markets near Malembo Pool. The Tio people who were there, having to begin with constituted the slaves for Afonso, soon controlled this commerce, drawing captives from the far interior and selling them to Portuguese, or, in the next generation to their mulatto agents, the so-called *pombeiros*, men who went deep into the interior and constructed a quite new pattern of commerce.

These arrangements suited all parties concerned. The Tio received payment for their services in *nzimbu* shells, which the Portuguese bought from Afonso. That king imposed his tax on the trade at Mbanza Kongo (São Salvador), through which all caravans of slaves had to pass. The increasing abundance of slaves in the market also reduced the inclination of Portuguese traders to kidnap Congolese subjects. By 1540 Afonso was boasting to the King of Portugal: 'Put all the Guinea countries on one side and only Congo on the other, and you will find that Congo renders more than all the others put together. . . . No king in all these parts esteems Portuguese goods as much as we do. We favour the trade, sustain it, open markets, roads, and markets where the pieces are traded.' (The word 'pieces' signified 'pieces of Indies': 'prime' male slaves, with no faults.)

There had been a slave trade to Congo, and slaves in the kingdom, before the Portuguese arrived. But the Portuguese market transformed it and caused an upheaval in the interior of Africa.

Perhaps 25,000 slaves were carried to São Tomé between 1500 and 1525: say 1,000 a year.[32] Many were thereafter sent on to Portugal, and some on to the Spanish Caribbean and this traffic probably exceeded that from the Senegambia and Cape Verde region by 1525. In 1530 about 4,000-5,000 slaves were being exported every year from Congo, and if there were no more that was because there were too few ships to carry them. In 1520, a Portuguese pilot visited São Tomé and found there planters owning as many as 300 slaves each. These were obliged to work the whole week, he reported, save for Sundays and holy days, 'when they work on their own plots – growing millet, yams, or sweet potatoes, also many vegetables. They drink either water or palm wine or sometimes goats' milk. They just have a small piece of cotton cloth which they wrap round themselves.' It seems that, on those days of 'rest', the slaves were obliged to grow what they needed to maintain themselves (including clothing) for the rest of the week. Carmelite monks protested at these conditions in the 1580s, but to little avail. There was one way in which life at São Tomé seemed benign, however: these slaves were not required to live in barracks, as would so often be the case in the New World; they could live with their wives in houses which they had built themselves.

Everything conspired to ensure prosperity in São Tomé. Slave captains from Portugal were in the mid-sixteenth century obliged to leave a proportion of their cargo on the island as a tax – unless they were going to Brazil, in which case they merely paid a tax in cash. But few as yet did: the first Brazil-bound African slaves were taken from the Cape Verde Islands, an easy stop on the way to South America, as well as to India.

The Portuguese *converso* merchant who had brought slaves back from Brazil with Marchionni, Fernão de Noronha, had now obtained the monopoly of supplying slaves and wine to Elmina, as well of the trade from the same rivers in the Bight of Benin which Marchionni had once owned, and he also controlled the pepper trade from both Brazil and Guinea.

Loronha was able to extend his monopoly for several years, but there were soon others associated with him, such as José Rodrigues Mascarenhas, also a *converso*, who held a monopoly of slaves from the River Gambia from 1500 onwards, and was succeeded by his son António. King Manuel I approved of converted Jews and afforded them benefits wherever he could.

Despite the developments in the Congo, Elmina remained the keystone of Portuguese activities in Africa. There was now a town beneath its walls: inhabited by half-Europeanized Africans, 'the Mina blacks', it became a self-governing republic at the disposal of the Portuguese governors. Those officials included three remarkable men in the 1520s: Duarte Pacheco Pereira, later author of a famous chronicle about the Portuguese empire, *Principio do Esmeraldo de situ orbis*; Braz Albuquerque, illegitimate son of the architect of Portuguese dominion in the East, who used his ample leisure in Elmina to edit his father's commentaries; and also João de Barros, who wrote his histories there, gaining for himself the designation 'the Portuguese Livy'. All of them traded slaves as well as gold, and grew rich on them. Daily they heard a mass for the soul of Henry the Navigator, and sought to use St Francis as the motor of conversion of Africa: a picture of him, painted with white lead, was said to have mysteriously turned black when it reached Elmina.

East Africa should not be forgotten. As a part of the remarkable Portuguese thalassocracy stretching to the Far East, Sofala (Beira), a hundred miles south of the mouth of the Zambezi, was already an important Portuguese trading post in the early sixteenth century. The Zambezi in those days seemed to the Portuguese to be an artery of wealth, perhaps running up to Ophir (the Faro Mountain), believed to be governed by a legendary monarch, held to live at what is now Harare. In 1507 the Portuguese established themselves even more substantially on Mozambique Island, a malaria-ridden spot which served, all the same, as the main stopping place between Lisbon and Goa. Later, Lourenço Marques and Antonio Caldeira, after having made their fortunes in São Tomé, founded an ivory trade in the region of the Bay of Delagoa, a preparation for a substantial slave commerce to Brazil and elsewhere in America.

The continuing popularity of slaves of all colours was one of the obvious characteristics of those days in both Portugal and Spain, above all in Lisbon and in Seville. In Lisbon, King Manuel I, for example, had incorporated many slave provisions in his Ordenaçoes Afonsinas, a revision of the Portuguese code, in contrast with his uncle King Afonso V's code of 1446, which had little to say of the matter. Black slaves were still plainly preferred by the Portuguese to Muslim ones, on the ground that they were less likely to rebel or run away. In Seville, Vespucci when he died had five slaves in his household, of whom two were black, one Canary Island, and two mixed Spanish and Canary (the two last may have been his bastards). One indication of the popularity of slaves is that the painter of The Virgin of the Sailors (La Virgen de los Navegantes), Alejo Fernández, thanks to his good husbandry, was able to endow his sons grandly – he had his own house, with black and Indian slaves as well as servants.[33] Nor were all the slaves black: a 'white slave', Juana de Málaga, evidently a Moor, was sold to Diego Velázquez, the first Governor of Cuba, in 1516, though it is unclear whether she was packed off to Santiago, the capital at that time of Cuba, or whether she remained waiting for her master in Seville. In 1514–22 the baptismal books in Sanlúcar de Barrameda show that 420 slaves were baptized at the parochial church, Our Lady of the O.* Two hundred and twenty of these were Africans, six (Caribbean) Indians, three Canary Islanders, and the rest 'blancos': that is, Moors. Possession of slaves in Sanlúcar, as in Seville, was not a privilege: blacksmiths, carpenters, tailors, and most town councillors enjoyed the use of slaves, and only a few years before (in 1496), the lord of the place, the Duke of Medina Sidonia, had had as many as fifty-two Canary slaves: the Medina Sidonias had for a time owned three of the Canary Islands. Many of these were domestic slaves; but some of them were employed to carry wheat and other supplies to the ships bound for the Americas.[34]

Nor were Portugal and Spain alone as slave countries: the institution was still flourishing in Italy and in Provence, where Marseilles held a large slave market.

*

* The designation apparently derives from the exclamation of surprise of the Virgin when the angel announced to her that she was to bear the baby Jesus.

So it was that the old institution of slavery was revived in the New World. The Renaissance in Europe had no humanitarian pretensions. Its 'hard, gemlike flame' reburnished the ideas and practices of antiquity, the institution of slavery among them. It was entirely logical that the discovery of the New World should be attended by a rebirth of the idea of forced labour. A Flemish diplomat, Ogier-Ghislaine de Busbecq, en route for Constantinople, in the mid-sixteenth century, even regretted the shortage of slaves in his day: 'We can never achieve the magnificence of the works of antiquity,' he sighed, 'and the reason is that we lack the necessary hands, that is, slaves.' He also went on to deplore the absence of 'the means of acquiring knowledge of every kind which was supplied to the ancients by learned and educated slaves'.[35] The Spanish historian and statesman of the nineteenth century Cánovas would comment: 'The idea of servitude, so opposed to Christianity, was thus fortified amongst us, and with it as its sister and comrade, the justification of tyranny entered into all spirits. . . . From philosophy, the nation, far from receiving doctrines of progress and sentiments of humanity, gathered nothing more than the resignation of stoics . . . and a greater sum of intolerance.'[36] Almost the only adverse comment to be found in the first years of the sixteenth century about the lavish renewal of slavery then under way was that of another Fleming, Clenard, who went to Portugal as tutor to a sixteenth-century Prince Henry, and who said that slavery made the masters idle; a fact which, in his opinion, explained 'the pompous radish-eaters' who 'paraded indolently in the streets of Lisbon, accompanied by an army of slaves whom they could not afford'.[37]

7

FOR THE LOVE OF GOD,
GIVE US A PAIR
OF SLAVE WOMEN

*'For the love of the Lord God, give us a pair
of slave women as alms, because we are
spending the pittance we have entirely on
hired girls.'*

An abbess to the Queen of Portugal,
sixteenth century

THE TRANSACTIONS of the Portuguese on the periphery of West Africa in
the early sixteenth century must be considered in continental perspective.
As yet, the traffic in African slaves to Europe, or the Indies, was small in
comparison with the ever-flourishing trade across the Sahara. In 1518,
while Charles V was granting his slaving licence for 4,000 slaves to his
friend Gorrevod, the great Emperor of the Songhai on the Middle Niger
was offering a gift of 1,700 slaves to Cherif Ahmed Es-Segli when he
established himself at Gao, on a higher bend of that river. Most of the
black slaves bought in Sicily in the sixteenth century were Bornus, from
what is now Nigeria, who had been carried to North Africa across the
Sahara. Only at the end of the sixteenth century did the trans-Saharan
traffic decline, as merchants and monarchs alike began to succumb to
Atlantic temptations.

All the same, in the second quarter of the sixteenth century about
40,000 slaves were probably shipped from Africa to the Americas or to
Europe and to the Atlantic islands, perhaps 1,600 a year; between 1550
and 1575, the figure may have reached 60,000, or nearly 2,500 a year.

The Old World was still the largest importer of these African slaves
until about 1550 – that is if the island of São Tomé, which received about
18,000 slaves between 1525 and 1550, is included. Five thousand went to
the North Atlantic islands and 7,500 to Europe. Probably a mere 12,500
went to Spanish America and a trickle only to Brazil. But many of the São

Tomé slaves were eventually taken to the New World; and, after 1550, the first market in the Atlantic slave trade was undoubtedly Spanish America – an empire which, between 1550 and 1575, probably received twice what it took in the previous quarter-century, or 25,000. São Tomé, then still enjoying a sugar boom, perhaps once more took 18,000, but again many of those were shipped onwards; for it was then that Brazil began to be seriously interested. That last territory perhaps received as many as 10,000 Africans in the third quarter of the century: sugar cane had begun to be planted there on a large scale.

Europe, with a purchase of probably no more than 2,500 over the twenty-five years after 1550, and the Atlantic islands, also with 2,500 or so, were then falling back. A few Moorish slaves continued to be taken to the New World in the mid-sixteenth century, but the Crown did what it could to prevent it, on the ground as usual that as Muslims they would be intractable.[1]

Every encouragement, meantime, was given by the Spanish Crown to those who wanted to carry slaves to the New World. In 1531 a decree in Castile permitted loans on easy terms to settlers there who wanted to buy slaves in order to found sugar mills.

The Portuguese were responsible for most of these shipments from Africa, the work being carried out by a series of enterprising merchants, in the tradition of Marchionni or Noronha, who regularly obtained licences for trading.

During this era of the High Renaissance in Europe the pattern for the entire history of the Atlantic slave trade was set. First, the initial bartering – or still, in a few cases, kidnapping – of slaves was the work of Portuguese captains, in the estuaries of one or another of the rivers of the West African coast. These men, in ships of about one hundred tons, would carry their slave cargoes, along with gold and other goods, to some important entrepôt of the Portuguese African enterprise: São Tomé; Santiago, in the Cape Verde Islands; or, now less and less important, Elmina. All those colonies were well established, their nursery gardens had expanded to include shrubs and fruit trees from the East as well as the West: yams, oranges, tamarinds, coconuts, and bananas from the first; pineapples, sweet potatoes, groundnuts, papayas, and above all maize (which took some time to become popular) from the second; the modern staple food of Africa, cassava or manioc, came later, from Brazil. Despite the regulations against them, the half-Portuguese half-African lançados, who remained on the upper Guinea and Senegambian coasts, increased in wealth and numbers, and in the end received a grudging if informal acceptance from the Crown. The Church approved, since their existence seemed to make possible the conversion of Africa. The lançados (some were of Spanish, Greek, or even Indian origin) were still the only foreigners to be settled permanently in Africa.

Many slaves in those days had a roundabout journey to the Americas. Thus some who were first quartered at São Tomé or Elmina might eventually be transferred to Santiago, in the Cape Verde Islands. There they might be sold to other merchants, including Spanish ones, especially from the Canary Islands. They might then go to Lisbon or to Seville, to Madeira or the Azores; or they might be carried directly across the Atlantic on Portuguese or, possibly, Spanish ships to the important ports of the empire; either to Cartagena, in what is now Colombia, or Portobelo in Panama, for shipment south to Peru, or to Santo Domingo, Havana in Cuba, and Veracruz in Mexico. By the end of the sixteenth century the direct route from São Tomé to Brazil or, even more adventurously, to Buenos Aires, a small new Spanish settlement on the River Plate, was the rule. The sugar kings of late-sixteenth-century Brazil were beginning to send directly across the south Atlantic to obtain what they wanted from the region of the Congo. Some of those last planters would club together to send a little fleet of, say, six ships across the south Atlantic. Such ventures enabled the people concerned to procure slaves at a lower price than if they bought them from merchants in Brazil.

Some slaves were also carried to the Americas in these years from East Africa, where the fatally romantic King Sebastian of Portugal was dreaming of founding an African empire comparable to the Spanish dominions of New Spain and Peru.

The monarchy of Benin had ceased to be a serious provider of slaves. After 1553 the Royal Factor in São Tomé prohibited all Portuguese trade with the place. A few Portuguese captains did continue to slip up the River Benin for illegal trade, but more important, on the next-door River Forcados, the merchants in still-prosperous São Tomé had made friends with a new polity, the monarchy of Ode Itsekiri, whose leaders became at the same time enthusiastic Christians and ardent slave traders.

Captains from Portugal not only carried most of the slaves from Africa north to the Cape Verde Islands, to São Tomé, or to Europe, but they took most Spanish slaves across the Atlantic, and often sold them in Cartagena or Veracruz. Portuguese traders were, too, to be found in viceregal Peru. Most sales involved one or two slaves, with a maximum of ten to twenty, yet all the same the overall numbers rose steadily.

An indication of the geographical origin of slaves in Spanish America is to be seen in an inventory of the possessions of Hernán Cortés in 1547. Cortés owned 169 indigenous Mexican slaves; he also had sixty-eight black slaves from a wide variety of places: Gelofe (Wolof, in Senegambia), Mandingo (Malinke, in the Gambia Valley), Bran (Bram, in Guinea-Bissau), Biafra, and even Mozambique. Many of these were *negros ladinos*: that is, they were Spanish-speaking and had either been born in Spain or had spent some time there. Fifty-six of these slaves worked at Cortés's experimental sugar mill at Oaxaca in southern Mexico. It is in some ways surprising that there were not more black slaves on that estate, for in 1542 Cortés had contracted in Valladolid with the Genoese Leonardo Lomellino to import 500 black slaves, a third of them women, from the Cape Verde Islands at seventy-six ducats each. Perhaps, though, one of Cortés's agents sold the surplus in the Mexico market.[2] Whether that transaction makes the great Conquistador a slave trader must be a matter for personal judgement.

Much the same geographical origin can be read in notarial registers, a little later, of slaves in Lima and Arequipa. These suggest that 80 per cent (1,207) were African-born and the rest came from Spain of, of course, enslaved African parents. Like those on Cortés's property, three-quarters of those from Africa came from the 'Guinea of Cape Verde' – Senegambia and Guinea-Bissau. But there were also some from the Congo, and five from Mozambique.

The most important merchant of Portugal concerned in the slave trade in the mid-sixteenth century was Fernando Jiménez, who though based in Lisbon had close relations living in Italy, and others in Antwerp. Despite his Jewish ancestry, the powerful reforming Pope Sixtus V was so appreciative of his services that he gave him the right to use his own surname, Peretti. Jiménez's descendants were among the largest contractors in Africa – above all, eventually, in Angola. The Jiménezes were run close in wealth and influence by another New Christian, Emanuel Rodrigues, and his family – including Simón, a dominant figure in the trade from Cape Verde. Other *conversos* in the slave trade included Manuel Caldeira, whose commercial great days were in the early 1560s, and who then became Chief Treasurer of the realm. In Lisbon in the mid-century there were altogether about sixty to seventy merchants in slaves, though only three large-scale ones – Damião Fernandes, Luis Mendes, and Pallos Dias – seem to have survived into the 1570s. In the mid-century Clenard not only noticed that the birth of a slave child in Portugal was greeted enthusiastically, but that some masters did business by encouraging female slaves to breed, 'as they do pigeons, for purposes of sale, without being in the least offended by the ribaldries of the slave girls'.[3] The same judgement was made by Giambattista Veturino when he visited the palace of the Duke of Braganza at Vila Viçosa: the slaves were treated, he said, 'as herds of horses are in Italy', the aim being to create as many slaves as possible for sale at thirty or forty scudi each.[4]

The mid-sixteenth century also saw for the first time the emergence of a number of Spanish slave merchants of significance. In those days the market was open, there were no monopolists, and the Spanish empire took in more slaves than the Portuguese one. Of course, the Spaniards still had as a rule to buy from the Portuguese, though sometimes they carried the slaves which they had obtained across the Atlantic in their own ships. About thirty Spanish ships were licensed for Africa in the 1550s, but they usually went to buy in the Cape Verde Islands – no further. Those who broke the law and tried to buy in Guinea were few and far between. One such trader who did finance an expedition to the African mainland met with disaster, for the seamen who had expected to buy slaves from Muslim traders found themselves enslaved by them.

The slave merchants of Seville also included New Christians, as was the case in Lisbon. For example, prominent in the 1540s was Diego Caballero, a *converso* from Sanlúcar, who began to make his fortune in Hispaniola in 1510 or so and much increased it when he went to Seville. Portraits by the fashionable painter Pedro de Campaña (Pieter de Kempeneer) of him and of his brother Alonso (probably the same Alonso Caballero who acted as 'admiral' to Hernán Cortés at Veracruz) can be seen in the Chapel of the Mariscal in the Cathedral of Seville, which Diego presented to that great church.

In the 1550s the outstanding mercantile family in Seville were the Jorges, also *conversos*. This dynasty was founded by Álvaro in the 1530s, and his sons Gaspar and Gonzalo, and then his grandsons, Gonzalo and Jorge, carried on the business. They had five ships which regularly made the Seville–Cape Verde–America voyage. The Jorges seemed the most powerful consortium in Spanish-American commerce for a time, their interests embracing wax, clothes, mercury (for use in the silver mines), wine, and olive oil as well as slaves. Some of these things came from their haciendas at Cazalla de la Sierra (wine) and Alamedilla (olives), in the sierra to the north of Seville and near Granada respectively. Ironically, these 'New Christians' were in the habit of referring to their old Christian rivals, solid old Castilian families without a drop of Jewish blood, as '*negros*'. The Jorges never seem to have recovered from one of the periodic forced loans levied by the Crown on merchants in Seville returning from America: seizing from them the then vast sum of 1,800,000 ducats of gold, in return for an annuity of a mere 3 per cent.

Old Christians were also engaged in the slave traffic in Seville: there was, for example, not only Juan de la Barrera, mentioned in the last chapter, but Rodrigo de Gibraleón of Seville, who was concerned with pearls as well as slaves. His son Antonio acted as his agent in Nombre de Dios, where he stayed till 1550, when his father died. In the 1560s the first merchant of the city was probably Juan Antonio Corzo, who was of Italian origin (though he did not derive from the old Genoese *sevillano* oligarchy). He first accumulated a fortune in Peru, selling linen, oil, saffron, and above all slaves. He returned to establish himself in Seville in 1558, when he had a network of trading posts, all run by members of his family. By 1566 his fortune was worth 31,000,000 maravedís.

By 1568 Corzo had been overtaken by Pero López Martínez, whose principal activity was certainly the sale of slaves, though like most of the other entrepreneurs mentioned he was also interested in other goods: mercury, cochineal, linen, and wine. With Gaspar Jorge and Francisco de Escovar, López Martínez is found agreeing to supply a hundred slaves for the building of the fortress at Havana in the 1570s – the famous la Cabaña, subsequently scene of so many miseries, and not only for black prisoners.[5]

Evidently, many people dabbled in the slave trade in Seville in the mid-sixteenth century. It was the new fashion. For example, the famous doctor of Genoese origin Nicolás de Monardes bought shares in slave ships. As usual, there were Italian merchants involved, in addition to Corzo: Juan Fernando de Vivaldo and Germino Cataño of Genoa and Seville, Tomás de Marín (Marini) of Sanlúcar, and Leonardo Lomellino, and there were also Girolamo and Giovanni Battista Botti (of Florence), the latter a creditor of Hernán Cortés. These merchants were more or less law-abiding in that they paid the regulation fee per slave on shipment. But extra slaves beyond those provided by the rules were often hidden on board the ship by the captain or the owner, and many more slaves were carried than are indicated by the official figures. Many captains carried cargoes of slaves across the Atlantic without registration and sold them profitably. Nor was the law of 1526 banning the import of Spanish-born slaves maintained. Heavy fines did not prevent these and other illegalities; and after a while even admirals stocked their ships with slaves, so much so that the first line of cannon was sometimes submerged when naval vessels entered the harbours of the New World.

There were, naturally, more African slaves in Portugal than in any other European country. In 1539 12,000 black slaves were sold in Lisbon alone – many of them, admittedly, to be exported later to Spain. In 1550 Lisbon boasted 10,000 resident slaves in a population of 100,000, and Portugal as a whole probably had over 40,000. In 1535 Clenard wrote, 'In Evora, it was as if I had been carried off to a city in hell; everywhere I only meet blacks.' He added that when a gentleman of Evora went out on his horse two slaves might go in front, a third would hold the bridle, a fourth would be available to rub down the horse; and other slaves would carry the master's hat, cloak, slippers, clothes brush, and comb.[6]

Such slaves were often bought almost as decorations, as continued to be the case throughout Europe till the eighteenth century. African slaves, however, still performed many more valuable services in sixteenth-century Portugal. King João III, father of the Brazilian empire, had a black slave as a jester; the naval foundry employed slaves; and so did the palace kitchens and gardens.

Portugal seemed indeed in those days to be a veritable Babylon. Portuguese viceroys in the East sent back slaves from wherever they could, some from Malacca, some from China. When, in 1546, Baltasar Jorge d'Evora of Lisbon made his will, he left two captives from Gujarat in India, and two Chinese slaves, of whom one was a tailor and one from the old Genoese mart of Kaffa in the Crimea. In 1562 Maria de Vilhena, in Evora, Portugal, in her will, freed ten slaves, of whom one was Chinese, three were New World Indians, two were Moorish, one was white from Eastern Europe, one was black, one brown, and one mulatto.

Spaniards also still employed slaves on a large scale. In the early sixteenth century every family of means in Andalusia had at least two slaves, black or white, African or Moorish, preferably the first. When the record states that the conquistador Juan Ruiz de Arce lived during his retirement in Seville a life of luxury on his Peruvian fortune, 'surrounded by horses and slaves', we can be sure that those last were mostly African slaves, not American ones.[7] In 1565, Seville was the home of over 6,000 slaves out of a population of about 85,000, blacks by then outnumbering Berbers or 'white slaves' (7 per cent of the population, compared with Lisbon's 9 per cent). The authorities in that city tried conscientiously to mitigate the harshness of the life of slaves by allowing them to gather on feast days to dance and sing, and to have their own steward (*mayoral*) to protect them, and defend them if necessary in the courts. The Church of Our Lady of the Angels established a hospital for blacks, and it received many donations – for example, from the Duke of Medina Sidonia, one of the two leading aristocrats in the city. Free blacks retained their own religious confraternity.

Slaves were sold in Seville by being advertised publicly in the streets. They were used as kitchen maids and as doorkeepers, as nursemaids and as porters, as valets, waiters, and cooks, as escorts when riding, and as entertainers, in singing and dancing. Sometimes slaves were better treated than regular servants were. The religious life of the slaves sometimes did concern their masters in Seville, and children of domestic slaves were usually baptized. Female slaves were often close to their mistresses: thus in the plays of Lope de Vega, such as *Amar, servir y esperar*, they appear often as confidantes and go-betweens in love affairs (as in those of Plautus in Rome). They might even be buried in family vaults.

In the mid-sixteenth century African slaves were to be found at work in the silver mines of Guadalcanal, to the north of the Jorges' property at Cazalla de la Sierra. The Franciscan friary of Las Cuevas in Seville, where Columbus's body remained for thirty years after his death, used Africans to look after their beautiful gardens.

Some slave owners leased out their slaves and lived on the proceeds. Many of these worked as stevedores in the Seville docks, in the soap factories for which the city was famous, or in public granaries, while others earned a living as porters, or street vendors, or bearers of sedan chairs, in print shops and in swordmakers' shops, even as agents for traders. Some served as constables for the municipality.

Blacks might often be mocked in the street, but they mixed easily, marriage between black and white was not forbidden, sexual relations were frequent, and slaves in Seville were received as full members of the Church. Prominent free blacks, of whom Juan Latino (who claimed to be a real Ethiopian by birth) was outstanding, played a full part in the intellectual life of Andalusia, such as it then was. Several mulattos also distinguished themselves (Juan de Pareja the painter, for example, and

Leonardo Ortiz, a well-known lawyer), even if a few crafts prohibited blacks from entry.

In the middle and late sixteenth century in southern Spain there were also one or two signs of what might be called a slave trade in reverse: the *criollo* slave – that is, a slave born in the empire but brought back to Spain – began to be popular in Andalusia. One such was Elvira in Lope de Vega's *Servir a un señor discreto*, the witty maid of Doña Leonor, daughter of a merchant with interests in the New World. Rich merchants of the Americas, such as Leonor's father, often brought back their slaves from the colonies: Don Álvaro, in Castillo Solórzano's novel *La Niña de los Embustes*, was caused to return from Lima to Seville with four black slaves.[8]

Sometimes such *criollo* slaves could gain their freedom in Castile, in which case they might even return to America (as, for example, occurred in the case of Ana, a freed slave of the Pineda family in 1538). The archives of the Casa de Contratación in the sixteenth century give evidence of several black freedmen and women who were determined to return across the ocean to seek employment in the New World, where they had been born as slaves.

Given the survival of the Canary Islands as a producer of sugar – there were seven mills at work – it was understandable that the modest trade in Berber slaves between Africa and the Canary Islands should have continued throughout the sixteenth century, the ships averaging 150 slaves each voyage, with the Canary Islanders mostly keeping to the geographical limits between the designated capes prescribed by the Spanish–Portuguese treaties; though in 1556 the Portuguese navy carried back to Lisbon as prisoners a group of Canary Islanders who had tried to trade slaves at Arguin. Las Palmas, in Gran Canaria, remained a significant slave market, and slaves, both black and Berber, were sold from there to Seville or Cádiz at profits of almost 100 per cent. African slaves were also shipped from the Canaries to the Indies on a small scale.

The institution of slavery survived elsewhere in Europe. In 1538 a Greek bought as a slave by an Italian and carried to France was declared free, '*selon le droit comun de France*'. That phrase expressed, actually, a pious hope, not a reality: for when in 1543 Khaïr-ed-din Barberousse, Admiral of the Caliph Selim I, arrived in Marseilles as an ally of Francis I, he brought with him slaves kidnapped in a raid on Reggio di Calabria and put them forward for sale. He found a market with no difficulty.

In Italy, Genoa, moved by a desire to avoid too many Africans in the city, in 1556 established rules against the sale of slaves, but all the same in a statute of 1588, when making arrangements for the division of goods lost at sea, the rules still spoke of slaves as among the frequent merchandise. In 1606 a Florentine traveller said that he did not need to go abroad to buy slaves because he could obtain a diversity of them at a modest price in his own city.

In the New World conditions were always harsher than those in Europe, since the slave owners were often more nervous, and perhaps less experienced, than those at home: further, the King in Spain explicitly provided for a change in the laws of Alfonso the Wise, the 'Siete Partidas', whereby slaves were proclaimed free to marry whom they liked; that generosity was not to be afforded to Africans in the New World. Already the complexities contingent on black slaves' marrying free Indians had begun to weary state lawyers. In the Americas, however, Africans were also beginning to be seen everywhere: as pearl-divers off New Granada, as dockworkers at Veracruz in New Spain, in the new silver mines at Zacatecas, as cowboys in the region of the River Plate; in gold diggings in Honduras, Venezuela, and Peru; and as blacksmiths, tailors, carpenters, and domestic servants in every city. African slaves worked for viceroys and for bishops, for private entrepreneurs in urban sweatshops making textiles, and on farms, while female slaves were often established as planters' maids, mistresses, wet-nurses, or prostitutes. The pattern was established of assigning to black Africans any difficult or demanding task.

We catch a glimpse of what these first North American Africans were doing in the first years after the Spanish conquest of Mexico: for example, in the new textile workshops which sprang up in the late 1530s, at first in the city of Mexico, then in the new city of Los Ángeles (Puebla), and finally in Antequera (Oaxaca) and Valladolid (Yucatán), founded to make up for the shortage of clothes brought over from the mother country. Some of these little factories employed Indians, but black slaves were sought after from the earliest days. Africans also helped to open up agri-culture: for example, in the Valle de Mezquital, to the north of the Valley of Mexico, the largest group of immigrants as early as the 1530s were African slaves. They came first to work on the local sheep stations, and then in the mines at Ixmiquilpan and Pachuca.

The first work of these early American Africans was usually as herds-men, in which capacity they were so active that they infuriated the Indians, who knew nothing of domesticated animals. Brutality was normal, and Indian villagers were often bullied or even killed by Africans: one Indian who went to the help of his wife who had been attacked by an African was tied to the tail of a horse and dragged to his death.

Other recollections of the first Africans in the New World sometimes placed them in an unattractive light in relation to the indigenous peoples. The well-intentioned Judge Alonso de Zorita, for example, recalled in his *Lords of New Spain* that about 1560 he saw 'a great number of Indians hauling a long heavy beam to a construction site. . . . When they stopped to rest, a black overseer went down the line with a leather strap in his hand whipping them all from first to last to hurry them on and keep them from resting. He did this not to gain time for some other work, but simply to keep up the universal evil habit of mistreating the Indians. . . . The black struck with force and they were naked.'[9]

The Indians all the same made clear that they supported the introduction of African slaves. For example, in the 1580s a group of indigenous people in Mexico told the Viceroy, Álvaro Manrique de Zúñiga (a cousin of Cortés's second wife), that they were themselves unable to work in sugar plantations, and that that 'difficult and arduous work' was 'only for the blacks and not for the thin and weak Indians'.[10]

A fillip to the African slave trade was naturally given by the trend towards the outlawing of Indian slavery in the Spanish empire, as a result of the agitation of Bartolomé de Las Casas and other Dominicans. An indication of the mood in 1544 is shown by a letter of Cristóbal de Benavente, public prosecutor of the Supreme Court in Mexico, to the King: 'Every day the gold mines are giving less profit, because of the lack of Indian slaves. In the end, if Your Majesty abolishes local slavery . . .', wrote Benavente, 'there will be no alternative to allowing blacks into the land, at least in the mines. . . .'[11]

The plantations now established in Brazil and in the Spanish Caribbean were beginning to show all the signs of the familiar commercial enterprise of later days: a greater number of men than women; other obstacles offered to the male slaves to prevent them from founding families; excessive work, especially during harvest; harsh punishments for minor offences; and deaths because of machinery working badly. Similar judgements could be made of conditions in the many mines opened in the sixteenth century from Mexico to Peru.

There seemed always to be a shortage of workers. In 1542 the town council of Mexico requested of the Crown in Madrid that because slaves were needed in 'the mines and other services' the King 'might be moved to give anyone licence and general permission in order that they may bring slaves over to this New Spain, paying in its ports the *almojarifazgo* [port duty], without having the need to get any other licence, because the existing arrangements are the source of much vexation'.[12] The request was not granted: general permissions without payment of taxes were not in the tradition of the Spanish Crown.

By the mid-sixteenth century Brazil had already begun its long life as a producer of sugar for the European market. A pioneer was the first Portuguese expeditionary, Martim Afonso de Sousa, to whom King João III had allocated the captaincy of São Vicente, to the south of Rio de Janeiro. His largest interest was the Engenho (Sugar Mill) São Jorge dos Erasmos, of which he was a shareholder along with a German, Erasmo Schecter, and which was administered from the beginning by German and Flemish overseers. More important still was the northern captaincy of Pernambuco, where Duarte Coelho, the King's captain there, reported five sugar mills in operation by 1550. One of them, Nossa Senhora da Ajuda, was the property of Coelho's brother-in-law, Jerónimo de Albuquerque, 'the

Pernambucan Adam', who had greatly helped good relations with the local Brazilians by marrying a Tobjara princess and setting up several of her relations as his mistresses.

The main labour force on these mid-sixteenth-century Brazilian plantations was still, admittedly, indigenous Brazilians: slaves certainly, but at least not as yet Africans, or at least not yet Africans on a large scale. Indian slaves were then seen by the new conquerors as essential: 'If a person comes to this land and contrives to get hold of a couple of them (even if he has nothing else he can call his own) he then has an honourable [!] means of supporting his family; for one of them will fish for him, another will hunt for him, and the others will cultivate and harvest his plantings; and in this way he is at no expense for food, either for them or for his family.' Yet by 1570 disenchantment with Indian labour had set in. The Portuguese captains sought slaves outside their captaincies. But still there were shortages; and Duarte Coelho wrote to the King in 1546 that, whereas in the past, 'when the Indians were needy', they used to come and work for practically nothing, now they wanted 'beads and feather caps and coloured clothing that a man could not afford to buy himself'. In the good old days, a Jesuit remembered, some tribes would sell 'an [Indian] slave for a chisel'.[13] But that was no longer the case in 1570.

So, little by little, in the new cities of the new empire, African slaves began to work much as they had done for a hundred years in Portugal – as servants, gardeners, cooks, seamen, and as symbols of wealth, and finally on plantations, with some of the attitudes of the Portuguese at home being emulated by colonists in dealing with the Africans.

There was still little criticism of slavery and the slave trade in these days of the High Renaissance. After all, antiquity continued to be the fashion. Michelangelo designed a monumental *Dying Slave* – a Slav, it would seem – now in the Louvre, but it is obvious that he worried less about the slavery than the mortality. Sir Thomas More had provided for slavery in 1516 in his *Utopia*. He thought it 'a suitable station in life for any prisoner of war, for criminals and also for the hard-working and poverty-stricken drudge from another country'.[14] More's friend Erasmus said nothing of the matter. Machiavelli was also silent. How should it be otherwise? The cultivated and wise Pope Leo X, the greatest Renaissance head of the Church, did, it is true, remark that, with regard to the enslavement of Indians, 'not only the Christian religion but nature herself cried out against a state of slavery'.[15] But Leo was not talking of Africans, and there would certainly have been one or two slaves from the coast of Guinea in the Vatican in his day.

Even more explicitly concerned with the Indians was Pope Paul III (Alessandro Farnese). Influenced by yet another Dominican friar engaged in humanitarian matters, Fray Bernardino de Minaya, Paul, in a letter to Cardinal Juan de Tavera, Archbishop of Toledo, forbade conquistadores in the New World to reduce Indians to slavery; and then in a bull, *Veritas Ipsa*, he proclaimed the complete abolition of slavery, stating firmly that all slaves had the right to free themselves. Indians were to be deprived neither of their liberty nor of their property, even if they were still pagans. The penalty for disregarding these injunctions was excommunication.

The declaration disturbed the Emperor Charles, for it seemed that the Pope was wishing to act in the temporal sphere. But it is obvious that Paul's mind was still centred on Indians in the New World, not blacks. Indeed, his subsequent bull *Sublimis Deus* of 1537 shows that he was merely trying to insist that 'the Indians are true men', even if he did make the (to the slave owners, dangerous) concession that 'all are capable of receiving the doctrines of the faith'.[16]

No serious study of slavery in antiquity was written in the sixteenth century. The first consideration of the matter seems to have been in 1613, when Lorenzo Pignoria of Padua published *De Servis et Eorum apud Veteres Ministeriis*, about the urban lives of Roman slaves, a work 'unsurpassed in its scope till the late nineteenth century'. But he sought to draw no modern moral.[17] Pignoria would no doubt have agreed with his contemporary Giles of Rome, when he recalled in 1607 that Aristotle had 'proved' that some people are 'slaves by nature and that it is appropriate for such people to be placed in subjection to others', a view that found general support.[18]

Neglect of the African dimension was not reserved to the Church of Rome: when certain serfs in Swabia appealed for emancipation in 1525 on the argument that Christ had died to set men free, Luther was alarmed. He did not believe that the earthly kingdom could not survive unless some men were free and some were slaves.[19]

All the same, some concerns were expressed by Portuguese and Spanish writers in the middle of the sixteenth century. The Portuguese, the major traders in slaves, even sought to lay down conditions in which slaves were to be transported. Thus in 1513 a decree limited the number of slaves who could be carried in a single ship (an echo of the old Genoese law). In 1519 another decree sought to govern conditions on the short journey from Africa to São Tomé. It also insisted that captains should maintain gardens on the latter island to feed slaves properly before they were embarked for the Americas. The best slaves were henceforth to be retained to work the plantations and grow the provisions of the future.

Even the Spanish Crown intervened in favour of humane treatment of slaves who, Charles V remarkably required in 1541, should be subjected to an hour every day of instruction in Christian precepts, and should work on neither Sundays nor feast days – regulations which were surprising even if they were very rarely observed.

The famous public argument at Valladolid in 1550 between Bartolomé de Las Casas, the apostle of the Indies, and the classicist Ginés de Sepúlveda on the subject of how the Catholic faith could be preached and promulgated in the New World was judged by a board of notables. Among these fifteen wise men was a Dominican theologian, Fray Domingo de Soto, of Segovia. De Soto was the most distinguished of the pupils of the recently deceased jurist Francisco de Vitoria, with whom he had lived for many years in the same Dominican monastery in Salamanca. A professor at Segovia as well as at Salamanca, de Soto served the Crown at the Council of Trent and is generally held, with Vitoria, to be the creator of international law. He was also a confessor of the Emperor Charles V.

De Soto was asked to make a résumé of the proceedings at the debate at Valladolid. That document supported Las Casas. But there was, as usual in such congresses, no discussion at all of black Africans.

A few years later, however, in 1557, de Soto published his *Ten Books on Justice and Law* (*De Justicia et de Jure*), in which he argued that it was wrong to keep in slavery a man who had been born free, or who had been captured by fraud or violence – even if he had been fairly bought at a properly constituted market. In speaking thus, de Soto must have been thinking in terms of black or Moorish slaves, of whom there were then certainly some in Salamanca. De Soto could not have been more influential. His work was dedicated to the heir to the Spanish throne, Don Carlos. Yet his words on slavery, written clearly in the greatest Spanish university, struck few chords at the time.[20]

One who did listen to him though was Alonso de Montúfar, Archbishop of Mexico, another Dominican, who wrote to King Philip II in 1560: 'We do not know of any just cause why the negroes should be captives any more than the Indians, because we are told that they receive the gospel in good will and do not make war on Christians.' Philip does not seem to have replied.[21] He had a little earlier, when still prince not king, asked a committee which included a Dominican, a Cistercian, and two Franciscans about the benefits of granting a certain banker, Hernando Ochoa, the right to carry 23,000 slaves to the Americas at eight ducats each. The discussion did not touch on whether it was legal or illegal to treat Africans in such a way but whether such a large contract would damage other businessmen.[22]

At much the same time, a Portuguese captain and military writer, Fernão de Oliveira, also criticized the slave trade, in his *Art of War at Sea* (*Arte de Guerra no mar*). His criticism is a real anticipation of the abolitionist movement, and the captain should receive due credit for such a pioneering work. He pointed out that the African monarchs who sold slaves to the Europeans usually obtained them by robbery or waging unjust wars. But no war waged specifically to make captives for the use of the slave trade could possibly be just. Oliveira denounced his countrymen for being the inventors of 'such an evil trade' as the 'buying and selling of peaceable freemen as one buys and sells animals', with the spirit of a 'slaughterhouse butcher'.[23]

Oliveira's work was published in 1555 in Coimbra, a city where, a few years later, in 1560, yet one more humane Spanish Dominican, Martín de Ledesma, wrote, in his *Commentaria*, that all who owned slaves gained through the trickery of Portuguese traders (the *lançados*, for example) should free them immediately, on pain of eternal damnation. He also pointed out that Aristotle's comments about wild men living without any order could not for a moment be held to apply to Africans, many of whom lived under regular monarchies.[24]

These arguments in Portugal were not quite without consequences. The Crown did try to persuade traders not to buy slaves who had been kidnapped, but on most occasions the distinction between kidnapping and war was an indistinct one; and the traders themselves continued to maintain that in buying slaves they were serving the best interests of humanity.

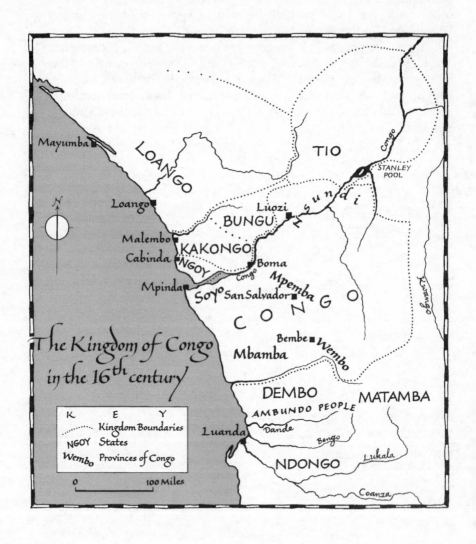

The Kingdom of Congo
in the 16th century

Mayumba

LOANGO

Loango

Malembo
Cabinda
NGOY
Mpinda
Soyo San Salvador

KAKONGO

Boma
Congo
Mpemba

C O N G O

Bembe Wembo

Mbamba

TIO

Luozi
BUNGU

Nsundi

STANLEY
POOL

Congo

Kwango

DEMBO
AMBUNDO PEOPLE

Dande

MATAMBA

Luanda

Bongo

NDONGO

Lukala

Coanza

K E Y
.... Kingdom Boundaries
NGOY States
Wembo Provinces of Congo

0   100 Miles

8

THE WHITE MEN ARRIVED
IN SHIPS WITH WINGS

*'One day the white men arrived in ships
with wings, which shone in the sun like
knives. They fought hard battles with the
Ngola and spat fire at him. They conquered
his salt pans and the Ngola fled inland to
the Lukala River. . . .'*

Pende oral tradition

IT HAD BEEN AGREED between the new Christian King of Congo, Diogo I,
and Portugal that the settlers on São Tomé should only trade in the
former's realm; and as a result ten leading Portuguese merchants (such as
Fernando Jiménez, Emanuel Rodrigues, and above all Manuel Caldeira)
took up the slave trade there, twelve to fifteen ships arriving every year
to carry off 400–700 slaves each. These ships were still too few to carry
the slaves available; captains overloaded, often causing revolts. The
Portuguese being unable to fulfil all the details of this treaty, King Diogo
of the Congo broke off relations in 1555 and expelled the seventy or so
Portuguese living in his realm, even though many had by then been
established there, mostly with African women, for many years. His position had been adversely affected since in recent years the Tio slave traders
at that cosmopolitan, overcrowded spot known as Malembo Pool had
been coveting European goods more than the *nzimbu* shells which he
offered them. Thus the King's income in European goods had declined.
But in 1567 the old relationship was restored with a new King of Congo,
Álvare.

Next year, in 1568, a savage, cannibalistic, and nomadic people, the
Jaggas, who originated on the southern banks of the River Kwango
(which now forms part of the boundary between the states of Angola
and Congo), invaded Congo, and drove Don Álvare to take refuge on
Hippopotamus Island, in the Congo estuary. The Jaggas had been

disrupted by the intensive slave raids of the Tio in their territory in the mid-century. In his refuge, Don Álvare's shortage of food became so severe that he and his counsellors sold slaves for bread. Some of his advisers were even constrained to sell their children as slaves to secure a day's subsistence. The King sent some slaves as emissaries to Lisbon, and asked King Sebastian to dispatch an army to restore him, which he did; and 400 Portuguese from São Tomé, led by Francisco de Gouveia e Sotomayor, a member of one of the most distinguished families in Portugal, re-established King Álvare in São Salvador. The use, and perhaps even more the sound, of gunfire was especially effective in this campaign.

The grateful Álvare thereupon sent to Lisbon to buy back his nobles, though a few of these, disappointingly, preferred to remain in Portugal 'for the love of God'. The actions of the Jaggas long remained, meantime, a terrible warning in the minds of the Portuguese, for it had been a shock to find a monarchy which they had supported, and which they thought had become Christian, overthrown so easily by ruthless nomads. Gouveia, on the other hand, was ordered by his master in Lisbon to build at the expense of Álvare a fort where the King, and the Portuguese residents of Congo, could find shelter, if there were to be future attacks by the Jaggas.

The Congo as a result fell more and more under Portuguese tutelage. Álvare avoided direct vassalage, but once he had used Portuguese troops to restore his authority, they remained. For Portugal, Congo was a dependency worth having: Pacheco Pereira wrote that in that realm 'they make some cloths of palms, with a surface like velvet, and some with fancy work like velvetized satin, so beautiful that there is no better work in Italy'.

There was, however, every year a greater emphasis on slavery within Congo, the only Christian monarchy of any importance in Africa, and the only one where literacy made any headway. King Álvare now used slaves as soldiers and servants, messengers and mistresses, builders and bearers, as well as workers on the land. In the short term, this strengthened the monarchy, reducing its previous reliance on chiefs and noblemen. King Álvare even felt so powerful that he could designate a son by a slave wife as his heir (but that son was in the event set aside when Álvare died in 1614, being supplanted by a half-brother, Bernardo II, who was also the son of a slave mother).

Mulatto traders were now to be found in all the most important Congo ports. Though trade between villages and between neighbouring peoples had existed for generations, the coming of the Portuguese had the consequence of creating, for the first time, a long-distance commerce, in which European goods (and some American ones) were carried along new routes.

The Portuguese in São Tomé were also making friends with Angola – that is, with the *Ngola*, the king of another Bantu state named Ndongo, composed of Mbundu people, whose small monarchy stretched from the River Dande (which runs into the sea north of what is now Luanda) to the River Coanza (the river on which Luanda would soon be built), and which had been loosely under the dominion of the kings of Congo. Ndongo had been from the early sixteenth century a minor source for slaves for the Congo in raiding expeditions. By the terms of the Congolese–Portuguese treaty these slaves could only be traded through the Congo port of Mpinda, but, more and more, Portuguese interlopers would obtain these slaves directly, at the mouth of the Coanza, just to the north of the Luanda islands; for the traders of São Tomé found the arrangements at Mpinda unsatisfactory, for they could never obtain enough slaves there.

As early as the 1550s there had been some rivalry between the kings of Congo and Ndongo as to who should be the main suppliers of slaves to the Portuguese; and, though Portugal was obliged formally to support Congo, her interests were becoming more and more concerned with Ndongo.

In 1559 Paulo Dias de Novães, a grandson of Bartolomeu Dias, the explorer of the Cape of Good Hope, left Lisbon with three ships, accompanied by two Jesuits and two lay brothers. He made for the island of Luanda in the estuary of the Coanza and dispatched a cousin, Luis Dias, with the Jesuits up the river itself to Pungo-Andungo, the then capital of Ndongo. There the Portuguese explained that their king wanted the new monarch, Ndambi, to convert to Christianity, as had occurred in Congo. Ndambi was cautious, and the negotiations on the matter were long drawn out. One of the Jesuits died, along with others among the explorers. So Paulo Dias, on the coast, lost patience and set out himself, with a small expedition. Having travelled 120 miles by river, and then perhaps 50 miles on land, he reached the capital. Ndambi thereupon imprisoned him and several colleagues, including Fray Gouveia, seized such European goods as he could find, and dispersed or killed other Portuguese.

Fray Gouveia, a kinsman of the first proconsul of Angola, died in captivity, though not without sending an important letter to his superior, in which he insisted that the only way seriously to convert heathen people was to conquer them.[1] Paulo Dias was released after six years. In 1575 he returned to Angola – with a permit from the King of Portugal at least, if not from the Ngola – to colonize. The terms of his contract gave him vast powers. He seems to have been convinced that with so many slaves available, the Portuguese in Angola would be able to build a civilization comparable to that of Rome in the Mediterranean. As a first step in this notable enterprise Dias set about building what became São Paulo de Luanda, the first Portuguese fortified town in West Africa south of Elmina, at the mouth of the Coanza, first on the island of Luanda, then on the mainland, near what is now the fortress of São Miguel.

A new *ngola*, Quiloanage, understandably took exception to these encroachments, though his capital was the local capital of the slave trade for many Portuguese buyers, and though the island of Luanda was not actually his, since it had been looked on as belonging to the King of Congo. After years of diplomatic manoeuvring, during which the slave trade to São Tomé and to Brazil flourished as never before, the *Ngola* was convinced by several local Portuguese traders, who distrusted Dias, that that proconsul planned to overthrow him. The *Ngola* thereupon killed his Christian slaves and thirty Portuguese. The result was war. After further setbacks, in a long campaign beginning in 1580 the Portuguese, with 350 Europeans – 'mostly rogues and cobblers', according to one chronicler – and many African mercenaries (including slave bowmen and slave lancers), using terrorism as much as open war, eventually defeated the *Ngola*, and established their colony on the coast firmly. But by then Dias was dead and many of his countrymen had also died, more of disease than in battle, as usually was the case in tropical wars. In the interior the *Ngola* glowered in temporary impotence, though relatively easy to restrain.

Luanda soon became the headquarters for all Portuguese operations south of Nigeria. By 1590 300 Portuguese were settled there. The colony attracted merchants from Portugal, especially those who like some converted Jews had been unable to secure opportunities in Portugal itself. The Crown sought to control such immigration but in the long run it was quite unable to do so.

With this good base at Luanda, a lovely port, and with relative peace established with both the King of Congo and the *Ngola*, there was nothing to prevent the slave trade from prospering, and it soon became the economic mainstay of Angola as well as of Congo. The best historian of Portuguese–African race relations, Charles Boxer, saw the slave trade as a reason, along with the high incidence of malaria, why a responsible Portuguese colony was not founded in Angola in the sixteenth century. Yet one of the main purposes of this entity was precisely to undertake a slave trade to Brazil.

Already in 1576 Frei Garcia Simães, SJ, had written: 'Here one finds all the slaves which one might want and they cost practically nothing. With the exception of the leaders, almost all the natives here either are born in slavery or are reduced to that condition without the least pretext. . . . After his victories the king gives entire villages over to his subalterns, with the right either to kill or to sell all the inhabitants.'[2] For the tail of an elephant, it was even said, one could buy three slaves. An English prisoner, Andrew Battell (in Angola from 1589 to 1603), described seeing thousands of slaves in Portuguese hands.[3] Between 1575 and 1592 over 50,000 may have been taken from Angola. In 1578 Duarte Lopes visited Luanda, and remarked that there was 'a greater Trafficke and Market for slaves that are brought out of Angola than in any place else. For there are yearly brought by the Portuguese above five thousand head of Negroes, which they afterwards conveigh away with them, and so sell them to divers parts of the world.'[4] Thomas Turner, an English captain, reported: 'Out of Angola is said to be yearly shipped 28,000 slaves and there was a rebellion of slaves against their masters, ten thousand making a head and barricading themselves but by the Portugals and Indians chased and one or two thousand reduced. One thousand belonged to one man who is said to have ten thousand slaves, eighteen sugar mills etc. his name is John de Paüs ... and here prospering to this incredibilitie of wealth. ... '[5] In 1591, one official assured the Crown that Luanda could expect to supply slaves to Brazil 'until the end of the world'.[6]

The Portuguese Crown naturally maintained a financial interest in all these undertakings. The African coast had been divided into several zones of exploitation. In these the collection of royal taxes or duties was farmed out to individuals, who in turn made arrangements with the traders and collected the dues concerned in return for licences.

The Portuguese influence on Africa had, of course, positive sides. By then they had introduced into Congo and Angola not only – at a certain superficial level, to be sure – Christianity, but many European techniques, and several important European or West Indian crops – rice, oranges, coconuts, onions, and above all manioc (cassava). The last-named crop would inspire a veritable agricultural revolution in the seventeenth century, enabling the population to grow to previously unattainable levels, therefore indirectly no doubt making available more candidates for the Atlantic trade. Another American transplant was maize, which had similar consequences a little later.

Nevertheless, there can be no doubt whatever that the main impact of the Portuguese in this part of Central Africa was the encouragement of the commerce in slaves. Though these things meant that São Tomé and Portugal itself (and the Spanish empire) could continue to be well supplied with the workers they coveted, the real beneficiary was Brazil.

In 1570 the Brazilian black population was only 2,000–3,000. Most slaves were still Indians. But these indigenous captives were becoming less easy to acquire because of the diseases brought by the Portuguese (the epidemic of dysentery, combined with influenza, of the 1560s was as destructive in Brazil as the smallpox had been in 1520 in Mexico and the Caribbean). It is true that Indians still accounted for two-thirds of Pernambuco's labour force on sugar plantations in the 1580s. But these Indians were poor workers, for they were quite 'unused to such continuous and back-breaking toil. In addition to the diseases which these inferior races always acquire upon contact with the whites, the ill treatment which they received was a cause of illness and death, notwithstanding the laws against it which were continuously promulgated.'[7] The 'expenditure in human life here in Bahia in these past twenty years', wrote a Jesuit in 1583, 'is a thing that is hard to believe; for no one could believe that so great a supply could ever be exhausted, much less in so short a time.'[8] But from this time, because of the Angolan connection, blacks, above all to work on the new sugar plantations, were every day more available.

Between 40,000 and 50,000 African slaves, nearly all from Congo or Angola, seem to have reached Brazil between 1576 and 1591. The population of black slaves in 1600 was probably about 15,000, mostly in sugar mills, whose labourers were by then 70 per cent black – though ten years later, in 1610, a Frenchman named François Pyrard de Laval visited Bahia and estimated that though the administrative region round that city boasted 2,000 whites and 3,000 or 4,000 black slaves, there were another 7,000 black or Indian slaves on the sugar estates. But certainly Indians were playing less and less of a part in the plantations. In 1573 there had been an understanding between the Jesuits, the Governor of Brazil and Maranhão, and the Auditor-General. The enslavement of an Indian would only be possible if the person concerned were to be captured in a just war, or if he had fled from his village and had remained absent for over a year. Although the arrangement was not adhered to, its mere existence increased the need for black slaves. Later, it was laid down that a just war was one which was so declared by the King. In fact the Crown and the settlers continued to quarrel over the issue of Indian slaves for many years more – the monarch taking a moral position, and insisting eloquently that enslavement damaged the chance of converting slaves to Christianity, while the settlers argued that in capturing Indians they were saving them from becoming cannibals.

The discrepancy between the figures for the population of slaves and for their import shows the position in all its brutality: slaves were expected to die after ten years or so and therefore, on any effective property, had to be replaced from Angola or Congo. From the very beginning it was thought essential on these sugar estates to replenish the slaves by making new purchases rather than by encouraging breeding: as a witness (the future Admiral Sir George Young) in a British inquiry in 1790 put the matter, 'All I ever understood was that purchasing slaves was much the cheapest method of keeping up their numbers; for . . . the mother of a bred slave was taken from the field labour for three years, which labour was of more value than the cost of a prime slave or new Negro.'[*][9]

Angola or Congo and Brazil were thus more and more linked. Currents and winds intensified the relationship: ships leaving Portugal

---

[*] *In the same inquiry in London, the question was put, 'Can any cause be assigned which impedes the natural increase of Negroes?' The answer was: 'the lascivious abuse of authority in white servants over the immature and unprotected females. . . . The women . . . have in general a sense of decency and decorum in their fidelity. . . . The men have none; they follow the examples of the white servants. . . . To their loose amours, many of them are sacrificed. Both sexes are frequently travelling all night going to or returning from a distant connection. . . .'*

for Angola had virtually to pass by Brazil, and those leaving Angola had to sail close to Rio.

In these years, Brazil was showing herself to be São Tomé's successor as Europe's most important sugar supplier, just as São Tomé had succeeded Madeira, the Canaries, and the Mediterranean islands. Brazil – that is, a narrow coastal strip – had about 120 sugar mills by 1600 and was then the richest European colony. She was also an international enterprise: Italian sugar equipment was to be seen, artisans from the Canary Islands and Madeira had been deliberately brought out, and as early as the 1540s Cibaldo and Cristóvao Lins, Lisbon representatives of the Fuggers of Augsburg, were marketing as well as producing sugar. Dutch merchants often provided the ships to carry the sugar home to Europe, as well as the capital for many of the plantations. Then it was the great market of Amsterdam which sold much of the sugar – still principally considered as medically desirable, rather than as a sweetener, since tea, coffee, and chocolate, which seemed in their early days of fashionableness to need sugar for taste, had not appeared on the European scene.

However, sugar was already sometimes coveted for the pleasure it gave, especially among the rich. A German travelling in England thought that though the Queen was majestic her teeth were unfortunately black: 'a defect to which the English seem subject, from their too great use of sugar'.[10]

These developments in Brazil mark the beginning of the American sugar revolution. It is usually thought that that occurred in the Caribbean, in the mid-seventeenth century. But the typical sugar plantation, with its characteristically male population, its slaves who were expected to die so young and who remained more African than American in their ways, was developed in Brazil three generations earlier.

As has been mentioned, sugar had already been known in the Caribbean earlier in the century. But in the haciendas of Hispaniola and Cuba, as in Mexico, that crop was grown alongside others, with cattle and tobacco. The modern sugar estate, producing nothing but sugar, for export and on a large scale, was an invention of Brazil.

Sugar is not a complicated crop: all that is necessary is fertile and well-irrigated land, and the digging with hoes of shallow holes in which a few pieces of stalk from mature sugar canes can be placed. The holes are covered with earth, and within about fifteen months the new cane is ready for harvest. In Brazil the cane would then be cut by slaves with machetes (that was the heavy work) and carried by ox cart to mills driven either by water, oxen, mules, horses, or wind. These would grind the juice out of the cane. That juice would be boiled, skimmed, and cooled. The brown crystals of the rough sugar would be separated from the viscous parts, molasses, which could be used to make rum or second-rate sugar. The good sugar would be held for a time in counting houses before being placed in hogsheads, carried down to the nearest port or river, and put on ships. The crushed stalks of the cane could, meantime, be used as fuel. A little over a year later, a second harvest, from the stumps of the old canes, could be reaped; and, although the cane produced would be less good than it was at the first harvest, the process could be repeated three or four times.

Occasionally the raw sugar was refined in the tropics, but usually that was done in Europe. The division of function had nothing to do with climate nor with labour: the home countries were determined to prevent colonial manufacturing.

The ideal sugar plantation seemed to be about 750 acres, certainly not less than 300 acres. The enterprise was best carried out with, say, 120 slaves, 40 oxen, and a great house in the centre, surrounded by the specialist buildings and slaves' quarters. On such properties, slavery, black African slavery, appeared the best kind of labour. In the late eighteenth century, a British inquiry into the sugar industry would state firmly that 'to cultivate annually 100 acres of cane requires 150 working negroes at least in the field'.[11] White labourers were less amenable than Africans, less strong, and were considered less suitable for tropical conditions: 'It is plain to demonstration that hot countries cannot be cultivated without negroes', George Whitfield, the Calvinistic Methodist, would stiffly write in the eighteenth century.[12] In 1848 a British planter, M. J. Higgins, a sugar merchant, would tell another British inquiry, of the House of Commons, that 'the labour which I have seen exacted from the slaves in Cuba [for which read 'Brazil' any time after 1570] would have been quite fatal to Europeans if that amount of labour had been exacted from them in that climate'.[13]

These were widely held views, but they were myths: many white men have worked hard in heat, even in cane fields, in the South of the United States and Queensland, as well as in Puerto Rico, Barbados, and elsewhere in the Caribbean. In the eighteenth century, the same British report already quoted about the working of the sugar industry asked, 'Would it be possible to cultivate to advantage the West Indian islands by the labour of Europeans or free negroes?' The reply was: 'It *would* be possible to cultivate cane by negroes *gradually* rendered free and when taught the experience of being paid in money . . . and Europeans, inured to the common labour of digging and carrying burdens, whose pride was not to be excited and inflated by a condition of men legally unprotected and too much below them, might also cultivate these lands very well, especially [but] for cotton, the labour of which bears no comparison with that required for canes. . . .'[14]

In late-sixteenth-century Brazil neither white slaves nor white labourers were easily available, even if a few Slavs or Turkish slaves might have been still found in the Mediterranean. Slaves from China, India, or elsewhere in the East were in theory an alternative, for the Portuguese could have brought them from their Asian outposts, but they would have been expensive to ship, and neither the trade nor the men were fully tried out. For the silver mines at Potosí in Peru the idea was once suggested of recruiting 'Chinese, Japanese, and Javanese, who come from the isles of the Philippines', and who, it was said, were 'a people more domesticated than the blacks, and very suitable for any kind of work'. In New Spain (Mexico), the scarcity of slaves from Africa did for a time lead colonists to use the Philippines as a source for a few workers: the Manila galleons which made their regular journeys across the Pacific from Manila to Acapulco after 1565 rarely failed to bring one or two slaves. But planters in Brazil were not interested: they were finding black slaves both hard-working and resilient, in every way adequate. Their value was reflected in relative costs: twenty-five dollars per African slave in 1572, only nine dollars per Indian.

Blacks were also reliable in skilled positions of authority on the estates, for many Africans had experience of agriculture, even of dealing with cattle. There was another side to the matter. The harvesting of sugar cane was laborious and repetitive. The typical Indian of the Brazilian forest had been used to hunting and fishing, as well as fighting. A semi-nomad, he had left the modest cultivation carried out (of manioc, above all, but also of tobacco, maize, and yams) to women. He served the Portuguese well as a soldier, but the Africans, with their remarkable reserves of toughness and good humour, were far more effective in the sugar fields; and so they would remain for the next three centuries; while African women made good cooks, nurses, mistresses, and wet-nurses.

Anyone black in a strange country, obvious by his features as well as his colour, often ignorant of the language of the Portuguese, could also be easily kept isolated.

The region of Brazil which acted as the host for these important changes was the north-east, the two northern captaincies of Pernambuco and Bahia. The latter was the capital of the colony from 1549, the most important port, and a growing centre for sugar: the Recôncavo, a beautiful strip of land about sixty miles long and thirty wide behind the Bay of All Saints, was the most sought-after district for the mills. There the most energetic of sixteenth-century governors, Tomé de Sousa, built a sugar mill for the Crown. The most successful undertaking, however, was probably the Engenho Sergipe, set up by the most effective of Sousa's successors, Mem de Sá, on the north shore of the bay. In 1601 the Jesuits built their first sugar mill nearby, and other religious orders followed.

Here began that curious society summed up in Brazil by the word *bagaceira*, or 'a life built round cane waste', so brilliantly romanticized in Gilberto Freyre's *The Mansions and the Slaves*, with 'the Great House' built of mud and lime, covered with straw or tile, with verandas on the sides, sloping roofs to give protection against tropical rains and sun, at once 'a fortress, a bank, a cemetery, a hospital, a school and a house of charity', all protected, at least in the sixteenth century, by a palisade against savage Indians.[15]

The men and women who created this first great sugar boom in the world lived well. Many stories are told of the opulence of the planters in old Brazil, their tables laden with silver and fine china bought from captains on their way back from the East, doors with gold locks, women wearing huge precious stones, musicians enlivening the banquets, beds covered with damask; and an army of slaves of many colours always hovering. These fortunes rested on sugar, and sugar on African slavery, but it was no less real for all that.

A few of these first sugar mills of Brazil were owned by converted Jews. Let us not exaggerate: of about forty mills in the region of Bahia whose owners can be identified in 1590, twelve were apparently New Christians. Yet the Inquisition thought that in 1618 twenty out of thirty-four mills were so owned. Some of these individuals were probably still practising Jews: the Holy Office discovered a synagogue on a plantation on the River Matoim, no distance from Bahia, in the 1590s. But they were adept at finding what they wanted to find: much more important, these *conversos* stayed in touch with their equivalents elsewhere, in Amsterdam, especially, and in Brazil itself; the most famous of them all, Diogo Lopes, the so-called Count-Duke of Brazil, remained most influential despite countless denunciations by the Inquisition.

It was not surprising, meantime, that by 1618 the phrase 'a new Guinea' was once more used, this time to speak of the north-east of Brazil.[16]

These plantations represented substantial investments. All the same, one must keep a sense of proportion here also: in the late sixteenth century the value of the slave trade to the Portuguese Crown was, through taxes per slave and so on, 280,000 cruzados, but the Eastern trade of Portugal yielded 2,000,000.

Spain's slave trading, in the last era when that country and Portugal were alone in the New World, had many upheavals. Thus the 1560s saw an economic collapse in the country. Both Crown and private merchants, slavers and silver kings alike, were ruined. One disaster followed another. A regular merchant ship belonging to the Jorges burned; in it they had loaded clothes for the New World, and there were other losses at sea. The Jorges were especially damaged. Then the Crown repudiated its debts. Since Phillip II had borrowed so much from so many, and had paid so little interest, several great men lost all they had. The slave trade to the empire lurched to a temporary stop. Between 1566 and 1570 only nine ships were licensed for Africa (they carried a mere 1,300 slaves). A few continued to carry slaves on the short journey from Africa to the Canaries, but these too were few. The price of slaves in Cartagena reached the record height of 60,000 maravedís a head.

In order to try and save something from the wreck for which he himself was partly responsible, King Philip II sought in 1568 to reach an agreement with his cousin and ally, Sebastian, King of Portugal, whereby that monarch, or his agents, would supply annually 2,000 slaves to be handed over to Spanish merchants in the Cape Verde Islands. The idea had been proposed by Alonso de Parada forty years before. The aim was both to supply labour to planters in the West Indies, who needed it, and to gain a secure royal income from the issue of licences. But the Portuguese seemed little interested. The only merchants to put themselves forward, Jimeno de Bertendona and Jerónimo Ferrer, offered inadequate terms. So throughout the 1570s the slave trade to Spanish America continued in the doldrums: between 1571 and 1575 a mere sixteen Spanish ships were licensed for slaves from Africa, of which four went direct to Guinea, most of the rest, as heretofore, to Santiago in the Cape Verde Islands, carrying a little over 2,000 slaves in all. The King made matters worse in 1574 by establishing a capitation tax on all slaves held in America. In the late 1570s only two ships were licensed by the Spanish Crown for Africa or the Cape Verde Islands (responsible for only about 300 slaves).

In 1576 another bank failed: that directed by Pedro de Morga. That failure dragged down several more *sevillano* shippers, such as Alonso and Rodrigo de Illescas and the brothers Sánchez Calvo, who were all linked to American commerce, above all in gold and silver, but had some interests in mercury, linen goods, cochineal, and slaves.

Demand for African slaves continued all the same. Planters in Peru, for example, wanted to make use of blacks on a regular basis. A few Genoese bankers continued to make money from trading slaves. Yet the Crown was deaf to suggestions by viceroys and others that Africans should be bought specially to work building bridges in tropical territory, where Indians from the highlands were ineffective. The Viceroy of Peru, the determined and ruthless Francisco de Toledo, tried to compensate for the shortage of labour by impressing all free blacks, mulattos, and ungainfully employed Spaniards into work in the silver mines which opened in 1545 in Potosí, or in the mercury mines established a little later at Huacavelica. But this compromise failed, for black Africans could scarcely survive at the high altitude of Potosí.

By 1580 Spanish officials in both Peru and Mexico had come to decide that a constant supply of black African labour was the only way of satisfying the motherland's appetite for precious metals.

The goddess Fortune turned a kindly eye on King Philip II after 1580. The royal line of Portugal died out, and King Philip 'bought, inherited and conquered' the country (as he put it himself). Easily disposing of a patriotic protest in Lisbon, the two realms were united. Though they remained separate entities, Philip, or the Council of the Indies, merged their policies towards commerce, especially towards the matter of trading slaves. Spain also took over the fort of Arguin, the oldest Portuguese trading post in Africa.

The benefit of this association to Spain cannot be overemphasized. By the 1580s Spain had already, through bureaucracy and perseverance, ensured the security of her colossal empire. Castile controlled most of the world's silver, as well as a large proportion of tropical America's indigo, tobacco, cochineal, and dye woods. After 1580, with Portugal subservient, the Spanish Crown dominated international trade, the world's gold supply, the production of marine salt and of pepper, spices from the East Indies, and, with Brazil, most of the sugar, too. One of the main aims of Spanish policy became to impose an embargo on foreign trade, especially Dutch and English trade, and much of the history of the next sixty years was concerned with that ultimately vain endeavour.

King Philip II decided to use the experienced Portuguese merchants to provide the Indies with slaves, including the Spanish Indies, and he therefore signed contracts with two of them, Juan Bautista de Rovelasco, a great capitalist of a Flemish family, and Francisco Núñez de Vera to take slaves from São Tomé to certain designated ports in the New World. Afterwards he turned to Pedro de Sevilla and Antonio Mendez de Lamego, both *conversos*, residents of Lisbon, who had been already concerned with slave trading for the Portuguese Crown. These two merchants obliged themselves, by a contract of 1587, to carry a specified number of slaves every year to the Spanish Indies, usually 500 but sometimes more, from their three main points of assembly: Santiago in the Cape Verde Islands, though it was sacked by Francis Drake in 1585 and by Antony Shirley (Fellow of All Souls, Oxford; spy; and traitor) in 1596; second, São Tomé, still prosperous (despite a destructive slave revolt in 1574); and third, Luanda, which, being more remote, was more secure, and which would provide more Africans for the Americas than anywhere else in the coming century (84 per cent, according to one estimate, of those sent between 1597 and 1637).

Though Sevilla and Mendez de Lamego could conduct trade themselves, they also had to sell licences to anyone who asked for one. Their position was immensely powerful, since they had already a similar contract to carry slaves to Brazil. The two also agreed to provide the King, free of all charges every year, with two choice black slaves, whom the King could pass on to whomsoever he liked. A subcommittee of the Council of the Indies, a Junta de Negros, a mixed commission of eight men from the Council of the Indies and the Treasury, was set up to resolve all the problems relating to the slave trade. It was usually composed of powerful noblemen or bureaucrats known in other parts of the administration, for whom the activity provided a useful extra income.

The consequence was a reinvigoration of the slave trade to the Spanish as well as to the Portuguese empire. It was much needed, or so it seemed: as early as 1570 Fray Diego de Salamanca, the Bishop of Puerto Rico (where there were about eleven sugar mills), had sent a familiar-sounding report in the form of a letter to the King saying that 'the most important cause of the decay and decline of this island is the lack of slaves'.[17] But New Spain's production of sugar, though never so important as that of Brazil, was thriving, the Jesuits' plantation at Xochimalcas near Guanajuato having 200 slaves in 1600. The equipment invested in such mills was considerable: one plantation, La Santísima Trinidad, also in New Spain, owned by a certain Hernández de la Higuera, had about 1610 not only a *casa grande* on two floors, a chapel, and a mill, but a boiling house with seven boilers and two refineries, tended by 200 slaves, the whole being valued at 700,000 pesos, a colossal sum for that time. Almost all the sugar equipment came from heretical Holland. At Tlaltenango in the early seventeenth century about half the black slaves were born on the property, incidentally a level of reproduction rarely repeated in the history of European sugar growing in the New World.

The contractors Sevilla and Mendez de Lamego took their task seriously. They obliged themselves to carry to the empire 3,000 slaves in six years, or 500 slaves a year. Their investors seem to have included the Medici and the Strozzi of Florence. But they failed to fulfil their commitments.

In the 1590s, after several years of further generous agreements with other Portuguese merchants to carry slaves to his empire, the King revived the monopoly system which had been tried so unsuccessfully by his father, Charles V, in his youth. As with Charles, the Crown's desire to make money played an important part in the decision. Several schemes had already been devised to secure new monopoly arrangements. Thus in 1552, as has been mentioned, the Crown contemplated contracting with Hernando Ochoa for 23,000 slaves to go to the Indies over seven years, with the payment of eight ducats tax a head to the Crown. But Ochoa did not carry the plan through, partly because of the opposition of the merchants of Seville to the idea: they believed that they as individuals could perform the task better. Then in 1556 the famous Manuel Caldeira of Portugal secured a contract to dispatch 2,000 blacks to whatever part of the Indies that he desired, to be carried in Portuguese or Spanish ships. Perhaps the high royal share of this scheme prevented it from working (each licence was to cost taxes equivalent to two-fifths the value of each slave).

In 1595 a new monopoly contract was at last concluded between the Spanish Crown and Pedro Gomes Reinel, a Portuguese merchant who was already the king of the slave trade in Angola. Gomes Reinel bought this favour for 100,000 ducats a year for nine years. He agreed to arrange for the carriage of 4,250 blacks a year to the Spanish Indies, of whom, it was coldly stated, 3,500 had to be landed live. The slaves were to be fresh from Africa, and none could be mulatto, mestizo, Turkish, Moorish, or of any blood other than African. The King reserved the right to grant licences for another 900–1,000 slaves to other people. So Gomes Reinel's was not exactly that of a full monopolist: and he too could sell licences at thirty ducats to merchants – in practice, nearly all Portuguese slave traders – who desired to enter the trade. He could not reasonably refuse anyone. He himself kept, however, what he hoped would be a monopoly right to carry slaves to the new port of Buenos Aires. All the ships which he licensed had to be registered in either Seville, Cádiz, the Canaries, or Lisbon. Buenos Aires, incidentally, had presented herself as a new city needing slaves more than anything: a sad letter forwarded by the superior of the Franciscans there told the King in 1590 that the inhabitants believed: 'We are so poor and needy that we could not be more in want, in proof of which we do our ploughing and digging with our own hands. . . . Such is the need from which the settlers suffer that their own women and children bring their drinking water from the river. . . . Spanish women, noble and of high quality, because of their great poverty, carry their drinking water on their shoulders . . . as if it were the tiniest village in Spain.'[18]

What, of course, they thought they needed were – African slaves.

Though Gomes Reinel was to be the contractor, some slaves would still be brought by other Portuguese, from São Tomé and the Cape Verde Islands. Gomes Reinel also had to pay a fine of ten ducats a slave for every licence not used. All the same, he expected to make a fortune, for there was a large difference between what he had paid for his contract and the sum for which he could, separately, sell licences. Yet his costs were great, too: he had to pay agents in Spain, Africa, and the Indies; he had to make appropriate presents or bribes to royal officials throughout the empire; the costs of the slave journeys were greater than he supposed that they would be; and he had to pay taxes. Then there was much bureaucracy: for example, during the time that this contract lasted, all the licensing, of all ships and cargoes, had in theory to be performed in Seville, and the final checking of all ships had to be done in Bonanza, the little port on the Guadalquivir, just next to Sanlúcar de Barrameda.

This first important state slaver of the new era, Gomes Reinel, was probably a *converso*. He seems to have been more a typical courtier than a merchant, one of the few Portuguese who spoke and wrote Castilian to perfection. On the other hand, he was audacious. Thus he had coolly ruined the banker Cosme Ruiz Embite by recalling a loan actually contracted in the slave trade.

At all events, Gomes Reinel at first seemed to have solved the problems of providing slaves for the Spanish and Portuguese crowns. The years of his monopoly saw a new peak of licensed trade to Africa: 188 boats were approved. About half (90) went to Guinea, and thence carried over 25,000 slaves, or 5,500 a year. In Gomes Reinel's day, the Spanish Crown, no doubt impressed by the Portuguese experience, made a famous concession to the sugar planters of the empire by granting that sugar mills could not be attached for debt or for unpaid mortgages. This 'privilegio de ingenios' lasted several hundred years – almost as long, indeed, as the Spanish empire itself.

Of course there was a substantial contraband trade in slaves, particularly between the Caribbean ports. Many ships sailed directly from Africa to the Caribbean without having registered in Seville, though sometimes sailing north-west to take on water in the Canaries. Those vessels travelled outside the protection of the Spanish Crown. There were also many small smuggled imports to secondary ports – for example, Havana, Puerto Rico, Santo Domingo, and Jamaica – by the captains of slave ships and of naval vessels (including admirals). Captains would continue to stock more slaves than they registered (and were taxed) for, and sell the surplus where they could. For example, in 1574, the caravel *San Sebastián*, master Diego Rodríguez, carried from the Cape Verde Islands as many as 400 slaves, but with only 145 licences. Both naval vessels and cargo ships would often enlist Africans in Guinea as 'cabin boys' and sell them in America. Sometimes masters would register small boats and exchange them for big ones capable of carrying larger numbers of slaves. Port officials and even viceroys would often turn a blind eye to such infractions, provided they themselves profited: and Luis de Velasco, Viceroy in Mexico in 1591, thought that instead of seizing slaves carried illegally the authorities should merely collect the extra tax owed.

In 1600 Gomes Reinel died, and the contract for trading slaves was transferred to João Rodrigues Coutinho, who was then Governor of Angola, and extended to 1609. The contract was the same as that afforded to his predecessor, except that anyone who broke any of the rules would be fined 100,000 maravedís, of which penalty two-thirds would go to the contractor. No foreigner was to be allowed into the trade, and Rodrigues Coutinho had to sell licences openly in both Lisbon and Seville. He was also required, in order to hold the slave contract for Angola, to build forts at such places as the Kisama salt mines and at Cambambe (both far inland), and at the Bay of Cows, in Benguela, to the far south.

This new monopolist was an aristocrat, born at Santarém, a knight of Henry the Navigator's Order of Christ, and he lived in Madrid, where he was a member of the King's Council of Portugal. He was one of the few major Portuguese slave dealers of this era who were not *conversos*, and several of his brothers and sisters were monks or nuns. When appointed Governor of Angola he had undertaken to take 2,500 horses there, to assist the troops which were helping to pacify the place after the death of Dias. He had also lived in both Elmina and Panama, a colony that, as he knew, needed its black slaves for the back-breaking carriage of goods across the isthmus. Rodrigues Coutinho invested all the money which he made from the slave trade in seeking to complete the conquest of Angola, a task which obsessed him.

When he died, in 1603, a long way up the River Coanza, in pursuit of the ever-elusive final victory over the Kingdom of Ndongo, his brother Gonzalo Vaz Coutinho succeeded him with the slave contract. He had been responsible for much of the detailed work in his brother's time; he, too, was a *caballero* of Henry the Navigator's Order of Christ; and he had been Governor of the island of São Miguel in the Azores. He was a man with many interests. Thus he offered himself to develop the copper mines near Santiago de Cuba, taking with him 250 Castilian colonists and 900 slaves. To do this, he asked to be named *Adelantado* (military commander) of Cuba, and Governor of Santiago, Bayamo, and Baracoa, and for the titles to pass to his descendants for three lives. This extravagant suggestion by a Portuguese adventurer was not approved.

In the first quarter of the seventeenth century the total number of slaves exported from Africa probably approached 200,000, of which about 100,000 went to Brazil, over 75,000 to Spanish America, 12,500 to São Tomé, and only about a few hundred to Europe. The average per year must thus have been about 8,000.[19]

The African element in the population of New Spain was beginning to seem the dominant one in most big towns where Europeans lived – outnumbering the mestizos. The blacks were also important in all mines, and dominant in all sugar properties, particularly in supervisory roles: indeed in 1600 King Philip III finally forbade the use of any Indians in plantations. Since there were never enough African slaves to keep the sugar estates in being, that was tantamount to a royal discouragement of business in New Spain.

The Casa de Contratación in Seville, with a bureaucratic insistence worthy of the twentieth century, was still determined to guarantee that all imports, including human ones, should enter the Spanish empire via Cartagena, or Portobelo, where their own representatives were. This rule was, however, an inspiration for a considerable smuggling trade in which most royal officials participated with enthusiasm, as Francisco de Salcedo, Archbishop of Santiago de Chile, complained to the King. The episcopal démarche seems to have been the explanation why in 1622 the Crown established an internal custom house 400 miles inland from Buenos Aires, at Córdoba.

Africa was not in these years a mere silent participant in the supply of slaves to two distant European empires. The overthrow at the Battle of Tondibi of the great Songhai empire by a Moorish army sent down the great Western caravan route by the Sultan from Marrakesh had immeasurable consequences for the international market in slaves. Despite their victory, Berber (Moorish) control was far from certain, even of the main Songhai cities of Gao and Timbuktu, and internecine disputes disturbed the completeness of the pashas' triumph. The consequence was that, quite independent of the growing European demand, every day there were more slaves available in the interior of Africa. The victors after Tondibi may themselves have limited their loot to 1,200 prisoners, as well as forty camel loads of gold dust. But the Saharan slave trade thereafter much increased.

On the coast of West Africa these were the years when in consequence of the Atlantic trade several fishing villages at the estuary of the Niger began to turn into city states, their economies based on trading slaves to the Europeans. A famous hunter, Alagbariye, on an expedition for game to the coast, is said to have come upon the site in Nigeria on which Bonny now stands and, aware of the potentialities for trade, brought his people there, much as Huitzilopochtli the Mexican warrior god was held to have seen in Tenochtitlán the ideal site for a city. Such developments led to the villages in the delta of the Niger becoming important slave markets in the seventeenth century, though they were never as important as Angola or Congo. Once Bonny and the city states had been established there was little room for free men; slaves abounded, and not just for the benefit of the Europeans.

Some of these cities eventually became strong monarchies: Bonny, to begin with, but also New Calabar and Warri as well as Bell Town and Aqua Town, in the Cameroons; and there were some strong commercial republics, such as Old Calabar and Brass. But the powers of the Bonny kings were always limited: 'Although in many respects they appear to exercise absolute power, unrestrained by fixed principles,' wrote one English slave captain, 'they may be properly termed heads of an aristocratic government. This is evinced by having a grand palaver [consultation] house, in which they themselves preside, but the members of which, composed of the great chiefs and great men, . . . [are] convened and consulted upon all matters of state urgency.'[20]

Imports of African slaves to Europe and the Canaries were coming to an end. The explanation was that the high birth rate of the sixteenth century satisfied the demands for labour in Spain, Italy, and southern France; and when the population declined in the seventeenth century the economies in those countries were in poor condition. Brazilian sugar farmers could afford black slaves; Lisbon noblemen could do so less and less. Yet indigenous Indian slaves were still to be found in Portugal in the early seventeenth century, and the slaves of Lisbon in 1620 may still have been over 10,000, about 6 per cent of a total population of 165,000. Perhaps, too, a tenth of the population of the Algarve were slaves at this time. In 1600 Catalonia and the Mediterranean coast of Spain were still importing slaves as a result of maritime raids against Arab towns, and the authorities there were often occupied by the flight of slaves to France. (But this dimension diminished during the seventeenth century, when naval engagements were won by Moors more often than by Spaniards.) In Seville there was actually an increase in the population of the black quarter of San Bernardo. The parish had even to be divided into two (the new section was San Roque, whose church was finished in 1585). Perhaps there was here, as there had been in Portugal, a deliberate encouragement of black births for a time; in Palos, at least, masters apparently sought to persuade slave women to have a child every two years.

Meantime, another firm declaration against the slave trade then so vigorously under way had been made in Seville by Tomás de Mercado, a Dominican friar who when young had been to Mexico. He wrote an account of the commerce between Spain and the New World. He knew from personal observation in what vile conditions slaves were carried on ships. So he could be more direct on the matter than de Soto and others had been. In his *Tratos y contratos de Mercaderes*, published in Salamanca in 1569, he admittedly accepted the institution of slavery. He recognized too that prisoners captured in war had, throughout history, been enslaved, and even considered that slaves were usually better off in America than they were in Africa. But he also described vividly how so many slaves were obtained through kidnapping or trickery, even if the kidnappers and tricksters were usually Africans. The high prices offered for slaves by Europeans, he pointed out, also encouraged the African monarchs to raid each other's land, and even persuaded fathers to sell their children, sometimes out of spite. Overcrowding on slave ships while crossing the Atlantic was so atrocious that the smell alone was enough to kill many: 129 slaves on a recent ship, he said, had died the first night of the voyage. No official regulations about loading slaves, such as the Portuguese had tried to introduce, could be expected to work. So, he argued, indulgence in the slave trade to the Americas automatically caused men to incur deadly sin. Those who engaged in the trade in Seville, such as the Jorges and other distinguished merchants, should urgently discuss the matter with their confessors.[21]

These stern words had no effect. The Arenal in Seville remained full of ships clearing for the Cape Verde Islands, if not for Africa.

A few years later Bartolomé Frías de Albornoz, a lawyer born in Talavera in Spain who had emigrated to Mexico and lived there, went further than Mercado had done, in his *Arte de los contratos*, published in Valencia in 1573. Frías de Albornoz was the first professor of civil law in New Spain and is now considered 'the father of Mexican juriconsultants': a paternity which has certainly had an extended progeny. In his book, he doubted whether prisoners of war could ever be legally enslaved. Unlike Mercado, he thought that no African could benefit from living as a slave in the Americas, and that Christianity could not justify the violence of the trade and the act of kidnapping. Obviously, he thought, clergy were too lazy to go to Africa and act as real missionaries.[22]

Clearly these expressions of doubt needed a reply; and they came, in the form of a revelation. A Dominican friar, Fray Francisco de la Cruz, told the Inquisition in Lima that an angel had told him that 'the blacks are justly captives by reason of the sins of their forefathers, and that because of that sin God gave them that colour'. The Dominican explained that the black people were descended from the tribe of Aser – he must have meant Isacchar – and they were so warlike and indomitable that they would upset everyone if they were allowed to live free.[23]

Similar views to those of Frías de Albornoz were nevertheless expressed by a Jesuit, Frei Miguel García, who, arriving in Brazil about 1580, and being among the earliest members of the order to reach that dominion, was horrified to find that his society owned Africans who, as he thought, had been illegally enslaved. He decided to refuse to hear confession from anyone who owned African slaves. He and a colleague, Frei Gonçalo Leite, returned to Europe in protest. But nothing more was heard of them. A comparable protest was expressed in 1580 by the historian Juan Suárez de Peralta, a nephew by marriage of Hernán Cortés, who wondered why no voices were raised on behalf of the black Africans when so many were so raised in favour of the Indians: 'There is no difference between them other than that one is darker in colour', he sensibly pointed out.[24] But his book, like Las Casas's *History of the Indies*, in which that author spoke similarly, was not published till the nineteenth century.

A ferocious attack on the slave trade was also made at the end of the sixteenth century by the Portuguese Bishop of the Cape Verde Islands, Frei Pedro Brandão. He tried to end the traffic and proposed that all blacks should be baptized and then declared free.

These disparate challenges to the ancient institution, like all others, fell on deaf ears. Spain, and Portugal with her, was entering an intellectually dead period. The assumption was that the status quo had to be maintained. The age of adventure was over, and that of considerate philanthropy had not arrived. Printing had come, but there was no method of general communication. Albornoz's book was condemned by the Inquisition as being unduly disturbing. Anyway, what was written in a Dominican monastery, however important, could not be expected to be read by merchants on waterfronts.

All the same, these isolated denunciations enable the Catholic Church to present herself as a prefiguration of the abolitionist movement more plausibly than is often allowed. Throughout the seventeenth century, letters of protest on the matter of the slave trade continued to arrive at the sacred Congregation for the Doctrine of the Faith in Rome from Capuchins, Jesuits, and bishops.

Mercado and Albornoz might have no effect, but they had successors. Thus, in the early seventeenth century, a Jesuit named João Álvaras wrote – privately, of course – 'I personally feel that the troubles which afflict Portugal are on account of the slaves we secure unjustly from our conquests and the lands where we trade'.[25] Fray Alonso de Sandoval, a great Spanish Jesuit traveller who was born in Seville but educated in Lima, asked some embarrassing questions in his book *Naturaleza . . . de todos los etíopes*, which was published in his birthplace in 1627. He concluded that slavery was a combination of all evils. In 1610 he had written to Frei Luis Brandão, the Rector of the newly established College of Jesuits in Luanda, to ask if the slaves whom he had himself seen in Brazil had been legally procured or not. Brandão replied delphically: '. . . there have been fathers in our order eminent in letters, [and] never did they consider this trade as illicit. . . . We and the fathers of Brazil buy these slaves without any scruple. . . . If anyone could be excused from having scruples, it is the inhabitants of those regions for, since the traders who bring those blacks bring them in good faith, those inhabitants can very well buy them from such traders without any scruple, and the latter . . . can sell them.' He then warned Sandoval, 'I find that no black will ever say that he has been captured legally . . . in the hope that they will be given their liberty'. He added: 'In the fairs where these blacks are bought, there are always a few who have been captured illegally, because they were stolen, or because the rulers of the land order them to be sold for offences so slight that they do not deserve captivity; but these are few in number and to seek, among the ten or twelve thousand who leave this port every year, for a few who have been illegally captured is an impossibility. . . .'[26] Sandoval published this letter, but the exchange seemed surprisingly to have convinced the Jesuits of the legality, *grosso modo*, of the trade in slaves.

The only tangible consequence of all these discussions was a decision by Philip III, King of Spain as of Portugal, to insist that all slave ships carry priests.

Despite this official neglect of criticism of the new trade in black slaves, it is hard not to feel that there were, by 1600 or so, enough hostile voices to have brought the trade to an end within the next generation or so had it not been for the entry into the business of the Northern European Protestants, as will be discussed in the next chapter.

There were also in these years just a few indications that the institution of slavery itself was not accepted as a permanent state of affairs. In 1571, for example, the *Parlement* of Bordeaux declared that 'all blacks and Moors which a Norman merchant [probably from Honfleur] has brought to this town to sell should be placed at liberty: France, mother of liberty, does not permit any slaves'.[27] A little later, a slave travelling between Genoa and Spain with his master was set free in Toulouse on the ground that any slave who entered that city was automatically free. Jean Bodin, the philosopher of sovereignty, was personally present on the last occasion, and he used what he saw to support his argument in his *Six livres de la république* that an all-powerful sovereign could abolish slavery altogether.[28] But the decisions at Bordeaux and at Toulouse were isolated events of little significance. Whatever was said by Bodin, slavery persisted sporadically in France; and Frenchmen would soon show that they were quite ready to participate in the international slave trade, if they could only find a way.

There was, in the early seventeenth century, just one expression of uncertainty about the slave trade emanating from West Africa itself. Thus an ex-slave captured by the Moroccans at the great Battle of Tondibi, Ahmed Baba, established himself as a lawyer in Tuat, a great market town of North Africa. Some of his admirers approached him, shocked by the increasing quantities of 'ebony' passing through their oases in the Saharan trade. To be sure, they were worried not about the slave trade as such but, rather, that there just might be some 'brothers', Muslims, included by mistake in some of these caravanserais. Ahmed Baba then wrote a study concluding that slavery was certainly permissible if the slaves were captured in a just war, but all captives had to be asked before being enslaved whether they would accept Islam.[29] If they did they should be freed. A free man, therefore, might just have supposed in 1620 that Islam was a more tolerant faith than Christianity.

Book Two

THE INTERNATIONALIZATION OF THE TRADE

9

A Good
Correspondence
with the Blacks

Spain and Portugal assumed in the sixteenth century that they could together retain the Atlantic as a private lake. But from the beginning those imperial nations were troubled by pirates or interlopers in their trade in both Africa and the Americas.

The first seizure of a shipment of gold from Elmina by a French 'pirate' was as early as 1492. In 1525 a French ship anchored off Mpinda, just to the north of the River Congo, and King Afonso welcomed what he thought were two new friendly Europeans in his capital; the Portuguese complained bitterly, and did all they could to prevent any repetition of the unwelcome incursion. But by the 1530s French captains, mostly from Dieppe, that grand arsenal, both of shipping and of robbery on the high seas, had become intolerable to the Portuguese. The most feared figure – shipbuilder to the King of France, but pirate to the Spaniards as well as to the Portuguese, Jean Ango, of Dieppe, later Viscount of that city (one of his captains seized Cortés's treasure fleet in 1522) – secured royal approval to plunder Portuguese shipping as early as 1530. In 1533 two of his ships attacked two Portuguese vessels off the River Mahin, near Benin, and by 1539 French merchants were already buying the pepper, though not so far as is known the slaves, of that city.

The Portuguese sought to provide naval escorts for their trading ships. By then, however, it was almost too late: France had begun to displace the Portuguese on the Rivers Sénégal and Gambia. A Portuguese renegade, João Affonso, sailing under a French flag as Jean Alphonse, was among the first to carry out what is now spoken of as a triangular trade, sailing to the Grain Coast for pepper, and across to 'France Antarctique', then a promising French settlement at Rio de Janeiro, for wood. As well as attacking Portuguese ships, he probably carried slaves on a small scale. Another French adventurer, Balthazar de Moucheron, appreciating the possibilities of African trade, tried to make a permanent settlement on the coast of Guinea. He attacked the Portuguese at Elmina with a small force, but failed to dislodge the paramount power. Other French attempts, to gain possession of Príncipe and São Tomé, were equally unsuccessful. All the same, France was plainly determined to play a part in the destiny of Africa – as well as in that of Brazil. The records of Le Havre, Dieppe, and Honfleur suggest that nearly 200 ships from those pretty Norman ports set sail for Sierra Leone between about 1540 and 1578; and at least fourteen vessels left La Rochelle, then France's main Atlantic-facing port, for Africa between 1534 and 1565. In 1544 Estevan Darrisague of Bordeaux hired his ship, the *Baptiste de Saint Jean de Luz*, to a well-known captain, André Morrison, to make another triangular voyage: Guinea, Brazil, Bordeaux. Morrison made what trade he could: such were the rules in those days. No document survives to show that he carried slaves; but nothing proves that in the easiest stage of the journey, later so well known, from the Congo to Brazil, he did not.

During the disastrous Huguenot wars of the last half of the century French commerce was quiescent; but no sooner had peace returned than trade to Africa revived; and in 1594 a ship of fifty tons, *L'Espérance*, from La Rochelle, certainly took slaves from Cape Lopez, near Gabon, to Brazil.[1]

Long before that, the English, too, had become engaged in the tempting African waters: the first adventurer there was William Hawkins, of Tavistock in Devonshire, who sailed to the Guinea coast in the 1530s. In 1532 he even brought an indigenous chief back to England from a voyage to Brazil. This individual was intended for show; Hawkins left behind one of his seamen in the new continent as a hostage, who returned later, though the chief died on his way home. That was not a slaving journey.

There was a similar voyage to Guinea, precisely to the Gold Coast and to Benin, in 1553, led by two quarrelsome captains – Thomas Wyndham, originally of Norfolk, and Antônio Anes Pintado, a renegade Portuguese, perhaps a *converso* (he was denounced as a 'whoreson Jew' by his English colleague, but that may have been a typical East Anglian insult) – with the intention of breaking into the trade in gold: an aim which they fulfilled, for their ships brought back 150 pounds of it, though both captains died on the journey. This expedition sailed some way up the Nun River entrance to the Niger and later visited Benin where, following in the footsteps of the French, they bought pepper direct from the *Oba*. The captains resisted the temptations of the slave trade. Wyndham, who had previously sailed and swashbuckled with William Hawkins, was not the last member of his family to be associated with the African trade; but he was the first Englishman to sail into the perilous waters of the Bight of Benin.

Another expedition, the next year, of Captain John Lok, who returned from West Africa with gold, ivory, and Guinea pepper (malaguetta), also brought back to England some Africans, from a village between Cape

Three Points and Elmina, as showpieces, but these men were sent home eventually. The voyage was financed by sober merchants of the City of London, many of whom had become interested in trade in Morocco as the Portuguese began to withdraw from there: indeed, by the mid-sixteenth century the English controlled much of that country's external commerce. Even Queen Mary was interested. The success of Lok's expedition led to several other journeys – for example, two of a similar nature led by Captain William Towerson between 1555 and 1558, though, again, they do not seem to have been concerned with slaves.

These English voyages greatly disturbed the Portuguese, and so in 1555 a special ambassador, Lope da Sousa, was dispatched by a worried and elderly King João III to remind Queen Mary of the papal grants of Portuguese monopoly in Africa, and so prevent any further English inter-lopers from going to Guinea. The Privy Council in London accordingly forbade such undertakings. But that prohibition did not even last for as long as the loyal Catholic Mary was on the English throne. The Portuguese Governor of Elmina is found writing home to Lisbon in April 1557 asking the King of Portugal to be sure to send a fleet every year to help him protect the castle against these intolerable foreign ships, whose captains 'glut the whole coast with many goods of all kinds', even buying half of the available gold from the region of Elmina.[2] These successes of the French and the English were due to the low prices for their goods which they could offer in comparison with the Portuguese. The latter built new small forts at San Sebastián da Shama and at Accra, to the west and east respectively of Elmina, to try and prevent further Northern European trading. But they were ineffective.

Under Queen Elizabeth, more English captains set off to Guinea: for example, there was Richard Baker, whose journey is said to have inspired Coleridge's 'Rime of the Ancient Mariner'; there was even discussion of founding an English trading post; and then in 1562 Captain John Hawkins initiated the English slave trade. No doubt his father, by then dead, had passed to him useful information about currents, geography, people, and markets.

John Hawkins decided to go to Africa at a time when the Spanish government seemed to be beginning to crack under the weight of too many commitments: 'and being, among other particulars, assured that Negroes were very good merchandise in Hispaniola, and that [a] store of Negroes might easily be had upon the coast of Guinea', Hawkins resolved 'to make trial thereof'.[3] That positive assurance derived from a previous visit to the Canary Islands. His backing was at least as distin-guished as that available to slave traders of Lisbon; for he gained the support of his father-in-law, Benjamin Gonson (Treasurer of the Navy), Sir Thomas Lodge (Lord Mayor of London, Governor of the Russia Company, and a trader to both Holland and 'Barbary' – that is, Morocco and North Africa), Sir William Winter (Master of the Ordnance of the

Navy), and Sir Lionell Duckett (later Lord Mayor): 'all which persons liked so well of his intention that they became liberal contributors and adventurers [that is, investors] in the action'.

The Queen, Elizabeth, approving Hawkins's expedition, expressed the pious hope that the slaves would not be carried off without their free consent, a thing 'which would be detestable and call down the vengeance of Heaven upon the undertakers'. In so speaking, she amply demonstrated her ignorance both of Hawkins's intentions and of conditions in Africa.

Hawkins sailed with three ships from England in 1562. He stopped at the Canary Islands, where he picked up a pilot, then went to the River Cacheu and there or subsequently, in the River Sierra Leone, he captured at least 300 blacks, partly, as he said, 'by the sword, and partly by other means'. In fact, he seized most of his slaves from six boats already packed by Portuguese *lançados* and ready to be sent to the Cape Verde Islands.

Hawkins then sailed across the North Atlantic to the north side of Hispaniola, specifically to Isabela, Puerto de la Plata, and then Monte Cristi. He pretended that he had to careen his ships and that he could only pay for services rendered by selling slaves. This subterfuge eventually enabled him, in those shabby tropical cities, after some tortuous negotiations, to exchange the slaves for 'hides, ginger, sugars, and some quantity of pearls, but he freighted also two other hulks with hides and like commodities', which he sent for sale to the mainland of Spain. That commerce was illegal by Spanish law, and set the scene for many subsequent acts of smuggling: 'and so, with prosperous successe and much gaine to himself, and the aforsayde adventurers', he returned to London in September 1563. He had been away nine months. He lost the merchandise in the hulks, for they were confiscated in Spain. But all the same, his City friends 'made a good profit'.

In 1564, fired by success, Hawkins set out on a second voyage; he was supported by one or two of those who had helped him before (such as Gonson and Winter), but also by three influential noblemen, Lords Pembroke, Leicester (the Queen's favourite), and Clinton, as also by Benedict Spinola, one of those ubiquitous Genoese merchants to be found in every prosperous European city in the sixteenth century. The Queen must have approved this ruthless combination of aristocracy and bourgeoisie, for she herself sent a ship with Hawkins, the 700-ton *Jesus of Lübeck*, which her father had years before bought from the Hanseatic League. The time seemed especially favourable for another impertinent journey to the Spanish empire, for there had just arrived in England a refugee French Huguenot, Jean Ribault, who had tried unsuccessfully to establish a colony in what is now Port Royal, South Carolina.

The new expedition again made for the River Sierra Leone, probably went also to Ceberro (Sherbro) Island, to the south and, every day, went on shore: 'to take the Inhabitants, . . . burning and spoiling their townes'. This was a most unpopular action with the Portuguese, since at that time they were in the habit of negotiating carefully for all their slaves. Hawkins once again seized some blacks from Portuguese ships; he also traded with two monarchs, and set off for the West Indies, this time with 400 African captives. He sailed to the Venezuelan coast, where he eventually sold his slaves, first on the pearl island of Margarita, then at Borburata, near the modern Puerto Cabello, at Curaçao, an island off the mainland which had recently been occupied, and at both Rio de la Hacha and Santa Marta, on the Guajira peninsula in the modern Colombia, where the Spaniards were duplicitous and the English arrogant. Once again Hawkins tried to excuse himself by saying that the only way that he could pay for anything was to settle his account in slaves. He returned home, after paying the right taxes, via the new temporary French colony in Florida, 'with great profit to the venturers of the said voyage, as also to the same realm, in bringing home both gold, silver, pearls and other jewels': 50,000 ducats' worth in gold, according to Guzmán de Silva, the Spanish Ambassador in London, to whom Hawkins boasted that he had made a profit of 60 per cent. The adventurer was later knighted: he took as his crest a black female African.

There were soon rumours of a third Hawkins voyage. Guzmán de Silva tried to prevent it by complaining personally to Elizabeth. The Queen thanked the Ambassador, but what Guzmán called 'the greed of these people' was great, and several of the Queen's Council themselves took shares in the new expedition. In the event, however, Hawkins delayed and Captain John Lovell of Plymouth set off from London (the ships loaded by Hawkins), seized some Portuguese ships stocked with slaves off Cape Verde, in Hawkins's style, and then sailed to the north coast of South America, where he sought to sell them at Rio de la Hacha. But though Lovell made common cause with a French pirate and slaver, Jean Bontemps, and though they both seized Borburata, after the usual pretence of an accident needing repair, the trade was bungled, and it would seem that Hawkins received nothing.

Yet this failure whetted Hawkins's appetite for more profits, and soon his third journey was really under way. The preparations were, of course, noticed by the Spanish Ambassador, who made his usual complaint. All the same, Hawkins set off with six ships, of which two this time belonged to the Queen. The young Francis Drake was on one of the ships (he had earlier sailed with Lovell). The little fleet went down to Africa, and despite setbacks eventually secured between 400 and 500 blacks, partly by kidnapping ('Our general landed certain of our men . . . seeking to take some negroes'), mostly by the customary Portuguese method of negotiation with African rulers. They also seized a Portuguese slave ship which they rebaptized *Grace of God*. Then they sailed across the Atlantic and after the usual plea that they had suffered damage in bad weather and needed repairs for which they could only pay in slaves forced the sale of their captives in several now familiar Spanish ports – Borburata, Rio de la Hacha, and Santa Marta. Hawkins also burned Rio de la Hacha in a pointless act of war. Finally, on their return voyage, they were – genuinely, for once – driven off course by storms, and the expedition put in to Veracruz, the main port of New Spain (Mexico), the only harbour where a ship of the size of the *Jesus of Lübeck* could be repaired. Here, in September 1568, they were trapped by a Spanish fleet bringing a new viceroy (Martín Enríquez, later known for having welcomed both the Jesuits and the Inquisition into his dominion). Hawkins conducted himself intemperately, a fight ensued (though England and Spain were not at war), some of the English ships were destroyed, and such money and goods as Hawkins had on board were seized. Two of his ships escaped at night; one of them set down a number of English sailors in Pánuco, in northern New Spain, where they were captured. Several spent years in a Mexican jail, but three were strangled, then burned at the stake. Others were set down in Galicia, in Spain, with similar consequences. Hawkins, with Drake, managed to escape to England, having lost several ships (including the *Jesus of Lübeck*) and their profits, but not, curiously, their reputations. All the same, the first stage of England's participation in the Atlantic slave trade had come to a discreditable and bizarre end.

A more tolerant Portuguese attitude towards other Europeans in West Africa soon followed. For example, in 1572, they granted to the English the right to trade peacefully on the coast of Guinea – for gold, not slaves, for the time being. Then, after 1580, the defeated claimant to the throne of Portugal, Father Antônio of Crato, lived in London as an English puppet, and gave his authority to English ships trading in Portuguese-Spanish waters.˙ But the only consequence in the short term was the issue, in 1588, of a charter to the so-called Sénégal Adventurers in London. They were to have an English monopoly of trade with the Sénégal region for ten years. They did little, seem not to have been engaged in slaving, and sank into obscurity.

In Africa the Portuguese in these years were complaining less about French and English invasions of their privileges than about the Spaniards, united politically though they may have been. Thus in 1608 we find the municipality of Santiago in the Cape Verde Islands petitioning the Crown to end the practice of allowing ships proceeding directly from Spain and the Canary Islands to go to the upper Guinea coast; and there were other such demands – to no avail. A modest illegal trade in slaves continued to be carried on by Spanish merchants.

˙ *Philip II became King of Portugal in 1580, since the main line of monarchs in Lisbon had died out. Philip had a good claim to the throne through his mother. The crowns, though not the laws, of the two countries remained united till 1640.*

After the French and the English, the Dutch now made their appearance in Africa. In 1592 a Dutch captain, Bernard Ericks, bound for Brazil, where his countrymen had begun to trade in the 1570s, was captured by the Portuguese, and held for some time on the island of Príncipe, to the north of São Tomé. Here he learned of the interesting profits which could be earned from the African trade, and once free he set about establishing a Dutch company, which sent him back to Guinea. Ericks made the journey successfully, 'running along the whole Gold Coast, where he settled a good correspondence with the Blacks, for carrying on the trade with them in future times. . . . These people, finding his goods much cheaper and better than what they used to have from the Portuguese [the Portuguese merchants often used goods which they had bought in Amsterdam but raised the price], and being disgusted at the violence and oppression of their tyrannical government, besides their natural love of novelty, provoked the Portuguese to use them worse than they had done before.' Thus the Netherlands entered the history of Africa.[4]

This adventure by the Dutch was to begin with concerned with gold and ivory; then after the decline of the elephant in West Africa in the early seventeenth century, with gold; and only thereafter with slaves.

Holland had by 1600 been at war for thirty years with Spain and Portugal. King Philip II had sought to prohibit Dutch shipping from entering both Spanish and Portuguese ports. These exclusions acted as a stimulus to Dutch interference in Spanish-Portuguese trade: the Dutch republic was then creating what soon became the largest merchant marine in the world. Amsterdam, its capital, with its gabled roofs, its crowded harbour, its 10,000 ships (the property of sophisticated partnerships), and its merchants sustained by the rich pasturages of the Rhine delta, was becoming the world's greatest centre of finance and insurance. To some extent this trade was directed by Sephardic Jews who had found refuge there from the Spanish and Portuguese Inquisitions, and who knew very well the size, and the nature, of the Spanish and Brazilian markets. Great wealth, too, would soon enable the Dutch to establish the only standing army in Europe comparable to that of Spain.

The fact that Bernard Ericks had been on his way to Brazil explains much. The Dutch entry into the trade there had begun in collaboration with German merchants from the Hansa ports. By 1600 the Dutch had secured half the carrying trade between Brazil and Europe. Dutch capital was also invested in Brazilian sugar plantations, to which they sold good Italian-made sugar equipment (such as large copper cauldrons which the Venetians had used in the eastern Mediterranean). Dutch ships, as we have seen, had already begun to carry raw sugar from Brazil to refineries in Holland, and then to export the finished product throughout the Continent, even to countries with whom the country was at war.

The Dutch enterprise in Africa began seriously in 1599, after which their vessels were relieved of duty if they brought back gold from there. Twenty ships were soon sailing there annually. Similar journeys began to be made to the Caribbean, primarily, in the first instance, to look for salt needed by the Dutch fisheries. By 1600 many Dutch captains were sailing annually on their own Carreira da Mina, often financed by the same men who were founding their great Dutch East India Company. In 1602, the year when that enterprise was registered, there was even a publication: Pieter de Marees's account of the Guinea coast.

These Dutch merchants were by then well equipped to trade with the coast of Guinea: not only did they carry cheaper, and better, cloth than the Portuguese had usually done, they could offer the East Indian cloth (such as muslin) and Swedish iron ingots, which the every year more sophisticated African traders were known to covet.

In 1600 Pieter Brandt, another enterprising Dutch captain, made an even more ambitious journey. He sailed to Mpinda. He and others who followed him became, because of the quality of their wares, immediately popular there with the Sonyo (a cultivated people then theoretically subject to the kings of Congo). The Portuguese managed eventually to persuade the Sonyo to exclude these interlopers. Brandt then made his way north to Loango Bay. The kings of the Vili, the most powerful rulers in that region, had until then maintained their distance from the Portuguese, though the latter had sometimes bought copper and ivory from them (the copper came from a metalliferous region a hundred miles inland, in the valley of the River Niari).

The Dutch, thanks less to Brandt than to another adventurer, Captain Pieter van der Broecke, soon established themselves precariously on the Loango coast. For van der Broecke had good relations with the King of the Vili. He and his friends bought ivory, for which there was much demand in seventeenth-century Amsterdam, especially among merchants in their fine tall houses on the 'Herrengracht.

The Dutch trade in slaves was slower to get under way, though a few pioneer voyages had been made in the 1590s, when several merchants of Amsterdam brought slaves there to be told that they could not sell that cargo in that city – apparently for moral reasons. The same occurred in 1596, when a captain from Rotterdam, Pieter van der Haagen, brought 130 African slaves to Middelburg, the capital of Zeeland. The city council considered the matter and decided, again on moral grounds, that slaves could not be sold in that port. Next year, Melchior van Kerkhove took two ships to 'Angola' – then a term meaning anywhere south of Cape St Catherine – in order to buy slaves and sell them in Brazil or the Caribbean. But his ships were captured by the Portuguese. Then in 1605 another Dutch merchant, Isaac Duverne, agreed with planters in Trinidad, Cuba, to carry to them 500 captives from Angola. But it is not clear whether he did make the purchases in the end.

In 1607 a Dutch West India Company was founded on the model of the already successful East India Company, but at first it failed. An older United Company, meanwhile, turned itself into the Guinea Company in 1610 and two years later even built a fortress at Mouri, on the Gold Coast, only about fifteen miles east of the colossal Portuguese castle at Elmina. Mouri soon became the headquarters of the Dutch struggle against the Portuguese. It was renamed Fort Nassau.

Negotiation, as well as war, characterized Dutch aggrandizement. Thus in 1617 they bought from the Portuguese the strategically useful island of Gorée, on which they built two forts; and on the Rio Fresco, nearby but on the mainland, they built a factory, or deposit for goods. So the Dutch now had excellent access to both Senegambia and the Gold Coast. But they still do not seem to have bought slaves on any regular basis.

In 1621, with war beginning again with Spain (and Portugal, still united to Spain as a dual monarchy) after a twelve-year truce, the Dutch West India Company (the 'Oude' Company, to historians) was re-established, and given a monopoly for twenty-four years of Dutch trade to Africa and the West Indies. Influenced by Calvinist zealots from Zeeland and Holland, this body was run by a Council of Nineteen (the Heeren XIX), of whom the Chairman was appointed by the States General. Part of the capital came from public funds and, though its soldiers were paid by the company, the government supplied both them and the war *matériel*. The company was divided into five chambers deriving from different parts of the Netherlands, each being responsible for a different proportion of the capital and enjoying a corresponding control over the enterprise. The Amsterdam chamber was the dominant one, for it owned most of the capital. The successes of this body would be enormous, as much in war as in trade.

The man behind the new foundation was a visionary, originally from Antwerp, Willem Usselinx. Before the Dutch rebellion against Spain, he had been an apprentice to merchants in most of the great ports of Europe. He had seen the return of the Spanish treasure fleet to the Arenal at Seville, the Portuguese casting anchor in the Azores, and Brazilian sugar being unloaded at Porto. He fled from Antwerp to Amsterdam in the 1570s, and joined the brilliant circle of the geographer Petrus Plancius. To this group, Usselinx often expanded on the need for the Dutch consciously to seek to take over the imperial mission of Portugal, as well as to succeed to Spanish greatness. In numerous letters and speeches he demanded that the States General persuade or, if need be, force the Spaniards to allow Dutch commerce and settlement, particularly in areas where there were no colonies already established. He was among the first Europeans to see that the Americas could contribute much to the home continent, as the example of Brazil, already penetrated by Dutch capital, seemed to prove. He also thought (with no personal knowledge of the people concerned) that the indigenous Indians could be persuaded to accept the Dutch as their leaders more easily than they could Latins, for he was a Calvinist and an enemy of the pope. Of course, he opposed the idea of encouraging colonial industry, as did everyone else in his day. But he did suggest the emigration of agricultural labourers, including Germans and Balts, who already were contributing much to Dutch maritime power as seamen. He was critical of slave labour, thinking, as Adam Smith would do a century and a half later, that it was both uneconomical and – most unusually for his time – inhuman. Indeed, he believed that free white workers would work better than slaves, even if they might have to be in sugar mills all night.

To begin with, as a result of Usselinx's insistence, the new West India Company continued to eschew trading in slaves. Some enterprising shareholders proposed the traffic. But the directors decided, after discussion with theologians, that a trade in human beings was not morally justified. That might seem odd, for at that time, Calvinists usually accepted slavery as unthinkingly as Catholics did, agreeing that it derived from the curse of Ham.* But the first work of literature to criticize slavery outright had already been written in 1615 in Amsterdam by the brilliant poet Gerbrand Brederoo, who, in his *Moortje, The Little Moor* (based on a free French translation of Terence's *Eunuch*), talked of the traffic in slaves as 'Inhumane custom! Godless rascality! That people are being sold to horselike slavery. In this city there are also those who indulge in that trade.'[5] So those directors of the West India Company who were not influenced by their pastors were affected by their visits to the theatre.

Despite the playwright and the pastors, however, a few independent merchants of Amsterdam were by 1620 engaged in slaving. The most prominent of these was Diogo Dias Querido, originally a citizen of Oporto in Portugal who had lived for a time in Brazil. He had black servants – or were they slaves? – in his house in Amsterdam, and he trained them there to serve as interpreters on the African journeys which he promoted. Dias Querido, a Sephardic Jew, was important in Dutch foreign trade for many years: as well as carrying slaves on a small scale to Brazil, he imported sugar from both the latter and São Tomé, and sold it in Livorno and in Venice. Still, only twenty to forty ships sailed annually to Guinea from the Netherlands during the 'twelve years truce' between 1610 and 1622, and only two or three of them did so on behalf of Dias or other merchants interested in slaving.

At first, these doom-laden Dutch initiatives had little effect on Spanish-Portuguese imperial ways. The Portuguese in Luanda were certainly perplexed as to what to do about Dutch activities in Loango, to the north

* See page 23.

of their own city, but they thought that force was the only answer to such incursions, and the Crown in Madrid was reluctant to act. The court in those days, if it thought about black Africans at all, was probably more concerned about Yanga's revolt of 1607–11 in New Spain, a rebellion of slaves born in the Americas, who were less submissive than African-born *bozales*. The upheaval lasted many years, until a conciliatory viceroy allowed the escaped slaves to survive in their own community, San Lorenzo de los Negros, near Córdoba, in the Sierra de Orizaba, on the assumption that they would not attack white communities and travellers. Another black revolt, supposed to threaten the capital of New Spain in 1612, was only arrested by the execution of thirty-six blacks. In Brazil, the Governor-General was preoccupied with the lesser planters' continuing insistence on using Indian slaves, thousands of whom were captured in the interior, on the ground that they could not afford Africans: a poverty which led to the extraordinary expeditions of the *bandeiras*, freely organized bands of bandits, in search of Indian slaves which, between 1600 and 1750, did so much to discover the heartland of central South America, and ruin the Indians at the same time.

Perhaps the Dutch appearance on the international commercial scene seemed in New Spain less remarkable than the fact that there were by now mulatto slaves in Spanish America. The disastrous final expulsion of the Moors from Spain in 1610 did not disturb the domestic slave trade, since Moorish slaves were excepted from the rules, though obliged after 1626 to accept Christianity. In Cádiz there were in 1616 300 Moors, as well as 500 black slaves, most of them employed in building fortifications against new attacks by the English. Lisbon in 1620 still numbered over 10,000 slaves – almost all black: Moorish slaves would indeed be prohibited in 1641, while in 1606, and again in 1618, limitations were placed on sending slaves back from the Americas (one could only send males over sixteen years old). Neither religious corporations nor individuals had yet abandoned slaves in Europe.

Further, the Portuguese dominance of the slave trade was causing much bad blood with their nominal friends the Spaniards. Spanish merchants accused the Portuguese of being thieves who stole Spanish silver; of being Jewish heretics who continued to practise Judaism behind a mask of Christianity, and who were even filling the Americas with Africans educated to follow those heretical beliefs. As a result, the Council of the Indies of Madrid introduced a law in 1608 which made it difficult for foreigners to trade in Spanish America; but it was never applied to slave traders.

Because of all these difficulties, negotiations in the Junta de Negros in Madrid for a new contract (*asiento*) to carry slaves into the Spanish empire continued very slowly, as if the Dutch fleets and merchants did not exist. Thus, in 1611, the Casa de Contratación in Seville proposed the division of this legendarily valuable private treaty into two: one to apply to ships whose captains would buy slaves in the Cape Verde Islands, with an obligation to register all cargoes in Seville; the other concerning the carriage of slaves from Angola direct to Brazil and the Indies. The scheme was not accepted, since the first obligation would have added a long extra stage to an already formidable journey. The merchants of Seville, however, argued that to allow slave ships to leave direct for the Americas from Lisbon or the Canary Islands, as well as from Seville, would enable many captains to escape paying taxes. Anyway, the *sevillanos* insisted, officials in Lisbon and the Canaries were less punctilious than those of Seville. They wanted the ships to come to Seville, where the slaves would be listed for purposes of taxes, sold, and placed on Spanish vessels for the transatlantic crossing. The Portuguese argued that the adoption of these new ideas would ruin Portugal.

But seeing the slave trade primarily as an item in tax revenue, the supreme authority, the Council of the Indies, eventually conceded victory to the *sevillanos*. All slaving ships destined for the Spanish overseas empire were henceforth to be inspected at Seville. Africans destined for the New World would be taken first to Seville, and then transferred to one or another of the caravels in the annual convoys. Only if there were no Spanish ships available would Portuguese traders be able to carry slaves to the Spanish New World.

But there were no candidates for a new contract on these conditions. The old *asentista*, Vaz Coutinho, continued, therefore, provisionally to sell licences for his own profit. Then, finally, in 1616 (after discussion of other candidates, and again against the complaints of *sevillano* merchants), a new contract was granted to another Portuguese millionaire, and *converso*, Antônio Fernandes Elvas. He agreed to pay 120,000 ducats a year for the privilege of arranging the annual import – through licences, of course – of between 3,500 and 5,000 slaves into the Spanish colonies. He already had a similar contract to supply Brazil with slaves from Angola, for which he had paid 24,000,000 reals; while a cousin, Duarte Pinto D'Elvas, had had the same right to trade slaves from the Cape Verde Islands – an assignment which Antônio now took over, too, at a cost of over 15,000,000 reals.

Elvas had been born rich, he was a member of the prosperous Portuguese *converso* community in Madrid, and he had married a wealthy woman, Elena Rodrigues de Solís (also of Jewish origin, whose brother was at that time rotting in the Inquisition's prison in Cartagena de Indias). He had been Treasurer to King Philip II's daughter, the Infanta María, and had numerous properties in Lisbon, where he preferred to live, as well as a luxurious *quinta*, Mil Fontes, just outside that capital. Elvas agreed, in order to satisfy the Spanish complaints, that in theory he would take his Caribbean-bound ships to Seville for inspection before they set off for the colonies. Further, his blacks would be delivered only in Cartagena and Veracruz, a limitation which made taxes easier to collect.

So Elvas now became responsible for nearly all the legal slave trading from Africa to America. There were spectacular consequences, for after some bad years (between 1611 and 1615, only nine slave ships had been licensed by Vaz Coutinho, carrying a mere 1,300 slaves), 139 ships were licensed between 1616 and 1620, most (104) going to Angola – Luanda – carrying nearly 20,000 slaves. Between 1621 and 1625, 125 ships were licensed for America, the West Indies, and West Africa, from the Tropic of Cancer to the Cape of Good Hope, again mostly (82) to start from Angola (carrying more than 17,000 slaves).[6]

Thus more slaves went annually to the Indies under Elvas's aegis than ever before: an official named Benito Banha Cardozo wrote in 1622, 'Most people being employed [in Luanda] in the slave trade, they neglect everything else.' In the New World, the colonists found themselves receiving blacks from all parts of Africa. In her will about this time, for example, in Cartagena de Indias, María de Barros left four American-born Africans, three Angolans, three 'Ararás' (Dahomeyans), two 'Lucumís' (Yorubas), one Congolese, and one from Biafra.

As usually happened with these contracts, Elvas's *asiento* led to difficulties. That entrepreneur was probably the first merchant to make a financial success of the contract. But that in itself excited extraordinary jealousy for him, and not only among the *sevillanos*. Accused of cheating the King, he defended himself inadequately and went to prison, where he died. After war began again with Holland, in 1621 (largely as a result of the Spanish Crown's determination to reimpose its embargo on Dutch trade, to be sure), the *asiento* passed to Manuel Rodrigues Lamego, who gained a new contract for eight years in 1623, against the claims of Elena Rodrigues de Solís, Elvas's widow. Slave ships were henceforth to be permitted to register at Lisbon, not just at Seville, and thereafter most did so: the biggest shippers of slaves were, after all, still the Portuguese.

Rodrigues Lamego was another *converso* merchant, already enriched by the slave trade in Angola, both a friend and a relation of bankers in Brazil and the north of Europe, including many in Holland. Like his predecessor Elvas, Lamego was the proprietor of several rich farms in Portugal. But like other New Christian merchants at that time he lived in constant fear of the Inquisition, whose activities were often venomously promoted by less fortunate, jealous merchants in Seville. Lamego's brother, Antônio, suffered an auto-da-fé in 1633. His son, Bartolomé Febos, was in constant danger of a similar tragedy, for he was intimately linked with the powerful *converso* commercial network of Madrid. Like Elvas, Lamego made money from the *asiento* even though, between 1626 and 1630, only fifty-nine ships were licensed for Africa, mostly for Luanda (they carried a total of about 8,000 slaves). Much of the demand for slaves was in these years beginning to be met by interlopers, many of them Spanish and Portuguese – minor traders who had been kept out of the national arrangements with the powerful Portuguese merchants.

But even the official figures picked up in the next quinquennium: between 1631 and 1635, eighty ships were licensed – mostly (sixty-four) for Angola (carrying over 11,000 slaves). There were, again, a few more between 1635 and 1640: eighty-three ships were then licensed, as ever the majority (seventy-six) bound for Angola (carrying in theory over 11,000 slaves).

These increases, both official and illegal, were the consequence of the permission granted by Philip IV in 1627 to Portuguese businessmen to trade wherever they liked in the 'Iberian' empire. The fact that so many of them were *conversos* did not disturb the King, nor his Prime Minister, the great Olivares, for (perhaps because of the little drop of Jewish blood which he himself enjoyed through his great-grandfather, Ferdinand the Catholic's secretary, Lope Conchillos) the Prime Minister had always been well disposed towards that minority.

Of course, illegalities, smuggling, and corruption continued undisturbed. There were innumerable cases of ships arriving in Cartagena de Indias whose captains, for fiscal purposes, declared that they carried fewer slaves than they really did – say, 200 slaves instead of 500. The chief dealer in Cartagena was in those days a Portuguese, Jorge Fernández Gramaxo, who had begun to trade slaves in 1594 for his uncle, Antônio Gramaxo. By 1610 Jorge was defrauding the Spanish Treasury on so large a scale that he seemed 'enough in himself to destroy the Indies'. Once a representative of Gomes Reinel, and later of Vaz Coutinho, he had several properties outside Cartagena, where he stored illicitly introduced slaves on a large scale (much as, in the same country, in much the same region, in the twentieth century, his spiritual successors would keep cocaine), and he maintained an extensive correspondence with Amsterdam, Seville, and Lisbon. He began to be accused by the authorities of illegal, treasonable contact with foreign states (the Netherlands, in particular); but he escaped all charges since, again like some modern drug dealers, he was a local benefactor. He eventually obtained the position of commander of the fortifications in Cartagena and, from then on, he could not be challenged. He died in 1626 a very rich man, leaving his fortune to his nephew, Antonio Núñez Gramaxo, who dissipated it.[7]

Perhaps the most flagrant example of smuggling, though, was that of João Correia de Souza, Governor of Angola who, after a singularly disastrous administration of that province, himself set off on 3 May 1623 to Cartagena, in a vessel with 300 slaves, as well as a good deal of silver. He sold everything without registering the fact, thanks to the useful connivance of the Governor of Cartagena, a friend for many years.

Despite these irregularities, the Crown in Madrid – still for a few more years the united Crown of Portugal and Spain – remained concerned to promote the traffic in slaves. The tone had been set for the new century when in 1607 the King of Spain told a new Governor of Angola, Manuel Pereira Forjaz that, during his proconsulate, the buying of slaves was to be encouraged, so as to swell the tax returns to the Royal Treasury. The King coupled this instruction with a reminder that no white man should ever be allowed to go inland to slave markets, for African middlemen could usually buy cheaper than Europeans could. By that time, indeed, most slaves bought in Angola were bought from the half-African, half-Portuguese *lançados*, traders who could live in two worlds – one pagan, the other Christian – with no difficulty.

Typical of those active in slaving in those last years of the Portuguese-Spanish control of the Atlantic slave trade, as of the Americas as a whole, was Diego de la Vega of Madeira (he originated in the Castilian market town of Medina del Campo), who made a fortune by selling contraband slaves for use in the Peruvian silver mines. After working for years with the Angolan slave merchants, he, like Elvas, ended in prison in Lisbon, as a smuggler, and also on a grand scale. (His ruin was caused by the government's prohibition in 1622 of the overland route from the new colony of Buenos Aires to Chile and Bolivia, insisting that slaves for Peru and Pacific colonies should henceforth be sent by a long roundabout route which they could easily control – and tax – via Panama.)

More disconcerting at first sight to the Portuguese than the growing Dutch challenge to them was new warfare in the Kingdom of Ndongo in the hinterland behind Luanda after 1608. This fighting was caused by a series of brutal attacks on the Mbundu people of Ndongo by the nomadic, palm-wine-drinking, and often cannibalistic Lunda. To enable them to retain their mobility, the Lunda never raised children. Even the monarch, with his long hair embroidered with shells, and his daily anointment with the boiled fat of his enemies, would slaughter his own offspring, by all his twenty or thirty highly perfumed wives. To maintain their numbers, the Lunda adopted adolescents from the peoples whom they conquered. These novices were slaves, and wore iron collars as a sign of that status, until they were able to present the severed head of an enemy to the King. An English sailor, Andrew Battell (of Leigh-on-Sea, in Essex) – who was imprisoned for many years by the Portuguese, first in Brazil, then in Luanda – observed the Lunda at this time, precisely when they fell on Benguela, a new coastal settlement 250 miles to the south of Luanda, on the northern bank of the sluggish River Kuvu.* After their victory, the Lunda lived off the cattle and pigs which they had captured – and off the profits of selling the population to Portuguese traders.

Eventually, though in a different territory, the Lunda would settle down, adopt a conventional attitude to families and procreation, and

---

* *A new colony had been founded by the Portuguese at Benguela, with an ex-Governor of the first city, Manuel Cerveira Pereira, in command. The venture was not solely concerned with the possibility of trading slaves, but it was probably uppermost in the mind of the new conquistador.*

become a formidable empire in Central Africa, trading slaves in traditional style on a large scale.

The Portuguese about 1620 had three ways of obtaining the slaves whom they desired. First there was the usual, most common, method, of trade with chiefs or kings, as happened almost all the way along the African coast. This commerce depended, in the region of Luanda, on the finding of slaves by *pombeiros* – at first Portuguese but by the seventeenth century usually Luso-Africans or Africans who would negotiate with African monarchs, such as the *Ngola*, who seems to have been happy to trade in that way, even when he was at war. Second there were slaves obtained as a by-product of war, or even in consequence of wars nominally conducted to seek, say, silver mines – a method often resorted to by governors keen to make the most money out of a short appointment in Angola. The third method was tribute.

A new Portuguese governor of Luanda, Luis Mendes de Vasconcelos, embarked on a campaign designed to finish with the threats of the continuously hostile Ndongo, for good or evil. He captured that monarchy's capital at Kabasa, and the *Ngola* fled. In the event, though, Mendes de Vasconcelos, through his military victory, damaged the slave trade: in defeating the *Ngola* he had weakened the monarch, who at that time had been the most effective purveyor of slaves for the Brazilian slave ships.

This governor's service to the slave trade was, however, far from negligible, as befitted the son-in-law of one of the leaders of the business in the previous century, Manuel Caldeira. Thus he defeated a native chief named Bandi, on whom he imposed an annual tribute of one hundred slaves. Mendes de Vasconcelos also forbade any Portuguese or mulatto trader to enter the interior for slaves. Only the black *pombeiros* could do so. These traders would vanish for a year or so, and come back with trains of up to 600 chained slaves, many carrying ivory or copper on their bowed heads.

The next governors (João Correia de Souza, Pedro de Souza Coelho, and then Bishop Simão de Mascarenhas) sought to patch up relations with the *Ngola*. They had come to realize that to ensure the slave trade, which seemed every year as necessary as it was profitable, they required some stable African state in the region of Luanda with which to deal. The King of Congo was now feeble, the Lunda unpredictable; the *Ngola*, for all his faults, seemed to offer the best hope. The Portuguese were in the end successful in making peace, largely thanks to their skilful diplomacy with the *Ngola*'s remarkable sister, Nzinga (baptized Dona Ana de Souza), who was living in Luanda as Ambassadress. Then in 1623 Nzinga succeeded as *ngola*, though not before poisoning, perhaps eating the heart of, her nephew, the late *ngola*'s son. Nzinga would have liked to re-establish the old slave trade with the Europeans but, instead, Portugal unwisely went to war with her, since she had begun the practice of harbouring captives escaped from the coast. The Portuguese went so far as to establish a puppet *Ngola* (Ari, baptized as Dom Felipe I), who agreed to pay to the settlers a tribute of one hundred slaves a year, as well as to allow the Jesuits to build a church at his capital, now Punga a Ndongo. Fairs for the sale of slaves were reopened. But warfare with Nzinga continued, usually sporadic, sometimes bitter. That princess adopted some of the techniques of the Lunda, cannibalism and infanticide among them. She eventually established herself as the strongest military power in southern Angola, and the Portuguese failed to deal effectively with her. She never became the reliable purveyor of slaves for whom successive governors of Luanda hoped. Nor could the puppet *Ngola* produce slaves in the quantity which the Portuguese required; the latter sometimes even had to make do with old or young slaves, instead of men in the prime of their lives.

In these years the prize Portuguese colony of São Tomé, in the Gulf of Guinea, almost on the equator, survived as an essential entrepôt, seemingly unchanged, despite the periodic threats of Dutch fleets. In 1617 Fray Alonso de Sandoval, the enlightened Jesuit from Seville, described how Portuguese or Spanish ships were still bringing cargoes of slaves there from all over the West Coast of Africa. Many of these slaves came now from the 'Caravalies' (the Kalbarai Ijo, from both New and Old Calabar, centres of the trade from the Bight of Benin until overtaken by Bonny later in the century). The Calabars were cities without kings, addicted to war between themselves, sometimes for the specific purpose of obtaining slaves for the external market.

But in the Americas Angolan slaves were dominant, so much so that another Jesuit, Fray Diego de Torres, in 1615 ordered a grammar in Angolese for the benefit of those from that territory who were working in the mines of Potosí.

The Spanish-Portuguese empire in those early days of the seventeenth century was a vast enterprise, such as was scarcely to be seen again in history. But its size, pretensions, power, and apparent prosperity prompted attacks on it. In 1623 the newly reformulated Dutch West India Company planned a remarkably imaginative onslaught. Having temporarily seized Benguela, they planned first a naval attack on Bahia, the port of the sugar empire of the Brazilian north-east; then the fleet would turn across the Atlantic to join another one, direct from Holland, and both would strike at Luanda, the largest European settlement in Africa, and the main source of Brazil's slave labour.

The idea of this venture, breathtakingly audacious but fraught with risk, derived from a property speculator of Utrecht, Moucheron, who may have known how to bribe mayors in Zeeland but knew little of the problems of empire. To begin with, however, all went well. The Dutch were instantly successful in the first part of this strategy, seizing Bahia in 1624. 'When we entered Bahia', wrote Johann Gregor Aldenburg, one of the Dutch commanders, 'we only met blacks, for everyone else had fled from the city.'[8] The Dutch immediately put these slaves into an armed company to fight their old masters.

Though Bahia was soon recaptured by a large Portuguese-Spanish expedition (the slaves who had fought for the conquerors were hanged 'in a peculiarly abominable manner'), the Dutch shortly took Olinda and Pernambuco, to the north, and there further developed the sugar-plantation system which, through investment and commerce, they already knew well. A new empire, New Netherlands, seemed to have been achieved. The 'time of the Flemings' in Brazil had begun.

In Africa, however, the Portuguese held on at Luanda. That seemed for the time being of minor significance, since having conquered one of the largest economies dependent on slaves the Dutch West India Company was now having to revise its earlier doubts about the morality of the African trade. Their capture of Pernambuco was the turning point in this reconsideration. Those who still opposed the commerce in human beings were unable to suggest how the new possessions could be made to pay other than by the use of slaves. The earliest mention of the traffic in the records of the West India Company occurs in 1626, when that body's Zeeland Chamber, the most Calvinist of the different colleges within the undertaking, gave permission for the dispatch of a ship to 'Angola' – presumably, Loango, where the Dutch already had three trading posts – and the transport of slaves to the region of the Amazonas, a new Dutch settlement on the river of that name. The same Zeeland Chamber soon also allowed Dutch settlers in both Guiana and Tobago, as well as northern Brazil, to import slaves. The first reports from Brazil had, after all, told not only of the serious decline in the Indian population of the place, but of the difficulty of ensuring that those who existed worked effectively.

The transformation in Dutch trade, however, was slow. The West India Company began by obtaining most of their slaves from ships which their captains captured in war – war, of course, with Portugal, for the ships of the two nations constantly fought in these years: for example, between 1623 and 1637 2,336 slaves were so obtained, and sold in the New World, for an average price of 250 guilders each.

The Dutch by then also had trading posts in North America: the first, on Manhattan Island, was set up in 1613; settlements were also made in the Caribbean by the West India Company before 1630. By the mid-1630s they had several entrepôts there – in Curaçao, a barren island in a convenient place off Venezuela, as well as St Eustatius and St Thomas, both previously uninhabited, in the Leeward Islands.

Black slaves began to be carried by the company to the colony of New Netherlands in North America in 1625-6: in 1628 the Reverend Jonas Michaëlius, of New Amsterdam, the first minister of the Dutch Reformed Church in North America, was already complaining that Angolan slaves were 'thievish, lazy, and useless trash'. The following year, the Dutch

West India Company baldly declared that it would 'endeavour to supply the colonists with as many blacks as it possibly can'.[9]

As for Brazil, though the majority of the colonists continued to be Portuguese, numerous new settlers flooded in from Holland, including some Sephardic Jews whose families had had commercial connections with the territory for some generations. Slaves seemed to everybody to be the key to prosperity there; a governor of New Holland would remark in 1638, 'It is not possible to establish anything in Brazil without slaves.' Those Portuguese sugar planters who fled before the Dutch invasion had made the same point in a different way when they carried (in the words of an eyewitness) 'their pretty *mulata* mistresses riding pillion behind them, while they left their white wives to struggle on foot through the swamp'.[10]

Still, most slaves taken to New Holland – they averaged 1,500 a year in the late 1630s – continued to be captured at sea from Portuguese ships.

The new masters of Brazil could not leave their labour force so ill provided for. In 1636, a cousin of the Stadtholder of the Netherlands, Johan Maurits of Nassau, was appointed Governor-General of Brazil (he was later known in his homeland for the Mauritshuis, which houses the greatest collection of paintings in the country). An enlightened and far-sighted ruler, he was determined to make a financial success of New Holland. Olinda under his aegis became the finest city of the colony, possibly on the continent: royal palaces and four-storey town houses soon looked out across broad avenues to botanical and zoological gardens, synagogues and Calvinist churches.

Prince Johan Maurits first set about trying to improve the lamentable relations of the Europeans with the Indians; and at the same time tried, in the spirit of Las Casas and the first Spanish colonists in the Caribbean, to increase the supply of slaves from Africa. In 1637, to ensure the latter, he sent a naval force across the Atlantic to Elmina. Taken completely by surprise, it fell easily. This was the end of an era, for the Portuguese had been there 160 years. So the daily masses for the soul of Prince Henry the Navigator ended, the Portuguese church was converted into a warehouse (though a new chapel was soon built, as demanded by the Dutch Reformed Church), the rules for the pay and conduct of governor and officers drawn up in 1529 were abandoned, and the daily issue of four loaves of bread to each member of the garrison was forgotten. Salaries, to the local Africans, were thenceforth paid in florins, not reals, and a lay preacher replaced the royal chaplain. The Portuguese had, however, been singularly unsuccessful in converting the local natives, and African Catholics were scarcely to be found outside the region of the castle. So the Dutch conquest meant less to the people of Elmina than might at first have seemed likely.

The victors thereafter made a determined effort to exclude the Portuguese altogether from the Guinea coast: the other Portuguese fort on the Gold Coast, at Axim, which had been developed recently to produce gold as well as to sell slaves, was surrendered to them in 1642.

The pioneers of Western European endeavour in Africa thus retained, in the whole vast region north of the equator, only one recently fortified place on the River Cacheu, a little to the south of the River Gambia.

Johan Maurits wanted another Dutch fleet to complete the grand designs of the 1620s and capture Luanda. The West India Company was at first reluctant, and instead Hendrickx Eyckhout was sent out to the Dutch settlements at Loango Bay to increase the supply of slaves from that territory for Brazil. Cornelius Hendrickx Ouwman, who took his place in 1640, found it hard work to do this: only 205 slaves were sent to Pernambuco/Olinda in 1641, though there was no shortage of ivory, redwood, and copper. Dutch naval ships could also still lay their hands on some slaves by seizing Portuguese shipping in the waters of São Tomé or Luanda. But Ouwman, having been in Loango for a year, insisted that only the capture of Luanda could remedy the position. In May 1641 the Brazilian directors of the West India Company at last agreed with the adventurous plan, and a fleet was sent under Admiral Jol. He seized Luanda in August, São Tomé in October, Benguela in December. Now the Dutch in New Holland could surely have access to all Luanda's sources of captives, including those available from the monarchy of Queen Nzinga which, a director of the new Angolan administration in Luanda, Pieter Mortamer, wrote, was now 'overflowing with slaves for sale'. King García II of Congo also aligned himself completely with the new masters, and promised to revive trade with them, though not in slaves, since he had apparently had enough of the practice, as he remarked in unusually modern terms: 'Instead of gold and silver and other goods which function elsewhere as money, the trade and the money are persons, who are not gold or in cloth, but who are creatures.'[11]

The man who from the first had opposed this new policy of trading Africans by the Dutch West India Company, Usselinx, now left his home country, determined to found a rival enterprise. He went first to the King of Denmark, Christian IV, and when rejected in Copenhagen went to King Gustavus Adolphus of Sweden. That ambitious monarch authorized Usselinx to found 'a South Company', to trade with Africa, which, after Usselinx's death, also did its best to enter the slave trade.

The Danes soon became keen to found an Africa company of their own, and in 1625 a Dutch merchant settled in Copenhagen, Johann de Willum, received a licence to operate in the West Indies, Brazil, Virginia, and Guinea, a vast chain of territories which, however, in the seventeenth century, seemed to be one. The partners of the company were only allowed to load their ships at Copenhagen, where all cargoes had to be unloaded on their return. But little happened for the time being.

The Spanish and Portuguese officials in these difficult years of their countries' defeat, withdrawal, and decay must have realized that the Dutch invaders were merely the precursors of other countries. For example, France had long before these events in Africa put down roots in America – in Canada in 1603 and, in the next generation, in several islands in the Caribbean, beginning in 1625, with Saint-Christophe and Tortuga – the latter in collaboration with some English pirates. In 1627 Bélain d'Esnambuc, acting in the name of Cardinal Richelieu, disembarked on the first island a contingent of 300 Norman emigrants. In 1635 a new Company of the Isles of America was established in Paris by François Fouquet, a merchant interested since his youth in North American trade, father of Louis XIV's financier, Nicolas, and himself a member of the Conseil de la Marine; and Liénard de l'Olive received permission to occupy Guadeloupe and Martinique. These colonizations were completed quickly, and tobacco began to be grown on Guadeloupe in the first year of settlement. St Lucia, St Vincent, the Grenadines, and Grenada were also declared French, though an attempt to consolidate this little empire by occupying the intermediate island of Dominica was obstructed by the Caribs, who perilously survived there.

The question immediately arose, how were these new colonies to be worked? In 1626 a French company had been formed in Rouen for trade to Sénégal to bring back ivory and gum. Behind this enterprise we detect the influence of Cardinal Richelieu, Superintendent-General of Commerce and Navigation, who was determined to increase the maritime activity of his country. This new Compagnie de Saint-Christophe received permission to buy forty slaves. Thereafter Captain Thomas Lambert of Rouen was to be found frequenting the mouth of the River Sénégal. Soon two further French companies were formed – one for trade between Cape Blanco and Sierra Leone, the other to operate from Sierra Leone to Cape Lopez. In 1637–8 Lambert's expedition to the Sénégal reached what became Terrier Rouge, a hundred miles up the river, where the French offered iron bars, Indian cottons, linen, brandy, beads, and silver trinkets, for gum, gold, and pepper, but apparently no slaves. Were there moral scruples, were there religious doubts? Did the captains recall how, in the 1570s, a court in Bordeaux had ruled against the possibility of selling slaves there?* It is not altogether clear. The greatest historian of the Atlantic slave trade, Elizabeth Donnan (whom no student of the matter can think of without gratitude), once wrote: 'Just when the French scruples against trading in slaves were discarded is not clear, but by the time that French planters called for negro labour for their growing sugar plantations [say 1640–45], French merchants were willing . . . to provide such labour'.[12]

The matter may have been affected by the fact that France still had slaves at home, especially in the navy, and Marseilles still had a slave market. A *négrillon* of twelve years born in Cartagena de Indias was, for example, buried at Perpignan in 1639.

*

*See page 148.

Like the Dutch and the French, the English were also beginning to work on the periphery of the great Spanish-Portuguese empire. Thus settlers from London, having made several journeys of reconnaissance, settled in Bermuda in 1609. The English were soon in Virginia and Massachusetts and, in the next few years, founded various Caribbean ventures: in 1625, Barbados, for instance; by 1632, Antigua, Nevis, and Montserrat in the Leeward Islands were considered English possessions.

Some of these colonies needed slaves, or so it seemed, especially in the islands. The indigenous inhabitants, the Caribs, had almost all been stolen for that purpose a hundred years before by the first Spanish conquistadores on the bigger islands of the Caribbean. The descendants of the cattle and pigs which the Spaniards had inadvertently brought, and which roamed the empty islands and provided food for the new settlers, were not an adequate substitute. Or could workers from England and France be induced to settle in the lands over which their country's flag now flew?

Actually, before the new European settlers entered the African slave market the business was initiated on the mainland. In 1619 John Rolfe, the Norfolk-born first Recorder of Virginia, already a grower of tobacco, who had been recently left a widower by Princess Pocahontas, noted, 'About the last of August came a Dutch man of war that sold us twenty negroes.'[13] This comment is usually held to be the first reference to the import of black slaves into what became the United States, though Pánfilo de Narváez, Menéndez de Avilés, and Coronado had all taken slaves with them in their expeditions of conquest in Florida and New Mexico the previous century and it is anyway unclear what transpired in 1619. The early history of Anglo-Saxon America lacks the ample written records which distinguish the arrival of the Castilians in Mexico and Peru. Probably the ship concerned was not a man-of-war but a privateer, whose captain had captured the slaves from a Portuguese ship in the West Indies.

Even before that, King James I in London had granted to an active entrepreneur and favourite of the court, Robert Rich (shortly to be Earl of Warwick), and to thirty-six others, control over British African trade, through the formation of a Company of Adventurers to 'Gynny and Bynny' (Guinea and Benin). This was the first incorporated English company to concern itself with Africa. Rich already owned a tobacco plantation in Virginia, and was probably hoping to secure black slaves to work it.* A 'list of the living in Virginia' of 1624 included twenty-two blacks, several of them presumably coming to the New World as personal slaves of certain passengers on ships, such as Rich's own *Treasurer* (1619),

---

* *Rich had been one of the performers in Ben Jonson's* Masque of Beauty, *and went on to write one of the most sycophantic letters ever penned, to Oliver Cromwell: 'Others' goodness is their own; yours is a whole country's.'*

but also the *James* (1621), the *Margaret and John* (1622), not to speak of the *Swan* (1623).

The English attitude to slaving was at that time not quite clear. For example, a merchant named George Thomson went out, on behalf of Rich's Guinea Company, to explore the River Gambia. He was primarily interested in gold. Thomson lost his vessel to the Portuguese, and a certain Richard Jobson (of whom nothing is recorded except that he despised the Irish) went to relieve him, to find that Thomson had been murdered by one of his own men. Jobson reported that the natives on the Gambia were afraid of him, because their compatriots had 'been many times by several nations surprized, taken and carried away'. Jobson was offered slaves by an African merchant, Buckor Sano, but, speaking for himself and not for the Guinea Company, he declared proudly that 'we were a people who did not deal in such commodities, neither did we buy or sell one another, or any that had our own shapes.' The African merchant seemed to marvel at this, and 'told us it was the only merchandise they carried down into the country, where they fetched all their salt, and that they were sold there to white men, who earnestly desired them. . . . We answered, "They were another kind of people different from us." '[14]

Jobson made various explorations in the Gambia region, looking for gold, but this journey and two subsequent voyages of his were financial failures, and after a loss of £5,000 the Guinea Company gave up.

Jobson's protests were exceptional. The Anglo-Saxons turned out to be as ready to trade slaves as their French neighbours were. John Hawkins had in no way lost his reputation after his slaving expedition, for he had become Treasurer of the Navy and remained a national hero. Some private slaving had also already been carried out by English ships on the Guinea coast: English ships carried sugar from São Tomé to Lisbon, and there is a record of an English vessel carrying slaves from São Tomé to Elmina under contract in 1607.

The consequence of this commercial failure of Thomson and Jobson was that in 1624 several independent London traders complained that they had lost business because of the monopoly grant of 1618. Had they not already built European-style houses and factories in the estuary of the River Sierra Leone? This was the first mention of such a thing, but the Crown must have been interested. So some English trading revived on the Guinea coast. Did the ships carry slaves? Surely: in May 1628 there was a new report of black slaves arriving in Virginia: John Ellzey, collector of the Admiralty Tenths for Hampshire, wrote to Edward Nicholas, Secretary to the Admiralty with the Duke of Buckingham, 'The *Fortune* has taken an Angolan man [a vessel] with many negroes, which the captain bartered in Virginia for tobacco. . . .'[15] The next year, one of the independent traders, Nicholas Crisp, a Gloucestershire man whose father had been Sheriff of London, was found complaining about the French seizure of his ship *Benediction*, which had been carrying on its 'accustomed trade' with 180 slaves on board. In 1632 King Charles I granted a licence to transport slaves from Guinea to a syndicate of separate traders (that is, a group which had nothing to do with the company of 1618). This was headed by that same Nicholas Crisp, the other directors being all prominent men about the court: Sir Richard Young, Sir Kenelm Digby, George Kirke, Humphrey Slaney, and William Clobery.

Of these men, Crisp was original in many ways other than maritime enterprise ('The art of brick-making, as since practised, was his own, conducted through incredible patience by many trials'); Digby, son of a conspirator in the Gunpowder Plot, was a genius; and Slaney was a Bohemian by birth. They received an exclusive right (among English traders) to trade in Guinea, Benin, and Angola for thirty-one years. Crisp had already built a British factory at a place which came to be known as Cormantine (Kormantin), on the Gold Coast: and it would remain the English headquarters, indeed the only English fort, though not the only English settlement, till 1661. He was the foremost member of the company.

This enterprise certainly traded slaves. Thus in 1637 the ship *Talbot* was found equipped to 'take nigers and to carry them to foreign parts'; and, the same year, Crisp, interloper turned gamekeeper, was himself complaining that new interlopers – English ones, that is – were threatening his monopoly. In 1644 he lost control of his company. As a monarchist (he 'gave thousands' to the King during the Civil War) he could scarcely be surprised at being accused by his opponents of owing the state £16,000, to settle which debt his share of the Guinea Company was seized. Other English merchants were now beginning to be interested: for example, Samuel Vassall (a trader of French extraction, much concerned with Massachusetts, of which he, with his brother, John, was one of the first promoters). Crisp's Guinea company was denounced by Vassall and other rivals before the Council of State in 1649, for having gained their monopoly by the 'procurement of courtiers'.[16]

The next year Crisp himself went to Guinea, to Cabo Corso (Cape Coast), with what he understood from the King of Fetu was a permission to build there. He bought the land for £64 worth of goods; 'whereupon the people gave several great shouts, throwing the dust in the air and proclaimed that this was Crisp's land'. Fourteen days later, though, Henrick Carloff, an adventurer in the service of the Queen of Sweden, appeared offshore, and the King of Fetu allowed him, too, to build. The English were soon turned out, and so it was the Swedes who built the first castle at Cabo Corso.

When denounced as monarchists in 1649 Crisp and his friends defended themselves by saying that they had brought £10,000 from the Africa trade into England, that they had founded a trading post in 1632, had purchased Winneba in 1633, and had even taught English to the son of the King of Aguna.

*

By the late 1630s a few African slaves were to be seen in most of the European North American colonies. In 1638, for example, there were some recorded in the territory which would become Pennsylvania. Equally, that was when slaves are known to have been first in Maryland: an official, Richard Kemp, wrote to the Governor that he had bought, among other things, 'ten negroes . . . for your lordship's use'.[17]

The *Desire*, 120 tons, built at Marblehead (Massachusetts) but registered at Salem, was probably the first ship constructed in North America to trade for slaves, though she merely went to the West Indies, not to Africa; she was also the first ship to carry black slaves to Connecticut, in 1637. According to John Winthrop the younger, the Suffolk-born first Governor of that colony, William Pierce, its master, 'brought some cotton and tobacco and negroes etc., from thence and salt from Tortugas [off Hispaniola]. . . . Dry fish and strong liquors are the only commodities for [exchange in] those parts.'[18] Pierce also kidnapped, and apparently left behind, some Indian captives at Providence Island (the Islas Providenciales, in the Caicos Islands, in the Bahamas).

In these years, it seemed possible that the demand for agricultural labour in both French and English North America and the Caribbean could be satisfied by white indentured servants: men and, to a lesser extent, women who, in return for a free passage and an opportunity for possession of land in future, bound themselves to work for a specific number of years with employers. The English government approved: Francis Bacon, when Lord Chancellor, had coldly told King James I that, through this kind of emigration, England would doubly gain: 'the avoidance of people here, and in making use of them there'.[19] These chances of a successful escape from half-feudal Europe, with its wars and obligations, seemed a great chance, not only to the English poor but to the French: the so-called *engagés*, from France, went to the French Caribbean on similar lines. For a generation, too, 'Newlanders' travelled along the Rhine Valley trying to persuade discontented German peasants to seek their fortunes across the ocean, as did similar agents in Bristol and London. Kidnapping for this purpose also became frequent; men and women were given drink, or children sweets, by planters' 'spirits', to persuade them to agree to work in America. Conditions on these emigrant ships were almost as bad as those on slavers. Long before Australia was discovered, convicts, too, were sent.

But the era of the *engagé* or indentured servant was short. Within a generation it came to be realized that the treatment of such men and women was harsh, and that the feudal conditions which many had sought to avoid in Europe were being copied in the New World. Wages in both France and England were also increasing. Indentured servants found it hard to find good land after their ten years of service were over; and slaves began to look cheaper to the planter: a slave could be had at the end of the seventeenth century for £20, whereas an indentured labourer might cost £10–15 as well as the cost of the journey. Africans were anyway tougher than white yokels. They stood up to tropical diseases better than farmers' boys from Normandy or East Anglia.

In the new circumstances, meantime, in which all Northern Europe seemed seeking entry into a formerly closed Iberian world, the Spanish Crown tried to manage affairs by maintaining all its old techniques (it was still responsible for the affairs of Portugal): thus in 1631 a new *asiento* was let to Melchor Gómez Angel, another merchant of Lisbon with *converso* origins. The contract reduced the number of slaves to be carried to 2,500 a year; but, as usual, no one kept to the rules. *Asentista* boats went to non-*asiento* ports; the King's uncle, the Cardinal Infante Enrique, was allowed to send an extra 1,500 slaves a year for Buenos Aires, through a licence to Nicolás Salvago of Seville. The entry of Spain into the Thirty Years War meant that the Caribbean became – for the first time – a war zone: Portuguese slave merchants lost twenty ships, mostly to the Dutch, who were ever more active against all Portuguese possessions, especially in Africa. Nevertheless, the slave traffic could still be described by the 'Visitor to New Spain', Medina Rosales, a kind of official inspector-general, as 'the most considerable and important [*cuantioso*] commerce that there is in the Indies'; and in 1638 the Viceroy of that dominion, the Marquis of Cadereita, wrote that the slave traffic 'is the biggest income and most secure of all which His Majesty has in his realms'.[20]

The *asiento* continued in the hands of Portuguese *conversos*: passing in 1637 from Gómez Angel (he seems to have lived in Andalusia, on the Guadalquivir, perhaps at Lebrija) to a relation, Cristóbal Méndez de Sosa.

But the Inquisition was still concerning itself with the alleged Judaizing activities of all Portuguese merchants, whether or no they were involved in the slave traffic. The traders of Seville were thereby enabled to have their revenge on the traders in Lisbon, whose economic dominance they had so long resented. Thus 1636 saw the trial of Francisco Rodrigues de Solis of Lisbon, brother-in-law of the monopolist of the 1620s, Antônio Fernandes Elvas. Sent to Cartagena de Indias to liquidate his affairs there, he fell into the hands of the Inquisition and was accordingly submitted to an auto-da-fé. There was in 1638 a big auto-da-fé in Cartagena, of João Rodrigues Mesa of Extremós, Portugal, who had sold a great number of Angolans since he arrived in the city in 1630. A large crowd of slaves, free blacks, mulattos, and some Spaniards threw oranges at him and other condemned men before they were burned.

Subsequent autos-da-fé would ruin the Portuguese slave-selling network in the New World. For example, in 1646 Antonio Váez de Acevedo, buyer and provider of slaves at Veracruz, and in 1649 his brothers, Simón and Sebastián Váez Sevilla, were humiliated (though not burned), in the terrible auto-general of that year. Sons of a butcher from Castellobranco, in north-east Portugal, who had acted as executioner and then become a stevedore in the port of Lisbon, Antonio had provided most of the African slaves who were sold in Mexico; Sebastián had been Purveyor-General to the recently founded Spanish Caribbean naval squadron, the Armada de Barlovento; and Simón had become one of the richest men in Mexico thanks to his slave dealings. Friend and protégé of the Viceroy, the Marquis of Villena, as well as holder of several governmental positions, on excellent terms at one time with bureaucrats of the very Inquisition which condemned him, Simón Váez had also prospered from the trade with China, via Acapulco. He had married Lorena de Esquivel, an old Christian – but philo-Semitic, according to the Holy Office, for had she not, years before, broken a pot in anger when a ham was cooked in it? In consequence of such minor matters were great fortunes lost. No doubt, Simón Váez and his brother Sebastián were secret Jews: as early as 1625, one of Simón's accountants, Hernando Polanco, had denounced him for never permitting cooking with lard, and for arranging that his wife always arrived too late for mass. On the other hand, hostility towards the Portuguese merchants, Jewish or non-Jewish, was evidently a strong motive in the persecution in Mexico which was pressed ferociously by the temporary Viceroy, the brilliant and unbending Bishop of Puebla, Juan Palafox.

Simón Váez, betrayed by people who had worked for him, communicated during his seven years in prison with his friends and relations through some of the slaves whom he had sold so well; but to little avail. The auto-da-fé of 1649 was watched by it was said 30,000 people of every rank of society: how agreeable it must have been for the Indians and the African slaves to observe the parading of the great merchant, with his wife, his brother, and other relations, men and women, half naked and shaved, who, a few years before, had 'driven through the city in coaches, receiving judges and their wives at their parties, respected as if they had been the grandest nobles of the kingdom'.[21]

Similar trials of *converso* slave merchants were also held in Lima, above all that which, beginning in 1635, ended by incriminating the most important slave merchant there, Manuel Bautista Peres. Peres had been active in slaving since 1612, having been at first a captain of slave ships from Africa. He had been in Lima since 1620. In later years, he obtained slaves through his brother-in-law, Sebastián Duarte, who regularly bought Africans in Portobelo or Cartagena for shipment to Peru. Peres was looked upon as the leader of the Portuguese in Lima, and known there as '*el capitán grande*'. His fortune was estimated at 500,000 pesos, a large sum for that time. He owned silver mines in Huarochiri, fifty miles inland from Lima, where his house was so luxurious as to be nicknamed the de Pilatos. He conducted himself as a serious Christian, and priests educated his children; yet it was said that he held secret theological meetings which showed him to be Jewish. Peres never confessed to Judaism, and he tried unsuccessfully to kill himself with a dagger, but he and Duarte were both burned alive all the same.

The Inquisition of Cartagena de Indias had a similar bout of accusations. Thus Luis Gómez Barreto, also a *converso*, also a slave trader, who played an important part in the city between 1607 and 1652, was in the end seized and tried. His ceaseless travelling, in pursuit of the best slaves, between São Tomé and Luanda or between Guinea-Bissau and Benin, sometimes returning to Spain, and making four journeys at least to Lima, availed him nothing in the end. Then Manuel Álvarez Prieto, taught to be a practising Jew in Angola, was also tried for it in Cartagena de Indias.˙

The slave trade to the Americas in the sixteenth and early seventeenth centuries – until the 1640s, when sugar took over from tobacco in the Caribbean plantations – was still on a fairly small, and therefore a relatively human, if not humane, scale. It was probably still smaller in many years than the Arab trans-Saharan trade in black slaves. The commerce in slaves also still flourished with respect to captured Christians, from all over Europe. William Atkins in 1622 described how he and some other English Catholic schoolboys bound for Seville were, despite being encouraged to fight by a draught of aquavit mixed with gunpowder, captured by a Morisco captain in the service of the King of Morocco (of Marrakesh). He was imprisoned with 800 Spanish, French, Portuguese, Italian, Irish, and Flemish slaves in Salé, on the Atlantic coast, near what is now Rabat, where slaves were sold in the streets with the seller calling out, 'Who buys a slave?' and the captives being beaten to walk faster by a peezel, a bull's penis.[+22]

These slaves were treated with at least as much brutality as the African slaves were by Europeans: Atkins described how a Frenchman, 'catched in the creeks of the river, with hopes to have escaped over in the night time', was 'found by his patron, [who] first cut off his ears, then slit his nose, after that beat him with ropes till all his body which was not covered with gore was black with stripes, and lastly drove him naked, thus disfigured, through the streets, for an example and a warning to other slaves not to try and escape. In the end, they threw him into a dungeon with a little straw under him, loaden with irons.' A Breton sailor caught trying to escape not only had his ears cut off, but was forced to eat

---

˙ *In Luanda, another* converso, *Gaspar de Robles, for a long time dominated the trade in the early seventeenth century. He went to New Spain, where the Inquisition seized him, as it had done Manuel Álvarez Prieto in Cartagena.*

† *They were held in a dungeon known by the term* matamoros, *a Hispanicization of the local word* matamoura, *grain silo (which served as a prison) but also, ironically, the Spanish for 'Killer of Moors'. They narrowly escaped being made eunuchs to 'wait upon the King's concubines in their chamber'.*

them. Eight hundred English captives were held as slaves at Salé in 1625, over 1,500 in 1626. It will be recalled that Defoe caused Robinson Crusoe to be a slave here for two years in the 1650s. He escaped to become, however, a would-be slave trader in Brazil.

10

THE BLACK SLAVE
IS THE BASIS
OF THE HACIENDA

*'The Black Slave is the basis of the hacienda
and the source of all wealth.'*

José de los Rios, Procurator-General
of Lima, 1646

THE REVERSES in Brazil and Angola were not the only ones suffered by the joint Spanish-Portuguese Crown in these years. In 1640 both Catalonia and Portugal rebelled. After many battles, the Catalans were reabsorbed by Spain, leaving behind a train of resentment which has never disappeared. The Portuguese, on the other hand, escaped into self-assertive independence under the rule of the Braganza kings. These events brought an end to the imperial Spanish Crown's collaboration with the Portuguese merchants in the slave trade to their empire. Had it not been for the revolution, the old *asentista* Cristóbal Méndez de Sosa would probably have gained anew the rights which had expired. Instead, he and others like him removed to Lisbon. There was for the time being no new *asiento*. The Spanish slave trade remained suppressed for ten years.

These events seemed to promise catastrophe. José de los Ríos, Procurator-General of Lima, wrote in 1646: 'The shortage of blacks threatens the total ruin of the entire kingdom, for the black slave is the basis of the hacienda and the source of all wealth which this realm produces.'[1] Without African labour, he went on mournfully, all economic activity would collapse: market gardens, cornfields, vineyards, sugar mills, mines. For the agriculture of the region of Lima was then heavily dependent on African workers; the vineyards of the valleys of Pizco and Ica employed 30,000 slaves, and the owners constantly needed them replenished. Similar complaints were made by owners of silver mines in New Granada and in New Spain. Everyone in the Americas also remembered how the great protective fortresses of the Spanish empire had been largely the work of black African labour: San Juan de Ulloa, Havana, Cartagena – 100 or 200 slaves had made all the difference to the defence of the empire.

An illegal trade in slaves did flourish, so much so that some less important parts of the Spanish empire, such as Buenos Aires, remembered that 'it was when the metropolis ceased to send them that the colonies were best supplied with slaves'.[2] But old hands, in rose-coloured haciendas, in Lima or Mexico, in Cartagena de Indias or in Jamaica (still Spanish for a few more years), or pearl merchants in Margarita, looked back with nostalgia to the old days, when the empire was regularly served by the great Portuguese *converso* merchants.* The last few years had been unsatisfactory in many ways. There had never been enough slaves, but what was to come would surely be worse. For in these years the interlopers were mostly heretic Dutch.

The Dutch presence was the paramount one in both Africa and the Caribbean in the 1640s. They were in these heady years the dominant world power, Portugal's successor on both sides of the Atlantic, with innumerable possessions in the East too. Their painters at home, such as Rembrandt and Vermeer, were at the summit of their powers; and distinguished artists also travelled to Brazil to depict the Dutch triumph there.

In Africa, Elmina, once the magnet of Portuguese power in the Gulf of Guinea, remained with the Dutch at the temporary peace of 1640. They reinforced the place, building nearby Fort Conradsburg, and they soon had a chain of similar castles on the Gold Coast. Their sale of slaves increased by leaps and bounds. Whereas between 1636 and 1640 the average number of slaves sold in Pernambuco varied between 1,000 and 1,800, the subsequent six years 1641 to 1646 saw the figures change thus: 1,188, 14,337, 2,312, 3,948, 5,565, and then back to 2,589. 'Without Negroes and oxen nothing can be expected from Pernambuco', the Heeren XIX, the supreme authority of the West India Company, were told in 1640;[3] and in 1648 Frei António Vieira, himself grandson of a black woman, and the greatest defender and friend of the indigenous Indians, would write: 'Without blacks there is no Pernambuco and, without Angola, there are no blacks'. Vieira also pointed to the uncomfortable fact that the Portuguese had been fighting a people whiter than they, the Dutch, and embarrassingly asked whether 'we are not as dark compared with them, as the Indians to us'?[4]

The Dutch, having established themselves in Luanda, took care to maintain their older relations with the Vili, on the Loango coast. The trade from there was now put to better use than ever, in that the fine cloths of the place, the much prized redwood, and the *nzimbu* shells could be

---

* *In default of indigenous labour, African slaves, especially boys between fifteen and sixteen years old, had learned to dive for pearls, and also to take them to the mainland in large canoes.*

exchanged in Luanda for slaves almost as easily as Dutch textiles and Swedish iron bars. The local kings all rejoiced at the thought of a new European master. The King of Congo even sent an ambassador to Maurits of Nassau in Brazil in order to ensure that the slave trade to that country would be just as the Portuguese had had it. He sent presents, including two other slaves for the Governor, and a few more for his council. Other African ambassadors went to Amsterdam to seek Dutch help against Portugal. The King of Congo placed images deriving from the Dutch Reformed Church on the altar of his Catholic cathedral. The invincible Queen Nzinga (in retreat, her kingdom was known as Matamba) also became a Dutch ally, and undertook several small wars locally in order to provide the Dutch with more slaves than she could otherwise supply.

Yet the Portuguese were resilient. After the Dutch capture of Luanda the Governor, Pedro Cesar de Menzes, led the old colonists a few miles north to the Bengo River, where the Jesuits had established plantations, and where they sought to prevent their old African friends (and enemies) from collaborating with the conquerors. Failing to do this, the Governor and his friends moved much further into the interior, to the fort of Massangano, on the River Cuanza. There Cesar de Menzes was able to count on the backing of the puppet *Ngola*, Ari, of Ndongo.

Given the interruption of the Portuguese slave trade to Brazil, certain noblemen of Lisbon (Gaspar Pacheco, Francisco Fernandes de Furna, Antônio Lopes Figueroa, and Ruy da Silva Pereira) had, in the meantime, presented a new plan to their King. It was adopted in 1643. The idea was to arm Flemish boats, crew them with Portuguese, and send them round the Cape of Good Hope to Mozambique, to fetch both slaves and valuable woods: the same dues would be payable in Rio on the slaves as if they had come from Angola. So 4,000–5,000 slaves were soon being exported every year in this way to the Americas, mostly to Rio, but also to other markets. Mozambique, so remote, so exotic, became the last resort of the European slave traders, and the tiny island of that name soon became much used, and not just by the Portuguese.

After a while the Dutch and Portuguese in Angola came to a working agreement: the former, in Luanda, would tolerate the settlement at Massangano and sell it food, provided that the Portuguese supplied them with slaves. The Dutch conquerors were in fact disappointed: they had expected to find in Portuguese Africa a self-sustaining export trade of 16,000 slaves a year, and their failure to achieve that without much greater efforts than they had expected forced them into all kinds of bargaining. They demanded high prices (in slaves) for their food, while the Portuguese colonists waged war to gain slaves, for all the world as if they were local Africans.

Portugal, newly independent again after 1640, was a more formidable power than a nation tied to the coat-tails of the King of Spain. The Portuguese-Brazilian settlers still living in New Holland – the *moradores*, those who had stayed on under Dutch rule – staged a rebellion. In a short and effective campaign they expelled the Dutch from all their old territory, except for Recife-Pernambuco. Then in 1648 they sent fifteen ships, under a brilliant general, Salvador Correa de Sá, across the South Atlantic to reconquer Luanda and São Tomé. This expedition was immediately successful, for the Dutch were as ill-prepared in 1648 as the Portuguese had been in 1641. So the latter's enclave at Massangano (which had been besieged by Holland's African allies) was relieved. Correa de Sá, now the new Governor of Angola, destroyed the Dutch outposts (to the north of the Congo, at Pinda, and even at Loango), while García, King of Congo, as a punishment for his welcome to the Dutch, was obliged among other things to accept Portuguese sovereignty south of the River Dande (fifty miles north of Luanda), to deliver annually 900 basketfuls of palm cloth, worth 1,000 slaves, and to give up all those Angolan slaves who had recently taken refuge in his kingdom.

Given these wars and other reversals of fortune, some of them explicitly inspired by disputes over the source of labour for the Americas, it is scarcely surprising that much the same number of slaves were exported from Africa in the second quarter of the seventeenth century as in the first: about 200,000, of whom 100,000 probably went to Brazil and 50,000 to Spanish America. For the first time (in the 1620s and 1630s), the English and French Caribbean appeared as major consumers: nearly 20,000 and 2,000 respectively to the English in Barbados and the Leeward Islands, and 2,500 to the French in Martinique and Guadeloupe. The average number of slaves exported per year from all parts of West Africa might have been about 8,000, many of whom, in the last part of this era, were brought in Dutch boats, including those taken to the Spanish empire. Probably Angola was the most frequent source, if by that word one understands the whole region south of St Catherine's Bay.[5]

Despite their military failures, Dutch merchants in the 1650s, however, still dominated the market of slaves for the West Indies. Their superior position there reflected their global standing. Holland remained the world's dominant economic power, in Central Europe as in the Baltic. The Dutch East India Company was still prospering, and much of world trade was in its hands; like Antwerp a century earlier, and London a century later, Amsterdam was a market for everything under the sun. She held her position by keeping her costs low. It was cheaper, for example, for French merchants to buy Baltic goods in Amsterdam for exchange with Africans than to obtain them direct from where they were made.

As for slaves, the Dutch were soon back in the region of the Congo, if not at Luanda. They had, after all, an old association with Loango, principally concerned with ivory and copper, and that was now revived, though in the 1650s and 1660s transformed to concentrate on slaving. By 1670 the Overseas Council at Lisbon was talking of the Dutch activity at

Loango as if it were still a real threat to the Portuguese slave traffic, since many slaves exchanged at Loango Bay were taken from what had previously been Angolan sources of supply. Other captives were taken from Allada (Ardra), in the commercially promising territory of the so-called Slave Coast.

Though the Dutch soon lost all their possessions in Brazil, they retained settlements in the north of South America, in the Guyanas, on the Rivers Demerara, Essequibo, Berbice, and after 1667, Suriname, as well as islands in the Caribbean: Curaçao, off Venezuela, to which had been added nearby Aruba and Bonaire. They also held islands in the more northerly Leeward group: St Eustatius, St Thomas (taken by the English in 1667), Saba and half of San Martin.

Of these Caribbean colonies, Curaçao was every year richer and more important. It had no gold, and now no native population. It was too dry to be a plantation colony. It was tiny. But there was a fine harbour, at Willemstad. The Spaniards had used the place primarily to obtain dyewood. They took some cattle there, too. The Dutch first used Curaçao as a naval station. They planted oranges, from whose juice they distilled the famous liqueur. Then in 1641 their West India Company began to use the island as a collecting point for slaves captured from foreign ships. A large prison warehouse was built, capable of housing over 3,000 captives. In the 1650s the bleak spot was an important slaving centre, with 500 or 600 slaves being taken there every year direct from Africa, ready for illicit sale to the Spaniards above all but, also illegally, to the English and French. In 1659 the Governor of Curaçao, Matthías Beck, wrote to his superior in New Amsterdam, Peter Stuyvesant, that the trade with 'our nearest neighbours', the Spaniards, was looking promising, despite differences of religion.[6] During the last quarter of the seventeenth century the Dutch West India Company, reconstituted in 1674 primarily as a slave-trading organization, was sending three or four ships a year to the Caribbean from West Africa, without counting its shipments to the Guyanas.

There were also Dutch settlements in North America until 1664. These seemed to require at least some African slaves as a labour force. On 26 July 1646, for instance, instructions to the Director-General and Council of New Netherlands (that is, the Dutch colony in North America) provided that 'for the promotion of agriculture . . . it is deemed proper to permit . . . the conveyance thither of as many blacks as they are willing to purchase at a fair price. . . .'[7] Two years later the colonists of North America were authorized to send food to their fellow Dutch colonists in the Guyanas, and carry away slaves in return. New Amsterdam, on Manhattan Island, was to be allowed to trade with Angola; and there was talk of converting that city into a slave mart to serve the English mainland colonies, just as Curaçao and St Eustatius were beginning to serve the Caribbean islands. Still, only two substantial shipments of slaves from the Guyanas to Dutch North America seem to have been made: one was of an unspecified number of slaves in 1654, in the West India Company's *Witte Paert*; the other, of 290 in the *Gideon*, in 1664. For the rest, the Dutch in North America bought slaves in small numbers from Curaçao, of whom some were probably sold down the coast to the English in Maryland or Virginia.

Among the Dutch merchants concerned in this new trade, the de Wolffs were outstanding. The most prominent of these men was Abel de Wolff, born in Amsterdam in 1636, whose interests embraced Baltic grain, wine from Bordeaux, whaling, gold and ivory, and salt in New York, as well as slaves. His father, Dirck de Wolff, had been a baker in Haarlem before rising to the board of the Brokers' Guild in Amsterdam. Most Dutch merchants in North America were ruined when New Amsterdam fell to England in 1664, but Abel de Wolff survived – partly because of his interest in whaling in Greenland, but partly thanks to his investment in the slave trade. In 1670 de Wolff's profits from the Africa trade exceeded 50,000 florins. Some of his partners and friends (for example, Gerrit Zuyuck and Tobias van Hoornbeeck) also survived, moving into the trade in slaves to Suriname, to the east of the main Guyana settlements, a colony founded by the English in 1651 but captured in 1667 by the Dutch, who retained it. The British had made the place prosper; the Dutch failed to do so to begin with until, however, a Society of Suriname was founded in 1682, and a more substantial slave trade began; 22,000 African captives had been taken there by 1700.

When in 1654 the quarter-century of Holland's control of northeastern Brazil came to an end with the expulsion of the last Dutch troops from Recife-Pernambuco, certain Dutch colonists, including some members of the Jewish community, moved to Barbados. A paper entitled 'Touching Barbados', written in England in the 1660s, stated: 'The Dutch losing Brazil, many Dutch and Jews repairing to Barbados began then planting and making of sugar. . . . Likewise, the Dutch, being engaged on the coast of Guinea . . . for negro slaves, having lost Brasille, not knowing where to vent them, they trusted them to Barbados'.[8] To a lesser extent, they also sold to the larger (French) island of Guadeloupe. Brazil had been the major zone of large-scale cultivation of sugar cane in the Americas. Now the Caribbean began to perform that function, and did so in a way which seemed, from an economic point of view, more efficient than Brazil.

There had been sugar in Barbados before the coming of the Dutch; and sugar survived in Brazil. Jean Aubert, of Rouen, originally a surgeon, introduced the cultivation of sugar cane into the French Antilles in 1640, at Saint-Christophe. All the same, the small number of Dutch colonists in Barbados did have an effect out of all proportion to their number. For the result was the transformation of most of the only recently colonized Caribbean islands. The best indication of what occurred can be seen in Barbados itself. There, in 1645, rather more than 11,000 impoverished white farmers of English stock were established, owning about 6,000 slaves, and mostly growing third-rate tobacco. By 1667 there were 745 owners of plantations growing sugar, and over 80,000 slaves. The island was held to be nearly twenty times richer in 1667 than it had been before the coming of sugar. The changes in the price of land were even more remarkable, for 500 acres which had been sold at £400 in 1640 fetched £7,000 for only a half-share as early as 1648. The white small farmers, who either did not wish to or could not turn over to sugar, lost almost everything. They emigrated where they could – many to the North American mainland, particularly Carolina, which retained its air of being a kind of Barbados-over-the-sea for a long time. Some whites survived on the island to become the ancestors of the twentieth century's 'red-legs'. Meantime, the planters who carried out this sugar revolution, such as James Drax, eventually went home to England as rich men, and their families began to think of their Caribbean sugar properties as if they were gold mines. Most of the smaller British islands in the Caribbean went through the same kind of experience as Barbados, though a little later.

The slaves who made these transformations possible were, in the first instance, mostly bought by English planters from the Dutch, but then they began to be carried in ever greater numbers by English traders themselves, in circumstances to be discussed in the next chapter.

The conversion of the Caribbean into the archipelago of sugar which it remained for 200 and more years was largely a French and English enterprise; but, in the beginning, it was inspired by Dutch ideas deriving from Brazil, and it was powered by slaves made available by Dutch merchants.

The investment in slaves and sugar equipment was so great, the strategic risks seemed so considerable, and the need for a regular supply of slave labour was so compelling that all the main colonizing nations organized privileged national companies of the kind which seemed such a success in the case of Holland. Private traders, it was thought, would build no forts in Africa, much less keep them up; would pay no taxes, make impolitic agreements with African rulers, and then perhaps betray them, to the home country's disadvantage. So not only the French and the English developed these enterprises, in emulation of the Dutch, but even small polities, such as those of the King of Denmark, and the Duke of Courland in the Baltic states, established companies which combined African with West Indian interests. These companies soon developed bureaucracies of a kind not seen again till the advent of the great nationalized businesses of the early twentieth century.

Thus the Caribbean and the slave trade came to be a treasure house of three monopolies. First, sugar was the dominant crop. Second, the colonies were formally supposed to trade exclusively with their own home countries: 'to be immediately dependent on their original parent', as an English pamphleteer of the eighteenth century, Malachy Postlethwayt, put the matter. Third, the trade of the countries concerned with its colonies was supposed to depend on a national monopoly company. To protect these 'mercantilist' colonies, every country had its version of the British Navigation Acts, which aimed to ensure that nothing in the colonies could be bought which was not made in England: neither a hat nor a hammer.' Governments, anxious for popularity among the business community, also supported the Atlantic trade: for example, from 1651 to 1847 British West Indian producers were protected by duties against 'foreign sugar' coming into England.

Colbert's 'colonial system' in France was the most elaborate of these schemes. It was based on the notion that colonies were to be economic children whose interests were to be entirely subordinate to the fatherland. The dependencies would produce sugar, or later on coffee, or perhaps indigo, for the home market. That production would require black slave labour. Nothing else would suffice. The colonies were not to produce anything other than things specifically agreed with the government at home and, in general, the colonists would depend on goods produced at home for their survival. Nobody in the colonies could make anything for sale. Nor could currency be imported into the colonies. Instead, a theoretical Caribbean coinage was devised: a recipe for both inflation and the surreptitious use of foreign coin, such as Spanish 'pieces of eight'. The principle was 'l'exclusif': French colonies could 'exclusively' trade only with France, and in French ships.

Planters protested. Naturally, and in all the empires, there were numerous acts of defiance by private or independent merchants. Dutch and British captains, as adept in those years at breaking other nations' laws as their own, became specialists above all in smuggling slaves, but also other goods, into the Spanish colonies, whose masters in Madrid had still no African possessions.

The reason for the sudden interest in sugar in Europe requires an explanation. The usual one is that in Britain, Holland, and France, every day richer, the rise in demand derived from the cult in the 1650s of drinking coffee, tea, and chocolate, and that that itself led to a growth in the processing of sugar.† Yet tea, coffee, and chocolate were taken in their original habitats without sweetening.

' There were in England three such acts: that of 1647, which attempted to ensure that no plantation should allow its products to be shipped save in English ships; that of 1650, which provided that all foreign ships trading with plantations had to be licensed; and that of 1651, the Navigation Act proper, which provided that no goods from Asia, Africa, or America could be imported into any English territory, colonies included, except in English-built ships directed by an English master, and manned by a crew at least three-quarters English in origin. Between 1660 and 1672, further laws provided that most colonial produce had to be sent to England and, on the English ships which carried the goods, three-quarters of the crew had to be English.
† The first coffee house in London seems to have been opened in 1652, tea houses existed by 1658, and chocolate soon followed.

The truth seems to be that, in the seventeenth as in the twentieth century, the desire for sugar, in milk as in tea, is strong among poor people in the first step of their rise from primary indigence. A report of the Food and Agriculture Organization of the United Nations in 1961 declared: 'The large increase in consumption that takes place in low income countries as soon as personal income rises can be related apparently to the double function which sugar performs . . . first, a source of calories . . . [and second] as an appetizing element, in a generally drab and almost always monotonous diet. . . . Sugar is craved because it adds taste, variety and attractiveness. . . .'[9] Western Europe and, to a lesser extent, North America were in the seventeenth century for the first time experiencing the charms of this product on a grand scale. It was not only the classic beverages which gave sugar its frame: rum had a wonderful history of success in Britain; so did jam.

Conditions on the plantations growing sugar were harsh. The condemnation can be made equally of Portuguese, English, Dutch, French, and later, Spanish sugar plantations. As early as 1664 a French priest, Antoine Biet, expressed his horror at the beatings in Barbados given by English overseers to slaves for the slightest offence.[10] But the French acted similarly: it is childish to suppose that any nation conducted itself much 'better' than its rivals. During the long eight-month sugar harvests, slaves were everywhere sometimes forced to work continuously for almost twenty-four hours. The length of the working 'day' also increased the risk of accidents deriving from the primitive machinery. Sometimes, to begin with, slaves on these new plantations (in Cayenne, Guadeloupe, Barbados, and Jamaica, say) were allowed to build houses for themselves and live with their wives and even to form families. But as plantations became bigger, these possibilities diminished. The captives began to live as if they were soldiers in a barracks; women were few, for the planters considered that they were too weak to be effective in the canefields, and too expensive to maintain if they had children.

The Dutch inspired, and served, this confederation of sugar in its first days. They still had, in their West India Company, the oldest, apparently the best managed, and the richest of the monopoly companies. They had a fine line of forts in both North-west Africa (Gorée, Arguin) and in the Gulf of Guinea, above all at the old Portuguese master-castle of Elmina, and, although gold was still the main export from the last named, more and more slaves every year derived from there or from the next door Slave Coast to the East. In the pursuit of gold from the Gold Coast Dutch traders continued to import slaves as porters for African mines, as the Portuguese had done, both from the Slave Coast and from Angola. In 1679 the Dutch West India Company was discussing ways of increasing shipments of slaves, with the Loango coast designated as the most important area for development. With that in mind, they planned new trading posts at the two small ports of Malemba and Cabinda, each with a factor and a small staff. Perhaps, they hoped, 4,000 slaves could be shipped from there every year. A warship would be sent to the coast to seize interlopers, foreign or Dutch. In fact, though, the idea of a permanent establishment at Loango was abandoned as soon as it was conceived. By the turn of the century, Dutch traders were still trading for slaves in that region from boats anchored offshore.*

France was also beginning to see an ever greater need for slaves in the West Indies and even in Canada. Thus in 1643 a new Company of the Isles of America had been formed to manage the French possessions in the Caribbean, and it contracted with a Rouen merchant, Jean Rozer, for sixty Africans to be delivered at the harbour of Guadeloupe at 200 livres each. The first Governor-General of the French islands on behalf of this company, Charles Houel, later said that he had paid for these slaves out of his own pocket, and unsuccessfully demanded the entire island of Marie-Galante as compensation, since the company seemed unwilling to recompense him.

Meantime, French smugglers, with the support of the Crown, had begun to make temporary settlements in western Hispaniola. Finding the land fertile, they established plantations there. Thus what became the French colony of Saint-Domingue (now Haiti) began its brilliant but ultimately tragic history. (The French position was recognized formally by Spain when, at the end of the century, the influence of France was at its most potent in Madrid.) Years of great prosperity lay ahead.

Yet in the 1660s the French West Indies hardly seemed promising. The Company of the Isles went bankrupt, and most of its possessions were sold off to private people, who ran them as little duchies under the French Crown. The first Caribbean island to be colonized by France, Saint-Christophe (called by the English St Kitts), was even bought by the Order of St John of Jerusalem. There were other eccentricities.

Still, in 1664 a more effective Company of the Western Islands was founded by the protectionist statesman Colbert. This enterprise was intended to manage all French activities both in the Caribbean and in Africa. It bought out the dangerously independent private owners: France could scarcely have allowed a new feudal regime to establish itself in her empire just when she was busy reducing the power of nobles at home. To cover the initial investments, the company raised 3,000,000 livres from private investors; another 3,000,000 was promised from the King personally; the state contributed another 2,000,000. One essential task was to deliver slaves to the colonies.

Despite the egoistic nationalism symbolized by the expression 'l'exclusif', already mentioned, the new company immediately arranged that

---

* *The Dutch involvement in the Spanish empire at the end of the seventeenth century is discussed in chapter 12.*

the first slaves would be delivered to the French Antilles by that Danish adventurer Henrick Carloff, who had so successfully chased out the British from Cabo Corso.ˑ He agreed to deliver slaves for six years from his private forts in Guinea: he would give the company 7 per cent of them as a tax; and he would sell the rest, in French possessions, just as he liked.

The scheme proved inadequate to the demand. Carloff was a man of vast schemes, never fulfilled. Once again the Dutch West India Company, and Dutch interlopers, too, were asked to sell slaves to the French colonists without impediment. (Interlopers from the Netherlands made 14,000 sales between 1688 and 1725.) In 1669 Colbert decided to try again to exclude the Dutch from the French islands. So several French slaving expeditions were sent to the River Sénégal, with government backing: there was, for example, that of Jean Clodoré, himself the Governor of Martinique, Sieur d'Elbée, Commissaire de la Marine, who left a vivid account of his experiences.[11] In 1670–72 the carrying capacity of the French slave trade was officially 1,000 a year. That figure suggests how many illegal slaves were being carried, for the real number of imports from all sources, including from French interlopers, approached 5,000. The merchants responsible for the increase were principally from La Rochelle, still the leading French Atlantic port in these early years of the traffic; the place began to dispatch vessels to Africa for slaves in 1643 and between 1670 and 1692 sent forty-five such ships. But other ports were also involved: André l'Espagnol, for instance, sent the *Pont d'Or* from Saint-Malo in Brittany in 1688; and Bordeaux dispatched her first slave ship, the *Saint-Etienne*, to Africa in 1672, with a captain from Honfleur on board, with some of the King's counsellors in Paris being among the investors. The Hamel brothers were similarly active in Dieppe.

In 1672, partly as a result of this lively illegal trade, Colbert lost patience with the company and it in turn lost its right, and its obligation, to sell slaves. Next year, a new company was formed, the first of many companies to be named 'de Sénégal', being headed by a group of Parisian entrepreneurs (Maurice Egrot, François François, Claude d'Apougny, and François Raguenet). This body bought the ownership of French facilities in north-west Africa, mainly the fledgling forts or trading posts on the River Sénégal. The change marked the end for the moment of the French government's efforts to organize trade with all Africa and the Caribbean through one large company.

The new arrangements worked better. Between 1675 and 1700 Martinique may have taken 40,000 slaves, Guadeloupe 8,000, and the new (still formally illegal) settlement of Saint-Domingue over 7,000. France's equally new mainland colony of Cayenne (French Guiana) perhaps took 2,000.

ˑ *See page 176.*

Henry the Navigator, whose captains looked for gold, but found slaves (*c.* 1440)

Pope Pius II (Piccolomini), who declared that baptized Africans should not be enslaved (1462)

Above: Charles II of England, who backed the Royal African Company, on a golden 'guinea'

Left: Ferdinand the Catholic, who, as Regent of Castile, first approved the dispatch of African slaves to the Americas (1510)

Louis XIV of France, who started the practice of giving bounties to French slave traders

William IV, who as Duke of Clarence opposed abolition in the House of Lords

María Cristina, Queen Mother of Spain in the 1830s, whose slave interests in Cuba were vast

Humphrey Morice: Governor of the Bank of England, MP, London's major slave trader *c.* 1725

John Blount: the brain behind the South Sea Company, whose main business was to ship Africans to the Spanish empire

Above: Thomas Golighty, Mayor of Liverpool, JP, who traded slaves up till the last legal minute in 1807

Left: Sir Robert Rich, among the earliest entrepreneurs to carry slaves to Virginia

Henry Laurens: a major slave trader in Charleston, South Carolina
who in the 1760s opposed the traffic, before becoming President of
the Constitutional Congress (1776)

Philip Livingston, of New York, who traded slaves in his youth, signed the Declaration of Independence in his maturity, and founded a chair of Theology at Yale in his old age

Aaron Lopez of Newport, born in Portugal, the only important Jewish slave trader in the Anglo-Saxon world

Colonel Handasyde Perkins of Boston, whose firm specialized in carrying slaves from one Caribbean island to another (1790s)

Antoine Walsh of Nantes, who conveyed 10,000 slaves from Angola to the Americas, and Bonnie Prince Charlie to Scotland

Pierre-Paul Nairac, the most active slave trader of Bordeaux, who was refused a peerage because he was a Protestant

Joaquim Pereira Marinho, among the last great slave traders of Brazil, a philanthropist in Bahia

Julián Zulueta of Havana, the greatest merchant in the last days of the Cuban trade, carried his vaccinated slaves by steamer to his plantation

King Tegbesu of Dahomey, who made £250,000 a year from selling Africans in about 1750: far more than any English duke's annual income

King Álvare of Congo, who provided slaves to the Portuguese, c. 1686

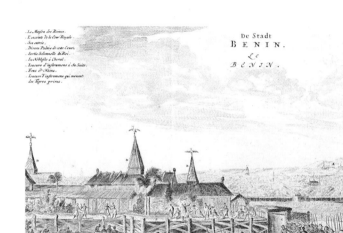

De Stadt
BENIN.
Le
BÉNIN.

Above: The King
of Benin, *c.* 1686,
whose ancestors
refused to sell men;
but his descendants
sold everyone

Left: Francisco Felix
de Sousa (Chacha),
a Brazilian who
dominated the slave
trade in Dahomey
in the 1840s

To ensure that these colonies received their slaves, Jean, Count of Estrées (nephew of Gabrielle, the beautiful mistress of Henri IV), seized the strategically well-placed island of Gorée, just south of Cape Verde, from the Dutch in 1677. The brilliant young Captain Jean Ducasse captured the old Portuguese fort of Arguin in 1678. Two thousand slaves a year was now declared as the goal for carriage in French slave trade companies these years, but it was a target never met.

The new Sénégal Company, after six successful years, was enlarged and given new responsibilities: a monopoly of the whole African coast. That was its downfall. For like its predecessors, it failed to cope with these extensions of authority and, overextended, and with too many officials in Paris, went bankrupt.

Colbert sought then to found yet another new company, formed of civil servants, not merchants – he had an extraordinary enthusiasm for bureaucracy – but that, too, was inadequate. Ships sank, pirates captured other vessels, captains remained unpaid, planters failed to pay or paid late, many slaves died. In 1681 the new company also declared itself bankrupt. It handed over its assets to one more monopoly company, 'la Nouvelle Compagnie de Sénégal'. This enterprise started its brief life with a capital of 600,000 livres. But it soon faced fresh debts, fresh crises. In 1682–4 its captains were carrying annually 1,520 slaves from the region of the River Sénégal, but that was its best performance. Further, its zone of activity was in 1684 restricted to trade north of the River Gambia, for a 'Compagnie de Guinée', headed by Colbert's son, Jean-Baptiste, the Jesuit-educated Marquis of Seignelay, was set up to trade south of that landmark. In selling slaves in the West Indies, the two new companies cooperated. But the new company of Sénégal still seemed incapable. French private investors were unenthusiastic. If they were interested in the slave trade, they preferred to back interlopers. Funds, therefore, for the companies could only be gained by borrowing from the Crown, a stratagem which demonstrated their lack of independence. In 1685, to confuse matters exceedingly, a supplementary Sénégal Company was founded, with instructions to furnish 1,000 slaves annually to the West Indies, receiving the right to trade south of the Gambia for twenty years. Five years later, the French Antilles boasted 27,000 slaves (mostly working in one or other of the 400 or so sugar mills), alongside fewer than 20,000 French settlers and a mere 1,500 free blacks or mulattos. One or two thousand slaves were brought into these colonies every year in the late seventeenth century, probably 3,000 in the early eighteenth.

The Sun King himself, Louis XIV, now entered the debate. He asked his council in Paris in 1685 whether 2,000 slaves could really be needed annually in the West Indies. The reply was that 2,000 slaves did indeed constitute the minimum required, particularly since expansion was always occurring. King Louis then suggested that French vessels should simply be sent to the Cape Verde Islands, where they would buy slaves from the Portuguese, as the Spaniards had often done, and go thence to the Indies. But the colonists insisted, in petitions, that the easiest solution to their problems was to be allowed to buy slaves in other islands in the Caribbean. The King was unenthusiastic, but soon that plan was privately if illegally accepted, war with Holland making it in many ways inevitable. Ducasse, the victor of Arguin, now Governor of Saint-Domingue, was told that because of the war he might find slaves wherever he liked.

The King should have known all about the capacity of slaves, for his own galleys were still powered by them. Thus in 1685 Michel Misserel, an enterprising merchant of Toulon, engaged himself to supply 150 Turks for those galleys. They had to be between eighteen and forty, and in good health. The French Consul in Candia acted as an agent for the King in providing most of these. In 1679 the Company of Sénégal provided 227 African slaves for the same purpose. The racial mixture was looked on as unimportant: at that time, the French royal galleys contained Russians, Poles, and Bulgars, as well as blacks. Some of the Turkish soldiers captured by the Austrians after the siege of Vienna ended their days in these vessels, and there were 2,000 helping with the fortifications at Cádiz; earlier in the seventeenth century, the Turks had enslaved hundreds of Christians after their victories in Hungary and the Balkans.

Meantime, the French Crown was begged by its Governor in Canada, the Viscount of Denonville, to authorize the direct shipment of slaves from Africa to his colony. The Attorney-General in Paris, Ruette d'Auteuil, supported him. For Denonville had, he said, failed to carry out his instructions to turn the savage indigenous Indians into Frenchmen; on the contrary, the settlers in Quebec were every day becoming more savage. Ruette thought that only the provision of Africans could reverse the tendency. The Governor believed that the survival of slaves in New England and New Netherlands proved that Africans could sustain Canadian winters. They could be kept warm on the St Lawrence in coats of beaver skin, which the traders would naturally be delighted to sell to the planters. The King supported these ideas, but the traders never did much: French Canadians could not afford many African slaves, and most of the slaves whom they owned in the early eighteenth century were Indians.

The New Sénégal Company, directed by Parisian interests, soon confessed itself ruined. It sold itself to one of its directors, Claude d'Apougny, who shortly organized yet another enterprise. This was explicitly not to meddle with the Guinea Company, which had been successful in maintaining French commercial interests south of the River Gambia. The new body sent out first Jean-Baptiste de Gennes, then the formidable André Brüe to Africa to restore the position. Gennes expelled the English from Fort James on the River Gambia, which France held till the Treaty of Ryswick in 1697, when it was returned to the English. Brüe, however, built a port at Albreda, on the northern bank of that waterway, long a thorn in the side of the English, and established a trading post also at Vitang Creek, a southern tributary. He then began a long period of successful rule, basing himself at Saint-Louis, at the mouth of the Sénégal, establishing further trading counters, talking to kings and chiefs, trading slaves, exploring the country, and even making friends with the English.

This increase in the slave trade from West Africa coincided with some turbulent events in the region which the French were beginning to consider their own. Thus a Muslim reform movement led by a prophet-king, Nasir-al-Din, seized power in what would now be thought of as southern Mauritania. A Muslim army swept south over the River Sénégal and, in support, the local Muslims there, previously living in enclaves outside the societies concerned, captured many capitals, such as Jolof and Futa Toro. Opposition to enslavement of Muslims inspired this movement, though doubtless a desire to convert the inhabitants to Islam and to recapture the rich valley of the Sénégal for its own sake played a part. The French, however, allied with the local non-Muslim monarchs, and drove out those whom they saw as usurpers; and Nasir-al-Din was killed in 1673. But the fear of a possible revival of a Muslim threat continued to hang over those desirable northern rivers.

11

LAWFUL TO SET TO SEA

*'We hereby for us, our heirs and successors
grant unto the same Royal African
Company of England . . . that it shall and
may be lawful to . . . set to sea such as
many ships, pinnaces and barks as shall be
thought fitting . . . for the buying, selling,
bartering and exchanging of, for or with
any gold, silver, Negroes, Slaves, goods,
wares and manufactures . . .'*

*Witness the King at Westminster the seven
and twentieth day of September [1672]*

BY THE KING

Charter of the Royal African Company

IN THE YEAR that the Stuarts were restored to the English throne, 1660,
that monarchy had already substantial interests in the Caribbean and in
mainland America. Jamaica had been captured from Spain in 1655, but
the heart of this American empire was still, for the moment, the rich sugar
island of Barbados. Its geographical position made it a natural lodge gate
to the Americas. It was also a place much used by the North American
colonists, who bought all manner of things there, slaves included. Thus in
1645 the young Reverend George Downing went down from Harvard,
as chaplain of a merchantman, and wrote to his cousin, John Winthrop
(still Governor of Connecticut): 'If you go to Barbados, you shall see a
flourishing island, [with] many able men. I believe that they have bought
this year no less than a thousand negroes and, the more they buy, the
better able are they to buy for, in a year and a half, they will earn (with
God's blessing) as much as they cost."

---

* *Downing, a villainous individual, later served Cromwell in London as Scoutmaster-
General and then as Minister to Holland, where, remaining after 1660, he betrayed several*

Emmanuel Downing, father of George, then comfortably settled in the port of Salem, Massachusetts, also wrote to Winthrop in 1645, saying, 'I do not see how we can thrive until we get a stock of slaves sufficient to do all our business.'[1]

At this stage North American slaves were still few, almost all of them obtained by purchase in the West Indies. One journey, though, was made in 1645 from Boston, Massachusetts, to West Africa, where a certain Captain Smith seized some slaves. But these were afterwards returned, since the merchant concerned apparently did not wish to disturb good commercial relations with Africa by an act of kidnapping.

In 1651, in the face of what seemed the obvious need for Africans, at least in the Caribbean if not in New England, a new Guinea Company in London was founded, in which, not surprisingly, the chief interloper of recent years, Samuel Vassall, was the major shareowner. Vassall was a Londoner but was, in the sense that so many prominent merchants, especially slave traders, were, also a citizen of the world. Nowadays we take it for granted that private persons and politicians travel; in the seventeenth century, the only people who did so were merchants and seamen; statesmen and monarchs stayed at home. Thus we find Vassall one of the early 'incorporators' of Massachusetts. He also collaborated with Lord Berkeley (to whom Burton dedicated his *Anatomy of Melancholy*) to develop Virginia. Vassall had an adventurous life, being once committed to prison for 'seducing the King's people' (that is, forcing English workers as indentured labourers to embark for the Americas against their will). He had endless debts and lawsuits, and several terms of imprisonment. An MP, for the City of London, he was also a commissioner concerned in the establishment of the Providence plantations in Narragansett Bay.

The eclipse of the monarchy of Charles I, and the coming of a Puritan administration, had had no effect on the City of London's desire to make money from slaves; nor did the change in the regime after the Restoration of 1660 alter that ambition.

The territory in which these Londoners were to trade was smaller than that allowed to their predecessors as monopolists, Nicholas Crisp and his friends: it was limited on the one hand to a stretch of land on the Gold Coast sixty miles on each side of the fort of Cormantine, and on the other hand to the banks of the River Ceberro (by now happily Anglicized as 'Sherbro'), near the River Sierra Leone. This company did not prosper, for its ships were attacked at sea by the Royalist Prince Rupert, then leading a piratical monarchist fleet to the West Indies in alliance with the Portuguese. They were also attacked by the buccaneer Captain Carloff and his Danes. The losses of the company perhaps reached £300,000.

---

regicides to Charles II. Downing Street in London is inappropriately called after this double-faced traitor, whose name for a time was a synonym for infamy.

All the same, the trading of slaves by London-based ships now started on a regular basis. One instruction of 1651 by the Guinea Company demanded of a captain that he bring back to England 'fifteen or twenty lusty negers' – presumably for use at home in England. Another asked a captain to 'put aboard . . . so many negers as your ship can carry' – a cargo also apparently for London. Yet a third letter requested, more conventionally, 'We pray you buy as many lusty negers as she well can carry, and so despatch her to the Barbados'.[2]

In 1660, after the Restoration, a new company, that of the Royal Adventurers into Africa, was founded in London. The impulse for this was given by that same Prince Rupert who, in his days of impecunious exile, had attacked the old Guinea Company's ships. King Charles, with whom Rupert had quarrelled, was anxious to find a role for him, and seems to have been genuinely pleased at the idea of the new venture. For Rupert had been, with his brother Maurice, not only to the Cape Verde Islands and the River Gambia (where Rupert had been wounded), but also to the West Indies, where he fought the Cromwellians at Nevis (Maurice was drowned off that island). They were the first members of a European royal family to go to West Africa; and the last till the nineteenth century.

This new company was, as was then thought the best economic course, given a monopoly of the English African trade for 1,000 years. The Royal Adventurers, each of whom invested £250 in the enterprise, included most of the important Cavalier politicians: for example, the King's friend the Duke of Buckingham, and the rich and generous Lord Craven (the benefactor of the Winter Queen). Other backers included three members of the future 'Cabal', Lord Ashley, the Duke of Albemarle (General Monck), and Lord Arlington, as well as Lords Berkeley (son of Vassall's partner), Crofts (the Duke of Monmouth's guardian), Henry Jermyn (a prominent Catholic and, despite 'his looks of a drayman', the Queen Mother Henrietta Maria's *cavaliere servente*), and Lord Sandwich, the admiral who had brought back King Charles II from exile in Holland. The King's brother, the unemployed Duke of York, became President, and Princess Henrietta ('Minette'), the King's sister, also had a share.

There were, in fact, on this list of investors, four members of the royal family, two dukes, a marquess, five earls, four barons, and seven knights. Though the company was managed by a committee of six (headed by Lord Craven), it seemed more an 'aristocratic treasure hunt than an organized business'. But once the patentees tried to trade – for gold principally, to begin with, slaves playing a minor role – they found themselves impeded by the Dutch.

A new charter was issued for the company of Adventurers in January 1663. Shareholders this time again included the King, and the Duke of York (with £2,000 invested). Among those who had not figured in the list of subscribers three years before were the new Queen, Catherine of

Braganza (as a daughter of the restored King of Portugal, she should have known all about the African trade: indeed, her colossal dowry of £330,000 was financed by a special levy on Lisbon merchants, including slave traders),* the Queen Mother, Henrietta Maria, and Samuel Pepys. The last wrote: 'There was walking in the gallery some of the Barbary Company [Salé in 'South Barbary' was the northernmost point where the company could trade], and there we saw a draft of the arms of the company, which the King is of, and so is called the Royal Company, which is, in a field argent, an elephant proper, with a canton on which England and France is quartered supported by two Moors.'³ (A canton is a section of a coat of arms occupying less than a quarter of it.) The young John Locke, philosopher of toleration, then teaching at Oxford, was another subscriber. For the profits which could be made from trading slaves had by then been appreciated in England.

The commitment by the court to the African trade was strong. In 1663 it was agreed that some of the gold brought back from the Gold Coast should be turned by the Royal Mint into coins with an elephant on one side. They were popularly called 'guineas' from the beginning. Soon established at a rate of twenty-one shillings, the coin was made until 1813, and the unit of currency continued in use till the abolition of the old shilling in 1967.

Neither the new King nor his brother – the one flippant, the other feeble – had any hesitation about embarking on the same course as their Continental brother princes; nor do any of the standard biographies of these self-centred monarchs devote any attention to the matter. They were children of their age. If they ever considered the plight of African slaves, for which there is no evidence, they would have accepted the Catholic Church's acceptance of the commerce, and supposed that it was better for an African to be in the New World at the behest of a Christian master than in Africa working for an infidel.

The company set about restoring the English forts on the West Coast of Africa, and seeking to recover what the Dutch (or Swedes) had taken. The cost of refurbishment was £300,000. Forty English ships set off for Guinea in the first year. Robert Holmes conquered the Cape Verde Islands, and recaptured Cape Coast and several other Dutch possessions on the Gold Coast, before crossing to seize New Amsterdam, in New Holland, in North America, a city soon after renamed after the leading shareholder in the Royal Adventurers, the Duke of York. Cape Coast was hereafter the English headquarters in Africa.

A quarter of this new African trade was, to begin with, devoted to slaves: in 1665 the company estimated its annual return from gold as £200,000, from slaves as £100,000, and from ivory, wax, hides, woods,

* The dowry also included Tangier, and privileges for English merchants in the Portuguese empire.

grain (pepper) as another £100,000. Lord Windsor, the sickly first civilian Governor of the new English colony of Jamaica, was told in 1663 that the company would soon deliver 300 slaves to his colony; his colleague of Barbados, Lord Willoughby of Parham, was informed that he could expect to receive 3,000 slaves annually at £17 each. The estimate was not far out: in the seven months after August 1663, 3,075 captives were delivered to Barbados.

The company had assured the King that 'the very being of the plantations depends upon the supply of negro servants for their works'.[4] So its agents began to trade slaves seriously. Slavery, as an expanding English business, dominated the first formal letter of the company to Willoughby in Barbados. The plan was also unfolded of selling to the Spaniards on a large scale. Spanish merchants were to be allowed to go to Jamaica (from which they had only recently been expelled as masters) or Barbados to buy slaves whom the company would have brought there. That the Crown of England was learning from that of Spain how to profit from the traffic is shown by a rule that ten Spanish pieces of eight were to be paid as tax to the government for every slave exported to the Spanish empire.

These innovations constituted a challenge to the Dutch. Those serious traders still desired to establish exclusive European rights to trade on the coast of Guinea. To confirm their rights, they sought to bring the rulers in Africa to their side by presents, and bribes. Hence what the English call the Second Dutch War, inspired by rivalries over the slave trade as much as anything else. Admiral de Ruyter, greatest of Dutch admirals, soon reconquered most of the forts on Guinea, and established Fort Amsterdam on the site at Cormantine. The English company lost money, and failed to provide the planters in the West Indies with anything like the number of slaves which they had come to believe they needed. Prices rose: whereas formerly the slaves had been bought for £12–£18 each, they were now sometimes sold at £30.

There were many demands for a free trade in slaves. In 1667 Lord Willoughby in Barbados added his support when he said that unless English captains were allowed to go to Guinea for blacks as and when they liked the plantations would be ruined.

In fact, with the Adventurers in parlous financial straits (they owed £100,000 to creditors by 1668), licences began to be sold to private individuals to trade within the monopoly. For the next five years the greater part of the English trade was to be in the hands of such independent merchants; and they never forgot the advantages which they then enjoyed.

In an effort to improve efficiency, the Adventurers founded a daughter company, the Gambia Adventurers, to exploit the Rivers Gambia, Sierra Leone, and Sherbro. Though that was a success, by 1668 the original Adventurers, ruined by the Dutch War ('beaten to dirt . . . to the utter ruine of our Royall Company', as Samuel Pepys put it), were scarcely much more than a holding company, in which the English interest in Africa was vested, being pressed for a mere £57,000 pounds by their creditors.⁵ They did what trading they could through the ubiquitous Afro-Portuguese *lançados* who still dominated the banks of the River Gambia.

The troubles of the Royal Adventurers continued, so much so that in 1672 – a year when half Lombard Street seemed to be ruined – the company was wound up and, in its place, the Royal African Company (hereinafter RAC) founded: it paid £34,000 for the assets of the Adventurers, with which money the old company would pay off its creditors at eight shillings in the pound, its shareholders at £20 a head. The history of these English companies was, therefore, very similar to that of the comparable enterprises in France. The new RAC would retain its predecessor's handsome premises, Africa House, in Broad Street (later it moved to Leadenhall Street), and some of the staff remained the same, as did many of the shareholders. But there was a new flotation, and 200 people subscribed the large sum of £111,600. Though the RAC desired to import gold, ivory, dyewood, hides, and wax, it was more concerned with slaves from the beginning than the previous company had been. Its charter, like that of its predecessor, gave it a licence for trade lasting 1,000 years – 1,000 years of carrying gold to England and Africans to America would surely enrich a multitude. The boundaries of the RAC's operations were also wide: from Cape Blanco in the north to the Cape of Good Hope in the south.

The charter had some engaging provisions. The RAC was required to provide the King and his successors with two elephants whenever they should set foot in Africa (they never did). The company would also have a monopoly of all African trade till 1688, and thereafter they would be able to extract a fee from other English traders on the coast.

The Governor, and largest shareholder, was James, Duke of York. Thus the company maintained the royal connection which the Adventurers had had. But there were in this company more merchants than noblemen. The directors also included four proprietors of plantations in Carolina (Lord Shaftesbury – the minister to whom Britain would owe the Habeas Corpus Act – and Lord Craven; Sir George Carteret, Commissioner for Trade and Plantations; and Sir John Colleton, a landowner in Barbados as well as Carolina) – as well as the ever-active Lord Berkeley, 'the first peer . . . to collect directorships'. The shareholders included fifteen of the lord mayors of London in the years between the Restoration and the Glorious Revolution, twenty-five sheriffs of London, and, like the Royal Adventurers, the philosopher of liberty, John Locke (he took £400 of stock to begin with, and £200 more in 1675).

The RAC's African posts were to be on the Gold Coast: at Cormantine, Cape Coast, Anashan, Commenda, Aga, and Accra. Cape Coast was confirmed as the headquarters, with a garrison of fifty English soldiers, thirty slaves, a resident Commander responsible for all English actions in West

Africa, and some other officials. The RAC was also soon exploring the possibilities of trade in slaves as far south as the Dutch reserve of Loango Bay; and, though it soon established an interest there, the long-standing liking in the Vili kingdom for Dutch textiles obliged British slave traders to buy their cargoes in Rotterdam or Amsterdam before setting out.

The RAC was one of the largest early joint-stock companies, combining the idea of incorporation (an ancient method of organization for charitable purposes) with the modern one of the association of capital. But since the sum raised by the company, though large, was less than what was needed to finance the activities envisaged, and since new building was necessary on the West African coast, the company had to borrow from the beginning, and interest on this loan accounted for much of the budget. Commerce was not helped by having a royal duke as the chairman. Nor did the King pay what he had offered. In the West Indies turnover was slow, too, because it seemed necessary to extend credit to planters who bought slaves. Then, to buy slaves on the scale needed to make a profit, the RAC's captains had to have £100,000 worth of goods per voyage (for example East Indian cloth, Swedish iron bars, Dutch guns, or French brandy) for exchange. They rarely achieved that.

Another difficulty was that the company, largely an enterprise of London merchants, was from the beginning of its life denounced and often outmanoeuvred by interloping merchants and captains from 'outports' – principally Bristol, a great port from the Middle Ages onwards which by 1700 had become Britain's premier sugar and West Indies harbour. The city's distilleries and sugar refineries (active as early as 1654), on the River Avon and near Frome, were kept busy by the import of much raw sugar and molasses. (Bristol was also Britain's chief port for shipping, and kidnapping, indentured servants, many of whom originally came from Ireland.)

The RAC had, however, its defenders. Thus Charles Davenant, Commissioner for Excise, probably the ablest economist of the day (son of William Davenant the playwright), argued that the company was 'in the place of an academy, for training an indefinite number in the regular knowledge of . . . the African trade':[6] a university of the slave trade, so to say.*

By the end of the seventeenth century as much as three-fifths of the income of the RAC derived from the sale of slaves.† Between its foundation and 1689 the company indeed exported just under 90,000 slaves – about 24,000 from the so-called Windward Coast, or the modern Liberia; nearly 20,000 from the Gold Coast; 14,000 from Whydah, on the Slave

---

* According to Aubrey, William Davenant was the son of Shakespeare by the wife of an innkeeper in Oxford.
† The other two-fifths being gold from Senegambia and the Gold Coast; camwood and beeswax from Sierra Leone; and gum, used for textiles, from the Sénégal Valley.

Coast (an important slave entrepôt from then till 1850); and a little over 10,000 slaves each from Senegambia and Angola. Six thousand slaves came from Benin and the two Calabar rivers. The largest number of these, over 25,000, went to Barbados; nearly 23,000 went to Jamaica (that island's own enslaved population increased from 550 in 1661 to nearly 10,000 in 1673); nearly 7,000 went to Nevis; and the rest were sold either to the Spaniards or to English North Americans. The RAC sold 75,000 slaves to British North America between 1673 and 1725. These figures would suggest that over 5,000 slaves left Africa every year in ships of the RAC, about 4,000 arriving. In one way or another, the British Caribbean perhaps imported nearly 175,000 slaves in the last twenty-five years of the seventeenth century, instead of a total of under 70,000 in the preceding quarter-century.[7]

In 1671 Sir John Yeamans, a Barbados planter of Bristol origin who became the first Governor of Carolina, and who indeed founded Charleston, brought slaves from Barbados to clear his plantation on the River Ashley – the first notice of an introduction of slaves to that colony (he was accused of wishing to subordinate Carolina to Barbados, a charge he angrily rebutted, though Carolina for a long time continued in the shadow of Barbados). But some English colonists were also buying from the Spaniards. In 1674, Andrew Percival, who also had a plantation on the Ashley, was ordered by the colony's proprietors to 'begin a trade with the Spaniards for negroes'.

The English New Yorkers were even more imaginative: they established, in the first years after the capture of Manhattan, a fruitful relation with the pirates who infested the East India route and had their headquarters at Madagascar. How many slaves were thereby brought by the formidable journey from there may never be known, for these importers never made a legal entry. But several New Yorkers, we know, did well out of this improbable trade. For example, Frederick Philipse (born Flypse), a Dutch entrepreneur, came to America in 1647 from Friesland as a carpenter with the Dutch West India Company. Adolphus Philipse, his son, was described, at the end of the century, as returning in a ship from Madagascar with 'nothing but negroes'. Frederick Philipse, who bought the Yonkers plantation and built Castle Philipse, as he also did the manor hall of Yonkers, had his respectability as a long-standing member of the Council of New York bruised by a quarrel, precisely because of his Madagascar trade, with the powerful East India Company. Philipse's dealings in slaves began in the 1680s, and prospered in the 1690s. That was because of a friendship established by letter with an adventurous New Yorker, Adam Baldridge, who had set himself up on the island of Sainte-Marie, off Madagascar's east coast. Rum and gunpowder were Philipse's cargoes for exchange.[8]

Philipse had successors, both among the new Anglo-Saxon and the old Dutch merchants of New York, which remained, however, in those days behind both Boston and Philadelphia as the commercially powerful city of the continent.

These were good years for the RAC. The Gambia Adventurers' licence ended, and the RAC entered into possession of its monopoly. In 1683 the RAC was allowed to raise its prices for slaves, previously fixed at £18 a head. The company was successfully competing with the Dutch. In West Africa a new fort was embarked on at a lovely, sheltered bay, Dick's Cove (Dixcove), to the west of the Dutch ports at Axim and Elmina. Increasingly, English merchants now went direct to the Baltic for Swedish iron and amber, so useful to exchange for slaves in Africa, rather than buying such things in Amsterdam, where prices had increased vertiginously. Glass beads were also obtained directly, in London. The cheap fabric imitating the East Indian textiles known as 'annabasses', which was popular in Africa, had been bought in Holland till 1677. But after that the RAC's Court of Assistants ordered its Committee on Goods – the bureaucracy was already considerable – to promote the manufacture of the stuff in England; and so the 20,000 or so pieces of this material shipped from England to exchange for slaves in Africa in the 1680s were of English manufacture. The same thing occurred in respect of scarlet cloth and 'boysadoes', a heavy material which had also previously been made in Holland. Birmingham knives and guns manufactured, say, by John Sibley & Co., also took over from the Dutch trade. Serges in the Indian style, such as says (once of silk, now of a very fine wool) and perpetuanas (a very durable woollen), were henceforth made in Devonshire, carried by sea from Exeter, and then dyed in London. Thus the RAC stimulated what would become English manufacturing superiority in the eighteenth century.

The Glorious Revolution of 1688 placed the RAC in a difficult position. Coincidentally, the date was when its exclusive licence came to an end, or had to be renewed. But the company could hope for little from the new regime. The removal of royal support was evident. The last instruction to a naval officer to seize interlopers found trading in the zone of the company's monopoly was dated the day that King James left London in early December. Several of the old directors, such as Henry Jermyn, now Lord St Albans, fled to France with him. Thereafter the company limited itself to encouraging interlopers to obtain proper licences and trying to persuade them to seek their cargoes to the east of the River Volta, where there were no English forts.

The RAC traded over 16,000 slaves between 1690 and 1700. But there was now every year more competition from interlopers. Even Edinburgh was engaged: for example, in 1695, George Watson, first accountant of the newly formed Bank of Scotland, collaborated with the London-based Scottish firm of Michael Kincaird and James Foulkes, and some others (Robert McKerral of Dublin, William Gordon, Alexander Lorimer, who was concerned in Anglo-Dutch trade, and James Foulis, manager of the London branch of the Bank of Scotland), to fit out a slave ship of 120 tons.

The RAC learned of these activities from their agents, whom they had at almost every port of England, as in the empire: a report by Sir Henry Morgan – the one-time brutal pirate who, by an appointment as curious as it was scandalous, had become Lieutenant-Governor of Jamaica – explained, with the intolerance of the robber turned policeman, that, 'notwithstanding our vigilance, some interlopers do escape and, landing their negroes, distribute them in plantations near adjacent and so avoid seizure'.[9] (When Morgan withdrew from Portobelo in 1668, one of his prizes had been a consignment of thirty slaves.)

The inquiries into the best manner in which to carry out the African trade were extensive. The government received a vast number of petitions from anyone remotely connected with it: clothiers of Somerset, dyers of London, artificers of Bristol, as well as merchants of Virginia and Maryland and planters of Barbados, all of whom inveighed against the company. In the circumstances it was hardly surprising that in the summer of 1698 the RAC, with only a quarter-century used up out of the presumed thousand years of privilege mentioned in its charter, lost its monopoly. Interlopers henceforth were able to practise as 'separate traders'. A new Act giving them legal status declared, though, that the forts maintained on the Gold Coast by the company were 'undoubtedly necessary' and that all who traded to Africa should help in their maintenance. So the separate traders had in theory to pay an *ad valorem* tax of 10 per cent on all exports to Africa – to the RAC, whose position was thus to that extent preserved. The independent traders were also to pay 10 per cent on all direct imports to Britain from north-west Africa between Capes Blanco and Monte. Exports to the Americas, including slaves, were to be free of taxes. In return, the traders were to have rights at the company's forts. Governors and other officials at the forts would, however, be appointed by the Crown, and be paid well enough for them not to be tempted to trade in slaves, an injunction which was never kept.

The 'Ten Percenters', as the English independent traders came to be known, complained about these 'impositions'. The arguments were many and bitter. Taxes were not paid or, if they were, paid late. The tax was altogether remitted in 1712. Thereafter it was the turn of the company to rail at the interlopers' bad behaviour: how could they dare to say that the serge which they offered the Africans was superior to the company's? Why did they not contribute to the cost of maintaining the forts and factors on the Gold Coast?

With these changes, Bristol, home of interlopers, fully entered the slave trade – though this is to anticipate, there were to be over 2,000 separate slave voyages to Africa from that port up to 1807.[10] Many smaller English maritime towns entered into the business too. All the heroic Elizabethan ports of Devon, such as Barnstaple, Bideford, and Plymouth, sent a slave ship or two in the next few years, as did Lyme Regis and Poole, Dartmouth and Falmouth, Exeter and her neighbour Topsham, Portsmouth and Weymouth, not to speak of Berwick and Whitehaven, as well as Lancaster and Deal, the last of which was the city of the tragic *Luxborough*, accidentally burned on her journey home from Jamaica, leaving her crew, under Captain Kellaway, to survive in a yawl, eating their (dead) companions' flesh and drinking their own urine. The Irish ports of Dublin and Belfast, Kinsale and Limerick were also active in the trade in a mild way. Some of these lesser ports had already sent slave expeditions to Africa before this date: the *Speedwell* of Dartmouth took 170 slaves to Barbados from Mozambique in 1682.[11]

The majority of the slaves whom the English carried worked on sugar plantations by the end of the seventeenth century: 'The pleasure, the glory and grandeur of England', Sir Dalby Thomas, the first Governor of the English fort at Cape Coast under the new arrangements, would write, 'has been advanced more by sugar than any other commodity, wool not excepted.'[12]

The success of these changes is borne out by the figures. Ten Percenters would carry 75,000 slaves between 1698 and 1707, as against 18,000 by the RAC. The RAC tried to continue its fight for strict insistence on the rules; in 1699, Charles Chaplin, its man at the new city of Kingston, Jamaica, seized the *Africa*, James Tanner captain, for not paying the 10 per cent tax. But one such action had little effect.

A characteristic merchant among the Ten Percenters of these years was Isaac Milner of Whitehaven, who moved to London but all the same showed his old home town the way into the African trade. He sent twenty-four expeditions from London or Whitehaven to Africa between 1698 and 1712, and throughout this time was an active agitator against allowing the RAC any trace of privilege. He was interested in the wine trade from Madeira and Lisbon, too.

It was understood that the North American colonies would continue to buy in the Caribbean. None of these English colonies needed slaves as yet on a large scale. But all the same, these captives were beginning to be found in New England. Each of these colonies has its separate slaving history.

For example, in Connecticut, there is little evidence of trading slaves in the seventeenth century; in 1709 the Governor wrote to the Commissioners of Trade and Plantations in London: 'We have made strict enquiry what number of negroes have been imported June 1698–December 1707, and find that there hath not been one vessel, either of the Royal African Company's or of separate traders, that hath imported any negroes hither in that space of time, nor any since or before, that we can hear of. There are but few negroes in this Government and those we are supplied with [come] from the neighbouring provinces, for the most part, except that, some-times, half a dozen in a year may be imported from the West Indies.'[13]

In Massachusetts as late as 1680 her elderly Governor, Simon Brad-street, had said that the colony had only about 100 or 120 slaves, and added, 'There hath been no company of blacks or slaves brought into the Country since the beginning of this plantation, for the space of fifty years, only one small vessel about two years since, after twenty months' voyage to Madagascar, brought hither betwixt forty and fifty Negroes, most women and children sold here for £15 and £20 apiece.' He must have been referring to slaves brought direct from Africa, for many had by then come into the colony from the West Indies: a French refugee in 1687 reported, 'There is not a house in Boston, however small may be its means, that has not one or two [slaves]. There are those that have five or six. . . .'[14]

New Hampshire, meantime, had nothing in the way of a slave trade till about 1708. In that year Governor Joseph Dudley wrote, 'There are in New Hampshire negro servants to the number of 70. . . . About 20 of them in the nine years past have been brought in. . . . '[15] After that there are several mentions of direct journeys to Africa, though the ships concerned were probably based in Boston or Salem.

Only in 1683 was there news of black slaves in New Jersey. There was then a dispute between the collector of the port of New York and a master who had returned from Madagascar with slaves. The latter thought that if he brought his slaves to New York they would be seized; so he took them into Perth Amboy, New Jersey, where he sold them.

Among the so-called border colonies, Virginia had begun a long history as the home of tobacco plantations. Even so, in 1649 she had a mere 300 slaves. The annual import was fewer than twenty. Her needs were modest and were, for the moment, confined to the requirements for house slaves. The work on tobacco plantations was mostly done at first by European indentured labourers. But slaves soon began to play a part. In 1670 Virginia had about 2,000 Africans, though there had been no ships importing them for several years. Natural increase must explain the change. That in turn must have been inspired by the Virginian climate or the relatively benign treatment offered by tobacco planters (characteristics of Virginia throughout its history as a slave-employing territory). Virginia was, however, in 1700 still largely a colony of white yeomanry. Edmund Jennings, Acting Governor of Virginia in 1708, wrote to the Board of Trade: '. . . before the year 1680 what negroes were brought to Virginia were imported generally from Barbados, for it was very rare to have a negro ship come to this country direct from Africa'.[16] All the same, there was increasing interest. In 1681 William Fitzhugh, an English-born lawyer, planter, and merchant who died in 1701 leaving 54,000 acres in Virginia, wrote to a friend, Ralph Wormley, also a landowner: 'I request you to do me the favour, if you intend to buy any for yourself, and it be not too much trouble to you, to secure me five or six, whereof three or four boys, if you can.'[17] In the 1690s these planters were beginning to find

Africans better tobacco workers than the Europeans; and indentured servants were increasingly hard to find. Their plantations were beginning, too, to have the same imbalances between male and female which marked sugar plantations in 'the islands', as well as the same system of allocating slaves of different sexes to live in separate barracks, which obstructed the possibility of family life.

As for Maryland, that colony for many years constituted too small a market to bid for an entire cargo of slaves: she procured her slaves in ones and twos from Virginia or the West Indies. The territory did not have slavery by law for many years, even if an Act of 1664, 'concerning negroes and other slaves', recognized their existence, in the indirect English way. Governor Charles Calvert wrote in 1664 to his father, Lord Baltimore, the proprietor of the colony, that although he had tried to find someone to sell him 100 or 200 slaves from the Royal Company of Adventurers in London, 'I find we are not men of estates good enough to undertake such a business.' But, he added, he 'could wish [that] we were, for we are naturally inclined to love negroes, if our purses would endure it'.[18] In the 1670s there was a hardening of the position: the Maryland Assembly passed an act stipulating that just because slaves became Christian they should not presume themselves free; and even the children of Christian captives might be considered slaves. No doubt this declaration reflected a shortage of labour: even in 1670 there still was no regular direct trading from Africa to North America. Only in 1685 did a serious slave trade to Maryland tentatively begin: in that year, instructions from the RAC's Committee on Shipping (the ever-active Lord Berkeley was on it) asked a sea captain, Marmaduke Goodhand, to deliver 200 slaves to be shared among Edward Porteus (a merchant of Gloucester County, Virginia), Richard Gardiner, and Christopher Robinson (a future secretary of the colony), on the Potomac River. Next year, there was a reference to a consignment of 'slaves and sugar' in Maryland from Barbados. The intention had been to load tobacco, as if the transaction were normal; and there are some other, isolated references to slaves arriving at Annapolis or smaller ports on Chesapeake Bay.

Meantime, in 1670, just after the foundation of Carolina, and the proclamation of its somewhat feudal constitution, influenced if not written by the prudent shareholder of the RAC, John Locke, with a modest paragraph about slavery as an institution to be accepted, there is the first mention of slaves there: an early colonist, Henry Brayne, wrote to Lord Ashley, the Cabinet minister and director of the RAC who was also one of the fathers of the state: 'I have put on . . . enough for my people which is one lusty man, three Christian servants and an overseer I brought out of Virginia. . . .'[19]

For some time there were few African slaves in this new colony, but by 1699 at least direct trade between it and Africa had begun. In that year, Governor Blake and others in Carolina gave to Captain William Rhett 'all such sums of money, goods, wares, merchandise, negro slaves, gold, elephants teeth, wax effects, and things whatsoever which the said captain William Rhett had in his hands in account of their being part owners of the ship *Providence* . . . whereof the said William Rhett is commander'; and Captain Daniel Johnson was arrested and thrown into Marshalsea Prison in London for failing to pay the appropriate dues for landing slaves in Carolina in 1703.[20] But in those days one in four slaves in the colony was an Indian. The year after that, a report to the Board of Trade from Governor Sir Nathaniel Johnson (a promoter of silk cultivation) estimated that with a total population in Carolina of 9,580 'souls', there were 1,800 African male slaves, 1,100 African female slaves, and 1,200 African child slaves, alongside 500 Indian male slaves, 600 Indian female slaves, and 300 Indian children – of whom many of the latter had been captured by Johnson himself in an expedition in 1703.

Still, no country was then free from the threat of being embroiled in the trade. Just when the British were beginning to take slaving in Africa seriously, a British resident in Constantinople, Thomas Bendish, reported in 1657 to the Protector, Oliver Cromwell, that some Venetians there had a stock of English slaves (perhaps initially captives of the Barbary pirates) whom they brought every year to that city to be sold for eighty to a hundred dollars apiece. Bendish redeemed some but lacked the money to free them all.[21] Doubtless they were eventually bought by a Turkish nobleman who liked their pink complexions.

12

HE WHO KNOWS HOW
TO SUPPLY THE SLAVES
WILL SHARE THIS WEALTH

*'Everyone knows that the slave trade is the
source of the wealth which the Spaniards
draw from their Indies, and that he who
knows how to supply the slaves will share
this wealth with them.'*

Benjamin Raule of Zeeland
to the Elector of Brandenburg, 1680

SPAIN LIMPED ALONG for some years after the defection of Portugal from
the combined realm in 1640 without a policy for the supply of slaves to
her imperial possessions. King Philip IV approved a return to the policy
of separate licences, with no *asiento*, such as had prevailed before 1580.
But this arrangement worked even worse in the seventeenth century than
it had in the sixteenth, because the presence now of the Dutch, the French,
and the English in the Caribbean led to smuggling on a large scale.
Despite that there were continuous shortages. Thus in 1648 Pedro Zapata
de Mendoza, the Governor of what was now the biggest entry port for
slaves, Cartagena de Indias, in present-day Colombia, wrote home to
Madrid that no Africans had been brought in for seven years. He recalled
that in addition to the disastrous consequences for the economy, the
losses of taxes were considerable: 'A ship full of blacks brings more to
the Treasury than galleons and fleets put together.'[1] Most of the few
slaves who entered those territories in these years were imported illegally
from Dutch captains: the letters of Beck, Vice-Director of the Dutch
West India Company, were in the 1650s full of the possibilities of landing
slaves on the north coast of Cuba, where there were no coastguards and
few fortresses, or at Portobelo, with due arrangements. In Africa a few
Spanish ships traded illegally in Portuguese territories such as the Cape
Verde Islands or in the Rivers Cacheu and Bissau, causing a good deal of

irritation, even scandal, there, but not sensibly affecting the problems of the Indies.

Yet there were all the same in 1640 probably about 330,000 African slaves in Spanish America, of which half, or 150,000, were in Peru and the Andean region, 80,000 in New Spain, about 45,000 in what is now Colombia, over 25,000 in Central America, perhaps 16,000 in the Spanish Antilles, and about 12,000 in the modern Venezuela. These were the estimates of Fernando de Silva Solís, a captain who wrote to the King that having spent twenty-five years in the Indies, he knew that the annual demand for slaves in the Empire was nearly 9,000.[2] Slaves from Africa had come to seem essential in the silver mines of Potosí in Bolivia and Zacatecas in New Spain, in pearl fishing, in building fortresses, and on sugar plantations which, if none were at that stage anything like so efficient as the Anglo-Saxon and French ones, were all the same well established.

The increasing reliance of Spanish planters on Dutch, French, or English interlopers meant above all that the Crown was losing what it had always considered to be essential taxes. So in 1651 for the first time since 1580, Spanish merchants were given the opportunity of supplying the empire with Africans. The trade was to be handled, from 1651 till 1662, by the Consulado, or Universidad de Mercaderes, of Seville, a guild of great merchants. This body had been set up a century before, in 1543, when Spain had seemed to constitute a lively economy, to arrange with the Casa de Contratación the dispatch and outfitting of fleets to the Americas.[*]

Four years later, in 1655, Spain suffered the loss to the English of Jamaica, which had been for some years, with its long and unfrequented coastline, a centre of the illicit slave trade in the Caribbean. The event was a bad defeat for the Crown, but for the merchants of Seville, who had not yet organized a slave trade from Africa, it was a blessing in disguise. Jamaica, English though it in theory now was, became a prosperous slave mart, stocked now by the new masters without any apology, as by the Dutch – a mart to which the Spanish ex-masters of the place could return and buy fruitfully. The reliance on English heretic suppliers was, it was true, a bitter thing for good Catholic Spanish colonists. But they had for years accepted the humiliation of buying from the Dutch; and, a harbinger of what was to come, two English merchants, Burchett and Phillips of Barbados, had already in 1642 offered to supply the Spaniards with 2,000 slaves a year – acting, as it turned out, as intermediaries for the Dutch.

In 1662 Spanish merchants from Cartagena de Indias proposed to Humphrey Walrond, President of the Barbados Council, that they buy slaves from him for Peru. Although such sales were quite illegal by both

---

[*] *The most prominent of the businessmen who took advantage of this opportunity were Juan Rodrigo Calderón, Juan de Salcedo, and Jacinto Núñez de Loarca.*

Spanish and English law, Walrond allowed the Spaniards to buy 400 slaves at between 125 and 140 pieces of eight per head. The explanation was that Walrond, one of the most curious individuals in the bizarre history of the West Indies, was virtually a Spanish agent since, a cavalier, he had passed the years of the Commonwealth in the Spanish service, for which he had been named a marquis, and even a grandee of Spain, by Philip IV.*

Weary of these unsatisfactory arrangements, disgusted with the inactivity of the *sevillanos*, and anxious to return to those rules which had seemed to work so well before 1640, the Spanish Council of the Indies in 1663 established a new *asiento*, in favour of Domingo Grillo and Ambrosio and Agustín Lomelin – all three Hispanicized Genoese merchants whose families had had many years of contact with Spain and Portugal. Ancestors of Lomelin had been rich and influential in Madeira in the fifteenth century, and another member of the family, Leonardo, had contracted to supply slaves to Cortés in 1542. Once a Lomelin had been Portuguese Consul in Genoa at the same time as a cousin was selling sugar in Madeira. The Grillos, too, had had a remarkable mercantile history in the fifteenth century, in Spain as well as in Genoa. Their ships had already been on the coast of Angola as interlopers.

The idea of employing these Genoese came from yet one more influential Dominican at the Spanish court, Fray Juan de Castro, whose innocent title of Regent of the Order of Preachers gave him access to everyone on both the Council of the Indies and the Junta de Negros. Castro had known the new *asentistas* when they had been treasurers of the Santa Cruzada, a lucrative fiscal responsibility. Grillo and the brothers Lomelin pledged themselves to deliver in Veracruz, Cartagena, and Portobelo 24,500 *piezas de indias* in the next seven years, on which they would pay duty of 300,000 pesos.† But they were not to take their slaves from merchants whose countries were at war with Spain. So their schemes, adequate though they were for illegal interlopers, were confused. In practice, the Spanish colonists continued to obtain what they needed from the Dutch island of Curaçao, so conveniently close to Cartagena, and to a lesser extent from Jamaica and other English islands. They established a network of agents in London and Amsterdam to assist them to find the slaves whom they had promised. Meantime, as a price for the contract, Grillo and the Lomelins agreed to build two galleons for the Spanish government at their own cost.[3]

The Spanish Ambassador to The Hague, Esteban de Gamarra, warned his king that these Genoese were going to seek slaves everywhere under the sun – the 'trade is now being introduced by way of Curaçao . . .

---

* *Walrond was Marquis of Vallado, an obscure mountain hamlet near Oviedo.*
† *A pieza de indias was now a male slave in the prime of life and in good health; two children could make up one pieza de indias, and two or even three old women could also.*

[where], as I understand it, they have now established large stores with every kind of merchandise there which they deliver during the night, using long boats, taking back silver bars and other products. . .'.[4]

Dutch Sephardic Jews played a certain part in this slave traffic from Curaçao. They had excellent contacts with Portuguese New Christians, in both the Caribbean and Brazil. Firms directed by *conversos* in Amsterdam were also concerned. By 1702 the Dutch Sephardic community on Curaçao of perhaps 600 accounted for more than a third of the wealth of the island. Curaçao flourished, and perhaps 4,000 slaves were exported from there every year between 1668 and 1674. Yet in 1668, because of difficulties over sales, over 3,000 slaves had to be held in the island's 'storage'.

All the same, the English were evidently, in the long run, more satisfactory to the Spanish buyers than the Dutch. Grillo recognized that reality by arranging a subcontract with the Royal Adventurers of London for an annual delivery of 3,500 slaves, to be obtained chiefly from Old and New Calabar, in the Niger delta. An effort was made to keep the contract secret, for Grillo knew that the Spaniards would not like it. But that contract was not fulfilled, and the truth came out. Grillo for a time turned back to Portugal and to Holland for what he needed.

Grillo had been helped by a decision in 1666 by the Portuguese Overseas Council that the Genoese could trade, among other places, in Angola for slaves to be sold in Spanish America, on condition that they paid to the Crown in Lisbon dues of 1,000,000 or 2,000,000 reals, as had been previously demanded by Spain. But as so often, the *asiento* made for unhappiness, even among those to whom the privilege was granted. Thus Agustín Lomelin died on the way from Veracruz to Mexico, a victim of a revolt of slaves whom he was leading to the capital, the only example of a great slave merchant being killed by his cargo; and thereafter his brother, Ambrosio, lost interest as well as money. In 1667 Grillo, then acting alone, took the radical decision to appoint as the administrator of the *asiento* an important Dutch banker, Baltasar Coymans, then established in Cádiz as representative of his brother, Jan Coymans, one of the biggest bankers in Amsterdam. Of course, he realized that most of the slaves would come from Curaçao, many of them directly through the Dutch West India Company. Thus it was that Amsterdam became the unofficial headquarters of the Spanish traffic in slaves.

In 1670 Grillo's *asiento* was cancelled. By that time he had earned the hatred of the very Dominican who had promoted his and the Lomelins' cause in the first place, Fray Juan de Castro, whose hopes of profiting from shipbuilding in Havana had not been fulfilled. For the next five years the supply of slaves to the empire was vested in a joint concession to Antonio García and Sebastián de Siliceo, both Portuguese businessmen living in Madrid; to the Consulado of Seville; and to Juan Barroso del Pozo, an independent merchant, also of Seville. All employed the

Dutch in Curaçao to supply their ships, and also used Dutch banks in Amsterdam for the financing. When, a year or two later, García took over the contract alone, he bought all his slaves in Curaçao, borrowing the money he needed from Coymans's bank in the Dutch capital, which thus continued their dominance of the commerce behind the scenes, as if they were supercapitalists in a play by Shaw – or in a pamphlet by Marx.

The Spanish government did what it could to oppose this reliance on the heretic enemy, and in 1676 awarded an *asiento* to last for five years to another consortium of merchants of Seville, organized by the Consulado of that city, with the explicit instruction that no slaves were to be bought in Curaçao. Many merchants in Seville, Cádiz, and Sanlúcar de Barrameda, some of them women (such as Jerónima Vabas or Juana Balcano), invested money for the purpose. But the Consulado had difficulty in finding the right number of slaves, and in 1679 confessed its failure and shamefacedly handed back its contract.

Despite these failures, over 60,000 slaves were carried between 1650 and 1675 to Spanish America. The Dutch West India Company was no doubt the largest single supplier to its old enemy; certainly by the last quarter of the seventeenth century slaving had become the mainstay of that company which, it will be remembered, had, in the first place, entertained doubts about entering into that business at all.

The constant changes of *asiento* in the late seventeenth century are curious. It is surprising that the Spanish court did not seek to approach the Pope to revise his concessions in the fifteenth century to the Portuguese to control trade in Africa; they must have realized that there was no effective alternative to seeking their own slaves in Africa. Yet they seem to have made no effort to change the status quo. After the failure of the *sevillanos*, for example, the contract went in 1679 to Juan Barroso del Pozo (the independent merchant of 1670) and his son-in-law, Nicolás Porcío, yet one more Hispanicized Italian. The scheme, like everything related to the *asiento*, was complex; in ten years they had to import black slaves from Africa in such quantity as would fill 11,000 tons of shipping, and in return for that privilege they would have to pay over 1,000,000 pesos in taxes and be responsible for 200,000 escudos of government expenditure in Flanders. It was recognized that they would buy their slaves in Curaçao.

This arrangement lasted only till 1685. Barroso and Porcío operated on a small scale, though Porcío moved to Cartagena. They seem to have imported only 883 slaves in all, nearly all from Curaçao, though their eight ships could easily have brought in four times that number, and though Porcío seems to have had an interest in the now more promising Jamaica.

Spanish settlers were privately every year more busy in Jamaica buying slaves illegally, including many from the RAC. In 1684 Sir Thomas Lynch, the Governor there (he had been on the island in several capacities since its capture in 1655), wrote home to London about the difficulty of preventing the Spaniards from buying slaves from English interlopers. He thought it difficult to keep any contract with Spain, for, he wrote, 'their ill conduct will ruin any that trust them'. He admitted that 'particular Spaniards may be in their senses, but the Government is out of it. . . . Altogether, if we can get negroes, it is very likely that, let who will have the *asiento*, they will come to us. . . .'[5] Next year, an Order in Council in London, though forbidding foreign vessels to go to English colonial ports, made an exception for Spanish ones, which 'shall come to buy Negroes at Jamaica or Barbados . . .'.[6]

Often in these days there were piracies involving slave ships en route to Spanish harbours: for example, in 1677 a Scottish pirate, James Browne, with a mixed Dutch, French, and English crew, seized a Dutch slave ship off Cartagena, killed the captain and several of his men, and took the 150 slaves back to Jamaica. Browne was hanged for piracy, but his crew was pardoned; the slaves, however, remained at the Governor of Jamaica's disposition.

In 1685 Barroso died and Porcío, his son-in-law, was forced to abandon the *asiento* from which he had profited so little, partly because of illness and partly because the Governor of Cartagena, Juan de Pando, had himself reached a close understanding with the Dutch in Curaçao. Pando gave it out that Porcío was insane, seized his ships, and had him consigned to a prison. Porcío appealed to the Supreme Court, the Audiencia, at Panama, and carried his case to the Council of the Indies in Spain. He was prospering there when Baltasar Coymans – the banker from Amsterdam, the power behind recent *asentistas* – entered the lists. He was supported by several members of the Council of the Indies, including its President, the Duke of Medinaceli, as by the friends of the Governor of Cartagena. No doubt money changed hands. The Dutch Ambassador in Madrid had lobbied extensively for Coymans. At all events, Coymans won the contract.

The *éminence grise* had thus come into the limelight. The great privilege was at last formally in the hands of a heretic – as the Dean of the cathedral at Cádiz, Pedro Francisco de Barroso, Porcío's brother-in-law, took a great deal of trouble to point out. This might have seemed the triumph of Holland; but in truth that once aggressive state was now in decline, the Dutch West India Company (with which Jan Coymans had worked in respect of his sales of slaves in the Spanish Indies) was near bankruptcy, and though the Dutch had sustained themselves successfully in war and trade when their rivals were Catholics, whether Spaniards or Portuguese, they were now being outmanoeuvred by their Protestant neighbours, the English.

Baltasar Coymans received the *asiento* with qualifications: his firm had to make a large payment, in cash, to the Spanish Ministry of Finance, and he also, like Grillo and Lomelin, had to promise to build ships for the

Spanish navy, four of them this time. To cover his expenses, which were in the nature of a loan, the Crown exempted certain of the slaves whom Coymans would bring in from the regulation duty. Even so, by this time the Inquisition, apparently alerted by Dean Barroso, as well as by the Papal Nuncio in Madrid, had begun to interest itself in the matter. The Nuncio had a paper prepared on the subject for him by Miguel de Villalobos concerning the dangers implicit in giving power to a heretic. Villalobos pointed out that in the East, the Dutch, making much of a far smaller opportunity than would be open to Coymans in the West, had been able to put an end to the propagation of the true faith. The Nuncio intrigued with the King's confessor, the Bishop of Sigüenza, and both of them let the King know that in their opinion the Pope would be bitterly opposed to the new *asiento* if he only knew of it.

The Nuncio had gone too far. What business was it of his? Anyway, in Rome itself, business with heretics went on all the time. Why should the Nuncio find intolerable in the Spanish Indies what the Holy Father himself countenanced in the shadow of St Peter's? A committee of the Council of the Indies approved the confirmation of the *asiento*, but at the same time King Charles II of Spain, in a rare act of self-assertion, insisted on mounting an inquiry into the implications of the affair. This report, after a good deal of argument, declared: 'First, the introduction of blacks is not only desirable, but absolutely necessary. . . . The fatal consequences of not having them are easily deduced, for . . . they are the ones who cultivate the haciendas, and there is no one else who could do it, because of a lack of Indians. [If there were no slave trade] the landed properties, the main wealth of which consists chiefly of black slaves, would be lost, and America would face absolute ruin. . . .'

There followed a more curious passage: 'As to . . . whether this slavery is permitted [by God, or the Church], there are many authors who discuss it. . . . The Council is . . . of the opinion that there cannot be any doubt as to the necessity of those slaves for the support of the kingdom of the Indies nor as to the importance to the public welfare of continuing and maintaining this procedure without any change; and, with regard to the question of conscience, its [desirability is proved] . . . because of the reasons expressed, the authorities cited, and its long-lived and general custom in the kingdoms of Castile, America and Portugal, without any objection on the part of His Holiness or ecclesiastical state, but rather with the tolerance of all of them. . . .'[7]

This document suggests that the moral dimension was at least recognized to exist in Spain, even if not faced. The effect of the declaration was, however, weakened by a statement by the Supreme Council of the Inquisition, which took the view that the contract with Coymans would not guarantee the purity of the faith, and would enable the introduction into the Indies of Africans who could be subversive of order. The Vatican's important Congregation for the Propagation of the Faith took the same view, by talking of 'the spiritual ruin' to be expected if the *asiento* went to a heretic. The next stage was that a special committee of the Council of the Indies recommended that the *asiento* to Coymans should indeed be annulled.

But Coymans was already at work, using Jamaica, the English depository, as well as Curaçao, the Dutch, to obtain his captives. Yet even Jamaica could not fully meet the demands. The recent establishment of tobacco in Cuba increased those requirements, even if sugar was still managed in an elementary way. Instructions in 1685 to a new Governor of Jamaica (Sir Philip Howard) included permission to allow a Spanish agent, Diego Maget of Cartagena, to settle 'in Jamaica, in order to continue the Negro trade' on behalf of Coymans. In 1689 the Council and Assembly of Jamaica – it must be remembered that these English islands always had parliaments, whose decisions could often be unpredictable – were found protesting that the Spaniards received the 'choicest negroes', and the Jamaicans only the 'refuse'; and, when Jamaican planters had gone aboard the ships to buy slaves, 'their ready money has been refused because it was not pieces of eight'.[8]

It does not seem as if Baltasar Coymans had the definite intention of using any of his twelve or so ships (such as the immodestly named *Rey Baltasar*, specially built for the trade, in Amsterdam, or the *Profeta Daniel*) for the purpose of introducing Dutch or other Northern European goods into Spanish ports as well as slaves, but obviously some smuggling did occur, giving support to the fears of Dutch imperial expansion expressed by the civil servants in Madrid. Coymans had no doubt committed this pardonable offence in the past, since he specifically had introduced into his contract a clause forgiving him for all previous illicit business. As a result of the intervention of the Council of the Indies, Coymans also agreed to carry Capuchin friars on his boats, and he seems to have tried to do so.[*]

But then this imaginative Dutchman inconveniently died, and his long-time assistant and heir, Jan Carçau, a Dutch-born Spanish resident (and a Catholic) was soon in a jail, chained, in Cádiz for fraud. Coymans's contribution to the slave trade had been much less than the Spanish government had hoped, for the legal import was less than 500 slaves in the two years 1685–6, even if the smuggled number must have exceeded that. Coymans had encountered difficulties in securing permission for his ships to leave Cádiz, one excuse after another being used by the port authorities – the need to carry post, passengers, even troops – in order to delay departures of which they heartily disapproved. Then Coymans had been obliged to maintain a large bureaucracy in the main ports of the

---

[*] *Capuchin friars, mostly Italians, had reached Congo, precisely the Sonyo community, in 1645, to embark on a determined effort at evangelization which continued till at least 1700.*

empire. With numerous quarrels preventing the free supply of slaves to the Spanish empire, the 'storage' in Curaçao in 1687 was again over-crowded – so much so that a special ship had to be sent to Africa to bring food for the 5,000-odd slaves.

Despite the interest of Jan Coymans, Baltasar's brother, and, behind him, the Dutch West India Company, Coymans's company now lost the *asiento*: first it was returned to Nicolás Porcío who claimed that he had been unfairly outmanoeuvred by Coymans; and then to Bernardo Marín de Guzmán, a merchant of Caracas who had many connections with old Spain. The former used Curaçao much as Coymans had done; the latter struck out on his own for supplies, for he employed the new Portuguese joint-stock Cacheu Company (founded in 1676, on the initiative of Duarte Nunes, a Portuguese merchant established in Hamburg) of which he, Marín de Guzmán, had previously been the agent and which backed him strongly.* The Crown was also in favour of this, for it seemed to mean that Spain would thus escape from the embarrassing reliance on heretics. But Marín de Guzmán died mysteriously in 1696 – murdered by a Dutch agent, it was rumoured.

In 1690 an Order in Council in London, meantime, had given freedom to both Barbados and Jamaica to trade in blacks with Spain. The Governors of the two islands were even asked to give protection to all Spanish merchants who came to them; the year before, a Spanish agent, Santiago Castillo, representing Jan Coymans, arrived in London to nego-tiate with the RAC a regular arrangement for the sale of slaves. The aim was, as it were, to make regular an accepted illicit practice.

This was a remarkable concession to free trade. But it lasted a very short time. A reconstituted Cacheu Company asked for the *asiento* and, after the usual complicated negotiations in Madrid, obtained it, by offering a loan of 200,000 pesos to the Spanish Crown, as well as under-taking to deliver to Spanish America 30,000 slaves in the following six and a half years. The agreement showed that the old Spanish resentment of Portugal after 1640 had died away; and *converso* connections between merchants in Portugal and Holland probably still enabled the former to obtain their goods for the African trade in Amsterdam both more easily and more cheaply than would otherwise have been the case. (The Huguenot French merchant and captain Jean Barbot wrote in the late 1670s that 'the Portuguese . . . have most of their cargoes from Holland, under the names of Jews residing there . . .').[9]

Still, the Portuguese company failed to supply what it had promised. In these circumstances Simon and Louis de Souza, agents for this com-pany, as so many of their predecessors as *asentistas* had done, approached

---

* *This was not the first Portuguese privileged company; the Companhia da Costa de Guiné had had a short-lived and obscure existence for a few years after 1664, organized by the brothers Lorenzo and Manuel Martins.*

the Dutch West India Company to help them find the necessary slaves. This request certainly maintained the fortunes of Curaçao but, as ever, demand there exceeded supply. In the end, the Cacheu Company did manage to carry 10,000 slaves to Spanish imperial ports legally, of whom just over half came direct from Africa. But hundreds of slaves were illegally imported: some were landed without payment of duties at Cartagena, on the plea that they were dead or dying – an early version, it might be said, of Gorki's novel *Dead Souls*; and over 2,000 went into the small port of Rio de la Hacha, one of John Hawkins' old markets. This was too much for the new Governor of Cartagena, Juan Díaz Pimenta, who arrested the Portuguese company's agent, Gaspar de Andrade, and closed his offices. Litigation followed, the Governor being amply justified by evidence of the purchase of slaves in Jamaica and Curaçao. It even seemed, after a while, that the defrauding of the Spaniards had been the main purpose of the Portuguese company, though King Pedro II is said to have been the main investor in it. As King Louis XIV would say, in the early 1700s, 'The English and the Dutch are the only ones to have profited . . . '.[10]

In Portuguese America – that is, Brazil – the usual estimates of African slaves imported for the first half of the seventeenth century seem exaggerated: one historian thought in terms of 200,000, or 4,000 a year, but his evidence is questionable. There were, after all, still thousands of Indian slaves available then from the raids of innumerable *bandeirantes* in the interior for all but the hardest work in the sugar plantations. Nonetheless, 350,000 African captives were almost certainly taken to Brazil in the second half of the century.[11]

The end of the sixty-year association with Spain incidentally seems to have had little effect on Portuguese trading to Brazil; thus a single contractor held the right to trade slaves from Angola from 1636 to 1644 (Pero Avoiz de Abreu), and he retained his place during the Dutch occupation there; he was followed by a succession of well-established Lisbon merchants.[*] The same continuity was to be seen in the less valuable trading of slaves from the Cape Verde Islands, where Gaspar da Costa was the contractor, from 1637–43. Private merchants maintained the trade from Lisbon or Porto till the end of the century, when a national company was established, in much the same way as had happened in the other European countries. This was indeed the Cacheu Company, from the river of that name, between the Gambia and the Sierra Leone, whose activities in respect of Spain have already been touched upon.

The Governors of Angola after the expulsion of the Dutch, João Fernandes Vieira and André Vidal de Negreiros, revived the old relations

---

[*] *Tomas Figueira Bultão and Diogo Sanches Caraçe, then Antônio da Gama Nunes and Jeronymo Teixeira da Fonseca.*

with the kings of Congo (ever more dependent, in a disintegrating realm), re-established the *Ngola* of Ndongo as a useful puppet, made peace with the still-resilient Queen Nzinga (she did not die till 1663), sought a way of connecting Angola with the Portuguese colony in Mozambique by land, and above all began a process whereby Angola became more and more a commercial dependency of Brazil, rather than a colony of Portugal. Frei Antônio Vieira would, in his famous *Sermões*, at the end of the century, pronounce that, though Brazil certainly had its body in America, its soul was in Africa (he encouraged the black slave to resignation).

Congo was for a generation at the end of the century the best source of slaves for Brazil. The Portuguese had gone to war against the kingdom in 1665, King Antonio I had been executed after a victory (his head had been taken in unchristian triumph to Luanda), and though the place remained nominally independent, it had in effect accepted the suzerainty of Portugal. That meant that the latter could extract from the territory such slaves as they wanted. Congo then began to break up; different members of the old Christian dynasty (the so-called *infantes*, each with his incongruous Christian name, a Pedro Constantino and even a Pedro del Valle de Lagrimas) fought each other, while the nominal monarch survived only as a ghost of his former eminence, and despite the emergence of a prophetess who claimed to be in touch with St Anthony of Padua (in order to bring the wars to an end) several small, autonomous principalities traded slaves without interruption.

Within a few years, the puppet Kingdom of Ndongo also declined, and after a rebellion was extinguished as an independent entity; the breakaway monarchy of Matamba, founded by Queen Nzinga, was in much the same condition after 1681, and that monarchy agreed to protect Portuguese *pombeiros* entering the realm in search of slaves. Beyond, the once equally ferocious Lunda kingdom had also allowed itself to be tamed, and by 1700 was the biggest slave producer for the Portuguese, with whom its people happily exchanged wine and clothes in return for souls.

Meantime, the Sonyo confirmed their independence from the Christian kings of Congo, though the astounding role there of the Capuchin order seemed to limit this freedom. The sons of the Sonyo king, for example, were named the 'ten masters of the Church', acting as interpreters, chanting mass, and assisting with confessions. This spiritual presence did not, however, interfere with a steadily rising export of slaves.

At the very end of the seventeenth century the Brazilian market was transformed by the discovery of large deposits of gold. Just as Brazil had been the first in the Americas, in the late sixteenth century, to develop sugar-plantation agriculture, so she was the first to experience a 'gold rush', in Minas Gerais, in 1698: nothing like it had been seen before and 'nothing like it was seen again, until the California gold rush of 1849'.[12] To begin with, Indian slaves were used to open up the mines, but they as usual proved themselves (or contrived to prove themselves) inferior to blacks, in endurance, commitment, and docility; and so the demand for Africans increased accordingly, as more and more gold was discovered, often in more and more remote places: the Mato Grosso, for instance, as well as Goiás and Cuiabá. The demand for labour so far exceeded supply that the mines' owners even absorbed the extra taxes on slaves imposed by officials always looking for ways of replenishing the treasury, as of enriching themselves. Most of the work in this adventure was soon being performed by Africans, under the supervision, of course, of Brazilian masters. The mine owners made their petty distinctions aamong different slaves; thus the captives from Guinea were found to be stronger and better for this new back-breaking work than those from Angola. Slaves imported from Whydah, on the Slave Coast, were also thought for some years to have a magic gift for discovering new deposits of gold.

Slaves for Brazil were now easily, and directly, carried across the south Atlantic from Angola, Congo, or possibly Mozambique. But many, perhaps most, still came from the Gulf of Guinea – or 'Mina', as the Portuguese came to call that territory (a fond diminutive of lost Elmina). One estimate gives an overall figure of over 150,000 carried to Brazil in the first ten years alone of the eighteenth century, of whom fewer than half, about 70,000, were said to have come from Angola, and 80,000 from Mina.[13] Most of the few settlers in Luanda in these years were engaged in one aspect or another of slave trading, and in the 1680s there were seldom fewer than twenty slave ships in the harbour. (The Portuguese had been permitted by the Dutch to return to Axim in Guinea, though not to Elmina – on condition of a 10 per cent duty on all trade goods brought to the coast. Thereafter, Portuguese traders also set themselves up at four ports on the Slave Coast: Grand Popo, Ouidah, Jaquin, and Apa.)

Though the journeys of most of these ships were still organized in Lisbon, increasing numbers were now often sent across the Atlantic directly by merchants from Rio. That was, in some ways, the most important long-term consequence of the gold rush in Minas Gerais. Daniel Defoe caused his character Robinson Crusoe to participate in one of these early direct journeys from Brazil to Africa, and it was on the outward journey that Crusoe was shipwrecked.[14] Later on some of these Rio-based traders would also smuggle slaves to Spanish settlers at Buenos Aires, on the River Plate. Though these merchants made money, and sometimes a great deal of it, their long-term position was weaker than it seemed, because they naturally could not offer the elaborate range of European goods which the Lisbon captains, with their connections in England and Holland, could guarantee. Brazil, however, had two successful direct exports, which accounted for a majority of the slaves taken to the place in these years: first, there was the sweet molasses-dipped third-rate tobacco which was especially favoured in Benin; second, they produced a strong, rough cane brandy, *gerebita*, which was extraordinarily popular in Angola.

As well as the trade to Brazil, there was also in Angola still a flourishing coastal slave trade with Guinea and São Tomé, and even from Luanda to the southern city of Benguela. Municipal councils in the different parts of Luanda, the Governor, the Bishop, and most government and ecclesiastical officials were paid indirectly in 'black ivory': it was in return for such services that the councillors were awarded a third of the available shipping space for themselves in 1716.

On the other side of the Atlantic, travellers to Bahia at the end of the seventeenth century were astonished at the numbers of slaves, especially domestic ones, as they were amazed at the frequency with which black girls, lavishly adorned with jewels, but slaves all the same, became the mistresses or even wives of Portuguese settlers. For example, the French traveller La Barbinais noted in 1729: 'The Portuguese born in Brazil prefer the possession of a black or a mulatto woman to the most beautiful [white] one. I have often asked them whence comes such a bizarre taste, but they do not know the answer themselves. I believe that, being brought up and fed by these slaves, they acquire these inclinations with their milk.'[15]

Scandinavians were also by then implicated in the slave trade from Africa. One initiative was taken by Louis de Geer, a financial genius from Liège, who had made a fortune from Swedish ironworks during the Thirty Years War. He was inspired to interest himself in Africa by Samuel Blommaert of Amsterdam. His first voyage returned to Gothenburg by way of West Africa and the Caribbean with a good cargo of tobacco and sugar, as well as ivory and gold; other journeys followed. Though Swedish in name, these expeditions were mostly led by Dutch captains, who had been rejected by their own Africa company, and the capital behind the schemes came from de Geer's friends in Amsterdam. A company was formed in 1649, the charter being a copy of the Dutch West India Company's of 1621 except that, so far as possible, the firm would use Swedish ships, crewed by Swedes, and built in Sweden. If forts were built in Africa, Swedish soldiers would man them.

The company commissioned Henrick Carloff, that restless captain originally from Rostock, in the Duchy of Mecklenburg, on the Baltic Sea, to make African settlements. He indeed did begin to do so, at Cape Coast (Carlosburg), between Elmina and Nassau, the cornerstone being apparently laid by a Swiss, Isaac Melville. Some of Carloff's subsequent adventures have been described earlier. The English, the Dutch, and the Portuguese had trading stations nearby and they, of course, protested at the newcomer's arrival. Carloff cleverly renewed an old document which a Swedish predecessor had made with the King of Fetu, and built fortified trading stations at Anamabo and Takoradi, as well as on a smaller scale Gemoree and Apollonia. For several years these settlements were successful, largely because the Dutch and English were at war with one another.

Next, following in the wake of Carloff, a Baltic aristocrat became concerned. This was the Duke of Courland (Lithuania), then a dependency of Poland, though the Duke descended from the grand masters of the Teutonic Knights. In 1651 seamen acting for that faraway nobleman seized St Andrew's Island in the River Gambia: that was the origin of Fort James (James Island) which, after 1658, fell first to the Dutch, and in 1660 to the English, being conquered by that same Admiral Robert Holmes who would sweep so successfully through the Dutch forts on Guinea before turning aside to seize New Amsterdam. The Duke of Courland had intended to trade slaves: 1,000, 'or indeed more', to be sold in America – more precisely, in Tobago, where the Duke sought to set up a sugar colony in 1654. But there is no evidence that such a traffic ever began.

The year 1651 also saw the Danes committed to begin an adventure in Guinea which would last over 200 years. The plan was conceived in Glückstadt, a fortified city of Holstein on the Elbe (then part of Denmark), which had been renowned for its generous reception of Portuguese Jews. These seem to have taken the initiative in launching the Danish African trade, Simon and Henrik de Casseres being the first to receive 'sea passes' to go to trade at Barbados, from the patron of the city, Count Dietrich Reventlow. Danish ships were recorded in Africa from 1649, and a charter for the Glückstadt Company was drawn up in 1651. Jens Lassen, Secretary to the Exchequer in Copenhagen, went so far as to ask for a permission to enter the slave trade from Bernardino de Rebolledo, the astonished Spanish minister, and a ship owned by Lassen and some partners, the *Neldebladet*, was the first Danish vessel to carry slaves from Africa to the West Indies, bringing back sugar, ivory, gold, and palm oil to the Elbe. The success of this voyage stimulated further journeys.

In 1657 Carloff, who had by then quarrelled with his Swedish employers, sailed from Denmark on a new ship, the *Glückstadt*, with a Danish force, and seized the Swedish establishments which he himself had founded at Takoradi, Ursu (Accra), and Anamabo. He even captured a Swedish ship, laden with gold and probably slaves, too, the *Stockholm Slott*. Carloff returned to Europe; the Swedes requested his arrest as a pirate; the Danish authorities allowed him to escape, with his stolen property; and war between Denmark and Sweden followed. Carloff, however, slipped back to Guinea and founded his own fort, Christiansborg, at what became Accra, and later also built Fort Friedrichsburg. The Swedes sent a naval vessel to Africa to reconquer what they had lost, but were unsuccessful. Henceforth the Swedes, preoccupied by their ambitions in Poland, disappeared from the history of Africa, if not entirely from that of the slave trade. But Carloff remained, to desert the Danes in turn as he had deserted the Swedes, and then to act, as indicated earlier, as an agent for French slave labour in the 1660s.

The Danes, meantime, after several naval battles with the Dutch, carried on a modest slave trade from several of the forts that Carloff had won for them, as also from Friedrichsburg and Christiansborg. An average of a ship a year left the latter in the 1670s, carrying about 4,000 slaves to the Caribbean in the twenty-five years between 1675 and 1700. (Carlosburg, however, beside Cape Coast, had by then been finally lost to the English.)

The Danish arrangements were far from regular. When Carloff died his successor at Christiansborg Castle, Johann Ulrich, was murdered by a Greek butler in 1679, and Ulrich's successor, Pieter Bolt, sold the place on his own responsibility to the Portuguese and the local Africans for a mere £36 in gold. It was not till 1682 that with the help of the Dutch the Danes recovered that castle; and they then lost it again to Africans in 1692. But they once more recovered it, and would hold it throughout the eighteenth century. Their main preoccupation was to send slaves to St Thomas, the tiny sugar-island colony which they had by then acquired in the Caribbean.

Yet one more Northern European people entered upon the African scene: the Brandenburgers. Once again, as in the case of the Danish involvement in Africa, Dutch interlopers seem to have taken the initiative, in this instance to influence the Great Elector Frederick William. So the Germans entered African commerce with an expedition led by one of these men from Holland, Captain Joris Bartelsen, sailing under the Brandenburg flag. His idea was to carry slaves from Angola to Lisbon and Cádiz. He was also instructed to bring home to the Great Elector in Berlin 'six slaves aged between 14 and 16, handsome and well-built'.[16]

Though nothing came of this journey, settlements in the name of Brandenburg were made by another Dutch interloper, Benjamin Raule from Zeeland: at Gross Friedrichsburg, subsequently Princestown, near Axim; at Fort Dorothea, at Akwidah; and at a trading post at Takoradi. The Brandenburgers also established themselves in 1685 at the abandoned Portuguese post at Arguin, the first European commitment in West Africa, their hold on which was confirmed by the Treaty of Ryswick (they carried on much contraband from there). From these bases German captains were ready to sell slaves to São Tomé and to the Dutch Guyana colony on the Berbice River, and even to bring them back for use in Berlin. In the Caribbean the Germans, who had no American possessions, carried most of their slaves to the Danish island of St Thomas.

These Brandenburgers came to Africa in substantial strength – more so than the other Europeans. At their smallest forts, there was a captain and under him nearly a hundred men, sixteen six-pounder cannon, and 1,500 hand grenades. After a while, they sought a West Indian base: they tried for Tobago, as the Duke of Courland had earlier done, but the Dutch opposed them, and they did not press the matter.

In consequence, no doubt, of this failure, the Brandenburgers soon tired of African adventure and, after some delays, sold out to the Dutch in 1720, when Gross Friedrichsburg became, more modestly, Fort Hollandia.

By 1700 all the chartered national companies, ambitious 'nationalized industries', set up to trade with Africa and carry slaves to the New World seemed to be financial failures. They were usually unable to attract sufficient capital, and so governments were continually forced to subsidize them; the officials on their payrolls could not prevent high costs, deriving from the maintenance and defence of forts in Guinea, as well as from their own salaries; they failed to secure employees willing (or able) to surrender their private interests; and their obligations – for example, to provide a specific number of slaves every year to a specific buyer – meant that they had to trade, whatever the conditions. They were constantly criticized – above all, by independent traders excluded from their monopoly, and by manufacturers, who objected to the terms according to which they exchanged goods for slaves, as by political opponents of monarchical power. Even the Dutch West India Company was out-manoeuvred on every side by interlopers. The same was equally true in relation to its English, French, and Portuguese equivalents.

In consequence of these failures the commanders of the settlements in Africa which depended on the companies were by 1700 beginning to adopt a policy of 'live and let live' rather than conquest: born of weakness and exhaustion, not principle. The monopoly companies could not defeat the interlopers, any more than the English could annihilate the Dutch, or vice versa. What was true of nations was true of different groups within them.

At the end of the seventeenth century there were in that region of Africa which had the largest number of foreigners, the Gold Coast, nearly 400 Dutch citizens, about 200 English, about 85 Danes, and the same number of Brandenburgers. There were still some small Portuguese settlements on the Rivers Cacheu and Bissau, between Cape Verde and the River Sierra Leone, as on the Cape Verde Islands themselves. The French and English had forts on the Rivers Sénégal, Gambia, Sierra Leone, and Sherbro, as also at Gorée. The Dutch, Portuguese, and English had trading stations too at Whydah (Ouidah) on the Slave Coast (the kings there would only permit Europeans to establish mud forts at three miles inland from the shore). All the nations concerned except the Portuguese eschewed anything in the nature of real colonies. Most European governments even deplored the idea of their employees' making gardens and plantations, on the ground that the land was leased, not owned. Thus in 1678 the local Chief Agent of the RAC recommended that all trading for slaves should be conducted from sloops, offshore: 'Once settled ashore, a factor is absolutely under the command of the King where he lives, and is liable for the least displeasure to lose all the goods he has in his possession, with danger also to his life'.[17] (As late as 1752 the British Board of Trade would forbid the Company of Merchants Trading to Africa – a successor to the RAC, as will be seen* – to introduce any kind of cultivation into the Gold Coast, since they 'were only tenants of the soil which we hold at the good will of the natives'.)[18] The Portuguese African establishments south of the equator – in São Tomé, Congo, and Angola, as well as in Mozambique, where a steady flow of slaves for the Americas now derived – were more solid enterprises. Luanda was a real imperial outpost with a governor, a bureaucracy, and, of course, a bishop, each with appropriate public buildings.

The last quarter of the seventeenth century had seen a great increase in the export of slaves from all these African ports. The best historian of the statistics of this matter thought that there might have been nearly 370,000 exported between 1650 and 1675, or a little less than 15,000 a year, and for the years between 1675 and 1700, his estimate was just over 600,000, an annual average of over 24,000. A majority of these slaves were now going to the islands of the Caribbean.[19]

The impact on West Africa was, of course, colossal, but it is not easy to give an impression of the consequences so far. For example, the ivory trade had for a long time been a rival of the trade in slaves in the European mind (in the seventeenth century, the region of the Rio del Rey, on the east side of the delta of the Niger, was exporting 40,000 pounds of ivory a year). But two centuries of uncontrolled hunting had greatly diminished the number of elephants. Gold, on the other hand, was still a real rival to slaving. Then, too, most European traders entered into several departments of African commerce: thus the Portuguese used cola nuts from Sierra Leone to buy slaves in Senegambia; the Dutch shipped beads and cloth from Benin to the Gold Coast. So it is hard to distinguish between the impact of European trade as such and the impact of the trade in slaves.

Yet there were obviously political changes in Africa because of the slave trade. Just as the medieval Arab trade in slaves had inspired new cities on the bend of the Niger such as Timbuktu, so the Atlantic trade in slaves was consolidating new polities: for example, in Ashanti and Accra, on the Gold Coast, in Dahomey and Lagos, on the Slave Coast, as in the oligarchies of the delta of the Nile. In Senegambia, the region of the Wolofs, the Damel (ruler) of Lat Sukaabe would inspire reforms which led to the increase in the number of slave warriors; while the Bambara kingdom, founded about 1710, on the Middle Niger, would soon become an 'enormous machine to produce slaves'.[20] The decay of

* See page 265.

the Kingdom of Congo was a good example of the impact of slaving on an indigenous monarchy.

The emergence of the Ashanti kingdom on the Gold Coast shows how hard it is to decide absolutely about the impact of the Atlantic commerce. The Ashanti, living about one hundred miles north of Elmina on the Gold Coast, also to the north of the gold mines of the Akan forest, had been for many years dependants of the Akans. By 1700 the Akans were conquered by their vassals who, led by Osei Tuti, the first 'Asanta-hene' or independent monarch of the Ashanti, using guns obtained from the English and Dutch, would soon establish his people as the dominant one on the Gold Coast. Osei Tuti's new capital was Kumasi, a city built near the ancient trading town of Tafo, and the symbol of the power of the new empire was the famous golden stool. The Ashanti people soon traded slaves extensively with the Dutch. Yet they would probably have become an important power even if it had not been for the slave trade. They were, after all, concerned with gold more than with slaves for a generation after their emergence from the Akan yoke. Between 1675 and 1700 three-quarters of the value of Dutch imports from Guinea was gold, and only about 13 per cent slaves. Thereafter slavery did play a big part: a director of the Dutch West India Company reported in 1705 that the Gold Coast was 'changing completely into a slave coast, and the natives no longer concentrate on the search for gold, but make war on each other to acquire slaves'.[21]

By 1700 it should have been evident that no chartered company had a future. But all staggered on, as state enterprises usually do, and new ones even came to be founded. It should have been obvious too to the Spanish Crown that the pursuit of the ideal monopoly contract (*asiento*) for trading slaves was as vain as the search for a Fountain of Eternal Youth; and it should have been evident to potential candidates eager to obtain that contract that it was an enterprise as unlucky as it was unprofitable. But not only were such new privileges granted, they were sought after ever more enthusiastically. Indeed, during the War of the Spanish Succession, which began in 1701, the issue of which nation afterwards would have the *asiento* was one of the most important questions at stake.

In 1700 the Portuguese still had the privilege, but as has been seen their control of it had been racked by controversy. Further, most of the goods carried on the outward journey were as often as not French, provided by powerful French merchants in both Portugal and Spain. So it was not surprising that in 1701 the Cacheu Company should have been induced, by a handsome payment of 1,000,000 pesos, to hand back the *asiento* to the Spanish Crown. The new French-born King of Spain, Philip V, grandson of the King of France, immediately gave the opportunity to France. Future profits were to be divided among the two Bourbon Kings of Spain and France and Jean-Baptiste Ducasse, the hero of Gorée, now

Governor of the extraordinarily successful sugar colony Saint-Domingue. He had been a French special envoy in Madrid, and was an experienced trader in Africa, for he had earlier worked for the Sénégal Company as a captain of slave ships as well as an effective administrator (his favour with Louis XIV was due to his actions in seizing both Cartagena de Indias and Jamaica during the wars of the 1690s).* In consequence of these arrangements, King Pedro of Portugal allied with England and the Habsburgs against the Bourbons, and Philip V immediately cancelled all payments which he had agreed to make to his Portuguese colleague.[23] This marked a real triumph for France: after all, one of the long-standing aims of Colbert had been to gain control of the Spanish imperial market.

The French, under the new arrangements, were to take their slaves from Angola and the island of Corisco, off Gabon. They were to enjoy a ten-year monopoly, from 1702 to 1712; 4,800 *piezas de indias* were to be delivered every year to any port in the Spanish Indies to which entry was not specifically prohibited. On nearly all the slaves, a duty of thirty-three and a third écus would be levied. Three thousand slaves would also be taken to the French Indies; and whatever company performed these duties in France it would have to pay the King of Spain 600,000 livres.

Louis XIV, on the advice of his astute Chancellor Louis Pontchartrain – another hero of Saint-Simon – assigned the prize of the *asiento* to the Guinea Company (at that time one of three surviving French African companies, the others being the Royal Company of Sénégal of 1696, and the Royal Company of Saint-Domingue).†

The treaty was unpopular in Spain. France had been mocked continually during the seventeenth century, and it seemed that now the imperial economy was being handed over to the object of the national derision.

---

* *Saint-Simon, in his memoirs, reserved for this son of a seller of hams in Bayonne some of his most respectful sentences: 'gentle, polite, respectful', he was also possessed of 'much fire and vivacity'; he was 'never false to himself'.*[22]

† *The King would pay a bounty of thirteen livres per slave delivered live to the Americas, in order to encourage the traffic. The company was relieved of paying any duty on any goods carried. Two hundred thousand pesos would be paid to the Spanish Crown for the contract, and they would pay a duty per slave of thirty-three and a third pesos, which was 4.5 per cent lower than the one levied on the Portuguese. Further, 17 per cent of the duty was to be deducted per head of 4,800 slaves actually delivered: an enticement which suggests how little the expectation was that the contract would be fulfilled. The company would not, actually, have a complete monopoly, for trade to Cayenne and to the Windward Isles was to be allowed to other French traders. All merchants of the Breton port of Nantes might also go to Guinea, if they paid the company twenty livres per head on the slaves whom they took to Saint-Domingue, and ten livres if they went to the other French islands. Merchants from Martinique might import 400 or 500 slaves a year, provided that they paid thirteen livres to the company and sent 100 slaves to Guadeloupe. A final section of this exceptionally complicated understanding provided that the two kings, Louis XIV and Philip V, grandfather and grandson, would take a quarter each of the stock in the company, while the rest would be available for French investors. The company also agreed to give King Philip a loan to buy the stock which he had reserved to him.*

Any dandified courtier in Madrid seized by the townspeople and asked if he could pronounce '*ajo*' (garlic) or '*cebolla*' (onion) ran the risk of being beaten for the crime of being French if he could not. The Council of the Indies thought that the treaty would make it easy for the French merchants to import all manner of goods into the empire, as well as slaves, and thought that 'Spanish national interests' – the modern phrase was used – would undoubtedly suffer. The King made a mild effort to mollify the offended commercial leaders of his new country by prohibiting the Guinea Company's ships from docking at Pacific ports and reducing the number of slaves to be landed at Buenos Aires. Those provisions had little effect: and Spanish officials both at home and in the Indies did all they could to impede the new contractors. Even the Council of the Indies, in 1702, forbade the import of slaves from the Gold Coast or Cape Verde Islands into the empire, on the specious ground that they were barbarous, difficult to convert to Christianity, and liable to eat human flesh 'with voracity'. When one of the company's vessels, *La Gaillarde* of La Rochelle, reached Cartagena in 1703, with thirty-six ill among 103 male slaves on board, the Governor there, Díaz Pimenta, charged them all the full duty. There were other minor vexations which the Spaniards delighted to devise in order to humiliate or to obstruct their new patrons.

At the same time, the illegal trade continued. The Guinea Company later claimed that in its years of privilege it carried a total of 10,000 or 12,000 slaves, but the real figure imported at that time into the Spanish empire approached 40,000. Demand seemed greater than ever in the course of the War of the Spanish Succession. The new gold mines of El Choco in New Granada, if never so significant as those in Brazil, used up slaves at a high rate. Though Holland was at war with France, the Dutch West India Company sold many slaves to the Guinea Company at Curaçao, and knew that they could have sold more, had they had them: representatives of the French *asentistas* (Gaspar Martin, Jean Chourra, Louis Chambert) visited them with that in mind. (The accounts of the Dutch West India Company show that almost 20,000 slaves were sold in Curaçao to Spanish buyers between 1700 and 1729.)

Jamaica, the main entrepôt of France's most important enemies, the English, was at this time even busier, dealing both direct with the *asiento* company and through interlopers. Yet there was English indignation (especially among the directors of the RAC) that France should have secured the great contract. After all, Britain was by then more important as a slaving nation than France. In 1701 the slave population of Martinique, Saint-Domingue, and Guadeloupe was a mere 44,000, many of whom must have come from Jamaica or Barbados. Over twice as many were imported into the British colonies in the first ten years of the century alone.

In May 1702 an infuriated RAC suggested to the Admiralty that if the French could only be prevented from obtaining slaves to fulfil their contract, the Spanish colonists might be forced to buy from England. The African Company's factor in Jamaica, Lieutenant-Governor Peter Beckford (a sugar planter of Gloucestershire origin, then at the beginning of his family's rise to vast wealth), wrote to the Secretary of State, James Vernon, suggesting that the English should station frigates off Portobelo and Cartagena de Indias, and on the African coast, in order to 'constrict the French trade'.[24] English merchants, he thought, should also be prevented from making contracts with the French or from delivering slaves to them. Next year the RAC itself, in the same vein, suggested to Vernon's successor, Lord Nottingham, that since French slave ships spent about two months on the African coast collecting slaves a mere three British ships of war and one fireship could spoil their entire traffic.

The British government did not pursue this tactic, but the war did mean fighting between British and French ships. Thus a new Lieutenant-Governor of Jamaica, Handasyd (an enemy of Beckford, whom he accused of murder), wrote in 1703 to the Board of Trade and Plantations in London: 'We have a dismal account of the great losses of the merchant ships by [French] privateers of Martinico [Martinique] which, as I have been informed, are twenty-eight in number and have taken seventy-odd sail of ships and sloops. Some of them are laden with negroes.' He added: 'Our number of slaves augments daily but, to my great grief, the number of white men daily decrease.'[25]

The British and the French were in competition everywhere, even for the trade of Loango Bay. With the Dutch in retreat from those harbours, the French desired to destroy all their rivals in the region and establish their own monopoly. For they had been informed that given proper supervision 2,000 slaves could be bought annually at Loango, and the same number again in the two nearby small ports of Cabinda and Malemba. The rivalry of great powers was, however, destructive for the trade there; and in 1706 a Dutch captain reported that though there were many slaves available in those ports no one was there to buy them.

In 1707 the British government, largely to satisfy the RAC, drew up a draft contract between Queen Anne and the Archduke Charles, the British candidate to be King of Spain, to supply slaves to the Spanish empire, this being sent to James Stanhope, their minister in Spain. The British would pledge themselves in ten years to find the 48,000 slaves which the French had undertaken to carry but, thanks to the war, had been unable to deliver. Advances would be paid, rather like a modern contract for a book ('The contractors are to advance by way of anticipation 200,000 pesetas [in pieces of eight] or £45,000 English money, to be paid in two payments, the first two months after his Catholic Majesty's approbation of this contract, the second two months after the first, which sum the said contractors shall not be reimburst'). But those were matters for the peace to resolve.

The French themselves had more ambitious plans. That same year Louis XIV sent an emissary – a rich young official, Nicolas Mesnager – to Holland to propose a collaboration of all the maritime powers to provide slaves for the Americas. A similar plan was proposed by King Philip V: Spain, Britain, Holland, and France were to have each a fourth part. This remarkable idea for a European Common Market in selling slaves failed: since the Dutch refused to think of making common cause with the French, nothing was done.

The British maintained their pressure on Spain. By 1710 they were selling well over 10,000 slaves a year to the Indies, the Spanish empire included; the French sold fewer than 13,000 in the twelve years 1702–13. The former were obviously in the dominant position. The Spaniards and the French were also falling out. For example, in 1712, the Guinea Company asked the Crown of Spain for 5,000,000 pesos in debts, interest, and damages. Many colonists in the Spanish empire and several officials in Spain were coming to think that recourse to England was the only way that their empire could be properly stocked with African labour. At the same time, in London, 'this abstruse trade' now seemed 'the most beneficial of all others to the nation'.[26] There were innumerable petitions to the House of Commons from gunmakers, cutlers, dyers, sailmakers, weavers, and tuckers, manufacturers of wrought iron from Birmingham, serge makers, merchants from Edinburgh and from Chester, not to speak of manufacturers of Welsh flannel, at the horrible thought that the government might, as a result of the forthcoming peace, limit rather than extend their participation in the trade to Africa, and hence in the traffic of slaves.

The consequence was that when the Treaty of Utrecht came to be drawn up in 1713, to conclude the War of the Spanish Succession, the British were able to insist on taking over the *asiento*. Though a Bourbon ruled in Madrid, British ships would carry Africans to the Americas to work in the haciendas, the palaces, the mines, and the tobacco and sugar farms of his great empire. A new French Company of Sénégal, run by merchants from Rouen, could do little more than complain. It was a victory for British diplomacy beside which the concurrent acquisition of Gibraltar and Minorca seemed modest.

Book Three

APOGEE

13

NO NATION HAS PLUNGED
SO DEEPLY INTO THIS GUILT
AS GREAT BRITAIN

*'No nation in Europe . . . has . . . plunged
so deeply into this guilt as Great Britain.'*

William Pitt the Younger,
in the House of Commons, April 1792

IN 1713 THE TREATY OF UTRECHT, a Dutch name for a Latin peace, presented several gifts to Britain: two places from which to command the Mediterranean, Gibraltar and Minorca; Newfoundland and Nova Scotia, two deserts of ice, as Voltaire would later describe Canada; and, the greatest prize, the El Dorado of commerce, as it then seemed, the endlessly sought after contract (*asiento*) to import slaves, and a few other goods, to the Spanish Indies. No knowledge of the financial failure of earlier contractors dimmed the satisfaction now felt in Britain.

The architect of this British triumph was Lord Lexington, the British Ambassador in Madrid, on the advice of a commercial expert, a friend of the Jacobite Bolingbroke, Manuel Manasses Gilligan, who was henceforth to receive 7.5 per cent of the profits, almost certainly for the benefit of his patron. Lexington, who was also a Jacobite, would no doubt have played a part in a new Stuart regime had one succeeded in 1714.

The government in Britain sold the new privilege, as expected, for £7,500,000 to the South Sea Company, an enterprise which had been formed only two years before, as a Tory reply to the Whiggish Bank of England, precisely to export merchandise in perpetuity to the Spanish empire. The 'South Sea' of the title signified generally the Pacific but also the Atlantic face of South America. Robert Harley, then Chancellor of the Exchequer, in effect Prime Minister, was the new company's first Governor. South Sea House was eventually established in the heart of the City of London, at the corner of Threadneedle Street and Bishopsgate. The hope was that the national debt would be wiped out by the abundant

Spanish trade; thus £9,000,000 worth of unfunded government securities were compulsorily exchanged for shares in the South Sea Company.[1]

The genius behind this company, 'the Earl of Oxford's masterpiece', was a financial adventurer, John Blunt, son of a Baptist shoemaker from Rochester, who had made a fortune from manufacturing sword blades, conveniently married a daughter of a director of the RAC, Richard Craddocke, and was said to live with his prayer book in his left hand and a company prospectus in his right, without letting either know what the other held. Daniel Defoe wrote a powerful pamphlet in favour of setting up the Company. 'There has not been in our memory an undertaking of such consequence', he said, though he did not mention the main purpose of the enterprise once in his forty pages. (It has been suggested that the idea of the company originated in his brain.)[2]

A torchlight procession through London greeted the news of the grant. Happy days had, it seemed, come again! The moment had been foreshadowed in Queen Anne's speech to Parliament of 6 June 1712: 'I have insisted and obtained that the *asiento* or contract for furnishing the Spanish West Indies with negroes shall be made with us for thirty years.'[3]

The occasion was a special triumph for London, with its hundred joint-stock companies, its stockjobbers, its 200 coffee houses, its 5,000 or so traders, with their handsome counting houses, its large foreign communities (Huguenots, Dutchmen, Germans, and Scotchmen), its eighteen newspapers, its unnumerable pamphleteers, its inventiveness, and its curious disposition to catch speculative fever.

The South Sea Company had the same kind of obligations which had been assumed by other *asentistas*: in addition to its requirement to carry 4,800 slaves annually for thirty years, it had to pay the Spanish King thirty-three and a half pesos in silver for each captive delivered safe and sound, and also to pay him an advance of 200,000 pesos. All the ports of the Spanish Indies made available to France in 1701 were to be open to the company's ships. In addition to taking slaves, the company was to be allowed to send one 'permission ship', of 500–600 tons, every year to Portobelo, Cartagena, and Buenos Aires, carrying British goods. But the slaves constituted the most important item of the planned commerce.

Spain ensured that she did well out of the affair: officials in Madrid, such as the President of the Council of the Indies and the five members of the Junta de Negros, all received handsome fees. King Philip V was allocated 28 per cent of the stock in the company, and Queen Anne in England 22.5 per cent, but as in the arrangement made ten years before with the French Guinea Company the company would lend the King of Spain 1,000,000 pesos with which to buy his shares.

The scheme was not universally popular in England; and the planters of Jamaica opposed it, since they thought it likely to ruin their thriving illegal trade to the Spanish empire (before 1713, Jamaica had provided the Spaniards, as even Robert Harley admitted, 'one year with

another, with three or four thousand negroes, in return for which, and for
flower [*sic*], woollen and other goods, there has been received of them in
gold and silver and the produce of New Spain 200,000 or 250,000 pounds
yearly'). The youthful but skilful new British Envoy in Madrid, George
Bubb, thought the same: 'I have perused the *Asiento* treaty,' he wrote to
the Secretary of State, 'and I do think it one of the worst that I ever saw
and the most calculated for captiousness and chicane.'⁴ (This individual,
who when he inherited money from an uncle took the name of
Dodington, later became known as the most unctuous English place-
hunter of the mid-eighteenth century.) The merchants of Bristol were also
far from pleased by what they thought of as a confirmation of London
merchants' privileges.

But the plan went ahead. The South Sea Company agreed to buy in
Africa the slaves required from the old RAC; take them to Jamaica, where
the weakest, the 'refuse' slaves, would be eliminated (left to die uncared
for on the dock, in many cases); and then carry the prime slaves to
Spanish markets. A second contract specified how the RAC would
provide the 4,800 slaves. In the event, these rules were not observed:
a third of the company's ships would go to Loango Bay, a quarter to
the Gold Coast, a little less to Dahomey, and the rest mostly set off
for Senegambia. Some ships went as far as Mozambique and even
Madagascar.

The new South Sea Company established factories at Barbados
(directed by Dudley Woodbridge) and at Port Royal, Jamaica (controlled
by John Merewether), for the shipment of slaves onwards to the
Spaniards; slaves for Buenos Aires (now, for the first time, a port to
reckon with) were carried direct across the South Atlantic in a trade
amounting to two or three ships a year. In the entrepôts of Barbados and
Jamaica the slaves would be 'refreshed' and made to look healthy after
their Atlantic voyage. The company would hire sloops or packet-boats
locally in Jamaica or Barbados for the short onward journey to the
Spanish ports. The enterprise also had agencies in Cartagena de Indias,
Panama, Veracruz, Buenos Aires, Havana, Santiago de Cuba, and, after
1735, Caracas. Each of the factors in these places was free with his
presents to Spanish officials. Instructions to the one in Havana, for
example (this was Richard O'Farrill, whose parents hailed from Longford, in Ireland, though they had established themselves in Montserrat),
included the provision that he was 'to take special care of what Negroes
come to your hands for the Company's account. . . . You are to sell for
ready money as much as possible. But, where you are under an absolute
necessity of trusting, you are to make strict enquiry after the ability and
honesty of the parties, taking such security as you think will be punctu-
ally performed and to be very cautious and circumspect that the
Company may not Sustain any losses thereby. . . . You are to keep a
regular and exact account of what negroes come by each ship, how many

Men Women Boys and Girls and their ages and how they are disposed of to whom and at what price. . . .'⁵

With this contract a long-standing British ambition was fulfilled, although as is often the case no sooner was one aim achieved than another took shape. On 15 December 1713, at a meeting in the Board of Trade, London, Colonel Cleland, that body agent for Barbados, suggested to the Lords Commissioner of Plantations (in effect the administrators of the colonial empire) that 'we should endeavour to exclude all other nations from the negro trade etc on the coast of Africa. . . . Mr Kent replied that [that] . . . would be of extraordinary benefit, were it to be practicable. . . .' There was some discussion about the desirability of supplying Brazil, but 'these gentlemen all agreed that our carrying negroes to the Brazils would be prejudicial to the British plantations in America'.⁶ The Portuguese trade was, of course, as they all knew, a considerable undertaking, for in those days the slave-powered mines at Minas Gerais were exporting a larger quantity of gold than anywhere else in the world.˙

Apart from the mysterious Manasses Gilligan (for whom read, surely, Bolingbroke), among those who stood to gain by all these arrangements was, first and foremost, Queen Anne, with her substantial portfolio. When that monarch died in 1714, her successor, King George I, took over her shares, and bought more, as did his heir, the Prince of Wales, who became Governor in 1715, following Harley's impeachment. After a family dispute, the King made himself Governor, in 1718: 'You remember how the South Sea was said to be Lord Oxford's brat,' the Duchess of Ormonde wrote to Jonathan Swift, who was also a shareholder, 'now the King has adopted it and called it his beloved child.'⁷ In 1720 an imaginative scheme was also devised whereby the King's two illegitimate daughters by his German mistress, Melusina, the Duchess of Kendal (known as 'the Maypole' because of her spare frame), would be allowed £120 for every point the stock increased.

The directors of the South Sea Company who would gain substantially included John Blunt, the instigator of the whole enterprise, politicians such as Bolingbroke, and later, the Duke of Argyll and Edward Gibbon, grandfather of the historian. Another director was the fascinating Sir John Lambert, a Huguenot exile financier who travelled between England and France with apparent ease, and who had interests in the slave trade from Nantes as well as that from London. Shareholders with over £10,000 worth of stock included the Earl of Halifax, the founder of the Bank of England; the politician James Craggs; the Master of the Rolls,

---

˙ *The RAC in 1721 devised a plan for selling slaves to the Portuguese. The slaves were to come from Gambia, and those not disposed of for Africa were to be delivered to a certain Playden Onely, Lisbon. Apparently 150 were so delivered; there, the Duke of Chandos hazarded, 'we are given to understand they'll come to a good market'.*

Sir Joseph Jekyll – and, after 1719, the Duke of Chandos, a scandalous financier but a good administrator, who had organized the supplies for the army in Marlborough's wars. Smaller stockholders included Defoe, Sir Godfrey Kneller (the portraitist of all his fellow investors), and Sir Isaac Newton.[8]

The South Sea Company was not as great a success as had been hoped. First, its capacity as 'a shield for illicit trade' – in the words of Bolingbroke – was exaggerated. The executive directors of the company were always interested in that side of the matter. Ships of the company did regularly arrive at Cartagena and at Buenos Aires with not only slaves but goods of all sorts, for which, instead of paying duties, the captain paid a present to the Governors. A Frenchman living in London, the androgynous *malouin* Guillaume Eon, the King of Spain's representative on the Board of Directors of the company, was paid £1,000, plus an £800 pension, to ensure that he avoided seeing such irregularities. The Viceroy in Mexico also expected to receive similar agreeable *douceurs*. But the 'permission ships', the annual authorized vessels with English goods, encountered many difficulties, since they were only entitled to go to the New World when a fair was held at one of the two main points of reception of slaves, Mexico and Portobelo (for transit to Lima); and these fairs were held irregularly, nothing like so often as once a year.

Another trouble arose because the Jamaican Assembly, a more independent body than foreigners usually believed, imposed a local tax of £1 on every slave exported from Jamaica, that to include even those intended to be trans-shipped to the Spanish world. The Council of Trade and Plantations in London tried to pronounce against any duty on slaves merely landed for 'refreshment'. But the Jamaican Assembly maintained its opposition, since its members thought that they were being robbed of the profits from its old illegal trading to Spanish ports. So the company began to consider trading direct to the Spanish empire without the much-needed stop in the British West Indies.

The company was also imprudently slow in replying to the numerous requests from private traders for special licences: Neil Bothwell, for example, who wished to export English-carried slaves from Santo Domingo; William Lea, who hoped to do the same in Guatemala; a certain Durepaire, who desired a similar trade to Puerto Rico; and Antonio Francisco de Coulange, who wanted to sell a mere twenty slaves a year bought in Danish St Thomas.

Another difficulty still was that private, independent, and, even by English law, illegal trade continued. Naval officers indulged themselves in this business, and the company confessed in 1723 that it could do nothing about the matter: 'As to what you write concerning our men of war protecting and carrying on the private trade,' the directors wrote to their man in Portobelo, 'we are not insensible, [for], however beneficial it may be to the nation in general, it is a great damage to the Company in particular, but it is not in our province to complain of it.' Between 1738 and 1745 even sailors made complaints: for example, 'This deponent, at his arrival at Anamabo [on the Gold Coast] in February . . . on board [HMS] *Spence*, saw there negro slaves of both sexes to the number of seventy and upwards at one time, together with diverse sorts of trading goods, lying on deck and in the captain's cabin, that were, as this deponent verily believes, bought on the said coast in order for trade.'[9]

All the old contractors – the Dutch, Portuguese, and French – also continued, where and when they could, to carry slaves to the Spaniards. Thus Captain Goldsborough, who sailed a company ship to Buenos Aires in 1731, complained that because of Portuguese interlopers it was 'impossible to sell fifty negroes in six months'. The company's agents did seize many illegally introduced slaves, as it was in their power to do: 231 at Portobelo in the three years 1716 to 1719. But those agents were often too fearful to act, and some of them were also actively interested in the illegal traffic.

The main supplier to the South Sea Company, the RAC was also troubled by the old problem of independent traders. In 1714 Gerrard Gore, that company's man in Cape Coast, reported, 'The English interlopers continue to infest that Coast. . . . Anamabo is Seldom without Five or Six of them, and Shidoe constantly frequented by them. . . .'[10] These ships were mostly from Bristol, whose merchants much resented the monopoly companies, dominated as they were by London investors. Their costs were, of course, less than those of the company, for they still did not contribute to the upkeep of the forts, though they believed themselves to be more sensitive to the desires of the African monarchs than the RAC's men were.

Then there were pirates – among whom the worst was a Spaniard, Miguel Enríquez, who made his headquarters in Puerto Rico and who preyed on both English and French shipping, with 'the greatest cruelty', often marooning the crews of slave ships on uninhabited islands, to die of thirst and hunger while he stole the slaves.

War again interrupted trading in 1718, and the *asiento* was closed till 1721. The company's property was seized in the Indies. When peace came again, the contract was revived (to the fury of the Spanish Prime Minister, Cardinal Alberoni, who hated the Treaty of Utrecht), and the confiscated property restored, though Spaniards made new difficulties for the South Sea Company, stipulating now that all the slaves imported had to come direct from Africa; otherwise they would be tainted with heresy. In 1727 another short war with Spain again interrupted the trade, and again the company's properties were seized for two years.

Finally, as a correction to any swift triumph in the history of the new slave-trading company, there was the speculation in shares of 1720. Change Alley, the centre of London's gambling for stocks, saw its wildest days. For the historian of the slave trade, the affair is chiefly interesting for the fact that the list of shareholders for the so-called Third Money Subscription in 1720 reads like a directory of contemporary Britain. Most of the House of Commons (462 members) and 100 members of the House of Lords (out of its total of 200) were included. So were Alexander Pope, Sir John Vanbrugh, John Gay, and all the royal family, including the bastards. The Speaker of the House of Commons, Black Rod in the House of Lords, and the Lord Chancellor were all on the list; and some distinguished names from France were introduced by the sophisticated Sir John Lambert. The Swiss canton of Berne had a large holding of South Sea stock – an unusual investment in the slave traffic. So had King's College, Cambridge, and Lady Mary Wortley Montagu. Whether all these shareholders realized that the main purpose of the South Sea Company was to carry slaves to the Spanish empire is far from obvious. But all would still have thought, had they considered the matter, with Kings Charles II and James II, that it was better for black slaves to be given work by Christians in the Americas than by godless princes in Africa.

Several investors made money before the collapse of the company. One of these was the King's mistress, the Duchess of Kendal; and another was the bookseller and philanthropist Thomas Guy who in 1720 had as much as £45,000 of the original stock. When the price of shares rose to £300 Guy began to sell, and he sold his last share at £600. With the fortune so accumulated, Guy was able to leave money for his hospital for 'the poorest and sickest of the poor'.

But most people were less fortunate, for the price of a share rose to £1,000 in June 1720 and fell to £180 in September. Banks, directors, great insurance companies, statesmen, noblemen saw their imagined fortunes collapse. Some of the most powerful men in the country were ruined; at their head, the Duke of Portland, son of William III's favourite, who was afterwards forced to seek a colonial governorship. His move to Jamaica, the main South Sea slave entrepôt, seemed a suitable denouement to this affair. Britain's other main slaving centre, Barbados, equally appropriately, went to another lord who had lost a fortune: Lord Bellhaven, who lost his life, too, when the South Sea ship the *Royal Anne*, taking him to his new office, sank off the Scilly Islands. Sir Isaac Newton lost £20,000 and, it is said, could not bear to hear the words 'South Sea' for the rest of his distinguished life. The playwright John Gay and the fashionable portraitist Kneller were also hard hit. Given the connection between the company and the national debt, as well as the royal implication in the business, the country itself would have faced bankruptcy had it not been for the cool head of the new first minister, Sir Robert Walpole, the intelligence of his banker Robert Jacombe, and the admirable new Governor of the Bank of England, who rejoiced in the forbidding name of John Hanger.

Still, the South Sea Company survived, and between 1715 and 1731 sold altogether about 64,000 slaves: Portobelo-Panama receiving most,

with about 20,000; Buenos Aires rather surprisingly coming next; while
the old great port of the trade in the Spanish world, Cartagena de Indias,
was third, with about 10,000 slaves. Most of these slaves came through
Jamaica. A Spanish captain, Antonio de Cortayre, wrecked off that island
in 1718, was obliged to live there for nearly a year, and saw over 200 small
ships leaving Port Royal, most of them going to the Spanish empire,
carrying from thirty to fifty slaves, as well as, to be sure, other, illegal
goods.

Britain and France had, in these early years of the golden eighteenth
century, comparable experiences. Whereas the former lost her head over
the South Sea Company, the latter did so with respect to the Mississippi
Company. It is hard not to think that the two countries were affected by
the same virus of self-deception. In both instances, too, the slave trade
was an unacknowledged actor in the crisis.

In 1708 the financier Antoine Crozat had obtained a monopoly of
commerce in the huge French dominion of Louisiana, a territory which
then stretched from the Gulf of Mexico to what is now Illinois. That
concession allowed him to bring in a cargo of blacks from Africa every
year – which seemed quite an adventure, since when he began to trade
there were apparently only ten slaves in the province. But Crozat, who
had taken the precaution of going to India and the Middle East though
not the Antilles, lost 1,200,000 livres on his investment and gave up his
interest to John Law's Mississippi Company – formally the Company
of the West, though the old name remained.* John Law was a brilliant
Scottish adventurer. He had fled to the Continent from London to avoid
the consequences of a conviction for killing a certain Beau Wilson in a
duel in Bloomsbury Square. In Amsterdam he acquired a knowledge of
finance as well as a fortune from gambling. Having impressed the Regent
Orléans, he was permitted to found a bank which transformed the French
economy by offering loans at a low rate of interest; he also issued paper
money, which greatly prospered in contrast to the old French metallic
currency. In 1718 Law, established magnificently in the Place Louis-le-
Grand (the Place Vendôme), bought the privileges of the Company of
Sénégal (formed in 1709 from the ashes of the company of the same name
of 1696), to which he added, in 1719, the French East India Company, the
China Company, and the Company of Africa trading into Barbary. These,
together with the Company of the West, were combined into a 'New
Company of the Indies' (Nouvelle Compagnie des Indes), which was
floated as 'a mighty salvation' for the French people. As a consequence,
Louisiana enjoyed a short reputation as being a new El Dorado, the site of
fabulous riches, and the company was, formally at least, in possession

---

* Crozat's fortune enabled his bachelor brother, Pierre, 'Crozat la pauvre', to become the
most formidable art collector of the age.

of an empire – though only 500 slaves were introduced into the vast colony in 1719. In the Rue Quincampoix, the French equivalent of Change Alley, multitudes seethed in an orgy of speculation, much as they had in London. All Frenchmen of foresight wished to make themselves 'Mississippians': 'I must say,' wrote Lady Mary Wortley Montagu, 'I saw nothing in France that delighted me so much as to see an Englishman (or, at least a Briton) absolute in Paris: I mean Mr Law, who treats their Dukes and Peers extremely *de haut en bas*.'[11]

In 1720 Law added to his conglomerate the Company of Saint-Domingue and also the Guinea Company. The Nouvelle Compagnie des Indes was by then the largest commercial organization which the world had yet seen, and even now must be seen as one of the largest undertakings of all time. At one moment in 1720 Law's company had sixty-two ships at sea, as well as a monopoly of coining money, and it also managed the French national debt. Shares issued at 500 livres reached 10,000 and, as in London, great fortunes were made overnight. Law was allowed to introduce a complete reform of the fiscal system of the country. The Royal Bank was even merged with the company. But as soon as people began to wish to realize their gains, Law's paper money collapsed in value, and Law himself fled to Brussels, passing from being the hero of France to the villain in a matter of days.

For a time, Law's extraordinary mergers seem to have galvanized the French slave trade. Though the founder had fled, the company remained. A monopoly of trading Guinea Coast slaves was granted to it. It was required to deliver 30,000 slaves in the next twenty-five years, on each of whom it would receive a bounty of 143 livres from the Crown.

Law's company, though it had its headquarters in the new city of Lorient, also had close ties with Nantes. The private traders of the latter city, in theory opposed to monopoly, in practice gained from it, for they obtained licences from the privileged company. The new multiheaded company was still sending four slave ships to Africa in 1740, mostly large: about 300 tons on average.

Despite the disappointments caused by the South Sea Company, the British slave trade grew immeasurably in the early eighteenth century. In 1720 nearly 150 ships were engaged, mostly from Bristol and London, but a few also set out from Liverpool, Whitehaven, and lesser ports, such as Lancaster, Chester, and even Glasgow.* Even the fortunes of the old RAC revived, thanks to the interest of the Duke of Chandos, struggling to

* The Act of Union between England and Scotland of 1707 had enabled Glasgow to participate in the 'extensive and increasing trade with the West Indies and American colonies [which] has, if I am rightly informed' – the speaker was the hero of Sir Walter Scott's brilliant creation, Rob Roy – 'laid the foundation of wealth and prosperity, which, if carefully strengthened and built upon, may one day support an immense fabric'.

recover his wealth after losing heavily in the South Sea Bubble. This nobleman, who received his title in 1719, was a patron of Handel, and the builder of a colossal house, Canons, at Edgware. Swift said of him, 'All he got by fraud was lost by stocks. . . .'[*12]

At a committee meeting of the RAC in 1728 – attended by the Duke and the Subgovernor, Edward Acton – Sir Robert Davers, the new government agent for Barbados, and himself an independent trader to Africa, 'agreed . . . that he should be furnished with sixty adult negroes from 14 to 30 years of age, half men and half women; as also 30 boys and girls, or as many more as his agent shall desire to have, from 10 to 14 years of age and this to be done between December and July . . . that they be negroes of Cape Coast, Whydah or Jaquin,[†] that they be delivered to Sir Robert Davers's agent at Barbados out of the first three ships of the company's which shall arrive . . . all merchantable negroes to be approv'd of by his agent . . . that the sums to be paid for each Negroe be in sterling money . . . for each Man £23, for each Woman £22, for each boy and girl £21. . . .' A later report of the RAC, on the state of the slave trade, included the unusual recommendation 'that all endeavours be used to teach the Negroes to read and write . . .'.[13]

The consequence of all this activity was that in the ten years between 1721 and 1730 the British carried well over 100,000 slaves to the Americas, much the same number as in the previous decade: of these, nearly 40,000 went to Jamaica, over 20,000 to Barbados (many were taken thence to Cuba and elsewhere in the Spanish empire), about 10,000 to mainland colonies such as South Carolina, and nearly 50,000 to British Caribbean colonies. Among shippers, London was still ahead: an average of about fifty-six ships a year left between 1723 and 1727, while Bristol sent thirty-four ships and Liverpool eleven.

The prince of London slave merchants in those days was Humphrey Morice, of Mincing Lane, Member of Parliament, and Governor of the Bank of England between 1727 and 1728. Morice had been an effective spokesman for the independent traders in the complaints against the Royal African Company. In 1720 he had eight ships in the trade, all named after his wife or daughters, often loading gunpowder and spirits in Rotterdam. He seems to have preferred to sell the slaves whom he bought in the Gold Coast to the Portuguese on that same continent, rather than send his ships across the Atlantic: 'You may take Brazil tobacco in payment', he told Captain William Clinch in 1721.[14] But sometimes his captains took their cargoes of captives to Virginia or Maryland (almost all

---

[*] He was attacked as 'Timon' by Pope, in his 'Epistle to Lord Burlington', but the poet apologized, and began talking sycophantically of 'Gracious Chandos . . . beloved at sight'. The Duke raised a statue to King George I in his grounds, which, according to a biographer, later 'helped to make Leicester Square hideous'.

[†] These last were ports on the Slave Coast, for which see page 351.

the slaves imported there in the early eighteenth century were brought in London ships), or Jamaica. Morice was a pioneer in medical treatment of both crews and slaves: he usually had a surgeon on board his ships, and for reasons of health captains also had to buy limes before the Middle Passage across the Atlantic – long before Dr James Lind published his famous recommendation on the benefits of the regular use of that fruit, in his *Treatise on the Scurvy* in 1754.

The 1730s saw Bristol overtaking London as Britain's main slave port (though London continued a centre for marine insurance, as for finding the right cargoes, and some merchants of the city maintained ships in the slave trade until the 1790s). Bristol was sending nearly fifty ships a year to Africa between 1728 and 1732, carrying well over 100,000 slaves on them. In comparison, London and Liverpool, a rising star in slave commerce, sent in the same years forty and forty-four ships respectively. Merchants from Bristol were also pioneers in the business of carrying slaves to Virginia, and in moving slaves from one North American colony to another.

The most prominent merchants in Africans in Bristol were Isaac Hobhouse, who undertook forty-four slave voyages between 1722 and 1747; James Day, with fifty-six voyages between 1711 and 1742; Richard Henvill, who began slaving in 1709; and later James Laroche, of Huguenot origin, from Bordeaux, whose father had come to England in the train of Prince George of Denmark about 1705, and who was far the biggest slave trader of the city, sending out 132 slave voyages between 1728 and 1769.[15]

In the Caribbean there were similar changes. Jamaica had by now overtaken Barbados as the prize colony of the English. Being – as settlers there noticed, with a taste for accurate mathematics not always evident in their returns – twenty-six times bigger than Barbados, it seemed to have a chance of becoming richer than all other British islands. About the turn of the eighteenth century the European population there stood at 7,000, that of slaves at 45,000. In 1712 her production of sugar already exceeded that of Barbados. The richest planter of the island, Peter Beckford, was also the most powerful: at his death in 1735 he owned nine sugar plantations and was part owner of seven more. His son, William, returned to London, for which city he was returned as an MP, the most powerful businessman in the City of London, of which he would be twice Lord Mayor, becoming one of the few close friends of the elder William Pitt. But he always maintained his 22,000 acres of sugar land in Jamaica, and the pride of his family, Drax Hall, in the central parish of St Ann, had both a windmill and a watermill.

These were, of course, great days for British trade and manufacturing. The commercial prospects of the colonies in both North America and the West Indies seemed limitless. Nearly all the increase in British exports of commodities which occurred in the sixty years after the Act of Union in 1707 went to markets outside Europe. Continental European customers for British goods also grew, if more slowly, and about 1750 half the goods exported to Africa (cloths, iron bars, brandy) constituted re-exports from the Continent of Europe.

In the 1730s British ships carried perhaps 170,000 slaves in all – for the first time, probably, more in ten years than the Portuguese carried to Brazil. Perhaps 40,000 slaves went to the Southern mainland colonies in North America (Virginia, Maryland, and the Carolinas; Georgia formally held out against employing slaves till 1750). This was four times the total of the previous ten years. Forty-two thousand probably went to Jamaica, a little under 30,000 to Barbados, and 60,000 to other places. Probably one-third of the British slaves taken to the Americas were still intended, via Jamaica, for the Spanish empire.[16]

The contraband traffic sponsored by the South Sea Company, as much in manufactured goods as in slaves, had by the late 1730s reached such a scale that Spain's imperial economy was beginning to suffer. In 1737 the Casa de Contratación told the King that the merchants of Seville could not sell any of their clothing in the empire because of the quantity of smuggled English goods available. The Spanish government did what it could to limit the damage. In 1733 the Viceroy of Peru was even ordered not to take gold or silver to ports where the company's ships might dock. A small fleet of coastguard sloops was also established, off Cartagena and Havana. The War of Jenkins's Ear of 1739 was inspired by one of these coastguards' alleged treatment of Robert Jenkins, captain of the brig *Rebecca*, off Cuba. In 1739 the British and Spanish governments, in an attempt to preserve peace, called an end to all such search-and-seize operations. But the South Sea Company refused a Spanish request for an examination of its books, and instead demanded handsome compensaton for the impounded property. War followed in November, and the company never recovered its position afterwards.

Bristol's pre-eminence in the slave trade lasted barely twenty years. Just as London, with the relative decline of the RAC, had given way to Bristol, so now Bristol gave way to Liverpool.

The rise of Liverpool is a remarkable history, in which the slave trade played an important, perhaps even a decisive part. That was certainly the claim of General Bonastre Tarleton, an MP who came from a slave-trading family, in a speech of 1806 defending the commerce in which he described how the place had thereby risen from being a fishing hamlet, 'to become the second place in wealth and population in the British Empire'. The city's maritime business had begun with the Irish trade, and by 1670 she was already trading in a small way to North America and to the West Indies, as well as Madeira and the Canary Islands. Liverpool's merchants were at first all interlopers, men operating on a small scale and without much attention to accurate returns. Already by that time, the city had many local industries which led easily to good exports: linen, glass, leather, various metal goods, as well as shipbuilding.

During the French wars of the first years of the eighteenth century, Liverpool already seemed a prosperous port, with fine streets and many grand houses of stone, in which the richer merchants lived. The leaders of the corporation were generally supporters of the Protestant succession, the merchants being mostly Anglicans and Whigs, but many of the seamen were dissenters. Defoe in 1726 rightly called Liverpool 'the Bristol of this part of England'.[17] Its new wet dock, the first commercial one in England outside London, opened in 1715.

Liverpool's entry into the slave trade occurred in the 1690s, though the first slave ship of which there is record was the *Liverpool Merchant* of 1700: it carried 220 slaves to Barbados. From the beginning, as in other ports, the trade interested the city's powerful men: Sir Thomas Johnson, the architect of the new wet dock, Member of Parliament, and Mayor, had a 50 per cent interest in the *Blessing*, the second Liverpool slave ship of which anything is known. Whereas Bristol carried many slaves for Jamaica to be sold to the Spanish merchants who regularly visited that island, Liverpool specialized, in the years after 1713, in a direct and illegal slave trade to the Spanish empire, especially to Havana and Cartagena de Indias.

By 1740 Liverpool was sending thirty-three ships a year to Africa, and thereafter the total grew. The reasons were various. Thus, Liverpool was better placed for the Atlantic trade than London, and was less exposed in time of war to the French than was Bristol. By often landing their goods on the homeward voyage on the Isle of Man, 'a vast warehouse of smuggled goods', Liverpool captains were able to evade duty on the returning cargo. Her traders also found cargoes for the slave trade in that island, such as brass, arms, and gunpowder. In addition, Liverpool merchants could avoid the risk of meeting marauders by sending their ships round the north of Ireland and into the Atlantic by that route. The captains and crews seem also to have been treated more austerely by their owners than Bristol and London ones: 'The generality of their captains were at annual salaries', a historian of Liverpool would comment, 'or, if at monthly pay, four pounds were thought great wages . . ., no cabin privileges were allowed, primage [bounties] was unknown among them and, as to port allowances, not a single shilling was given'.[18] Liverpool merchants, themselves often ex-captains or seamen, would pay crews less well than those in Bristol: one reason why the former were able to sell their cargoes for 12 per cent less than the rest of the kingdom, and return with an equal profit. In Africa, Bristol merchants tended to remain faithful to safe old anchorages in the Gold Coast and Angola, while their Liverpool confrères struck out anew to seek Africans in Sierra Leone, Gabon, and the Cameroons.

In 1753 four families had private carriages in Liverpool. Three were owned by slave merchants. The outstanding man among these was Foster Cunliffe, who had come to Liverpool from the Lancashire countryside.

He associated with a trader, Richard Norris, who turned to slaving about 1720. Cunliffe made a fortune and was Mayor three times. Most years in the 1730s he would send four or more ships to Africa. We are told that he was 'stern and obstinate', but also philanthropic, being President of the Liverpool Infirmary, and a sponsor of the Blue Coat school. In a chapel of St Peter's Church, Liverpool, Cunliffe was described as 'a merchant whose sagacity, honesty and diligence procured wealth and credit to himself and his country; a magistrate who administered justice with discernment, candour and impartiality; a Christian devout and exemplary . . .'.[19] Before he died he secured his son Ellis's election to Parliament, in a contest in which the candidate is said to have been 'helped by his father's popularity'. The Cunliffes also had excellent commercial representation in North America, with a headquarters at Oxford, on the east side of the Chesapeake Bay, as well as a large store at New Town (the modern Chestertown), Maryland. His chief representative there was for many years Robert Morris, father of the financier of the American Revolution.[*]

Ellis's fellow MP for Liverpool, Charles Pole, was a slave merchant too, as was his predecessor, John Hardman ('the great Hardman'), and also his successor, Richard Pennant, later father of the Welsh slate trade, who owned properties in Jamaica, with all of whose leading families, such as the Beckfords, he was connected by blood (he became Lord Penrhyn in 1780).

Liverpool was in no way shy about the benefits brought her by the slave trade. The façade of the Exchange carried reliefs of Africans' heads, with elephants, in a frieze, and one street was commonly known as 'Negro Row'.[†]

Bristol did not produce lasting dynasties among slave traders: her most astringent historian sharply comments that five of the leading twenty-six Bristol slavers died bachelors and a further ten died without male heirs.[20] But several Liverpool slave merchants founded great families, many of whom continued rich and influential after the trade in slaves had ended (for example, the Leylands, the Cunliffes, the Bolds, and the Kennions). The fortunes of several important Liverpool slave merchants became the basis of banks and new manufactures, such as those of the Leylands, the Hanlys, and the Ingrams.

Liverpool was also the main outlet for Manchester's new products. The latter's cotton goods early in the eighteenth century dominated the West India market, and were also much sought after by Spanish buyers. Costs of transport between Liverpool and Manchester, already low, were transformed by the opening of the Bridgewater Canal after 1772 (the price of transport changed from forty shillings a ton by road to six shillings by canal).

[*] *See pages 272–3.*
[†] *For blacks in England, see chapter 23.*

The consequence was remarkable: Manchester's export trade was negligible in 1739, standing at £14,000 a year. Twenty years later, it had increased to over £100,000, and by 1779 it stood at over £300,000. A third of this business went to Africa, principally items exchanged for slaves, and half either to the West Indies or the North American colonies. The favourites were cotton goods, especially the coarse striped annabasses copied from India. English dyeing, like French dyeing, was poor, and could not at first achieve the bright colours of the Indians. Manchester, however, was clever in marketing its cotton checks ('Guinea cloths'), which enjoyed every year a greater success in Africa.* Every year too more and more (nearly three-quarters by 1750) of the goods traded by British slave merchants to Africa were manufactured in England.

The outstanding manufacturer of cotton checks was Samuel Touchett, who was also an occasional slave merchant. The son of a pinmaker in Warrington, he was one of the three first patrons of Lewis Paul's unsuccessful spinning machine. He was an insurer, too, on a large scale. He helped to equip the British expedition which captured the settlements on the River Sénégal from the French in 1758, and subsequently sought unsuccessfully for a monopoly of trading there. He next went to London as the representative of the family firm, becoming 'the prime mover in parliamentary agitations' and the man who presented Manchester's many petitions to the government. He became a Member of Parliament in the interest of the Duke of Newcastle, and a friend of the corrupt but charming Paymaster-General, Henry Fox. He had a partnership in West Indian business, through which he sent ships with slaves to Havana when the British captured it in 1762. After the British occupation of Florida in 1763, he bought land there. Finally, he advised Charles Townshend, the Chancellor of the Exchequer, to introduce the taxes which led to the American rebellion (his advice was listened to, since it was supposed that he knew everything about America as well as finance). His career was so various that it might have been he, instead of his chancellor, whom Edmund Burke compared to 'a tesselated pavement without cement'.

In both Liverpool and Bristol the success of the slave trade was naturally a fillip to shipbuilding; and by the end of the century the leading Liverpool firm of shipbuilders, Baker and Dawson, had become the largest slavers, with a special licence to sell to the Spanish colonies.

This new trade by British captains and merchants meant, in the absence of any laws to the contrary, that Africans were now being sold in Britain on a small scale. Many advertisements were to be seen for black boys 'fit to wait on a gentleman' or for, for instance, 'a healthy negro girl

---

* Raw cotton came to Manchester at first from, above all, the West Indies and the Levant, then from India, later still from Brazil – and finally, of course, after the invention of the gin, from the United States.

aged about fifteen years, speaks good English, works at her needle, washes well, does household work, and has had the smallpox'.[21] In Liverpool these slaves were frequently advertised for sale on the steps of Silvester Moorecroft's new red-brick Custom House, the assumption being that what prevailed in the West Indies should prevail at home. Lord Chesterfield had a slave boy at The Hague in 1728, when he was British Ambassador, as did Charles Lennox, the radical, and tolerant, third Duke of Richmond. Black boys were often treated as toys by duchesses. When they grew old, they were usually sent to the West Indies. Newspapers often advertised for runaway slaves. In 1690 *Williamson's Advertiser* spoke about 'a negro named Will, aged about 22, he had a grey suit, and speaks English well. Whoever secures him, and gives notice to Mr Lloyd [the founder of Lloyd's Insurers] at his coffee house in Tower Street shall have a guinea reward'. Most slaves were, of course, recaptured, for their black colour caused them to stand out. But some humane people assisted the runaways, and the act of escape was looked on as a civil offence, not a crime.*

Meantime, the failure of France to gain the *asiento* in the Treaty of Utrecht in 1713 had had a remarkable effect on the French slave traffic. A sense of realism seized French commercial policymakers after the collapse of Law's great schemes. The old Guinea and Sénégal companies were abolished, and though Law's company survived, trade to Africa was opened to all French merchants who wished to go there, provided admittedly that they derived from one of five privileged ports: Rouen, La Rochelle, Bordeaux, Saint-Malo – and, above all, 'fortunate' Nantes, the 'eye of Brittany'.[22] It is true that thereafter each merchant had to pay a tax of thirty livres on each slave taken to Saint-Domingue, and fifteen livres on those carried to Martinique and Guadeloupe. The possibility of raising money through taxation of slaves was, indeed, the justification of the Crown's limitation to five ports (other cities were naturally angry at the limitation). The money gathered by taxation was to be spent on forts and trading posts in Africa. But alongside these taxes, the arrangements encouraged the French slave trade by helpful concessions: all French manufactured goods, for example, as well as all imported East Indian goods used for buying slaves, were declared exempt from export duties; and 'sugars and other types of merchandise from the islands, purchased from the sale of slaves', would receive a reduction of 50 per cent of the tax concerned on entry into France. These imports would not be taxed at all if re-exported to among others Holland or Germany.

The two nerve centres of the French slave trade in the eighteenth century were Saint-Domingue and Nantes. The former was of course the territory on the west of Hispaniola which had been officially ceded to

---

* *See chapter 23 for implications.*

France by Spain at the Treaty of Ryswick in 1697. Thereafter it experienced an extraordinary rise in its fortunes as a plantation colony, producing sugar principally, to serve the coffee, chocolate, and tea houses of eighteenth-century Europe. In the early eighteenth century it expected slave ships every other month; by 1750 once a week was more likely. Its success dazzled Paris, whose merchants, bankers, and officials believed that they had not discovered, but created, a real El Dorado.

The merchants of Nantes were Saint-Domingue's complement in the home country, for it was they who provided most of its labour. Nantes, neither entirely Breton nor Angevin, nor even part of Poitou, had been because of its position in the estuary of the Loire, with the numerous islands nearby, a promising port for several generations. Set fifty miles from the sea, at a point where the Loire is joined by the Erdre (soon to be canalized in its urban section), the former river linked Nantes with a valuable hinterland, even with Paris, through the Orléans Canal. But until the mid-seventeenth century Nantes had limited its commerce to the French coast, with occasional excursions to Newfoundland for fish. Now Nantes entered the international trade with a vengeance. The Compagnie de Sénégal had used that port as the main one for the sale of its goods, and the place soon gained an advantage over other harbours because of its specialization in importing Indian goods, which could then be taken to Africa (especially cottons). In the late seventeenth century, a few slave ships probably left for Africa. One certainly did in 1707. Afterwards, between 1715 and the revolution, Nantes sent out about 800 slave ships. Already in the 1720s it was the main French port for the commerce, being responsible for half the annual French expeditions.

The family of Montaudoin, headed by the brothers Jacques and René, were the greatest names in this trade in Nantes. They were responsible for half of it from the city for the first few years after 1713.* When some Poor Clares visited René to seek charity, he might open a chest full of gold and say: 'Plunge in your hands.'[23] The Montaudoins equipped 357 ships between 1694 and 1791, which probably make them the largest of all private traders. Closest to them in the African trade were the de Luynes, with 182 ships; the Boutelhiers, with 171 ships; and then the Bertrands, the Drouins, the Grous, the Michels, and the Richards. Most mercantile enterprises in these days in Nantes, however, had, as in Bristol and Liverpool, about twelve shareholders.

Among the interesting leaders of this business in Nantes was Antoine Walsh, an Irish Catholic immigrant, but one of the most powerful figures of the French slave trade. Altogether he sent fifty-seven expeditions to Africa. He married Marie, a daughter of Luc Shiell, another major slave trader of the early eighteenth century, also of Irish origin (a sister of hers married

---

* *The Montaudoins hailed from Paris, their first known ancestor to settle in Nantes being Jean, an artisan who came in 1616.*

another famous merchant of Nantes, a Grou). Haughty towards bureaucrats, contemptuous of small sums, Walsh was a romantic Jacobite, as well
as a man of commercial vision. His father had carried King James II of
England from London to France on one of his ships; and in 1745 he himself
accompanied Prince Charles Edward to the Highlands on another, the *Du
Teillay*. After the '45 he saw the great opportunities presented by buying
slaves from the African coast then known as Angola – really, the coast of
Loango – and with the help of Parisian bankers (Tourton and Baur, and
Paris de Montmartel) he established a company, with a capital of 2,000,000
livres, to send ten ships in 1749, whose purpose was to carry 2,000 slaves to
the colony of Saint-Domingue and elsewhere in the Caribbean. Walsh had
a reputation for choosing poor crews and for losing many slaves en route,
but perhaps that cannot be attributed personally to him.

Walsh overreached himself. He lived on the elegant Île Feydeau, an
island whch seemed to be anchored to the city of Nantes by two noble
bridges; he bought a nearby great property, Serrant, for his brother
François-Jacques in 1749, for the then colossal sum of 824,000 livres; and
he lost money as the Chairman of the Société d'Angola, partly because in
the Americas slaves from Angola were considered inferior to those from
the Gold Coast. Though it failed, Walsh's Société d'Angola was an original enterprise in that it sought to operate by stationing three large ships
permanently off Loango Bay, Cabinda, and Malemba, the purpose of
which was always to have European goods available to buy slaves, and
from which five smaller vessels would set off annually for Saint-
Domingue. The Société carried, in the end, 10,000 slaves in seven years.

Dutch merchants were as numerous as Irishmen in Nantes: handling
the trade with Northern Europe, they formed a 'nation' to such an extent
that the Abbé Expilly, in the 1760s, thought it hard to 'distinguish the true
character of the native population'.[24] They provided the merchants of
Nantes with much of their regular cargoes: iron bars from Sweden, East
India cloths, as well as the always sought after cowries from the Maldive
Islands in the Indian Ocean.

The sugar brought home to Nantes from the French sugar islands was
usually refined nearby. So Nantes could export much sugar: 25,000,000
livres' worth a year, above all to the Dutch, but also to Germany, Spain, the
Netherlands, Sweden, Italy, Denmark, and even to Guinea.

Another tropical import to be processed at Nantes was cotton. There
was a direct connection with Africa. For the first direct link between a
slave trader in Nantes and the manufacture of cotton occurred in the late
1720s, when René Montaudoin, the great slaver, and a director of the charity of La Sanitat, the Nantes general hospital, suggested that the workshop
there should be geared to the manufacture of cottons – partly for use in the
slave trade. Later, Montaudoin and some associates set up an annexe to
that hospital, which they named La Providence, specially to manufacture
cotton. The printers of Nantes soon devised methods whereby they could

copy on locally produced cloth the Indian designs; and these pretty '*indi-ennes*' also played an essential part in the cargoes sent to Africa. Finally, Montaudoin and his friends founded La Grande Manufacture, a factory in the modern sense of the word, which made the first dyed cottons; it used indigo from the Americas as a dye. Another new firm in Nantes was the Royal Glass Manufacture, directed at first by Joseph de Wansoul, from Liège, one of whose first purposes was to make bottles for the slave and West India trade.

Many of these successful merchants in slaves, cotton, sugar, and glass, such as the Grous, bought rural properties within a day's journey of their counting houses which not only afforded them the illusion of calm but enabled the development of vineyards, which were able to produce the cheap brandies needed for the Africa trade. Just so had the Jorges of Seville used their *finca* at Cazalla de la Sierra to make the wine which they exchanged for slaves in Cape Verde 200 years before.

Traders from Nantes tried to obtain their slaves from the Gold Coast and Whydah on the Slave Coast, but the English and the Dutch dominated the first, and trade in the second was for a time in the doldrums after Dahomey's seizure of it,˙ so that the captains of Nantes became more and more interested in the free trade of the coast around Loango Bay. By 1740 about a third of Nantes vessels went to that region.

Bordeaux, though in the eighteenth century the premier colonial port of France, never approached the activity of Nantes in the slave trade (except in 1802, the year of the Peace of Amiens). Still, in the 1730s it was sending one slave ship out a year, the *Heureuse-Paix*, the *Henriette*, or the *Union*, mostly owned by a single merchant, Jean Marchais, son of a tailor, with experience of 'the islands', interested in selling wine, as well as 'ebony'. Other shipping magnates of Bordeaux began to devote attention to the slave trade after 1750, among them David Gradis, Pierre-Paul Nairac, Isaac Couturier, and Laffon de Ladébat. Most of these merchants were men who came from far afield: from Gigounet, near Castres (Tarn), like Nairac; from Portugal, like Gradis; from Ireland, like Jean Valentin Quin; or from La Rochelle, like Elie Thomas. Nearly all of them were, like their counterparts in Nantes, Catholics, but a few Protestant (Nairac) and Jewish (Gradis, Samuel Alexandre) entrepreneurs also played a part.

'*Une seule passion dominait mon père,*' a nobleman from Saint-Malo, wrote Chateaubriand, '*celle de son nom.*'[25] But another interest ran that heroic passion close: making money, and particularly from the limited but all the same steady slave trade of Saint-Malo in which Chateaubriand *père* first served as a captain, of the *Apollon*, a ship owned by a friend, which carried 414 slaves from various African harbours to Saint-Domingue in 1754, and in which he subsequently engaged himself, as the owner of the

˙ *See page 356.*

Renoncule, captained by his brother, Pierre du Plessis, and the *Amarante*, which both set off in 1763. La Rochelle, Le Havre, Honfleur, Saint-Malo, Lorient, and Marseilles, in that order, all made contributions to the eighteenth-century French slave trade, each sending over a hundred slaving expeditions to Africa during the century.*

As a result of all these African voyages the number of black Africans living in France grew, as it did in England. In 1691 the *Oiseau* had arrived in La Rochelle with two slaves from Martinique. They were not sent back, *'la liberté étant acquise par les lois du royaume par des esclaves, aussitôt qu'ils touchent la terre . . .'.*[26] But there was some hesitation about this judgement, and though these two slaves went free their price (300 livres each) was maintained on the list of goods of the captain. A new law of 1716, hastily introduced by the Regent Orléans, enabled masters to keep in France slaves brought home from the colonies. A decree of 1738 refined the conditions in which blacks could be retained. Black slaves in France would be obliged to learn a trade. They could not stay in France more than three years; otherwise they would be confiscated by the King, which might mean that they would go to the galleys of the navy. Nor could these colonials maintain slaves in their French houses. These changes marked a step away from what had seemed France's refusal to accept the institution of slavery inside her borders: though masters were, in theory, not allowed to sell or even to exchange them in France.

In Nantes, in consequence, there were soon innumerable black men and women: they seemed, with the children, the parrots, and sometimes the monkeys, in many cases to be part of the family. Slave merchants, living in their fine town houses, with the face of Neptune over the front doors, in the Rue de la Fosse near the docks, or on the even more elegant Île Feydeau, would give such *'négrillons'* or *'négrittes'* to members of their households as tips. In 1754 an *ordonnance* provided that colonials could bring into France only one black apiece. But that rule was often forgotten. At the beginning of the revolution there were enough *'nègres'* in Nantes for a black battalion, *les hussards de Saint-Domingue*: they were a band of executioners, assassins, and pillagers who helped to make the city at that time one of the most bloody in France. Similar small populations of blacks survived in Bordeaux and La Rochelle.

Between 1721 and 1730 the French shipped fewer slaves than either the British or the Portuguese, but they still were responsible for carrying at least 85,000. During the 1730s the French were busier. They probably shipped over 100,000 slaves. Between 1738 and 1745 Nantes alone would carry 55,000 slaves in 180 ships, the chief buyers being the *nouveau riche* planters of Saint-Domingue (about three-quarters of the total) and Martinique (about a fifth).[27]

---

* *La Rochelle sent 400 (the main mercantile family being the Rasteaus, who sent about thirty négriers to Africa) and Le Havre nearly 350.*

Almost all French ports were allowed to engage in the slave trade after 1741, though this relaxation in no way affected the other Colbertian principles on which the French empire had been set up: neither slaves nor anything else could be sold to other empires.

The Netherlands scarcely seems in conventional history to have been an important Atlantic power in the eighteenth century. But that would not be quite the impression as seen by a trader in slaves. The Dutch still maintained four colonies on the north coast of South America, distant remembrances of the old days, when they had controlled half Brazil – those on the banks of the Rivers Essequibo, Demerara, and Berbice, as well as the far larger Suriname. During the eighteenth century the colony on the Essequibo received 15,000 slaves, that on the Demerara (where a serious settlement began in 1746) 11,000, the Berbice 14,000, and the Suriname, where cotton was beginning to be grown, about 150,000. In addition, the Dutch West India Company developed the tiny Leeward Island of St Eustatius as a slave mart, as an addition to, and after a while as a substitute for, their old centre of Curaçao. Some slaves were also still carried to Brazil by the Dutch West India Company: perhaps 3,500 between 1715 and 1731.

Still, that West India Company lost its formal monopoly in Africa in 1734, as in the West Indies in 1738, and Dutch interlopers, now legal free traders, came into their own. Thereafter any Dutch citizen who wanted to make money trading slaves could do so, on payment of a fee. Many independent firms took advantage of this opportunity, particularly in the late 1740s, when Holland was neutral in the War of the Austrian Succession, leading to a golden time for the Dutch trader. This was the era when merchants from Zeeland, especially Middelburg, moved into the forefront of the traffic. The most important firm there was the Middelburgische Kamerse Compagnie (Middelburg Commerce Company), which sponsored over one hundred voyages to Africa in search of slaves, carrying over 30,000 of them. About 1750 the Dutch still had their forts at Gorée and on the Guinea coast, with others at Elmina, Nassau, Axim, Accra, Anka, and Benda. But soon their decision to ally with the enemies of the Ashanti brought them into difficulties, for Ashanti power was every year increasing, partly at least because of the shipment of weapons to them in exchange for slaves made possible precisely by the company.

The example of the British in entering the slave trade on a major scale was everywhere emulated by nations that looked to them as the economic leaders of Europe. Thus the Danes were further developing their interest in the traffic. In 1725 their West India Company began to allow the introduction of slaves into their small islands by private traders. In 1733 they added St Croix to their Caribbean possessions, which already included St Thomas and St John (the latter island acquired in

1719). This new colony was larger than those other holdings, and the economy there was turned over from the production of cotton to that of sugar. Though the government failed to persuade Danish colonists to emigrate (St Croix was colonized by English Catholics from Montserrat, led by Nicholas Tuite), it carried on a good trade in illegal slaves to the Spaniards. The sugar plantations also required their own African captives: say 9,000 in 1755, 24,000 in 1775. A substantial number of the slaves taken to St Croix came from elsewhere in the West Indies, instead of direct from Africa. St Thomas, mountainous and tiny, was a transit slave camp rather than a plantation island, for which its beautiful harbour, Charlotte Amalie, prepared it. Probably over 25,000 slaves passed through the place in the second half of the eighteenth century.

Though on a small scale, Danish investors in sugar made fortunes as their counterparts did elsewhere. The Schimmelmann family, which directed the Danish economy during much of the late eighteenth century, accumulated its riches through sugar plantations in St Croix (Henrik Schimmelmann would be Minister of Finance between 1768 and 1782, his son Ernest after 1784).

Finally, among the innovations of these years, an Ostende Company, founded in 1723, showed that the Austrian Netherlands had no intention of being mere spectators in what they assumed was the great international bazaar of African slaves. This re-entry of a Habsburg dominion into the slave trade was not, however, without its sorrows. For example, the Moors of Algiers were continuing their slave operations; and in 1724, a boat from Ostende, bound for Africa, the *Keyserinne Elizabeth*, was captured at the entry into the Channel by two corsairs, and the crew of one hundred white Europeans was taken to be sold at Algiers.

Despite the activities of the English and the French, the Portuguese remained the largest shippers of slaves across the Atlantic till the 1730s. In 1724 a new Portuguese monopoly company was set up to serve Brazil; between 1721 and 1730 nearly 150,000 slaves were probably carried to the latter colony, just under 80,000 from Mina, just under 70,000 from Angola. The urgent perceived need for slaves in the gold mines in Minas Gerais largely explains this. English manufactures, as well as those brought from India by the Dutch and the English East India companies, which Brazilian gold bought in Lisbon, were ideal goods to exchange for slaves in Angola.

Only a minority of ships which slaved in Angola now had contact with Portugal: for the trade with Brazil was becoming horizontal, not triangular. As for Africa itself, most of the slaves shipped from Angola now derived from inland, far beyond the tributary Kingdom of Ndongo, further even than Matamba (the monarchy deriving from Queen Nzinga)

---

* These are now the United States Virgin Islands, bought by President Wilson, for $25,000,000 in 1917, just before he drafted the Fourteen Points.

or the once-violent Lunda in Kasanje. The other monarchies just mentioned, even Kasanje, were now mere corridors through which the slaves passed. Though the wars which marked the first hundred years of Portuguese involvement in Angola were generally over, and though the Portuguese governors were more effective in control of their large territories, there were perpetual disputes between the governors (and other officials sent out from Portugal) and the settlers in Luanda. The latter thought that the governors neglected their responsibilities in order to make fortunes quickly from the slave trade. In the end, Portuguese Angolans were able to persuade Lisbon in 1721 to place a ban on the trading of slaves by the governors in return for huge increases of salary. Perhaps as a result of these and similar disputes so typical of colonial society in the Americas as well as in Africa the rate of export of Portuguese-Spanish slaves was less in the early eighteenth century than it had been in the early seventeenth: instead of 10,000 a year, the average between 1710 and 1720 was about 6,000.

In the 1730s Brazil still received well over 150,000 slaves, mostly (100,000 at least) from Angola, but nearly 60,000 from Guinea (Mina). Rio was still the most important slave-receiving port, taking about twice the number of those sold in Bahia. Buyers in both cities seemed, though, perpetually short of labour: the Viceroy there wrote to the Governor of Pernambuco in 1742 that the trade was declining so much 'that, unless we find a good means of reorganizing it, I am afraid that it may finish altogether. The consequence would be the ruin of Brazil, which cannot subsist without the service of slaves. . . . The mining people here who come and look for blacks which they need ruin themselves by paying prices both exorbitant and intolerable. The proprietors of sugar mills and the tobacco planters are in the same boat.'[28]

Diamonds had been mined in Brazil since the 1720s, and those jewels, like the produce of the gold mines of Minas Gerais earlier on, were generally worked by African slaves. Just as slaves hid much gold from their masters, large diamonds were often secreted by slaves in ingenious ways: and it was widely said that the Church of Santa Efigenia in Rio was established from the proceeds of gold dust washed out of their hair by slave girls who knelt at the font.

The early eighteenth century marked the end of North America's novitiate in the traffic in slaves. In the seventeenth century, too poor or too concerned with primitive agriculture, colonists there had been slow to participate in any substantial way. A few slaves acting as servants had always been seen in all the colonies; but it was not till the owners of plantations in the Carolinas, learning from their own experience in Barbados, realized that they could make considerable profits from rice and indigo that anything like a regular trade in slaves began. Those in Virginia made a similar discovery with regard to tobacco. So from then on Africans were sought on a regular basis. Then the small independent farmer began to fail, as had happened in Barbados and elsewhere in the West Indies when those colonies had embarked on growing sugar. It was the conventional wisdom of the age that these new tobacco plantations could not be served by a few indentured servants; and that white men did not work well in the rice fields, at least not so well as blacks. Slavery seemed the only solution to the problem, as it had appeared in the West Indies, and before that in Brazil.

Independent traders from Britain, including several from minor ports, such as Exeter or Dartmouth, began to serve these 'plantation colonies' with slaves in the first ten years of the new century. All the same, there were some hesitations among the settlers of the thirteen colonies – less on moral grounds, to be sure, than on those of prudence. Would not a colony with many slaves incur rebellions, as everyone knew occurred from time to time 'in the islands'? So a bill was introduced into the Assembly of South Carolina which demanded the payment of £2 duty per slave. Yet the same document stated firmly that 'the plantations and estates of this province cannot be well and sufficiently managed, and brought into use, without the labour and service of negroes and other slaves', even though such people might have 'barbarous, wild, savage natures, such as renders them wholly unqualified to be governed by the laws, customs and practices of this Province'.[29] So Carolina had a divided mind on the matter. The same might have been said in Virginia. In poor North Carolina the Reverend John Urmstone wrote in 1716 to the Secretary of the Society for the Propagation of the Gospel asking him to arrange for three or four Guinea slaves, three men 'of middle stature about 20 years old and a girl of about 16 years. Here is no living without servants, there are none to be hired of any colour, and none of the black kind to be sold good for anything under £50 or £60.'[30] (He wrote often, without success.) In his *Natural History of North Carolina*, published in 1737, John Brickell declared that slaves were reckoned 'the greatest riches in these parts', and that the planters 'were at great pains to lay in store of gold and silver with which to purchase negroes in the West Indies and other places'. All the evidence, he insisted – rightly, as it happened – was that slaves in North America were treated far better than those in the Caribbean, where the life of a slave was rendered inhuman by conditions on sugar plantations.[31]

Over 3,500 slaves were carried to South Carolina between May 1721 and September 1726. In 1732 there were in that colony probably 14,000 white people, while the blacks there numbered about 32,000: the first time a black majority was registered in an English colony on the mainland. The cultivation of rice in South Carolina, which inspired these changes, had its ironies. For seed rice had been introduced from Madagascar, and slaves from both there and Senegambia were perfectly informed of how to produce it before they came to the Americas. The clearing of the cypress swamps in South Carolina and the subsequent harvesting of the new crops were thus tasks performed by experienced workers.

At a hearing before the Board of Trade, Mr Samuel Wragg (a merchant of Carolina, who traded slaves himself, and who would be ennobled for encouraging emigrants to the colony) testified that Carolina was importing 1,000 slaves a year, largely since the rice trade had increased from 1,500 to 25,000 barrels a year, and so a 'negro can make £10 clear profit for his master'.[32]

By 1730 we also find 6,000 slaves in North Carolina – though most of them were probably not shipped, but carried in as a result of purchase in Virginia. The colonists mostly paid by barter: food, livestock, and even pitch. The colony complained it since it had no direct deliveries – from Africa – which 'the People are able to pay for' they received 'the refuse refractory and distemper'd negroes, brought from other governments'.[33]

Pennsylvania started to import slaves within three years of its foundation, in 1684, when 150 Africans were brought in and used to clear trees and build houses. Most of the first settlers exhausted their supply of cash in buying these captives. In the early eighteenth century there were few further supplies, but by the 1730s, thanks to the reduction or disappearance of import duties, the commerce increased considerably. The lead was taken by a Quaker, Isaac Morris, though he mostly bought his captives in the West Indies.

What troubled the merchants involved in this trade in the eighteenth century were the duties imposed by colonial governments, taxes which were designed to reduce the number of imports for fear of rebellion. Thus 1733 saw petitions of English merchants against the 'exorbitant duty' imposed on slaves imported into South Carolina. The merchants who protested included some of the most powerful men in the trade: Isaac Hobhouse, from Bristol; Ben Whitaker and Richard Acland, of London; and Charles Pole, of Liverpool.

But though slow in the uptake, and with some hesitations, British merchants in the eighteenth century encouraged the trade in African captives to begin in earnest to North America. Advertisements for 'prime young slaves' or 'strong hearty stout negroes' were soon everywhere to be seen; there were sales of 'parcels of very likely negroes', sometimes with the enticement 'of the very blackest sort'; and, often, there were combined sales of 'negroes, cocoa and sugars'. In 1721 the Boston Gazette describes the sale of 'several lusty negro men, arrived lately from the island of St Jago' (Cape Verde Islands);[34] in 1724 an Irish-born merchant, Thomas Amory, with Portuguese and French connections, wrote from his wharf in Boston, Massachusetts, then the largest city of the thirteen colonies and much the most important port, to a customer in North Carolina: 'In the fall, we expect negroes directly from Guinea, a vessel having sailed from here and one from [Newport] Rhode Island.'[35] Boston from then on experienced, every year, several sales of slaves direct from

Africa. We hear of the schooner *William*, the brigantine *Charming Betty*, as well as the *Charming Molly*, bringing 'parcels' of such cargoes to the city, though without specifying exactly whence the slaves came. On 19 June 1732 Godfrey Mallbone of Rhode Island is found selling 'choice young negro Gold Coast slaves' in Boston. Ships from more northerly ports, for example, such as Salem, also in Massachusetts, were soon setting off direct for Africa, in imitation of their English rivals.

Amory's letter, incidentally, suggests that even at the beginning of the North American slave trade though the shippers of slaves in British North America were as a rule from New England the biggest customers were in the South or the Caribbean; and, within New England, the colony of Rhode Island was from the beginning pre-eminent.˙

The success of Rhode Island in this traffic derived from the fact that it possessed excellent harbours but had little soil. The place lacked the grasslands of Connecticut or Massachusetts, and did not have easy access, as those colonies did, to the fisheries of Newfoundland. There was little to do there except to trade, build ships, and distil rum. Thus in the eighteenth century the tiny, barren colony had a Venetian economy, or one comparable to that of Hong Kong in the late twentieth century; the port of Newport was the centre of activity; and slaving, though far from the only commerce, figured importantly.

Regular sailing for Africa seems to have begun from the harbour of Newport in 1725, when three ships set off, though sporadic sailings had occurred before, 1700 being the earliest year recorded for that port, when we also hear of three ships sailing for Africa. They were largely owned by two Barbados merchants. Newport had excellent rum distilleries and, from at least 1723 its ships carried that liquor to Africa as their special contribution to the cargoes exchanged for slaves. Another mark of this activity was that the ships concerned were smaller than the usual European ones, carrying seventy-five to a hundred slaves, which their crews loaded as quickly as they could in African ports, in order to reduce the risk of sickness or death to both themselves and their captives.

Rum was an immediate success in Africa; and North American captains were therefore especially sought after. The pioneers in these activities were John and William Wanton, Abraham Redwood, the benefactor of the Redwood Library, and Henry Collins, the 'Lorenzo de' Medici of Newport'. By the mid-century, Samuel and William Vernon, sons of a famous silversmith (Samuel Vernon I, with his distinctive mark of a fleur-de-lis within a heart), were pre-eminent.

So Newport became a major commercial port, and her captains were selling slaves all over the British empire, particularly to planters in the

---

˙ *The Rhode Island slave trade and the American slave trade were 'virtually synonymous',
wrote its historian, Jay Coughtry, thereby underestimating the trade from New York,
Maryland, and South Carolina.*

Caribbean. This trade was in many ways an extension of Rhode Island's earlier dealings in the same places for wood and food. The commerce naturally led to Jamaica and Barbados becoming the principal suppliers of Rhode Island's imports of molasses, which it needed in order to make its rum.

Providence, Rhode Island, was also concerned in the trade from 1736, when James Brown, a near-illiterate merchant at that time (judging from his letters), anxious for money with which to expand his spermaceti candle-making business, fitted out the first Guineaman, the *Mary*, to set out from that harbour, his son Obadiah serving as supercargo. But that was an isolated instance: the next slaver from Providence was the *Wheel of Fortune*, sent by Obadiah in his own right as a merchant, but not till 1759.[36]

New York was now far behind the ports of New England. Only fourteen voyages to Africa for the purpose of buying slaves seem to have been made from there between 1715 and 1747, the ships travelling across the Atlantic and directly back. The merchants concerned included descendants of old Dutch families, such as the Schuylers and van Hornes, but also Anglo-Saxon or Scottish ones, such as the Livingstons and Walters: alliances of the two social groups occurred, as when Arnot Schuyler and John Walter of New York jointly invested in the *Catherine*, which brought back 260 slaves from Africa in the 1730s.[37]

Meantime, it should not be assumed that the Americas in those years constituted the only market for West African slaves. The Moroccan Sultan Mulai Ismail carefully established a large black slave army about 1700, with 180,000 soldiers, and 20,000 of them were still under arms when he died in 1727. Such figures would suggest that at least 4,000 black slaves were exported from West Africa to Morocco in the first quarter of the eighteenth century; and Egypt was probably taking as many.

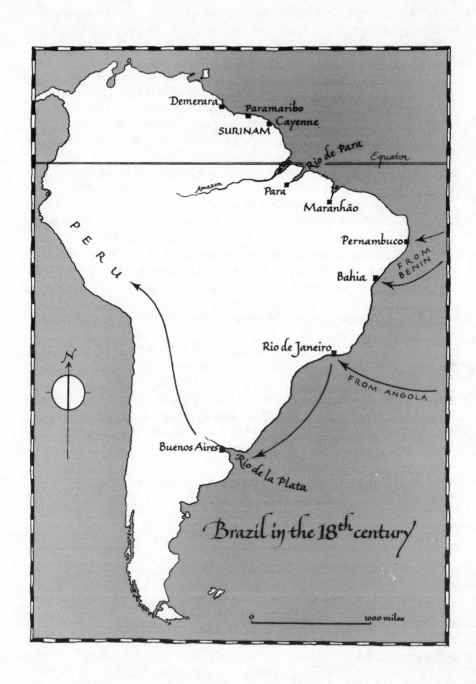

Demerara
Paramaribo
Cayenne
SURINAM
Rio de Para
Equator
Amazon
Para
Maranhâo
Pernambuco
FROM BENIN
Bahia
PERU
N
Rio de Janeiro
FROM ANGOLA
Buenos Aires
Rio de la Plata
Brazil in the 18th century
0   1000 miles

14

BY THE GRACE OF GOD

*'Louis, by the grace of God . . . we have been
informed that le sieur Jacques-Alexandre
Laffon de Ladébat, trader in our city of
Bordeaux, has carried on his commerce in
Africa and in America and is distinguished
by his zeal, by the extent of his operations
and by the commerce of the slave trade . . .
that, since 1764, he has arranged to send to
our islands of America over 4,000 slaves,
through fifteen vessels which he has sent to
the coasts of Africa . . . that at present
without cease he has seven ships employed
in the slave trade or in the provisioning of
our islands. . . .'*

Letter by King Louis XV with respect to
the ennoblement of a Bordeaux merchant

THE LATE EIGHTEENTH CENTURY saw the beginning of that industrial
revolution, which still has not spent itself two hundred years later. It
marked the subsequent beginning of a transition from a life predominantly rural to one decidedly urban; and a new language in which social
and political history could be discussed was devised in France. The last
half of the century also saw several wars in which the national identity of
the leading nations was created or reaffirmed, with a new generation
of heroes: the framers of the Constitution of the United States; Nelson's
captains; the French revolutionary generals; the enlightened despots and
their advisers in Prussia, Spain, and Portugal. It was the age of medical
advances symbolized by vaccination against smallpox; but it was also the
age of sugar.

We observe in England the consequences, in the fat faces in the
portraits of the beauties and the kings, of the ostlers and of the actresses.
In 1750, already, 'the poorest English farm labourer's wife took sugar in

her tea'. She baked sweet cakes, and spread treacle on her bread, as well as her porridge. Mrs Hannah Glasse's famous first cookery book in England, *The Art of Cookery Made Plain and Easy* and subtitled *Excelling any Thing of the Kind ever yet published*, whose first edition was in 1747, shows that sugar was no longer to be considered primarily a medicine, at least in a supposedly advanced country such as England. 'Take . . . three quarters of a pound of the best moist sugar . . .' was part of her recipe for 'a cake in the Spanish way'. Jane Austen's *Sense and Sensibility* records a moment of anxiety when impending poverty threatens the heroine's family's purchases of sugar. The pudding, hitherto made of fish or light meat, now embarked on its unhealthy history as a separate sweet course. Sugar began too to be used as a preservative, as an addition to salt. Fifty years later the typical poor family in England would give as much as 6 per cent of its income to sugar. In 1848 a planter with property in both Demerara (Guiana) and Grenada declared to a committee of the House of Commons that the consumption of sugar had 'almost become a necessary of life'. The saccharine soul of Britain's golden age seems thus clear. How could the supply of sugar be assured? As yet, the idea of obtaining it from beet was still a secret in the brain of an obscure Silesian; so the plantations of the West Indies seemed, therefore, the source of all comfort.

France was in a condition similar to Britain. By now two-thirds of French exports carried by sea went to the West Indies, and as in the case of England sugar was the most valuable single import. Sugar stimulated the talkers in the great coffee houses of Paris and of Bordeaux. It gave energy to the *philosophes* in the drawing rooms of great ladies and humour to *petits marquis* in the cold drawing rooms of Versailles. It would afford courage to the soldiers as well as the generals of the Grande Armée. Prince Talleyrand's nostalgia for an epoch when the *'douceur de vivre'* survived employed an appropriate metaphor; and, of course, sugar in France, as elsewhere, depended on the imports of African slaves into the Caribbean.

Britain was in these years dominant in the Atlantic commerce in slaves. Between 1740 and 1750 her ships probably took to the Americas over 200,000 slaves: far more than any country had carried in any ten years before. Of these British shipments, nearly 60,000 were probably delivered to Virginia and the Carolinas. Over 50,000 slaves went to Jamaica, and 30,000 to Barbados, with well over 60,000 to other colonies. In the single year 1749 British merchants sent out about 150 ships in the trade, with a capacity for at least 50,000 slaves: seventy ships from Liverpool, nearly fifty from Bristol, eight from London, as well as twenty or so ships from minor harbours, such as Whitehaven, Lancaster, and Glasgow. Those secondary ports should not be ignored, for Lancaster was investing heavily in these years in the traffic, and that tiny port became Britain's fourth largest slave trader, with twelve ships so occupied in 1756, her example encouraging some of her poorer neighbours on

Britain's north-western coast, such as Preston, Poulton, and even bleak Ulverston, to follow her lead. South Carolina was an especially appreciative market, as can be seen from the papers of the Charleston merchant Henry Laurens. Well might Malachy Postlethwayt – a hack economic writer, author of *The Universal Dictionary of Trade and Commerce* – say, approvingly, in a book published in 1745 to support the Royal African Company, that the British empire was then 'a magnificent superstructure of American commerce and naval power, *on an African foundation* [author's italics]'.[1]

In 1750 the slave trade was made even easier for British merchants: an act made the commerce entirely open, so that it was henceforth 'lawful for all His Majesty's subjects to trade and traffick to and from any port in Africa . . .'.[2] A new holding company representing all merchants trading to Africa was established to look after British forts and trading posts. This was to be directed by a board composed of traders from Bristol, London, and Liverpool, which set about devising a new form of regulation to maintain those places. The eventual arrangements were a good example of the English approach to the mixed economy: the Crown gave the new company an annual grant of £10,000 to maintain the forts, but the company – that is, the merchants – ran them, and were also responsible for the appointment of governors. Every trader to Africa was thereafter supposed to pay £2, to either the Town Clerk of Liverpool, the Clerk of the Merchants' Hall in Bristol, or the Chamberlain of London, as a fee for using the African ports. Like many of the best English institutions, the company had the character, therefore, of a club.

The 1750s saw few changes in slave deliveries, at least until the outbreak of the Seven Years War. Britain again delivered over 200,000 slaves in these ten years: about sixty-five ships a year left from Liverpool, twenty-five from Bristol, ten from London; ships from Liverpool were now carrying over half the slaves exported from Africa by Europeans. The Brazilian trade was not far behind, and accounted for 170,000, over half from Angola, about 50,000 from Mina, and the remainder from Mozambique round the Cape of Good Hope. The French, much affected by the war, in which they lost so much, shipped about 90,000. That conflict virtually brought their commerce to a temporary end. From 1757 to 1761 only two slave ships left French ports (both from Bayonne). The English seized over a hundred ships from Nantes, causing the ruin of several famous shippers there (Michel et Grou, Trochonde Lorière, Rollet du Challet, Struickman, Desridelières-Leroux, and others). But there were some successful French attacks on English ships: Captain William Creevey, father of the courtly diarist Thomas Creevey, recalled how his slaver, *Betty*, was sunk off Spain while en route to Gambia.

The war affected slaving in other ways. Thus in 1758 a British expedition sent on the urgent recommendation of Thomas Cumming, of the Company of Merchants Trading to Africa, captured both Sénégal

(2 May) and Gorée (27 December), and soon all the most important French anchorages in Africa, with their six factories, were in Britain's hands.

The victors began immediately to export slaves from those ports. Yet, war or no war, some merchants of France were prosperous: between 1748 and 1757 and then 1761 and 1765 a single merchant, Guillaume Grou, sent from Nantes forty-three *négriers*, to carry over 16,000 captives. The government in Paris showed itself so determined to revive the trade that it introduced bounties for slave ships leaving France for Africa, and increased the existing bounties for every slave landed in the West Indies. French planters were, however, still dissatisfied, for the shortages were continuous and harvests had to be brought in whatever the cause of the conflict. They bought slaves illicitly from English or Dutch merchants – sometimes from ships 'obliged' to take refuge in a French harbour, sometimes from English ships which secretly landed slaves on the indented south coast of Saint-Domingue.

There was, meantime, one unexpected benefit to France of the failure of Bonnie Prince Charlie's (and Antoine Walsh's) efforts to recover the British throne for the Roman Church: a Jacobite manufacturer from Manchester, John Holker, fled to France, and convinced both merchants and officials there of the desirability of using, and stealing, English techniques for dyeing and printing textiles: hence his factory in the Rouen suburb of Saint-Sever in the Seine Valley. Many of his imaginative products found their way onto slave vessels. So did those of Julien-Joseph Pinczon du Sel des Monts, who at Salleverte, near Rennes, planned his new manufactury of textiles for the benefit of the shippers of Nantes's African trade. His *Considérations sur le commerce de Bretagne* endeared him to the *états* of the region, and they gave him a large subsidy. Another new manufacturer was André Langevin, who had himself been a minor slave dealer, but who in 1759 became an *indienneur* to serve his old colleagues and rivals in that trade with cloths.

In these years Spain was too backward and too poor to look on sugar as the recipe for prosperity. The aristocrats could buy it from France, the poor ('*les nègres de l'Europe*', in Chamfort's phrase) could be overlooked. Yet sugar was being produced in the Spanish empire, and slaves were still held to be needed in a hundred anchorages there. When after 1739 the War of the Austrian Succession between Spain and Britain caused the South Sea Company's contract again temporarily to lapse, the Spanish Crown made a contract for slaves with a Havana merchant of Basque origin, Martín de Ulibarrí, the first Spanish *asentista* for two generations; and, when nothing seemed to transpire, began a series of separate agreements with different companies which, the government hoped, would meet the demand in different markets. Thus after 1746 the new Royal Havana Company was given a twenty-year licence to introduce merchandise to that port, including the right to sell 500 slaves at 144 pesos each. The company sounded new; but its directors were all members of well-known Cuban oligarchic families, who themselves had sugar mills near at hand. Other companies were given similar licences: the much more successful Guipúzcoa (Caracas) Company, for example, which made much money carrying cacao to serve the new chocolate craze in Madrid, carried nearly 12,000 slaves to the port of Caracas between 1754 and 1765; and a special concession enabled Ramón Palacio to import 2,000 or more blacks into Chile and Peru.

The changes which these arrangements made were modest: none of the new companies went to Africa to look for slaves, they merely continued to buy in Jamaica, or elsewhere in the Caribbean. The Spanish government must have known that was likely, if only because the Havana Company's agent, José Ruiz de Noriega, travelled to that island specifically to make the necessary plans with George Frier, who had previously been the South Sea Company's representative at Cartagena.

Peace after 1748 brought the revival of the South Sea Company's contract, but two years later its directors, such as Sir Peter Burrell MP, being by then passive or lazy, by mutual agreement between Spain and Britain brought the venture to an end. Neither the British government nor those directors felt that the once-promising arrangements concluded in 1713 now had prospects. Spain even paid £100,000 for the British renunciation of the opportunity.

Spain had then to consider its needs anew. Another Basque merchant, Martín de Aiostegui, was in 1754 asked to try and satisfy the demands of the empire. But despite his initial enthusiasm he failed to produce any slaves at all. France was then again temporarily if informally allocated the *asiento*, and Antoine Walsh, Prince Charles Edward's friend and financier, prepared to supply blacks from his 'floating factory', off the coast of Angola. His plan was that there would be a fortified assembly point in Saint-Domingue, from which slaves would be distributed to the French and Spanish markets. But again little transpired. As a result, in 1753 the Spanish Crown gave permission to Spanish companies to bring slaves directly from Africa to Cuba. The papal rule limiting trade with Africa to Portugal was at last, unceremoniously, put aside, at a time when the Spanish and Portuguese governments were also reconsidering Pope Alexander VI's division established at Tordesillas in 1493.

All the same, nothing was done immediately in the light of this liberal decision. Spanish merchants had gone down the West African coast occasionally in the seventeenth and early eighteenth centuries, but the Crown had no African factories, no navy on the coast, and little commercial experience in the territory. Still, when similar rights were offered to a Catalan company, the Barcelona Company, to provide slaves to Puerto Rico, Santo Domingo, and Margarita, some long-term voyages were planned, and in 1758 the first boat for many years, *La Perla Catalana* of Barcelona, did arrive in San Juan direct from Africa.

The opportunities offered by the trade in slaves, and especially the dominance of Britain in the business, were reflected in North America, where, in these last years before the revolution of the 1770s, slave merchants were beginning to be men of wealth. They were never as rich as those found in Liverpool or Nantes, or even in Middelburg in the Netherlands, but relatively speaking they were important. In South Carolina, for example, there was Henry Laurens of Charleston, who has already been briefly mentioned. Laurens was a trader of Huguenot stock (his grandfather, André, came from La Rochelle, in the late seventeenth century a major slave port, and so perhaps the commerce was in his blood). South Carolina was already known, at the time of Laurens's birth, for the production of rice and indigo for the home market; a biographer of his explained, 'The very trying summer climate, supplemented by the unhealthy nature of the tasks, made African slavery inevitable.'[3] Laurens began to trade slaves in company with George Austen, also of South Carolina, in 1748, when he told Foster Cunliffe, the Liverpool slave merchant, that 'there is a good prospect of good sales for negroes in that province, as rice [this year] promises fair to be a good commodity'. He told other English slave merchants of his plans to enter the traffic in slaves (for example, Isaac Hobhouse of Bristol). He, Laurens, wanted to buy slaves from English or other traders and then resell them – mostly, but not entirely, to Carolina planters. In return for a commission of 10 per cent, Laurens would also arrange to give security in England, and collect all slave-trading debts, but he did not propose any limit on the length of time that he would be offered credit. Laurens's principal partner in England was Devonshire, Reed and Lloyd of Bristol, but he also used the imposing Augustus Boyd of London who, with his son, John, would form one of the best collections of paintings in England.[*] After a few years, though, Laurens's English partners, especially those in Liverpool, began to turn their business over to other traders who would offer 'immediate remittance'; and so Laurens was run close, as the main dealer, by rivals such as Samuel Brailsford and Miles Brewton. Laurens sent a few ships direct to Africa, but most of his profits derived from buying captives from captains who had been sent by his friends in England, and then reselling them.

There was plenty of money to be made by all these men, for the 1750s marked a breakthrough in slaving in South Carolina. In 1754 the Governor, James Glen, reported that 'negroes are sold at higher prices here than in any part of the King's dominions . . . a proof that this province is in a flourishing condition, for these importations are not to supply the place of Negroes worn out with hard work, or lost by mortality. . . . But our number increases even without such yearly supply. I presume 'tis indigo that puts all in such high spirits. . . .'[4] The proportion of slaves which came from natural increase in South Carolina was

---

[*] *See page 295.*

certainly high: one plantation's stock of slaves there grew in Laurens's day from eighty-six to 270 in thirty-eight years, only twelve or fourteen of them being replaced by purchases. Yet Laurens reported in 1755, 'Never was there such pulling and hawling for negroes before. Had there been a thousand, they would not have supplied the demand'.[5] The firm of Austen and Laurens was concerned with wines and spirits, beer, deer-skins, rice, indigo, and indentured servants, as well as slaves, but it carried in 1755 about a quarter of Charleston's slaving business: 700 slaves that year. Laurens made a profit of 10 per cent on every slave imported, 5 per cent on other produce.

That same year Laurens wrote to Captain Charles Gwynn of the *Emperor*, then at Jamaica: 'If you had arriv'd about the middle of April, or anytime since, we should have made a glorious Sale of your cargo, our planters are in full spirits for purchasing Slaves, and have made almost all the money loaded up for that purpose. Indigo has kept up at almost an exorbitant price in England, so has rice. . . . Capt. [William] Jeffries [on the *Pearl*, owned by Thomas Easton & Co., of Bristol] arrived here the 10th instant with 251 pretty slaves. . . .' Most sold at between £270 and £280 each, 'a very great price for Angola slaves'. Laurens was able to tell Easton that he had made £52,294 on this voyage.[6]

In another sale at Charleston, Laurens sold slaves from the *Orrel*, owned by John Knight of Liverpool, to a most diverse group: to, for example, Peter Furnell of Jamaica; to Gedney Clarke, Collector of Customs at Barbados; to William Wells, Jr., of St Kitts; to Devonshire, Reed and Lloyd of Bristol, presumably for resale in North America; to the art collector and slave dealer Augustus Boyd of London; and to Robert and John Thompson, two brothers who were the leaders of the trade in slaves from Lancaster. The sale shows the extent to which these traders in captives, even in then parochial North America, were far from being provincial men; like Bartolommeo Marchionni of Lisbon in the fifteenth century, or Coymans of Amsterdam in the seventeenth, they thought in intercontinental terms.

Laurens is one of the most interesting men in the long history of the Atlantic slave trade, since, a great gentleman who loved his own slaves, in later life he repented of his involvement in the traffic. But he never did much against it, and bought one or two more slaves from an English friend, Richard Oswald of London, even after he had become convinced of the need for change. Having made his fortune, and established himself at Mepkin, a fine property on the Cooper River, inland from his city, Laurens withdrew from active slaving about 1764; he later entered politics, became the President of the Continental Congress, and after a year in prison in England became a peace commissioner, in 1782, with Benjamin Franklin and John Jay in Paris, where Richard Oswald was a senior British negotiator.*

* *See page 484.*

Despite the significance of Charleston as a market, Rhode Island, and particularly Newport, was in the 1750s and the 1760s still the North American colonies' most important slaving zone. Newport, which always welcomed enterprising people without asking whence they came, also used more slaves in small businesses, farms, or homes than any other Northern colony. If, as seems likely, Rhode Island carried just over 150,000 slaves from Africa either to the Caribbean or to North America, probably 100,000 were financed by merchants of Newport. About 110 slavers cleared Newport for Africa in the 1750s, 165 in the 1760s. These figures were, of course, small beer in comparison with those of the major slaving ports of Europe.

One successful merchant of Newport interested in slaving was the 'active, alert, shrewd, bold, and masterful' John Bannister, whose ancestors had been merchants in Boston, and who, like many others, came to Newport after 1733 as a protest against the prejudices he encountered in that austere city. Like Laurens in Charleston, Bannister was as much at home in old as in New England. He even built ships for merchants in England, such as Joseph Manesty of Liverpool (owner of the *Duke of Argyll*, presumably called after the duke who had been a South Sea director, of which the Reverend John Newton was once captain).* Another important slave merchant was Abraham Redwood, who was among the first North Americans to carry commercial logic to its geographical conclusion by not only trading in Newport and Africa but owning a plantation in Jamaica, to which his own ships took slaves from Africa. Quaker merchants were involved, too, in Rhode Island slaving; for example, Joseph Wanton, who became his family's fourth Governor of Rhode Island, saw no difficulty whatever in buying and selling slaves in the 1770s.

The most interesting of these merchants of Rhode Island with slaving interests in the second half of the eighteenth century was, however, Aaron Lopez of Newport, who, unusually in the United States at that time, was Jewish Portuguese in origin. He had concealed his Judaism in his youth in Portugal and came to North America in 1752 (and to welcoming Newport a little later). He was to begin with a general trader, operating from a shop in Thames Street, selling everything from bibles to violins, being especially concerned in the trade in candles made from whale spermaceti. He always kept his spermaceti works, but he entered the slave trade in 1762, in collaboration with his father- and brother-in-law, Jacobo and Abraham Ribera; and spermaceti candles often figured among their cargoes to Africa. By 1775, Lopez was the largest taxpayer in Newport and owned over thirty ships. It is not quite clear how many slaving ships he financed; his accounts seem to list only fourteen direct voyages to Africa, but over fifty to the West Indies, from which his

---

* See chapter 15. 'Bannister's Wharf' survives in Newport to this day.

captains sometimes presumably returned with slaves, and delivered them in North America – for example, in South Carolina. Lopez, like Abraham Redwood, was as philanthropic as he was successful. The *Dictionary of American Biography* exhausts its approbatory adjectives in describing Lopez as 'beneficient to his family connections, to his nation, and to all the world', as 'almost without a parallel'. Again like Redwood, he was also the proprietor of an estate in the British West Indies, in his case in Antigua.

Trading in slaves was carried on elsewhere than in Rhode Island: for example, in Maryland, where the Galloway, Tilghman, and Ringgold families were prominent. They or their colleagues sold 100,000 slaves in one way or another by the end of the eighteenth century, perhaps many from natural increase, but also many bought from captains hailing originally from Liverpool or London. Thomas Ringgold and Samuel Galloway, with houses on opposite sides of Chesapeake Bay, sent at least one ship direct to Africa, all the same, as well as several to the West Indies.

Nor can New York be neglected as a slave port. At least 130 slave voyages seem to have been mounted from that city to Africa between 1747 and 1774, William and Garret van Horne and John and Stephen van Courtlandt being prominent alongside Nathaniel Marston and Philip Livingston, the latter's sons also being investors (Marston and Livingston seem the only merchants to have had investments in as many as four ships). Thus it was not surprising that in the region of the Sherbro River, in what is now Sierra Leone, John Newton of Liverpool, then the captain of a slave ship, should have exchanged slaves with Captain William Williams of New York in the *Rebekah*, a sloop. Trading in slaves, of course, constituted only a tiny proportion – 2 per cent perhaps of the total commerce of the city – and many more ships, nearly 600 between 1715 and 1764, went to the West Indies than to Africa. Even so, between a third and a quarter of New York's 400 merchants were concerned in one way or another in the slave trade in the mid-eighteenth century.

Merchants from Massachusetts were also implicated: families from Boston who invested in the slave trade in the eighteenth century included the Belchers, the Waldos and the Faneuils; there were also the Crowninshields and the Grafton brothers of Salem; and, further north still, the Pepperells of Kittery, a little port just in Maine. Still, all these enterprises were on a small scale. Boston shipping destined for Africa rarely totalled ten a year before 1774, in comparison with nearly sixty destined for Britain and sometimes nearly 200 for the Caribbean.

Pious Pennsylvania was also sending ships in the 1760s to Africa for slaves. The supply of indentured servants there had been exhausted. This led to new initiatives being taken by merchants already interested, such as Thomas Riche, or the powerful firm of Thomas Willing and Robert Morris. The latter company is of special interest, since Morris, the future 'financier of the revolution', even if he did help to send the patriotic-sounding *Granby* across the Atlantic to Africa, was the son of an agent of the well-connected slave merchant Foster Cunliffe, of Liverpool, at Oxford, on the Chesapeake Bay. Perhaps a dozen ships left the City of Brotherly Love for Africa in the ten years before the War of Independence, and perhaps 1,000 slaves a year were imported.

Few slaves were in these days sold in New England, except for Rhode Island, and fewer still of those came direct from Africa. For there was no work on which slaves could be easily employed there, and the captives in New England were mostly domestics.

One important change came in 1750. For the first fifteen years of its existence, between 1733 and 1748, the Trustees of Georgia had forbidden the import of slaves. The Scottish settlers of Darien, on the southern coast, and the Salzburgers of nearby Ebenezer supported this prohibition, but the Anglo-Saxon settlers in Savannah bitterly opposed it: they had been raising their tall glasses after dinner to 'the one thing needful' for twenty years. The trustees were harassed, and there had been much illegal import. In 1750 the Anglo-Saxons won the debate and Georgia declared slavery legal. Thereafter, the colony was soon transformed: there were 1,065 slaves in 1753 and 7,800 in 1766.

The Seven Years War, of 1756–63, was Britain's most successful engagement in a world conflict. Her defeat of France in both Canada and India was accompanied by her conquest of the French sugar islands of Guadeloupe and later Martinique, as well (as we have seen) as their slave suppliers in Africa.* Havana also fell to the English in 1762.

Cuba had previously had a small number of African slaves, say 32,000, working on about a hundred small sugar plantations. John Kennion, the Liverpool-born Unitarian commissary, or general supplier, to the commanders who conquered the island, was given an exclusive right to import to the place 2,000 slaves a year, of whom 1,500 were to be men, 500 women. Kennion already had plantations in Jamaica, as did many go-ahead English slave merchants of the day. But though this unitarian Liverpudlian sold many slaves during the nine months of British occupation – probably 1,700 – his competitors sold as many: 'The acquisition of Havana will give great spirits to the planters in Georgia and Carolina to purchase negroes', wrote Henry Laurens to John Knight in Liverpool; 'a cargo from Angola lately sold at higher prices than we ever knew, considering the quality.'[†] Many of the most respected names

---

* *Minorca had earlier been captured by France, and Pitt's friend the sugar king, William Beckford, Lord Mayor of London 1762–3 and an MP, apparently advised that France would certainly exchange Martinique for Minorca at the peace.*

† *Two hundred and seventy slaves were sold in Havana by Laurens's rivals, the Charleston firm of Smith, Brewton and Smith.*

in the Anglo-Saxon world of commerce turned their ships towards Havana in 1762 and 1763 (including Samuel Touchett, the cotton pioneer and MP, of Manchester, and Sir Alexander Grant MP, of Glasgow and London).

All these merchants found that Kennion's privileged arrangements formally excluded them. The glut in slaves in Cuba meant that prices of smuggled slaves plummeted. The old state monopoly company had before the war sold *piezas de indias* at 300 dollars each. The new merchants could only sell at 90 dollars. The British army also sold off in Havana the thousand or so slaves which it had brought to serve as porters and general assistants in the campaign.

The *criollo* planters of West Cuba were delighted by the British occupation: this was before the age of patriotism. As well as slaves, they bought from the conquerors a vast quantity of cloths, clothes, and sugar equipment. This brief extension of the British empire to Cuba marked, as the inspired Cuban economist Francisco de Arango would later recognize, a turning point in Cuban history, the import of so many Africans being the motor of an economic change which made Cuba, by the end of the century, a formidable sugar producer: 'The tragic event of its surrender gave Havana life in two ways', Arango wrote; 'the first was considerable riches, with the great import of blacks, utensils, and cloths which were brought in during only a year. . . . Second, it showed our Court the importance of this.'[8] The occasion also demonstrated the charm of Cuban sugar to a wide audience: 'The Havana sugar which I have for sale is exceeding good and very clear', Henry Laurens wrote from Charleston in April 1763.[9]

Thus it was that Cuba was launched on her astonishing career as the world's grandest sugar bowl; and soon few, apart from historians, would remember the old days before 1763, when the poorer island had a more balanced economy, in which a trade in hides and tobacco competed for labour and investment with shipbuilding.

The attitudes of the Spanish *criollo* planters of Havana were shared by their French counterparts in Guadeloupe. Into the latter island the English conquerors introduced even more slaves than they did in Havana (probably over 12,000), and over a longer period, for the occupation lasted seven years. The economy of the island was transformed.

The possibility that the peace might return some of these conquests to their original owners distressed businessmen in London. Thus in November 1762 145 merchants of Liverpool petitioned Lord Egremont (the Secretary of State for the Southern Department) to keep at least Guadeloupe after the peace, because of their great success in selling slaves there: 'The possession of that island has increased their trade beyond all comparison with its former state, in the demand of British manufactures for slaves. . . . The West-Indian and African trade is by far the largest branch of the great and extensive commerce of this kingdom

... the most beneficial commerce, not only to themselves but to the whole kingdom, as the export is chiefly of the manufacturers of this kingdom, British ships and seamen solely employed. . . .'[10]

The protests were to no avail. The policy of 'Take and Hold', advocated by William Pitt and those who had won the war, did not move those more tranquil souls concerned to make the peace. Lord Egremont succumbed to what the polemicist Junius described as 'a fatal lethargy'. Thus though Britain gained Canada and India at the peace, she abandoned the one opportunity afforded since 1600 to any great power of uniting the Caribbean under a single flag.

At the Treaty of Paris there was a most notable transfer of 'people and provinces' in what Woodrow Wilson, at another peace made later in the same city, would call 'the great game of the balance of power'. For though Britain returned to France Gorée, off Africa, and Guadeloupe, Martinique, Belle Isle, Desirade, St Lucia, and Marie-Galante, in the Antilles, as well as Havana to Spain, she retained Fort St Louis, at the mouth of the River Sénégal, and other trading points on that great river; and in the West Indies, she kept several islands: St Vincent, Dominica, and Tobago, with a total population of perhaps 20,000, together with Grenada (a new sugar island, with 12,000 slaves in 1750). The huge French territory of Louisiana, Crozat's old concession, passed to Spain, with its 6,000 slaves, while the almost empty Spanish colony of Florida also fell to Britain.

Both the French and Spaniards reacted to this peace by a determination to compensate for their losses. The French Prime Minister, Choiseul, sought immediately to develop new French interests in Africa so as to free its colonies in the West Indies from reliance on Britain, formally or informally, for the supply of slaves. That the provision of slaves was an essential part of French commercial policy he was left in no doubt. Thus in 1762 the Chamber of Commerce of Nantes declared: 'The African trade is precious not only because of gold and ivory, it is infinitely more so because of the blacks that it makes possible for only they are capable of carrying through the hard work which the agriculture and manufacturing [of sugar] demand. . . .'[11] Choiseul agreed: 'I look upon this trade as the motor of all the others. . . .' Equally, the same body in La Rochelle declared in 1765: 'The African trade has always been looked on rightly as very advantageous to the nation. More than 100 ships [that is, from La Rochelle] are annually employed in this navigation. . . . They each introduce 300 blacks. The Ministry has been shown that this commerce brings into the kingdom 11,470,330 livres solely from the expeditions. . . . If foreigners [for example, Perfide Albion] were to introduce blacks into our colonies, our manufactures, our sailors, and our farmers would be deprived of innumerable outlets. . . .'[12]

The fifteen years of peace between 1763 and 1778 (the year when France entered the American Revolutionary War against Britain) were good for the slave trade in all the main commercial nations, including British North America. The continuing popularity of coffee, tea, jam, and chocolate partly explains the matter. Two-thirds of the slaves shipped to the Americas in the 1770s worked on sugar plantations, and 84 per cent (160,000 out of 190,000) of the slaves in Jamaica were employed to produce sugar on the large plantations established there. Slaves in these years also seemed essential to all important European military operations in the Americas: 500 from Jamaica went with Admiral Vernon's disastrous expedition to Cartagena de Indias and twice that in 1762 to Havana with General Lord Albemarle. So it is unsurprising that Britain should have carried something approaching 250,000 slaves across the Atlantic between 1761 and 1770 – of whom about 70,000 went to the Southern mainland colonies, where they would be sold by Henry Laurens or his successors to the owners of rice or indigo plantations. These British-shipped slaves were carried by merchants and captains primarily from Liverpool, which city sent over a hundred ships to Africa in 1771 for the first time, carrying more than 28,000 slaves. The largest ship of these, the *Prince of Wales*, was alone responsible for 600. London transported 8,000 slaves in fifty-eight ships; and Bristol a few more, nearly 9,000 in twenty-three ships; even Lancaster carried 950 in four. In the single year 1774 the British slave trade seems to have accounted for 40,000 captives, these captives coming mostly from the Bight of Benin, the Niger Delta, and the Loango coast.

These were golden days for British West Indian society in particular: the governing class was small, but the large slave populations seemed resigned to their productive if ignominious lot. Visitors noted the pretty landscapes – a tropical version of Gloucestershire, with, however, hedges of Cape jasmine and pomegranate, logwood and lime, to point the contrast. How agreeable it was to hear, from travellers' vivid accounts, of the feasts, with turtle on the table, accompanied by thirty-two different fruits. Meantime, the slaves, in their Sunday suits, would be making the best of their hard lives with amazing forbearance, even with high spirits, having often survived dangers at sea which would have made Dante blench.

In these same years, however, France was beginning to overtake Britain as a sugar producer. In 1767, for the first time, her colonies exported more of the ever desirable commodity than did her rival: 77,000 tons against 72,000. She also shipped for the first time over 100,000 slaves in a period of ten years. She did not seem to have much missed her old slaving harbours on the River Sénégal. The average number of slaver ships leaving French ports every year was fifty-six, a modest increase only, it is true, over previous figures, but the new ships were bigger, averaging 364 slaves per boat. The merchants were also much assisted by the government's policies directed towards using the slave trade as a means of economic revival. Thus after the Peace of Paris France refortified

Gorée, refurbished the French trading points on the River Gambia and at Whydah, established forts at Lahous, Quitta, and Apollonia (on the Windward Coast), and even opened an inquiry into the reasons why their trade in blacks had been bringing less profit than that of Britain. Finally, in 1767, Law's old Compagnie des Indes lost its monopoly. Henceforth the government used the ten livres paid by traders for a licence much as their English rivals did, to maintain their forts in Africa.

Nantes remained the great French slaving port, followed by Bordeaux. The latter sent five ships a year to Africa in the early 1760s, eight a year in the 1770s. Other ports were struggling to enter, or re-enter, the profitable business. For example, merchants from Le Havre, such as the Foäche family and their relations by marriage the Bégouens, were heavily engaged. The Foäches established a younger son (Stanislas) in Saint-Domingue, as firms in Nantes had long done, to receive the slaves dispatched by the head of the family (Martin-Pierre and his wife, Catherine). Le Havre was able to make herself France's third most important slaving port in these years, ahead of La Rochelle. The new promising circumstances encouraged René-Auguste de Chateaubriand, of Saint-Malo, to re-enter the trade: he sent the *Saint-René* to Africa in 1768, just at the moment when his wife was giving birth to the future author of the novel *René*.[13] Saint-Malo dispatched seventy-five ships, all told, to Africa in the first fifteen years after the peace of 1763. Outstanding among those who entered the French trade at this time was Jean-Baptiste Prémord, of Honfleur, who in 1762 contracted with the London owners (Richard Oswald, Alexander Grant, and their friends) of Bence Island, in the Sierra Leone estuary, to buy 1,500 slaves a year for five years – a figure which was not reached. But Honfleur went ahead in the trade in Africans, thanks largely to Prémord's determination, and sent forty-four ships to Africa between 1763 and 1777, another seventy-two between the latter date and 1792. Rouen also played a part.

The Crown was delighted. In 1768 King Louis XV expressed himself pleased in particular at the way *'les négociants du Port de Bordeaux se livrent avec beaucoup de zèle au commerce de la traite des nègres'*.[14]

The great success in these years of Loango Bay, with Cabinda and Malemba nearby, as a slave harbour was due to its remaining a zone of free trade. The rulers of Loango retained their independence and traded with all comers. Here, in the 1760s, the French did the best, if only since they seemed the most numerous. They also now supplied what Loango judged to be the best goods, and they paid the highest prices for the captives. By the 1780s two-thirds of the French slave trade was from Loango, whose total product was then between 10,000 and 15,000 slaves a year.

The chief buyers of these French-carried captives were the planters in Saint-Domingue (three-quarters), who also bought many slaves illegally from the British. There were over 200,000 slaves in Saint-Domingue in

1765, and it was generally assumed that 15,000 slaves had to be introduced every year just to maintain the labour force at the right level. The French government, meantime, did what it could further to support the commerce by raising the bounty per slave when it was delivered to 100 livres, a figure which would be increased further in 1787 to 160.

The government in Paris, never completely able to escape the tradition of Colbert, who so hated the thought of free trade, could not bring itself to abandon the idea of monopolies; and so part of the French trade, that from the newly fortified Gorée, was allocated to a new Company of the Coast of Africa (it became in 1776 the Guyana Company, on the mistaken assumption that it would sell slaves exclusively to the new colony of Cayenne-Guyane). This company was given the exclusive right to trade slaves from Gorée for fifteen years.

That African slavery was regarded as the solution to all problems of labour in Brazil was confirmed by the formation of two new chartered companies in Lisbon: the Maranhão Company, established in 1755, and the Pernambuco Company, founded in 1759. The first was most interested in Bissau and Cacheu, and specialized in large ships, such as the *Nuestra Senhora da Esperança* or the *San Sebastião* – able to carry between 500 and 800 slaves each voyage. The second – its ships had the same devotional names – dealt largely with Luanda, the main Portuguese settlement in Angola, where, for its first twenty-two years of trading, 1761–83, it rapidly became the major buyer. Both companies were concerned primarily with slaves, though they had other interests, and both were exempt from the export duties levied on their competitors. There had been a Maranhão Company in the seventeenth century, but it had not been successful: the price of slaves had been too high for the settlers on the Amazon, who had then been able to kidnap Indians with great ease and without much cost. Now, however, the Indian tribes had either been destroyed or had escaped further into the green interior. Furthermore, Pombal, the Prime Minister, a man whose own monarch thought that he had 'hairs growing on his heart', was determined to introduce a new era for the Indian in Brazil. His law of 1755 on the matter did break new ground so far as the surviving Indians were concerned. But it meant a greater emphasis than ever on black slaves.

Black slavery was thus now the characteristic form of labour in Brazil, in both the rural and the urban scene, even if the mining of both gold and diamonds was in decline, and if the old gold province of Minas Gerais was being turned over to agriculture. Sugar and tobacco were Brazil's most important crops, and both began to seem as valuable as exports of precious metals. Large concentrations of slaves, mostly from the Gold Coast, seemed essential in plantations: for example, as always, at Recôncavo (near Bahia), at Pernambuco, on the coast near Rio (Baixada Fluminense), and soon at São Paulo.

The Maranhão Company imported 25,000 slaves between 1757 and 1778 (28,000 loaded), nearly 14,000 to Pará, nearly 11,000 to Maranhão, about half deriving from Bissau, half from Cacheu, and the exports carried to Africa to pay for these included many new products from the Amazon region: sarsaparilla, for example, a berry whose juice was believed falsely to cure syphilis, and coffee, as well as cotton and hardwoods. The peak year of that company was 1764, when there were nearly 2,000 'chegados vivos' (live captives).

The Pernambuco Company, on the other hand, brought into Brazil between 1761 and 1786 nearly double what was sent by the Maranhão Company. Nearly all were landed at the city which gave the firm its name. Here the peak year was 1763, when about 4,000 slaves were imported. Most of these derived from Angola. In 1781 José da Silva Lisboa wrote from Bahia: 'the African trade is of great importance here and is directed to the supply of slaves, yet nevertheless the profit which should accrue to it is seldom realized. Its staples are tobacco, either waste or second-rate leaf, and strong spirits. More than fifty cargoes a year depart from Bahia in corvettes and smacks; eight or ten corvettes go to Angola with European goods while others go to the coast of Guinea [both] to buy slaves. . . . The investment risked in entering this business is small. . . . A cargo may consist of sixty slaves. . . . If few die . . . the voyage is lucrative. . . . More than 25,000 slaves have arrived for use in agriculture this year, 15,000 entering Bahia alone and 10,000 at Rio. . . .'[15]

The Brazilian slave trade accounted for about 160,000 slaves between 1760 and 1770. The Viceroy, the Count of Arcos, wrote in 1757 to Pombal in Lisbon that he thought slaves the most important merchandise in the Americas: 'Without them, the colonists would receive irreparable damage to a commerce which is already in a state of decay.'[16] But this was still a bad period in Brazil, with prices of commodities low, and it is at first sight surprising that the figures for imports were as high as they were. The explanation is that traders from Rio took many of the slaves whom they had bought for sale (illegally, of course) to Buenos Aires, a city which, to Lima's disgust, was becoming the largest port in the Spanish empire; or to other harbours on the River Plate. The payment which they received was, above all, in silver, so much desired in eighteenth-century Europe. The French naturalist Bougainville, on his way to the South Seas in 1766, thought that thirty of the coasting ships which he saw in the Bay of Rio were about to take slaves south to Buenos Aires in return for silver or hides.[17] The coming of a final peace between Portugal and Spain in 1777 (which settled the frontiers of Brazil to the Portuguese satisfaction) legalized this traffic.

The position in Angola was transformed by permissions in 1758 and 1762 to merchants in both Luanda and Benguela to trade freely inland. Further, an energetic governor of the colony, Francisco Innocêncio Sousa Coutinho, a protégé of Pombal, tried, in the true spirit of enlightened despotism, to diversify the economy of the place, even to reduce the colony's reliance on the slave trade. He set up an iron foundry and a leather factory, and gave money for numerous agricultural schemes aiming to establish plantations in Africa, instead of in Brazil. He tried to arrange that ships returning to Portugal from Goa would automatically call at Luanda, to sell Indian goods: satin, dinner services, enamel vases. He also persuaded the government in Lisbon to abolish the arrangements by which the slave trade was indirectly administered, the duties being collected by inefficient and easily corrupted tax farmers. That contract had, in the past, accounted for 20 per cent of the taxes received from the trade.

Yet a single governor, however energetic, could not hope to change habits which had persisted for 200 years. In 1780, too, there were twelve or so influential slave merchants in Luanda (whose population was probably 4,000), and about four or five in Benguela (whose population was then about 2,000). These traders were among the most important individuals of the places concerned, and they operated in well-known internal market places, such as Dondo, buying from African merchants who would assemble their captives, usually by now from the far interior, and march them down in 'coffles' of about a hundred. There were about eleven slaving establishments at Dondo by the 1790s. These men were difficult to outmanoeuvre, much less restrict.

These merchants of Angola operated a transatlantic system, buying goods in Rio de Janeiro or Bahia with the money from the sale of their slaves and carrying them across the South Atlantic for further slave purchases. Benguela was a pioneer in this practice. By the end of the century about twenty slave firms were active there, the directors being usually rich enough to live in the beautiful, melancholy houses, facing the sea on the south side of the city, known as *sobrados*. Portugal, meantime, was playing less and less of a part in all this commerce, and her statesmen knew it: Martinho de Melo Castro, Secretary of State in Lisbon, wrote in 1770, 'One could not without great sorrow see how our Brazilian colonies have absorbed commerce and shipping on the African coast to the total exclusion of Portugal; and what the Brazilians do not control, foreign nations do.'

Spain, at that time also modernizing after her fashion, had still not lost all belief that a magic property was communicated by the grant of the famous *asiento*. The first new contract after the peace of 1763 for importing slaves to the empire was that by the new Captain-General of Cuba, the Count of Ricla, to Martín José de Alegría, of Cádiz, allowing him to bring in 7,000 slaves to Cuba, of whom 1,000 had to be sold to the Crown (whose officials in Havana had embarked upon a lavish programme of public works). 'The prosperity of this island depends mainly on the import of African slaves. . . . The King [too] will derive much more revenue from the import duties on slaves . . .'[18] Thus General

O'Reilly, who was responsible for overseeing the new defences, wrote from Havana in a letter to Spain in April 1764.

Then came the concession of a new large-scale *asiento* in the old style to the Cádiz Slave Company, a society directed by an imaginative and persistent Basque, Miguel de Uriarte, of Puerto de Santa María, supported by numerous fellow Basques resident in Cádiz. Uriarte wanted a ten-year contract, to sell slaves at 300 pesos a *pieza*, wherever he thought desirable. His scheme was traditional in structure. Ships would be sent from Cádiz full of European goods to West Africa, where the goods would be exchanged for slaves. He suggested that neither his ships nor his goods should incur taxes. He proposed taking all his slaves first to Puerto Rico, whence they would be distributed to other Caribbean ports, just as Walsh had thought of assembling all his slaves in Saint-Domingue.

Much discussion followed, Uriarte being forced to admit that he would have little chance of obtaining slaves direct from Africa, given that the coast between the River Sénégal and the Cape of Good Hope was so well covered by competing Europeans. All the same, a report was prepared in Havana which sought to explain how the innovative English procured and sold their slaves. It seemed desirable to learn from the leaders in the profession.

Arguments about these and other requests took a long time in Madrid. At one moment the issue was confused by the presentation of a request to carry slaves to the Spanish empire by the immortal Beaumarchais, at that time in the Spanish capital gaining material for his incomparable plays, looking for business, seeking to avenge the honour of his sister, and making love to the Marquesa de Croix, the wife of the enlightened Spanish Viceroy in Mexico.[19]

Yet in the end Uriarte triumphed over his competitors, including Beaumarchais, though with the numerous bureaucratic conditions always associated with the *asiento*. He was obliged to carry 1,500 slaves a year to Cartagena de Indias and to Portobelo, and 1,000 to Havana, though Havana could have taken more and Cartagena been satisfied with less; 600 each to Cumaná (near Caracas), Santo Domingo, Trinidad (the island), Santa Marta (Hawkins' old market near Cartagena), Puerto Rico, and the pearl mart of Margarita; and, finally, 400 each to Honduras and Campeche. The slaves would be obtained by sending Spanish ships to the Cape Verde Islands, to the River Sénégal (even though it was in English hands), or to Gorée, the French fortress. But they could also be carried in foreign ships for distribution from Puerto Rico. The absence of Veracruz from this list showed that the need for labour in New Spain was already being filled by the growing indigenous population there.

The company was then formed, and in 1767 the *Venganza* was duly from Cádiz sent to Africa. Though it sought to buy 600–700 slaves, it only managed to find 250, at a high price, almost all in the Cape Verde Islands. The failure was repeated a year or two later, with another vessel, the

Fortuna. The company then decided to change its tactics and obtain from the Caribbean all the slaves that it could, assemble them in Puerto Rico, and then sell them off. This system was put into practice; Puerto Rico became for a few years a major slave centre and, in the first seven years of the new *asiento*, from 1765 to 1772, nearly 12,000 slaves were sold. But about 1,500 died, either en route to or waiting at Puerto Rico, and the price obtained (and previously fixed) often did not even cover the price of purchase.[20]

The company survived into the 1770s, but it never made money. The Spanish planters throughout the empire, and especially Cuba, wanted to trade directly with Jamaica, legally or illegally: ill-paid colonial officials were far too used to receiving presents from smugglers to permit Uriarte anything like a real monopoly.

Later, one more *asiento* was drawn up, in which Uriarte's partners Lorenzo de Ariostegui and Francisco de Aguirre formed a new company after 1773. But by then it was almost impossible to maintain any such monopolistic arrangements. They were out of date. Jamaica was, as a later witness – Philip Attwood, the first English merchant to be established in Havana, a representative there of the Liverpool firm of Baker and Dawson, shipbuilders and slave traders – reported in 1787, responsible for at least three-quarters of the slaves sent to Cuba in the 1770s; and Cuba was by then the main buyer in the Americas on a large scale.[21]

Cuba was making headway as a sugar producer as well as a receiver of slaves. Production there in the 1770s was seven times what it had been before the English occupation of 1762–3. This change was simply the result of more plantations being cut out of the wild, more land being planted to cane, and therefore, of course, of more slaves being imported for the harvesting and for the clearing of virgin land: which in turn meant more capital being invested, and more money being borrowed, usually from those merchants in Havana who were themselves interested in sugar.

There was also expansion in North America, where a direct slave trade from Africa had opened in 1766 to Florida, a new colony for Britain after 1763, a development of which slave merchants soon took advantage. A note in the *Massachusetts Gazette* of 24 December 1767 reads that Captain Savery had just arrived in London 'from St Augustine, on the brigantine *Augustine*, having carried there seventy negroes from Africa, the first ever imported directly from thence into that province . . . . Upwards of 2,000 were contracted for, by the noblemen and gentlemen in Great Britain . . . to be imported there from Africa the ensuing summer.'[22] This ship was probably owned by Richard Oswald, the outstanding member of a circle of traders of London, already touched on,* who had also established plantations in Florida, to the south of St Augustine on the

* *See page 484.*

Atlantic coast (near Ponce de León Bay) in 1765: he was the main slaver among those early settlers, and spoke of the place as a 'paradise' and 'a new Canaan'. It was, however, a Canaan from which no milk and honey would flow for many years, despite Oswald's slaves, for the land produced almost nothing.

Richard Oswald was the Glaswegian merchant based in London with whom Laurens had often traded slaves. The intimate adviser of Lord Shelburne, to whom he had been introduced by their mutual friend, Adam Smith, Oswald had been a commissary of the British armed forces in Germany during the Seven Years War ('Oswald's loaves' were famous there). He was a prominent dealer in slaves, selling them from Bence Island, in the Gambia River, which he had bought in 1747 with several London mercantile associates.* He also tried to breed Africans in Florida, where he speculated in land with Benjamin Franklin. The size of his fortune, however gained, is clear in that, with an offer of £60,000, he was much the largest single contributor to the government loan of 1757 (the next-largest was the cotton-check merchant Samuel Touchett, with £30,000).

Originating in Caithness, Oswald had spent some years in the 1730s and early 1740s on the Chesapeake Bay, dealing in tobacco for his cousins, the founders of the firm which he himself came to dominate. He married an heiress in Jamaica, also of Scottish origin, Mary Ramsay. The most obvious symbol of his achievement was the large property which he bought in 1764 – Auchincruive, near Ayr, where the Adam brothers built him a fine rural palace. By the time of his death in the 1780s Oswald also owned two plantations in Jamaica and several commercial tracts alongside the James River in Virginia. He died leaving £500,000, as well as a name as a 'truly good man', in the phrase of Franklin.[23]

The American war, like all conflicts of the eighteenth century, had an adverse consequence for the trading of slaves. Between 1771 and 1780 Britain carried fewer than 200,000 slaves – the figure being down from the 1760s precisely because of the fighting which, beginning in 1774, had a disastrous effect on Liverpool, as on the British West Indies. The trade to Barbados almost ceased, as did that to Antigua. The French, on the other hand, shipped only a little less than 100,000 slaves in the 1770s. The traffic of neutrals also kept up well, the Dutch Leeward Island of St Eustatius becoming again, as it had once been in the 1720s, a 'golden rock', where slaves were always available, and where the colonists of the British West Indies bought the food needed for their slaves and themselves alike. St Eustatius ('Statia' to the English) also supplied the rebel North American colonies with food till it was captured by Admiral Rodney in 1781. Other neutrals, the Portuguese or Brazilians, carried about 160,000 slaves in these years.

* *For the pleasures of Bence Island, see chapter 17.*

In this war, as had occurred on other occasions, many slave ships on both sides were turned into privateers. As in the Seven Years War, ex-slavers often preyed on slavers as well as other privateers. But though that did not help the planters, it saved the merchants and the captains. There were some curious incidents. For example, Captain Clement Noble, on the Liverpool slaver *Brookes*, armed fifty of his slaves to fight the French off Barbados; they fought 'with exceeding spirit', the Captain reported, before he proceded to Montego Bay, Jamaica, to sell them.[24]

One alarming foretaste of the future – alarming to the merchants, that is – was also to be observed in the city of Liverpool during this war. Many merchants were unable to maintain old levels of employment. So there were riots in Liverpool over wages, inspired by crews of slave ships, an unheard-of development for those days. We hear how 'the crew of the *Derby*, given only 20 shillings when offered 30, rioted, and were sent to jail. But that evening, 3,000 sailors assembled, broke open the jail, released their friends, and stopped all ships [even the slave ships] from sailing. In the meantime, constables fired – seven were killed and 40 wounded. The sailors this morning again assembled, upwards of 1,000, all with red ribbons in their hats, and . . . about one of the clock assailed.'[25] In this attack four persons were killed; the house of Thomas Ratcliffe, a prominent slave merchant, was wrecked, and those of Thomas Yates, John Simmons, and William James (a Member of Parliament, who had twenty-nine vessels engaged in the slave trade) were also damaged. The rioters found the black page of the last-named hiding in a grandfather clock. The affair shows the crews of slave ships to have been in the lead of organized labour acivities.

On the other side of the Atlantic there were different kinds of upheaval. At Newport, Rhode Island, 2,000 citizens, including the most effective trader, Aaron Lopez, left the city during the prolonged British occupation, and died soon after. The magnificent house of the leading slaver, William Vernon, abandoned by its owner, was used first by the English and then the French as their headquarters, the Vernons them-selves having taken a major part in protesting against the British policies before the war.

Yet these disturbances seemed temporary. The long-term prospects for the slave trade appeared excellent in, say, 1780, provided only that the nations could live in peace. Thus on 12 April 1775 David Mill (Governor of the British fort at Cape Coast, a member of an influential West Indian planters' family) wrote: 'The trade has rather fallen off in the last six weeks, attributed in great measure to the Fantees being down to Leeward settling a dispute between the Accras and Akims. It is, however, likely to be equally as good as last year; a good number of slaves having already been shipped for the West Indies.'[26] All the commanders of the British forts – John Dixon in Commenda, Thomas Trinder in Fort James, Accra, and Lionel Alson in Fort William, Whydah – reported that trade was bad because of difficulties among the Africans, not because of the war; and Richard Miles, Mill's successor at Cape Coast, reported that 'a greater number of slaves' had been purchased there in 1780 than ever before and that 'the present prospects looked good'.[27]

In the 1780s the slave trade, indeed, was not only restored, but attained its highest levels, even if to begin with the extension of the Navigation Acts to ban trade between the West Indies and the new United States adversely affected the economies of the British West Indies. The French and Spanish empires were also excluded from trading with the new country. All the same, all these colonies recovered their poise; the increase in Jamaican sugar production, for example, continued steadily in those years, after a steep decline at the end of the 1770s.[28]

So in the ten years between 1780 and 1790 at least 750,000 slaves were carried across the Atlantic: perhaps 325,000 by Britain, Liverpool being as ever the dominant city. If Newport, Rhode Island, ruined by the long British occupation in the years of the revolution, was no longer in the forefront of the United States trade, the nearby ports of Bristol and Providence, as well as Boston and Salem in Massachusetts, not to speak of Philadelphia and Charleston, made up for it. Perhaps forty ships a year sailed from the new United States for Africa in the 1780s: again, nothing in comparison with old Europe, but what seemed a good beginning to independent commerce.

We could do worse than linger on this new slaving port of Bristol, Rhode Island. Pre-eminent among the merchants there was Simeon Potter, who had begun life as a cooper on board ships sailing to the Caribbean for molasses and mahogany. By 1744 he was a captain, and sailed as a privateer in the wars of the forties and fifties. By 1756 he had made enough money to retire from the sea, and invested his savings in slaving voyages which were undertaken by his brother-in-law, Mark Antony de Wolf (or D'Wolf), and that adventurer's sons. This de Wolf had signed on in Guadeloupe as a sailor during one of Potter's journeys, though he is said to have been of United States stock – perhaps descended from a bastard line of the Dutch de Wolffs of New York in the 1670s.*

Simeon Potter's first slave journey was that undertaken by Mark Antony's son Charles in the *Phoebe* in 1757. Potter's instructions to his captain William Earle in his slaver *King George* seven years later indicate his character as well as his literacy: 'Worter [sic] yr. rum as much as possible and sell as much by the short mesure [sic] as you can.' Five of Mark Antony's sons, Potter's nephews, afterwards engaged in the slave trade, beginning in the 1780s. Of these, the youngest, Levi de Wolf, abandoned the business after one journey, apparently in disgust. His brother Charles had no qualms: he once told the local parson of the Congregational

* See page 187.

church, 'Parson, I've always wanted to roll in gold.'[29] He proceeded to lie down on a pile of canvas sacks full of that metal. William and John de Wolf, after making money in the slave trade, became respectively an insurer and a farmer. The great success, though, of the family was James de Wolf, later a United States Senator and cotton manufacturer, who made a fortune between 1780 and 1808 in carrying and selling slaves, as will be seen in a subsequent chapter.*

In the 1780s French captains, meantime, carried 270,000 slaves. Nantes, still dominant, was responsible for 35 per cent of this trade in 1785. But that port was pursued closely by ever more ardent rivals, such as Bordeaux, La Rochelle (seeking to compensate for the loss of the Canadian fur trade after 1763), Saint-Malo, and Honfleur.

The French profited greatly from the American Revolution, and recovered their old headquarters on the Sénégal at the peace in 1783. They re-established their interests, thereafter, in the trade south of that river. Ships leaving French ports for the Antilles averaged fifty-three a year during this war, in contrast with a mere eleven during the Seven Years War. Pierre-Paul Nairac, the leading slave merchant of Bordeaux, in 1777 paid the largest taxes in his city; as did Pierre Meslé at Saint-Malo, the leading slaver there. Businessmen in France were confident. One of the leading shippers of Nantes would write, in the early 1780s, to his brother: 'The slave trade is the single branch of commerce which presents a perspective of benefits.'[30] Marseilles also entered the slave trade seriously after 1774, though one slave ship had gone to Guinea from that city every four years or so since 1700. The single colony of Saint-Domingue, the 'Eden of the West', was now importing nearly 40,000 slaves a year; and, if the *grands seigneurs* of that rich colony slept *au pied du Vésuve*, as Mirabeau would shortly put the matter, their feasting hours in their lovely houses were full of gaiety.[31]

Spain, too, was expanding her slave traffic. In 1777 she gained from Portugal the neglected islands of Annobón and Fernando Po, in the Gulf of Guinea, in order to have bases from which to supply her colonies with the much-needed slaves in the now permitted direct trade to Africa. Portugal also agreed that Spain should be able to engage freely in the slave trade from Cape Formoso, at the mouth of the Niger, and Cape Lopo Gonçalves, south of the estuary of the Gabon (she did not occupy them, though).

So it was that in 1780 the African trade in slaves seemed an essential part of the economies of all advanced countries, both a traditional thing and one which was being adjusted to meet all modern opportunities: the cotton cloth of Lancashire – above all Touchett's cotton checks, the very symbols of the new industrial process – were exported to secure African slaves. In France, too, cotton, unknown before 1700, was as we have seen

* *See page 533.*

being developed, and also in imitation of Eastern fabrics, in order to please the Africans: hence the pretty *'indiennes'* of Lille and Saint-Denis, as well as of Nantes, not to mention the cotton velvet of Evreux, Amiens, and Dieppe. Bordeaux seemed to be within reach of overtaking Nantes as the major slaving port of the country, making special efforts on the east coast of Africa, where her merchants were busy carrying slaves to Île de France and Bourbon, as well as round the Cape of Good Hope to the Americas. French slave merchants even brought themselves sometimes to carry the popular and cheaper English cottons. The French also were expanding their African interests; for example, in 1778, Jean-François Landolphe created a trading post at Ughoton, on the Benin River, where the Portuguese had first begun to deal in slaves and pepper in the 1480s, nearer the sea than the capital, in succession to the Dutch there.[32] Merchants in Nantes were adapting effectively to the times by christening, as the Montaudoins did, their ships the *Jean-Jacques* and even the *Voltaire*. (Liverpool merchants were less imaginative and remained with ships named the *Charming Nancy* or the *Betty* until the end of the traffic; but James de Wolf, of Bristol, Rhode Island, did own a slave ship which he called the *Monticello*, presumably to honour Thomas Jefferson.) All forward-looking planters of sugar realized that the new Otaheite cane, brought from the South Seas, would further increase the yield of well-organized sugar plantations and, for that reason, the planters in French colonies were already producing more than their Jamaican neighbours.

North American colonists continued to hold Indian slaves throughout the eighteenth century. But for reasons unrelated to morality, some colonies prohibited their import: for example, Massachusetts, Connecticut, Rhode Island (between 1712 and 1714). The same prohibition later occurred in Jamaica (in 1741). The fear was that indigenous captives could, through their restlessness, inspire wars with the tribes from which they came. Other Europeans restricted the use of Indian slaves to certain tribes: the French in Canada seem to have used only the Pawnees.* These restrictions seem to suggest the need for an even greater emphasis on African labour.

Until this time, few in Europe or the Americas doubted that however vile the condition of a slave might be in a sugar plantation or a gold mine in Jamaica or in Brazil such a life was superior to anything which the person concerned might encounter in Africa. But these years of the greatest level of the Atlantic slave trade also saw the beginning of a discussion whether it was, after all, the right way for civilized men to make a fortune.

---

* *The 1750s also saw the final formal prohibition of the enslavement of Amerindians in Brazil.*

Book Four

THE CROSSING

15

A FILTHY VOYAGE

*'Your captains and mates . . . must neither
have dainty fingers nor dainty noses, few
men are fit for these voyages but them that
are bred up to it. It's a filthy voyage as well
as a laborious [one].'*

Sir Dalby Thomas, the commander
of the Royal African Company at
Cape Coast, the Gold Coast, c. 1700

*'Look at that shipbuilder who, bent over his
desk, determines, his pen in hand, how
many crimes he can make occur on the
coast of Guinea; who examines at leisure
the number of guns he will have need of
to obtain a black, how many chains he
will need to have him garrotted on his ship,
how many strokes of the whip to make him
work. . . .'*

Abbé Raynal, Histoire philosophique
et politique des Indes, 1782

THE ATLANTIC SLAVE TRADE was, for much of its long life, a governmental enterprise in the countries concerned. The Portuguese Crown set the tone, in establishing the principle that expeditions to the coast of Africa had to be approved by its Casa da Guiné, and were subject to taxation. Certain merchants were given licences to trade in slaves and other 'merchandise' in Africa, the assumption being that they would sell sublicences to other traders. An early beneficiary, as we have seen, was the formidable Lisbon Florentine Bartolommeo Marchionni, who had the privilege of trading on the Slave River, Benin, between 1486 and 1493, and in the 'rivers of Guinea' between 1490 and 1495. In the sense that he operated on the grand scale, but with governmental backing, he was the characteristic European slave merchant.

By the sixteenth century it had been laid down that a Portuguese trader to West Africa, for gold as well as slaves, should discharge charitable obligations in Lisbon and also help to maintain the clergy in the Cape Verde Islands; should send at least twelve ships to Africa within three years; should undertake not to sell or barter European weapons to the Africans; and should accept that the settlers in the Cape Verde Islands would trade freely on the mainland opposite, with their own produce; and bring back as many slaves as they personally needed. For many years, traders in slaves who went to West Africa were also supposed to stop at Santiago, in the Cape Verde Islands, and pay duties; though they often did not, and so an official was appointed to collect those taxes on the African River Cacheu. Later, the Portuguese Crown generally agreed to farm out the collection of all these taxes to various businessmen, who made money in consequence, in Angola as well as in the Cape Verde Islands and elsewhere, till a change of policy was introduced in 1769 by the great reformer Pombal. All the same and despite the participation of many entrepreneurs, the prime mover in the slaving business was the state.

There were similar obligations in Spain with respect to merchants who bought slaves from the Portuguese before taking them to the New World; a licence was required from the very beginning, and there was, on top of that, a tax of two ducats for every slave delivered. Later, as has been amply shown, the *asiento*, or contract, to deliver slaves to the Spanish empire was another much-valued source of income for the Spanish Crown.

In different ways, the French, the English, and the Dutch Crowns developed similar financial interests in the slave trade, and monarchs from King Louis XIV of France to King George I of England, the Kings of Sweden and Denmark, not to speak of the Stadtholder in Holland and the Duke of Courland, divided though they might be on every other matter, had a mutual interest in the prosperity of the slave traffic.

The main trading nations also created privileged companies concerned to carry slaves from Africa to the New World; the Portuguese, for example, founded the Cacheu Company, in the seventeenth century, and the Maranhão and Pernambuco companies in the late eighteenth century; Holland had its very grand West India Company, and Britain established the Royal Adventurers, the Royal African Company, and, in the end, the South Sea Company. Spain, too, had numerous companies with a privileged status in the eighteenth century; and the reader will sensibly have forgotten how many Guinea companies were founded by France after Colbert established the first one in the 1670s. There was also John Law's extraordinary New Company of the Indies. Even the Scandinavian countries had their special, if more modest, enterprises. All these firms sought to establish numbers of slaves to be carried, as well as the prices at which they were to be sold, and interfered in other ways with the free working of the market. Only the Portuguese tried to interfere in order to lay down rules concerning how the slaves were to be treated and transported.

The only nation free from this curious mixture of capitalism and state management was the United States, one of the smallest of slave carriers.

These state companies were directed by a diversity of individuals, half bureaucrats, half entrepreneurs, but in the end it was recognized almost everywhere that private enterprise, with as few restrictions as possible, brought the best results.

The individual slave trader who played such a part in the eighteenth century, in particular, is a person of consuming interest. The typical 'slaver' – we can, oddly enough, use the noun for the individual and for his ship – is easy enough to picture, in his substantial counting house, with meeting rooms on the ground floor of that building, bedrooms for the family on the first floor, and above rooms for his clerks. The fine *hôtels* of the Montaudoins in Nantes, and the Nairacs in Bordeaux, with the head of Neptune over the big door, are admired today; and, though one can only imagine their equivalents in London (where the redevelopment of the late twentieth century finished what the Luftwaffe began), there are streets in both Liverpool and Bristol where houses of old slave traders still stand. Stanislas Foäche can be traced in Le Havre (just), and Jean-Baptiste Prémord in Honfleur, as can Coopstad, Rochussen, and Michiele Baalde in Rotterdam. The noble houses of slave merchants of Spain's golden age, such as the Caballeros and the Jorges, the families of the Genoese Corzo and Pero López Martínez, survive in old Seville. Across the Atlantic the splendid mansions of Nicholas and John Brown in Ower Street in Providence, George de Wolf (Linden Place) in Bristol, and the Vernon family in Clarke Street, Newport, are still visited – even if Philip Livingston's house in Duke Street, New York City, has vanished, along with his splendid country mansion in Brooklyn Heights.*

A typical slaving expedition in the eighteenth century would require a substantial sum to fit out: perhaps 250,000 livres in France, the same kind of sum, the admirable historian of the trade from La Rochelle, Jean-Michel Deveaux, has pointed out, as would be needed to buy a large house (*hôtel particulier*) in a fashionable street in Paris, such as the Rue Saint-Honoré.

The typical slave trader was interested in all kinds of commerce as well as slaves: he might be a banker, such as Pierre Cornut, who financed the second slave voyage from Bordeaux in 1684; or always also concerned in whaling, in order to make spermaceti candles, as was the case with the

---

* *Yet Livingston Road in Brooklyn survives to point the modern traveller in the direction of the old manor.*

Browns of Providence and Aaron Lopez in Newport, Rhode Island; or he might be a man such as the giant John Brown, who drew his brothers into the slave business and then became interested in the China and Baltic trades, insurance, and banking, in gin as well as in slaving; while Richard Oswald of London was first interested in tobacco, from Maryland, and did well as a commissary feeding the British troops in Germany in the Seven Years War. All the Basque merchants, such as Arioseguí or Uriarte, who led the Spanish slave commerce in the second half of the eighteenth century, were general traders, for whom slaving was an important but not a dominating part of their commercial activities. Jacques-François Begouën-Demeaux reached Le Havre in the 1720s, made a fortune, and then embarked on the slave trade about 1748. He always limited his interest to a third share. Richard Lake, who both bought and sold slaves in Jamaica, was known also as 'a great coffee planter', very generous in his manners, and hospitable, too. Etienne Dhariette, the first large slave merchant of Bordeaux, had, in the 1670s, an interest in 133 ships which left his city for the West Indies as well as Africa, many carrying *engagés*, French indentured labourers – masons, surgeons, and coopers – to the 'islands', even if he soon saw that he could make more money carrying blacks than whites. The same was true of the Liverpool slave merchant Foster Cunliffe, who operated so successfully in Chesapeake Bay as well as Liverpool. Samuel Sedgely of Bristol was a slave trader who interested himself in carrying convicts to Maryland, as did Lyonel Lyde, one of the partners of Isaac Hobhouse, who had interests in copper. Sugar and tobacco, rice and indigo were traded by many of these merchants in the New World, as well as East Indian cloth, silk, iron bars from Sweden, copper goods, and linen in the Old.

The purchase of plantations in the West Indies was a preoccupation for some English and North American slave traders: Abraham Redwood, Aaron Lopez, James de Wolf, and George de Wolf all had them, as did Simeon Potter, the father of slaving at Bristol, Rhode Island. The London Scotsman Sir Alexander Grant, one of the dealers in slaves whose ships turned to Havana in 1762, had been a country doctor in Jamaica, to begin with, but had seven plantations on that island, totalling 11,000 acres, at his death in 1772; his ships carried his own sugar back to England, and their captains bought slaves at the mouth of the River Sierra Leone (from a property of which he was also part owner, Bence Island). John Tarleton of Liverpool most unusually had an estate and a store in Curaçao. The wife of Richard Oswald, Mary Ramsay, inherited land in Jamaica, to which her husband carried slaves; he himself not only owned part of the island off the River Sierra Leone on which to assemble his cargoes bought in Africa, but like Samuel Touchett of Manchester also had property in the then undeveloped Florida, where he bred slaves.

In much the same way, many families of Nantes had relations or agents in the French Caribbean, especially in Saint-Domingue, where, for example, the Walshes of Nantes had plantations. The Gradises of Bordeaux also had their cousins, the Mendèses, looking after their interests there.

Merchants had themselves been captains of ships in the trade. The most distinguished example was, no doubt, Captain Jean Ducasse, 'the hero of Gorée', who became one of the main beneficiaries of the French *asiento* of the early eighteenth century. Another was Manuel Bautista Peres, the Portuguese *converso*, a captain of slave ships from Angola in the early seventeenth century before establishing his great fortune in Lima. About a quarter of the slavers in Nantes had once been ships' captains, or were sons of such – for instance, Louis Drouin, the 'second-richest man in Nantes', was the son of Captain René Drouin. The most successful slave merchant of La Rochelle, Jacques Rasteau, had been a captain when young. Slave captains who became merchants in North America included Godfrey Mallbone and Peleg Clarke in Newport and James de Wolf in Bristol, Rhode Island, along with Joseph Grafton in Salem, Massachusetts. Obadiah Brown, founder of the firm which became Nicholas Brown & Co., went as supercargo on Providence's first slave voyage, in 1736. In New York, Jasper Farmer, who in the 1740s captained the Schuyler family's *Catherine*, later himself invested in slave ships trading to Africa. In England, Captains James Bold and John Kennion, both of Liverpool, became rich merchants, the latter being the monopolist in Havana during the British occupation. Patrick Fairweather, of Liverpool, was a slave captain in the 1770s but by the 1790s owned his own ship, the *Maria*. The most successful slave merchant in Liverpool in the 1790s was John Dawson, who had begun life as a captain of privateers, capturing the French merchant ship *Carnatic* in 1778 on the high seas, and bringing it back, full of diamonds, to the Mersey. He married the daughter of the powerful shipbuilder Peter Baker, several times mayor, and he and Baker collaborated in the late 1780s to carry a great number of slaves to Cuba, owning over twenty ships, some of them capable of carrying 1,000 slaves.

Sometimes ships were captained by men who either owned them or had a share in them. This happened often in the early Portuguese days, and continued till the late eighteenth century: and later examples were Thomas Hinde of Lancaster and William Deniston and Peter Bostock of Liverpool, as well as John Rosse of Charleston.

The most powerful merchant at the end of the eighteenth century in London was Richard Miles, who had been employed by the Company of Merchants Trading to Africa at several British forts on the Gold Coast, and ended his official career as Commander of Cape Coast Castle. He had always, by his own statement to a select committee of the English Privy Council, 'traded the whole time on his own account'. He was a cultivated man, who could speak Fanti.

In some ways, though, the concept of a slave trader acting as an individual is misleading. For most 'independent' slave voyages were financed by partnerships, with say six or more merchants participating in the cost of the voyage, perhaps associating again on other occasions; in smaller ports, such as Whitehaven in England, professional men, spinsters, pawnbrokers, and milliners were all investors in the trade. The same was true of La Rochelle especially when, in the late eighteenth century, slaving vessels accounted for over a third of the number of voyages which set off from the town. The most frequent type of association, in Liverpool as in Newport, in Nantes as in Rio, leading to a slave voyage was one of relations, the only tie which could be trusted to endure. So the slave trade seemed, to a great extent, a thing of families: the Montaudoins, the Nairacs, the Foäches, the Cunliffes, the Leylands, the Hobhouses, the de Wolfs, the Browns. Many partnerships were between father and son: for example, Guillaume Boutellier *et fils* at Nantes, David Gradis *et fils* at Bordeaux, Jacques and Pierre Rasteau at La Rochelle. Often, though, a trader would have many partners in his working life: Isaac Hobhouse, the most interesting slaver of Bristol – he never travelled, he said, because he had 'such a feeble constitution . . . that I stir little abroad' – traded in company with seven major associates, two of them his brothers.[1]

Complete outsiders might also seek shares. Carter Braxton, a planter of Virginia, later a revolutionary statesman, wrote in 1763 to Nicholas Brown & Co. of Providence, Rhode Island: 'Sirs . . . I should be very glad to be concerned in the African Trade and will be a quarter of the voyage, if you choose it. . . . I should choose to be insured, and whatever Expence came to my Share more than the slaves sent, I would remit by return of the vessel that bro't the slaves. The whole of the voyage I leave you to conduct and you may begin to prepare if you please, . . . [for] the price of Negroes keeps up amazingly.'[2]

Nearly all Liverpool slave voyages were financed by people who lived in Liverpool – though Liverpool society embraced many conditions, and though there were one or two exceptions from further afield, such as manufacturers from Sheffield, or gunmakers from Birmingham who also invested. French firms often depended on silent partners from far away: in order to survive the difficult years of war, Henry Romberg, Bapst et Cie of Bordeaux relied, for instance, on Frederick Romberg and the Walckiers brothers, of Brussels – one of the rare involvements of the latter city in the transatlantic slave trade. Financiers in Paris, such as Dupleix de Bacquencourt, Duval du Manoir, and Jean Coton, Tourton et Baur invested heavily in, first, Law's New Company of the Indies, later in Antoine Walsh's Société d'Angola and the Société de Guinée. Eventually these hardheaded men turned to invest in private firms. Thus two-thirds of the Begouën-Foäche partnership of Le Havre after 1752 belonged to Parisians.

Successful slave owners would often buy substantial country properties, as of course most merchants did. Jacques Conte, the slaver who led the revived trade in slaves at Bordeaux during the Peace of Amiens in 1802, established his agreeable chateau at Saint-Julien-Beychevelle, in the heart of the great vineyards of the Médoc. Richard Oswald, as has been noticed, found rural happiness at Auchincruive in Ayrshire, a house designed by the brothers Adam, while his partner, John Boyd, had himself built a vast pile at Danson Hill, near Bexley Heath. Thomas Leyland of Liverpool established himself in Walton Hall, outside Liverpool. Another slave merchant of Liverpool, George Campbell, erected a strange, ecclesiastic-looking house with gargoyles, which he appropriately named St Domingo, at Everton. John Brown's house at Providence, Rhode Island, was the best house in New England; and, in a few years, the same would be said of James de Wolf's clapboard mansion, Mount Hope, about twenty miles away, overlooking the port of Bristol: 'Spacious and substantial. Nothing was wasted, and nothing stinted', wrote the historian of the family; while the *United States Gazetteer* would add, 'For elegance of style, for the general splendor of its appearance, and the beauty and extensiveness of the various improvements, it will rank among the finest in our country.' There was a deer park.

Equally, in South Carolina, Henry Laurens bought at least eight properties, including his own favourite, the Mepkin plantation, on the Cooper River; his chief rival in the slave trade, Samuel Brailsford, bought the Retreat plantation, on Charleston Neck, in 1758. Long before, the Jorges had bought property near Constantina – in the Sierra Morena, to the north of Seville – where they made a strong wine which they used in the slave trade.

Some slave merchants founded good collections of pictures: in London, for example, the Boyds, George Aufrère, and Oswald. Oswald had a good collection of Dutch masters, including a Rubens; Aufrère claimed to possess a Dürer, a Raphael, and a Rembrandt; but Boyd owned what he considered to be three Brueghels, nine Rubenses, a Velázquez, four Turners, and sixteen Morlands. It was said that Baltasar Coymans had many pictures in his house in Cádiz, including 'some marine landscapes'; his dining room was full of maps.[3]

Other slave traders invested in manufactures; thus the Browns of Providence 'introduced the cotton manufacture into the country', said their historian, who added amiably that that 'was financed originally by the transfer of funds acquired in maritime pursuits' – not all slaving, admittedly. In Nantes the greatest slaving family, the Montaudoins, were the first into the manufacture of cotton. John Kennion of Liverpool – the would-be monopolist of Havana in 1762 – interested himself in the same in Rochdale; and the omnifarious Samuel Touchett, whose achievements in manufacturing cotton led him into slave trading, invested in Paul's spinning machine. Brian Blundell of Liverpool invested in coal; Henry Cruger and Lyonel Lyde, both of Bristol, interested themselves in iron; and Joseph and Jonathan Brooks of Liverpool were the biggest builders of the city and built the famous town hall, designed by John Wood, with its sculpted heads of slaves on the frieze. Samuel Sedgely of Bristol was also concerned in the shipment of convicts to Maryland. John Ashton, a slave trader in Liverpool in the 1750s, helped to finance the Sankey Brook Canal, which linked his city so creatively with Manchester. Still, the profits of the slave trade never seem to have been a decisive reason for an industrial development, even if many successful slave merchants participated in them.

Some slave merchants would end their lives as bankers: the best example is Thomas Leyland, who founded his own bank, Leyland and Bullins, in 1807, and died leaving the then splendid sum of £600,000 in 1827.

All Christian denominations were involved in the slave trade. But usually the dominating religion of the port concerned decided the religious complexion of the merchants. In Liverpool, London, and Bristol, for instance, most slave merchants were Anglicans; in Nantes, Bordeaux, Lisbon, and Seville – and, of course, in Bahia and Luanda – most were Catholics. But in La Rochelle the slave merchants were mostly Huguenots, as they were Calvinists in Middelburg, and there were important Huguenot slaving firms elsewhere: the Dhariettes and the Nairacs in Bordeaux, as well as the Ferays in Le Havre. The Nairacs believed that they were not ennobled, and the Laffons de Ladébat were so, because of their religion, though the former had sent twenty-five ships to Africa between 1740 and 1792 and the Laffons a mere fifteen.

Quakers were important in the slave trade in the eighteenth century in New England, especially in Newport, where the Wanton family was still trading slaves in the 1760s. Friends were also prominent in the slave trade in Pennsylvania, often carrying slaves from the West Indies to their own city. Among these, William Frampton seems to have carried the first slaves to Philadelphia in the 1680s; he was followed by James Claypole, Jonathan Dickinson (he carried Africans from Jamaica to Philadelphia on his ship *Reformation*), and Isaac Norris (who, however, had some doubts about the commerce: 'I don't like that kind of business', he wrote to Dickinson as early as 1703), as well as William Plumstead, Reese Meredith, John Reynell, and Francis Richardson.[4] In England the Quaker gunmaking firm of Farmer and Galton of Birmingham sent at least one ship, the *Perseverance*, to carry 527 slaves to the West Indies.[5]

In Brazil the slave merchants of Bahia had their own religious brotherhood, which organized a regular procession at Easter, beginning at the Church of San Antônio da Barra, whither a bust of St Joseph, long venerated at Elmina as the patron of the slavers, was brought in 1752.

The Bishop of the Algarve in 1446 may have been the only prince of the Church to send out a caravel to Africa. But other spiritual potentates were shareholders in voyages. The Cardinal Infante Enrique, brother of King Philip III of Spain, was through his secretariat a formidable trader in slaves to Buenos Aires during the early seventeenth century. Both the Jesuits and their traditional enemies were much involved. In Bordeaux at the end of the eighteenth century most Freemasons appear to have been slave merchants.

For a time, in both Spain and Portugal, the slave trade was dominated by Jewish *conversos*: for example, Diego Caballero, of Sanlúcar de Barrameda, benefactor of the Cathedral of Seville; the Jorge family, also in Seville; Fernão Noronha, a Lisbon monopolist in the early days in the delta of the Niger, and his descendants; and the numerous merchants of Lisbon who held the *asiento* for sending slaves to the Spanish empire between 1580 and 1640. The most remarkable of these men was Antônio Fernandes Elvas, *asentista* from 1614 to 1622, connected by blood with nearly all the major slave dealers of the Spanish-Portuguese empire during the heady days when it was one polity.

Yet these men had formally become Christians. The Inquisition may have argued, and even believed, that many of them secretly practised Judaism, tried some of them in consequence, and left a few of them to be punished by 'the secular arm'. Some no doubt were indeed secret Jews, but it would be imprudent to accept the evidence of the Holy Office as to their 'guilt'. That body, after all, was said to have 'fabricated Jews as the Mint coined money', as one inquisitor himself remarked.[6]

Later, Jews of Portuguese origin played a minor part in the slave trade in Amsterdam (Diogo Dias Querido), in Curaçao, in Newport (Lopez and the Riberas), and in Bordeaux (the Gradises, Mendèses, and Jean Rodrigues Laureno).˙ In the late seventeenth century Jewish merchants, such as Moses Joshua Henriques, were prominent in the minor Danish slave trade of Glückstadt. But more important there is no sign of Jewish merchants in the biggest European slave-trade capitals when the traffic was at its height, during the eighteenth century – that is, in Liverpool, Bristol, Nantes, and Middelburg – and examination of a list of 400 traders known to have sold slaves at one time or another in Charleston, South Carolina, North America's biggest market, in the 1750s and 1760s suggests just one active Jewish merchant, the unimportant Philip Hart. In Jamaica, the latter's equivalent was Alexander Lindo, who later ruined himself providing for the French army in its effort to recapture Saint-Domingue.

Old enemies of the Jews, gypsies played a minor part in the slave trade, in the cities of Brazil in the eighteenth century, where they gained a name for sadism and were suspected of stealing children to sell as slaves.

˙ *The firm of Gradis in Bordeaux was founded by Diego Gradis, a Portuguese immigrant, in 1695, and it was later run by his son David. In 1728, they had capital of 162,000 livres. David left 400,000 livres when he died in 1751, but his business, by then directed by his own son, Abraham, was worth 4,000,000 livres in 1788 (Abraham gave 61,000 livres to the Bordeaux synagogue in 1777). The Gradises had about half their fortune invested in Saint-Domingue or in Martinique. By 1788 typically, since they were among the richest families of Bordeaux, their interests were moving towards viticulture instead of commerce.*

Many slave traders were Deputies, or Members of Parliament, or their equivalent. In England, for example, in the eighteenth century, the list includes Humphrey Morice, George René Aufrère, John Sargent, and Sir Alexander Grant, all of London; James Laroche and Henry Cruger of Bristol; Ellis Cunliffe, Charles Pole, and John Hardman of Liverpool as well as Sir Thomas Johnson, Mayor of Liverpool, who was partly responsible for one of the first slave ships to leave his city, the *Blessing*, in 1700. French deputies to the National Assembly in 1789 included the biggest slave trader of Bordeaux, Pierre-Paul Nairac. The slavers in the Continental Congress in Philadelphia included Thomas Willing, Mayor of that city; Henry Laurens of Charleston; Carter Braxton, of Richmond, Virginia; and Philip Livingston of New York. John Brown of Providence became a Congressman for Rhode Island, and James de Wolf of Bristol would become a United States Senator. Caleb Gardner and Peleg Clarke, both slave captains, served in the Rhode Island Assembly. Back in England, most mayors of Liverpool in the second half of the eighteenth century were traders in slaves. Miles Barber, the Mayor of Lancaster in the 1750s, was the richest of that little port's slave traders.

Slave traders were often philanthropists. Foster Cunliffe is recalled on a plaque in St Peter's Church, Liverpool, as 'a Christian devout and exemplary in the exercise of every private and public duty, friend to mercy, patron to distress, an enemy only to vice and sloth . . .'. Brian Blundell of Liverpool was a founder of the Blue Coat School. Robert Burridge, last of a slave-trading family in the Dorset port of Lyme Regis, was similarly remembered for his charity towards the aged, the infirm, and 'such poor as generally receive the Lord's supper'. Philip Livingston of New York founded a professorship of divinity at his own old university, Yale, as well as helping the establishment of the first Methodist society in America. John Brown in Providence founded the admirable university which now bears his name. Abraham Redwood's library in Newport still stands secure as a monument to that trader's munificence. René Montaudoin in Nantes gave away thousands to charities. Even the hardheaded Isaac Hobhouse of Bristol left a guinea to be paid to each of the twenty poor men and women who lived in the street adjoining the quay at Minehead, where he had been born.[7]

The slave trade engaged the interests of many foreigners in the places concerned; at the beginning, in Lisbon and Seville, Florentines took a decisive part. These included Columbus's friends the Berardi brothers, whose headquarters was Seville, and of course Bartolommeo Marchionni. That entrepreneur's Seville agent in the early 1500s was Piero Rondinelli, also of Florence. Another Florentine interested in the slave trade in the mid-sixteenth century was Giacomo Botti, an associate of Hernán Cortés, to whom that conquistador left his best bed. Then there were the early imperial privileged monopolists (Gorrevod, and the Welsers' representatives) while, from the beginning, many Genoese were to be found in the

Spanish trade, culminating with Grillo and the Lomelins, who obtained the *asiento* as late as the 1660s. Coymans in Cádiz was, of course, Dutch. In Nantes, George Reidy and Benjamin Thurninger came from Switzerland, and Irish immigrants, such as the Jacobite Antoine Walsh, were at the top of a long list of foreign-born slave merchants of the eighteenth century. (Other Irish slave dealers were to be found in Havana: Richard O'Farrill of Longford, for example, in the early eighteenth century, and, far more wealthy, Cornelius Coppinger of Dublin in the 1760s, the gaunt ruins of whose castle still bleakly stand near Glandore, County Cork.) An important investor in Nantes was the firm of Peloutier (Germans in origin) and Bourcard (or Burckhardt), connected with the Basel firm of Christoph Burckhardt, who formed a partnership in 1756 to manufacture calicoes for the slave trade. In Rhode Island, Aaron Lopez and his brother-in-law, Abraham Ribera, were originally Portuguese as well as Jewish. Henry Laurens in Charleston had a Huguenot grandfather, as did James Laroche in Bristol, England, and George Aufrère of London.

The colossal slave trade from Angola to Brazil was, by the late eighteenth century, generally organized by Luso-Africans, descendants of *lançados*, Portuguese adventurers who had stayed behind to live with Africans. They would obtain the slaves from, or in, the interior, hold them in 'barracoons'* at Luanda, on the coast, and then treat directly with Brazilian captains, from Rio de Janeiro and Bahia.

Aristocrats, such as the Duke of Chandos in London, the father of the writer Chateaubriand in Saint-Malo, and the Espivents and de Luynes of Nantes (though the latter originated in Orléans), were frequently involved. Many independent merchants in France were ennobled because of their mercantile success, such as happened in the case of nearly all the biggest slave merchants of Nantes. Philip Livingston of New York, grandson of the founder of Livingston Manor, and John van Courtlandt, who descended from Stephanus van Courtlandt, proprietor of a vast Hudson River property, should surely be accepted as aristocrats in a broad sense.

None of these slave merchants financed more than a hundred voyages to Africa for slaves. The maximum probably would have been the eighty organized by the Montaudoin family of Nantes. Out of over 1,130 *négriers* in France in the eighteenth century, more than half sent only one or two expeditions to Africa, and only twenty-five families invested in over fifteen voyages.[8]

Several slave merchants testified before British inquiries into the business during the late 1780s or 1790s. They contributed details about what was happening, but few general reflections. If they had had the time to consider the matter, they would surely have agreed with the much-repeated view of (among others) Jean Barbot, the Huguenot who traded

---

* *The word almost certainly derives from the Portuguese* barraca, *meaning shed.*

slaves in the 1680s, that however unpleasant it was to be a slave in the Americas it was better than to be one, or even to be a free man, in Africa. They would have accepted the declaration of Sir Dalby Thomas, the English Commander of Cape Coast Castle, who in 1709 in an essay entitled 'A True and Impartial Account of What We . . . Believe for the Well Carrying On of This Trade' gave a bleak picture of morality in Africa: 'The native here has neither religion nor law binding them to humanity, good behaviour, or honesty. They frequently, for their grandeur, sacrifice an innocent man. . . .' He thought that 'the blacks are naturally such rogues, and bred up with such roguish principles, that what they can, they get, by force or deceit . . .'.[9] Even more violent judgements were made in France: 'At bottom, the blacks are naturally inclined to theft, robbery, idleness, and treason. In general, they are only suited to live in servitude and for the works and the agriculture of our colonies', wrote Gérard Mellier, Mayor of Nantes in the late eighteenth century.[10] William Chancellor, surgeon on Philip Livingston's *Wolf*, wrote in 1750 that the slave trade was a way of 'redeeming an unhappy people from inconceivable misery'.[11]

One or two doubts occurred, all the same, to some prominent North American slave traders. A few Quakers in Philadelphia in the early eighteenth century questioned the ethics of what they were doing – but many of them (such as Jonathan Dickinson and Isaac Norris) continued trading slaves nonetheless. In 1765 Stanislas Foäche wrote home to Le Havre from Saint-Domingue, '*La vente* [of slaves] *m'a donné de cruelles inquiétudes, elle a achevée de me faire blanchir. . . .*'[12] That reflection did not prevent him from remaining a dealer in slaves in the doomed colony for another twenty years. In 1763 Henry Laurens, the largest slave merchant of Charleston, South Carolina, who a few years before had been openly talking of making 'a glorious sale of the cargo' wrote to John Ettwein, future Moravian Bishop of North America, to say that he had often 'wished that our economy and government differed from the present system but, alas – since our constitution is as it is, what can individuals do? Each can act only in his single and disunited capacity, because the sanction of laws gives the stamp of rectitude to the actions of the bulk of the community. If it were to happen', Laurens went on, 'that everybody . . . were to change their sentiments with respect to slavery, and that they should seriously think that the saving of souls [was] a more profitable event than the adding of house to house and laying field to field . . . those laws which now authorise the custom would be instantly abrogated. . . .' Later, Laurens abandoned the trade, explaining to William Fisher, a merchant of Philadelphia, to whom he had often sold rice, that he did so 'principally because many acts [were reprehensible], from the masters and others concerned, from the time of purchasing to that of selling them again . . .'. Laurens was the first prominent person from the South of what soon became the United States to express any compunction about the slave traffic: 'I hate slavery', he later told his son, John, one of the heroes of the Revolutionary War, in 1776. But that was after he had made his fortune.[13]

At much the same time, in 1773, Moses Brown resigned from the family firm of Brown of Providence, became an abolitionist, and freed his own slaves; he often attacked his brother John for remaining in the business.* Then in 1788 the son of a prominent slave trader of Bordeaux also turned against the traffic in a sensational way.† But these instances are as nothing against such a vast background of commitment, justification, and neglect of humane consideration.

Most merchants in these slave ports knew the nature of their cargoes. Thus Nantes had a large black population in 1780, including several hundred captives introduced as a result of recent laws making slavery legal in France. The population of Liverpool in 1788 included about fifty black or mulatto boys and girls, mostly not slaves but the children of African merchants who had sent them to England for their education. There were more blacks in Bristol, and far more still in London, some free, most of them living in limbo between liberty and bondage. Middelburg in Zeeland, the biggest slaving port in eighteenth-century Holland, also had its black minority, as did, on a larger scale, Lisbon and Seville. In North American slaving ports there were also slaves but, except in Charleston, fewer than might have been supposed. For example, there were merely seventy-three in Bristol, Rhode Island, very few owned by the family which became in the 1780s the dominant one in both the trade and the town, the de Wolfs.

The typical slave voyage is assumed to have been triangular. That geometric figure is supposed to have been emblematic of its special character. But there were many exceptions, such as the journeys made directly between Brazil and Angola. There were also numerous direct voyages between the English North American colonies and Africa in the late eighteenth century, and similar journeys later still between Cuba and Africa. For the first hundred years of the Atlantic slave trade the Portuguese, as has been shown, sailed between Lisbon and different harbours in Africa; they carried some slaves from Benin to Elmina, or to São Tomé or the Cape Verde Islands. Many expeditions in the eighteenth century ended with the sale of the ship in the West Indies, or its return to Europe in ballast. Still, the classic journey, probably responsible for three-quarters of all the voyages, was one which began in Europe, picked up slaves in Africa in exchange for European manufactures, carried the slaves to the Americas, and then returned to Europe with certain tropical American goods which slaves would probably have helped to harvest.

* See chapter 25.
† See page 520.

In the fifteenth century the Portuguese had founded this commerce by using single-decked caravels, with square or lateen sails, of fifty to a hundred tons burden. Each would have been able to carry about 150 slaves. They used even smaller vessels – of, say, twenty to twenty-five tons – for trading slaves between Benin and Elmina, Benin and São Tomé, or even São Tomé and Elmina. The Portuguese also had some vessels as big as 120 tons: three-masted, square-rigged roundships. Ships in the small-scale Spanish slave trade from the Barbary Coast to the Canary Islands in the late fifteenth and sixteenth centuries were probably between thirty-five and forty tons, able to carry no more than about forty slaves each.

A typical slave ship sailing from, say, European ports to Africa and the West Indies would not, in the eighteenth century, have been a specialist vessel. Rather, it would have been a typical wooden cargo vessel, perhaps in the seventeenth century a flute ship (a half-armed ship of war) and, in the eighteenth, a frigate (a square-rigged vessel with three masts, two complete decks, and fine lines). Some slave ships had castles, a few were fast, and others just manoeuvrable. In the mid-eighteenth century, vessels from the merchant fleet of the country concerned were used as opportunity offered and, where necessary, adapted. Every ship was, in its way a work of art of complexity, joinery, and design, in which several different woods would have been creatively combined as if the shipwright had been a cabinetmaker. The ships of Clément Caussé of La Rochelle, for example, were masterpieces. All ships were subject to damaging attacks by barnacles or shipworm, for only in the late eighteenth century did ships of Northern Europe begin to be given copper-sheathed hulls: an innovation which not only protected vessels from shipworm but increased their speed.

A French slave vessel of about 1700 would have been between 150 and 250 tons burden, eighty to ninety feet long, twenty to twenty-five feet wide, sixty-five to seventy-five feet on the keel, with ten to twelve feet of hold – that is, the size of an average modern fishing schooner. British ships were usually smaller. Slave ships could easily have been bigger and carried more slaves, but the nature of coastal and riverine trading in Africa dictated a range of 100 to 200 tons. At the end of the eighteenth century the best-known shipbuilder of Nantes, Vial du Clairois, would declare that the ideal *négrier* was between 300 and 400 tons, with ten feet of hold, and four feet four inches between decks. To show the diverse character of the trade, however, the ships of the *asentista* Baltasar Coymans should be recalled: they ranged from the *Profeta Daniel*, of 430 tons, to the *Armas de Ostende*, of thirty-one.

A high proportion of British slave ships, nearly half the total, were naval prizes, obtained easily at the conclusion of wars, the rest being built in British shipyards. In the 1790s, about 15 per cent of all British shipping was intended for the Guinea trade, but almost all of that shipped slaves.

The typical European slave ship, if such a vessel can be hypo-
thesized, would by 1780 still have been less than 200 tons burden. Its
owners would not expect it to make more than about six voyages to
Africa, or indeed to last more than about ten years: only one vessel out
of nearly 800 which sailed from Nantes between 1713 and 1775 both
made six journeys and lasted ten years. This was the *Vermandieu*,
belonging to N. H. Guillon, which was active between 1764 and 1775. The
longest-lasting Dutch ship was the *Leusden*, which made ten voyages
between 1720 and 1738, and carried nearly 7,000 slaves. Ships from Brazil
to Angola generally made even fewer voyages – an average of two per
ship – though one or two made more than twelve; and four ships
belonging to the Pernambuco Company made over ten voyages, one of
them, the elaborately named *Nuestra Senhora da Guia, San Antônio e Almas*,
twenty.

To begin with, all the Portuguese ships which dominated the early
slave traffic had the names of virgins or saints; how many Our Ladies of
Misericordia or of *Conceição*, *São Miguels*, and *São Tiagos* traversed the
green sea of darkness in that epoch we shall never know exactly. In
the eighteenth century those names still held their lead among
Portuguese and Brazilian ships: out of forty-three ships which carried
slaves under the flag of the Company of Grão-Pará and Maranhão, all
had the names of saints except for two (those were the *Delfim* and the
Africana); and, out of fifty ships of its sister Pernambuco Company all but
ten had religious names. In one list of slave ships to Bahia, *Nossa Senhora*
appeared 1,154 times, with fifty-seven different suffixes, above all *Nossa
Senhora de la Conceição* (324 times); while male saints were used 1,158
times, of whom *San Antônio* (of Padua, but with his identity moved to
Lisbon) was the most popular (695 times). *Bom Jesus* appeared 180 times
(above all, the *Bom Jesus do Bom Sucesso*).

After 1800, however, pagan deities became frequent among
Portuguese and Brazilian ships – the *Diana, Venus, Minerva, Hercules*
appearing frequently – while religious names declined. (In the nineteenth
century they would appear on the Bahia list only a few dozen times out of
1,677 voyages.)

In the Anglo-Saxon world the most frequent names of ships were
Christian names, especially girls' names, sometimes, in the comfortable
Anglo-Saxon way, with a qualification: the *Charming Sally*, for instance. In
the three years 1789, 1790, and 1791, 365 ships left Liverpool, London, and
Bristol to go slaving in Africa; of these, 121 had girls' names, Mary, Ann,
Margery, Diana, Hannah, Fanny, Isabella, Ruby, and Eliza being the most
popular. But sometimes there were more sophisticated Anglo-Saxon
designations; for example, the *Othello*, owned by William and Samuel
Vernon of Newport. The *Reformation* and the *Perseverance* also appeared;
both belonged to Quakers, one to the Dickinsons in Philadelphia, the
other to the Galtons of Birmingham.

In France, however, most ships received the name of some kind of quality. Thus over a quarter of the slave ships leaving Bordeaux were called the *Confiance*, the *Cœurs-Unis*, the *Paix*, or some such concept. Neither the *Amitié* (one belonging to Rasteau, in La Rochelle) nor the *Liberté* (one belonging to Isaac Couturier, in Bordeaux) was unknown. But even in France feminine Christian names were the second most frequent apellations: a fifth of them in Bordeaux, again commonly, as in England, with a qualifying adjective: the *Aimable-Cécile* or the *Aimable-Aline*. Among the last slave ships sailing from Nantes before the revolution in Saint-Domingue there were the *Cy-Devant*, the *Nouvelle Société*, the *Soldat Patriote*, the *Ami de la Paix*, and the *Egalité*. The last vessel before the revolution closed down business for a time was the *Subordinateur*, belonging to Haussman & Company.

Portuguese vessels in the early days might have about twenty officers and men in the small caravels, and sometimes sixty in a *nau*. Matters changed over the years. Assuming a burden of 150 tons in the late eighteenth century, the captain, officers, and crew might number thirty on an English ship; while there could be forty-five on the somewhat larger Dutch or French ships. These crews would undertake formally to serve, obliging themselves to obey the captain as if he were their commander in battle. They must have realized that their chances of survival were poor; worse than those of their slave cargoes.

On early Portuguese ships, there would always be a notary, to supervise the trade and prevent illegal trading.

The complements on French ships were more numerous at the beginning of the eighteenth century than at the end. Thus in 1735 the *Victorieux*, of Nantes, belonging to Antoine Walsh's father-in-law, Luc Shiell, 250 tons, employed ninety-nine crew members, or one man per two and a half tons. In the late eighteenth century, the proportion was more likely to be one man per five tons, as it usually was in England.

The captain on an English slave ship would probably be paid £5 a calendar month (100–200 livres in France). René Auguste de Chateaubriand of Saint-Malo, on the *Apollo* in 1754, received 150 livres and also gained a 5 per cent bonus on slaves delivered live: a rather high percentage, for a bonus of 1 or 3 per cent was normal. The other officers, the mates, the surgeon, and the cooper and carpenter, would all receive between £1 and £4 a month. As to the crew, experienced seamen might be paid £2 a month, inexperienced ones 30s, boys £1 only. Half of these wages would customarily be paid in advance, before leaving home, the rest 'at the port of delivery of the said vessel's negroes in America in the currency there'. On ships from other European countries, payments would be similar. On all vessels, coopers were well paid, because of the need to carry so much water: 300 barrels, say. Carpenters, whose task was to refit vessels from carrying cargoes to carrying captives, often received more than the other specialists.

Most of the crew would be men in their twenties, the captain and the mates in their thirties, but some of the specialists might be older, even in their fifties; and there were many boys in their teens.

Sometimes, especially on Rhode Island ships in the late eighteenth century, and on Brazilian ships from the sixteenth century onwards, members of the crew were free blacks, and sometimes the sailors might themselves be slaves, rented out as shipboard labour by their masters. The caravel *Santa Maria das Neves*, for example, carried seven blacks out of her fourteen crew when she travelled between the River Gambia and Lisbon in 1505–6. At that time, African slaves often crewed ships between Guinea and São Tomé. In the mid-sixteenth century a French geographer, André Thevet, thought that the whole crew of one of the Portuguese ships which he saw were slaves; for that reason alone, he said, the captain would not engage in any close fighting. In the late eighteenth century almost half of the 350 Brazil-bound ships for which records survive included slaves in their crews. These blacks could become able seamen, but never officers or captains.

Most officers and some of the specialists had extra rights: for example, to carry a slave or two of their own (four such 'privilege slaves', say, for a captain, a boy for an ensign). The Royal African Company allowed a captain the right of two slaves free of freight for every hundred whom he carried; if 150, three; if 500, five; and so on; 'the captain marking his own slaves [with a burning iron or a silver mark] in the presence of all his officers . . .'.[14] The South Sea Company offered its captains four free slaves for every 104 slaves delivered live, and would then offer to buy them at £20 each. The purpose was, of course, to encourage the captains to interest themselves in the well-being of their cargoes. The first mate in that company had a similar privilege of carrying one free slave; the second mate and surgeon, one between them, etc.

The captain had to be a man of parts. He was the heart and soul of the whole voyage, and had to be able, above all, to negotiate prices of slaves with African merchants or kings, strong enough to survive the West African climate, and to stand storms, calms, and loss of equipment. He had to have the presence of mind to deal with difficult crews who might jump ship, and he had to be ready to face, coolly and with courage, slave rebellions. A good captain would always discuss with his officers all the problems which might arise. Thomas Clarkson, in his *History of the Abolition of the Slave Trade*, records the exploits of several brutal masters of slave ships, including murderers, but courage, patience, and serenity were frequent. French sea captains had to take exams before assuming a command. Many captains carried little libraries of useful books: for example, on the *Créole* of La Rochelle in 1782, the captain had, besides six volumes dealing with naval construction and maritime techniques, and six commercial works, the twelve volumes of the complete works of Rousseau, a history of Louisiana, the voyages of Père Labat, and the

Histoire Philosophique of Raynal. The latter, despite its ferocious criticisms of slavery, was much read by slave captains (the father of Chateaubriand referred to the abbé as *'un maitre-homme'*).[15] The French adventurer Landolphe, who tried unsuccessfully to develop the region around the River Benin as a slave colony in the 1780s, read Diderot's *Encyclopédie*, which criticized the institution of slavery in a lapidary manner, on the banks of that waterway.

A captain was sometimes a man who would become an owner, as has been mentioned, and that was often his ambition. After a few voyages as captain of another merchant's ship he might have made enough money (by, for instance, the sale of his privilege slaves) to invest in other men's voyages, or to buy a ship of his own. Occasionally, of course, a captain was an owner already, and sailed as such. Robert Champlin of Newport sailed as captain on ships owned by his brothers Christopher and George.

All the same, to be a slave captain was not really a profession: even experienced captains rarely went to Africa more than three or four times. Deputy captains would always have to be ready to take over command, in case, as sometimes happened, their masters died; that happened about once in every ten voyages, at least in the Dutch West India Company's experience.

Captains made even more statements of what they thought about the trade than did the merchants. For example, Hugh Crow, who captained several voyages of slave ships owned by the Aspinalls of Liverpool, thought that 'the abstraction of slaves to our colonies [was] a necessary evil'. He seems to have been sincerely convinced that the African slaves in the West Indies were happier than when they lived as slaves in their own country, 'subject to the caprices of their native princes'. Had he been a slave, Crow said, he would have much preferred to have been a black slave in the West Indies than even a free man at home in England – than, say, a fisherman, a coal miner, or a factory worker, or a man sent to jail 'for killing a paltry hare or a partridge'. 'Think of the wretched Irish peasantry! Think of the crowded workhouses', he amiably concluded his memoir.[16]

Joseph Hawkins of Charleston, South Carolina, went to Africa as a slave captain in 1793. Though initially dubious, he confessed when he reached a slave barracoon, where many slaves had been kept waiting for sale, that he became 'fully convinced [that] the removal of these poor wretches, even to the slavery of the West Indies, would be an act of humanity, rather than one exposed to censure. . . . The slaves [whom] I had purchased were young men, many of them being eager to escape from their bondage in Ebo, [and] preferred the evil "they knew not of" to that which they then felt; but', he admitted, 'the majority were evidently affected with grief at their approaching departure. . . .'[17]

Both Captain Thomas Phillips of London, at the end of the seventeenth century, and Captain William Snelgrave of Bristol, at the beginning of the eighteenth, felt some remorse about their activities but, like some merchants in the same frame of mind, continued nonetheless in the business, both writing accounts of what they did. The comments of Phillips, a Welshman, are remarkable for their time. Speaking of the slaves, he said: 'Nor can I imagine why they should be despised for their colour, being what they cannot help. . . . I can't think there is any intrinsic value in one colour more than another, that white is better than black, only we think it so, because we are so, and are prone to judge favourably in our own case. . . .'[18]

John Newton, Captain of the *Duke of Argyll* (belonging to the Manesty brothers of Liverpool), the future Vicar of St Mary's Woolnoth, thought a great deal about his old trade, but unlike Crow did not seek to justify it. On the contrary, he explained that he knew of 'no method of getting money not even that of robbing for it upon the highway, which has so direct a tendency to efface the moral sense . . .'. All the same, Newton only abandoned the trade because of bad health. He had a vision which led him to become a clergyman, but when he was still a slave captain he was already a Christian: he wrote to his wife, on leaving Africa on the *Duke of Argyll* for the West Indies with a cargo of slaves, of 'innumerable dangers and difficulties which, without a superior protection, no man could escape or surmount, [and which] are, by the goodness of God, happily over'. He had to face a slave rebellion two days after he wrote that sentence. He added that he overcame the emergency 'with the Divine Assistance'. Newton would customarily read prayers twice a day to his slave crews. He was an autodidact: he taught himself Latin and read Virgil, Livy, and Erasmus while still captaining a slaver. That did not prevent him from sometimes putting the 'boys . . . siightly in the thumb screws to obtain a confession'. Newton was still a slave captain when he wrote his best hymn, 'How Sweet the Name of Jesus Sounds'.[19]

Some interesting reflections were made by Captain Crassous on the *Dahomet* of La Rochelle, as in 1791 he touched at Las Palmas in the Canary Islands, and pitied the poor Spaniards who, unlike the French, still lived under a violent and arbitrary government. He hoped that one day the example of 'the French Revolution would awake poor Spain from its slavery [sic] and lethargy'. He then set off for Mozambique to buy Africans for Saint-Domingue.[20]

The surgeon on the slave ship was in charge of all matters relating to health, carrying with him such supposed medicaments as gum camphor, pulverized rhubarb, cinnamon water, mustard, and bitters, and was always involved in major decisions about the voyage. Several surgeons, such as Alexander Falconbridge, or Thomas Trotter on the *Brookes*, or William Chancellor on Philip Livingston's sloop *Wolf* in 1750 (he found Africa beautiful but despised the Africans), contributed priceless information as to how the slave trade worked. The surgeon, a most important member of any ship's company, would receive the same income as a first

mate or carpenter, £4 on an English ship.* But it was not legally necessary
to carry a surgeon, and many slave ships economized by neglecting to
have one: including most of those flying the flag of the United States.

Some other officers on slavers recalled their experiences; one such
was Jean Barbot, who travelled on slave ships from La Rochelle in the
1680s. He hoped that officers tempted to be brutal would 'consider [that]
those unfortunate creatures [the slaves] are men as well as themselves,
though of a different colour and pagans'.[21] Edward Rushton, second mate
in a ship belonging to Richard Watt and Gregson of Liverpool, had his life
saved by a slave, and then went blind, after treating slaves suffering from
ophthalmia, when bound for the island of Dominica. He subsequently
became an abolitionist, a poet, and a bookseller. His *West Indian Eclogues*
included the line 'Oh, for the power to make these tyrants bleed!': a sentiment which endeared him to reformers, even if it caused difficulties for
him in his native Liverpool.

Ordinary seamen on slave ships were usually young men of low
achievement and aspirations, primarily because of the poor pay, the vile
conditions, and the danger. The names of sailors on North American or
English ships indicate nothing except dour Anglo-Saxon ancestry: for
example, in Frederick Philipse's *Margaret* in 1698 we find sailors called
Burgess, Lazenby, Powell, Ransford, Harris, Dorrington, Upton, Herring,
Dawson, Whitcomb, Whore, Oder, Laurence, and Crook. Members of
Parliament would have had much the same surnames.

Sometimes sailors such as these were lured on board slave ships by
'crimping': that is, being plied with drink at an inn until, penniless as well
as intoxicated, they could be carried off as part of a bargain between
innkeeper and captain. A carpenter in the navy, James Towne, told a
House of Commons committee on the slave trade: 'The method at Liverpool [to obtain sailors] is by the merchants' clerks going from public
house to public house, giving them liquors to get them into a state of
intoxication and, by that, getting them very often on board. Another
method is to get them in debt and then, if they don't choose to go aboard
of such guinea men then ready for sea, they are sent away to gaol by the
publicans they may be indebted to.'[22]

John Newton was convinced that the slave trade ruined the sensitivi-
ties of all crews: 'The real or supposed necessity of treating the Negroes
with rigour gradually brings a numbness upon the heart and renders
those who are engaged in it too indifferent to the sufferings of their

---

* *At least at the end of the eighteenth century, if he was on board a Liverpool ship, a ship's
surgeon might have been trained at the Liverpool Royal Infirmary, the medical school
from which the University of Liverpool developed. The fact that so many Liverpool ships
carried trained doctors led to the growth of tradition of tropical medicine there, which in
turn led eventually to the Liverpool school of that science, and therefore, indirectly, in the
late nineteenth century, to Sir Ronald Ross's nomination of the mosquito as the agent of
malaria.*

fellow-creatures.' He also thought that 'there is no trade in which seamen are treated with so little humanity'. Officers certainly treated sailors as badly as, or worse than, they treated the slaves. Thus James Morley, once a cabin boy on the *Amelia* of Bristol, in answer to a question at a House of Commons inquiry, 'How have the seamen been generally treated on board the Guinea ships in which you have sailed?' replied, 'With great rigour and many times with cruelty.' He recalled how he once accidentally broke a glass belonging to Captain Dixon: 'I . . . was tied up to the tiller in the cabin by my hands, and then flogged with a cat, and kept hanging there some time.' Most seamen, Morley thought, slept on the deck: 'They lie on deck and they die on deck.'[23] Many witnesses in these inquiries testified that the crews were atrociously treated. In 1761, on board the *Hare*, Captain Colley of Liverpool killed the carpenter, the carpenter's mate, the cook, and another man with a handspike. 'I have been on a number of ships,' remarked one sailor, 'and always found the same treatment as we had on board our own, that is, men dying from want of provisions, from being hard worked and from being inhumanly beat. . . .'[24] A French novelist, Edouard Corbière, would in *Le Négrier* point out that a slaving voyage was a colossal challenge to the patience and endurance of the crews: 'How many wounds were caused in the characters, the customs, and even the passions in these men so often so diverse who find themselves gathered together in the middle of so many perils in this narrow space we call a ship.'[25] Chancellor, the surgeon on Philip Livingston's ship *Wolf*, doubted, on returning to New York, whether he could ever 'have satisfaction for the misery I have undergone on this voyage'.

Deaths were rarely less than a fifth of the crew, sometimes more: the *Nymphe* in 1741 lost twenty-eight out of forty-five; the *Couéda* arrived at Cap François in 1766 with only nine crew members. Perhaps the worst record was that of the *Marie-Gabrielle* of Nantes, which in 1769 lost thirty-one sailors out of thirty-nine. The *Deux Pucelles* of Nantes lost all her officers in 1750. Analysis of the Dutch slave trade suggests that about 18 per cent of crews died on all their recorded voyages – in comparison with 12 per cent of the slaves. Something like the same statistic must have been true of the English trade: for example, over 20 per cent of English crews died on Bristol and Liverpool slavers even in the 1780s. But the crews had a longer time on board the ships than the slaves did.

Slave ships had to be armed. Both the Gulf of Guinea and the Caribbean were infested with pirates. So the average armament of a 200-ton French slaver of about 1700 might have been fifteen to eighteen cannon. Some ships, such as those belonging to the Montaudoins, had even more weapons. Later, the risk of pirates became less and, in the 1730s, ships of 200 tons might have only eight to twelve pieces. Slave ships which sailed in time of war would be more heavily armed, but they would often have military commissions and be technically corvettes or auxiliary frigates.

All ships were insured, often internationally. Insurance seems first to have been undertaken in Antwerp, but Amsterdam, London, and Paris soon followed, and then the slaving ports themselves would develop their own companies on the initiative of merchants who might have small stakes in the business themselves. English companies would usually insure the few United States ships. French traders at Nantes and La Rochelle estimated that insurance averaged 7 per cent of the cost of the ship in time of peace, but the percentage would rise to 35 per cent in tense international conditions, even if the ship concerned travelled in convoy. In La Rochelle,the slave ships were often insured in other cities: Nantes, for example, or even Amsterdam, Hamburg, and London. At least one insurer – Duvivier, of La Rochelle – himself became a major dealer in slaves. An important London marine insurer, Hayley, of Hayley and Hopkins, explained in 1771 to Aaron Lopez of Newport that 'the premium for a winter voyage from Jamaica is never less than 8 per cent and upon vessels not known in the trade can seldom be under 10'.[*][26] Still, some North American insurers (Tench Francis, for example, the leader of the bar in Philadelphia) did business before 1774, and after the revolution, many merchants turned to Boston. Samuel Sanford founded the Newport Insurance Company. When that enterprise became infiltrated by opponents of the slave trade, the Bristol Insurance Company was founded, and that was followed by the Mount Hope Insurance Company, founded by the de Wolfs, themselves large-scale slavers. Rates varied from 5 to 25 per cent.

Slave captains would usually receive precise instructions from their owners as to what to do, and where to go. A characteristic instruction was that to Captain William Barry of Bristol, who was told in the 1730s: 'As the wind is inclining to be fair, you are ordered with your men (which we allow to be twenty in number, yourself included) to repair on board the *Dispatch*, brigantine, of which you are . . . Commander and to lose no time but to sail directly . . . to the Coast of Africa: that is, to that part of it called Andony [on the Bight of Biafra, north of Fernando Po] (without touching or tarrying at any other place), where you are to slave . . . The cargo of goods are of your own ordering and, as it's very good in kind and amounts to £1,330 8s 2¼d, we hope it will purchase you 240 choice slaves, besides a Quantity of teeth [of elephants] . . . provided they are large. . . .'[27]

A ship such as this would be expected to be at least a year abroad, to cover 12,000 miles in the voyage, and to anticipate hurricanes in the

---

[*] *That Hayley married Mary, a sister of the orator of constitutional liberty John Wilkes, another of whose sisters, Sarah, was the inspiration for Miss Havisham in Dickens's* Great Expectations.

Caribbean, tornadoes on the coast of Guinea, and almost everywhere rot
and pirates, barnacles and leaking. An average voyage, throughout the era
of the trade, varied from between fifteen and eighteen months. The fastest
journey in the classic era of the trade, in the mid-eighteenth century, was
probably that of Michel and Grou's *Sirène* from Nantes, which took only
eight months and thirty-two days, carrying 331 slaves from Sénégal to
Léogane in Saint-Domingue in 1753; only two slaves died.

Each trading port had its peculiarities. Thus merchants from Liverpool often bought provisions in Ireland, so that they could tell the
authorities on the Liverpool dock that they were merely leaving for
Kinsale. Sometimes Bristol ships would pick up the spirits for their
cargoes in Jersey, a big smuggling port. London ships might go for that
purpose to Rotterdam. The captains of Dutch ships from Middelburg or
Amsterdam would usually join them when they were already in the open
sea. Many French ships would stop for water, wine (sometimes to be used
in barter), and fresh food in Portugal (say, Lisbon) or Spain (say, Cádiz).
Some French slave ships also put in at Madeira or Tenerife, more often at
Praya, in the Cape Verde Islands. Hugh Crow wrote that in his experience
English slave ships also usually made for the Canary Islands 'in the first
instance'.

Ships would usually leave with live turkeys, chickens, and even
cattle on board, for future killing. A year and a half's supply of biscuits
would perhaps be taken: say, four or five tons of them. Captains would
also try to carry enough wine to provide the crew with a litre and a
quarter a day per man. Water would, of course, also be embarked, but no
more than necessary to reach Africa. Flour would be available to be made
into bread by the ship's baker. Smoked meat was Ireland's chief contribution to these voyages, as hard cheese was one of Holland's. Some fishing
would be done to supplement the rations.

There were two classic passages for slave ships to West Africa from
Northern Europe: first, in French terminology *la petite route* – that is, via
the Cape Verde Islands – after which the captain would stay close to
the coast. *La grande route* entailed the captain's keeping well out into the
Atlantic before striking east-south-east to Angola or the Congo. *La petite
route* was customary in winter and was, of course, always used when the
vessels were making for the Gulf of Guinea. Most of this journey was in
sight of the coasts. *La grande route* was more prudent between March and
August, when the south-east trade winds could cause many difficulties,
and that itinerary was, of course, normal when the destination was
primarily Central Africa. Ships on their way to Mozambique, or other
ports in East Africa, would also naturally follow this second route, but
would try to avoid any wind or current which would make it hard to
clear the Cape of Good Hope.

Portuguese ships bound for Angola would always take *la grande
route*, or a variation of it which meant that, after touching at the Cape

Verde Islands, they would pick up the winds blowing down the coast of Brazil – much as Cabral had sailed on that first extraordinary journey in 1500. They might then touch at Pernambuco or Rio, but most did not; rather, they would head back into the open sea north of the Brazilian mainland, and make for Angola.

North American traders, of course, made quite different voyages, for a journey which would usually take from seven to twelve months, from home in New England to Africa and then to market, which might often be the West Indies, or perhaps Charleston, South Carolina, and rarely New England itself.

Ships leaving Europe were sometimes seized by pirates off the north-west coast of Africa, especially the terrifying ones of Salé. So in the early eighteenth century sensible slave captains would try to carry a 'Turkish pass'. This was bought from pirates in Algeria to enable captains to pass without molestation. But there were often captures of slave ships. In 1687, for example, a large Dutch slave ship en route for Africa was sunk because the captain did not have a pass.

It was because of those perils, as well as the dangers of disease and rebellion, not to speak of enemy action, that captains and crews usually forbore to think of the slaves themselves.

16

GREAT PLEASURE
FROM OUR WINE

*'The Wolofs are great drunkards and derive
great pleasure from our wine.'*

Valentim Fernandes, c. 1500

THE CARGOES FOR THE SLAVE TRADE changed over the centuries,
depending on the character, the purse, and the imagination of the European supplier who responded to a great variety of constantly changing
African demands. Although the cargo must always have cost about two-
thirds of the total outlay of a slave voyage, there were many differences as
to how goods for the trade were carried and financed. For example, by
the late eighteenth century, because of the exceptional nature of the
Angolan–Brazilian commerce, Portuguese merchants would carry goods
to Angola and return with some African product as ballast, leaving the
Luso-Africans who ran the Angolan side of the Brazilian business to
exchange the European goods for slaves as and when seemed best. In the
early days, when the Portuguese were still carrying slaves from Benin
direct to Portugal, or to Elmina, the royal factor in São Tomé would
instruct captains bound for Ughoton, the port of Benin, that even for the
best slaves they should not pay more than fifty manillas (bronze leg
bracelets). But by the next century such an all-or-nothing approach would
have been inconceivable: thus in 1628 no fewer than 218 different types of
goods for trading were to be found in Elmina. In the late eighteenth
century a bill of lading from Newport, Rhode Island, might run: 'Shipped
by the Grace of God, in good order and well-conditioned, by Jacob
Rod[rígues] Rivera and Aaron Lopez, on their joint account, . . . upon the
good ship called Cleopatra, whereof is master under God for the present
voyage James Bourk, and now riding at anchor in the harbour of
Newport, and by God's grace bound for Africa, to say, two hundred and
thirty-four hogsheads New England rum; two barrels wine, six barrels
tarr, six barrels pitch, six barrels turpentine, two half barrels [gun]-
powder, sixty-four kegs water bread [water biscuits], six casks Indian

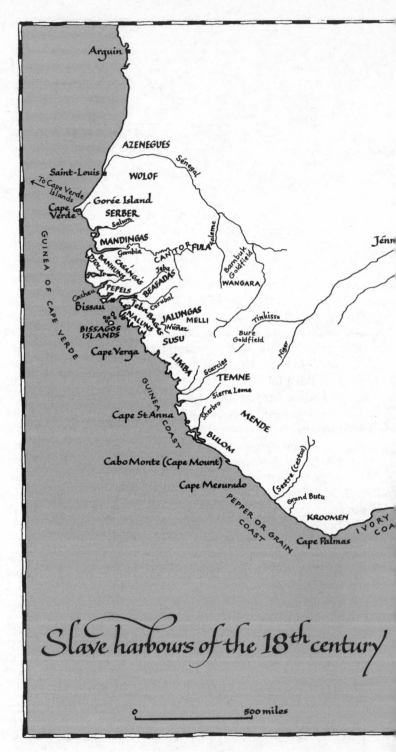

Slave harbours of the 18th century

corn, one tierce [a large cask] gammon, one thousand hogsheads' hoops, six hundred and seventy feet white oak boards, three hundred and thirty red oak boards, eleven hogsheads and one small cask calavants [chick-peas], two hogsheads' black-eyed peas, six tierces and two hogsheads rice, twenty barrels common flour, ten barrels superfine flour, thirty sheep and provender, eight casks common ships' bread, six hogsheads and four tierces hard-baked bread, twenty-eight barrels beef, twenty-four barrels pork, one firkin [a small cask] butter, and two cases window frames and shutters, two masts and two pieces timber, one bundle sailors clothes, twelve pounds chocolate; and, half a hundred weight sugar . . .'[1]

A surgeon in the British navy, John Atkins, reported following an expedition in 1721 whose purpose was to destroy pirates such as the murderous Captain Roberts: 'The windward and the leeward parts of the coast are as opposite in their demands [with respect to slave goods] as is their distance. Iron bars which are not asked for to leeward are a substantial part of windward cargoes. Crystals, oranges, corals, and brass-mounted cutlasses are almost peculiar to the Windward coast; as are brass pans from the Rio Sethos to Apollonia [the Gold Coast] and cowries . . . at Whydah, [and] copper and iron bars at Callabar; but arms, gunpowder, tallow, old sheets, cottons [that is, Indian cottons] . . . and English spirits [whisky] are everywhere called for. Sealing wax and pipes are necessary in small quantities, they serve for dashees [tips]. . . .'[2]

These reports show how varied the business of trading slaves was. As for the nature of the exchange, at Whydah, Dahomey, in 1767, a slave might be bought for sixteen anchors* of brandy; or twenty cabess of cowries;† or 200 pounds of gunpowder; or twenty-five guns; or ten long cloths; or ten blue bafts (lengths of coarse blue cotton made in India); or ten patten chints (chintz); or forty iron bars.

On the coasts of Malemba and Cabinda (semi-independent ports in what is now Angola), 'the negroes, before striking a bargain, go and mark off . . . in the captain's store, which is on the sea side, the pieces of stuff they choose to take; & he who has sold four slaves at fifteen goods a head goes to receive 60 pieces of the stuffs marked off. . . . It is customary to give for each slave . . . the "over and above", for example, 3 or 4 guns and as many swords, 15 pots of brandy, 15 pounds of gunpowder, and 12 knives. . . .'[3]

In places such as Loango Bay, when slaves were said to cost 'thirty', it did not mean thirty pieces of stuffs, but '30 times the ideal value which they fix on, and call a piece. So a single piece of stuff is sometimes estimated at 2 or 3 pieces, and sometimes several objects must form a single piece. . . .'[4]

---

* A measure of 8½ imperial gallons.
† A cabess was 5,000 cowries.

Overall, the cargo carried by most slave traders, and most sought after in Africa, reckoned in terms of cost in Europe, was cloth: woollen, and later cotton, cloth, made in Europe, in India, or just possibly elsewhere. The typical exchange for a slave in the sixteenth century between Congolese and Portuguese merchants was a piece of textile large enough to clothe a single individual, only about two yards of stuff. One type of cotton cloth, guinée cloth, *une pièce de guinée*, was once a currency on the River Sénégal, as cloth had been in ancient Mexico before the coming of the Europeans. An African-made cloth was also for a time similarly used in Angola, and the cloth of the Cape Verde Islands, especially the large blue 'barafula', was also for a time a currency in the exchanges of settlers there with the mainland. But normally the cloth was worn, since most men in Africa dressed in some kind of loincloth, and all but the poorest women in Africa wore an upper garment, as well as a cloth of about one and a half to two cloths long wrapped round the waist. Rich men had even larger loincloths.

West Africans had cloth of many different kinds before the Europeans arrived in their harbours, and early Portuguese visitors admired its quality. The dyes, especially the indigo dyes from the River Núñez, were excellent. Most West African communities had a tradition of spinning and weaving, and so the European products were merely added to an existing industry. Some cloths used in the slave trade were actually African: for example, the 'high cloths', woven in the Cape Verde Islands by the Afro-Portuguese settlers (or their slaves), cloth from Benin and elsewhere in what is now southern Nigeria, as well as 'Quaqua' cloths from the Ivory Coast, were exchanged for slaves by European traders on the Gold Coast. Sometimes, as in the case of the cloth of Allada (Dahomey), the Africans merely treated European cloth with their own dyes to make the bright products which European traders were then able to sell in, for example, Barbados.

But there was too little African cloth, and the choice offered by the Europeans was attractive. People in the region of Guinea preferred white cloth, those in Angola blue.

In the earliest days, when the slave trade was controlled by the Portuguese, the most popular items were *lambens*, which were full-length cloaks bought in North Africa. They had armholes and an opening in the centre for the head, comparable to a Peruvian poncho. Sometimes, they were striped: red, green, blue, white. One good *lamben* from Algeria might be exchanged for a prime male slave. These were known to West Africans before the arrival of the Portuguese caravels, because the Sahara trade had brought many such desirable objects from the Mediterranean, though never enough to satisfy demand.

During the two centuries when they dominated the slave trade the Portuguese carried to Africa many different textiles from Europe, including, long before those nations entered the traffic, woollens from England and Holland.˙

A manifest of the ship *Santiago*, which set out in 1526 for Sierra Leone and Cacheu (the River São Domingos, as it was then known) and brought back to Lisbon 125 slaves, included as its most important items 1,600 cubits of vermilion or yellow cloth, 357 *varas* of handkerchief material, 24 cloths from the Portuguese province of Alentejo, 8 *varas* of hemp for sacks, and 120 bells, as well as 2,345 brass manillas and 1,240 bracelets of tin.

The Northern Protestant countries, entering the slave trade in the seventeenth century, each had its special textile to offer to the Africans. Thus the English speciality was in the early days woollen cloth, then and now a protection against the fierce cold wind of the Gulf of Guinea, the harmattan (when 'the sharpness of the air . . . obliged all persons whatsoever, white or black, without exception . . . to keep to their houses or chambers'), and for use as blankets during those harsh nights of shivering known to the English as 'rigours'. So woollens were always a staple in West Africa: particularly serges and says, a fine woollen cloth, sometimes mixed with silk, originally produced in the villages near Lille, Arras, Valenciennes, and Armentières, but using wool from Spain, Scotland, Germany, or Friesland. Later, says were made by the English, who also produced perpetuanas (a tough cloth like tweed, woven in Devon), bays (baize), bridgwaters (from Bridgwater, in Somerset), or Welsh plaines (a simply woven cloth made in the Midlands as well as in Wales).

Each of these products has its own history, and in England their manufacturers were to be found among those who protested first against the exclusion of 'interlopers' from the legal slave trade towards the end of the seventeenth century, and also against the idea of abolition at the end of the eighteenth. Perhaps 85 per cent of English textile exports went to Africa before 1750, and over 40 per cent during the following twenty years. In the 1780s the percentage was much lower, varying between 11 and 32 per cent because of the much increased European market. England after the Methuen Treaty of 1703 also dominated Portugal and its empire, being able to export cloth there without paying duty, in return for the much more modest Portuguese right to carry their wine similarly freely (that meant port wine). Much English cloth went to Lisbon to be traded in turn for slaves by Portuguese merchants.

Though the Germans played a tiny part in the Atlantic slave trade as principals in the business, their cloths were important in it, just as their brass manillas had been earlier on. German linen goods were specially in demand in the harbours of the Bissagos Islands, and the African trade as

---

˙ *They brought not only cloth but a new strain of cotton from the Americas,* Gossypium barbadense. *African cloth was made from this on a large scale on the upper valley of the River Sénégal.*

a whole was a useful outlet for all German textiles, made in Westphalia, Saxony, and Silesia.

Dutch woollen goods for the slave trade were mostly made in Leiden or Haarlem. Linen also played an important part in the Dutch trade, particularly secondhand linen sheets which were sold for clothing. Barbot noted that everyone on the Gold Coast seemed to wear a cloth from Holland which passed between the thighs, and 'whose ends hung down to the ground behind and before. . . . When they go through the streets, they take a length of Leyden serge or perpetuana two or three ells in length, which they pass over their necks . . . like a mantle'.[5] Noblemen and merchants alike on the same stretch of land were often seen wearing Chinese satin, taffeta, or coloured Indian cloths – apparel made possible since in the seventeenth century the Dutch began to take with them to Africa such exotic offerings as Japanese silk dressing gowns or other silks from China or India. The Dutch East India Company brought back many such things from the East, especially from India, and many of them were immediately transferred to the slave trade.

In the beginning, English and French merchants bought these Indian textiles from Holland for their slave cargoes. Ships from London, for example, might make a special detour to Rotterdam on their outward journey, if they had not bought the goods in London. Ships from La Rochelle might also plan to pick up at Le Havre all their supplies from Holland, England (knives and forks), Sweden (iron bars), Rouen (hand-kerchiefs), Honfleur (cider), and Amsterdam (sheets), as well as Dutch chains and razors.

For a long time Indian goods were banned from the English and French home markets. But obtained through the Dutch, and then the British, East India companies, they were much appreciated in West Africa: partly because of their bright colours, partly because of their durability. In good years in the late seventeenth century, £20,000 worth or so of East Indian goods would go to Africa on British ships alone, principally as fabrics. The merchants of Bristol gave a special emphasis to these goods: they accounted for over a quarter of the value of all goods shipped from England to Africa between 1699 and 1800. Among the most successful of these textiles were bafts, or in French *guinées bleues*. Baft was originally made in south-eastern India, in the neighbourhood of Madras and Pondicherry, the two main English and French trading points in old India. This heavy cloth was dyed a dark, almost indigo, blue. It became a favourite of the Muslim traders on the River Sénégal who, indeed, would sometimes downright insist on it.

East Indian cloths all had of course their special traders: among them in London Peregrine Cust, of the Company of Merchants Trading to Africa in 1757, and John Sargent, member of a circle of trading partners which included the protean Richard Oswald (though he also traded extensively in the Baltic and Germany for linen). Sargent found his original opening through the well-connected Huguenot émigrés, the Aufrère family. He had his equivalents in Lisbon and Nantes, and even in Bremen and Copenhagen.

In the second half of the eighteenth century, as has been shown, manufacturers in Manchester and Rouen tried to copy the Indian products. But English and French dyeing, even at Rouen, was at first inferior to that of the Indians, and could not achieve the bright colours of the latter. In the end, however, Mancunian manufacturers, in particular, showed themselves very clever with cotton checks ('Guinea cloths'), a local imitation of an Indian cotton which enjoyed a greater success in Africa every year. In Lancashire in the 1750s the largest of the early manufacturers (William and Samuel Rawlinson, Samuel Taylor) did especially well in this line of business. After 1760 coarse annabasses, made in Manchester, became especially sought after on the West African coast. Many loads of this fabric were bought by the Portuguese and the French for use by their captains. Such European cloths often kept their Indian names ('nicanee' or 'cash-toe'), or a variant of them, even if they were made in Lancashire. Rouen had a good line in Simaoises as well as indiennes which stocked ships at Le Havre or Honfleur as well as at Rouen itself.

New England, too, produced coarse cottons, though that commodity was never so successful in the slave trade as rum.

After cloth, metals played the most important part in the European slave traffic in Africa.

In the fifteenth and sixteenth centuries copper and brass objects were welcome in Africa in every shape and type: particularly brass bowls, but also chamber pots, cauldrons, jugs, or mere sheets of copper. West Africans had some knowledge of metalworking, and many of the objects were melted down by the natives. Thus the bracelets, manillas, often made in south Germany especially for the trade, bought by Portuguese or their Genoese representatives in Antwerp, and used as anklets, were often exchanged in Africa for slaves, and, like some cloths, they were also sometimes used as a currency in the neighbourhood of Whydah, on the Slave Coast between the River Volta and Lagos, and also in the delta of the eastern Niger. As early as the mid-sixteenth century German metal traders were established at Lisbon, so that the Portuguese could buy direct from them, rather than have to buy at Antwerp.

Copper was the chief metal attraction for West Africa till about 1520. Thereafter an age of brass lasted till about 1630, when iron began to establish itself as Northern Europeans, in touch with the Swedish iron foundries, embarked on the slave trade. But brass remained popular: brass pots, kettles, and pans, made in Birmingham, Liverpool (the Holywell works), and North Staffordshire (the Cheadle Company), were still being used until well after 1700. Other brass objects, such as wire made by Baptist Mills of Bristol, 'Guinea rods', also had their day.

In the eighteenth century, iron bars (usually nine inches long) became not just an article of trade but a trading medium too, at least in the Gulf of Guinea (in Congo and Angola they never enjoyed the same appeal as they did in the north). For a time, one such iron bar in Guinea was reckoned as equal to four copper ones. In 1682 the Royal African Company was exporting to Africa about 10,000 such iron bars a year. Most of these came from Sweden, the rest from Germany. In 1685 all but six of thirty-five ships dispatched to Africa by the RAC carried iron bars as part of their cargoes. The people of the Gambia had a particular interest in these cargoes: a quarter to half of the RAC's exports to the territory were of that commodity, though few went to Angola in the company's day. In 1733, at the height of the slave trade, an English ship from Bristol to Bonny stocked up with £1,226 worth of goods to buy 250 Negroes at Bonny, of which iron was the most expensive item. Much of this was transformed in Africa for use in agriculture: as hoes, for example.

The demand for these bars naturally meant profits for those who carried them from Scandinavia to the slaving ports. Some of these merchants themselves became interested in the slave trade in consequence; one such was Anthony Tourney (Tournai), who enjoyed a most fruitful association with the London slave merchant and banker Humphrey Morice. The same occurred in the case of George Aufrère, the Huguenot trader who made his first fortune selling East Indian cloths to London merchants. Tourney and Aufrère later invested in slave ships.

These imports of iron did not have much effect on African production, for the interior empires had learned the art of smelting not long after the Europeans had done so. These products therefore did not destroy an African native tradition of metallurgy. But nails from Spain, iron from Sweden, copper from Hamburg, Ostend, or London made the mineral dimension of the slave trade an international undertaking in its own right.

Gold played a modest part in the slave trade. Yet Brazilian gold – in dust or bars – was carried by Brazilian traders to the Bight of Benin from the late seventeenth century onwards. They exchanged it for slaves. They had no legal right to do this, so it was a contraband trade, even if it was tolerated. These traders even exchanged gold for slaves with the English at Cape Coast, thus performing the unusual feat of carrying gold to the Gold Coast. Some of the slaves bought with Brazilian gold were taken to Brazil to mine that very commodity in Minas Gerais. At the end of the eighteenth century, other Brazilians, from the colony's northern cotton-growing regions, also took gold to Angola.

A few coins from either Europe or the Americas made their way to Africa. The Mandingos particularly liked Portuguese silver coins, or Spanish copper coins called *patacas*, which they made into bracelets or necklaces. Then the French Sénégal Company carried pieces of eight to Bissau, and the Royal African Company took guinea coins to the River

Gambia. Dutch twenty-eight-stuiver pieces, as well as Spanish dollars (thalers), were used on a small scale as a medium of exchange on the Gold Coast in about 1700. But paper money and credit notes were never acceptable in Africa: Captain William Snelgrave, in Dahomey in the 1720s, reported that the agents there 'did not like a bit of paper for their slaves, because the writing might vanish from it, or else the notes might be lost, and then they should lose their payment'.[6]

Throughout the sixteenth and seventeenth centuries shells, especially cowries (commonly known as 'bouges', from the Portuguese *búzios*) from the Maldive Islands in the Indian Ocean and conch shells, were to be specially reckoned with in the slave trade – above all, the standard cowrie, *Cypraea moneta*. Cowries (the word derives from the Hindi *kauri*) had been adopted as a common, though not a single, currency throughout much of the Indian subcontinent by the tenth century AD, and began to be carried across the Sahara to West Africa in the eleventh, when they were in use in markets in the valley of the Niger. Cowries were to be found in Venice. In the fourteenth century, there are several references to cowries in use as currency in the Mali empire: one of them in 1352 by the astonishing traveller Ibn Battuta, who in 1344 had even been to the Maldive Islands, where he had married four wives. Cowries were already in Arguin when Ca'da Mosto arrived. At the end of the fifteenth century the Portuguese penetrated the Indian Ocean, and were themselves taking the shells from the Maldives by 1520. They even had a small fort there in 1519. The Dutch reached the Maldives in 1602, the English in 1658.

In the early sixteenth century slaves were sometimes sold for cowries alone. The standard price for a male slave destined for São Tomé in the River Forcados in 1520, for example, was 6,000 cowries, and though thereafter traders demanded many other things, cowries always played a part in the trade in that region – sometimes a third, sometimes even a half. Often prices of slaves were reckoned in terms of cowries, in the 1770s perhaps 160,000 cowries per slave.

In the eighteenth century, while these shells were still being used as currency in India, they had the same role in much of West Africa, especially at Whydah, the biggest importer of cowries in the eighteenth century. Between 1700 and 1800, over 25,000,000 pounds of cowries seem to have been imported into West Africa by European traders. The peak year was probably 1722, when over 700,000 pounds of cowries were taken to West Africa by English and Dutch captains alone. The RAC found that cowries were essential for trading for slaves in certain places, particularly at Whydah and in the Bight of Benin. African dealers might insist that a quarter, sometimes as much as a half, of the cost of slaves was paid in this way.

Cowries in West Africa were often strung in forties, which were known as tockies (from the Portuguese *toque*). Five tockies made a *galhina*, a chicken, and 125 tockies made a cabess (from *cabeça*, a head). In the mid-seventeenth, as in the mid-eighteenth century, one cabess, or 5,000 cowries, seems to have equalled in value one iron bar.

Cowries had many virtues as a money. They made possible an international currency, which circulated in the markets of large and small polities, while a single shell had the virtue of having a very low value indeed (the least valuable coin in Britain, the farthing, was equivalent to between twenty-five and thirty-two cowries in the delta of the Niger about 1780). Cowries are attractive to look at and to handle, they are hard to break, and they neither fade nor wear. They are impossible to counterfeit, as King Gezo would tell the explorer Richard Burton, hard to hoard, and can be put to no other use. The only disadvantage to cowries as a unit of account was that they were cumbersome to transport; all the same, the camels, the donkeys, and the slaves of West Africa became accustomed to carrying them over the centuries.

After cloth, metals, and shells, weapons of various kinds (including swords) were probably the most important goods in the trade, though not before the middle of the seventeenth century: the Portuguese (and the Brazilians) were forbidden by law to export them. The Portuguese had done their best to avoid the exchange of any such arms for any African product (except for horses in the fifteenth century),* and officials had been posted in the harbour of Lisbon to check against infringements. This rule was in keeping with one of the strictest rules of medieval commerce, which was not to sell weapons to any heathen or infidel. Early in the eighteenth century, in 1718, a new Portuguese royal decree repeated the prohibition on the export of arms 'because these people are pagan'. Yet the Afro-Portuguese *lançados* liked to have good German swords to accompany their antiquated taste in dress, and some of these – cutlasses from Söllingen, near Düsseldorf, for instance – made their way to Africa. (Tradition had it that the art of making swords reached Söllingen from Damascus.) By the late sixteenth century handguns were reaching West Africa along the caravan routes from the Maghreb. One could obtain not only muskets but Turkish musketeers in Bornu, in what is now northern Nigeria, by the 1570s, and the great Moroccan army successfully sent south in 1591 to conquer the gold-bearing territories of the central valley of the Niger also included musketeers.

The Portuguese maintained their prohibition until the end of their participation in the slave traffic. They also banned the export of paper to Africa: for they realized that the pen could be mightier than the cutlass (who in their senses wanted Africans who could write?). But the arrival in West Africa of the Dutch, and even more of the English, altered matters.

---

* *Exchange of slaves for horses reappeared in the eighteenth century, according to the books of Nicholas Brown of Providence. Thus in 1765 his firm exchanged forty horses in Surinam for rum, sugar, molasses, and 'one negrow garl'.*

So did the fact that the then new flintlock musket was both a more effective and a more easily transportable weapon than the arquebus.

From 1650 onwards West Africans developed a taste for, and a habit of using, muskets. The 'Angola gun', a long-barrelled flintlock musket, soon dominated the market between Cabo Negro and Benguela. Short French guns with iron ramrods, 'decent sham Dane guns with wooden ramrods', and cheap 'Bonny guns' were all to be found in eighteenth-century African palaces. Willem Bosman wrote, about 1700: 'For some time, we have been selling many weapons. We are obliged to do this in order to remain at the same level as the foreigners and interlopers [that is, presumably, the English and the French], but I would prefer that this commerce had never started here and that, in the future, it would not be carried on.'[7] It was too late. By 1780 many African monarchies looked on muskets as necessary for self-defence, knowing that they could only be obtained by trading slaves.

In the eighteenth century the cargo of the Dutch Middelburgische Kamerse Compagnie was usually 14 per cent gunpowder and 9 per cent guns per slave. Perhaps 6,000–7,000 guns were imported into Luanda alone every year in the 1780s, but many more were exchanged for slaves on the Loango coast. London and Birmingham gunmakers both contributed substantially. Lord Shelburne, then secretary to Pitt the Elder, even thought in 1765 that 150,000 guns had been sent to Africa from Birmingham alone, thus enriching such businesses as the Quaker firm of Farmer and Galton in Birmingham, and Thomas Falkner and John Parr in Liverpool, not to speak of Richardson and Co., gunpowder makers at Hounslow, and Samuel Banner of Birmingham, who made swords as well as firearms. The total number of guns exported from Europe in the second half of the eighteenth century approached 300,000 a year. A Liverpool merchant with the appropriate name of Henry Hardware declared in 1756 that gunpowder and arms were a 'necessary part' of the cargoes of ships trading to Africa. It was often said then that a slave had the value of one Birmingham gun, just as in the fifteenth century a horse had bought a dozen slaves. But three guns per slave was a more normal equivalence; and in some places it was as high as five or six. The fact was that the price of slaves trebled between 1680 and 1720, while that of guns fell, so that several large well-armed states were able to develop along the Gold and Slave coasts: Ashanti and Dahomey above all.

Of course, the Africans had preferences, and it would appear that among the guns offered by English traders 'tower guns' (guns planned for a tower) were much the favourite, followed by round muskets, Danish guns, and 'Bonny muskets'. Further, the Bonny River area was probably the territory most anxious for guns in exchange for slaves: the Vili traders in Loango were also very interested, and it seems possible that as many as 50,000 guns arrived every year in those ports in the last quarter of the eighteenth century, to be dispersed throughout Central Africa.

No doubt these guns were often employed to protect agriculture, as decoration, and for trade, but their use in enabling the Africans who obtained them to gain more slaves was also considerable.

Many of the guns were inferior: King Tegbesu of Dahomey once complained that a consignment which he had bought from the English burst whenever they were put to use, and hurt his soldiers; and he made a similar complaint about French guns. After a visit to the Galtons' factory in Birmingham, Lord Shelburne made the considerate comment, 'What is shocking to humanity is that above half of them, from the manner they are finished in, are sure to burst in the first hand that fires them.'[8]

Gunpowder was also popular: 'an article on which there is the greatest gains of any in the trade', reported the captain of a Liverpool ship in 1765. In the 1770s and 1780s the quantity of gunpowder imported to Africa from Britain exceeded 1,000,000 pounds annually, and in 1790 it would exceed 2,000,000.

Alcohol was a great attraction for the slave trade, though, as happens in 'Western culture', it was also used to promote good bargains. West Africans had their own palm wine. Some peoples made wine from honey, or a kind of beer from millet. But palm wine became 'sour, so that it cannot be drunk after ten or twelve days', Jean Barbot wrote, and after 1440 most Africans, especially those in the Gambia region, came to prefer Portuguese wine, of which muscatel – sold in *pipas*, two hogsheads each and carrying 500 litres – was the chief attraction of the sixteenth century. Large casks of Madeira and port were also features of early slaving journeys. 'The Wolofs are great drunkards,' Valentim Fernandes noted in 1510, 'and derive great pleasure from our wine.'[9] Wine continued to be provided by the Portuguese, and when the Spaniards re-entered the slave trade in the late eighteenth century barrels of wine figured largely on the lists of the Cádiz Company, to be exchanged for slaves in Africa. The slave merchants of La Rochelle, Bordeaux, and Nantes always sent wine to Africa as part of their cargoes, La Rochelle being then a great producer, and even known as the 'city of Bacchus'.

But by the seventeenth century the distilling process, that great invention of Catalan Benedictines, came into its own in the slave trade. Spirits were especially sought after on long voyages. French 'brandies' played a great part, being often carried on Dutch and English ships. Bordeaux and La Rochelle were especially well placed to send wonderfully strong eaux-de-vie. Brandy was specially made, in Porto, for African sale. Barbot recalled that three 'anchors' of that brandy would buy for him a young male slave. The Brazilians made themselves popular, too, in Africa, with the sale of *gerebita* – a cane brandy, made from the foam skimmed off the second boiling of cane juice, which, being 50° or 60° proof, seemed superior to all other liquors. Alcohol constituted a fifth by value of Portuguese cargoes at the end of the eighteenth century; and each *pipa* of this Brazilian spirit might buy ten slaves. This liquor, the product of a hundred or more small stills in Rio or its surroundings, was Brazil's largest export to Angola. The records of the Middelburgische Kamerse Compagnie in the eighteenth century show that alcohol constituted over 10 per cent by value of the cargoes for slaves.

On the African side we hear of many rulers such as the King of Barsally (Gambia), of whom it was said, 'It is to that insatiable thirst of his after brandy that his subjects' freedoms and families are in so precarious a situation: for [being intoxicated] he very often goes, with some of his troops, by a town in the daytime, and returns in the night, and sets fire to three parts of it, and sets guards to the fourth to seize the people as they run out from the fire; he ties their arms behind them, and marches them to the place where he sells them, which is either Joar or Cohone [both were markets on the river].'[10]

In the late seventeenth century Anglo-Saxon rum began to replace brandy as a slave cargo, at least on English and North American ships. Rum was cheaper than brandy and was held to be less destructive to the liver. This era began when English interlopers, principally from Bristol, began to carry the new cargo direct from Barbados. Jean Barbot wrote that on his return to Cape Coast on the Gold Coast in 1679 he found 'a great alteration: the French brandy, whereof I had always had a good quantity abroad, being much less demanded, by reason that a great quantity of spirits and rum had been bought on that coast . . . which obliged them all to sell cheap'.[11] Frederick Philipse of New York stocked his ship *Margaret* with sixteen casks of rum, among other things, in 1698. In 1721 the RAC's factor at Cape Coast told his masters in London that rum had become the 'chief barter', even for gold. In 1765 two refineries were established in Liverpool specifically to supply slave ships with rum. There were also by then distilleries in Massachusetts and Rhode Island.

Once a direct slave trade began from North America to Africa distillers in the former territory began to see rum as one of their most important products. In 1770, just before the American Revolution, rum represented over four-fifths of New England's exports by value. About 11,000,000 gallons of Rhode Island rum were exchanged for slaves in Africa between 1709 and 1807, with about 800,000 gallons being the annual average marketed in the last few years before 1807. Each slave ship might carry fifty to a hundred hogsheads. An especially strong 'Guinea rum' was by then distilled in Newport for the Africa market. The rum trade on the coast of West Africa was by then a 'virtual monopoly of New England'.[12] In 1755 Caleb Godfrey, a slave captain from Newport, Rhode Island, bought four men, three women, three girls, and one boy for 799 gallons of rum, two barrels of beef, and one barrel of pork, together with some smaller items; and in 1767 Captain William Taylor, acting for Richard Brew of Cape Coast, bought male slaves at 130 gallons each, women at 110, and young girls at 80. By 1773 the price was higher: 210 to 220 gallons per slave was paid by the captain of Aaron Lopez's *Cleopatra*.

When the American Revolution interrupted the slave trade, the shortage of rum on the West Coast of Africa caused as much heartache among the European factors and governors as among the African dealers. Governor Richard Miles of Cape Coast had to make do with Caribbean rum for some years, but it was not the same thing. Richard Brew was equally distraught. The Africans with whom Rhode Island captains had traded, especially along the Gold and Windward coasts, had also become addicted to North American rum, a fact which gave captains from Rhode Island a remarkable advantage when the traffic recovered in the 1780s.

Rum was also used to pay African workers; in 1767 Captain William Pinnegar paid canoemen who took the slaves to their ship one and a half gallons each for their services.

Gin, cider, and beer also played their part in the slave traffic. Bristol merchants, for example, had for a time specialized in trading gin for slaves in the eighteenth century; the captain of the *Bance Island*, leaving Charleston for the River Sierra Leone in 1760, carried cider and 'Vidonia' (Canary Island) wine. Beer and cider, indeed, may have been traded more in the slave trade than the records suggest, especially on ships from Bristol.

Tobacco was another product with a long life in the slave business. The main producer of the tobacco which the Africans liked had been Bahia in the sixteenth century: 'Bahia had tobacco, and wanted slaves; the coast of Mina had slaves and wanted tobacco' – 'in rolls, not in leaf', wrote Captain Dampier in 1699. From 1644 this trade was authorized by Portuguese royal decree to be direct: a commerce which escaped the control of Lisbon. The Governor of Bahia in 1779, the Marquis of Valença, said, 'The truth is that the tobacco of Brazil is as necessary for the trade in slaves as those same slaves are for the maintenance of Portuguese America.'[13] This gave the Brazilians a near monopoly of the Portuguese trade with West Africa in the eighteenth century.

The reason for the permission was that this tobacco was not even of second-best quality, but of a poor grade, third class, as it appeared to the Portuguese; they called it '*soca*'. This tobacco's charm was accidental: it had been treated with molasses to prevent it from crumbling, and the Africans found it to their taste.

The commerce was among the most long-standing in the history of the Americas: it began in the late sixteenth century, and was still popular in 1800. Many Northern European captains bought this tobacco from Brazilian ships offshore to add to their own cargoes. French captains from La Rochelle or Nantes might even stop off at Lisbon to buy supplies of the tobacco for their own trading, though in theory the harbour master in Lisbon was supposed to refuse entry to them.

*

Even in the rum-laden vessels from North America, the *gerebita*-stocked ships from Brazil, and the textile-heavy vessels from Liverpool, there were always other items in a typical slave cargo: for example, handkerchiefs, smoked codfish, pots and kettles, silk hats and shaving bowls. Traders in Bristol, Rhode Island, would customarily obtain these and other things from general merchants in Boston, such as Samuel Parkman. These miscellaneous items – such as beads from Venice (or Dutch copies), silver bells, pewter, pretty bits of glass, and bracelets – were much in demand in Africa. The ships of the Cádiz Company often carried porcelain made in Seville in their cargoes to Africa in the 1770s: for example, '3,200 *docenas de loza de Sevilla*', that is, 3,200 sets of china, were carried in the *San Rafael*, one of the first slave ships to leave Cádiz after the end of the *asientos*, in 1766, under Captain Juan Antonio Zabaleta. In 1757, the slave ship from Nantes *Jeune Reine* carried twelve large rosaries, forty-eight chaplets, and 108 reliquaries.

Beads were probably the most important of these trivia. Yellow and green glass beads were desired by the Sapes in the sixteenth century, and so were red cornelians by the people of Calabar in the seventeenth. Daniel and Claude Jamineau – Huguenots in London in the eighteenth century, the most successful dealers in beads – perhaps did best out of this business. One slave merchant reported receiving a prime Negro in return for thirteen beads of coral, half a string of amber beads, twenty-eight silver bells, and three pairs of bracelets. In a good year in the late seventeenth century, about £3,000 worth of beads and glass would be carried by the RAC: bought in Amsterdam, and made in Venice. The Dutch soon began to make beads themselves, in more colours, sizes, and qualities than those from Venice, some loose, some threaded, white, large and small, crystal, garnet, some amber or coral, and speckled white. Beads made in Venice were however still being sent by the Portuguese to Angola in the late eighteenth century. Different parts of the African coast, of course, had different tastes: the rulers of the River Gambia wanted amber beads; in Whydah and the Niger Delta, small Venetian beads were required.

Some beads had always been known, and even made, in Africa. For example, the aggry bead of hard glass had apparently been made, from an early date, at Ife in the territory of the Yoruba.

In the earliest days of the Portuguese slave trade with West Africa Pacheco Pereira spoke of horses as if they had been the main item of cargo. The French traveller Lacourbe mentioned Arab horses being sold for twenty-five slaves each at the end of the seventeenth century. Barbot thought that horses sold for twelve to fourteen slaves; and the official Pruneau de Pommegorge, at the end of the eighteenth century, claimed to have seen an African buy a horse for a hundred slaves and a hundred oxen. At that time, horses were still close to being a currency, and a historian of Islamic Africa wrote that slaves and horses were the gifts most favoured by Muslim kings in the interior.

Non-slave transactions, of course, accounted for much of the income of traders to Africa: two-fifths in the case of the RAC in the late seventeenth century: redwood from the banks of the Rivers Sierra Leone and Sherbro; ivory, wax, hides, gum, and gold turned into guineas by the mint. These shipments were usually carried out by a direct trade to Africa and back. But in the late eighteenth century slaves dominated all the European nations' West African commerce. One English trader settled on the Gold Coast, Richard Brew, explained (from his fortress, Brew Hall) in 1771: 'Formerly, owners of ships used to send out double cargoes of goods, one for slaves, one for gold . . . How strangely things are reversed now. . . . We scarce see a ship go off without her complement of slaves. . . .'[14] Brew spoke, of course, as a self-confident trader of Anglo-Saxon stock at a time when Britain and North America still happily constituted a single and powerful Atlantic polity.

17

SLAVE HARBOURS I

*'Friends who meet occasionally remain
better friends than if they are neighbours –
on account of the nature of the human
heart.'*

King Caramança to Diogo da Azambuja,
builder of Elmina, 1482

THE ANCHORAGES where slaves were obtained in Africa over the centuries
extended from opposite the Canary Islands, all the way down the West
Coast of Africa, then round the Cape of Good Hope, to include Mozambique and Madagascar. These harbours all had eras of prosperity and of
decline, but from the beginning of the trade to the Americas in the
sixteenth century to the end of it in the nineteenth slaves from most
regions could always be found. For example, in a list given in the will of
Hernán Cortés in Mexico in 1547 slaves from both Mozambique and
Senegambia were present. Slaves from the same places were among those
at work on the steam-powered sugar mill Alava belonging to Julián
Zulueta in Cuba in 1870.

To a great extent, the Atlantic slave trade was also an affair of rivers:
those vast, marvellously beautiful waterways, which often rise in the very
heart of the continent, and which fascinated travellers from Ca'da Mosto
in the 1450s to Livingstone 400 years later, were the means of transport by
canoe of millions of black captives to the Atlantic, at the sight of which the
slaves were, of course, usually as surprised as they were fearful.

The northernmost zone of Africa used as a slave harbour was the
stretch of 500 or so miles facing the Canary Islands between Agadir and
Cape Bojador, which the Treaty of Alcaçovas of 1479 between the
Spaniards and the Portuguese had allocated for commerce and fishing
to the former. Here the Spanish colonists on the Canary Islands carried
out numerous raiding expeditions in the late fifteenth and early sixteenth
centuries, and made as well some negotiated purchases of slaves; and
from there several thousand Berber slaves were taken, either to work
thereafter on the Canary Island plantations or to be shipped to Spain

herself. But the Spanish fort near Cape Juby, the nearest point to the Canary Islands, had been overrun in the 1520s by the Berbers and by the late eighteenth century the ancient traffic which it had assisted was scarcely a memory.

The first zone of intensive trading for slaves was well to the south of this, at Arguin, in the bay beyond Capo Blanco. It was from here that Portugal first took slaves, mostly Azanaghi, in the 1440s. The Portuguese Crown built ten years later a polygonal fortress above a 200-foot cliff and in the 1560s it was still profitable to Portugal. Between 1441 and 1505 anything between 25,000 and 40,000 slaves were carried from there to Portugal, many of them being first exchanged 200 miles inland, at the oasis of Wadan, on the westernmost caravan route from sub-Saharan Africa to Morocco. The Portuguese, as it were, diverted these slaves from their regular route northwards.

The Spaniards took over Arguin when in 1580 they merged their empire with that of Portugal, only to lose the trading post in 1638 to the French, who demilitarized it, for the caravan route now ran much further to the east than Wadan, and the place had ceased to be the golden market which it had seemed in the days of Prince Henry the Navigator. In the late seventeenth century the least important of European slave traders, the Brandenburgers, seized Arguin and established a garrison of twenty to serve as an intermediate trading post on the way to their headquarters at Prince Town, on the Gold Coast. When the German interest waned the Dutch bought Arguin, but in 1721 they too lost it to the French, with whom it unprofitably remained. Such vicissitudes, with no consideration of the local people in what is now Mauritania, were common among European settlements in West Africa.

The French concentrated on expanding their trade, in ivory and gum as well as slaves, well to the south of Arguin, along the Sénégal. That river had seemed for a long time to be a West African Nile, because of the way the waters rose as a result of the heavy rains in the interior between June and October. The current appeared to carry the river a long way out to sea. The French trading port was protected by a large, mud-built, badly designed fortress, Saint-Louis, built on an island of that name at the mouth of the river. Around that edifice lay a cemetery, a hospital and, of course, a church, as well as a few brick houses for the small white or mulatto population, and also numerous huts in which Africans lived. There were in about 1780 600 French officials and soldiers and a few European-born residents, as well as an undefined number of mulattos: especially *mulatas*, '*les signares*' (that is, '*senhoras*'), descendants of Portuguese settlers of the old days, whose combination of good looks and commercial enterprise made Saint-Louis an attractive place to the visitor. Here the French Governor did all he could to ensure the effectiveness of the trade in slaves as in that of gum, which his countrymen obtained from the acacia forests along the north side of the river, and

which was required as a dye in the French calico-printing industry. He
issued austere regulations: for example, a provision stipulating that no
brandy be issued to those who did not attend evening, as well as
morning, prayer. The charm of this region for trading slaves was not only
that it faced the Atlantic but that it was also connected, by good waterways in savannah country, to more ancient caravan routes to the Maghreb
than could be easily tapped at Arguin. There were also both artificially
constructed and natural salt pans. The Bambuk gold fields were acces-
sible by water, 300 miles inland. The tropical forest did not begin till
about 500 miles to the south, and so the valley of the Sénégal was well
north of the tsetse-fly zone. Thus cattle could be bred there, and meat
dried, for use on Atlantic journeys. At one time in the early seventeenth
century the cattle imported did so well in this region that the export of
hides brought in more money than slaves did. The Portuguese, it may be
remembered, had looked on the River Sénégal as the dividing line
between the Moors and the blacks and as early as 1506 the German
printer and traveller who took the name Valentim Fernandes noted
that though 'one exchanges here very little gold', there are 'plenty of
black slaves'.[1] The statement could have been repeated at the end of the
eighteenth century.

The first slaves sold here were said to be Wolofs (Jolofs), the people
who dominated the territory. But, as in the case of most names in Atlantic
Africa, many who were called 'Wolof' in America would originally have
come from the far interior, from places well beyond the head of navigation on the Sénégal. The Wolof kingdom itself had probably been created
in the fourteenth century, and it had a nobility which was Muslim, with a
capital between the Rivers Sénégal and Gambia. The Wolofs for a long
time dominated the first of these rivers and its banks, and their tributaries
included a few monarchies on the coast (Walo, Cayor, Baol, Sine, and
Salum) as well as the more numerous Serers, their kinsmen, to the south.
The Portuguese made an unsuccessful attempt to place a Christianized
Wolof, Bermoi, on the throne of his ancestors, but already in the sixteenth
century the power of that kingdom was in decline; power, such as it was,
had passed to the subordinate princelings. Later, a number of rebels from
the Songhai empire on the Niger, the Mande and Fulani, made their way
towards the coast and established themselves in the hills of Futa Toro, just
to the south of the Sénégal where previously the Wolofs had been all-
powerful. Many of the slaves traded in the middle of the sixteenth
century were originally captured by these people, whose monarchy came
to be thought of as a new empire. By 1600 this 'Empire of the Grand Foul',
as the English liked to refer to it, seems to have extended over the whole
of the upper Sénégal, including the gold fields of Bambuk.

Other Fulani, known as the Mane, carried out similar advances, but
from the south-east, establishing themselves in the sixteenth century in
numerous little kingdoms along the coast which had previously, and

immemorially, been ruled by monarchs from the places concerned rather than by these Muslim interlopers.

These political changes took place without overt European influence; rebels from the Songhai empire would probably have sought power by the use of force and prosperity through the slave trade whether or no there had been buyers of Africans for the markets in the Americas.

The River Sénégal was difficult to ascend before the days of steam because of the current and a downstream-flowing wind. The most reliable way of travelling upstream was by cordelling, pulling the ships by tow from the shore, or by kedging, taking an anchor ahead in a canoe and pulling the ship up by the capstan. Usually this work was done by African labourers, the so-called *laptots*, the word being a Gallicized form of Wolof but coming to mean any African who worked with Europeans.

Like most European forts, Saint-Louis changed hands often, being captured by the English in 1693, then regained at the subsequent peace by France. The English captured it again during the Seven Years War, but lost it once more to the French in 1779. The English, when they were formally in control, left much trade on the Sénégal in the hands of Afro-French boatmen. Several ports on the river, such as Podor, a hundred miles inland, had from the early eighteenth century belonged to French privileged companies, such as Law's Compagnie des Indes, which established what was intended to be a monopoly there – not just for slaves (the Compagnie des Indes ceased slaving after 1748) but also for gum. To serve these interests, the French had an islet at Saint-Joseph, a mud-built fort on the upper river which could hold 250 slaves at any one time in its *captiverie*. This was a curb to the slave trade, for it set a limit for buying slaves during the dry season: to ꞏenlarge the prison would have been expensive; and to hold slaves without a prison was inconceivable. Slaves arriving in the 'high season' might, however, be shipped directly downriver to Saint-Louis, whose cellars could hold 1,000 slaves. Dr Christian Wadström, Chief Director of the Assay Office in Sweden, who visited Africa in the 1780s to 'make discoveries in botany, mineralogy, and other departments of science', thought that at least that number of slaves was shipped annually down the Sénégal. Several French independent traders had by then set themselves up in Saint-Louis on a permanent basis. Typical was Paul Benis, an illiterate sailor who learned Wolof and was a prosperous merchant by the mid-1780s. The Nantes-based firm of Aubrey de la Fosse also had a permanent manager in Saint-Louis, responsible for exporting 300 slaves each year.

The interior of this region, the Senegambia, was relatively stable throughout most of the era of the slave trade. Most people spoke the Fulbe language. English witnesses to the Privy Council's court of inquiry in London in 1788–9 described the absolute governments of this zone as being largely under the influence of the Moorish merchants inhabiting the desert on the north side of the River Sénégal. In the late eighteenth century, though, the old stability seemed to be breaking up, and there was frequent combat between the surviving ancient coastal monarchies and the Muslims, the latter seeking to expand, or consolidate, their power, as a means of avoiding their own enslavement, though in no way opposing the enslavement of infidels.

Few Senegambians saw Europe, or Christianity, as constituting a political threat between 1440 and 1780: especially in the first part of the eighteenth century, the external danger was from the Moroccans, with their powerful slave army and, after 1750, the Bambara, a black Muslim people on the middle Niger. Islam had been encroaching for centuries since, before the Portuguese had arrived, Senegambia had been a frontier region – not quite as Spain had been before 1492, since there were Muslim rulers who ruled traditional peoples. Enclaves of powerful and rich Muslim merchants also still lived in the centre of cities attached to ancient deities.

Crops from the new American continent, such as peanuts, tobacco, manioc, and, above all, maize, had been grown since the sixteenth century, but the irregular rainfall had prevented them from being culti-vated in any but a piecemeal fashion. Various kinds of millet, therefore, remained the staple food; cotton was grown, too, and cattle, sheep, and goats were plentiful.

The trader in slaves sailing south along the West African coast would, a hundred miles south of the estuary of the Sénégal, and before reaching the River Gambia, come upon a peninsula of high land rising gradually to two conical hills known as the Paps (like the Paps of Jura). This was Cape Verde, after which, to the south, the coast of Africa begins to turn slowly to the south-east, the observation of which caused the Portuguese at first to think that their long-desired circumnavigation of the continent would be easier than it turned out. The place was green enough in the rainy season, but otherwise yellow and dry. In the early days of the traffic, this territory, on which Dakar was built in the nineteenth century, was a big source of slaves for the Portuguese, and for some Spanish smugglers also.

In the archipelago off Cape Verde, the main island, Santiago, was for hundreds of years a depot for slaves. There were also large natural deposits of salt (on the island of Sal), as well as orchilla, a lichen, for dyes. In the sixteenth century cane, indigo, and cotton were grown, and cattle bred. The islands had greatly benefited from the fact that in the early days the coast of the mainland opposite had been looked on by the Portuguese Crown as a dependency of the archipelago. In 1582 the combined populations of the two most important islands, Santiago and Fogo, comprised over 1,600 Europeans, 400 freed captives, and nearly 14,000 slaves. But the islands declined in the seventeenth century, as did all this region, principally because the Islamic affiliations of the coastal peoples made slaves from there distrusted by both Spanish and Portuguese potential buyers. Nor were those *berberiscos*, or slaves, of 'the Levante' very dark, and Spanish planters preferred their slaves pitch-black. *Berberiscos'* introduction into the Spanish empire was repeatedly prohibited for religious reasons.

Still, there were in the eighteenth century many years of renewed success for the Atlantic trade from the Cape Verde Islands, particularly after the creation of the two Portuguese monopoly companies, founded on the recommendation of Prime Minister Pombal; even in the 1780s, after the collapse of those enterprises, slaves exported each year to Brazil may have amounted to about 2,200, most of them probably originally from far up the River Sénégal.

Uninhibited friendships between Portuguese and blacks from the earliest days had resulted in a mulatto population on the Cape Verde Islands, though there remained families who considered themselves white (few visitors shared that opinion). The families of most of the mulattos, *morgados*, had long before broken free of direct Portuguese control, even if formally they remained Catholics, and under the political direction of the enfeebled (unpaid) Portuguese Governor, who was in titular control of all the Portuguese possessions in northern West Africa. But that relative independence did not lead to economic success. In the early seventeenth century Praia, the main town on Santiago, was described by its own governor as the 'charnel house and dung heap' of the Portuguese empire; while in 1804 a North American trader would report that he found 'nothing but beggars from the Governor down to the lowest Negro'.[2] Spanish trading here for slaves as well as for local dyes was continuous, even though successive Portuguese decrees forbade it. Those Spanish illegal traders were popular because they had better goods to offer than did the Portuguese.

Just to the south of Cape Verde itself was a bay which Ca'da Mosto had looked on as beautiful, probably because in his day the palm trees came down almost to the beach. Here lay Gorée, a long island with two forts, Fort Saint-Michel and Fort Vermandois (later Saint-François), built on a gloomy basalt excrescence; in the eighteenth century it was an entrepôt as well as a centre of supplies so important that it gave its name to the main quay in Liverpool's new harbour, and to a poor parish in Bristol, Rhode Island, for a time one of the most prosperous United States slave ports. Gorée had been much prized by European captains from the seventeenth century onwards, for there they could find water from good wells, as well as food for the slaves, not to speak of an interpreter and information about the state of the markets, from European or mulatto traders, living in fine houses, surrounded by *mulata 'signares'*, pretty black girls. Dr Wadström said that in 1788 one of these mulattos told him that the slaves of Gorée held in *captiveries* below these fine houses numbered nearly 1,200, but the Swede thought, 'I have reason to believe that it was not so many.'[3] Among the permanent residents there were eccentrics: for example, the Chaplain in the 1780s, Father Demanet, who under the cover of founding a sisterhood of the Sacré Coeur had at his disposal the prettiest *mulatas* of the region.

Sheltered by the curve of the northern coast of Cape Verde above it, Gorée was easy to approach; there were no difficulties at the bar, the climate was pleasant, and the rainy season short. The sea nearby abounded in fish. Its history was similar to that of Arguin. Thus it was first occupied by the Portuguese. The Dutch seized it in 1617, and built a fort. The Portuguese took it back, after a siege, only to lose it again to the Dutch, who refortified it in 1647. The English captured it in the First Anglo-Dutch War during the reign of Charles II, the Dutch won it back, and it was then taken by Marshal d'Estrées and a French expedition. After this, France held Gorée, except for a period after 1693 when the English captured it, and for a few years during the Seven Years War, when the same occurred. But Britain returned it to France in 1763.

The French made Gorée into the most spacious of all the West African European establishments after Elmina on the Gold Coast. They had room to build the zigzag 'lines of fortification' recommended by great fortress architects in Europe, such as Vauban. Gorée was the first slave harbour of West Africa to use a real currency as opposed to iron bars or cowries: in this case, the silver dollar, or the Dutch twenty-eight-stuiver piece. The mercantile house of David Gradis *et fils* of Bordeaux was well established at Gorée, but so were others from the same city.

The large River Gambia was barely a hundred miles south of Gorée. By 1780 it had enjoyed for many generations a most varied character. It was lined, like most of those nearby, by mangroves, at least to the limit of the tides. It had a much smaller alluvial plain than the Sénégal but, all the same, was tidal for at least 150 miles upriver, as far as the Barkunda Falls; so the salt had a bad effect on agriculture on the floodplain of the lower river. The river had for a long time been fancied as likely to lead to an African El Dorado because at the market town of Cantor, 200 miles inland, Mandingo merchants would exchange gold found further inland still, at Bambuk; but the early promise disappointed. After 1586 no Portuguese ship seems to have sailed up to Cantor, the sale of gold being thereafter in the capable hands of Berber middlemen, who would gauge whether it was worthwhile selling to Europeans on the coast, or to merchants from the Maghreb.

The lower part of the river was in 1780 largely in the hands of Afro-Portuguese settlers, *lançados*, as they had been called in the fifteenth century, some of them deriving from the Cape Verde Islands. In the eighteenth century, these adventurers still managed several towns on the Gambia, particularly Tankula and Sika, which served as the headquarters of a far-reaching trade, in slaves above all. The furthest place inland where they were established was Cantor. Jean Barbot described dining lavishly but primitively there with one of these traders, a Senhora Catarina, in 1680. The 1730s constituted a peak in their trade. Then the central part of the river began to be controlled by Mandingo merchants, who had impressed the early Portuguese explorers with their intelligence and their energy; while the upper river was dominated by travelling Muslim scholar-merchants, known as 'marybuckes' (marabouts).

The low-standing previously uninhabited St Andrew's Island at the mouth of the Gambia was in 1651 bought from the local Ñomi chief by Baltic Germans sent by James, Duke of Courland. These representatives of the ancient Hanseatic League thought that possession of this place would give them control over the river, and so enable them to levy tolls on all those, European and African alike, who used the waterway. A fort was built out of local sandstone, a Lutheran pastor appointed, and cannon on the island were placed so as to command both channels to the north and south. The plan, as indicated earlier,* was to sell slaves to the Duke's colony in Tobago, but the scheme did not prosper.

The Dutch bought out the Duke of Courland in 1658, and the Baltic Governor left for Jamaica, 'with his goods and slaves', but the island was seized in 1661 by the English, who renamed it Fort James, after the Duke of York, the future James II, then Lord High Admiral. Thereafter the mouth of the river remained under the influence of Britain, though the French three times captured the island, devastated it, and then abandoned it, lacking the will to occupy it permanently. A Welsh pirate captured the island in 1715 and traded extensively; afterwards the RAC strengthened the fort considerably.

Fort James was lost by the British to the French in 1779. They did nothing with it, and even at the coming of peace in 1783 left it unoccupied. So the English resumed their control, and a governor was appointed by the Company of Merchants Trading to Africa (subordinate to the Governor of Cape Coast). The English had founded two factories a considerable way up the river, at Joar and Cattajar; the French, determined to keep a foothold on this waterway, had one at the Mandingo town of Albreda, begun in 1681 on the estuary. It was a constant source of annoyance to the British, for it took a lot of the trade of the river.

The whole of the region roughly known as Senegambia, which includes the modern Guinea-Bissau and Guinea, as well as Gambia and Sénégal, may have exported about 60,000 slaves in the course of the eighteenth century, carried in about 340 ships, so averaging about 176 slaves per vessel and 600 a year. This was probably a little less than the exports of the late sixteenth century.

Next in the slaving journey from north to south down the West Coast of Africa came a series of rivers, the Casamance, the Cacheu, and the Gebo, much used by the Portuguese from the fifteenth century onwards.

* See page 223.

At almost every estuary there was a trading centre for slaves, sometimes in direct contact with the Cape Verde Islands, sometimes acting as a clearing house for the bigger places, such as those on the two rivers, Cacheu and Gebo, both estuaries being guarded from the incursions of foreigners on the ocean by the offshore Bissagos Islands. This region remained Portuguese throughout the era of the Atlantic slave trade, though many Spanish captains came down here to buy slaves illegally. The French also were trading slaves quite successfully here by the late seventeenth century. There were two crumbling forts, *praças*, in the 1780s: one, built in 1591 at Cacheu, on the river of that name, was originally established by the *lançados*, and its defence in the eighteenth century seemed merely to consist of a wooden palisade, garrisoned by raga-muffins; the second, on the estuary at Bissau, on the mouth of the modern River Corubal, founded in 1587, had been formidably restored in 1641, and refortified by the Maranhão Company in 1766 at the cost of many lives and of continuing enmity from the local Pepel people. Cacheu in its time 'bustled as the centre of the Hispano-Portuguese slave trade', and had a population of about 500 Europeans and 1,000 blacks in various degrees of dependence. There were a few dependent garrisons (*presidios*) elsewhere, mostly staffed by Cape Verdians, convicts from Portugal, or *lançados*. Cacheu was for a time in the seventeenth century also a major boat-building place, since the local *cabopa* tree yielded planks said to resist shipworm; and even the despised mangrove had a fibre which could be used for caulking. When Barbot visited this river in 1680, he found that it was healthier than the Gambia, and that there were there about 400 huts or houses, mostly made of 'clapboards in the Portuguese style', as well as four Catholic churches.

When the Portuguese started trading slaves from the River Cacheu, in the fifteenth century, the mixture of peoples on the river (Balanta, Pepel, Djolas, Casangas, Banhuns) – some Muslim, some not – made the area a slave traders' paradise, for wars were frequent and could easily be stimulated. Slaves were still being traded in the late eighteenth century, as they would be in the mid-nineteenth.

In contrast to Cacheu, which always remained Portuguese, Bissau fell more and more under the influence of the French in the eighteenth century: but in 1755 the new Portuguese company formed for the devel-opment of northern Brazil, the Company of Grão-Pará and Maranhão, again began to export slaves on a large scale. The company was well endowed and could afford to devote much effort to construction. This enabled Bissau to enjoy a bout of prosperity which continued even when the monopoly company, having carried 28,000 slaves out of the two rivers in a little over twenty years, lost its licence in 1778.

Offshore, the Bissagos Islands had always been a good source for slaves, since the military-minded indigenous people there had long expe-rience in raiding the mainland, twenty-four men using seventy-foot canoes (*almadias*) hewn from silk-cotton trees. After a while, however, the peoples whom these islanders had been wont to seize, such as the Beafadas or the Pepels, became themselves skilled slave traders. Indeed, the Beafadas gained such a reputation for slaving that they were fancifully accused by their neighbours of introducing the idea into the world.

By the eighteenth century the Bissagos Islands were dominated by mulattos or octoroons, and they customarily retained there a substantial store of slaves, always ready for sale when a slave ship should come. Since the European demand at that time was overwhelmingly for men, and since the peoples on the islands raided one another indiscriminately, the islands had a large female majority, almost as if here at last were the famous islands of the Amazons so much sought by the early Spanish conquistadores. Much of the actual trading on these islands was done by women.

The two Rivers Pongas (Pongo) and Núñez – the 'rivers of the south', between Bissau and what became Sierra Leone, in what is now the state of Guinea – were also reliable slaving harbours from the fifteenth to the eighteenth centuries; in the latter era, they may even have been responsible for a tenth of the total African exports of slaves, the best trading year apparently being 1760, at the time of the consolidation of the theocratic Muslim state of Futa Jallon in the mountains inland, which sent thousands of refugees fleeing to the coast. But, then, the zone had always been a major slaving territory. On this river there was once a rare example of an African ruler seeking to prevent or at least to resist the slave trade; but the alliance of a few villages formed by this individual – Tomba, a Baga – failed, and he was himself swept into slavery.[*]

In the eighteenth century several European companies or individuals owned islands at the mouth of one or another of these rivers. For example, in 1754 Miles Barber of London bought one of the Los Islands (Idolos), close to the mainland (off what is now Conakry), planted rice, and built a trading post, with '*deux captiveries*', on the east coast. The water was good, and the fish abundant. Barber had another eleven establishments on the West Coast of Africa, and probably himself was selling about 6,000 slaves a year to the New World in the 1780s, 4,000 from the Los Islands, as well as beeswax, ivory, and some dyewood. His establishment was sacked by Americans during the War of Independence, but immediately after the peace his company started selling slaves again, a French captain, Rousseau, being the biggest buyer, on behalf of the Sénégal Company. Three thousand slaves were packed off from here to the French West Indies annually in the 1780s. In the late eighteenth century, when ships from North America began to come often to Africa, Barber's establishment was one of their favourite ports of call.

Only a short way south of the Los Islands lay the River Bereira, where about 1780 a most remarkable woman, Betsy Heard, had established

---

[*] *For Tomba's future history, see pages 392 and 423.*

herself. She was the daughter of a Liverpool-born entrepreneur who had come to the Los Islands in the mid-eighteenth century and an African (the daughter of a slave), and after a conventional English education near Liverpool Betsy returned to the town of Bereira, where she remained the unofficial queen of the river till the end of the century. Her success as a dealer in slaves was due to the Islamic jihad in Futa Jallon. Bereira itself was seized by an Islamic people, the Morians, who sought to force the population to convert to Islam. This did not affect Betsy Heard's commercial success – after all, Muslims never shrank from business – and in the 1790s she was known as one of the most successful traders. Next to her, to the south, was the River Scarcies, where a Mande-speaking people, the Susu, who had fled from the upper Niger in the late Middle Ages, had set up a series of trading stations principally concerned with the salt trade to the Niger. But they had slaving interests also.

Another example of a private exploitation of an island in this region was Bence Island, called after a Squire Bence of the late seventeenth century, one of several islands in the estuary of the River Sierra Leone, which had been an English post for several generations. Most of these islands were for many years infested by pirates. In the 1670s, though, Bence Island was established as the local headquarters of the RAC. Its buildings were destroyed in 1728 by Africans, led by a Luso-Senegambian, and the place was then maintained for a few years by slavers from London. One of these, George Fryer, sold the island in 1748 to the London Scottish syndicate of Sir Alexander Grant, Augustus and John Boyd, father and son, and Richard Oswald, all of them, as we have seen, rising, internationally active merchants from Scotland who had become established in London – alongside John Mill and John Sargent, both of London; Sargent was one of London's largest buyers of East Indian goods and, therefore, one of the largest providers of cargoes to the slave traders.

The fortification of Bence Island was a square enclosure, with all the guns facing the sea, and the English traders relied for security on a 'good understanding with the natives'. Grant and Oswald gave the island a luxurious central building with 'a very cool and convenient gallery', even establishing nearby a golf course, served by African caddies dressed in kilts especially woven in Glasgow, on which waiting captains could play an unusual version of their national game. About thirty or forty white clerks, and their assistants, mostly Scotch and some of them relations of the owners, managed Bence Island in its heyday, under the direction of another Scot, James Aird. The place was easily captured by the French in 1779, who reduced it to 'a heap of ruins'. It was returned at the Peace of Paris (Richard Oswald was a British negotiator in Paris, but he seemed to be uninterested by then). After Oswald's death, in 1784, his nephews, Alexander and John Anderson of Philpot Lane, London, ran the island till the early nineteenth century, selling slaves on a large scale at least till 1800, Danish buyers figuring prominently among the clients in the last days.

Bence Island was a 'general rendezvous' of slaving from the 1760s onwards. The captives were bought from African kings with no difficulty, most of them being obtained some miles up the River Sierra Leone, and held for a time in 'outfactories' established on the Banana Islands, on the Los Islands, and near the Sherbro River. In these places European or mulatto middlemen had often settled: not only descendants of Portuguese *lançados* but English versions of them. There was, for instance, James Cleveland, who had settled on the Banana Islands, to the south of Sierra Leone, and Harrison and Matthew who, like Miles Barber, were to be found on the Los Islands. Cleveland ruled ruthlessly in his little kingdom in the late eighteenth century, with many Africans terrified of being seized by him in compensation for unpaid debts and then sold as slaves.

These middlemen would assemble slaves beforehand and so could offer captains the benefit of being able to buy slaves quickly. That in turn would reduce the time that they had to spend on the African coast. French merchants from Honfleur, Le Havre, and Rotterdam frequented Bence Island, but the main clients were the proprietors who sent their own ships from London to pick up 400 or so slaves, and set off for North America, Grenada, St Christopher or Jamaica, where several of them had plantations. Florida was another market after the English gained the place in 1763.

There was once a ferocious rebellion here: 'Armed only with the irons and chains of those who were so confined, the slaves audaciously attacked the lock-keeper, at the moment he made his entrée to return them to their dungeon after a few hours of basking in the sun. But this bringing on themselves the close fire of the musketry ... which they probably neither saw nor contemplated ... may have contained their only wish, a relief from the misery by the hand of death. ...'[4]

A fort was also built on the nearby but more swampy York Island. The region was from an early time full of mulattos of English ancestry. A note to the Royal African Company in 1684 reported that there 'every man hath his whore'; and the Prussian Otto von der Grüben noted prudishly that most officers, including the Governor, had 'concubines', who gave them children.[5]

The dense forest of the Guinea coastland began near what is now Conakry. Here the first landmark to the south was the estuary of the River Sierra Leone (so named by the Portuguese, apparently because of the lionlike mountains behind) which, despite treacherous rocks at the mouth, afforded the best harbour on this largely surf-bound coast. It had, therefore, been one of the main ports of call for ships bound for the southern Guinea coast, and even for India, from the early sixteenth century. In consequence, it had become also a headquarters of *lançados*. In canoes they would search the nearby creeks and rivers for slaves, and have them all available in the estuary of the Sierra Leone. Sometimes the urgent demands of the trade entailed long journeys into the interior. A headland to the south of the estuary known as Cape Tagrin marked where John Hawkins had bought his slaves in 1564. The main African peoples here were the Bulom, the Temne, and the Limba on the coast, and inland the Susu, the Fula (Fulani, Fulbe, Peul), and the Loko. Each of these peoples was independent, and for all of them rice was by the eighteenth century the staple crop. They provided a little gold and a good deal of ivory to Europeans. Here, too, the RAC had had a trading post till it was overrun in 1728 by men belonging to the powerful mulatto trader José Lopes de Moura, allegedly the grandson of a Mane ruler and the dominant African in the region of Sierra Leone in the eighteenth century. Afterwards, no permanent European trading post was established. When the cities of Futa Jallon, where the River Sierra Leone rises, were violently converted to Islam, several of the coastal peoples adapted, and Muslim traders established themselves in most of the ports. Anyone who owed them anything and did not pay was seized and sold as a slave. Thus in 1751, partly as a result, Captain Nye reported to the RAC that there was a 'prodigious trade' in slaves in the locality, especially at George Island.

To the south lay the River Sherbro, whose banks were swampy and thus hard to travel up; it was scarcely surprising that there should have been many small monarchies, Sherbro (or Bulom) people near the coast, Mende inland. On the River Sherbro, the English began to establish themselves as early as the 1620s, though Wood and Company, the first to be interested, were concerned not with slaves, but with the export of hard red camwood for making cabinets. In the eighteenth century there were already many half-African, half-English families; and by 1700 slaves were extensively traded at the mouth of the river, just short of Cabo Monte. The earliest English settlers had built a small fort, a stone house inside an earthwork, but that was in ruins by 1726. They were then being helped by useful mulatto intermediaries, the Caulker family, descendants of Thomas Corker of Falmouth, the RAC's last factor on the coast, who had married a lady from the locally famous Ya Kumba family, Senhora Doll, the 'Duchess of Sherbro' to the slave captains whom she entertained. She and her descendants established a small standing army of free blacks with whom they exercised control over a large tract of land on the riverside; they held slaves for long periods in camps until they could make an effective sale. Here, too, was that 'Black Liverpool' (the second place so named – the other being to the north, near the River Pongas), where John Newton once refused to buy a woman slave because she was 'long breasted'. In the mid-eighteenth century, Nics (Nicholas) Owen, from Ireland, set himself up on the banks of the Sherbro River as an intermediary, trading slaves from a large boat in an attempt to revive his family's ruined fortunes. Later, Henry Tucker, another formidable mulatto entrepreneur, a descendant of a John Tucker who worked for the Gambia adventurers in the 1600s, with his seven wives, his retainers, his silver, his riches, and his plantation, on which he grew food to sell to slave captains, dominated the region. Later still, on one of the Plantain Islands, at the mouth of the Sherbro River, the villainous Mrs Clow, 'P.I.', the African wife of an Englishman, severely ill treated John Newton while her husband was away buying slaves.

The British government in 1785 thought of relieving its country's overcrowded prisons by sending convicts to Sierra Leone. The prisoners were saved from this fate by Edmund Burke, who spoke violently against sending the men concerned to what he assumed would be certain death in West Africa. The supposedly more salubrious site of Botany Bay in Australia was accordingly selected as an alternative.

The river south of Sierra Leone was the Gallinas, which was not much used for trading slaves in the seventeenth and early eighteenth centuries, but by the 1780s was already the centre of operations of several famous Portuguese traders. There were several towns established on the banks of the river, and the only commerce seems to have been trading slaves, held in barracoons, in each of which some 500 or 600 slaves could be assembled, till their sale to the Europeans.

Further south again, at Cabo Monte (Cape Mount), a Dutch fort had been built in the early seventeenth century in order to protect some experimental sugar plantations established there. But the local Africans destroyed this settlement, and neither from there nor from the next door Junko were there slaves to speak of; ships stopped there only for indispensable supplies. The trade could, however, be taken up again between Junko and Sestre (Cestos), the centre there being the tiny port of Sanguin. Sestre was a very old slave market: the Portuguese in the 1480s had bought slaves there for two shaving bowls a head, a price which by 1500 had increased to five.

This zone, as far as Cape Palmas, was known as the Pepper or, occasionally, the Grain Coast, so named since peppercorn, or paradise grain, malaguetta, was grown there. That product had been much sought after in the fifteenth century, but by 1780 interest in it had long ago evaporated. A few slaves could usually be obtained in this stretch of land, chiefly by kidnapping, for the peoples there were reluctant to trade, and attacked Europeans. The population in these densely forested coasts was anyway small. Another impediment to trading, of every nature, was an absence of harbours. The coast was surf-bound, and a strong easterly current made it hard to land. All this territory had been a favourite place for French pepper traders in the sixteenth century, before they began to trade slaves.

The next important line of shore was the so-called Ivory Coast, between Cape Palmas and Cape Three Points. It received the name, which it retains in the twentieth century, because of the quantity of elephants' tusks obtainable there in the sixteenth. Cape Palmas, where the coast of Africa turns eastwards till it reaches the Bight of Biafra, was the territory of the Kroomen, known to be good linguists and expert sailors. European captains often hired them for boat work or as interpreters. There were several lagoons near the town known to the French as Cap Lahou (earlier, Cap de la Hou and, after 1787, Grand Lahou, to distinguish it from Half Lahou and Petit Lahou), which were a promising source of slaves during the eighteenth and early nineteenth centuries. The trade in ivory was in the 1780s considered more important, for it was held to be 'the best in the world'.

The local people, the Avikam, sold numerous slaves, ranging from individuals who were already slaves inside Avikam society to others who came from a long distance away in the hinterland, whom they themselves had bought with salt or European goods. The Avikam obtained, by theft or purchase, as many female slaves as they could, in order to boost births, so as in turn to be able to sell the children. This seems to have been the only zone in Africa where such a policy was coherently pursued. The region of the Ivory Coast produced about 3,500 slaves a year in the 1770s, the largest embarkments being from Drouin, St-André, and Cavailly.

The Dutch fort at Axim was about thirty miles short of Cape Three Points. Here the Dutch maintained cotton plantations – and they also did so at Shama, a little further on. For a time they even had sugar plantations, at Butre, from whose product, briefly, they made rum.

The Gold Coast, the modern Ghana, lay between Cape Three Points and the River Volta. The coast, which ran gently east-north-east in its general direction, was, as far as the modern city of Accra, hilly, with rocky knolls near the shore. Further inland there were higher mountains, which could often be seen from out at sea. In the eighteenth century there were along the Gold Coast a hundred European trading posts and fortresses, of different sizes and pretensions, the most important being those of the Dutch. This was perhaps because there was in this zone an almost complete absence of dense forest, which only began again to the east of the Volta, near Allada. Throughout most of the era of the slave trade there were about a dozen small kingdoms here, with the capitals a little way inland. These monarchies remained masters of the territory into which the Europeans did not dare to penetrate far. The kings, however, had made arrangements so that by the late eighteenth century much of the coast had been divided between the English, the Dutch, and the Danes. The Portuguese had by then lost all their interests here, and the French never succeeded in establishing themselves, though they tried to, in the west, at Assini. The slaves exported were the product of the many small wars between the coastal states, probably as a rule not the consequence of conflicts undertaken specially to obtain them.

This remarkable line of European forts had mostly been built of mud and brick, the latter material brought out as ship's ballast in great quantities. Only the Portuguese brought out stone – for Elmina, in 1481. Most of these forts were obtained from the African local rulers on perpetual leases, in payment of an annual rent, even though some were bought by, or given to, the Europeans; and, in a few instances, the Europeans had merely imposed themselves. The reluctance of the African ruler Caramança, near what became Elmina, to make a contract with the King of Portugal is well known; others probably shared his views, even if those were not recalled by a great Portuguese chronicler such as Barros.* The companies concerned would seek a monopoly of the local commerce and, in return, guarantee to defend the African town against attack. The arrangements often irritated the Africans, but they accepted them as the price of being able to trade and receive the European goods which they coveted. Occasionally, as in the case of a threatened attack by an internal empire, such as the Ashanti, that guarantee counted for something. The Europeans' possession of these places did not mean that they were the masters of the country. Africans controlled the communications of the garrisons with the surrounding country, and they alone knew the roads through the tropical forests to the northern markets, which the Europeans never risked because of the threat of sleeping sickness, which was so easily contracted in the jungle.

In these forts, a melancholy if brutal social life, characterized by excessive alcohol, bell-ringing for periods of commerce and of guard, ignorance of local conditions, slave labour, and the fear of death, was carried on. Palm oil and palm wine soothed many anxieties, as did rum, brandy, and gin. Of course, there were occasional happy times: thus when the first Dutch Governor of Elmina went home in 1645 he gave a party to say good-bye in the garden of the castle, and invited the prominent local Africans, as well as some ships' captains and his own staff. They 'were entertained with ten casks and some bottles of wine, a cask of brandy and three cows . . . and, by the evening, were merry and each went off to his house in great satisfaction'. There were also prostitutes: every village from the Ivory Coast to Allada had 'three or four whores', noted the Dutch geographer Olfert Dapper.[6]

Till the late seventeenth century few slaves were shipped from the Gold Coast, for the European traders there were concerned with gold and ivory. The slave trade of Elmina continued to indicate an import of captives, not an export, till 1700. Between about 1480 and 1550 over 30,000 slaves had been carried there in Portuguese ships, chiefly coming from São Tomé or from one of the five 'slave rivers' of the Bight of Benin. Some of these were put to work in the rivers of the forests behind Elmina, to look for gold, and others were treated by their African masters as just another item of merchandise, and sold to the ever-hungry northern slave

---

* According to Barros, Caramança asked the Portuguese to leave and simply to go on trading as they had always done, for 'friends who meet occasionally remain better friends than if they are neighbours – on account of the nature of the human heart'.

markets. Some such slaves may even have reached the Mediterranean, having begun their slave life in São Tomé under the auspices of Portugal.

But by 1700 that particular African slave trade was in decline. By 1740 slaves on the Gold Coast intended for the Americas had replaced both gold and ivory as the most important item of export.

The biggest fort here was still Elmina, which the Dutch had, of course, captured from the Portuguese in 1637. It was the African head-quarters of the Dutch West India Company, and there lived the company's African Director, surrounded by a staff of about 400 civil servants, soldiers, sailors, and craftsmen, mostly eating salted food, suffering from malaria or the 'penitential worm', and served by about 300 'castle slaves'. The region of Elmina, unlike the upper Guinea coast, had in Portuguese days been relatively free of those *lançados*, the half-caste intermediaries who penetrated the interior: 'The Mina negresses pregnant by white men', the best historian of Portuguese race relations wrote, 'seem to have indulged in abortion or infanticide; and mulattos were much less numerous than in Upper Guinea.'[7] Yet there was by 1700 a town at Elmina of about 1,000 Africans, living in the shadow of the castle.

The original designs for the castle, by Diogo da Azambuja in the fifteenth century, had long ago been modified by Portuguese, as well as Dutch, accretions. Yet Elmina was, according to Jean Barbot, 'justly famous for beauty and strength, having no equal in all the coasts of Guinea. It is built square, with very high walls of a dark brown stone, so very firm that it may be said to be cannon-proof.'[8] In the late seventeenth century a hundred white soldiers, many of them Germans, served there, alongside a hundred black ones. The great cistern beneath the castle, which Azambuja had built, still supplied water to all trading captains who needed it. Elmina was, however, no longer such a great entrepôt as it had been in the sixteenth century, when so many African merchants had used to gather there in order to buy the new things which the Portuguese had brought in their fine ships: including slaves from the island of São Tomé. Neither the Portuguese nor the Dutch had been able to employ the castle, overpowering though it was, as a means of dominating the neighbourhood: the power of the governor scarcely extended beyond the city. From the 1660s onwards, as has been mentioned, Brazilian captains, who carried the much sought after molasses-dipped tobacco direct from Bahia to their own favoured coast of Dahomey and Whydah, were required by the treaty to leave 10 per cent of their cargo, including slaves, with the Dutch at Elmina.

In the hinterland behind Elmina lay the kingdom of Ashanti, which had come into being at the end of the seventeenth century, created around a market place, Kumasi, 120 miles inland, ideally placed between the north-going inland trade routes and the coast. The Ashanti, like the Fanti on the coast, were descended from a people named the Akan. For a long time the Dutch had treated with, and assisted, the Ashanti's previous suzerains, the Denkyera. Then about 1701 they saw that the military advantage now lay with the Ashanti, who in their capital of Kumasi had adapted themselves to the use of guns; and the Dutch began to court them, sending an emissary to their monarch, the Asantehene, that same year. A Dutch representative remained in Ashanti for most of the eighteenth century; and an equivalent Ashanti stationed himself at Elmina, being the broker for all local trade, for which he received a regular income.

In the eighteenth century the Ashanti kings were providing a substantial proportion of the European slave exports from Elmina, certainly over 1,000 slaves a year in the 1770s. The Dutch at Elmina were still the closest European friends of the Asantehene, and one of the latter even sent fourteen of his children to the Netherlands to be educated. The Ashanti, as well as the Dutch, were keen to keep the roads open through the jungle from their capital to Elmina and Axim (the second most important Dutch fort) on the coast, because there were many gold-bearing reefs on the way; and the 'great road' to Elmina was the most important line of land communication in West Africa. Along that road there also travelled slaves and slave traders, as well as the Ashanti collector of the *kostgeld*, which the Dutch had agreed to pay to one or another local potentate from as early as 1642, and to the Asantehene after 1744.

By the end of the eighteenth century the most effective traders in these territories were the *tapoeijers*, or Afro-Dutch mulattos. Officials had been allowed by the Dutch West India Company to trade on their own account from the mid-century, and gradually came to use *tapoeijers* to find slaves for them. After 1792 *tapoeijers* would be allowed to trade on their own account, and two of them, Jacob Ruhle and Jan Niezer, were for a short time the richest and most powerful men on the coast, the latter becoming the recognized agent of the Ashanti in Elmina. (Niezer's father was Johann Michael Niezer, of Würzburg, who came out to the Gold Coast as a surgeon to the Dutch West India Company. The boy Niezer worked with a well-known merchant of Vlissingen, Looyssen, who exchanged manufactures with him in return for slaves, and subsequently started himself selling Africans to the Americas: his first ship took a cargo of 125 to Demerara in 1793.) Jan Niezer and his wife, Aba, a Ga, lived in a grand house which he named Harmonie.

The biggest English fort was that at Cabo Corso ('Short Cape', corrupted as Cape Coast), founded by the Swedes under Henrick Carloff in 1655. This was the best landing place on the whole coast, for nowhere else could ships reach so close to land. After changing hands often, belonging for short periods to both the Dutch and the Danes, it was finally captured in 1664 by the English, who enlarged it. The new fortification consisted of outworks, platforms, and bastions; with apartments for the governor-in-chief, the director-general, the factors, clerks, and mechanics, as well as the soldiers. There were magazines, warehouses, storehouses, granaries, guard rooms, and two large water tanks, or cisterns, built of English brick and local mortar. 'Slaveholds' were established to confine 1,000–1,500 captives: 'The keeping of the slaves thus underground is a good security against any insurrection', Jean Barbot wrote.[9] There were also vaults for rum, not to speak of workshops for smiths, armourers, and carpenters. The fort was guarded by seventy-six cannon in the late eighteenth century and there was in the armoury a substantial quantity of small arms, soldiers' coats, blunderbusses, buccaneer guns, pistols, cartridge cases, swords, and cutlasses. The castle had gardens capable of producing plantains, bananas, pineapples, potatoes, yams, maize, cauliflowers, and cabbages, and it also had ponds of fresh water. There were attractive walks, planted with orange trees, limes, and coconut palms. There was, of course, a chapel.

Yet the English seemed for many years the poor relations among the Europeans: they had too few men, their forts were shabby, and they had too few goods. The government's subsidy, paid to the Company of Merchants Trading to Africa after 1750 to maintain the English forts, was also too small. European visitors to Elmina could not fail to notice the grandeur in which the Dutch Governor lived, in comparison with life in the English headquarters.

The RAC employed a chief factor, of whom the most intelligent was Sir Dalby Thomas, who had wished to establish a real colony at Cape Coast; and the most interesting was the engaging Nicholas Buckeridge, who became the lover of the corpulent Queen of nearby Winneba. After 1750 the Company of Merchants Trading to Africa named Cape Coast's commander the 'Governor' and a succession of experienced men followed one another in control: Thomas Melvill being the first, David Mill the richest, and Richard Miles the strongest. At the end of the century the Governor was the curiously named General Morgue, whose correspondence about the slave trade with the Graftons of Salem fills many pages in the letterbooks of that firm.

The English also built a large new fort in the 1750s at Anamabo, twenty miles to the east of Cape Coast. Here – uniquely, as it happens – was a specifically designed cellar prison for slaves waiting to be carried overseas, which, for all its gloomy atmosphere, did have the merit of maintaining a constant temperature.

The main Danish fort in the late eighteenth century was Christiansborg, in Accra, with a garrison of about thirty-five officers, some of them Germans. The Danes had bought the site in 1661 from the paramount local king for the equivalent in goods of a hundred ounces of gold; and nine subordinate trading posts to the east depended on it. The architect was Christian Cornelissøn, who designed as fine a castle there as was to be seen in all European Africa. But 'there was a most vile harbour' for landing, and ships had to anchor a long way offshore to the east. Even there, the anchor had every day to be raised because the bottom of the sea was strewn with sharp rocks. For a time in the late seventeenth century this fortress had been in Portuguese hands, but in the next generation the place was firmly Danish. Accra had the name in that era of being one of the best places to slave, for the small local wars were continuous, so that many prisoners were available.

The governors of all these European forts, English as well as Dutch, Danish as well as Brandenburger, traded slaves privately (and illegally): 'Governor Melvill to his death,' it was reported, 'and the other officers of the committee, during his command, carried on the Negroe trade, and sent them from Africa to America for their own accounts, without the least reserve or restraint; also . . . Governor Senior, and the officers under him, did the same.'[10] Richard Brew, an Irishman, became Governor of the English fort at Anamabo in 1761, when he already had a slave ship at sea, the *Brew*, fitted out in Liverpool: he would eventually set up as a private trader in a spacious house near Accra which he named Brew Hall ('Castle Brew'), and provided it with mahogany panels, chandeliers, and an organ. His friendship, based on a deep appreciation of the merits of Newport rum, was so close with the Vernons of that city that they once envisaged taking over Anamabo as a North American trading station. Richard Miles, when Governor of another British fort, at Tantumquerry, was in close touch with the French dealers. In six years he bought and dispatched to the French colonies at least 3,000 slaves. He later became Governor of Cape Coast, where he had seven children by his 'wench', but in the 1790s, leaving those descendants on the Coast of Africa, he established himself as one of the most important slave merchants of the city of London.

These forts depended on supplies from home for even simple needs: recall, for example, agent Bradley's request in 1679 from Cape Coast for 'Timber Baulks, Planks, Deales, Sparrs, all sorts of nayles, locks, Crow[bar]s, Shovells, Pitch, Tarr, and Plaister of Parris, Rigging for shippes . . . sheathing board, Twine, some small anchors, Pick Axes, and workmen, [such as] bricklayers, smiths, armourers, carpenters, and chirurgeons to be sent to other places and a mate for this; Borax for soldering . . . 30 or 40 sheets of good lead . . . two pairs of bellows for the smith and hides to mend them, four dozen of good sheepskins for sponges, and staves for ditto, four or five dozen of sayle needles, 1,000 of ten inch tiles . . . quills' ink, penknives, two quire paper books, and other and good writing papers, wax and wafers [as well as] parchment skins for drums heads. . . .'[11]

One of the difficulties for captains when trading in these territories for slaves and other cargoes during the seventeenth and eighteenth centuries was that they did not always know whether their home governments were at war with one another. But even when they were not the French and the English were always quarrelling: thus in 1737 the French Captain Cordier on the *Vénus*, of Bordeaux, began to trade at Anamabo,

and stayed there twenty-one days, despite the bitter opposition of twelve
English captains present. Then two coastguard ships of the English
arrived, and the English commander took 'his launch to board the *Vénus*
to oblige it to leave, saying that that port was not for them, that his
countrymen had paid large fees to the King of Anamabo to trade there,
and that the French had paid no such taxes. . . . Captain Cordier was
forced to raise anchor and leave the harbour. . . .'[12]

Given the European investment of men and money on the Gold
Coast in the eighteenth century, it is surprising that there should not have
been more serious efforts to try and encourage the development of agriculture. If plantations could only have been organized to grow sugar,
coffee, rice, and cotton, it might have been possible to concentrate slaves
to work there, rather than carry them across the ocean by such extraordinary efforts. Thus Sir Dalby Thomas made the imaginative suggestion
that cotton, pepper, and 'mineral' plantations might be founded, in 1705;
his Dutch colleague Willem de la Palma went further and sent to
Suriname for 'twelve experienced blacks to teach the slaves here the
method of the cultivation of sugar cane'.[13] But these puny efforts were
unsuccessful: no sooner did the slaves set to work than they escaped.
Barbed wire, that fine invention of the mid-nineteenth century, which
would have prevented such flights, had not yet been devised.

18

SLAVE HARBOURS II

*'At 5 a.m. at Aqua landing; it was a fine
morning, so I go on board the Cooper and
come ashore. I make an agreement for two
slaves with captain Osatam. After 9 o'clock
at night I send 5 of my people to go to
Yellow Belly's daughter, the mother of Dick
Ebrow's sister, to stop one of my house-
women from giving [any slaves] to the ship,
because her brother gave one of my fine
girls, which I gave my wife, to Captain
Fairweather, who did not pay me. . . .'*

Diary of Antera Duke, 17 June 1785,
in Old Calabar

BEYOND THE SWAMPY ESTUARY of the River Volta the coast continued in
a generally eastern direction, but as far as the modern city of Lagos
and beyond there lay a series of lagoons, which enabled almost continuous transport, and much fishing, by canoe. Behind the lagoons lay a
savannah-like landscape, extending almost to the sea, allowing the
breeding or at least the use of cattle, horses, goats, sheep, chickens, guinea
fowl – and, after the arrival of the Portuguese, pigs. (Dogs were also
fattened and eaten in this region at the end of the seventeenth century, as
they had been in ancient Mexico.)

All European travellers noted both the large population – the inhabitants of the towns were said by Spanish missionaries to be so numerous
in 1660 that 'the squares, streets and roads form a continuous ant-hill' –
and the 'prodigious number of palm trees', from which palm oil (from the
fruit) and palm wine (from the sap) derived (though the indigenous
Africans here preferred to drink beer made from sorghum).

At the end of the eighteenth century this coast was dominated by the
powerful King Kpengla of Dahomey, whose state had been built up by
his father and grandfather. The story of the family's capture of authority
is intimately linked with that of the slave trade, which was in the 1780s by

far the biggest economic activity of the kingdom. Kpengla's grandfather
Agaja, the creator of the country, was described by a French slave captain
as 'slightly bigger, and having wider shoulders, than Molière'; Kpengla's
father, Tegbesu, who sold over 9,000 slaves a year, chiefly to the French
and Portuguese, was estimated as having an annual income in 1750 of
about £250,000 – a figure which far exceeded that of the richest merchants
of Liverpool or Nantes. (The richest English landowner might expect, in
the eighteenth century, an income of £40,000 to £50,000.)[1]

There had been almost no slave exports from the so-called Slave
Coast in the sixteenth century. Instead, seawater was boiled to make salt,
smiths created iron weapons, beads were made, and both cotton and
palm leaves were, from very early days, woven to make clothes. About
1550 the Portuguese began to trade there, and by 1600 regular commerce
had begun, with some merchants established more or less permanently:
Pieter de Marees, the first Dutch traveller in the region, wrote, 'The
Portuguese do a lot of trade here.'[2] The Dutch themselves were on this
coast by the 1630s, and set up a trading post. The Danes, the Swedes, and
the English followed – the Company of Adventurers founded a trading
post next to the Dutch one – while the French eventually set up their base
at Whydah.

This territory was inhabited by two peoples, the Aja and the Yoruba,
both of whom had established a multiplicity of kingdoms, some with a
capital on which depended a number of subject towns and hamlets,
others being autonomous cities. The Aja occupied the coastal stretch of
land, and their main political entities, each with a recognizable monarch,
were Allada, or Ardra, about forty miles inland; Popo and Whydah on the
coast; and Dahomey, whose capital, Abomey, was about 120 miles inland.
Allada was the 'father-state' of all these places, though its kings usually
found it impossible to control their nominally subject cities once the Europeans arrived.

The peoples of this region were sophisticated. They had a currency
based on cowrie shells ('They prefer them even to gold,' Barbot wrote),
and they traded salt, cotton, wooden carvings, and some iron products at
large markets.

Yet further inland lay the Oyo empire, the main Yoruba monarchy, to
whose ruler, the *alafin*, the Aja had been for a time subservient. The Oyo,
also known in the seventeenth century as the Ulcumy, or Lukumi, as the
slaves sold there were designated in Cuba, came into being in the
fifteenth century, and their rise was marked by the skilful use of cavalry.
The Oyo supplied Allada with slaves, receiving European goods in return
– muskets included, once the Dutch and English had appeared. Unlike
the coastal polities, they had always supplied slaves to their Arab neighbours to the north.

The European trading posts were never here as formidable as those
on the Gold Coast. In 1670 the French were refused permission by the

King of Allada to build a post in the 'European fashion', since that would have enabled them to instal cannon and so become masters of his realm, as the Portuguese had become on the Gold Coast through the establishment of Elmina (that monarch had been educated in a convent on São Tomé). The modest European trading posts for which permission was granted were obliged to set themselves up inland and were thus incapable of resisting African attacks very long should they occur. Most Europeans, therefore, traded from ships, which were sometimes anchored permanently in lagoons in unhealthy conditions. The monarchs of Allada tried to ensure that the Europeans concentrated all their commerce in their kingdom. They failed, as completely as the Capuchin monks who visited them in the 1640s failed to turn them into Christians.

The Dutch reached Allada first among the Europeans, but seem not to have traded in slaves. Then the Chevalier Dubourg and François D'Elbée led a French expedition to that city in 1670 and persuaded the King to supply four shiploads of slaves a year, the loading to occur at Offra or at Jaquin, on the coast.* Dubourg died in Allada, but D'Elbée carried the slaves to Martinique on his vessel, the *Justice*, of Le Havre. Thereafter the slave trade prospered, though Allada's raids in search of captives in the interior were sometimes obstructed by the Kings of Dahomey, and though the Aja never found as many slaves as did their subordinate neighbour, the King of Whydah. Further, the people of Allada became accustomed to selling slaves in lots, so that the European buyers had to take good and bad slaves together, whereas elsewhere slaves could be bought singly, and so could be carefully selected.

Whydah was by 1700 de facto independent, and its ruler was soon priding himself on being able to produce several thousand slaves a year. An important part in the rise of the place had been played by the Danish adventurer Henrick Carloff, who established a trading station which he named Pillau just outside Whydah, in the hamlet of Gléhoué (Glehue), on behalf of the French (the original Pillau, now Baltisk, had been his birthplace on the Baltic Sea near Königsberg). Here France maintained from 1671 its only permanent sub-Saharan outpost: a reflection of the popularity of the slaves from the port. Pillau was managed by about eleven Europeans, who supervised the work of a hundred Africans. It was a more elegant emporium than most European lodges in West Africa, for orange trees were planted in the large courtyard, onto which looked a fine dining room. Had it not been for the malaria and the yellow fever, Whydah would have been 'one of the most delicious countries in the universe', wrote the French writer Prévost, for 'the green of the fields, the grandeur of the trees and the multitude of the villages formed a charming perspective'.[3] Outposts were also established at Whydah by the Portuguese (São João Bautista), in the 1670s, the Dutch in 1682, the English the following

---

* *Offra was often known to the Europeans as Little Ardra (Allada).*

year, and even the Brandenburgers in 1684. All these newcomers enjoyed an unusual kind of free trade. The King kept the place open to ships of all flags, and there was an enlightened agreement, after 1704, that the vessels of one country should not interfere with those of another, even if the two were at war.

The Slave Coast was soon sending about 16,000 slaves a year to the Americas, about half the African total at that time. The Portuguese especially prized slaves from Whydah who, they thought, had a magic nose for knowing where gold deposits were. In fact, much of the success of the gold mines of Minas Gerais depended on the resilience, if not the magic, of slaves from Whydah, mostly obtained from merchants representing the Oyo empire, and most of them being from the Yoruba linguistic group.

Petley Weyborne, who having been an interloper from Bristol became an agent of the RAC, described the English establishment about 1700: 'This morning I went ashore at Whydah, accompanied by my doctor and purser, Captain Clay, the present captain of the *East-India Merchant*, his doctor and purser, and about a dozen of our seamen of our guard, armed, in order here to reside till we could purchase 1,300 slaves. . . . Our factory lies about 3 miles from the seaside, where we were carried in hammocks which the factor, Mr Joseph Peirson, sent to attend our landing, with several arm'd blacks that belonged to him for our guard; we were soon trussed in a bag, toss'd upon negroes heads and conveyed to our factory . . . low near the marshes . . . a very unhealthy place. The white men sent to live there seldom return to tell their tale: [it] is compass'd about with a mud wall, about six feet high and, on the south side, is the gate; within, is a large yard, a mud-thatched house, where the factor lives, with the white men; also a store house, a trunk [a prison] for slaves, and a place where they bury their dead white men, called, very improperly, the hog-yard; there is also a good forge and some other small houses. . . .'[4]

As for payment, Whydah merchants, including the kings, were especially interested in importing cowries as a price for the slaves: 'Each ship brings its thirty to sixty or even eighty thousand weight', wrote a French official 'Pruneau de Pommegorge' in the late eighteenth century.[5]

A third harbour of interest, after Allada-Offra (later Allada-Jaquin) and Whydah, was opened at Popo, and for a generation or more the people there vied with those of Whydah and Offra in promoting the slave traffic. A Danish surgeon, Paul Edmond Isert, was much impressed by the three-storey mansions belonging to the African slave merchants which he saw at Popo. Dutch, French, English, and Brandenburger lodges were soon to be found there.

Though the Europeans were relatively peaceful in the harbours of the Slave Coast, their new African friends were not. Sometimes the princes employed European mercenaries, and sometimes the Europeans interfered in local politics to ensure a succession to one of the thrones of the ruler who they thought would collaborate best with them. That occurred in 1671 even in Allada, as well as in 1703 in Whydah (when the Director of the English fort, Peter Duffield, imposed his candidate). The issue behind these conflicts was often the requirement to kidnap as many neighbours as possible, in order to fulfil the demanding export opportunities. For a time, Allada was successful in persuading the other cities of the region to exclude Whydah from the slave-raiding territories in the north, and the foreign representatives all had to report that captives had become scarce between 1714 and 1720. The French, English, and Dutch collaborated to send weapons to assist Whydah against Allada, but the King of the former, the youthful Huffon, was unable to put these to good use. After a while a modus vivendi was established, Allada allowing enough slaves through to maintain Whydah's prosperity.

To the north-east of these feuding but wealthy little ports lay two inland kingdoms: the Weme (Ouémé), on the river of that name – the only river of any significance here; and Dahomey, with its capital at Abomey, whose territory was separated from the coastal zone by an extensive swamp known as 'the Lama'. It does not seem as if there was a kingdom at all in Dahomey before about 1625, and the place may have been founded by an exile from Allada. In the early eighteenth century King Agaja, one of the most formidable African rulers with whom the Europeans came into contact,* and his captains were 'great admirers of fire arms [that is, muskets] and have almost entirely left off the use of bows and arrows'.[6] The Dahomeyans also had a high standard of discipline in comparison with their neighbours. Much blood was shed, and prisoners were regularly sacrificed with an almost ancient Mexican sense of dedication.

In the early eighteenth century Agaja conquered his near neighbour, the King of Weme, and so gave notice that his was a power to be reckoned with. That led to an appeal for help from a defeated candidate in a struggle for succession in Allada and that in turn led to Dahomey's conquest of that monarchy too. Bullfinch Lambe, the representative of the RAC, was present at the final battle for Allada, and saw 8,000 captives being counted afterwards, among the bodies, where, 'had it rained blood, it could not have lain thicker on the ground'.[7]

Some of the other local leaders (for example, the King of Jaquin) then submitted to Agaja who, after careful preparations stretching over three years, turned on Whydah, at that time on the brink of civil war. King Huffon put up no resistance and fled; 5,000 people were killed, and over 10,000 enslaved. All the European posts were sacked, and their directors imprisoned. The Dahomeyans, it is true, were next year defeated by the Oyo, for whose cavalry, despite their firearms, they were no match. But they retained what they had won on the coast on condition of paying a tribute to their own conquerors.

On the throne since 1708.

The trade in slaves from Whydah was in the doldrums for several years after the Dahomeyan conquest. The exiled Whydah people, the Dahomeyans, the Oyo, and the Europeans all struggled for control. The English and French commanders were both killed. But soon after concluding a treaty with the Oyo, King Agaja revived the commerce of slaves with the Europeans from Whydah. That he wanted to keep all the captives on whom he could lay his hands in order to work them on his own farms appears to be a myth: what he seems to have disliked was having to treat with middlemen to deal with the Europeans. Nor did he want his own Dahomeyans enslaved. The King did interrupt the old deliveries of slaves from the far interior and tried to control them. But he sold the captives whom he obtained in war on a considerable scale, and began again, with alacrity, the business of raiding the territories to the north, which his predecessors in control of these ports on this so-called slave coast had also carried out. The slave trade from Dahomey was not the royal monopoly which it is sometimes represented to have been – many chiefs were also permitted to trade – but King Agaja until 1740, and then his son King Tegbesu, and his grandson King Kpengla after him, all played a decisive part in this commerce. New trading posts were built, and the old rhythms of trade were revived on a larger scale than that before 1725. Hundreds of Dahomeyans assisted in the regulation of the slave trade, being usually paid in cowries.

Europeans of all the slave-trading nations would thereafter often embark on the regular journey from Whydah 120 miles inland to the King's palace at Abomey, to observe the royal celebrations and the human sacrifices, to admire the exhibitions of silks and textiles, or to stand aghast at the place set round with skulls 'as thick as they can lie one by another', while their agents negotiated at the coast.

These monarchs of eighteenth-century Dahomey imposed law by brutality: they cut off the head of anyone who stole a single cowrie. The kings carried out periodic arbitrary, ruthless, and effective purges of provincial officials. Tegbesu and Kpengla were also surrounded by an ample court of soldier-women ('Amazons', according to most Europeans), and were tyrants to be placated and not fought, a perennial subject of fascination for European traders.

In the late eighteenth century Dahomey went through a depression as a slave-trading centre, and the kings tried many expedients in order to revive the commerce. For example, since the monarch and his family had come, like so many other Africans, to appreciate the Brazilian market more than any other, attracted by that sweet if third-rate Brazilian tobacco, King Adandozan (Kpengla's successor) sent an emissary to Bahia in 1795 to suggest that his realm should become the exclusive source of supply of slaves from the coast of Mina for Brazil. The Governor of Bahia rejected the idea, not only because he thought that monopoly would increase prices, but because he was fearful of the political consequences of bringing many slaves from the same place, all speaking the same language. The King then sent an emissary to Lisbon, only to receive the same polite rejection of his ideas. Despite the rebuff, Whydah recovered and in the 1790s was once more seen as one of the most important slaving centres, especially favoured by the last generation before the French revolution of slave captains from Nantes. The incompetent English representative at Whydah, Lionel Abson, wrote in 1783 to Richard Miles, the Commander at Cape Coast, 'Since I have been on the coast, I have never seen the quantity of Frenchmen arrive that has lately.'[8]

By that time a new port, Porto-Novo, had opened on the extreme east end of this windward coast, on the sea, not the lagoon, and there a branch of the old rulers of Allada managed to establish themselves. Another group of Allada exiles set themselves up at Badagry, as a result of the initiative of a Dutch freelance captain, Heinrik Hertogh, the founder of the city. Both Porto-Novo and Badagry were prosperous in the late eighteenth century, though the latter was destroyed in 1784 by the King of Dahomey. Popo continued to be a resort of exiles from Whydah, and sometimes these outcasts attacked their old home – once, in 1763, being repelled only thanks to the intervention of the British Commander of the trading post, William Goodson. Beyond, originally a colony of Benin, to the east, lay Onim, the island on which the modern Lagos stands. Onim was an important slave port in the late 1780s, obtaining most of the cargoes from merchants from the lagoons to the west. The freedom of action of these ports, despite Dahomeyan power, was due to the protection of the Oyo empire.

That enterprise, indeed, always in the background of Dahomeyan politics, was now the principal supplier of slaves to all these ports, using a large market, Abomey-Calavi, as its chief trading centre. Abiodun, the Emperor (*Alafin*) of the Oyo after 1774, had been a trader in potash before his accession, and looked on the new city of Porto-Novo as, as he put it, his own 'callabash'. By the 1780s it was in consequence more prosperous than Whydah. The Oyo not only ensured that the merchants there had prisoners of war to sell but also bought slaves from their Arab northern neighbours and resold them to their southern ones, including the Dahomeyans, whose independence was thus shown to be becoming as limited in commerce as it had been for so long in politics. The Oyo still dominated the region, directly or indirectly, at the end of the eighteenth century, despite repeated efforts by the Dahomeyans to escape their shadow. Only in the 1790s did Oyo power begin to decline, and the *Alafin* went so far as to ask for the assistance of King Kpengla of Dahomey in certain military activities, a move which was to prove his and his people's eventual undoing.

Perhaps 2,000,000 slaves were exported from this stretch of coast between the River Volta (Little Popo) and Lagos-Onim between, say, 1640 and 1870, about half (900,000 or so) being carried by Portuguese or

Brazilian traders, with the British (say 360,000), the French (perhaps 280,000), the Dutch (say 110,000), the Spaniards, and the North Americans following behind.

Next in his journey along the slave harbours of Africa the late-eighteenth-century traveller would come to the five 'slave rivers' encountered by the Portuguese in the late fifteenth century, of which the largest, the Rio Fermoso, or Benin, led to the city and kingdom of that name. That monarchy, apparently of Yoruba origin, had been, through its port of Ughoton, a major exporter of slaves at about the turn of the sixteenth century. This was the territory where the Florentine merchant Bartolommeo Marchionni had from the King of Portugal a lucrative licence to trade slaves in the late 1480s. But Benin was not a major slave zone after 1530, and the *Oba* (King) tried to cut off the traffic completely in 1550. Cloth, an excellent pepper, and elephants' tusks then became the main exports. The Portuguese had earlier tried hard to convert the *Oba* of Benin and his subjects to Christianity, but neither the Franciscans in the sixteenth century nor the Capuchins in the late seventeenth met with more than politeness.

Because of the risks to health, including the currents and the sand-bars, this part of Africa was considered a dangerous zone by European seamen. One famous rhyme went:

> *Beware and take care of the Bight of Benin;*
> *Few come out, though many go in.*

The beautiful River Benin (Fermoso) itself seemed especially hazar-dous. That was where, appropriately, the first English captain to go to the place, Thomas Wyndham, had died in 1553.

Another Northern European, the Dutch traveller Pieter de Marees, about 1600 thought that the King of Benin had a great many slaves, and that it was the women's task to carry water. But they may have been more servants than slaves and anyway they were not for sale, or at least not to Europeans. The success with which Benin avoided trading in slaves after 1550 showed that such restraint could be exercised if an African king really willed it.

In the late seventeenth century some slaves began to be sold again by the *Oba* or his chiefs to the Portuguese. In the 1720s his slaves were also being bought by Dutch, French, and eventually and above all, English traders, when the prices of ivory and cloth had fallen. The *Oba* even removed his ancestor's sixteenth-century ban on selling males. Though he maintained the trade as a royal monopoly, the business fell into the hands of the *Ezomo*, a grand vizier of the kingdom. This official, sitting in his throne room encrusted with cowries, supported by his own captives, and who had his visitors' feet washed in a large brass bowl before presiding at, for example, a yam festival, including human sacrifices, was henceforth the potentate with whom the European traders had to deal in Benin.

The French, led by the Burgundian captain Jean-François Landolphe – who had long experience of the slave trade and had worked for the Compagnie de Guyane – set up a short-lived factory at Ughoton, on the lower Benin River, in 1778, for trading goods (ivory and cloths) as well as slaves, and then established another more effectively near the river's mouth in Itsekiri territory in 1783. (Landolphe brought home to Paris a nephew of the *Olu*, or King, of the Itsekiri in 1784.) But yellow fever took its toll of the French traders; Landolphe was outmanoeuvred by Liverpool shippers; and he never fulfilled his plans of making Benin a port where he could buy 3,000 slaves a year.

There was a strong English interest in this territory by the mid-eighteenth century, some of the demand being satisfied by Itsekiri traders. Thus five ships left Liverpool in 1752 to buy 1,280 slaves in Benin.

All the same, neither the *Oba* nor his *Ezomo* organized a major slave-trading network in the style of Ashanti or Dahomey (or, as will be shown, Calabar), and they were never able, because unwilling, to satisfy European demand.

Beyond Benin, on the Rio dos Forcados, 'the swallowtails', was a principality called Ode Itsekiri, ruled by a family of princes who were related to those of Benin. They had in the 1560s begun to take the place of Benin as a supplier of slaves to São Tomé and then to the Americas. The Itsekiri, like their neighbours and rivals, the Ijo, were known for their long, powerful war canoes, with which they dominated the lower waters of the Benin River, and with which they ensured a regular supply of captives to sell to whomsoever would buy from them.

Even worse than the rivers of Benin in terms of health was the Rio Reale, the Bonny River to the English, on the Bight of Biafra, for in the late eighteenth century the death rate from malaria, at least on the British ships which slaved from there, was over ten a voyage, twice as bad as in any other slave region. The captains were trading in the estuaries of the delta of the great Niger, here to be seen also in the form of the Cross River and the Old Calabar River, between which innumerable creeks provided an elaborate network of waterways into the interior. The entire territory was most unhealthy. The nineteenth-century traveller and entrepreneur Macgregor Laird would call the lower reaches of the Niger 'one extensive swamp, covered with mangrove and palm trees [from which] the fen-damp rose in the mornings, cold and clammy to the skin, like the smoke from a damp wood fire'.[9]

The Bight of Biafra was an important zone of slave trading as early as 1700: at least 4,500 slaves a year were exported in 1711–30, and perhaps a third of all the slaves carried by Britain in the eighteenth century came from these ports, as did possibly a quarter of all the slaves carried to

North America. The main anchorages here were Old Calabar, at the mouth of the estuary (called Iboku by the Efik); Adiabo, ten miles up the River Calabar; and Mbiabo, on the Cross River (Curcock to Europeans). Lower down, near the sea, was Duke Town, called after its leader, Duke Ephraim, which later became the core of New Calabar. Beyond were Bonny and Opobo, still rather small cities at the end of the eighteenth century.

The Portuguese knew of the Cross River and its tributary the Calabar but they did not trade there, and in 1600 the Dutch traveller Pieter de Marees advised traders to avoid the place, because there was nothing to be gained, with always a danger of being wrecked. There was, indeed, a large reef in front of the Old Calabar River. But by the 1600s the English had learned to avoid that, and were trading extensively, buying slaves for Barbados, as well as monkeys and ivory for England. By 1700 so many English ships were 'gone to old Calabar' that other Europeans knew that 'you cannot have trade there'. The slaves of Calabar were considered the least satisfactory, since they were rebellious. In the course of the next hundred years the place became, however, with its many rivers, one of the most favoured of slave regions, for the French and Dutch as well as the English.

The Efik traders, an Ibibio-speaking people, had moved south-east to these waterways in the seventeenth century (according to legend because of a quarrel over an axe); when they matured from fishermen to become traders, in slaves among other things, they founded a powerful commercial brotherhood, known as the Egbe. The leaders of this association, realizing the importance of having a trading language with the Europeans, developed an engaging version of English, which used the words of that tongue with a syntax based on Ibibio. James Barbot, a slave captain at the end of the seventeenth century (a brother of Jean, the writer), spoke of these leaders as Duke Aphrom (Ephraim), King Robin, King Mettinon, King Ebrero, and even Old King Robin. The titles were allusions to leaders rather than monarchs. Most slaves sold in Old Calabar in the seventeenth century came from the relatively near at hand Ibo hinterland but, a hundred years later, they were often bought at fairs many miles inland. The strong preference for exchange was for copper bars to begin with, then iron ones. For a time, copper bracelets constituted a kind of currency. Some of the sons of these traders visited England and, in consequence, schools were established at home in Old Calabar for 'the purpose of instructing . . . the youth belonging to families of consequence'. Material for building houses was also obtained from Europe, and one black African trader called his house Liverpool Hall: Antera Duke, one of the slave traders, noted in his diary in the late eighteenth century, 'After 10 o'clock, wee go chop for Egbo Young house, Liverpool Hall.'[10]

The most famous of the Efik slave traders about 1780, Eyo Nsa (Willy Honesty to the English), was not in fact an Efik, for he had himself been brought to Old Calabar as a slave. He became a successful general in the Efik service, especially in fighting the pirates at the mouth of Ikpa Creek. He married an Ambo princess and in later life became rich as a slave trader. He, himself, had an immense household of slaves, whom he sold when the price was right.

Imports from Europe were seized on in the region of Calabar as wonderfully helpful to the local economy. Old wooden agricultural implements could be tipped with European iron and so made more efficient. The salt-boiling communities recognized that they benefited from the import of brass 'neptunes' (large basins) and the imports of textiles were most useful to a people which had previously produced little. On the other hand, in this zone the population declined constantly from the 1690s till 1850, presumably as a direct consequence of the trade in slaves: the most serious decline in population in Africa in these years. (This whole territory was, however, one of the few areas of Africa where there was always a shortage of land, so a drain of slaves may have been advantageous.)

The sacred Aro shrine at Arochuku, the so-called Long Juju, was the focus of slave dealing in this part of Africa at the end of the eighteenth century. The oracle was offered slaves as fees or fines, and the priests then sold them. This trade came to be dominated by mercenaries, the Akpa, their power based on firearms, the first such to be used inland of the Bight of Bonny.

An English traveller, John Adams, said that here was a 'wholesale market for slaves, as not fewer than 20,000 are annually sold here; 16,000 of whom are . . . Heebo [Ibo], so that this single nation has not exported less than . . . during the last twenty years . . . 320,000'.[11] He probably exaggerated. More important, he failed to realize that the majority of the slaves sold by the Ibo at Bonny were brought from the interior, and were, therefore, of many origins. Nor did he notice the even more interesting characteristic of the slaves exported from the Bonny River: that they included the highest percentage of females in all West Africa.

In 1789 some account of how the trade was managed here was given to the British Privy Council by Isaac Parker, an English shipkeeper who jumped ship in Duke Town in 1765. He told how he had gone on an expedition to find slaves with a dealer named Dick Ebro – it was a journey of kidnappers, pure and simple. His African friends armed some canoes and went up the river, 'lying in the bushes in the day when they came near a village, and taking hold of everyone they could see. These they handcuffed, brought down to the canoes, and so proceeded up the river, till they got . . . forty-five, with whom they returned to New Town. . . . About a fortnight after, they went again, and were out eight or nine days, plundering villages higher up the river. They seized on much the same number as before, brought them to New Town, gave the same notice and disposed of them as before among the ships [that is, the slavers].'[12]

This zone reached its peak as a slave exporter in the years 1711–20, when there were exports of over 150,000. Exports continued high throughout the eighteenth century, never falling below 70,000 in a single space of ten years. The territory's importance in the Atlantic slave traffic continued well into the nineteenth century. Canoes, sometimes eighty feet long and carrying 120 people, were the chief instruments of the traffic.

Beyond the delta of the Niger, the coast of Africa at last begins to turn south again and there, in the Cameroons, in the late eighteenth century, Liverpool merchants from England pioneered a new branch of the slave trade. Further on, and well to the south, the River Gabon, just north of Cape Lopez, was also coming into full activity as a slave region in the 1780s. This area seemed to the Reverend John Newton to possess 'the most humane and moral people I ever met with in Africa', perhaps 'because they were the people who had the least intercourse with Europe at that time'. But off the coast the Dutch had for a long time used the island of Corisco (the word in Portuguese means 'flash of lightning') as a trading centre, though not specifically for slaves.

In the late sixteenth and early seventeenth centuries the main slave emporium in this whole region was São Tomé, that tragic island-prison of 400 square miles nearly 170 miles off the mainland. The equator runs through the island's southern tip. For generations, slave traders from there had dominated the Niger Delta, the Cameroons, and the northern Congo. From there the Hispano-American markets were accustomed to buying slaves whom they spoke of as *casta de São Tomé*', *'novos'*, *'Terra Nova'*, or merely *'Congos'*. São Tomé was, by nature, a delightful place, for it was dominated by a high, wooded mountain, the vegetation was lush, and fresh fruit (including pineapples and grapes) and vegetables were always available. Numerous lemon trees grew in the valleys, and there were plenty of wild turkeys, geese, ducks, and even partridges, as well as fish. In its capital were four churches. For a short time in the seventeenth century, the Danes had a lodge there. But the place remained Portuguese, and there was always a Portuguese governor. For many generations slave ships provisioned there and took on water. Prices were high, but São Tomé was too convenient to be avoided.

The nearby smaller island of O Príncipe (so called because the taxes of the island had been settled on the heir to the throne of Portugal) had similar benefits, if on a more modest scale. Its water was good, and it contained innumerable monkeys and two churches.

All these territories, like the Cape Verde Islands, had created as a result of continual contact between the Portuguese and the Africans a thoroughly mulatto population.

To the south, on the mainland, there were various minor trading places, such as Cape St Catharine, and then several harbours belonging to the Vili Kingdom of Loango: Mayumba, the large harbour of Loango itself, and the two smaller ports, Malemba and Cabinda, beyond. The charm of the Loango kingdom for traders was that despite Portuguese opposition the *maloangos*, the strong monarchs of the Vili kingdom, were able, over many generations, to maintain free trade to all the Europeans (much as the kings of Dahomey had done). Thus the Dutch had established a trading post at Mayumba and at Loango in the late sixteenth century, and the French were the favoured customers in the eighteenth. At first these Europeans had concerned themselves with ivory, redwood, copper, and palm cloth, but the Dutch began to trade a few slaves in the 1640s and by 1670 the Vili traders were finding slaves more profitable than ivory. The Dutch West India Company was that year carrying 3,000 slaves a year from Loango. The King, the *Maloango*, now entered into the commerce with a will, usually obtaining slaves along the rivers to the south, and dealing with the Europeans through a special official, the *Mafouk*, in each of his main ports. The slave traders of Loango were soon competing successfully with those from Luanda, and obtained many slaves from the same sources. The success of the region was such that the British decided to establish a fort there, and appointed a governor, Captain Nurse Hereford, who left England for Cabinda with nine staff and six soldiers in 1721. The fort was built, but it was destroyed by the Portuguese with the help of Congo soldiers. Despite this setback the British colonies, including those in North America, were probably getting a fifth of their slaves from this region in the eighteenth century. In the 1760s, and again in the 1780s, energetic Portuguese governors of Angola tried to prevent this by sending expeditions there; but the soldiers sickened, many died, and the remainder were expelled by a French squadron in 1784.

In the 1770s a Portuguese journey of inquiry sent up from Luanda reported that there were seventeen ships on the Loango coast: nine French, four English, and four Dutch. Twenty thousand slaves were said to be carried from there by these carriers every year, but 14,000–18,000 would be a probable annual average between 1765 and 1790. Many of the slaves were Monteques or Quibangues, who had been seized in the far interior and carried to the coast along waterways earlier developed for trade by copper and ivory merchants.

The Vili state of Loango was in decline in the late eighteenth century, partly because of the adverse effects of the slave trade. This commerce had opened up many opportunities for merchants outside the old oligarchy which had once run the place, and the *Maloango*'s power declined in relation to that of the port officials, the *Mafouks*. A symbolic change occurred. In the past when a *Maloango* died he was succeeded by his sister's son. But a new ruler could only be chosen when the late *Maloango* had been buried. In the late eighteenth century, the last *Maloango* was not buried for fifty years, so no successor was installed. The kingdom began to split up into small entities.

To the south of the Vili Kingdom of Loango the more ancient and long-Christian Kingdom of Congo was now a weak monarchy, dependent on Portugal, with a large mulatto community in all the important towns. Congo had exported many slaves in the seventeenth century, but that enterprise seemed beyond the capacity of the incoherent princelings. The now independent Sonyo were, however, trading extensively, and there was some slaving in the estuary of the Congo itself, where a people named the Zombo became the main traders in the mid-eighteenth century.

To the south of the Congo lay the great centre of Angola. 'Casta Angola', 'Manicongos', 'Loandas' (from Luanda), or 'Benguelas', the last from the city of that name, were the products of that market when as slaves they reached their destinations. From the middle of the seventeenth century the coasts here produced a steady supply of slaves, for Brazil above all but also for the whole of Latin America. Perhaps three-quarters of the slaves imported into Brazil derived from Angola. A study of African slaves in Mexico in the eighteenth century suggested that two-thirds of them were originally from Angola, too.

The main exporting harbour here was Luanda, the city on the island in the estuary of the River Cuanza, established in 1575, for two centuries the biggest European town in Africa (though still with only 400 'whites'), which probably supplied 5,000–7,000 slaves a year in the seventeenth century, and 7,000–10,000 a year throughout the eighteenth, in twenty or thirty ships; but Benguela, 200 miles to the south, was supplying about a quarter of the Brazilian trade in the late eighteenth century. The majority of the slaves carried by the Portuguese Pernambuco-Paraíba Company derived from here.

Luanda was described by a Portuguese, Pacheco Pereira, as long ago as 1504. He spoke of the little 'low and level and sparsely wooded islands' at the mouth of the Cuanza, where African women busied themselves looking for the shells known as *nzimbus*. (By now, only slaves judged inferior could be bought for these once-prized objects.) Luanda, like Benguela, was set in decidedly dry territory, and needed supplies of food to be brought from remote places. Drinking water was also always in short supply. Thus the slaves carried from here to Brazil, and elsewhere, were often suffering from malnutrition and dehydration even before they were put on the ships which would carry them across the sea.

Luanda in the eighteenth century was on the estuary not just of a river but of a huge network of trading waterways which penetrated far into the interior of Africa. Near the coast these constituted a narrow corridor, along the lower Rivers Bengo and Cuanza, but in the interior the ways broadened, and there were also footpaths which connected the rivers with Kasanje in the middle valley of the Kwango, and the internal monarchies of the forest.

The slave trade from these southern ports was a complicated affair. First the slaves themselves were procured, almost always bought in the interior, by Luso-Africans – mulattos of half-Portuguese, half-Angolan descent – who kept their captives in barracoons, waiting for ships to take them to Brazil. In contrast with what obtained elsewhere, these merchants were the owners of the slaves till they were sold in the Americas. The captains of the slave ships were usually paid wages by these merchants and so had not themselves a direct economic interest in the lives of their charges. In the eighteenth century, these seamen were usually Brazilians, not Portuguese. The Portuguese officials in Luanda had an interest in the trade, since government income (hence their own salaries) depended on duties levied on slaves: and those taxes were farmed out to Lisbon merchants until 1769, but paid direct to officials of the exchequer thereafter.

Benguela was, for most of the eighteenth century, almost a colony of Brazil, and with the hand of Lisbon's law running lighter evasions of rules, such as the law of 1684 about the treatment of slaves on the journey across the Atlantic,* were the more easily accomplished. There the so-called *arqueação* – the capacity tonnage – permitted under that law seemed no more than an invention for giving money to the officials in charge of the measurements.

Benguela's slave trade grew greatly after the 1760s, thanks to the growth of farming in southern Brazil, as well as to the activities of French interlopers. Most slaves from Benguela were marked out from Africa as being destined for Brazil but they were often smuggled into Cuba or other parts of the Spanish empire. The Overseas Council in Lisbon was so perturbed by the risk of losing taxes through the growth in the trade from Benguela that it even forbade all sailings from there to Brazil – an unusually ineffective decree.

These two Portuguese cities of Luanda and Benguela were, in the eighteenth century, managed by a powerful white or mulatto slave-owning and -trading class of merchants. This oligarchy was sustained largely by Brazilian food and alcohol. The slaves were brought down to the sea in 'coffles'† of about a hundred each, of which one or two would typically come every week, and were held on the coast till an appropriate buyer appeared. Now no African monarchy threatened the Portuguese dominion, but the Portuguese themselves had long before ceased to be aggressive, or curious, imperial adventurers. In 1760 the expulsion of the Jesuits had exacerbated the intellectual decline. The dedication of the enlightened and energetic Governor Coutinho‡ had little permanent effect. An intelligent historian, Fernando da Silva Correa, reported about 1789 that 88 per cent of the income of Luanda derived from the trade in slaves.[13]

---

* *See page 417.*
† *From the Arabic* kafilah, *meaning a string of men, or animals, forced to travel together.*
‡ *For whom see pages 278–9.*

Behind these kingdoms, and still acting as serious traders in the eighteenth century, lay the Lunda people, whose headquarters was on the River Kasai, about 600 miles inland. The Lunda wars of expansion had taken them as far as Lake Tanganyika in the east and the River Kwango in the west. These conquests led to a great channel of tribute being opened for slaves from the heart of Africa. The Lunda were a commercially active people by the mid-eighteenth century; their old capital, Mussumba, was the site of a great fair, and one at which the trading of slaves was the most profitable business. A trade route ran from Mussumba to the coast at Loango, bypassing Angola and Congo, sometimes providing the Vili with slaves from what is now Zambia.

The Mbundu Kingdom of Ndongo, ruled by the *Ngola*, the ruler from whom Angola takes its name, survived. The *Ngola*'s capital, Kabasa (whence he still purported to govern from a series of interlocking huts roofed with peacock feathers), lay in fertile and hence prosperous territory, its palm trees produced wine, its women were concerned with raising cattle, and the currency had become rock salt, obtained in square blocks from the mines of Kisama. The River Cuanza gave easy access to the interior.

The Portuguese colonists in Angola had a great many slaves of their own; some individuals are said to have enjoyed the service of as many as 3,000. These were employed either in farming or in fishing, and some were hired out, or performed the functions of barbers or even doctors, while no Portuguese in Angola in the late eighteenth century would have dreamed of going outdoors without two slaves who carried a hammock, while a third would carry a parasol.

Angola would seem thus primarily maintained for trading slaves, who indeed were everywhere to be seen. Many came from the centre of the continent, or even further away: Captain Louis Grandpré, a French explorer, in 1787 met a black African who, he realized, must have come from East Africa, since she remembered 'seeing the sun rising over the water'.[14]

Benguela was the last slave-trading harbour on the long coast of West and West Central Africa. But from the earliest days of the terrible traffic slaves were often carried across the Atlantic from Mozambique and Madagascar, and also from the Portuguese Asian possessions. There was a substantial trade in slaves to the Indian islands, too: 125,000 are said to have left Mozambique in European ships for those harbours between 1720 and 1800. French interest in this East African trade was considerable. For example, the *Trois Cousins* left Saint-Malo on 11 January 1784 for India and Mauritius. On its return, the ship reached West Africa on 2 June 1785, and at Malembo, just to the south of Loango, bought 888 slaves, who were carried to Cap François, in Saint-Domingue, where 700 were delivered live. But the main trade of East Africa was still under the auspices of the Portuguese, who had had a decisive influence in the whole region since they first opened it up in the early sixteenth century. As early as 1520 Simão de Miranda had been in control of the captaincy of Sofala and Mozambique, and concerned himself to send home slaves to Portugal. By the eighteenth century this commerce, directed to the Americas, was more important on that coast than anything else.

Many captives were also obtained from Madagascar, 'a vast island abounding with slaves', in the words of William Beckford, Lord Mayor of London, who needed them for his sugar plantations in Jamaica.[15] In the seventeenth century these were sometimes shipped eastward, via Manila across the Pacific to Acapulco, where they were sold as 'chinos'.* But this trade died out because even the Spaniards found that distance excessive. In the late eighteenth century English traders from Bristol were much involved. The South Sea Company, inadequately supplied by the RAC, dispatched slaves to the Americas from Madagascar in considerable numbers. Like Frederick Philipse of New York they were warned off by the East India Company, which looked on Madagascar as one of its reserved trading zones. But Bristol merchants continued such activities. New England merchants intervened, too, and the taste for slaves from here was strong in Charleston. One advertisement there ran: 'The character of the slaves from the East coast of Africa is now so well-known that it is unnecessary to mention the decided preference they have over all other negroes.' The port of Quelimane also entered the international slave trade about 1780. The pioneer was a French Portuguese, Pedro Monero, one of those innumerable personalities of mixed blood to be found in powerful positions throughout the chequered history of the Atlantic slave trade.

---

* *Not to be confused with the small number of Chinese and Filipinos, also known as chinos, who, after the opening up of the Pacific by Miguel de Legazpi in 1564–5, began to be carried to Mexico in the 'Manila galleons'.*

19

A GREAT STRAIT FOR SLAVES

*'[The King of Whydah] often, when ships
are in a great strait for slaves and cannot be
supply'd otherwise, will sell 300 or 400 of
his wives to complete their number. . . .'*

Captain Thomas Phillips, 1694

BY THE END of the eighteenth century something approaching 80,000
black African slaves were being carried every year across the Atlantic.
The question how those slaves were obtained troubles people now, and it
troubled them at the time. In 1721 the Royal African Company of London
set afoot one of those inquiries for which Britain is still famous: it asked
its agents in Africa to discover how slaves were originally taken, how
many days they spent on their march down to the coast from their own
country, whether they had become slaves in any manner other than by
'being taken prisoners in war time [and] whether they have any other
method of trading for them than this bringing them down to the coast of
Africa to sell to the Europeans'.[1] The conclusion was obscure even after
the meticulous gathering of evidence.

The overwhelming majority of slaves were certainly obtained by
the European traders in Africa by purchase or negotiation with local
rulers, merchants, or noblemen. Some were obtained directly through
European wars, principally in Angola; except during the first days of the
Portuguese on the coast, up till 1448, only a small number were obtained
by Europeans by kidnapping.

The Africans from whom the Europeans obtained most of the slaves
to be shipped acquired them much as ocurred in antiquity in the Mediterranean, or in medieval Europe: first, as a result of war; second, in
consequence of enslavement as a punishment for the people concerned;
third, from poverty, resulting in someone's being constrained to sell his
children, or even himself; or, fourth, from kidnapping, which was as
frequent among Africans as it was rare among Europeans.

African monarchs also often bought slaves (who might earlier have
been obtained in any of these ways) from dealers, in order to sell them
again to Europeans (or to other Africans, and especially Arabs).

Different observers made different judgements, often decisive, as far as they themselves were concerned. In the fifteenth century the Venetian Alvise Ca'da Mosto reported that most slaves had been captured in war, many of them having been for a time integrated into the local economy, whereas others were regularly sold to 'Moors' in exchange for horses. Over a hundred years later, in 1600, Pieter de Marees, however, thought that the slaves on the Gold Coast were, firstly, 'poor people who are enslaved because they could not earn a living; secondly, persons who owe their King some fines which they cannot afford to pay; thirdly, they are young children who are sold by their parents because they do not have the means to bring them up'. Jean Barbot, after two slave voyages in the late seventeenth century, believed that 'The slaves [whom the African monarchs] possess and sell are prisoners of war ... or, if from among themselves, are condemned to slavery for some crime. But there are also those who have been kidnapped by their compatriots, these being mainly children who had been stationed in the fields to guard the mill, or who had been seized when travelling along the main roads.'[2] A little later Willem Bosman, of the Dutch West India Company, was of the view that war explained the existence of slaves: 'It sometimes happens, when the inland countries are at peace, here are no slaves to be got. So ... the trade of this place is utterly uncertain.'[3] In 1730 Francis Moore, an experienced English trader in slaves, for he had been a factor of the RAC at Fort George on the River Gambia, described how the Mandingos, then the middlemen in the slave traffic in the region, brought down to the coast 'slaves to the amount of two thousand, which, they say, are prisoners taken in war: they buy them from the different princes who take them'.[4] Some years later John Newton, who spent some years at Bissau as well as serving on slave ships, as mate as well as captain, believed that most slaves came from wars, that the wars would cease if the slave trade ceased, but that the Europeans did not especially foment these conflicts.

In 1789 a witness at another British inquiry into the nature of the traffic, this time of the Privy Council, Sir George Young, captain in the Royal Navy (subsequently an admiral of the blue), thought that the greatest number of slaves were taken as prisoners of war, 'one village that was stronger than another seizing that which was weaker, and disposing of the inhabitants to the ship'.[5] James Penny, a Liverpool captain who had made eleven slaving voyages to Africa, told the same investigation: 'At Bonny ... traders go up into the country to purchase slaves ... in large canoes with two or three principal persons, about fifty men in each. The canoes go in a body altogether, to defend themselves if attacked. At the head of these two rivers there is a mart for trade where the black traders purchase these slaves of other black slave traders, who bring them from the interior country.' When asked if he had ever observed whether these slaves had marks of any fresh wounds, Penny replied, 'Not often'; but he had *sometimes* done so.

He added: 'From the great number of slaves which [*sic*] are annually exported ... one would be led to imagine the country would in time be depopulated; instead of which no diminution of their numbers is perceived; and from every account we have been able to acquire from the natives themselves, who travel into the interior country, it is extraordinarily populous; but how such a number of slaves are procured, is a circumstance which I believe no European was ever fully acquainted with. The best information ... is that great numbers are prisoners taken in war, and are brought down, fifty or a hundred together, by the black slave merchants; that many are sold for witchcraft, and other real or imputed crimes; and are purchased in the country with European goods and salt; which is an article so highly valued and so eagerly sought after by the natives, that they will part with their wives and their children and everything dear to them to obtain it, when they have not slaves to dispose of and it always makes part of the merchandise for the purchase of slaves in the interior country. ... Death or slavery were, and still are, the penalties for almost every offence. ... The fate of prisoners was also in a great measure determined by the season of the year, and the occasion they had for their services. If they were taken after the harvest was over, they were seldom spared; but those who were captured before the commencement of the rice season experienced a different fate, as they were reserved to cultivate the rice ground; and sold, after the harvest, to those tribes bordering the sea who had no other means of acquiring slaves than by purchase; or were kept as labouring slaves and forever fixed to the spot.'[6]

Thirty years later, Eyo Honesty II of Creek Town, on the Old Calabar River, told the English missionary Hope Waddell that slaves came 'from different countries and were sold for different reasons – some as prisoners of war, some for debt, some for breaking their country's laws, and some by great men who hated them. The king of a town sells whom he dislikes or fears; his wives are sold in turn by his successor. A man inveigles his brother's children into his house and sells them. The brother says nothing, but watches his opportunity and sells the children of the other.'

After taking into account these differing views, based on partial if personal observation, and asserted with conviction by many persons of contrasting experience, it is a relief to find some statistical evidence. This derives from an analysis of the origins of slaves brought to Sierra Leone, then a colony of freed slaves, made by a dedicated philologist, Sigismund Koelle, in the 1850s. It could not be accurate for the whole era of slave trading throughout West Africa, from Arguin to Mozambique, but the figures show that 34 per cent of Koelle's informants were taken in war, 30 per cent had been kidnapped (by Africans), 11 per cent had been sold after being condemned by judicial process (adultery figured largely because that was one of the few 'crimes' to which people would confess),

7 per cent had been sold to pay debts, and another 7 per cent had been sold by relations or friends. (The remaining 11 per cent were slaves who fitted into more than one category: for example, refugees who were kidnapped.) Of those stated to have been taken in war, most had been victims, in one way or another, of a recent Fulani Islamic jihad, the greatest manufactory of slaves in the later eighteenth century – though the Fula and the Mande had both been sellers of slaves on a substantial scale for generations before the jihad.

During the debates in North America and England about the abolition of the trade in slaves the philanthropists would often insist that wars were deliberately undertaken by Africans to obtain slaves for the Europeans. Yet wars were frequent before the Europeans arrived in West Africa, and were probably sometimes undertaken in order to obtain slaves even then: Ca'da Mosto, for example, remarked, 'The black chiefs are continually at war with one another'; and Pacheco, as has been seen, said the same when talking of Benin. In the late eighteenth century King Kpengla of Dahomey and King Osei Bonsu of Ashanti were both asked by European visitors (Archibald Dalzell, a friend of the slave trade, in the case of Kpengla, Jean-Louis Dupuis, an opponent of it, in the case of Osei Bonsu) whether they went to war to provide the Atlantic slave trade with captives; they both said that they did not, and had their own political motives for their conflicts. They may have been lying, but it is unclear why they should have done so. Yet the kings of Dahomey more than once appealed to their European trading partners for arms to enable them to carry out the raids on their northern neighbours which alone could provide the slaves needed to fill the European boats.

There were certainly some occasions when wars were undertaken to provide slaves for sale, to Europeans as to Arabs. For example, a governor of Cape Verde, de Almada, thought in 1576 that the ruler of Cayor, on the River Gambia, had embarked upon fighting his neighbour simply to enable him to pay a debt which he owed to a merchant of Cape Verde. Even if the war concerned might have had an indigenous origin, it might very well have been pursued further than it was because of the potential sale of captives offered by the Atlantic trade. This was specially so in the region of Senegambia, a mainstay of slaving in the early seventeenth century. Then there were certainly instances of war being undertaken by Europeans in order to obtain slaves. One such conflict was that embarked upon by Mendes de Vasconcelos, the Governor of Angola, in 1620, so helping to swell the large exports of slaves in those days. The Portuguese also sometimes acted as military advisers to African rulers – to those of Congo, as of Benin, both in the sixteenth century – and their arms were useful in achieving victories, and hence slaves. Sometimes, in the monarchies of West Africa, if there was a big demand for slaves, or poverty in the region, a chief might exaggerate some slight, and order the alleged guilty party's village to be razed and the people of it reduced to slavery. Sometimes such a thing no doubt occurred because the African chief desired European goods. In the early eighteenth century the RAC plainly convinced itself that wars were good for business: for example, an agent of that body, Josiah Pierson, in Cape Coast in 1712, commented that 'the battle is expected shortly, after which 'tis hoped the trade will flourish'.[7]

In the late eighteenth century the *Newport Mercury* reported that there had been a time 'when the Akims and the [A]shanties were fighting, the worthy Fanties [people on the coast] were very busy pillaging and stealing the Akims, who were so reduced by famine, that they have given themselves up in great number to any body which would promise them victuals, so that slaves became very plenty. . . . Neither did they confine themselves to stealing the Akims only: for the Shanties began to pillage the Fanty Crooms [towns] and plantations, by which conduct the Fanties picked up about 1,000 of them, 300 of which we [the Royal African Company] purchased in eight or nine days, in Castle Brew [the head-quarters of Richard Brew].'[8]

On the other hand, a witness at a House of Commons inquiry, John Matthews, a lieutenant in the Royal Navy, who knew the West Coast of Africa well, said: 'That slaves are often captives taken in war is a position I readily accede to; but that those wars are undertaken merely for the purpose of procuring slaves is by no means the case; for . . . the king or chief of a tribe has not power to make war upon any other tribe without the consent and approbation of the principal people of his nation; and it can scarcely be conceived that such consent could be obtained to a measure that would draw down upon them the resentment of the neighbouring states.' The fact was, he went on, quite fairly, 'the nations which inhabit the interior parts of Africa . . . profess the Mahometan religion; and, following the means prescribed by their prophet, are perpetually at war with the surrounding nations who refuse to embrace their religious doctrines. . . . The prisoners made in these religious wars furnish a great part of the slaves which are sold to the Europeans; and would . . . be put to death if they had not the means of disposing of them. . . .'[9]

All the same, the Swedish mineralogist Christian Wadström commented: 'The wars which the inhabitants of the interior parts of the country . . . carry on with each other are chiefly of a predatory nature, and owe their origin to the yearly number of slaves, which the Mandingos, or the island traders, suppose will be wanted by the vessels which arrive on the coast. Indeed, these predatory incursions depend so much on the demand for slaves that, if in any one year, there be a greater concourse of European ships than usual, it is observed that a much greater number of captives from the interior parts of the country is brought to market the next.'[10]

The variations were considerable. For the Bight of Biafra, for instance, there is nothing to show that raids and war produced more than a small percentage of slaves exported in the eighteenth and nineteenth centuries. War, though it was always being waged, was on too small a scale to produce many captives. In some places in that part of Africa the locally accepted rules even prevented prisoners from being sold as slaves. Instead, the prisoners might be eaten; or the heads of enemy captains cut off as trophies, as Europeans cut off the heads of animals which they killed when hunting. Alexander Falconbridge, a ship's surgeon in Bonny in the 1780s, wrote: 'I never saw any negroes with recent wounds; which must have been the consequence at least with some of them, if they had been taken in battle. And it being the particular province of the surgeon to examine the slaves when they are purchased, such a circumstance could not have escaped my observation.'[11]

Nevertheless in Central Africa – whence, after all, most slaves were exported, through Congo and Angola – there can be no question but that the slave trade stimulated wars. The guns traded by the Northern Europeans exacerbated the aggressive characteristics of anyway aggressive peoples. The constant raids of the Lunda on their neighbours, those of the Jaggas on theirs, and the Angolan troops – white, mulatto, or black – on the borders of their dominions are to be explained largely by the demand for slaves. Many of the problems of Central African monarchies would no doubt have occurred without the Atlantic slave trade. But the connection between the trade and the collapse of some kingdoms and the rise of others is certain; there had before 1500 never been a large slave trade in this region to the north, as had occurred in the land known so generally as 'Guinea', and one historian of the 'kingdoms of the Savannah', Vansina, has said that 'the trade explains most of the history of the kingdoms of Central Africa between 1500 and 1900'.[12]

The Dutch, meantime, persuaded themselves that their trade had a peaceable effect on the Africans: reports of the Dutch West India Company show that its employees thought that peace was essential to get the slaves to the coast: 'That the fire of war among the natives there has been to a large degree extinguished is very sweet and pleasant news', ran one report.[13] Yet the Dutch in the seventeenth century, unlike the Portuguese before them, had no hesitation about exchanging guns, principally muskets, for slaves. The English and French were similarly unconcerned.

There was often little difference in practice between a war of two peoples and a raid by one leader on his neighbour's town or village. Nor was there much difference between capturing prisoners on the field of battle and seizing them in a village after it had been captured. Still, kidnapping of individuals by kings in 'general pillage' was performed almost every day in Africa, at least in the dry season, in Dr Wadström's opinion, and practised by all the kings on the coast. This was certainly sometimes encouraged by Europeans. For example, the militaristic Bissagos

Islanders in their devastating canoes were seeking no territory and no strategic alterations when in the sixteenth and seventeenth centuries they launched their raids on each other and on the mainland: the whole purpose was to obtain slaves for the Portuguese. In the late eighteenth century Sir George Young thought that in Senegambia slaving was 'excited by the French officers and the mulattos that accompanied the embassy by means of a constant intoxication'. The surgeon John Atkins described how the King of Whydah was 'as absolute as a boar, making sometimes fair agreements with his country neighbours, ... but, if he cannot obtain a sufficient number of slaves that way, he marches an army, and depopulates. He and the King of Ardra [Allada]', added this witness, 'commit great depredations inland.'[14]

In such raids old men and women, as well as children, were considered valueless and often killed. Sometimes, as the German explorer Heinrich Barth recorded as late as the 1850s at Bornu in northern Nigeria, men in the prime of life to the number of 170 were left to bleed to death after a raid. The British naval officer Sir George Young once found a beautiful infant boy who had been kidnapped the night before and whom the Africans could not sell. They had said that they would throw him into the sea; at this, Young bought the boy for 'a quarter cask of vidonia [Canary Island] wine', and presented him in England to the Prime Minister, Lord Shelburne (who, he believed, still seems to have owned him ten years later). In Angola most slaves were obtained through kidnapping (by black middlemen); but razzias were common in the north, where such raids accompanied the consolidation of the Sokoto caliphate.

Occasionally kings of Africa would resort to raids among their own people so as to satisfy the European demand for slaves, but this was unusual: had it not been through such a practice that the Akwamu empire had collapsed? All the same, in the 1730s, a king on the River Saalum, between Cape Verde and Gambia, often attacked his own villages at night, set fire to the houses, and seized the escaping residents for slaves; the Ashanti Kings Kusi Obudum and Osei Kodwo in the 1760s also permitted the defeated King Ebicram to raid their dependent cities in regions of Akwapim and Accra.

Kidnapping by merchants or individuals was a 'general way of procuring single slaves', in the words of Wadström. The consequence was that, if people had to travel at all, they travelled in large, and armed, groups. Wadström explained: 'Every town having their own *cabiceers* or ruling men ... [are] all so jealous of the others' panyarring [that is, kidnapping] that they never care to walk even a mile or two from home without firearms; each knows it is their [own] villainies and robberies upon one another that enables them to carry out a slave trade with Europeans; and, as the strength fluctuates, it is not infrequent for him who sells you slaves to-day to be a few days hence sold himself at some neighbouring town. . . .'[15]

Children were almost always left with neighbours if their parents were away, and many of them spent numerous hours sitting in trees watching for kidnappers. Olaudah Equiano, a slave from the region of the Gambia, and one of the very few who lived to describe their experience of the trade, explained: 'Generally, when the grown people in the neighbourhood were gone far in the fields to labour, the children assembled together in some of the neighbours' premises to play; and, commonly, some of us used to get up a tree to look out for an assailant or kidnapper.... One day, as I was watching at the top of a tree in our yard, I saw one of those people come into the yard of our next neighbour but one, to kidnap, there being many stout young people in it. Immediately ... I gave the alarm of the rogue, and he was surrounded ... so that he could not escape till some of the grown people came and secured him. But ... one day, when all our people were gone out to their works as usual, and only I and my dear sister were left to mind the house, two men and a woman got over our walls and, in a moment, seized us both and, without giving us time to cry out, they stopped our mouths, and ran off with us into the nearest wood. Here they tied our hands and continued to carry us as far as they could.' Equiano explained that when they reached a neighbourhood which he recognized he tried to cry out, whereupon his captors put him in a sack. He was soon separated from his sister and sold to an African chief, who was reasonably kind. He escaped from him, returned home, was captured again, resold, and subsequently sold again to people who sold him to the English.[16]

Wadström described how this 'pillage' was 'practised by individuals who, tempted by the merchandise brought by the Europeans, lie in wait for one another. For this purpose, they beset the roads, so that a travelling negro can hardly ever escape them.... A Moor [a Muslim] seized a negro and ... brought him to Sénégal and sold him to the [French Sénégal] company. A few days afterwards, this Moor was himself taken by some negroes in the same manner and brought to be sold in his turn. The Company [of Sénégal] seldom buy Moors: but, as they were obliged, in consequence of their privileges, to supply the colony of Cayenne with a certain number of slaves, and as several ships then in the road ... could not complete their cargoes, they made the less scruple to buy him.... Chance so directed that the Moor, after he had been purchased, was carried on board the same ship in which the negro lay. They no sooner met than a quarrel took place between them, which occasioned for some days a great tumult in the vessel. Such encounters frequently happen on slave ships', added the Swede, 'and the uproars occasioned are seldom or never quieted, till some mischief has been done.'[17]

Willem Bosman, speaking from forty years' experience on the African coast, wrote in the early eighteenth century that 'nine parts in ten of the slaves are of other countries'.[18] That comment suggested that the tenth part would have been obtained from the people who were doing the selling. There were two possibilities: either that the slaves became so as a result of being enslaved as a punishment; or that they were sold as slaves because of the poverty of their parents. Sir George Young thought that punishment was, indeed, the second most usual way of making slaves available. Judicial enslavement was certainly frequent in Angola. Debtors, murderers, and adulterers were also often punished in West African societies by being sold into slavery. Sometimes, the most minor offences were so punished: 'Every trifling crime is punish'd in the same manner', wrote Francis Moore of the RAC in the 1730s. Insolvency was sometimes treated in the same way. The mere existence of the Atlantic slave trade, Moore thought, meant that more and more offences were punished by slavery, and there being an advantage to such condemnations, 'they strain for crimes very hard, in order to sell into slavery. . . . In Cantor [on the Gambia] a man seeing a tiger [presumably a lion] eating a deer which he had killed and hung up near his house, fired at the tiger and the bullet killed a man; the King not only condemned him, but also his Mother, three brothers and three sisters to be sold. . . .'[19]

Bonny, on the way to becoming the largest slave market in the delta of the Niger at the end of the eighteenth century, was usually provided with slaves in consequence of fines levied by the oracle Chukwu. These slaves were demanded from convicted individuals or even families. It was then said that the oracle had eaten them. In fact, they were passed to the merchants on the coast by the Aro priests – a clerical commitment which was certainly not excelled by the Jesuits. Votaries who consulted the oracle and whose questions were thought to be stupid were also sometimes seized as slaves, an unusual treatment of folly. It has been suggested, perhaps with exaggeration, that more than half the slaves from the delta ports passed through this medium.

Sale as a slave was a frequent punishment in all parts of Africa for repeated theft. Kidnapping another for purposes of sale was also often rewarded by being enslaved oneself. Adultery by a woman, or by a man if he were to seduce a wife of an important man, could also lead to enslavement. In 1821 an Efik was sold at Calabar for 'ravishing his father's wives'. Oddities were also often sold into slavery: twins, the mothers of twins, children with deformities, even girls who menstruated before the expected age.

Thomas Poplett, of the Company of Merchants Trading to Africa, in Gorée during its control by the British during the Seven Years War, reported that very often slaves in his neighbourhood were supplied by villages in the region of the Sénégal in default of tribute: 'To furnish the revenues . . . every village pays a regular custom to the King. . . . This . . . is paid in slaves, powder, shot, brandy, tobacco and other merchandise brought from Europe; when this custom is not paid regularly, the King gives notice to pay it and, if not then paid within a certain time, he comes down with a force, and breaks the village; that is, he takes a great number of the inhabitants prisoners, whom he detains for some time; if the duties are paid, he restores the prisoners; if not, they are sold as slaves.' Captain Phillips recalled in 1694 that the King of Whydah 'often, when ships are in a great strait for slaves and cannot be supply'd otherwise, will sell 300 or 400 of his wives to complete their number . . .'.[20]

The sale of children sometimes occurred when a family had nothing to eat. The children might be pawned. Domestic slaves might also be sold: indeed, in the 1850s, 30 per cent of Sigismund Koelle's informants had been domestics before they were sold by masters.

The Europeans kidnapped some Africans. But most European traders, especially if working for a great national company such as the RAC, were always determined to keep on good terms with the Africans and therefore to avoid random kidnapping, which would deprive the African trader of his payment; but the 'separate traders', the interlopers, men from Nantes or Bristol in the early eighteenth century, 'had little concern for the future in comparison with their desire for immediate profit', and so sometimes broke the rules. Sometimes those who kidnapped came to grief: Dr Wadström described how, on the island of Gorée, the captain of an English ship, which had been for some time on the River Gambia, enticed several natives on board and then sailed away with them. 'His vessel was . . . driven back to the coast from which it set sail, and was obliged to cast anchor on the very spot where this act of treachery had been committed. At this time, two other English vessels were lying in the same river. The natives, ever since the transaction, had determined to retaliate. . . . They accordingly boarded the three vessels and, having made themselves masters of them, killed most of their crews. The few who escaped to tell the tale were obliged to take refuge in a neighbouring French factory.'[21]

In general, therefore, experienced slave traders from Europe avoided seizing Africans without negotiation and payment, because such a practice damaged future prospects. But this prudent self-denial did not apply to the *lançados*, those interesting Afro-Portuguese settlers whose families had lived in the estuaries of the rivers of Guinea for three centuries. They conducted themselves as if they were Africans and raided coasts for slaves in the region of Bissau or Cacheu. Captain Towerson, the first English trader to go to the Gold Coast, was told by the King of Shama in the 1550s that 'the Portugals were bad men and . . . they made them [the Africans] slaves if they could take them'.[22]

Yet Europeans always obtained a few slaves by 'stealing' them. In 1702, the Africans near Cape Mesurado complained to Willem Bosman of the Dutch West India Company that 'the English had been there, with two large vessels and had ravaged the country, destroyed all their canoes, plundered their houses, and carried off some of their people as slaves'.[23] In 1716 the monarch of Fooni received five men from the RAC's chief agent on the River Gambia, whose mission was to 'take a place up the river named Geogray and to "panyar" [kidnap] the people and make them slaves'.[24] Two years later, Bennet, the RAC's man at Commenda, on the Gold Coast, was accused of encouraging his gunner, an African, to seize black girls and boys in order to sell them to English captains. John Douglas, on the *Warwick Castle*, a slave ship, reported that he went ashore at Bonny in 1771 and 'saw a young woman come out of the wood to the waterside to bathe; afterwards, I saw two men come out of the wood who seized the woman, secured her hands behind her back, beat her and ill-used her, on account of the resistance she made, and brought her down to me, and desired me to put her on board, which I did; for it was the captain's orders to the ship's company whenever anybody came down with slaves, instantly to put them on board the ship'. Richard Drake, a garrulous captain of the nineteenth century, wrote that on the first ship on which he served, about 1805, Captain Fraley of Bristol usually conducted his trade by barter, 'but he also organised hunting expeditions on his own account . . . on the small rivers which emptied into the Gambia. . . . It was customary for parties of sailors and coast blacks to lie in wait near the streams and little villages, and seize the stragglers by twos and threes when they were fishing or cultivating their patches of corn.'[25] General Rooke, in command at Gorée when it was in British hands after the Seven Years War, told the Select Committee of the House of Commons in 1790 that when about 150 Africans came to greet him as Governor, three English slave captains suggested that they should carry them all off to the West Indies, asserting that every previous governor would have accepted the idea straight away.

Still, there was always a sense, let us say, of priorities among slave traders. Francis Moore explained that besides the slaves whom the merchants brought down from the interior, many were bought along the River Gambia: 'These are either taken in war, as the former are, or else men condemned for crimes, or else people stolen, which is very frequent. . . . The Company's servants never buy any of the last if they suspect it, without sending for the *alcalde* or chief man of the place, and consulting with them about the matter.' In 1765 Captain Charles Thomas, who had taken the *Black Prince* directly from Virginia to Guinea, was furious at the suggestion that he 'clandestinely carried off by force several free men from the coast of Africa. . . . It gives me much concern that I should be accused of an action which I should condemn in another.'[26]

Fairs where slaves could be bought and sold, and which were available to the coastal peoples, thrived long before the coming of the Euro-peans to the coast of Africa. The large markets of Senegambia, for instance, included Bambuhu, Khasso, Segú, and Bambarena. In the late eighteenth century, near the last named, the local ruler maintained and guarded something like a slave village, where captives could be held until they were able to be sold. Sometimes, naturally, slaves were born in these villages; and Mungo Park, the redoubtable botanist and son of a farmer on the Duke of Buccleuch's estate at Fowleshiels near Selkirk who travelled in the region in the 1790s, thought that African merchants preferred those who had been brought up in such circumstances since, never having known freedom, they did not think of running away.

In this so-called western Sudan most slave traders in the eighteenth century were Muslims. Islam of course still prohibited the enslavement of its own devotees, but still blessed that of pagans by Muslims. By about 1780 most of the Muslim states in the interior depended on slave labour. There were slaves in households, in workshops, in the fields, in the harems (as eunuchs and as concubines), in the civil services, and in the armies. Some slaves rose to high positions, as they had done under Rome or in Muslim Spain, though even privileged slaves always risked injustice at the whim of their masters. Kings and noblemen lived by slave raiding and slave trading. If there had been no slaves, women would have had to work, and so would not have been kept in seclusion. That would have been a serious crime according to the Koran and would, indeed, risk hellfire for the criminal.*

Slaves in the Muslim world had some undoubted advantages. They alone were socially mobile in the society concerned. Transport in a slave coffle was a terrible experience but, once settled, slaves could make a life for themselves better than they generally could in the Americas. Household slaves were always, not just occasionally, treated as members of the family. Slaves in slave villages would usually have their own plots on which they could grow plants. Though there was always a legal distinction between a freeman and a slave, there was little economic or social difference. Slaves could even own slaves, and some slaves also participated in slaving expeditions. None of this affected the Atlantic slave trade directly, but the presence in the African interior of a vast slave society encouraged coastal monarchies, whether or not they were Muslims, in their own slaving activities.

Thus in the far interior of what is now Nigeria there were many markets (including some full-scale fairs) where slaves were sold and bought. For example, just below the confluence of the Rivers Niger and Benue, near Igala, the capital of Idah, there was an important island market at which 11,000 slaves were sold a year – 300 a session. These

---

* One speciality remained a characteristic of the Muslim slave trade, which did not occur in its sister commerce of the Atlantic: a continuing interest in eunuchs, to guard the harems of the monarchies of Africa and the Ottoman empire. Some eunuchs became civil servants. The gelding of fully grown young men was a normal practice in the western Sudan even though, unless the surgeon was a member of the reputedly skilled Mossi tribe (who inhabited what is now Upper Volta and northern Ghana), the loss in life was considerable.

markets might serve the Atlantic slave trade, or the trade to the Muslim north, or both.

Of markets such as these Mungo Park would write: 'There are indeed regular markets, where . . . the value of a slave in the eye of an African purchaser, increases in proportion to his distance from his native kingdom. . . .' For that purpose, the slave was frequently transferred from one dealer to another, until he lost all hopes of returning to his native kingdom.

The slaves purchased by the Europeans on the coasts were, Park thought, usually of this description: 'When a free man is taken prisoner, his friends will sometimes ransom him by giving two slaves in exchange; but, when a slave is taken, he has no hopes of redemption. . . . The slaves which Karfa [an African trader who befriended Park] brought with him were all of them prisoners of war. . . . Eleven of them confessed that they had been slaves from their infancy; but the other two refused to give any account of their former condition.' They were all very inquisitive; and they viewed Park with looks of horror, and repeatedly asked if his countrymen were cannibals. 'They were very desirous to know what became of the slaves after they had crossed the salt water. I told them that they were employed in cultivating the land; but they would not believe me; and one of them, putting his hand on the ground, said to me . . . "have you really got such ground as this to set your feet upon?"' [27]

From these internal markets the slaves would be marched under guard, in coffles of about a hundred people, to the ports. The slaves would often be chained together in twos or threes, and sometimes they were forced to carry goods (water, sorghum, ivory, wax, hides) or even stones on their heads in order to discourage them from trying to escape.

Slaves were, of course, harshly used in Africa before they were bought by Europeans. Barbot reported how most of them were 'severely and barbarously treated by their masters, who subsist them poorly, and beat them inhumanely, as may be seen by the scabs and wounds on the bodies of many of them when sold to us. They scarcely allow them the least rag to cover their nakedness, which they take off them when sold to Europeans; and they always go bare-headed. . . . When dead, they never bury them, but cast out their bodies into some place, to be devoured by birds, or beasts of prey'. [28]

Both the RAC and Barbot, like all Europeans, were admittedly at the mercy of wild stories: and Africans who sold the captives would give out that in the interior of the continent, 'there were cruel, and ferocious, irreconcilable enemies who drank human blood and ate their prisoners . . . '. Such exaggerations were put about by merchants who transported their slaves by means of the yoke of a so-called *bois mayombé*, by which if the slave pulled the supervisor could tug and choke, even strangle, the slave. They did not want European enquiries into any of their activities.

Many of the slaves on the coast near the estuary of the Gambia, Willem Bosman wrote, were Brumbrongs and Petcharias, people who each have a different language, 'and are brought from a great way inland. Their way of bringing them is, tying from each other, thirty or forty in a string, having generally a bundle of corn or an elephant's tooth upon their heads. In their way from the mountains, they travel thro' very great woods, where they cannot for some days get water, so they carry in skin-bags enough to support them for that time. . . . They use asses as well as slaves in carrying their goods, but no camels or horses.'[29]

A French officer, Meinhard Xavier Golbéry, travelled in Sénégal in the 1780s. Visiting twenty African peoples in the hope of extending French influence there, he described seeing 'whole chains of captives arrived from all parts, at the market of the trade, and we were astonished to learn that many of these caravans of slaves did not arrive at Galam in the Sénégal . . . and at the factories of the rivers Sherbro, Gabon, Volta, Benin, and Zaire [Congo], before they had performed marches of sixty, seventy, and eighty days; and by calculating these routes, it was evident that they must have come from the most central regions of Africa. We may, therefore, be convinced', he added, 'that the interior of this continent is not so desert a place as has been long imagined. . . .'[30] The probability is that the slaves concerned derived from near Timbuctu.

The costs of a slave on the coast would have to be shared by a multitude of people who would have to pay tolls, taxes, and so on en route, so that, quite possibly, the original enslaver, the kidnapper, or the original captor in a half-forgotten skirmish, might receive only 5 per cent or so of the price obtained on the coast.

Wadström noted in Senegambia: 'The unhappy captives, many of whom are people of distinction, such as princes, priests, and persons high in office, are conducted by the Mandingoes in drives of twenty, thirty, and forty, chained together either to Fort St Joseph on the River Sénégal or . . . to places near the River Gambia. . . . These Mandingoes perform the whole journey, except at certain seasons of the year when they are met by the traders belonging to the coast, who receive the slaves from them, and give them the usual articles of merchandise in exchange. . . . I was curious enough to wish to see some of those that had just arrived, [and] I applied to the director of the Company who conducted me to the slave prisons. I saw there the unfortunate captives, chained two and two together, by the foot. The mangled bodies of several of them, whose wounds were still bleeding, exhibited a most shocking spectacle. . . .'[31]

Portuguese *pombeiros* (usually mulattos) entered the tropical forests to the east of Luanda and Benguela innumerable times, but none of them left an account. The only European to accompany an African slave caravan for any length of time, and to write of it, was Mungo Park. His heroic journey, to Segú, the capital of the Bambara, the great slave market, where he saw on 20 July 1796, 'with infinite pleasure . . . the long sought for, majestic, Niger, glittering in the morning sun, as broad as the Thames at Westminster, and flowing *eastward'*, thereby correcting the geographical errors of centuries, needs no commemoration.'[32]

Park reported in 1799 (on behalf of the African Association, an initially scientific, latterly commercial body founded in 1788) that a typical slave coffle in the upper valley of the River Sénégal would spend about seven to eight hours on the road every day, and would start at daybreak, continuing till the early afternoon – before, that is, the worst heat of the day. An average march would be twenty miles a day in good circumstances. Some caravans would comprise 1,000 slaves, which would necessitate several hundred porters and guards. The leader of the coffle, the *saatigi*, would be chosen by discussion.

Park wrote that the slaves whom he saw were usually secured by placing the right leg of one and the left leg of another into the same pair of fetters. If the fetters were connected by a string, these men could walk, though slowly. Every four slaves might also be fastened together by the necks, with a strong rope of twisted thongs, and at night additional fetters would be put on their hands. Sometimes, a chain would be passed round their necks. Those slaves who protested were imprisoned in a thick billet of wood about three feet long, and a smooth notch being made upon one side of it the ankle of the slave was bolted to the smooth part by means of a strong staple, one ring of which was passed on each side of the ankle. All these fetters and bolts were made from African iron.

In some respects, the treatment of slaves was, Park thought, far from being harsh or cruel. They were led out in their fetters every morning to the shade of a tamarind tree, where they were encouraged to play games of chance, and asked to sing, to keep up their spirits. (Among the freemen accompanying the caravan were six singing men, whose musical talents were used both to divert the slaves and to obtain a welcome from strangers.) In the evening, the irons were examined and hand fetters put on; after which they were conducted to two large huts, where they were guarded during the night by domestic slaves of the coffle's leader.

When Park and the coffle left the town of Kamalia, they were followed for about half a mile by most of the inhabitants of the town, some of them crying, and others shaking hands with relations who were about to leave them for ever; and when they had gained a piece of rising ground from which they had a view of the town all the slaves were ordered to sit in one place, with their faces towards the west, and the townspeople were asked to sit down in another place, with their faces towards Kamalia. The schoolmaster pronounced a prayer. When this ceremony was ended, all the people belonging to the coffle sprang up and, without taking formal farewell of their friends, set off. Since many of

---

* *It was not commemorated at all, though, on 20 July 1996, at a time when many far less important discoveries were amply recalled.*

the slaves had remained for years in irons, the sudden exertion of walking quickly, with heavy loads upon their legs, occasioned spasmodic contractions of those limbs, Park recalled, and the procession of slaves had not journeyed a mile before it was found necessary to detach two of them from the rope and allow them to walk more slowly.

Bala was the first town beyond the limits of the Mandingo kingdom. The slaves marched towards the town in a procession. In front walked the singing men, and they were followed by other free people. Then came the slaves, fastened, in the usual way, by a rope round their necks, four of them to a rope, and a man with a spear between each two groups of four. After them came the domestic slaves and in the rear the free women. In this way they walked until they came within a hundred yards of the gate of the town. Here the singing men began to chant loudly, intending to flatter the vanity of the inhabitants by extolling their well-known hospitality to strangers and their particular friendship for the Mandingo. When they entered the town, the procession went to the centre of the place, where the people gathered round the coffle to hear its history. This was related by two of the singing men. They related every circumstance which had befallen the coffle. When that account was ended, the chief of the town gave the leaders a small present, and all the people of the coffle, both free and enslaved, were invited home by some person or other and accommodated for the night.

The next town which they approached was Koba. Before they entered it, the names of the people belonging to the coffle were called over, and one freeman and three slaves were found to be missing. All presumed that the slaves had murdered the freeman and escaped. It was therefore agreed that six people would go back to the last village, both to find the body and to collect news of the slaves. The remaining slaves waited, lying down in a cotton field, forbidden to speak except in a whisper.

Towards morning the six men returned, having found no sign of the missing man or the slaves. Since no one had eaten for the last twenty-four hours, it was agreed that the expedition should continue to Koba and seek provisions. They accordingly entered the town before daylight and the leader bought food, in the form of groundnuts, which they roasted and ate for breakfast. About eleven o'clock the freeman and slaves who seemed to have deserted the coffle entered the town. One of the slaves, it appeared, had hurt his foot . . .

The expedition was later joined by some Serawoolli traders. A slave dropped a load from his head, for which he was whipped. The load was replaced; but the slave had not gone more than a mile before he let it fall a second time, for which he received the same punishment. After this, he travelled in great pain. The day being remarkably hot, he became exhausted, so that his master was obliged to release him from the rope, for he lay motionless upon the ground. A Serawoolli, therefore, undertook to remain with him and try to bring him to town during the cool of the night. About eight o'clock the same evening, the Serawoolli returned and said that the slave was dead. The general opinion was that the Serawoolli had killed him, or left him to perish on the road: the Serawoollis were known to be more cruel to slaves than the Mandingo were.

At about ten o'clock the next morning the coffle met another one of some twenty-six people and seven loaded donkeys; the people explained that they were returning from the valley of the River Gambia, which was not far away. Most of the men in the new coffle were armed with muskets, and several wore broad belts of scarlet cloth, no doubt from Manchester, over their shoulders, with European hats on their heads. These men explained that there was little demand for slaves on the coast, for no trading vessel had arrived for some months past. On hearing this, the Serawoollis separated themselves and their slaves from the coffle. They could not, they said, maintain their slaves in the estuary of the Gambia until a vessel arrived, and were unwilling to sell their captives at a loss. They therefore left for the north towards the Sénégal. Park with his group continued on his way through the wilderness, and travelled through a rugged country covered with extensive thickets of bamboo.

One of the slaves belonging to the coffle who had travelled with great difficulty for the previous three days was found unable to continue. His master, a singing man, proposed to exchange him for a young slave girl belonging to one of the townspeople at the next village. The girl concerned was ignorant of her fate until all the bundles carried by the slaves were tied up in the morning and the expedition was ready to depart. Then, coming with some other girls to see the coffle set out, her master took her by the hand and delivered her to the singing man. 'Never', said Park, 'was a face of serenity more suddenly changed into one of the deepest distress. The terror which she manifested on having the load put upon her head and the rope fastened round her neck, and the sorrow with which she bade adieu to her companions, were truly affecting.'

Park wrote that he parted for the last time with 'my unfortunate fellow travellers, doomed as I knew most of them to be to a life of captivity and slavery in a foreign land', with great emotion. 'During a wearisome peregrination of more than five hundred British miles, exposed to the burning rays of a tropical sun, these poor slaves, amidst their own infinitely greater sufferings, would commiserate mine; and frequently, of their own accord, bring water to quench my thirst and, at night, collect branches and leaves to prepare me a bed in the wilderness.'[33]

When slaves came from the far interior, as they so often did, the long journey to the coast weakened the captives terribly; many died from shortage of food, exhaustion, exposure, as well as dysentery or other diseases. Raymond Jalamá, a merchant of Luanda, estimated in the late eighteenth century that nearly half of the captives might be lost through either flight or death between the moment of capture and arrival at the sea.[34] Whatever the truth of the matter, as a modern historian points out with respect to Angola, where either warfare or kidnapping caused the initial capture, 'the victims would have begun their odysseys [across the Atlantic] in exhausted, shaken, and perhaps wounded physical condition'.[35]

20

THE BLACKEST SORT
WITH SHORT CURLED HAIR

'[Slaves] of the blackest sort with short curled hair and none of the tawny sort with straight hair.'

Instruction to English captains trading
with Madagascar as to what the Spanish
buyers wanted

THE PATTERN OF EUROPEAN TRADING IN AFRICA was early set by the Portuguese, before the end of the fifteenth century. Captains sailing down the coast of West Africa would expect to stop at numerous ports, where they would go ashore with their interpreter (perhaps brought from Lisbon or the Cape Verde Islands) and, observed by a notary, bargain with the local ruler for the slaves whom he would be offering. From early on, the Portuguese would often have the benefit of being able to use the services of the *lançados* (or *tangos-mãos*), bilingual expatriates who would often gather slaves together before the ships arrived. This was done on a regular basis at Arguin and in São Tomé, and afterwards, on a far larger scale, in Angola.

Still, there were many variations to this classic pattern of negotiations. West Africa was not a single nation, and the idea of it even as a continent seems inadequate.

Also from early on, different Europeans had set up their regular establishments in Africa. The Dutch, the English, and then the French had their trading places, especially in the region of the Rivers Sénégal and Gambia and on the Gold Coast. Those forward-looking peoples were, as we have seen, followed by the Danes, the Swedes, and the Brandenburgers. Yet the purchase of many slaves, perhaps most, continued to be negotiated between a captain on a ship and an African trader in an estuary.

Most of the slaves bought by Europeans over the centuries were sold by kings, nobles, or their agents; but there were always small traders, selling slaves in twos or threes. The negotiation would often be conducted on the monarch's behalf by a special official – for example, the *Mafouk*, as he was known in Loango. Many African kings required a tax of, say, 120 iron bars before giving permission for the captain to start slaving. In the 1730s the King of Barra, 'a truculent monarch of the Mandingo people', demanded a salute from all who entered and left his river; the same was required by the *Maloango* in Loango. The King of Allada would insist that the first slaves bought were slaves he himself owned; thereafter his colleagues would expect to have priority. The ceremony of entering negotiations for purchase was always, and everywhere, complex, even if the captain of the slave ship had been to the same place before, and had previously experienced, say, the dropping of a little salt water into his eye, or the taking of it into his mouth and spitting it out – which gesture had, in Sierra Leone, to be answered in the same way, or else no trade would follow. In Angola the style of purchase was different from that in 'Guinea'. In the former, the *Mafouk* and some 'courtiers' would usually come on board the slaver to arrange matters, drink a little eau-de-vie, receive a present – a dache,* in the form of a cloak, some silk, a barrel of eau-de-vie, or perhaps some handkerchiefs and sheets. James Barbot, buying 648 slaves in the River Calabar in 1699 as part-owner and supercargo of the *Sun of Africa*, recalled giving the King a hat, a firelock, and nine strings of beads. To other courtiers he gave hats, fishhooks, and textiles.

There were many other variations in the details of the traffic. Thus in the early days of the trade in Loango, business was conducted in two stages. First, the Portuguese would exchange their goods, their cloths or their brandy, their trinkets or their beads, for palm cloth – sometimes the best 'painted cloths', either dyed or with coloured strands woven into it, sometimes second-quality *songa*, or even cheap cloth, obtained from the peoples of the forested north of the Congo. The exchanges would be effected by *pombeiros*. These cloths, used as clothing as well as a currency, would then be exchanged for slaves.

Each of the European peoples had their eccentricities, too: Willem Bosman reported, of his fellow countrymen the Dutch, that some of their traders seemed 'utterly ignorant of the manners of the people [and] don't know how to treat them with that decency which they require'. Yet he also wrote: 'The first business of one of our factors [of the Dutch East India Company] when he comes to Fida [Whydah] is to satisfy the customs of the King and the great men, which amounts to about 100 pounds in Guinea value. . . . After which, we have free licence to trade, which is published throughout the land by the crier. But yet before we can

---

* *The origin of this word, still used in West Africa, may be* doação, *the Portuguese for* 'gift'; medase, *Akan for 'thank you'; or* dachem, *a Portuguese corruption of* datjin, *a small Chinese gold weight.*

deal with any person, we are obliged to buy the King's whole stock of slaves at a set price ... commonly one third, or one fourth higher than ordinary. After which, we have free licence to deal with all his subjects of what rank soever.'[1]

Thomas Phillips, commander of the *Hannibal*, of London, described how, having traded all along the Gold Coast, he was eventually received in 1693 at Whydah: 'As soon as the King understood of our landing, he sent two of his ... noblemen to compliment us at our factory where we designed to continue that night and pay our devoirs to His Majesty next day ... whereupon, he sent two more of his grandees to invite us there that night, saying that he waited for us and that all former captains used to attend him the first night ... whereupon we took our hammocks, and Mr Pierson [the factor], myself, Captain Clay [commander of the vessel *East-India Merchant*], our surgeons, pursers, and about twelve men, armed, for our guard, were carried to the King's town which contains about fifty houses. . . .'[2]

Phillips assured the King of Whydah that the Royal African Company of England had much respect for him, for his civility, and his fair and just dealings with their captains; and that notwithstanding there were many other places that begged their custom they had rejected all of them out of good will to him, and therefore sent him and Captain Clay to trade with him and to supply his country with what he needed. The King replied 'that the African Company was [obviously] a very good brave man, that he loved him, that we should be fairly dealt with and not imposed on. . . . After examining us about our cargo, what sort of goods we had, and what quantity of slaves we wanted etc., we took our leaves and return'd to the factory, having promised to come in the morning to make our palavera [agreement] ... about prices.'

They attended the King with samples of their goods, and made their agreement about prices, though with much difficulty, for the King demanded very high ones. At that point, they had warehouses, a kitchen, and lodgings assigned to them, but none of their rooms had doors till they made them themselves, and put on locks and keys: 'Then the bell' was ordered to go about to give notice to all people to bring their slaves to the trunk.'†

Captains Clay and Phillips agreed to go to the trunk in turns to buy the slaves in order to avoid the quarrels between Europeans which were usually used by the Africans to raise their prices. 'When we were at the trunk, the King's slaves ... were the first offered to sale ... though they

---

* *A hollow piece of iron in the shape of a sugar loaf, the cavity of which could contain about fifty pounds of cowries; a man carried this about, and beat it with a stick, making a small dead sound.*

† *An underground dungeon, usually damp, with nothing in the way of beds, not even wooden boards, without water, and rarely cleaned. Since slaves were often chained, they often had to lie in their own excrement.*

were generally the worst slaves . . . and we paid more for them than any others, which we could not remedy, it being one of His Majesty's prerogatives.' For every slave the 'nobles' sold them, publicly, they were obliged to pay part of the goods they received for him or her to the King, 'as toll or custom, especially the bouges [cowries], of which he would take a small dishful out of each measure; to avoid that, they would privately send for us to their houses at night and dispose of two or three slaves at a time and we, as privately, would send them the goods agreed . . . for them; but this they did not much practice for fear of offending the King should he come to know of it. . . . Sometimes after he had sold one of his wives or subjects he would relent, and desire us to exchange for another. . . .'[3]

A little later, Captain William Snelgrave wrote of arriving in Abomey, the capital of Dahomey, in 1727: 'On our coming into the court . . . we were desired to stay a little till the presents were carried into the house that His Majesty [that is, Agaja] might view them. Soon after, we were introduced into a small court, at the further end of which the King was sitting crosslegged on a carpet of silk spread on the ground. He was richly dress'd and had but a few attendants. When we reached him, His Majesty enquired, in a very kind manner, how we did; ordering that we should be placed near him; and, accordingly, fine mats were spread on the ground for us to sit on. The sitting in that posture was not very easy to us, yet we put a good face on the matter, understanding by the linguist [the interpreter] that it was their custom.

'As soon as we were placed,' Snelgrave went on, 'the King ordered the interpreter to ask me what I had to desire of him. To which I answered that, as my business was to trade, so I relied on His Majesty's goodness, to give me a good dispatch and fill my ship with Negroes.'

A certain Zunglar, who had been the King's agent at Whydah, on the coast, before his conquest of that port, then said that, 'His Majesty, being resolved to encourage Trade, though he was a conqueror . . . would not impose a greater Custom [duty] than used to be paid to the King of Whydah.' Snelgrave answered that 'as His Majesty was a far greater Prince, so I hoped he would not take so much. . . .' The King replied that 'as I was the first English captain [whom] he had seen, he would treat me as a young Wife or Bride who must be denied nothing at first.' (Subsequently Agaja caused much trouble to English traders, killing Testesole, the new Governor of the English fort at Whydah, for helping the enemies of the Dahomeyans.)[4]

Sometimes 'courtiers' in these monarchies knew foreign languages; one or two of them had been to France or England. (A certain Cupidon was, for example, found by the captain of the *Dirigente* in 1750 to have spent some years at Saint-Malo.)

In addition, many were artful negotiators: a Dutch West India Company director writing to Holland said, 'One has to be fair to the negroes and say that, as merchants in whatever branch, they are very cunning; one generally notices how one merchant tries to do as much damage to the other as possible.' The Africans often knew more of the Europeans than the Europeans knew of them; thus Thomas Phillips, of the *Hannibal*, reported that his opposite numbers 'know our Troy weights as well as ourselves'; and, 'the Blacks of the Gold Coast', wrote Jean Barbot, 'having traded with the Europeans since the fourteenth century [*sic*] are very well skilled in the nature of all European wares and merchandise vended there. . . . They examine everything with as much prudence and ability as any European can do'.[5]

Ships in the eighteenth century would frequently stop at numerous places on the West African coast. An extreme example of this was the voyage in 1738 of the French vessel the *Affriquain* of Nantes, of 140 tons, belonging to Charles Trochon. She reached the Banana Islands off the River Sierra Leone on 21 November of that year, and obtained twenty-one men and two women. Soon after, the slaves revolted, the captain, Nicolas Fouré, was killed, along with one sailor, and many other members of the ship's company were wounded. A new captain, Pierre Bourau, took over, nine slaves were killed, and two were so badly wounded that they died soon after. Bourau then made a phenomenal number of stops, almost as if he were conducting a river bus. Thus on 11 December the *Affriquain* was at Cape St Ann, and reached the river Gallinas on 14 December. She stayed at Cabo Monte (Cape Mount) from 16 to 21 December, sailed to 'the little cape' there on the 21st, and on the 24th went to Petites Mesurades (Mesurado), in what is today Liberia. On the 26th the *Affriquain* moved on to Grand St Paul, on the 29th to the Grandes Mesurades, where she remained till 6 January 1739. Then she set off for the Rivers Petite Jonque, Grande Jonque, and Petit Bassam, and was at the River Grand Bassam by the 8th. On the 9th she reached Grand Cories, and on the 10th the River Sestre; here she remained till the 16th, when she moved on to Petit Sestre. On 17 January the *Affriquain* moved to Sanguin; on the 18th to Bafo, to Tasse, and to Sinaux. On the 21st she had reached Sestre-Crous; on the 23rd Crous-Sestre. On the 26th the ship was at Grand Sestre, and on the 29th at Cape Palmas, where the coast of Africa turns east, at the beginning of the Ivory Coast. She then spent some days off the estuary of the River Canaille. On 4 February the *Affriquain* was at Tabo, the next day at Drouin, and then St-André. On 8 February she was at Cap Lahou; on the 10th she continued to Jacques-Lahou, Petit Bassam, and Grand Bassam (the site of the modern Abidjan, capital of the Côte d'Ivoire). On 11 February the vessel went to Issiny (Assini), where the French had once tried unsuccessfully to establish a trading post; on the 13th to Cap d'Apollonis, the beginning of the Gold Coast. On the 14th she was at Pamplune; on the 25th at Axim, the first Dutch fort; on the 16th at Dixcove ('Dick's Cove'), the first English fort ; on the 19th at Fort Botro; and on the 20th at Takoradi, the modern port of the Gold Coast. On the

22nd she went to Shama, and on 1 March she was at the Dutch headquarters at Elmina, where she stayed six days before moving on to Cape Coast, the British command post. On the 7th she lay outside that fort. By that time, Captain Bourau had bought 340 Africans, and lost one member of his crew by desertion. The *Affriquain* then sailed for Saint-Domingue, touching at the island of O Príncipe on the way.[6]

After the middle of the eighteenth century such journeys became unusual; European purchases of slaves were more often made in little boats detached from the main slave ship, capable of going up the rivers, where they would set up a stall and a depot for slaves. 'When the adventurer arrives upon the coast with a suitable cargo', John Matthews of the British navy said in 1787, 'he despatches his [small] boats, properly equipped, to the different rivers. On their arrival at the place of trade, they immediately apply to the head man in the town, inform him of their business, and request his protection; desiring that he will either be himself their landlord, or appoint a suitable person, who becomes security for the person and goods of the stranger, and also for the recovery of all money lent, provided it is done with his knowledge and approbation.

'This business finished, and proper presents made (for nothing is done without), [the captains] proceed to trade either by lending their goods to the natives who carry them up into the country, or by waiting till trade is brought to them. The former is the most expeditious way, when they fall into good hands; but the latter is always the safest.'[7]

Quite often, too, by the 1770s, a slave ship would take all its slaves from the same source. The time spent on the coast shortened, and hence there were fewer deaths among the crews. The Dutch in the early eighteenth century might require 228 days for trading, the French 154 days. But by the 1790s English slavers would average only 114 days. On the other hand, the Portuguese liked to collect the slaves whom they obtained on islands in rivers – from barracoons, such as those at Luanda and Benguela, or from entrepôts such as São Tomé, where they might be employed in agriculture before being shipped to Brazil. Sometimes, as with the English in Gambia and certain French companies, such as Michel et Grou, or Rollet du Challet, in Sénégal, or Walsh, off Loango, ships were kept as floating depots, and maintained as prisons until the merchants came. This enabled the quick departure of slavers. For most vessels at this time two to four months' trading was rapid and happy, four to six normal; over six implied a difficult voyage.

The first three months of the year, January to March, were the calmest for sailing down the West African coast, or crossing the Atlantic; the last three, October to December, were the worst, because of the fierce heat and the thick fogs, which were so frequent 'that it is not possible to see from one end of the ship to the other'. Most slavers tried to visit the coast of Africa in the dry, moderately healthy season – say, March to June – so as to have slaves ready for the sugar harvests which, in the Caribbean, usually began in December. There were other considerations: yams, the inland Africans' customary subsistence, were not fit to be taken from the ground before July. Different times of the year suited different zones – and different slavers. The best months in the River Calabar seemed to be May and June, because of continual rains, which the traders found more acceptable than fog. But some people – including Captain Phillips of the *Hannibal*, in 1694 – thought that the summer was considered 'the most malignant season by the blacks themselves who, while the rain lasts, will hardly be prevailed upon to stir out of their huts. . . .'[8]

The prisons or barracoons, the 'trunks' in which slaves were kept waiting for purchase, varied between the harsh and the atrocious. For example, in the English headquarters at Cape Coast, 'in the area of this quadrangle . . . are large Vaults, with an iron grate at the surface to let in light and air upon these poor wretches, the slaves, who are chained and confined there till a demand comes. . . .' John Atkins, the surgeon of 1721, recalled how at Bence Island, Sierra Leone, 'slaves are placed in lodges near the owner's house for air, cleanliness and Customers better viewing them. I had every day the curiosity of observing their behaviour which, with most of them, was very dejected. Once, on looking over some of old Cracker's [Caulker's] slaves, I could not help taking notice of one fellow among the rest, of a tall, strong male, and bold, stern aspect. As he imagined, we were viewing them with a design to buy, he seemed to disdain his fellow slaves for their readiness to be examined and, as it were, scorned looking at us, refusing to rise or stretch out his limbs, as the master commanded; which got him an unmerciful whipping from Cracker's own hand, with a cutting manatea strip [a whip made from the hide of a manatee], and had certainly killed him but for the loss he himself must sustain by it; all of which the negro bore with magnanimity, shrinking very little, and shedding a tear or two, which he endeavoured to hide as tho' ashamed. All the Company grew curious at his courage and wanted to know of Cracker how he came by him; who told us that this same fellow, called Captain Tomba, was a leader in some country villages that opposed them and their trade, at the River Núñez; killing our friends there, and firing their cottages. The sufferers this way, by the help of my men, says Cracker, surprised and bound him in the night about a month ago, he having killed two in his defence before they could secure him; and from thence he was brought thither and made my property.'[9]

Both sides would try and cheat each other. The Africans would often mix brass into the gold dust when selling metal. Ill slaves might be painted, and great trouble was taken to conceal infirmities of any kind in the captive. The Europeans, for their part, often watered the brandy, the wine, even the rum: King Tegbesu of Dahomey used to keep beside him a pot of watered brandy which he had been constrained to buy from Europeans and would offer it to any European trader who complained that his subjects robbed; he would say that if watering were discontinued theft would vanish from Dahomey. Gunpowder was also often fraudulently weighed by such simple techniques as adding a false head to the keg; linen and cotton cloths were often opened and two or three yards, according to the length of the piece, cut off from out of the middle, where the fraud might not be noticed until the cloth was unfolded; a piece of wood might be placed inside to make up the weight.

There were often disputes. For example, in March 1719 the RAC's agent, William Brainie, in charge of Fort Commenda on the Gold Coast, described how an African trader with whom he had often dealt, John Cabess, came in 'bawling and saying that [the traders who had arrived in the castle] . . . were fools, and he . . . did not deign to trade, for, having seen two slaves and asked the price of them, they had told him six ounces [an ounce of gold was worth about four pounds sterling] each and that he had offered them four ounces, and told them it was the highest price we could give for which he believed he could get them or a little more. I answered John to all this that I did not take it well in him that he should offer to bargain for anything . . . without my knowledge, yet, however, seeing he had offer'd four ounces for the slaves (tho' it was the utmost farthing the company allowed for the very best), I, to save his credit among the tradesmen, would give so much, provided the slaves were good, whereupon they were sent for but, when they came, [I] found two old fellows not worth £4 each, which made me very angry with John, and gave me suspicion that he designed to put the other money into his own pocket, for which I checked him and told the traders [that] the slaves were not worth buying. However I bid them privately return to me after John was gone, having something to talk to them of. They accordingly did [so] and then, upon enquiry, I found they had agreed with John Cabess for ten pees [pieces] each slave, whereby he designed to put Six pees in his own pocket. . . .' Similar arguments continued for centuries.[10]

On all European voyages the ship's surgeon usually played an essential part in the selection of the slaves. Indeed, his was the decisive voice in advising captains whether or not to buy. Much the same procedure was followed, whatever the nationality of the purchaser. As in most matters affecting the slave trade, the pioneers in this examination, the so-called *palmeo*, were the Portuguese. This included a measurement of the slaves to see if they reached the ideal of, say, seven palms high (about five feet seven inches). If they did, and were the right age and were also in good health, they could be considered 'a piece of Indies' in themselves, and not a fraction of that. John Atkins in 1721 commented, as did many others, that the slaves were 'examined by us in like manner as our brother traders do beasts in Smithfield'. Another English witness testified 'how our surgeon examined them well in all kinds to see that they were sound in wind and limb, making them jump, stretch out their arms swiftly,

looking in their mouths to judge of their age. . . . Our greatest care of all is
to buy none that are pox'd, lest they should infect the rest. . . . Therefore
our surgeon is forc'd to examine the privities of both men and women
with the nicest scrutiny, which is a great slavery [*sic*]. . . . When we had
selected from the rest such as we liked, we agreed in what goods to pay
for them. . . .' In the early nineteenth century Captain Richard Willing
employed a mulatto overseer 'who could tell an unsound slave at a
glance. He handled the naked blacks from head to foot, squeezing their
joints and muscles, twisting their arms and legs, and examining teeth,
eyes, and chest, and pinching breasts and groins without mercy. The
slaves stood in couples, stark naked, and were made to jump, cry out, lie
down, and roll, and hold their breath for a long time.'[11] French captains
behaved similarly. The surgeons would examine the potential slave
minutely. They, too, made use of the notional term *pièce d'Inde* for the
perfect *'nègre'*, and he was paid for in full. Women slaves had to have
their breasts *'debout: Il faut choisir les nègres, surtout point de vieux peaux
ridées, testicules pendants et . . . graissés, tondus et rasés. . . .'* The lack of a
tooth rendered a slave defective.[12]

The Portuguese also began the practice, in Arguin in the 1440s, of the
carimbo, the branding of a slave with a hot iron, leaving a mark in red on
the shoulder, the breast, or the upper arm, so that it was evident that he or
she was the property of the King of Portugal, or some other master, and
that a proper duty had been paid. This procedure survived from the
Middle Ages – indeed, from antiquity: the Romans used to brand their
slaves but when Constantine the Great ruled that slaves condemned to
work in mines or fight in the arena were to be marked on the hands or
legs, not the face, many slave owners substituted bronze collars for
branding.

Each European nation during the slaving centuries had special procedures. Thus slaves landed at São Tomé were branded with a cross on the
right arm in the early sixteenth century; but later this design was changed
to a 'G', the *marca de Guiné*. Slaves exported from Luanda were often
branded not once but twice, for they had to receive the mark of the Luso-
Brazilian merchants who owned them as well as the royal arms – on the
right breast – to signify their relation to the Crown. Sometimes, baptism
led to the further branding of a cross over the royal design. Slaves of the
Royal African Company were marked, with a burning iron upon the right
breast, 'DY', Duke of York, after the Chairman of the company. In the late
eighteenth century a 'G' would indicate that the slave concerned had been
marked by the Compañía Gaditana, the Spanish Cádiz company concerned to import slaves into Havana in the late 1760s. Captain Thomas
Phillips, an interloper, described how 'we mark'd the slaves [whom] we
had bought on the breast or shoulder with a hot iron, having the ship's
name on it, the place being before anointed with a little palm oil, which
caused but little pain, the mark being usually well in four or five days'.[13]

The South Sea Company later branded its slaves with the distinctive mark of the port in the Spanish empire to which they were being shipped – Cartagena, Caracas, Veracruz, and so on – this new brand being made of gold or silver: preferably the latter, because 'it made a sharper scar'. That enterprise's Court of Directors in London in 1725 specified that the slaves should be marked on the 'left shoulder, heating the mark red hot and rubbing the part first with a little palm or other oil and taking off the mark pretty quick, and rubbing the place again with oil'.[14] Willem Bosman reported of his Dutch colleagues and himself, 'We take all possible care that they are not burned too hard, especially the women, who are more tender than the men.' A Dutch instruction of the late eighteenth century to the Middelburgische Kamerse Compagnie was more specific: it insisted that, 'as you purchase slaves, you must mark them at the upper right arm with the silver mark CCN ... the area of marking must first be rubbed with candle wax or oil; ... the marker should only be as hot as when applied to paper the paper gets hot. . . .' The French had a similar technique: 'After discussion, the captain inscribes on a slate the merchandise for exchange, a specific officer delivers, while the bought African waits in a prison before being attached to a ring and taken to the canoe which will carry him to the ship. The surgeon stamps the slave on the right shoulder with an iron which gives him the mark of the shippers and the ship – it will never come off (if the slave is of second rank, he is stamped on the right thigh).'[15] In the eighteenth century sometimes the initials of the shipper were marked, '*une pipe sous le téton gauche*'.

A German surgeon who travelled with the Brandenburg Company's slave ship the *Friedrich Wilhelm* in 1693 gave one of the most vivid descriptions. He discussed carrying out his duties in Whydah: 'As soon as a sufficient number of the unfortunate victims were assembled', wrote Dr Oettinger, who was from Swabia, 'they were examined by me. The healthy and strong ones were bought, while the *magrones* [the word was from the Portuguese *magro*, 'weak'] – those who had fingers [!] or teeth missing, or were disabled – were rejected. The slaves who had been bought then had to kneel down, twenty or thirty at a time; their right shoulder was smeared with palm oil and branded with an iron which bore the initials CABC [Churfürstlich-Afrikanisch-Brandenburgische-Compagnie]. . . . Some of these poor people obeyed their leaders without a will of their own or any resistance. . . . Others on the other hand howled and danced. There were . . . many women who filled the air with heart-rending cries which could hardly be drowned by the drums, and cut me to the quick.'[16] Pieter de Marees in 1600 reported that in those days the Africans also branded their slaves.

By the eighteenth century the Portuguese forbade the embarkment of any slave who had not been baptized. That had not always been the rule: most of the slaves taken to Portugal in the fifteenth century were not christened. That did not hinder some slaves from being received into the

Church afterwards, a consummation which in turn did not prevent their remaining slaves – even if the enslavement of a Christian had been condemned by Pope Pius II.* But King Manuel the Fortunate, in the early sixteenth century, ordered all Portuguese captains to baptize their slaves on pain of losing them – unless the slaves themselves did not want it (as was the case with the small number of Muslim slaves, mostly by then brought from West Africa). All slave children in Portugal were to be christened, whatever happened. King Manuel made it possible for black slaves in Portugal to receive the sacrament from the hands of the priest of the Nossa Senhora da Conceição, a church in Lisbon destroyed in the earthquake of 1755. Captains of ships could baptize slaves about to die on board their ships. This procedure was regularized by Pope Leo X, at the beginning of his pontificate, in a bull of August 1513, *Eximiae Devotionis;*† he also asked for a font to be built in Nossa Senhora da Conceição for the baptism of slaves.

In the early seventeenth century it became customary for slaves in Africa to be baptized before their departure from Africa. This requirement was first laid down by King Philip III of Spain (II of Portugal) in 1607 and confirmed in 1619. The slaves had as a rule received no instruction whatever before this ceremony, and many, perhaps most, of them had had no previous indication that there was such a thing as a Christian God. So the christening was perfunctory. In Luanda the captives would be taken to one of the six churches, or assembled in the main square. An official catechist, a slave, say, who spoke Kimbundu, the language of Luanda, would address the slaves on the nature of their Christian transformation. Then a priest would pass among the bewildered ranks, giving to each one a Christian name, which had earlier been written on a piece of paper. He would also sprinkle salt on the tongues of the slaves, and follow that with holy water. Finally, he might say, through an interpreter: 'Consider that you are now children of Christ. You are going to set off for Portuguese territory, where you will learn matters of the Faith. Never think any more of your place of origin. Do not eat dogs, nor rats, nor horses. Be content.'[17]

Portuguese governments tried to make these ceremonies less rudimentary, for it was against canon law to baptize adults who had not been properly instructed. It was laid down that the slaves should receive an initiation into Christianity on the boats during the crossing. The same King Philip who had laid down that slaves should be baptized decreed that Portuguese slave ships should carry priests to attend to the spiritual needs of the slaves. But the shortage of priests prevented the fulfilment of this pious rule and even when priests were available their commitment to the cause seems to have been lukewarm.

---

* *See page 72.*
† *This bull was a product of the Fifth Lateran Council.*

Baptisms of slaves bound for Brazil were carried out, before sailing, in Angola and the Congo but those from 'Mina' – that is, the Gold and Slave Coasts – were often not baptized till they reached Brazil.

Slaves were drawn not only from all parts of Africa but from all classes within the different peoples, including the highest: a queen in Cabinda created a legend in Rio de Janeiro as the slave 'Teresa the Queen'; she had been caught in adultery and sold by her husband. When she arrived in Rio she still wore the gold-plated copper bands on her arms and legs which proclaimed her royal status, and her companions showed her respect. She refused to work, and behaved imperiously, until whipped into submission as if she had been a commoner. The mother of King Gezo of Dahomey, who had been a slave before she had been a queen, was also sold into slavery, also in Brazil, by her stepson, Gezo's predecessor. When her own son Gezo came to the throne, he instituted an abortive search for her.

Different colonists had different preferences as to where they would like their slaves to come from. For example, whereas Virginian planters seem not to have been interested in ethnic origins (an attitude which bore some relation to the role of natural increase in the growth of the Virginian slave population), South Carolinians preferred slaves from Madagascar or Senegambia (mostly Malinke or Bambara in the eighteenth century), because these knew about the cultivation of rice. Similarly, some Spanish buyers preferred Angolans, because the work which was going to be required of them, such as copper mining (for instance, in the royal mines at Prado in Cuba), was something of which they had experience in Africa. Senegambians were generally prized, because they were good at languages; many were bilingual, in Wolof and Mandingo, before they reached the Americas. Because of these skills, Wolofs were often used as interpreters on slave ships, lending a distinct Wolof character to the 'emerging pidgin'. These Senegambians were the preferred slaves of the Spaniards in the late sixteenth and early seventeenth centuries, because they also seemed intelligent, hard-working, and even enthusiastic, never losing an opportunity to dance and sing. The French in the eighteenth century thought them 'the best slaves also'.[18]

Physical characteristics played a major part in these considerations. Thus South Carolinian planters were prejudiced against short slaves. Barbadian planters made clear to the RAC in 1704 that they preferred 'young and full breasted women'. Some French seem to have specially prized the Congolese, because they were 'magnificent blacks', in the words of Captain Louis Grandpré, 'robust, indifferent to fatigue . . . sweet and tranquil, born to serve. . . . They appeared content with their lot. If they had tobacco and bananas, they made no complaint.'[19] When the South Sea Company of London assumed the responsibility for serving the Spanish market in the early eighteenth century the company's agents were made aware that the buyers wanted slaves 'of the blackest sort with short curled hair and none of the tawny sort with straight hair', according to an instruction to the captains trading with Madagascar.[20] The same prejudice in favour of jet-black slaves existed in Brazil, where the most highly prized were said by an English visitor to have been those who were 'blackest in colour, and are born near the Equator'. Thomas Butcher, the South Sea Company's agent in Caracas in the 1720s, reported a demand from the powerful cacao growers there for slaves 'of the finest deepest black (Congo and Angola slaves being best liked here)' but 'without cuts in their faces, nor filed teeth, the men to be well grown of a middle stature, not too tall nor too short ... the women to be of a good stature ... without any long breasts hanging down'. The prejudices against slaves with 'a yellow cast' continued throughout the South Sea Company's interest in the matter.[21] The planter Caldeira Brant in Brazil insisted in 1819 that slaves from Mozambique were 'the devil', but he bought them all the same, because of their fine colour. *Moçambiques* seem to have divided Brazilian buyers: some desired them, because they were 'equally intelligent and more pacific than "Minas", faithful and trust-worthy, they bring a high price'.[22] But others disliked them, because of the scars which they had on their faces.

There were other preoccupations, more political than aesthetic or economic. In the eighteenth century slaves from the Gold Coast seem to have been the most popular amongst all the buyers in the Americas: 'The negroes most in demand at Barbados', wrote Captain Thomas Phillips of the *Hannibal* in 1694, 'are the Gold Coast or, as they call them, Corman-tines, which [*sic*] will yield £3 or £4 more a head than the Whidaws ... or ... Papa [papaw, Popo] negroes.' Christopher Codrington, from the *hauteur* of his fine plantations of Antigua, agreed: Cormantines 'are not only the best and most faithful of our slaves, but are all really born heroes'.[*][23] John Atkins in the 1720s also reported that slaves from the Gold Coast were 'accounted best', whereas a slave from Whydah was 'more subject to small pox and sore eyes'; which last comment was echoed by Thomas Phillips, who considered those slaves 'the worst and most washy of any', and also 'not as black as others', while 'an Angolan negro is a Proverb for worthlessness'.[24] Henry Laurens of Charleston, though speci-fying that in a good slave cargo there 'must not be a "callabar" among them', agreed that 'Gold Coast or Gambia are best, next to them the Windward Coast are preferred to Angola's': that is, slaves from the Calabar rivers were thought rebellious, whereas those of the Gold Coast were considered the most capable of responsibility. The Dutch agreed:

---

[*] *Codrington, a high-minded planter, had two plantations on Antigua, named 'College' and 'Society' respectively, of which the first was called after All Souls in Oxford, the second after the Society for the Propagation of the Gospel, to whom he left both plantations to be used to finance a college on the island.*

their colonists always disliked 'Calabarries' as too prone to run away, or as being 'crazy and retarded', or 'unwilling to work and [liable] to die more easily' and also to be 'cowardly'.[25] Like Laurens, Codrington, and the others, they preferred slaves from the Gold Coast and the Slave Coast. French colonists in the Caribbean, who disliked Bantu slaves from Central Africa, also preferred those from Guinea: 'The Negroes from the Gold Coast, Popa, and Whydah ... are the most valuable for the laborious cultivation of the sugar-cane.' They had a characteristically intellectual reason for this preference: these Africans 'are born in a part of Africa which is very barren. ... On that account, when they take the hoe in hand, they are obliged to go and cultivate the land for their subsistence. They also live hardly; so that, when they are carried to our plantations, as they have become used to hard labour from their infancy, they become a strong, robust people and can live upon the sort of food the planters allow them ... : bread made from Indian corn, and fish, such as herrings and pilchards sent from Britain, and dried fish from North America, being such food as they lived upon in their own country. ... On the other hand, the Gambia, Calabar, Bonny, and Angola Negroes are brought from those parts of Africa which are extremely fertile, where everything grows almost spontaneously. ... On that account, the men never work but live an indolent life and are in general of a lazy disposition and tender constitution.'[26]

The predilection for Gold Coast slaves was not universal: in the late eighteenth century in Barbados and other English islands of the eastern Caribbean, slaves from the Gold Coast were looked on as 'prone to revolt'; William Pitt, speaking in the House of Commons in favour of the abolition of the slave trade in a debate in 1792, quoted from the historian of Jamaica, Edward Long, in arguing that because of their rebellious nature a tax amounting to a prohibition should be imposed on Cormantine Africans. Much the same disposition to rebel was assumed by the Portuguese to exist among slaves from the Bissagos Islands. Spanish colonists, who usually had recourse to shippers rather than their own merchants, had the view, in the earliest years, that the clever Wolofs (*Gelofes*, they called them) were rebellious and dangerous.

The French preference for slaves from the Gold Coast was tempered by their belief that they were subject to *'une mélancolie noire'* which led them to suicide, for they were convinced that after their death they would return to their own country. Jamaican colonists on the other hand had, like most people, a basically favourable view of the Akan (Gold Coast) peoples, but a hostile one of the Ibo and those from the Niger Delta ('Bight slaves' or 'Calabars').

The slaves least prized were undoubtedly the Angolans, though more of them were traded than any other people. In the 1750s Henry Laurens looked on them as 'an extream bad sort of slave'. Much earlier, the Dutch in New Netherlands – that is, New York – considered Angolan slave women to be 'thievish, lazy and useless trash'. Dutch traders were also contemptuous about slaves from the Bight of Benin; slaves from there seemed 'very obstinate when they are sold to white men but, once they are on board and out of sight of land, they become very dejected and in too poor health for the voyage'.[27]

Brazilians always had their own views, but their views changed. Thus to begin with they actually preferred slaves from Angola to those from 'Mina', because the former were more tractable and easier to teach, and because there were more of them and therefore they fitted in better with their comrades who had already arrived. They had a shorter distance to travel from Angola than their confrères from Guinea, and so survived the passage from Africa better. But by the eighteenth century Brazilians came much to prefer 'Minas' to Angolans, whom they began to consider inappropriate for working in mines or on plantations, and whom they thought good only as domestics. They thought slaves purchased at Allada or Whydah the best for sugar plantations, because they were stronger – even if they were often sullen, 'not so black and fine to look at as the North Guinea and Gold Coast blacks', and 'most apt to revolt aboard ships'. Slaves from between Cape Verde and Sierra Leone were considered in Brazil as lazy but 'clean and vivacious, especially the women, for which reason the Portuguese buy them and use them as domestic slaves'.

One thing in particular probably saved the Europeans from more revolts: the Muslim Hausas, from what is now the north of Nigeria, were difficult to obtain, for they were the preferred slaves of the Maghreb, the men for their intelligence and the women for their neatness, meticulousness, good looks, and cheerfulness. When in the nineteenth century many Hausas were, for internal African reasons, imported into Brazil the incidence of slave revolts greatly increased.*

All these preferences, often arrived at so lightly, were expressed in prices: Gold Coast slaves were sold in the 1740s for £50 each in Jamaica currency, as opposed to slaves from Angola, Bonny, and Calabar, who might not raise as much as £30.

Prices for slaves in Africa of course varied over the centuries. In the 1550s the average price per slave was the equivalent of about £10; it rose to £14 by 1600 and fell back to £5 in the 1670s. But the price had risen again, to £25, in the 1730s, then to £30 to £50 in the 1760s; here the figure remained till the Napoleonic Wars when, as a result of events which will be amply explored in succeeding chapters, the price fell back to £15 (in the mid-nineteenth century, the average price was down to about £10, where it had been four centuries before). These prices were low in terms of other goods: even in the eighteenth century the cost of a slave was only about four times the value of his subsistence for a year. But, as will be

* See Chapter 29.

THE BLACKEST SORT WITH SHORT CURLED HAIR

later suggested, the rise in prices of slaves at the end of the eighteenth century damaged the trade considerably.

African slaves were not the only ones available in the obvious harbours. In consequence of Portugal's and Holland's international activities, a few Malays were sometimes to be come upon in Guinea. Thus we hear, for example, of slaves for sale at Accra 'of a tawny complexion, with long black hair. They all go clad with long Trowsers and jackets . . . and can write and read . . . are now and then exposed for sale at the European forts.'[28] They had been imported by the Dutch from the Orient. The implication of this passage describing them (in William Smith's *Journey to Guinea*) is that they were much prized.

Whatever the preferences of buyers, they were often not satisfied. On many plantations in the New World the labour force still came from a dozen peoples. One of the best-documented estates at the end of the seventeenth century is Remire, in the French colony of Cayenne, where there were between 1688 and 1690 twenty-eight slaves from Allada (on the Slave Coast), three from the Gold Coast, six from the Calabar rivers, eleven from near the River Congo, and nine from near the Sénégal.

Throughout the slave trade, women and children were less sought after than men in the prime of life. This was a contrast with the Arab trade in West African slaves across the Sahara, in which women were more important – as they were in some African coastal slave markets (Benin in the sixteenth century, Senegambia in the late seventeenth), where they, because of their part in agriculture, as in bearing children, fetched a price double that of men.

In the New World the reverse was often true. A decree in Lisbon of 1618 sought to ban female slaves absolutely, as well as males less than sixteen years old. Two men to one woman was the proportion which the Royal African Company customarily sought. In the Dutch trade between 1675 and 1695 18,000 women slaves seem to have been carried, compared with 34,000 men. The explanation is that planters preferred slaves whom they could work hard and then discard, or leave to die, without the trouble of having to rear their families. Most sugar plantations from the beginning to the end of the slave era were undertakings which, it was supposed, needed a constant annual replenishment to maintain the labour force.[*]

The same judgement applies to slave children: only 6 per cent of slaves shipped from Luanda between 1734 and 1769 were children, only 3 per cent of those shipped from Benguela, and only 8 to 13 per cent of those shipped overall by the Dutch West India Company. Probably a figure of 10 per cent would be a generous estimate for all the slave centuries. In the late eighteenth century more children were shipped to both North and South America, because of an increase in the demand for children as

---

[*] *The one exception to these procedures was in the Bonny River where, uniquely in West Africa, only a little under half the slaves exported were women.*

servants; and it later came to be thought that children, like women, were more efficient than men in cotton fields, in Demerara, for example.

Thomas Tobin, a Liverpool slave captain of the 1790s, describes rejecting some slaves on the grounds that they were too young. Sir Robert Inglis, Member of Parliament for Oxford University, an old-fashioned Tory, asked the then elderly Tobin, presumably with irony, before the Hutt Committee in the 1840s, 'Notwithstanding all the advantages of the Middle Passage, with decks five feet four, and a surgeon on board, you have no reason to believe that any negro ever went voluntarily from the coast of Africa to the West Indies?' Tobin replied, ' . . . there was no objection on the part of the females and the boys; the stout, able men, might appear not to wish to go; but, if they were not taken by the captain of the ship, they knew they would not be at liberty, because they would [have] come down for 100 miles or 200 miles, and they would . . . still be slaves. Besides, they could not know of the advantages . . . until they had been some time on board; and then they became reconciled.' Tobin said that he recalled that he 'had known the young ones get hold of you by the knees and beg you to take them to your country'.[29]

An important part in all these negotiations for slaves was played by interpreters: 'these linguists [who] are natives and freemen of the Country, whom we hire on account of their speaking good English, during the time we remain trading on the coast; and they are likewise brokers between us and the black merchants. . . .'[30] 'Linguists' were often taken on board the ship and were in many ways more important than the sailors. Thus Captain Joseph Harrison, on the *Rainbow*, belonging to Thomas Rumbold and Co. of Liverpool, found an excellent free African as linguist, whom he named Dick. It later happened that a sailor named Richard Kirby (also called Dick) reported that African Dick to be 'no better than a slave', and recommended that he be sold as such in Barbados. Thereupon Dick the interpreter grew sulky. The captain found out what had transpired, and established that Kirby was the culprit. Dick the linguist demanded satisfaction, but Captain Harrison said that he had no power to beat any white person; instead, though, fearing an insurrection of slaves, he desired Dick to take his own satisfaction. This he did: administering three- or four-and-twenty lashes. Kirby died soon after, and Harrison was not punished, since it turned out that the dead man had had a lethargic disorder, a flux or a dropsy.[31]

Sometimes during the shipment the traders were attacked. For example, in 1730 unknown blacks assaulted Adrien Vanvoorn's 150-ton ship *Phénix* from Nantes, while the captain, Laville Pichard, was negotiating the purchase of slaves, and set it on fire off Queta, at the mouth of the River Volta. The consequence, as on most other such occasions, was that numerous slaves died.* Usually, everyone came off badly from such

---

* Still, the vessel crossed the Atlantic with 326 blacks, of whom 182 died en route, or during the sale at Martinique.

affairs. The snow* *Perfect* (Captain William Potter of Liverpool, bound for Charleston, South Carolina) was, in 1758, 'cut off by negroes, in the River Gambia, and every man on board was murdered. . . .' Similarly, the *Côte d'Or*, a 200-ton vessel belonging to Rafael Mendez of Bordeaux, was stranded on a sandbank near Bonny in 1768. Over a hundred rafts approached, each with thirty to sixty blacks on board, most of them carrying sabres, knivre, or rifles. These men boarded the ship and stole everything in sight. Only the appearance of two English ships saved the crew, who were taken to São Tomé.

The RAC had many disasters in the early eighteenth century. For example, in 1703 Africans seized the company's fort at Sekondi, on the Gold Coast, and beheaded the chief agent. The same year an agent of the RAC in Anamabo was held prisoner for eighteen days, until he bought his freedom with 'good words and a great deal of money'. In 1704 three agents of the same company were stripped naked and held prisoner on the Senegambian coast. In 1717 Captain David Francis reported, 'My boats and people are seized at almost every port I send them.'[32]

Then there was a famous massacre at Calabar in 1767, which had a different conclusion (and which was mentioned by William Wilberforce in his first speech in the House of Commons proposing the abolition of the traffic). The captains of five Liverpool ships, and one each from Bristol and London, lay in the Old Calabar River. A dispute was under way at that time between the rulers of Old and New Calabar. The English captains offered themselves as mediators, and suggested that the inhabitants of the old city should come aboard one of their ships. Nine canoes left Old Calabar, led by Amboe Robin John, a leader of that city, each canoe carrying nearly thirty men. When these craft approached the English vessels the English captains fired and seized the canoes, arresting three leaders, while onshore the warriors of New Calabar came out from behind the bushes and fell on those who were trying to swim to safety. Amboe Robin John was forced into a canoe and had his head cut off; his brothers were sold in the West Indies.[33]

Once or twice slaves ready for embarkation also rebelled. Thus in 1727 at Christiansborg, the Danish castle on the Gold Coast, a group of slaves seized the slave overseer and killed him. They escaped, but half were caught. The ringleaders were broken on the wheel and then beheaded. A harsh response followed a sale of Ashanti slaves in Elmina in 1767. These six captives had been personal servants of a recently dead director-general of the Dutch West India Company, and they would have been freed if the Asantahene had paid some debts which he owed the company. But he did not, and the Dutch decided to sell the men concerned to traders: 'We put their feet in shackles', the report goes on,

---

* *A snow was a small sailing vessel resembling a brig, with a main- and a foremast, as well as a trysail mast just behind the mainmast.*

'and, on the day that they were to be sold, the slave dungeons were thoroughly searched for knives and weapons, but apparently not enough. . . . The result . . . was that, when the company slaves were ordered into the yard to take hold of each, they [the personal slaves] retreated and, in a savage and inhuman manner, cut their own throats and, when they did not succeed the first time, they repeated the thrusts three or four times, the one who had used a knife giving it a comrade who was not provided with one. One negro even cut the throat of his wife and then his own. . . . The yard of the noble company's chief castle was thus turned into a bloodbath. . . . The remaining Ashanti who were unharmed were brought up to the hall, sold in public, and then taken on board of a waiting English ship.'[34]

Many more slaves died during the often long time of waiting for shipment than did so in such rebellions or protests. Sometimes the time spent waiting to be shipped was as long as five months – perhaps longer than the voyage to the Americas. Thus in 1790 Captain William Blake bought for James Rogers and Co. of Bristol (England) 939 slaves, of whom 203 died, 'of natural causes', while still on the West African coast.

The embarkment of the slaves was a complicated affair. Captain Thomas Phillips recalled in 1694 that at Whydah, 'when we had purchased to the number of fifty or sixty, we would send them aboard, there being a cappasheir [an official], entitled "the captain of the slaves", whose care it was to secure them to the waterside, and see them all off; and if, in carrying to the marine, any were lost, he was bound to make them good to us, the "captain of the trunk" being oblig'd to do the like. . . . These are two officers appointed by the King [of Whydah] for this purpose, to each of which every ship pays the value of a slave in what goods they liked best for their trouble. . . .' There was, likewise, a 'captain of the sand', appointed 'to take care of the merchandise [whom] we have come ashore to trade with, [so] that the negroes do not plunder them, we being forced to leave goods a whole night on the sea-shore for want of porters to bring them up; but notwithstanding his care and authority, we often came by the loss. . . .'[35]

Willem Bosman reported that to save extra charges by the sellers he would send his slaves to the ships at the first opportunity, 'before which their masters strip them of all that they have on their backs, so that they come aboard stark naked, as well women as men; in which condition they are obliged to continue, if the master of the ship is not so charitable . . . as to bestow something to cover their nakedness . . .'.[36]

'When our slaves', wrote, again, Captain Thomas Phillips, 'were come to the seaside, our canoes were ready to carry them off to the long-boat . . . if the sea permitted, and she convey'd them aboard ship, where the men were all put in irons, two and two shackled together, to prevent their mutiny or swimming ashore. The negroes are so wilful and loth to leave their own country, that they have often leap'd out of canoes, boat and ship, into the sea, and kept underwater till they were drowned, to avoid being taken up and saved . . . they having a more dreadful apprehension of Barbados than we have of hell though, in reality [this was a very frequent comment], they live much better there than in their own country; but home is home etc. . . .'[37]

Some slave captains found that there were always a few slaves, usually from 'a far inland country, who very innocently persuade one another that we buy them only to fatten and afterwards eat them as a delicacy'.

Captain Snelgrave tried to come face to face with these anxieties: he said, 'When we purchase grown people, I acquaint them by the interpreter, "That now they are become my property." I think fit to let them know what they may [have been] . . . bought for, that they may be easy in their minds: for these poor people are generally under terrible apprehensions upon being bought by white men, many being afraid that we design to eat them; which, I have been told, is a story much credited by the inland Negroes.

'So, after informing them that they are bought to till the ground in our country, with several other matters, I then acquaint them, how they are to behave themselves on board towards the white men; that, if anyone abuses them, they are to complain to the linguist, who is to inform me of it, and I will do them justice; but, if they make a disturbance, or offer to strike a white man, they must expect to be severely punished. . . . When we purchase the negroes, we couple the sturdy men together with irons; but we suffer the women and children to go freely about; and, soon after we have sailed from the coast, we undo all the men's irons.'[38]

At the end of the eighteenth century an interesting account of slaves leaving home was given by the slave captain Joseph Hawkins of South Carolina. He had been trading in one of the rivers which constitute the delta of the Niger. He set off for the sea, and 'the slaves were out on board [deck] and necessarily in irons brought for the purpose. This measure occasioned one of the most affecting scenes that I had ever witnessed: their hopes, with my assurances, had buoyed them up on the road; but a change from cordage to iron fetters rent their hopes and fears together; their wailings were torturing beyond what words can express; but delay at this stage would have been fatal. . . . We were passing through a narrow part of the river, two of them found means to jump overboard, a sailor, who was in a small boat astern, seized one of them by the arms and, the end of the rope being thrown to him, the slave was taken [back] on board, though not without some difficulty.

'The others who had been at the oars, seeing their fellows, one of them seized, and the other struck on the head with a pole, set up a scream which was echoed by the rest below; those that were loose made an effort to throw two of the sailors overboard; the rest, except the one on the boat and at the helm, being asleep; the noise had now aroused them, and the scream impressed on them some degree of terror. They seized on the guns and bayonets of those that lay ready, and rushed upon the slaves, five of whom from below had got loose, and were endeavouring to set the rest free, while those we had to deal with above were threatening to sacrifice us to their despair. . . . We at length overpowered them; only one having escaped and one being killed, the rest were immediately bound in double irons and [we] took care from thence till our arrival at the ship not to suffer any of them to take the air without being made fast. Five of the sailors were considerably but not dangerously hurt. . . . We reached the ship in five days [where we found that] the officers had all provided themselves with three or four wives each. . . .'[39]

Slave women sometimes benefited from the fact that the crew were unable to maintain themselves without women. Thus Captain Yves Armés of the *Jeannette* from Nantes in 1741 found an English ship off West Africa where *'la coutume entre eux [est] d'avoir chacun leur femme'*. Some captains tried to restrain this. Thus Captain Newton, the future clergyman, recalled, 'In the afternoon, while we were off the deck, William Cooney seduced a woman slave down into the room and lay with her brutelike, in view of the whole quarter deck, for which I put him in irons.'[40]

But now the darkest time in the life of the slave and also of the sailor was about to begin.

21

IF YOU WANT TO LEARN
HOW TO PRAY, GO TO SEA

Portuguese proverb

*'It is perfectly impossible to make a slave
voyage a healthy voyage.'*

> Captain Denman to William Hutt's
> committee in the
> House of Commons, 1848

*'Whether it was my ship or any other ship
the whole of the officers and crew were
employed altogether in endeavouring to
keep the slaves in a healthy state and in
good spirits.'*

> Thomas Tobin, a one-time
> Liverpool slave captain, to
> the Hutt Committee, 1848

THE CROSSING of what the Spaniards of the fifteenth century spoke of as
'the great Ocean Sea' was the characteristic experience of the Atlantic
slave trade. Otherwise, the journey of a captive to the coast from his
remote origin, in the interior of Africa, among the ruined cities of the
Songhai empire, or in the Congo kingdom before the emergence of
the Ngola, for example, would have been much the same if the slave was
being carried to a Mediterranean port or an American one, to Elmina or to
Brazil. It would have been as harsh. But it was the sea, the vast, mysterious, terrifying 'green sea of darkness', which gave the Atlantic slave
trade its special drama.

No slaves before 1750 left any description of what it was like to see
the ocean for the first time after being taken on the long journey from the

interior of Africa. But certainly many Africans thought that the Europeans were people who had no country, and who lived in ships. One slave who later did tell his story was Olaudah Equiano, a remarkable slave captured by the British and carried to the West Indies in the 1760s. 'The first object which saluted my eyes', he wrote, 'was the sea, and a slave ship, which was then riding at anchor. . . . These filled me with astonishment, which was soon converted into terror, when I was carried on board. I was immediately handled and tossed up, to see if I were sound, by some of the crew, and I was now persuaded that I had got into a world of bad spirits and that they were going to kill me. Their complexions too, differing so much from ours, their long hair and the language they spoke . . . united to confirm me in this belief. Indeed, such were the horrors of my views and fears at the moment that, if ten thousand worlds had been my own, I would have freely parted with them all to have exchanged my condition with that of the meanest slave in my own country.

'When I looked round the ship', Equiano continued, 'and saw a large . . . copper boiling . . . I no longer doubted my fate . . . I fell motionless on the deck and fainted. When I recovered, I found some black people about me who, I believed, were some of those who had brought me on board, and had been receiving their pay; they talked in order to cheer me, but all in vain. I asked them if we were not to be eaten by those white men, with horrible looks, red faces and loose hair. They told me I was not, and one of the crew brought me a small portion of spiritous liquor in a wine glass. . . . I took a little down my palate, which . . . threw me into the greatest consternation at the strange feeling it produced, having never tasted any such liquor before. . . .'

Equiano testifies to the widespread suspicion, throughout Africa, that the white (or 'red') people – presumably followers of the Lord of the Dead, Mwene Puto (an Angolan devil) – had seized the slaves in order to eat them. Some Africans were certain that the red wine which the Europeans drank so merrily derived from the blood of the blacks, that the olive oil which they used so carefully came from squeezing black bodies, and even that the strong-smelling cheese of the captain's table derived from Africans' brains.

Equiano asked if these people, the crew, had 'no country'. Did they live in this 'hollow place'? Did they have women and, if so, where were they? How did the ship sail? The answers which he received to these sharp questions were unsatisfactory, and inadequate.[1]

The crossing of the Atlantic was now due to begin. Ships carrying slaves did not alter much over the generations. Thus in the seventeenth century, in the era of the Portuguese *asiento*, an average vessel arriving in Cartagena de Indias would seem to have carried 300 slaves. The typical French slave ship in the eighteenth century was responsible for about 400, and a Portuguese ship 370. The usual load on an English ship was less: about 230 slaves at the end of the eighteenth century. But there were innumerable exceptions: thus the *Comte d'Hérouville* of Nantes (owned by René Foucault *aîné*, captained by Jean-François Cadillac) in 1766 carried live only one adult slave and one *'négritte'* to Martinique. Many ships sailed for the Indies with fewer slaves than they had been expected to carry; some were more crowded than planned.

If conditions were good the crossing of the Atlantic took, on Portuguese journeys in the seventeenth century, nearly thirty-five days from Angola to Pernambuco, forty to Bahia, and fifty to Rio. At the end of the eighteenth century such voyages across the South Atlantic seem because the vessels were larger to have been cut to average only thirty days. In the 1670s British ships from Guinea would take some forty-four days to reach the Caribbean. But Dutch boats in the West India Company usually took eighty days to reach Curaçao, with the shortest journey twenty-three days, the longest 284. Most French journeys across the Atlantic, like those of the British, lasted two to three months, seventy days being normal for ships from Honfleur, but journeys lasting longer were frequent. These journeys were relatively easy, since, in normal circumstances, the captains sailed in a large circle around a mid-Atlantic area of high pressure.

The shorter journeys from West Africa to Portugal in the fifteenth and sixteenth centuries would of course have taken less time: perhaps twenty days to a month, from Arguin to Lisbon; from São Tomé the time could have been as much as three to six months.

In the eighteenth century a record for a slave journey across the Atlantic was set in 1754 by the *Saint-Philippe*, of Nantes, 340 tons, which, owned by the Jogue brothers, carried 462 Africans from Whydah to Saint-Domingue in only twenty-five days.

The longest journey in the eighteenth century seems also to have been French, that of the *Sainte-Anne*, of Nantes, belonging to Louis Mornant, which in 1727 took no less than nine months to travel from Whydah to Cayes Saint-Louis, Saint-Domingue, fifty-five slaves being lost en route.

When the vessel set off the captain would believe that with good fortune the south-east trade winds would almost automatically take the ship, before the wind, across the Atlantic. But before those winds could be picked up, while still in sight of Africa, the male slaves were usually held in chains, in pairs, the right ankle of one connected to the left ankle of the other.

Jacques Savary, a brilliant Angevin businessman who had been a protégé of Louis XIV's onetime favourite, Fouquet, and was a theoretician of commerce, wrote in his *Le Parfait Négociant* at the end of the seventeenth century: 'From the moment that the slaves are embarked, one must put the sails up. The reason is that these slaves have so great a love for their country that they despair when they see that they are leaving it for ever; that makes them die of grief, and I have heard merchants who engage in this commerce say that they die more often before leaving the port than during the voyage. Some throw themselves into the sea, others hit their heads against the ship, others hold their breath to try and smother themselves, others still try to die of hunger from not eating, yet, when they have definitely left their country, they begin to console themselves, particularly when [the captain] regales them with the music of some instrument. . . .'[2] Captain Thomas Phillips of London wrote, from personal experience, about the same time: 'When we come to sea, we let them out of irons, they never attempt to rebel. . . . The only danger is when we are in sight of their own country. . . . We have some thirty or forty Gold Coast negroes . . . to make guardians and overseers of the Whydah negroes, and sleep among them to keep them from quarrelling.'[3] A hundred years later, in 1790, Ecroyde Claxton, a ship's surgeon, told the House of Commons committee of inquiry that once, he remembered, a slave did manage to throw himself overboard as a protest. A great effort was mounted to recover him. The slave, 'perceiving that he was going to be caught, immediately dived under water and, by that means, made his escape, and came up again several yards from the vessel, and made signs which it is impossible for me to describe in words, expressive of the happiness he had in escaping us'.[4]

As for the character of the ships, the Dutch thought that they had the best-managed ones: 'Though the number [of slaves] sometimes amounts to six or seven hundred, yet by . . . careful management . . . they are so regulated that it seems incredible: and, in this particular, our [Dutch] nation exceeds all other Europeans; for the French, Portuguese and English slave ships are always foul and stinking; on the contrary, ours are for the most part clean and neat'.[5]

Overcrowding was normal. With regard to Portuguese ships, Father Dionigio Carli de Piacenza wrote, in the late seventeenth century, 'Women who were pregnant were assembled in the back cabin, the children were huddled together on the first entrepôt, as if they were herrings in a barrel. If anyone wanted to sleep, they lay on top of each other. To satisfy their natural needs, they had bilge places [sentines] over the edge of the sea but, as many feared to lose their place [if they did such a thing], they relieved themselves where they were, above all the men [who were] cruelly pushed together, in such a way that the heat and the smell became intolerable.'[6] A hundred years later James Morley, who had served as a gunner on the slaver *Medway*, told a House of Commons committee of inquiry that he had seen the slaves 'under great difficulty of breathing; the women, particularly, often got upon the beams, where the gratings are often raised with bannisters, about four feet above the combings [the raised borders along the hatches which prevent water from running below] to give air, but they are generally driven down, because they take the air from the rest. He has known rice held in the mouths of sea-sick slaves until they were almost strangled; he has seen the surgeon's mate force the panniken [bread] between their teeth and throw medicine over them so that not half went into their mouths – the poor fellows wallowing in their blood . . . and this with blows of the cat [the cat-o'-nine-tails].'[7]

The Portuguese, it is fair to recognize, tried to lay down rules for the carriage of slaves. Thus the same King Manuel of Portugal who in the early sixteenth century had insisted on baptism for these cargoes ordered that the captives – they were then still being carried mostly to Europe, not to America – should have at the least wooden beds, under a roof to give protection against rain and cold. The same monarch tried to establish standards for adequate supplies of food, such as yams – though the provision of sticks to gnaw in order to calm the pangs of hunger, as well as to clean the teeth, scarcely seems to constitute the height of generosity.

Even these tepid suggestions of humanity were rarely put into effect, and each early Portuguese slave ship carried on it much the same locks, manacles, chains, and head-rings to secure the slaves which they had 300 years later.

The law of 1684 sought to make a clear provision for the *arqueação* – that is, the requirement of officials to measure the capacity tonnage of ships, taking into account the need to define the difference between the hold, reserved for cargo, and the decks, for slaves. The regulations did not take into account headroom, but all the same there were provisions for 'comfort' which could be interpreted as requiring it.

As a result of these and other rules the Portuguese are often supposed to have been the most humane of the European shippers of slaves: Jean Barbot wrote of them as 'commendable, in that they bring along with them to the coast a sufficient quantity of coarse thick mats to serve as bedding under the slaves aboard, and shift them every fortnight or three weeks with fresh mats which, besides it is softer for the poor wretches to lie upon than the bare deals or decks, must also be much healthier for them, because the planks or deals contract some dampness more or less, either from the deck being washed so often to keep it clean and sweet, or from the rain that gets in now and then . . . and even from the very sweat of the slaves; which, being so crowded in a low place, is perpetual'.[8] The Swedish mineralogist Wadström, who knew the northern slave harbours such as Bissau or Cacheu well, also wrote, in the 1790s: 'The Portuguese slave ships are never overcrowded and the sailors are chiefly . . . *negros ladinos*, who speak their language and whose business it is to comfort and attend the poor people on the voyage. The consequence is that they have little or no occasion for fetters, so constantly used in the other European slave ships, and that they perform their voyage from Angola etc., to Brazil with very little mortality. . . .'[9] By the eighteenth century, good conditions were further assisted on Portuguese ships by allocating to each sailor the care of about fifteen slaves. These men were paid a new crown for every slave delivered alive.

All the same, the Portuguese were perfectly able to balance profit against hardship. Dr Wadström also testified: 'Some slave merchants were sending a few ships to Mozambique for slaves. They told me that, though in the long, cold and stormy voyage round the Cape of Good Hope, many more of the slaves died than even in the passage from the coast of Guinea to the West Indies, yet . . . their cheapness in Mozambique fully compensated for their increased mortality.'[10]

Thus though the Portuguese may have approached the whole business of the slave trade more humanely than their Northern European confrères, in practice there was not much difference between them. For example, only in the latter half of the eighteenth century did Northern European attitudes to hygiene, modest as they were, begin to reach Lisbon, Luanda, and Rio. Perhaps the real difference was psychological. The Portuguese, with their slave sailors, had no great sense that a black captive was an unusual person – he was just one more suffering soul in God's inexplicable scheme – whereas, for the white Protestants of the North, Africans were as exotic as they were alarming.

The slave Equiano wrote of this first stage of the journey across the Atlantic: 'The stench of the hold while we were on the coast was so intolerably loathsome that it was dangerous to remain there for any time, and some of us had been permitted to stay on the deck for the fresh air; but now that the whole ship's cargo were confined together, it became absolutely pestilential. The closeness of the place, and the heat of the climate, added to the number in the ship, which was so crowded that each had scarcely room to turn himself, almost suffocated us. This produced constant perspirations, so that the air soon became unfit for respiration . . . and brought on a sickness among the slaves, of which many died, thus falling victims to the improvident avarice, as I may call it, of their purchasers. This wretched situation was again aggravated by the galling of the chains, now become insupportable; and the filth of the tubs, into which the children often fell, and were almost suffocated. The shrieks of the women, and the groans of the dying, rendered a scene of horror almost inconceivable.'[11]

Zachary Macaulay, the indefatigable abolitionist, travelled as a passenger on an English slave ship about 1795 to discover what such a voyage was like. Macaulay, characteristically, kept his notes in Greek to fool the crew. The captain 'told us that a slave ship was a very different thing to what had been reported. He accordingly said a few things to the women [slaves], to which they replied with a cheer. He went forward to the forward deck and said the same things to the men, who made the same reply. "Now," he said, "are you not convinced that Mr Wilberforce has conceived very improperly of slave ships?"' Macaulay was shown where to sling his hammock and asked if he would not mind a few slaves sleeping under it: the smell, he was told, would be unpleasant for a few days but, 'when we got into the trade winds, it would no longer be perceived'.[12]

An examination of the diagram of the Liverpool slave ship *Brookes* of 1790 (so called since it was owned by a famous family of builders in Liverpool of that name) or of that of the 232-ton Nantes vessel the *Vigilant* of 1823 (owned by François Michaud)* suggests that the British in the 1780s and French in the 1820s would hold their captives in a space five feet three inches high by four feet four inches wide. Dr Thomas Trotter, an Edinburgh physician (he later wrote a well-known thesis, *Drunkenness and Its Effects on the Human Body*) who served on the *Brookes* as surgeon in 1783, was asked about conditions by a committee of the House of Commons. The question was put to him: 'Had they [the slaves] room to turn themselves, or in any sort to lie at ease?' Trotter replied: 'By no means. The slaves that are out of irons are locked "spoonways", according to the technical phrase, and closely locked to one another. It is the duty of the first mate to see them stowed in this manner every morning; those which do not get quickly into their places are compelled by the cat and, such was the situation when stowed in this manner, and when the ship had much motion at sea, that they were often miserably bruised against the deck or against each other. . . . I have seen their [the slaves'] breasts heaving and observed them draw their breath, with all those laborious and anxious efforts for life which we observe in expiring animals subjected by experiment to bad air of various kinds.' The *Brookes*, on the voyage in which Trotter participated, carried over 600 slaves and lost sixty en route.[13]

About the same time as Trotter's statement, Thomas Clarkson, the celebrated opponent of the trade, talked to a witness who told him: 'The misery which the slaves endure in consequence of too close a stowage is not easily to be described. I have heard them frequently complaining of heat, and have seen them fainting, almost dying for want of water. Their situation is worst in rainy weather. We do everything for them in our power. In all the vessels in which I have sailed in the slave trade, we never covered the gratings with a tarpawling, but made a tarpawling awning over the booms . . . [but some were still] panting for breath, and in such a situation that the seamen have been obliged to get them immediately onto deck, fearing lest they would otherwise have fainted away and died.'[14]

From time to time there were suggestions that the provision of better conditions on board these ships might reduce the losses or, rather, increase the profits: 'We find the covetousness of commanders crowding in their slaves above the proportion for the advantage of freight is the only reason for the great loss to the company', the factors of the RAC wrote home to the directors from Cape Coast in 1681. 'If Your Honours would be pleased to beat them down in their number though you gave

---

* The *Vigilant* *sailed for Bonny, picked up 344 slaves, and was intercepted by the British naval vessels* Iphigenia *and* Myrmidon *on her way to Cuba.*

them five shillings per head extraordinary, Your Honours would be considerable gainers at the year's end.'[15] But the RAC did nothing: in London it was difficult to conceive of inhumanity in Africa, and 'tight-packing' remained the rule.

All the European nations lodged the two sexes of their slaves apart, as usual following Portuguese practice, ordinarily 'by means of a strong partition at the main mast, the forepart is for men, the other behind the mast for the women. If it be in large ships carrying five or six hundred slaves, the deck in such ships ought to be at least five and a half or six feet high [being] the more airy and convenient for such a considerable number of human creatures; and consequently far the more healthy for them.' Female slaves were treated better than the men, not being chained. The reason for these arrangements was not only to prevent the male slaves from seducing the women but also that black women were often said to do what they could to urge the men to assert themselves and attack the crew.

These slave decks were usually between the hold and the main deck of the ship. Any lowering of the slave deck, or extending it towards the bow or stern of the ship, in order to allow more room for the slaves, had the effect of reducing the area in which food and water casks could be stored. But on some ships a second tier of wood would be set up within the slave deck, so as to allow a second assembly of captives to be carried in two narrower compartments.

Most slavers had portholes, but the ships were normally too low in the water for them to be opened except in calm seas. Hatchways opening onto the deck allowed the slaves what air they could expect, without giving them any chance of escape.

Several distinguished scholars have recently shown that despite the comment of the RAC cited above, there was no close relation between 'tight-packing' and mortality. A meticulous analysis of statistics suggests that tightly packed ships in fact did not have a significantly larger number of deaths than more humanely stored ones: 'the number ... taken on board in itself did not relate to [the] mortality experienced by African slaves' during the crossing. The disadvantage of overpacking was not, it seems, that it in itself led to a greater incidence of disease, but that it was usually accompanied by a reduction in the space available for storing food for the voyage; and that, of course, caused malnutrition. An epidemic would, after all, sweep through even a lightly loaded ship; and if there were no epidemics, and the captain was clever as well as fortunate, he might be able to land most of his cargo even on a tightly packed vessel.[16]

A windsail, a funnel of sailcloth used to ventilate a ship, was some-times employed to try to force air through the slave deck, but its effectiveness of course depended on there being enough wind.

Officers and crew (and passengers, if there were any) also travelled in narrow circumstances on board these ships. The sailors would sleep in hammocks, or perhaps bunks, slung or built into any available corner. On the *Brookes*, for example, the crew's quarters lay aft of the slaves' compartment, and on the deck above were quarters for the officers, with a good cabin for the captain – on the *Brookes* this measured nearly fourteen feet long by about five feet broad and six feet high. Sometimes, if the ship was overloaded, the sailors would sleep in the boats, on the deck, or in gangways. The officers and the captain would often make less room for themselves by loading as many personal slaves as they could beneath their bunks or in their cabins. This was specially noticeable on voyages between Luanda and Rio about 1800 when at least twelve of these illegal slaves, depending on the size of the crew, would often travel. Sometimes captains and officers concealed these personal slaves from the officials in Luanda who had inspected the ship for weight and slave per ton; or they would bring in the slaves over the gunwale at night, after the formal inspection, perhaps stopping at one of the bays along the coast below the city to take on the smuggled cargo.

After eight days the ships would usually be out of sight of land, and the slaves would be allowed on deck. Great efforts were then made to maintain good spirits as well as good hygiene. Thus the captives would be organized in groups for the cleaning of the ship and required to sing while doing it. Jean Barbot wrote that on the French ships from La Rochelle on which he had served, 'thrice a week, we perfume betwixt' decks with a quantity of good vinegar in pails, and red hot bullets in them, to expel the bad air, after the place has been well scrubbed with brooms: after which, the deck is cleaned with cold vinegar'.[17] Captain Phillips of the *Hannibal* recalled that the Gold Coast slaves whom he used as the ship's non-commissioned officers took care 'to make the negroes scrape the decks where they lodge every morning very clean, to eschew any distempers that may engender from filth and dirtiness; when we appoint a guardian we give him a cat o' nine tails as a badge of his office, which he is not a little proud of'. Female slaves were often asked to work the corn mill, the corn being put, perhaps with rice or peppers, into the bean soup. About 'a fortnight after leaving', recalled Thomas Tobin of Liverpool for the benefit of the House of Commons, to whose committee he was testifying, 'I endeavoured, by keeping them in a good humour, to knock perhaps a dozen out of these irons on a morning; then the next morning the same; the men took it in good heart and they used to draw lots themselves to see who should be let out the next morning, until they were about half out, and then we let them all out.'[18]

Brutality was neither normal nor inevitable. It was in everyone's interest to deliver as many live slaves as possible to the Americas. An instruction of the Dutch Middelburgische Kamerse Compagnie in 1762–86 specifically insisted: 'Do not permit any Negroes, slaves, or slave women to be defiled or mistreated.'[19] That order went on to demand that 'care be taken that the doctor and supercargo check the mouths and eyes of the slaves every morning'. Jean Barbot, after his own slave voyages, recommended good treatment of slaves in order to 'curb their brutish temper', but also 'to lessen the deep sense of their lamentable condition, which many are sensible enough of, whatever we may think of their stupidity'. He also thought that, generally, on board ship, 'all possible care is taken to preserve and subsist them [the slaves] in the interest of the owners'.[20]

Yet the eighteenth century was a violent age; human life was not held in much respect. One description of a sea passage of a slaver was that, 'once off the coast, the ship became half bedlam and half brothel'. Captains often treated their own crews with criminal sadism, too. Captain William Lugen, of Bristol, was tried at Charleston for murder, because one of his female captives had a baby and the woman died. The crew committed the 'poor infant to the people of its own colour; but they, like true savages, handed it upon deck, and refused to admit it among them; their reason being that they believed the illness to be infectious. The infant was then left in the broiling heat of the sun and in the agonies of death (the surgeon said that it could not live the day). The captain ordered it to be thrown overboard.' He was later acquitted of murder, as 'there could [have been] no premeditated malice'.[21] On a French ship in the eighteenth century (probably the 1770s) the captain reported that the second captain, Philippe Liot, had 'mistreated a very pretty negress, broke two of her teeth, and put her in such a state of terror that she could only be sold for a very low price in Saint-Domingue, where she died two weeks later'.[22]

Thomas Tobin, the slaving captain of Liverpool who gave evidence to the House of Commons recalled, on the other hand, how if the slaves whom he was transporting 'had been in a nursery in any private family, they could not have been treated more [kindly]'. The whole ship's company, he said, was 'constantly employed . . . making everything [as] comfortable as could possibly be for the slaves. . . . They came up at about eight o'clock in the morning, and people were appointed over the hatchways with cloths, and they were rubbed down by themselves.'[23] Captain Thomas Phillips of the *Hannibal* wrote in 1694: 'I have been informed that some commanders have cut off the legs or arms of the most wilful [slaves], to terrify the rest, for they believe that, if they lose a member, they cannot return home again: I was advised by some of my officers to do the same, but I could not be persuaded to entertain the least thought of it, much less to put in practice such barbarity and cruelty to poor creatures who, excepting their want of Christianity and true religion (their misfortune more than fault), are as much the works of God's hands, and no doubt as dear to him as ourselves.'[24]

Food en route to the Americas was of course simple, with, as usual, a few national differences: manioc (or cassava) was a staple food on

Portuguese traders in Benin *c.* 1500, who obtained five slaves for a horse

Above: Newport slave traders carouse in Surinam *c.* 1755. Those still sober include Esek Hopkins, later Commodore of the United States Navy, and Joseph Wanton, later Governor of Rhode Island

Left: John Newton, the slave captain who wrote the hymn 'How Sweet the Name of Jesus Sounds'

Hugh Crow from Liverpool: one of a thousand captains from there who sailed for Africa to obtain slaves

Pierre Desse, a slave captain of Bordeaux in the illegal days, *c.* 1825

'Captain Jim' de Wolf, of Bristol Rhode Island: in his youth a slave captain, then a merchant, later a United States senator and cotton manufacturer

Robert Surcouf, corsair of Saint-Malo, who revived the French slave trade after 1815

Lisbon: at least 100,000 slaves were brought here from Africa in the fifteenth and sixteenth centuries

Liverpool: the largest slaving port in Europe: her merchants sent 4,000 slaving voyages to Africa between 1700 and 1807

Nantes: France's main slaving port, sent 2,000 voyages to Africa for slaves

THE COUNTY PALATINE OF LANCASTER.

1. S.t Nicholas Church.
2. Water Street.
3. The Old Tower.
4. The Beacon.
5. The Exchange.
6. The Tobacco Pipe.
7. The New Church.
8. Yeram.
9. S.t Peter's Church.
10. The Dock.
11. The Custom House.
12. The Charity School.
13. The Coppers House.
14. The Glass House.
15. Lawhill.
16. The Sugar House.
17. The Bowling Green House.
18. Eastham Ferry Boat.
19. Rock house Ferry Boat.
20. The River Mersey.

Elmina, the Portuguese stone-built castle on the Gold Coast, captured by the Dutch in 1637. Slaves were exported from here for 350 years

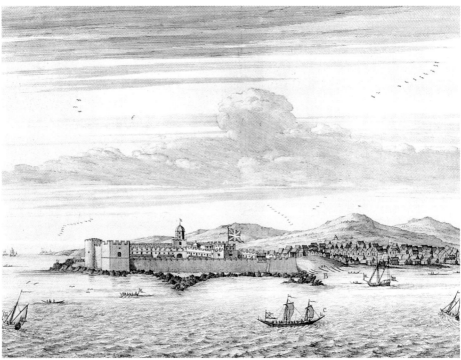

Cape Coast castle, built by Heinrich Carloff, became the English headquarters on the Gold Coast in the 1660s

Rio de Janeiro: the major slave port of Brazil, its merchants sent for and
received several million Africans *c*. 1550–1850

Havana: in the nineteenth century the largest slave port in the world, both as receiver of slaves and as a planner of voyages. Here the British are seen moving into the city after their defeat of Spain in 1762

Portuguese boats; maize (already known to the English as 'Indian corn') on English and Dutch ones; while it was oats, brought from France, on French ones. Rice or millet (grown in Africa) was also often available. To these, kidney beans, plantains (that is, coarse bananas), yams, potatoes, coconuts, limes, and oranges might be added. The food of the slaves was not much inferior either in quantity or in quality to that of the crew. It was also probably better than what the slaves would have enjoyed during the months of waiting or travelling in Africa.

By the late eighteenth century, a typical ration per day for a slave on a ship might be three pounds ten ounces of yam, ten ounces of biscuit, three and a half ounces of beans, two ounces of flour, and a portion of salted beef. One plantain and one ear of corn might be added three days out of five. A mouthwash of vinegar or lime juice might be given in the mornings, to avoid scurvy (as people had begun to realize was necessary after James Lind's celebrated treatise of 1754, though the Admiralty did not specify the need for such a juice till 1794; and surgeon Trotter of the *Brookes*, previously mentioned, was a pioneer in the practice).

Once again, the Portuguese had laid down precise regulations in 1519 about the food for the journey of a slave vessel and, for a time at least, those rules were maintained. The law of 1684 elaborated them. But captains bound for Rio from Luanda or Benguela in Angola often refused to buy what was needed. They even bribed officials in the port to permit them secretly to use the space which would have been taken up by food to add to the complement of slaves.

Supplies were almost always less than what was needed. An Irish sailor, Nics Owen, sailing with Captain William Brown from Sierra Leone to Newport, Rhode Island, in 1753, found that the ration for the crew was one ounce of salt meat every twenty-four hours, with just a half-biscuit in addition.

The Dutch fed their slaves 'three times a day with indifferent good victuals and' – so the crews insisted – 'much better than in their own country'. On the other hand, on French boats, a stew of oats would be cooked daily in a large copper, to which dried turtle meat (such as could be obtained in the Cape Verde Islands) or dried vegetables were added. Fresh vegetables and water were bought whenever the ship touched land. On English ships, meals were usually distributed to the slaves in tens in 'a small fat tub, made for that use by our coopers . . . each slave having a little wooden spoon to feed himself handsomely. . . .' Captain Phillips recalled that these meals were held on the main deck and forecastle, so 'that we may have them all under command of our arms from the quarterdeck in case of any disturbance; the women eat upon the quarterdeck with us, and the boys and girls upon the poop'. Meals on English ships were usually given twice a day, at ten in the morning and five at night: 'The first meal was large beans, boil'd with a certain quantity of Muscovy lard which we have from Holland. . . . The other meal was of pease, or of

Indian wheat "dabbadabb" [Indian corn ground in an iron mill], which we take for that purpose, as small as oatmeal, then mixed with water and boiled well in a copper furnace till as thick as pudding, to which salt, palm oil, and malaguetta [pepper] were added to relish.' It was thought that malaguetta pepper would give 'our negroes in their messes [something] to keep them from the flux [that is, acute diarrhoea] and dry bellyache'.[25]

The RAC always carried its own dry 'bisket', from England, as well as horsebeans and lard, and would buy maize on the Gold Coast before going to Calabar. In the early eighteenth century these English ships would also take with them baskets of potatoes, barrels of salt, hogsheads of palm oil, pepper, rice, chests of corn, and sometimes quantities of Suffolk cheese, vinegar, 'English spirits' (gin, presumably), and tobacco.

Different observers left contrasting impressions of slaves' desires. Jean Barbot found that slaves had 'a much better stomach for beans ... than Indian wheat, mandioca [manioc] or yams'. Thomas Phillips also recalled, 'These beans, the negroes extremely love ... beating their breasts eating them and crying "Pram, pram," which is very good.' On the other hand, Barbot said about 1700, 'A ship that takes in 500 slaves must provide above 10,000 yams, which is very difficult, because it is hard to store them, by reason that they take up so much room; and yet no less ought to be provided, the slave being of such a constitution that no other food will keep them: Indian corn, beans and mandioca disagreeing with their stomachs.'[26] A hundred years later, Thomas Tobin said much the same, save that he often needed 15,000 yams.

Sometimes it was necessary to force slaves to eat to prevent them from committing suicide by self-starvation. Barbot, who was, so he said, 'naturally compassionate', had nevertheless 'been necessitated some-times to cause the teeth of those wretches to be broken because they would not open their mouths'. Wilberforce instanced a captain who had ordered his mate to offer a recalcitrant slave a piece of yam in one hand and a 'piece of fire' in the other. For those recalcitrants, a special pair of scissors, or *speculum oris*, was carried. The blades were forced between the teeth of the rebel, and then the attached thumbscrew was turned in order to force the jaws apart.*[27]

The hour of meals was the most dangerous time for the crews: four o'clock in the afternoon was 'the aptest time to mutiny [, the slaves] being all on deck. . . . Therefore, all that time what of our men who are not employed in distributing victuals to them ... stand to their arms; and some with loaded matches at the great guns that yawn upon them, loaden with cartridge, till they have done. . . .'[28]

Dinner being ended, reported Jean Barbot, 'we made the men go down between decks, for the women were almost entirely at their own

---

* There is a reproduction of one of these, with other such things, in Clarkson's history of the abolition of the slave trade.

discretion, to be on deck as long as they pleased, nay, even many of the males had the same liberty by turns ... few or none being fettered [when at sea]. ... Besides, we allow'd each of them, between their meals, a handful of Indian wheat and mandioca and now and then short pipes and tobacco to smoke upon deck by turns and some cocoa nuts ... and the women [put] a piece of coarse cloth to cover them and the same to many of the men, which we took care they did wash from time to time to prevent vermin. Towards evening, they diverted themselves on the decks as they thought fit, some conversing together, others dancing, singing and sporting after their manner, which pleased them highly and often made us pastime, especially the female sex who, being apart from the males on the quarterdeck, and many of them young sprightly maidens, full of jollity, and good humour, afforded us abundance of recreation.' Both sexes were indeed 'encouraged to sing and dance as much as possible', the captain of a French vessel declared; 'for this purpose, two drums might be made available. Slaves who danced well might be given a small ration of eau de vie, as well as a little piece of meat or a biscuit. This gave them something to look forward to. They were never given pipes (for fear of fire), but a little tobacco in powder is all right for the same purpose.' Sometimes these dances were executed under the menace of a whip. Thomas Phillips recalled, 'We often at sea in the evening would let the slaves come up into the sun to air themselves, and make them jump and dance for an hour or two to our bagpipes, harp and fiddle.'[29]

It was asserted in the 1790s by an English slave captain, Captain Sherwood, that on slave ships there was as a rule adequate water. That was sometimes true, usually not. An average man may be supposed to require, in one form or another, a quart of water to drink every day, and a quart and a half in food. Africans were accustomed to drink more than Europeans. The Portuguese in 1519 laid down that adequate water should be provided on these vessels, and their law of 1684 specified what that meant: enough water should be carried to give each slave a daily *canada* (one and a half pints) for both drinking and cooking, which was, however, only half the ration established as necessary earlier in the century. Liverpool ships would often carry enough water to provide two pints a day, and ships from Nantes three pints or even slightly over a full gallon.

The space needed to provide adequate water was considerable: a Portuguese ship carrying 300 slaves would have to ship thirty-five barrels (*pipas*) by law. Jean Barbot said that at 'each meal we allowed each slave a full coconut shell of water and, from time to time, a dram of brandy'. In fact, a double supply of water was often shipped. Thus the ship *Brookes* carried in the 1780s 34,000 gallons of water for its 600 slaves and forty-five sailors. Yet a ration of three pints of water per slave per day would have required only 12,000 gallons.

These voyages were usually very hot as well as very crowded. Many slaves suffered from dysentery and therefore lost liquid at a rate which made even the ration of water prescribed by Portuguese law inadequate. Dehydration in conditions of over 100 degrees Fahrenheit below decks was frequent.

The RAC during the early years of the eighteenth century tried to provide machines 'to make salt-water fresh . . . to render the voyage much the shorter and . . . lessen the mortality of the Negroes'. But they were quite unsuccessful.

Water was often carried in most unhealthy ways. For example, on the voyage between Angola and Brazil, it was often stored in the same barrels which had been used to bring over Rio's special cane brandy, *gerebita*, on the outward journey, a preparation which fouled any liquid unless the barrels were thoroughly cleaned first. Water in Luanda and Benguela was anyway notoriously bad, as well as in short supply.

Despite the efforts of provident captains, illness was rife on slave ships. The enlightened Dominican Tomás de Mercado, whose treatise of 1569, *Tratos y contratos de Mercaderes*, included, as we have seen, one of the earliest criticisms of the slave trade,˙ recalled a Portuguese ship which lost 100 slaves out of 500 in a single night from an unrecorded disease.[30] Later, if the surgeons found any slaves indisposed, they would cause them 'to be carried to the *lazaretto*, under the forecastle, . . . a sort of hospital. . . . Being out of the crowd, the surgeons had more conveniency and time to administer proper remedies; which they cannot do properly between decks, because of the great heat that is there continually, which is some-times so excessive that the surgeons would faint away and the candles would not burn; besides that, in such a crowd of brutish people, there are always some very apt to annoy and hurt others, and all in general so greedy, that they will snatch from the sick slaves the fresh meat or liquour that is given to them'. Thus Jean Barbot, who added, 'It is in no way advisable to put sick slaves in the long boat upon deck, as was impru-dently done on the *Albion*, for they being exposed in the open air, and coming out of the excessive hot hold, and lying there in the cool of the nights for some time, just under the fall of the wind from the sails, were soon taken so ill of violent cholics and bloody fluxes that, in a few days, they died. . . .'[31]

An English surgeon in 1790 thought that two-thirds of the deaths on a slave journey were due to '*banzo*', a mortal melancholy, as it was described in a Brazilian dictionary, or 'involuntary suicide'.

In truth, dysentery, or 'the flux', was the worst of the diseases on the ships: a third of deaths were probably so caused, or from dehydration induced by it. Smallpox was probably the second most common cause of death, and earlier on it was probably even more destructive than the flux:

˙ *See page 146.*

'The negroes are so incident to the smallpox', wrote Captain Phillips at the end of the seventeenth century, 'that few ships that carry them escape without it and, sometimes, it makes vast havoc and destruction among them; but, though we had a hundred at a time sick of it, and . . . it went through the ship, yet we lost not a dozen by it . . . though it will never seize a white man.'[32] That latter immunity, it should be said, was something to which Europeans had become accustomed after the epidemic which had been so destructive in Mexico in the days of Hernán Cortés. Scurvy (known as *mal de Loanda* on Portuguese ships) was also to be found regularly, as well as skin diseases. Several kinds of ophthalmia occasionally also had devastating effects.

Losses aboard slave ships were usually recorded, though most of the early 'death books' for the Portuguese and Spanish deliveries of slaves during the first two centuries have long been lost. Fairly low figures, naturally, are recorded in the fifteenth and sixteenth centuries for Portuguese ships going direct to Lisbon: say 5 per cent maximum if the ship was coming from Arguin. But the average was far higher in the journey from São Tomé, in the unhealthy Bight of Benin: perhaps as high as 30–40 per cent. Tomás de Mercado, in 1569, thought that the average mortality on a slave voyage was 20 per cent. Brazilian historians have suggested losses of 15–20 per cent in the sixteenth century for the trade to Brazil and 10 per cent in the nineteenth. But there were sometimes much bigger losses. In 1625, for instance, five ships sent to Brazil by the Governor of Angola, João Correa de Sousa, carried 1,211 'pieces' and lost 583; another sixty-eight slaves died soon after the disembarkation. That meant a loss of over 50 per cent.

When the Northern Protestants entered the slave trade in the seventeenth century figures of deaths were better recorded. The RAC is known to have lost 14,388 slaves (24 per cent out of the 60,000 or so shipped) on voyages carried out by 194 ships between 1680 and 1688. Early in the eighteenth century that figure diminished to 10 per cent. By the 1780s the death rates on English vessels had declined further to about 5.65 per cent. The statistics between 1715 and 1775 in Nantes suggest that the highest loss was 32 per cent in 1732, the smallest 5 per cent in 1746 and 1774. Ships from Honfleur in the late eighteenth century lost 8.7 per cent. William Wilberforce, however, in his speech in 1788 beginning the long series of parliamentary debates on the question of the slave trade, talked of 12.5 per cent as normal, a figure which derived from an inquiry into the deaths on British ships examined by the British Privy Council. In 1791 the House of Lords estimated a loss of 8.7 per cent in 1791 and 17 per cent in 1792. But Thomas Tobin, a slave captain himself, giving evidence to a House of Commons committee many years later, thought that 3 per cent mortality was the average on his own ten voyages in the 1790s. A rate of 9 per cent may, however, be a reasonable estimate for the eighteenth century, with the Dutch having the lowest mortality among European slave traders.

As was natural, ships making the longest journey (for example, from East Africa) had the highest rate of mortality. Thus the captain of the South Sea Company's ship *George*, which lost all but ninety-eight of her 594 slaves in 1717, attributed the disaster to the 'length of the voyage', as well as to 'the badness of the weather'.

Many deaths on slave journeys across the Atlantic derived from violence, brawls, and, above all, rebellions. There was probably at least one insurrection every eight to ten journeys. On French ships though there seem to have been only about one every twenty-five voyages. Most such risings of slaves occurred when the ship was still off the coast of Africa or close to it, at the time of embarkation; or between embarkation and sailing. But there were still some in the open sea.

Every trading nation experienced these attacks. Usually they were mastered by the crew without serious losses to themselves. There were few examples of successful slave risings. But there were some. For example, in 1532, on the Portuguese ship *Misericordia*, commanded by Captain Estevão Carreiro, with 109 slaves being shipped from São Tomé to Elmina, the slaves rose and murdered all the crew except for the pilot and two seamen. Those three survivors escaped in a longboat and reached Elmina, but the *Misericordia* itself was never heard of again. The slaves did not know how to sail and, as occurred in most such instances, the ship was almost certainly lost. In 1650 a ship sailing from Panama for Lima was wrecked off Cape San Francisco, in what is now Ecuador. The captives killed the surviving Spaniards, and their leader, a determined slave who had taken the name Alonso de Illescas, established himself as the lord of the Indians in the region of Esmeraldas. Then in 1742 the galley *Mary*, with Captain Robert as master, belonging to Samuel Wragg of London and Charleston, was driven ashore, plundered, and destroyed in the River Gambia by the local people. The slaves on board rose, murdered most of the crew, and kept the captain and mate prisoners in the cabin for twenty-seven days. They eventually escaped to the French fort on the River Sénégal.

A rebellion with a curious ending occurred on the *Marlborough* of Bristol in 1752. This ship was owned by Walter Lougher and Co. The captain shipped about 400 slaves, some from Bonny and some from the Gold Coast. About twenty-eight of the latter were on the deck. The sailors were below, washing the slave decks. The slaves seized some arms and shot most of the crew of thirty-five, except for the boatswain and seven others. These were ordered to sail the vessel back to Bonny, which they did. There the Bristol slaver *Hawk* tried to capture the ship, but failed, for the ex-captives were by then well able to use firearms. A fight broke out between the Gold Coasters and the men from Bonny. The former emerged on top, after a hundred captives had died. The Gold Coasters set off for Elmina, guided by the Bristol survivors. None was seen again. The remaining slaves from Bonny lived to tell the tale.

But usually the rebellions were quelled, and brutally. Thus Willem Bosman recalled how in the late seventeenth century the anchor of an English ship was being carried onto his Dutch vessel and placed where the male slaves were kept. But the slaves 'possessed themselves of a hammer; with which, in a short time, they broke all their fetters in pieces upon the anchor; after which, they came up on deck, and fell upon our men, some of whom they grievously wounded, and would certainly have mastered the ship if a French and English vessel had not very fortunately happened to lie by us; who, perceiving by our firing a distressed gun that something was in disorder aboard, immediately came to our assistance with chalops* and men, and drove the slaves below deck.... Some twenty of them were killed.'[33]

There was also an important rebellion on the *Robert* of Bristol, Captain Harding in command. The ringleader of the slaves was that Tomba who may be remembered as having been harshly treated before setting out from Africa.[†] 'Tomba ... combined with three or four of the stoutest of his countrymen to kill the ship's company, and attempt their escapes, while they had a shore to fly to, and had near effected it by means of a woman-slave who, being more at large, was to watch the proper opportunity. She brought him word one night that there were no more than five white men upon the deck, and they asleep, bringing him a hammer at the same time (all the weapons that she could find) to execute the treachery. He encouraged the accomplices what he could ... but could now at the push engage only one more and the woman to follow him upon the deck. He found three sailors sleeping on the forecastle, two of whom he presently despatched, with single strokes upon the temples; the other rousing with the noise, his companions seized; Tomba coming soon to their assistance and murdering him in the same manner. Going aft to finish their work, they found, very luckily for the rest of the company, that the other two of the watch were, with the confusion, already made awake, and upon their guard; and their defence soon awakened their master underneath them who, running up and finding his men contending for their lives, took a handspike, the first thing he met with in the surprise, and redoubling his strokes home upon Tomba, laid him at length flat upon the deck, securing them all in Irons. . . .

'Captain Harding, weighing the stoutness and worth of the two slaves, did, as in other countries they do to rogues of dignity, whipped and scarified them only; while three other, abettors, but not actors, nor of strength for it, he sentenced to cruel deaths; making them first eat the heart and liver of one of them killed. The woman he hoisted up by

* *A chalop or shallop was a small open boat propelled by oars or sails and used in shallow waters.*
† *See pages 339 and 392.*

the thumbs, whipped and slashed her with knives, before the other slaves, till she died. . . .'[34]

In 1727 William Smith described how one night, 'the moon shining very bright . . . we heard . . . two or three Muskets fired aboard the [adjacent ship] *Elizabeth*. Upon that, I ordered all our boats manned and, having secured everything in our ship, to prevent our own slaves from mutinying, I went myself in our pinnace (the other boats following me) on board the *Elizabeth*. In our way, we saw two negroes swimming from her but, before we could reach them with our boats, some sharks rose from the bottom and tore them in pieces. We came presently along the side of the ship, where we found two men-negroes holding by a rope, their heads just above water; they were afraid, it seems, to swim from the ship's side, having seen their companions devoured just before by the sharks. These two slaves we took into our boat, and then went into the ship where we found the negroes very quiet, all under deck; but the ship's company was on deck, in a great confusion, saying that the cooper, who had been placed sentry at the forehatch-way, over the men-negroes, was, they believed, killed. . . . We found the cooper lying on his back quite dead, his skull being cleft asunder by a hatchet which lay by him.

'At the sight of this I called for the linguist and bid him ask the negroes . . . Who had killed the white man? . . . One of the two men-negroes we had taken up along the ship-side impeached his companion, and he readily confessed he had kill'd the cooper with no other view but that he and his countrymen might escape undiscovered, by swimming on shore. . . . We acquainted the negro that he was to die in an hour's time for murdering the white man. He answered: he must confess it was a rash action in him to kill him, but he desired me to consider that, if I put him to death, I should lose all the money I [*sic*] had paid for him.

'To this, I bid the interpreter reply that, though I knew it was customary in his country to commute for murder by a sum of money, yet it was not so with us; and he should find that I had no regard to my profit in this respect; for, as soon as an hour glass, just then turned, was run out, he should be put to death. . . . The hour glass being run out, the murderer was carried onto the ship's forecastle, where he had a rope fastened under his arms, in order to be hoisted up to the foreyard arm, to be shot to death. . . . As soon as he was hoisted up, ten white men who were placed behind the *barricado* on the quarter deck fired their musquets and instantly killed him. This struck a damp upon our negro-men who thought, on account of the profit, I would not have executed him. The body being cut down upon the deck, the head was cut off and thrown overboard . . . for many of the blacks believe that, if they are put to death and not dismembered, they shall return again to their own country after they are thrown overboard.'[35]

An insurrection off Accra was experienced by Captain Peleg Clarke of Newport, Rhode Island, in 1776. That captain wrote to John Fletcher, the ship's owner in London: 'I am sorry that I have so disagreeable a story now to tell which is [that], about the 8th of last month, our slaves rose on board and a large number of them jumped overboard, out of which twenty-eight men and two women were drowned. Six men were taken up by the Moree town people which [sic] Mr Klark, the [Dutch] governor of the fort at that place, took out of their hands, and has them in his fort. I endeavoured to get them, but the townspeople ask eleven ounces [of gold] per head for taking them up, so I could not settle it with them, and, being obliged to return to Accra again in order to settle, I have begged the favour of Mr Mill [one of a famous mercantile family of Guinea and the West Indies] to settle it for me. . . .'[36]

Slave rebellions were often reported in the press, once that medium took shape. The *Newport Mercury* reported in 1765: 'By letters from Capt. [Esek] Hopkins in the brig *Sally* belonging to Providence [the ship belonged to Nicholas Brown & Co.] arrived here from Antigua from the coast of Africa, we learn that, soon after he left the coast, the number of his men being reduced by sickness, he was obliged to permit some of the slaves to come upon deck to assist the people: these slaves contrived to release the others, and the whole rose upon the people and endeavoured to get possession of the vessel; but was happily prevented by the captain, who killed, wounded, and forced overboard eighty of them which obliged the rest to submit.'[37]

The most brutal punishment for a slave rising seems to have been the treatment meted out to the ringleader of a revolt on the Danish vessel *Friedericius Quartus* in 1709. This individual had his right hand cut off and shown to every slave. Next day, his left hand was cut off, and that, too, exhibited. On the third day, the man's head was cut off, and the torso hoisted onto the mainyard, where it was displayed for two days. All the others who had taken part in the rebellion were whipped, and ashes, salt, and malaguetta pepper were rubbed into their wounds.[38] Here is an account by one of the executioners on the *Affriquain* of Nantes, whose journey to numerous ports in Africa has been described:* 'Yesterday, at eight o'clock, we tied up the most guilty blacks, that is those who led the revolt, by their arms and feet and, lying them on their backs, we whipped them. As well as that, we put hot plasters on their wounds to make them feel their faults the more.' The captain left the slaves to die of their injuries.[39] A Dutch captain suspended the Ashanti rebel Esserjee from a crossbar by his arms (his hands had been already cut off); here he was abused by the crew till he died. Captain John Newton recalled that, after rebellions, he had seen slaves sentenced to 'unmerciful whippings, continued till the poor creatures have not had power to groan under their misery, and hardly a sign of life has remained. I have seen them agonising for hours, I believe for days together, under the torture of thumb screws.'[40]

*

* *See pages 390–91.*

Other perils for the slave ship came from storms, calms, and pirates.

In the case of storms, slaves were often called on to help an over-worked or exhausted crew. Thus we hear how, 'in the midst of these distresses, the vessel, after being three weeks at sea, became so extremely leaky, as to require constant exertion at the pumps. It was found neces-sary, therefore, to take some of the ablest negroes out of the irons and employ them at this labour, in which they were often worked beyond their strength.'[41]

The most disgraceful slave voyage was occasioned by a storm. In 1738 the Dutch vessel *Leuden* was stranded by weather on rocks off the Suriname coast, at the mouth of the River Marowijne (now the border between Suriname and French Guiana). The crew closed the hatches of the slave decks to avoid pandemonium and then escaped with fourteen slaves who had been helping them; 702 slaves were left to drown. Even more costly, though less shameful, was the case of the Danish *Kron-Printzen*, which was lost in 1706 in a storm with no fewer than 820 slaves on board.

Whatever the outcome, a storm was, of course, always a much-feared eventuality. Off Mozambique a Portuguese captain reported: 'Suddenly, the weather closes in, and the sea rises so high and forcefully that the ships obey the waves without course or control, at the mercy of the winds. It is then that the din from the slaves, chained to one another, becomes horri-ble. The clanking of the irons, the moans, the weeping, the cries, the waves breaking over one side of the ship and then the other, the shouting of the sailors, the whistling of the winds, and the continuous roar of the waves ... Some of the food supplies are pushed overboard.... Many slaves break their legs and their arms, while others die of suffocation. One ship will break apart from the fury of the storm and sink.... The other drifts on, dismasted, ruined by the force of the ocean ... on the verge of capsizing.'[42]

As for calms, the Capuchin friar Carli described being on a boat from Benin to Bahia in the late seventeenth century when the boat remained still for days. Everyone was afraid. The seamen prayed to St Anthony on their knees, having fixed his statue to the deck.

There was also much evildoing by Europeans against Europeans, even while the slavers were still in Africa. For example, Matthew and John Stronge of Liverpool reported in 1752 how they sent their snow *Clayton* to the River Bonny, how it took on board 324 slaves, and how, two days after leaving, it was seized by 'nine Englishmen, who had before robbed their own captain, and another ship; after cruelly wounding the said captain, they turned him adrift in their boat and ordered the mate ... to steer the vessel to Pernambuco in Brazil. But soon after their arrival [there], he, getting on shore, discovered the matter to captain John de Costa Britto, Commander of the *Nazarone*, a Portuguese man of war.'[43] Captain Britto sold the slaves, now reduced to 200 by sickness, and gave the money forthcoming to the Portuguese treasury. The brothers Stronge spent many years trying unsuccessfully to be reimbursed by the King of Portugal.

Captain John Jones, Master of the *John and Mary* of Virginia, and bound there with a cargo of 175 slaves, was in 1724 at anchor about six miles off Cape Charles, at the end of Chesapeake Bay, when a 'ship bearing British colours bore down on him, he [being] . . . not at all apprehensive of any pirate . . . did not offer to make sail, but was surprised to find himself attacked, with a command to strike his colours and come on board in his boat and, at the same time, to see about seventy small arms pointed at his ship, threatening to fire into her if he did not immediately do so.

'At his going on board in his boat, he, with four of his men, [was] immediately secured, [and] was carried into the great cabin to a person called the Captain, who ordered about fourteen men, mostly Spanish, to take possession of the *John and Mary*, to get under sail and to follow him. . . . About eleven in the forenoon of the same day, they met the Brigantine *Prudent Hannah*, of Boston. . . . The Spanish ship gave chase to her and, coming up with her, commanded the Master, Captain Mounsell, to come on board. He came in his boat, with only his cabin boy, and his boat was immediately sent back with five Spaniards to take possession. . . . On the six of June, the Spaniard, with his prize standing off ENE from the capes of Virginia about eight leagues, made a sail which proved to be the *Godolphin* of Topsham, bound for the Rappahannock River in Virginia.' The Spaniards hoisted an English ensign, and put out a pendant and a Union Jack and stood off to intercept that ship and, under these colours, fired a great gun for the *Godolphin* to bring to, which she did, and the master (Theodore Bane) being commanded off in his boat, the Spaniards . . . took possession. . . .

'The three captive captains . . . received the following information from several English and Irish men of that [sixty-strong] crew: viz, that "the said ship belonged to the Governor . . . of Cuba, that she was called the *San Francisco de la Vela*, that the captain is Don Benito . . . that he is a knight of one of the Spanish orders, that the ship is a Bristol-built galley, first taken by the Sallee Orders [the Moroccan pirates], retaken from them by a Spanish man of war, sold at Cales [Cádiz?] by some merchants and by them freighted to the West Indies . . . and hired to Benito . . ."' Captain Jones, it appears, lost 'his scripture, about £350 sterling in gold dust, 1000 gallons of rum, about £200 worth of the remains of the Guinea cargo, together with 38 of his choicest slaves. . . .'[44]

Occasionally slavers themselves turned pirate. In 1723, for example, the RAC noted, 'Our merchants have advice that the ship *Baylor*, Capt. [William] Verney, having been slaving on the coast of Guinea, and

---

* *That river's estuary was important in the slave trade to Virginia.*

thence set sail for Virginia, turned pirate, the negroes being thrown over-board.'[45]

This long voyage, known to history as 'the Middle Passage', with its innumerable tragedies, did, however, in the end reach its term.

22

GOD KNOWS WHAT WE SHALL DO WITH THOSE THAT REMAIN

'God knows what we shall do with those that remain, they are a most scabby flock. . . .'

Henry Laurens, c. 1756, Charleston

'On avait pourtant réussi le miracle de ne perdre que vingt noirs. Mais le cargaison était en piteux état.'

René-Auguste de Chateaubriand

'On Thursday last arrived from the coast of Africa, the brig Royal Charlotte *with a parcel of extremely fine, healthy, well limb'd Gold Coast slaves, men, women, boys and girls. Gentlemen in town and country have now an opportunity to furnish themselves with such as will suit them. . . . They are to be seen on the vessel at Taylor's wharf. Apply to Thomas Teckle Taylor, Samuel & William Vernon. . . .'*

Newport Gazette, 6 June 1763

AFTER FORTY TO FIFTY DAYS AT SEA, or in some cases, as we have seen, many more, the appearance of birds, or perhaps of grass smelling of marsh, would suggest to the captain of a slaver that he was near the Antilles; or, after a different length of time, by different routes, the coast of Brazil or of Virginia. Then, according to the nationality of the vessel, familiar ports might come into view.

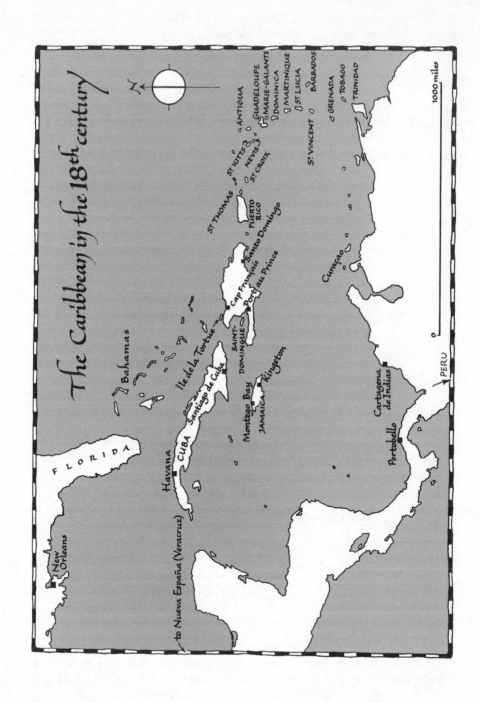

The Caribbean in the 18th century

FLORIDA

New Orleans

to Nueva España (Veracruz)

Havana
CUBA
Santiago de Cuba

Bahamas

Île de la Tortue

SAINT-
DOMINGUE

Montego Bay
JAMAICA
Kingston

Cap Français
Port au Prince

Santo Domingo
PUERTO
RICO

S.t THOMAS
S.t KITTS
NEVIS
S.t CROIX

ANTIGUA
GUADELOUPE
MARIE-GALANTE
DOMINICA
MARTINIQUE
S.t LUCIA
S.t VINCENT
BARBADOS
GRENADA
TOBAGO
TRINIDAD

Curaçao

Cartagena
de Indias

Portobello

PERU

1000 miles

The attention of those harbours would be caught by firing a gun, and that would attract a pilot and the visit of the doctor. The distant, but all the same vile, smell of vomit, sweat, stale urine, and faeces wafting over the port concerned would let its citizens know that a slave ship had arrived.

As usual, the arrival of the slaves in the fifteenth century in Portugal set the tone for what happened next. Once a ship carrying slaves had anchored off Lisbon, in the old days, several officials (the Director of the Casa da Guiné, the Treasurer of the Port, a magistrate, a collector of taxes, and their guards and clerks) would be carried out to the ship to inspect the cargo; the slaves would be assembled on the deck and listed. They would then be taken to the Casa dos Escravos, where they would be divided into lots for the purpose of deciding the taxes due. The Director and the Treasurer would carefully examine each slave, who would be naked. A price would be fixed. This would be hung round the slave's neck, on parchment. Buyers would then also make their inspections, much as the ships' surgeons or others had made on the coast of Africa. Slaves were then sold as the merchants who had financed the expedition thought best, though sometimes they would ask the director of the Casa da Guiné to undertake the sale. Most slaves were sold through a broker, who would take 2 per cent of all payments. Then there would be taxes to pay, and perhaps a present to the officials of the port, which sometimes amounted to a tenth of the value of the slaves carried.

That was the pattern. But every port in the Americas, from Brazil to New England, as well as in Lisbon, had its different way of marking this 'ceremony of arrival'. Nearly everywhere, in contrast to Lisbon, the slaves were assembled onshore in a camp (not on board ship), where they would be fed, cleaned, and otherwise looked after, in such a way that they would lose all trace of the 'fatigues' of the journey. Meantime, the vessels themselves would be disinfected or fumigated (by slaves, of course).

The main Brazilian port for slaves from the seventeenth century to the nineteenth was Rio de Janeiro, 'the most magnificent harbour in the world', as it appeared to travellers who approached it by sea. Bahia, the old capital, was only half as prosperous, and by 1750 was beginning to be overtaken by Pernambuco, Recife, and Maranhão. All the same, slaves were sold there: 'Who would believe it?' Amadée-François Frézier, a French engineer who travelled to South America in the early eighteenth century, in order to look at Spain's and Portugal's imperial fortifications, wrote of Bahia. 'There are shops full of these wretches, who are exposed there entirely naked, and bought like cattle.' The traveller added, 'I cannot think how they can combine this barbarity with the sayings of religion, which give [the slaves] the same soul as the whites.'[1]

'There being no difference between negroes and goods', in the words of a Portuguese official in 1724, the sale of slaves in all these harbours was methodical, simple, and well organized.[2] Few slaves went on from these ports to remote distances, for the sugar plantations of the north-east and even the gold mines of Minas Gerais were close at hand. In Rio, at the end of the eighteenth century, most slave dealers lived and dealt in large houses in a long street, the Rua Vallongo, which ended in a beach in the north-eastern part of the city. The site was pretty, and travellers noticed red-tiled houses wedged between the tree-covered Livramento and Conceiçao hills. But every house seemed to have a large 'ware-room', in which 300 or 400 slaves were 'exposed for sale like any other commodity'. The merchants would live on the first and second floors, while the slaves would be lodged on the ground floors, in large rooms opening onto patios kept fresh by sea breezes. There the slaves would be prepared to be sold, being shaved, fattened, and if necessary painted (to give the illusion of health), often by slaves of their own nation. Food in African style (*pirão*, or manioc stew, and *angu de fubá*, cornmeal mush) might be prepared, in an effort to make the slaves feel at home. Some religious instruction might casually be available. Tobacco and snuff were sometimes given to slaves who behaved well, or to cheer them if they seemed melancholy. Slaves would also be made to dance and sing, in order to raise their spirits, in the same way as aboard the ship which had brought them from Africa.

Buyers would again patiently examine the wares, feeling the Africans' limbs and bodies much as butchers handled calves. The slaves were often asked, as they had been told to do before leaving Africa, to show their tongues and teeth, or to stretch their arms. A 'guide for the plantation owner' published in the nineteenth century (Imbert's *Manual do Fazendeiro*) insisted that it was important to pay attention to the slave's penis in order to avoid acquiring an individual in whom it was underdeveloped or misshapen and, therefore, bad for procreation. The slaves would be ranged according to sex, age, and, sometimes, provenance. Often slaves would be sold at auction by one or other of the houses which specialized in the business, the bidding being at the door of the customs house. Occasionally the merchants would seek to sell their slaves by hawking them, chained, from house to house. Usually the purchase in Rio meant the slave would be rebranded with the name of the new owner, and a 5 per cent tax, the *siza*, was paid by the buyer to the government.

But in these showrooms the deaths due to heat, overcrowding, or illnesses contracted on the ships were just as frequent as in African trunks or on the ship, so that quite distant neighbours complained incessantly about the smell. Numerous huts were soon put up on the swampy shore; there, however, even more slaves would die in the next fifty years, of 'scurvy, scabies, buboes [plague] and dysentery'. It remains curious that, leaving aside questions of common humanity, merchants who had gone to such trouble and expense to find and transport their captives did not take better care of them.

This avenue of tears, the Vallongo, today the Rua Camerino, had been allocated to the slave merchants by a philosophically minded viceroy, the Marquis of Lavradio (he also brought rice for the first time to Brazil), in 1769; previously, he wrote, the slaves had done 'everything which nature suggested in the middle of the street where they were seated on some boards that were laid there, not only causing the worst kind of stench on those streets and their vicinity, but even providing the most terrible spectacle that the human eye can witness. Decent people did not dare to go to the windows, [and] the inexperienced learned there what they had not known and should not know.'[3]

The counterpart of Rio de Janeiro as the main port for receiving slaves in the Spanish empire was Cartagena de Indias, which in 'its best days', in the early seventeenth century, received at least 3,000 slaves a year, in about twenty ships. When a slave ship arrived there, it would undergo an elaborate (but nevertheless ineffective) inspection to ensure that there was no contraband. The log of the ship would be checked, and there would be a visit to the vessel by the Royal Health Inspector, the *Protomédico*, to see if there were diseases on board. If there were, the ship would be quarantined. But since slaves were always in such demand, the common procedure was that the obviously sick slaves would be held on land, in barracoons outside the walls of the city, and the healthy slaves would be received by the Chief Constables of the place, and by a representative of the Spanish government, or even, according to the circumstances, by the Governor. There were in Cartagena many documented instances of kindly behaviour at the point of arrival, by priests and others: above all, by the Catalan-born Jesuit Fray Pedro Claver, the 'saint of the black slaves', who in the early seventeenth century made a point of greeting affectionately the slaves at Cartagena, embracing and welcoming them, as well as assuring them that the colonists did not intend to boil them down for oil or for anything else.* On innumerable occasions Claver entered the infested holds of the ships where the slaves were kept, and not only brought the captives spiritual comfort but bandaged their wounds and sores; sometimes he carried out the sick on his own shoulders. He also baptized slaves who had not been so welcomed into the Church before leaving Africa, as were most who left the Gold and the Slave Coast. Perhaps he christened as many as 100,000 slaves during his ministry, which lasted from 1616 to his death in 1654.[4] Some Spanish priests also made noble efforts to bring dying slaves into the Church; others still tried to make up for the ineffectiveness of the baptisms which had been carried out in Africa by rechristening the captives, and giving them medallions to put round their necks.

Disembarkations also had their terrible side at Cartagena; for the barracoons in which the slaves were held were often 'veritable cemeteries'.

* *Claver was canonized by Pope Leo XIII in 1888.*

Fray Alonso de Sandoval, a Jesuit who was one of the inspirations for Fray Pedro Claver, described how he entered a patio in Cartagena to find two dead slaves, 'stark naked, lying on the bare ground as if they had been beasts, face up, their mouths open and full of flies'.[5] Sometimes slaves were held in estates outside Cartagena especially prepared to receive those who had been fraudulently disembarked on the coast before the ships entered the harbour, in order to avoid the port dues. Smuggling was, of course, at the heart of all American commerce, and in no region was this more true than in the territory of New Granada. But even smugglers wanted their merchandise to seem at their best, and so they would expect slaves to be well fed before sale. Physical defects which had escaped the eagle eyes of ship's surgeons in Africa (eye defects, for example, or skin marks) lowered the price, but moral ones (a disposition to drink, thievery, or flight) did not seem to do so.

Before sale, slaves were usually submitted to yet another *palmeo* – that is, another careful examination, including a measuring and grading – and were also, as in Brazil, branded again by a *carimbo*, a silver iron designed to show that the slave had been legally imported.

Many buyers in the seventeenth century would come to the slave market in Cartagena, some from as far as Mexico, others from Lima. Cartagena was a stepping stone to both – above all, to Lima via Portobelo. Another long journey would then begin for the slaves, much of it by sea, followed by a long march by land if the destination was the City of Mexico. Subsequent resales, such as those held in the Zócalo in Mexico City, the main square, under the arcades, must have seemed almost merciful affairs. Here, and in similar places far removed from the original dock, prices greatly varied: a prime male slave in the early seventeenth century might cost 250–275 pesos in Cartagena, 370 in Mexico, 500 in Lima, and as much as 800 in Potosí. Specialized slaves – bricklayers, agents of estates, dressmakers, cooks – would naturally cost more.

Buenos Aires by 1750 had become one of the most important slave harbours of the Spanish empire. It was a deposit for Córdoba, itself a centre of distribution for Potosí and upland Peru. At least 7,800 slaves carried by the South Sea Company to Buenos Aires were taken by that enterprise's local agents to Chile, Bolivia, or Peru between 1715 and 1738, the caravans of walking slaves being conducted by Englishmen on horse-back (who had, most unusually, been given permission to travel in the Spanish empire), accompanied by some Spaniards, one of them a surgeon. These terrestrial extensions of the oceanic Middle Passage added the new horrors of cold to those of excessive heat encountered on the way from Africa: in one caravan of 408 slaves dispatched in 1731 thirty-eight men and twelve women died of cold before they reached Potosí.

Curaçao and St Eustatius were the two main Dutch harbours of the Caribbean at the turn of the eighteenth century. Tiny though they were, they were much frequented by private merchants, interlopers, and independent traders of all nationalities, who sold to planters in the English, the French, and above all the Spanish islands. Curaçao had its golden age in the seventeenth century; a hundred years later, St Eustatius had its turn to act as the 'golden rock', selling annually 2,000–3,000 slaves. In both places, smuggling was as important as legitimate trade. Another important Dutch port was Berbice, New Amsterdam, in what was then the Dutch colony of Suriname. Here Dutch servants might often be seen inspecting the slaves before the auction. The Africans would be obliged 'to go through every kind of motion, as if their limbs would be pulled out of joint, or their jaws cracked open. . . . One lady was not satisfied till she had forced a wench to screetch by squeezing her breast cruelly.'[6]

French journeys were concluded in much the same way as those of other countries. A vessel from Nantes or Bordeaux, or Honfleur or La Rochelle, bound for the El Dorado which Saint-Domingue seemed to the French to be after 1750, would pass by the Virgin Islands or Puerto Rico. There would then appear the northern coast of Saint-Domingue, the luxurious capital, Cap Français, 'Le Cap', where the merchants' local agents would hire a large field with some huts. There, as elsewhere in the slaving world, a combination of a few days' idleness and good food would make the slaves ready for sale. The captives in Saint-Domingue were usually given strong drink to enliven them. The checking of captives seems to have been more rigorous in the French colonies than elsewhere; in Louisiana, an agent of the importing company (the Compagnie des Indes) would examine the assets of the planter to determine whether he could pay.

Saint-Domingue was a relatively new colony. Other customs prevailed elsewhere. Father Labat described how on arrival at Fort-de-France in Martinique slaves would be ordered to bathe in the sea, and their heads would be shaved. Their bodies would be rubbed with palm oil, and they would be persuaded to eat often, and little: 'This good treatment, together with the clothes which they are given, and along with a certain kindness [douceur] which is showed them, makes them affectionate and causes them to forget their own country, and the unhappy state to which slavery has reduced them.'[7] Sometimes, in Saint-Domingue, sales were effected on board the ship (it was easier to prevent flight there), sometimes in the field hired by the merchant where the slaves would have been 'refreshed'.[8]

Then there were taxes. In 1715 Achille Lavigne, captain of the *Grand Duc de Bretagne* of Nantes, owned by the Bertrand family, complained that he was obliged on his arrival in Martinique to pay not only 2,750 livres to the Governor, Abraham Duquesne, but 3,000 too to the *Intendant*, M. Caucresson, and 1,000 livres to M. Meunier, the *Commissaire*, 'which

---

[·] *The* intendant *and the* commissaire *were important officials in France, and the offices had been extended to the empire.*

sums they forced him to pay, without which he would not have been able to make his sale of blacks in the said isle . . .'.'[9]

The best way for a captain to ensure a good sale was to have a subsidiary office in the American port and use a good agent there. This technique was well developed by French traders. Thus Jacques-François Begouën-Demeaux, probably the richest slave trader of Le Havre in the second half of the eighteenth century, was represented by his brother-in-law, Stanislas Foäche, in Port-au-Prince; and the Nantes firm of Riedy et Thurninger had a subsidiary company at Cayes Saint-Louis in 1791. The Charauds of Nantes were ill-served in the New World till they bought a fifth share in Guilbaud, Gerbier et Cie of Cap Français.

Ten to twenty days were needed at Saint-Domingue to dispose of 500–600 slaves. Since fifty *négriers* arrived each year at Saint-Domingue in its prosperous days, the slave markets must have been continuous.

English ports such as Jamestown in Barbados, Charleston in South Carolina, or Kingston, by the late eighteenth century the main port of Jamaica, were less ceremonious and bureaucratic than their French or Dutch counterparts, but also apparently less careful of hygiene and less concerned to prepare the slaves before sale. Thus sanitary arrangements seem to have been unknown in Kingston: 'Dunghills abounded and, from these, the ruts in the streets and lanes were filled up after very heavy rain. In the early morning, negro slaves might be seen bearing open tubs from the various dwellings and emptying their indescribable contents into the sea.'[10]

After a sale in Kingston in 1773 of slaves intended (illegally) for Cuba, Thomas Dolbeare reported on the slaves carried by the *Ann*, belonging to Aaron Lopez and Jacobo Rodrigues Ribera, of Newport, Rhode Island: 'Fifty-seven were sold the first day averaging £63 – clear of duty, fourteen the third day at £51, twenty-two the fifth day at £32, the remainder at £8 only. Had there been five times as many, and the negroes good, they would have sold at the price they did the first day, there were a number of old men, but the boys went off very high. . . . I have acted from principle, gentlemen,' Dolbeare concluded, in his letter to Lopez, 'in the sale of this cargo and I hope it will be satisfactory. . . .'[11]

Slaves imported to Jamaica for subsequent sale in the Spanish empire were, however, normally treated more carefully. As usual, they would as a rule be fattened and acclimatized. The South Sea Company of London made elaborate arrangements to restore them to health after the voyage from Africa. At one time, it was thought best to bathe sick slaves in water in which the leaves of herbs had previously been soaked. These slaves might receive two meals a day, and were sometimes given rum to drink and occasionally pipes to smoke. Then, after about a month, they would be sent by small ships to Cartagena or another of the great Spanish ports.

Occasionally, after these English journeys, the sale of slaves would be a 'scramble': Dr Thomas Trotter, surgeon in the *Brookes*, recalled how 'people who wish for slaves are ready, when the signal is given them, to open the sale to apply their tallies to the slaves [whom] they wish to purchase, by rushing all at once among them. This unexpected manoeuvre had an astonishing effect upon the slaves; they were crying out for their friends with all the language of affliction at being separated.' Equiano, the eloquent slave autobiographer, left a description of how this kind of sale was carried through. He was sold in Barbados 'after the usual manner, which is this: on a signal given (as the beat of a drum), the buyers rush at once into the yard, where the slaves are confined, and make choice of that parcel they like best. The noise and clamour with which this is attended, and the eagerness visible in the countenances of the buyers serve not a little to increase the apprehensions of the terrified Africans. . . . In this manner, without scruple, are relations and friends separated, most of them never to see one another again.'[12] Sometimes, though, merchants were much more considerate: Jean Barbot, for example, described how in 1679 he sold an entire family to a single master, 'since he did not care to separate them'.[13]

Slaves who excited no interest, or were too ill to do so, 'refuse slaves', were often left to die unattended on the quayside of the port of entry into the Americas. James Morley, a gunner, a sailor in the trade in the 1760s, recalled seeing such captives 'lying about the beach at St Kitts, in the market place, and in the different parts of the town, in a very bad condition, and apparently nobody to take care of them'.[14]

Sometimes, too, there were incipient rebellions among the cargoes at the port of arrival. Also at St Kitts, on 14 March 1737, one slave captain 'found a great deal of discontent among the slaves, particularly among the men which continued till the 16th about five o'clock in the evening when, to our great amazement, above a hundred slaves jumped overboard, and it was with great difficulty we saved as many as we did; out of the whole, we lost thirty-three of as good men slaves as we had on board. . . . The reason (I have learned since) of this misfortune was owing to one of their countrymen who came on board, and told the slaves, in a joking manner, that they were first to have their eyes put out and then to be eaten. . . .'*[15]

Charleston, South Carolina, was the biggest port of entry for slaves in North America (even if the merchants were established in Rhode Island or in Bristol, England). Outside the port, ships carrying slaves would have to wait at the pesthouse on Sullivan Island for ten days for clearance; and if they turned out to be suffering from smallpox they would have to wait a month or so in quarantine. The sales were usually in the open-air exchange behind the post office, at the foot of Broad Street, a short walk from the wharf where the slaves arrived; the women in blue flannel dresses, the men in blue cotton trousers. In winter, humane traders sometimes gave the slaves shoes and warmer clothing.

* *For a similar joke which went horribly wrong, see page 718.*

Henry Laurens, the most interesting of the slave traders of this city, described in 1755 how 'our common method of selling slaves, arrive at what time they will, is for payment in January or March following. If they are a very fine parcel, purchasers often appear who will provide the ready money in order to command a preference. The engagements we enter into in the slave trade are . . . to load the ship with such rice as can be got, pay the coast commissions and men's half wages, and to remit the remainder [to Bristol, for example] as the payments shall grow due.' Apropos of a sale in Charleston which did not do well, Laurens wrote to Samuel and William Vernon, his partners in Newport, Rhode Island, that on 29 June 1756 he had put up for sale some slaves from Sierra Leone who had been brought in one of the Vernons' vessels, the *Hare* (which he, Laurens, had insured): 'We had as many purchasers as we could have wished for had we had three times the number for sale but, in taking a transient view of them, before they were landed, many of them became extremely angry that we should invite them down from eighty or ninety miles distance to look at a parcel of "refuse slaves", as they called them and, with some difficulty, [we] prevailed on them to wait the sale. . . . We were willing to believe that Captain [Caleb] Godfrey obtained the best [slaves] he could but, really, they were a wretched cargo, such a one as we would not have touched could we have been excused from it for three times our commission.

'We have this day sold forty-two to the amount of £7,455-12 shillings [in] currency,' Laurens went on, 'in which are included that sold at vendue [auction] for only £35-12 shillings. They seemed past all hopes of recovery. God knows what we shall do with those that remain, they are a most scabby flock. . . . Several have extreme[ly] sore eyes, three very puny children and, add to this, the worst infirmity of all others with which six or eight are attended, viz. old age. . . . Poor Godfrey seems very distressed that he should not have been able to do better. . . . We had a sloop arrive with a hundred and fifty prime slaves from the factories at Gambia and Bance [Bence] island the evening before the sale of your negroes which would not have at all injured your sale had they been good, for we did not discover what a prime parcel they were till after the first day's sale was over.'[16] (These were the years when William Vernon and Abraham Redwood, also of Newport, were buying slaves in Africa at the rate of 115 gallons of rum a man slave and 95 gallons for women.)

In Charleston in 1755 most people thought that the new war – the Seven Years War – would dampen the prices of slaves. On the contrary, with respect to a cargo of slaves imported by Captain Robert Bostock of Liverpool, on the *Prince George*, ''twas so much the reverse that some of the buyers went to collaring each other' – so Laurens reported – 'and would have come to blows, had it not been prevented, in contending for the choice which gave the seller an excellent opportunity to make them pay what price he pleased and, through them, he got £300 for some.'[17]

Still, a year later, Laurens would write to Richard Oswald, part-owner of the factory on Bence Island, off the River Sierra Leone, that he had not sold all the slaves whom he had sent: 'We still have several remaining of your nine, two of them [from] Gambia which [*sic*] we would part with on very moderate terms could we find the person who would make the offer, but nothing will tempt them but prime young people.'[18]

English slave traders, like their French counterparts, would by the eighteenth century usually have their representatives in the New World. For example, Isaac Hobhouse of Bristol, who sold so many slaves in Virginia, had agents all over North America, many of them deeply involved in the local tobacco trade, or perhaps indigo.

Many captains of slave ships looked on their task as, as a rule, complete when they had delivered their slaves to the West Indies. But it was often impossible to realize the proceeds of the sale of slaves fast enough to provide the ship concerned with a return cargo of sugar. Merchants and captains could not be certain of the prices which they would receive at home for goods taken on their own account. Planters might take several years to pay for the slaves. Sometimes the European merchant preferred to have remittances from the West Indies in bills of exchange than to have sugar, indigo, cotton, or ginger in exchange for the slaves, because the prices of these goods in London were either unpredictable or low. Planters might prefer to give their own bonds for five years to pay for slaves, instead of bills of exchange for twelve to eighteen months. These could be used to make payments, but the planters sometimes were obliged to stop payment when owing considerable sums to suppliers (assuming they were English) in London or to manufacturers in Manchester and Birmingham. So, sometimes, the return journeys of many slave ships, belonging to all the major countries concerned, were in ballast. Captains might be told by their owners that they should return quickly 'unless a freight offers . . . worth staying a fortnight for'. But such return journeys were unusual: out of 300 ships which left Jamaica in the last years of the eighteenth century, only twelve left in ballast.

North American and Caribbean planters mostly had bank accounts at home (whether that meant England, France, or Holland). They usually did one of three things when they made their purchases: they paid in cash for the slaves, in money 'of the islands' (the French livre there was worth a third less than its equivalent in France); they asked for credit from the merchant, which might be a matter of up to two years (even ten years, exceptionally); or they might settle the bill in merchandise, rarely for the entire amount, frequently for a small percentage. This last might, according to the colony concerned, be sugar (first and foremost), semi-refined or raw; indigo (in decline after 1750); cotton; and coffee (first mentioned in the Caribbean in 1730 and popular with captains of slave ships thereafter). Irregularly, there were reports of ginger, vanilla, tobacco, and skins. Snuff also played a part.

Full payment upon delivery of the slave was rare. Although the value of the debts was expressed in colonial currencies, payments were often made in commodities which had a clear value in Europe. Probably the most normal procedure in the 1780s was for 25 per cent of the bill to be paid immediately, either in cash or cargo, with the rest to be paid over eighteen months. The planter would give the agent of the merchant a series of bills due on certain dates, usually at intervals of thirty, sixty, or ninety days. Portions of the bills were sometimes paid with receipts for earlier sales of slaves, the balance still owed in a bill of exchange drawn on a guarantor in Europe.

Payment for slaves brought to the Spanish colonies as part of the *asiento* was almost always in silver: pieces of eight.* That was why the Spanish market had always been so attractive, and indeed why Havana would become a popular market for United States slavers once the trade was authorized there after 1789: 'Get what hard cash you possibly can,' one Rhode Island captain was advised by his ship's owner.

Portuguese sales in Brazil were complicated since the slaves themselves were, by the late eighteenth century, usually owned by Angolan merchants until their sale in Rio or Bahia or elsewhere. Payments in kind or in cash were made into the bank of the merchant concerned in Brazil. The transaction was, therefore, simpler than the practice of Northern European merchants.

The heart of the matter was the hunger of the colonists for slaves. They were always buying up to, or beyond, their limit, as if this transaction was their last chance of obtaining essential labour. Thus planters borrowed, and extended the system of agricultural credit beyond all bounds. Most slaves sold in Charleston and elsewhere in British North America in the eighteenth century were bought on credit. Many slave merchants, therefore, did not know when they would be paid. That eventually led them, especially those in Liverpool, to insist on 'immediate remittance', which caused a merchant's colonial agent to send back on the slave ship a receipt for the purchase in the form of bills of long maturity drawn by the factors on their guarantors in England.

In the American port, however the bill for the slaves was settled, and whether the place concerned was part of the British, Spanish, French, Dutch, or Portuguese empire, the captain would reorganize his crew, for some sailors would not want to return to Europe, and few journeys would have been completed without deaths among the ship's company. Those sailors who planned to go home, having usually been away a long time, always wanted to do so quickly, as indeed did the captain.

* *A piece of eight was a peso, or Spanish dollar, equal to eight reals.*

The average return voyage from the West Indies to Europe across the Atlantic might take between two and three months. Then would begin the sale of such merchandise as had been brought home; and the reckoning of the profits, if there were any.

The question of profits is a complex one. Henry Callister, a Manx agent in charge of the warehouse of the Liverpool slave merchant Foster Cunliffe, on Chesapeake Bay in the 1740s, wrote to his brother, Anthony, on the Isle of Man, 'The Africa trade is quite dangerous for life and health, though most profitable.' His neighbours the merchants Thomas Ringgold and Samuel Galloway disagreed: 'There are more disasters in those voyages than any other whatsoever', the former wrote to the latter in 1762.[19] What is the truth of this matter?

To put matters at their simplest: in 1783 the firm of Giraud et Raimbaud of Nantes sent its 150-ton ship the *Jeune Aimée* to Angola and obtained 264 slaves, whom it sold in Saint-Domingue. The price of the ship had been 6,000 livres; with other expenses (wages for the crew, the cargo, the slaves at Mayombe), the initial costs came to about 156,000 livres. The slaves and some other goods were sold for a total of over 366,000 livres. The profit, then, was 210,000 livres, or about 135 per cent. That was, however, the ideal voyage, the voyage of which merchants dreamed, the voyage which caused them to risk so much, in money and lives (including so many European sailors' and captains' lives). It was that kind of voyage also which inspired captains who themselves thought, with reason, that one day they, too, might become merchants; and, it fired the imagination of younger officers who thought that they too one day might become captains. But when John Newton was asked in the House of Commons in 1790 if he thought that the trade was profitable, he replied: 'My concern in it was not profitable to my employers [Joseph Manesty of Liverpool]: there were gainful voyages, but the losing voyages were thought more numerous. It was generally considered a sort of lottery in which every adventurer hoped to gain a prize.'[20] Those who heard that the RAC was buying slaves in Africa for a little over £3 a head and selling them in the Americas for £20 often did not take into account that the company had to manage its forts in Africa, and transport its cargo from London to be exchanged there. Some slave merchants ruined themselves. For example, Noblet Ruddock of Bristol, after 'managing' thirty slave voyages between 1698 and 1729, more than any other single merchant in that city except one (James Day), was bankrupt by 1726 (he later became a mere slave factor in Barbados).

Sometimes, though, and despite the scepticism of Newton, 'miracles' did occur. Thomas Leyland, thrice Mayor of Liverpool, made a profit of £12,000 from a voyage of the ship *Lottery*, whose captain was John Whittle; in 1798 the ship carried 460 slaves from the River Bonny to Barbados. Indeed, Leyland's accounts suggest that he had repeated successes: Captain Cesar Lawson in the *Enterprize* in 1803,[*] Captain Charles Kneal in the *Lottery* in 1804, Captain Charles Watt in the *Fortune* in 1805 all performed very well, bringing back an average profit of about £40 per slave delivered.

For most of the history of the slave trade profits were made by independent traders. National privileged companies, on the other hand, often made losses, because they were staffed at home, and in Africa, by officials who all assumed that they were there to make a private profit out of the enterprise. On the other hand, sometimes even privileged companies were fortunate. Accounts of the RAC's journeys to the Windward Coast in Africa – between Sierra Leone and Cape Three Points – are available for 1680 till 1687. There were ninety-five voyages. In these eight years, three cargoes showed a net loss; the largest profit was 141 per cent; the average was 38 per cent. In the early eighteenth century, the South Sea Company also seems to have made a profit of nearly 30 per cent on its trade with Buenos Aires; and no director complained then that the costs of the traffic were too heavy.

But the real profits at that time were made by 'interlopers', who would usually sell slaves in the West Indies, or on the mainland of both North and South America, to New Englanders as to Brazilians, for more than twice what they cost on the Congo coast. These traders did make considerable profits, sometimes as much as 200 per cent, as, for example, one ship from Nantes did. Usual figures for Nantes in the early eighteenth century ranged from 50 to 100 per cent. The news of such great profits became well known; it is that which presumably led Humboldt to suggest that a profit of 100 per cent was normal, and some polemicists to assume an average profit of 300 per cent.[†]

The prices on the two sides of the Atlantic at the end of the eighteenth century were drawing closer. The cost of slaves in Africa, as we have seen, was about the equivalent of £50 by 1780: ten times what it had been a hundred years before. It can hardly be surprising, therefore, that profits fell: in the second half of the eighteenth century, the merchants of Luanda who traded with Bahia sometimes found that slaves were 'sold for less than they cost'. The accounts of Aaron Lopez in Newport, Rhode Island, suggest a remarkable change from earlier in the century: out of fourteen voyages which he financed to Africa between 1760 and 1776 between four and seven of them only made a profit. Reasonably accurate information survives for twenty-five slavers sent from Nantes in 1783–90. Ten made profits, six of them gaining more than 19 per cent; six lost money; one expedition broke even; and eight were apparently about to lose money when payments ceased at the end of 1792, thanks to the revo-

[*] *See Appendix 5.*
[†] *Alexander von Humboldt, traveller, naturalist and polymath, author of* Voyage aux régions équinoxiaux du nouveau continent.

lution in Saint-Domingue.* In the last sixty years of British slaving, the annual returns seem to have been less than 10 per cent. Another estimate for the British slave trade between 1761 and 1807 was a profit of 9.5 per cent, with a high level of 13 per cent achieved in 1791–1800 and a low one of 3.3 per cent in 1801–7.[21] John Tarleton of Liverpool told a British inquiry in 1789 that '10 per cent ought to be the net profit in the African trade'. The average profit in the accounts of the Liverpool slaver William Davenport was 10.5 per cent over seventy-four voyages, and his overall annual profit averaged 8 per cent. In this connection, an analysis of the profits made by the London Scottish circle of Richard Oswald, Augustus Boyd, and Sir Alexander Grant who, it will be remembered, traded extensively from Bence Island, off Sierra Leone, seems to suggest that their nearly sixty slave voyages made a profit of £30,000, a benefit of a mere 6 per cent.

Of one hundred journeys by Dutch ships in the second half of the century forty-one seem to have registered losses. A careful analysis of Dutch slaving expeditions undertaken both by the Dutch West India Company and by interlopers suggested profits of little more than 3 per cent, with an annual gain of 2 per cent at most on investments. A study of the Middelburg company suggested that between 1761 and 1800 it must have had an annual profit of only 1.43 per cent, though it had cleared over 8 per cent in 1751–60.

A similar study of the Maranhão Company of Brazil in the mid-eighteenth century suggested a profit of 30 per cent, but that figure did not take into account many costs.

From the early eighteenth century onwards there were always voices within the Danish West India Company arguing that the slave trade bought losses: Frederik Holmsted, the company's bookkeeper from 1708, was a critic of the trade for that reason.[†]

To summarize: considerable profits were made in the slave trade in the seventeenth and early eighteenth centuries. At the end of the latter era, however, prices of slaves rose considerably in Africa, so that profits averaged 8 to 10 per cent, the same kind of percentage obtained in ordinary commercial undertakings. But some skilful, or lucky, merchants continued to prosper greatly. At all times, the costs of the privileged companies in salaries, upkeep of forts, and other bureaucratic activities limited their profits. The decline in profitablity of the traffic at the end of the eighteenth century was undoubtedly in the minds of some traders in slaves by 1780; but that does not seem to have had much effect on the extraordinary course of events then about to transpire.

For which see page 521.
† But the company never listened. Its directors always believed that the colonies in the West Indies – St Thomas, St John, and St Croix – had to be served.

Book Five

ABOLITION

23

ABOVE ALL A GOOD SOUL

*'One cannot put oneself into the frame of
mind in which God, who is a very wise
being, took it upon himself to put a soul,
above all a good soul, into such an entirely
black body.'*

Montesquieu, L'Esprit des lois

'THE ATTRACTIVE AFRICAN METEOR', as a pamphleteer employed by the
bakers of Liverpool later described the Atlantic slave trade, was at its
height in the 1780s.[1] Well-equipped ships carried about 70,000 or more
Africans every year to enthusiastic ports all along the coastlines of
North and South America and the Caribbean. Perhaps half that number
was carried by captains from that most modern and freedom-loving
of nations, Great Britain. About two-thirds of the captives sent from
Africa were taken to colonies making sugar, the most sought-after of
tropical products. There may have been 3,000,000 slaves altogether in the
New World. William Pitt, the British Prime Minister from 1783, thought
that the West India trade, which depended so heavily on slaves, was
responsible for four-fifths of the income reaching Britain from across
the seas.[2]

Many subsidiary trades depended on the traffic in slaves – cotton in
Manchester and Rouen, wool from Exeter, rum from Rhode Island,
brandy from Rio de Janeiro, wine from Bordeaux and La Rochelle, guns
from Birmingham and Rotterdam. All those concerned knew the 'African
trade' to be an important outlet.

Every few years, new developments, maritime or technological,
appeared, to make things easier for the many practitioners. Thus in the
1770s slave vessels began to sail with copper-sheathed bottoms, which
resisted shipworm and sailed faster.* Even in Luanda, that white man's
grave in Angola, a prudent Portuguese governor was introducing new
standards of hygiene on vessels bound for Brazil, and insisting that his

---

* *The first naval vessel to be copper-sheathed was the frigate* Alarm, *in November 1761.*

own officials should inspect the ships, rather than leave the task to local men.

Imperial authorities in Europe were becoming less concerned with national exclusiveness. After 1783 France opened up her slave ports in the Caribbean to foreign traders, providing that they paid a tax. The liberal Viceroy of New Granada, Archbishop Caballero y Góngora, inspired an active commerce in slaves between Cartagena and the English Antilles in the mid-1780s.

The biggest French slaving port, Nantes, which sent more than 1,400 slaving expeditions to Africa in the eighteenth century, and was in the 1780s challenging Liverpool as the largest carrier of slaves, had 'that sign of prosperity which never deceives, namely new buildings. The *quartier* near the Comédie [the new theatre] is magnificent, all the streets at right angles and of white stone,' wrote Arthur Young. 'I doubt whether there is in all Europe a better inn than the Hôtel Henri IV.'[3] We catch a glimpse of these remarkable aristocrats of commerce, the slave traders of Nantes, in a memoir of Francis Lefeuvre: 'They form a class apart, never mixing, save when business requires it, with the other merchants who approach them only with signs of a profound respect.... They are important personages, leaning on high, gilt-topped canes ... dressed in full city regalia, their hair carefully arranged and powdered, with suits made of dark- or light-coloured silks according to the season; wearing long waistcoats, and breeches, also of silk, and white stockings and shoes with large gold or silver buckles. They carry a sword.... What should be most admired is their fine linen and the resplendence of their shirts, which they send to be washed in the mountain streams of Saint-Domingue, where the water whitens clothes much better than in French rivers.'[4]

In England, Temple Luttrell, MP for Milborne Port, reflected the accepted wisdom when he declared in the House of Commons in 1777: 'Some gentlemen may ... object to the slave trade as inhuman and impious; let us consider that, if our colonies are to be maintained and cultivated, which can only be done by African negroes, it is surely better to supply ourselves ... in British bottoms.'[5] Not for nothing, it might be added, was he the grandson of a governor of Jamaica.

Ambitious European powers were expanding their Caribbean interests. Sweden, in 1784, received an island, the barren Saint-Barthélémy, in the Lesser Antilles, with about 408 slaves and 542 French settlers, from King Louis XVI, in return for permitting French trading privileges at home in Gothenburg. The Governor of this new colony sought to build a Swedish slave trade, though that idea foundered.

But as already hinted, a phenomenal change was on its way. In Britain, in the Anglo-Saxon colonies, in France, and then in the many places where French and English ideas were influential, hostility was growing towards both the slave trade and the very existence of slavery.

The seventeenth century, otherwise so productive of political ideas, had little critical to say of the slave trade. Milton, it is true, wrote some fine lines in *Paradise Lost* which insisted that:

> Man over men
> He [God] made not lord, such title to himself
> Reserving, human left from human free.[6]

But it is obscure whether he thought of Africans as included within that generous comment. Both Grotius and Hobbes considered slavery to be as reasonable as Sir Thomas More had. Locke saw slavery as a 'state of war continued between a lawful conqueror and a captive'.[7] He probably inspired a paragraph accepting slavery in his draft of the 'Fundamental Constitutions' or 'Grand Model of the new colony of Carolina'; and, as has been seen, he was also a shareholder in the Royal African Company. George Fox, the founder of the Quakers, preached brotherhood by letter to the slave owners of the West Indies, and denounced slavery in Barbados; but in Pennsylvania he, like his disciple William Penn, the founder of the colony, owned slaves.

There had been for some time considerable unease over the matter of slavery in the Catholic Church. But the proclamations by crown or pontiff continued to denounce the enslavement of the mild Indians rather than the competent Africans. Firm statements of King Philip III of Spain (II of Portugal) spoke in 1609 of 'the great excesses that might occur if slavery were to be permitted in any instance'.[8] But that monarch was evidently speaking of Indian slaves. Pope Urban VIII (Barberini), in a letter in 1639 to his representative in Portugal, condemned slavery absolutely, and threatened with excommunication those who practised it. This denunciation derived explicitly, however, from the journey of Spanish Jesuits to Rome to protest against the enslavement of thousands of Brazilian Indians by the *bandeirantes* of São Paulo.[9]

Still, the proclamation of Pope Urban's statement caused an uproar in Brazil. The Jesuits, who were known to have urged it, were expelled from their college in Rio. But, again, the controversy affected only the Indian slaves. It is true that missionaries, in letters to the Congregation for the Doctrine of the Faith, often described the evil effects of black slavery on their own work, and there was a further meaningless papal condemnation of the institution in 1686. But in the Atlantic-facing ports Catholics were as deaf to such statements as were Protestants. There is no record in the seventeenth century of any preacher who, in any sermon, whether in the Cathedral of Saint-André in Bordeaux, or in a Presbyterian meeting house in Liverpool, condemned the trade in black slaves. La Rochelle and Nantes were far apart in matters of religion, but they were as one on the benefits of the trade in slaves. The greatest preacher of the age, António Vieira, was the friend of Amazonian Indians – but not of African slaves, whose plight he seems never to have mentioned, in any of his astounding sermons. Indeed, like Las Casas 150 years earlier, he urged solving the problem of shortage of labour in Brazil by importing more African slaves, in order to enable the Indians to live better.

As will be recalled, the Dutch West India Company at first pronounced against the idea of trading slaves. Early seventeenth-century Amsterdam, indeed, took a humane attitude to such things. The work of Brederoo has been discussed.· But by the mid-1620s these hesitations were forgotten – a reminder that humanity can diminish as well as grow, in the seventeenth as well as in the twentieth century.

Meantime, there had been just a few irritants to the slave traders in France. When it was proposed that Africans should be introduced into the French empire, Louis XIII is supposed to have paled and said no, since slavery was forbidden on French territory. He was, however, persuaded that in removing these unhappy beings from paganism the *négriers* would convert them to the religion of Christ. On his deathbed he apparently said that 'since the savages would be converted to the Christian faith, they would become French citizens, capable of all the responsibilities, honours, and donations' of a Frenchman;[10] and France in the seventeenth century became used to seeing blacks, mostly from the Antilles, but some from Africa direct, for example the slave Aniaba, christened by Bossuet, the black servant of Queen Anne of Austria. In 1642 the Protestant synod at Rouen had to reproach 'over-scrupulous persons who thought it unlawful for Protestant merchants to deal in slaves':[11] a helpful remark for the commerce, since Rouen was about to embark on a long, if minor, life as a slave port. In 1698, a theologian, Germain Fromageu, presiding over a tribunal in Paris for cases of conscience, denounced the many slave traders and owners who did not ensure that their slaves were fairly procured – that is, by war, not kidnapping. Still, these were pinpricks, and the French trade in slaves, as has been seen, enjoyed profits throughout the eighteenth century.

In spite of the denunciations of Indian slavery by the Pope and others, there was little difference in the Europeans' treatment of Indian and African slaves. Indians captured by the Anglo-Saxon colonists of North America were sometimes punished by being shipped to the West Indies. Such hesitations as the colonists felt about enslaving Indians derived from *raison d'état* as much as from piety: it was thought dangerous to antagonize certain peoples. For that reason – not, it would seem, from delicacy of sentiment – Massachusetts, Connecticut, and Rhode Island all banned the import of Indian slaves, in the early eighteenth century; Jamaica (where the indigenous population had long since died out) did the same, though not till 1741.

Some criticism could be heard in England during the second half of the seventeenth century of the profitable trade in English indentured

· *See page 162.*

servants: but in 1670 a bill prohibiting the export of convicts was rejected, and another, against the theft of children, was never properly discussed. Judge Jeffreys, showing a humanity for which he is not generally renowned, wanted to imprison a mayor of Bristol who permitted the kidnapping of servants, but the merchants who benefited were not restrained.

All the same, at the beginning of the Anglo-Saxon adventure in North America there were a few doubts about the morality of the slave trade, even of slavery as such. The Massachusetts Body of Liberties in 1641, for example, made a Delphic statement: 'There shall never be any Bond-Slavery, Villeinage, or Captivity amongst us, unless it be lawful captives taken in just wars and such strangers as willingly sell themselves or are sold to us . . . provided this exempts none from servitude who shall be judged thereto by authority.'[12] But, of course, the concept of a 'just war' was less clear than it should have been.

In 1644 a New England ship returned from Africa with two slaves; a legal dispute showed that the slaves had been kidnapped, not bought, in Africa. The magistrates in Massachusetts ordered the slaves returned to Africa and the responsible seamen arrested. An early act of the General Court of Rhode Island also included the tart reflection that though there was 'a common course practised amongst Englishmen to buy negers, to that end that they might have them for service for ever', Rhode Islanders were adjured to prevent 'black mankind or white being forced by covenant bond or otherwise . . . to serve any men . . . longer than ten years'.[13] This was an instruction which Rhode Islanders in particular would find it hard to fulfil.

These documents are ambiguous, giving to some modern writers evidence that slavery was abhorrent to the early settlers, and to others proof that Massachusetts was as conscious of the need for slaves as any other colony. In truth, the availability of indentured servants from Europe blunted the need for slaves until in the early eighteenth century people in England began to worry about underpopulation more than overpopulation; the indentured servant, however, with his commitment to work for only ten years, usually seemed more expensive than the black slave.

These attitudes in North America were given some support by a petition of the Reverend Richard Saltonstall, who in 1645 denounced not only the murder of certain black slaves who were said to have been brought to New England from Africa, but also 'the act of stealing negers, or of taking them by force . . . on the Sabbath Day', as being 'contrary to the law of God and of this country.'[14] But Cotton Mather, a Unitarian, one of the founders of Yale University, and a constant advocate of fair treatment of slaves, seemed in several of his 450 published works uncomfortable about the 'fondness for freedom' in so many captives' minds: as

---

* *The publication of these laws in 1672 left out the words 'and such strangers'.*

slaves in America, he said, voicing an opinion shared by thousands of Europeans, 'they lived better than they would have done as free men in Africa'.[15] All these contradictions derived from the fact that there were no laws in English North America stating positively that slavery was legal, but it was assumed to be so from immemorial usage.

These dignified ambiguities in North America did not last. Joseph Dudley, a cold, ambitious, and effective governor of Massachusetts, was found reporting that the province had 550 slaves in 1708, mostly in Boston and mostly bought in the West Indies. In Rhode Island, hostility to slaves (if it was indeed ever profound) came to be limited by the desire of its assembly to realize duties on their import. Slaves came there, though 'the whole and only supply to this colony is from . . . Barbados'.[16]

Some English Protestant voices were heard attacking slavery in the late seventeenth century – just when English participation in the trade was beginning. The Puritan Richard Baxter, for example, compared English slaveholders to Spanish conquistadores: an accusation intended to be highly insulting. It was better, he thought, to call those who owned slaves demons than Christians. Then the remarkable Aphra Behn, the first Englishwoman to make a living as a writer, praised, in 1688, in her *Oroonoko, or the History of the Royal Slave*, a noble Cormantine from the Gold Coast, a man with a face of 'perfect ebony', killed after leading a doomed slave revolt in Suriname – the Dutch colony which Mrs Behn had known as a child, where her alleged father had been Lieutenant-Governor during its short-lived time as an English colony. A dramatic version of the novel in 1696 (by Thomas Southerne) presented these noble slaves' predicament to fascinated audiences in both England and France for nearly a hundred years. Oroonoko, it is true, offered 'gold or a vast quantity of slaves' in return for his own liberty – thereby indicating an egotism which would not please later opponents of slavery. Yet Aphra Behn's contribution to the preparation for the abolitionist movement can scarcely be exaggerated. She helped to prepare literary people's minds for a change on humanitarian grounds. She was more influential than popes and missionaries.[17]

In the early eighteenth century the indications that some kind of ethical dimension should affect the trade grew more and more frequent. Thus in 1707 a secretary of the Royal African Company, no less – Colonel John Pery – wrote to a neighbour, William Coward, who was interested in promoting a slave voyage, that it was 'morally impossible that two tiers of Negroes can be stowed between decks in four feet five inches'. He went on to admit that any limitations would risk the profitability of the expedition: to add one tier in such circumstances was feasible.[18]

Twenty years later, in 1729, the ship's surgeon Dr Thomas Aubrey would recall that his captain on the slave ship *Peterborough* had asked: 'What the devil makes these plaguey toads die so fast? To which I answer: 'Tis inhumanity, barbarity and the greatest of cruelty of the commander and his crew. . . .' He advised slave merchants to be as careful of slaves as if they had been white men. 'For, though they are heathens, yet they have a rational soul as well as us; and God knows whether it may not be more tolerable for them in the latter day [of Judgement] than for many who profess themselves Christians.'[19]

The eighteenth century in England was scarcely a sentimental era, yet it produced a positive anthology of poetry which directly or indirectly condemned slavery. These verses were in the style of the famous and successful Scottish poet James Thomson, who, in his immensely popular *Seasons* (first published 1726–), would describe a shark, which was following a slave ship,

> Lured by the scent
> Of steaming crowds, of rank disease, and death,
> Behold! he, rushing, cuts the briny flood,
> Swift as the gale can bear the ship along;
> And from the partners of that cruel trade,
> Which spoils unhappy Guinea of her sons,
> Demands his share of prey – demands themselves![20]

The reflection gains poignancy if it be recalled that Thomson was the author, in 1740, of the most famous patriotic verse in English, 'Rule, Britannia!', where it was famously stated that (even if they might be slave merchants) the British would never be slaves.

Daniel Defoe, Richard Savage, William Shenstone, and even Alexander Pope asked, just as explicitly,

> Why must I Afric's˙ sable Children see
> Vended for Slaves, though form'd by Nature free . . . ?

and imagined, as Pope did,

> Some happier island in the wat'ry waste,
> Where slaves once more their native land behold.[21]

Sir Richard Steele, in 'Inkle and Yarico', also spoke of the issue of slavery in touching terms. So did Laurence Sterne in *Tristram Shandy*.

Yet such allusions were partly persiflage. It was a fashionable thing for these elegant gentlemen to affect outrage at the sufferings of Africans. Their contemporaries were always talking of slavery in one context or another: 'the slave of pomp' is a frequent figure of speech in the works of

---

˙ *The romantic 'Afric' figures often in poems such as these reaching, via Milton, Swift, and Gay, its consummation in the preposterous line of Bishop Heber's hymn, which speaks of 'Afric's sunny fountains'.*

Savage, as is 'slave to no sect' in Pope. But they had little idea of the implications of what they were saying, even though such publications as John Atkins's *Voyage to Guinea, Brasil, and the West Indies*, of 1735, candidly described the business of slaving (Atkins had been a surgeon in the navy). Defoe, a polemicist more than a poet, did not pursue the subject (which he touched on in *Robinson Crusoe*): iniquity in England consumed his attention. He himself had been anyway concerned in the creation of one of the largest of slave-trading enterprises, the South Sea Company. The poet Thomson accepted the sinecure of Surveyor-General to the Leeward Islands, which included several prosperous slave-powered islands, such as Nevis and St Kitts. Yet the contributions of these writers were, in the long run, very important. They helped to create a state of mind in which cultivated people in Europe's most free country, which was also the biggest slaving nation, began to deplore the institution of the trade in Africans if not of slavery itself.

The Church of Rome continued to make intermittent hostile complaints. In 1683, for example, Alderamo Cardinal Cibo, the Papal Secretary of State, wrote to the Capuchin mission in Angola from Rome, in the name of the Sacred College, that he understood that 'the pernicious and abominable abuse of selling slaves was yet continued ... and requiring us to use our power to remedy the said abuse; which, notwith-standing we saw very little hope of accomplishing, by reason that the trade of this country lay wholly in slaves and ivory'.[22] All the Capuchins did was to try to stop Protestants, such as the Dutch and English, from buying slaves. But that venture was equally impossible. It is true that in 1684 two Capuchin friars did start talking in Havana against the slave trade. The Governor sent them home to Spain on the first boat, and the Council of the Indies declared that they should never be allowed to return to America. Then, at the very end of the seventeenth century, the Bishop of the Cape Verde Islands, Frei Victoriano Portuense, denounced the frequent failure to baptize slaves: 'Knowing the manifest injustices by which the people are made slaves in Guinea, the only excuse ... is to say that these Gentiles are being taken out to receive the light of the church.' But he added, perhaps speaking ironically: 'My scruples are not so great that I totally condemn this trade, seeing that it is tolerated by so many men of letters and great theologians.'[23]

A curious conversation occurred in the Congo in the late seventeenth century between Father Merolla, an Italian Capuchin friar, and an English captain (the Capuchins were in those years the most exemplary of the religious orders, the only missionaries who worked in the fever-stricken interior of the Congo). The latter accused the former of trying to persuade the King of Congo not to sell slaves to him. Father Merolla said the King of Portugal had given orders not to make any such sales to heretics. The English captain said that the Duke of York, the President of the Royal African Company, was a Roman Catholic. Father Merolla said he was sure that the Duke did not want his representatives to sack African towns and kidnap slaves, as one English captain had done the previous year. He thought that he would write and tell his fellow countrywoman Mary of Modena, Duchess of York, how badly the English were conducting themselves. The captain became furious. In the end, however, the King of Congo did trade privately with the English, behind the back of the Capuchins.[24]

Still, the only place where any government actually intervened to ameliorate conditions in the slave trade remained Portugal. Many provisions about the good treatment of slaves had been issued to the governors of Angola, but these usually took the form of general admonitions to protect the slaves, rather than specific standards. In 1664, a law in Lisbon specified the minimum amount of water which should be carried on a slave ship from Angola. In 1684, as has been seen, another decreed formal restrictions on the ratio of slaves per ton of shipping: the slave-carrying capacity of each ship would thenceforth be listed in its registration papers. The figure varied from 2.5 to 3.5 slaves per ton, depending on the character of the ship (if a decked ship, or one with portholes, etc.). Child slaves (*molleques*) could be loaded at five per ton, but they could be carried only on the open, weather decks. Adequate water – a *canada*, or one and a half pints a day – should be provided for each slave. Other clauses of the law concerned the provision of food, and the duration of the voyages. This might have seemed a beginning of better times for slaves, but bribery of officials prevented the enactment of these rules; and anyway, as suggested earlier, a *canada* was inadequate.*

In all the richer parts of the New World Dominicans and Jesuits, Franciscans and Carmelites still had slaves at their disposal. The French Father Labat, on his arrival at the prosperous Caribbean colony of Martinique in 1693, described how his monastery, with its nine brothers, owned a sugar mill worked by water and tended by thirty-five slaves, of whom eight or ten were old or sick, and about fifteen badly nourished children. Humane, intelligent, and imaginative though Father Labat was, and grateful though he was for the work of his slaves, he never concerned himself as to whether slavery and the slave trade were ethical. He was required, on one occasion in 1695, to buy twelve slaves from a consignment which had arrived at Basse-Terre from Africa, having been brought by a ship belonging to a M. Maurelet of Marseilles, one of the least active of the French slave ports. Labat made the purchase without self-reproach, though he did later comment on the sad condition of these captives who, he thought, had arrived 'tired, after a long voyage'. The only occasion on which he used the word 'infamous' to describe what he saw was when he observed an African dance. He was convinced that the Church had a special responsibility to 'inspire in the Africans the

* *See page 419.*

cult of the true God', to purge them of idolatry, and to make them 'perse-
vere to the death in the Christian religion which we had caused them to
embrace'.[25]

Once again the Vatican spoke out against slavery at the beginning of
the eighteenth century: knowing that the dominions of the King of
Portugal still had the largest number of slaves in the Christian world, the
saintly and active Umbrian Pope Clement XI caused the Congregation for
the Doctrine of the Faith to ask his nuncios in Madrid and Lisbon to act so
as to bring about 'an end to slavery'. But there was no response whatsoever. Clement had anyway offended the Bourbon kings of France and
Spain by taking the side of the Habsburgs in the War of the Spanish
Succession. The Inquisition was at that time still more concerned about
the possibility that some slave dealers were secret Jews than about the
trade. For example, with regard to the *asiento* of the Portuguese Cacheu
Company, at the end of the seventeenth century, the Holy Office at Cartagena de Indias denounced to the Spanish Crown three Portuguese agents
who were responsible for the traffic there – Felipe Enríquez, Juan Morín,
and Gaspar de Andrade – for being 'of the hebraic nation'. These men had
allegedly even been seen, in Cartagena, after a delivery of slaves, both
killing lambs and keeping the Sabbath in the Jewish manner. But the
accusations never bore fruit; the persons concerned were able to escape
castigation easily.

In English America the voices of doubt about, or hostility to, slavery
were a good deal more frequent. In 1676, for example, a Quaker, William
Edmundson, a wild friend and companion of George Fox, the society's
founder, dispatched a letter from Newport, Rhode Island, to Quakers in
all slave-owning places. He put forward the theory that slavery should be
unacceptable to a Christian. It was 'an oppression on the mind'. This
caused the aged Roger Williams, the father of the colony, to denounce
him as 'nothing but a bundle of ignorance and boisterousness'.[26]
Edmundson also justified rebellions of slaves in Barbados, where two
Quakers (Ralph Fretwell and Richard Sutton) had been fined by the
Governor for the crime of 'bringing Negroes into their meetings for
worship'. There were similar accusations, and similar fines, in Nevis.

Twelve years later, in 1688, in Germantown (Philadelphia), a group
of German Quakers originally from Krisheim, in the Rhineland, signed a
petition against the idea of slavery, not just the trade.* In both 1696 and
1711, at the society's annual meetings in Philadelphia, 'advice' was given
to guard against future imports of Africans, and instruction to ensure
good treatment of those already bought. Cadwallader Morgan, a Quaker

---

* *These Germans had opposed the slave trade from early on: some Germans held slaves, but
most of them thought the institution evil. The German press in North America differen-
tiated itself from the English one in this respect, and generally did not carry
advertisements for the sale of slaves, nor notices about escaped ones.*

slave merchant, after some soul-searching, decided, 'I should not be concerned with them.'[27] Can one say that this was the beginning of the abolition movement in Pennsylvania? Scarcely, for the protests were ignored, Friends remained prominent as slave traders as well as owners of slaves, and few took into account the 'advice' for years afterwards. Though they had compunction about the matter, Jonathan Dickinson and Isaac Norris, both Quakers of Philadelphia, continued to trade slaves. There was even a ship belonging to members of the sect in the early eighteenth century called the *Society*. (Her captain was Thomas Monk, who loaded 250 slaves in Africa in 1700, and lost all but twenty-two of them in the Middle Passage.)[28]

But other Friends made isolated, if neglected, protests in that colony over the next thirty years. In 1716 a Quaker tract written in Massachusetts arguing that the slave trade adversely affected white immigration had included the radical statement that the slaves had a perfect right to liberty, and so might resort to armed rebellion. The Friends asked: 'Are not we of this country guilty of that violence, treachery and bloodshed which is daily made use of to obtain them?'[29] Benjamin Lay, a hunchback originally from Colchester in England – who had settled in Abington, near Philadelphia, after living in Barbados and seeing scenes of cruelty to slaves, 'which had greatly disturbed his mind' – was driven by seeing a naked slave hanging dead in front of a fellow Quaker's house (killed because he had tried to run away) to a series of eccentric but sensational protests: for example, dressing in homemade cloth to avoid using material made by slaves, and breaking his coffee cups to discourage the use of sugar. Lay once stood at the door of a Quaker meeting house with one leg bare and half buried in deep snow. To those who sympathized, he said: 'Ah, you pretend compassion for me, but you do not feel for the poor slaves in your fields who go all winter half-clad.' He also once filled a sheep's bladder with blood and then plunged a sword into it at a Quaker meeting, saying, 'Thus shall God shed the blood of those persons who enslave their fellow-creatures.'[30]

All these protests were individual actions by unrepresentative people. A more characteristic reaction was that of some Baptists in South Carolina who wrote home to England to ask for guidance as to how to treat a brother member of their Church who had castrated his slave. They received the reply that they should not risk dissension in the movement over 'light or indifferent causes'.

Still, it was not only these dissenters who were concerned: in 1700 a conventional judge in Boston, Samuel Sewall, wrote a pamphlet, *The Selling of Joseph*, which despite receiving 'frowns and hard words' made the first reasoned criticism of the slave trade, and indeed of slavery itself. (Sewall, a Presbyterian, was one of the judges who had in 1692 condemned the witches of Salem; he himself may once have been concerned in the slave trade.)

In 1754 the annual meeting of the Society of Friends in Philadelphia at last took a definite step against the traffic in slaves. Recalling in an open letter that it had often been 'the concern of our annual meeting to testify their uneasiness and disunity with the importation and purchasing of negro and other slaves', this time they said plainly that 'to live in ease and plenty by the toil of those whom violence and cruelty have put in our power' was inconsistent with both Christianity and common justice. After several paragraphs giving vivid examples, the document appealed to Quakers to make the case of the Africans 'our own and consider what we should think, and what we should feel, were we in their circumstances'.[31]

This change was the consequence of further agitation in the Society coincident with the doubts about how to react to Indian raiding on the colony of Pennsylvania, inspired by such candid, dedicated, and determined Friends as William Burling of Long Island, Ralph Sandiford of Philadelphia, and above all John Woolman, a tailor from New Jersey, who in 1754, after a visit to Quaker slaveholders in Virginia and North Carolina, had published his candid pamphlet *Some Considerations on the Keeping of Negroes*. Woolman thereafter devoted his life to visits, usually on foot, to prominent Quaker slaveholders to try to convince them, by calm and rational appeals, of the 'inconsistency of holding slaves'.[32] He even went to Newport, Rhode Island, the great slaving port of North America, where he addressed his fellow Quakers on the matter, and seems to have had some effect. In 1758 the yearly meeting of Quakers at Philadelphia agreed with Woolman that no Quaker could keep a slave without risking damnation, since no master could be expected to resist the temptation to exploit the slave. That same year the Quakers in London at their annual meeting also condemned both slavery and 'the iniquitous practice of dealing in negro and other slaves', and threatened to exclude from a place of responsibility within the Society of Friends anyone who participated in the trade. Another resolution, at the Quakers' annual meeting in England in 1761, decided, since 'divers under our name are concerned in the un-Christian traffic in Negroes', to condemn the practice, and to disown those who did not desist. This was strong stuff for Quakers. Once they were committed, there was, however, no drawing back; the yearly meeting of 1763 in Phildelphia further condemned all who invested in the trade or supplied cargoes for it.[33]

Thus a prominent Bostonian could later write: 'About the time of the Stamp Act [1765], what were before only slight scruples in the minds of conscientious persons, became serious doubts and, with a considerable number, ripened into a firm persuasion that the slave trade was *malum in se*.'

The direct consequence of this Quaker activity was that in 1767 a proposal was, for the first time, introduced into a real legislature against the slave trade: in the House of Representatives of Massachusetts.

Though this bill failed, a substantial duty was laid thereafter on each slave imported.

Another point of view was, meantime, developing slowly in British North America. This was that the import of slaves into the Americas should be restricted, not because of doubts about the morality of the slave trade, but from fear of the consequences of having too many slaves: rebellion above all. After 1770 this opinion had as much influence over the growth of the abolition movement as philanthropy. For example, even in South Carolina, as early as 1698 an act was passed to encourage the use of white servants, because of 'the great danger' of revolution and upheaval which the presence of too many slaves might pose. In 1730 William Gooch, Lieutenant-Governor of Virginia, a Suffolk-born landowner who later fought in the British siege of Cartagena de Indias, wrote home to London that there were 30,000 slaves in Virginia (in a population of 114,000), 'and their numbers increase every day as well by birth as by importation. And in case there should arise a man of desperate courage amongst us, exasperated by a desperate fortune, he might with more advantage than Catiline kindle a servile war.* Such a man might be dreadfully mischievous before any opposition could be formed against him, and tinge our rivers, wide as they are, with blood. . . . It were therefore worth the consideration of a British parliament . . . to put an end to this unchristian Traffick of making merchandise of our fellow creatures. . . . We have mountains in Virginia to which they may retire as safely . . . as in Jamaica. I wonder whether the legislature will indulge a few ravenous traders to the danger of public safety. . . .'[34]

This view was also expressed, privately, in 1736, from his lovely estate of Westgrove, near Jamestown, Virginia, by Colonel William Byrd, son of the London-born merchant of the same name who had 'imported, used and sold many slaves [from Barbados]', in a letter to Lord Egmont, the President of the Trustees of the newly founded colony of Georgia.† He envied Georgia's prohibition on the import of slaves – a ban which would be only briefly maintained – and commented: 'I wish, my Lord, we could be blest with the same prohibition. They import so many negroes hither that I fear this colony will some time be confirmed by the name of New Guinea. I am sensible of many bad consequences of multiplying these Ethiopians amongst us. They blow up the pride and ruin the industry of our white people who, seeing a rank of poor creatures beneath them, detest work, for fear it should make them look like slaves. Another unhappy effect of many negroes is the necessity of being severe. Numbers make them insolent and then foul means must do what fair will not. We have, however, nothing here like the inhumanity which is practised in the islands

---

* *Did he mean Spartacus?*
† *This was the eccentric John Perceval, who also had plans to make himself King of the Jews.*

[the West Indies] and God forbid that we ever should. But these base tempers require to be rid with a taut rein, or they will be apt to throw the rider. . . . Private mischiefs are nothing if compared to the public danger. We have already 10,000 men of the descendants of Ham fit to bear arms.'[35]

Similar views were also expressed in Georgia itself; thus certain Scottish colonists of Darien declared that it was shocking 'to human nature that any race of mankind . . . should be sentenced to perpetual slavery; nor in justice can we think otherwise of it, than they are thrown amongst us to be our scourge one day or another for our sins; and as freedom to them must be as dear as to us, what a scene of horror must it bring about. . . .' George Whitfield, who spent some time in the colony as secretary to Governor Oglethorpe, wrote an open letter to the other Southern colonies in which he complained not so much about the slave trade (of which matter, he curiously said, he was not capable of deciding the legality) as about the fact that the settlers treated their slaves worse than they did their horses.[36]

Slave revolts were understandably on everyone's mind. More than a dozen major ones took place during the eighteenth century in Jamaica, where escaped slaves carried on guerrilla war in several colonies in the forested mountains. There had been a slave revolt on Long Island in 1708, and others in the city of New York in 1712 and 1733; in 1739 a group of slaves in South Carolina seized arms and began to march south to Florida – to, that is, as they ignorantly supposed, freedom.

The official position in South Carolina was interesting for a different reason. Advising the King to reject the petitions of merchants of London and Bristol in 1733 against a duty on the import of slaves, the council chamber of that colony insisted: 'The importation of negroes, we crave to inform Your Majesty, is a species of trade that has exceedingly increased of late in this province where so many negroes are now trained up to be handicraft tradesmen, to the great discouragement of Your Majesty's white subjects, who come here to settle with a view to employment in their several occupations, but must often give way to a people in slavery.'[37] Lewis Timothy, printer of the Laws of South Carolina, and for a time a partner of Benjamin Franklin, wrote in the *South Carolina Gazette* (which he owned) in 1738 that the slave merchants were ruining the colony by persuading so many planters to buy Negroes: 'Negroes may be said to be the bait proper for catching a Carolina planter, as certain as beef to catch a shark. How many under the notion of eighteen months' credit have been tempted to buy more negroes than they could possibly expect to pay for in three years?'[38]

Several colonial assemblies in North America would soon vote to impose prohibitive duties on the import of slaves, precisely out of anxiety lest the import might grow out of control and public order be threatened. In 1750, for example, Pennsylvania imposed a duty on the import of slaves which was supposed to be prohibitive. In Virginia in 1757 Peter

Fontaine, the Huguenot Rector of Westover, wrote to his brother Moses about their 'intestine enemies, our slaves', though he added: 'To live in Virginia without slaves is morally [sic] impossible.... A common labourer white or black if you should be so much favoured as to hire one, is a shilling sterling or fifteen pence currency a day ... that is, for a lazy fellow to get wood and water £19-16s-3d per annum [sic]; add to this [only] seven or eight pounds more and you have a slave for life....'[39]

In 1769 New Jersey also imposed a prohibitive duty of £15 a head on imports of slaves. In 1771 a duty of £8–£9 brought the trade to an end in Maryland for a time. North Carolina, unlike its southern neighbour never a big employer of slaves, experienced some protests. Thus the freeholders of Rowan County resolved 'that the African trade is injurious to this colony, obstructs the population of it by freemen, prevents manufacturers and other useful immigrants from Europe from settling amongst us, and occasions an annual increase of the balance of trade against the colonies'. Three weeks later the Provincial Congress resolved: 'We will not import any slave ... nor purchase any slave ... imported or brought into this province by others from any part of the world after the first day of November next.'[40] Slaves who arrived after the date concerned were to be reshipped to the West Indies. About the same time, the Rhode Island Assembly prohibited the import of slaves and determined that any slave brought in would be freed. But the Assembly was then too weak to ban slave traders operating out of Newport. None of these prohibitions, it is worth emphasizing, was decided upon for reasons of humanity. Fear and economy were the motives.

What became the main argument against slavery and the traffic in Africans, outrage at the very idea of slave traffic, was slow to gather civilized support, even in England, France, and North America. Elsewhere the process was still more lethargic, being confined to isolated statements by writers whose works, however well intentioned and high-minded, gained little currency. Among these, for example, were two Portuguese polemicists: first, André João Antonil, who in *Cultura e Opulencia do Brasil por Suas Drogas e Minas*, published in Lisbon in 1711, demanded amelioration, not abolition; and, second, Frei Manuel Ribeiro da Rocha, who in *Ethiope Resgatado, Empenohado, Sustenado, Corregido, Instruido e Libertado*, published in Lisbon in 1758, went so far as to demand an end to the slave trade and the substitution of free for slave labour. He remarkably argued that all slaves should be prepared for eventual freedom, for he thought the slave trade was illegal 'and ought to be condemned as a deadly crime against Christian charity and common justice'.[41] However contemptuous the Anglo-Saxons might be later about such Portuguese attitudes to the slave trade, this was a denunciation before anyone in Britain or North America had gone nearly so far.

Just one indication is available to show that in these years the moral side of the slave trade was at least being considered by some practitioners. In August 1736 Antonio de Salas, the Spanish Governor in Cartagena de Indias, wrote to his King, Philip V, to complain that the South Sea Company was importing 'black Christians' into the Spanish empire, specifically from the region of the River Congo. The King understood the point: it was not lawful, he replied, 'to enslave anyone born free, nor is it lawful that any Christian should enslave another'.[42] But now that the slaves had arrived, he declared, they were better off in the hands of the Spaniards than in those of English Protestants. It seems that those slaves remained in Cartagena, and the outbreak of war with England in 1739 prevented Philip from having to reconsider his policies. Anyway, the collection of laws relating to the Indies which had so painstakingly been put together in Madrid in the 1680s contained only brief references to black slaves.

The great wave of ideas and emotions, known in France and those who followed her as the Enlightenment, was (in contrast to the Renaissance) hostile to slavery, though not even the most powerful intellects knew what to do about the matter in practice. For example, the playwright Marivaux, the great Voltaire, the brilliant Montesquieu, the assiduous Diderot, and the contributors to the *Encyclopédie* as well as Jean-Jacques Rousseau, all condemned, or mocked, or denounced, slavery; but they assumed that all they had to do was to launch ideas into the cafés and governments would follow their advice, even if it was merely implicit. As early as 1725 Marivaux wrote his one-act play *L'Île des esclaves*, in which two haughty Athenians, shipwrecked on an island inhabited by escaped slaves, exchange places with their own servant-slaves. Marivaux's affection for the slaves derived from his contempt for antiquity. The theme of this work was: 'The difference in human conditions is only a test to which the gods make us submit.' His Athenians are cured of inhumanity when they return to Athens. Though now the play seems mild, it was a success, being played twenty times in Paris and once in Versailles.[*43]

The grand figure of the Enlightenment was, of course, Voltaire, who laughed at 'those who call themselves whites ... [but] proceed to purchase blacks cheaply in order to sell them expensively in the Americas.'[†] He also mocked the Church of Rome for having accepted slavery. In his *Scarmentado*, in 1756, he depicted a variation on the theme of Marivaux: a shocked European slave captain finds his ship and crew seized by Africans. The crew are enslaved. What right have you, the captain asks, to violate the law of nations and enslave innocent men? The African leader replies: 'You have long noses, we have flat ones; your hair is straight, while ours is curly; your skins are white, ours are black; in consequence,

---

[*] *J. M. Barrie plagiarized the idea for his* The Admirable Crichton.
[†] *'Ceux qui se disent blancs vont les acheter des nègres à bon marché, pour les revendre cher en Amérique.'*

by the sacred laws of nature, we must, therefore, remain enemies. You buy us in the fairs on the coast of Guinea as if we were cattle in order to make us labour at no end of impoverishing and ridiculous work ... [so] when we are stronger than you, we shall make you slaves, too, we shall make you work in our fields, and cut off your noses and ears.'[44] Voltaire caused Candide to observe a young slave who had an arm and a leg cut off as the price demanded for the sugar which had to be sent to Europe. He also criticized slavery in his *Dictionnaire philosophique* in 1764, in rather an indirect manner, and argued that 'people who traffic in their own children are more condemnable than the buyer; this traffic shows our superiority.'*[45] Not surprisingly, in view of that remark, he seems to have gambled in the slave trade himself. He certainly accepted delightedly when the leading *négrier* of Nantes, Jean-Gabriel Montaudoin, offered to name one of his ships after him.[46]

Montesquieu, more profoundly, believing as usual in the deter-mining influence of climate on manners, thought that slavery, if inappropriate for Europe (at least then!), might have a natural basis in tropical countries, where 'heat enervates the body' and no one could be expected to work unless he was made afraid of punishment. Unlike Voltaire, Montesquieu was much interested in the question, as was natural in one who had been President of the *Parlement* of Bordeaux, a slave port. The core of his argument in *L'Esprit des lois* was that slavery was bad both for the master and for the captive: for the first, because the institution led him into all kinds of bad habits, causing him to become proud, impatient, hard, angry, louche (*voluptueux*), and cruel; and for the second, because the condition prevented him from doing anything virtu-ously. Montesquieu added an ironical passage: 'If I were to try and justify our right to make slaves of the blacks, this is what I would say: The Euro-peans, having exterminated the peoples of the Americas, have had to enslave those of Africa, in order to ensure the clearance of a great deal of land. Sugar would be too expensive if one could not get slaves to produce it. The slaves I am talking about are black from head to toe, and they have such ruined noses that one can't begin to complain of them. . . . One cannot put oneself into the frame of mind in which God, who is a very wise being, took it upon himself to put a soul, above all a good soul, into such an entirely black body.' He continued: 'The blacks prefer . . . a glass necklace to one of gold, to which properly civilized [*policées*] nations give such consequence. [So] it is impossible for us to suppose these creatures are men because, if one were to allow them to be so, a suspicion would follow that we are not ourselves Christian.'[47]

The author of *L'Esprit des lois*, like Marivaux, may not seem to be radical in the twentieth century. But his mocking insistence that slavery

---

* '*Un peuple qui trafique en ses enfants est encore plus condenable que l'acheteur; ce négoce démontre notre supériorité.*'

had to be discussed seriously was very important at the time. His remarks influenced everyone who thought of the matter thenceforth, even the modest reflections of the great Gibbon on the subject, in chapter II of his *Decline and Fall of the Roman Empire*. They also inspired an impassioned essay, *Les Chaînes de l'esclavage*, for the Académie Française in 1774 by the young Jean-Paul Marat, a tutor in Bordeaux in the early 1760s to the children of Pierre-Paul Nairac, the greatest slave merchant of that city.

Jean-Jacques Rousseau, more extreme than anyone else with regard to the issue of slavery as to everything, insisted that the essence of the institution was its dependence on force; and so, in his *Discours sur l'origine et les fondements de l'inégalité* (1755), he condemned slavery absolutely, describing it as the final manifestation of the degrading and idiotic principle of authority. In his *Du Contrat social* (1762), he added: 'However we look at the question, the right to enslave is null and void, not only because it is illegitimate, but also because it is absurd and meaningless. The words "slavery" and "right" are contradictory.'[48] Then Diderot's great *Encyclopédie* (in the volume published in 1765), in its article on the slave trade (by Louis de Jaucourt, a hard-working and self-effacing scholar who had spent three years at Cambridge before studying at Leyden), stated, without equivocation: 'This purchase [that is, of slaves] is a business which violates religion, morality, natural law, and all human rights. There is not one of those unfortunate souls ... slaves ... who does not have the right to be declared free, since in truth he has never lost his freedom; and he could not lose it, since it was impossible for him to lose it; and neither his prince, nor his father, nor anyone else had the right to dispose of it.' The *Encyclopédie* also stated firmly that if any slave entered France and was baptized he automatically became free. That was a procedure which was explained by 'long usage' which had 'acquired the force of law'.[49]

These firm statements made anti-slavery part of new French radical thought; and, for once, radical thought coincided with Catholic thinking: in 1741 Pope Benedict XIV (Lambertini) repeated the prohibitions on slavery discussed a century before by Pope Urban VIII, in the brief *Immensa*. Benedict was, like so many of his predecessors, concerned primarily with prohibitions on Indian slavery in the New World, but the declaration clearly covered black slavery, too; and the Papal Nuncio in Lisbon later reported, among the causes for his distaste for the Jesuits in the Portuguese dominions, that the Society of Jesus 'engaged in a slave trade'.[50] But Benedict had even less importance than Urban in the commercial mind. Presumably some slave merchants thought that they had satisfied their consciences when they christened their ships *Liberté*, *Ça-Ira*, and *Jean-Jacques*, instead of *Saint-Hilaire* or *Saint-François*, and other saints' names favoured in the past.

24

THE LOUDEST YELPS
FOR LIBERTY

'How is it that we hear the loudest yelps for liberty among the drivers of negroes?'

Dr Samuel Johnson

'Il est surprenant de voir des hommes vendre leur liberté, leur vie, leurs concitoyens aussi tout étourdiment que font ces malheureux noirs. Passion! Ignorance que de morts vous faites au genre humain.'

Voltaire, Essai sur les mœurs, *ch. 197*

IN 1752 a prince, known as William Ansah Sessaracoa, from Anamabo, on the Gold Coast, returned home to Africa after a stay in England. Visits of that kind had been made before, but no previous African had been so successful in English society. The expedition had arisen because the Prince's father, John Corrantee, had entrusted his son and a friend to a Liverpool slave captain to go to England to learn manners. The captain treacherously sold these African noblemen as slaves. The captain died and the officers on the slave ship informed the authorities in Jamaica what had happened. The Prince and his companion were then taken to England and were looked after by the Earl of Halifax, then President of the Board of Trade and Plantations.* They were educated, were introduced to the King and, according to the peerless letter-writer Horace Walpole, became the 'fashion at all the assemblies'.[1] They even went to the presentation of one of the many theatrical versions of Aphra Behn's *Oroonoko*, at Covent Garden:

---

* *He had a great fortune, which he had inherited from his wife's grandfather, Sir Thomas Dunk, a clothier of Kent, whose woollens could scarcely have been absent from the ships of London slave dealers at the turn of the eighteenth century.*

'The dialogue between Oroonoko and Imoinda so affected the Prince that he had to retire weeping . . .' Horace Walpole reported. The visit under-pinned the existing disposition of humanitarians to romanticize the 'noble negro', the Prince unjustly enslaved – forgetting the humbly born slaves whose sufferings were as many and as great.

By this time the combination of popular poetry and of journalism was beginning to have its effect on cultivated imaginations in England and in North America on the subject of slavery. Several authors were crit-ical of the institution in the periodical press in the mid-eighteenth century. The existence of that press was the main reason for the circula-tion of these ideas, which soon began to be taken up in elected assemblies. The fourth estate began to discuss the matter of slavery before the other three did. The relative freedom of expression in Britain explains why, despite the imaginative force with which French philosophers wrote, 'abolitionism' prospered first in the Anglo-Saxon countries (though under Louis XV and Louis XVI criticism of the slave trade was not as a rule itself censored, any criticism of the Church or the established order of things in France risked persecution). The ease with which corres-pondence could be carried on in North America and Britain was another important explanation for the rise of the movement.

Thus in 1738 the English *Weekly Miscellany* published an article which declared that if Africans were to seize people from the coast of England one could easily imagine the screams of 'unjust' which would be heard. In July 1740 the *Gentleman's Magazine* included a letter by a certain '*Mercatus Honestus*', addressed to 'the Guinea merchants' of Bristol and Liverpool. It declared that men were born with a natural right to liberty; that they could only forfeit that by taking away the property of another; that the loss of liberty by a parent was no reason that a child should be enslaved; that the merchants in Guinea dealt with men, women, and children; that they stimulated war among Africans; that the blacks in Africa were more virtuous there, at home, than after they had been brought to America; and that the treatment of the Africans in the West Indies was shocking. The cheerfulness which the slaves showed in dying, the letter continued, proceeded not from ignorance but from 'a natural nobleness of soul'. The writer suggested that some who carried on the trade – 'among whom there are no doubt wise and good men', he added with a good dose of English hypocrisy – should give their reason for it.[2]

A reply appeared in the *London Magazine*. The inhabitants of Guinea, the writer argued, 'are in the most deplorable state of slavery under the arbitrary powers of their princes both as to life and property. In the several subordinations to them, every great man is absolute lord of his immediate dependents. And lower still; every master of a family is proprietor of his wives, children and servants, and may consign them to death or a better market. . . . Such a state is contrary to nature and reason, since every human creature hath an absolute right to liberty ... yet it is not in our power to cure the universal evil and set all the kingdoms of the world free from the domination of tyrants. ... All that can be done in such a case is to communicate as much liberty and happiness as such circumstances will admit, and the people will consent to: and this is certainly by the Guinea trade. For by purchasing, or rather ransoming, the negroes from their national tyrants, and transplanting them under the benign influences of the law and Gospel, they are advanced to much greater degrees of felicity, tho' not to absolute liberty. ...'[3]

There was a further rejoinder in the December issue of the *Gentleman's Magazine*. Thomas Astley, who had edited a famous collection of voyages in 1745, wrote, in relation to Captain Snelgrave's argument,* that if the Africans benefited from slavery in the Americas then they themselves should be asked to make the decision as to whether to go there. But as yet there was no public controversy on a large scale, for, though influential, the *Gentleman's Magazine* had a tiny circulation, as did the *London Magazine*. No parliamentarian as yet touched the issue.

In 1750, as has been explained,† and despite some forceful statements by certain Georgians about the iniquities of the institution, the trustees of the colony decided to allow slavery and the slave trade after all. Many prudent people at home in England were pleased at that decision, though others were critical, Horace Walpole among them. 'We, the temple of liberty, and bulwark of Protestant Christianity,' he wrote to his favourite correspondent, Sir Horace Mann, the British Envoy in Florence, 'have this fortnight been [in Parliament] pondering methods to make more effectual that horrid traffic of selling negroes. It has appeared to us that six and forty thousand of these wretches are sold [annually] in the English colonies alone. It chills one's blood.'[4]

Walpole's comments show what an educated Englishman of the mid-eighteenth century was beginning to think. They suggest, if not opposition to the trade, a clear sign that the morality of the matter, that 'morally speaking' in the words of Captain Pery earlier in the century, was now discussable. The same implication might well have been drawn from a British naval report of 1750 which insisted that government money would be well spent in sending out good instructors to the forts of the Gold Coast, 'for the Africans are very tractable to learn trades'.

The issue of the legality of freedom was thus already on the agenda, so to speak, of English public opinion: and in 1755 Professor Francis Hutcheson's *A System of Moral Philosophy* was published. The author, an Irish Protestant who had become Professor of Philosophy at Glasgow, had actually died some years before. His main interest was

---

* In his account of a journey to West Africa, to which several references have been made.
† See page 272.

the definition of happiness; and it was he who coined the phrase made famous by Bentham concerning the desirability of ensuring the 'greatest happiness of the greatest numbers'. The originality of his work with regard to slavery lay in his conclusion that 'all men [without exception] have strong desires of liberty and property', and that 'no damage done or crime committed can change a rational creature into a piece of goods void of all right'.'⁵ Four years later, another professor at Glasgow, Adam Smith, who when young had been to Hutcheson's well-delivered lectures, wrote in his *The Theory of Moral Sentiments*, 'There is not a negro from the coast of Africa who does not . . . possess a degree of magnanimity which the soul of his sordid master is scarce capable of conceiving.' Many of Smith's pupils at Glasgow, like Hutcheson's, absorbed these views.⁶

But the arguments were not always so straightforward. Five years later still, the *Gentleman's Magazine* published an article complaining that Africans in the neighbourhood of London 'cease to consider themselves as slaves . . . and no more willingly perform the laborious offices of servitude than our own people'.⁷ Late eighteenth-century London had, after all, many 'St Giles' blackbirds' – from the region near St Giles' Church. When the *Gentleman's Magazine* said that slaves could not breathe in Britain, it implied that they, and all blacks, should be required to leave.

Other Scottish intellectuals took up the matter. One of them was George Wallace, a lawyer who published his *System of the Principles of the Laws of Scotland* in 1761. He was influenced by Montesquieu, as he admitted, and he was almost paraphrasing *L'Esprit des lois* when he wrote, 'An institution so unnatural and so inhuman as that of slavery ought to be abolished.'⁸ Another Scotsman of considerable influence was Adam Ferguson, Professor of Philosophy at Edinburgh. In his *Institutes of Moral Philosophy*, based on his lecture notes and published in 1769, he argued that 'no one is born a slave; because everyone is born with all his original rights. [Further], no one can become a slave; because no one, from being a person, can, in the language of the Roman law, become a thing, or subject of property. The supposed property of the master in the slave, therefore, is a matter of usurpation, not of right.'†⁹

---

* *In these ideas Hutcheson was influenced by the enlightened third Earl of Shaftesbury, Anthony Cooper, a man supposed by Voltaire to have been 'the greatest English philosopher' and whose work* Characteristicks of Men, Manners, Opinions, Times *(published in 1701), gave a generous picture of the idea of benevolence. This was recognized by the slave captain John Newton, who found the book by chance when in the great Dutch slave port of Middelburg. But the modern reader cannot find much of interest in Shaftesbury except a few important phrases such as 'moral sense', which occurs in his* Inquiry Concerning Virtue, *of 1712.*

† *Ferguson had been chaplain to the Black Watch, in which capacity he had, to the astonishment of his colonel, charged the enemy at Fontenoy at the head of his men.*

What Wallace did for Montesquieu in Scotland, Sir William Blackstone did in England. That judge's *Commentaries on the Laws of England*, published in Oxford between 1765 and 1769, stated the case against slavery more directly than Montesquieu had done.* Thus he derided the three causes of slavery named in Justinian's Code of Laws – slavery following on defeat in war, by selling oneself, and by being born a slave. He declared, too, that the law of England 'abhors and will not endure the state of slavery within this nation', and went on to insist that 'a slave or a negro, the moment he lands in England, falls under the protection of the laws and, with regard to all natural rights, becomes, *eo instanti*, a freeman'.[10] The effect of this firm statement was, however, much weakened by the qualification in the second edition of the book that, even so, 'the master's right to his service may probably still continue'; and 'probably' was itself altered to 'possibly' in the fourth edition, published in 1770.[11] These changes were almost certainly due to the influence of Blackstone's friend and benefactor Lord Mansfield, at the time Lord Chief Justice of England, a tolerant but cautious man. (Mansfield himself had in his household a mulatto girl, Dido, daughter of his nephew, Rear Admiral Sir John Lindsay, by a slave mother, whom he had captured in a Spanish vessel during the siege of Havana.)

Blackstone's fluent work had immediate success. His remarks about slavery probably influenced Isaac Bickerstaffe when he wrote his immensely successful play *The Padlock*, performed in 1768. A song, sung by Mungo, a slave, includes the verse:

> *Dear heart, what a terrible life am I led*
> *A dog has a better, that's shelter'd and fed*
> *Night and day 'tis de same,*
> *My pain is dere game.*[12]

In the same mood, in 1766, Horace Walpole wrote his *Account of Giants Lately Discovered*, which mocked the slave trade by suggesting that a newly discovered tribe of Patagonian giants should be enslaved and used in the sugar trade, bearing in mind the experience of planters in North America that a slave could be worked to death after four years, because by then he would have earned his purchase price.[13]

Perhaps more important, though, in the late 1760s was the clear sign that the Quakers, who had already pronounced against their members' participation in the slave trade, were beginning to carry the argument about slavery beyond their own movement. Friends still traded slaves, and certainly still owned them. But Anthony Benezet, a 'worthy old Quaker' as Granville Sharp called him, from Philadelphia (if born in Saint-Quentin in

---

It should not, however, escape the present generation that this classic statement of the nature of English law was profoundly influenced by a great Frenchman.

France, and briefly educated in England), was talking to the world beyond Friends' House, and to England as well as to North America, when between 1759 and 1771 he wrote a series of works such as *A Caution and Warning to Great Britain and the Colonies* and then *Some Historical Account of Guinea*. These and other studies were remarkable for their use cf material taken from far outside the normal range of Quaker reading. For example, the first cited Montesquieu, Wallace, and Hutcheson; it also used numerous first-hand accounts of trading slaves in Africa, including those of Bosman, Barbot, and Brüe. Benezet, a tiny ugly man with no presence, was also influenced by his reading of Wallace's work. He was affected too by the determination and dedication of John Woolman. Benezet had begun to work on the question of the slave trade in the 1750s, and the decisions of the Quakers in Philadelphia owed a good deal to his persuasion. The quiet persistence of these two men led Quakers to form 'little associations in the middle provinces of North America, to discourage the introduction of slaves among people in their own neighbourhoods': including people who were not members of their Society. Perhaps the energies of Benezet and Woolman were especially fired by the knowledge that in the late 1750s and 1760s the import of slaves into Philadelphia was higher than it had ever been; or perhaps the wide experience of Benezet, himself from a persecuted minority, was the prime cause of the ignition of his exertions.*

A retired teacher when, only in 1766, he began his work of agitation, Benezet had once been in business in Philadelphia, though not the slave business, as a young man. In the second edition of *A Caution and Warning*, published in 1767, he quoted (and took as his theme thereafter) a West Indian visitor's comment that 'it is a matter of astonishment how a people [the English] who, as a nation are looked upon as generous and humane, . . . can live in the practice of such extreme oppression and inhumanity without seeing the inconsistency of such conduct'.[14]

Benezet did, it is true, argue, falsely, that the troubles of Africa all derived from the Atlantic slave trade. But, as Las Casas knew, and many others have realized since, exaggeration is the essence of successful propaganda. Benezet then embarked upon a campaign of converting fellow Quakers to his way of thinking, largely by correspondence. Nor did he confine his letters to Quakers; for he wrote to Edmund Burke and the Archbishop of Canterbury, and to John Wesley.

Dr Benjamin Rush – a Presbyterian, not a Quaker – on Benezet's encouragement wrote some admirable and still-readable pamphlets in the 1770s, and helped to form, in Philadelphia, the first society devoted to abolition.

---

* *Benezet's favorite quotation from Montesquieu was that philosopher's comment that slavery 'is neither useful to the master nor slave; to the slave since he can do nothing through principle (or virtue); to the master because he contracts with his slave all sorts of bad habits and insensibly accustoms himself to want all moral virtues.'*

In the history of abolition, Benezet, like Aphra Behn and the half-forgotten Tomás de Mercado, should have a place of honour. He was not only a link between the writings of the moral philosophers, such as Montesquieu and the Quakers, but also one between America and Britain; and indeed between the Anglo-Saxons and the French.

Still, for the moment, the thrust of the humane influences in England was legal, not religious; and it is in the context of someone who had read Blackstone, not Benezet, that the case of the slave Somerset, heard in 1771 before Lord Mansfield, should be considered. The judgement determined unsensationally, it is true, that there could be no slaves in England. Though the case had nothing directly to do with the slave trade, and though the significance of it has been dismissed by some modern historians as sentimental, the occasion was, all the same, a turning point in the history both of the traffic and of the institution.

The story is well known, so need only be summarized. The case was initiated by Granville Sharp, then a junior clerk in the Ordnance Office, who came from a family of successful Anglican clergymen. Grandson of an Archbishop of York, Sharp is a good example of those patient English philanthropists whose capacity for dull, hard, meticulous, and above all effective work is even now so striking an aspect of English public life.

Sharp had in 1765 befriended a slave, Jonathan Strong, in the streets of London. He had been badly wounded by his master, David Lisle of Barbados. Sharp and his brother William, a surgeon, helped to restore Strong to health and he went to work for an apothecary. But then he was accidentally seen by Lisle, who without physically repossessing him sold him to a planter in Jamaica, on the understanding that the price of £30 would not be paid till Strong was on a ship ready to sail to Kingston. Two slave hunters captured Strong and took him to a private prison, the Poultry Compter. Sharp secured Strong's release on the ground that he had been confined without warrant. The Jamaican planter who had bought Strong then sued Sharp, while Lisle challenged him to a duel. Sharp was left to his own devices. This obliged him to investigate the law of slavery. He was disturbed to find that English law did not really deal with the matter.

In the days of Queen Elizabeth a certain Cartwright had brought back from Russia a slave, who was declared free, on the ground that 'England was too pure an air for slaves to breathe in' – a view which was remembered in 1772 by one of the lawyers, Serjeant Davy, during discussion of the case of Somerset. But that judgement may have been spurious, and certainly black slaves were to be seen in Elizabethan and Jacobean London. It was true that in 1672 Edward Chamberlayne had written, in *The Present State of England*, 'Foreign slaves in England are none since Christianity prevailed. A foreign slave brought into England is, upon landing, *ipso facto* free from slavery but not from ordinary service.' That work was, however, a copy of a similarly titled book about France, where the same statement, similarly false, was made.

There were several late seventeenth-century judgements on the matter, inspired by the increase in the slave trade. The Court of King's Bench and the Court of Common Pleas both found that slaves could be reclaimed in England. But, in the case of *Smith* v. *Brown and Cooper*, in 1706, the Lord Chief Justice Sir John Holt apparently determined that 'one may be a villein in England, but not a slave'; and even 'as soon as a negro comes into England, he becomes free'. But Holt's judgement received little attention, and one of those who sat with him, Mr Justice Powell, thought, on the contrary, that 'the laws of England take no notice of a negro'. The judgement was anyway, as it seemed, reversed in 1729, when Sir Robert Walpole's Attorney-General and Solicitor-General, Sir Philip Yorke and Mr Charles Talbot (a patron of the poet Thomson) gave it as their opinion, in reply to a deputation of West Indian planters, that a slave in England was not automatically free, nor did baptism 'bestow freedom on him, nor make any alteration in his temporal condition in these kingdoms'. A master could also legally compel 'a slave to return to the plantations'. These were decisions which Yorke confirmed twenty years later in a judgement, when Lord Chancellor (and Lord Hardwicke), in the case of *Pearne* v. *Lisle*.

Yorke had the reputation of being one of the hardest men ever to become Lord Chancellor, as his conduct in relation to the execution of the Jacobite peers showed, as also in the case of Admiral Byng.˙ But Talbot was known as a man of wit and charm. Their decisions are difficult to explain. It also became evident that even baptism did not make a man free, as had come to be assumed (by, for example, the slave Olaudah Equiano, who in 1761, two years after being christened, was sold at Gravesend and then spirited away by Captain James Doran on his vessel, the *Charming Sally*).

So there seemed in England in the 1760s no clear law on the matter: one judge had said one thing, another another. There was no Code Noir as there was in France, explaining the way that slaves were to be treated. The opinion of Yorke was however so well known that it was spoken of as if it had been a judgement. In 1788 an inquiry in the House of Commons into the condition of slavery in Barbados led to the following declaration being made: 'The general power which a master exercises ... over his slaves is rather by implication (from slaves being bought as chattels in the same way as horses or other beasts) than by any positive law defining what the power of a master shall be in this island.' In practice, therefore, the law of a master over a slave was 'unlimited'. The further question 'What is the protection granted by the law to slaves in Barbados?' received the answer 'Effectually none.'[15]

˙ *Admiral John Byng's squadron was defeated off the island of Minorca. He was court-martialled and executed on his own quarterdeck, the distant view of which tragedy caused Voltaire's Candide to return to France.*

That lack of 'positive law' about slavery seemed to obtain in England too. The matter was important, for all the black slaves in London might sue if they thought that they were free. Some people of African origins *were* free: Francis Barber, for example, Dr Johnson's servant, was so, having been emancipated by his previous owner, Colonel Bathurst; a black valet in the service of Sir Joshua Reynolds was also. Some blacks were, however, not free. Had not King William III, of 'glorious memory', owned a favourite black slave whose bust was still to be seen at Hampton Court? Slaves as such were often put up for public sale in Bristol or Liverpool. There was some ambiguity about the legal status of the black domestics in the homes of returning West Indian planters, such as the Halletts of Stedcombe, a property outside the minor slaving port of Lyme Regis. But when John Hallett had died in 1699 and gave freedom to 'my boy Virgil' on his deathbed, he presumably believed that he was granting something real.

Most black slaves then in England had been brought back by sea captains. But, whatever their status, there had been a constant increase of them to England in the early eighteenth century, and many were hired out by their masters to shipowners, or even slave captains, as casual labour.

Granville Sharp acted as if the judgements of Attorney-General Yorke had no authority. He based his arguments on the Habeas Corpus Act of 1679, and insisted that a master had rights in a slave only if he could prove that the captive in question had *in writing* willingly 'bound himself, without compulsion or illegal duress'. Whatever might be the custom in the colonies, in England, he argued, an African slave immediately became entitled to the King's protection.

Sharp's arguments made headway, and his opponents in the case of Jonathan Strong did not press their suit. His success, and his subsequent pamphlet, *A Representation of the Injustice and Dangerous Tendency of Tolerating Slavery in England*, published in 1769, made him a natural recipient of other complaints by blacks in England who were either kidnapped or threatened with kidnapping.[16] Sharp put this matter further to the test in the case of the slave Thomas Lewis, who, belonging to a West Indian planter, escaped in Chelsea. When he was recaptured, and shipped to begin the journey to Jamaica, Sharp served the captain on his boat with a writ of habeas corpus. The case came before Lord Chief Justice Mansfield, who put to the jury the question whether the master had established his claim to the slave as his property. If they decided affirmatively, he would rule whether such a property could persist in England. The jury decided that the master had not established his claim. So the main question was left unsettled. Lord Mansfield said, rather curiously, that he hoped that the question whether slaves could be forcibly shipped back to the plantations would never be discussed.

In 1772 Sharp acted similarly, as indicated above, on behalf of the slave James Somerset, who had been brought from Jamaica to England by his master, Charles Stewart of Boston, in 1769. He escaped in 1771, was recaptured, and was then put on board the *Ann and Mary*, whose captain was John Knowles, bound for Jamaica, where he was to be sold. On this occasion, there could be no doubt about the master's right to the slave. But Sharp succeeded in arranging the transfer of the case to the Court of King's Bench. There, after a long trial which spread over several months, in which the fundamental questions were well put by defending counsel, Lord Mansfield decided that there was no legal definition as to whether there could, or could not be, slaves in England. He was not the most convincing of friends of liberty, since he evidently wished to avoid pronouncing on the fundamental question; to begin with, he urged a settlement out of court, and even suggested that Parliament might introduce a law to secure property in slaves. When none of these things availed, after further procrastination Mansfield decided the case on the simple ground that slavery was so 'odious' that nothing could be suffered to support it even if positive law about the matter did not exist. Somerset therefore was freed. Mansfield, as he himself said in 1779, 'went no further than to determine that the master had no right to compel the slave to go into a foreign country'.[17] He did not make a general declaration of slave emancipation in England. Blacks continued to be kidnapped in Britain and taken back to Jamaica or elsewhere if their masters could so arrange it.

Admittedly, the agent of the North American colonies in London[*] taunted the English for freeing old slaves in England while continuing to make new ones on the African coast. Yet the new judgement affected public opinion. Provincial newspapers, even the *Liverpool General Gazette*, carried good accounts of the case.

After the 'Mansfield judgement', there was, of course, general celebration among the many blacks present in the Court of King's Bench, which was then in Westminster Hall. But little changed in the Caribbean, and in Africa. A young sugar planter who went out to Nevis or Jamaica in the late 1770s would have written much as John Pinney did ten years before, when, after his first visit to a market where slaves were being sold, 'I can assure you I was shock'd at the first appearance of human flesh exposed to sale. But surely God ordained 'em for the use and benefit of us. Otherwise, his Divine Will would have made itself manifest by some particular sign or token.'[18]

The case of Somerset had the consequence of putting Granville Sharp and Anthony Benezet in touch with each other, and they now embarked upon correspondence. The latter came to London in 1773 and argued publicly that if the trade in slaves could be abolished, 'I trust the sufferings of those already amongst us ... would be mitigated.'[19] The visit of Benezet to London, as also that of John Woolman (he would die of

---

[*] *British colonies usually had representatives in London to act on their behalf.*

smallpox in York after addressing the Quakers there), testified to the growing transatlantic dimension of the opposition – a thing made easy by the English origins of several of the leading North American Quakers. In 1774 William Dillwyn, a pupil and amanuensis of Benezet, also came from North America with the declared aim of helping the English Quakers to organize their movement in favour of abolition. The same year, inspired by letters from Benezet (indeed, he used Benezet's words *in extenso*), John Wesley published his *Thoughts upon Slavery*. Influenced by his own memories of Georgia, where he had lived forty years before, as by conversations with the German Moravians there, he castigated the slave trade. He also eulogized the Africans. They seemed to him capable of a sensibility which the captains of slave ships could not approach. He asked those captains rhetorically: 'Do you never feel another's pain? Have you no sympathy? . . . No pity for the miserable? When you saw the flowing eyes, the heaving breasts, or the bleeding sides or tortured limbs of your fellow beings, were you a stone or a brute . . . ?' In America – Georgia, no doubt he meant – one saw 'mothers hanging over their daughters, bedewing their naked breasts with tears and daughters clinging to their parents till the whipper soon obliges them to part'. Was that not a proof of Africans' humanity? Wesley said that it would be better for the West Indies to be sunk 'in the depth of the sea, than that they should be cultivated, at so high a price'.[20]

Where Wesley, as the great Methodist, struck a new note was his prediction that the time for repentance would soon come for England, whose worst crime, he insisted, was its indulgence in the slave trade. Given the appeal of Methodism, which already extended much further than that of the Quakers, and the attention which anything written by Wesley received, this pamphlet constituted the most serious onslaught on slavery, as well as the trade, that had yet been made.

Dr Johnson had been keenly interested in the growing controversy. He dictated to Boswell a note on the matter: 'It is impossible not to conceive that men in their original state were equal. A man may accept life from a conquering enemy on condition of perpetual servitude; but it is very doubtful whether he can entail that servitude on his descendants. . . . The sum of the argument is . . . [that] no man is by nature the property of another. [So] the defendant is by nature free. The rights of nature must be seen [to be] . . . forfeited before they can be justly taken away. . . . That the defendant has by any act forfeited the rights of nature we require to be proved.'[21]

Boswell spoke, however, for what was still conventional opinion when he commented that he entered his 'most solemn protest against [Johnson's] general doctrine with respect to the slave trade. For . . . his unfavourable notion of it was owing to prejudice, and to imperfect or false information. . . . To abolish a status which in all ages God has sanctioned . . . would not only be robbery to an innumerable class of our fellow subjects, but it would be extreme cruelty to the African savages, a portion of which it saves from massacre or intolerable bondage in their own country; and introduces into a much happier state of life. . . . To abolish this trade would be', he added with a surrealistic extravagance, 'to shut the gates of mercy on mankind.'[22]

Still, Johnson had always opposed slavery, and once, when he was with 'some very grave men at Oxford', his toast had been, 'Here's to the next insurrection of the negroes in the West Indies.' Boswell professed himself shocked. Johnson's 'violent prejudice against our West Indian and American settlers', wrote Boswell, 'appeared whenever there was an opportunity'. Towards the end of the great doctor's *Taxation No Tyranny*, he wrote, 'How is it that we hear the loudest yelps for liberty [in the American colonies] among the drivers of negroes?' In conversation with John Wilkes, he once mockingly asked, 'Where did Beckford [Lord Mayor of London] and Trecothick learn English?' Both were from famous West Indian as well as West Country families.[23]

A different but even more effective criticism appeared in Adam Smith's *Wealth of Nations*, published in 1776. Though, curiously enough, that work did not mention the trade in slaves at all, Smith recognized that the discovery of America was one of the two greatest events in history (the other was the unveiling of the route to India), and he did speak of slavery. Following his *Theory of Moral Sentiments* of seventeen years before, Smith argued that the institution was just one more artificial restraint on individual self-interest. If a man had no hope of gaining property, Smith thought, he would obviously work badly, for 'it appears . . . from the experience of all ages and nations . . . that the work done by freemen comes cheaper in the end than that performed by slaves'. That sentence was immensely influential, but it was even less sustainable than Smith's contention that Irish girls had good complexions because they ate potatoes.[24]

In 1775, prompted by Quakers, a commission of the House of Commons was appointed to take evidence on the slave trade. After it had done so, in 1776, David Hartley, MP for Hull, son of a doctor who like Pope had written an 'Essay on Man', introduced a debate on the theme 'that the slave trade is contrary to the laws of God and the rights of men'. He was seconded by a philanthropist, Sir George Savile. The subject was thus clearly put on the political agenda in England, though Hartley was an inappropriate standard-bearer for a great cause: a dull, self-opinionated, vain, charmless, and naive windbag, it was he who inspired the comment 'No one can have a complete idea of a bore who has not been in Parliament.'[25]

On the other side of the Atlantic, the American Revolution delayed a full debate on the matter. That upheaval, of course, began as a tax rebellion: a revolt against paying taxes imposed by a distant, unrepresentative legislature. It was unrelated to the matter of slavery. After all, there were still fewer slaves in the mainland British colonies than in the 'islands': only 22 per cent of the population of the thirteen colonies in 1770, whereas in 'the islands' the percentage was over 90 per cent. About 80 per cent of the slaves in the mainland colonies, too, had been born in America. In contradistinction to the rest of the Americas, natural increase seemed already, in the mainland colonies, the determining element in the size of the slave population.

Still, from the point of view of the abolitionist Quakers, the language used by the rebels against the Crown had an uneasy ring. In December 1771 the weekly *Boston Gazette* published a letter 'from an American' to King George III. This included an attack on the doctrine that the acts of the British Parliament could bind North Americans; 'to say the contrary is to say that we are slaves, for the essence of liberty is to be subject only to laws made by ourselves; and, being subject to laws made by other people, is the essence of slavery'. This surely dangerous language was repeated incessantly: 'the endless and numberless curses of slavery'; 'my sons scorn to be slaves'; the 'British plan of slavery'; 'abject slaves as France and Poland can shew in wooden shoes'; or 'to receive them is worse than death – it is SLAVERY!' These comments by such contemporary leaders as Joseph Warren of Massachusetts, or John Dickinson of Maryland, were an interesting reminder, as Dr Johnson realized, of how men could use metaphors without reflection: especially since Dickinson came from a family concerned in slaving, and his father-in-law, Isaac Norris, was also concerned in the trade.

The rebellion began with a decision by the so-called Association, a union of the colonies, to end commercial intercourse with the mother country. Since the slave trade was an important part of that, it was one of the first branches of business to come to an end. This was a move opposed by the merchants of Liverpool and Bristol, sustained by the President of the Board of Trade in London, the Earl of Dartmouth, who said, 'We cannot allow the colonists to check or discourage in any degree a traffic so beneficial to the nation.'[26]

After several declarations by the assemblies of individual colonies, the Continental Congress in October 1774 resolved that no more slaves should be introduced into the United States after 1 December of that year, and trade with other nations engaged in the traffic would be prohibited. But this statement was swiftly forgotten and – except in Georgia, whose leaders were so naive as to suppose that it would be acted upon – it was indeed hardly commented upon.

---

* *It was he who nominated John Newton to the curacy of Olney. Richardson, when asked by Newton who was the original of his* Sir Charles Grandison, *replied, 'Dartmouth, were he not a Methodist.' He is described in the* Dictionary of National Biography *as 'entirely without any administrative capacity'. But he was all the same one of the promoters of Dartmouth College.*

The events in Massachusetts were interesting. There, before the war, the Assembly had made two attempts to stop the import of slaves, on the usual ground that to have too many might risk a black rebellion. But the idea was thwarted by the Governor, General Thomas Gage. The colony, or commonwealth, therefore, entered the War of Independence with no law limiting the trade. Then on 13 September 1776 a resolution was introduced into the new House of Representatives there which declared – in a direct echo of the French *philosophes* – that the 'selling and enslaving of the human species is a direct violation of the natural rights vested in all men'. If any sale were to be made henceforth, it would be 'null and void'. (The author must have read Diderot's *Encyclopédie*.) But on 16 September a second draft was written. That transformed the original phraseology, and stated merely, 'Any blacks taken on the high seas and brought as prisoners shall not be allowed to be sold.'[27]

Slavery was in truth taken for granted by most American rebels. So was the slave trade. Thus Samuel Phillips Savage, who presided at the famous meeting in Old South Church in Boston which decided that tea should not be landed if duty had to be paid, was an insurer of slave ships, though, to be sure, of other ships as well. Prominent slavers or ex-slavers, such as Philip Livingston or Henry Laurens, our constant point of reference, and the merchants of Newport and Philadelphia, supported the revolution with their purses: at their head, Robert Morris, the Liverpool-born 'financier of the revolution', who as a partner of Willing and Morris of Philadelphia had himself been concerned in slaving in the 1760s.* The Board of Naval Commissioners of the Eastern states included, as its senior member, William Vernon of Newport, one of the best-known slave merchants of that city.

Several seamen who now enjoyed their hour of glory had also been concerned in the slave trade; for example, Esek Hopkins, a slave captain of Newport, who had sailed to Africa and Suriname for the Browns of Providence, became, first, Commander-in-Chief of the Rhode Island forces in 1775, and later the first Chief of the American Congressional Navy, even though it was an office from which he was dismissed in ignominy. The brave John Paul Jones, captain of the famous *Bonhomme Richard*, had had a long service as a mate or second mate on board slavers sailing from Fredericksburg, on the Rappahannock River, in Virginia. James de Wolf of Bristol, Rhode Island, carried out operations at sea against the British which made him a hero; and so began one of the great slave-trading careers, and fortunes. Even Benjamin Franklin, the most

---

* *Morris was also an associate of Anthony Bacon, one of Liverpool's most astute merchants, who had provided slaves to the British colonies in the 1760s on the government's behalf – though he had moved on to iron before the American Revolution and, the founder of the South Wales iron trade, was soon making money out of providing guns for the British Army in North America.*

thoughtful of North Americans, was cautious about abolition: 'Slavery is such an atrocious debasement of human nature', he rather curiously said, 'that its very extirpation, if not performed with solicitous care, may sometimes open a source of serious evils.'[28] The Quakers were, meantime, discredited in these years because of their refusal to support armed action in the war against the English, even if they did, in 1776, call on all Quaker slave owners to resign from their community.

Still, the discussion leading to the Declaration of Independence included critical talk of the slave trade, and Jefferson's first draft of that document contained, among other general statements, a condemnation of King George III as waging 'cruel war against human nature itself, violating its most sacred rights of life and liberty in the persons of a distant people who never offended him, captivating and carrying them into slavery in another hemisphere': a statement as historically inaccurate as it was unfair, even though the King would later appear enthusiastic for the trade. Jefferson eventually explained that these words were finally omitted 'in complaisance to South Carolina and Georgia, who had never attempted to restrain the importation of slaves and who, on the contrary, still wished to continue it'. He added, 'Our northern brethren also, I believe, felt a little tender under those censures; for, though their people had very few slaves themselves, yet they had been pretty considerable carriers of them to others.' The Articles of Confederation were in the end silent on the question of the slave trade.[29]

So it was scarcely surprising that it should have been the loyalist Earl of Dunmore, Governor of Virginia, who was the only commander to free slaves in an attempt to win black support for his side. But though some of these ex-slave warriors were inspired to wear emblems saying 'Liberty for Slaves', they were not much help militarily. The British government rejected Dunmore's audacious scheme for reconquering the Southern colonies with a black army, even though many more slaves fought on the British side in the conflict than on that of the rebels (as many as 50,000 may have been evacuated by the British to Canada or Nova Scotia; some of them later returned). The American revolutionary army also did use blacks (free blacks, at Lexington and Bunker Hill), then banned them, and afterwards allowed their re-enlistment. John Laurens, son of the repentant Henry, tried to found an army of 3,000 slaves in South Carolina, but failed to receive Congressional support.

Meantime the rich British Caribbean colonies, led by Barbados and Jamaica, refused any idea of standing alongside the mainland colonies. They feared for their slaves. Britain was relieved: in 1773 British imports from Jamaica alone were five times the combined import from the thirteen colonies.

One further contemporary comment should be noted. Edmund Burke, the philosopher-statesman, as is well known, supported a policy of conciliation with the American colonies. But he was at that time a

Member of Parliament for Bristol, still one of the foremost slaving ports of Britain; and his fellow member Henry Cruger, a North American by birth, had often invested in slaving voyages. In his speech in the House of Commons in March 1775 advocating negotiations with the colonists, Burke opposed the idea of punishing the colonists by liberating their slaves. An offer of freedom, he said, 'would come rather oddly, shipped to them in an African vessel, which is refused an entry into the ports of Virginia and Carolina with a cargo of 300 negroes. It would be curious to see the Guinea captain attempting at the same instance to publish his proclamation of liberty and to advertise his sale of slaves.'[30] But while the fighting for one kind of liberty was going on, there was not much thought given to the idea of liberty for slaves.

Once the war was over the subject of slavery began immediately to be discussed. Several states accepted not just an abolition of the slave trade, but actual emancipation. The motor of these remarkable changes was once more the Quakers, who recovered their standing at the peace; and the Society of Friends, at that time, was a transatlantic movement, in which members on both sides of the ocean were in constant touch. New polemicists took up the cudgels: David Cooper, for example, pointed out that Washington and his friends had asked God to deliver the Americans from oppression, when 'sighs and groans' were to be heard in consequence of worse oppressions.[31]

Thus Pennsylvania abolished slavery in 1780. The law admittedly applied only to future generations, and delayed freedom for any slaves till after they had reached the age of twenty-eight; participation in the slave trade by Pennsylvanians was not prohibited until 1789. Between 1780 and 1800 similar acts of gradual or qualified emancipation were carried through, not without opposition, in Massachusetts, New Hampshire, New York, New Jersey, and even in Rhode Island. Upper and Lower Canada, still British, with their small store of slaves, followed suit. By 1786 slaves could only legally be introduced into Georgia. How ironic, considering that that was the state which had legalized slavery as lately as 1750!

There were numerous qualifications to these seeming acts of philanthropy. Rhode Island might have abolished slavery, but that did not mean that it outlawed slave merchants: indeed, in its act of 1774 prohibiting the importation of slaves Rhode Island had preserved the interests of its traders by providing that if they were unable to dispose of their slaves in the West Indies they could bring them to the home state for a limited period of a year, and then re-export them at will. In New York all existing slaves were to remain so, and slave merchants were still legally able to operate from that state's ample shores.

Enlightened opinion in England, with a somewhat larger number of slaves to consider than in the United States (there were probably close to 800,000 in the West Indies alone, and in the new United States about

650,000), was, meantime, beginning to think not that slavery or the slave trade should be abolished, but that it was desirable to make slavery less cruel and better regulated. In 1780, for example, Burke conceived a scheme to make the slave trade and slavery humane, as well as to civilize the coast of Africa. He retreated, however, when he thought of the strength of the West Indian interest in the House of Commons.* But the opposition of Scottish thinkers to slavery as such continued. Thus the historian William Robertson, who was a member of a debating society in Edinburgh to which both Adam Ferguson and Adam Smith belonged, explained in his *History of America*, published in 1777, that the slave trade was 'an odious commerce no less repugnant to the feelings of humanity than to the principles of religion'.

More energetic opposition to slavery was now being expressed in France, which in these years seemed further from social upheaval than did England. In 1769 the poet Charles-François Saint-Lambert created, in his novel *Zimeo*, the curious personage of Wilmouth, the philanthropic Quaker; while in 1770 Louis-Sébastien Mercier, in *L'An 2440: Rêve s'il en fut jamais*, describes how the hero, awakened from a sleep of 772 years, finds a Paris where all injustices have vanished; where Greek and Latin are spoken in the street; and where he sees a 'singular monument', made of marble, depicting, 'on a magnificent pedestal, a black, bare-headed, his arm outstretched, with a proud look, his attitude noble, imposing. Around him was the debris of twenty sceptres. At his feet, one could read the legend "to the Avenger of the New World".' The book was, of course, proscribed.[32]

Then, in his *Histoire philosophique et politique des Indes*, the Abbé Raynal (and his collaborators, who included Diderot) again argued that slavery was contrary to nature, and so universally wrong. The book now reads confusedly, though the language is eloquent and, at the time of its first publication – in Amsterdam, in 1770 – its effect was electric. Raynal had been a Jesuit, a journalist on the *Mercure de France*, and had frequented the salons of Paris, including that of the famous Mme de Geoffrin. One of his biographers has suggested that he himself had invested in trading slaves. All the same, he first described polemically the vile conditions in which most Africans lived in the New World, and said that the women were given such hard work that they could not think of having children. He thought that whereas the Spaniards made their slaves the companions of their indolence, the Portuguese the instruments

---

* *Some years earlier (despite his admiration for Montesquieu), he had shown that he was in no way concerned about the slave trade when he wrote to a friend, Harry Garnet: 'I shall only trouble you with one point more which is to recommend to your very serious consideration the consequences which will probably attend any project for altering the present constitution of the Royal African Company. The act upon which it stands was made by the most experienced men upon the most mature deliberation.'*

of their debauches, and the Dutch the victims of their avarice, the English treated them as purely physical beings, and would never become familiar with them, never smile at them, or even talk to them. The French, Raynal thought, were less proud and so less disdainful, according their slaves a kind of a morality which enabled them to forget their intolerable condition. The Protestants, the Abbé went on, allowed their captives to stew in their 'mahommedanism' or their idolatry, provided they worked, whereas the Catholics thought themselves obliged to afford some sort of baptism, if only rudimentary.

Raynal did think it necessary to try to make the conditions of existing slaves more supportable. Give them more music, he argued, let them dance, let the women be encouraged to have families so that there would be some labourers accustomed from childhood to the light of the Americas. 'I shall . . . prove', Raynal said proudly, 'that there is no reason of state which can authorize slavery. I shall not be afraid to denounce to the tribunal of reason and justice those governments which tolerate this cruelty, or which are not even ashamed to make it the basis of their power.' He then systematically destroyed the arguments of all who, 'executioners of their brothers', sought to justify slavery, reserving a final thrust at those who argued that the enslavement of Africans was 'the only way to conduct them to the eternal beatitude through the great benefit of holy baptism. O pious Jesus,' Raynal continued, 'would you have predicted that your sweet doctrines could be made the justification of such horror?'

The gradual disappearance of slavery in Europe, Raynal argued, had been the result not of religion but of the decisions of various monarchs who had thought that they would thereby ruin their feudal tenants. The Americas had offered an unlimited new field for the exploitation of human beings; and European expansion into America had been from the beginning marked by oppression. The slave trade, since the Renaissance, was to be attributed to a generation of pirates from both France and Britain. 'Whoever justifies such an odious system deserves mocking silence from the philosopher,' said the Abbé, 'and a stab with a dagger from the black.'

Raynal thought that the abolition of slavery would come as a result of a revolution of slaves led by a hero who would render 'the Americans drunk with long-awaited blood' (such as had indeed nearly happened in a terrible slave rebellion on the Danish island of St John in 1731). The Code Noir, which was supposed to govern the treatment of slaves by their masters in French territories, would disappear and, in its place, there would be a Code Blanc, which would, he thought, be terrible enough if it were only to reflect the right of vengeance.[33]

Though the clergy of Bordeaux demanded that Raynal's work be prohibited because of its outrage to religion, and the *parlement* of Paris even ordered it burned by the public executioner, his influence quickly spread throughout society. Thus it was because of having read him that a Huguenot merchant, A. Triquier, spoke out firmly in a meeting of the Academy at Marseilles in 1777: 'But how can we pass over in silence the means which we have invented to ruin America after having devastated it? . . . Barbarians that we are!' Raynal, too, had addressed his fellow Europeans as 'barbarians', adding, 'Will you persuade me that a man can be the property of a sovereign, a son of a father?' God, after all, was the Father, not the master. The speaker gained a prize for this lecture.[34]

Still, for the moment, administrative action in response to the issues raised by the Quakers, by the *philosophes*, by Granville Sharp, by a few enlightened Portuguese friars, and by Raynal was confined to trying to draw a line between what pertained in the empires concerned, and what happened, or was allowed, at home. In 1773, in what was presented as an enlightened measure, 'people of colour' from Brazil were forbidden to enter Portugal. (Portugal had abolished slavery at home in 1750.)

The last public sale of a black slave in England appears to have been in Liverpool in 1779. In 1777 a royal declaration forbade the entry of any black into France, because '*They marry Europeans, they infect brothels, and colours are mixed.*' Whether this law had any effect is doubtful: six years later, in 1783, a ministerial *circulaire* complained that black servants were still being disembarked: 'They are daily confiscated; and their masters insist that they have not heard of the law of 1777.'[35]

25

THE GAUNTLET
HAD BEEN THROWN DOWN

'The matter had now become serious. The
gauntlet had been thrown down and
accepted. The combatants had taken their
station, and the contest was to be renewed,
which was on the great theatre of the
nation.'

Clarkson, History, *vol. II*

THE PEACE CONFERENCE between the new United States and Britain was held in Paris. Benjamin Franklin was the first United States negotiator. Though he was much involved in business throughout his life, and though he once advertised the sale of slaves in his newspaper, he had become a firm opponent of the slave trade, if not yet of slavery itself.* His British counterpart was David Hartley, the dull Member of Parliament who had first raised the matter of the abolition of the slave trade in the House of Commons. But the deputies of these negotiators included two old partners in the slave trade, Henry Laurens of Charleston and Richard Oswald of London (and Bence Island). Since his withdrawal from the slave trade Laurens had been President of the Continental Congress. Oswald, chosen for his riches and knowledge of America, was a merchant with whom Laurens had often traded slaves, and had become the intimate adviser of the Prime Minister, Lord Shelburne (to whom, curiously enough, he had been presented by his fellow Glaswegian, Adam Smith). Oswald had looked after Laurens's children when they boarded in London, had worked for Laurens's release when he was imprisoned in the Tower of London in 1781, and had even speculated in land in East Florida with Franklin (to whom he seemed a 'truly good man').[1]

---

* He had also, as long ago as 1729, published a pamphlet by Ralph Sandiford, the early Quaker opponent of slavery.

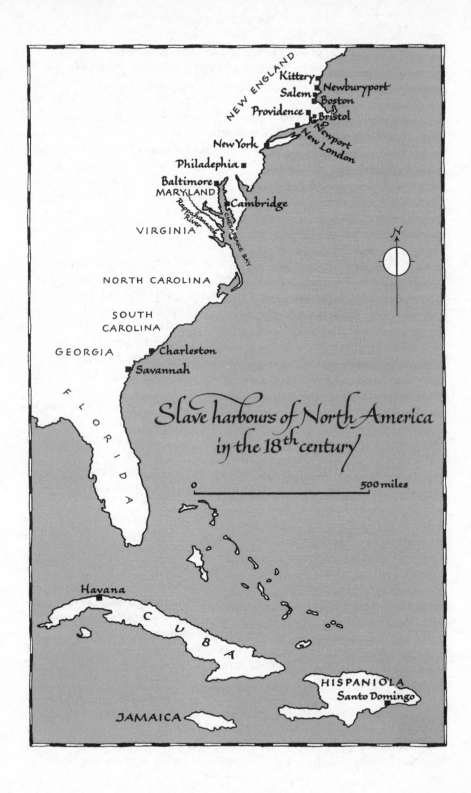

Slave harbours of North America
in the 18th century

The association between Laurens and Oswald at opposite sides of the table at the famous Peace Conference of 1783 in Paris is a symbolic association in the history of the eighteenth century. Both men were Atlantic dealers, men whose activity was not limited to one country, and both had much to lose from a separation of North America from Britain, and even more from a bad treaty marking that separation.

With this sponsorship of the peace, it is scarcely surprising that the slave trade should afterwards revive as if nothing had happened. A member of a large firm in Nantes, Chaurand Frères (it fitted out eleven slavers between 1778 and 1790), understandably wrote in 1782: 'The slave trade is the only branch of commerce which presents perspectives of profit. The need of the colonies for slaves is so great that they will always be received with pleasure.'[2]

The new Otaheite cane from the South Seas seemed a prescription for revived success even in old sugar plantations, and there was already talk of how James Watt and Matthew Boulton's new Birmingham-made steam engines could simplify the business of boiling the sugar. The trade in slaves led to the production not just of sugar, but also of coffee. Saint-Domingue exported about 12,000,000 tons of those benign beans a year in the late 1760s, and was selling over 72,000,000 by 1789. In the 1780s the consumption of coffee by the French increased in proportion to their interest in political freedom.

British business and British politicians, too, seem to have had no doubt about the importance of the slave traffic. In 1787 the Board of Trade would be told that the British probably carried 38,000 slaves from Africa that year.

In North America, despite disapproving legislation, merchants were dealing in slaves with more energy than ever. This was the era in particular of the rise of Bristol, Rhode Island, which began to replace the old dominating harbour, Newport, which took some time to recover from occupation by the British for two years. Several slave ships also left Boston in these years for Africa with 'positive orders to take slaves only'. The tall figure of Colonel Thomas Handasyde Perkins of that city had recently established a good business selling slaves in Saint-Domingue. Baltimore merchants (Samuel and John Smith, William van Wyck, John Hollins, Stewart and Plunkett) were also all busy buying (and selling) slaves in the West Indies, as well as landing cargoes in Charleston.

It is true that in all the big slaving nations people had begun to talk of abolition, but the concern seemed confined to unorthodox sects, such as the Quakers in Britain and North America, and intellectuals in France. Few anxieties troubled the slaving princes in Madrid, Lisbon, and Rio de Janeiro. Still, there were some disquieting signs. The success of the Abbé Raynal's book was disturbing; and even in New England, Moses Brown of Providence, as a young man himself active in the family firm of Nicholas Brown, which had sent ships to Africa for slaves, wrote discouraging words to the merchants Clarke and Nightingale of the same city after he had heard that they were thinking of moving into the promising new slave trade with Cuba. He wanted them not to do so: 'As I have entertained a respectful opinion of your humanity . . . and remembering how it was for me, when our company were engaging in that traffic that, altho' the convictions of my own conscience were such as to be averse to the voyage, yet in reasoning on that subject with those who were for pursuing it, my holding slaves [myself] . . . weakened the arguments [he had since freed his slaves], that I suffered myself, rather than break my connexions, to be concerned but, as I have many times since thought that, if I had known the sentiments of others, or had their concurring testimonies to those scruples [which] I then had, I should have been preserved from an evil, which has given me the most uneasiness, and has left the greatest impression and stain upon my own mind of any, if not all my other conduct in life. . . . Under these considerations, I felt some engagement for your preservation from so great an evil as I have found that trade to be. . . . You are men of feelings, and abilities to live without this trade, why then should you be concerned in it against your own – against the feelings of your friends . . . ?'[3]

But, despite this appeal, Clarke and Nightingale entered the trade, believing like many other established firms that the high risks were acceptable, especially if they carried slaves bought in Africa direct to Havana; and the beautiful yellow-painted clapboard house which Nightingale built in Power Street, next to John Brown's brick mansion, remains to remind the modern visitor of his financial success. John Brown himself was engaged in a ferocious argument with his brother and others on behalf of the slave traders; and it was no secret that the anonymous polemicist in favour of the slave trade 'A Citizen' was none other than that substantial merchant.

Still, the intellectual preparation for abolition continued. Among some in England after the loss of the American colonies, anti-slavery became a 'means to redeem the nation, a patriotic act'. In 1782, for example, William Cowper published his poem 'Charity', which, inspired by his friend John Newton – the repentant slave captain, by then Vicar of St Mary's Woolnoth, in London – denounced the slave merchant who 'grows rich on cargoes of despair':

> Canst thou, and honour'd with a Christian name,
> Buy what is woman-born, and feel no shame?
> Trade in the blood of innocence, and plead
> Expedience as a warrant for the deed . . . ?

Cowper at that time had, however, little renown, though later the wide distribution of his works would make him almost as well known as the once ultra-popular James Thomson.

When peace returned after 1783 the persistent though now septuagenarian Anthony Benezet revived his campaign by correspondence. He
had some remarkable successes. For example, he persuaded Benjamin
West, the fashionable American painter who was President of the Royal
Academy in England, to present a letter on the subject, with some
pamphlets, to Queen Charlotte, though what that solid Mecklenburg
matron made of the documents is apparently unrecorded. No doubt she
passed them on to her husband, the King, who never permitted sentiment
to hamper his support of the trade.

Opinion in both Britain and North America was next affected by the
case brought in 1783 relating to the Liverpool slaveship *Zong*. The *Zong's*
master was Luke Collingwood, and it was owned by William Gregson
and George Case, who were well-known merchants of Liverpool (of
which city both partners had been mayors).* This ship sailed in
September 1781 with 442 slaves from São Tomé. Collingwood mistook
Jamaica for Saint-Domingue. Once they had lost the way, water became
short. Many slaves died or became ill. Collingwood called together his
officers and said that if the slaves on board were to die naturally the loss
would be that of the owners of the ship; but if, on some pretext affecting
the safety of the crew, 'they were thrown alive into the sea, it would be the
loss of the underwriters'. The first mate, a certain Kelsall, thought that
'there was no present want of water to justify such a measure'. But the
opinion of Collingwood prevailed, and 133 slaves, most of whom were
sick and not likely to live, were flung into the sea. Fifty-four were thrown
overboard on 29 November, forty-two the next day, and, despite the
coming of rain (which alleviated the shortage of water), twenty-six on
1 December; while another ten jumped in of their own accord.

A case deriving from this scandal came to court in 1783, since the
insurers (Gilbert et al.) disagreed with the captain's judgements about
the finances, and refused to pay anything to the owners. The latter
brought a suit against the insurers, demanding to be paid £30 for each
slave, and were backed by the King's Bench, whereupon the underwriters
petitioned the Court of Exchequer. Lord Mansfield, still Lord Chief
Justice, allowing a second trial, remarked: 'The matter left to the jury was
whether it was from necessity [that the slaves were thrown into the sea];
for they had no doubt (though it shocks one very much) that the case
of slaves was the same as if horses had been thrown overboard.' By the
time of the trial, Captain Collingwood was dead. The barrister for
the owners argued, 'So far from a charge of murder lying against these
people, there is not the least imputation – of cruelty, I will not say – but

---

* *Gregson, Mayor in 1762, was for long one of the most prominent men in his city; he was
a member of the council from 1760 till 1800, and he held the corporation account in his
bank. His partner, George Case, his son-in-law, was a member of the council for fifty-seven
years, and Mayor in 1781.*

[even] of impropriety.' The persistent Granville Sharp, all the same, tried to 'prosecute the murders' before the Court of Admiralty, but failed: the Solicitor-General, John Lee, deplored his 'pretended appeal to humanity', and declared that a master could drown slaves without 'a surmise of impropriety'.'⁴

By then Sharp was considered a person of consequence, and as a result of his and Benezet's fruitful correspondence he had by now the support of most of the bishops of England in his campaign against slavery. He accordingly sent a copy of the proceedings of this trial to both the new (short-lived) Prime Minister, the Duke of Portland, and to the Lords of the Admiralty. Sharp heard nothing from these grandees but, as usual, he was not cast down by the apparent setback.

Such events as the massacre on the *Zong* had occurred before, but now there was much more concern about the question of slavery and there were now methods whereby protest could be articulated. Thus Thomas Day, the eccentric rationalist, had already composed a poem, *The Dying Negro*, which denounced the inconsistency of the North Americans in fighting for liberty while maintaining slavery. Now he wrote a *Letter on the Slavery of the Negroes*, making the same point in a more coherent way.⁵ The Bishop of Chester, Dr Beilby Porteus, preached a sermon before the Society for the Propagation of the Gospel adjuring them to free the slaves on the Codrington properties.† (The Bishop knew what he was talking about, being the eighteenth child of a Virginia planter who had returned to England.) A famous polemical divine, Dr George Gregory, also included a bitter denunciation of the slave trade, in the manner of Raynal, in his *Essays Historical and Moral*. (He, too, wrote from experience, having been a clerk to the Liverpool alderman and merchant A. Gore.)

From then on the case against the slave trade began to be stated in England with ever-greater effectiveness, by a whole new school of active polemicists and theologians. The enemies of slavery were in touch with one another, and could boast of several successes. Thus in 1783 a bill was introduced into the House of Commons forbidding officials of the Royal African Company from selling slaves – a motion which caused the ever-active Society of Friends to submit a passionate appeal for a general prohibition on the commerce (Sir Cecil Wray introduced the appeal). Lord North, the amiable Home Secretary at this time, accepted the spirit in

---

* The tragedy of the Zong influenced Turner in 1840 to embark on his most impassioned painting. Perhaps he learned of the event in his father's barber shop in Maiden Lane. (He was, after all, eight years old in 1783.) The painting, Slave Ship, now hangs in the Boston Museum of Fine Arts.

† The Society was at that time firm in its support for slavery. When Anthony Benezet wrote to them asking them to abandon slavery, he received the answer, 'Though the Society is fully satisfied that your intention in this matter is perfectly good, yet they most earnestly beg you not to go further in publishing your notions, but rather to retract them. . . .'

which this document was presented, but said that it was impossible to abolish the trade, since it was 'necessary to every country in Europe'.[6] That year, 1783, was the last in which the Liverpool Quaker timber firm of Rathbone and Son supplied timber for the Africa trade – for the third voyage of Thomas and William Earle's ship, the *Preston*. The Rathbones thereafter became one of a small but lively group of abolitionists in Liverpool.

Next year, 1784, the first petition to the House of Commons was presented by a municipality, the town of Bridgwater, in favour of an end of the slave trade. At about the same time Dr James Ramsay published two pamphlets, first the *Essay on the Conversion and Treatment of the African Slaves* and second, *An Enquiry into the Effects of the Abolition of the Slave Trade*.

Ramsay, born near Aberdeen, had been a naval surgeon; his vessel encountered a slave ship on which an epidemic of plague was raging. Ramsay went on board, saw the terrible conditions in which the slaves were living, and resolved to do what he could for them. Injury obliged him to seek work onshore, and he became a clergyman on the tiny but prosperous island of St Kitts, where several thousand slaves were at work making sugar. Ramsay spent nineteen years there, in the course of which he made himself hated by the planters because of his sermons (an echo of Fray Antonio de Montesinos so long before in Santo Domingo) which denounced both slavery and the slave trade. He then returned to England, to take up a living in Kent, at the village of Teston, where his old naval captain – Sir Charles Middleton, now a naval commander, a Member of Parliament, and an agriculturalist (an innovator in the cultivation of hops) – had a property.

Ramsay's arguments were curious, since he admired the discipline of sugar plantations, such as those which he had seen on St Kitts, and liked the relation of master and servant which had often marked them. But he thought that slavery inspired a society 'where power becomes right'. His support for the cause of abolition was important, for up till then the most active opponents of slavery, such as Sharp or Benezet, had had no personal experience of the West Indies.

Publications in France, where there was no censorship on matters relating to slavery (even if there was in respect of criticisms of the Church), were making much the same points. The Swiss economist Jacques Necker, just dismissed as Minister of Finance in France, included, in his highly successful study of the country's finances a scathing account of 'how we preach humanity yet go every year to bind in chains twenty thousand natives of Africa'. That essay sold 24,000 copies in a very short time.[7] (All the same, a slave ship bearing that minister's name would go to Africa from Nantes in 1789, and two others also named *Necker* left Le Havre and Bordeaux in 1790.)

Benezet – now old, his work of bringing the enemies of slavery together in a working alliance almost done – published yet another pamphlet, *The Case of Our Fellow Creatures, the Oppressed Africans*. Over

10,000 copies of this were published, and the English Quakers, who had by now formed a special committee to discuss ways of enlightening the public mind about the slave trade, distributed copies to members of the House of Commons.* Whenever Quakers met they now talked of the iniquity of the trade; and, profiting from the general mood of tolerance in Britain, they made it their business to lecture influential schools: Westminster, Winchester, Harrow, Charterhouse, St Paul's, and Eton, for example.

The climate in Britain with respect to the slave trade was now transformed in a special way. In 1785 the eminent divine Dr William Paley published his *Moral Philosophy*, based on his lectures at Cambridge, which included a condemnation of the business in severe terms. As with Dr Gregory's pamphlet on the matter, the tone was that of the violent Abbé Raynal, not the ironic Montesquieu. This book, as Thomas Clarkson later wrote, 'was adopted early by some of the colleges in our universities into the system of their education . . . [and] found its way also into most of the private libraries of the kingdom'.[8] That same year Clarkson himself, son of a headmaster at Wisbech in the Isle of Ely, a clever and determined graduate of Cambridge, then aged twenty-four, and intended for the Church (his prospects were brilliant, he himself recalled later), won a famous Latin essay prize at his university on the subject of whether it was lawful to make men slaves against their will. The subject ('*Anne liceat invitos in servitutem dare?*') had been chosen by the Vice-Chancellor, Dr Peter Peckard, a Whig theologian who in a recent sermon at St Mary's Church had talked of slavery as a crime. To prepare for the essay, Clarkson read Benezet's *Historical Account of Guinea* and papers made available by a recently deceased slave trader whom he had known. Seeking to get the prize essay published in English, Clarkson went to London. On the way, at Wades Mill – near Ware, in Hertfordshire – he experienced a revelation: 'If the contents of the essay were true, it was time some person should see these calamities to their end.' Clarkson took the essay to a Quaker bookshop run in London by James Phillips. Phillips (whose mother, Catherine, had preached the Quaker message throughout the unpromising territory of Carolina) published Clarkson's work, as *An Essay on the Slavery and Commerce of the Human Species*; and he introduced Clarkson to many others (such as Dr Ramsay; William Dillwyn, Benezet's pupil; and Granville Sharp) who, from different perspectives, were determined to destroy slavery. Clarkson was surprised to learn of the work on the subject now close to his heart which had been done by these men. With this meeting, inspired by a Quaker bookseller, of the disparate members of the abolitionist movement in London, the campaign against

---

* *The members of the committee were William Dillwyn, George Harrison, Samuel Hoare, Thomas Knowles, John Lloyd and Joseph Woods (author of a famous pamphlet,* Thoughts on the Slavery of the Negroes).

the commerce in slaves began in earnest. Clarkson determined to 'devote myself to the cause', even dropping his plans to enter the Church, after talking at length to Dr Ramsay at Charles Middleton's dining table in Kent in the summer of 1786.[9]

In 1787 a Committee for Effecting the Abolition of the Slave Trade was founded in London; Clarkson and his Quaker friends took the lead. Granville Sharp and Ramsay disagreed with the emphasis on the abolition of the trade: they wanted the campaign to deal with slavery too. But the younger, now more energetic, and dedicated Clarkson thought that an end to either the trade or to slavery would finish the other, and his ideas prevailed. He assumed that if the trade were abolished planters would immediately take care to look after the slaves well. The abolition of slavery itself would have threatened the institution of property and perhaps, if one remembered how the North American rebellion had begun over taxes, would risk the loss of the British West Indies. This decision was in keeping with the mood of the times; Charles James Fox would tell the House of Commons in 1806, 'Slavery itself, odious as it is, is not nearly [so] bad a thing as the slave trade.'[10] Further, it was thought open to question whether the British Parliament could legally act on the issue of slavery in the West Indian colonies, each of which had its independent legislature; but it could certainly act with regard to any branch of commerce. The journey of the slave in the trade was rightly seen as the part of his life where he suffered the most.

In retrospect, this plan seems to have been flawed: if the principle of slavery was accepted, the idea of buying slaves could be made to seem logical.

The establishment of Clarkson's committee, however, marked the transition of what had hitherto been the Quaker cause of abolition into a national, even an international, movement. The emblem of the campaign – designed by the master potter Josiah Wedgwood, a committed supporter – was an inspired piece of propaganda, worthy of the Roman Church, or of a modern political party. It consisted of a picture of a chained Negro on bended knee with as legend the question: 'Am I not a man and a brother?'

Clarkson was the right man to inspire this movement. He had a nose for both the telling piece of information and for finding the right backing. Thus he gained support in all sorts of circumstances: from the socially influential dandy Benet Langton to the Bishop of Chester. Through Ramsay he had the support of Sir Charles Middleton, who was Comptroller of the Navy and would become Lord Barham. As a result of the committee's activity letters poured in from all parts of the country. Deans and doctors, majors and great businessmen, tutors of colleges, bishops and squires, prebendaries and archdeacons, not to speak of backwoods members of Parliament, such as William Smith of Sudbury, testified their interest.

In May 1787 Clarkson, then aged twenty-seven, met the politician William Wilberforce, a year older than he, and on the urging of Lord Barham, and through the mediation of Benet Langton, asked him to assume the political leadership of the movement for abolition.

Wilberforce, MP for Hull, where he had a property, was like Clarkson a Cambridge graduate, as was his equally young intimate friend, the Prime Minister, William Pitt.

Wilberforce came from a mercantile family long settled in Hull. That city was not quite unknown as a port in the slave trade, but Wilberforce's forebears were involved in Baltic commerce. Wilberforce himself was a well-educated and independent man, eloquent, charming, and rich. Mme de Staël once called him 'the wittiest converser in England'. Most remarkably, he was as religious in temperament as he was socially successful. On a Continental holiday in 1784–5 with a clever divine, Dr Isaac Milner, Professor of Natural Philosophy at Cambridge, he had had a spiritual conversion, prompted by reading the Nonconformist Philip Doddridge's *On the Rise and Progress of Religion in the Soul*, one of those influential works whose contemporary success baffles a later age. In 1787 Wilberforce was already a leader of evangelical thought.

Wilberforce had the advantage of a most agreeable voice, for which he was known as 'the nightingale of the House of Commons'. He had already read Ramsay's pamphlets, had met the Reverend John Newton, knew Hannah More (the Bristol-born philanthropic playwright), and had concerned himself, in a superficial way, with the question of slavery. After some hesitation, he agreed to lead the parliamentary side of the abolitionist movement, though not without having consulted Pitt, who, with the best brain that has ever graced English politics, became equally convinced of the evil of the slave trade and the desirability of ending it speedily. (Clarkson thought that Wilberforce, before he talked to Pitt in February 1787, had had 'but little knowledge of it'.) The critical conversation between the two – the statesman and the parliamentarian, old Cambridge friends, both young men still under thirty – was 'at the root of an old tree at Holwood, just above the steep descent into the vale of Keston', near Croydon. Many serene and pastoral scenes in England had been financed by the efforts of slaves on sugar plantations in the West Indies. Now a tranquil place would in return ultimately inspire a transformation in those islands.

Pitt's support for the cause may need some explanation. Was it, as was argued by Dr Eric Williams, that Britain's economic interests were now concerned with the East, not the West, Indies? Could it be that the West Indies were in decline, after the American War of Independence? Those economic arguments neglect the fact that statesmen are as often influenced by idealism as by ambition. Nor were the West Indies in a poor condition: both imports to, and exports from, the British West Indies were increasing during the 1780s. The British Africa trade was also at its apogee. The British share of the European slave traffic was higher than ever, and many merchants were doing well. Then the portfolios of several outstanding opponents of abolition, such as Pitt's dear friend Henry Dundas, as well as Alderman Newman and William Devyanes, included shares in East, not West, Indies trade. All three, indeed, were directors of the East India Company, and the last-named became its chairman. Moral conviction was in truth the determining element in the unusual chapter of British parliamentary history about to begin.

When on 24 May 1787 Clarkson, the heart and soul of the campaign for abolition, presented the Committee for Effecting the Abolition of the Slave Trade with evidence on the unprofitability of the business, he used rational arguments: an end of the traffic would save the lives of seamen (he had obtained much detail from a scrutiny of Liverpool customs records), encourage cheap markets for the raw materials needed by industry, open new opportunities for British goods, eliminate a wasteful drain of capital, and inspire in the colonies a self-sustaining labour force, which in time would want to import more British produce.

Clarkson set himself to gathering further information and spent the autumn of 1787 doing so. Though no one thought that the government would in the foreseeable future introduce a bill for the abolition of the trade, individual members, including officials, were (thanks to the help of Pitt) encouraging, and gave him access to invaluable state documents, including customs papers of the main ports. Clarkson went to Bristol. He described how on coming within sight of the city, just as night was falling, with the bells of the city's churches ringing, he 'began now to tremble at the arduous task I had undertaken, of attempting to subvert one of the branches of the commerce of the great place which was then before me'. But his despondency lessened, and he entered the streets 'with an undaunted spirit'.[11] He inspected a slave ship, he talked to seamen, and he met Harry Gandy, a retired (and repentant) sailor who had been on a slave ship; but all retired captains avoided him as if he 'had been a mad dog'. The Deputy Town Clerk of Bristol obligingly told him, however, that 'he only knew of one captain from the port in the slave trade who did not deserve to be hanged'. Clarkson followed up the case of the murder of a sailor, William Lines, by his own captain. From Quaker informants Clarkson found evidence of the brutalities committed on a recently returning slaver, the *Brothers*, whose captain had tortured a free black sailor, John Dean. He received the testimony of a surgeon named Gardiner, about to sail to Africa on the ship *Pilgrim*. He talked to a surgeon's mate who had been brutally used on board the slave ship *Alfred*; and he gained information at first-hand of the terrible affair of the Calabar River in 1767.[*] He also saw the inns where young men were made drunk, indebted, or both, and then lured to serve as sailors on slavers.

* See page 403.

Clarkson went to Liverpool, too. In contrast to his experience in Bristol, Ambrose Lace and Robert Norris, both retired slave captains, did talk to him; the former had commanded the *Edgar* at the massacre at Calabar twenty years before. Clarkson also talked to slave merchants. He held a curious court in his inn, the King's Arms, at which, by now well informed, he engaged in argument with practitioners of the trade. Here, too, he pursued a murder case: in this instance, the affair of the steward, Peter Green, a flute-player, who had been whipped to death by his captain in the Bonny River with a rope, for no good cause. Clarkson was once threatened with assault on the quay, but his foresight in hiring a retired slave-ship surgeon from Bristol, Alexander Falconbridge, as his assistant and bodyguard preserved him from death.

The activities of these abolitionists secured an interest in France. The worthy Jacques-Pierre Brissot de Warville – the celebrated writer into whose hands the attackers of the Bastille would deliver the keys of that prison – and Etienne Clavière, who had much money at his disposal from speculation, announced their intention of establishing a society similar to that existing in England, even though, they explained, it might take some time. But Marshal Lafayette, then at the summit of his reputation, gave his support and suggested that a French committee should be formed there and then. Within months, the Société des Amis des Noirs was indeed set up; the enlightened aristocrats the Duke of La Rochefoucauld and the Marquis of Condorcet, the traveller Volney, the chemist Lavoisier, and the two most famous radical priests, the Abbé Sieyès and Père Grégoire, all became members. The Swiss pastor of Lyons, Benjamin Frossard, echoing Adam Smith, wrote in a book, *La Cause des esclaves nègres*, published in 1789, that the slave produced less than the free man, 'despite the whip'. But these men did little till visited by Clarkson.*

The consequence of Clarkson's agitation in London was that in February 1788 a committee of the Privy Council was set up to investigate the slave trade. To secure such a committee was a great victory, and Clarkson himself prepared the case for the abolitionists, working with both Pitt and Wilberforce. Some witnesses testified in favour of the trade, several describing at length the benefits to the Africans, while one witness even described the holds of slave ships as 'redolent with frankincense'. To Clarkson's astonishment, one of those whom he had interviewed extensively in Liverpool, and expected to speak on his behalf, the captain and merchant Robert Norris, testified in favour of the trade; no doubt he had been bribed to change his attitude. The main thrust of his argument was the same as had been used so often through the centuries: that the slave trade saved Africans from a worse fate in their own countries. Another witness – Samuel Taylor, one of the biggest Manchester cotton manufacturers – claimed that the value of the goods, principally cotton checks and

---

* *Clarkson's visit to Paris is discussed on page 320.*

other East Indian imitations, supplied by his city 'for the purchase of Negroes only', accounted for £180,000 and 'employed immediately about 18,000 of His Majesty's subjects. . . . This manufacture employs a capital of at least £300,000.' He added that about three-quarters of his own trade was in goods for Africa and, with the profits from it, he had 'raised and supported a family of ten children'.[12] Meantime, the *Boston Gazette* commented, a little prematurely: 'The African trade is come into the House of Commons, it is, of course, to go as soon as come. For to those who make a comprehensive judgement on the subject, how is the argument for the abolition of the slave trade to be maintained?'[13] Clarkson, for his part, devoted much attention to the sufferings of the crews on slave ships which, with a sure ear for politics, he believed would be the best argument to move the imagination of the members of both the House of Commons and the House of Lords.

Simultaneously, the Committee for Abolition began further to arouse 'the general moral feeling of the nation' by a wide distribution of pamphlets and books by Benezet, Clarkson, and Ramsay and a study of the slave trade by the Reverend John Newton, as well as the poems *The Black Slave Trade* by Hannah More and Cowper's *The Negro's Complaint*. Local abolitionist committees were founded, innumerable high-minded men recruited, and remarkable journeys of enquiry carried out. This was the first major public campaign in any country for a philanthropic cause. That it coincided with celebrations of the centenary of the Glorious Revolution gave a happy sense of good timing.

A proposal was made that a new African colony should be founded to receive some of the freed slaves to be seen in London. These constituted a serious concern, for the West Indian planters would not accept them: they thought that they would stimulate rebellion. Nova Scotia was tried out, but most of the slaves who had been sent there because they had fought on the side of Britain during the American Revolution hated the climate. A Swedish botanist, Dr Henry Smeathman, who had spent three years on the islands off the estuary of Sierra Leone as the guest of Richard Oswald and his associates, proposed that the rivers there, with 'their extraordinary temperature and salubrity of the climate', rendered the place ideal for a colony of freed slaves. A year before, incongruously, he had pronounced the unsuitability of the place as a penal colony: the convicts would die, he thought, at the rate of a hundred a month.

The discrepancy between these two judgements did not disturb Granville Sharp, the most enthusiastic friend of the idea of such a colony, who hoped to found a society free of the evils of a monetary economy. The government agreed to give support. In 1787, just as Clarkson was beginning his campaign, 'the Sierra Leone plan' was therefore launched: the government gave £12 per African towards the cost of transport, a ship was chartered, the sloop-of-war *Nautilus* was commissioned as a convoy, and on 8 April the first 290 free black men and 41 black women, with 70 white women, including 60 prostitutes from London (women 'of the lowest sort in ill health and of bad character'), left for Sierra Leone under the command of Captain Thomas Boulden Thompson of the Royal Navy.* A stretch of about nine or ten miles by twenty miles, 'a fine tract of mountainous country covered with trees of all kinds' between the famous slaving rivers Sherbro and Sierra Leone, in the words of Sharp, was bought for about £60 in goods from the local overlord of the Bulom shore, a Temne chief known to the English as 'Tom'. Here, in the expectation of the ever-idealistic Sharp, would be set up a 'free settlement', where 'the ancient English frankpledge'† would be the basis of all regulation. There would be nothing so imperial as a governor: the ruler would be selected by free vote.

Adam Smith had insisted that freemen would work better than slaves. But he was confounded, for malaria, drink, idleness, war with the local Africans, and above all rain ruined this high-minded enterprise. Half the settlers died in the first year. 'Frankpledge' or no, settlers deserted and, worst of all, some went to work for nearby slave dealers. Agriculture did not flourish. From London, Sharp wrote to the settlers: 'I could not have conceived that men who were well aware of the wickedness of slave dealing, and had themselves been sufferers (or at least many of them) under the galling yoke of bondage to slave-holders ... should become so basely depraved as to yield themselves instruments to promote, and extend, the same detestable oppression over their brethren.'[14] Even Henry Demane, one of the Africans whom Sharp had rescued from slavery by sending a writ of habeas corpus to a vessel already under sail from Portsmouth to Jamaica, became a dealer in slaves.

Worse was to follow. Voltaire, not Burke, would have felt justified. Encouraged by slave traders, who resented the new settlement, King Tom's successor, 'King Jemmy', gave the settlers three days to leave their town, and then burned down the place (the quarrel occurred because an American slave captain had kidnapped a number of Temnes). The colonists fled and re-established themselves at a new 'Granville Town'. A Sierra Leone Company was founded, the directors being leading abolitionists (such as the benign host of the 'Clapham Sect', Henry Thornton, and Wilberforce, Captain Sir George Young, and Clarkson, as well as Sharp). Over 1,000 of the blacks who had been quartered in Nova Scotia, after the American War of Independence, went out to Sierra Leone in 1792, with another hundred white people, under the leadership of Lieutenant John Clarkson, a brother of the philanthropist.

---

* *Captain Thompson later fought at the Nile and Copenhagen, where he lost a leg, was made a baronet, and became Comptroller of the Navy.*
† *A system of law in which all members of a community take responsibility for the achievements of, or the damage caused by, the others.*

Sierra Leone now ceased to be a 'province of Freedom' and became a colony under a governor, even if one appointed by Sharp's committee. Of course, the personality of this official counted for everything. The first to be named was William Dawes, who had been a subaltern of marines at Botany Bay – an experience which suggested somewhat gloomy conclusions for the 'hundredors and tithingmen' who, by Granville Sharp's inspiration, still constituted the free society of the frankpledge. But matters changed for the better when in 1794 Zachary Macaulay – the pompous yet effective and humane son of the minister at Inverary, Argyll, a bookkeeper when young, afterwards a manager on a sugar estate in Jamaica – took command in Sierra Leone, which he enthusiastically reported to be 'a more agreeable Montpellier'. His feelings for the sufferings of slaves had been awoken in Jamaica, and on his return across the Atlantic, without humour, taste, or a moment's relaxation, he devoted the rest of his life to seeking to ameliorate their conditions. But very difficult times continued in Sierra Leone; and in 1794 a French flotilla, guided by a New York slave trader, Captain Newell, bombarded, then pillaged, the city of Freetown, despite the protest by Macaulay that it was a humanitarian colony. He received the reply: '*Citoyen, cela peut bien être, mais encore vous êtes anglais.*'[15]

Zachary Macaulay was a successful governor. He rebuilt the place after the French onslaught, and surrounded himself with interesting men, such as the Swedish botanist Adam Afzelius, the missionary Jacob Grigg, who came to Africa in order to convert the heathen to Christ but died as a slave trader, and John Tilley, who managed a nearby slave factory yet worked with Macaulay as a patriot in times of war. A botanical garden was established on the initiative of Sir Joseph Banks, in collaboration with the director of the newly founded one in Kew Gardens.

After Macaulay left in 1799 the thriving community which he had built up declined. In 1800 the colony was saved from chaos only by the arrival of a contingent of 550 Jamaican blacks (Maroons), whose ancestors had taken to the hills after the British capture of Jamaica in 1655, and whose independence had long been recognized informally by British governors on the condition that they returned runaway slaves.

Sierra Leone became a full dependency of the Crown in 1808. The Reverend Sydney Smith, the curate of the Whigs, would say later that this colony had always two governors – one who had just arrived and one who had just returned – for the death rate was notable.

The same year that Clarkson met Wilberforce and Pitt in England, 1787, the new Constitution was signed in the United States, and then adopted, with its odd circumlocutions on the issue of slavery as well as the slave trade.

This famous document delayed a discussion in the new republic on the principle of the slave trade for twenty years. It provided – in article I, section 9 – that the 'Migration or Importation of such Persons as any of the States now existing shall think proper to admit, shall not be prohibited by the Congress prior to the Year one thousand eight hundred and eight, but a Tax or duty may be imposed on such Importation, not exceeding ten dollars for each Person.' That provision, of course, was intended to apply to slaves as well as immigrants.

The wording meant, on the one hand, that the slave trade received a federal lease of life for twenty years; but on the other it did mean that the matter had to be discussed. Many of those who supported the compromise spoke, like James Iredell (author of the famous 'Marcus' letters, in favour of the Constitution), of the slave trade as something 'which has already continued too long for the honour and humanity of those concerned in it'. (Iredell was the English-born nephew of a merchant of Bristol.) James Wilson, a Scotch-born delegate from Pennsylvania, one of the most influential members of the Constitutional Convention, pointed out that the clause would allow the United States Congress to prohibit the slave trade after 1808. George Lee Turberville, a Virginian planter and friend of Washington, in a private letter to Madison, did refer to the trade at this time as 'another great evil'; while Luther Martin of Baltimore thought it absurd that the United States should permit states to continue to carry on 'the only branch of commerce which is unjustifiable in its nature and contrary to the rights of mankind'.[16]

The compromise on slavery occurred because the delegates as a whole, and especially the leaders, agreed with Roger Sherman of Connecticut, the most experienced of those present, who made the simple observation that it was 'better to let the southern states import slaves than to part with those states'. The 'morality and wisdom' of slavery, declared another delegate from Connecticut, Oliver Ellsworth, a future chief justice of the Supreme Court, 'are considerations belonging to the states themselves'. Let every state 'import what it pleases', he continued. The leaders of South Carolina and Georgia had made it evident before that they 'would not perhaps otherwise have agreed to the new Constitution'.[17]

In addition, as had become clear in the 'special committee', with one member from each of the thirteen states, the Northern states were 'very willing to indulge the Southern ones at least with a temporary liberty to prosecute the slave trade, provided that they would in their turn gratify them, by laying no restriction on the navigation acts'. Finally, the states which were interested in a continuation of the slave trade were united, whereas the friends of liberty were divided. At that time, the latter were 'animated by no very strong and decided anti-slavery spirit with settled aims', whereas the delegates from Maryland, Virginia, and North Carolina, as well as those from South Carolina and Georgia, were quite opposed to the inclusion of any philanthropic sentiment in the matter of the slave trade in the Constitution, even though Virginia and Maryland had closed their ports to slaves from Africa in 1778 and 1783 respectively,

North Carolina had done the same in 1786, and South Carolina had done so, as an experiment, in 1787.

There was criticism outside the narrow political world which had reached this compromise. Samuel Bryan of Philadelphia, 'Sentinel', wrote in the Quaker *Independent Gazetteer* that, in the Constitution, 'the words, dark and ambiguous ... are evidently chosen to conceal from Europe that, in this enlightened country, the practice of slavery has its advocates among men in high stations.'[18] In *The Federalist* James Madison of Virginia replied, in more cautious terms than theretofore: 'It ought to be considered a great point gained in favour of humanity that a period of twenty years may terminate forever, within these states, a traffic which has so long and so loudly upbraided the barbarism of modern policy.' He added, quite fairly: 'Happy would it be for the unfortunate Africans if an equal prospect lay before them of being redeemed from the oppression of their European brethren!'[19]

There was a good deal of sporadic opposition to this clause of the Constitution. For example, General Thompson of Massachusetts asked: 'Shall it be said that, after we have established our own independence and freedom, we make slaves of others?' George Mason, a planter of Virginia, and himself a slave owner, engaged in an argument with Madison in which he declared himself against allowing the Southern states to enter the Union unless they agreed to discontinue the slave trade. But there was also opposition of a different kind: 'Negroes were our wealth, our only natural resource; yet behold how our kind friends in the north were determined soon to tie up our hands and drain us of what we had'! Thus Rawlins Lowndes of South Carolina, who had been born in St Kitts, had opposed independence from Britain and now openly opposed a federal constitution.[20]

. The two other clauses of the Constitution which mentioned slavery were also compromises: first the peculiar 'three-fifths clause' (article I, section 2, paragraph 3), whereby members of the House of Representatives were to be elected in proportion to the populations of their states, taking into account three-fifths of the slaves who were there; and then the 'fugitive slave' clause. But it was the article on the trade in slaves which excited most attention.

The Constitution did not mean that individual states could not abolish the slave trade or slavery itself before 1808; and several soon did so, in their own fashion. Thus New Jersey abolished slavery, and even imposed a duty on slaves who had been brought into the state since 1776. Moses Brown, Samuel Hopkins, and the Quakers of Rhode Island petitioned the legislators of that state to end the slave traffic and, to their surprise, a bill prohibiting the residents of the state from participating in it was passed. In 1788, as a result of more Quaker pressure, the legislature of Massachusetts also passed an act 'to prevent the slave trade'. Its preamble denounced the 'lust for gain' of those engaged in the 'unrighteous commerce'. Connecticut abolished the trade in 1788, the prime mover being the theologian Jonathan Edwards, at that time Pastor of the White Haven Church at New Haven, an ally of the abolitionists of Rhode Island nearby: that was necessary if the prohibition in Rhode Island was to have a chance since if there had been no prohibition in the next-door state the Bristol and Providence slavers could easily have moved their business there. New York also abolished the trade in 1788. Even Virginia declared that illegally imported slaves were free. Delaware next prohibited African slavery and imposed a fine of £500 per slave imported. Pennsylvania did the same, raising the fine to £1,000.

Nobody thought that these prohibitions would be easily put into practice. The intermeshing of state and federal law was poor. The issue was bedevilled by problems of jurisdiction. A debate in Charleston on the import of slaves into South Carolina in 1785 had also suggested the kind of resistance to the very idea of abolition which would be met in North America at the local level: John Rutledge, the most gifted leader in South Carolina, and later Chief Justice of the state, proclaimed, unequivocally, that he 'had been of opinion, for many years, that Negroes were the reason for an increase of our wealth; what number of slaves had been imported since the peace?'[21] General Charles Pinckney, an aide to George Washington, a future minister to France, and an unsuccessful federalist presidential candidate in 1804 and 1808, thought that 'this country is not capable of being cultivated by white men. . . . Negroes are to this country what raw materials are to another country. . . . No planter can cultivate his land without slaves.'[22] (Pinckney was himself a substantial planter, at Belmont, Virginia, and in Charleston.)

Had it not been for the destruction caused by the war, and the urgent demand for slaves in the South, the traffic in slaves might have been outlawed in 1787; and the history of the United States would have been different. But three states (North and South Carolina, and Georgia) continued to look on the trade as legal; and merchants in the Northern states continued to serve them. Thus began what W. E. B. Dubois, still the foremost historian of the abolition of the trade in the United States, described as 'that system of bargaining, truckling and compromising with a moral, political and economic monstrosity, which makes the history of our dealing with the slavery in the first half of the nineteenth century so discreditable to a great people'.[23]

The leaders of the states which had abolished the slave trade expected that state prosecutors, customs officials, and even private citizens would bring to book those who broke these laws. No such action followed till in May 1789 a private citizen, William Rotch, a whaler and a member of the Providence Society for Abolition in Rhode Island, charged the owners of the brig *Hope* (John Stanton, Caleb Gardner – the 'revolutionary hero' who had piloted the French fleet into Newport in 1780 – and Nathaniel Briggs) with sailing from Boston to carry 116 slaves from Africa to Martinique. A case was heard, in the course of which the defence claimed that the defendants could not be tried because they were not citizens of Massachusetts. In the end, the prosecution won. But the case had taken so long, and the punishment was so derisory, that the victory seemed to all concerned a Pyrrhic one.

The Society to Promote Abolition in Philadelphia, which had been formed before the War of Independence, was meantime enlarged, with Benjamin Franklin as its president, and a mixture of Quakers and others, including Benjamin Rush, the founder of medical science in the United States and Surgeon-General to the Continental Army during the war, were placed on its committee.* Moses Brown also founded a Providence Society for the Abolition of the Slave Trade. All these societies were attacked by slave interests in journals such as the *Providence Gazette*, in which the most powerful influence was John Brown, Moses Brown's elder brother and now head of the firm of Nicholas Brown.†

There was as yet no sign whatsoever that these humane ideas had any echo at all in Portugal or in Spain, nor in their empires. Indeed, the Spanish government, as always in search of ready cash, was still toying with the idea of monopoly companies; and a new Company of the Philippines (largely composed of entrepreneurs previously involved in the old Caracas Company) was given an exclusive contract to exploit the new Spanish islands of Fernando Po and Annobón. These had been bought from Portugal in 1778, in order to trade slaves there; and in 1786 that company was also given the right to import slaves into the region of the River Plate (the modern Argentina, Uruguay, and Paraguay), Chile, and Peru. But the Spaniards did not settle the new islands, all the same; and the company procured most of its slaves from large English houses. Their London agent made an arrangement with the big Liverpool shipbuilders turned slave merchants, Baker and Dawson, to import 5,000–6,000 slaves a year at $155 each. (Peter Baker, the biggest shipbuilder for the navy, had embarked upon the slave trade about 1773. His daughter Margaret married James Dawson, who captained some of his father-in-law's ships – among them the *True Briton*, which carried over 500 slaves from Africa to Jamaica in 1776, despite an insurrection and the outbreak of war.)

In 1788, when Baker and Dawson's contract came up for renegotiation, the firm made a bid to introduce 3,000 slaves into Cuba every year. But their terms were unsatisfactory. The Spanish government, in no way

* *Rush had been converted to the cause of abolition in the 1770s by Benezet, and published two pamphlets on the matter before the War of Independence.*
† *Meantime, Moses Brown himself was interested in new things: in 1789, he agreed to finance Samuel Slater of England, who had worked with Jedediah Strutt, a partner of the great Arkwright, to set up a water mill to make cotton textiles. Thus the industrial revolution in Rhode Island began.*

showing that it was disconcerted by the new mood in London – or in North America, come to that – and at last despairing of monopoly companies, on 28 February 1789 allowed as many slaves to be brought into Cuba, Santo Domingo, Puerto Rico, and Venezuela as the planters liked for the next two years. Slaves had, it is true, to be landed at specific ports (to assist collection of taxes), a third of the slaves had to be women, and as well as a government subsidy of four pesos per slave landed a tax of two pesos was levied for slaves intended for domestic labour. Foreign captains were limited to twenty-four hours in Spanish ports, their ships had to be of less than 300 tons, and they were not allowed to land in certain places, such as Santiago de Cuba, where the Crown feared that it was too easy for captains to escape the attention of officials. The policy was extended to the viceroyalty of New Granada (that is, Cartagena de Indias) in 1791, and to the remaining Spanish imperial territories, including Peru and the River Plate in 1795.

For some of the old slave centres, such as Cartagena de Indias, this liberalization of the laws came too late. From 1791 to 1794 only 262 slaves were legally imported there; even if the real figure, taking into account contraband, was higher, the old slave trade to the South American mainland was in full decline, for reasons which had nothing to do with Anglo-Saxon abolitionism. For by this time in both New Spain and New Granada (Mexico and Colombia) the indigenous, or mestizo, population was growing fast, and the need for African slave labour seemed less. But merchants in Cuba seized the opportunity: in consequence, 4,000 slaves were introduced in a single year, half of them by Baker and Dawson, as a result of the skilful salesmanship of their agent in Havana, Philip Allwood. In addition, the great landowners of the territory which would become, after independence, Venezuela, 'los amos del valle' (to recall the title of Herrera Duque's fine novel), with their large plantations of cacao in the valley of Caracas, were equally pleased, for they had always hated the silly restrictions on their imports of slaves which the old regulations had necessitated. They too were prominent customers of Barker and Dawson.

More comfort still was given to the British traders in slaves by the arrival in England in 1787 of five planters and businessmen from the Spanish empire. These included the Count of Jaruco, from Cuba, who came to buy modern sugar-processing equipment, and to discover how the British managed their sugar refineries and also their trade in slaves. No doubt Jaruco and his comrades discovered that most English sugar planters lived away from their properties. The Cubans also took back from England a steam engine which was for the first time put to use on one of Jaruco's sugar plantations.

William Walton, the Spanish Honorary Consul in Liverpool, told Lord Hawkesbury, the experienced President of the Board of Trade and Plantations (himself a West Indian proprietor), how these visitors had 'been down to Manchester to look at the kinds of goods and their prices usually sold to the English African merchants, [and] since that they have been at Liverpool to view the town and the ships employ'd in the slave trade . . . how many hands each vesell carried . . . the list of cargoes necessary to purchase slaves on different parts of the Coast . . . which goods might be procured in Spain, which must be purchas'd in England, and which were East India goods; [and] whether the slave trade had been profitable to the Town of Liverpool at large. . . .

'They likewise particularly enquir'd whether captains and doctors experienced in the Slave Trade might not be prevailed upon, by proper encouragement and great advantages given them, to go out to Cádiz and undertake the purchasing of the cargo, navigation of their vessells, and management of their Slaves. . . . They told me that the Court of Spain propos'd to have a slave trade of her own. . . .'[24]

The Spaniards were naturally disturbed by hearing of the campaign to bring to an end the British slave trade, on which their empire so greatly depended. They began to realize that sooner or later they might have to do without the supplies of Africans from Liverpool merchants. So they returned to found enlightened societies in Cuba, such as the Sociedad Económica de Amigos del País, a club concerned to promote liberal ideas without any risk of a political or social upheaval; they also promoted the first Cuban newspaper, El Papel Periódico; and they inspired a development board known as the Junta de Fomento. They instigated schools, and interested themselves in all technological innovations. Nor did Jaruco and his friends see a reason to consider the abandonment of either slavery or the slave trade just because the British were having what seemed to be a temporary fit of conscience. They were looking forward to achieving in Cuba the wealth of Jamaica or Saint-Domingue, preferably on a larger scale, a possibility to be entertained because their territory was much bigger. They would go to any lengths to secure the slaves which they believed were necessary to make that possible.

The enlightened government of King Charles III in Madrid was anxious to do all that it could to assist these schemes and first reacted by promulgating a new slave code: the Código Negro Español, based largely on precedents extracted from previous laws of the Indies (especially the Código Carolino of 1785 and the French Code Noir of 1685). It contained several benign provisions. Masters were now absolutely obliged to instruct their slaves in the Catholic religion, not just baptize them and leave everything else to chance, and to feed them according to standards fixed by a specially designated 'protector of slaves'. Masters who abused slaves were subject to fines, and even risked their confiscation. There were to be only 270 working days a year, the rest being holidays and feasts. Nevertheless, on working days slaves could still be legally obliged to work from sunrise to sundown, unless they were older than sixty or younger than seventeen. The recalcitrant slave could still be punished with twenty-five lashes or by being placed in stocks and irons. Nor was this revised document generally implemented. Spanish laws, even under the rule of King Charles III, were still more an indication of what intelligent civil servants in Madrid hoped might occur than a reflection of what did happen in the colonies.

While Cuban liberals were in England studying how their traffic in slaves, and slavery itself, could be expanded, William Pitt, the Prime Minister of the country which they were visiting, was converting the question of the abolition of the British slave trade – not, for the moment, that of slavery itself – into a major political matter. For in May 1788, with Wilberforce ill, Pitt himself raised the subject in the House of Commons, and announced that he was planning to place it on the agenda of the next session of Parliament. The great Burke used the opportunity to speak out against the very idea of slavery, which he called 'a state so improper, so degrading, and so ruinous to the feelings and capacities of human nature that it ought not to be suffered to exist'; the fact that the declaration was the opposite of what he had said on the subject twenty years before was a sign that even great men were having to change their views. Charles James Fox spoke in similar vein. But the Member for Liverpool, Bamber Gascoyne, through his mother a man with substantial economic interests in that city,˙ now made the first of many speeches against changing the existing order, saying that those of his constituents 'who were more immediately concerned in the trade, were men of such impeccable characters that they were above the reach of calumny'. Gascoyne was a close friend of the premier slave merchant, Peter Baker, to whose house he had indeed been carried in a chair on his election in 1780. Abolition of the trade, he said, was 'unnecessary, visionary and impracticable'.[25]

Then as later, Pitt was unable to secure a majority of his Cabinet and party for abolition, and so the motion was introduced as a Private Member's action, with a free vote. Pitt had a great ascendancy, but he did not have a large personal following.† Radicals such as the eloquent Lord Brougham, the persistent Sir James Stephen, and the tortuous Sir Philip Francis thought that Pitt could have pressed the matter of slavery more strongly than he did. Was he not the most powerful statesman of his age? Had he not then been in power for several years? Could he not have overridden his Cabinet? John Somers Cocks, Member for Reigate, said in 1804:

˙ *Gascoyne's mother was Mary, daughter of Isaac Green of Childwall Abbey. His father, another Bamber Gascoyne, had been an MP most of his life and was himself son of Sir Crisp Gascoyne, a London brewer. Gascoyne's daughter, Frances, married the second Marquess of Salisbury, who took the additional name of Gascoyne, in view of the fortune which thereby passed. As a result, Bamber Gascoyne was grandfather of the Lord Salisbury who became Prime Minister in the 1880s.*

† *Pitt's most recent biographer, John Ehrman, suggests that the Prime Minister did try to secure abolition's presentation as a government measure in 1800, but failed to carry the idea through.*

'It had frequently occurred to him that if the Right Hon. gentleman had employed the fair, honourable influence of office, the great object which he professed to have had so cordially in view would long ere this time have been obtained.' But Pitt could not have done that without difficulty. His friend and manager, on whom he relied for so much, Henry Dundas, was as determinedly against change as was the long-serving Lord Thurlow, the Lord Chancellor ('No man was ever so wise as Thurlow looked,' Fox once said). Lord Hawkesbury, another influential senior minister, was also hostile to abolition. Later on, issues of peace, the French Revolution, and war would overshadow the issue of slavery. King George III may have made some intervention too which prevented Pitt from taking the kind of initiative that Somers Cocks thought desirable. That may explain the mysterious paragraph in Clarkson's *History*: 'A difficulty, still more insuperable, presented itself, in an occurrence which took place in the year 1791 but which is much too delicate to be mentioned. The explanation of it, however, would convince the reader that all the efforts of Mr Pitt from that day were rendered useless, I mean as to bringing the question, *as a minister of state*, to a favourable issue' (emphasis added). To support this interpretation, the agent for Jamaica, Stephen Fuller, who was also a Member of Parliament, wrote that he was convinced that more was owed to the King than was generally realized in securing 'the defeat of the absurd attempt of abolishing the slave trade' (he was writing in 1795).'[26]

The French historian Gaston Martin thought that Pitt's attitude derived from a wish to ruin French commerce. Eric Williams added, 'It can be taken as axiomatic that no man occupying so important a position as Prime Minister of England would have taken so important a step as abolishing the slave trade purely for humanitarian reasons.'[27] That seems as inaccurate as it is harsh. Pitt assured Granville Sharp that his 'heart was with us'. Clarkson, always quick to denounce treachery, recalled that year after year Pitt 'took an active, strenuous and consistent part' against the slave trade. Clarkson always had access to him, and gained a great deal of help from him. Whatever papers Clarkson wanted, Pitt supplied. Pitt was genuinely interested in the 'civilisation of Africa': and hoped, by imperial expansion, to assist it. His speeches confirm his concern: he concluded his first declaration in the House of Commons on abolition with the ringing words: 'When it was evident that this execrable traffic was as opposite to expediency as it was to the dictates of mercy, of

---

* Professor J. A. Rawley has argued that Pitt's conduct might be explained by his government's purchase of over 13,000 slaves, from Africa as well as from the Caribbean, to make up a shortage of men in its West Indian regiments between 1795 and 1807. That could have been so, though had it been, it would surely have been noticed explicitly, or Pitt would have mentioned it to George Canning, or one of his other younger followers. Further, the crucial year was 1791, not 1795. Yet John Ehrman, the biographer of Pitt, in a personal letter to the author, thought that Pitt did not owe anything much to the King in 1791.

religion, of equity, and of every principle that should actuate the breast
... how can we hesitate a moment to abolish this commerce in human
flesh which has for too long disgraced our country and which our
example would no doubt contribute to abolish in every corner of the
globe?'[28]

Sir William Dolben, the much respected if aged MP for Oxford
University, had, meantime, visited a ship in the Thames which had been
used for carrying slaves. No captives were there, but he could see the
'equipment'. He saw that, 'when the slaves were transported, they were
chained to each other hand and foot, and stowed ... like herrings in a
barrel'. Appalled by the evidence, Dolben, a high-minded Anglican, introduced into the House of Commons a bill restricting their number by
tonnage of the carrier. The Portuguese, after all, had had such restrictions
for a hundred years, as he no doubt knew from a mention in the Report of
the Privy Council commissioned in 1788 of that fact. Dolben was power-
fully supported by Henry Beaufoy, Member for Great Yarmouth, who
came from a Quaker family, though he was by then an Anglican. Bamber
Gascoyne attacked the idea of restriction, and he was supported by a
fellow Member for Liverpool, Lord Penrhyn, as well as by one of the two
members for Bristol, Matthew Brickdale, a clothier and undertaker, and
by the Member for Dorchester, William Ewer, an ex-governor of the Bank
of England.* All thought that to insist that ships carry anything less than
two men per ton would ruin the trade. Penrhyn denied that cruelty even
existed. It was absurd to think that 'men whose profit depended on the
health ... of the African natives would purposely torment and distress
them during their voyage'.[29]

During the hearing of evidence at the bar of the House of Commons,
witnesses from Liverpool did all they could to discredit the bill,
suggesting not only that the existing mode of transport was suitable for
the Middle Passage, but even that the voyage to the West Indies from
Africa, with so much merrymaking on the deck, was 'one of the happiest
periods of a Negro's life'. Dolben's bill was carried in the Commons,
however, with Pitt making a statement that he considered the slave trade
an iniquity; but the House of Lords amended it severely, after receiving
many petitions from slaving interests.

In the course of these debates some curious statements in favour of
the slave trade were heard. The great Admiral Lord Rodney (master of a
devoted black servant, who had long attended him) said that in all his
victorious years in the West Indies he had seen no evidence to show that
the Africans were treated with brutality. Africans on ships complained

---

* Penrhyn (it was an Irish title, if a Welsh place) was Richard Pennant, son of another
Richard Pennant of Penrhyn Hall, a merchant of Liverpool, and grandson of Edward
Pennant, Chief Justice of Jamaica, and Bonella, daughter of Joseph Hodges, also of
Jamaica. Lord Penrhyn was also known for his road-building in North Wales.

more frequently of cold than of heat, Rodney thought. He added that 'he should rejoice exceedingly' if he heard that the English labourers were 'half so happy as the West Indian slaves': a statement which led Lord Townshend to suggest ironically that Parliament should set about putting 'the English yeoman on a footing with the West Indian negro slave'. A general, Lord Heathfield, the defender of Gibraltar in the late war, said that the bill was unnecessary, since his soldiers had been allowed seventeen cubic feet of air in tents, whereas African slaves had thirty in their ships. Lord Thurlow, the Lord Chancellor, then made a speech which left the impression – or so it seemed to Clarkson – of 'taking the cause of the slave merchants conspicuously under his wing'. Lord Sandwich, who had been First Lord of the Admiralty, said that he did not think that one slave the less would be carried across the Atlantic were the British to abolish the trade.

The bill passed the House of Commons thereafter, in its amended form, by 56 to 5, and the House of Lords (thanks to Pitt's intervention, in the background) by 14 to 12, though not before the Duke of Chandos, who may have had the same financial interests in slaving as his grandfather had, had asserted that when the slaves (who, he thought, must read the English newspapers avidly) heard of the measures taken to ameliorate the conditions of the Middle Passage, 'they would burst out into open rebellion' leading to a 'massacre of the whites'.[30]

In the debate in the House of Lords, Thurlow, disgusted by Pitt's attitude, sneered at 'a five days' fit of philanthropy which had sprung up'. The remark was misleading, not least because the slave trade had begun to obsess the public. The extent to which the Anti-slavery Committee, through its Quaker connections, had awoken opinion was astonishing. An abolitionist movement in Liverpool even held meetings. Two-thirds of Manchester's male population signed a petition demanding an end to the slave trade. Another hundred towns followed. The Reverend, and ex-Captain, John Newton published his *Thoughts upon the African Slave Trade* with success. In March 1788 John Wesley delivered another famous sermon in the New Rooms at Bristol on the immorality of slavery: an oration interrupted by an inexplicable shaking of the building, surely a sign of divine wrath, it was supposed, which stopped the proceedings for six minutes. That same year, the painter George Morland exhibited *The Slave Trade* (also called *The Execrable Traffic*), the first depiction of the commerce in visual form, at the Royal Academy; its sentimental picture of weeping Africans saying goodbye to their families brought tears to many fashionable eyes.

All the same, opposition to reform was also organizing itself. In Liverpool the town council paid £100 to a local Spanish resident, the sometime Jesuit 'Raymond Harris', really Raimundo Hormoza, for his curious pamphlet *Scriptural Researches on the Licitness of the Slave Trade*. John Tarleton, Member of Parliament for Seaford, from a family of

Liverpool slaving merchants, who failed to convince Pitt in a conversation of the merits of his views, wrote to Lord Hawkesbury, to re-emphasize his and his friends' unaltered support of the traffic, though he cheerfully added that his own firm would engross the largest share of trade even under Dolben's conditions. (Tarleton himself, with his partner David Backhouse, invested in thirty-nine Liverpool ships between 1786 and 1804, of which half were slavers.)

The Privy Council's committee of inquiry, meantime, had made progress. Captain Perry of the Royal Navy visited Liverpool on behalf of the committee and looked at several ships, including the *Brookes*, whose master was Clement Noble; this vessel – of 297 tons, and capable of carrying 609 slaves – belonged to its builder, James Brookes. (It may be recalled how Noble had armed some of his slaves to fight the French off Barbados in the late war.) Perry sent his description of it to Clarkson, who had a meticulous sketch made of how the slaves, during the Atlantic crossing, were fitted into their places at night as if they were sardines in a box. The diagram was much used. A rising young clergyman, Thomas Burgess, compared the design to Dante's *Inferno*. The picture inspired William Grenville, later Prime Minister, a cousin of Pitt's, to say: 'In the passage of the negroes from the coast of Africa, there is a greater portion of human misery condensed within a smaller place than has ever yet been found in any other place on the face of this globe.' Many years later, Wilberforce caused the sketch to be shown to Pope Pius VII, who was also much affected. The fact that the design was slightly erroneous, since it omitted the space needed for gaining access to the slaves in order to feed them or to remove the dead, was irrelevant to the impact it made.

In fact, the passage of Dolben's act had a decisive effect on the British slave trade, for it reduced the slaves-per-ton ratio. This, and the subsequent bonuses offered to captains and surgeons who reported a modest loss of life, had a benign effect. It did not mean, however, that fewer ships participated in the trade. On the contrary, the new law led to an increase in the number. But each English ship now carried a smaller quantity of slaves than the French ships did.*

---

* *The act provided that vessels should carry only five slaves per registered ton of shipping up to 201 tons and one slave only for every ton beyond that; every slaver had to carry a surgeon, who was to keep a register of slaves shipped; and a premium of £100 was to be paid to the master and £350 to the surgeon on each vessel whose cargo showed a loss of less than 2 per cent; half was to be paid if the mortality was between 2 and 3 per cent. Incidentally the variability of the meaning of 'tons' in the years covered by this book was considerable. For most of the period commercial contracts used 'tons burden', an estimate of carrying capacity, while government contracts and shipwrights' contracts of sale used 'measured tons' calculated by a formula from certain dimensions (usually length of keel, breadth, and depth of hold). Because the measurements assumed all ships had the same hull form, in an English ship of the seventeenth century for example measured tons often exceeded tons burden by about a third, while in the late eighteenth century the reverse was true; measured tons overestimated sharply built*

The idea of the abolition of slavery or of the slave trade was still confined to the European and American nations. There were at least 4,000 slaves in Egypt, and a minimum of a hundred new ones were imported every year, but no one yet thought that their plight could be mitigated by Quaker philanthropy. The same was true of the 3,000 or 4,000 slaves imported annually into Tunis from Timbuktu across the Sahara in these years (they came, the British Consul-General in Tangier reported, largely from Bambara on the middle Niger, where the King would still 'give from twelve to twenty eunuchs for a horse'). The slave trade to Tripoli was also prospering. Hiring French, occasionally Venetian, sometimes English ships, the traders sold extensively to Chios and Smyrna, to Constantinople, and even to Athens, Salonika, and the Morea. We should suppose an average annual sale of these slaves, originating in Fezzan, of 2,000 in the 1790s, each fetching seventy sequins – with eunuchs selling best. Indeed, the evidence is that the slave trade to North Africa increased in these years, since prices began to fall in West Africa at the end of the century. Slaves from sub-Saharan Africa were found in Morocco, tending date palms, mining salt, and looking after camels. The East African slave trade was also growing. It used to be thought that the coming of Mehmet Ali to Egypt after Napoleon's invasion of that country was a stimulus to the slave trade there; but there was a rise in imports before Napoleon arrived. When Jeremy Bentham sailed from Izmir to Constantinople in 1785 he reported that 'our crew consists of 15 men besides the captain . . . beside 18 young negresses (slaves) under the hatches.'[31] The pioneer of philosophical radicalism did not seem in any way surprised.

---

small ships (such as slave ships) while underestimating those with fuller lines. Governments encouraged the use of measured tons; Britain made registration of ships compulsory in 1786, after which date all official statistics are in registered (measured) tonnage. Other countries introduced similar legislation at different times.

26

MEN IN AFRICA OF AS FINE
FEELINGS AS OURSELVES

*'Why, might there not be men in Africa of
as fine feelings as ourselves, of as enlarged
understandings, and as manly in their
minds as any of us?'*

Charles James Fox, in the House of
Commons, April 1791

IN 1789, JUST BEFORE THE FALL of the Bastille transformed the political
history of the world, debates on slavery and the slave trade were held in
the legislatures of both the United States and Britain, ex-enemies whose
interest in both the commerce and in abolition was coincidentally
stronger than anywhere else. The two debates by chance began within
one day of each other but, given the slowness of communication, neither
paid attention to the other.

The first and most important of these debates, taking into account the
level of participation in the traffic, was that in the House of Commons to
discuss the report of the Privy Council on the subject of the slave trade.
Those who had read that admirable two-volume document, with its
wealth of detail, its muster rolls of sailors, its statistics, and its testimony
from participants, gained an intimate knowledge of how slaves were
obtained in Africa, how they were transported to the Americas, and how
they were treated there. Much of the information in the report was the
consequence of the inquiries of the tireless Clarkson, who never allowed
inconvenience to interrupt his pursuit of truth. No scholar in search of an
explanation of the Maya glyphs, no explorer of the source of the Nile, has
devoted more trouble than he to a great cause: 'O Man!' he once allowed
himself to reflect. 'How often, in these solitary journeyings, have I
exclaimed against the baseness of thy nature, when reflecting on the little
paltry considerations which have smothered thy benevolence, and
hindered thee from succouring an oppressed brother.'[1] By that time,
though, Clarkson was far from solitary, for he was the captain of an army

of philanthropists, the largest until that date ever to have been gathered to voluntary service in a great cause.

The debate in the House of Commons was introduced on 12 May by Wilberforce, in a fine speech lasting three and a half hours which set out to show how all the evidence supported the case against the trade. We should imagine him, small in build, rising from the front bench of the chamber, the daylight coming in from the west window. Wilberforce began by declaring that if guilt existed for the slave trade all the people listening to him 'were all of them participators in it'. He did not argue against slavery as such but suggested that the abolition of the trade would lead to planters being forced to treat their slaves better. It was nonsense that the slave trade was the nursery of the navy, as Lord Rodney had insisted during discussion of Dolben's bill; rather, it was the grave. The orator dwelt at length on the Middle Passage: 'So much misery condensed in so little room was more than human imagination had ever before conceived. Think only of six hundred persons linked together, trying to get rid of each other, crammed in a close vessel with every object that was nauseous and disgusting, and struggling with all the varieties of wretchedness . . . yet . . . this transportation had been described by several witnesses from Liverpool to be a comfortable conveyance.' Wilberforce made fun of the way in which some witnesses who had spoken in favour of slavery had depicted the crossing. Could it really be true that, when sailors had to be flogged, that punishment was administered out of the hearing of the Africans, lest it should depress their spirits? Was it usual for the 'apartments' where the slaves slept to be 'perfumed after breakfast with incense'? Wilberforce thought that France would soon follow Britain in abolishing the trade, so any suggestion that, after abolition, that country would take up the British trade was nonsensical.

But there was opposition: from members who again exhibited all the prejudice, and expressed all the received opinions, which had grown up over generations. Bamber Gascoyne even said that he was 'persuaded that the slave trade might be made a much greater source of revenue and riches . . . than it was at present'. His fellow Member for Liverpool, Lord Penrhyn, said that, were the Commons to vote for abolition, 'they actually would strike at seventy millions of property, they ruined the colonies and, by destroying an essential nursery of seamen, gave up the dominion of the sea at a single stroke'. The members of Parliament for London also strongly opposed abolition, a reminder that the capital still had a substantial stake in slaving. For example, Alderman Newman, a banker and sugar grocer, grotesquely said that if the trade were to be abolished the City would be filled with men suffering as much as the poor Africans. Alderman Sawbridge, a stalwart of metropolitan radicalism in his youth, opposed Wilberforce on the ground that abolition would not serve Africans: 'If they could not be sold as slaves, they would be butchered and executed at home.' George Dempster, Member for the Scottish seat of Perth Burghs, insisted (despite his friendship with Scottish liberals such as Hume and Adam Ferguson) that neither Wilberforce nor Pitt nor anyone else who did not own plantations had any right to interfere with the interests of those who did. John Drake, Member for Amersham, thought that abolition would be 'very prejudicial' to the interests of the nation. Crisp Molineux, a West Indian planter, and Member for Garboldisham, thought that his fellow entrepreneurs were really the greatest slaves – to their high responsibilities. If abolition became law, he thought, all sensible merchants would go to France, where they would be well received.˙ John Henniker, Member for New Romney, read out in the House of Commons a long letter from the ruthless but effective King Agaja of Dahomey to the first Duke of Chandos, which showed, to his satisfaction at least, that, 'if we did not take the slaves off their hands, the miserable wretches would suffer still more severely'. He concluded with a quotation from Cicero.

But Wilberforce was supported by Burke, who used the occasion to state, characteristically, that 'he was not over fond of abstract propositions'. Whatever he might have thought before, he now at least had no doubt that the slave trade was 'an absolute robbery'. He insisted that Africa could never be civilized while the trade continued.† Pitt also spoke magisterially, committing himself to abolition for the first time as an individual, and suggested that a British termination of the traffic might, through negotiation, lead to a similar consummation in other countries. France in particular would agree that it was 'highly becoming for Great Britain to take the lead of other nations in such a virtuous and magnificent measure'.[2]

The anticipation, or fear, that legislation would follow was evident. The same day that Parliament debated the trade, many petitions (fast becoming the main tactic of extra-parliamentary pressure) were presented to the House of Commons against abolition, including one from the West Indian traders of Bristol. That document insisted that 'it has been found . . . with great exactness that the African and West India trade constitute at least three fifths of the commerce of the port of Bristol and that if, upon such a motion [as proposed by Wilberforce], a Bill should pass into law, the decline of the trade of . . . Bristol must inevitably follow', with the 'ruin of thousands'. The trade, the meeting held at Merchants' Hall in Bristol had concluded, was also a thing 'on which the welfare of the West Indian Islands and the commerce and revenue of the kingdom so essentially depend'.[3]

˙ Molineux, whose property was in St Kitts, was a special enemy of the Reverend Ramsay, and, when that philanthropist died, in the summer of 1789, from calumnies inspired by the planters, his friends thought, the MP wrote to his illegitimate son in St Kitts: 'Ramsay is dead: I have killed him.'

† This was a speech which the generous Charles Fox later described as 'the most brilliant and convincing speech that ever was . . . delivered in this or any other place' ('O si illum vidisse, si illum audivisse . . .').

This document was written by a committee chaired by the sugar merchant William Miles, an ex-mayor, the self-made chairman of a bank and of the second-biggest sugar refinery in Bristol. Miles, who had made his first fortune in Jamaica in the middle of the century, was not himself a slave merchant, though he did act as a guarantor for slave journeys. He was supported by five aldermen, all of whom were bankers. The petition was presented by Burke's colleague as a Member for the City, that Henry Cruger, of New York, whose family had been prominent in the colony's politics until the revolution and who had often invested in the trade.

Liverpool, too, presented her opposition. The Mayor was Thomas Earle, who had engaged in many slave ventures: he had a share in the *Mars*, for instance, which sailed for Africa that year, as well as the *Othello* and the *Hawke*. His petition stated firmly that 'the enterprising spirit of the people', which enabled them 'to carry on the African slave trade with vigour', had taken the city to 'a pitch of mercantile consequence' which could 'not but affect and improve the wealth and prosperity of the kingdom as a whole'. The sailmakers of Liverpool also expressed their horror at the idea of an end to the traffic ('Their principal dependance in the port of Liverpool is upon the outset and repairs of the shipping employed in the African trade'). So did the bakers of that city, for they, too, depended, they said, 'chiefly for employment on the great number of ships fitted out in that port to supply the West India islands with negro slaves from the coast of Africa and from the great number of people, whites and blacks, to be fed on board during a long voyage'. After all, 'almost every man in Liverpool is a merchant and he who cannot send a bale will send a bandbox. . . . The attractive African meteor has from time to time so dazzled their ideas that almost every order of people is interested in a Guinea cargo'; for it was well known that 'many of the small vessels that import [only] a hundred slaves are fitted out by attornies, drapers, grocers, tallow chandlers, barbers, tailors, etc., [who] have one eighth, some a fifteenth, and some a thirty-second share. . . .'[4]

At that time, a quarter of the ships in Liverpool were probably engaged in the African trade. The city had five-eighths of the African trade of Britain and three-sevenths of the European; in 1792, the tonnage engaged in slaving would have been far greater than it had been in 1752. In the years 1783–93, about 360 firms of Liverpool had engaged in the traffic in one way or another. William Gregson, with a part share of six slavers in 1791 – a formidable figure in Liverpool politics, an ex-mayor, owner of the brutal Captain Collingwood's *Zong* – made the patriots' point: 'Whenever it is abolished, the naval importance of this kingdom is abolish'd with it.'[5]

Nor was it just Liverpool which was worried: hardly a manufacturing town, much less a trading one, in England did not have some interest in the slave trade. Manchester, for example, annually sent £180,000 in goods to Africa in exchange for slaves. Another rising commercial town, Birmingham, also considered its fortunes tied to the slave trade: 'A very considerable part of the various manufactures in which the petitioners are engaged', ran one appeal from there, 'are adapted to, and disposed of for, the African trade, and are not saleable in any other market.'[6] The gunmakers presented a similar petition, talking of 'the fatal consequences which must inevitably attend such a measure' – although, a real sign of the times, an alternative position was taken up by a group of persons led by the ironmasters' chief spokesman, Samuel Garbett, and including several future bankers, the Quaker Lloyds.[7]

An alliance against abolition was now in being at Westminster. This included the articulate members of the royal family, of whom several were willing to speak and vote in Parliament; most of the admirals, active and retired; many landowners who feared any innovation; and, of course, the main commercial interests in London: people interested in cotton as well as sugar, for cotton, above all from Dutch settlements, was needed in the new industrial revolution even more than sugar. At that time, 70 per cent of the cotton used in Britain came from tropical America, principally Suriname, and less than 30 per cent came from Turkey or elsewhere in the Old World. The West Indian islands were still considered in London the most brilliant of diamonds in the British imperial crown: Pitt estimated the income from West Indian plantations as £4,000,000, compared with £1,000,000 from the rest of the world; and even Adam Smith thought that 'the profits of a sugar plantation in any of our West Indian colonies are generally much greater than those of any other cultivation . . . known in Europe or America'.[8]

Some signs of the newly organized opposition to the idea of abolition were visible when there was a further debate on the slave trade in the House of Commons in January 1790. Bamber Gascoyne, of Liverpool, was still the main spokesman for the trade; he sought procedural delays to prevent the establishment even of a committee of inquiry into it. A leading role began to be played, too, after the election of 1790, by Colonel Banastre Tarleton, brother of John Tarleton, the Liverpool merchant who had protested against Dolben's bill, and who was one of the few heroes of Britain's unsuccessful war in North America. Banastre Tarleton had succeeded Lord Penrhyn as the Member for Liverpool, and had a slave ship belonging to the family firm called after him: the *Banastre*, of ninety-three tons burden. Once, in a debate in 1791, he suggested that people (such as, presumably, Wilberforce) who were looking for philanthropic work should concern themselves with the poor laws rather than devote their time to ruining a trade of great benefit to the country.*

---

* *Tarleton had fought bravely in the American War, and his crippled hand, with two fingers lost in action, became an asset in elections. He was the lover of the actress Perdita Robinson, ex-mistress of the Prince of Wales, but afterwards he and his wife were thought excessively uxorious: they not only customarily sat on the same chair but ate off the same plate.*

In these early days of his campaign, Wilberforce, however, always had the support of Pitt, Fox, and Burke, who spoke often, brilliantly, and effectively. The combination should have been devastating, yet they failed to convince a House of Commons in which slaving interests were so well represented.

That body now did set up its own special committee of inquiry, at which many of the important problems were again posed. For example, Dr Jackson, who had been a physician in Jamaica, was asked the pertinent question 'whether it was more the object of the overseers to work the slaves moderately and keep up their numbers by breeding; or to work them out, increasing thereby the produce of the estate, and trusting for recruits to the slave trade?' He answered, accurately: 'The latter plan was more generally adopted, principally, I conceive, owing to this reason, that imported slaves are fit for immediate labour: slaves that are reared from childhood are liable to many accidents, and cannot make any return of labour for many years.'[9] Evidence was also given by the much-travelled Swedish mineralogist Dr Wadström, who had been to Gorée and Sénégal, and assured his questioners that, 'if the slave trade were abolished, they [the Africans] would extend their cultivation and manufactures . . . particularly if some good European people had enterprising spirit enough to settle among them in another way than is the case at present'.[10] The Reverend John Newton came forward to testify that, in his opinion, the Africans 'with equal advantages . . . would be equal to ourselves in capacity'.[11]

What must have vividly struck those members of Parliament who studied this absorbing if terrible document was the account of the endless brutalities, whippings, and tortures executed as a matter of routine, and without any legal limitation, to the slaves at work on plantations in the West Indies. For example, Major-General Tottenham gave evidence with regard to Barbados. In reply to the question, 'Did it appear to you that the slaves in the British islands were treated with mildness or severity?' he said: 'I think in the island of Barbados, they were treated with the greatest cruelty. . . . I will mention one instance. . . . About three weeks before the hurricane, I saw a young man walking the streets in a most deplorable situation – he was entirely naked – he had an iron collar about his neck, with five long spikes projecting from it. His body before and behind his breech, belly and thighs were almost cut to pieces with running ulcers in them, and you might put your finger in some of the weals. He could not sit down, owing to his breech being in a state of mortification, and it was impossible for him to lie down, owing to the projection of the collar round his neck. . . . The field negroes are treated more like brutes than human beings. . . .'[12]

The second important debate in May 1789 was that in the United States House of Representatives. This was the first meeting of that body, and the members who assembled in City Hall in New York numbered a mere sixty-five. Here the discussion could not concern itself with the abolition of the trade, since the Constitution had left that aside, as a federal matter at least, till 1808. Instead, the debate concentrated on possible duties to be imposed on slaves imported. Thus Josiah Parker, of Virginia, moved that a tax of $10 should be laid on every slave imported; the Irish-born O'Brien Smith, of South Carolina, wished to postpone a matter 'so big with the most serious questions for the state which he represented'; and the experienced Roger Sherman of Connecticut could not 'reconcile himself to the insertion of human beings as an item of duty'. James Jackson of Georgia thought that all these matters should be left to individual states, and later declared that the blacks were 'better off as slaves than as freemen'. In the end, the bill was withdrawn, amid rising bad temper: only James Madison spoke in a way likely to be remembered, when he said, 'By expressing a national disapprobation of this trade, we may destroy it, and save ourselves from reproaches, and our posterity the imbecility ever attendant on a country filled with slaves.'[13]

A further debate on slavery was held in the Congress of the United States in 1790, as it had been in England. This discussion, held in New York like its predecessor, occurred in response to numerous petitions from Quaker societies. Michael Stone, of Port Tobacco, Maryland, mocked the 'disposition of religious sects to imagine that they understood the rights of human nature better than all the world besides'. Aedanus Burke, of South Carolina, born in Galway but a traveller to the West Indies before he went to live in Charleston, thought that 'the rights of the southern states ought not to be threatened' in any way. When a petition was brought in – from the Pennsylvania Society for the Abolition of Slavery, and signed by Benjamin Franklin – that same Burke said that the mere discussion of the plan by a committee of Congress 'would blow the trumpet of sedition in the southern states'. A colleague of his, Thomas Tudor Tucker, a surgeon from Bermuda who had been educated in Edinburgh, said ominously that the Southern states would not submit to a general emancipation without 'civil war'. William Loughton Smith, also of South Carolina, like so many of his colleagues educated in England, said that he considered the idea of ending slavery as 'an attack upon the palladium of the property of our country' (he was a planter). The scheme was then sent to a committee, on which there were no members from any Southern state. This body's final report concluded that 'Congress [did] have authority to restrain the citizens of the United States from carrying on the Africa trade *for the purpose of supplying foreigners with slaves*' (my emphasis). It also declared that Congress would be within its rights to insist on proper regulations for the humane treatment of slaves on their passage to the United States. The consequence was that Congress did prohibit foreigners (Cubans as well as Englishmen and other Europeans) from fitting out slave ships in the United States, and prohibited the United States' slave trade to foreign ports. Everything else was left pending till 1808.

Little enough transpired. The Congress of the United States, in February 1790, might hear a Quaker praying that God would inspire the new Congress against the wickedness of the slave trade. But the enemies of abolition were powerful. James Jackson – English-born, like so many friends of slavery, now a senator for Georgia where he had previously been a congressman and a grower of rice and cotton on his plantations – argued that slavery was permitted by the Bible. The trade itself was expanding too. In the first six months of 1792, regardless of the new law, thirty-eight North American captains were recorded as arriving in Havana, Cuba, with slaves – that is, six a month on the average. Warren, Providence, and Bristol, Rhode Island, were now competing successfully in these years with their neighbour Newport as the new nation's premier slave ports. William Ellery, a prominent Newport merchant who had become a collector of customs in the city, wrote in 1791, 'an Ethiopian could as soon change his skin as a Newport merchant could be induced to change so lucrative a trade as that in slaves for the slow profits of any manufactory'. (In 1759 Ellery, as a young man, had himself taken a ship, with '82 barrels, 6 hogsheads, and 6 tierces of New England rum', to Africa.)

Congress's passage of the law condemning the foreign slave trade, of course, made many of these Rhode Island merchants technically criminals. The punishments for breaking the law were the surrender of the vessel concerned, and fines of $1,000 for each merchant or captain engaged and of $200 for each slave transported. The Quakers saw these penalties as constituting a triumph, but they had little effect on the Rhode Island shippers. The young United States was less law-abiding than its founding fathers assumed that it would be. The active men who came of age in the 1770s had, after all, been raised in a fiscal atmosphere in which lawbreaking, smuggling especially, was a defensible practice. British attempts to enforce the Sugar Acts had made illegal trading appear patriotic. Anyway, trading to Africa itself was not illegal, so there was no need for a slave captain to conceal his first port of call. The question of the final destination was more complicated, and some captains did what they could to remove from their vessels incriminating 'equipment', such as slave platforms, shackles, and swivel guns, as well as letters and other documents relating to the traffic, before returning home. Some slavers sold their ships in Havana, and returned as passengers on other vessels. Other merchants devised two sets of papers.

All these subterfuges were probably necessary. Customs officers and federal agents in Rhode Island brought several cases against slave traders. There were a few instances of foreign slave ships being captured and condemned. This befell 'two French ships from the coast of Guinea, with near

800 slaves on board', at New London, Connecticut, in 1791. Yet the trade continued. Thirty-two ships left Newport, Rhode Island, for Africa in 1795. Among these was the *Ascension*, commanded by Captain Samuel Chace, who bought goods in Rotterdam and the Île de France (Mauritius), with which he bought 283 slaves in Mozambique. These were sold at Montevideo, Havana, and Buenos Aires. This vessel was owned by the ex-sea-captains Peleg Clarke and Caleb Gardner, in partnership with William Vernon. The biggest merchant in Rhode Island, however, was Cyprian Sterry of Providence. The Society for Abolition sought to persuade the United States Attorney to prosecute both Sterry and John Brown, who was known as a man of 'magnificent projects and extraordinary enterprises'. Sterry agreed surprisingly to withdraw from the trade. The case against Brown began, and was heard in 1797. His ship, *Hope*, was confiscated and sold, but no charges were preferred against him. In a second trial, Brown escaped because the prosecution case collapsed.

A few days after the second parliamentary discussion in London of the slave trade, in early 1790, Thomas Clarkson set off for Paris as the representative of the English abolitionists. The revolution in France had begun, and was still enjoying its *'illusion lyrique'*.˙ He was received with enthusiasm by all the friends of liberty of Africans: La Rochefoucauld, Lavoisier, Condorcet, Petion de Villeneuve, Clavière, Brissot, Lafayette. All these men were now engaged in French Revolutionary activities. La Rochefoucauld had also raised the question of the liberty of slaves in the States-General of June 1789, while Lavoisier was busy on the commission working out a new system of weights and measures, and Condorcet was commissioner of the money supply. Petion de Villeneuve was at the height of his influence in the National Assembly, while Clavière was financial adviser to Mirabeau, apparently the man of the future. Brissot was the editor of the famous *Le Patriote français*, and Lafayette was talking grandiosely of a scheme for an 'ideal' plantation in Cayenne. Clarkson saw them all, and showed them the diagram of the slave ship *Brookes*. When Mirabeau saw this, he ordered a cabinetmaker to make a model of it in wood. It was a ship in miniature, about a yard long, and 'little wooden men and women, which were painted black to represent the slaves, were seen stowed in their proper places. . . . The Bishop of Chartres† . . . told me that . . . he had not given credit to all the tales which had been related of the slave trade, till he had seen this diagram after which there was nothing so barbarous which might not readily be believed. . . .'[14] The effect was, indeed, prodigious: a first example of

---

˙ *The expression by André Malraux with regard to the early stages of the Spanish Civil War.*

† *Jean-Baptiste-Joseph de Lubersac, who had already demonstrated his liberalism by voting in the States-General for the abolition of hunting rights.*

political propaganda using a visual aid to create a scandal. Clarkson was everywhere well received. After all, the Declaration of the Rights of Man of August 1789 had stated plainly 'Men are born free and are equal before the law.' Article VII had declared that nobody could be seized except by due process of law. How then could slavery be justified? Necker, back in power, talked of Clarkson to the King, who, however, was thought to be in too poor health to be able to stand seeing the picture of the *Brookes*. Clarkson also saw veterans of Africa such as Geoffroy de Villeneuve, who had been aide-de-camp to the humane Chevalier de Boufflers at Gorée (he had been sent to that exile because of a ribald song about the Queen), had been up the Sénégal with Dr Wadström, and also had been 'all over the kingdom of Cayor on foot'.

A Société des Amis des Noirs had, it will be remembered, already been founded in Paris. It included both La Rochefoucauld – 'the most virtuous man in France', in Lafayette's phrase – and Lafayette himself, as well as Mirabeau. It now gathered much support. One of its leaders was still Condorcet, who urged France to follow the example of America, whose leaders, he believed, already knew that they would 'debase their own pursuit of liberty if they continued to support slavery'. In Bordeaux, André-Daniel Laffon de Ladébat, son of a great *négrier*, had in August 1788 bravely denounced the slave trade as 'the greatest public crime'.[15] This view gained some backing, but not enough to interest the Constituent Assembly when it first met. The Société was represented by its planter-enemies as a nest of British agents. Members were threatened with death if they persisted in their activities. Ex-Secretary of State for the Marine Massiac organized a club to carry out these and other menaces. Clavière told Clarkson that he was being accused of conspiring to foment an insurrection in Saint-Domingue. Clarkson believed that two senior members of the Committee on Abolition were agents of slave traders in Nantes; and Mirabeau told him that all the members of the Assembly with whom he had talked of abolition had been canvassed by the slave traders. Clarkson in France was also discouraged by the strange affair of Samuel de Missy, an honest Rochelais, who had been a *négrier* and joined the Société des Amis des Noirs, but resigned from it when denounced by the Chamber of Commerce at La Rochelle, saying that he could see that his membership might plunge the port into misery.

In March 1790 the matter of the slave trade was at last debated in the Constituent Assembly, some weeks after Clarkson had gone back to London. Inspired by information largely deriving from the English – France had as yet carried out no inquiry into the slave trade – the Société put forward three Girondin speakers: Vieuville des Essarts, Petion de Villeneuve, and Mirabeau, the so-called 'Shakespeare of eloquence', who prepared a powerful speech. He described in great detail the more brutal aspects of the slave trade and then mockingly asked his audience, in the spirit of Montesquieu, '*Et ce commerce n'est pas inhumain?*' The repetition several times of this ironic statement had the effect of a refrain. But Mirabeau unwisely chose to rehearse the speech at a meeting of the Jacobin Club. It was a triumph but afterwards his enemies, led by the demagogue Antoine-Pierre Barnave (often a friend of liberty, a word he would indeed die proclaiming, on the scaffold in 1793), managed to prevent the orator from speaking in the Chamber. They secured the passage of a decree which included the alarming phrase: 'Whosoever works to excite risings against the colonists will be declared an enemy of the people.'[16]

Still, the trade in slaves was eventually discussed in the Assembly. Ten deputies came from the West Indies. Mirabeau asked why such small islands should send so many members. The reply he received was that in the French empire (in emulation of the three-fifths clause in the Constitution of the United States) the slaves were counted in apportioning representation (though they could not vote). If that argument was accepted as valid, Mirabeau demanded, why should not the horses of France also be reckoned?

Some free mulattos were among these West Indian deputies. They were rich men who had done well in business, but both slave merchants and planters thought that they should not sit. Arthur Dillon, soldier and scion of an ancient Irish family who represented Martinique, said that the white colonies would revolt in fifteen minutes if the mulattos were seated. The matter was shelved.

Shortly afterwards, a delegation from the newly founded and revolutionary Armée Patriotique of Bordeaux reached Paris and told both the Jacobin Club and the Assembly that 5,000,000 Frenchmen depended on the colonial commerce for their livelihood, and that both the slave trade and West Indian slavery were essential for the prosperity of France. Another committee was then entrusted to make a report on slavery. That body, however, did little more than denounce attempts to cause risings against the colonists. Mirabeau was shouted down when he tried to oppose this. The assembly voted for the committee's proposals for inaction, and until 1793 the French slave trade continued to receive a subsidy in the form of a bonus for every slave landed. Nantes in fact enjoyed its best year ever as a slave city in 1790, sending forty-nine ships to Africa. For the slave merchants in that politically radical city, the word 'liberty' seems to have signified the idea that the slave trade should be open to all.

There was tumult in the West Indies in consequence of these events, and Vincent Ogé, a radical mulatto, appealed to the authorities in Saint-Domingue to insist that the mulatto members in Paris should be seated. ('*Périssent les colonies plutôt qu'un principe,*' he told the Assembly in Paris when he was allowed briefly to address it.) When he was not listened to, Ogé, who had political ambitions and had obtained weapons from the North Americans, raised a standard of insurrection in Saint-Domingue, near Cap François. After several skirmishes, he was defeated. He fled and escaped to the Spanish end of the island, where he was arrested and handed back to the French Governor, who had him broken on the wheel. This disaster gave new support for the mulatto petitioners in France, and that in turn increased turmoil in the colonies. The debates in Paris on the matter became impassioned. Robespierre entered the discussion with an advocacy of full freedom for slaves, himself adding, '*Eh, périssent vos colonies si vous les conservez à ce prix . . . !*'

Early in 1791 the National Assembly condemned slavery in principle, but insisted that any immediate extension of the rights of man to slaves would be certain, at least at that stage, to be accompanied by many evils; all the same, the children of all free parents, regardless of colour, would be looked upon as full citizens. The colonists saw that concession, modest as it was, as a betrayal. This was the first such condemnation in any European legislature.

The leaders of the free blacks and some of the slaves in Saint-Domingue had themselves been following these arguments, insofar as they could. As a result of the large-scale imports of slaves by French traders in the 1780s, they constituted an immense majority of the population in the rich colony: say, 450,000 blacks compared with fewer than 40,000 whites, and 50,000 mulattos. The free blacks and the mulattos were prepared to strike again at the colonial government, but the slaves made their rebellion first. They did so on 22 August 1792. Henceforth the machete and the firebrand ruled. The sugar plantations were set ablaze.

Too late, on 28 August, the Constituent Assembly in Paris declared anyone who arrived in France to be free, whatever his colour. This was twenty years after Lord Mansfield's decision in England, but 220 years since a judge in Bordeaux had first made a similar judgement. A deputy for the latter city, Béchade-Casaux, anxiously wrote home: 'The States-General are still occupied by the declaration of the Rights of Man which must serve as a preamble to the Constitution. I am fearful lest that may lead to a suppression of the slave trade.'[17] Thereafter, though, events moved so fast in Paris as to cause the complete neglect of affairs in Saint-Domingue. The worst outrages in Paris in August 1792 were admittedly preceded by a riot in the city over shortages of sugar, themselves caused in part by events in Saint-Domingue. But few appreciated the interconnection, and in the colony events moved ever more swiftly to catastrophe. The slave traders of Nantes, who had about 60,000,000 livres' worth of property in the colony (the Bouteillers, the Drouins, the Charauds, the Arnous who had been the big investors of the 1780s), lost all they had there in the only completely successful slave revolution in history.

Eventually, in 1794, on 4 February, the Convention in Paris declared the universal emancipation of slaves (though not actually outlawing the trade). The event was celebrated in the Temple of Reason (Notre-

Dame), as in many great 'fêtes révolutionnaires' up and down the country. Hundreds of engravings denouncing slavery were published; and songs were composed. In Nantes, a black officer eloquently gave his thanks to the Republic. The most elaborate celebration was at Bordeaux. The Convention's representative, the implacable Tallien, made a wonderfully enthusiastic speech in Bordeaux's Temple of Reason (before and afterwards, the Cathedral of Saint-André). Two hundred black people were present. Afterwards, the organizers of the meeting took one of these men or women by the arm, and walked with them in a procession to the Hôtel Franklin, where a colossal banquet was held.*[18]

By this time, the pioneers of the French abolition movement, Mirabeau, Clavière, La Rochefoucauld, Brissot, Lavoisier, Condorcet, and Petion, had died, the first in his bed, the second by his own hand in prison, the third at the hands of an assassin, the fourth, fifth, and sixth under the guillotine, and the last eaten by wolves during an escape from sanctuary. All that can be said of their achievements is that the French bounty on the carriage of slaves had been abolished.

But France had become engulfed in such terrible events that it was no longer easy for men to consider great moral issues. 'The revolution', Clarkson had to admit, 'was of more importance to Frenchmen than the abolition of the slave trade.'[19] Mirabeau had had at the end other pressing considerations, though, 'a host in himself', according to Lafayette, to his death he maintained his interest in the question of slavery. That did not prevent Bernard Aîné et Cie from dispatching from Nantes a slave ship bearing his name, five months after he died prematurely in April 1791, with the purpose of carrying 300 slaves from Angola to Martinique.

The French Revolution and its attendant outrages greatly helped the friends of the slave trade in Britain. Any change in the status quo could now be easily presented by them as potentially subversive of public order. Enlightenment was easily represented as certain to lead to barbarism. The legal reformer Samuel Romilly wrote: 'If any person be desirous of having an adequate idea of the mischievous effects produced in this country by the French Revolution ... he should attempt some reform on humane and liberal principles. . . .'[20] So it was scarcely surprising that when in April 1791, after many months of gathering more evidence (in the course of which Clarkson visited no fewer than 320 ships, in different English ports, travelling nearly 7,000 miles in 1790), Wilberforce's motion to introduce a bill into parliament to abolish the slave trade was at long last introduced, it should have been obstructed.

---

* Tallien in Bordeaux fell in love with the granddaughter of one of Bordeaux's prominent négriers, Dominique Cabarrus: she 'sweetened his life', and dictated his career; shortly afterwards, he married her.

Yet there was no reasoned justification of slavery, nor of the traffic. The speeches concentrated on the impracticability and unwisdom of abolition, rather than, as in 1789, on the benefits of the trade. Thus 'tunbellied Tommy Grosvenor', an elderly Member of Parliament for Chester, acknowledged that the slave trade was 'not an amiable trade but neither was the trade of a butcher an amiable trade, and yet a mutton chop was, nevertheless, a good thing'. Alderman Watson of London, a director of the Bank of England, argued, as so many had done, that the natives of Africa were taken from a worse state of slavery in their own country to one more mild. Banastre Tarleton pointed out that the African monarchs themselves had no objection to the continuance of the slave trade. John Stanley, the agent for Nevis and Member for Hastings, spoke strongly against abolition, which he described as unjust to planters and traders, injuring them without recompense. There were many allusions to France: whether she would steal the British trade if the British abolished it, or whether Britain should wait till France acted.

Some inspiring speeches were also made: 'While we could hardly bear the sight of anything resembling slavery, even as a punishment among ourselves, should we countenance the exercise of the most despotic power over millions of creatures who, for aught we know, were not only innocent but meritorious?' James Martin, a banker who was Member for Tewkesbury, teased the House of Commons for being so eager to condemn the proconsul, Warren Hastings, for his bad conduct in the East, while doing nothing about this abominable practice in the West. The trade was carried out with humanity? It was a new species of humanity, said John Courtenay, Member for Tamworth, an erudite Irish wit of 'the school of Diogenes'. Both Fox and Pitt spoke for Wilberforce. The former called on the House to 'mark to all mankind their abhorrence of a practice so enormous, so savage, and so repugnant to all laws human and divine'. He made fun of the fact that many slaves captured in Africa were said to be being punished for adultery: 'Was adultery then a crime which we needed to go to Africa to punish? Was this the way in which we were to establish the purity of our national character? . . . It was a most extraordinary pilgrimage, for a most extraordinary purpose.' Burke said that 'to deal and traffic, not in the labour of men but in men themselves, was to devour the root, instead of enjoying the fruit, of human diligence'; yet, in Burke's constituency of Bristol, when the vote was lost (88 to 163 against Wilberforce) in the House of Commons, church bells rang, cannon were fired on Brandon Hill, there was a bonfire and a fireworks display, and a half-holiday was granted to workmen and sailors.[21] 'Commerce chinked its purse,' Horace Walpole wrote to Mary Berry, 'and that sound is generally prevalent with the majority.'[22]

The year 1791 was a good one, in fact, for the English slave trade. English shippers were making substantial inroads into the now open Cuban slave market. We find thirty English ships registered as having delivered slaves in Havana that year, including, in September, Captain Samuel Courtauld (of the Delaware branch of that Huguenot family) on the *Vela Ana*; and, in March, Captain Hugh Thomas on the *Hammond*.[*23]

The campaign continued, however, despite the parliamentary reverse. In 1792 no fewer than 500 petitions against the slave trade were prepared from all over Britain. In Birmingham a prominent Quaker raised the question whether it was right to accept financial support for the rebuilding of the Friends' meeting house from the gunmakers Farmer and Galton, who had been concerned with the supply of weapons for the slave traffic, and indeed in the traffic itself. A campaign for a national boycott of slave-grown sugar was even launched.

Wilberforce, Clarkson, and the abolitionists were also much cheered by astounding news from Denmark. In March 1792, after a report from their Great Negro Trade Commission (three of whose members were directors of the Danish monopoly Baltic-Guinea Company), the Danish government abolished the import of slaves from Africa to their islands. The Danes had, for 150 years, participated on a small scale in the slave trade, although, on balance, it had been unprofitable, and although the forts in West Africa were only maintained in order to serve three tiny colonies in the West Indies. In the previous fifteen years Denmark had sent about a hundred ships to Africa. The Danish West Indian sugar islands had, however, been of importance to many merchants of Copenhagen, including the powerful Schimmelmann family, of whom Ernest was in 1792 the humane, far-seeing, and able Minister of Finance; he was also, influenced by his love of England, the leading promoter of abolition (even though he still owned four plantations on St Croix). Before the establishment of the commission, he had unavailingly sent a professor of divinity, Daniel Gotthilf Moldenhawer, to Madrid to offer an exchange of Denmark's forts on the coast of Guinea; in return, the Spaniards would cede Crab Island (Bique), in the Caribbean, to Denmark. The Danes had also launched several intelligent schemes to create cotton plantations on the Gold Coast, thereby rendering the Middle Passage unnecessary.

The cautious royal statement in Copenhagen on abolition was definitive: 'We, Christian VII, ... from the result of ... enquiries, ... are convinced that it is possible, and will be advantageous to our West India islands, to desist from the further purchase of new negroes, when once the plantations are stocked with a sufficient number for propagation and the cultivation of the islands.' The trade, therefore, was to be prohibited after 1803. There were to be no taxes on imports of female slaves between 1792 and the deadline, and no more taxes were to be levied on female field slaves already in the country.[24]

Until 1803, any country, however, could import any number of slaves into the Danish islands, though none were to be exported any more from

---

[*] *The latter captain's deliveries can be seen in plate 56.*

them. In fact, many continued to be so, for the island of St Thomas, close to Puerto Rico, remained a transit market for the Spaniards, and that trade seems to have reached its peak only in 1800. The truth about this commerce is difficult to disentangle, since some ships which were really North American, or English, sailed under Danish flags even after 1808.

The Danish commerce was abolished because the price of slaves in the Danish West Indies was low, because the government thought it certain that the British would abolish the trade shortly, and because it seemed that on the two or three ships which were sent every year from Copenhagen too many members of the ships' companies died. The Danish forts on the Guinea coast, such as Christiansborg Castle at Accra, were also expensive. The Danes believed that they could arrange for the number of slaves needed by encouraging natural increase.

The Danish trade flourished between 1792 and 1802. Many slaves taken to the Danish West Indies islands at St Croix and St Thomas were re-exported, often to Cuba, where nearly 200 Danish ships seem to have gone between 1790 and 1807, carrying well over 12,000 slaves.

Much encouraged by this news, in April 1792 Wilberforce tried again to carry a bill abolishing the trade. This was the occasion for one of the greatest debates in the history of legislative assemblies. 'Africa, Africa,' said Wilberforce, to begin with, 'your sufferings have been the theme that has arrested and engages my heart. Your sufferings no tongue can express, no language impart.' The orator pointed out how Denmark had now abolished the slave trade. Could Britain really be far behind? He described how, only the previous year, six British captains, to the outrage of a French captain present, had fired on an African settlement on the River Calabar, merely in order to secure lower prices of slaves. The record of the debate then states: 'The House, in a burst of indignation, vociferated "Name! Name!" Mr Wilberforce for a long time resisted. At last, the cry overcame him and he gave the following names of ships and captains: the ship *Thomas*, of Bristol, Captain Phillipps; the *Betsey*, of Liverpool, Captain Doyle; the *Recovery*, of Bristol; the *Wasp*, Captain House; the *Thomas*, of Liverpool; and the *Anatree*, of Bristol.'

Many declarations were made, as before, in favour of the status quo; the first such was that by James Baillie, a Scotsman from Inverary, the agent for Grenada, who had lived both on that island and on St Kitts. He owned a plantation in Demerara and talked, in this his only speech in the Commons, of the 'wild, impracticable and visionary scheme of abolition'; he thought that there was brutality on innumerable ships, not just slave ships, and in innumerable European armies; and that there was more wretchedness in the parish of St Giles in London, where he had a house, than in the colonies. He also thought that the revolution in Saint-Domingue had been directly caused by the unfortunate discussion of abolition of the slave trade. Then Benjamin Vaughan, a Unitarian merchant who confessed to being 'a West Indian by birth', profession, and private fortune, also vindicated the planters.* The future Lord Liverpool, the long-serving Prime Minister in the next century – then plain Robert Jenkinson – pointed out that no major foreign slave-trading nation had shown any inclination to follow the British example; Denmark was of no importance. Banastre Tarleton once more inveighed against the folly of allowing a 'junto of sectarians, sophists, enthusiasts, and fanatics' to destroy a trade which brought in £800,000 a year and employed 5,000 seamen, as well as 160 ships.

But the speeches attacking the slave trade were of a high quality. Thus Robert Milbanke, Lord Byron's future father-in-law, argued, in the spirit of Adam Smith, that where slavery was used as a form of labour, 'every operation was performed in a rude and unworkmanlike manner'.

Then came what turned out to be the decisive oration: Henry Dundas, the 'indispensable coadjutor' of the ministry (Treasurer of the Navy and the leading politician on the Board of Control of the East India Company), in effect minister both for Scotland and for India, whose control over Pitt was both so profound and so inexplicable, introduced, in his broad Scottish accent, and ungraceful manner, 'as a compromise', the word 'gradually' into the motion. His intention, he said, was to propose a middle way. He conceded that the trade 'ought to be ultimately abolished but, by moderate measures, which should not invade the property of individuals, nor shock too suddenly the prejudices of our West India islands'. The cooperation of the planters with any new law was surely essential. Dundas agreed that newly imported slaves were likely to inspire revolts. He also talked airily of the imperial network of investments in undeveloped lands as a major argument against immediate abolition. He suggested one or two further amendments: a prohibition on the import of elderly slaves, and an agreement, such as had occurred in the United States, to abolish the foreign trade. Dundas had, in 1778, taken the side of the slave Joseph Knight, in a Scottish version of the Somerset case. He had been on the side of the angels then. But time, power, and age seem to have taken their toll, and the reasonableness of his procrastination scarcely concealed that he now sided with the West Indian interests.†

---

* *Vaughan later became an extreme radical, fled to France on being suspected of treachery, and eventually went to live, and die, in the United States.*
† *Dundas originally proposed 1 January 1800 as the date to end the trade, but others, including Pitt, 'saw no reason why 1793 was not preferable'. The years 1794 and 1795 were also canvassed. This was the occasion when Lord Carhampton, whose grandfather had been Governor of Jamaica, said that 'gentlemen might talk of inhumanity but he did not know what right anyone had to do so inhumane a thing as to inflict a speech of four hours long on a set of innocent, worthy and respectable men'. Dundas was a formidable parliamentary opponent for the abolitionists: Lord Holland recalled how 'he never hesitated in making any assertion and, without attempting to answer an argument, he either treated it as quite preposterous or, after some bold misstatements and inapplicable maxims, confidently alleged that he had refuted it.'*

Charles James Fox ridiculed Dundas. Advocates of 'moderation' reminded him of a passage in Middleton's life of Cicero: 'To break open a man's house, and kill him, his wife and family in the night is certainly a most heinous crime, and deserving of death, but even this may be done with moderation.' Fox pointed out that if a Bristol ship were to go to France and the democrats were to sell the aristocrats into slavery, 'such a transaction . . . would strike every man with horror . . . because they were of our colour'. Fox thought that if the plantations could not be cultivated without slaves, they ought not to be cultivated at all.

Pitt, the Prime Minister, next made what was by all accounts the most eloquent speech of his career. Though confessing himself exhausted – it was already five o'clock in the morning when he began to speak – he described the trade as 'the greatest practical evil which has ever afflicted the human race'. He analysed Dundas's position without losing track of his own. How was the slave trade ever to be eradicated if every nation was 'prudentially to wait till the concurrence of all the world?' For the last twenty minutes of this speech, Pitt, his friends thought, 'seemed to be really inspired'. He imagined how a Roman senator, looking at the world of the second century AD, and speaking to 'British barbarians', might say, 'There is a people that will never rise to civilisation.' He adjured the House – immediately, and without any delay – to restore Africans to 'the rank of human beings'. Towards the end of his oration, he quoted two lines of Virgil:

> *Nos primus equis Oriens afflavit anhelis;*
> *Illic sera rubens accendit lumina Vesper . . .*

and the first rays of the early-morning sun are said to have entered the House of Commons behind the Speaker's chair at that moment.*

The Commons then voted (it was 3 April) 230 to 85 in favour of Dundas's amended motion 'that the slave trade ought to be *gradually* abolished'. The vote was taken at half-past six in the morning. Returning home by foot across a still sleeping London, Fox, Charles Grey (the future Prime Minister of the Reform Bill), and William Windham (who later deserted the cause of abolition, for reasons still unclear) agreed that Pitt's speech 'was one of the most extraordinary displays of eloquence they had ever heard'. They had been present, as they believed, at the supreme moment of parliamentary democracy.[25]

The votes on these motions, if inadequate for Wilberforce, Fox, Burke, and Pitt, constituted a remarkable change from what had happened the previous year. Yet the main event in recent politics was the revolution in Saint-Domingue, an occurrence which was already causing

---

* *Alas, Pitt's biographer John Ehrman says that he knows of no evidence that the sun did so rise.*

a real shortage of sugar, and not just in France. Perhaps the impact of that terrible event was to make the members realize that an end had to come one day to the system of slave plantations. Of course, Saint-Domingue was referred to in the debate. Whence, for example, asked Samuel Whitbread, the Nonconformist brewer, did the slaves there learn the cruelties they practised? Where, he answered himself, but from the French planters?

In the subsequent debate in the House of Lords on this same motion, the Lord Chancellor, still old, obstinate Lord Thurlow, wondered why, if the slave trade were such a vile crime, it had taken the House of Commons till 1792 to realize it. The Duke of Clarence, the future King William IV, chose to make his maiden speech on this occasion, and stated, probably with the support of his father, King George III, that he had unequivocal proof that the slaves were not as a rule treated in the manner which had so agitated the public mind. He had, after all, been in Jamaica as a midshipman in the navy, and when ill had been cared for by a famous mulatto nurse, Couba Cornwallis. Slaves in his opinion lived in a state of humble happiness. All the same, and despite this royal sermon, the Lords supported Dundas's amendment. (In the course of the debate, Lord Barrington, grandson of a Bristol merchant trading to Virginia and Maryland, Sir William Daines, made the interesting comment that slaves appeared to him so happy that he often wished himself in their situation.)[26]

What Dundas's amendment signified in practice was less than clear. Britain had committed itself to abolish the slave trade, at some indefinite time in the future. The date seemed to depend on Dundas himself, who made it every day evident that his motion for delay was a ruse for indefinite postponement. The suggestion that the final date should be 1796 was soon agreed; but nobody expected that commitment to be fulfilled. The most brilliant orators in British history had been outmanoeuvred, as had the parliamentary leader, Wilberforce, of the most powerful movement of agitation which any country had experienced. The consequences would have become immediately apparent, no doubt, and Wilberforce, Clarkson, and their friends would have acted differently, had it not been that, when Parliament resumed in early 1793, war with revolutionary France was about to begin (which it did in February, just after the execution of King Louis XVI). Wilberforce's opposition to the conflict lost him support everywhere; Pitt's responsibility for leading the nation at war caused his attention to shift to matters other than humanitarian.*

Now, too, every attack on the slave trade could be represented as an attack on ancient British institutions, apparently everywhere under attack, precisely because of the French Revolution – and the war. This did not seem the moment for any adventure. Lord Abingdon, in his youth a

---

* English political history may not be understood unless it be realized that Parliament in those days sat between January and August, never in the autumn.

friend of liberty – and of John Wilkes – in April 1793, in the House of Lords, specifically linked the demands for abolition of the traffic with the disastrous obsession with the rights of man which had so damaged France: 'What [else] does the abolition of the slave trade mean more or less in effect than liberty and equality?' In this debate, the Duke of Clarence again declared how impolitic and unjust it would be to abolish the slave trade, and described Wilberforce as either a fanatic or a hypocrite. ('William made a most incomparable speech', remarked his brother, the Prince of Wales.)[27]

So, for the moment, such merchants as Richard Miles and Jerome Bernard Weuves in London, with their ships the *Spy* and the *Iris*, or Sir James Laroche and James Rogers in Bristol, with the *African Queen* and the *Fame*, as well as John Tarleton, Daniel Backhouse, Peter Baker, James Dawson, and Thomas Leyland in Liverpool, with the *Eliza*, the *Princess Royal*, and the *Ned*, could sleep in peace a few more years; and their captains, Samuel Courtauld and Hugh Thomas included, could sleep happily in their high-strung hammocks. Their equivalents in North America, Rio de Janeiro, and even Havana in Cuba seemed equally confident. True, the vast French slave trade had collapsed as a consequence of the revolution and the war, but the years of the middle 1790s were good ones for France's neighbours.

The slave trade did particularly well in 1793 in, for example, Britain's prime colony of Jamaica, which imported a record number of 23,000 captives that year. The total for 1791–5 was just under 80,000, far more than in any other quinquennium (even if at least 15,000 were re-exported to Cuba). In 1791 Jamaica employed 250,000 slaves, and in 1797 it would employ 300,000. The output of sugar increased, too: Jamaica produced 60,000 tons in 1791, over 70,000 by 1800 – its greatest year ever being 1805, when it was the biggest exporter of sugar in the world, producing nearly 100,000 tons.[28] For the first time, too, in the years after the revolution in Saint-Domingue, Jamaica was producing substantial quantities of coffee: 22,000,000 tons in 1804. By then, Britain was also exporting (re-exporting) as much coffee as it did wool.

Jamaican planters were, of course, horrified at the possibility of abolition of the traffic: they not only busied themselves with reinforcing resistance to the idea in Westminster, but began to do what they could to encourage the breeding of slaves at home. Thus a Jamaican law of 1792 offered incentives to both proprietors and overseers of estates who could show a natural increase during the year. The wife of the Governor of Jamaica, Lady Nugent, recorded in her diary that Lewis Cuthbert, a planter, told her that, at his Clifton plantation – on the Liguanea plain, now part of Kingston – 'he gave two dollars to every woman who produced a healthy child.'[29]

Then, as many opponents of abolition had argued in debate in London, the supposition that the British might be about to bring their slave traffic to an end did have the effect of stimulating their rivals. When the Dutch Minister to London heard of the first vote against the slave trade in the Commons, he sent a special messenger home to Amsterdam so that his countrymen would be able to take advantage of the opportunity. But though this did inspire a brief revival of the Dutch slave trade, the French conquest of Holland, and the subsequent establishment of the Batavian Republic, under French influence, in 1795, made the continuation of such activities on any large scale unthinkable. Yet the thought of abolition was unacceptable in Holland: a few years later, the Fiscal at Elmina, on the Gold Coast, Jan de Maree, would write that it would do 'irreparable damage to our richest source of trade'.[30]

The news from the United States was equally discouraging for the cause of abolition. Despite the successful prosecution of the brig *Hope*,[†] other such lawsuits proved unsuccessful and, the law notwithstanding, the slave traders of Rhode Island continued unperturbed. The Quakers tried their usual tactics of persuasion by correspondence, but for once they were ineffective. Dr Samuel Hopkins of Newport told Moses Brown that a printer who had promised to print one of his pamphlets had explained to him later that 'he had consulted his friends and they tell him that it will greatly hurt his interest to do it, that there is so large a number of his customers either in the slave trade or in such connection with it, or so disposed with respect to it, to whom it will give the greatest offence, that it is not prudent for him to do it. . . . In vain do I tell him that he has fallen from his profession.'[‡][31]

The Spanish colony of Cuba, too, was expanding, not withdrawing in any way from, her slave interests, and here traders of Liverpool such as Baker and Dawson, and Thomas Leyland, were deeply engaged. There were 500,000 acres of land in sugar cane in Cuba in 1792 in comparison with little more than 3,000 in 1762, there were 530 sugar mills throughout the island, and the slave population, though far behind its neighbours, was over 80,000. French refugees to Cuba from Saint-Domingue were establishing coffee farms both in East Cuba and near Havana, often using more slaves than the sugar planters. Steam engines were being introduced for the first time into the sugar plantations. But this technological innovation seemed to have no effect on the planters' need for slaves from Africa.

---

[*] *The trade in the Dutch empire had never recovered after the Fourth Anglo-Dutch War, in the early 1780s; and the many slaves needed by the Dutch colonists in Surinam were often carried there by North Americans.*

[†] *See page 519.*

[‡] *In 1792, Kentucky entered the union as a new slave state. When the South (Georgia and the Carolinas) relinquished claims on the territory to the west of them, they had stipulated that any new state there should be slaveholding. By now, the Northern and Southern populations in the new nation were more or less equal, and expansion was expected to be a lateral matter.*

In 1792 Francisco de Arango and Ignacio, the Count of Casa Montalvo, young, well-educated members of the planter oligarchy in Cuba (both of them were sons of men who recalled the British occupation of Havana), set off on another voyage of enquiry to England. Arango, then in his twenties, was the most intelligent *criollo* of his generation; later, he would be known as the 'Colbert of Cuba'. He accepted that the trade in slaves was a 'miserable' thing, but what he wanted was an adequate supply of slaves to enable his island to compete with Jamaica, and then to end the traffic.* Arango told Spanish ministers that the high price of sugar after the collapse of French production in Saint-Domingue could make Cuba as rich as Mexico. All that was needed was freedom to introduce slaves into Cuba for eight years. As a consequence, for the first time, in 1792, a Cuban vessel, *El Cometa*, Captain Pedro Laporte, set off from Havana, with slaving cargoes such as aguardiente (cane brandy), tobacco, and some white sugar, to Africa direct, and without losing a single sailor brought back 233 slaves, of whom 87 were women. This expedition was repeated in September of the same year, under a French captain, Pedro Lacroix Dufresne.[33]

So it was that during these very years when the issue of abolition had been so sensationally raised in Britain, the world's major commercial power, the slave trade was growing as never before on an island in which that nation, like the United States, already had many interests. Official statistics suggest that in 1790 about fifty ships entered Havana, bringing 2,270 slaves. Of these, six were North American (including James de Wolf's *María*), two Dutch, thirty Spanish, seven English, one 'Anglo-American', whatever that may mean, two French, three Danish, and two unknown. The next year, free-for-all slave trading in Havana was extended till 1798. Both the old subsidy and the per-capita tax were removed, as was the requirement that a third of the slaves imported had to be women. The maximum tonnage of foreign slavers was raised to 500 tons, too. Agents of foreign slave traders, such as Allwood, the representative of Baker and Dawson of Liverpool, were able to establish themselves legally in Havana – including, after 1792, French agents, who, in theory, had been excluded from the first arrangements (even though, illegally, many French slavers had come in: perhaps thirty-two between 1790 and 1792). Allwood, meantime, remained the largest importer: the Captain-General of Cuba, perhaps bribed, evaded the order of the government in Madrid to expel him for attempted corruption of officials.

---

* *The Countess of Merlin, a niece of Montalvo, would express in the 1840s what Arango seems to have thought fifty years earlier: 'Nothing is more just than the abolition of the slave trade; nothing is more unjust than the abolition of slavery.'[32] She thought the latter a violation of the rights of property, an attack on something which all governments had always supported, and even helped to finance.*

Whereas Liverpool merchants more than maintained their interest, those from the United States seem to have compensated in Cuba for losing some of their markets in North America itself. Indeed, in the 1790s, United States slave ships sailed more often to Cuba than to anywhere else – South Carolina, Rhode Island, and Georgia were far behind. There was another innovation in the traffic in the 1790s for North Americans: it became for a time profitable for traders to buy slaves on one Caribbean island and sell them on another. This was, for J. and T. Handasyde Perkins of Boston, as they pointed out themselves, a 'business which we are particularly well situated to effect. . . . We will do the business at 5 per cent.'[34] Sometimes that meant taking from Savannah, Georgia, a cargo of rice or indigo to exchange for slaves in the Windward Islands and sell them in Cuba. That was done, for instance, by Captain William McNeill in the Perkins' *Clarissa*.

This North American trading to Havana was, of course, illegal, under the federal law which forbade the trading of slaves to foreign states. So the merchants ran risks of prosecution at home. A lawsuit in Salem was, indeed, once brought against Sinclair and Waters, the owners of the *Abeona*, by a private individual, Stephen Cleveland. The owners lost the case, but refused to pay the fine of £4,000. Three of their vessels were then seized by the court. The owners appealed. The court became entangled in discussion of its own competence, and the case did not prevent the *Abeona* from sailing again.

In these years Salem, whose merchants had done little with respect to the trade in the past, became the most important Massachusetts slave port. The brothers Joseph and Joshua Grafton were the first leaders, though John White and George Crowninshield soon caught up; the latter found the business rather expensive: 'We find prime slaves were not to be purchased for less than 200 galls. rum each', they wrote thoughtfully to Captain Edward Boss, who wanted to take out one of their ships to the African slave harbours.[35] Whatever the price, Boss was all the same to be found with the sloop *General Green*, with slaves to sell in the River Suriname in 1794.

Among the captains often in Havana in these years was James de Wolf, the outstanding captain and merchant in this era of North American slave trading. De Wolf, with his 'florid cheeks, a blunt nose, gray eyes, an upper lip as sheer as a carpenter's plane, and big, capable sailor's hands', was one of five brothers of Bristol, Rhode Island, who were all for a time slave captains or merchants. They were sons of Mark Antony de Wolf, who, it will be recalled,* had captained slave ships for his father-in-law, Simeon Potter, in the early 1770s. The de Wolfs entered the trade in their own right after the American Revolution. James de Wolf, a hero of several naval fights against the British, was an outstanding individual. Before he was twenty he was master of his own ship; before he was twenty-five he had made enough money from the slave trade to last him the rest of his life. Though operating from a house on Mount Hope, a hill outside the little port of Bristol, he would sometimes go down to Charleston or Savannah to superintend the landing of slaves from his ships. He sensibly married the daughter of William Bradford, the owner of Bristol's large rum distillery (and a United States senator), when rum was still the main slave cargo on the African coast. Simeon Potter, writing to his successful nephew in 1794, explained how, despite the new federal law which prohibited the citizens of the United States from carrying slaves to other nations, there were ways in which vessels could still be fitted out for the trade. James profited from this advice, and he or other members of the family sent eighty-eight journeys to Africa for slaves between 1784 and 1807. In order to benefit from this form of labour the more, James de Wolf bought a sugar plantation in Cuba – one of the first North Americans to invest in that island after it became legal to do so in 1790.[36]

It was not simply Cuba in the Spanish empire where planters and traders were now taking advantage of the new conditions: the slave trade to Lima also expanded in the 1790s, slaves being bought as a rule in Buenos Aires or Montevideo and taken overland to Peru. The greatest merchant there was José Antonio del Valle Cortés, a well-connected mayor of Lima, who had become Count of Premio Real for his services in the colony's fight against the Inca rebellion of Tupac Amaru; between 1792 and 1803 he sold an average of 270 slaves a year on the Lima market. Del Valle's son Juan Bautista bought a substantial hacienda, Villa, south of Lima, where he put 1,500 African slaves to work his cane fields. Sales in Caracas also increased, the buyers being the cocoa farmers of the valley: 350 slaves a year were sold there at the end of the century, another of Baker and Dawson's representatives from Liverpool, Edward Barry, being the major seller.[37]

Though the international news was, therefore, far from promising, the abolitionists found some encouragement at home. For example, they gained comfort from a financial crash in Bristol. Some of the outstanding merchants were ruined – among them James Rogers, the most vociferous in his denunciations of abolition. The last in the great series of admirable Scottish philosophers, James Beattie, published the second volume of his *Elements of Moral Science*, in which (as usual among British writers of the era, following Montesquieu) he firmly stated, 'All the men upon earth whatever their colour are our brethren.'[38] Further, though the new war with France delayed innovation in politics, it had the same consequence for commerce as had occurred during all the wars of the century. Indeed, because of the fighting, and the conversion of so many merchant ships into privateers, no ships left Liverpool for slaving in 1794.

Yet there were always new merchants ready to seize any opportunities which opened up as a result of the renewed war in Europe. The

United States, not France, was the obvious candidate now for succession to Britain as the world's major slaver, should abolition be carried through in London. Zachary Macaulay, who was still in Sierra Leone, wrote from there in 1796 to the Reverend Samuel Hopkins in Newport, 'You will be sorry to learn that, during the last year, the number of American slave traders on the coast has increased to an unprecedented degree. Were it not for their pertinacious adherence to that abominable traffic', he added, rather optimistically, 'it would, in consequence of the war, have been almost wholly abolished.'[39]

Despite the war and the contrived hostility of Thurlow and Dundas, as well as of the Duke of Clarence (with all that that suggested), Wilberforce held fast to his mission. He was still supported by both Pitt and Fox, even if the former's mind had to be on the war. In 1794, when it was supposed that the trade would end in 1796, he successfully introduced a bill providing for a ban on British merchants' sale of slaves to foreign markets. The same opponents as usual spoke against him (Tarleton, Sir William Young, Alderman Newman). There were some new voices, too, such as that of Edmund Lechmere, Member for Worcester, who thought that, 'since all Europe was in a state of confusion, it would be highly imprudent to adopt any untried expedient'. Also among the Tory opposition there appears for the first time the name of Robert Peel, Member for Tamworth, the first cotton king to sit in Parliament, who thought that the Africans were not yet sufficiently mature to deserve liberty. Wilberforce on this occasion persuaded the Commons to vote for him, but the House of Lords as usual defeated him, the names of the lords who opposed being, apparently, not recorded.

It thus became clear, seven years after the first debate on the matter in the House of Commons, that the parliamentary effort to end the slave trade would constitute a long struggle.[40] As Lord Shelburne – Pitt's predecessor as Prime Minister, and the first such statesman to write an autobiography – once put it: 'it requires no small labour to open the eyes of either the public or of individuals but when that is accomplished you are not got a third of the way. The real difficulty remains in getting people to apply the principles which they have admitted and of which they are now so fully convinced. Then springs the mine composed of private interests and personal animosity.'[41]

27

WHY SHOULD WE SEE GREAT BRITAIN GETTING ALL THE SLAVE TRADE?

> *'Why should we see Great Britain getting all the slave trade to themselves? Why should not our country be enriched by that lucrative traffic?'*
>
> John Brown, Member of the House of Representatives from Rhode Island, 1800

CAPTAIN JAMES DE WOLF   St Thomas, April 1 1796
This will inform you of my arrival in this port safe, with seventy-eight well slaves. I lost two on my passage. I had sixty-two days' passage. I received your letter and orders to draw bills on thirty days sight, but I have agreed to pay in slaves – two men slaves at twenty-eight joes and one boy at twenty-five joes and another at twenty joes.* I found times very bad on the coast. Prime slaves are one hogshead and thirty gallons of rum or seven joes gold and boys one hogshead of rum. I left captain Isaac Manchester at Anemebue [that is, Anamabo] with ninety slaves on board all well. Tomorrow I shall sail for Havana, agreeable to your orders. I shall do the best I can and without other orders load with molasses and return to Bristol.
>   *I remain your friend and humble servant,*
>   *Jeremiah Diman.*

PERSISTENCE IS THE MOST important quality in politics. It was possessed in heroic measure by Wilberforce who, in the spring of 1795, again inspired a motion in the House of Commons which would have enabled

---

* *A 'joe' was a 'Johannes', a gold coin of Portugal, called for King João, worth eight dollars at the time.*

the country to go ahead with the abolition of the slave trade at the time which Henry Dundas had once suggested, at the beginning of 1796. But by now the public mood seemed in favour of indefinite delay. The consequences of the revolutions in France and Saint-Domingue, the war, and the social problems at home caused the opposition to abolition to become far stronger. That year was one in which many people supposed that a revolution in the French style would break out in England, and the abolitionists were uncertain what to do. Yet, as usual, Wilberforce was supported by Fox and Pitt. All, of course, spoke well, even if Pitt's other preoccupations had somewhat dimmed his advocacy of 'practical justice and rational liberty' – in comparison only, however, with what had prevailed in 1792. Dundas spoke of the desirability of further delays: 'The propriety of abolishing the slave trade he thought no man could doubt; yet he thought it equally clear that this was not the period for its abolition.'[1] As noted (in a letter to his sister) by the young George Canning, Pitt's most brilliant protégé, now in Parliament for the first time, Wilberforce's motion, 'to the disgrace of the House, was negatived by . . . 78 to 61, in defiance of plain justice and humanity. . . . For my own part, the slave trade is a question upon which I find it so difficult to conceive how there can exist but one feeling. . . . When the question is put to me "Shall such enormities go on – for any purpose, under any circumstances, to any degree?" I feel myself compelled at once, without looking to the right or the left, or taking any other than a straightforward view of the matter to answer with an unequivocal and unqualified "No" . . .

'Of the leaders,' Canning continued, 'I rather suspect that Sheridan has some little doubts upon the subject; but he was not present – indeed, I do not think he would divide against the measure, even if he thought against it much more decidedly than I suspect him to do.˙ Of us younger ones – Jenkinson [the future Prime Minister, Lord Liverpool], is a slave trader, so is Charles Ellis [he had been born in Jamaica where he had a plantation] . . . so is Granville Leveson [later the first Earl Granville, a gambler known later, when Ambassador to Paris, as 'le Wellington des joueurs']. . . . Seeing Leveson . . . I began to remonstrate with him jokingly upon his savageness in dividing so improperly.'[2]

Some businesses had anticipated the vote going the other way. Thus Alexander Houston and Co., one of the leading West Indian houses of Glasgow, assuming that the slave trade would end, speculated in the purchase of slaves. But in the event they had to maintain an army of unwanted Africans in Jamaica, of whom disease killed many, and the firm in consequence went bankrupt in 1795: the biggest financial disaster in

---

˙ *Sheridan had, however, in 1790 told the House of Commons that 'he required no further information to convince him that the power possessed by the West India merchant over the slave was such that no man ought to have over another'.*

the history of Glasgow till that date, and the worst in the history of the British slave trade.

The next year, 1796, Wilberforce yet again put his case to the legislature, securing permission, by 93 to 67, to introduce a bill on the subject.˙ Yet again, Fox and Pitt spoke eloquently for abolition. Yet again, Dundas insisted that, evil as the slave trade was, it was not possible for Parliament to give effect to the bill at that moment. Sir Philip Francis told the House that if he had not voted in favour of abolition in 1789 he would have inherited a great fortune from a lady who had property in the West Indies. Wilberforce lost his bill, which demanded abolition of the trade as from 1 January 1797, on the bill's third reading by only four votes, 70 to 74.[3] It was believed that the abolitionists lost some votes because of the rival attractions of a new comic opera presented that night.

The list of those who, all the same, voted with Wilberforce included as usual the greatest names in English political life: Pitt, Canning, Fox, Sheridan, as well as Francis. Yet their speeches had now become a little repetitious, lacking new information, partly because Clarkson, the essential linchpin, the packhorse, the patient traveller, the interviewer – indeed, the slave, as it would have been put at that time – of the abolition movement, had collapsed. 'All exertion was then over,' he himself reported; 'the nervous system was almost shattered. . . . Both my memory and my hearing failed me. . . .'[4] He had done the work of a hundred men and, according to his own account, had travelled on a large scale all over England in search of evidence. His place would soon be taken by James Stephen, the equally possessed son of a supercargo who had lived at the minor slave port of Poole, had been a lawyer at St Kitts in the Caribbean, and saw, in England's current discomfiture by France, a divine retribution for her part in the slave trade. (Stephen's hostility to slavery had been inspired by seeing two slaves condemned in St Kitts to be burned alive.)

The interest of British public opinion in the matter of slavery was maintained up to a certain point by another lawsuit comparable to that of the *Zong*, though with a different conclusion. This was *Tatham v. Hodgson*. A ship left Liverpool for Africa and picked up 168 slaves. She then set off for the West Indies. The voyage took over six months because of bad weather, and 128 slaves died en route – most of them as a result of starvation, since the captain had laid in food for only the usual six to nine weeks. The question was whether the loss of slaves could be attributed to the perils of the sea, in which case the insurance company would pay the owners. Lord Kenyon – the new Lord Chief Justice, after Mansfield's retirement – asked sharply whether the captain of the ship had also

---

˙ *This is the only roll call of voting members in the Houses of Commons and Lords on this issue which seems to have survived.*

starved to death. The answer was no. In the end, Kenyon's judgement was that the shipowners were not entitled to call on the underwriters to make good their loss.

In 1797 and 1798 Wilberforce was again defeated. On these occasions he had new supporters – such as Benjamin Hobhouse, though he came from Bristol slave-trading stock* – and new enemies, in the shape of Bryan Edwards, member of the Jamaican Assembly, as well as of the House of Commons, and the author of a competent history of the British West Indies. Edwards had the audacity to invoke the recent work of Mungo Park to support his contention that all Africa was in a condition of absolute slavery, and suggested to Wilberforce that if he were desirous of exercising his humanity he should look to Britain, where 'he would even meet a race as worthy of his benevolent attention as those in the West Indies, namely the chimney sweeps'.† Another critic was Canning's friend Charles Ellis, who in 1797 proposed that the governors of West Indian colonies should be instructed to encourage the West Indian legislatures to improve the conditions on plantations until the slaves' natural increase made the trade unnecessary. Pitt was, for a time, attracted by this idea but, in the end, sided as usual with Wilberforce.[5]

In 1799 Wilberforce again put the question, being supported again by the same brilliant band of fine orators. A new opponent of Wilberforce was John Petrie, a merchant and banker who had four estates in Tobago, and who in his only speech in the House of Commons argued that abolition would be the scourge of Africa. Dundas, with whom the spirit of inspired gradualism was turning to that of outright hostility, now argued that the future of a subject as important as the trade in slaves should be decided by the legislatures of the colonies themselves – a view effectively mocked by Canning, now in the government as Undersecretary at the Foreign Office. Pitt on this occasion said ironically that the opponents of abolition evidently thought that 'the blood of these poor negroes was to continue flowing; it was dangerous to stop it because it had run so long; besides, we were under contract with certain surgeons to allow them a certain supply of human bodies every year for them to try experiments on, and this we did out of pure love of science.' On this occasion, the motion to abolish the trade was defeated by only 74 to 82.[6]

Wilberforce also introduced a bill, making the more modest suggestion that slave traders should be excluded from the colony of Sierra Leone because of its freed citizenry. This rather obvious measure passed the

---

* He was father of Byron's friend John Cam Hobhouse, and nephew of Isaac Hobhouse the slave trader of the first part of the eighteenth century.
† High society, meantime, was diverted by the song of the popular musician Ferrari, with words by the much-loved Duchess of Devonshire, based on one of the most affecting incidents in Mungo Park's Travels.

Commons, but even that failed to pass through the Lords: the Duke of
Clarence assumed the lead of those who opposed the idea, and was
presented for his pains with the freedom of the city of Liverpool.

One bill which did pass the House of Commons in 1799 restricted
still further the number of slaves per ton of British shipping (the average
number of slaves per ship henceforth was to be 289). Slaves would now
be fitted into an average space of eight square feet instead of five to six
square feet. As the future Prime Minister Lord Liverpool argued would
be the case, in his opposition to this modest proposal, the profitability of
these regulated ships was declining in comparison with Britain's
competitors: for example, in 1806 the Royal Navy captured as a prize 413
slaves on board a Dutch ship which, under British regulations, would
have been allowed to carry a maximum of only 260.

As the new century began, Wilberforce and his friends realized
bitterly that ten years after the formation of the abolitionist movement
British ships were still carrying over 50,000 slaves a year to the Americas,
and that the years 1791–1800 had seen the British slave trade at its most
grandiose – nearly 400,000 slaves had been landed from about 1,340
voyages. Despite the high prices of slaves in Africa, the trade was more
profitable than it had been in the 1780s: the average profit per voyage
was probably 13 per cent. In 1798 almost 150 ships, the highest ever, left
Liverpool for Africa.·

The British economy appeared even more to depend either on
slavery, or on slave-produced goods, in the first years of the nineteenth
century than when the movement for abolition had been launched. In
1803, for instance, less than 8 per cent of the cotton used in Britain
derived from 'free areas', such as Turkey. The rest came from slave-using
plantation colonies such as Louisiana, Brazil, or Demerara-Suriname (the
latter was the great cotton success of the early 1800s, the 'most rapidly
developing colony in the world', where most cotton plantations were
owned by English investors). Between 1790 and 1806 the slave population
increased in the British empire by at least a quarter, and if the new West
Indian islands, conquered or merely occupied, were added to the total,
the increase would be about a half. Liverpool merchants such as Baker
and Dawson (so often mentioned), John Bolton, and John Tarleton (of
Tarleton and Backhouse) figure as major investors, not only in trading
slaves to Demerara, but in employing them when they got there and
carrying steam engines there, too. James Stephen, now Wilberforce's
brother-in-law, wrote in a tract published in 1804: 'I see my country still
given up without remorse to the unbridled career of slave-trading specu-
lators,' and added, 'The monster, instead of being cut off, as the first burst

---

· *Liverpool sent to Africa 135 ships a year between 1798 and 1802, carrying an average of
37,086 slaves a year; and 103 between 1803 and 1807, carrying 25,953 a year; compared
with London's mere eighteen and thirteen, and Bristol's mere four and one respectively.*

of honest indignation promised, has been more fondly nourished than before; and fattened with fuller meals of misery and murder. . . .'[7]

One modern historian, Seymour Dreschler, was, therefore, quite correct to comment, more drily: 'In terms of both capital value and overseas trade the slave system was expanding, not declining.'[8]

It need scarcely be added that neither the Portuguese Crown nor the Brazilian ascendancy had for a moment contemplated an end of their traffic in slaves. How could they? The income to the Portuguese state from the trade, as a result of per-capita taxes on slaves, was higher than ever before. In 1770, for instance, the tax on slaves amounted to 150 contos, whereas other receipts did not attain a twentieth of that. In 1801–10 about 200,000 slaves were carried to Brazil, over three-quarters from Angola and 50,000 from the Gulf of Guinea. About 10,000 were carried every year to Rio alone. Many of these were children, because of a lack of other supplies. Even Portugal had been still importing slaves in the 1770s, perhaps several thousand a year, though it was illegal. (The first prosecution for importing slaves to Lisbon came in 1798.) No one in Brazil would have disagreed with a statement by the merchants of Bahia to the King of Portugal, in the 1790s, that 'the arms of slaves . . . are those that cultivate the vast fields of Brazil; without them, there would perhaps not be those things as important as sugar, tobacco, cotton and the rest which are transported to the Motherland, and which enrich and augment national commerce and the royal treasury of Your Majesty. Any objection to the slave trade [such as, it might have been added, were being made by a few hypocrites in the parliament of His Majesty's oldest ally] . . . are attacks on the population, the commerce and the income of Your Majesty.'[9]

The most promising new market for slaves in these years, however, was still Cuba. Philip Baker, of Baker and Dawson, took care in 1795 to inform the Commons that he had £500,000 invested in eighteen slave ships – for the service of Spain (that is, Cuba). The new circumstances there had encouraged the establishment, in Havana, of a new breed of slave traders. Havana previously had never had such merchants, for the planters on the island had usually traded there directly with the English, French, Dutch, or other captains. But now an oligarchy of merchants took shape which imported slaves and resold them to planters or, in some cases, sent ships themselves to other Caribbean ports to buy them. The new names included Santiago Drake, whose interests included both trading in slaves and using them on plantations (born James Drake in England, he had gone to Havana when the old regulations were dismantled in 1792); his relations, the del Castillo family, one of whose members, José del Castillo, was dedicated to commerce of all kinds in Havana, whereas his cousins, the Marquis of San Felipe and his brothers, grew sugar at their fine hacienda at Bejucal; Santiago de la Cuesta y Manzanal, a giant who would have a great future in public life and die a marquis;

the de Poëy family; Cristóbal Durán (who specialized in carrying slaves from North America to Cuba); Clemente Ichaso; and Francisco Antonio de Comas. Many of these new Havana merchants had North American associates or even partners. For example, Santiago Drake had as a partner Charles Storey in that most northerly of Massachusetts ports, Newburyport, and he also had connections in his home country. Apart from him and the de Poëys, who were originally French, most of these merchants were born in Spain, even if they soon took their place among the business leaders of Cuba.

The new merchants were certain that their mission was to bring as many slaves to Cuba in as short a time as possible. For that reason they turned a little away from the English suppliers who had sold them so many slaves in the past: the latest English law restricting the slaves per ship seemed unbusinesslike. Between 1796 and 1807 the United States dominated the Cuban slave trade, and, in that last year, thirty-five out of the total of forty-four ships which officially entered Havana were registered as North American, though sometimes these supposed United States ships were really British: 'A large proportion, perhaps all the American slave ships which are now fitted out in our ports, are owned by British subjects,' James Stephen noted.[10] But when the world was at peace – as it was in 1802, after the Peace of Amiens – English ships, such as William Jameson's *Fame*, and Henry Colet's *Minerva* (in May 1802), still occasionally brought substantial cargoes to Havana: 380 and 246 slaves respectively.

One interesting change occurred in Havana in the 1790s. Las Casas, the Cuban Captain-General (that is, Governor of the island), ruled that only slaves direct from Africa could be brought to Cuba: those who had been working for many years in other Caribbean islands were potentially suspect as bearers of evil liberal ideas. For a time, this rule was interpreted as being an instruction to those buying from foreign captains; but it was already recognized in Cuba not only that 'the need for labour of this kind is not temporary but permanent', but also that 'the entry and departure of foreigners to and from our ports is not convenient while we are in a position to reach another agreement'. By 1798, following the pioneering voyage of Lafuente in *El Cometa* of 1792, ships were beginning to leave Cuba direct for Africa quite often, if not regularly. For example, a vessel captained by Luis Beltrán Gonet purchased 123 slaves on the River Sénégal. In 1802 José Maria Ormazabal, on behalf of Francisco Ignacio de Azcárate, a Basque merchant established in Havana, went to Africa in the schooner *Dolores*, and brought back 122 slaves after a voyage of fifty-eight days, making a profit of 75 per cent. This direct traffic was still technically illegal, and several of the captains, crews, and financers were not Spanish, but in 1804 the Spanish government changed its mind. Any Spanish citizen was, for another twelve years, to be allowed to import slaves from Africa free of all duty. Foreigners were permitted to do the same, though only for six years. Sugar mills – this decree was proclaimed with an eye to Cuba, especially – were to be provided with slave women, so that reliance on imports would, it was optimistically hoped, eventually cease (planters never liked such provisions, and as usual did their best to avoid them). This reform was the result of a note sent from the King of Spain to the Council of the Indies in April 1803 which declared firmly, 'American agriculture, which, because of its impact on the commerce and navigation of European nations and the prosperity of the colonies themselves, is so important, cannot exist without the slave trade.'[11]

In consequence, even official figures suggest that in the years 1790–1810 about 150,000 slaves were imported into Cuba; nearly 14,000 in 1802 alone.

In these years, the cause of abolition in the United States suffered new complications. On the one hand, all three Southern states where the import of slaves had been left as legal in 1787 formally prohibited it: Georgia in 1798 (which provision endured, although scarcely fulfilled); South Carolina in 1788, for five years, and when that prohibition ran out it banned the trade for another two years, a law which continued to be extended, though with modest penalties, till 1803; and, finally, North Carolina, whose legislature, though the state had in 1790 repealed its prohibitory duties on slaving in 1794, influenced by hideous stories of events in Haiti, introduced a bill to prevent the further import of slaves.

On the other hand, there were several further lawsuits against slave traders. During the second half of 1799 alone there were six actions for breaking the federal law of 1794. But the prohibitions on importing were not really maintained; most of the lawsuits did not prosper, for the confiscation of the slave ship, which was the usual penalty, was customarily easily circumvented by the ship's being bought back at an artificially low price by the old owner; the government's attempts to prevent this usually proved futile. Other cases were lost on technical grounds.

A new act of 1800 tightened the federal law, making it technically illegal for both residents and citizens of the United States to have any share in a slave ship on its way to a foreign country. The Congress voted for this law overwhelmingly, the Senate by 67 to 4. The debate in the lower house was interesting for a speech by John Brown of Rhode Island, the famous merchant of Providence, who alleged that in 1794 his fellow members had been 'drilled into [passing the act of that year] by certain members who would not take no for an answer'. He was certain that the existence of an act in the United States against the slave trade would not prevent the exportation of a single slave from Africa, because shippers from other countries would take them. He believed: 'We might as well enjoy that trade as leave it wholly to others. It was the law of that country [Africa] to export those whom they held in slavery – who were as much slaves as those who were slaves in this country. . . . The very idea of making a law against this trade, which all our other nations enjoyed, was ill policy. He could further say that it [abolition] was wrong when considered in a moral point of view since, by the operation of the trade, the very people much bettered their condition. . . . [In addition] all our distilleries and manufactures were lying idle for want of an extended commerce [in slaves]. He had been informed that, on those coasts [of Africa], New England rum was much preferred to the best Jamaica spirits. . . .'[12]

There was a moment when despite the opposition of John Brown it seemed that this act really might spell the end of the traffic from Rhode Island and elsewhere in New England; but the federal courts were still inactive, partly because of local threats of violence and bribery. The law seems to have had no effect on United States' slave trading to Cuba. Then in 1804, as a result of skilfully conducted local intrigues, an abolitionist, Jonathan Russell, was removed from the decisive post of Collector of Customs at Bristol, Rhode Island, and substituted by Charles Collins, a brother-in-law of James de Wolf. This was a disastrous appointment, since Collins had not only once been a slave captain, but was still part-owner of the slave ships *Armstadt* and *Minerva*; the very day when he was sworn in to his new post the latter ship landed 150 slaves at Havana. Collins remained collector for twenty years. Not surprisingly, there were for the moment no more prosecutions in Rhode Island for breaking the law on trading slaves.˙

Partly in consequence of the trade originating in Rhode Island, an apparently uncontrollable traffic seemed to swamp the states which still thought themselves in need of slave labour: in particular, South Carolina, which in December 1803 reopened her own slave trade, allowing about 40,000 new slaves to enter legally until a federal prohibition took effect in 1807. These slaves were almost all from Africa, for the legislators in the state, like the Captain-General in Cuba, feared a slave rebellion if West Indian slaves should come. According to customs-house returns, scarcely likely to exaggerate, the shippers came primarily from Britain (nearly 20,000 slaves, in ninety-one ships), Rhode Island (nearly 8,000 slaves, in eighty-eight ships), Charleston itself (2,000 slaves, in thirteen ships), and France (over 1,000 slaves, in ten ships).

The main firm in Charleston in these days was that of John Phillips and John Gardner, both of whom had come down from Newport to make their fortunes, and certainly seem to have done so: they sent twenty-five ships direct to Africa in the last four years of the slave trade.

˙ *For example, the government confiscated the* Lucy, *belonging to Charles de Wolf. The surveyor of the port of Bristol was ordered to buy the ship for the government at a reasonable price. The day before the sale, the surveyor was visited by Charles and James de Wolf, with John Brown. They advised him not to go to the auction. The day of the auction, the surveyor was kidnapped by some of the de Wolfs' seamen, and kept in hiding till the* Lucy *had been sold back to its old owner at a negligible price.*

A representative of the de Wolf family (Henry or 'Gentleman Jim', for example, young men still in their teens) would probably be there to receive the cargoes which their uncle James de Wolf had commissioned.

The national response was modest. Representative David Bard, a pastor from Pennsylvania, was admittedly outraged at the resurgence of the traffic. He said: 'Had I been informed that some formidable foreign power had invaded our country, I would not, I ought not, be more alarmed . . . while we see the flood gate open and pouring innumerable miseries into our country.' He then proposed a tax of $10 a head on the slaves imported: scarcely a severe penalty, since, at that time, the price of a slave was $100.[13]

As many Africans were probably introduced into the United States in the last twenty years of the eighteenth century and the first eight years of the nineteenth century as in the entire era since the 1620s.

An impression of the African consequences was given by Captain Matthew Benson of Rhode Island, who had himself once traded in slaves but was now concerned primarily with camwood and gum. He wrote home to Nicholas Brown & Co. of Providence in 1800, from the coast of Sierra Leone, to say that there the 'American hive continues its swarming beyond all previous periods. Not a week passes without arrivals. The quantity of rum, tobacco and provisions arriving since the tenth of the current [month] is almost incredible.'[14] In 1806 the United States' slaving fleet was said to have been almost three-quarters the size of the British one. These vessels of the former, unlike those of the latter, were of course unregulated by anything like the Dolben bill, and so could carry as many slaves as their captains thought fit.

The early years of the nineteenth century thus looked distinctly unpromising for the abolition of the trade, much less that of slavery itself. No one could be certain what the Congress of the United States would decide in 1807, the year when there was, by the terms of the Constitution of 1787, certain to be a new debate; nor whether anything which might be decided would be effective in practice. The slaveholding states of the United States were now responsible for about 45 per cent of the seats in the House of Representatives. The slaveholders were already looking to the Senate to admit new slave states. At the same time, the old enthusiasm for abolition in England had diminished. The campaigners were growing older, the attentions of Pitt were absorbed by the war, and little really had happened in respect of abolition. The novelty of the cause had worn thin. King George III looked on Wilberforce's activities as a jest: 'How go on your black clients, Mr Wilberforce?' he once asked that statesman at a levée.[15] The standing of the navy stood high, and the navy, from Nelson to the Duke of Clarence, was generally in favour of the traffic. The former once said that he was 'bred in the good old school, and taught to appreciate the value of our West Indian possessions, and neither in the field nor the Senate shall their just rights be infringed, while I have an arm to fight in their defence, or a tongue to launch my voice against the damnable doctrine of Wilberforce and his hypocritical allies'.[16] In this atmosphere, it is scarcely surprising that between 1801 and 1807 266,000 slaves were carried by Britain, without taking into account those carried in foreign-owned vessels which were really British. The war might have tired the abolitionists, but not the slavers.

Then, in 1802, France revived the trade: Napoleon greeted the Peace of Amiens by reintroducing slavery itself into the French empire. This law, of 30 Floréal in the year X, did not inspire the slightest opposition in the passive 'tribunate' in Paris. Article III of the new document stated simply that the slave trade, which had never been abolished, would continue according to the rules obtaining before 1789. Napoleon had previously seen the Deputies for Nantes, Bordeaux, and Marseilles, and they had talked to him of the urgent national need to revive the slave trade. Pierre Labarthe, in his *Voyage à la côte de Guinée* of 1802, praised Napoleon for this return to 'the principles of a wise policy'.[17]

No doubt the deputies' influence was considerable. Perhaps also Josephine, the brilliant daughter of Martinique, gave her counsel. But the First Consul was not sentimental: his colonies required labour as much as his merchants required profits. The Council of Commerce in La Rochelle had earlier rejoiced that '*les temps déplorables de la démagogie*' – in which entire colonies had been allowed to perish in order to preserve a principle – '*sont à la fin passés.*' The Council of Commerce of Bordeaux, too, composed of nine men of whom five were *négriers* (Dominique Cabarrus, Mareilhac, Chicu-Bourbon, Gramont, and Brunaud), also stated firmly that 'the supreme object of African commerce has always been to sustain our western colonies. . . . Cultivation cannot be usefully carried on except with the strong arms of Africans. *De là, la nécessité de la traite*': always provided, in their opinion, that it was not a *traite* managed by one of those terrible privileged companies which in the past had so damaged honest traders.[18]

Bordeaux, for a short time, was the biggest slave port of France, sending between February 1802 and January 1804 fifteen ships to Africa, among them such prettily named vessels as the *Grand d'Alembert*, the *Incroyable*, and the *Harmonie*. The dominant trader in this new phase of the history of the Gironde was Jacques Conte, the Protestant son of a sea captain from the peninsula of Arvert (Charente-Maritime), who had first made a fortune from seizing merchant ships as a privateer: 152 in all. The slave trade was popular. Men advertised themselves to work on board the new generation of vessels: '*Un citoyen des bonnes moeurs, âgé de 32 ans, appartenant à une famille connue . . . s'emploierait sur les côtes d'Amérique ou d'Afrique [comme] subrécargue.*'[19] Local papers published numerous advertisements announcing that the merchant concerned had the ideal cargo necessary for the journey.*

---

* *The same year as the restoration of slavery, the entry of blacks into France was finally forbidden.*

The French restoration of the institution of the trade removed in England the stigma of Jacobinism from the abolitionist cause; and, by the same token, it soon came to seem pro-British or anti-patriotic to oppose slavery in France.

Napoleon, having in 1800 forced Spain to return Louisiana to him, sent an army to Saint-Domingue to reconquer it, and it seems as if, for a time, he anticipated a new French empire in the Americas, without rights for slaves. Another French army reconquered Guadeloupe from the rebel Victor Hugues. But the failure of General Leclerc to re-establish French power in Saint-Domingue weakened Napoleon's imperial desires, as well as placing power in the new republic of Haiti in the hands of the despot Dessalines, who cut himself off from the world (even if he did, on proclaiming himself emperor, receive a crown from the United States, brought on the *Connecticut*). The incompetence of Dessalines did not make the new country seem a good example for the future of other once successful sugar colonies.

The resumption of the war in Europe in 1803 persuaded Napoleon to withdraw from his Caribbean ambitions. He even sold Louisiana to the United States, thereby doubling the size of the Union (for the territory stretched far to the north) and, in the long run, making possible the United States' growth to its modern place as a world power.

The slave history of Louisiana after its sale is instructive. It was soon accepted that slaves should move into Louisiana as easily as into Mississippi (where, in 1798, the bill introduced to establish it as a state contained a specific declaration that the anti-slaving clause of the Constitution should not apply, since slavery was a legal institution in the surrounding country). At that time, Louisiana was a small producer of sugar – a mere 5,000 tons – and thus scarcely a big slave consumer. But a substantial proportion of the large numbers of slaves imported during these years into South Carolina found themselves eventually in Louisiana.

A federal law soon condemned the Louisiana slave trade. But despite protests to President Jefferson (notably by Representative James Hillhouse and by the pamphleteer Tom Paine, now back in the United States) slavery itself was permitted. The Marquis of Casa Calvo, the last Spanish Governor of the colony, wrote after his return to Havana: 'Truly, it is impossible for lower Louisiana to get along without slaves. And it will be very damaging to their interests if they cannot obtain the hands necessary for their work which will infallibly decline. It is not easy to adduce a reason for this conduct [of the government of the United States] in the colony which was making great strides towards prosperity and wealth. The inhabitants are so angered that it is with difficulty that they will be able to be amalgamated with the rude citizens of the United States.'[20]

The same opinions were expressed by an official, John Watkins, sent to travel in Louisiana by the territory's first United States Governor,

William Claiborne: 'No subject seems to be so interesting to the minds of the inhabitants of all that part of the country which I have visited as that of the importation of brute negroes from Africa. This permission would go further with them, and better reconcile them to the government of the United States, than any other privilege that could be extended to this country. They appear only to claim it for a few years. . . . White labourers, they say, cannot be had in this unhealthy climate.'[21] Few, in fact, thought that the planters of Louisiana, with their growing cotton production, would obey federal laws on slavery. That distrust was correct.*

By chance, Napoleon's revival of slavery coincided with a fresh impetus for the cause of abolition.

First, in 1803, the Danes carried out their agreement of 1792 to abolish the slave trade. True, as might have been expected, the number of slaves carried in their last years exceeded all past levels, so that by 1802 the few small islands of the Danish West Indies counted over 35,000 slaves (in comparison with about 28,000 in 1792).

Then in 1802 a brilliant young Spanish geographer, Isidoro Antillón, read before an academy of Spanish law in Madrid a dissertation against the commerce and enslavement of Africans. Though his essay was largely an adaptation of the ideas of Montesquieu, it was certainly the first faint indication of abolitionism in a country whose colonial merchants were every year expanding the traffic.[22] There had been just a whiff of the same even in Cuba a few years before, when a Jesuit, Fray José Jesús Parreno, was expelled from the island for mentioning the matter in a sermon (his manuscripts were seized). Even in Portugal and Brazil some enlightened spirits were beginning to question the basis of the traffic in slaves on which the latter dominion seemed still absolutely to depend. In 1794, for example, a Capuchin brother, José de Bolonha, was expelled from Bahia, since he too had publicly maintained that the African trade was illegal, on the ground this time that so many slaves were kidnapped. Two years later, Bernardino de Andrade, who had been an official of the Grão-Pará and Maranhão Company, wrote rather optimistically from Guinea-Bissau to his Secretary of State in Lisbon that if the slave trade could only be replaced by other enterprises, the people of Upper Guinea might end 'their interminable dissensions and return to agriculture'.[23]

Probably without knowing of these Latin initiatives, the patient Wilberforce revived his efforts in 1804; this time the bill, his fourth, actually passed the House of Commons, by 49 votes to 24 – a victory achieved because many of the (new) Irish members voted for him.† In the debate,

---

* The settled portion of 'Louisiana' would be admitted to the Union as a state in 1812. The great stretch of land to the north and west became known as the 'Missouri Territory'.
† The independent Irish Parliament, 'Grattan's Parliament', had come to an end after the Act of Union of 1800.

Wilberforce had some entertainment in mocking the remarks of the historian of Jamaica, Edward Long, which had included the outrageous reflection, 'An orang-outang husband would by no means disgrace a negro woman.'[24] (Long was still the proprietor of a 500 acre sugar estate in Jamaica, Lucky Hill, in the parish of Clarendon, which made him £4,000 a year.) As usual, in those debates, Wilberforce found new enemies, such as John Fuller, Member for Sussex, a planter in Jamaica (he had inherited the Rose Hill plantation) who insisted that 'he had never heard the Africans deny their mental inferiority'. Another new enemy of reform was William Devyanes, a banker and Member for Barnstaple, sometime Chairman of the East India Company, who had spent years in Africa and told the House of Commons that an African king had assured him that, 'if the slave merchants did not purchase from him and others their prisoners taken in war, they would be killed'. (Devyanes, however, was known as an 'active philanthropist'.) But the House of Lords, whither the crafty Dundas had now been translated as Lord Melville, as usual proposed a delay, such as was equivalent to the defeat of the bill. Once again, the ineffable Duke of Clarence spoke for procrastination. Wilberforce wrote to a friend, Lord Muncaster, a Westmorland peer, that 'it was truly humiliating to see, in the House of Lords, four of the Royal Family come down to vote against the poor, helpless, friendless slaves.'[25]

Wilberforce was, however, encouraged by his success in the House of Commons. The signs were suddenly propitious to his cause. As so often in politics, patience had its rewards. Dundas, without whose skilful obstructions the trade would have been abolished in 1796, if not 1792, was impeached in April 1805.[*] Pitt's prejudiced Lord Chancellor, Thurlow, was dying. Whatever the attitude of the royal family and the House of Lords, the mood of the new generation in the House of Commons was evidently inclined to abolitionism, thanks to the propaganda of Clarkson, Sharp, and Stephen. Though Pitt was in the last year of his life, he was still concerned, and indeed was anxious to avoid the risks of a new Saint-Domingue in newly captured Caribbean territories such as Trinidad, Tobago, St Lucia, and St Vincent.[†] An order-in-council also forbade the import of slaves to the three new rich Guianan colonies of Essequibo, Demerara, and Berbice (which Britain had temporarily

---

[*] *For mismanagement of funds when Treasurer of the Navy.*
[†] *Pitt was constrained to act because of an issue which had been raised during the short-lived previous administration, in 1801. Some investors pressed Lord Addington, when Prime Minister, to sell off the Crown lands in the recently acquired Trinidad and St Vincent, to increase government revenue and encourage the clearing of new land. That would have given an impetus to the slave trade there. Canning, speaking as a private member of Parliament, not as a minister, hoping to force the Addington administration out of office, warned the Commons of the risks of stocking Trinidad with slaves. He asked for a suspension of the plan to sell off the land, urging an agricultural reform by which Trinidad would become a model island. Addington backed down.*

acquired) after 1 December 1805, but only beyond 3 per cent per year of the existing populations. A full ban on the import of slaves from Africa would take place after 1 January 1807. In order to prevent illegal import, there would also be a register of all slaves.

This modest restriction, following what had transpired in respect to St Vincent and Trinidad, was a turning point in the history of abolition; the new rule inspired fury among the cotton planters of Demerara, and led to the import for the first time there of Chinese labour, and to the hiring of some free blacks.

All the same, the next year, Wilberforce was to his surprise again obstructed, this time by a delaying amendment to a new version of his bill by Isaac, the brother of his old enemy Bamber Gascoyne of Liverpool (the voting on the second reading was 70 to 77). For the first time in this long series of debates, Pitt, preoccupied by personal as well as national problems (he was deeply distressed by the impeachment of Dundas), declined to speak on the matter.

Britain and the United States now moved as if together, though of course there was no possibility of deliberate cooperation. For after several interesting debates as to whether it was right to deal with the slave trade exclusively by taxing imports of slaves, President Thomas Jefferson, in his annual message in December 1806, condemned those 'violations of human rights which have been so long continued on the unoffending inhabitants of Africa', and urged Congress to take advantage of the end of the constitutional limitation of twenty years, which would come in 1807, to abolish the slave traffic absolutely.[26] This was a remarkably firm statement for a president who was so often ambiguous, especially on the question of slavery. At one stage of his life, when most influenced by the French *philosophes*, he did once more talk of the relation of master and slave as 'a perpetual exercise of the most boisterous passions, the most remitting despotisms on the one hand, and degrading submissions on the other'.[27] But he himself always employed, and sometimes sold, slaves, and never endorsed outright the cause of abolition. He had also approved the fatal appointment of Collector of Customs Collins, a designation leading to the worst evasions of the law.

The day after Jefferson's statement, Senator Stephen Bradley of Vermont (also known as the inventor of the stars and stripes on the flag of the United States) introduced a bill which would eventually prohibit the African slave trade. The ensuing debate concerned itself with important details. What, for example, was to be done with illegally imported slaves if they were identified as such? Surely they could not be sold, because, if that were done, 'we punish the criminal, and then step into his place and complete the crime'. But could they become free Africans inside the United States? Or should they be returned to Africa? If so, could their old homes be found, and how could they be prevented from being sold again as slaves? Punishment of those found guilty of illegal importing and the limitation of the interstate traffic naturally concerned the Congress, too. It was also admitted that violations of the law would be certain to occur, at least at first. Speakers from the Southern states suggested that no federal law against the slave trade could be put into effect in the Carolinas and in Georgia, where the trading of slaves would be seen at the most as a misdemeanour, not a crime: Peter Early of Georgia asked, 'What honour will you derive from a law which will be broken every day of your lives?'

As to punishments of illegal traders, the argument came up against the difficulty of correlating them with existing severe penalties for theft; and Representative Joseph Stanton of Rhode Island, no doubt thinking of old friends at home, declared: 'I cannot believe that a man ought to be hung [sic] for only stealing a negro.'

But in the end a bill in favour of abolition of the slave trade passed the Senate on 27 January 1807, and in the House of Representatives on 11 February. President Jefferson signed it on 2 March. It stated unequivocally that from 1 January 1808 it would be illegal to introduce into the United States any 'negro, mulatto, or person of colour, as a slave'. The law also prohibited any United States citizen from equipping or financing any slave ship, to operate from any port in the United States. Sales of slaves to Cuba as to Brazil would henceforth be as much a crime as a sale to South Carolina. The question of the treatment of freed slaves was resolved by leaving the matter to the legislatures of the states concerned. Punishments would be a fine of $20,000 for equipping a ship, as well as the loss of the ship; for transporting slaves, a fine of $5,000 and the loss of the ship; and for carrying illegal slaves, a fine of $1,000 to $10,000, as well as imprisonment for five to ten years, accompanied by the forfeiture of both ship and slaves. Anyone who bought illegally imported slaves would be fined $800 a slave, and would forfeit the ship.[28]

The shortcoming of the act passed in Congress was that no special machinery was devised for its enforcement. Most of the Southern states, admittedly, did pass acts which were concerned with the disposal of illegally imported slaves. Thus Georgia and the new Alabama-Mississippi Territory (in 1815), and North Carolina (in 1816) caused the slaves to be sold by auction for the benefit of the state. For the rest, the Secretary of the Treasury, responsible for the collection of customs, was theoretically in charge, but he had no special police at his disposal. In 1820 Secretary William Crawford, a Georgian, would tell Congress, 'It appears, from an examination of the records of this office, that no particular instructions have ever been given by the Secretary of the Treasury, under the original or supplementary acts prohibiting the introduction of slaves into the United States.'[29]

The discussion in the Congress of the United States on the final abolition was quite different from its equivalent in the House of Commons in London, since the legislature of the United States was concerned with something on which everyone present was to some extent informed from personal experience: every senator or congressman (even Bradley of Vermont, the one state in the Union which had never known slavery) had known a slave. On the other hand, in London, only a small minority of lords or members of Parliament had had experience in the West Indies, and practically none by then in North America.

In the early part of 1806 the abolitionists held a series of discussions in London with the new 'Government of All the Talents' – that is, with the Prime Minister, Lord Grenville (Pitt had died); with Lord Henry Petty, the young Chancellor of the Exchequer; and with Charles James Fox, who was at last Foreign Secretary. Grenville, son of Pitt's 'Gentle Shepherd', who, through his Stamp Act, had done so much to lose the American colonies for Britain, had been an enemy of slavery since the first discussion in the House of Commons on the trade in 1789. He, like Fox, had spoken against the trade in nearly all the debates of the 1790s. Petty – the Chancellor of the Exchequer, son of Shelburne – was only twenty-five, but had the reputation of having been 'a friend of democrats' at Cambridge (he would later be the politically long-lasting mid-Victorian Lord Lansdowne). The Attorney-General, Sir Arthur Pigott (son of John Pigott of Barbados, having been also Attorney-General in Grenada, he knew the Caribbean background), then introduced a bill forbidding British captains to sell slaves to foreign countries. This was a stepping stone to full abolition, but it was introduced quietly, so that Sir Robert Peel, the cotton manufacturer and slave-owning Member for Tamworth, had to admit, in a speech on the third reading, that he had not been present during the earlier discussions because he had not realized the bill's importance. The Commons voted 35 to 13 in favour. In May 1806 this bill passed even the Lords (by 43 to 18). By then a new economic argument had been added to the purely humanitarian one: the West Indies were in debt, there was a large sugar surplus, and the 'saturated' old colonies did not want new slaves. The abolitionists were now cock-a-hoop: Clarkson, recovered from his mental maladies, could comment, 'There was never perhaps a season when so much virtuous feeling pervaded all ranks.'[30]

Further debates were held in June 1806. Fox and Grenville then moved, in the lower and upper houses respectively, resolutions which pledged Parliament to abolish the slave trade 'with all practicable expedition'. Both houses were persuaded also to urge the government to negotiate with other countries in order to achieve a general abolition of the traffic: British abolition would lead to an international British crusade. The recent death of Pitt, and the sword of Damocles hanging over Dundas, cast a shadow over the debates. In the Lords the new Lord Chancellor, the brilliant but mercurial Thomas Erskine, redeemed the dismissive comments of his predecessor, Thurlow, in 1792, by saying first that he had personally changed his mind in favour of abolition, and that 'it was our duty to God and to our country, which was the morning star of enlightened Europe and whose boast and glory was to grant liberty and life, and administer humanity and justice to all nations, to remedy that evil'. So a motion in favour of abolition was carried in both houses, by 114 to 15 in the Commons, and 41 to 20 in the Lords. The debates showed, Canning wrote enthusiastically, 'what a government *can* do if it pleases'.[31]

An act was quickly passed enacting that after August 1807 no new ships should be employed in the slave trade. In the debate in the House of Commons Isaac Gascoyne declared that he had no doubt that after the abolition, 'great distress, public and private, will follow ... and that a number of our most loyal, industrious and useful subjects will emigrate to America'. Wilberforce introduced the argument that were the slave trade to be abolished planters would be constrained to look after their slaves much better; indeed, 'to do everything which was likely to have the effect of increasing the population' – a point further stressed by Henry Petty, who said, 'Where provisions are abundant and labour not excessive, the natural population of every place will answer its demands.' George Rose, a Member of Parliament for Christchurch, an old ally of Clarkson and agent for Dominica, yet who had a financial interest in the continuing traffic in slaves, thought that there was a danger that abolition of the trade would lead to the emancipation of the slaves: 'I can think of no man living, who looks at the matter without prejudice, who can be of the opinion that the negroes will be in a better state after emancipation than they are at present.' He even refused to think that the Middle Passage was 'a period of misery; now one half of the evidence shews it to be very different'.*[32]

Grenville, in the Lords, percipiently asked, 'Can we flatter ourselves that the mischief which [the slave trade] has created will not be remembered for many ages, to our reproach?' He piously hoped that 'we shall never be the objects' of slavery. He also thought that 'we are really inexcusable' for not having abolished the trade long before. He pointed out that the trade was the worse because it was 'not founded in necessity'. Those who justified the slave trade said that the Africans had condemned the men to be slaves: by that assertion, 'we are made the executioners of the inhuman cruelties of the inhabitants of Africa'.[33]

Grenville as Prime Minister then felt able, in January 1807, by a most curious chance the same month as the Congress of the United States took its similar step, to introduce a bill for full abolition in the Lords. This stated that the trade was 'contrary to the principles of justice, humanity and sound policy'. In his speech on the second reading, Grenville spoke of the trade as not only detestable but 'criminal' – an interesting adjective for a prime minister to use in relation to something which had been

---

* *Of Rose at his death, John William Ward wrote, 'I had grown accustomed to him in the House of Commons just as one grows accustomed to an old, clumsy, ill-contrived piece of furniture.'*

supported by governments of Britain for many generations. Since he was a peer, he had to initiate the bill in the House of Lords; but, given the past hostility of that house to abolition, that arrangement was perhaps as well. His bill declared that 'all manner of dealing and trading in the purchase, sale, barter or transfer of slaves . . . on, in, at, to or from any part of the coast of Africa' be prohibited. The envisaged punishments were similar to those specified in the United States: a malefactor would in future have to pay £100 for every slave found on board, as well as suffer the confiscation of the ship concerned. Grenville argued that abolition was necessary to ensure the survival of the older Caribbean colonies: 'Are they not now distressed by the accumulation of produce on their hands, for which they cannot find a market? And will it not be adding to their distress . . . if you suffer the continuation of further importations?'[34]

There was, of course, still opposition: not only from the Duke of Clarence, but also from Lords Westmorland, St Vincent (at that time in command of the Channel Fleet), and Hawkesbury, of whom the first, furious at Wilberforce, said, with too much candour for comfort, that many of the noble lords owed their seats in that upper house to the slave trade. Hawkesbury wanted to suppress the words 'contrary to the principles of justice [and] humanity' in the text of the bill, and simply leave 'contrary to sound policy' as the theme. One royal duke, that of Gloucester, a liberal and old acquaintance of Wilberforce's, spoke in favour of abolition (he later became President of the Africa Institution).[35] The bill passed (100 to 34), and then went to the Commons. There Sir Charles Pole, Groom of the Bedchamber to the Duke of Clarence, an admiral, said that the 'immediate abolition of the slave trade would be the most barbarous proceeding even to the negro himself'. He spoke as Member of Parliament for Plymouth, a port which had scarcely taken part in the slave trade, but the naval tradition there was strong. T. W. Plummer, Member for Yarmouth in the Isle of Wight ('little Bacchus Plummer', according to the diarist Creevey), who had been in shipping – his firm was the agent for Lady Holland's Jamaican plantation – said that he was as much an advocate of liberty as any man, but thought it was dangerous to propagate such ideas 'among a people so unintelligent and so easily provoked to revolt as the negroes'. A new London member, George Hibbert, Chairman of the West India Dock, Member for Seaford, who had once traded in slaves himself and had property in Jamaica, insisted that more acts of cruelty occurred every week in London than in a month in Jamaica. Thomas Hughan, Member for Dundalk, and one of Ireland's few West Indian merchants, said that the bill was 'fraught with ruin to the colonies and to the empire'. William Windham, then Secretary for War and Colonies, was the only member of the administration who opposed abolition; he said that it was not the time to embark 'on such a dangerous experiment'. John Fuller, Member for Sussex, one of the richest and most boisterous county members, who had opposed abolition continually, said, 'We might as well say, "Oh, we will not have our chimney swept, because it is a little troublesome to the boy."' Despite such trenchant, candid opposition, the bill passed on 23 February by 283 to 16, for the first time with a large number of members voting. The final debate was remarkable for an elegant comparison by Sir Samuel Romilly between Napoleon and Wilberforce; at the end of it, the whole house rose to give the latter unprecedented applause. He deserved it: Wilberforce's achievement is one of the most remarkable examples of the triumph of an individual statesman on a major philanthropic issue, and at the same time one more reminder that individuals can make history.[36]

The bill received royal assent on 25 March. The trade was to be illegal from 1 May 1807.

There was, of course, discomfiture among the slave traders: for example, in Africa itself, Tucker and Gudgeon, on the River Sherbro; Crundell and Mason on the Gallinas; William Peel in Bullam; Goss in the Plantaines; and J. N. Dolz in Havana – not to speak of the Andersons, who had succeeded Richard Oswald and his friends as proprietors of Bence Island, opposite the estuary of the Sierra Leone. The African kings with whom the English had dealt so long could not believe the news: resentment on the Gold Coast even led to riots. Was not the slave trade the mainstay of Dahomey, Bonny, and Lagos, to say the least? The Atlantic slave trade had shaped too many African societies for the staple article in commerce to be so easily dropped overnight. The King of Bonny told Captain Hugh Crow of Liverpool in 1807, 'We think that this trade must go on. That is the verdict of our oracle and the priests. They say that your country, however great, can never stop a trade ordained by God himself.'[37]

Many ordinary petitions were also laid against this decision of the legislature of the world's largest slave trader: for example, one from Joseph Marryat, member of Parliament for Horsham, a substantial West Indies merchant and father of 'Captain Marryat', the novelist. But they were to no avail: 30 April 1807 was the last date when a slaver legally sailed from a British port; and all the Duke of Clarence, the future King William IV, could do was complain, 'Lord Grenville, at one blow, destroys . . . the maritime strength of the nation.'[38]

James de Wolf, 'Captain Jim', also took a last slave voyage to Africa in 1807 in his ship the *Andromache* and then, foreseeing the likely ruin which would come to his town once slaving was abolished, invested his fortune in the Arkwright textile mills to the north of Providence.

It was widely supposed, since the British and the United States agreed about the matter, and since recent victories in war had given Britain control of so much of the Atlantic and the Caribbean, that the slave trade as such would soon be brought to an end. Grenville had said as much when introducing his motion to abolish the trade: 'Did not the noble lord [Eldon] see that, if we gave up the trade, it was not possible for any other state, without our permission, to take it up? Did we not ride everywhere unrivalled on the ocean?'[39] The eloquent Henry Brougham, now moving to the centre of the political stage, which he would often dominate, had argued in 1803 that, since 'we have been the chief trader, I mean the ringleaders in the crime', it was to be expected that British abolition would lead to imitation by other states.[40] Alas, many tears were still to be shed, as some English opponents of abolition had anticipated, before the aspiration contained in those fine words could be fulfilled.

Book Six

THE ILLEGAL ERA

28

I SEE . . . WE HAVE NOT YET BEGUN THE GOLDEN AGE

'I see clearly that we have not yet begun the golden age.'

A Tuscan diplomat, after the failure of the plans for suppressing the slave trade, at the conference of Aix-la-Chapelle, 1818

THE CONFUSION IN AFRICA after the abolition of the slave trade by Britain and the United States was considerable. In 1820 the King of Ashanti asked a British official, Dupuis, why the Christians did not want to buy slaves any more. Was their God not the same as that of the Muslims, who continued to buy, kidnap, and sell slaves just as they had always done? Since the Koran accepted slavery, some Muslims even persuaded themselves that the new Christian behaviour was an attack on Islam.

Further, French, Portuguese, and even Spanish traders still acted as if they thought that slavery was ordained by God, just as the Anglo-Saxons had done up till 1807; though, of course, in the Napoleonic Wars, the first was an enemy of Britain, while the other two were formally allies.

It was years before these African attitudes began to change. There were, after all, more slaves in Africa in 1807 than in the Americas, even though there were also many more gradations of enslavement in the former continent. Mungo Park, travelling in Senegambia, had thought that 'labour is universally performed by slaves',[1] i.e. that territory, and guessed that 'three-quarters of the population were slaves'. Probably slaves had constituted three-quarters of West African exports in the eighteenth century. 'The slave trade has been at all times popular and is now', commented an English businessman, John Hughes, after a visit to Cacheu-Bissau, or Portuguese Guinea, in 1828, adding, 'I believe that every native African . . . would indulge in the slave trade if allowed to do so.'[2]

In the region of the Rivers Sénégal and Gambia, much political power lay with the slave soldiers, the so-called *ceddo*, of the local aristocracies, who had from the early eighteenth century themselves gained wealth from selling slaves. The abolition of the Anglo-Saxon section of the European slave trade caused increased activity on the part of the *ceddo*, anxious to take advantage of what might seem the last days of the European interest in slaves; and the phenomenal rise, in the region of Senegambia, of the power of mullahs, at the expense not only of the *ceddo* but of noblemen and the temporal power, partly derived from the collapse of the European traffic. (These mullahs were at least as interested in slaving as their predecessors.) On the other hand, the emerging Sokoto caliphate in the Hausa city states, a Sunni enterprise in the north of what is now Nigeria, had for a time been hostile to the Atlantic slave trade. One leader there seems to have offered himself as a kind of 'Muslim Wilberforce' to Africa in an attempt to stop the enslavement of free Muslims. But that prophet limited himself to saving his co-religionaries and anyhow he soon gave way to more traditional individuals, for whom slave trading and slave raiding were normal activities sanctioned by time and the Koran. The Hausa slave trade continued inland unabated, and about a quarter of the population of the caliphate may have been slaves at the end of the nineteenth century. Among the Ashanti, the most powerful of the kingdoms in Guinea, every man of property had slaves even if, since there were no plantations, their condition was more like being a member of 'a family of friends'. The labouring people were still 'mostly slaves' in the 1840s. 'Many of the chiefs possess . . . many thousands of slaves', remarked the Reverend John Beecham, a Methodist missionary in the Gold Coast in 1843.[3] Slaves were still sacrificed at the death of kings in West Africa, often in a dramatic fashion, and in the kind of numbers which would have earned the approval of the ancient Mexica: perhaps 1,000 or more on the occasion of the death of the King of Ashanti in 1824. Slaves dominated the military in certain kingdoms. Even in European settlements, 'castle slaves' who had worked in the forts, including those in Cape Coast, remained, receiving payments till they died: they had only rarely been subjected to the indignity of being shipped to the New World. In Dahomey, a French visitor thought that two-thirds of the population were slaves: a statement which admittedly loses much of its force if it be realized that some argued that the inhabitants of Dahomey were legally 'all slaves to the King'.[4]

Further along the coast, in the delta of the Niger, most of the population seem to have been of slave descent. 'There are not ten free people in Bonny', a British businessman, J. A. Clegg, would tell a House of Lords select committee in 1843; and he continued: 'At one time, there was not a chief in Bonny who was not a slave trader.' These slaves had attained their status by climbing within the curious system of 'houses', or associations of families, which remained the most important social authority in the delta. Inland, the Aros, the economic dictators of the region, were continuing to exploit their influence effectively and were reluctant to abandon the commerce which had brought them such riches. Slaves were for them, as for innumerable Africans, the main capital asset. Abolition by

Britain brought for many in the Gulf of Guinea a fall in income, particularly for those who had depended on the tolls paid by African slavers and merchants, as well as the original enslavers, all the way up the rivers which had been the old routes of the traffic. Aristocracies often lost, with abolition, their only source of income.

A British trader, Francis Swanzy, recalled in 1843, 'As soon as a man had made a little money he bought a slave; the people expended much money on the acquirement of slaves, which gave them power'; while a French traveller, René Caillé, thought about 1820 that a peasant's first aspiration was to own ten to fifteen slaves.[5]

The abolition of the British slave trade and the subsequent efforts of the British to ensure that other Europeans followed their example made available for domestic African economies many slaves who would otherwise have been exported to the Americas. In the region of upper Guinea the masters employed more and more slaves to farm the goods approved of by the English as the 'legitimate trade', such as palm and cola nuts. The number of footloose slaves in West Africa even became a threat to established rulers and, just as slaves were held originally to have helped the development of states, they now assisted their disintegration; for example, in the Oyo empire, slave soldiers of northern origin came together under the flag of an Islamic jihad and hastened the demise of that power.

The slave trade from black Africa across the Sahara to the southern Mediterranean and Egypt continued after 1808 as it had throughout the era of the Atlantic trade. This accounted about 1800 for something in the region of 2,000–3,000 captives a year, which probably expanded after 1820 to at least 8,000. The Oyo in 1810, before their fall, invaded the Mahi country to their east and brought back 20,000 slaves for sale at Lagos, and some of these went north across the Sahara, not west to the Americas. The slaves exported to North Africa continued to include a substantial minority of much sought after and expensive eunuchs, favoured as civil servants throughout the Muslim world in the nineteenth century. In the internal areas most affected by the Sahara trade merchants might refuse in the 1820s to accept payment for goods in anything but slaves, who therefore became something like a currency around Bornu, near Lake Chad. Al-Nasiri, a Moroccan historian of distinction, complained of 'the unlimited enslavement of blacks, and the importation of many droves of them every year, for sale in the town and county markets of the Mahgreb, where men traffic them like beasts'.[6]

To the south, in the Portuguese (and, before 1792, French) zones of Loango, Congo, and Angola, the slave trade continued after 1808 with if anything greater intensity: for the traders there began to fear that the British might use their superior naval power in order to insist on the end of the trade, so it seemed necessary to stock up with slaves while that was still possible.

The British House of Commons rebuked the committee of the still-surviving Company of Merchants Trading to Africa for failing to convince Africans that abolition was for the good of the local population. The committee replied, not unfairly: 'Can the wildest theorist expect that a mere act of the British legislature should, in a moment, inspire ... [the] unenlightened [sic] natives of the vast continent of Africa, and persuade them, nay more, make them practically believe and feel that it is for their interest to contribute to, or even to acquiesce in, the destruction of a trade not inconsistent with their prejudices, their laws, or their notions of morality and religion, and by which alone they have been hitherto accustomed to acquire wealth and purchase all the foreign luxuries and conveniences of life?'[7]

Western European philanthropists talked much of persuading Africans to exchange the slave trade for other commerce. The charter of the newly founded Africa Institution, whose first president was the abolitionist Duke of Gloucester,* made evident that it aimed at 'diffusing useful knowledge and exciting industry among the inhabitants'. But when people tried to put the ideas of the institution into effect in Africa itself, they seemed a challenge to the existing order. Captain James Tuckey, an Irish-born geographer, during a journey 'to solve the problem of the Congo' on the river of that name in 1816, wrote baldly: 'The native merchants do not wish Europeans to penetrate into the country lest they should interfere with their business.'[8]

How could the peoples of West Africa who had been used to selling slaves to Anglo-Saxons build a new life? Dealing in salt was one possibility, a trade surviving indeed from the pre-Portuguese era: Captain John Adams, writing in the late eighteenth century, described how at Warri, inland on the River Forcados, 'neptunes, or large brass pans, are used during the dry season for purposes of evaporating sea-water to obtain its salt ... and a great trade is carried on in this article with the interior of the country'.[9] But Europeans did not want African salt, so it could not be a real rival to the trade in slaves.

More promising was palm oil, especially from the territory just behind the delta of the Niger, in which trade the towns along the Rivers Bonny and Calabar would eventually play as big a part as they previously had with respect to slaves. Palm oil also was produced in the eastern part of the Gold Coast by the Akuapem people, who had been known as farmers in the days of the slave trade. It had been in use in Benin when the Europeans reached there in the fifteenth century, and in the 1520s Portuguese sailors had been allowed to bring back a duty-free allowance of it of two jars apiece on their slaving voyages.

---

* *Known in the royal family as 'Silly Billy', presumably because he was enlightened; the first Secretary of the Africa Institution was the zealous ex-Governor of Sierra Leone, Zachary Macaulay.*

The most important use of palm oil in 1800 was soap; and, after that, candles. In Africa it was also made into a kind of gin (in the Gold Coast, when the question was asked whence came the capital used in the cocoa business, 'palm oil and gin' was the usual answer). Palm oil was, too, an essential ingredient for lubricants. The coming of railways and other new machinery in the nineteenth century in Europe and North America caused an increase in demand for produce on a large scale. The industrial revolution relied on this African export far more than it had on slaves.

Some of the Liverpool merchants who had been busy with slaves until 1807 made a remarkable transition to this business: among them, the Aspinall brothers; George Case, Gregson's partner in the owner-ship of the *Zong*; Jonas Bold, whose brother Edward was a pioneer in trading palm oil in the Benin River; and, above all, John Tobin, whose family were pioneers of Old Calabar. Tobin and Horsfall imported 450 tons of palm oil to England in 1807; in 1830, 4,000. Since the average price was £14 per ton in Calabar, and £28 in England, the profits began to be as high as they had been in the slave trade. The method of trading, too, was similar, to begin with, to what had happened in connection with slaves: textiles, iron bars, muskets, alcohol (especially rum), *manilla* bracelets, and cowries were all exchanged for the raw material. The irony was that many palm-oil groves were tended by slaves. European philanthropists thought that that labour force would eventually be substituted for by wage earners. But that liberal, or capitalist, alternative took several generations to develop.

Another possibility for 'legal trade' was gum, especially from acacia trees along the sandy north of the River Sénégal. That product, sought after in all Europe, had already brought in for the region of that waterway half what the slave trade had done in the 1790s; by 1820, before effective French abolition of the slave trade, it was already equal in value to the trade in slaves.

Hides and beeswax were an equivalent to gum on the River Gambia, and by the 1820s those products too exceeded in value the income from slaves. Ivory, gold, rice, timber (especially camwood), pepper, peanuts (later to play a great part in the valley of the Sénégal), and rice were other old African items of commerce which were renewed.

Yet though the King of Bonny might sell palm oil to his newly moral-istic old British friends, he was quite ready to continue to sell slaves to the Portuguese; indeed, to anyone who would buy them. Hugh Crow, one of the last Liverpool captains to go legally to West Africa – in 1807, with Thomas Aspinall's *Kitty Amelia*, to carry 400 slaves to the West Indies – was told by the King of Bonny (in Crow's customarily condescending rendering of the statement): 'We tink trade no stop, for all we Ju-ju man tell we so'. The King of Dahomey sent an ambassador to the Vice-royalty of Brazil in 1810 to reassure his customers that for his part the traffic would be maintained.[10]

He need not have worried. For the Governor of Bahia had had a clear instruction from Lisbon that 'it is far from being the royal intention to restrict this commerce in any way. On the contrary, the royal authorities wish to promote and facilitate it in the best way possible.' The Bishop of Pernambuco, José Joaquim da Cunha, had in 1808 denounced the 'insidious principles of a sect of philosophers' concerned to preach abolition; he went on to insist that 'the commerce of slavery is a law dictated by circumstances to barbarous nations'.[11] Thereafter, several African kings found it convenient to have informal embassies in Brazil, directed, to be sure, by persons of Portuguese blood, to ensure the smooth working of the trade in the new circumstances. The long-standing exchange of slaves for third-rate tobacco between Bahia and the 'coast of Mina' continued: 8,000 slaves were carried from the latter coast to Bahia in exchange for tobacco in 1807 alone; in 1810 Rio recorded its largest annual import of slaves, 18,677, in forty-two ships.

So, despite the high-minded efforts of the British, and despite the numerous acts of emancipation, soon to be introduced in some of the newly independent Latin American countries, the number of African slaves in the Americas in 1822 was probably twice what it had been in, say, 1780. Adam Smith's contention in The Wealth of Nations that slavery was an uneconomic system had been widely read, but it was also almost everywhere rejected. In Brazil, as in Africa, wage labour was not generally available, and slave-powered agriculture seemed to prosper.

It therefore became appreciated soon after 1808 in London, if less so in Washington, that the abolition of the trade in slaves would be incomplete unless the British and American acts of 1807 were followed by similar denunciations in the other slave-trading countries. Since they had abolished the slave trade themselves, it was scarcely in British interests to allow their commercial rivals to stock their colonies with slaves. That country's diplomats, therefore, set about trying to convince other governments that they, too, should abolish their slave trades, in the hope that, eventually, that would lead to an end to slavery itself in the respective empires. A long crusade, usually misunderstood by other peoples, thus began.

The abolitionists, whether they were in power (and many in Britain were now inside the administration, as civil servants, if not as ministers) or whether they were still acting as a pressure group outside the government, faced three major challenges: first, one from Portugal, and her empire in Brazil; second, one from Spain, and her American empire, which in 1807 still seemed, from Mexico to Chile, unchanged and loyal; and, third, one from the United States. The war with France had for the moment put paid to the slave trade of the latter country, while the other European countries constituted lesser problems. Britain herself was the most law-abiding of nations in the early nineteenth century, so that when the act condemning the trade was passed the business generally closed. But there was still some small-scale trading, and some indirect connections which would give rise to concern.

Brazil was still the main market for slaves from Africa, as had generally been the case since the late sixteenth century, except for the second half of the eighteenth, when she had been overtaken by the clients of Britain. Half the population of the huge colony were slaves (nearly 2,000,000 out of about about 4,000,000 in 1817). Slaves performed much of the productive work, working in mines, on sugar and coffee plantations, carrying sacks full of the produce of those enterprises to ships, and also acting as servants in the grand houses of the rich, as water carriers, or carrying their masters and mistresses, or merely escorting them along the ill-lit streets. The import of slaves was the most important part of Rio de Janeiro's international trade, and accounted for a third of all commerce. Masters still believed that their supply of slaves needed constant replenishment, for the low birthrate continued as a result of the traditional, and deliberately contrived, shortage of women (two women to eight men at best were imported). In 1817, a British traveller, H. M. Brackenridge, reported once again that the natural increase of blacks was discouraged 'from the calculation that it was cheaper to import full-grown slaves than to bring up young ones'.[12]

Slavery still existed everywhere throughout the Spanish empire. But by now the old nerve centres of that colossal enterprise, the Viceroyalties of Mexico and Peru, as well as the lesser territories of Chile and Argentina, employed more indigenous Indian labour than black slaves (10 per cent only of the Mexican population was black or mulatto in 1810, and most of them were free; if a quarter of the population of Buenos Aires were black in 1810, Chile had only 5,000 black slaves all told). The only large employers of slaves in 1810 in the Spanish empire were the Cubans, followed by the Venezuelans (as they were soon to be).

Cuba had many things in common with Brazil. A lenient attitude to manumission, in both places, had made possible the rise of large free black populations. The colonists of both territories considered a substantial slave population essential for the economy. Both colonies depended economically on European countries whose national identities were protected during the Napoleonic Wars by Britain. But Cuba's slave population was still small: a mere 200,000 in 1817, compared with Brazil's 2,000,000. Cuba was an island, if a large one. That fact of geography dominated its history, as the historian Michelet would unsubtly emphasize with respect to Britain. ('L'Angleterre, c'est un île,' he would tell successive generations of students in Paris.)

Thirdly, though Cuba was every year more prosperous, this 'pearl of the Antilles' was nouveau riche, in comparison with Brazil, which had been receiving immense numbers of slaves from across the Atlantic for several centuries and had specialized in sugar even in the days of Philip II. By contrast, Cuba had until the eighteenth century primarily constituted a depot for Spanish treasure fleets.

Yet the most important product in Cuba was now sugar. Before the 1770s planters in Cuba had neglected their opportunities for its production, though the soil was as suitable for its cultivation as that of Jamaica or Saint-Domingue; and there was much more land. Still, by 1788, Cuba was already producing about 14,000 tons a year. By 1825 that figure had trebled to over 40,000 tons, grown on about 2,000 plantations. Soon Cuba would be exporting more sugar than all the other islands of the Caribbean put together – an increase made possible by the ceaseless growth in demand for the product in the United States and Europe; and this sugar was grown on slave-powered plantations.

As for Venezuela, the great landowners, the Uztarizes, the Toros, and the Tovares, the families who made money in the place, still needed slaves for their plantations of cacao in the beautiful valleys of Caracas and Aragua. In 1800 the slave population had admittedly been under 10 per cent of the total population, but, then, the *criollos*, or whites born in the New World, could only have been about 20 per cent; the rest were mulattos, or free blacks. All the same, the landowners remained the masters of the colony, and Humboldt commented that these men were conservative in politics simply because 'they believed that, in any revolution, they would run the risk of losing their slaves'.[13] They had, after all, vivid memories of recent slave revolts, such as one in their own country which in 1795 had proclaimed 'the law of the French Republic', had caused much destruction, and had even led to the temporary occupation by rebel slaves of the town of Coro, on the coast opposite Curaçao.

Another problem facing abolitionists after the Act of 1807 was the United States. The trade was prohibited. Several later acts of Congress refined the definition of the crime and toughened the penalties. But it was not till 1862, in the time of President Lincoln, that anyone was executed for the offence; in the meantime the United States enjoyed a modest illegal international trade in slaves for fifty years.

This mostly flowed through Texas (part of the Spanish empire till 1821, then of Mexico till 1835, and independent till 1846), Florida (Spanish till 1818), and South Carolina. In Florida, in particular, slaves could easily, and legally, be landed at Pensacola and then shipped up the Escambia River into Alabama, or escorted by land into Georgia. Baltimore shipbuilding firms such as Samuel and John Smith, William van Wyck, John Hollins, and Stewart and Plunkett were still involved after 1808, as they had been before, in building ships for the trade and buying slaves in the West Indies. Underwriters in Boston still insured slave ships: thus N. P. Russell wrote to Messrs J. Perkins in 1810: 'At your particular request, I have offered to the underwriters in my office the two African risks, viz: the *San Francisco de Asis* and the schooner *Carlota*. . . .'[14] Some Rhode Island slave merchants, including members of the de Wolf family, continued as such: (General) George de Wolf, not his uncle, James, was the biggest shipper in these illegal days though he was concerned principally to import slaves into Cuba, not the United States. He celebrated his new wealth by building a magnificent house, with Corinthian columns and Palladian windows, Linden Place, in Bristol, Rhode Island. In Providence in the same state in 1816 an unidentified correspondent wrote to Obadiah Brown, philanthropist and pioneer of cotton manufacture, saying: 'The impunity with which prohibited trade is carried on from this place has for some time past rendered it the resort of many violators of commercial law. . . . The African slave trade is one of this description now most successfully and extensively pursued.'[15] The truth is still concealed by deliberately contrived confusion. For example, in late 1809, the Africa Institution of London reported the coast of West Africa to be 'swarming' with ships flying Spanish flags which derived from the United States. The Smiths of Newport, not to speak of Francis Depan and Broadfoot of Charleston, as well as John Kerr of New York, all seemed to be implicated. So, judging from a letter written by James de Wolf of Bristol to his brother John, was the well-known merchant Samuel Parkman of Boston: 'I learn that Parkman of Boston sends you a schooner to Bristol [Rhode Island] to be outfitted for an expedition to the eastward, and that you have refused to have anything to do with her, which, in my opinion, is a very proper determination of yours.'[16]

On 11 January 1811 the United States Secretary of the Navy, Paul Hamilton (himself a slave owner and planter who had earlier urged the legislature of South Carolina to abolish the slave trade), wrote to Captain Campbell, the naval commander at Charleston: 'I hear, not without great concern, that the law prohibiting the import of slaves has been violated in frequent instances at [the port of] St Mary's [Georgia], since the gunboats have been withdrawn. . . . Despatch them [the gunboats] to St Mary's with orders to use all practical diligence';[17] and President James Madison, whose opposition to the slave trade had been continual, if occasionally tactical, told Congress, in his message of 10 December of that year: 'It appears that American citizens are [still] instrumental in carrying on a traffic in enslaved Africans, equally in violation of the laws of humanity and those of their own country.' He added: 'The same just and benevolent motives which produced the interdiction by force against the criminal conduct will doubtless be felt by Congress in devising further means of suppressing the evil.'[18] 'Doubtless' turned out to be rather a strong word in the circumstances. Sometimes, it is true, a slaver would be caught by an enterprising customs officer (such as the *Eugene*, captured off New Orleans), but its disposal was another matter.

Louisiana, newly acquired from France, was an especially difficult problem: Governor William Claiborne was quite unable to enforce the abolition of the trade in slaves, and dealing with the smuggling of them 'proved to be one of the most troublesome problems in the administration of the prohibitory legislation'.[19]

As for South Carolina, as early as 1804 Representative William Lowndes of that state said: 'With navigable rivers running into the heart of it [the state], it was impossible, with our means, to prevent our eastern brethren [that is, New Englanders] who, in some parts of the Union in defiance of the general government, have been engaged in this trade, from introducing them [slaves] into this country.'[20] Several other states of the Union, such as North Carolina, had always been dependent on slaves brought in by land (mostly from South Carolina), not by water, so there are no entries recorded in the books of the customs.

The United States Slave Trade Act of 1807 only prohibited the international slave trade. It condemned neither the internal nor the coastal traffic. There was no limit to the number of slaves who could be so traded, nor any regulation as to the way they should be carried. The size of this commerce was large: slaves were carried either by sea or, more often, by land, to New Orleans or Charleston, and there sold to shippers who might take them elsewhere in the United States or even (illegally) to Cuba. Thus the *Virginia Times* would boast in 1836 that 40,000 slaves had been sold for export the previous fiscal year. The journey from Virginia to the market in New Orleans might take as many days as the Middle Passage from Africa.

The mention of Virginia raises an interesting subject. From the beginning of agriculture there in the seventeenth century proprietors on tobacco plantations had, as has been pointed out, increased their stock of labour from home-bred slaves without excessive recourse to the international market. By 1800 slaves on some plantations were being deliberately bred there for sale. The idea had often been practised in the West Indies (for example, in Jamaica and on the estates of the Society for the Propagation of the Gospel) and in Portugal as an alternative to the slave trade. The Gadsdens of Charleston, the Campbells of New Orleans, and Nathan Bedford Forrest of Memphis were the outstanding names in this new business, but there were others, in Alexandria, Savannah, and Richmond, though most of them saw the breeding of slaves as an incidental, rather than a dominating, business.

The United States was more successful in producing slaves by natural increase than any other slave-employing society in the Americas. Was this because special attention was coldly paid to 'breeding women', to those who were 'uncommonly good breeders'? Did some Virginian slave owners realize that slave children were, as it were, a return on capital which could increase their wealth? The testimony is slight and a little tainted: Richard Drake described seeing such a breeding farm near Alexandria, Virginia, but no one has been able to decide on the reliability of his vivid account of thirty pregnant women and the huts swarming 'with piccaninnies of different shades'.[21] The argument that female slaves would have more children if well treated had been often used during the debates on abolition; for example, Captain Thomas Wilson, of the British navy, who had had experience of both the West Indies and mainland America, did so in evidence to the House of Commons in London in 1790: 'I always thought them [the slaves of North America] better treated and clothed – they appeared more domestic and happy – marriages are more frequent among them – there are fewer imported in proportion.'[22]

The concern whether a slave population could be maintained by breeding was still a consideration of the abolitionists after the 1790s; though, usually, the answer which they received to their questions about the West Indies was of the order of 'I understood from one planter to whom I spoke on the subject that the slaves in general were too hard-worked to breed.'[23] Dr Harrison, a doctor who, like Captain Wilson, had experience in both Jamaica and the North American colonies (before 1778), explained, 'In South Carolina, the slaves were well fed, well clothed, less worked and never severely whipped; in Jamaica, they were badly fed, indifferently clothed, hard worked, and severely whipped.' In Brazil, 'the Portuguese do not hesitate to tell you that it does not pay them to breed slaves, and bring them up, as the woman is kept away from her usual duties for so many years that it would not remunerate them for loss of time, and the cost of feeding them. Besides that, the mortality among children is said to be great.'[24] Later, with the coffee boom in Brazil after the 1830s, that attitude would change, since 'children of a very tender age can go and pick coffee'. But even then, J. B. Moore, the Chairman of the Brazilian Association of Liverpool, said that he was not 'aware of any distinct establishment [in Brazil] for the breeding and sale of home-grown slaves'.[25]

In 1790 slavery in North America, as opposed to North American participation in the slave trade to Cuba and elsewhere, seemed to be in decline. But Eli Whitney's fateful invention of the cotton gin, on Mrs Nathanael Greene's plantation at Savannah, Georgia, during the spring of 1793, and the realization that with this removal of the great hindrance hitherto to the large-scale cultivation of cotton (the taking of the lint from the seeds) 'one negro could produce fifty pounds of cleaned cotton a day', was already transforming the position. The figures are remarkable if well known; in 1792, the year before Whitney's invention, the United States exported a mere 138,328 pounds of cotton, which placed it on the same level as a producer as Demerara (Guiana); in 1794, already, the figure had leapt to 1,601,000; in 1800 it exported 17,790,000; and in 1820 cotton exports reached 35,000,000 pounds.

This triumph, depending on the cultivation on a large scale of green seed-cotton in Georgia and the Carolinas, marked the conversion of this crop into the most important item in North American exports, and caused an unprecedented demand for slaves; especially women, since it was supposed that the sensitive harvesting of cotton demanded female labour.

This latter perception had demographic consequences. In 1790 there were only 500,000, well-acclimatized slaves in the United States, most of them of the second or third generation. Between 1800 and 1810 slaves within the United States increased by a third, and there was an increase of nearly another third in the next ten years, to 1820. By 1825 the slaves in the United States numbered over a third of all slaves in the Americas. This trend would continue. But the slave trade into the United States was tiny. Why should the smallest slave importer have the largest slave population? The reason for the increase in slaves in North America must have been linked to the use of female slaves on the cotton plantations.

United States shippers continued to provide slaves to Cuba and other parts of the Spanish empire and also, though in smaller numbers, to Brazil. In 1807, for example, in the nine months for which the record survives, thirty-five United States ships entered Havana, out of a total of thirty-seven (the other two were technically 'Danish'). The fact that the licence to foreigners to import slaves into Cuba ended in 1810 mattered little: the appropriate officials in Spain considered what should be done, and some of them (the Consulado of Cádiz, for example) expressed humane hopes, but with the country at war the best course seemed to be to do nothing; and in the meantime the trade to Cuba continued without impediment. The official returns for Havana list only five United States ships between 1808 and 1819.* But there were certainly others, under a variety of flags, and landing slaves in a variety of ports. In May 1808 Captain Madden's *Pitter* carried sixty-two to Matanzas, where Captain Wilbey delivered eighty-six in the *Venus* in February 1809. Numerous ships which sound by their name to have been Anglo-Saxon – for example, the *Rebecca*, under Captain Colquhoun, in March 1810; or Captain Beale's *Tripe* in June 1810 – were probably from the United States.

Continuing English involvement in the trade is more difficult to analyse. A few dealers established in West Africa or islands off the shores continued to play a part. Some English captains sailed under United States flags, and later under Swedish, Danish, and even French ones. More important, probably, several prominent firms participated in the trade after 1807 by investing in or even owning theoretically Spanish- or Portuguese-owned ships.† British sailors helped to teach Cuban-based

---

* *Captain Coburn's* Catalina, *carrying 103 slaves in November 1810; Captain May-berry's* Eagle, *carrying only three slaves to Havana; Captain Dunbar's* Rosa *in June 1812, carrying 116 slaves; Captain Intoch's* American, *carrying twelve slaves; and Captain Perry's* Thistle, *in September 1819, bringing 698 slaves.*

† *For example, McDowal, Whitehead and Hibbert; M. R. Dawson; and Holland and Co., both of Liverpool; and Clark and Co. of London.*

Spaniards the tricks of the trade. Many English firms still supplied the 'trade goods' for slave voyages of Portuguese and Spanish ships. But most important English firms did drop out. They even abandoned the slave trade between the Caribbean islands.

The first move in the British policy of seeking to restrict the international traffic in slaves came as early as April 1807, when Lord Strangford, the British Minister in Lisbon,˙ sought to persuade Portugal to abolish the traffic; or at least to ensure that the Portuguese trade remained within its existing limits. The Portuguese Foreign Minister, Azevedo, however, thought that it was impracticable for his country to adopt any measures on the subject. Lord Strangford, the father of George Sydney Smythe, the model for Disraeli's Coningsby, should have known all about the slave trade, since his American-born mother was a Philipse of New York, a great-granddaughter of a famous merchant in slaves, Frederick Philipse, of a hundred years before; but perhaps the significance of that genealogy was hidden from him, for the family had recently been through many vicissitudes. Strangford had gone on, however, in August 1807, to persuade Dom João, the Regent of Portugal (his mother, Queen Maria, was mad), to reject Napoleon's ultimatum demanding that he close Portuguese ports to the English or be invaded. This defiant act led him and the Portuguese court, and a great number of businessmen, to sail in English ships to Brazil. Strangford had let it be known that England would 'occupy Brazil' if the royal family were to allow themselves to fall into the hands of Napoleon.

The change of residence was a great success for Brazil. The mere presence of the Regent and the court transformed Rio. No matter that the Regent himself was an easy-going and amiable bourgeois prince. Rio began to think of herself as a capital. From then on, all the trade which used to go to Lisbon went to Rio. A bank was founded in that city, not to speak of a mint and a public library, as well as a botanical garden and a new theatre. There were newspapers, and a Portuguese edition of *The Wealth of Nations*, with its scepticism about the value of slavery, was published. To cap the arrangements, the Regent agreed to sign, under the kind of courtly duress which diplomats from London could then inspire, a commercial treaty with Britain (giving that country a 'most-favoured nation' status, with a preferential tariff for her goods), as well as a treaty of alliance, by whose article 10 the Regent agreed to cooperate to ensure the 'gradual abolition of the slave trade'. Dom João also undertook that Brazil would thenceforth take slaves only from those parts of Africa which were already part of the Portuguese zone of influence. That meant

˙ *Described by Byron as*
> *Hibernian Strangford with thine eyes of blue*
> *And boasted locks of red or auburn hue.*

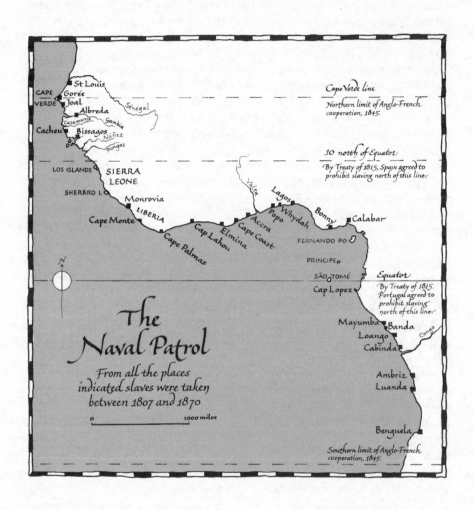

The
Naval Patrol

From all the places
indicated slaves were taken
between 1807 and 1870

0 _____ 1000 miles

St Louis
CAPE VERDE
Gorée
Joal
Albreda
Senegal
Casamance
Cacheu
Bissagos
Gambia
Núñez
Pongas
LOS ISLANDS
SIERRA
LEONE
SHERBRO I.
Monrovia
LIBERIA
Cape Monte
Cape Palmas
Cap Lahou
Elmina
Cape Coast
Accra
Popo
Whydah
Lagos
Bonny
Calabar
FERNANDO PO
PRINCIPE
SÃO TOMÉ
Cap Lopez
Mayumba
Banda
Loango
Cabinda
Ambriz
Luanda
Benguela
Volta
Congo

Cape Verde line
Northern limit of Anglo-French
cooperation, 1845.

10 north of Equator
By Treaty of 1815, Spain agreed to
prohibit slaving north of this line.

Equator
By Treaty of 1815,
Portugal agreed to
prohibit slaving
north of this line.

Southern limit of Anglo-French
cooperation, 1845.

that they could trade legally in Loango, Angola, and Mozambique, at São Tomé and Principe, and at Whydah but not at Lagos, where there was no Portuguese fixed presence. The treaty was in some respects vague: for example, there was no guarantee that Portugal, once re-established at home and at peace (if that were to happen), would legislate against the slave trade. For the time being, too, the increased quantity of British manufactured goods now brought into Brazil, legally, could continue to be used in the trade to Angola, and in exchange for slaves: a weakness in the schemes devised in London which the Foreign Office had overlooked. Whether the Regent envisaged that anything serious would come from his signature on the document is a matter for the imaginative novelist rather than for the historian: though he would not have known the figures, Dom João must have realized that, after his arrival, the import of slaves had increased in Brazil (from, say, 10,000 to 20,000 a year), a good business in which he himself is said to have invested.

With this treaty, meantime, the British demonstrated that almost overnight they had changed their international posture: from having been the great practitioners of the trade in slaves, they had become philanthropic opponents of it on moral grounds. The transformation puzzled all those with whom they came into contact. Opportunistic motives were naturally suspected. The French, the North Americans, and the Spaniards thought that the new British crusade was a way of consolidating their navy's command of the sea. For immediately after the passage of the bill prohibiting the slave trade a British West Africa Squadron was established to ensure the implementation of the law: to ensure first and foremost that no British captain, from any British port, traded slaves along 3,000 miles of African coast. The act of 1807 also permitted the seizure of pirates, and any vessels which carried false papers would automatically be judged pirates, at least according to English law.[*] A bounty of £60 per male, £30 per female, £10 per child would be paid by the Admiralty to naval officers and some other beneficiaries, including Greenwich Hospital, for every slave liberated (these rules meant that captains of slavers would never be indicted as pirates, because, had they been so, the bounties would not have been paid).

After the report of some transgressions by English merchants (for example, the discovery of the *Commercio del Rio*, a fully equipped Spanish slave ship, in the Thames), the penalties for breaking the law were made more severe. In 1811 a new bill, the consequence of more agitation by the abolitionists, steered through Parliament by the mercurial Henry Brougham, made slaving a felony, and punishable by transportation (to Australia) for fourteen years. Brougham instanced the ship *Neptune*

---

[*] *This would cause a lot of trouble later – for example, when, in 1816, the ship the* Nueva Amable, *carrying 388 slaves, was seized off Sierra Leone, as a French ship under the cover of false Spanish papers.*

which, as well as carrying wood and ivory from Africa, had taken thirteen slaves to the isle of Principe. Then the *George* was also observed setting off to carry slaves. The navy stopped a ship with 109 slaves, called the *Marqués Romano*, which turned out to be the Liverpool vessel *Prince William*. Other Spanish disguises were the *Galicia* and *Palafox*, in reality the *Queen Charlotte* and the *Mohawk*. The judges at Sierra Leone had found that over 1,000 slaves had been produced for emancipation at their court.[26]

This further legislation seems to have had a decisive effect on would-be British slavers. Transportation, after all, was tantamount to a life sentence. Few accusations of British slave trading were subsequently made, although surreptitious investment in the Spanish and Portuguese ships continued, and though British goods remained popular among slaving captains.*

The first British West Africa Squadron at first consisted of only two ships, the frigate *Solebay* (thirty-two guns, Commodore E. H. Columbine) and the sloop *Derwent* (eighteen guns, Lieutenant E. Parker). They made a trial journey to the West African coast in 1808. The two ships were small, slow, and incapable of restraining a multi-million-dollar commerce. Then in 1811, after the Anglo-Portuguese Treaty, which seemed to permit the use of naval power against Portuguese or Brazilian slavers plying between Brazil and Africa, a larger flotilla was dispatched, under Captain Frederick Irby, a veteran of Camperdown and the Glorious First of June. He had at his disposal the *Amelia* (thirty-eight guns), the *Ganymede* (twenty-four), the *Kangaroo* (sixeen), and the *Trinculo* (eighteen). His task continued difficult because both of the length of the coast which he had orders to supervise and of the ambiguity of the laws under which he was operating. Since the country was at war, Britain claimed the right to board and search the ships of all neutral and enemy nations: that included those of the United States as well as France. But the two largest slave shippers were then Spain and Portugal.

A story from one of Irby's voyages explains much. Having been told that forty-five Portuguese ships were loading slaves between Cape Palmas and Calabar, Irby set off from his headquarters at Sierra Leone just after Christmas 1811. On 31 December he met the Portuguese brig *São João*, full of slaves. Irby intercepted and sent her, with an escort on board, to Sierra Leone. A few days later, he met another Portuguese vessel, the *Bom Caminho*. She had no slaves on board, so she was released, even if Irby observed that she had recently bought two canoes, which (he

---

* *The continuing inadequacy of the law was, however, shown when the Governor of Sierra Leone arrested, and brought to trial, several factors established nearby who were clearly concerned in the slave trade, three of them English (Dunbar, Brodie, and Cooke). But the sentence of transportation was quashed on the ground that the court was unable to try the prisoners.*

believed) must have been intended for carrying slaves from Cape Coast to the ship. Irby reported this to the (British) Governor of Cape Coast, and warned him never to sell canoes again if they could be used for slaving. He continued to Whydah, where he saw three Portuguese brigs were openly trading for slaves. But since the Portuguese had a trading post there Irby could do nothing. A little further on, near Lagos, at Porto-Novo, the British found three more Portuguese ships, in the process of buying slaves. There was there no permanent Portuguese post, so he thought that he was entitled to seize them and sent them off, again with an escort of British officers on board, to Sierra Leone. Irby did the same at Lagos itself, again sending three ships to Sierra Leone, though leaving three others. After a brief stop at São Tomé, Irby returned to Sierra Leone.

These and similar actions caused fury among the Portuguese, though the captains of their merchant ships were quite unprepared to fight the navy of their ancient ally. But many ships of countries other than Portugal had left the ocean because of the continuing war; and their slavers for a time habitually used the Portuguese flag.

The colony of Sierra Leone, so long a centre of the trade, and the recently bankrupt philanthropic colony of a private company, now became the headquarters of Britain's anti-slaving activities. A prize court under the Admiralty had been set up at the new city of Freetown, on the estuary of the River Sierra Leone, with a judge and officials fully imbued with Wilberforcian ideals. It seemed for a time possible that, in this new role, Sierra Leone might, after all, become 'the cradle of African civilisation'. When a slave ship was captured, the naval officer concerned would send her there with a prize crew. If the vessel were condemned, as it almost always was, it would be confiscated and sold, and the slaves would be maintained at government cost for a year. After that, they had to shift for themselves, unless they volunteered to go to the British West Indies as apprenticed labourers. Almost all, however, remained in Sierra Leone, which thus became a microcosm of African tribal differences. The Governor of that colony, usually a retired naval officer, was at the same time made generally responsible for all British interests in West Africa.

It seemed to be an ideal solution. But difficulties began when Irby, acting as 'the new champion of the cause of humanity and justice', in Ambassador Strangford's words, or, in the new style of English 'global moralism', to use the French historian Pierre Verger's phrase, interpreted (or misinterpreted) parts of the Anglo-Portuguese Treaty as showing that Portugal considered the slave trade to be generally illegal. Irby and his captains captured twenty-four nominally Portuguese or Brazilian slave ships in four years, 1810–13, of which twelve came from Bahia. There were continuous outcries from Lisbon. The new Foreign Secretary, Lord Castlereagh, had to write to the Admiralty in May 1813 'to desire that your Lordships will be pleased to instruct His Majesty's cruisers not to molest Portuguese ships carrying slaves *bona fide* on the account and risk of Portuguese subjects from the ports of Africa belonging to the Crown of Portugal to the Brazils'. Irby and the prize court judges in Sierra Leone protested in turn. What was the former to do? The question was not soon to be answered. James Prior, of the navy, wrote, also in 1813, that all other considerations in Bahia faded 'into insignificance in comparison with the slave trade; Portugal and Spain, England and France, Wellington, Bonaparte, the Prince Regent can all vanish into the land of shades; what does it matter provided that their dear traffic, the subject of their dreams, day and night, can be maintained? This attachment, no power of reason can shake, only the argument of force can have any effect.'[27]

British naval captains had also to stand by if they saw ships from the United States at work on the African slave coast. The United States might have abolished the international slave trade, but it had no intention of allowing British naval officers to inspect its ships, criminal or no. Nor, for the time being, was it thinking of a naval patrol of its own off Africa.

There was a hectic anxiety about the slave trade in these years which contrasted with its stability before 1788. No one knew how long it would continue. Planters who had always used slaves now bought them at inflated prices, since they feared that they might not find any more. The problems worsened (for the slave users, that is) as several Latin American countries, anxious for British commerce, recognition, and protection, and themselves no longer dependent on the institution of slavery, hastened to abolish their slave trades. Britain, with a virtual monopoly over all tropical produce, then had the only navy which could intervene in every continent. Thus Brazil, Argentina, even Mexico and several other ex-Spanish colonies were her virtual dependencies: her Foreign Secretary in the 1820s, Canning, would candidly say, in 1824, 'Spanish America is free and, if we do not mismanage our affairs sadly, she is English.'[28]

Bolívar thought that abolition of slavery was the key to Spanish American independence, and liberated his own slaves. The Supreme Junta of Caracas, the first government of an independent Venezuela, abolished the trade in slaves in 1811; and in New Granada (Colombia) in 1812, the liberator Miranda promised freedom to any slave who would fight the Spaniards for ten years (scarcely a generous concession). In Buenos Aires, the first revolutionary triumvirate, in a rare lucid moment, in 1812, prohibited the slave trade in the grandiose terms to which their compatriots had become used, though a clandestine commerce continued for a few more years. (The liberator, San Martín, thought that, in his army, 'the best infantry soldier we have is the black and the mulatto'.[29]) His equivalent in Uruguay made a special appeal to blacks to rally round him, even calling on the slaves in Brazil to do the same. In Chile the Revolutionary Congress in 1811 agreed to a proposal by a humanitarian liberal, Manuel de Salas, to abolish the domestic slave trade – a proposal which aroused the old guard who, as elsewhere, thought that the measure would shake the social order; even though that was anyway shaky. Then Morelos, in

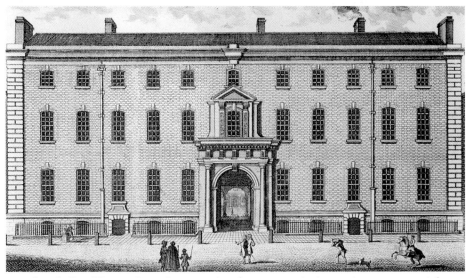

South Sea House. In quiet counting houses, as in imposing commercial edifices such as this headquarters of the South Sea Company, the slave trade was planned

Rochefort: in this French Atlantic harbour (depicted by Joseph Vernet for King Louis XV) copper pots and other cargoes were shipped to exchange for slaves in Africa

Above: The most important cargoes in the slave trade were cloths such as this 'indienne' made in Nantes in imitation of Indian textiles

Left: Metal, such as these copper bars, also figured substantially in the slave trade

Bottom left: Cowrie shells from the Maldive Islands in the Indian Ocean were a currency in West Africa. One slave might cost 25,000 of these. Here is a headdress made from the shells

The *Wanderer*: 'you'd think she could fly instead of sailing'. The last ship to bring slaves to North America (1859)

A typical Liverpool slave ship depicted on a plate

Above: Black captives like this Egyptian slave from Ethiopia were sought after in the Mediterranean from time immemorial

Right: A slave ship in the eighteenth century built for Pierre Rasteau of La Rochelle

In Africa, slaves were captured in raids, for both the Atlantic and trans-Saharan trade

Slaves were transported to the port or market in long marches lasting for weeks, as graphically described by Mungo Park *c.* 1790

Above: The brand of the Cadiz Company, *c.* 1768. 'G' is for Gaditano (the adjective for Cadiz); 'R' is for Rey, King

Right: Branding a slave, with the initials of the buyer *c.* 1820

Slaves being taken by canoe to Dutch ships, near Elmina

Above: Inside a slave cabin, *c.* 1815

Left: A rebel slave at bay, *c.* 1830

Captain Kimber sued Wilberforce when the latter talked of his activities
depicted in this cartoon *c.* 1790

What the captains most feared: a slave rebellion *c.* 1820

Death of Capt. Ferrer, the Captain of the Amistad, July, 1839.

Don Jose Ruiz and Don Pedro Montez, of the Island of Cuba, having purchased fifty-three slaves at Havana, recently imported from Africa, put them on board the Amistad, Capt. Ferrer, in order to transport them to Principe, another port on the Island of Cuba. After being out from Havana about four days, the African captives on board, in order to obtain their freedom, and return to Africa, armed themselves with cane knives, and rose upon the Captain and crew of the vessel. Capt. Ferrer and the cook of the vessel were killed; two of the crew escaped; Ruiz and Montez were made prisoners.

Above: The rebellion on the *Amistad* (1840) was one of the very few successful slave rebellions

Left: Sales of slaves were carefully registered. This shows a list of slaves imported into Havana in 1791

The Rua do Valongo in Rio de Janeiro, *c.* 1800, a notorious slave market

his rebellion in New Spain (Mexico), ordered all masters to free slaves within three days, and promised that such emancipated captives should have equality with Spaniards. But at that time there were few black slaves in the country; in any case, Morelos was soon defeated. Only in Cuba, as in Brazil, did a continuing demand for slaves seem to characterize the new era – and, partly for that reason, independence was delayed for nearly another century. Francisco de Arango, bewailing the decline in the introduction of slaves into Cuba in 1809 to a mere 1,162, insisted that no foreigner could provide Cuba on the scale which she required: 'All our hopes', he declared, 'centre on ourselves alone, and our entire attention must be directed to that end.'[30]

Ourselves alone, *nosotros solos!* The new leading merchants of Havana who dealt in slaves, mostly *peninsulares*[*] in origin, now led by Santiago de la Cuesta y Manzanal, Francisco Hernández, and Juan Magín Tarafa, with the support of the Governor, soon set about carrying out the suggestions of Arango. In 1809 they jointly dispatched a brigantine, the *San Francisco*, to London, with instructions to buy goods there which could be exchanged for slaves in Africa. Other ships followed: the *Zaragoza* went direct to Loango, the *Junta Central* to Calabar. The Intendant[†] of Havana, Juan de Aguilar, wrote to the Council of the Indies explaining how he was trying to encourage more direct journeys from Africa to Cuba, in Spanish ships, captained by Spaniards. Further, for all Arango's declaration of insular self-reliance, the Cuban slave dealers were in close touch with North American shipbuilders and merchants, in Baltimore and Philadelphia.[31]

But this new traffic brought Spain immediately into difficulty with the British, theoretically allies of Spain, just as the Portuguese–Brazilian commerce had done. The British Foreign Secretary had, in both 1808 and 1809, asked his representative in Spain to urge the desirability of a gradual abolition of the Spanish slave trade throughout the Spanish empire. Wilberforce also wrote to the Minister in Spain, the Marquis Wellesley, and they talked about the matter in 1810. But if in the capitals the British were diplomatic, at sea they were less so.

Thus in the two years 1809 and 1810, Irby and his naval patrol intercepted nine ships out of about twenty-four which left Cuba for Africa to seek slaves, and sent most of them to Sierra Leone, where they were declared prizes and sold off, their slaves being liberated there. Most British officers believed that the Spanish slave trade was carried on by non-Spaniards and that therefore these vessels were fair game. True, there

---

[*] *That is, men born in Spain. The tension between them and criollos, men and women born in the colony but of Spanish blood, constituted the main problem of the later Spanish empire, and explains the movement for independence.*
[†] *This was a new official established in Spain in imitation of a similar one in France, and transferred to the empire, in order to improve the efficiency of the administration.*

were some North Americans among the captains of these ships. But had not the United States abolished the trade as well as the English? So it was assumed that those accused would have to prove by their own laws that they were innocent. The Spanish Ambassador in London – Pedro Alcántara de Toledo, the Duke of Infantado, a friend of King Ferdinand VII – complained: the slave trade had not been abolished by Spanish law. A British tribunal could not cause British laws to apply to Spanish ships. The British government, triumphant in the long war, paid no attention. Her insensitivity to the national pride of a great nation fallen on hard times in the long run damaged the abolition cause.

The seizure of these ships was usually attended by a complex drama. Take, for example, the case of the brigantine *Hermosa Hija*, which belonged to Francisco Antonio Comas, of Havana. This vessel left Havana for Africa in 1810 and had almost returned again, with its cargo of several hundred slaves, when the British hired vessel *Dark*, under Captain James Wilkins, captured her. Wilkins put on board a prize crew and gave orders that the boat be taken to Sierra Leone. Within twenty-four hours the Spanish crew had mutinied and overthrown the British sailors, and for four days the ship was sailed back to Cuba. Then the British managed to recover control, and chaining both slaves and Spaniards set off again for Freetown. There the Spaniards were accused and condemned, not of slave trading but of the more serious crime of insurrection.

Cuban slave merchants had other difficulties than those presented to them by moralistic British naval officers. Once, one of their vessels was seized by Haitians, and the slaves were set free in that liberated but unfortunate country. The War of 1812 between Britain and the United States also made it legitimate for the British to seize ships with North American flags. But it also legalized privateering, and United States ships, including some owned by the de Wolfs of Bristol, captured British merchantmen. The traders in slaves often found themselves caught in the crossfire between the navies of the two Anglo-Saxon powers. The Caribbean was full of pirates in the early nineteenth century, no less brutal, if less picturesque, than those of the past. For example, a French corsair, Dominique You, in the barque *Superbe*, captured the United States ship *Juan*, with 134 slaves on board, belonging to Cuesta y Manzanal of Havana; another French pirate, Captain Froment, in the *Minerve*, seized the sloop *Hiram*, with sixty-one slaves intended for David Nagle also in Havana. Another coup of a different nature was that of the French Captains Brohuac and Morisac, who before 1808 seized a British merchantman on her way to Jamaica and sold the 220 slaves whom they had found on board in Cuba.

All the same, for abolitionists, the first promising news after 1808 did seem to come from Spain. In full war, with Napoleon's armies in control of most of the country, the new liberal constitution made possible a legislative assembly representing the empire as well as the peninsula. José Miguel Guridi y Alcócer, an eloquent deputy for Tlaxcala, New Spain (he was a priest also), on 26 March 1811, presented to the Cortes of Cádiz the first formal Spanish project for the abolition, not of the slave trade, but of slavery as such, which, he said, adapting his Wilberforcian ideas to Latin phraseology, was contrary to natural law. He demanded the immediate abolition of the trade, freedom for all children of slave mothers, wages for surviving slaves, and the automatic right of slaves to buy their freedom if, through one way or another, they could lay their hands on any money. He hoped, too, to guarantee better treatment for all who remained in slavery. But in reply a deputy from Bogotá, José Mejía Lequerica, said that although he agreed that the abolition of the trade was an 'urgent necessity', that of slavery itself required much more thought. The Cortes decided to refer the matter to its commission on the new constitution. It remained there. Then on 2 April the radical Deputy Agustín de Argüelles (who had had, he said, 'the sweet satisfaction' of having been in the House of Lords in London in 1808, on the night when it passed the bill of abolition) proposed the condemnation of the trade. He insisted that 'Spain ought to be in line with Britain.'[32] The British should be assured of that, so that the two most enlightened opponents of Napoleon could work together. Argüelles, it seems, had heard that the British Ambassador, Henry Wellesley – brother of the Marquis Wellesley, then British Foreign Secretary, as of the Duke of Wellington – was about to make a request to this effect and had persuaded him to hold his hand, so that the idea of abolition could be made to seem a Spanish one.

This discussion caused panic in the Spanish empire, above all in Cuba, whose planters were horrorstruck, and whose Captain-General, the Marquis of Someruelos, Salvador de Muro, a subtle administrator whose motto was 'know everything, pretend much, punish little', sent back a message to the Cortes on 7 July 1811, which requested the government to treat the idea of abolition of the trade with reserve, 'in order not to lose this important island'. The municipality of Havana on 20 July sent a ninety-two-page memorandum to the Cortes, blaming Bishop de Las Casas for the slaves in Cuba in the first place: but 'the slaves have come and are here, to our misfortune; not by our fault, but of those who first initiated and encouraged this commerce in the name of law and religion'. Now the economy of Cuba depended on both slavery and the slave trade, and that fact had to be faced. There was not a property on the island which had the slaves which they needed. The document was well written, showed a surprisingly detailed knowledge of the debate on abolition in London, and indicated that the *criollos* in Cuba would be formidable enemies of the British abolitionists. The precise knowledge which the author also had of the growth of 'slave philanthropy' (*filantropia negrera*) was a warning to the government of Spain not to take the loyalty of Cuba for ever for granted.[33]

Then, also in the Cortes, as Deputy for Cuba, there was the economist Francisco de Arango, who made a skilful rearguard defence of the existing position – much in the style of Henry Dundas in 1792. Though accepting the injustice of the trade, Arango opposed, as equally unjust, an overhasty resolution of the problem, arguing that the Cortes should wait till a constitution for Spain had been worked out, and suggesting that since Britain and the United States had in effect given their planters twenty years' notice of their plan to abolish the trade Spain should be allowed to do the same. The planters of Cuba, and other places which had come to depend on slaves, should, in the meantime, encourage the import of female slaves for the purposes of reproduction.

The following year, on 23 November, in another debate in the Cortes (on a bill to remove the purchase tax known as the *alacabala* on the sale of slaves), Isidoro Antillón – the gifted geographer who had first among the Spaniards suggested the abolition of the trade, ten years before – proposed the full abolition of slavery. Arango again skilfully secured that the proposal was lost, by confining discussion of it to the oblivion of a secret session. The friends of slavery, of whom there were many, came to realize that they could influence opinion when they hinted that the abolitionists were covert allies, or even agents, of the English. That accusation made everything much more difficult, even if the English were allies of Spain. All the same, the municipality of San Juan in Puerto Rico did instruct its Deputy, Ramón Power y Giralt, to support all measures in Madrid which favoured the immigration of Europeans and the gradual extinction of slavery, which they termed 'the worst of ills from which this island suffers'.[34]

These debates were signs that abolition might be proposed in the Spanish Cortes, but the violent reaction in Cuba suggested that the planters were unlikely to conduct themselves in the law-abiding way which had characterized their companions in Jamaica. There was an indication that that lawlessness might spread to the mother country too when Antillón, some days after his speech, was beset in the streets of Cádiz by three thugs, who inflicted wounds so severe that he died a year later. It would be, however, difficult to say that this was the first murder of an abolitionist, for the identities of Antillón's assailants were never made clear.

The British government was determined to prevent the use of the Spanish flag by its subjects to carry slaves to Cuba. So Henry Wellesley was in May 1811 ordered to ask Spain 'to take all necessary action' to prevent the use of Spanish colours and documents by British as well as American slave captains. The British navy would be available to assist the Spanish government in putting its new regulations into effect. Suspicious ships – for example, off Tenerife – could be captured and judged, unless 'the whole concern' were positively shown to be the bona fide property of Spanish subjects.

The Spanish government, needing British help against Napoleon, gave a conciliatory reply. It said that it would instruct the authorities in Tenerife to act as appropriate, in the light of Brougham's accusations. But, not surprisingly, they gave no sign whatever of enthusiasm for the offer of British naval assistance.

In November 1813 the Portuguese, under the influence of their British friends, who insisted on the benefits of Sir William Dolben's Act of 1788 (itself an adaptation of an old Portuguese law), agreed to a new limitation on the number of slaves carried: five per two tons of ship in any ship up to 201 registered tons; in larger ships, there could be only one slave per ton beyond that.

This measure had several consequences. First, it favoured Portuguese merchants who had re-established themselves in Rio de Janeiro, sometimes with British financial backing and occasionally with equipment bought from Liverpool slave traders. At the same time, brandings with hot irons, which had been used in Africa to identify slaves since the fifteenth century, gave way for a time to marking with a metal bracelet or a collar, though in 1818 the old system was restored, using a silver implement, on the ground that captains cheated the customs by substituting healthy slaves whom they shipped on behalf of others for captives of their own who died.

The new rule also gave the British navy a pretext to inspect Portuguese ships. So by 1814 Captain Irby and his West Africa Squadron thought that they would shortly be able to bring to an end the slave trade, by threat and by bullying in support of the new Portuguese law.

The impression was confirmed by the Treaty of Ghent of December 1814, which ended the War of 1812 between Britain and the United States. By that document's article 10, Britain and the United States agreed 'to use their best endeavours' to end the slave trade. But the United States still had no intention of permitting the British navy to inspect American ships. No one in the new country could forget that the issue of search-and-seize had indeed helped to cause the War of 1812. After that war, the United States attached a meaning to the phrase 'freedom of the seas' with which Britain never agreed. In 1817 John Quincy Adams, then Secretary of State, would tell the United States Minister in London that the 'admission of a right in the officers of foreign ships of war to enter and search the vessels of the United States in time of peace under any circumstances whatever would meet with universal repugnance in the public opinion of this country'.[35] The British Minister in Washington, a few years later, asked Adams, after he had become the sixth President of the United States, whether he could think of an evil greater than the slave trade. The President replied that he could: to grant the right of search, and 'so to make slaves of ourselves'.[36] Yet, at that very time, some of those fast Baltimore clippers which, 300 US tons burden, and 100 feet long, had been built as privateers during the late war with Britain, were being adapted as slave traders, often being sold to traders in Havana, carrying a crew of forty.

Meantime, the worthy English abolitionists were beginning to irritate the statesmen whose imaginations they had almost captured. On 29 July 1814 the Duke of Wellington complained to his brother Henry Wellesley, the new Minister to Spain, that the pressure by Wilberforce and his friends to secure the end of the trade was so strong that they seemed to want Britain 'to go to war to put an end to that abominable traffic; and many wish that we should take the field in this new crusade. . . . I was not aware till I had been here [in London] some time of the degree of frenzy existing . . . about the slave trade.'[37] Lord Castlereagh was just as annoyed: he knew that 'morals were never well taught by the sword'. All the same, he, too, wrote to Wellesley in Madrid: 'I believe there is hardly a village [in England] which has not met and pronounced upon it [the traffic]'; and his correspondent, passing on his government's desire to bring the trade to an end, told the Spanish Foreign Minister, the Duke of San Carlos, that the Pope, Pius VII, following his re-establishment in the Vatican after his Avignon-like exile, was going to try and persuade all the Catholic nations to abolish the trade. The Duke was incensed: it was 'inconsistent with his duty as head of the Catholic Church, by which he was bound to use his best endeavours to make converts to the Catholic faith; and that every Negro became a Catholic from the moment he set his foot in any of the Spanish possessions'.[38]

Still, at the Congress of Vienna, Wellington and Castlereagh sought on Britain's behalf to secure a joint declaration from all the nations present that they wished to abolish the slave trade, though the delegations of both Spain and Portugal opposed the plan. Castlereagh also proposed an international police force to suppress the slave trade: a notion very far ahead of the times. The Spanish Plenipotentiary, Pedro Gómez Havelo, Marquis of Labrador, for his part, repeated Francisco de Arango's argument, that the British colonies had had twenty years to consider abolishing the trade, and so it was not unreasonable that Spain should wish to allow its colonists to stock up, even doubling the number of their slaves. Spain's participation in the war, the Marquis insisted, had prevented its sending slave ships to Africa for some time (a scarcity not noticeable in Havana). Anyway he thought it too soon to abolish the trade.

The problem of the French slave trade now also became a preoccupation. The overthrow of Napoleon in 1814 had brought the Bourbons back to Paris and, of course, an end to the war. Neither the restored Louis XVIII nor his Foreign Minister, the astute Talleyrand, was an enthusiast for the abolition of slavery or of the slave trade – though the latter did secure an agreement from his monarch that he would be willing to 'discourage the efforts of a few of his subjects to renew the commerce in slaves'. That was not what England had expected. Nothing less than full condemnation was now adequate. But the government of the Restoration was the heir of Louis XV, not of Montesquieu. France thought that any agreement to allow the British to inspect and, if necessary, seize ships suspected of slaving would give Britain command of the seas; and the suggestion, at the Congress of Vienna, that the return of the French West Indian colonies of Guadeloupe and Martinique (occupied by Britain during the war) might depend on their abolishing their own trade understandably infuriated the government.

The British perhaps thought that restoration France would show herself so grateful to them for defeating Napoleon that she would accept British policy towards the slave trade, and bring it immediately to an end. The French government, facing a hundred pressing problems, hesitated. This vacillation infuriated the determined British abolitionists. So in 1814 the British anti-slavery movement excelled itself in relation to France. No fewer than 800 petitions were sent to the British government urging it to persuade the restored French monarchy to end the slave trade. Three-quarters of a million people signed. Similar appeals for support were sent to the Tsar of Russia, a form of communication with which that autocrat was unfamiliar. There were public meetings on an unprecedented scale. Samuel Whitbread, the brewer and a philanthropic, though distrusted, Member of Parliament, thought that 'the country never has, and I fear never will, express a feeling so general as they have done about the slave trade'.[39] Yet while these firm views were being presented to the governments of both Britain and France, the latter administration was beginning to receive other petitions, from its maritime citizens: the merchants of Nantes, for example, were restoring their relations with Guadeloupe, Martinique, and Cayenne, while the Chamber of Commerce of that first city of *négriers* was explicitly demanding the re-establishment of the slave trade in order to revive the sugar industry in the islands. All Frenchmen remembered how, a short time ago, the trade had not only been honoured, but even subsidized, by the state.

Still, at the First Treaty of Paris, signed on 30 May 1814, the restored government of France agreed to join Britain in doing everything possible to secure the suppression of the traffic in slaves. Abolitionists in Britain were distressed, not only that the collaboration was unspecified, and that the treaty restored to France most of her colonies (though not Tobago, St Lucia, and Mauritius), but also that Talleyrand had secured that King Louis XVIII would agree only to abolish the slave trade within five years. With respect to the latter qualification, in the House of Commons on 6 June Wilberforce, still most active in the abolitionist movement, declared, grandiosely, that Lord Castlereagh had brought back the angel of death under the wings of victory. What ruin, he declared, could not be accomplished in five years! If France were to set about reconquering Saint-Domingue (for which adventure many in Paris were still hankering), there would be still more demand for slaves. Lord Holland thought that 20,000 slaves would be exported a year from Sénégal alone if France were permitted her five years. Madagascar, he knew, was also full of slaves ready for export.˙ Lord Grey, Fox's old lieutenant, meantime told a meeting in June 1814 that some English slave merchants were hoping for a return to the slave trade with the same provisions as in France.

All the same, and though the French government was already doing what it could (by tax concessions) to encourage French slave merchants to make the best of those five years, King Louis had made a crucial admission. How crucial it is easy to see from the outrage of French maritime interests. The Harbour-master of Bordeaux in these years, Auguste de Bergevin, had been thinking not of abolition, but of persuading the government to revive the old bounty on delivery of slaves; and sixty shipbuilders of Le Havre protested their 'douleur' at government policy, while Nantes talked of British hypocrisies.

In October 1814 Wilberforce wrote to Talleyrand asking for his support in general terms over the slave trade, but especially over the French commerce. He dispatched similar letters from Clarkson to both Tsar Alexander I and the Duke of Wellington. That to the Tsar ran in part: 'It is to be presumed you are totally ignorant of what takes place on the continent of Africa. [But] not to put an end to crime when you have the power makes you accomplice to it. . . . Divine providence has restored you to your former comforts and to your hereditary dominions. . . . Let the era of your own deliverance be known in the history of the world as that of the deliverance of others also. . .'.[40] Talleyrand replied that Wilberforce's argument had convinced him, yet he had still to convince France. The ex-Bishop of Autun was perhaps more influenced by a pamphlet of the historian Sismondi, *De l'intérêt de la France à l'égard de la traite des nègres,*† which argued that the economic interests of the country would be served better by an end to the slave trade. Even more important, Sismondi suggested that France could (and should) never hope to recover Saint-Domingue.

Finally, in February 1815, the governments of Britain, France, Spain, Sweden, Austria, Prussia, Russia, and Portugal were prevailed upon, by Castlereagh, to sign a general declaration that, since 'the commerce known by the name of the African slave trade is repugnant to the principles of humanity and universal morality', those powers possessing colonies accepted that it was their 'duty and necessity' to abolish it as soon as possible. The timing, however, like the detail, was a matter for negotiation. Indeed, it was conceded that no nation could be made to

---

˙ *Lord Holland's Jamaican-born wife, the admirable Elizabeth Vassall, had in 1800 inherited from her grandfather Florentius Vassall two prosperous Jamaican sugar plantations: 'Sweet River', and 'Friendship and Greenwich', with some 300 slaves. The Vassalls were an enormous family, descended from Samuel Vassall, the slave trader of the 1650s, with Bostonian connections.*

† *His* Histoire des républiques italiennes du moyen âge *had already made him famous.*

abolish the trade 'without due regard to the interests, the habits, and even the prejudices' of its subjects.[41]

Despite that extraordinary qualification, this statement seemed a triumph for Castlereagh, for humanity, and for Britain. These negotiations were accompanied, too, by what seemed further positive achievements with respect to both Portugal and Spain. Thus Britain and Portugal concluded a new treaty in January 1815; the former agreed to pay the latter £300,000 to compensate for the thirty or so ships illegally seized (as the Portuguese thought of it) since 1810; Britain also gave up hope of recovering a previous loan of £600,000; in return, Portugal would abandon her slave trade everywhere north of the equator – a measure by which the ancient traffic from Whydah or Benin to Bahia would in theory be ended. She also agreed to draft a treaty at some time in the future to set a date for the complete abolition of the Portuguese slave trade. Suspected slave ships north of the equator would be taken before either a mixed commission in Sierra Leone, or another in Rio de Janeiro (there would be a judge and commissioner from each nation in each place, the secretary appointed jointly). Ships of each power could be inspected by those of the other, though it was at that time inconceivable that a Portuguese naval vessel would take any action against a slaver.

The shortcomings of the arrangement became evident. For example, the new courts took a long time to be established. The Portuguese government explained that it was hard to secure good men willing to undertake such unprofitable tasks in a bad climate. Nor did the treaty say anything about the trade from East Africa, and it was that which a new generation of Brazilian slave merchants – such as José Nunes da Silveira, with his brig *Delfim*, capable of carrying nearly 400 slaves – was now exploiting.

Wilberforce thought this new treaty 'full of hypocrisy, wickedness and cruelty' and told Castlereagh as much. All the same, the British navy was given its instructions to seize Portuguese slavers anywhere north of the equator.

Those captains were also ordered to seize ships of Spain if there was any indication that the slave ship concerned had any contact with a British insurer, investor, or even port. Often, though, the seizures of Spanish ships which were made had not even that modest justification. Still, in July 1815 Spain – in a Treaty of Madrid with Britain, distinct from the Congress of Vienna's final document – expressed, as the reformer Argüelles would no doubt have liked, conformity with the British over the iniquity of the slave trade, promising also to prohibit Spaniards from supplying foreign countries with slaves. Spain agreed to limit slaving, even for the benefit of her own empire, to the seas south of the line drawn ten degrees north of the equator; and added that she would abolish the trade completely in eight years. It is true that, for the time being, the Spanish commitment went no further than this statement of intent, and she made no immediate move to carry this first agreement into their domestic law. The Spanish government continued to complain about British high-handedness. Another Spanish ambassador to London, the Count of Fernán Núñez, declared that two ships belonging to a merchant of Barcelona had been seized by the English frigate *Comus* in the Old Calabar River. The captains concerned were conducting themselves entirely legally, however: the trade did not end for several years more, and there was no British 'equipment' or stores on board.

The abolitionists remained dissatisfied, but even they could not fail to be impressed by what seemed yet more good news from France. There had still been no sailings by slave ships since the peace, and the return of Napoleon to France in March 1815 had a most positive effect. In the course of 'The Hundred Days', on 29 March, the Emperor, who in 1802 had shocked so many of his foreign admirers by permitting the revival of slavery with no qualifications, now, equally with no qualifications, abolished the French slave trade, having been influenced, on the one hand, by his enlightened minister, Benjamin Constant, and, on the other, by his hope that he would thereby win over British opinion. Further, the consequence was that, on 30 July, Louis XVIII, after Wellington and Blucher had destroyed 'l'Usurpateur' at Waterloo, felt obliged to confirm the policy of his enemy and, contrary to what he had agreed in 1814, with no delay; so in November 1815, in the Second Treaty of Paris, Britain, France, Austria, Russia, and Prussia engaged themselves to concert their efforts for the 'entire and definite' abolition of a trade 'so odious and so strongly condemned by laws of religion and nature'. The declaration of February was also attached to the Final Act of the Congress of Vienna. Pope Pius VII's representative played a part in these discussions, enough to cause that Pope to feel he had assisted the enlightened cause – though not enough for that intervention to be recorded by Castlereagh.

But the battle for abolition within France was still far from won. French shipowners on the Atlantic coast, in the old slave ports, had been ready to dispatch their ships to Africa, and several had already declared their cargoes and destinations before the return of Napoleon, while they were still supposing that abolition would wait for five years. They argued that, in the national interest (the restocking of the Caribbean colonies), they should still be allowed to set off, and with the approval of the Ministry of Marine. In the summer of 1815 a few ships did indeed leave for Africa, including the *Belle* of Bordeaux, Captain Brian, financed by Jean-Marie Lefebvre and the Hourquebie brothers, a Calcutta-built vessel (seized from the English in 1806) which would be intercepted in September 1815 off Dessada, Guadeloupe, by the British naval vessel HMS *Barbadoes*, with 501 blacks from Angola on board.

The instructions to Captain Brian of the *Belle* show how everything had been arranged for the reception of the slaves at Guadeloupe: 'You will address yourself to Mesdames Bosc and Briard, with whom you will arrange to sell your slaves at the highest price possible.'[42]

The French government was meantime divided: the Ministry of Foreign Affairs inclined towards abolition, since it wished to please the English; the Ministry of Marine, beset by shipbuilders, and by shipbuilders' friends in the ports, such as the presidents of the chambers of commerce, wished to allow at least some ships to depart. While the government vacillated – and France was still within two months of the disaster of Waterloo – Robert Surcouf of Saint-Malo, a shipbuilder of great reputation as a 'corsair' (he had captured many English ships during the war), and a man whose family had been concerned in the slave trade during the *ancien régime*, sent his *Affriquain* – 212 tons, twenty-nine crew, Captain Pottier – to Angola on 15 August 1815. The government did nothing. To denounce Surcouf, who was Colonel of the National Guard of his city, would have been to act against a national hero. Other slave merchants soon followed Surcouf's example. The Ministry of Marine had no idea what to do. Its indecision suggested to the shipbuilders that, after all, the trade was open. Surcouf – 'simple, brusque, generous, and brave beyond the call of duty', as his hagiographer calls him – was, therefore, the father of this new stage of the French slave trade.*[43]

The British navy then played into the hands of the French slave merchants. It seized three French ships: the *Hermione* as well as the *Belle*, both of Le Havre; and the *Cultivateur*, of Nantes. It is true that several other ships arrived at Africa and eventually at their Caribbean destination; and that others soon set sail, without approval, and reached their markets. But the outrage in France caused by the seizures extended far beyond the ports. French feeling was inflamed; for in French maritime life a ship was supposed to be something sacrosanct: '*Le navire, c'est un pays.*' How could the English be allowed to set foot on a French merchantman? The builders of slave ships, with their excellent relations in the ministries and, to some extent, even among the politicians – the Minister of Marine after 1815, Baron Portal, was a Bordeaux man with experience of the sea – used their opportunity to advantage, gaining, if not approval for their mercantile activities, at least official neglect. In 1816 no fewer than thirty-six ships left French ports on slaving missions: a small figure in comparison with the eighteenth century, yet an important beginning to the new stage of French commerce, in which the denunciations of the slave trade by Montesquieu, Voltaire, and the Abbé Raynal, and even the very existence in the past of an old Société des Amis des Noirs, were forgotten.† Whatever their talk of serving the national interest, the French

---

* *Surcouf was responsible for at least three more voyages, all in the vessel* Adolphe: *whether this armateur was teasing Benjamin Constant, a leading opponent of the slave trade, by using this, the name of his great novel, is unknown. Surcouf has a fine street called after him in Paris, and a statue in Saint-Malo looking out to sea.*

† *The Minister of Marine for a time in 1815 was the Marquis de Jaucourt, a nephew of the* philosophe *of the same name who had written the article about the slave trade in Diderot's great* Encyclopédie.

slavers from Nantes were in these voyages serving Cuba as much as, or even more than, the French Caribbean. These vessels seem to have visited and taken on slaves nearly everywhere on the West African coast from the Cape Verde Islands to Angola; and they also went to Madagascar and Zanzibar.

In 1817 the quarrel with England came to a head with the seizure of the French slaver *Louis* on her way between Africa and Martinique by HMS *Princess Charlotte*, after a regular battle in which twelve English sailors were killed. The *Louis* was from Nantes and its captain, and probable owner, was Jean Forest. She had obtained only twelve slaves between New Sestos and Cape Mesurado when, about forty miles off the shore, she met the *Princess Charlotte*. There was a subsequent judgement, then a condemnation at Sierra Leone. Captain Forest, well advised, appealed to the Admiralty Court in London, where Sir William Scott gave a decision in favour of France. For that honest judge wrote, 'I can find no authority which gives us the right of interruption to the navigation of states in amity upon the high seas.' No government, he added, could force the way to the liberation of Africa by trampling on the independence of other states in Europe. Sir William, who had already declared his irritation with the language of the Portuguese treaty of 1811, concluded that 'to procure an eminent good by means that are unlawful is [not] consonant with private morality'.[44] The British government then had to order its navy to cease to interfere with French merchant ships, even if they were plainly slavers. The naval officers complied, with reluctance, for there was nothing which they enjoyed more than to continue action against the French, even if the Bourbons were back in Paris.

This setback to naval hopes was accompanied by others in relation to Spain. It is true that the British navy did stop and seize several further Spanish slave ships. In June 1815 W. H. G. Page, a lawyer who was acting as the Cuban planters' agent in London, complained to the Foreign Office that over 200 ships belonging to Spaniards had been seized or condemned, all illegally. He tried to ensure that Spanish slave shippers whose vessels had been wrongly taken would be compensated. He was unsuccessful. All the same, the Spanish trade prospered, and when in February 1816 the Council of the Indies, the powerful body which had advised the Spanish Crown for three centuries about imperial questions, proposed to King Ferdinand that the slave trade should be immediately abolished, the subtle Cuban Arango, a new member of that body, asked what the haste was. Had there not always been slavery? The Cubans believed that they needed slaves, and there were plenty of merchants ready to provide them, whatever the British might formally desire. The Spanish *apoderado* (representative) of the Consulado de Havana in the post-war years, Francisco Antonio de Rucavado, a confidant of Arango, wrote in 1816 that he was 'himself persuaded that there was no just reason for fearing that there would be an end to the traffic'; in September

1816 the Treasurer of Cuba, Alejandro Ramírez, a Castilian with wide experience of the West Indies and Guatemala, told the Intendant of Santiago de Cuba that there it was 'not necessary to obtain permission from the captain-general for expeditions to Africa to fetch slaves'.[45]

A sign that even in Britain there were hesitations about over-hasty abolition in the Spanish empire was given in the rejection of a bill introduced into the House of Commons in May 1815, which would have proscribed the slave trade as an investment for British capital (the Foreign Slave Trade Bill). Alexander Baring – Member of Parliament for Taunton, a director of the Bank of England (married to the daughter of William Bingham, the richest senator in the United States), a man of 'singularly large and enlightened views', according to Sir Charles Webster, the historian of that time, 'the greatest merchant perhaps England ever had', according to Disraeli, and until then a declared abolitionist – opposed this measure on the interesting ground that it would 'extinguish' Anglo-Spanish commerce.*

The debate on this bill produced some other remarkable statements: for example, that of Joseph Foster Barham, Member for Stockbridge, who argued that British capital was responsible for the Spanish slave trade (a statement apparently supported by Henry Wellesley), not to speak of half the Danish and a great part of the Portuguese. The bill was eventually defeated in the Lords, as so many earlier bills had been in the days of the great campaign of Wilberforce.[46]

---

* Baring later became President of the Board of Trade and as Lord Ashburton in 1841 concluded an important anti-slaving treaty with the United States. His father-in-law, Senator William Bingham, had begun his career as British Consul in Saint-Pierre in Martinique and had then been the Continental representative in the West Indies throughout the American Revolution, laying there the foundation of his fortune in 'ownership of privateers and constant trade'. He subsequently became a founder of the Pennsylvania Bank, later the Bank of North America, under the one-time Philadelphia mayor and slave trader, Thomas Willing. For other connections between Barings Bank and Cuba, see pages 647 and 684.

29

THE SLAVER IS MORE CRIMINAL
THAN THE ASSASSIN

*'The négrier [slaver] is more criminal than
the assassin because, slavery being only an
agony cruelly prolonged, death is preferable
to the loss of liberty.'*

L'Abbé Grégoire, Des peines infamantes
à infliger aux négriers (1822)

BRITISH MERCHANTS, we know, had been the greatest of slave traders in
the eighteenth century. In the nineteenth, their government embarked
upon a crusade to destroy that very commerce. Appropriately, the Prime
Minister of England under whom this campaign began was Lord Liverpool, whose father – being then merely Lord Hawkesbury – had been presented with the freedom of the great slaving city of Liverpool in June 1788
to thank him for his parliamentary support of the slave trade. In May 1796,
when Hawkesbury was created Earl of Liverpool, the corporation invited
him to quarter the arms of the city with his own. As a young man, the
second Earl of Liverpool had had most of the attitudes of his father, voting
constantly against abolition, as George Canning had as constantly complained. But as Prime Minister, Liverpool abandoned his past prejudices
and, remarkably, his administration, after the peace of 1815, embarked on
one of the most moral foreign policies in British history, precisely intended
to bring the slave trade to an end on a global scale.

Liverpool's first Foreign Secretary was Lord Castlereagh. Like his
Prime Minister, he had been less than enthusiastic about abolition in the
years leading up to 1807. Grenville, the final architect of abolition, would
remark to Samuel Rogers, the poet, 'What a frightful mistake . . . to send
such a person as Lord Castlereagh to the Congress of Vienna! a man so
ignorant that he does not know the map of Europe; and who can be won
over to make any concessions by only being asked to breakfast by the
Emperor.'[1] Yet, in the end, Castlereagh's conduct of Britain's diplomacy in
these years was a triumph of aggressive liberalism. Though a Tory, he

THE SLAVER IS MORE CRIMINAL THAN THE ASSASSIN 591

thought that it was desirable to try and formulate general principles. His circular dispatch of 1 January 1816, for example, was a sketch for a European 'confederacy' of great powers to preserve the peace of the world on which many later, less well-written documents, such as the Covenant of the League of Nations and the Charter of the United Nations, have been based. Lampooned by radicals for his conduct in Ireland – who does not recall Shelley's lines 'I met Murder in the way/ He had a mask like Castlereagh'? – this statesman did much for the cause of black slaves. Public opinion in England had, of course, been awoken by the devoted leaders of the abolitionist movement, and those men, such as Wilberforce and James Stephen, were in personal touch with the Foreign Secretary. Castlereagh, on the other hand, had to deal with four nations – France and the United States, Spain and Portugal – whose statesmen resented Britain's intervention in their affairs, and saw Castlereagh's well-meaning declarations as a 'grab for world power'. The leaders of those countries did not understand the quasi-religious enthusiasm which had come to possess Britain with respect to abolition, nor how Castlereagh himself had become 'something of an enthusiast for the cause in which he had to fight'. John Quincy Adams, who became Minister to London after the Treaty of Ghent, recorded the passionate language with which Castlereagh spoke: 'He passed immediately to . . . the slave trade which, he said, was now carrying on to a very great extent, and in a shocking manner; that a great number of vessels for it had been fitted out in our southern states; and that the barbarities of the trade were even more atrocious than they had been before the abolition of it had been attempted.'[2]

Castlereagh used the declaration secured at Vienna to institute a permanent conference of the European powers in London. This was to be a centre of information, as well as of action, about trading slaves. The first meeting of this body was held on 28 August 1816. Fourteen meetings were held before a new full conference of foreign ministers at Aix-la-Chapelle in 1818, two more in 1819. Alas, the conference did little more than collect information, in which most powers seemed uninterested. They complained too that it did nothing for the cause of Europeans kidnapped by Barbary pirates in the Mediterranean which interested them more. Castlereagh therefore turned his attention to private negotiations with each of the countries concerned.

In September 1816 he wrote to the remarkable Greek who was Secretary of State in St Petersburg, Count Capo d'Istria, that he had been hoping that the Tsar would support 'with force' the additional, second article of the Treaty of Paris on the slave trade. 'In laying down the maxims of Christianity as to the rule of conduct between state and state', Castlereagh said, 'it would have been unworthy to have assumed a less benevolent principle towards Africa.' He added, with curious firmness, 'As the preamble stands, we may defy moral criticism, if our execution shall correspond to the principles we profess.' His intention was to secure

the support of Spain and Portugal for an alliance whose purpose would
be the final suppression of the slave trade. But he soon convinced himself
that the governments of both countries were 'well matched in dishonesty
and shabbiness'; and Castlereagh never appreciated the difficulties under
which these two nations laboured, the need to face revolutionary movements of independence in South America being an all-consuming matter;
while both governments knew that too many concessions to Britain on
the slave trade would jeopardize the loyalty even of Cuba, and certainly
of Brazil.[3]

Having been informed by the Africa Institution of London, in
December 1816, that 60,000 slaves were still being carried across the
Atlantic every year – 15,000, they said, in North American ships flying
Spanish flags – Castlereagh, at the conference of five nations at Aix-la-
Chapelle in 1818, remarkably proposed that the international right of
search of slave ships – a *sine qua non*, in Britain's eyes, for effective control
– should be complemented by 'the vigilant superintendence of an armed
and international police on the coast of Africa. . . . To render such a police
either legal or effective in its object, it must be established under the sanction, and by the authority, of all civilised states.'[4] This right of search had
its origin as long ago as the fourteenth century; the novelty was to
propose that it be introduced in time of peace.

The conference at Aix was also the first to be held of the great powers
of Europe when they were not at war to try and resolve their difficulties:
an innovation which has been persistently followed in later days. But
there were few supporters among other foreign ministers for the scheme
which Castlereagh proposed, which still appeared as a way whereby 'Perfide Albion' could morally justify her mastery of the seas, if not of the
world – though Tsar Alexander had already thought of establishing a
'neutral institution', with a court, international fleet, and headquarters all
of its own, in Africa. He had even suggested that the main nations might
concede to this body 'the right of visit' of suspected slave ships without
arousing national jealousies. But nothing came of this, the Tsar lost interest, and the Tuscan diplomat was right who wrote home to Florence from
this conference: 'I see clearly that we have not yet begun the golden age.'[5]

For the moment, the only international police consisted of the British
navy acting alone, often in dubious legal circumstances. The third
commander of the British West Africa Squadron, Captain Sir James Yeo,
an experienced if unlucky commander in both the American and the
Napoleonic Wars, reported that many North American merchants were
obviously continuing to trade after 1815, carrying slaves to both Brazil
and Cuba, some of them using those fast ships with twenty or more guns
which had been built as privateers in the Anglo-American War of 1812.
Their technique was to make a nominal sale of their ship in Tenerife or in
Havana to a Spanish merchant, who would provide a captain of his own
nationality with the real master continuing as passenger.

An expanded British naval squadron seemed necessary and so, in 1818, Sir George Collier went to West Africa with one frigate, three sloops, and two gun-brigs. His instructions from the Admiralty, like Irby's, were, 'You are diligently to look into the several bays and creeks . . . between Cape Verde and Benguela.'[6] That was an impossible task. Leaving aside that there were several hundred such bays, and several thousand such creeks, between those points, most of the territory was in the zone of trop-ical calm, where sailing breezes were rare, and where the prevailing wind, if such existed, was westerly or south-westerly – that is, blowing onto the shore. The current was from west to east. All these factors made it much easier to sail down the coast than to sail back, as everyone had known from the earliest days of European exploration. The steamy heat, the dazzle of the decks, the cramped conditions, and the simple diet made this work of patrol exhausting in the extreme.

In addition, there could be no real patrolling if the navy were to keep to the open sea. Ships had to sail close inshore to know what was happening and, often after dark, send boats upriver. These vessels would be met by mosquitoes at every turn – mosquitoes which, of course, some-times brought malaria. Naval captains were also frequently obstructed by sandbars at the mouths of rivers.

There were other difficulties. For example, Collier wrote to the Admiralty that: 'It is only by great cunning (or great accident) that they [the slavers] can be surprised with slaves on board. In some instances, while the boats [of the naval ship] have been rowing to the slave vessel, the relanding of the slaves has been effected, and then [they have been] paraded on the beach, compelled to dance and make every sign of contempt for the boats' crews. . . .'[7] On one occasion, Collier himself was fined £1,500 for wrongly detaining a ship, the *Gaviao*, which, in his judge-ment, had slaves on board and was found north of the equator. In the summer of 1822 HMS *Myrmidon* stopped sixteen slavers, of which only one was acting illegally according to the treaties.

Sir Robert Mends, another experienced officer (he had lost an arm in a battle of the American Revolution, while still only thirteen years of age) who succeeded Sir George Collier as commander, wrote from his flagship, the *Owen Glendower*, in which he would die in 1823, off Cape Coast: 'The traffic in slaves has not decreased. Nor do I see how it can whilst it is supported by European protection in the most open and avowed manner. . . .'[8]

Disillusion was thus never far away from serving officers, as well as sailors, in the West Africa Squadron. The failures of the squadron to bring back a swift and overwhelming victory, as the navy had been used to expect during the Napoleonic Wars, led, too, to a fall in the size of rewards available. In 1824 rates were cut to £10 a head for a slave liber-ated. To compensate for this, the Crown gave the sailors concerned in the capture half the proceeds of any sale of a confiscated slave ship.

British consuls also reported all manner of ships actively slaving in harbours north of the equator: for example, the Brazilian *Volcano do Sud*, whose crew, when captured by an English ship-sloop, HMS *Pheasant* (sixteen guns), in 1819, murdered the boarding party and delivered their cargo of 270 slaves at Bahia as if nothing had happened. Further, the Portuguese legal ban on trading slaves from north of the equator was a stimulus to trading to the south of it, and that included commerce from East Africa and Mozambique. In 1824 fifteen slavers, with 500 slaves on board each of them, were reported to be leaving East African ports for Brazil, where their cargoes were sold for $200 each. Inland merchants in Mozambique had bought them for no more than a few beads each, if they were not kidnapped, and then sold to the Portuguese traders for, say, $20. The excuses used by Portuguese captains to justify slaving were also without end: thus, in 1822, HMS *Morgiana*, Captain Knight, captured a Portuguese ship, the *Emilia*, just north of the equator, with 396 slaves on board. The captain of that *Emilia* declared that he had loaded his vessel at Cabinda, well south of that line. But the slaves themselves said that they had only been on board the ship a short time, the water casks seemed much fuller than would have been the case if the *Emilia* had come from Cabinda, and the slaves had clearly been branded only a short time previously.

In the circumstances, therefore, it became obvious that abolition could only be achieved if naval force was supported by diplomacy; and what seemed to be several achievements of this kind were soon registered. For example, in 1817, Radama, King of eastern Madagascar, made a treaty by which, in return for his agreement to end the slave traffic, Britain would pay him $10,000 a year for three years. Castlereagh made similar treaties with the Imam of Muscat and, in 1822, with the Sultan of Zanzibar. These were modest arrangements which would, however, be followed by many other, more far-reaching, undertakings in Africa.

It was on the basis of information collected by a new 'Slave Trade Department' in the Foreign Office from consuls, naval officers, and travellers that in September 1822, at the last regular meeting of European powers following the Congress of Vienna, in the lovely city of Verona, the Duke of Wellington, the British representative, was able to insist that thirty-five European vessels had entered African waters north of the equator in order to slave in the first seven months of 1821, and 21,000 slaves had been bought. Should not the slave trade be treated as piracy? But at this meeting the idea of joint international naval action about the slave trade was blocked by Chateaubriand, speaking for France. It was not, that great writer now Foreign Minister insisted, that France needed slaves for her own colonies of Martinique and Guadeloupe; nor even that the illegal slaving lobby in Nantes and Bordeaux was overpowering, though it was powerful (Ducudray-Bourgault, President of the Tribunal of Commerce in that city, was a *négrier*). Nor was Chateaubriand speaking thus because of his father's role as a slave trader; those were matters on which the brilliant statesman chose to dwell neither in his speeches nor in his memoranda. He was simply expressing the traditional French hostility to allowing Britain a free hand on the ocean. He was bored with the question raised so ardently by the English: 'It's very singular,' he wrote, 'this perseverance of the Cabinet of St James in introducing to a discussion about more important and more pressing matters, this remote . . . question of the abolition of the slave trade.'[9]

George Canning, veteran abolitionist since his first days in Parliament in the 1790s, succeeded Castlereagh in 1822 as Foreign Minister in London, when the latter tragically killed himself, when out of his mind. Witty and arrogant, impudent and cultivated, this determined opponent of slaving had been for years Member of Parliament for Liverpool: a fact which showed how life had changed in that commercial city. Canning entered office believing innocently that 'two or three years might suffice to sweep the African and American seas of the atrocious commerce with which they are now infested'. He proposed that the powers should boycott the produce of countries still engaged in the slave trade.[10]

Canning's foreign colleagues refused to take him seriously. His 'proposed refusal to admit Brazilian sugar . . . was met (as might be expected) with a smile; which indicated on the part of continental statesmen a suspicion that there might be something of self-interest in our [that is, British] suggestion. . . .' Canning then pointed out to the Duke of Wellington that the slave trade had become even more inhumane since formal abolition, because of the methods used to conceal the cargoes, 'which it hardly ever seems to occur to its remorseless owners . . . consists of sentient beings'. Wellington was to press this 'scandal of the civilised world' on all the attendants at the congress. Canning then suggested prohibitions on the use of Portuguese and Brazilian flags by foreigners, an international declaration that the slave trade constituted piracy, and a boycott of all Brazilian products. None of these ideas bore fruit.

The setbacks caused the new Foreign Secretary to fall back, for the next seven years, on Castlereagh's own policy of last resort, namely, direct negotiation with individual countries. He thus embarked on a large number of dispatches, numbering over 1,000, on the subject of the slave trade. It was Canning who, in relation to the slave trade to Cuba, defined in what circumstances a naval captain might reasonably suppose that a merchant ship was a slaver, even though no slaves were on board: ships anchored, or 'hovering', off the coast of Africa which contained greater supplies of food and drinking water than could be consumed by the crew, say, of thirty; spare planks in the hold which could easily be used to make a slave deck; and, more obviously, supplies of shackles and handcuffs, as well as hatches fitted with open gratings instead of closed tops.

There remained, meantime, some inconsistencies in the British position, which were seized upon by their enemies as indication of hypocrisy, if not of perfidy. Thus, when the new Republic of Central America formally abolished slavery in 1825, numerous black slaves fled there from next-door British Honduras (Belize) whither, after a difficult debate in the Congress, they were handed back on the insistence of the British Governor. It became more and more obvious that to attack the slave trade so vehemently, but at the same time to maintain the institution of slavery, was illogical. Then any celebration that there might have been in abolitionist circles that, at last, in 1820, slave-grown sugar had been overtaken as the main import into Britain, was effectively dampened by the knowledge that the crop's successor as the prime import was cotton – above all, from the United States – another slave-made product.

As was the case with sugar, Britain imported far more cotton than she needed to clothe herself. It was the export of cotton goods made in Lancashire to the Continent of Europe which made that county great in the nineteenth century; and Lancashire's demand for cotton not only assisted, but helped to cause, the settlement of the American South-west with slave plantations. Throughout the first half of the nineteenth century, until 1860 and the Civil War, Britain took half or more of the total United States cotton crop: in 1800, the United States sent Britain about 30 per cent of her cotton imports; in 1860, 88 per cent. British credits to, and investment in, the business underpinned the rule of 'King Cotton'. Not surprisingly, therefore, Britain's Continental enemies, such as the slave traders of Nantes, mocked their island neighbour by saying that she was 'as chivalrous as a ball of cotton'.

In March 1824 Britain passed a bill declaring that any British subject found guilty of trading slaves should be deemed guilty of 'felony, piracy and robbery, and should suffer death without benefit of clergy and loss of lands, goods and chattels as pirates, felons and robbers upon the seas ought to suffer'. Strong language, it might be said, for a commerce which until eighteen years before had been carried on by the best men in British commercial life and which, for over 200 years, had been practised by royal dukes, peers, and lord mayors. No prosecution, however, was brought against a British subject under this head, though there continued to be a few English-born slave merchants and seamen in the trade to Cuba, Brazil, or Suriname in the mid-nineteenth century (for example, Captain John Discombe, captain of the *Eliza*, probably an English ship, declared a prize at Freetown in 1819; William Woodside, captain of the *Beym*, captured at Gallinas in 1825; Jacob Walters, captain of the *Hoop*, an English ship, also seized at Gallinas, in 1826; Neil Williams – or was he Guillaume Neil? – found at Old Calabar in 1829, on board the *Jeune Eugénie*, with fifty slaves on board and all his ship's documents in English). English traders also procured slave ships for Pedro Blanco, the Spanish chief trader of the River Gallinas, about 1830, and a certain Jennings, who was known to supply cauldrons, shackles, etc., for Pedro Martínez, also of Spain. But, for all such hypocrisy, and philistinism, the British in the nineteenth century remained generally law-abiding. The modification of the Navigation Acts in 1825 to permit free trading anywhere in the world by the British West Indies was an earnest of this proposition.

These economic innovations rendered unimportant the various, often grudgingly slow or meaningless declarations of emancipation by new Latin American sovereign states, whose slave populations were tiny. Venezuela abolished slavery in 1821.˙ Colombia and Chile also abolished slavery after their independence the same year; while Mexico outlawed slavery in 1829. All these countries, as well as Argentina, pledged the assistance of their navies to help Britain, but though the symbolism was useful, in practice those forces counted for nothing. It may be a satisfaction, though, to friends of Latin culture to recall that the institution of slavery formally vanished in what had once been the continental Spanish empire long before it did in the United States.

Britain's efforts to bring an end to the slave trade also included conventional diplomacy with the main powers involved. Each of these countries responded after her own fashion to the British pressure. Each shared the common view, expressed most forcefully by France, that British abolitionism was hypocritical. That this interpretation was shared by many high-minded men, who were not English, is indicated by a comment by Goethe, whose compatriots were not engaged in the slave trade, who had no personal interest in the matter, but who, in a conversation with Eckermann, would remark: 'While the Germans are tormenting themselves with philosophical problems, the English, with their great practical understanding, laugh at us and win the world. Everybody knows their declamations against the slave trade; and, while they have palmed off on us all sorts of humane maxims as the foundation of their proceedings, it is at last discovered that their true motive is a practical object, which the English always notoriously require in order to act, and which should have been known before. In their extensive domains on the west coast of Africa, they themselves use the blacks, and it is against their interest for blacks to be carried off . . . so they preach with a practical view against the slave trade. Even at the Congress of Vienna, the English envoy denounced it with great zeal; but the Portuguese envoy had the good sense to reply quietly that he did not know that they had come together to sit in judgement on the world or to decide upon principles of morality. He well knew the object of England; and he had also his own which he knew how to plead for and to obtain.'[11]

If the great Goethe had this interpretation of English motives, it is unsurprising that the same idea was held by those actually concerned

---

˙ In qualified terms: slave children were to serve their mothers' owners until they grew up; boards would decide on the freed slaves' occupations; and the emancipation of adults depended on the payment of compensation to the owners, such sums being raised from taxes.

with slaving in Havana, Nantes, Rio de Janeiro, and Charleston, many of whom were additionally convinced that the English were determined to prevent the sugar and coffee production of their neighbours from flourishing by any means that they could.

In 1818 a new British–Spanish treaty dealt with the slave trade. This agreement was made on the basis of another recommendation by the Council of the Indies, in the teeth of the opposition of the Cuban interests, on behalf of whom Arango, with his colleague Rucavado, acted in Madrid. The British at this time purported to think that since the Spanish decree of 1804 permitted the trading of slaves for only a further twelve years (by foreigners for six), the commerce was actually illegal in Spain. But the government in Madrid disagreed.

In some ways complementing the Portuguese–British treaty of 1815, but in other respects going further, the new Anglo-Spanish Treaty provided that all Spanish subjects would be prohibited from engaging in the slave trade after 30 May 1820. Captains and masters thereafter captured with slaves would be imprisoned for ten years in the Philippines, and their cargoes declared free. Naval vessels of both nations undertook to report any merchant ship of either nation suspected of carrying a slave cargo; and, if one were found, the ship would be taken before a mixed tribunal at Sierra Leone (that is, not an exclusively British court), or if in American waters at Havana (the arrangements were similar to those provided for British–Portuguese collaboration). The 'right of search' was, of course, in Castlereagh's mind 'indispensable. It is the basis of the whole', he thought. But the need to establish that slaves were on board before that right was exercised would be a hindrance to the patrol, as time would show.

Another clause of the treaty provided that when a tribunal declared a ship a prize that vessel would be sold, and the two governments would share the profits; the slaves found aboard would receive a certificate of freedom. These *emancipados*, as they were known, were then to be delivered to the governments at the city where the tribunal had made its decision. Finally, in a provision which caused much criticism in London, the British agreed to pay £400,000 as compensation for the losses suffered hitherto by the Spaniards. The sum was questioned by the House of Commons, even if Brougham said that the agreement was cheaply bought.

Many Spanish slave ships had been seized in the eight years 1810–17, and some Spanish lives had been lost in resisting capture. The Cuban planters' man in London, W. H. G. Page, persuaded Dr Joseph Phillimore, Member of Parliament for St Mawes (and also Regius Professor of Civil Law at Oxford), to raise the question of compensation for those ships illegally confiscated. But the Foreign Office thought that all such claims should be referred to the Spanish government. Britain implied to the Spanish Ambassador, still the Count of Fernán Núñez, that she was reluctant to make any concessions to Spain, even over obvious wrongdoing by British naval officers, until the slave trade had been fully abolished in Madrid. Admittedly, the ships intercepted by the British navy constituted only a tiny percentage of those which set out: in the eighteen months from January 1816 to September 1817 alone about 150 set off for Africa from Havana, nine from Trinidad, thirty from Santiago de Cuba, and sixteen from Matanzas.

The King of Spain did not, however, pass on his £400,000 to the *negreros* of Cuba. He bought five frigates and three ships of the line from the Tsar of Russia in which to send out more soldiers to recapture his dominions in South America. The chance of making this desirable purchase (a '*negocio escandaloso*' for some) was one of the reasons why the treaty was signed in the first place.

The British had been active in Madrid before this treaty was signed. Charles Vaughan, the British Minister, talked to every member of the Council of State. He also distributed copies of a pamphlet, *Bosquejo del comercio en esclavos*, by the liberal writer Blanco White. But he had to pass on to London the news that the planters of Havana had offered $2,000,000 to the Spanish government to be allowed to maintain the trade legally, and another $500,000 every year afterwards while the private permission remained. In the event, it was the influential General Castaños y Aragoni – the Captain-General of Catalonia, who at Bailén in 1808 had inflicted on Napoleon his first defeat in Europe – who persuaded the King to concede over the issue in the interest of maintaining good relations with Britain. Spain, he said, needed British help against the United States' threats both to New Spain and to Florida.

Wilberforce praised God for the agreement; and if, in the debate on the matter in the House of Commons Sir Oswald Mosley, the Whig Member for Midhurst, declared that 'it was not for us to teach Spain humanity', the enlightened Sir James Mackintosh commented that 'the Right of Search was practical abolition'. But it soon became clear that the treaty in practice would mean less than it seemed at first sight.[12]

Before signing this document, José García de León y Pizarro, Spain's new Foreign Minister, wrote to the authorities in Puerto Rico and Cuba (now provinces, instead of colonies, of Spain), urging that they seek to arrange that slave ships in the next three years should carry women as at least one-third of their cargo, so that, 'by propagating the species, the abolition of the slave trade may be less noticeable in the future'. The tone of Pizarro's letter suggests that he at least hoped to cajole what remained of the empire into a genuine acceptance of abolition. But his 'Virginian solution' was rejected by a Cuba determined to develop her sugar industry in the same style as that of her neighbours in Jamaica, Brazil, and Saint-Domingue. For the other surviving parts of the empire, such as Mexico, Madrid's concession was of no great importance.

The news of the treaty reached Havana in February, and a longer letter from the Foreign Minister arrived in March (since the treaty had been signed in September, and Havana was then only four weeks away by fast ship, it would seem that the ministers in Madrid took an inordinately long time wondering how to express themselves). The Governor, General José Cienfuegos, nephew of the enlightened statesman of the previous century, Jovellanos, summoned a meeting of the Real Consulado. Representatives of the old families of Cuba were all there: Ignacio Pedroso; the Marquis Cárdenas de Montehermoso; Manuel de Ibarra; and Ciriaco de Arango, a cousin of the economist. Also present was a member of the new generation of dealers in slaves, mostly peninsular-born but now a major economic power in Havana, Santiago de la Cuesta y Manzanal, the well-known merchant of giant physique, who appeared 'so large that he looks as if he kept all his money within himself for safety'.[13]

The minutes of the meeting show several expressions of loyalty, as befitted citizens of that 'ever-faithful' (*siempre fiel*) island, which designation the Captain-General had recently secured formally for the colony. But the gathering unanimously requested the Governor to refrain from publishing the Anglo-Spanish Treaty as it was and suggested a committee to reflect on the matter. The committee would include Santiago de la Cuesta, who would know what was happening in the field.[14]

The committee duly reported. It requested the government to provide time in which the planters could seek the slaves whom 'in so many ways we need for the reproduction of the black species',* basing this ideal on the rules of 'convenience, humanity, and philanthropy ... mentioned in the treaty'. The law was, meantime, published in the official gazette of Havana, the *Diario del gobierno de la Habana*, on 17 March.

The slave merchants, planters, and officials of Cuba now reached agreement that the formal abolition of the slave trade by Spain would not be allowed to interfere in practice in the traffic. The French, after all, had shown the way.† There had been a number of discussions about the future of the trade the previous year. Now both the Governor and the Treasurer, Alejandro Ramírez, apparently assured Santiago de la Cuesta (who in turn informed his colleagues in the commerce) that, whatever the government in Madrid might do to please the English, matters would be different in the Caribbean. After all, most Spanish planters had been smuggling slaves – from the English in Jamaica above all – so as to avoid taxation: what more easy than to continue the practice, in order to evade the new treaty with the English, who had so curiously changed their mind on the matter of slaves? Perhaps, too, that Anglo-Saxon change of mind was just temporary; the merchants of Havana knew enough of England to realize that whatever the government in London desired, there were investors and merchants in that city only too willing still to help Cuba in its efforts to achieve an adequate labour force. It seems also

---

* 'Los esclavos que por tantos caminos nos hacen falta para la reproducción de la especie negra.'
† *See page 586.*

that the Spanish government secretly decided to permit its subordinates in Cuba to break the law on slave trading: a later captain-general of Cuba, General Tacón, wrote in 1844 to the then Ministers of Foreign Affairs and of the Navy that in 1818 the King had sent a confidential order to his predecessor in Cuba and to the same official in Puerto Rico, instructing them to overlook the illegal importation of slaves since, without slaves, he accepted, the agriculture of the islands could not make progress.[15]

The Spanish Crown, through its Cuban representatives, was also doing what it could to increase foreign investment in, and foreign immigration to, Cuba, by concessions on taxes. Many North Americans had been long established on the island, and now more came. Some entered the slave trade; others were content, for the time being, to maintain their sugar plantations; one such such was the ex-king of the Rhode Island traffic, James de Wolf, on whose estates, Mariana, Mount Hope, and San Juan near Matanzas, he employed slaves whom he himself had earlier imported or whom he obtained through his nephew George, who was still active in the commerce in slaves, and whose sugar plantation, the Arca de Nöe, Noah's Ark, lay to the south-west of Havana, near Batabanó.[16]

In those days, hostility towards 'la perfidia inglesa' was shared by almost everyone in Cuba, including the Captains-General, such as Cienfuegos and his short-serving successor, Juan Manuel Cagigal (both of them had had their first experience of dealing with England during the siege of Gibraltar in 1783). The Treasurer, the able Alejandro Ramírez, the real master of the island for many years, was in matters of foreign policy a traditionalist who always looked on England as the eternal enemy, this hostility being exacerbated rather than soothed by that country's help in the Napoleonic Wars.

The Spanish colonial officials had other things, too, with which to concern themselves: the fear of revolution, either in the style of the Haitians or in that of the rest of Latin America. The loyalty to Spain of the Cuban planter class could be secured only if they were assured of slaves.*

Whatever the secret expectations of the planters, the signature of the treaty with Britain, as might have been expected, was a stimulus to importing slaves before the legal deadline: in three years, 70,000 Africans entered Cuba through Havana alone, over 100,000 in the whole island. The ships which brought these slaves mostly flew a Spanish flag, but one also came in flying a Dutch flag, several purported to be Portuguese, one was United States, and one was French. Many of the ships with Spanish flags were, however, United States slavers, including several from George de Wolf's fleet from Bristol, Rhode Island. Barnabas Bates, at that time Postmaster in Bristol, wrote in 1818 that the system was that 'cargoes

---

* What most angered Ramírez was when United States vessels used the Spanish flag: as, for example, they did in the case of a schooner built in Bristol, Rhode Island, in 1816. That led to a protest to Ramírez of thirty Spanish merchants.

suited to the African market are procured here in Bristol, and taken aboard vessels suited to the purpose, and then cleared for the Havanna by the Collector [that is, Charles Collins]. The master there effects a nominal sale of the vessel and cargo to a Spaniard, takes on board a nominal master and proceeds to Africa. . . . When the vessel has made one voyage, she can proceed on another without returning to the United States. A new cargo is then sent out to her in the Havanna. . . . There is one [ship] lying here ready for sea called the *General Peace*, lately owned by Thomas Saunders, of Providence. . . . The crew talk familiarly of their destination, and one man against whom I had a claim boldly told me that I must wait "till he could go and catch some blackbirds".' '[17]

The legal Spanish trade did not end without one remarkable occurrence: the entry into action in 1819 of a corvette of the Haitian navy, the aptly named *Wilberforce*, which seized the Spanish slave ship *Yuyu* (otherwise known as the *Dos Unidos*) coming from Africa with a cargo of slaves. On 26 March 1820 the Captain-General of Cuba demanded of the *mulâtre* President Jean-Pierre Boyer of that island (he had temporarily reunited Santo Domingo with the ex-Saint-Domingue) that he give up the slaves which he had liberated. There was no reply. A further request from Cuba also went unanswered. Only in January 1821 did Boyer reply, in a conciliatory fashion, but he refused to give up the slaves. By that time, the slave trade to Cuba was formally illegal, the number of slaves actually in Cuba probably approaching 200,000.

Spain, secretly satisfied to find that the Cuban planters seemed to prefer riches and dependence to independence with no defence, tried to encourage, for the first time, European immigration into Cuba, including non-Spanish immigration. A tax of six pesos was also imposed on each male slave imported in these last years of the legal trade, and the revenue was to be used for bringing free white labour. Female slaves were exempted from the tax, to encourage imports of them.

Another faithful Spanish colony, Puerto Rico, always poorer, remained with a strong white (80,000) or free black or mulatto (85,000) population, against a limited number of slaves (17,500), in a population of over 180,000.

In 1820 the Spanish government, as everyone had anticipated would happen, made numerous demands of the English to delay the enactment of their anti-slaving treaty. Ships already at sea should surely be allowed to deliver their cargoes. Did not a ship setting out for Africa for slaves for Cuba have to count on a journey of ten months?

˙ *At that time, the* General Peace *had been sold to George de Wolf. His uncle by marriage, Charles Collins, was still Collector of the Customs in Bristol, Rhode Island, and was a frequent visitor at his plantation in Cuba: no doubt to arrange the details of the illegalities, so that the chances of prosecution were modest. All the same, George de Wolf was ruined in 1825, and dragged much of the town of Bristol down with him. He escaped to pass his last years in Cuba.*

The Cubans – planters, merchants, officials – were assisted in these moves by the tacit support of the King; by the dismissal of that minister, Pizarro, who had been so (unwisely) proud of having introduced an end to the slave trade; and by his replacement by the Marquis of Casa Irujo, a firm friend of the slave dealers. The Cubans' agent in Madrid, General de Zayas, seems to have done his job well.

On 20 May 1820, when the slave trade to Cuba was formally supposed to end, a new deadline was agreed delaying the measure till 31 October, but the Cubans, through their friends in Madrid, again argued that five months was too short a time. Only on 10 December were the newly appointed British Commissioners in Havana told by the Captain-General of the island that orders had been received to carry out the treaty. That was a direct consequence of a liberal revolution in Madrid, and indeed it is hard to believe that anything would have occurred had it not been for that upheaval.

So tribunals were established at Sierra Leone and at Havana: at the last named, the Spanish judges were to be, however, Alejandro Ramírez and Francisco de Arango – the first the Treasurer who had laid careful plans with the slave traders for the evasion of the treaty; the second, the theoretician of the slave trade in Cuba.

The Spanish navy would send only two ships or so as its contribution to the naval patrol, and neither they nor the few English ships in the region could do much, even if they had wished to, in Havana. It was impossible to distinguish at sight slave ships from the others leaving Cuba, and it was impossible to have to check each suspicious one.

A typical incident occurred in March 1821, only a few months after the treaty had come into force. The British Commodore Collier intercepted the Cuban-based schooner *Ana María*, in the Bight of Benin. She turned out to be carrying 500 slaves. Collier's boat crew boarded this vessel, whose captain insisted that he was a North American. Papers proclaimed him to be a Spaniard, Mateo Sánchez. This individual locked himself into his cabin and a fight ensued, during the course of which fifty female slaves jumped overboard, to be eaten by sharks. Collier was still able eventually to liberate the other 450 slaves in Sierra Leone.

A new liberal Cortes in Madrid, after the Revolution of 1820, had meantime appointed a commission to propose measures to stop all violations of the treaty of 1817, and to decree that that document should be included in the new criminal code. But this new Cortes naturally included members from the colonies, including three from Cuba, who had instructions to point out that a further delay of at least six years was necessary for any effective prohibition on the trade. It was desirable to stock up the haciendas with slaves, and to provide 'African women for the conservation of the species and the plantations. . . . Of all the provinces of the Spanish empire', the document went on, 'the most concerned . . . in this business is the island of Cuba. No other one has undertaken the African slave trade directly with its own ships and capital. Therefore, the damages caused by the sudden cessation . . . would be incalculable.'[18]

The Cuban deputies at the Cortes, however, included Fray Félix Varela, Professor of Philosophy, a real liberal who had passed his childhood in Florida. He ignored his instructions from Havana: the first Cuban to say anything publicly against the slave trade, he boldly stated that until slavery was abolished the Antilles would always be in danger of slave revolts, for the Haitian and continental revolutionaries had many plans for the liberation of his island. How could one expect the slaves to be tranquil while the *criollos* and others rejoiced in their new freedom under the constitution of 1820? 'The barbarian is the best soldier when he finds someone to lead him. Santo Domingo showed that there would be no lack of leaders [in Cuba]. The general wish of the people of Cuba is that there should be no slaves. They only want to find some other way to supply their necessities.' Varela proposed the liberty of slaves who had served fifteen years with the same master, and the liberty for all born after the publication of the decree. He also wanted the establishment of a lottery whose winner would be allowed to buy his freedom, and the foundation of philanthropic committees charged with directing abolition and protecting slaves.[19]

This speech received no attention in Spain, but much publicity in Cuba. The historian José Antonio Saco, a pupil of Varela's, himself soon to be a deputy from Cuba, recalled that he heard someone in the Cortes say, 'Any deputy from Cuba who asks for the abolition of slavery ought to have his tongue torn out. . . .' Another priest-deputy to the Cortes from Cuba, a canon of the cathedral, Fray Juan Bernardo O'Gabán, was persuaded to write a pamphlet against Varela (*Observaciones sobre la suerte de los negros*) in which he insisted that the slave trade was a means whereby the Africans could be rendered civilized. So, if humanitarianism were truly understood, 'wise legislators would compel the Africans to work, and protect, not oppose, their transition to America'.[20]

The question was left unresolved until, in April 1823, the French army of '100,000 Sons of St Louis', inspired by Chateaubriand, destroyed the revolutionary government in Spain. Liberals in Madrid were swept away, exiled, and even executed; and Varela and those who thought like him emigrated, as so many enlightened Cubans have had to do since, to the United States. With that counter-revolution, any chance of a swift end to Cuban slavery ended.

In an effort to maintain her own policy, the British navy extended its network of patrol ships to the coasts of Cuba and Brazil. Yet many slavers entered the ports of Cuba (twenty-six at least in 1820 and 1821, perhaps ten, four, and seven respectively in 1822, 1823, and 1824), and it was not till the last of these years that the British captured a slave cargo off the island and the slaves, the so-called *emancipados*, were freed.

After the capture of this first vessel, a new controversy broke out. The Commander-in-Chief in Spain, General Francisco Tomás Morales (he had commanded the last Spanish army in Venezuela, which he had withdrawn to Cuba), was found to be a major shareholder in the condemned ship: a fact which, as the British Judge Kilbee pointed out, in one of his many reports to London, 'speaks volumes as to the state of the slave trade'. Kilbee had already convinced himself that, 'with very few exceptions, all the employees under the government [in Havana] are directly or indirectly engaged in the traffic'.

Then arose the difficult question of the *emancipados*: these ex-slaves, beneficiaries of English philanthropy, were supposed to be handed over to members of the clergy, to widows, or to other benign proprietors who promised to look after them. But after a few consignments, the disposal of such unwilling emigrants from Africa became yet one more business. The Captain-General was unenthusiastic about releasing a large number of free blacks into Cuba, and handed over their distribution to Joaquín Gómez, originally of Cádiz, one of the prominent slave dealers of the island. In this way, the planters naturally came to control the *emancipados* exactly as if they had been slaves.

New laws, it is true, provided that these Africans were to be instructed in the Christian religion, taught a craft and so made capable of sustaining themselves, and after four years made free. But in practice the masters had no incentive not to overwork them. In addition, they were customarily re-employed by those who had had their services at the beginning.

The seizure by HMS *Lion* of a second Cuban slave ship, *El Relámpago*, in late 1824 was the beginning of an argument between the British and the Spaniards which lasted half a century. One hundred and fifty *bozal* slaves – that is, slaves from Africa – were on board, all entitled to certificates as *emancipados*. Judge Kilbee wrote out some provisions which would have given each freed man, or woman, a trade. But an astute new Spanish judge on the mixed court, Claudio Martínez de Pinillos, who had succeeded Ramírez, insisted on the political dangers of releasing the *emancipados*. If these Africans (filled with English ideas of freedom) were placed at liberty, they would constitute a dangerous example to others on the island. The Cuban authorities explained additionally that they could not return the *emancipados* to Africa, because of the cost, the difficulty of finding ships, the folly of returning such souls to 'the darkness of paganism', and the certainty of exposing the persons concerned to resale into slavery. Martínez de Pinillos, an able economist who was now Treasurer of Havana as well as a judge, had helped when still in Spain to draft the decree on free trade in the Americas, which had it been issued only a few years earlier might have saved the Spanish empire from dissolution. In Cuba he devised a way to raise the annual income of the colony from 2,000,000 pesos to 37,000,000 in a space of only twelve years. That was why he was taken so seriously.[*]

The Council of the Indies in Madrid, however, refused Martínez de Pinillos's ideas on the treatment of *emancipados*. One of the members, Manuel Guazo, suggested that the Africans should be brought to Spain and asked to build roads. But the Archbishop of Toledo was hostile to the idea. Others suggested they should be dispatched to the Balearic Islands or the Mosquito Coast in Central America to work under the guidance of priests. The Havana City Council argued that the captured slave ships and their *emancipados* should be carried back by the British to Sierra Leone. But the Spanish Foreign Minister in the end decided that the Africans should be taken to be employed as domestic servants in Spain. The journey would be paid for by the sale of the captured slave ships concerned and, if necessary, more money would be raised by a tax in Cuba.

This decision was issued as a royal decree in 1828. But the Cuban planters still thought that the scheme would cost too much. Joaquín Gómez, the slave dealer who had become Subprior of the Consulado of Havana, thought that twenty pesos a head was the minimum cost of taking the *emancipados* back to Spain. Martínez de Pinillos then suggested that these 'free men' should merely be distributed as theretofore among institutions or individuals of the island, 'to be employed, either as servants or as free labourers'. There was no indication as to how the Africans were to be distinguished from slaves if they were asked, as many were, to work on a sugar or coffee plantation, and the evidence is that they were not so distinguished. But for a few years this was the interim solution preferred.

The Spanish navy, of course, was supposed to be fulfilling the same task as was the British, but between 1820 and 1842 its vessels stopped precisely two ships, both Portuguese, and therefore the slaves within them were not subject to the jurisdiction of Judge Kilbee and his court. Yet though the British tally of ships seized was far higher, it made little impact on the number of slavers arriving: at least thirty-seven in 1825, perhaps bringing over 11,000 slaves, and some fourteen in 1826, bringing over 3,700. Kilbee reported to Canning in 1825, 'It is not from being in possession of better sources of information than formerly that I am enabled to state the number of slaves landed . . . but merely [because] transactions of this nature are now public and notorious, no mystery being found necessary.'[21]

The British government, for all its investment in intelligence, seems never to have realized the true picture of the Spanish scheme of things, and

---

[*] *He was also the pioneer of the first railway in the Spanish world, which extended from Havana to Güines, built in 1830 making use of a loan from Alexander Robertson of London, of £450,450.*

persisted in its efforts to seek formal agreements which it supposed would be honourably maintained by the other party. This was a policy which Castlereagh as Foreign Secretary in London pursued also with Portugal, with whom he arranged a new treaty, in July 1817. That constituted a modest extension of the undertakings previously concluded between the two countries. The navies of both countries were now to be able to board merchant ships suspected of illegal trading; and that meant, above all, the British navy, for the Portuguese had no stomach for such work. Still, ships found to have slaves on board illegally were to be detained, and their captains sent for trial, either in Sierra Leone or in Rio, by the usual creation of a mixed court, British and Portuguese judges being present in both places. The ships would be sold. Slaves found aboard would be freed as *emancipados* and employed as servants or free labourers to private persons of 'known integrity' or in public works. Two months after the treaty, the government of Portugal promulgated a domestic law which announced punishments, but only for illegal traders and captains: confiscation of the ship, heavy fines, and exile to Mozambique. South of the equator, slaving was still to be legal for another five years. The law of 1813 had specified that surgeons were to be carried on every slave ship; but now amateurs, 'negro bleeders', were to be enough. The law of 1813 had limited slaves to five for each two tons of displacement up to 201 tons, and only one slave for each additional ton. But after 1818, five slaves would be carried per two tons regardless.

Further, as in Cuba, the law relating to *emancipados* proved impossible to apply, and most of the Africans concerned were treated as if they were still slaves: while the sentence of 'exile to Mozambique' merely enabled the criminal to share in the continuing use of that territory as a slaving colony.

The treaty, though, caused fury in Brazil. The planters and merchants there, in circumstances wholly different from those in Cuba, began for the first time to contemplate independence. There seems never to have been any secret assurance from Lisbon to Rio that the trade in slaves would go on, as there had yet been in the case of Spain and Cuba; whatever the intentions of Portugal, the merchants of Brazil were determined to go on trading in slaves in their old harbours. Most of them took the British official opposition to the traffic lightly: were not Brazilian planters still being afforded credit by British banks to buy slaves? Were not British goods extensively used in stocking up ships which left Rio or Bahia for African shores? Just after the signature of the Anglo-Portuguese Treaty of 1817, the import of slaves increased 'beyond all former example', as the British Minister, Henry Chamberlain, put it in May 1818, adding that twenty-five ships had 'arrived here since the beginning of the year, none of them bringing less, and many more, than 400. . . .' Comparable figures were repeated annually.[22]

It would be a mistake to suppose that Brazilian independence was inspired only by anger over the slave trade. All the same, when in 1823 Dom Pedro, the Regent, so dramatically proclaimed the independence of the country, and his own place as first Emperor, he was sustained by a public opinion whose resentment of the government in Lisbon had been enhanced by its acceptance of English pressure on the subject of the slave trade.

Thereafter, Britain had to deal not so much with Portugal but with the new empire of the south. The first move was made by a Brazilian. In November 1822 Canning was approached in London by an unofficial Brazilian representative of Dom Pedro, General Filisberto Caldeira Brant (the future Marquis of Barbacena), about the possibility of diplomatic recognition. Canning explained that Brazil's involvement in the slave trade would have first to be considered. These remarks fell on unexpectedly favourable ears for Brant, like his master Dom Pedro, personally opposed the slave trade, and even talked of the desirability of the abolition of slavery altogether: they were interested in the replacement of slaves by European labour partly out of philanthropy but also because they feared what would befall Brazil were there to be a permanent black majority. In a later discussion, Canning implied that if Brazil were to offer abolition of the traffic he could promise that Britain would recognize Brazil. Brant, for his part, said that he was prepared to wager, but not to promise, that if there were to be recognition and if Britain were to agree to admit Brazilian sugar the traffic would be abolished within four years. Canning then asked for the backing of his own Cabinet for an arrangement along these lines, arguing that 'the great mart of the legal slave trade is Brazil'.[23] But Brant never obtained authority from his government. Dom Pedro's chief minister, Bonifacio de Andrada e Silva, was probably more hostile to slavery than anyone in the country, but he feared the social consequence of immediate abolition.* Soon Dom Bonifacio was forced from office, partly because of his critical views on slavery. Still, the Brazilian Assembly debated the matter openly and remarkably concluded by only asking for a minimum of four years before the abolition of the trade. A treaty along those lines was ratified in 1826. The agreement was similar to that made with Spain, with respect to Cuba; it provided for the end of the slave trade in three years. After 1830, therefore, trafficking in slaves would be considered piracy by the new Brazilian government. A commercial treaty was also signed, which gave Britain a privileged position in Brazil and, of course, Britain recognized the new country.

But a long debate in the Brazilian Assembly followed over whether to ratify these documents. The Brazilian Minister for Foreign Affairs, the

---

* This statesman, a scientist and traveller in the mould of Humboldt, had studied under Volta and Lavoisier, had visited France as well as Turkey, and had built canals in Portugal before returning to a political life in Brazil in 1819.

Marquis of Queluz, a Portuguese-born aristocrat who had in 1821 published a criticism of the slave trade, explained in a remarkably frank letter to the Chamber of Deputies that in accepting the British demands the government was 'acting for the good of the nation in conceding willingly what would have been taken from it by force'. Most speakers in the debate, whatever the merits of the matter, complained that Brazilians had been constrained to accept abolition by Britain: it was not the Chamber of Deputies which was making the law, but the 'English who dictated it, the English who are imposing it on us, and the English who are to execute it against the unfortunate Brazilians'. Thus Raimundo da Cunha Matos, who had spent many years in Africa, and who believed that 'the moment had not come for Brazil to abandon the importation of slaves'. Few Brazilians believed in Britain's humanitarian motives. Most thought that she must want to ruin Brazilian agriculture in order to benefit the British West Indies. Britain, they even thought, desired to break Brazil's links with Angola in order to help London to 'become lords of Africa'. As for the working conditions of slaves, Brazilian deputies pointed to the thirty-five saints' days, as well as Sundays, when the slaves of their country could dance and sing, and contrasted those with the hard life which they believed obtained in slave communities in British colonies in the Caribbean. In the event, however, the treaty was ratified, and the new country braced itself for abolition in 1830. In Luanda, merchants wondered how they would in future pay for the goods to which they had become used. What legal trade could there seriously be? Beeswax? Ivory?[24]

Meantime, the slave trade to Brazil, threatened with a speedy conclusion, rose to new heights just as it had done in Cuba in similar circumstances: slaves imported into Rio totalled over 30,000 annually in 1826, 1827, and 1828, and reached 45,000 and nearly 60,000 in 1829 and 1830. In Brazil, capital was 'everywhere embarked in the purchase of Negroes', a British observer remarked; and another traveller, the Reverend Robert Walsh, journeying from Rio to Minas Gerais in 1828, recalled meeting every day caravans of slaves 'such as Mungo Park described in Africa, winding through the woods, the slave merchant, distinguished by his large felt hat and poncho, bringing up the rear on a mule, with a long lash in the hand. It was another subject of pity to see groups of these poor creatures cowering together at night in the open ranches drenched with cold rain, in a climate so much more frigid than their own.' There was, he thought, 'such a glut of human flesh in the markets of Rio that it has become an unprofitable drug [unsaleable surplus]'.[25]

Paradoxically, the defenders of the trade began to insist that Africans were needed in order to civilize Brazil: 'Africa civilizes Brazil,' declared Bernardo Pereira de Vasconcelos. At the same time, 'heaping barrels of gunpowder into the Brazilian mine' was a frequent metaphor of the abolitionists, who began to exhibit, by implication, something like racial prejudice when they insisted that it was necessary for Brazil to end the slave trade in order to ensure the survival of a white population.

In May 1830 Dom Pedro, in his annual speech from the throne, confirmed that the Brazilian slave trade would soon be declared illegal. But a year later, convinced of his own unpopularity, he abdicated in favour of his six-year-old son; and though one reason for his bad reputation was his continuing link with the now hated Portuguese, another was his treaty on abolition with Britain. Yet this resignation did not prevent a new Brazilian government in November 1831 from passing legislation which would make the import of slaves illegal. Canning's one-time interlocutor, General Brant, introduced the bill into the Senate. Article 1 stated that all slaves entering Brazil would automatically be free. The police were given powers to examine ships which they suspected of bringing in captives. Fines, imprisonment, rewards, bounties were all prescribed. Various regulations followed, including one which enabled Africans who thought that their import had been illegal to present themselves to judges.[26]

This radical measure was not passed primarily for philanthropic reasons. It was partly done 'to show the English', as the phrase was: to indicate good intentions but not necessarily to promise good actions. Most rational Brazilians thought that the commercial benefits of being on good terms with Britain overshadowed everything. Others were frightened by recent slave revolts in the province of Bahia. It had seemed for a moment as if African religious wars might repeat themselves in Brazil. Recent revolts had been directed by intelligent men able to read and write Arabic. In the slave quarters of Bahia at this time, there sometimes seemed more literate people than there were in the 'Great Houses'. 'It was not uncultivated blacks who arrived here [in those days]', wrote the historian Nina Rodrigues, 'but highly civilized members of warrior peoples, who knew how to read and write in Arab script, and who sometimes had entered into the service of masters less refined than themselves. In addition, they had the religious spirit of Islam. . . . They were difficult to turn into docile machines for cultivating the land. . . .'[27] There had been a Hausa rising in Brazil in 1807, a more general Islamic one in 1809, and less easily identifiable rebellions in 1814, 1816, 1822, and 1826; thereafter an upheaval almost every year. Many whites were killed before the rebellions were at last crushed.

The Netherlands signed a treaty with Britain similar to that which the latter had arranged with Spain and Portugal, and also in 1818. It provided for abolition to be guaranteed by a British naval right of visit and search. There would be a court in Suriname (as well as in Sierra Leone) to balance those in Havana and Rio. It was agreed that a Dutch naval squadron should be established to the same purpose. This arrangement was achieved without much trouble by the British Minister at The Hague, Richard le Poer Trench, Lord Clancarty, who persuaded Castlereagh to permit him to give presents to those who helped; in the end, though, and despite Holland's virtual abandonment of the commerce in slaves, it was only the intervention of the new Anglophile King Willem of the Netherlands which led his Cabinet to act as the British desired.˙ Though no slavers had set out from the Netherlands for Africa after 1808, some Dutch merchants did continue to participate in the illegal trade to Suriname, as suggested by Heine in his poem 'Das Sklavenschiff' (as did some French ships, such as the *Legère* of 1823, whose Captain Dubois escaped prosecution on the curious, if romantic, ground that his father had been murdered in the Vendée). Meantime, the Dutch were busy on the Gold Coast in pursuit of 'legitimate commerce', and a fine proconsul, Governor Daendels, busied himself with widening the main road from Elmina to Kumasi.[28]

But even the Anglo-Dutch Treaty was evaded. For example, the Dutch judge at Sierra Leone, Van Sirtema, intervened on the side of the slavers. This was shown when in 1819 HMS *Thistle*, commanded by Lieutenant Hagan, arrested the Dutch ship *Eliza* off the Grain Coast. She had certainly been carrying slaves, but they had all been unloaded save for one, who provided the overt reason for Lieutenant Hagan's action. Van Sirtema preposterously ruled Hagan out of court on the legalistic ground that the treaty spoke of 'slaves', not 'a slave'.†[29]

The Dutch agreed in 1823 that a vessel could be condemned if she was obviously equipped for slaving, even if she had not yet purchased a slave. This 'equipment' was as Canning had defined it.‡ Several Dutch ships were condemned under these clauses in 1825–6. For some Dutch slaving continued. The sugar planters of Suriname needed slaves after the Napoleonic Wars, or thought that they did. Their production of sugar was modest in comparison with that of Cuba and Brazil, but they were deeply involved in the crop. Often Dutch ships concealed themselves under French flags. Crews on such ships were often, indeed usually, not Dutch. Then there were some incidents such as that of the *Fortunée*, which in 1827 was seized by a British naval vessel and taken to the Anglo-Dutch court in Sierra Leone, since the ship's papers had been thrown overboard and the crew had been ordered to learn some strange Christian names which

---

˙ *Some, such as the statesman Van der Oudermeulen, had wanted to revive the trade in slaves at that time to Suriname (Oudermeulen was a son of the famous governor of that colony).*

† *The case was repeated when the Portuguese judge ruled out of order the action of HMS* Myrmidon *in arresting a Portuguese vessel,* San Salvador, *with only one slave on board. On that occasion, the court found that the slave, who was sent back to the mainland when the* Myrmidon *came in sight, still belonged to the seller, the formidable merchant of Havana, Joaquín Gómez.*

‡ *See page 595.*

could be taken for Dutch. All together twenty-three ships were charged before the Anglo-Dutch courts, all but one at Freetown, the remaining one in Paramaribo. The latter, the *Nueve von Snauw*, was in 1823 declared a legal prize, the fifty-four slaves on board were freed, and the one English member of the crew was tried in Barbados.

Dutch planters seem not to have been able to afford slave prices after 1830. All the same, the interfering activities of the British judges in Paramaribo continued to incense the local planters, and the last British judge there, Edward Schenley, left fearing for his life, after having denounced some slave owners for cruelty. *In absentia*, after his return to England, he was found guilty of the slander for reporting ill of planters, in reports published in England.

British abolitionists, who to the outside world now seemed to include ministers as well as polemicists, had also to deal, in relation to the slave trade, with the complex position of the United States. Britain wanted to influence policy in Washington but found it difficult to do so. The United States had not been represented at the conferences organized by Castlereagh after the Napoleonic Wars, for the traditional reason that the country was determined to avoid 'entangling alliances' and was not concerned to look for 'monsters' to destroy. For example, when approached on the question of the slave trade in 1818 by Castlereagh, Richard Rush, the cultivated Pennsylvanian (son of the abolitionist Dr Benjamin Rush), who had previously been Secretary of State and was then Minister in London, insisted, on the instructions of Secretary of State John Quincy Adams, that 'nothing but the actual finding of slaves on board was ever to authorise a seizure or a detention' by a British naval ship. The 'peculiar situation and institutions of the United States' prevented the kind of agreement which Britain desired. The 'admission of a right in officers of foreign ships of war to enter and search the ships of the United States in time of peace, under any circumstances whatever, would meet with universal repugnance in the public opinion of this country'.[30] Had the British been able to realize the feelings which the United States still had about Britain's continuing claim in time of war to be able to impress into her navy sailors on board seized merchant ships, North American statesmen might have been more willing to accept the British position on the right of search. For, after all, Britain was proposing a *mutual* right; and the scheme was to be limited to a specific coast and to specific ships.

Actually, Britain's request did not seem unreasonable to everyone in the United States. In 1817, for example, a committee of the House of Representatives urged the opening of negotiations leading to a grant of the right of search, and in 1819 a great lawyer, then young, Judge Story, denounced the clandestine continuation of the slave trade before a grand jury in Boston. He recalled the passage in the Constitution where all men were declared free and equal, with inalienable rights. How could it be that slaves were excluded from that clause? He bravely concluded, with regard to the slave trade: 'If we tolerate this traffic, our charity is but a name, and our religion is no more than a faint and elusive shadow.'[31]

The territories where the trade was tolerated in that time were still Louisiana and East Florida. Slaves were concentrated at Galveston in Texas (still part of Mexico), and then bought by enterprising merchants in New Orleans. Many of these captives were procured, in the first instance, by pirates, who, using armed vessels, would capture bona fide Spanish slavers on the high seas. In March 1818 the Collector of Customs of Brunswick, Georgia (McIntosh), told the Secretary of the Treasury that 'African and West Indian negroes are almost daily illicitly introduced into Georgia'. Collector Chew of New Orleans assured the government that 'to put a stop to that traffic a naval force suitable to these waters is indispensable', for, otherwise, 'vast numbers of slaves will be introduced to an alarming extent. . . .'[32]

Florida was still Spanish.* Many settlements there had become bases for trading slaves to North America, especially Amelia Island, just off the coast at Jacksonville, a kind of Curaçao of the nineteenth century. So great was the trade there that 'three hundred sail of square rigged vessels were seen at one time in the Spanish waters waiting for cargoes'. Another centre was Barataria Bay, south of New Orleans, a site well known for many kinds of contraband goods in the years leading up to 1820, by law a part of the United States but a private, if illegal, fief of Jean and Pierre Lafitte, two Bayonne-born adventurers. Their technique was to send pirates out to capture Spanish slavers and bring their cargoes, via the bayous, the lakes and creeks to the west of the Mississippi, to the mainland. Jean Lafitte, first established in a blacksmithery in New Orleans about 1810, is a familiar figure in the history of the slave trade, a criminal with good manners, as much noted for his lavish hospitality as for his ruthlessness. Lafitte owed much of his success to his skilful manipulation of a British offer of pardon for past offences in return for help against the United States in the siege of New Orleans in 1814.

The government sent Commodore Daniel T. Patterson and Colonel George T. Ross to destroy the settlement of Barataria Bay. But there were always new opportunities for determined traders. For example, Commodore Louis Aury, another pirate, established himself first at Galveston Island, off what is now Houston, then at Matagorda, also in Texas but further to the south-west, and finally also at Amelia Island, in order to smuggle slaves (he was legally an officer in the navy of New Granada, though law was not a matter to which he gave a high priority). In 1817 Governor David Mitchell of Georgia (a Scot, having been born in

---

* Though not West Florida, which had been cavalierly absorbed by the United States in 1803.

Muthill, Perthshire) resigned his charge in order to become United States agent for the Creek Indians and so, apparently, share in the smuggling traffic between Georgia and Louisiana, where he received slaves. (He was detected and charged in 1821, but acquitted.)

The technique here, it became clear – in the words of Richard Drake, who participated – was for 'the kaffle [sic; that is, koffle], under the charge of negro drivers . . . to strike up the Escambria river and thence across the [unmarked] border [of Florida] into Georgia, where some of our wild Africans were mixed up with various squads of native blacks and driven inland until sold off, singly or in couples on the road. . . . The Spanish possessions were thriving on this inland exchange of negroes. . . . Florida was a sort of nursery for slavebreeders and many American citizens grew rich by trafficking in Guinea negroes and smuggling them continually, in small parties, through the southern United States. . . . The business was a lively one.'[33]

The Lafittes, meantime, established themselves at a settlement on Galveston Island which they named Campeche, where they carried on their profitable activities for several prosperous years: sometimes capturing slave ships themselves, sometimes trading with pirates, such as René Béluche or Georges Champlin, who had seized ships on the high seas. Some of the pirate slaves were sold in the United States, the rest in Cuba.

When General Andrew Jackson seized Pensacola in Florida in 1818, one of his officers, Captain Brooke, captured in the harbour the slaver *Constitution*, with eighty-four Africans on board, bound for a United States harbour; and Lieutenant McKeever also captured the *Louisa* and the *Marino*, with only twenty-three slaves between them. All were plainly destined for the United States market.

There was one other source of slaves: Richard Drake claimed (in a work which owed much to the author's desire to be sensational, but has some merits all the same) that in those years before he had set himself up on one of the Bay Islands off Honduras, where he regularly kept 1,600 slaves ready for sale to dealers who came from Havana as well as New York, New Orleans, Florida, and even Boston. Some of these slaves, he claimed, 'were taken into the great American swamps, and there kept until wanted for the market. Hundreds were sold as "captured runaways" from the Florida wilderness. We had agents in every slave state [of the United States], and our coasters were built in Maine and came out with lumber. . . . If you should hang all the Yankee merchants engaged in [the trade], hundreds would fill their places', he added comfortingly.

Estimates of the numbers of slaves imported in these years to the United States vary considerably. General James Tallmadge, a congressman from New York and subsequent President of New York University, told the House of Representatives in 1819 that it was a 'well-known fact that about 14,000 slaves have been brought to our country this past year', and Representatives Henry Middleton and Wright, from South Carolina and

Virginia respectively, both of them owning substantial plantations using slaves, suggested the same figures. These estimates are probably exaggerations. The subject of this illegal slave trade has, remarkably, been avoided by historians of North America. Still, the most serious student of statistics of the trade suggests that about 50,000 slaves were introduced into the United States between 1807 and 1860; if so, the vast majority of them must have arrived in the ways suggested, and during the years 1807 to 1830.[34]

Largely as a result of the scandal of Amelia Island, the administration of President James Monroe in 1818 introduced a new Antislaving Act, offering a reward to smugglers of slaves who informed on their associates. Ships would also be forfeit, half of the proceeds of the sale going to the government of the United States, half to the informers. Those accused had to prove that the slaves whom they had with them had not been brought in illegally. This bill did not excite much attention, even during its passage through Congress, though it was alleged in the debate that James Bowie of New Orleans (he of the sheath knife) made $65,000 in two years as a result, by first smuggling slaves sold to him by Jean Lafitte, and then informing on him, and so gaining the reward.

In 1819 Representative Hugh Nelson of Virginia, son of the revolutionary Governor of that state, and owner of a fine estate at Belvoir in Albemarle County, with slaves, insisted on writing a death penalty into the Antislavery Act. This was cut out by the Senate. But in May 1820 a new bill was introduced which did prescribe that punishment. By the same document, the President was empowered 'to cause any of the armed vessels of the United States to be employed to cruise on any of the coasts of the United States or territories thereof, or of the coasts of Africa or elsewhere', to seize American slavers. He was also allocated $100,000 to enforce the act.

President Monroe sent a small flotilla of naval ships to the African coast. Thus Captain Edward Trenchard, with the *Cyane*, set off in January 1820; Captain George C. Reed followed, with the corvette *Hornet*, in June 1820; Captain Robert Field Stockton (son of 'Richard the Duke', Senator for New Jersey), with the schooner *Alligator*, left in April 1821; Captain H. S. Wadsworth, with twenty-four guns, left with the corvette *John Adams*, in July 1821; and Captain Matthew Perry, on the schooner *Shark*, left in August 1821. This was the first occasion when the new United States had taken any action in the matter of the slave trade as far from home as West Africa. The experience afforded an interesting lesson, but otherwise it was scarcely an effective change. Yet this was the first action of the United States as an international power, apart from her earlier modest role against Barbary pirates.

Of these captains, Captain Perry (brother of the hero of Lake Erie, and future instigator of trade with Japan) would report, 'I could not even hear of an American slaving vessel.'[35] He was, however, a man from Newport, where his statue now stands in a prominent public place, and his brother had married James de Wolf's daughter, so perhaps any surprise at his remarkable statement should be muted. Perry did, however, halt and search a French schooner, the *Y*, Captain Guillaume Segond, owned by the Governor of Guadeloupe, which he was sure, from her cargo (1,000 gallons of rum, 7,000 pounds of tobacco, and a trunkful of umbrellas), was a slaver. But he could not prove it. (He was right: Segond later picked up 400 slaves and delivered them safe and sound in Guadeloupe.) He also found an unquestionable slaver of the same provenance with 133 captives on board from the River Gallinas, south of the Sénégal, the *Caroline*. France was not then a party to any treaty to suppress the trade, and Perry had to let her go. His officers, however, shocked by the emaciated condition of the captives, offered jointly to reimburse Perry for any loss which he might incur for illegal capture. Perry declined but elicited from the slave captain, Victor Ruinet, a paper pledging himself never to trade slaves again; but in a year or two that master was to be found in command again, on the *Jeune Caroline* and the *Prince de Orange*. In the *Cyane*, Captain Trenchard, who had Quaker forebears, was more successful: he captured five North American slavers; Captain Reed, in the *Hornet*, one; and Stockton, in the *Alligator*, four. (Stockton also fought two duels, one with a British officer, and later became a senator, like his father.) All the ships had been bound for Havana, and were condemned, but the masters and crews were released.

Altogether, between May 1818 and November 1821, 573 Africans were captured by United States naval captains, from eleven ships. Sir George Collier, still commander of the equivalent British squadron, reported with unusual warmth that his North American counterparts 'have, on all occasions, acted with the greatest zeal . . . and it is extremely gratifying to me to observe that the most perfect unanimity prevailed between the officers of His Majesty's squadron and those of American vessels of war engaged in the same view. . . .'[36]

That statement had substance in 1821. But there was little subsequent action by the United States until after 1839 and even then, as will be seen, little further collaboration between the two English-speaking powers. Another North American captain, more observant or more honest than Perry, reporting that he had made ten captures, said, 'Although they are evidently owned by Americans, they are so completely covered by Spanish papers that it is impossible to condemn them. . . . The slave trade', he added, 'is carried out, to a very great extent. There are probably no less than 300 vessels [of different nations] engaged in the traffic, each having two or three sets of papers.' Secretary of State Adams agreed that the United States ships might collaborate off Africa with British naval ships; but the practical consequences of that concession were modest.

The United States did, however, create her own Sierra Leone. Following the formation in 1816 of a 'colonization society' under the auspices of Henry Clay, then Speaker of the House of Representatives, eighty-six black ex-slaves on the brig *Elizabeth* set off in February 1820, escorted by the United States naval corvette *Cyane*, under Captain Trenchard, to land at Sherbro Island, where, sixty miles south of Sierra Leone, Kizel, a black from New Bedford, had established a colony of eight families at his own expense. But twenty-five of the new immigrants died of fever, as did the government agent, the Reverend Samuel Bacon. The rest went on to Sierra Leone. They were later taken to Cape Mesurado, which settlement was the basis of Monrovia (named after President James Monroe). After some fighting between these survivors and slave traders who were busy embarking slaves onto ships at Tradetown, some miles away, a colony was established as 'Liberia'. Other little polities were also founded. All these places, like Sierra Leone, were, however, on too small a scale to make much of a contribution to the problems of slavery in the New World.

In 1820 and 1821 another committee of the House of Representatives actually recommended granting the right of search to Britain. But the Secretary of State, John Quincy Adams, was still hostile to the idea. He told Stratford Canning, the British Minister in Washington (the self-assertive cousin of George Canning): 'A compact giving the power to the naval authorities of one nation to search the merchant vessels of another for offenders and offences against the laws of another . . . backed by a further power to seize and carry into another port, and there subject to decision of a tribunal composed of at least one half foreigners, irresponsible to the supreme corrective tribunal of this nation . . . was an investment of power . . . so adverse to the elementary principles and indispensable securities of individual rights that . . . not even the most unqualified approbation of the ends . . . could justify the transgression.'[37]

True, in early 1823, Britain and the United States together agreed to regard the slave trade as piracy. For a few months Congress seemed to be contemplating a real agreement with Britain. On 28 February 1823 the House of Representatives requested the President to embark on negotiations with 'the European maritime powers' in order to denounce the slave trade as piracy, and asked him, too, to concede a limited right of search: a qualification which was, however, lost in the Senate. (The lead among those senators who opposed this was taken by the ex-prince of North American slavers, James de Wolf of Rhode Island.) Still, Secretary of State Adams thought that a denunciation of the slave trade under the law of nations was politically possible, and sent to London a draft treaty to that effect, allowing suspect ships to be seized by the navy of any country, but always to be tried under the laws of the country of the trading vessel. Here seemed a real opportunity.

Canning, the Foreign Secretary, agreed to the scheme, though both he and his cousin in Washington believed that it would be much better to offer a general right of search. He added to Adams's document a sentence to the effect that citizens of any country captured under the flag of a third power should be sent to their own capitals for trial, and that citizens of

that third country should be similarly treated. President Monroe laid the
amended draft before the Senate on 30 April 1824. A vigorous attack was
then launched on it. The Whig Senator Henry Johnson of Louisiana, in
particular, proposed numerous destructive amendments – for example,
one excluding the territorial waters of the United States from the treaty, as
well as all mention of the application of the right of search to citizens
hiring a ship of a third nation. Such exclusions were unacceptable to
Britain. Stratford Canning reported to his cousin that he believed that he
was 'engaged in a hopeless task' in trying to secure that general right of
search which alone, he maintained, could result in a swift end to the slave
traffic. The consequences of these discussions – between men who were
among the ablest ever to hold the portfolios of foreign affairs in both
Britain and the United States – were ineffective; and so Britain was
obliged to act alone for the next fifteen and more years. A determined
North American abolitionist, Charles Fenton Mercer, Representative for
Virginia, tried often, in the next few months, to persuade his government
to reopen discussions with Britain. He failed; it was one of the reasons
why, at the age of sixty, he resigned from Congress to become a bank
cashier in Tallahassee, Florida.

The reasons for Mercer's failure were twofold. First, the constant
interference by British cruisers with United States ships caused rancour
(even if they were slavers), since, as John Quincy Adams had warned,
United States legislators could not contemplate approving foreigners'
exposure of their country's negligence in enforcing its own laws. The
second reason was that despite the relatively small number of its imports
of slaves in the nineteenth century, slavery seemed in the United States an
institution 'more deeply entrenched', at least in the South, than ever. In
those years, the South was prospering, and wealth was growing faster
than in the North. Cotton planters were certain that slavery was efficient
as a system of labour. They thus became busy in the active protection of
the prized institution: in eleven states, for example, the death penalty was
now introduced for slaves who took part in insurrections, and in thirteen
it became a capital crime to incite slaves to rebellion. New barriers to
manumission were also devised.

As a last offer, President Monroe requested all governments in
Europe to negotiate with him in order to achieve an end to the slave
trade. But that well-intentioned move led nowhere. European governments distrusted conferences, and certainly did not like the idea of one
presided over by the United States.

It should not be supposed that France and the United States, jointly
antagonistic to the British though they were in these years, were also
always in understanding with each other. In 1821, for example, relations
reached a very low level. That was because Lieutenant Stockton of the
United States Navy had seized four vessels off Africa flying French flags,
which he was convinced were slavers from North America. He put United

States crews aboard and sent them to Boston. The French government was outraged and, in particular, raised the case of the *Jeune Eugénie*, which was certainly French, had sailed direct from Guadeloupe to Africa to buy slaves, and had, under the name of the *Jeune Catherine*, already been apprehended once by the British navy. The French Minister, Jean-Baptiste Hyde de Neuville,˙ called on Secretary of State John Quincy Adams in fury: 'In a loud and peremptory tone, rising from his seat and with vehement gesture [he] said, "Well sir, since you think it proper to report to the President what I came here to say to you in confidential conversation with you, I desire you to tell him from me, as my individual opinion that, if satisfaction is not made to France . . . *la France doit leur déclarer la guerre."'* These last words, Adams reported, 'he spoke in a manner nearly frantic, dwelling on the word *"guerre"* with a long and virulent emphasis and, without waiting for a reply, rushed out of the room, forgetting his overcoat. . . .' (Hyde later became a strong abolitionist, at least in words; in 1823, he castigated the trade in slaves as being 'barbarous in a way up till now unknown in the history of barbarity'.)[38]

The consequences were inglorious. President Monroe assured France that Stockton had made a mistake, and that positive orders had now been given that the naval vessels of the United States were in no circumstances to seize slavers flying any foreign flag. No one seemed to complain. The cause of abolition was quiet so far as the United States was concerned.

Meantime, France, too, had by then made what seemed to be an adjustment to prevailing international opinion. In 1817 the government of the Duke of Richelieu announced firmly that any vessel which tried to take slaves 'into any of our colonies', whether French or foreign, would be confiscated, and the captain forbidden to hold any command in future. On examination, the decree seemed to be directed as much against Britain as against slave traders: it was a statement announcing that France would assume all responsibility for her own trade. The decree also left what happened within France untouched, it did not condemn French captains who took slaves to Cuba or Brazil, and the announced punishment was inadequate. The merchants of Nantes and Bordeaux, not to speak of those of Honfleur and Le Havre, immediately realized the opportunities offered by the new document, and the decree seems, not surprisingly, to have stimulated the trade to Cuba and other third countries: in 1818, there were at least twenty-eight slave journeys, mostly from Nantes.[39]

Another French measure had similarly little effect. For example, the government allowed slaves to be introduced into the territory of the River Sénégal (which Britain only returned to France with Guyane in 1817), where they were immediately declared free and then placed under an

---

˙ *This official, grandson of a James Hyde who had fled Scotland after Culloden, was a strong monarchist and would later become Minister of the Navy.*

engagement '*à temps*', for fourteen years.* Some of these men and women subsequently served the French state in Cayenne and Madagascar. Many of them had been African slaves before they worked for the French empire, and their later conditions of employment scarcely differed from slavery. All the same, the concession was considerable in law, as it was in promise.

The slave trade as such was finally declared illegal in France in March 1818. The government was probably influenced by the intelligent Baron Seguier, Consul in London, who argued that the way to outman-oeuvre the British was to reach even further than them in hostility to the traffic. However that may be, the Minister of the Marine, Count Molé, introduced a short, two-article, law on the matter in the National Assembly with a quotation from Montesquieu (the first time that that creative thinker had been quoted in the French legislature): 'Why cannot the Princes of Europe, who make so many pointless treaties, make one in favour of charity and pity?' There was no dissent in the chamber on the matter. Molé wrote to the harbour-masters in known slave ports requiring them to carry out the law prohibiting the traffic.

But this change, however well intentioned, merely converted the previously tolerated commerce into a clandestine one. A new generation of slave traders in the old harbours of France had become accustomed to the business in the three years since 1815, and they had sympathetic friends everywhere in the ministries and in the various port authorities. The trade from Nantes, illegal as it now was, was protected by the general approval of the local commercial and financial community: the Banque de Nantes, for example, and the Société d'Assurance de Nantes were domi-nated by slave interests. If the number of ships leaving French territory for slaves from Africa had been about thirty in 1818, it was nearly sixty the following year.

Molé, however, also established a French naval patrol to prevent the departure of slave ships from Africa, even if it was some years before it acted effectively. Still, four ships (the *Moucheron*, the *Iris*, the *Ecureuil*, and the *Argus*) were dispatched, first to Saint-Louis in Sénégal, then to Gorée. They were to 'visit' all French ships suspected of being slavers. (Another purpose was undoubtedly to reassert the French presence after the seven years' occupation of the French colonies in Africa by the English.) But they were not expected to approach ships which had nothing to do with France.

The first 'visit' which they carried out was nevertheless that to an Eng-lish three-masted vessel in the River Gallinas. That did not result in a con-demnation. But later they did stop and seize the *Deux Soeurs* of Marseilles. In these affairs, only the captain could be charged. Neither the crew nor the

---

* *Other places returned to France included various other African 'comptoirs', such as Arguin, Gorée, Rufisque, Joal, Portudal, Albreda on the River Gambia, the island of Gambia in the estuary of the Sierra Leone, and one or two trading posts on the islands of Los and Bissagos, as well as some on the River Casamance.*

owners had anything to fear. Many captains were interrogated, but for many months none of the cases led to any other than formal denunciations. Further, a substantial number of French vessels were still going to Cuba, as Pío Baroja recalled in his admirable novel about Basque sailors, *Los Pilotos de Altura*. That was not even a crime. In 1821 the Commissar-General of the Marine in Bordeaux, Auguste de Bergevin, would write a letter to his Minister, Baron Portal, that, 'not for a year have I had occasion to take any sailor before the courts'. But the *Dauphin*, belonging to the shipbuilder Audebert, took 300 slaves to Santiago de Cuba in 1820, and the *Mentor*, belonging to the Spanish merchant Sangroniz, probably planned to do the same. Are we to assume that the complaisant attitude of the Commissar-General was due to the recent marriage of his daughter with the widower of a member of a one-time slaving family? Or was there a tacit understanding between the Minister, Baron Portal, himself a *bordelais* ex-shipbuilder, and an Anglophobe, and Bergevin? Benjamin Constant, then a liberal deputy, thought that the latter was probable. The author of *Adolphe* was, at that time, the most eloquent, as well as the most determined, enemy of the slave trade in the Chamber of Deputies.

Despite Constant's speeches, the illicit trade both from and to Martinique and Guadeloupe also continued: and in 1820 Sir George Collier, from his frigate off Africa, reported that in the first six months of that year he saw twenty-five or thirty slave ships flying the French flag. The year had begun too with the disagreeable incident of the British cruiser HMS *Tartar*, which pursued a slaver from Martinique, *La Jeune Estelle*. The captain of the latter, Olympe Sanguines, who had obtained fourteen slaves on the Pepper Coast, was determined to avoid both pursuit and condemnation. He accordingly threw overboard a number of barrels, in each of which two girl slaves, aged about twelve to fourteen, were placed. The affair shocked the British navy, but French opinion blamed 'the enemy', to use the phraseology of the Minister of the Marine, Baron Portal. When the incident was raised in the National Assembly by Benjamin Constant he was shouted down by fellow members, who accused him of calumniating the nation. Baron Portal was not, to say the least, an enthusiast for naval patrol, even by France. For example, in 1822 he abandoned a possible action against Captain Pelleport, shipbuilder as well as master of the *Caroline* of Bayonne, because that officer was the brother of Pierre Pelleport, the Commander-in-Chief in Spain.[40]

Still, the cause of anti-slavery was becoming fashionable in some salons of restoration Paris: the return of Madame de Staël, a fervent admirer of Wilberforce, in 1816 initiated the cult of '*le bon nègre*' in intellectual circles.˙ The Marquis of La Fayette, sole survivor of the

---

˙ *Beginning, admittedly, with her family and friends. Jean-Michel Deveaux has pointed out that the abolitionist movement was headed by Constant, an ex-lover; Auguste de Staël, her son; and the Duke of Broglie, a son-in-law.*

pre-revolutionary Société des Amis des Noirs, attacked the slave trade in
the House of Peers in 1819. Pamphlets were published which had considerable force, even though most of them were largely based on material
obtained from England – even, in the case of the Abbé Giuidicelly's
Observations sur la traite of 1820, from British naval captains' reports
(though the Abbé had himself been in Sénégal). Joseph-Elzéar Morenas, a
Provençal traveller in Africa (he had been *agriculteur-botaniste* in Sénégal),
in his *Pétition contre la traite* of 1820, reported that the Chief Pilot at Saint-
Louis had used his position to buy and sell slaves. The Abbé Grégoire, a
veteran abolitionist who had signed the death sentence on King Louis
XVI, in 1822 published his *Des Peines infamantes à infliger aux négriers*, in
which he launched a famous denunciation: 'I call *négrier* not only the
captain of the ship who steals, buys, chains, barrels, and sells slaves . . .
but also every individual who, by direct or indirect cooperation, is an
accomplice in these crimes.' These idealists allied with a new society, that
of 'Christian Morals' (*Société de la Morale Chrétienne*), which set out to
seek the same broad backing as that which the committee against the
slave trade of the 1780s had in England. Beginning as a purely Catholic
organization, it gathered the support of many Protestant pastors, as well
as politicized professors such as Guizot, businessmen such as Lesseps,
and philosophical monarchists such as Maine de Biran. Auguste de
Staël was the most active of members, conducting himself as the
Thomas Clarkson of France. This body financed thousands of petitions,
organized meetings, collected information, and distributed propaganda
of every kind.

A major change in France was marked by the coming to power of the
Duke of Broglie as Prime Minister. This nobleman owed his fortune to his
descent from Antoine Crozat, the monopolist of Louisiana under Louis
XIV, but his principles to his wife. As a member of this new Society of
Christian Morals, he opened his Prime Ministership with a speech in the
House of Peers as important in its way as Pitt's had been in England in
1788. It was the longest oration made till that time in that chamber.[41] He
wanted to absolve the English of the reputation of a contemptible Machi-
avellianism of which they had been so often accused. He talked of the
scandals of the commerce, above all that of the *Jeune Estelle*, which seemed
a scandal as terrible in French eyes as the *Zong* had been in English. He
talked of the 30 per cent profits usually made, much higher than those
earned in conventional voyages. He wanted to make any involvement
in the trade a crime, and to embark on the Christianization of Africa – an
anticipation, no doubt, of France's civilizing mission in that continent.

The consequences were less considerable than the abolitionists
hoped. Broglie thought that the existing laws were adequate – they had
only to be fulfilled. It is true that the fleet off Africa did receive orders to
act forcefully against French slave traders. But all the same, the conduct of Broglie was only the beginning of a national campaign, not its

conclusion; and the French navy still covered effectively a mere 200 miles, between Saint-Louis and Gorée.

The campaign continued. In 1823 the Académie Française declared the Abolition of the Slave Trade the theme of its prize poem, while the number of slave traders was 42 per cent less than the previous year. In 1824 Bergevin, who had ceased to be Harbour-master of Bordeaux and was now a deputy for Brest, sought imprudently, in a speech, to put the blame for any surviving slave trade in Bordeaux on 'Spanish firms settled in France . . . sending Danish or Swedish ships'. The idea was surrealistic, though the mere fact that Bergevin showed himself so defensive suggested that abolitionism was beginning to be effective. The next year, the Duchess of Duras, a daughter of a Martiniquaise and granddaughter of a sugar planter (she had herself lived in Martinique, as well as in London during the great days of the slave-trade debates in the 1790s), published her romantic story *Ourika*, in which a black slave girl adopted by the mysterious Madame de B— is the heroine. It met with an extraordinary success: Humboldt, Walter Scott, Talleyrand, and Goethe loved it.*[42] In 1825 Auguste de Staël openly purchased slave equipment, such as chains and manacles, in Nantes (which sent forty-eight slave ships to Africa that year, more than in 1790), and he ensured that attention was paid to these objects when he exhibited them in Paris. A year later, Victor Hugo wrote his *Bug-Jargal*, in which he recalled the memories of his grandfather, Trébuchet, a captain of Nantes and a survivor of the revolution in Saint-Domingue. Again the central figure is a black, but this time he was a revolutionary of imagination.[43] Morenas's serious but tedious history of the slave trade appeared in 1828, based on travels in Haiti as well as in the Sénégal. Its impact was lessened by its impolitic dedication to President Boyer of Haiti, head of state of a regime founded on a massacre of French colonists. The best of all these literary works was, however, Mérimée's brilliant and ironical *Tamango*, of 1829, about a successful slave revolt in the open sea. Against this background, the number of French naval cruisers rose to six, and between 1823 and the end of June 1825 these 'visited' twenty-five suspected slavers off the Île Bourbon in the Indian Ocean as well as the French Antilles and the African coast (now going as far to the south as Old Calabar and Bonny). Of these, eleven were condemned.

Still, much would have to happen before the slave trade from France ended, much less before France abolished slavery itself. For twenty years after the publication of *Tamango*, deputies and journalists in Paris would continue to rail, as did the Duke of Saint-James in the House of Peers against the hypocrisy of the English in giving a moral excuse for their

---

* *Ourika, a sad story of a love affair of a black girl with a French aristocrat (and is based on truth), is one of three brilliant stories by the duchess about impossible loves: one was Olivier, about a love for an impotent man; and Edouard, about one for a person of inferior position.*

desire to rule the world; and a number of French writers, such as the play-wright Edouard Mazères and the naturalist Jean-Louis Quatrefages, sustained the opposition to change, with increasingly anti-African diatribes, the mere repetition of which, in the twentieth century, might cause a scandal.

Despite the support of intellectuals, statesmen, and writers in Paris, the business of catching slavers was still not popular. The law of 1818 did not specify very severe penalties. Chateaubriand, as Foreign Minister, explained to the Duke of Wellington in 1822 that if an 'appalling sentence' were attached to conviction of this crime it would be unfulfilled. French captains, demoralized by the purges carried out in their service after Waterloo, were reluctant to carry out what still seemed, despite the speech of Broglie, to be the policies of the English. About thirty French officers expelled from the Napoleonic navy after the Restoration had taken to the slave trade. Some of these sailors of fortune confronted, outmanoeuvred, or bribed their old comrades acting inside the Restoration navy. (For example, Captain André-Joseph Anglade was captain of the *Amélie*, a French slave ship destined for Santiago de Cuba, seized by Captain Delassale d'Harader, in the frigate *Sapho*. After $600 had passed from one officer to another, Delassale allowed his old comrade to sell his slaves in Puerto Rico.) Monarchist officers did not have their hearts in the pursuit, much less the capture, of such men. In 1830, Nantes still had eighty ships engaged in the trade, mostly 130-ton schooners, and the French flag was still often carried by captains from other nations desirous of avoiding the British busybodies. If a British naval vessel were to seize a suspected slaver the chances would be that a French flag would be found on board for use in the event of a capture. A sixth of the long-distance shipping in Nantes between 1814 and 1833 was probably engaged in the slave trade, and nearly all the shipowners of that harbour at that time invested at least once in the traffic. Of the shipbuilders, the most important in Nantes were new names – Vallé *et fils*, Pierre-Thomas Dennis, and Willaume – which sent, in the years 1818 to 1833, respectively thirty, seventeen, and fourteen slaving expeditions. Only the Mosneron-Dupins remained, and they on a small scale, of the shipping families which had been prominent in the trade before 1794.[44]

A list of slaving expeditions from France after the formal abolition of the trade in 1818 suggests that about 500 expeditions to buy slaves sailed from French or French colonial ports between then and 1831; six voyages seem to have set out from Bayonne, thirty-nine from Bordeaux, twelve from Honfleur, four from La Rochelle, forty-six from Le Havre, one from Lorient, eighteen from Marseilles, 305 from Nantes, and nine from Saint-Malo. Each voyage from Nantes perhaps made an average profit of 180,000 to 200,000 francs: considerably higher than in the eighteenth century. Expeditions which began in the Antilles included forty-three from Guadeloupe, and even eight from Danish St Thomas, though those were still basically French enterprises (for example, Captain André Desbarbès of Bayonne's the *Vénus* of 1825). Thirteen expeditions began in one port or another on the Sénégal, and fifty-five from the Île Bourbon.[45]

These journeys were complicated. No captain, no shipowner, and no shipbuilder would now admit that he was shipping slaves. A master would insist, when leaving Nantes or Honfleur, that he was setting off for legitimate trade in Africa, or for somewhere more exotic: Sumatra, for example.[*] At the same time, complicity of officials was frequent, whether because they had money in the business themselves (such as Governor Schmaltz in Sénégal, or the Governor of the Île de Bourbon, General Count Boubet de Lozier) or whether, like so many, they opposed anything which Britain supported, and so could be easily bribed: among them, no doubt, the customs officer at Port Louis in Guadeloupe who, in 1820, lazily observed, at two in the afternoon, the arrival of a ship from Le Havre, the *Fox*, with 300 Ibo slaves from Bonny. Sometimes the complicity of officials went further than just corruption: several civil servants in Saint-Louis were owners of *captiveries*.

Many of these vessels still made for Cuba (especially after the formal abolition of the slave trade by Spain) or for Brazil, rather than for French colonies. There was also a shift in French interest, so far as Africa was concerned, to the area north of the equator such as Bonny.

The French government was seeking to control these activities without conceding to Britain the right to intervene. Richelieu, Broglie, and Molé had their hearts in the right place, but they were ineffective. Then in 1822 a new Minister of the Navy, an ex-cavalryman, the Marquis of Clermont-Tonnerre, either on the insistence of his able civil servants or on his own initiative, decided to take the crusade against the slave trade seriously and, given the shortage of naval ships, promised cooperation with England. The Cour de Cassation in 1825 ordered the pursuit of slave traders 'in the sacred interest of humanity'. From 1825 crews in the French navy were rewarded with 100 francs for every slave freed. In 1826 a special commissioner was even sent to Nantes to investigate suspected slave merchants and captains. A further anti-slave law was passed in 1827, declaring those who practised this *'réellement infame'* commerce to be criminals.[†] One French commander of the enlarged West Africa Squadron, Auguste Massieu de Clairval, a Protestant from Normandy, not only ordered his staff to treat freed Africans at Cayenne with compassion, but also told the captains in West Africa to present themselves at Freetown.

---

[*] *However, there was a modest slave trade in Sumatra, or off it to the west, on the island of Nias, in which some French merchants participated, taking 1,000 slaves from there every year to the Île Bourbon, as was testified by a Captain Rogers, a commander of a Dutch ship.*
[†] *The law was passed in the chamber, 220 to 64, and friends of the trade made the same kind of speeches which had been made in the House of Commons thirty years before, though many speakers could not refrain from adding that England's apparent philanthropy was a ruse to ruin France.*

The seizures by the French squadron in West Africa became more and more frequent, other ships were held after their return to France, investigations of captains and seamen followed, consuls and other officials were charged to report suspicious events, and even the sceptical English abolitionists came to accept that official France was at last taking seriously the pursuit of French *négriers*, both ships and men.

Eventually, after 1830, the bourgeois King, Louis-Philippe, an Anglophile, and himself a member of the Society of Christian Morals, agreed with a recommendation of another enlightened officer, Captain Alexis Vilaret de Joyeuse, to make trading in slaves a crime. A third abolitionist law was then prepared and introduced by a new naval minister, Antoine, Count Argout, an ex-Bonapartist and old friend of the Duke of Broglie. He was only minister for four months, but that was enough to conclude what one historian has named 'seventeen years of tautology, bad faith, good reasons and countertruths'.[46] Henceforth an attempt to carry out the traffic would be as severely punished as the act itself. Slave merchants would be imprisoned for two to five years if their ships were seized in France, for ten to twenty years if they were caught on the high seas, and would receive ten years of hard labour if apprehended after the slaves had been bought. Freed slaves would be given liberty in the American colony for which they had been intended. The bill was carried with only six opponents in the House of Peers, and in the Chamber of Deputies the vote was 190 to 37.

In addition, the French agreed to a treaty whereby the right of search was granted mutually with the British between certain essential latitudes. The two countries also gave each other warrants to inspect each other's merchant ships if slaving was suspected. There was, admittedly, no equipment clause, as there had been with respect to the Dutch–British arrangements. All the same, this era of collaboration began well, with the French in 1832 receiving fifteen licences by the British, and giving the English twenty-two such warrants.

Certainly, the ships intercepted by France were to be brought not before mixed tribunals but national ones. Some kind of French slave trade continued. But it was on a negligible scale. Perhaps twenty ships set off for Africa from the mainland of France between 1832 and 1850. The French navy was always represented as showing 'little cruising zeal', in the words of a British naval surgeon, Peter Leonard. But in fact, between 1832 and 1838, the French fleet 'visited' thirty-two foreign ships: five North American, one Brazilian, one Sardinian, four Spanish, ten English, and eleven Portuguese.

The relations between Britain and France continued, however, imperfect. For example, if a British captain were to ask a ship to halt, and a French flag were then hoisted, the British naval vessel could still exercise no control: 'At most . . . she may exercise the right to speak with [the French ship], and demand answers to questions addressed to her through a speaking trumpet ... but without obliging her to alter or impede her course.' The British could check whether the suspect ship had the right to carry the French flag: 'A boat may for this purpose be sent to the suspected vessel, after she has first been hailed to give notice of the intention. The verification shall consist in an examination of the papers establishing the nationality of the vessel. Nothing can be claimed beyond [that]. . . . Any search or inspection whatever is absolutely forbidden.' These arrangements would, of course, give rise to many misunderstandings in the years ahead.[17]

30

ONLY THE POOR SPEAK ILL
OF THE SLAVE TRADE

Comment at a luncheon in Havana in the 1830s,
reported in a letter of Domingo del Monte

> *'When we were in the barracoon, the*
> *country people said that the reason of our*
> *being stopped . . . was that the Spaniards*
> *said that the ships of war belonging to*
> *the English kept us from going to the*
> *Spaniards' country.'*

> James Campbell, once a slave,
> afterwards a mason in Sierra Leone,
> to Hutt Committee, 1848

IN THE 1830s four substantial societies of the Americas depended on black slaves: first and second those of a coffee empire, Brazil, and a sugar colony, Cuba, whose reliance on the slave trade was absolute, and where slavery itself lasted another three generations, till the late 1880s (Puerto Rico should be considered with Cuba, though its wealth was far less); third, that in the cotton republic in the South of the United States, which was scarcely involved in the transatlantic trade, though its slave population was essential to it; and finally, that in the British and French West Indies, where the slave trade had ended, in 1808 and 1831 respectively, where slavery itself would disappear, in 1838 in the British islands and in 1848 in the French, and where the old sugar eminence was now in precipitous decline.

Of these slave societies, Brazil, with her long history of reliance on slaves from Africa stretching back to the mid-sixteenth century, should take pride of place. For two years after 1831, when the slave trade had formally been abolished, few Africans were brought in because of the earlier heavy import when planters thought that slavery would soon end for ever. But then in the mid-1830s the trade recovered and was reorganized, on an illegal basis, to serve plantations of cotton, though they were stagnating; of sugar, especially in new plantations near São Paulo and Campos; and, increasingly, of coffee in Rio, Minas Gerais, São Paulo and, above all, in the valley of the River Paraíba. Coffee was the great new Brazilian product. Brought to Pará in the north as long ago as 1727, it became the dominant slave crop in the 1830s. The slave was needed – or at least used – for clearing and laying out the new plantations, weeding and cultivating the coffee plants, and then harvesting them.

Some of these coffee plantations were the result of investment by new European immigrants. They were places where slavery implied harder work than that encountered by the domestic slave in Rio, or even than in many of the old sugar plantations, where (as in the Soledada, in Minas Gerais) a captive might be asked to spend his time in an orchestra, playing the clarinet or the violin.

The transition from legal to illegal trade in slaves in Brazil was curious. A nineteenth-century Brazilian wrote that 'the date for the cessation of the slave trade approached, and then the planters, and the whole population, saw that no preventive measures whatever were being taken or attempted; the slave traders, therefore, wanted to take advantage of the time still left to them and they filled up their ships again and again with immense cargoes of slaves'.[1] The idea of continuing the slave trade in this semi-surreptitious manner distressed a few Anglophiles, including the royal family, but most of the officials of the new country, and all the merchants, recalled that Britain had been until recently the monarch of the trade, and knew that most of the British merchants who had recently established themselves in Rio sympathized with them. Indeed, there continued to be collaboration between slave dealers and British businessmen who often, even now, provided what they knew would be used as 'trade goods' for the exchange of slaves in Africa. There were also in Rio de Janeiro English slave merchants who became naturalized Brazilians. Thus the terrible slave warehouses of the city had a renewed trade; and so did the cemetery in the nearby Misericórdia hospital.

In these years most Brazilian slaves seem to have come from the now forbidden territory of Dahomey or Lagos, north of the equator, despite the presence of the British navy: three-quarters, according to the long-serving British Consul in Bahia, William Pennell, because, said his colleague Robert Hesketh in Maranhão, the slaves from the north (Dahomey, Benin, Bonny) 'were accustomed to hard work in their homeland'. All the same, Rio remained a good customer for slaves from Angola, especially Benguela.

The new slave trade included several interesting new procedures. There was, for example, the technique of sending two ships to Africa. One, slow and old, would carry the merchandise, and perhaps some money, which the slave dealers used to exchange for slaves. The other (and there might be two or three of them) would be fast and small, well equipped to carry the slaves, who would have been assembled beforehand in Africa, to avoid any delay between the arrival and departure, as had always prevailed in the past. Indeed, the stay in the African port might now be a matter only of hours.

Another technique was to discharge the merchandise and then prepare the return voyage with some worthless slaves paraded ostentatiously. The slave merchants hoped that the nearby British naval vessel would be drawn to that place, supposing that they would there catch the malefactor (as they saw him) red-handed. But the captain himself would return swiftly to where the good slaves had been assembled.

The reception of slaves in Brazil also differed in the nineteenth century from the eighteenth. Rio remained the most important port, but Bahia declined, its place being taken by Pernambuco, Maranhão, and Pará. Ships left Rio with ostensible cargoes of tobacco or rum for the legitimate African trade, or for another Brazilian port, but they returned with illegal cargoes of blacks. These *boçal* slaves were then kept in camps where an attempt would be made to teach them Portuguese, so that they could be easily sold alongside already acclimatized *ladinos* and locally bred *crioulos*: but 'again and again', wrote a traveller, 'I have seen troops of slaves of both sexes who could not speak a word of Portuguese . . . from twenty to a hundred individuals . . . marched inland for sale'.[2]

Rio de Janeiro, like Bahia, had long been both a slave-receiving and a slave-seeking port. The most prominent dealer in slaves in the 1820s in the first of these handsome harbours was Joaquim Antonio Rio Ferreira, who must have brought over 15,000 slaves across the South Atlantic between 1825 and 1830. Running him close was Joaquim Ferreira dos Santos. Others from that city who each carried over 5,000 slaves in those hectic years were Miguel Ferreira Gomes, João Alves da Silva Porto (he specialized in slaves from Mozambique), Lourenço Antonio do Rego, and Antonio José Meirelles. These men were great merchants in their own right, dealing in all kinds of goods, as well as slaves. They were not merely the representatives of Angolan merchants, as had tended to be the case in respect of slaves in the eighteenth century.

In the 1830s, when the business became formally illegal, ships no longer sailed direct into the harbours of Rio or Bahia to unload their live cargoes in the middle of the city. They made their deposits some way outside, and the slaves had often to endure a rough march – perhaps as much as fifty miles – to the markets, to prepare for which they were usually accommodated not in the old slave streets, such as the Rua do Valongo, but in new depositaries in, for example, the Rua da Quitada, the fortress of São João, or the Ponta do Cajú. Unpleasant though the Valongo had been, it was as nothing to the hardships in these new improvised quarters. Despite the introduction of vaccination against smallpox, deaths were still frequent, and the hospital of Santa Casa da Misericórdia seems to have buried 700–800 every month in the early 1830s. There was thus much to be said for the view that the illegalization of the Brazilian slave trade created worse conditions than ever.

Another change was that the buyers in the coffee plantations of the nineteenth century preferred young slaves to full-grown men and women. Such statistics as survive suggest that between two-thirds and three-quarters were boys.

As in the past, many captives were sold by auction. An American traveller, Thomas Ewbank, recalled an 'auction store at the corner of the [Rua dos] Ourives and [Rua do] Ouvidor', which he found full of 'cheeses, Yankee clocks, kitchen utensils, crockery-ware, old books, shoes, pickles etc.' These were sold every day, but once or twice a week slaves were also disposed of. Once Ewbank saw eighty-nine persons for sale. He saw the black-whiskered auctioneer: 'A hammer in his right hand, the forefinger of his left pointing to a plantation hand standing confused at his side, he pours out a flood of words. [The slave] had on a canvas shirt, with sleeves ending at the elbows, and trousers of the same, the legs of which he is told to roll above his knees. A bidder steps up, examines his lower limbs, then his mouth, breast and other parts. He is now told to walk toward the door and back to show his gait. As he was returning, the hammer fell. . . .'[3] A similar sight was observed in the late 1820s by an English clergyman Robert Walsh: 'The slaves both men and women were walked about and put into different paces, and felt exactly as I have seen butchers feel a calf. [The overseer] occasionally lashed them, and made them jump to show that their limbs were supple, and caused them to shriek and cry, that their purchasers might persuade themselves that their lungs were sound.' These auctions were legal, for no one questioned the internal trade in slaves, and officials did not as a rule interfere to demand the provenance of the person who had been put up for sale.

The illegal trade to Brazil seems to have been begun by Portuguese-born merchants, such as José Maria Lisboa, who in the early 1830s began to use old ships which were destroyed soon after landing the slaves. Even so, the profits of these merchants seem to have been much greater than they had been in the eighteenth century.* Lisboa bought slaves in Africa for 20,000 or 30,000 reis each and sold them in Rio for as much as ten times that. Another Portuguese to take advantage of the new opportunity was José Bernardino de Sá, who made a point of always using English goods – cotton textiles, especially – for his traffic, and who was among those who established a system of permitting payment for slaves by instalments. But the slave merchant in Brazil who carried through most changes necessary in the new era was José de Cerqueira Lima. He, too, had been born in Portugal, but by 1830 was already the owner of a

* See page 725.

luxurious palace in the Corredor da Victoria in Bahia which before independence in 1821 had been the residence of the Governor of the province.* This building had been adapted to communicate, by an underground passage, with the beach where new slaves were landed. Cerqueira was known for the variety of his business interests, as for the grandeur of his way of life. His most successful ship, the *Carlota*, named after his beautiful wife, made at least nine voyages to Africa in the 1820s. The fact that several of his vessels were captured by the British and taken to Sierra Leone (the *Cerqueira* in 1824, the *Independencia*, the *Bahia*, and even the *Carlota* in 1827, as well as the *Golfinho* in 1839) made no difference to his social standing in Bahia.

Almost as important during the illegal days in Bahia were João Cardozo dos Santos, the master and owner of the swift-sailing *Henri-quetta*, Domingos Gomes Bello, Antonio Pedrozo de Albuquerque, and finally Joaquim Pereira Marinho (a grand seigneur who became baron, viscount, and finally count in Portugal). The latter was interested in the sale of dried meat, as well as of slaves, and was a director both of the Joazeiro Railway and of the new Bank of Bahia. He was responsible for about half the slaving journeys from Bahia between 1842 and 1851. He sent at least thirty-six voyages to Africa for slaves, and would die – prosperous, locally philanthropic, admired, and envied – only in 1884.

A more curious figure in the oligarchy of slave merchants of Bahia was Francisco López Guimarães, whose son married the sister of the poet Castro Alves, who was famous for his passionate verses against slavery; when López Guimarães died, his widow married the poet's father. These unusual relationships interrupted neither the flow of the slave trade nor the production of verse directed against it.

In Rio, the equivalents of Cerqueira and Marinho were Manoel Pinto da Fonseca, a Portuguese merchant who was a specialist in providing slaves from Mozambique; Antonio Guimarães; Joaquim dos Santos; Joaquim and José Alves de Cruz Rios (father and son); and Francisco Godinho. Though most of these men had begun life humbly, they were, in their last years, largely because of their success in trading African slaves, able to live like kings. Pinto da Fonseca was a leading figure in society in Rio, the intimate friend of ministers and officials, especially of the chief of police in that capital.

Some of these businessmen, like Bernardino de Sá, had, as will be seen, interests in Africa in the form of factories or barracoons, where slaves in Angola or Mozambique could be held before they were shipped.

Lesser merchants, the so-called *volantes*, might sail themselves to Africa in small boats and bring back, say, forty slaves. The slave trade employed many thousands of people. For example, there were the owners and crews of boats who escorted the slaves ashore, the guards

---

* *This palace is now the Secretariat of Education and Public Health in Bahia.*

who took the slaves inland, and also the teachers of Portuguese whose task was to enable Africans to speak the language of the empire. Port officials, underpaid bureaucrats, small-scale judges and police chiefs, army officers and naval officers all shared in both profits and bribes, the last sometimes themselves made in the form of slaves. The secretary of the Portuguese legation in Rio was said to receive 1,000 milréis each time he allowed a slave ship to leave harbour under a Portuguese flag. A certain Colonel Vasques made the fortress of São João, at the entrance of the harbour of Rio, into a slave depot from which he himself landed over 12,000 slaves in 1838 and 1839, and the commander of the adjacent fortress of Santa Cruz did the same. Officials or magistrates who refused to collaborate could go in fear of their lives, as occurred in the case of Agostinho Moreira Guerra, a judge whose criticism of the slave trade led to threats of assassination and his resignation in 1834.

Two regents of Brazil,' Nicolau Vergueiro and Pedro de Araújo Lima, later Marquis of Olinda, seem to have been themselves engaged in trading slaves; the former was directly concerned through a company over which he presided and which bore his name.

For a time in the 1830s, all the same, the government seemed to condemn the trade: 'The shameful and infamous traffic in blacks continues on all sides', the Minister of Justice Feijo complained in 1832, because, he added, the authorities themselves were 'interested in the crime'.[1] Brazilian warships seized one or two slavers. But in the end the perceived needs of the planters, and the wealth of the merchants, succeeded in reducing such intervention to naught. Most magistrates and governors of provinces were prepared to connive at slave dealing, for they themselves were usually landowners and slave employers. Slave ships were openly insured.

Coffee was Brazil's biggest export in the 1830s, and slaves on farms providing those beans constituted the largest division of the captive labour force in the country. The convention, as so often noticed before in respect of the sugar industry, was that this army of Africans had to be constantly replenished, as a result of deaths from disease, overwork, and excessively brutal discipline. The owners continued feckless in their attitudes to their slave property: one planter asserted that the high death rate 'did not represent any loss to him for, when he bought a slave, it was with the intention of using him for a year, longer than which few could survive, but that he got enough work out of him not only to repay this initial investment, but even to show a good profit'. The shortage of slaves initiated yet one more innovation in the history of slaving: theft. In the 1820s and 1830s the newspapers of Rio were full of stories of gangs organized for stealing slaves in the capital, men working for the benefit of planters or ranchers in the north. *O Diario de Pernambuco* in 1828 reported:

' Dom Pedro, Emperor after 1831, was a minor till 1842.

'It is public knowledge that slave-stealing goes on in this city almost daily, and that there are men who make a business of this. Some entice and lure the blacks. . . . they meet in the streets, others take them into their homes and keep them there until they can be put aboard ship or otherwise be got out of the city; others make a deal with the first ones they meet and take them to some distant place to sell them.'[5] In 1846 Father Lopes Gama, in his *O Sete de Setembro*, would even accuse planters from illustrious families, including the Cavalcantis and the Rego Barroes, of slave-stealing.

By the late 1830s imports of slaves into Brazil had reached 'fearful and impressive' levels, according to the British Minister in Rio (whose legation was virtually the abolitionist headquarters in the continent). The illegal trade was now responsible every year for landing over 45,000 slaves. The law of 1831 was a dead letter. One conservative Prime Minister, Bernardo Pereira de Vasconcelos, declared, before he entered office: 'Let the English carry into execution this treaty which they have forced upon us by abusing their superior power; but to expect that we should co-operate with [them] . . . in these speculations, gilded with the name of humanity, is unreasonable.'[6] In 1836 a report was published in Rio which sought to show that the slave trade was to the benefit of the slaves; 'without slavery', the author went on to ask, 'what would become of America's export trade?* Who would work the mines? The fields? Carry on the coastal trade?'[7]

In the early days of the illegal trade planters in Brazil had feared British threats and the commercial consequences of a serious quarrel with London. But by the late 1830s they were more perturbed by fears of a successful black revolution, as had occurred in Haiti. They had reason to be anxious. For another serious rebellion of slaves, the 'revolt of Malé', with a strong Islamic undercurrent, broke out in 1835. It was repressed with brutality: whippings with 500 or even more strokes were common punishments for mullahs accused merely of teaching friends to read the Koran in Arabic. Even the planter-dominated legislature of Bahia began in consequence to talk of ending the slave trade, with the corollary that the large population of free Africans of Brazil should in consequence be expelled and re-established in a new Sierra Leone or Liberia in Africa. A distinction then began to be made between those freed slaves who had come originally from Africa, and who, it was thought, might reasonably be deported; and those who had been born in Brazil, of slave parents, who might be expected to remain. Some of the former, horrified at the unjust punishments which they had seen (they were usually carried out in public), did set off on return journeys to Africa. One of these was in 1836 on the English schooner

---

* *Citizens of the United States may wish to remind themselves that the people of Brazil and the Spanish empire, too, all regarded themselves as living in 'America'.*

Nimrod, hired by two rich Brazilian free blacks. It returned 150 slaves to Elmina, Winneba, and Agué on the Gold Coast. What then happened to them is obscure. But it was in this atmosphere that in the summer of 1837 Canning's ex-interlocutor, the Marquis of Barbacena, introduced a new bill on the slave trade into the Brazilian Assembly. He was unsuccessful; but he comforted himself that Wilberforce had had to wait for nearly twenty years between his first move against the trade and his triumph in 1807.

Cuba, alongside Brazil, was the other great consumer of slaves from Africa in the nineteenth century. In comparison, Mexico, independent after 1822, now could only afford about 3,000, concentrated in the regions of Veracruz and Acapulco. It was easy enough for the conservative *criollos* who ran that country after independence to prohibit the slave trade in 1824, and even to suppress the institution itself in 1829: Indian workers were available. But Cuba was different.

In the early part of the century it seemed that the island might be known as much for its coffee as for its sugar, but that dream vanished when the 2,000 or so coffee plantations in Cuba (which, for a time in the 1830s, exceeded the land under sugar cane) were ruined by hurricanes. Sugar had anyway captured the imagination of the Cuban *criollos*. There were nearly 1,000 sugar plantations in 1827, more than twice as many as in the late eighteenth century. The average number of slaves on these was about seventy, some of them being specialized drivers or engineers.[*]

The biggest Cuban sugar mill, San Martín, which belonged for many years to a company in which the Queen Regent of Spain was a prominent shareholder, employed 800 slaves and in 1860 produced 2,670 tons of sugar a year; in comparison, the biggest Jamaican estate, in the great days of that island's prosperity, a hundred years before, belonging to Philip Pittucks, had employed only 280 slaves and produced less than 200 tons. The difference was thus enormous.

Probably the slave population of Cuba was 200,000 in 1817, or two-fifths of Cuba's population. Slaves were everywhere to be seen, above all as servants in the city of Havana, whose 100,000 inhabitants made it one of the great cities of the Americas, ranking in size after the City of Mexico and Lima, and before Boston and New York. There was a relatively large number of free blacks: say, 24,000, perhaps 12 per cent of the total population. This was the consequence partly of a tradition of owners' granting favourite slaves their freedom on their deathbed, and partly of a custom enabling purchase of freedom, sometimes done on the basis of payments over many years (*coartación*). In 1825 Humboldt commented: 'In no part

---

[*] *The tobacco plantations of the west of the island, which produced Cuba's famous cigars, were usually worked by free black labour.*

of the world where slavery exists is manumission so frequent as in the island of Cuba.'[8] Mulattos, too, were more numerous than elsewhere in the Caribbean, the women being the heroines in a thousand songs about returning Spanish entrepreneurs, the *'indianos'* of many nineteenth-century novels.

Slaves in the city of Havana were often looked after well: 'You see pampered slaves exceedingly well treated, and indulged over much; but the contrast between them and the slaves on the plantations is as great as can well be conceived. . . . It is the worst sort of slavery I have seen anywhere', remarked the outspoken British Consul, David Turnbull, in 1850.[10] A businessman, Joseph Liggins, from the same country, in Cuba in 1852, said that his impression was that the slaves worked eighteen hours a day, and seven days a week during the six-month harvest. So 'the annual mortality is considerable and the deficiency is, of course, supplied by the slave trade'.[11] The priests made sure that the slaves were baptized at birth or capture, and absolved on their deathbed, but on no other occasion did the Church pay much attention. Despite the high-flown doubts of the Vatican on the matter, articulated every fifty years or so in the most direct of language, no priests in Cuba seem to have admonished their flock for buying, or even selling, slaves. Indeed, the sales of slaves were sometimes announced in church for the following Sunday, 'before the church doors'. The British commissioners in Havana commented in 1826: 'The exhortations of the clergy upon this subject [that is, the slave trade] are, we suspect, neither zealously given nor seriously listened to.'[12]

Slaves were similarly to be seen in Puerto Rico, though her landowners never embarked on the grandiose exploitation of sugar and coffee which characterized Cuba. The import of slaves into that island was about 1,250 a year in the 1820s. But that trade seems to have been extinct on a regular basis by 1835,[†] for economic rather than moral reasons. Still, as Lord Palmerston once pointed out, in relation to Cuba, 'a feeling which arises from other circumstances is perhaps as sure a foundation on which to build upon as one that arises from moral opinion.'[13]

The prosperous Cuban colony offered a good example, in the first half of the nineteenth century, of an old oligarchy adapting itself to a new industry. Some of the families who controlled the production of coffee and sugar in Cuba in 1820 had been landowners for generations. Several were noblemen, many more would become so (a good and cheap way of

---

[*] *Slaves could buy their freedom by the system of* coartación: *they had to make an initial payment to their master, and then buy freedom by instalments, recovering a percentage of the original payment at each step. For that reason, said the Spanish abolitionist of the 1860s, Rafael Labra, 'the position of the free Negro is much better than elsewhere, even among those nations which have for ages flattered themselves as being the most advanced in civilization'.*[9]

[†] *The last slave ship to arrive in Puerto Rico was apparently in 1843.*

keeping the planters loyal), and sometimes their titles were most agreeable: there was a Marqués de la Real Proclamación and a Marqués de las Delicias, as well as a Marqués del Prado Ameno. Their family connections were endless, their hospitality generous. They were adapting to new technology. In 1827 fifty out of the thousand or so sugar plantations were driven by steam engines. Steamboats carried slaves from Africa; and railways – introduced in Cuba before Spain – soon carried sugar to the ports.*

As in Brazil, the British attitude to the slave trade after 1820 was considered either absurd or Machiavellian. The British Commissary Judge Henry Kilbee wrote in 1825 to Canning: 'It is universally believed that abolition was a measure which Great Britain, under the cloak of philanthropy, but really influenced by jealousy of the prosperity of this island, forced upon Spain by threats or other means.' There were, of course, many who still remembered the thousands of slaves brought from Africa before 1807 by firms such as Baker and Dawson of Liverpool, and sold successfully by that company's Cuban representative, Philip Allwood. Many of the slaves so imported were still alive. Cuesta y Manzanal had also used experienced Englishmen to teach backward Spanish sailors how to carry out the trade when he and his partners first began to send ships to Africa for slaves.

In Cuba, after 1825, in the light of the unrest of slaves and the threats of rebellions by *criollos* against Spanish imperial authority, despotic powers had been given to the Spanish governors, the captains-general. Brazil had a parliamentary assembly, however ineffective it might seem, and a free press, however little it might feel inclined to criticize the status quo. True, Cuba sent deputies to the Cortes in Madrid, but that legislature was often bypassed, and was never strong, while the Cuban deputies were a tiny minority among many whose main attention was concentrated on pressing domestic problems. In any case, after 1838 the Cuban deputies were not seated any more.

In Cuba, the illegal slave trade began earlier than it did in Brazil, and it lasted longer. The Spanish official who managed the transition from legal to illegal trading in Cuba was the skilful and cynical Treasurer, Alejandro Ramírez. He dominated captains-general and slave merchants alike. Just after his death, a new captain-general, General Francisco Dionisio Vives, arrived in Havana and confirmed all Ramírez's innovations, in which he was afterwards helped by the new Treasurer, Claudio Martínez de Pinillos. Vives, who was sixty years of age when he went to Cuba, and who had served throughout the Peninsular War, could like his predecessors justify to himself as to the King of Spain his support for the slave trade by reference to the necessity of pleasing the planters at a time when

---

* *A priest in the excellent novel of the 1880s* Cecilia Valdés *asked why there were so many more slave rebellions on steam-powered sugar mills. The answer is that such modern institutions were more inhumane.*

there were possibilities of a liberal invasion from Venezuela inspired by Bolívar, and rumours of other plots which could have led to the independence of the island – something which every Spaniard hoped to prevent, because of the every day greater importance of Cuba in the Spanish economy.

Vives, an Anglophobe through and through, sometimes insisted to English and North American visitors that he had done what he could to prevent the continuation of the slave trade: had he not permitted in January 1826 the circulation of a letter from the Archbishop of Cuba to all parish priests that they should look on the trade as 'a true crime'? But privately he had written the previous year to his Minister of Foreign Affairs: 'I conceal the existence of the slave trade and the introduction of slaves as much as is possible, given the treaty obligations, because I am completely convinced that, if there is no slave labour, the island's wealth will disappear within a few years, for prosperous agriculture is dependent upon these labourers and, at the moment, there is no other means of obtaining them.' (No doubt he had seen, or knew of, the letter sent by the King in 1817 asking for the trade to continue, to which Governor-General Tacón referred in the 1840s.) [14]

When the British complained that though they had pointed out that a slave ship, the *Mágico*, had landed half its slaves before being captured by the British naval schooner the *Union*, Vives insisted that it was not his business to prosecute the slave trade when the captives had reached land. A similar dispute occurred with respect to the Spanish schooner *Minerva*, in August 1826. The ship was chased into the harbour of Havana by two British cruisers. One British captain then sought unsuccessfully to search the ship. Thwarted, he placed a watch, and at night he and his colleagues observed six boatloads of slaves being landed from the *Minerva* at a wharf. Vives refused to allow any case to be heard by the Court of Mixed Commission since the events complained of had not occurred on the high seas.

As well as privately backing the slave trade, Vives encouraged gambling, neglected dealing with robbery in the streets, smiled on corruption of every kind, and even turned a blind eye to piracy (a gang of Muslim pirates were for a time active in the bay of Havana). '*Si vives como Vives, vivirás*', it was said of him in Havana, 'if you live as Vives lives, you will live well'. He became Count of Cuba on his return to Spain in 1832: the only time that that appropriate title was granted.

Between Vives and Kilbee, the British judge in Havana, there was a permanent duel. Kilbee was energetic and ambitious, and wanted to offer rewards to informers who observed breaches of the treaty. He also wished slaveholders to prove that they had obtained their slaves legally. But Spanish officials insisted that since the trading of slaves within the island was not prohibited the scheme was pointless and the idea of rewards

* See page 601.

impracticable. Kilbee could point out innumerable cases of the law being broken. From merely reading *El Diario del gobierno* he could see that over forty slavers set out from Havana in the eight months from June 1824 to January 1825. The information was passed on to Canning in London, who in turn informed his Minister in Madrid, and asked him to tell the Foreign Ministry there that unless they supported Britain over the slave trade they could not expect help with their own weak position in the Caribbean in relation to the United States and France.

It is true that in 1826 the Spanish government proclaimed that any slave who proved his own illegal importation could claim to be free. Logbooks of ships coming from Africa were also henceforth to be given to the port authorities, so that the latter could assure themselves that no slaves had been introduced. Kilbee and his staff, isolated moralists in a labyrinth of evasion, were for a time encouraged by these innovations. But the port authorities were slow, and the logs always bland, even when there was evidence that, as in the case of the brig *Breves* in 1827, the vessel had landed 400 slaves on the coast near Havana. Kilbee reported to London that such things were 'regarded by the public as marks of the ingenuity displayed by this government in thwarting the attempt made by His Majesty's commissioners'.[15]

Nor had there been anything like a permanent solution of the problem of the *emancipados*. In the 1830s most of them had been allocated to individuals – perhaps 3,800 were disposed of in 1832 – and were working as slaves in all but name. The government ensured that as many as possible were allocated to work on public projects, such as aqueducts, or prisons. But the continuing threat, as it seemed to be, of the arrival of new free labour from Africa disturbed the *criollos'* peace of mind; the entry, for instance, of HMS *Speedwell*, with over 600 slaves from the slaver *Águila*, caused much anxiety. The new Treasurer, Martínez de Pinillos, begged the new British judge to send the men to Sierra Leone. But that needed an agreement between the governments of London and Madrid. In the short term the 'liberated' Africans were distributed in the old way, as labourers were throughout the island.

The British came to accept that they had some responsibility for suggesting a solution to this problem. Kilbee's idea was that these Africans should be taken to Trinidad, now part of the British West Indies, where labour was short. Spain would pay for the journey there, each shipload would have to have an equal number of men and women, and a month's notice was to be given. These conditions were difficult for the Cubans to fulfil, for few female slaves were ever brought to the 'ever faithful isle', but all the same, and under the impact of fear caused by an epidemic of cholera, about 1,100 such captives were sent, the fruit of British intervention against five ships during the years 1833–5.

By now, even in the imperial dictatorship which Cuba had become, there were dissentient voices. José Verdaguer, a Catalan judge in Havana for nine years, shared most of the British views. Then in 1830 a prize essay by Pedro José Morillas suggested that white labour was as effective as black. Several well-known sugar planters, such as the Aldamas and the Alfonsos, tried out the idea. There were a number of candidates: Gallegos, for example, who might be attracted by Cuba's relatively high level of living; Canary Islanders, contracting to work for a specified number of years only; Irishmen, who would soon work on the railways; and, above all, Chinese, who had first been seen in the West Indies in Trinidad as early as 1806.

Captains-general in Havana changed, but their policies remained the same. Thus General Vives was succeeded by General Ricafort, who survived only a year before giving way to General Miguel Tacón, in 1834. Tacón, the most remarkable individual to govern Cuba in the early nineteenth century, was, as Vives had been, a veteran of the wars against Spanish American independence. In the course of many terrible marches and countermarches in the tropics he had learned to despise the *criollos* in South America. He looked on them as illogical, self-centred, brutal, lazy, and narrow-minded. The death of his wife had made him misanthropic. In Spain, he had sided with the constitutional revolution of Riesgo, and he owed his appointment in Havana to the liberal statesman Martínez de la Rosa (in respect of whom the historian Sir Raymond Carr wrote, 'Liberty was no longer a furious bacchante, but a sober matron'). But in Cuba Tacón conducted himself, as did most similar generals, autocratically and ruthlessly, interested in making money where he could, and supporting the slave trade. 'Servile in Spain, tyrannical in Cuba', was the comment of the writer whom he exiled, José Antonio Saco. Tacón was said to receive half an ounce of gold per slave safely landed, and in his four years of government he was rumoured to have gained 450,000 pesos. Tacón was bitterly anti-British, hated the United States, feared Methodists and Baptists as revolutionaries, and even despised railways as 'Anglo-Saxon ironwork'.

George Villiers, the British Minister in Madrid, told the Spanish Foreign Minister that he knew 'the slave trade in Cuba has never been so prevalent as since the period when the present Captain-General was appointed. . . . the persons engaged . . . appear to be acting in the full confidence not only of escaping with impunity but almost of meeting with open protection'.[16]

Tacón saw abolitionism in truth as the real threat to the island and thought that in those circumstances no concessions on political liberty could be made. His secret agent, Captain José Ruiz de Apodaca (whose hatred of Britain was due to having been captured at Trafalgar), went to Jamaica and 'confirmed' that Britain was training Methodists as agents to destroy Cuba by inspiring a rebellion of slaves. Two prominent slave dealers, Joaquín Gómez and Francisco Martí y Torres, became not just Tacón's chief advisers but his best friends. The Captain-General charged the latter with the sale of *emancipados*. He and his friends devised a Cuban version of Gogol's *Dead Souls*: when a slave died (and 10 per cent a year did so), an *emancipado* was often given his name and his place. The price of an *emancipado* in 1836 was a third of the price of a slave. In these years, the governors of British islands, such as Trinidad, were crying out for the Cuban *emancipados* to be sent to them, but Tacón had found a better use for them. When Tacón left for home, the merchants of Havana appropriately presented him with a seven-foot black footman in token of their gratitude.

Captain-General Tacón was assisted in his support of the slave trade by a clever and charming official, the United States Consul in Havana, Nicholas Trist, who had arrived in Cuba in 1833, having previously been secretary to Thomas Jefferson, whose granddaughter he had married. He helped the Cuban slavers by making United States registration, and hence flags, easily available to all their ships – and by being distinctly unhelpful to Judge Kilbee of the Mixed Court at Havana. Trist owned property in Cuba. He poured out his prejudiced views to the British commissioners in an 'extraordinary' memorandum, in Palmerston's expression. His conduct was investigated by a United States minister in Madrid, Alexander Everett, and he was condemned, and later dismissed. All the same, he would be President Polk's emissary to Mexico in 1848 and draw up the Treaty of Guadalupe Hidalgo.[17]

Trist must have been responsible for securing the entry of a great many slaves into Cuba. Kilbee's successor as British judge at the mixed court of arbitration in Sierra Leone, Henry Macaulay, son of Zachary and a brother of the historian, told a House of Commons committee that in 1838 and 1839 there were about thirteen ships which he thought 'were not American . . . but [which sailed] under the American flag, and with American papers, supplied to them by American authority', almost always in Havana. 'The whole thing', said Macaulay, 'was a complete fraud. . . . In some cases the vessels that were boarded one day by the cruisers under the American flag were boarded afterwards with the Portuguese or Spanish flag hoisted, and full of slaves.'[18] But sometimes the traders were avowedly United States citizens, such as James Woodley of Baltimore who collaborated with a compatriot, William Baker, a resident of Cuba, in the dispatch of slave ships such as the *Cintra* (with a French captain) in 1819.

Some, perhaps many, of the slaves helped into Cuba by Trist were afterwards carried to the new independent Republic of Texas, still an ideal place for disembarking slaves intended for the United States slave market in New Orleans. (North American settlers in Texas had pursued independence partly in order to reinstate slavery, abolished by Mexico in 1829.) Tolmé, the British Consul in Havana, in 1837 thought that 1,500 slaves might have been secretly carried to Texas in the previous few years.

But for the masters of Cuba the era between 1820 and 1865 renewed, as the Countess of Merlin put it, 'the charms of the golden age'. There were some remarkable town houses, theatres, and hotels in which balls, bullfights, and even goosefights were held.[19] In October 1840 *Hunt's Merchant Magazine and Commercial Review* declared that Cuba was 'the richest colony in the world'. The island in the 1840s was producing two-thirds more sugar than the entire British West Indies, and twice as much as Brazil. Speculation in property was even greater than that in slaves. Immigration by adventurous merchants and gamblers was continuous from all countries, from Venezuela as well as from the United States, and above all from Spain. Nor was the life of slaves always as grim as it was on the sugar plantations. For example, Edouard Corbière, in his novel *Le Négrier*, published in 1832, says: 'These blacks, fat and portly, lazy and jolly, whom I saw joking all day in the streets seemed much happier than our workers in Europe and than most sailors. . . .'[20] A picture of the life of slaves in Havana in the late 1830s was given by 'Fanny' Calderón de la Barca, who with her husband, the first Spanish Minister to Mexico, stopped in Havana on their way to their designated legation. As well as recording dinners at which she was offered 350 dishes, by beautiful countesses dressed in satin, she was fascinated by the 'little black boys, like juvenile apes, their arms folded, standing behind the chairs' in spacious Spanish-style town houses, on marble floors. She loved, too, the French beds with blue silk drapery, attended by slave girls, dressed in white mantillas and white satin shoes. Two black orchestras might play Mozart and Bellini alternately in the moonlight* and, in front of the ocean, the guests would drink champagne from golden cups. There might then be heard 'that continuous hiss [with] which the languishing *habañera* calls upon her ebony attendants so that the uninitiated might imagine himself suddenly transported amidst a sea of serpents'.[21]

Among these charming people, and in these beautiful houses, listening perhaps to 'The Last Rose of Summer' played on the harp, there would be men who had made their fortunes, not just on sugar plantations but from trading in slaves: for example, that 'very civil and good-natured' giant the Count of Reunión, who had been, before his ennoblement in 1824, none other than the successful and innovatory slaver, Santiago de la Cuesta y Manzanal. Fanny Calderón was entertained lavishly by the Count of Fernandina (the word for Cuba in the early sixteenth century), whose wife seemed 'full of revolutionary and reformatory projects', even if her jewels were worth 300,000 dollars, while her husband's sugar and coffee plantation, La Angosta, was among the most successful of all. All believed that their slaves were fortunate; indeed, sometimes they must have been. For example, at a ball of the Fernandinas, the Calderóns were 'amused to see numbers of negroes and negresses helping themselves plentifully to sweetmeats, uncorking and drinking fresh bottles of

---

* *One had to be careful what was performed: to play* 'Suona la tromba', *from Bellini's* Puritani, *risked condemnation, because rousing words about freedom accompanied it.*

champagne, and devouring everything on the supper tables, without the slightest concern for the presence of either master or mistress'. The Countess of Fernandina, it seemed, had just offered an old slave his freedom, and he had refused it, to become later the master of other slaves in the household.[22] When the equally charming, equally epistolary Countess of Merlin, another traveller but Cuban-born,* returned home to Havana after many years in Paris in 1840 she found herself immediately surrounded by black African slaves and servants, as well as cousins: 'At last there arrive the blacks and their ladies, happy, affectionate, each presenting their right to look at me. This one had brought me up, that one had played with me, a third had used to make my shoes. Each of them owed their liberty to the care they had devoted to me in my childhood.' Then came her nanny: 'And then, *voilà*, in front of me, the good old woman, sitting on the best armchair in my room, her hands on her knees, head held high, devouring me with her eyes and replying to every question which I put to her about members of her family . . .'[23] But, of course, all these were domestics, not workers on plantations. The comments remind us that there was as big a difference between black Cubans as there was between them and white ones.

The slave trade seemed in these days essential to this island: it was taken for granted that the way to the wealth to which all aspired was to cultivate more and more land, and that could only be done by slaves. Despite Morillas's prize essay, European labour was considered impractical and less reliable. It was also thought in Spain that an increase in the black population would make it certain that the Cuban *criollos* would remain faithful to the mother country, since the planters would have to rely on Spanish armies to deter, and if necessary defeat, a slave revolt.

As in Brazil, the slave merchants dominated the economy. Also as in Brazil, men from the *madre patria* played a large part in this illegal stage of the commerce. Thus there was Joaquín Gómez, whom we have met before as a friend of General Tacón, a Freemason from Santander, who rejoiced in the inappropriate Masonic name of Aristides. Perhaps it was of him that the Reverend Abbot was speaking when he described the typical Havana merchant as arriving from Spain 'in poverty, [they] begin with a shop six or eight feet square, live on a biscuit, and rise by patience, industry and economy to wealth and, unlike the Yankees, never fail'.[24] In the mid-1820s Gómez was not only the pioneer of illegal trading from Africa but was also one of the first Spanish-born slave merchants to buy sugar mills (two of them, in the western province of Pinar del Río) which he would himself provide with slaves. He was later a founder-director of the first bank in Cuba, the Royal Bank of Ferdinand VII, and was the first Cuban planter to

---

* *She was daughter of that Count of Jaruco who had been the first to put a steam engine on his sugar plantation, and a descendant of that Cubanized Richard O'Farrill who, after the Treaty of Utrecht, had been the South Sea Company's factor on the island.*

introduce iron rollers imported from England for use in his mills. Captain-General Vives asked him to organize the distribution of freed slaves in Cuba, the *emancipados*. Gómez's palace, at the corner of the Calle Obispo and the Calle Cuba, was the site of legendary receptions. In the 1830s he became the special confidant of Tacón, with whom he would be seen daily walking, deep in conversation about the iniquities of the United States and the hypocrisy of the British. Gómez's slave vessels were still setting off for Africa in the 1840s. Late in his life he was blinded by a deranged doctor from Catalonia, a certain Verdaguer, who threw vitriol in his face when he was leaving church: the vengeance of God for his slaving activities, it was said. All the same, when he died in 1860, and despite his Masonic ties, Gómez left money to the Church for its distribution to the poor, including enough for the purchase of a new organ for the cathedral. His nephew and heir, Rafael de Toca Gómez, became first Count of San Ignacio, was a founder of the Banco Español (when the son of that noble-man died in 1881, he left a great fortune of 183,000,000 reales).

Associated with Gómez was a Gaditano, Pedro Blanco, whose activi-ties in Africa will be discussed later,* and whose nephews, Fernando and Julio, would carry on their own substantial slave trafficking, in Havana, sometimes carrying slaves to New Orleans, and becoming specialists in the swift interchange of flags which was such a necessary part of the commerce in mid-century. Then in the 1850s they turned themselves into respectable London general merchants, with interests in both Liverpool docks and Manchester textiles.

Another formidable slaver in Cuba of the early nineteenth century was the Catalan Francisco Martí y Torres. He had fought for a time in the Peninsular War alongside the *guerrillero* Marqués de Romana, but reached Havana as early as 1810, where he embarked on a career as a pirate in the agitated Caribbean. A Cuban Vautrin, he eventually found employment as a naval lawyer concerned to punish smuggling, a sinecure in which he placed himself at the orders of Joaquín Gómez, using his position to make a fortune from receiving bribes from the slave traders whom he was theoretically intended to control. He soon began to send slave ships himself to Africa and, like Gómez, helped to manage the sale of *eman-cipados* on behalf of Tacón. Later, he organized the dispatch (as well as the kidnapping) of innumerable Yucatec Mayas to work in Cuba, including children, in conditions tantamount to slavery; at the same time, he received honours for capturing pirates, he became a philanthropist, and, on behalf of Tacón, he built a theatre, whose grandeur rivalled all others in the Americas at the time.[25]

Though Martí died a multimillionaire, his fortune was surpassed by that of Juan Manuel de Manzanedo, a native of Santoña, in northern Spain, who emigrated to Cuba in 1823. By 1845 he had already amassed

* *See page* 689.

vast wealth, partly in providing sugar equipment to mills, partly by making loans, partly by selling sugar in Spain and England, and partly in financing slaving expeditions. He was a member of all the important institutions of Cuba, such as the Tribunal de Comercio and the Junta de Fomento (Development Commission). He returned to Spain, bought property in Madrid near the Puerta del Sol, acted as Cuba's representative in that capital, and became a deputy, a marquis, and then a duke (of Santoña). His services to the restored Bourbon monarchy after 1876 did not prevent him from acquiring a collection of 138 pictures, among them two Velázquezes, two Goyas, and a Leonardo, all to be seen on the walls of his palace in the Calle Principe. Manzanedo died worth about 180,000,000 reales, most of which sum was then invested in Spain.[26]

Julián Zulueta, a Basque from the tiny village of Barambio in Alava, Spain, was an even more powerful merchant. At the end of the 1820s, Zulueta came to Cuba to work for an uncle, Tiburcio de Zulueta, who owned coffee farms. Julián Zulueta became his heir and seems then to have dropped the particule. He married Francisca, niece of his partner, the slaver Salvador Samá y Martí, who had become Marquis of Marianao. In the 1830s Zulueta also became interested in slaves, partly because of his wife's family, but more because of the interest of another uncle, Pedro Juan Zulueta de Ceballos, a successful London merchant, for whom he, Julián, acted as the Cuban agent. Later, he became the slaver-planter par excellence of Cuba, ensuring, like Gómez, that slaves for whose journey he himself had arranged would be delivered direct from Africa to one of his properties, such as his large sugar plantation, the Alava, the name of the Basque province whence he came. Zulueta was the originator of the scheme to make up for the shortage of labour in Cuba with Chinese, from Macao, and he also financed the Caibarién Railway. He had too an office for the purchase and sale of slaves in New Orleans. He both lent money and made sugar on a large scale. He probably brought into Cuba most of the 100,000 or so slaves imported in the years 1858 to 1862.

At that time Zulueta was the chief shareholder in a company, the Expedición por Africa, which owned about twenty ships. One of these was the *Lady Suffolk*, which disembarked 1,200 slaves in the Bay of Pigs in May 1853.[*] Zulueta received them in person, though he sold some of them to his co-planter and fellow slaver, José Baró, Marquis of Santa Rita, owner of the Luisa and Rita mills, respectively the seventh and ninth best mills of Cuba, who controlled the manufacture and supply of the moulds used in Cuban sugar manufacture.

The British Consul denounced the affair of the *Lady Suffolk*, and the then Captain-General, the mildly humanitarian General Cañedo, ordered the arrest of Zulueta. That great merchant was in consequence detained for two months in the most disagreeable fortress of La Cabaña, and only

---

[*] *Presumably the ship was named after the mistress of King George II of England.*

eventually released on the appeal of his doctor. Despite this, honours fell to Zulueta in later life, since he led the Spanish interests on the island during the civil war which began in Cuba in the late 1860s. Zulueta became a senator for life in Madrid, and a marquis. When he died he was worth 200,000,000 reales, a fortune which made him the richest man in both Spain and the Spanish empire, unless the landed wealth of the old aristocratic families of Andalusia is reckoned. The correspondent of *The Times* (of London), a repentant revolutionary, A. N. Gallenga, sometime secretary to the Italian revolutionary Manzini, described Zulueta as 'a king of men . . . almost the father of the gods and of men . . . another Cosimo de' Medici'.[27] There continues to be a street named after Zulueta in Havana: his Alava sugar mill also survives; but he himself seems quite forgotten.

Other slave merchants in Cuba included Pedro Martínez, who moved into the shipment of sugar in the 1840s but retained slaving interests until the late 1850s. (In Africa, he had agencies at both Lagos and on the Brass River.) He was said then to be the owner of 'thirty ships engaged in the traffic'.[28]

Only a little less powerful and almost as rich were two merchants originally from Bordeaux, Pierre Forcade and Antonio Font, of Forcade y Font (Cádiz), of whom the first owned the sugar mill Porvenir, near the town of Colón, and the latter Caridad, near Cienfuegos, a city founded by the recent Captain-General of that name, on the south coast of the island. Forcade had owned the slave ship the *Orthézienne*, which had been among the first to leave France for Africa after the Napoleonic Wars, before he moved to Havana where, according to the protagonist in Pío Baroja's brilliant novel, *Los Pilotos de Altura*, he lived grandly with two houses and two families 'one with a Spaniard to whom he was married, the other with a very pretty Cuban'.

The roll of merchants in Cuba who financed slave voyages is thus long. It should include Antonio Parejo, who came from the mother country about 1840 with a 'very immense capital', apparently the portfolio of María Cristina, the Queen Mother of Spain, on whose behalf Parejo invested in the large San Martín plantation. Nor should we forget Manuel Pastor, founder of the Banco Pastor.

Occasionally in the 1840s, a change in prices for slaves in Brazil in comparison with those in Cuba would cause the slave traders of the two lands to collaborate. Thus Forcade in Cuba made common cause with Manoel Pinto da Fonseca in Rio de Janeiro. Francisco Rubirosa, a well-known dealer in slaves in Havana in 1840, moved to Rio in the late 1840s, became known as Rubeiroza,* and then returned to Havana in the 1850s.

Many leading merchants in Havana, including slave merchants, had close connections with London firms, several of which, as in Brazil, saw

* See page 703.

no reason why they should not supply goods for the slave trade, even if they seem to have hesitated before concerning themselves directly. One or two enterprises, such as Thomas Brooks, which established its agents in Havana in the 1840s, included slave merchants in the ample credits which they extended. Samuel Dickley of London lent 12,000,000 reales to Francisco Martí, the Catalan merchant, in 1834, enabling that pirate of finance to buy a new ocean-going vessel, which he surely used for the slave trade; and the same firm provided 10,600,000 reales for Salvador Samá, Zulueta's father-in-law. Dickley's biggest loan in Cuba, for 16,000,000 reales, was to Rafael Torices, who though an experienced slave merchant was at that time interested in the traffic in Chinese from Macao. Then Hudson Beattie of London lent to both Manuel Pastor and to Tomás Terry, a substantial merchant of Venezuelan origin, 'the Cuban Croesus', established in Cienfuegos. Both concerned themselves with slaves at different periods of their long and prosperous lives. Lizardi of Liverpool included Julián Zulueta among their creditors, and so did the firms of Simeon Himely and Aubert Powell. Other London firms, such as Barings, Kleinwort and Cohen, and Frederick Huth (the London banker, incidentally, of the Madrid land speculator, the Marquis of Salamanca, as well as of the Queen Mother) were chiefly interested in sugar from Cuba, especially after 1846, when the tariff against foreign-produced sugar was abolished by Sir Robert Peel. Kleinwort had a special relation with the Cuban family of English origin, the Drakes; while Barings were close to the Aldama family, who sought in 1840 to use non-slave labour on their plantations, without much success.[29]

Some of these London firms, however, had a Spanish or a Cuban origin: for example, Murrieta, a great wine producer which began as a business exporting wine from Cádiz to London; the Ayalas from Santander, who were sugar planters in Cuba, sugar importers in England, champagne makers in France, and stockbrokers in Madrid; and, perhaps above all, the firm of Pedro Juan de Zulueta, already mentioned in connection with Julián, which did for a time concern itself in slaves in Havana; this became evident at the trial of the founder's son and heir, Pedro José, for slave trading, partly in collaboration with his cousin Julián in Havana. (He was fortunate to be acquitted.)

These London connections make it understandable that over half of the Cuban capital invested abroad in the mid-nineteenth century was placed in England. This included some fortunes of slave traders, such as that of the brothers-in-law Gabriel Lombillo and José Antonio Suárez Argudín, who began to invest in textiles in Manchester and coal mines in Wales after 1830 (the year when the first of these two one-time slave

---

* When a United States brig the Tigris was brought into Boston Harbor in 1841 by a British naval vessel, the outcry was such that the owners might have been heroes, not criminals.

merchants was poisoned by the second, a crime of which he appears to have escaped the consequences, spending only a most modest spell in prison). In Spain the investments of these Cuban entrepreneurs were so substantial that the banking system of the country was really their creation. There was no bad conscience about the investment of such slave-based fortunes in Spanish concerns, any more than there had been in England and the United States a half-century before.[30] The British Minister in Madrid in 1836, George Villiers – subsequently, as Lord Clarendon, Foreign Secretary under Gladstone – wrote in that year to his brother: 'All those Spaniards who are not absolutely indifferent to the abolition of the slave trade are positively averse to it. We think that an appeal to human-ity must be conclusive. The word is not understood. . . . Cuba is the pride and hope and joy of Spain . . . the place where revenue comes, and whither every bankrupt Spaniard goes in order to rob *ad libitum*.'[31]

In 1835 John Eaton, the United States Minister to Madrid (previously a controversial Secretary of War under Andrew Jackson), told the Spanish Foreign Minister, the liberal Count of Ofalia (Narciso de Heredia), that the United States had no need to worry about British abolitionist activi-ties, since slaves in North America were well taken care of, the proof being that they multiplied as fast as whites.

Slaves were certainly traded within the United States. Firms such as Franklin and Armfield made money by buying slaves in Virginia and dispatching them by sea, just as in the old transatlantic slave trade, to New Orleans, for possible subsequent shipment to Natchez or other places up the Mississippi. The same firm also sent hundreds of slaves a year overland to the South. It was once suggested that the profit obtained by selling slaves gave the capital for westward movement. That cannot be true since slave movements from Eastern to Western states numbered only about 127,000 between 1810 and 1860, and were worth only $3,000,000. All the same, some slave owners in the American South, espe-cially in the border states and in states along the Atlantic coast, did breed slaves 'systematically', and for sale, thus encouraging polygamy and promiscuity, the progeny being usually sold to the South-western states.

It was in the international trade, though, above all the trade to Cuba and Brazil, in which United States sea captains were still chiefly engaged during the first half of the nineteenth century, rather than in a clandestine traffic to the United States. Probably most United States administrations desired to stop this commerce, but slaving interests remained strong in Congress, and still no government in Washington could accept that a British ship could capture a United States ship and condemn the master to death for slaving.[*]

---

[*] *See Appendix 2.*

Britain in the 1830s carried through a complete emancipation of slaves in her empire, as had most states of the United States and of the new independent South American nations. This occurred partly as a result of renewed agitation by the anti-slavery movement headed in Parliament by Thomas Fowell Buxton; partly because of the destructive Jamaican slave revolt of December 1831; and partly because the Whig government was ready, after the Great Reform Act of 1832, to turn its attention to something new. Between 1830 and 1832 the anti-slavery movement held thousands of meetings. Even so the Whigs were only willing to act when certain of Tory support; which in turn was forthcoming only when the leaders of that party knew that the planters of the West Indies (who still included many members of Parliament such as the elder Sir Robert Peel and Gladstone's father) were satisfied with the terms.˙

The ambiguities and the consequences of this famous measure have been amply discussed. Suffice it to say that the immediate consequence was to cause disillusion among the adult slaves: if they were to be free, why did they have to wait five years? The long-term effect was to cause the decline of British West Indian sugar: the number of sugar plantations in Jamaica, for example, fell from 670 in 1834 to 330 in 1854; and there was no compensating improvement in production, as would occur in similar circumstances in Cuba. Indeed, the amount of land devoted to sugar fell in those twenty years by nearly 170,000 acres on that island.

Though the end of slavery in the British dominions had an effect on international opinion, it did not inspire the final abolition of the international traffic, which Wilberforce and his friends had begun to attack a generation before. The abolitionists – with anti-slave societies in every big British town, distributing 35,000 items of propaganda every year, collecting innumerable sums of up to £50 each, organizing petitions – did not have precise figures any more than a historian does. But it seems that even in the 1820s slaves shipped from Africa to the New World totalled about 60,000–70,000 a year, or well over 500,000 in the ten years: more than the late-eighteenth-century peak. Gross profits per slave delivered were in these days above the levels of the eighteenth century: perhaps between three and five times higher than the past. Prices went down in Africa, and the interference – as it seemed to be – of the British raised prices in the Americas.

˙ *The act of 1833 provided for the emancipation of 750,000 slaves. Children under six were to be free from 1 August 1834; while adults and older children were to be apprentices for six years and then be free, though all would be legally free from 1 August 1838. The promise of £20,000,000 in compensation gained the support of the planters.*

31

ACTIVE EXERTIONS

'The Brazen *is still cruizing to leeward in the Bight of Benin, waiting the arrival of messengers from the interior. During her stay there she has succeeded in detaining, after a chase of 46 hours, the Spanish schooner* Iberia *with 423 slaves, and also the English palm-oil ship, for a slaving transaction, the master having, by depositions from his crew, disposed of four female negroes ... to the master of a Spanish vessel lying in the river. ...'*

Commodore Bullen to the Admiralty,
London, 28 January 1826

THE SYSTEM OF INTERNATIONAL LAW which Britain sought to inspire, and with which some other nations collaborated without enthusiasm, in the hope of bringing the slave trade to an end, was an unusual affair. There were by 1830 four mixed courts of arbitration in Sierra Leone, Havana, Paramaribo, and Rio. At the first of these places a British judge sat beside Spanish, Brazilian, and Dutch colleagues; in each of the other ports there was a British judge and one from the appropriate second nation. In the case of a difference between the judges the court would turn to two commissioners of arbitration, again one British and one from the country concerned. These would draw lots to decide as to which of the two the matter should be referred for final decision.

Since France and the United States did not recognize any English court, cases which the French wished to bring were taken to a court at Gorée, while all cases affecting United States citizens were heard in the port of the United States from which the offending ship had come.

Finally, the very few Englishmen accused of trading slaves were usually tried not by a mixed commission but a Court of Vice-Admiralty, which was also held at Sierra Leone. But the only instance of a trial of an established merchant, Pedro de Zulueta, was in London.

Ships seized by the British or indeed any other navy under the laws condemning the trade in slaves were looked on as prizes, to be sold to the highest bidder. Half the profit of the sale of the ship went to the government under whose flag she had been sailing, and half went to the prize's captors, the admiral of the fleet concerned receiving one-sixteenth, the captain two-sixteenths, the rest being divided among the crew.* Such was the bureaucratic and legalistic structure of the immense system of international philanthropy now so remarkably mounted.

Given the size of the vast territories which the British West Africa Squadron was supposed to cover, and the unwillingness of other powers to make more than a token contribution to the crusade (or, as was the case with France, a refusal to do other than act against suspected French slavers), the British West Africa Squadron was increased: Sir Francis Collier, an officer who had been with Nelson at the Battle of the Nile, had by 1823 under his command the *Tartar* (thirty-six guns), the *Pheasant* (twenty-two), the *Morgiana* (eighteen), the *Myrmidon* (twenty), the *Snapper* (twelve), and the *Thistle* (twelve).* This force had many functions: it was supposed to be ready for combat at sea, to blockade ports anywhere between Cape Verde and Benguela, to seize foreign slavers, and also to protect legitimate traders.

The British were weakened by the fact that even with Collier's reinforcement this West Africa Squadron was still composed of old ships, with tall, easily detected masts, all left over from the Napoleonic Wars. Lord Palmerston, in 1862, would complain that 'no First Lord and no Board of Admiralty have ever felt any interest in the suppression of the slave trade', and added: 'If there was a particularly old, slow-going tub in the navy, she was sure to be sent to the coast of Africa to try and catch the fast-sailing American clippers.'[1] Though Palmerston exaggerated, the truth was that the vessels of the world's most powerful navy were, as a rule, easily outdistanced by the slavers' 'small, fast-sailing pilotboat schooners'.

The British began to introduce steamers into the navy as early as 1822, but they were slow to be adapted to West Africa, for there were only

---

* After 1828, the Dutch appointed no new judges to the Anglo-Dutch Mixed Court, and Britain was left to act as she thought best.

† In 1816 the Royal Navy changed the way it counted a ship's guns. Before then the number of guns listed for rated ships excluded carronades, the short-range cannon firing a low-velocity heavy ball with a light charge, even though ships had up to a dozen, while they were usually counted for unrated ones (often all-carronade-armed or nearly so). After 1816 carronades were included for all ships. Thus in the style of the later ratings Commodore Columbine's squadron on page 574 would be the Amelia (fifty-six guns), the Ganymede (twenty-six), the Kangaroo (twenty-two), and the Trinculo (eighteen). At the same time the larger ship-sloops were reclassed as frigates; an example is Captain Leeke's Myrmidon of 1821 on page 699; the Myrmidon was just a standard 20-gun ship-sloop under a new rating, only half the size and less than half the firepower of Irby's flagship Amelia of 1808.

three possible coaling stations: Sierra Leone, Fernando Po, and Luanda. If the navy's first paddle steamer on the station, the small *Pluto*, was faster than most slavers, she was an exception. In the 1820s and 1830s, Captain Denman recalled, 'dull-sailing ten-gun brigs' were all that were available – 'the model of which might have been taken from a haystack'.[2]

The contrast with the slavers was indeed laughable. George Cogge-shall, a United States traveller, described slavers on the Danish island of St Thomas as being usually 'armed with great guns'. The only British naval ships which were effective in the 1830s were in fact captured ex-slavers, the *Black Joke* and the *Fair Rosamond*. The quality of these ships alone might have shown to the governments of the United States and France that the British maritime activities off the coast of Africa were scarcely a grand design for world domination.

The only parts of the West African coast which were in practice regu-larly patrolled were the Bights of Benin and Biafra. Even there, British frigates mostly cruised forty miles offshore between well-known slave ports and, because of the shortage of ships and of money, were constrained to neglect other harbours. Thousands of miles were open to the slave traders. An indication of the inadequacy of the patrol was given by the captain of a slaver captured in the River Gallinas, in 1833. He told the mixed court in Sierra Leone that he had previously made thirteen voyages without difficulty. Captain Vidal, on the River Bonny, in 1826, wrote home that 'there were [often] twelve sail of slavers even there, and twelve British merchant ships, at the same time taking on palm oil'. From 1827 to 1834 the great entrepreneur Macgregor Laird thought that the famous old slave mart of the delta was, at 'the lowest calculation', exporting over 28,000 slaves a year.[3]

What could realistically be done? In 1827 Captain William Owen of the West Africa Squadron, his eyes on both Brazilian and Cuban slave traders, argued that the only hope of bringing the trade to an end would be to establish a base on Fernando Po, in order to control the delta coast-line. That island belonged to Spain, but had not been much used by her. Owen suggested that two British naval steamers should be stationed there, and a settlement founded. Acting quite illegally, Owen detained two Portuguese slavers south of the equator, and used the slaves on board to begin to build an anti-slave fortress – on the questionable ground that to send them to Sierra Leone would risk their lives.

Owen's successor, Colonel Edward Nicolls (as 'Fighting Nicolls', he had fought in over a hundred naval battles during the late war), thought a better approach was to make treaties between Britain and the African slaving monarchs. He often acquired property for the Crown without permission, and obtained a voluntary cession of the stretch of land from Bimboa Island to the Río del Rey, in the Cameroons, from King William of Bimbia: 'The three little islands in the bay of Ambosey', Nicholls reported, 'may be made little Gibraltars with little expense.' He thought that Duke

Ephraim, the leading chief at Old Calabar, would soon abolish the slave trade in his territory if he were asked to do so formally and paid a subsidy. But the British government had at that time no imperial ambitions on the West African mainland.[4]

The fate of the slaves liberated off Africa (35,000 of them in the 1830s) by the British was also unfortunate, since most were sent to work as labourers near Freetown, while a few agreed to go to the British West Indies as free apprentices. Even in Sierra Leone, the slave trade was continuing: indeed, opposite the new city of Freetown, on the right bank of the River Sierra Leone, a chief was always busy instructing his assistants to dart 'across the river in canoes and make captures of one or other of the theoretically free blacks there'. The continual influx of 'raw liberated Africans', mostly males, also made for much instability in the colony which was to be the new 'cradle of African civilisation'.

The British navy, of course, had some triumphs: a signal one was the seizure of the Cuban slaver *Veloz Pasajera*, a big ship with 555 slaves on board, apparently owned by the major slave merchant Joaquín Gómez, by HMS *Primrose* (Captain Boughton), after a challenge and naval action in which nearly fifty Spanish sailors and three British were killed. But such encounters were sporadic; nor did they always go well. In September 1831, for example, Captain Ramsay, in the Bight of Benin, in HMS *Black Joke*, sent two tenders in chase of two suspected Spanish slavers, the *Rápido* and the *Régulo*, which he observed as they were emerging from the Bonny River. Both 'put back, made all sail up the river and ran on shore. During the chase, they were seen to throw their slaves overboard, by twos, shackled together by the ankles, and left in this manner to sink or swim. . . . Men, women and children were seen in great numbers, struggling in the water, by everyone on board the tenders; . . . One hundred and fifty of these wretched creatures perished in this way.' Ramsay said that he and his men also saw sharks making for, and tearing apart, many of the struggling Africans. The *Régulo* was overhauled, with 204 slaves still on board, but the *Rápido* had none left, and only two slaves were saved from the river.[5]

The treaties also seemed to be still inadequate. British captains could arrest vessels which carried slaves, but they could do nothing to a ship which merely planned to do so. Captain Joseph Denman recalled later: 'We had no power over the [intercepted] ship, till the slaves were on board. The consequence was that, if a man-of-war lay in a port full of slavers, as I have seen in Whydah, with ten or a dozen . . . at one time, as long as the man-of-war was in port, they would not ship their slaves; directly the man-of-war was out of sight, they shipped their slaves, and every vessel in the harbour would weigh their anchor and set sail. The cruiser would probably chase the wrong ship and, after 100 miles, would be laughed at by the master of that vessel, who would say that he had only put on sail for a *pasatiempo*.'[6] Nor had the British yet secured the right to search and capture Portuguese vessels south of the equator (though in 1833 HMS *Snake* stopped the *Maria da Gloria* outside the harbour of Rio and found her carrying over 400 slaves from Luanda, mostly children under twelve). Then once a ship was detained the procedure was complicated and sometimes destructive, resulting, through delays, in the death of many slaves in theory freed.

The eventual consequence was a new treaty with Spain which enabled the navies of the two powers to seize ships flying the flag of either of those countries if slave equipment were found on board – in effect, a licence for the British navy to act more effectively against Spanish slavers. The 'equipment' was carefully defined. The treaty also stated firmly, if extremely optimistically, that the Spanish slave trade was 'totally and finally abolished throughout the world.'[7]

The treaty had occupied British diplomats a long time: in 1835 it was nine years since Canning had first mooted the matter and defined the word 'equipment'. Yet the remarkable further delay in promulgating the law – even in Spain, much less in Cuba – encouraged the slave traders and planters of the latter island to think that it would never be put into effect.[8] Spain was then being torn apart by the First Carlist War; it was inconceivable that any government in Madrid should act in such a way as to distress its Cuban taxpayers and merchants. Slave merchants in Havana, learning from the practice of North Americans, or encouraged by Portuguese officials, carried Portuguese or United States flags for use at their convenience, or even assumed another nationality; and the British Consul in Havana, Charles David Tolmé (the first such official), reported that the slave traders intended to establish more and larger factories on the African coast, to be sure that there was always a good supply of slaves ready for purchase and that ships with the right 'equipment' were there to carry them across the Atlantic.

The British navy was more effective after the treaty of 1835. From 1830 to 1835, the British West Africa Squadron captured ten slavers a year; from 1835 to 1839, the total was thirty-five, mostly bound for Cuba.

The Anglo-Spanish Treaty of 1835 also provided that the unfortunate *emancipados* should henceforth be assigned to the government by whose cruiser they had been freed. The British wanted to use this clause to

---

* *The equipment defined was of ten kinds: (1) hatches with open gratings, not closed hatches; (2) divisions or bulkheads in the hold or on deck in greater number than were necessary for vessels engaged in lawful trade; (3) spare planks fitted for being laid down as a second or slave deck; (4) shackles, boats, handcuffs; (5) a larger quantity of water in casks or in tanks other than was necessary for the crew; (6) an extraordinary number of casks or of other receptacles for holding liquid; (7) a greater number of mess tubs than was required for the crew; (8) a boiler of unusual size; (9) an extraordinary quantity of rice or other articles of food; and (10) a larger quantity of mats than necessary for merchant ships.*

permit the transfer to Trinidad or Jamaica of all these freed Africans. In Cuba a protector of these liberated slaves was named, to ensure this. The first to hold this post was Dr Richard Madden, an Irish journalist, doctor, and traveller, who had lived in Jamaica administering the changes necessary to ensure the effectiveness of the abolition of slavery. (He had denounced this as a farce in his *A Twelvemonth's Residence in the West Indies During the Transition from Slavery to Apprenticeship*.) Madden spent most of his first years in Cuba seeking to recover the *emancipados* released before this new treaty of 1835 came into effect. Those whom he saved were thereafter in theory to be sent to British colonies. But Captain-General Tacón henceforth refused to allow newly emancipated slaves to land in Havana. So the British naval ship-of-the-line *Romney*, launched in 1815, was sent to Havana from Jamaica in 1837. Its position in the harbour – 'a bulwark of abolitionism in the heart of slavism', in the phrase of Fernando Ortiz but also, so it seemed, an insult to Spanish national pride – was in addition a humiliating reminder to the British that their policies had failed. Tacón also forbade the largely black crew to land in Cuba; and the prosperous merchants of Havana would see the isolated ship every evening, when they walked, with their families, along the Alameda de Paula.

The same year that Spain concluded her treaty with Britain, Portugal at last formally abolished the slave trade, a bill being introduced to that effect by the Marquis Sá de Bandeira, whose opposition to the commerce is to be explained by his wish to create for Portugal a new 'Brazil in Africa'. The bill prohibited any Portuguese from importing or exporting slaves for profit.[*] In fact, though, this bill constituted just one more dead letter: the Portuguese flag would still be used to cover numerous illegal imports into Brazil and many slaves into Cuba.

Three years later, in December 1838, Lord Palmerston, the intemperate and passionate British Foreign Secretary, infuriated by his failure to break the Brazilian slave trade, decided to 'cut the knot' (as he put it) with respect to naval patrols, and determined to permit the British navy to seize all ships flying a Portuguese flag, wherever they were, if they were found carrying either slaves or even just the equipment for the trade.

Contradictory, calculating, and often vulgarly nationalistic, bullying (above all of the weak), Palmerston was now the dominant influence over British foreign policy. He saw himself as the spiritual heir of Canning; and his support for the abolition of the slave trade was certainly dedicated (though he was equivocal on the subject of slavery itself). At the University of Edinburgh, he had listened to Adam Smith's views on free trade, through the teaching of one of Smith's followers, Dugald Stewart. He had

---

[*] *Portuguese subjects would be allowed to take ten slaves from one Portuguese territory to another; and slaves could still be legally imported into Portuguese Africa by land.*

travelled in Europe when a child and had even seen something of the French Revolution; but he never visited Spain and Portugal, the two countries of Europe whose politics he sought to influence (though he had apparently read *Don Quixote* in Spanish when still at school).

First elected to Parliament as long ago as 1807, a few months after the passage of the bill abolishing the slave trade, Palmerston worked immensely hard and made his clerks and ambassadors do the same. A recent biographer insists that he was never concerned to lead a crusade about the slave trade, and that the naval patrol concerned to stamp it out was not the cover for a grand design of universal empire. Palmerston had, as it happens, a contemptuous view of both Africans and Portuguese. He believed that African kings were 'half naked and uncivilised', and could not be asked to keep to slave or any other treaties; and he thought that 'the plain truth is that the Portuguese are of Euro-pean nations the lowest in the moral scale'. Talleyrand, French Ambassador in London in the 1830s, thought Palmerston's defect was that he 'feels passionately about public affairs . . . to the point of sacri-ficing the most important interests to his resentments': a bad case of *trop de zèle*. Palmerston considered that 'the Anglo-Saxon race will in process of time become masters of the whole American continent . . . by reason of their superior qualities, as compared with the degenerate Spanish and Portuguese Americans'; but he maintained that Britain ought to do all she could to prevent United States aggrandizement.

The shortcoming of Palmerston's policy with respect to the abolition of the slave trade was that he never realized that the governments with whom he was dealing – in Spain, Portugal, and Brazil – were weak and sometimes had to spend all such energy as they had staving off a civil war; or, indeed, winning one. In those conflicts the British, like the French, were sometimes engaged. That did not inspire Lord Palmerston to any tolerance of the countries' difficulties. Nor did he ever see that with every confession of weakness at home the Spanish government became more and more dependent on the revenues of the 'ever-faithful' isle of Cuba. Spain needed the investments at home of men such as Joan Guëll, who brought back his Cuban fortune to invest in Catalan industry. Santander became rich on the strength of supplying flour to Cuba. The Queen Regent, María Cristina, always had investments in Cuban sugar.

Palmerston's contemptuous ideas about other peoples were widely held by British officials: William Ouseley, British Chargé d'Affaires in Brazil between 1838 and 1844, believed the Brazilians were 'vain, mediocre and ostentatious people'. His successor, James Hudson ('Hurry Hudson', as he was known from a phrase of Disraeli), spoke similarly of the Africans: 'a little barbarian, speaking a monkey dialect', could not be expected to send to Africa for proof that he had not been born a slave. He also assured Palmerston that Brazilian governments were all 'equally vicious, corrupt and abominable'.

Palmerston's determination to promote his new, aggressive policy in 1838 was itself partly inspired by the arguments of a new school of Quaker abolitionists, who thought that the West Africa Squadron should be withdrawn as a failure. These Quakers, among whom was the dedicated Joseph Sturge, Alderman of Birmingham and a man who had to good effect travelled in the West Indies and the United States, had in 1839 founded the British and Foreign Anti-Slavery Society, intended to be a new and efficient organization to follow the emancipation of British slaves by the global abolition of slavery. The new body opposed the idea of force, thinking that, 'The extinction of the slave trade will be obtained most effectually by the employment of those means which are of a moral, religious and pacific character.'

At much the same time, a new Society for the Extinction of the Slave Trade was founded in London by Sir Thomas Fowell Buxton. Buxton – the pertinacious son of a Quaker, married to a Gurney of Norfolk, a brewer as well as a Member of Parliament – thought that, since the naval patrols had been shown to be ineffective, they should be maintained only to guarantee legitimate trade. Buxton was not opposed to the use of force – he was only half a Quaker – but was primarily concerned to secure the regeneration of Africa through agricultural development. He thought that Britain should set up a series of trading posts on and near the Niger as an alternative to slaving. His influential *The African Slave Trade and Its Remedy* of 1838 was read by the British Cabinet. Like Macgregor Laird, he sought positive ideas for the moral recovery of Africa as part of the campaign against the slave trade: ideas which would eventually lead, through occupation, to a notion of empire far removed from the intentions of the first abolitionists.

Both the Prime Minister, the relaxed Lord Melbourne, and the flamboyant Foreign Secretary, Lord Palmerston, were irritated by Buxton, as they now often were by embittered men such as Lord Brougham, who brought his vast if mercurial powers to mock his old friends in the government: 'We pause, we falter, and blanch and quail', jeered Brougham, on one occasion, 'before the ancient and consecrated monarchy of Brazil, the awful might of Portugal, the compact, consolidated, overwhelming power of Spain.'[9] All the same, the government accepted that Buxton's scheme should be explored, and Palmerston offered Spain £50,000 for the island of Fernando Po as a start. The government also sent a flotilla of three steamers up the Niger in 1841 under a naval officer to stimulate the idea of legitimate trade, carrying over 6,000,000 cowries with them as currency. Malaria and yellow fever, however, made the voyage a failure.[*]

---

[*] *It offered Charles Dickens a fine opportunity to make fun of the expedition's surreal negotiation with the* Oba *of Aboh. The voyage also inspired the figure of Mrs Jellyby, in* Bleak House, *whose eyes 'had a curious habit of seeming to look a long way off. As if . . . they could see nothing nearer than Africa.'*

Palmerston, arguing that the independence of Brazil rendered illegal any Atlantic slaving trade by Portugal, now put forward a high-handed bill in Parliament which would give the British navy the right to stop all Portuguese vessels, as well as those without a flag (vessels 'not justly entitled to claim the protection of any state'), if they were found carrying 'equipment' useful for slaving.

The new bill was attacked but it did pass the House of Commons. The Viscount of Torre de Moncorvo, the clever Portuguese Minister (one of the few European diplomats in the nineteenth century to know anything of the life of ports, since he had been Superintendant of Customs and Tobacco in northern Portugal before going to London), protested. Palmerston told him arrogantly that his government could declare war if it liked. Thanks to the opposition of the Duke of Wellington (who had been approached by Torre de Moncorvo), the bill was defeated in the House of Lords. Wellington's view was that the proposed legislation was an affront to an ancient ally, as well as a violation of international law.

But the bill was then reintroduced, only slightly amended, in the next session of Parliament, and passed in August 1839, despite further opposition from Wellington (the Duke thought it better to declare war against Portugal than to proceed with a general right of visit; he said that that gave the bill 'a criminal character').[10] The Duke was correct in his legal appraisal, but he neglected to take into account that, as Commander Riley of the British navy would tell a House of Commons select committee in 1849, 'anyone who has been on the coast for two months will know a slaver from her manoeuvres; a legal vessel will heave to for you';[11] and a businessman, Francis Swanzy, told another such committee that even 'an amateur could form an opinion [about what was and what was not a slave ship] by the raking of the mast, the colour of the sails, the squareness of the yards, her tautness and low hull'.[12]

The final form of the new law enabled British captains off Africa to send captured Portuguese ships (both those with slaves and those only with equipment), as well as those without nationality, whether north or south of the equator, in rivers as on high seas, to the nearest British vice-admiralty court; to land any liberated slaves at the nearest British settlement; and to hand over the masters and the crews of the ships concerned to be judged in Portugal. 'Equipment' was defined in the same way that the previous act, covering Spain, had done.*

The government in Lisbon offered to sign a treaty along these lines, but only if Britain were to cease pressing for payment of her debts. Palmerston rejected that idea out of hand. He wrote to the British Minister in Lisbon that he should 'impress ... that the conclusion of a slave trade treaty is a matter which now concerns Portugal only. . . .' So,

---

* See page 654.

he argued, Portugal was offering nothing.[13] He arrogantly sent instructions to the navy to treat similarly, and capture, all Brazilian slave ships, and send them to the Anglo-Brazilian mixed court. He planned to increase again the West Africa Squadron: there would be thirteen ships in 1841. These included one fast, new ten-gun brig, HMS *Waterwitch*.

The *Waterwitch* was responsible for capturing forty slavers: a record. The British navy was also now regularly assisted by a system of spies all along the African coast, 'servants of the kings or the chiefs of the place who secretly ... gave any information we wanted' – for payment, of course. Intelligent British naval officers, such as Captain Denman, thought that the slave trade 'has diminished to one-half of what it was before', he told a committee of inquiry in 1842.

Brazilian or Cuban ships now had to use a United States flag if they wished to avoid the British navy. That recourse, admittedly, was easily available to them. President Martin Van Buren, 'the little magician of Kinderhook', who had briefly been Minister to London in 1831, when he had met Palmerston, complained of this practice to Congress in 1839. He demanded a tightening of the law in order to prevent the state of affairs whereby twenty-three ships (belonging to Manzanedo, Zulueta, and Gómez) left Havana that year flying United States flags. But Congress was reluctant to take any such step. The House of Representatives at that time was full of slaveholders, and they did not wish to talk about the issue of slavery at all. A financial panic in 1837 also precluded initiatives in almost every field. The lengthy debate as to whether the slave trade should be permitted in the District of Columbia had made it plain that for the Southern members anyone who talked of an end of slavery, such as John Quincy Adams of Massachusetts, or William Slade of Vermont, was 'a fanatic' – even when those men complained that, on their way to the Capitol, they had been 'compelled to turn aside from their path, to permit a coffle of slaves, chained to each other by their necks, to pass on their way to the national slave market'. There were now nearly 2,500,000 slaves in the United States, seen by James Henry Hammond, of South Carolina, as 'the greatest of all the great blessings which a kind Providence has bestowed upon our glorious region'; his colleague, 'Waddy' Thomson, also of South Carolina, went so far as to insist that slavery was 'essential to the maintenance of human liberty'; while William Cost Johnson, from Maryland, believed that it was a blessing for Africans to keep them in slavery. Abolitionists, even in the North of the country, were still a minority; in proper Boston, a leading enemy of slavery, William Lloyd Garrison, had recently been paraded bound through the streets in mockery of his ideals.[14]

In 1840 or so distrust of the British was also even more profound in the United States than it had been in 1824. Was not British abolitionism active in Texas? The emancipation of the British slaves in 1833 caused alarm. The planters in the South believed that they needed their slaves more than ever, while the British, even if consumers of cotton, were seen as a threat to that form of labour. Painstakingly, Palmerston would explain to the United States Minister to London, or the British Minister in Washington would explain to the Secretary of State, exactly how the slave trade was now working, how the bogus flag was assumed, how the fraudulent captain conducted himself, and how essential it was that all American ships fitted out as slavers should be condemned. But the United States would always refuse to concede any right of search.

The United States' failure to act with respect to the slave trade was highlighted by the curious affair of Lieutenant Charles Fitzgerald's prizes. This officer in the British navy in the brigantine *Buzzard* sailed into New York in the summer of 1839 with two United States ships as captures, the brig *Eagle* and the schooner *Clara*, both with slaves on board. Both ships were owned by merchants of Havana; the crews were Spanish, or Portuguese, except for the two captains, who admitted that they 'had merely been hired for the purpose of protecting the vessels from capture or detention by British cruisers'. Two weeks later, another British naval vessel, HMS *Harlequin*, sailed in, with another United States slaver, the *Wyoming*, in tow. Some months later still, HMS *Dolphin* came in with two more slaving schooners, the Baltimore-built *Butterfly* and the *Catharine*. All but the last named had slaves on board at the time of the capture and, even on the *Catharine*, the presence of 600 wooden spoons, and 350 pairs of handcuffs, as well as planks cut ready to install a slave deck, vividly suggested the purpose of the voyage; in addition, the United States captain on that ship had on his person instructions from the owners telling him how to convince a boarding party that the Spaniards and Portuguese on board were passengers.

Despite support in New York and Baltimore in favour of the slavers, President Van Buren ordered District Attorney Benjamin F. Butler to prosecute if he could. Butler decided that the captains of the first two vessels could not be tried, because the ships were then owned by Spaniards. Captain Fitzgerald set off with those two, with their cargoes, first to Bermuda, where the Court of Admiralty refused to act, and then, back across the Atlantic, to Sierra Leone. Though Fitzgerald had by then lost the *Eagle*, the court there did condemn, and seize, the *Clara*.

Back in New York, the District Attorney denounced the *Catharine*, the *Butterfly*, and the *Wyoming*. The merchants of Baltimore who owned the ships were then arrested and tried (Robert W. Allen, John Henderson, John F. Strohm, and Francis T. Montell). A case was brought against Captain Isaac Morris, of the *Butterfly*, and Captain Frederick Pearson, of the *Catharine*. Judge Betts confiscated the *Butterfly* and released the *Catharine*, declaring that the presence of a suspect cargo could not lead to a conviction for slave dealing. The Chief Justice of the Supreme Court, Roger Brooke Taney, then took a major decision: though a Southern aristocrat by upbringing, an owner of slaves like his predecessor at the

Supreme Court, John Marshall, a supporter of the institution of slavery, and a man who had long practised law in Baltimore, he deplored the practices which, as he stated, had brought disgrace on the flag of the United States as it did on Baltimore. The subsequent condemnation and confiscation of the ships led to a change in practice and, for a time, no slaves seem to have been sold in that prosperous city.

In the last months of 1839, because of the scandal of the frequent use of United States flags by slavers, Van Buren sent cruisers to mount another patrol on the African coast for the first time since the 1820s. This force admittedly had two functions: first, as 'a measure of precaution to protect American vessels from improper molestation' – by whom, it is easy to guess: and, secondarily only (so it would seem), 'to detect those foreigners who may be found carrying, without proper authority, the flag of the United States'.

Two officers set out: Captain John S. Paine, in the *Grampus*, and Commander Henry Bell, in the *Dolphin*.* Both stopped several slavers with double papers. Paine sensibly agreed, in March 1840 at Sierra Leone, with the British naval commander, William Tucker, in HMS *Wolverene*, that whenever he fell in with a vessel which was manifestly a slaver, showing any flag other than that of the United States, he would detain her until a British cruiser could make a search. Commander Tucker, on the other hand, would hold every suspect cruiser showing a United States flag till Paine could do the same. When Paine reported this intelligent plan to Washington, he was told that it was 'contrary to the well-known principles' of the government: so Paine had to deal with the 3,000 miles of African coast alone. Serious Anglo-American cooperation was further delayed.

British naval officers in those days frequently did search ships flying the flag of the United States: justifiably in their view; illegally, and arrogantly, in the view of the United States. Take the case of the *Mary* which, owned by Joaquin Gómez, with a Spanish crew, and with papers which showed that she was a Spanish slaver, was flying a United States flag when she was apprehended by Captain Bond of the Royal Navy. Andrew Stevenson, the Virginia-born United States Minister to London, told Palmerston that Captain Bond's action 'would seem to want nothing to give it the character of a most flagrant and daring outrage and very little to sink it into an act of open and direct piracy'.

Palmerston replied that though of course he well knew that 'British ships of war are not authorised to visit and search American vessels on the high seas, yet if a vessel which there is good reason to suppose is in reality Spanish property, is captured and brought into a port in which a mixed British and Spanish court is sitting, the Commissioners ... may

---

* *Bell, a Southerner by birth, was later chosen by Admiral Farragut during the Civil War to hoist the Union flag over the town hall of New Orleans.*

condemn her, notwithstanding that she was sailing under the American flag.'[15] There had, in fact, been a great many such cases, such as the *Douglass*, the *Iago*, and the *Hero*. There was the *Tigris*, the *Seamew*, and *William and Frances*. There was the *Jones*. Each had its little drama, its minor international scandal.

So Andrew Stevenson replied: 'It becomes my duty, therefore, again distinctly to express to your lordship the fixed determination of my government that their flag is to be the safeguard and protection of all its citizens. . . . The violation of the law of the United States is a matter exclusively for its own authorities. . . .' On another occasion, Stevenson insisted that 'there is no shadow of pretence for excusing, much less justifying, the exercise of any such right [of search]. . . . It is wholly immaterial whether the vessels be equipped for, or actually engaged in, slave traffic or no, and consequently the right to search or detain even slave vessels must be confined to the ships . . . of those nations with whom it may have treaties.' Palmerston said he could not think that the United States seriously intended to make its flag a refuge for slavers. He suggested that a distinction might be drawn between right of search and right of visit: 'Unless some measures could be adopted for the ascertaining whether the vessels and flags were American, the laws and treaties for the suppression of the slave trade could not be enforced.' He proposed that 'the right existed of ascertaining in some way or another the character of the vessel and that by her papers, and not by the colours on the flag which might be displayed'.

'I at once assured him', said Stevenson, 'that, under no circumstances, could the government of the United States consent to the right on the part of any foreign nation to interrupt, board or search their vessels on the high seas.' Palmerston thought it absurd that a merchantman could exempt herself from search by 'hoisting a piece of bunting with the United States' emblems and colours upon it. . . . Her Majesty's Government would fain hope that the day is not distant when the Government of the United States will cease to confound two things which are in their nature entirely different, will look to things, not words, and, perceiving the wide and entire distinction between the right of search, which has, heretofore, been the subject of discussion between the two countries, and the right of . . . visit which almost all other Christian nations have mutually given each other for the suppression of the slave trade, will join the Christian league; and will no longer permit the ships and subjects of the Union to be engaged in undertakings which the law of the Union punishes as piracy.'[16]

Relations were for a time so bad between Britain and the United States in 1841 that Andrew Stevenson reported home that in London there was a 'general impression that war is inevitable'. At the same time, General Cass, the Anglophobe United States Minister in Paris, did what he could to prevent France from agreeing with Britain on any subject; in particular, he applauded when in 1841 France refused to ratify the so-called Quintuple Treaty which had been signed in London (Britain, France, Russia, Austria, Prussia), which declared the slave trade to be piracy and which authorized whatever ships of war might be available to search every merchant vessel belonging to one of the signatory powers 'which shall, on reasonable grounds, be suspected of being engaged in the traffic in slaves'. The French refusal to ratify prevented the right of search from becoming a common maritime policy in Europe.* Cass had sent Guizot, the French Foreign Minister, on his own initiative, a note warning the Europeans against using force to accomplish their ends.[17]

An effort was also made by Palmerston to extend the area of the cooperation between the British and the French to cover the whole Atlantic. This idea was also thwarted (probably by the influence of General Cass). The issue was inflamed by the rough British handling of the crew of the Nantes merchant ship *Marabout* – she was not a slaver – in December 1841. A wave of anti-British feeling swept through French public opinion, excited by a nationalist press. Thus even such journals as *Le Constitutionnel*, which for so long had been a defender of everything British, insisted on 6 January 1842 that 'philanthropy is only a pretext for Britain's action'; other journals mocked British 'holy philanthropy'. The incident had the most adverse consequences in France for the cause of abolition, which was still commonly represented by the defenders of slavery (and the slave trade) as an English conspiracy.

As in the case of Britain's relation to the United States, there were more serious problems at issue between Britain and France than the slave trade. The question of policy towards Egypt, for example, had nearly caused war between the neighbours in 1840. Between the United States and Britain, the matters at issue included the questions of the Maine boundary, the Oregon Territory, and the affair of the burning of the United States ship *Caroline* at Niagara in 1837. All these disputes interacted, and the inevitable bad feelings were made infinitely worse by the disputes over the slave trade.

Britain had her difficulties with Brazil, too. Though new Liberal governments in Rio did give some difficulties to the practitioners of the slave trade, they were soon overthrown – not without numerous little incidents between the British and the Brazilians, as when Lieutenant Cox, of HMS *Clio*, landed in the Piumas Islands, half a mile offshore from Campos, about 150 miles north of Rio, and captured a slave ship with 300 slaves. The next week, when taking water in Campos, Cox and his men were attacked by men working for the slave traders, four sailors were wounded, and the rest were imprisoned. The British Chargé d'Affaires

---

* *The French refusal was partly a matter of pique: a reply by Guizot, the Foreign Minister, to his colleague Palmerston, who had gone out of his way, in a demagogic electoral speech in the West Country town of Tiverton, to criticize the policy of France in Algeria.*

protested, and the sailors were released, but the Brazilian Foreign Minister, Aureliano, said, with some spirit, 'I would prefer that Brazil should be erased from the list of nations rather than she should subject herself to the disgraceful tutelage of another which should arrogate to herself the right of interfering imperiously in the internal administration of my country.'[18]

The continuance of the slave trade in Brazil became every day more linked in the Brazilian mind with the question of national sovereignty, as well as economic survival. Even ministers who were anxious to diminish, if not to abolish the slave trade, or who were friendly to Britain, naturally had to avoid the appearance of bowing to that power.

The slave trade to Cuba still seemed to be increasing. For example, in 1837 an English abolitionist, David Turnbull, who had travelled in the West Indies, including Cuba, thought that out of seventy-one slave ships operating on the coasts of Cuba forty were Portuguese (if probably owned by Cubans), nineteen Spanish, eleven United States, and one Swedish. A few ships in the trade were even built still in Liverpool. He added: 'Two extensive depots for the reception and sale of newly imported Africans have lately been erected . . . under the windows of His Excellency's [the Captain-General's] residence, one capable of containing 1,000, the other 1,500, slaves. . . . These were constantly full.'[19] The British commander off the coast, Captain Tucker, about this time reported that the Spanish Captain-General now received sixteen dollars for each slave landed, the commander of the naval force four, the collector of customs seven, and lesser officials lesser amounts. Slaves at this time cost over three hundred dollars.

Britain was still determined to maintain pressure on Spain. She demanded in late 1840 a census in Cuba of all slaves: if slaves introduced since 1820 were found, they would be confiscated. This idea caused renewed outrage. The Spanish Council of State in Madrid rejected the scheme as something which would be 'the renunciation of authority by the government of a free and independent nation and a public confession of its impotence'. They then went on the intellectual offensive: had not all the white nations in their time introduced slaves? And, the first official use of an argument which was often to be repeated, had not 'the situation in Spanish colonies [with respect to the treatment of slaves] always been better than in other ones?' The increase in slaves in Cuba, the Council added, untruthfully, had nothing to do with the slave trade, but 'derived from the marriage and raising of slaves', as it did in the United States.[20]

The municipality of Havana added for good measure that if a census such as Britain proposed were to be established there would be a rebellion of *criollos*. Mariano Torrente, an economist and littérateur, argued that Spanish slaves had a standard of living 'much more favourable than that of the peasants of Europe. . . . What right has Britain, having paid so

little recompense to Spain, to demand the destruction of the huge investment of blood and money in the Antilles? Having destroyed her own
prosperity in Jamaica, she now plainly wanted to do the same in Cuba.'[21]
Many other such statements were made which were no doubt approved
by the new Captains-General, first General Joaquín de Ezpeleta and then
General Pedro Telléz Girón, Prince of Anglona, who together ruled only
three years, between 1838 and 1841. It is obvious that, as in 1817, the
Spanish government told its representatives in Cuba to avoid carrying
out the terms of the treaty. Captain-General Tacón, in another section of
that extraordinary letter of 1844, previously noticed, said as much: the
government, said Tacón, 'did not allow any doubts that its will was to
resist, so far as it was possible, the demand of Her Britannic Majesty
to prevent whoever was continuing to infringe the first treaty'. Thus it is
not surprising that Cuban officialdom remained obdurately hostile in the
face of aggressive British philanthropy.[22]

During Captain-General Ezpeleta's time in Cuba, Pope Gregory XVI
entered the controversy on the question of slavery when on 3 December
1838 he issued a bull which in language which followed a pure abolitionist line prohibited Christians from carrying out the slave trade. The
bull complained that the slave merchants treated slaves 'as if they were
true and impure animals', and accused them of fomenting wars so that
there would be slaves to sell. Those who carried on trading slaves would
therefore be excommunicated. The bull eventually appeared in the *Gaceta
de Madrid* in 1840; and the British Consul, Tolmé, asked to have it
published in Cuba. The Captain-General, the Prince of Anglona, refused
to do so: as remarkable an action for a consul of England as for the representative of the Catholic King.

The next Captain-General, General Jerónimo Valdés, seemed at first
inclined to wish to fulfil the spirit of the bull of Pope Gregory. An
Asturian, he was a friend of the new liberal dictator of Spain, General
Espartero, whom he had supported in his coup of 1840; he had gained his
captaincy-general in consequence. As a law student, he had taken part in
the rising against the French at Oviedo in 1808; later he had been Chief of
Staff to the last Viceroy fighting against the independence of Peru; after
years of combat in the harsh valleys and harsher mountain roads of that
'chamber of horrors' (Bolívar's expression), he had commanded half the
royalist army at the terrible Spanish defeat of Ayacucho in 1824. Now
aged fifty-seven, he arrived in Cuba in 1841 and immediately told the
slave traders that after six months he would seize any slave ships which
arrived in any Cuban port. This public declaration, the first such made by
a Spanish official of his rank in Cuba, turned Valdés for a few months into
the darling of the British in Havana. But they soon changed their minds
when in October 1841 they heard the Captain-General had taken refuge,
as his predecessors had done, behind the lame defence that he could act
only at sea against slave dealers, and not on land. But then Valdés did

seize some illegally imported slaves, to whom he sent copies of his own
instructions ordering compliance with the law: an unheard-of action by
an official in Cuba. A Spanish naval vessel even brought a captured slaver
into the harbour of Havana in March 1842, and in June that year the
Captain-General declared it to be illegal to buy ships from abroad and
register them as Spanish: a serious blow to those who had been lately in
the habit of buying excellent, fast ships in Baltimore. But Valdés was a
tactician and a Spanish patriot, not an idealist. He was acting out of what
he perceived as a necessity, to try to seem to meet at least some British
demands, rather than court defeat by that nation's destructive abolitionism (as it appeared), and so risk losing Cuba for Spain altogether.

All the same, the idea of ending the slave trade was bound to cause
difficulties for a conscientious captain-general. Valdés wrestled with such
questions as whether planters should surrender newly purchased slaves
if they were found; whether plantations could be officially searched for
imported Africans; whether he should seize ships denounced as slavers
by the British; and whether all concerned in a slaving voyage should be
arrested, or whether it should be just the captain and the ship's owner.
The Captain-General sent a memorandum putting these and some similar
questions to Madrid in March 1843. But he never received an answer.

General Valdés had by then become the target for attacks by the slave
merchants. In him for the first time they encountered a governor who was
unhappy to collaborate with them and receive their bribes. A ferocious
campaign was in consequence mounted against him in Madrid. In 1842,
just to select one of the innumerable documents which supported the
slave merchants, the provincial deputation of Santander, on the north
coast of Spain, announced that, 'when from all sides of the kingdom a
deeply felt clamour is raised against the demands of the English government which, under the pretext of humanity, seeks the ruin of the Spanish
Antilles, the provincial *diputacion* of Santander cannot do less than unite
its voice to the many who feel the blood of Castile run in their veins. . . .'
The fact was, as Aston, the British Minister in Madrid, wrote to Palmerston in February 1841, the Spanish government still depended 'entirely
upon the revenues of that island [Cuba] for the means of meeting the
pressing exigencies of the state'. It was also supposed that behind
Britain's advocacy of abolition lay a real intention to capture the island:
Gaspar Betancourt Cisneros, an enlightened planter, wrote to his friend,
the writer Domingo del Monte, that Britain had the force, the knowledge,
and the will to ensure the end of the slave trade: if it did not act, it meant
that there 'are sinister designs which will be realized by sinister means'.[23]

Meanwhile the abolitionist David Turnbull had become British
Consul in Havana: an astonishing appointment. Turnbull had been a journalist for *The Times* in Madrid, where his interest in the slave trade had
been awoken by the clever British Minister, George Villiers, who had
negotiated, with great patience, the treaty of 1835. His real character is

difficult to gauge. His United States colleague, Campbell, described him as 'just a Glasgow bankrupt, with some talent, more pretension, a great fanatic and regardless of the truth'. To the Spaniards, he was an archfiend. Valdés hated him but, then, he had accused Valdés of being as anxious to profit personally from the slave trade as his predecessors had been. In the view of the British apostle of free trade, Richard Cobden, Turnbull interfered in Cuban affairs so as to 'embitter the feelings of Cuba and Spain more than anything else'. Yet to abolitionists he was a hero and even a martyr.[24]

These were, of course, nervous times in Cuba. There was restlessness among the slaves and several revolts on plantations. Partly because of Brazilian competition,' the slave trade declined in the early 1840s. Consul Turnbull was accused by the Spaniards, as Dr Richard Madden had been, of exaggerating the facts in his reports, of trying to provoke a slave revolt, of encouraging the *emancipados* to present their claims through the British consulate, even of inciting his *criollo* friends to declare an abolitionist republic under British protection. Some of these charges were true. He probably did secure the release of 2,000 *emancipados* while in Cuba.

Palmerston replied by insisting that instead of Spain's having the right to demand Turnbull's dismissal, Britain wanted the power to dismiss all Cuban officials, from the Captain-General downwards. Turnbull's opinions, Palmerston declared, were, after all, those of the whole British nation. This high-handed approach astonished the Spaniards. Yet, despite being seen everywhere as a man bent on fomenting a slave revolt, Turnbull stayed a year or so more.[†] Meanwhile, Valdés had antagonized the planters by merely asking what they thought of Turnbull's plan. The overwhelming answer had been to oppose any further concessions. Who wanted some 'fanatical Methodist' in Havana who would be, at the same time, the 'judge, the accuser, and the instigator of revolts by slaves'?

Before he left Havana, Turnbull, by then a refugee in the British hulk *Romney* in Havana Bay, declared that the degrading spectacle of slavery in the Antilles and Brazil would soon be swept away by public indignation. Captain-General Valdés calmly suggested that such a humanitarian spirit might turn his attention first to Ireland and India before he concerned himself with foreign countries. Valdés thought that to accept Turnbull's plan would be equivalent to abandoning the island; and he, for one, a veteran of fighting against Peruvian independence, would resign rather than have anything to do with such a surrender.

In fact, as the Captain-General knew, there were at that time a few stirrings within Cuba in criticism of the slave trade. The director of the

---

' See page 732.
[†] *Until, in June 1842, he was dismissed by Palmerston's prudent successor, Lord Aberdeen who told the Spanish Minister in London that he would not press the matter of the register of slaves for the time being.*

Economic Society, for example, a popular philosopher, José de la Luz y Caballero, had become an opponent; far away in Paris, the exiled historian José Antonio Saco maintained a constant stream of publications on the same theme. Then Domingo del Monte, a Venezuelan by birth, a friend of both Dr Richard Madden and of Consul Turnbull, argued that Spain was only permitting the continued import of slaves from Africa in order to prevent a rebellion of *criollos*. He saw the slave trade, therefore, as an instrument of Spanish oppression.

There was also the beginning of a new mood in Madrid. Two members of the British and Foreign Anti-Slavery Society called on the economist Ramón de la Sagra. They convinced him of their arguments against the slave trade, and de la Sagra wrote a letter published in *El Corresponsal* in December 1840 which demanded the suppression of the commerce as a step towards the abolition of slavery itself. The Cubans, he said, echoing Adam Smith, were making a great mistake to suppose that the labour of slaves was superior to that of freemen.

In 1842 Turnbull, who had left Havana only to go to the Bahamas, and who was now the British government-appointed 'superintendent of liberated Africans', returned in a sloop to Cuba with some free British blacks, intending to try and liberate some Bahamians who he thought had been kidnapped as slaves. He landed near Gibara, on the north coast of the island, but was this time explicitly accused of seeking to organize rebellion, imprisoned, deported, and warned never to return. He was perhaps fortunate not to be executed, as many Spaniards demanded. Lord Aberdeen˙ abolished his office (though appointing him for seven years to be a judge of the Anglo-Portuguese mixed court in Jamaica).

Following what seemed to the world to be a modest victory over British pressure, Spain tried to soothe her critics by introducing yet one more slave code (in 1842). On the one hand, it was stricter than previous arrangements: slaves on one plantation now could not visit neighbouring ones without permission, and working days were defined as being of ten hours except during harvest, when they would be sixteen. But at the same time there were tolerant concessions: slaves who reported a conspiracy would be declared free; and slaves of advanced age without means of support would have to be maintained by the masters for whom they had once worked. In an effort to force household slaves onto plantations, the government imposed a tax of one peso per domestic slave.

In the face of continued Brazilian and Spanish or Cuban obstructionism, and the complex attitudes of France and the United States, the British government had now altered its approach to the problem of the slave trade in Africa itself. It had earlier signed treaties with three potentates in East Africa: the King of eastern Madagascar, the Sultan of Zanzibar, and the Imam of Muscat. These each included provisions

˙ *See page 670.*

against the slave trade. Why not, thought John Backhouse of the Foreign Office, extend this scheme to West Africa? So naval officers were instructed to begin that process there.

The first opportunity for applying the new policies occurred in surprising circumstances on the River Gallinas. There in 1840 Captain Joseph Denman, the determined officer who was son of the then Lord Chief Justice in London, at the request of the Governor of Sierra Leone, landed sailors from three warships, the sixteen-gun brigs *Wanderer, Rolla,* and *Saracen,* at the Spanish slave station on the Gallinas estuary, browbeat the local king into accepting his intervention, destroyed the most important nearby slave barracoons (at Dumbocorro, Kamasura, Chicore, and Etaro), and freed 841 slaves waiting to be shipped. Palmerston was delighted: 'Taking a wasp's nest . . . is more effective than catching the wasps one by one', he triumphantly proclaimed. While Denman burned the barracoons, local Africans helped themselves to the stores (including those belonging to the notorious Mrs Lightburne:˙ cottons and woollens, of course, but also gunpowder, spirits, and other goods). The Spanish merchants escaped upriver. The intervention led to the signature by the son of the king of the region of the first of the new treaties.

This sensational action caused a shock all along the African coast – particularly when other British naval officers followed, with other attacks: Captain Blount landed higher up the River Gallinas; Captain Nurse did so on a slave factory on the River Pongas, to the north of Sierra Leone; Captain Hill landed at 'Mr François's barracoon' at Sherbro; Commander Tucker did the same at the island of Corisco, off Gabon (he seized much merchandise, as well as a Spanish factor, Miguel Pons); and Captain Matson destroyed eight barracoons, owned by Brazilian and Spanish merchants, at Ambriz and Cabinda in Loango-Angola. (Asked later by a House of Commons committee how he knew that one merchant concerned was engaged in the slave trade, Captain Matson tartly answered: 'The only proof was finding slaves chained in the factories.')[25] When Matson was charged in London for trespass by one of the slave owners, Juan Tomás Burón, he explained that the slaves numbered 4,000, worth £100,000.

Under Denman's influence, various treaties were afterwards secured with several other kings on the coast to achieve the abolition of the traffic in slaves, in return for a modest payment. The treaties with native kings would be balanced by a 'vigilant and unremitting blockade', followed up by destruction of the barracoons. Captain Matson later recalled that he received orders that, 'wherever we found slave barracoons erected, we should endeavour to obtain the sanction of the native chiefs to destroy them; failing to obtain that consent, we were in certain cases to do it

˙ *See page 686.*

without. However, it was never difficult to obtain that consent, for it was really obtained for a trifling subsidy, and [so] most of the barracoons on the coast were destroyed.'[26]

These actions caused another shock in Havana. The dealers in slaves there seemed to the new British Consul 'to be paralysed for a time. . . . [They] came to me expressing great regret and remorse that they ever engaged in such an enterprise; and [hoped] that by following legal modes of traffic, great good might be done.'

Matters, meantime, at last also improved with respect to the relations between the United States and Britain when New Englanders regained control of United States foreign policy. Daniel Webster, a great orator, took office in Washington as Secretary of State, and Andrew Stevenson, the Virginian at the London legation, gave way to Edward Everett, of Harvard. It is true that Webster had the bland view that since slavery was bound to end one day there was no point in discussing the question. But that did not affect his efficacy as a diplomat.

At the same time, Palmerston was succeeded as Foreign Secretary by the austere, cultivated, and subtle Lord Aberdeen – Byron's 'travell'd thane, Athenian Aberdeen'. His remarkable features expressed a 'charted tranquillity', in Gladstone's words, 'the absence from his nature of all tendency to suspicion', which made him in some ways a more effective diplomat on the issue of the slave trade than Palmerston. He sought to understand the Spaniards and Portuguese, whereas Palmerston despised them; he saw the point of view of Brazilians, and never threatened them. Yet he gave up nothing to them. He was the one man whom Gladstone loved. His one published work, *An Inquiry into the Principles of Beauty and Grecian Architecture*, distinguishes him from all other statesmen of his era.

The new British Minister in Washington was the experienced Lord Ashburton. As the enlightened banker, and head of Barings', we have met before this Alexander Baring, when speaking on the slave trade in the House of Commons as long ago as 1814. He had served in Peel's administration in 1834, and he had the great benefit of having known the United States in Jefferson's day. Neither Aberdeen nor Ashburton surrendered Palmerston's aims, but they altered his language. Thus Aberdeen suggested that British naval officers should renounce the right to visit United States merchant vessels if they merely thought slaves were aboard; and should offer reparation if a trespass were to occur. All the same, he did assert the right to visit such vessels flying the United States flag, not as Americans but as suspected Spaniards. The actual difference was non-existent, the difference of style considerable.

The Webster–Ashburton Treaty of 1842 (primarily concerned with boundary disputes) marked this new mood of reconciliation between Britain and the United States. By it, both countries bound themselves to 'maintain in service on the coast of Africa a sufficient and adequate squadron or naval force of vessels, of suitable numbers and description, to carry in all not less than eighty guns, to enforce separately and respectively the laws, rights, and obligations of each of the two countries for the suppression of the slave trade'. The treaty was to remain in being five years, and afterwards till one of the two countries declared that she wished to end it. An early draft of the treaty provided that British and United States ships should, in the spirit of the Sierra Leone agreement between Lieutenant Paine and Commander Tucker, cruise off Africa in couples. But Britain's unfortunate continuing refusal to abandon the right of impressment of seamen found on neutral ships in time of war ruined the chance of this innovation, and the treaty merely left a pious understanding that cooperation should occur on the spot 'should exigencies arise'. Even so, the treaty had its enemies in Washington, such as Senator Thomas Hart Benton ('Old Bullion'). The treaty was also criticized as feeble by Palmerston, in Opposition, in the columns of the *Morning Chronicle*. In a wild speech in the House of Commons he also deplored Ashburton as 'a half Yankee', a man with American loyalties.

At the same time Aberdeen was prepared to criticize Palmerston's behaviour towards the United States: 'I think the United States had cause to complain', he rather curiously said. Discussion and argument, however, continued for many years yet, in the privacy of legations and government offices, in Congress and Parliament, as in the press, about the exact nature of the right of visit.[27]

Finally, Aberdeen's Advocate-General wrote in 1842 an opinion that the activities of Denman and other naval officers in destroying barracoons could not be justified 'with perfect legality'.[28] Basically, here was a restatement of the judgement of Sir William Scott twenty-five years before. Aberdeen had now to instruct the navy 'to abstain from destroying slave factories, and carrying off persons held in slavery'.

The captains were displeased. In the opinion of Captain Matson, the change played into the hands of the slave merchants. It told the Africans, he explained bitterly to a committee of the House of Commons in 1848, that 'there had been a revolution in England; that the people had risen and obliged the Queen to turn out Lord Palmerston, because he wished to suppress the slave trade; that there was now a revolution going on in England to oblige the Queen to carry on the slave trade.'[29] In Africa itself, some of the treaties which the officers of the navy had laboriously secured in order to abolish the trade were placed in jeopardy.

Slavers, though, both men and ships, were faced, in the beginning of the 1840s, with some further impediments: in addition to the British naval squadron, the French maintained a force in West Africa, which was sometimes as large as the British even if it confined itself to deterrence (between October 1842 and March 1843 three French warships 'visited' twenty-five ships, of which twenty-three were English, one Swedish, one from Hamburg). Incidents abounded; the United States had its ships, so did the Spanish and Portuguese, and even the last named sometimes, at least for the show of the thing, felt it necessary to intervene. The same was true of the tiny Brazilian navy.

32

Slave Harbours
of the Nineteenth Century

'The slave trade has been the ruling principle of my people. It is the source of their glory and wealth. . . .'

King Gezo of Dahomey to Captain Winniett, United States Navy, 1840

Deponent Pepper said: 'I was a slave, and lived with my owner, don Crispo, at Gallinas. The barracoons were burnt; I ran away to the boats of the big ship. A man told me that if I went to the Englishmen they would make me free. Ran away the same day that the big ship arrived. Saw great many slaves, men, women and children, in the barracoon. I was brought from Cosso about four years ago by a black man, who sold me to the Spaniard, don Crispo. . . . Don Crispo buys slaves and sells them to the Spaniards. . . .'

Evidence in the first report of the Select Committee on the Slave Trade, 1849

IN THOSE PROGRESSIVE DAYS of the mid-nineteenth century, the effective slave merchants were concentrated in the New, not the Old, World: in Rio, Bahia, and Pernambuco; in Havana; and, to a lesser extent, in New Orleans and New York. These fine harbours had generally taken the place of the old ones of Bristol, Liverpool, Amsterdam, and Nantes. In contrast to what happened in the eighteenth century, most slave ships ended their journeys where they began. The long-lasting triangle of Atlantic trade had been replaced by relatively straight lines. The only Northern European cities to have substantial slaving operations after 1815 were, indeed, French ports such as Bordeaux, Le Havre, and Nantes, but even there the

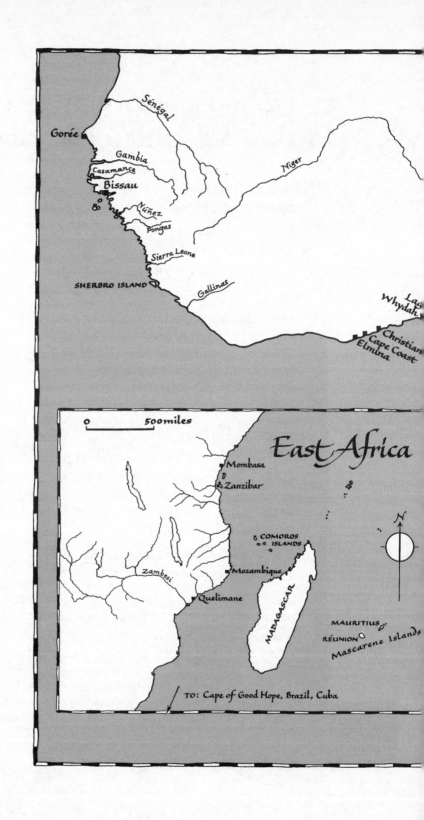

Sénégal

Gorée

Gambia

Casamance

Bissau

Núñez

Pongas

Sierra Leone

SHERBRO ISLAND

Gallinas

Niger

Whydah
Lag

Christian
Cape Coast
Elmina

500 miles

East Africa

Mombasa

Zanzibar

COMOROS
ISLANDS

Zambesi

Mozambique

Quelimane

MADAGASCAR

MAURITIUS

RÉUNION

Mascarene Islands

N

TO: Cape of Good Hope, Brazil, Cuba

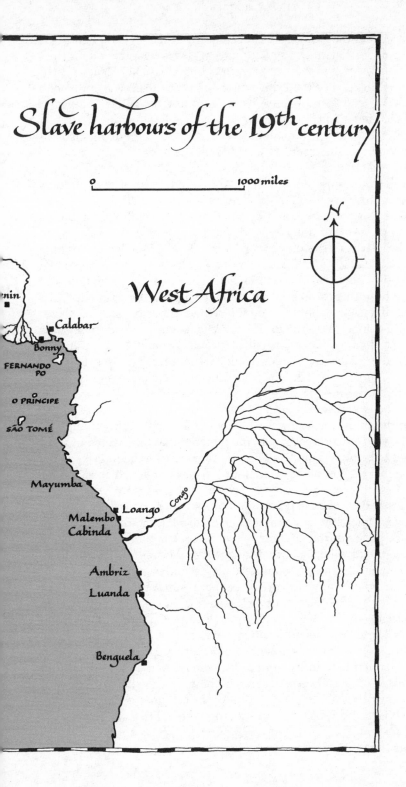

Slave harbours of the 19th century

0   1000 miles

N

West Africa

enin

Calabar

Bonny

FERNANDO PO

O PRÍNCIPE

SÃO TOMÉ

Mayumba

Loango   Congo

Malembo

Cabinda

Ambriz

Luanda

Benguela

trade more or less died out, as has been seen, in the 1830s. There were one or two suggestions that some trading in slaves was carried on from Liverpool in the mid-nineteenth century, but even the *Maid of Islay*, arrested by HMS *Alert* of the British naval patrol in 1848, was in the end found innocent; as was, more curiously, Pedro José de Zulueta's *Augusta* in 1843, in the High Court in London.*

In Southern Europe, matters were a little different: Lisbon's merchants continued to organize the dispatch of slaves from the rivers of Guinea to northern Brazil, and they also were still active in bringing slaves from Mozambique to the New World. But most of these traders went to Rio in the early years of the century, and remained there, seen by the Brazilians as Portuguese, and by the Portuguese as Brazilian. Still, a few slave ships were certainly being fitted out in Portugal for slaving in the 1820s. Similarly, Cádiz played a part in the new Spanish slave trade ('fitted out at Cádiz' is a frequent note by British commissioners in Havana about a ship arriving in Havana) and, to some extent, so did Barcelona, whose shipyards built several fine ships for the traffic to Cuba in the mid-nineteenth century. Announcements for the sale of slaves appeared in Spain as late as 1826. The merchants who owned these ships of Cádiz often had a connection with Havana. General Tacón, Captain-General in the 1830s in Cuba, would write of these last that the shareholders in many expeditions from Havana were anonymous, being backed by public opinion.

Crews and captains in these years came from even more unexpected places than the ships, including Sardinia and the Papal States, though all participants were always ready with the pretence that they were not what they seemed to be. A few English or Irish sailors were to be found. On the French schooner the *Oiseau* of Guadeloupe, for example, which sailed for Africa in 1825, the captain, second captain, and lieutenant when questioned said that they had been born in 'Europe', though actually Captain Jean Blais was Dutch; the mate came from Saint-Malo, the carpenter from Le Havre, the steward from Toulon, while the cook and one seaman came from Curaçao, and other sailors derived from Marseilles, Puerto Rico, Danish St Thomas, Germany, Saint-Barthelémy, and even India.[1]

Captains would now normally be paid substantially more than they were in the eighteenth century: for example, in the mid-century they might expect to receive $400, or £83 per voyage. Cuban captains were paid best. These nineteenth-century masters of the illegal trade were often rougher than their eighteenth-century predecessors. Often they were men left behind by normal life, semi-criminal survivors from the Napoleonic Wars, sailors ready for anything, like the hero of Edouard Corbière's novel *Le Négrier*, or the captain in Mérimée's *Tamango*, men capable, like Olympe Sanguines, of keeping their captives in barrels, the

---

* *See Appendix Two.*

easier to throw them overboard if a patrol vessel appeared. The brothers Amanieu of Bordeaux, who sailed on the *Cantabre*, should have been tried for murder for their actions against their brother officers. One brother, Joachim-Guillaume, was so tried at Brest. In February 1854 Cornelius Driscoll, an Irishman born in the United States, captain of the brig *Hope*, gave a speech to his crew which suggests the era well: 'Well, boys,' he said, 'you don't have to worry about facing trial in New York. . . . Let the cruisers take you if they will. I can get any one off in New York for $1,000. All you have to do is to get some straw bail, and you'll be free as birds. Look at me. I went to Africa, sold the *Hope* at Cabinda, and took my men over to the *Porpoise* while the Dagos put 600 "niggers" on board. But we saw what we thought was an English cruiser coming, so I went back with my papers to keep her away from the *Hope*. Made myself a pirate, they say. Some of my scurvy seamen informed on me afterwards and the marshal caught up with me in New York. . . .' But he escaped.

In 1845 Captain Peter Flowery was imprisoned at Salem for slaving. He had signed on in Havana as captain of the *Caballero*, ninety-six tons, had put out from New York to Africa, and had bought 346 slaves from Paul Faber* on the River Pongas. He landed them in Matanzas in Cuba and then, after his ship had been cleaned, sailed on to Havana, where the vessel had her name changed to the *Spitfire*; this ship Flowery registered before a public notary in Key West. He then sailed to New Orleans, where Juan Sococur, of Matanzas, chartered the *Spitfire* to sail to Africa. They sailed via Havana, where they took on appropriate cargo, with two 'passengers', Francisco Ruiz and Adolphe Fleuret, both slave traders. They set off to visit both Paul Faber on the Pongas, and Mrs Lightburne nearby. There they were betrayed by an ex-sailor, Thomas Turner, to Lieutenant Henry Bruce who, on the US brig-of-war *Truxtum*, escorted the schooner back to Salem, where Flowery was accused of launching a slave expedition. At a subsequent trial one witness said that the ship could not be a slaver, since slaves could not be 'very comfortably brought on boards laid over water casks', to which the defence counsel, District Attorney Rantoul, said, 'So the slaves thought too, I presume,' thereby showing that irony was not impossible at that time in North America.

Flowery was ably defended by J. P. Rogers but, thanks to Rantoul, was found guilty. He only served two years. Thereafter, he set off again, in the slave ship *Mary Ann*, whose crew abandoned him on finding, after setting out, the purpose of their voyage. The sailors put Flowery ashore in Africa. Under the command of a mate, they returned to New York, where they surrendered themselves to the authorities, only to be themselves charged with piracy.[2]

Crews also received much more pay in the days of the illegal trade than they had in the past: an average seaman in the legal trade in Brazil

* See page 686.

might receive $1 a day, but a sailor on a slaver find get $10. That explains why it was so easy to find crews. Seamen too might have their own slaves: Captain Birch, of the British navy, said that sometimes after he had captured a slave ship seamen 'came up and asked me to let them each take the slave that belonged to himself: he had paid for it. . . . They stamp them [that is, brand them] with their own mark'.[3]

Cargoes were just as diverse as in the past. When Captain Matson destroyed the barracoons at Cabinda in 1842 he found there *aguardiente*, cotton goods, muskets, rum, tobacco, powder – 'everything from red umbrellas to common small utensils of every kind . . . a great number of English production'. But a brother officer, Captain Broadhead, thought the trade in the 1840s was usually 'rum, tobacco, bale goods, powder, and muskets'. Captain-General Tacón thought that the cargoes usually sent from Havana in the 1830s were 'guns, powder, and tobacco', which, he added, 'were deposited openly . . . in warehouses and were earmarked publicly for Africa'; while the hero of Baroja's *Los Pilotos de Altura* said that the cargo was usually 'thirty or forty "pipas" of alcohol, usually *aguardiente*, and eight or ten loads of blue cloth'.[4] It seems that in Nantes the old favourites of the eighteenth century, locally produced *indiennes*, were still the most popular goods in the French clandestine trade; and well-known *indienneurs* of that city, such as Fabre and Petitpierre, did not hesitate to announce in the local press that they were supplying goods for the slave trade. The connection of the London general merchants Carruthers and Co. of Rio with Manuel Pinto da Fonseca, was evidently close. Carruthers sent the Consul a statement in favour of Pinto da Fonseca, whom they described as 'one of the most extensive general merchants in this market': a statement which, in retrospect, and in our present knowledge of those 'general' activities, could hardly have been more damning. The first British Minister to newly independent Brazil, Lord Ponsonby, thought in 1829 that 'one third of all [British] manufactures imported into Rio are eventually used in commerce with the coast of Africa.'[5]*

Not all this material was, of course, destined for the slave trade. But such an excuse could not have been made by Richard Parke and Singleton of Kingston, Jamaica, who supplied the cargo for a Havana slave ship, the *Golondrina*, in 1836 as they had surely done for other such vessels; and there were other merchants, in Brazil even more than in Cuba, who financed the trade by providing on credit goods to be traded in Africa. A witness at a select committee on the slave trade in London was asked in 1843 whether he was aware that many of the businesses in Brazil and Cuba concerned with the trade were 'in direct correspondence' with the

---

* *Ponsonby, an exceptionally good-looking man, was apparently sent to Rio by Canning to please King George IV, who was jealous of the attention paid him by Lady Conyngham, the royal mistress.*

first commercial houses in Liverpool and London, and that goods used in the slave trade 'were shipped to the orders of those houses in Brazil and Cuba?' The witness said that he was indeed aware of the fact, and thought, too, that 'there are houses in Manchester which make no other goods'.[6]

On the River Pongas, in Senegambia, iron bars were a currency in the nineteenth century; but when a ship exchanged slaves for a certain number of these, it could mean that the real exchange was against looking glasses, knives, guns, razors, scissors, gunpowder, china, red bonnets, sheets, and glasses. In East Africa, the goods offered for slaves were generally said to be 'powder, and every sort of merchandise; hardware and cutlery and beads'.

Merchants providing these goods could encounter difficulties in London if it could be proved that they sold their goods knowing how these were going to be employed; but the act of selling something to Pedro Blanco in Africa, or Joaquín Gómez in Cuba, would not of itself determine the matter. Anyone found with a consignment of shackles on board could be condemned for slaving: but by the 1840s that shipment was unnecessary, since blacksmiths in Africa were often able to make shackles from imported iron. Asked if any British merchant 'were to adopt any plan to prevent the slave dealers getting goods, and were himself to refuse to sell goods on that ground, do you think he could bring a general concurrence in his views by others?' Matthew Forster, both a Member of Parliament and a businessman, replied tartly, 'That man must know very little of trading competition, or of human nature, who could dream of such a thing; it is painful to hear the twaddle that is talked on the subject of the sale of goods to slave dealers on the coast of Africa. People forget that there is scarcely a British merchant of any eminence who is not proud and eager to deal as largely as possible with slave importers in Cuba and Brazil, and slave buyers and sellers in the United States.'[7]

The fall in the prices of manufactured goods in Northern Europe and North America in the early nineteenth century made the slave trade cheaper to fit out than it had been a hundred years before. A legitimate businessman concerned in Africa, William Hutton, explained in 1848 to a parliamentary inquiry in London that the slave dealers 'throw such quantities of goods into the market at such low prices, and of such good quality, that you would be perfectly surprised if you could see it'. Thomas Tobin, of a Liverpool firm which in the end did even better out of palm oil than it had once done out of slaves, estimated that the cost of such goods dropped by a third between, say, 1800 and 1848.[8]

A similar part was played by United States firms such as Maxwell Wright and Company of New York, Jenkins and Co. of Rio, and Birkhead and Pierce of Baltimore. United States entrepreneurs were, however, more concerned to sell ships to slave dealers than manufactured cargoes.

These came from numerous ports: Providence, Bristol, Salem, Beverly, Boston, Portland, even Philadelphia all made their contribution to ships for the Brazilian traffic. Thus, by irony, that part of the United States whose public men were most in favour of abolition also lent support for the traffic. Sometimes the individuals concerned seemed confused. For example, the owner of the *Bangor Gazette* in Maine preached abolition in his newspaper, while he was also apparently engaged in building slave ships in pretty ports in Maine such as Bath or Damariscotta.*[9]

In 1840 Joseph Fry, of the Quaker and chocolate family, was assured, perhaps exaggeratedly, that nine-tenths of the ships in the Cuban slave trade were then built in the United States: above all in Baltimore, 'where bonds that they shall not be employed illegally are regularly taken, and as regularly evaded or disregarded'.[10] Sometimes these vessels were very modern. Commander Charles Riley, for instance, a British naval captain who served off the Bight of Benin in 1848, described capturing a ship from Bahia, the *Rasparte*, of 105 tons, 'built to beat every vessel' under British command (he captured her because her captain took no trouble): 'I never saw anything so beautiful', he said, adding that she could sail across the Atlantic regularly in twenty-four days from Bahia to Lagos. Ships for the trade also continued to be made in Portugal.[11] A British captain captured one vessel built on the Douro in 1848. In the late 1840s steamers made their appearance in the Brazilian trade, and they came to be important in the Cuban commerce in the 1850s.

Theodore Canot (Theophilus Conneau), a captain who was later a slave dealer, described how in Havana Bay 'these dashing slavers, with their arrowy hulls and raking masts, got complete possession of my fancy.'†[12] Unlike their lumbering predecessors of the previous century, these could cross and recross the Atlantic several times a year, using a diversity of flags as the need arose. Thus the ship *Fanny* left Santiago de Cuba with a Dutch flag; arriving at Old Calabar, she carried a French flag; when pursued a little later, by a British frigate, she was using a Dutch flag once more. (She was almost certainly owned by Zulueta.)

The North American brandy merchant George Coggeshall once dined at Ponce, in Puerto Rico, with a captain and a supercargo of a recently arrived slave ship: 'They were intelligent, sociable men', he reported, who, 'when conversing on the slave trade, said that it was a most humane and benevolent traffic; that, in many parts of Africa, the negroes were cannibals and extremely indolent; that the different tribes were constantly at war with each other; that if there were no purchases for their prisoners, they would all be put to death; [and] that they were in

---

* A partial list of slavers suggests that a minimum of forty-four ships were built outside Maryland in the 1840s and 1850s, and twenty-three in Baltimore.

† Canot was son of an officer of Napoleon's army and an Italian mother, and educated in Florence. A brother of Canot, François, was doctor to Napoleon III in Ham Prison and in Paris.

the lowest state of degradation and of no service to the world. [But] on the contrary, when they were transported to the West Indies, they soon became civilized and useful to mankind.' Coggeshall said to one of these captains that it would be better if the slaves were carried in large, comfortable ships, rather than the crammed, small crafts in which they suffered so much. The captain replied that 'those who were engaged in the trade had been driven to every expedient in consequence of the persecutions which they had received from short-sighted and ill-informed philanthropists': that is, the British navy, government, and publicists.[13]

The African side of the Atlantic slave trade had changed in the nineteenth century almost as much as the American and European.

By now the main European peoples had established in Africa their special zones of influence. For example, in the far north of the slave-trading territories the valley of the River Sénégal was now French in character, and until the end of the trade in 1831 many slave captains from Nantes or Bordeaux dealt there, usually carrying their cargoes to Cuba. In 1819 there was still some local trading; indeed, we hear of a certain Labouret, an *armateur* of Sénégal itself, who had *captiveries* here. A ship-builder of Saint-Louis, Bourgerel, member of the Council of Justice of the colony, was engaged in the slave trade, sending the *Louise* to the nearby River Casamance in 1821, as well as sponsoring a good deal of other local traffic.*

By 1840, however, there was practically no trading of slaves on the River Sénégal, at least for the Atlantic market. African and mulatto trading continued till the 1860s. Devout local Muslim rulers, such as Ma ba Jaxoo, were determined to oppose the enslavement of their co-religionaries. But that did not prevent their followers from organizing as many raids as ever for slaves among 'pagan' peoples surviving nearby, partly for their own use, partly for sale along the old Sahara routes. For of course here, as elsewhere in West Africa, the French, like the other Europeans, claimed as their own only a small stretch of land: scarcely further than the city of Saint-Louis itself. Beyond that, Richelieu, like Colbert, and like all the ministers of the eighteenth century, had shown no enthusiasm for extending French political control. Legitimate French traders, often mulatto in origin, sought after 1830 to develop old lines of commerce in gum, wax, and ivory, as well as palm oil; by 1850 they were bringing in substantial profits. Gum, in particular, had a sensational success in the mid-nineteenth century. Ivory too also important because of an expanding European market, for pianos, billiards, and fans. The

---

* Saint-Louis, at the mouth of the river, had held out against the British in the Napoleonic Wars till 1809, and was not restored to the government of Louis XVIII till 1817. The return of the French, under the pedantic Colonel Schmaltz, was marred by the terrible shipwreck of the flagship the Méduse, to which subject the painter Géricault devoted his masterpiece.

territory was also beginning its adventure as a cultivator of peanuts, and by the 1860s that crop, too, cultivated by small farmers or migrant labour, was bringing in more than anyone had thought possible.

The Cape Verde Islands were often visited by slavers on their way to market. They were usually denounced as bleak: 'One might believe that, after the formation of the world, a quantity of useless surplus stones was cast into the sea', wrote Dr Theodor Vogel, a British member of the Niger expedition of 1841;[14] and another participant of that fantastic undertaking, the master-at-arms, John Duncan, thought that 'the meanest pauper in England is a king compared with the best and most opulent of them [the inhabitants]'.[15] All the same, a slave trade persisted in the islands. Slaves were brought from the mainland and then shipped to Brazil or Cuba, a Portuguese merchant, Brandão, and a French one named Antoine Léger being the outstanding operators in the place in the 1820s.

Gorée, the 'green, ham-shaped island' (in the words of the most intelligent of French governors, the Chevalier de Boufflers), below the hook of land south of Cape Verde itself, was no longer a slave port by 1835, though it remained a place where North American slavers would often pick up interpreters. After it was made a free entrepôt for certain non-European goods in 1821, United States rum and tobacco were available in great quantities.

A little below this island were several rivers whose slaving needs in the early part of the century were still provided for by the Wolofs, as had been the case almost continuously since the sixteenth century. One of the little ports here was Joal, where the disgraceful transactions described so acutely by Mérimée in his *Tamango* are said to have occurred.

The British had been for many generations loosely established in the estuary of the River Gambia. But in the Napoleonic Wars they withdrew from it, as did the French from their old trading port of Albreda. That left the river for some years at the mercy of North American slavers, who used it extensively for their trade in slaves to Cuba. After 1815 the British returned, and established their main post not at Fort James but on St Mary's Island, at the mouth of the river. By 1840 the settlement there, Bathurst, had become 'a very pretty little town', as Colonel Alexander Findlay, one of the governors, put it. British influence stretched at least 140 miles up the river, as far as Macarthy's Island, in a valley which had for generations been a valuable source of slaves. Slaving by, or at least for the benefit of, the French and Spaniards continued on the river in the 1820s. There were also frequent United States vessels. The French traders took to carrying their captives from an assembly point at their old headquarters at Albreda overland north to the River Salloum, which was outside British jurisdiction. They found other slaves from the Gambia at Vitang Creek, about fifty miles up the river, and marched them overland south to another French trading post on the River Casamance, where in the 1820s a black Portuguese governor, with a barracoon at Zingiehor, was active in the slave trade. Slaving had however almost ceased by 1840, the presence of a detachment of British troops at Bathurst playing an important part in securing this.

To the south of the Casamance the picture changed greatly, for a large network of slave dealers was still gathered in the labyrinth of creeks, islands, and mudbanks of the estuary of the Rivers Cacheu and Bissau. This territory had been a modest base for Portuguese slaving in the eighteenth century, but it grew spectacularly for that purpose in the first part of the nineteenth, though some hides and beeswax were also traded. The multitude of waterways, and the Portuguese control on land, made it difficult for the British navy to interfere in the place, though for a time it had a base on the fertile offshore island of Bolama, lying at the mouth of the Rivers Jeba and Grande. (Bolama was later abandoned on the ground that it was unhealthy.)

It was said that the factories in the Cacheu River were 'principally supplied by British vessels', and there is even a possibility that some London merchants (Forster and Co., for example) were indirectly concerned in the slave trade here in the early part of the century. In 1828 'the currency of the place, and in fact the representation of value . . . was according to the value of the slaves. The slave trade was the all engrossing object of the people there', reported an adventurous English businessman, John Hughes, who was obliged to flee because of threats to his life after the British detention of a Portuguese vessel.[16] Nor was the slave trade confined to large enterprises. Here the petty black or mulatto slave trader would often 'get into his canoe, with goods to the value of $100, and go up the Rivers Cacheu and Jeba . . . and bring down his two or three slaves'. A 'quite considerable' United States commerce was also reported by the Consul of that nation, Ferdinand Gardner, in Cacheu-Bissau in 1841; and the evidence for legitimate trade is missing.

The Fulbe and Mandingo traders were the most indefatigable providers of slaves in these years. They succeeded in restricting the Europeans to river traffic, and North American firms such as Charles Hoffman, Robert Brookhouse and William Hunt, all of Salem, and Yates and Porterfield, of New York, were the chief beneficiaries.*[17]

The Portuguese still maintained third-rate garrisons at the two fortresses at Cacheu and Bissau, half the soldiers being Cape Verdeans. Disease, underpayment, and inactivity rotted the lives of all who worked here. The Governor in the 1830s, Caetano José Nozolini, was, however, a remarkable official. Son of an Italian sailor who in the 1790s married a Cape Verdean heiress on the island of Fogo, Nozolini became a major slave trader at Bissau; he would send ships to Cuba as well as Brazil,

---

* *The missing pages in the log of Charles Hoffman's* Ceylon *in 1845–6 probably conceal an illegal traffic in slaves.*

perhaps buying goods from the British on the Gambia River, paying with bills drawn on such respectable London houses as Baring Brothers, and then exchange them in his own territory for slaves. When Captain Matthew Perry on the United States sloop-of-war *Orbel* seized $40,000 worth of property at Bissau in 1844, he found that most of it had been advanced by North American traders to Nozolini.

Nozolini was helped to reach his position by an alliance with the dominant merchant in Cacheu-Zingiehor, Honorio Barreto, a mulatto who succeeded him as governor in 1850. (He, too, traded in slaves.) But the strongest influence on Nozolini was his African wife, Mãe Aurélia Correia, 'the Queen of Orango', the largest island of the Bissagos Archipelago, a tyrannical *nhara* (that is, *senhora*) of these rivers. By 1827, though not yet in control, Nozolini was strong enough to deceive the British navy by shipping sixty-one slaves as members of his own family; it was some time before the Governor of Sierra Leone, Sir Neil Campbell, realized who these 'Nozolinos' [*sic*] were. Nozolini was strong enough to resist a demand from the French that he be charged for the murder of a French trader named Dumaigne, killed by some of his guards in 1835; and in the 1840s he was already cultivating peanuts on the island of Bolama, as well as assembling slaves there.[18] (The brig-of-war *Brisk* liberated 212 slaves from there in 1838.) At Nozolini's death his family succeeded him in the business: his son-in-law, Dr Antonio Joaquim Ferreira, was a pioneer of planting coconut palms at Ametite.

Just offshore in this zone lay Hen Island, previously uninhabited, which had been turned by Nozolini's predecessor as Governor, Joaquim Antonio Mattos, into 'a perfect receptacle, a nest, for the slaves'. These slaves were held in round houses, twelve to sixteen together. The place was raided in 1842 by the British Captain Blount, who felt free to act because it belonged, as it seemed to him, neither to Portugal nor to a native chief: just to Mattos, one of whose mulatto daughters was killed in the fray.[*][19]

On the River Grande, just to the south of the colony of Bissau, some curious scenes would unfold in 1842. Commander Sotheby, of HMS *Skylark*, received news that a Spanish slave ship was in the river. This information was denied by a local chief, who insisted that the Spanish merchant living there, a certain Tadeo Vidal, alias Juan Pons, traded only in groundnuts. Sotheby inspected eighteen creeks, and only when he offered a reward of 100 dollars was he told where the slave ship was. He found her, equipped for slaving but hidden in the mangroves. There was no sign of the crew. Sotheby thereupon blew up the ship. He was then informed that the Chief was hiding slaves, ready for shipment, and some of them escaped and joined Sotheby. Sotheby sent the Chief an ultimatum

---

[*] *Another monarch to have Spanish slave traders (Victor Dabreda, José van Kell) established in 1840 on his territory in this region was King Banco of Beomba, on the River Jeba.*

and said, 'Unless the slaves are brought down tomorrow, I will blow up the town.'[20] They were accordingly produced, and the mysterious Vidal was also brought in as a prisoner. He turned out to be the supercargo of the Spanish ship. The rest of the crew were visiting other creeks in search of slaves. Sotheby took both the Spaniards and the slaves to Freetown for trial and for liberation, respectively.

The next slave harbours to the south were the fever-ridden rivers Núñez and Pongas. The first of these was the favoured market of Fulbe slave caravans from the theocratic inland empire of the Futa Jallon, a sophisticated enterprise judged by Captain Denman, at least, as 'far superior' to any other African entity. The British established a trading post fifty miles up this 'exceedingly unhealthy' river, at Kacundy, but their presence did not seem to affect slaving unless there was a man-of-war there, though they did found some coffee farms. A local monarch named Sarah (according to John Hughes, 'one of the greatest barbarians. . . . He thinks nothing of tying a stone round a man's neck and throwing him in the river') once threatened a British trader, Benjamin Campbell, with death, on the ground that his presence was preventing slavers from going up the river.[21]

At the mouth of this River Núñez a mulatto family, the Skeltons (Elizabeth Frazer Skelton, 'Mammy Skelton', and her husband, William Skelton), established a new fort, which they named Victoria, in 1825. Elizabeth's father was a North American mulatto who had gone to Sierra Leone in 1797. Zachary Macaulay had refused to allow him to remain, since he knew him to be a slaver. The Skeltons sold their slaves on the nearby River Pongas. By 1840 the traders of the River Núñez had mostly changed to cultivating peanuts, and were apparently responsible for half the production of the region. The remarkable Mrs Skelton, a heroine to feminists if a villain to abolitionists, still dominated the upper river after her husband's death, when she was busy with nuts, not slaves.[22]

The River Pongas maintained its ancient importance in the slave trade because its estuary consisted of five separate waterways, separated from the sea by bars of sand and mud, behind which the commerce could be secretly carried on, protected by currents which made the place dangerous to inexperienced pilots. The headwaters of the river, like those of the nearby Núñez, were in the highlands of the Futa Jallon and so served very well as a commercial waterway for ivory, gold, and rice, as well as slaves. On the Pongas about twenty interesting European or mulatto slave traders were established. The most powerful of them in the 1820s had been John Ormond, 'Mongo John', the word *Mongo* indicating 'chief', perhaps the son of a French slave captain named Hautemont, or possibly that of a sailor, Ormond, of Liverpool, by a local girl. He began his working life as a mate on a ship belonging to Daniel Botefeur of Havana and then worked on Bence Island with Richard Oswald's nephews before abolition. At the riverside village of Bangalang on the

Pongas, Ormond had built a fine house furnished in European style, as well as a large fortified barracoon where his slaves would be chained while he awaited the arrival of ships from the Americas. With his brother, he dominated the slave trade in the region for a generation. He lived well, drinking to excess, with a harem, and his warehouses were full of gunpowder, palm oil, and gold, as well as alcohol. Ormond founded a secret society to protect himself, using young initiates as warriors. He would lend European goods to his subchiefs and if they did not pay the interest he would raid their villages and sell the captives. He committed suicide in 1828, when he had begun to lose control.[23] For a long time the slave trader Theodore Canot worked as Ormond's secretary, being paid 'a negro a month'. Another family of traders on the Pongas were the brothers Curtis, who were found in 1819 dealing with a French captain, François Vigne, of the *Marie*, from Guadeloupe, exchanging 306 slaves for 24,063 iron bars. (The ship was seized by HMS *Tartar*.)

Another trader on this waterway was Paul Faber, a North American, established at Sangha in 1809, at first a protégé of Ormond. With his black wife, Mary (a survivor of the Nova Scotian free blacks sent to Sierra Leone), and his mulatto son, William, he was still selling slaves in 1850 to Brazil, according to the British naval patrol, at an average of $65.50 each. The Fabers, like Mongo John, had a small slave army capable of fighting full-scale battles with rivals. Paul Faber was a slave captain as well as a trader, and would sometimes sell slaves in Cuba, cargoes which his wife had negotiated in Africa. Other traders here included at Faringura a Portuguese widow, Bailey Gómez Lightburne (Nyara Belí), her son Styles Lightburne, and her manager, Allen, a mulatto.[24]

Most of these adventurers produced local agricultural products, too, legitimate after their fashion. Thus John Ormond is said in 1827 to have had 5,000 or 6,000 slaves at work on his coffee farms, the Fabers were interested in rice and ginger, and the Lightburne heirs had about 6,000 slaves in 1860 working on groundnuts as well as coffee at Faringura.*

These traders organized their businesses more intelligently than their African predecessors of the eighteenth century: instead of a slave captain travelling along the coast picking up slaves here and there from a diversity of African harbours, he would more likely go to a single place and buy all he needed from a mulatto- or European-owned barracoon in one transaction.

To the south of the River Pongas there were the Îles de Los, known to the English as William (Tamara), Crawford's Island (Roume), and Factory Island (Kassa). North American slavers of the early part of the century

---

* *Mrs Lightburne's barracoons were destroyed by Captain Nurse and Commander Dyke of the British navy. After further attempts to trade more slaves in the 1850s, some successful, she went to Sierra Leone to sue the British officers. Failing to gain any satisfaction, she died of a broken heart.*

might pick up a pilot from here to help them through the confusing Bissagos Islands. In the eighteenth century there had been barracoons for slaves here, but they had been abandoned, for they were easy prey to British cruisers. Instead, stores of goods used in the slave trade were held, while three slave merchants of English origin ruled on Crawford's Island as little monarchs: W. H. Leigh, Samuel Samo, and a certain Nickson. They obtained their cargoes from the mainland coast opposite, where the city of Conakry, capital of Guinea, then only a village, now stands.

Further south lay the curious British colony of Sierra Leone, a green oasis at first sight, an oasis of the spirit too, yet a place which had not yet extinguished memories of the time when there had been important slave markets, including those of Bence and Banana islands. Unhealthy though it seemed to be for the Europeans who went there, Freetown, in Sierra Leone, was the capital of the British crusade against the slave trade. Up till 1840 425 slave ships had been escorted there by British warships, of which 403 had been condemned by the Mixed Court.* All the same, Freetown in those years was much frequented by North American traders, seeking both slaves and conventional goods; in 1809, the Governor even complained to the Foreign Secretary, Lord Castlereagh, that 'this has hitherto been an American and not a British colony'.

If a slaver was captured anywhere north of the equator she would be taken to Freetown under a prize crew. The crew would usually arrive exhausted, because so few hands were available to sail the prize, guard the captured crew, and attend, with some pretence of humanity, to the needs of the liberated cargo. Even if by sleeping on deck the crew escaped the prevalent dysentery or ophthalmia, they exposed themselves to mosquito bites. Having handed over their slaves to the prize authorities at the port, the sailors would then themselves go ashore happy. Within an hour or two, most of them would be drunk on local spirits. To sleep off the effects, they would lie all night in the gutters. By the time that they returned to sobriety, they would probably have been infected with malaria, if not yellow fever. If they had to stay in the town till they were drafted to another ship, the chance of death from one of those diseases was great. The danger of such proceedings became apparent in the 1820s, and henceforth leave ashore at Sierra Leone was prohibited to seamen, though not to their officers. But those regulations were not strictly followed.[25]

At the same time, the mortality of the slaves on board these prize ships en route to Sierra Leone was probably as high as when they were being taken across the Atlantic. There were many reports by captains describing tragedies, such as that referring to the *Rosalia* from Lagos in

---

* *Forty-eight ships had been taken to Havana and forty-three condemned by the court there; twenty-three were taken to Rio, of which sixteen were condemned by its court; only one vessel was condemned by the court at Surinam.*

1825: 'From extraordinary length of passage to Sierra Leone, lost 82 slaves and, with the exception of 10, by actual starvation.'

After a slaver had been escorted to Sierra Leone, and condemned by the Court of Mixed Commission, and while the naval officers were talking to the Proctor about their prize money, the slaves would be taken to an office in Kings Yard, and registered as British citizens. They would then be offered the alternative of going to the West Indies as apprentices, signing up with a regiment of black soldiers, or establishing themselves on a property in Sierra Leone, where they would be allocated a quarter-acre of land to cultivate under the care of a usually neglectful supervisor. The authorities in Sierra Leone would provide these men with only a small cloth to wear, a pot for cooking, and a spade.

There was then no procedure for baptizing the freed slaves so, as Lord Courtenay put it to a Select Committee of the House of Commons on the West Coast of Africa, 'Many of them remain a long time pagans.' An experienced witness, Dr Thomson, thought, 'Scarcely any of the immense numbers that are [taken] there . . . have risen to anything above mediocrity.'[26] Many problems were also caused by the ex-slave crews who were deposited there. In the late 1830s a scandal broke out because of the activities of a certain Mr Kidd who bought up the slave ships condemned by the Mixed Court and then resold them to slave traders on the River Gallinas, to the south. This practice was difficult to prevent until, after about 1840, those slave vessels were destroyed (in 'Destruction Bay'): sawn up, that is, in three bits, the material being sold piecemeal.

Until 1808 slave trading and conventional trade had continued, uneasily, side by side, in Sierra Leone and Africans could see no reason why that state of affairs should not continue indefinitely. An Englishman, Alexander Smith, an agent of the government, seemed, at least to a United States traveller, to constitute 'the first mercantile house in the economy in the illegal slave trade'; he told a North American trader, in the presence of the Governor, that 'just round that point' was a bay which was not subject to British rule.[27] In 1830 four freed Africans, by then British subjects, were condemned to death for selling slaves (to a French vessel, the Caroline, from Guadeloupe, with a French captain), though their sentences were commuted to five to ten years' forced labour.

Despite its climate, Sierra Leone had its elegancies: the streets were well laid out; many of the houses were of stone; shops, taverns, and chapels gave the place an air of well-being; there was a racecourse and a Turf Club, for dances and fêtes. St George's Church held regular Anglican services. The neighbouring Kru people continued to play many roles as sailors, working for slavers and the British navy alike, with equal competence.

Further still to the south of Sierra Leone, about sixty miles away, lay the famous slaving zone of Sherbro Island. Three English slave traders were arrested there in 1811, but their trials in Sierra Leone led to much confusion. The dominant family of traders in slaves, as in other cargoes, in the early nineteenth century, were still the Caulkers (Corkers). Canray ba Caulker, who flourished about 1800, acted as if he was an indigenous chief, for he often began raids and wars for control of the coast. Another merchant of Sherbro, also a mulatto, Henry Tucker, distinguished himself in 1844 by financing, organizing, and sending a ship to Cuba on his own, the *Enganador*, with 348 slaves whom he had himself procured. An English missionary, James Frederick Schön, visited the region in 1839, to find two Spanish slave dealers. While Schön was in the house of one of these men, 'a servant came in and said that he had bought five slaves of the Cossoo nation. He . . . asked him what he had paid for them. . . . It averaged seven or eight dollars for every slave. He . . . said that they were cheap, but that they were Cossoos, and that Cossoos were mere cattle.'[28] What he meant was they were unruly people, who had wrecked one of his ships and caused him losses.

While Schön was present several slaves who were chained together in the yard heard that an Englishman was there and came in to Tucker's house to ask for help. The slave dealer drove them out with a whip and curses. He told Schön that the English would be better employed helping the Poles against the Russians than liberating Africans.

South of Sherbro, many slave stations had been opened on the flat, mangrove-crowded banks of the sluggish River Gallinas, as on the innumerable islands which dotted the estuary. 'To one who approaches from the sea', wrote Theodore Canot, the spongy islands of the estuary 'loom up from its surface, covered with reeds and mangroves, like an immense field of fungi.'[29] As late as 1848 a British naval officer declared that in this river 'there is no trade but in slaves', nor had there been so, to his knowledge, for a long period.

In the 1820s the dominant slave trader was John Ouseley Kearney, a British ex-officer who carried on the slave trade openly under the Union Jack. He once told some English petty officers, 'I buy nothing but slaves. My object is to make a little money, and then I'll embark 300 or 400 slaves on board a large schooner . . . and go in her to the Havannah.' He had friends in Sierra Leone who kept him informed about all the details of the naval patrol.[30] By the 1830s Kearney's place on the Gallinas had passed to Pedro Blanco, of Cádiz, 'the Rothschild of slavery', according to Theodore Canot. Blanco, a native of Málaga, had, like 'Mongo John' and other successful slave merchants, originally been a captain of slave ships. For instance, in 1825, the British commissioners in Havana noticed him in charge of the brig *Isabel*, and he later brought in the *Barbarita* with 190 slaves. He was an educated man of great personal resource. He worked first with de Souza* in Dahomey and then, as a result of an incident with a British naval vessel off Nassau, spent some time in Cuba, on a sugar

* For de Souza, see page 696.

mill near Matanzas. In Havana, he informed himself of the commercial possibilities of illegal slave trading, and he visited Philadelphia and Baltimore, where he bought clippers. On one of these, the *Conquistador*, he left Havana for the Gallinas in 1822. There he set up an encampment on several islands. By skilful arrangements with the local monarchs, especially King Siaka (Shuckar), he was always able to have slaves available for captains, who thereafter never needed to wait and risk being observed by a British naval patrol. The slaves would be kept in a bamboo barracoon, be loaded under darkness, and be away before daylight.

On one island Blanco built a house for himself and his sister Rosa; on a second was his office, with his lawyer, five accountants, two cashiers, and ten copyists; on a third was his harem, usually with fifty beautiful girls; on a fourth island, the largest, he had his barracoons, capable of holding 5,000 slaves at any one time. He built lookout posts a hundred feet high on outlying islands from which his sentries would sweep the horizon with telescopes to warn their master of the approach of an English man-of-war. He had on his property workshops capable of making most items needed on a slave journey: manacles as well as slave decks.

Blanco made a great fortune, telling a United States officer in 1840 that if he could 'save one vessel out of three from capture', he found the trade profitable. 'This can easily be believed,' reported that captain, 'when slaves can be purchased at Gallinas for less than $20 in trade goods and sold in Cuba for cash for $350.' The scale of the traffic which Blanco promoted can be seen from the fact that in the single year 1837, though the courts in Sierra Leone condemned twenty-seven ships, seventy-two left Havana for Africa and ninety-two arrived in Brazil. Blanco was assisted in buying slaving equipment from England through an intermediary (probably Zulueta and Co.), just as his Cádiz associate, Pedro Martínez, was assisted in buying ships by an English contractor named Jennings. Some sharp questions were asked in 1842, such as how it was that an English firm, whose chairman was William Hutton of London, could have brought themselves to sell 200 guns to Blanco in 1838. (Hutton's lame answer was: 'We cannot always be responsible for what masters [of ships] do.') Papers confiscated by the British on one of Blanco's ships showed that he maintained commercial correspondents in both Baltimore (Peter Harmony and Co.) and New York (Robert Barry).

Blanco eventually founded a firm of conventional shippers, Blanco and Carballo, of Havana and Cádiz, before retiring in 1839, with his *mulata* daughter Rosita, first to Cuba (where Rosita was legitimized, if not accepted), then to Barcelona, where he arrived with over $4,000,000. While in Havana he carried on the slave trade as usual; the brigantine *Andalucía* brought 750 slaves to the beach of Guanímar, on the coast of the island, due south of Havana, in 1844. In Barcelona he became prominent in the new stock exchange, and finally retired to Genoa, where he died of a stroke brought on by madness in 1854. Blanco's last years were clouded by financial troubles: his firm failed about 1848, and Carballo, Blanco's partner of many years, drowned himself in Mexico.[*][31]

During the heyday of Pedro Blanco on the River Gallinas, King Siaka and his colleagues abandoned all such former legal trades as they had – camwood, palm oil, ivory, and cotton. They had even given up growing their own food. They imported what they needed from Sherbro Island. King Siaka was then a monarch 'wholly engaged in buying and selling of slaves'.

Captain Howland of Providence recalled seeing here in 1817 'a large number of slaves, mostly young men, women and children of eight, ten and twelve years of age, brought in by their black chiefs, or masters. There were several hundreds or thousands of them waiting for the rainy season to be over ... so that they could be shipped away.... One cargo was for a French vessel which was fitted out from Le Havre [probably the *Rôdeur*].... They are kept in a large pen, with no covering to shelter them from the sun, or rain, entirely naked except the adults, and they have only a small piece of bark cloth tied in front by a string round the waist. They are very emaciated, being allowed only a few palm nuts to eat once a day. I walked round among them and they made signs to me for food by pointing their fingers into their open mouths.... Some had their feet in the stocks, a log with a hole in the centre for the foot, and a peg in likewise to confine it.... Those white monsters, the French slavers, were branding them with a hot iron on the breast and shoulder with the initials of the owner.... I saw them brand a delicate female about twelve years old, I saw the smoke and I saw the flesh quiver, and turned away as I heard a suppressed scream. I did not stop to see the impression.... I observed that the black slave dealers were nearly as cruel to them as the white.... The dead slaves were thrown in the river where the crocodile was on daily watch for them.'[32]

Blanco's headquarters on the River Gallinas was destroyed by Captain Denman in 1841, but a year later many of his barracoons had been re-established. There were even new Spanish slave merchants established there: José Alvarez, Angel Ximénez ('the most intelligent of the slave traders', in the view of an English captain), and José Pérez Rola. It seems though that by 1848 the slave traders on the Gallinas, like those on the Núñez, were finding that they could make more money selling slaves (who would earlier have gone across the Atlantic) to the local planters in Africa than to Cubans or Brazilians.

Between the River Gallinas and the Gold Coast there stretched the Windward Coast which, apart from some modest activities at Capes

---

[*] *Blanco figures in Texido's novel in the style of Eugène Sue,* Barcelona y sus misterios, *as in Lino Novás Calvo's* Pedro Blanco, el negrero.

Mesurado and Monte, had never been great slaving territory. But a few slaves had always been taken from the Ivory Coast beyond, and in the mid-nineteenth century Cape Monte was for a time the headquarters of the slaver Theodore Canot (Conneau), who even built his own slaving vessel at New Sestos, one of the few successful slaving ports on the West African coast where there was no river. The landing was rough, and Canot needed the agile services of the local Kru, who took the boats full of slaves to the waiting slave ships.

Canot, according to his own account, became a slave captain in his twenties (with the *Estrella*, the *Aerostático*, the *San Pablo*) and made a fortune – which he soon lost in unwise speculations. After further adventures worthy of a picaresque novel, he established himself near Cape Monte about 1835. His establishment was destroyed in 1847 by an alliance of local people and the British commander of HMS *Favorite*, with the connivance of the captain of the USS *Dolphin*, an unusual example of British–North American collaboration. Canot then abandoned slave trading, and subsequently sold information about the traffic to British captains.[33]

It was at Cape Mesurado that North America's answer to Sierra Leone, Liberia, was finally established in 1823 (after the failure of a first colony at Sherbro). The United States naval lieutenant Captain Robert Stockton selected the land concerned, and bullied the local king, Peter, into a sale of it. Here, as in Sherbro, the early days were made difficult by a continuing local slave trade whose entrepreneurs made raids on the new polity, until in 1826 Jehudi Ashmun, the first important leader of Liberia, himself raided a large Spanish-owned barracoon at nearby Digby, and another at Tradetown, a little further on. The last action killed many slaves but also some slave traders, both Spanish and African, and it would seem that the attack shocked the neighbourhood into calling an end to the traffic. The naval support of the United States (two United States naval vessels were present) played a part in this. In the early 1840s Monrovia, though its population was a tenth of that of Freetown, already had two newspapers.

At Cape Palmas, by the River Bassa, in the early years after abolition, a British captain, Richard Willing, disguised by a Spanish name, established a settlement, New Tyre, with ample barracoons and with a Spanish factor. Here he assembled slaves from all over the coast, and then transported them, under a Spanish flag, to Brazil or even to Florida. According to the admittedly dubious evidence of the surgeon there, Richard Drake, they shipped 72,000 slaves to Brazil and the West Indies between 1808 and 1811. Later, the Philadelphia Colonization Society organized a small settlement near there, as did, further south, the Maryland State Colonization Society, giving the place the name of General Robert Goodloe Harper, a local hero in Baltimore. Yet another colony was founded in the name of the American Board of Foreign Missions, which consisted for several years merely of a planter of South Carolina, John Leighton Wilson, who freed the thirty slaves whom his wife had inherited and brought them to Africa.

Slaves continued to be carried from the region of Cap Lahou (now Grand Lahou) in the early nineteenth century, if on a reduced scale. Thus in 1843 two Brazilian brigs, suspected of *'opérations négrières'*, were discovered in the region of that landmark by a French navy by then interested in the repression of the trade. In 1848 recently imported slaves were found on Guadeloupe and Martinique from Cap Lahou, showing that the trade from there was still in being.

No doubt, in the far interior here, the decline of the Atlantic slave markets on the coast caused consternation, and sometimes worse: for example, a French official, Bregost de Polignac, reported that in 1843, after a war between the Bambara and the Sarakole had ended in victory for the former, the king concerned found himself arriving home with 800 captives. Finding it impossible to sell these men, he had most of them beheaded, though the executioner kept one captive out of ten as his personal slaves.

On the Gold Coast the dominant African power was still the Ashanti, who, just after the abolition of the slave trade in Britain, had for the first time broken through to the coast, placing most of the tribes there, above all Britain's old friends the Fanti, in some degree of subjection. The action infuriated the British and tempted the Commander at Cape Coast to intervene. A United States merchant, Samuel Swan of Medford, Massachusetts, reported, 'Since the abolition of the slave trade, the nations along the Gold Coast have been continuously embroiled in war', adding that, still 'nothing can be done' without 'American Rum'.[34]

The Danes and the Dutch on the Gold Coast had founded plantations of a sort. But costs were great, for salaries had doubled, because of loss of pay to which all had been previously entitled when they dispatched slaves overseas. As for the British, only in 1821 did the Crown agree to take over responsibility for the country's old forts, convert the slave vaults into cisterns, allow towns to be built on the old gardens, and eventually leave the castles to decay. Cape Coast had by then become the headquarters of a new colony.

The Danes, on the east part of the Gold Coast, were in a scarcely better position, though they made efforts to compensate for the end of the slave trade by raising crops for export. But that expansion exposed the Danes concerned to the sleeping sickness borne by the tsetse fly from the nearby wild territory.

In 1826 the British, with their diverse allies, including the Fanti, defeated the Ashanti, and drove them from the coast. By the mid-century that once-proud nation of warriors and slavers seemed more interested in selling cola nuts to their northern Muslim neighbours than slaves.* It is not evident that that change had much to do with British pressure. But

---

* *The cola nut had been important in West Africa for a remarkable number of uses – as a drink, as a yellow dye, as a medicine, as a religious symbol – and was specially valued by Muslims.*

the slave trade became smaller still as in the 1830s the British presence was strengthened on the coast, chiefly thanks to the efforts of Captain Charles Maclean, President of the British Council of Government at Cape Coast. Maclean, who was accountable to a committee of merchants who had elected him, was a 'dry, reserved, hard-headed Scotchman, of indefatigable activity'. He created an alliance of coastal tribes to resist the Ashanti, but he never recovered from the accusations, apparently false, that he had been concerned in the death of his wife, the poetess Letitia Landon, or 'L.E.L.' He was eventually made to resign, on the unproved accusation that he had himself dealt in slaves; remaining in Cape Coast as second-in-command to a new governor, he had the melancholy experience of seeing the alliances which he had founded unravel before he died in 1847.[35]

At the time of abolition the two most powerful and rich men in Elmina, Jacob Ruhle and Jan Niezer, both mulattos, took different paths: the first chose legality, and helped the British; the second decided to continue to trade slaves, on behalf of the Ashanti. Niezer prospered, since most Dutch governors were under his influence, the exception being the intemperate Governor Hoogenboom, murdered by young men of the town as he walked after dinner in his garden. Niezer was unpopular during the Ashanti invasion, which he assisted, but that action brought him profits. He was for many years the uncrowned king of Elmina, and as well as being Dean of the Dutch Reformed Congregation he was named, by the priests of the Benya shrine, 'Upper Great Ensign' of the Seven Quarters of Elmina: a duality of function as useful as it was unusual. His private army could be called upon to settle most difficulties in Elmina which Dutch officials could not resolve. He continued to sell slaves to the Spaniards, the French, and the Portuguese with impunity, till the arrival of a new and powerful Governor, Hermann Willem Daendels, who had restored the Dutch standing in the East Indies by building a road the length of Java, and who had now been instructed to bring an effective end to the Dutch slave trade, which, of course, King Willem had in theory abolished.* Daendels succeeded in ruining Niezer by an unusual method: he set up his own company, which traded everything except slaves, and drove Niezer to bankruptcy. Daendels also planned another road twenty-four feet wide from Elmina to Kumasi, the Ashanti capital, 'so good that merchandise could be carried on it by beasts of burden, such as elephants and camels'. Niezer was imprisoned on an invented charge after the two had had a quarrel, and Daendels freed his slaves.

The Governor was himself far from hostile to the slave trade in Africa; he merely had instructions to bring the international traffic to an end. Thus when approval for his great road (which he wanted to prolong to Timbuktu) was slow in coming, and when his envoy, Huydecoper, was

* See page 611.

delayed in his return from Kumasi, Daendels sent the Asantahene a request for 'twelve stallions, fifty oxen and bulls, and one hundred Donko slaves, with three cuts on both cheeks, including not more than twenty-five girls' – for use on his plantation, Orange Dawn. So he seems to have been far from convinced of the desirability of abolition. He wrote a letter to a Spanish slave captain whom he had met at Tenerife, on his way out from the Netherlands: 'My dear friend, it was with great but very pleasant surprise that I learnt that your ship has anchored off Apam, and that it is doing slave trade there. This means that the English are complaisant enough to furnish you with a cargo that you would never have obtained on this coast.'[36]

After Daendels died Niezer went to Amsterdam to plead his case. He won, and returned in triumph to Elmina, but his fortunes never recovered from the abolition of the trade in slaves. All the same, in 1817 about thirty Spanish or Portuguese slave ships were identified off the Gold Coast, and Niezer must have helped to load them. The next year, an English merchant, James Lucas Yeo, wrote: 'I find the trade almost as active in the neighbourhood of our forts as at any time.'[37]

By 1840 British commanders were established at seven points on the Gold Coast, Cape Coast still being the main one; Elmina and Axim, with some other old fortresses, remained Dutch (they were sold to the British in 1872); while Christiansborg in Accra and its dependent forts were Danish (till 1850, when they sold out to Britain).

Most of the coast between Cape Three Points and the Volta River was by then free of slaving, the decisive reason being the assertion of Dutch, Danish, and British sovereignty in the ports.* Yet Joseph Smith, an African merchant examined in 1848 before the British House of Commons, spoke of going on board a North American slaver, the *John Foster*, off Cape Coast; and at least one Dutch ship carried slaves to Cuba from Accra in 1830. In 1835 twenty-three ships suspected of being concerned in the slave trade stopped off at Cape Coast Castle, and others were found there in the next five years. The Governor of the Danish zone, to the east of the Gold Coast, Edward Carstensen, wrote in 1845: 'The slave trade found the country beyond the Volta too narrow. Gradually, among the blacks themselves, there grew up a lot of petty slave trade agents and commissioners who roamed the country in all directions in order to bring numerous heads to the market. . . . It came about that a great number of consignments could take place right from the fort of Elmina . . . [while] Dutch Accra has for a long time been the residence of several British trade agents, especially immigrated Brazilian negroes who have correspondents in Popo and Vay.' The same official

---

* *Cape Coast was taken over by the British Crown in 1821. But seven years later there was a plan to withdraw. A committee of London merchants was again put in charge, with a subsidy to maintain Cape Coast and the fort at Accra.*

wrote a year later: 'The Aquapim mountains, on the banks of the River Volta, has made it a staple place for the salt trade . . . but also a residence for slave trade agents.' Even British subjects, on the Gold Coast, sometimes held liberated slaves as 'pawns' – very little different from holding them as slaves.[38]

More important, the port of Popo, in what is now Togo, was still an active slave-trading harbour, as were many ports along the lagoons stretching from Dahomey to what is now Nigeria: in particular, Whydah and Lagos, short of the mouth of the River Benin. A British captain in the palm-oil trade, Captain Seward, gave evidence to a House of Commons select committee that to cover the Slave Coast from the River Volta to the Calabar adequately (naval patrol) would really require the permanent attention of fifty cruisers. This territory, another British captain pointed out, had 'water communication entirely round it, and by that . . . slaves [can be] . . . transferred from point to point and shipped anywhere on the beach, not just from Lagos, not just from Little Popo, but from any point, according to the position and arrangements of the slaves. . . .'[39]

Whydah, site of about six large slave barracoons in 1846, was the fief of yet one more opulent slave dealer, Francisco Félix de Souza, 'Cha-Cha' to the Africans, a Brazilian from Ilhã Grande, near Rio, who had first been employed in Dahomey, about 1803, as a clerk at the Portuguese fortress. He stayed on when others left, and after some disagreeable adventures with the new King Adandozan of Dahomey gained the favour of Adandozan's brother, Gezo, who when he came to the throne gave him the monopoly of the slave trade of the kingdom, on condition of paying a substantial tax on each slave exported. 'A little old man with a quick eye and an expressive manner', according to the Prince de Joinville, the son of King Louis Philippe (who later would escort the body of Napoleon from St Helena to Cherbourg), Souza bought slaves extensively from the nearby Aros. Like the Governor of Bissau, he had several slave ships of his own – for example, the *Atrevido*, a brig built in the United States, which in the 1830s would often make several journeys a year across the Atlantic, with slaves on board. He treated the captains who bought slaves from him with an eccentric but iron hand. He sold to Cuba as well as to Brazil. Surrounded by a staff of Maltese, Spaniards, and Portuguese, living in a palace which he had contrived in the old Portuguese fort, speaking several Dahomeyan languages well, Souza seemed an anachronism, yet he was generous, well mannered, and, according to most visitors, humane and good company. When he went out, he was customarily attended by a band, a guard, and a buffoon. Those who dined with him were impressed by his fine China teaset, his silver plate, and his gold spoons and forks. Joinville was told that Souza had 2,000 slaves in his barracoons, 1,000 women in his harem, and that he had fathered eighty male children: '*forts beaux mulâtres*', very well brought up, and dressed in white suits and panama hats.[40] As early as 1821 Commodore Collier of the

British West Africa Squadron described him as living 'in prodigious splendour'. Souza had good relations with the British: he brought out from England the frame of a wooden church in October 1841.

Helped by Souza, King Gezo established military suzerainty over much of the Slave Coast. Captain Broadhead said that Gezo thought he could raise '5,000 or 6,000 men if he chose it to oppose any force that might be sent against the place'.

The political reality behind this region was that by 1830 the once-powerful Yoruba empire of the Oyo had collapsed, and Dahomey, a tributary of that power since the 1720s, had become a free sovereign state. The Oyos' control over all the smaller principalities and towns had also failed. This was largely due to an internal rebellion, in effect a Muslim jihad, in 1817, in which insurgent slaves played an important part. Dahomey's own rebellion, in 1823, was directed by King Gezo ('a good king as kings go, and rather particularly good for an African', a North American naval officer commented). The final eclipse of the old empire, responsible for carrying so many slaves to European traders in the late eighteenth century, occurred about 1836.

An English businessman, Thomas Hutton, travelled the forty or fifty miles inland with Souza to see Gezo in Abomey in 1840. Like all visitors, Hutton was much impressed by Gezo's armed guard of tall, strong women, who were themselves sold as slaves if they rebelled. He observed the sacrifice of seven men who were torn to pieces by a mob who 'rushed upon them like bloodhounds, the throats of the poor wretches were severed and their misery quickly ended'. The same year, Captain Winniett of the United States squadron was told by Gezo that he disposed of about 9,000 slaves annually. He sold about 3,000 of these on his own account, and gave the rest away to his troops, who also sold them. Taxes paid on each slave exported afforded him a total income of about $300,000 – a significantly smaller income, it may be said, than that received by his ancestor Tegbesu. The King said that he was ready to do anything which the British government would ask of him 'except to give up the slave trade', for 'he thought that all substitute trades were point-less'. He said: 'The slave trade has been the ruling principle of my people. It is the source of their glory and wealth. Their songs celebrate their vic-tories and the mother lulls the child to sleep with notes of triumph over an enemy reduced to slavery. Can I, by signing . . . a treaty, change the sentiments of a whole people?'[41]

British naval officers made several attempts to persuade Gezo of the benefits of the palm-oil trade, bringing umbrellas and red silk tents as presents from Queen Victoria, but neither he nor his successor, King Gelele, could be convinced that it would be worth his while to abandon slaving. One reason was that the subsidy offered was too little: 'If instead of dollars [we] . . . could have offered pounds . . .', Dahomey might have accepted in 1848 the suggestions of the Chief Justice of Cape Coast, Judge

Cruikshank. King Gezo's return offer of two slave girls to do the Queen of England's washing seemed an inadequate reply.

When the naval blockade eventually made the shipping of slaves difficult from Whydah, Dahomey did turn over successfully to trading palm oil. The old social organization sustained the new business. In the past, the despotic King traded slaves through a class of noble merchants. The palm-oil commerce was easily introduced into this arrangement: the old nobles became landholders and used slaves whom they would previously have sent across the Atlantic to cultivate the palms. With this arrangement, Lagos and Badagry succeeded Dahomey as the chief slaving base in the region. Unlike the King of Dahomey, whose slaves were mostly obtained from war, the King of Lagos bought his captives from Yoruba merchants, who in turn had obtained them from the most remote places.

Lagos and the other ports of the region were protected from the British navy by a large sandbar. There were numerous interconnected lagoons there, making easy the transport of slaves from one creek to another by canoe. Admiral Hotham wrote in 1848, 'At certain times of the year, when the fresh breezes set into the Bight . . . a well-equipped slave vessel will escape even from a steamer.' One of the trading peoples there was the Muslim Filatahs, whose centre was the town of Rabba. The English Captain Allen said of them, after a journey up the Niger: 'Their whole occupation is slave-catching and selling; they make excursions every year during the dry season into the neighbouring states to take slaves. . . . All the tribes have to pay a certain sum [as tribute]. . . . Frequently the sums are so great that they cannot pay, and then they seize the [people as] slaves.' Rabba became an important city for slaving, for those gathered there were sold not only to Portuguese or Spaniards to take to the Americas, but to Arabs who would take them to Tripoli. [42]

Quite a part was played in the slave trade at Lagos by Italians who carried their cargoes to Brazil, and whose ventures were backed by the Italian (really at the time Sardinian) Consuls in both Bahia and Rio. The dominant trader in that port, however, was Domingos José Martins, born more Hispanically in Cádiz as Diego Martínez. He maintained an important commerce to Bahia in the 1840s, and his headquarters was first at Badagry, then at Porto-Novo. He lived less lavishly than Souza: his house at Porto-Novo was small, if with a large European garden. Usually dressed unpretentiously, in a blue calico shirt and trousers, he provided slaves for many years, fast and efficiently, for the swift modern schooners of the slave king of Bahia, Joaquim Pereira Marinho. Like Souza he had ships of his own, which he also used to carry slaves to Brazil. At the end of the 1840s he was explaining that it was 'so expensive to keep up his factory [of slaves] that he had now cleared away a considerable part of the country, and is forming a large farm [for palm oil], with the intention, as he says, of giving up the slave factory, which costs him so much and pays so little'. He retired to Brazil, found himself ostracized, and returned to Africa, this time to Lagos, where he became concerned in the legitimate trade in palm oil.[43]

The River Benin, as opposed to the Bight of Benin itself, was not much of a slaving waterway in the nineteenth century. It had always been a slow business to buy slaves there, and after the British abolition delay was risky, even to the adventurous Portuguese slaver. The dangerous bar had always been difficult for European traders and when it became necessary to cross it secretly, because of fear of British interference, the business declined rapidly. Only fifteen slave ships were to be found there between 1816 and 1839; by the 1840s the trade was at an end.

The Rivers Calabar and Bonny, or rather their creeks and mangrove swamps, on the other hand, continued to be the scene of much trading of slaves, particularly by French captains, most of the captives being Igbos or Ibibios. Captain Leeke, in a British frigate, was told in 1822 that in four months nineteen cargoes of slaves had been sent to the Americas from the Bonny, sixteen from Calabar. The British navy started visiting the rivers regularly at that time, however, and they afterwards became the scene of numerous heroic affrays. For example, in 1821, Captain Leeke, in HMS *Myrmidon*, decided to enter the Bonny by a back channel, the so-called Antony River, and explore the position. He sent Lieutenant Bingham in with small boats. He found six French slavers* busily stocking up but thought that he could do nothing in respect of them (because of Anglo-French rules since Scott's decision about the *Louis*). But one French captain told him that higher upstream there were two Spanish slavers. After some fighting, in which Leeke brought the *Myrmidon* into the main river, he seized the two slavers, with 154 and 139 slaves respectively. In 1822 Lieutenant Mildmay captured five Brazilian slavers in this river with remarkable courage; one of them, the schooner *Vecua*, had been abandoned by its crew, with 300 slaves chained in the hold. The departing crew left a lighted fuse over the magazine in the hope of destroying the British boarding party (as well, of course, as the slaves).[44]

How slaves were made here in the nineteenth century was vividly explained by a boy who lived to tell the tale: 'We came out into the street and when we walked about 50 yards from our house, we saw the city [Itokui, Erunwon, or Oba, in Nigeria] on fire, and before us the enemies coming in the street. We met with them and they caught us separately. They separated me from all my brethren, except one of my father's children born to him by his second wife. I and this brother were caught by one man. By the time we left the house of our father, I saw my father's mother pass the other gate. She, I had no hope of seeing again in the flesh, because she was an old woman. Doubtless they would kill her. . . . I was

---

* *Probably the* Actif, *Captain Benoît; the* Alcide, *Captain Hardy; the* Caroline, *Captain Pelliful; the* Eugène, *Captain Morin; and the* Fox, *Captain Armand – all of Nantes.*

brought the same day that the city was taken to Imodo, that is, the place where they made their residence when they besieged us. . . . When I came to that place, the man who took me in the city took me and made a present to the chief man of war . . . for the custom was, when any of their company went with war bands, if he catches slaves, half of the slaves he would give to his captain.'[45]

An English trader in Fernando Po, John Beechcroft, was found complaining in 1830 that at Old Calabar British merchant ships were outnumbered by nine French slave-trading vessels, whose captains laughed at his protests, knowing that he 'was not in a condition to enforce them, the French being nine to one against me, the smallest vessel having double the number of men that I had'. One of these captains was 'Gaspar, a Frenchman [from Guadeloupe in the *Heureuse Étoile*, who] arrived at Old Calabar and carried away hundreds of slaves in ships both well-armed and numerously manned'. All legitimate commerce ceased on his arrival, 'and a general scramble of robbery and plunder commenced to supply him with slaves'. British palm-oil ships were 'obliged to remain there, in expensive and sickly indolence, until the slavers and pirates are supplied with their unhappy victims'. The traffic in slaves was prospering in the 1840s. But a wreck of two ships at the mouth of the Calabar, and the capture of two others, weakened the local enthusiasm for the traffic; in 1841 a 'trifling present' was indeed made (five annual payments of 2,000 Spanish dollars) to the Kings of Calabar, and the commerce soon came to an end.[46]

High up these rivers in the 1840s there were slave barracoons. The English explorer John Duncan saw one at Egga. Slaves were brought there from different parts of the interior. Duncan asked how soon he could lay his hands on 600 slaves. He received the answer: 'The day after tomorrow.' Yet by then the overseas slave trade had run its course in the Bight of Biafra. Several witnesses testified in the 1840s in London that twenty years before they would see sixteen to twenty slave vessels in the river at a time, and they would sooner trade in slaves than with palm oil; 'but on my last voyage I was in the river three months, and there was not a slave vessel in the river'. One explanation was that the British allied with the new King of Bonny, Dappa Pepple, against the Regent, Alali, who had shown himself a typical old-fashioned autocrat, in alliance with French, Spanish, and Brazilian-Portuguese slave dealers. After several encounters between the British naval commander, Captain Craigie, and the Regent, the old order was overthrown, Alali resigned, and the King, henceforth a British puppet, signed a treaty in 1839. By this, the British promised to pay £2,000 a year or half the revenue which they had derived from the slave trade. But the British paid nothing in the first year, and King Pepple in 1840 returned to the slave trade. Still, Old Calabar and Bonny were both easily observed by British patrols, so they both began to turn over to palm oil. The newer ports of New Calabar and Brass were less conspicuous and still did much slaving in the late 1840s.

Brass, in particular, hidden in the recesses of the delta and approachable only by creek, with no direct outlet to the Atlantic, became the centre in these years of an important clandestine traffic. The controller of the network, with the King of Bonny and the Chiefs of Brass in support, was Pablo Freixas, a Portuguese partner of Diego Martínez, who was remembered locally for a long time for his exploits in defeating the 'English busybodies'. Still, the Chief at Brass, 'King Boy', was also active in the traffic. Captain Tucker, writing in the 1840s, reported, 'A constant supply of slaves are sent by canoe through the creeks to the Rivers Nun and Brass for shipment, 360 slaves having been taken by a Spaniard previous to my arrival in the river.' Tucker reported King Pepple as saying that he himself sold 3,000 slaves in the years 1839 to 1841, that he would continue to deal with Freixas, and that 'dollars and doubloons are plentiful in Bonny, which is always the case, after the arrival of a slaver in the Nun or Brass river, as most of the slaves shipped off from there are purchased at Bonny'.[47]

Captain Tucker eventually succeeded in negotiating another slave-trade treaty with King Pepple of Bonny. The latter was now promised £10,000 a year for five years. Pepple looked on the matter as concluded, but the British Parliament had to ratify the scheme. Palmerston, however, who had inspired the treaty, had now been replaced by Lord Aberdeen, who did not think the treaty wise. He wanted to go back to the treaty of 1839, which talked of only £2,000 a year. So it seemed to the Africans that the British did not wish to go through with the plan. They renewed relations with their Brazilian slave clients, only too pleased to revive the old traffic. Captain Midgley, of Liverpool, told a select committee of the House of Commons in 1842 that unless the British government acted with more energy than it had thitherto it would do well to 'keep out of the River [Bonny] altogether. [For] first comes a captain and makes a Treaty and then another comes and says the Treaty shall be null and void and tears it up.'[48]

Some other treaties were signed, and ratified, by the British in these years. In 1842 Eyo and Eyamba, rulers of the two leading towns of Old Calabar (Creek Town and Duke Town), made a treaty abolishing the slave trade in return for £2,000 for five years; a similar treaty was eventually made with Bimbia (Cameroons), where the subsidy was only £1,200 a year. The *Obi* Osai of Aboh declared, too, that he was willing to abandon the slave trade 'if only a better traffic could be substituted'. The *Obi* had been impressed by a Sierra Leone interpreter who put the case for the abolition, and who concluded a long speech by saying, 'Do you not see that it is harder to continue it than to give it up?' The *Obi* agreed.[49]

The *Obi*, impatient of contradictory European professions, put one part of the African case to the members of the Niger expedition in 1841: 'Hitherto, we thought that it was God's wish that black people should be slaves to white people; white people first told us that we should sell slaves to them and we sold them; and white people are now telling us not to sell slaves. . . . If white people give up buying, black people will give up selling.' All the same, there was suspicion: when Britain concluded the treaty against selling slaves in 1841, King Pepple of Bonny inserted a clause in the document stating: 'If, at any future time, Great Britain shall permit the slave trade, King Pepple and the Chiefs of Bonny shall be at liberty to do the same.'[50]

West Africa, or 'Guinea', largely as a result of British naval power, was thus very slowly in the mid-nineteenth century changing from an economy which was predominantly slave-trading to one based on commerce in raw materials. The discovery in 1830 that the River Niger entered the Atlantic in the Bight of Benin opened 'a great highway into the heart of Africa, coinciding with the invention of the steamship, which made journeys, and so [legitimate] commerce, up it possible'.

The internal slave trade, however, continued, and indeed probably expanded. Macgregor Laird went to Bocqu, above Ida, on the Niger, where there was a slave market every ten days; from here he supposed that '8,000 or 10,000 were sold annually' – the captives being mostly from the far interior, if still sometimes for 'onward shipment to Europeans'. Laird remembered seeing that 'the canoes were constantly passing by, with from four to six or eight slaves in them.'[51] The traveller Waddell described how King Eyo of Calabar 'did not employ men to steal for him; nor did he knowingly buy those which were stolen. He bought them in the market, at the market price, without being able to know how they were procured. . . . He admitted that they were obtained in various objectionable ways . . . but said that they came from different far countries of which he knew nothing. . . .'[52]

Perhaps two-thirds of the slaves carried to the Americas in the mid-nineteenth century came from south of the equator or from East Africa. Even just north of the equator the trade flourished at Sangatanga, at the mouth of the River Gabon, as well as on the island of Corisco, at the mouth of the River Mooney.

At the mouth of the Gabon in 1842 the local king ceded some territory to the French, and in 1843 Captain Montléon landed soldiers to establish a fortified post. In 1849 his successor founded Libreville, the French answer to Freetown and Monrovia, with some slaves rescued from the slave ship *Elisa*.

Offshore, of course, lay Fernando Po, Principe, and São Tomé. The first was now used, because of its calm waters (what a contrast with the surf on the coast of Guinea!), as a coaling station by British steamers. It was common enough to find there the crew of a slaver which had been deposited by an English captain after the capture of their ship waiting for transport to Calabar, and being well treated on an island generally considered to be 'the most healthy of any part on the station'. Palmerston offered Spain £50,000 for the place in 1841; but the offer was refused. Thereafter Spain tightened her control over the island, and it became a base of operations for Julián Zulueta, of Havana, and his London partners, including his cousin Pedro José. Many *emancipados* were later sent to Fernando Po from Cuba and Pedro José de Zulueta was responsible for ensuring their food: a task which he seems to have fulfilled with neither efficiency nor generosity even though in 1843 the Spanish government curiously named John Beechcroft, the English merchant, as acting Governor.

São Tomé still had its slave-powered Portuguese sugar plantations, as it had had ever since the fifteenth century. The island of Principe, meantime, in the mid-century seemed to be the private colony of the Portuguese Governor, José María de Ferreira, whose wife, a woman of vast girth, had invested deeply in Souza's interests in Whydah.

Some miles to the south of São Tomé, on the mainland, lay Cape Lopez, a great landmark, for from there the African coast turns southeast. The creeks here harboured a number of traders. Beyond, everyone agreed that the character of the slave trade changed. Sir Charles Hotham, commander of the British squadron, thought that here 'the speculation on the part of the Brazilian, is founded on the principle of employing vessels of little value, to be crowded to excess with slaves. . . . Here it is, therefore, that the traffic assumes its most horrid form. At this moment, the *Penelope* [the vessel which he commanded] has in tow a slaver, of certainly not more than 60 tons, in which 312 human beings were stowed. The excess of imagination cannot depict a scene more revolting.'[53] Among the traders with posts here about 1850 was one who had connections with Havana, and directed by José Pernea; one belonging to the Portuguese-Brazilian José Bernardino de Sá; and a third belonging to the Cuban Rubirosa.

There were many political entities on this coast, most of them now involved in slaving. First, there was Cape Lopez itself, where the French explorer Paul du Chaillu found in the years after 1810 a drunken and unpredictable monarch, Bongo, and his successor, Arsem, who quickly adapted to the need to camouflage his slave barracoons against British observation. These places were well arranged, slaves being chained together six by six, a method which best avoided the possibility of escape: 'It is rare that six men are sufficiently in agreement to make any attempt', he was assured. Arsem was in the habit of persuading captains who negotiated with him for slaves to drink blood before negotiations began. Captain Lancelot, who traded there in 1815 on the *Petite Louise* of Nantes, received a slave boy as a present, as did his officers. The slaves here, du Chaillu reported, came from the far interior of Africa, well beyond the point to which he had penetrated.[54]

Mayumba developed for the first time into a trading centre for slaves about 1815, after the legal abolition of the Portuguese traffic north of the equator. By 1840 this little port, with a population of no more than about 1,000 people, had some seven or eight barracoons for slaves in the hands of Spanish, Portuguese, or Brazilian traders. To the south there were one or two other small new slave harbours, such as Banda and Chilongo, and then the well-established Vili harbour of Loango, the city of Malemba, and the smaller port of Cabinda (Kabinda), for long a preserve of French and British. The withdrawal of the last-named from the trade after 1808 left the way open to Spaniards and North Americans interested in the Cuban trade – and some Portuguese or Brazilian traders who were pleased to sell slaves to Havana, even if their ships were registered as sailing for 'Pernambuco'.

In Loango Bay during the nineteenth century the political power of the Vili was in full decline. When German travellers visited the place in the 1870s they found the body of the last *maloango* – the King of the Vili – Buatu, still unburied since 1787, because no successor had emerged to initiate the funeral ceremonies. Independent slave dealers seem to have almost assumed sovereign authority: many of them began to place 'Ma' in front of their names to indicate the possession of land, and to wear such signs of princely status as animals' tails and shoulder decorations.

Cabinda, on its 'high, bold coast', not unlike 'the appearance of the land about Dover', in the imaginative phrase of Assistant Surgeon Peters, of HMS *Pluto*, became the biggest slave port in this region in the early nineteenth century. The people of Cabinda themselves were known as admirable sailors and good carpenters. So far as slaves were concerned, the place could draw on the facilities made available by the River Congo, on whose banks in 1845, near the mouth, there were about thirty barracoons – most of them the property of Cubans or Spaniards whose luxurious houses and gardens on the riverbank excited the admiration of British officers. One of these was Pedro Maniett, who 'so far as regards his communication with Englishmen, who have been even blockading and preventing his vessels coming there, has behaved in the kindest manner'; he even looked after English seamen wounded in one or another of the skirmishes which took place with slavers.[55] There were also a few Brazilian barracoons, many of them connected with or owned by individual merchants, of whom Manuel Pinto da Fonseca of Rio was the foremost. He was said to hold in his factory goods worth £140,000 in 1846, awaiting deals to buy slaves. These barracoons were by now often placed a few hours away from the mouth of the river, in order to avoid attack by the British navy. Even so, Captain Matson, in 1842, did destroy five barracoons there.

The slave merchants at Cabinda in the nineteenth century devoted great attention to loading slaves fast. A North American, Joseph Underwood, described how in 1845 'a sail [came] in sight ... at 1 p.m. She showed no colours. At ten past one, she came to anchor, a few yards from the *Sea Eagle* [Underwood's own vessel]. The brig had sliding sail booms rigged out and everything in readiness for making sail. The boats were soon alongside loaded with negroes. . . . They took on about 450 and, at 45 minutes past two, she weighed anchor and stood to sea . . . [bound for Rio].'[56]

The Congo River itself was an important source of slaves for Cuba as well as for Brazil in these years. This waterway provided perfect cover for slave ships hiding until the cruisers were out of sight. They could then load quickly, and escape by means of the fast Congo current. Another North American traveller, Peter Knickerbocker, wrote: 'The Congo river, at its mouth, is some twenty miles in width, and runs with the force of a mill sluice into the ocean; and the current continuing in strength and speed far out to sea, the slaver has greater facilities in obtaining a good offering at this point than any other slave mart on the coast. One dark night and an ebb tide will take him forty miles down the river and sixty miles [out] from the coast, let him sail ever so badly, and the probability of falling foul of a cruiser at this distance is very small.'[57]

Yet one more traveller, Montgomery Parker, wrote, with respect to North Americans' involvement in this territory, that 'numerous United States ships sail from Rio . . . Bahia and other ports in the Brazils and even from Cuba, under a charter to go to the coast of Africa, carrying an outward cargo and such passengers as the charterers may see fit to put on board and, to return to the port they sailed from, . . . they will make two or three trips to the coast [of Africa] and return each time, with a cargo of camwood, gums, ivory, etc., and soon they become pretty well-known to the armed cruisers of the various squadrons, who look upon them as legal and honest traders and cease to watch them as closely as they would a vessel that had come upon the coast for the first time. By and by, one of these vessels comes out again. The agents . . . find the coast is clear and that a good opportunity is offered to ship slaves. . . . They make an offer to the captain to buy his vessel. He accepts it . . . [and] goes on shore with his officers and crew . . . the slaves are hurried on board, the vessel is given in charge of a Brazilian master and crew, who are generally the passengers she has just brought over on her outward voyage and, with the Stars and Stripes still floating at the mast, she leaves the coast in safety.'[58] One such vessel sold in this way (or so it would seem) was Charles Hoffman of Salem's *Cipher*, sold at Cabinda in 1841. Other traders with interests here included Julián Zulueta of Havana, represented here by a certain José Ojea, and several of his Cuban or Spanish competitors such as Manuel Pastor or Manzanedo.

It is scarcely possible to estimate the number of slaves carried from these waterways in the mid-nineteenth century. But from the zone to the north of the Congo some 290 slave ships were seized by the British or other naval patrols; from the region to the south of it, the figure was only just a little less: about 280.

Further to the south lay the great slaving ports of Angola proper, at Ambriz and Benguela, the old city of Luanda lying between them. From these places and others on the coast, 500,000 slaves were probably shipped during the legal era, 1800–1830; and it would seem that over 600,000 may have been shipped in the illegal days after 1830. All these figures may be an underestimate.

Ambriz was a new centre for trading slaves to Brazil. Many Luso-Africans moved there from Luanda after 1810, for they could ship slaves in that port without the bureaucratic procedures usual at Luanda, and also avoid paying the taxes. The pioneer of this arrangement was Manuel José de Sousa Lopes, who made a speciality of selling slaves to Spanish buyers. The determined Captain Matson destroyed three barracoons there in 1842, but the trade recovered. About 1850 three prominent Brazilian or Portuguese traders had posts there: Manuel Pinto da Fonseca, Ferraz Coreira, and Tomás Ramos.

Luanda itself was not much concerned in slaving in the mid-nineteenth century, though there was still a large slave barracoon outside the city, at Lamarinas Bay. The conditions of keeping slaves in this imperial Portuguese city seemed even worse in the nineteenth century than in the eighteenth: 'The detention of the negroes on the coast,' wrote one visitor, 'in consequence of the market being overstocked, or of the nonarrival of the slavers which are to transport them to another shore, is a melancholy and notorious cause of mortality among them.'[59] Many slaves who went first to Luanda were ordered to walk on to Benguela for shipment. Ambitious slave merchants in Luanda in these days who did not go up to Ambriz often moved inland.

Benguela, with its close financial and commercial connections with Rio de Janeiro, was the home of those Angolans who, like the merchant António Lopes Anjo, after the independence of Brazil in 1822, would have preferred a political association with the new nation.

Behind these westward-facing ports, there was by the 1850s the beginning of a tug in a different direction. Arab traders from East Africa had already reached the Congo by the 1850s, bent on carrying slaves across the continent to Kilwa or Zanzibar. The supreme exponent of this new traffic was an Arab from the latter port, Tippoo Ti, known throughout Africa for his raiding parties with firearms. Governor D'Acunha of Luanda told one British captain, Alexander Murray, that 'these slave dealers did not hesitate to march armies of slaves completely across the continent from Benguela to Mozambique'.[60]

Throughout the centuries of the Atlantic slave trade, a steady flow of slaves went to the Americas from East Africa. By the 1820s these harbours, from Point Uniac in the south to Zanzibar in the north, a stretch of 1,000 miles, were probably shipping as many slaves as any other region – perhaps 10,000 a year in the 1820s, even 30,000 in the early 1840s, mostly from the cities of Mozambique, with their beautiful houses in which

formerly Portuguese merchants trading to India had lived, and Quelimane (Quilimane) – 'decidedly the headquarters', despite its dangerous
sandbar. East Africa was not ignored in the British crusade against the
slave trade, but it was considered of secondary importance, at least until
West Africa had been bullied, bribed, or persuaded into morality.

Richard Waters, the United States Consul to Zanzibar, who was on
Mozambique island in 1837, recalled seeing slaves in the harbour, 'mostly
children, from ten to fourteen years of age. . . . What can I say to those
engaged in this trade when I remember the millions of slaves in my own
country?'[61] The main item in the commerce of this island was now slaves,
ivory and gold dust being left far behind. The banks of the River Anghoza
were also 'a great depot for slaves'. 'The slave coast begins at Cape Lady
Grey', Captain Rundle Watson, commander of the British naval ship
Brilliant, told a House of Commons committee in 1850. Another slaving
port was Sofala, 'the Elephant's Shoal', at the mouth of the Zambezi. In
1827 Captain Charles Millett of Salem, a legitimate trader, found that in
the towns of Lindy and Kisawara, beyond Cape Delgado, there was 'no
trade except in slaves'. Here merchants of the Indian Ocean competed
with those of the Atlantic. Zanzibar was also a great slave mart, and it
also served the nearby islands in the Indian Ocean. A quarter of a million
slaves were probably carried from the island of Mozambique to those
islands in the first half of the nineteenth century.

The slaves brought here from the interior were treated at least as
badly as those in the Atlantic passage: 'Often 1,000 slaves are stowed in a
space hardly capable of receiving as many bags of rice', commented
Michael Shepard of Salem, adding, 'When they arrive in Zanzibar for sale
they are discharged in the same manner as a load of sheep would be, the
dead ones thrown overboard to drift down with the tide.'[62] A United
States tourist in 1849, Mrs Putnam, thought though that 'the slaves mind
no more about being sold than a pair of cattle would at home'.[63] (How she
knew she did not say.)

Most of these slaving harbours were, as usual, estuaries of rivers, up
which the 200-ton slavers could sail or steam. The agents were often
Hindus (Banyans) from the Portuguese port of Gujerat, and Arabs as well
as Portuguese were concerned to sell slaves to many places other than the
Americas. One of the biggest traders was a Christian from Goa who had
lived in Rio.

The most substantial merchants, nevertheless, were Mozambiques,
such as José do Rosário Monteiro, who began to build ships about 1784
and carried slaves to Brazil throughout the Napoleonic Wars; Manuel

---

* *Later, Waters, an anti-slaver from Salem, met a Spanish slave captain and said, 'I cannot
wish you a prosperous voyage for you are engaged in a business which I hate from the
heart.' The captain, 'quite a pleasant man', smiled and insisted that they were better off
where he carried them.*

Galvão da Silva, who was for a time Secretary to the Governor (whom he persuaded to invest in his ships); and finally João Bonifacio Alves da Silva, probably the biggest slave merchant in Quelimane, of which city he was also Governor for eighteen years.[64] The largest Portuguese firm of slave traders in East Africa after 1840 was the Portuguese Company, registered in New York, directed by Manoel Basilio da Cunha Reis, whose interests extended in the 1850s to Cuba. In the 1840s, the firm, however, sold its slaves mostly to Brazilians, and most would be carried to Rio de Janeiro in United States ships, perhaps to be made available to such princes of the traffic as Manuel Pinto da Fonseca or Bernardino da Sá. Portuguese bureaucrats were easily suborned by such businessmen: 'The small income of these officials renders the temptations to which they are exposed irresistible', wrote a British civil servant in 1850; 'banished for years to a pestiferous climate, the means for speedily escaping therefrom by enriching themselves sufficiently to give up their public situation is indeed very tempting.'[65]

Theodore Canot about 1830 sailed on a slaver from Cuba on a 'trim Brazil-built brig, of rather more than 300 tons', which anchored at Quelimane 'among a lot of Portuguese and Brazilian slavers.... We fired a salute of twenty guns and ran up the French flag. The captain in a full uniform [then] went to call on the Governor. Next morning, the Governor's boat was sent, for the specie; the fourth day disclosed the signal that called us to the beach; the fifth, sixth, and seventh, [they] supplied us with 800 negroes; and, on the ninth, we were underway.' (But the success of this journey was ruined by the outbreak of smallpox, in the course of which over 300 slaves died en route.)[66]

In 1846 Governor Abreu de Madeira was relieved from Quelimane for corruption; his successor abandoned his post, and 'escaped in a slave ship, with a large cargo of slaves'. The next Portuguese Governor of Mozambique, Captain Duval, seemed to the British 'one of the best persons we ever met' and within some years had, on fifty miles either side of the city, brought the slave trade to an end. What usually happened, said Captain Duval, was that 'governors would receive a box soon after they took up their office: on opening it, there were found to be four compartments.... [Inside] there was $1,500; $750 in one compartment, with a Crown on it and then, $250 in each of the others. These sums were from the leading slave trader in the place, for the Governor, his deputy, the Collector of Customs and the Commander of the troops.'[67]

After 1840 the Portuguese navy was mildly active in the region, with a brig and two schooners. They did stop some ships but, in general, 'the slavers laugh at them'.

The Mozambique Africans were usually seen by the Brazilians as 'a finer race of men' than those on the West Coast, 'an affectionate race of people who soon acquire a knowledge of the value of money'. But they were men from many races, for slaves often reached Quelimane from the far interior, along the Zambezi.

This trade diminished in the 1840s, thanks to the British, who after 1843 had powers locally granted by Portuguese governors which they never possessed in West Africa. They were able, for example, both to pursue all slave ships in parts of the coast where the Portuguese had not established a presence and to destroy barracoons at will. But then the slavers turned to buyers outside Portuguese territory – for example, in the sultanate of the Imam of Muscat (especially the Banyan barracoons), or in the Arab isles of Angoche, Comoro, and Western Madagascar. Madagascar prohibited the trade in slaves after a treaty between the Malagasy and the British in 1817, yet the evidence suggests a vigorous slave trade from the island throughout the nineteenth century, with about 3,000–4,000 slaves being exported every year, some to Mauritius or elsewhere in the Indian Ocean, the rest to various American harbours, especially Cuba.

The British capture and retention after 1815 of Mauritius did not affect the issue of slavery much, though the trade to the island from Mozambique prospered till it was legally abolished in 1813, and though it continued largely unchecked by the British authorities till about 1825. Nearby was Île Bourbon, which had remained with France after 1815. No slaves seem to have been carried from there, but many were, nevertheless, imported in the early nineteenth century, from both Mozambique and Madagascar, to assist in the harvesting of coffee and in the newly developed culture of cloves: 'They are also employed to draw merchandise about town in carts, instead of cattle', commented Dudley Leavitt Pickman, a merchant from Salem.[68]

Cuban vessels which used these harbours of East Africa were much bigger than those which frequented the West Coast, because small boats would not so easily pass by the Cape of Good Hope.

That passage past the Cape of Good Hope, incidentally, was trebly unpleasant for the slaves: first, because the journey from East Africa to Brazil was much longer than from Angola, sixty or seventy days being the average; second, because of the cold from which the slaves suffered when they rounded the Cape – in comparison with the great heat which characterized an Angolan slave journey to Brazil, where temperatures in the slave decks were often 130 degrees Fahrenheit; third, because of the storms.

As for the numbers of slaves carried to the Americas from these remote ports in the nineteenth century, fifteen to eighteen Brazilian slavers would arrive at Mozambique Island in the 1820s, and each would take about 500 slaves, though very often half would die en route. Perhaps 10,000 a year would be a fair estimate from that port. After 1830, when the slave trade to Brazil as well as to Cuba became such a curious illegal

---

* Cloves were introduced to Île Bourbon in 1779 by Pierre Poivre.

enterprise, the figure was probably higher, perhaps much higher, for these were years when the West African trade was declining. In 1819, for instance, five Spanish ships from Havana were to be seen in Mozambique before going on to Zanzibar, and such vessels were often to be seen there till the 1850s. It would seem that 15,000 slaves may have been exported from there during these years. About 10,000 may have left Quelimane.

33

SHARKS ARE
THE INVARIABLE OUTRIDERS
OF ALL SLAVE SHIPS

'Sharks ... are the invariable outriders of all slave ships crossing the Atlantic, systematically trotting alongside, to be handy in case a parcel is to be carried anywhere, or a dead slave to be decently buried ...'

Herman Melville, Moby Dick

'Next day we saw an English man-of-war [HMS Maidstone] coming. When the Portuguese saw this, it put them to disquietness and confusion. They then told us that these were the people which will eat us, if we suffered them to prize us; and they also enticed us, if they should ask, how long since we sailed, we must say it was more than a month. And they also gave us long oars and set us to pull. About ten men were set on one oar, and we tried to pull as far as we are able, but it was of no avail. Next day, the English overtook us and they took charge of the slaves. ...'

Joseph Wright, a slave, in Curtin,
Africa Remembered

'Sailing rapidly on a strong land breeze, the vessel was soon out of sight of the coast of Africa.'

Prosper Mérimée, Tamango

BOTH ENEMIES AND FRIENDS of the 'ebony merchants' – the phrase much used in France by the dealers in slaves – argued that conditions in the trade were worse during its illegal stage, since captains often packed many slaves into a smaller space than they would have in the past. The Duke of Wellington told the Congress of Verona in 1822: 'All attempts at prevention, imperfect as they have been found to be, have tended to increase the aggregate of human suffering. . . . The dread of detection suggests expedients of concealment productive of the most dreadful sufferings to the cargo.'[1]

Several witnesses at a long inquiry into the trade by a House of Commons committee in 1848 said the same. For example, J. B. Moore, Chairman of the Brazilian Association of Liverpool, thought: 'Year after year, I look upon it that the evils connected with the slave trade have been aggravated by our squadron being on the coast of Africa to prevent it . . . by increasing the sufferings of the slaves.' José Cliffe, a North American–Brazilian slave merchant, abandoned the trade because of the 'loss of life and increase of human suffering' which he regarded as a direct conse-quence of British philanthropy.[2]

Yet for the first twenty or thirty years after British and North Amer-ican abolition in 1808 the size and character of slave ships probably remained much the same as in the past. But in the mid-century some ships were used, including steamships, which were capable of taking 1,000 slaves across the Atlantic. On such slave journeys 'the suffering, though more intense, is of shorter duration', Captain Denman reflected in 1848. Still, one does not have to accept as true every sentence of the terrible account of Drake's life as a slave captain and surgeon to realize that confusion was frequent, and stowing of captives disgracefully done, so that there was often what he called 'a frightful battle among the slaves for room and air'. The crossing was, just as much as it had always been, 'a pestilence which stalketh the waters'.[3]

Vile conditions were as ever also encountered in Africa. Slave captains often genuinely supposed that they were doing slaves a real human service by carrying them off to Brazil or to Cuba, even if to slavery. Lord John Russell would tell the House of Commons in London in 1846 that a third of the captives intended as slaves for the Atlantic crossing died during the land journey on their way to the coast. But the time spent waiting in barracoons in Africa was probably longer in the 1800s than in the previous century for, as we have seen, the captains tried to pick up their cargoes in one sweep, rather than spend weeks negotiating: speed was necessary to avoid the interference of the British navy. Lord Palmerston commented: 'The liability to interrup-tion obliges these slave traders to make arrangements for a rapid embarkation.' Many children are said to have been carried on the illegal trade to Brazil, because their size permitted the loading of a greater number.[4]

The existence of these depots, however, to some extent made the control of the slave trade easier: most sites were well known, and they could be watched. These barracoons were flimsy constructions, usually of bamboo, maintained by Africans. 'Suppose that there were 500 slaves waiting in a barracoon', said the repentant slave merchant Cliffe. 'A cruiser is in the neighbourhood, and the slave vessel cannot come in. It is very difficult to get on the coast of Africa sufficient food to support them.' Thus 2,000 slaves were believed to have been murdered in 1846 in a barracoon at Lagos because, on the one hand, the slavers *Styx* and *Hydra* (ships with Italian flags) did not dare to brave the British patrol; and because, on the other hand, the king of the place had run out of food: the 'inducement . . . was simply that the feeding of so large a number of idle people was burdensome to him'. It was sometimes suggested that if the British navy (or anyone else) were to destroy all the barracoons, then the slave trade would have been fatally damaged. But the surgeon of the navy who has been quoted before, Dr Thomson, in evidence to the Hutt Committee, said, realistically, 'Whether there are barracoons or no, the slaves will be forthcoming.'[5]

Another picture of slaves waiting in a barracoon was given by an American naval commodore, Henry Wise, who wrote from Cabinda in July 1859 how 'in chained gangs, the unfortunate slaves are driven by the lash from the interior to the barracoons on the beach; there the sea-air, insufficient diet, and dread of their approaching fate, produce the most fatal diseases: dysentery and fever [often] release them from their sufferings; the neighbouring soil grows rich in the decaying remains of so many of their fellow creatures, and the tracks are thick-strewn with their bones . . . . On a short march', he continued, 'of 600 slaves, a few weeks back, intended for the *Emma Lincoln* [of the United States], 125 expired on the road. The mortality on these rapid marches is seldom less than 20 per cent. Such, sir, is the slave trade under the American flag.'[6]

However unpleasant the barracoon, slaves would no doubt have preferred to remain there than go to the 'finer country' talked about by the slave captains. An ex-slave, John Frazer, for example, described how in the nineteenth century, as in the eighteenth, the slaves often 'cried, they did not want to go'. 'Would they have preferred to have stayed in the barracoons?' Mr Richard Monckton Milnes, the aesthetic Member of Parliament for Pontefract, asked him. 'Yes,' said Frazer. (All ex-slaves who were questioned on the matter also said that they would prefer to remain in Sierra Leone than to return to their own birthplace, because, John Frazer insisted, Sierra Leone 'is a free country'.)[7]

Often in the 1840s the presence of the naval patrols made it difficult to embark slaves at the barracoons, as has been seen, and so the captives were forced to walk several miles, sometimes as many as forty or more, along the coast, to a secret rendezvous with a slave ship's canoes.

As in the past, slaves were obtained in Africa by the local dealers in many diverse ways and nobody agreed exactly how. Captain Matson, for example, thought that the practice of obtaining slaves by war and the destruction of villages had almost ceased; and that, on the contrary, 'one half of the slaves now supplied to the markets of Cuba and Brazil are obtained by purchases from their parents'. On the other hand, the Reverend Henry Townsend, of the Church Missionary Society, who lived for many years in Abeokuta, a city of 50,000 people near Lagos, thought about 1850 that war was a key to understanding the origins of slaves in that territory. For example, a quarrel might arise, and some fighting take place, 'and, ultimately, one of the towns was destroyed and the people carried into slavery, as many as they could take, and those who escaped joined those who had besieged them, and made an attack upon the others. And so they went from town to town, an army of the worst class of society attacked the towns, each town in succession, until the whole country was in a state of disorder.... The war first took place through revenge, and was then carried on through the slave trade giving them the means of carrying on that war, because they found then the profit of selling slaves which before they did not so well understand.'[8]

Several survivors of the trade of the nineteenth century gave evidence to the committee of the House of Commons, previously mentioned, in 1848. One of these was William Henry Platt, then a prosperous merchant in Sierra Leone. He came originally from the region of Benin, and was kidnapped when so small that he 'could hardly give an account of myself.... I and a friend went into a field to set traps for rice birds ... and then I was kidnapped. I think we took about three weeks to travel towards the sea, when I was embarked in one of the vessels for Brazil'. He waited for three nights on the coast and (presumably, for his account did not embrace that part of his life) was liberated by a British cruiser and taken to Sierra Leone. Platt had no desire to return to Benin, whose language he scarcely spoke by the time he gave evidence.[9]

One valuable piece of evidence derives from a slave later known as Joseph Wright who, in the 1820s, was loaded onto a ship at Lagos. Wright had been captured in the far interior and had been taken down to Lagos by canoe. 'Early in the morning', he wrote, 'we were brought to a white Portuguese for sale. After strict examination, the white man put me and some others aside. After that, they then made a bargain, how much he would take for each of us. After they were all agreed, the white man sent us into the slave fold [sic] ... [where] I was ... for about two months, with a rope around my neck. All the young boys had ropes round their necks in a row, and all the men with chains in a long row, for about fifty persons in a row, so that no one could escape without the other. At one time, the town took fire and about fifty slaves were consumed because the entry was crowded.... [Then] we were all brought down close to [the] salt water ... to be put in canoes. We were all very sorrowful in heart, because we were going to leave our land for another ... [and] we had heard that the Portuguese were going to eat us when they got to their country. . . . They began to put us in canoes to bring us to the Brig, one of the canoes drowned [*sic*] and half the slaves died. . . . They stowed all the men under the deck; the boys and women were left on the deck. . . .'[10]

Slaves were as always branded before their departure for the Americas. In this respect there was no difference between what happened in the legal, eighteenth century and the illegal, nineteenth: an iron with letters cut into it 'is put into fire on the beach, and a small pot containing palm oil is always at hand; the iron is heated, and dipped into this palm oil, and dabbed on the hip [men] or [just above] the breast [women] or wherever the slave dealer may choose to have his slaves marked. The palm oil is to prevent the flesh adhering to the iron.'[11]

Slaves bound for Brazil were still baptized before the crossing; and all continued as a rule to be examined by a doctor ('the doctor rubs them down to see if they are sound and picks out the best'), though many ships sailed without such officers: 'A respectable man would not go and a bad one would not be worth having.'[12] Sometimes, as occurred in the case of Mongo John, slaves were carefully inspected even before entering the barracoon.

As in the past, different peoples were preferred by different slavers. But in the nineteenth century, all agreed that a Kru, from the Windward Coast, made a bad slave, 'because they know that if he is enslaved he will commit suicide immediately'.[13]

As for the crossing itself, routes to and from Africa from Brazil or Cuba were more direct than they had been in the days of the triangular trade. But sometimes even Cuban shippers would stop at Bahia en route for the Bight of Benin in order to pick up that molasses-soaked tobacco which was still popular in the latter harbour. The haste with which packing was often done on the return journey sometimes caused ships to leave with inadequate water, resulting in several instances comparable to the *Zong*, with the slaves being thrown overboard.

It is improbable that before 1800 ships of only twenty-one tons burden would have been expected to carry ninety-seven human beings across the Atlantic, as was the case with the *Conceição* which reached Pernambuco in 1844. That ship's captain gave the slaves a mere fifteenth of the space thought right for a British soldier when engaged in crossing an ocean. James Bandinel, who directed the efforts of the Foreign Office in London against the slave trade for many years, agreed that the British methods of suppression did result in increased suffering by the Africans: 'In addition to the general horrible treatment, the slave traders have an additional motive, the fear of being taken, which induces them to start when their ships are half-provisioned; and . . . care is not taken of their health which was taken when the trade was allowed. . . .'[14] Commodore Sir George Collier, in HMS *Tartar* in 1821, found the slaves in the Cuban ship *Ana María* (captured in the Bonny) 'clinging to the gratings to inhale a mouthful of fresh air, and fighting with each other for a taste of water, showing their parched tongues, and pointing to their reduced stomachs, as if overcome by famine for, although the living cargo had only been completed the day before, yet many who had been longer on the boats were reduced to such a state as skeletons that I was obliged to order twelve to be immediately placed under the care of the surgeon. . . .' Four hundred and fifty slaves were discovered 'linked in shackles by the leg in pairs, some of them bound with cords; and several had their arms so lacerated by the tightness that the flesh was completely eaten through'.[15]

Very often in the nineteenth century there were no special slave decks. But men and women were always separated, the former in the hold, the latter in the cabin; the children as often as not were left on the top deck. Most slaves seem to have travelled naked.

Many other details of these voyages were the same as in the eighteenth century: the distribution of the slaves in tens at the two daily mealtimes, the washing of hands in salt water after eating, the punishment of slaves who refused to eat, the occasional distribution of brandy or tobacco, the rinsing of mouths with vinegar, the weekly shaving (without soap), the obligatory cutting of fingernails to limit damage in fights, and the daily cleaning of the decks. Then there was the systematic stowing of the slaves at night, 'those on the right side of the vessel facing forward and lying in each other's laps, while those on the left are similarly stowed with their faces towards the stern. . . . Each negro lies on his right side, which is considered preferable for the action of the heart.'[16] 'Constables' were as before chosen from 'superior slaves', and henceforth marked with a small rope or a row of beads round the neck. Sometimes billets of wood were available as pillows, the hatches and bulkheads were grated, and openings were made to give more ample circulation. Full-grown slaves seem normally to have been shackled to one another by the ankles.

Slave voyages in the nineteenth century usually took about twenty-five to thirty days between Angola and Brazil, or forty-five from the Bight of Benin or Biafra to the Caribbean; as earlier noticed, the voyage from East Africa could be far longer.

On these overcrowded ships such food and water as were available were often passed round in calabashes in the slave areas, avoiding thereby the necessity of taking the slaves up to the open decks, as had usually happened in the past. The slave merchant José Cliffe thought that in many voyages to Brazil slaves never left the hold at all.

Diseases continued to turn one out of every ten slave ships into a condition comparable to one of the most unpleasant circles in Dante's Inferno. Thus Captain Matson described finding a slave ship, the *Josefina*, after a chase of a few hours, and discovering that 'many of the slaves had confluent smallpox: the sick had been thrown into the hold in one particular spot, and they appeared on looking down to be one living mass; you could hardly tell arms from legs, or one person from another, or what they were; there were men, women, and children; it was the most horrible and disgusting heap that could be conceived'.[17]

One passenger, J. B. Romaigne, described a most surreal journey in 1819 on the 200-ton *Rôdeur* of Le Havre, a vessel owned by a merchant named Chedel, which was sailing from the River Bonny to Guadeloupe with 200 slaves. A virulent if apparently ephemeral form of ophthalmia broke out, causing most of the slaves and crew to become blind. The ship, without a helmsman, rolled about the ocean without a course and, after surviving a storm, encountered the *San León* of Spain, from whose crew they expected to gain help; but those sailors turned out also to be blind. 'At the announcement of this horrible coincidence, there was a silence among us for some moments, like that of death. It was broken by a fit of laughter, in which I joined myself and, before our awful merriment was over, we could hear, by the sound of curses which the Spaniards shouted at us, that the *San León* had drifted away. . . . She never reached any port.' Most of the crew of the *Rôdeur*, on the other hand, eventually recovered and made their way to Guadeloupe, though not before Captain Boucher threw overboard thirty-nine blind slaves.'[18]

Mortality on these slave journeys in the nineteenth century was usually lower than a hundred years before. José Cliffe thought that the average number of deaths on ships to Brazil in the 1840s might be 35 per cent. But Thomas Thomson, who spent years in Brazil, thought that figure exaggerated, and that 9 per cent was more likely – a figure which was lowered by Admiral Sir Charles Hotham to 5 per cent. In the 1840s the House of Commons published similar, though more detailed, figures for shipments to Rio, Bahia, and Havana between the 1810s and the 1840s. Their estimate was 9.1 per cent. Most vessels in the nineteenth century certainly travelled faster than their eighteenth-century equivalents, partly because of their copper-sheathed hulls. They were designed both to carry more water than their predecessors, and to catch more rainwater.

Slave captains were still ruthless if a case of smallpox was discovered and Canot described how a slave found suffering from that infirmity might be murdered at night, if it was thought that thereby the whole ship could be saved from contagion. But vaccination was already known, and seems to have been performed in Angola on most slaves after 1820.

The death rate among crews was, on the other hand, in the nineteenth century about the same as in the eighteenth: perhaps 17 per cent (malaria and yellow fever being the usual killers). But there seems to have been an improvement in the 1840s.

---

* Dr Grillé, the Duchess of Angoulême's optician, wrote a thesis on the epidemic, and the affair became public knowledge. The abolitionist Morenas pointed out that in the second edition of this work the 'jet en mer' was omitted.

There were also fewer rebellions or mutinies in the nineteenth century than in the past: first, because perhaps there were more children carried; second, because the journeys were shorter. But one of the most remarkable of all slave rebellions occurred in the mid-nineteenth century. A slave cargo was being carried west along the north coast of Cuba, from Havana to the small port of Guanajay, in a Baltimore-built vessel, 'a matchless model for speed of about 120 tons', the *Amistad*. The captain was Ramón Ferrer. The fifty-three slaves were mostly Mendes, originally from about sixty miles inland on the River Gallinas, where they had been embarked, perhaps by Pedro Blanco. The owners of the slaves, Pedro Mantes and José Ruiz, were on board. The ship was owned by a syndicate which was sending the slaves to be 'refreshed', apparently before marketing them, on one of the Bay Islands, off the coast of Honduras.*

A mulatto chef unwisely joked to the slaves, a little before they reached Guanajay, that on arrival they would all be killed and salted as meat. The wit was not appreciated. A certain Cinqué led a revolt, broke the slaves' irons, and threw captain and crew overboard. Cinqué then ordered the owners, Mantes and Ruiz, to sail the ship back to Africa, towards the rising sun. These two Cubans arranged between them to sail their ship off course at night so that after two months with water and food very short, they were able to anchor off Long Island, at Culloden Point, New York. The vessel was first held as a smuggler. The slaves were sent to jail at New Haven, and the ship was seized. The Spanish Minister in Washington demanded that both ship and merchandise be handed over to him, as provided by a treaty of 1795 between his country and the United States. But abolitionists, led by Joshua Levitt and Lewis Tappan, became apprised of the case, and a lawsuit followed. The central issue was whether the blacks had lawfully been made slaves. John Quincy Adams, the ex-President, now the serving Congressman for Massachusetts and the leading abolitionist in the House of Representatives, was persuaded to represent Cinqué and his friends, and he successfully argued before the Supreme Court that they had not lawfully been made slaves; so they were released into freedom – or, rather, to Sierra Leone. Some senators tried to have the owners indemnified, but they failed.[19]

The suppression of the mutiny on board the *Kentucky*, under Captain Fonseca in 1844, must have been the worst of many such occurrences of the century. After a rising of slaves had been suppressed, forty-six men and a woman were hanged, shot, and thrown overboard; before they were killed, 'they were . . . chained two together and, when they were hanged, a rope was put round their necks and they were drawn up to the yardarm, clear of the sail. This did not kill them, but only choked or strangled them; they were then shot in the breast, and the bodies thrown overboard. If only one of two who were ironed together was to be hung, a

---

* *See page 614 for the Bay Islands trade.*

rope was put round his neck, and he was drawn up clear of the decks, beside of the bulwark, and his leg laid across the rail, and chopped off, to save the irons. . . . The bleeding negro was then drawn up, shot in the breast and thrown overboard. The legs of about one dozen were chopped off in this way. . . . All kinds of sport were made of the business.'[20]

There were also sometimes rebellions of the crews. For example, the vessel *Céron*, owned by Gervais Rives, left Bordeaux in December 1824 under Captain Jean-Baptiste Métayer. In March 1825 the *Céron* entered the River Bonny and began to buy slaves. But the negotiation was protracted ('s'éternisa' was the graphic expression of a French historian), many seamen died, and it was not till September that the ships left Africa, with 380 slaves for Santiago de Cuba. About three-quarters of the way across the Atlantic, the crew, led by a chef who had come on board at Paimboeuf, near Nantes, attacked the officers. The captain, the second captain, the supercargo, the lieutenant, the *maître d'équipage*, the master carpenter, and one other were murdered. The ship then anchored at San Juan, Puerto Rico. Half the crew denounced the mutineers, who were arrested, but the ship then left for Danish St Thomas, where it was intercepted by a French cruiser. All the same the slaves were sold – bought, it seems, by a trader from Mayagüez, Puerto Rico.

A new dimension to the slave trade in the nineteenth century was created by the role of the British navy as a self-appointed world policeman; and to a lesser extent by the navies of the United States, France, and, in the end, even of Spain and Portugal.

The work of the naval officers responsible, as has been mentioned, was often tedious. Captain Eardley Wilmot pointed to this in a statement before a parliamentary committee in 1865: 'The incessant rolling, which is most trying, the constant rumbling of the heavy surf upon the beach which becomes tedious from its monotony, the low and uninteresting appearance of the land, all have an effect upon the best organised mind which is sometimes distressing, and we have, I grieve to say, examples of the effect of these trials in the invaliding of officers and others from mental disorganisation.'[21]

But there were also moments of exhilaration – a pleasure fully shared, it would seem, by the African traders. A British surgeon who knew both Brazil and Africa said that he thought the presence of the navy even stimulated the slave trade: 'The blacks, like other people, are fond of excitement. [The slave trade] . . . is now more a gambling transaction than it has ever been. It requires great activity and a great combination of means to effect the escape of the slaves, and of the slavers, from the coast. . . . The excitement is one of the great inducements of the natives to keep it up. . . . It is the sort of wild excitement which is most palatable to the African character. . . . All parties are kept in excitement while there is a cargo waiting. . . . The prohibition lends not only a charm to it with the Africans, but a direct stimulus' – and, he might have added, to the British navy, too.[22]

Until 1835, as has been shown, the British had no standing with respect to the activities of the citizens of Spain (with Cuba), Portugal, and Brazil, unless slaves were actually found on board the ships. If the slaves were loaded at night, the captain of a slaver could hope to escape the attention of the British navy, whose captains, learning the technique of their prey, would accordingly stand out offshore about thirty-five or forty miles when day dawned. The navy came to know, too, that 'one bright light from the shore indicated that a slaver could safely come into port; two bright lights meant not to come in'; and three such were the 'signal to run away as fast as you can'. The lookout on the masthead of such a naval ship would be promised a reward of, say, eight dollars, if a sail were sighted which proved to be that of a genuine slaver.

An especially intoxicating chase, in 1841, was that of the *Josephine*, 'the fastest slaver out of Havana', though Portuguese owned. At dawn on 30 April the British naval vessel HMS *Fantome*, Captain Butterfield (a ship designed by the naval Surveyor Sir William Symonds), sighted – off Ambriz – a strange brigantine. Butterfield gave chase and 'immediately shook out all reefs, set fore and maintop with studding sails and main royal flying jib, and went eleven knots'. By the afternoon, the mate of the *Fantome* could see the *Josephine* cutting away her anchors, and throwing a gun overboard, to lighten the ship. By nightfall, the distance between the ships was reduced to six miles. The *Fantome* was now trimmed so that every ounce of speed could be obtained: 'At 1 a.m., I took in scudding sails and main royal, and carried through a tremendous squall of wind and rain – a thing I should never have attempted in any other . . . vessel; and gallantly she went through with it. [Though] the slaver was very nearly lost, . . . the *Fantome* kept gaining on her prey by moonlight.' At dawn on 1 May, when off the island of Ana Bona (Annobon), Butterfield 'fired two shells . . . to bring the stranger to. I slackened sail as requisite. We hove to and boarded and detained the Portuguese brigantine *Josephine*, with 200 slaves. Sent Mr. W. S. Cooper, senior lieut., and eight men to navigate the prize into Sierra Leone. . . .' The two vessels had covered 240 miles in twenty-four hours.[23]

The chase by the *Rifleman* in 1849 (under Commander S. S. L. Crofton) off Brazil raised a different issue. Crofton sighted a suspicious-looking sail fifty miles south of Rio. He entered Brazilian territorial waters to give chase. The quarry was thereupon run ashore, with all sails set, as darkness fell. When the *Rifleman* reached the stranded ship, heavy seas were breaking over her. The slaver's crew had abandoned ship and left the cargo of slaves to die; some were washed overboard, others died because they had been manacled to the deck. Two midshipmen from the *Rifleman*'s boat crew remained on board the wreck, and at daybreak a hawser was brought. Hutchings, the second master of the *Rifleman*, lashed himself to the slaver's stern, and as each successive wave broke over him passed the remaining slaves one by one from the slaver to the deck of the *Rifleman* by swinging them along the hawser in a cradle. 'This tedious and dangerous service occupied the entire day.... [Thus] Commander Crofton rescued 127 Africans from death and slavery....' [*24]

Then there was the chase in 1852 of the *Venus* off Havana. It appears to have belonged to Antonio Parejo. It was thought to be the fastest ship in the slave trade at this time. But Captain Baillie Hamilton, in the *Vestal*, a fast British twenty-six-gun frigate, was in Havana Bay. The captain of the *Venus* determined to slip away while the *Vestal* was undergoing repairs. One morning, before dawn, Hamilton was onshore and told that during the night the *Venus* had sailed from Havana. Within minutes, the captain was back on board his ship. He sailed off in pursuit, the men on a nearby United States warship cheering as if a race had been engaged. Hamilton saw several ships on the horizon. He identified the *Venus* by her white colour and the spread of her canvas. The *Vestal* gained on her prey, but a tornado sprang up. The two vessels were parted. When the sky was clear again, there was no sign of the *Venus*. Hamilton assumed that her captain had sought refuge in one of the Bahama channels, perhaps hoping that those dangerous waters would deter pursuit. As Hamilton neared the shoals, he caught sight of the *Venus*, with two other vessels which he presumed were also slavers. They were trapped, but the *Vestal* could not go close, since she had a deep draft. Hamilton steered as near as he could, and fired a shot at an extreme range. He scored a hit. The master of the *Venus* hove to, and allowed a boat crew from the *Vestal* to board. Hamilton in person accompanied this boat and, putting a revolver to the head of the Spanish captain, said that he would shoot him if he did not make a course in the direction of the two other ships. He obeyed, and all three were captured, each with slave equipment. Hamilton brought all three of them back to Havana.[25]

There were also some outright naval battles. For example, the *Pickle* (with Lieutenant J. McHardy as captain), cruising in 1829 off northern Cuba, saw a heavily laden ship. He nearly reached this stranger by nightfall. No colours were hoisted even after a warning shot. As she came alongside, the *Pickle* was raked by musketry and cannon. The British crew had only one long eighteen-pounder and two eighteen-pound carronades (that is, short pieces of ordnance), whereas the Spanish ship had sixteen guns. Three British seamen were killed, eight wounded. All the same, a close battle ensued, at pistol range. After half an hour the Spaniard's mainmast fell and she surrendered, her captain and most of her crew being wounded. A prize crew was put on board. They put the Spanish crew in irons and released 350 slaves.[26]

The British sometimes suffered. For example, in 1826, HMS *Redwing* captured a Spanish schooner, the *Invencible*, with slaves in the hold. A prize

---

[*] *Neither Crofton nor Hutchings appears in the* Dictionary of National Biography, *unlike many less valiant officers.*

crew was put on board, and the ship set off for Freetown. Soon this vessel captured another slaver, a Brazilian schooner, the *Disunion*, carrying slaves from the Cameroons. But both were shortly met by a Spanish pirate and themselves seized and taken to Havana. There the slaves were sold, but the ships set adrift. The *Disunion*, with five Brazilians, eventually reached Rio. Of the *Invencible*, with her British prize crew, no more was ever heard.[27]

The case of the *Felicidade* in 1845 had a different conclusion. This Portuguese ship was captured by HMS *Wasp*, en route for Luanda, empty but equipped for slaves. The *Wasp* put a prize crew on board. Two days later, another Brazilian vessel was sighted and, when chased and captured, was identified as the *Echo*, with 400 slaves on board. The *Wasp* had been left behind, so the prize crew on the *Felicidade* sent a detachment to take over the *Echo*. The two prizes separated. The remaining British sailors on the *Felicidade* were attacked by the original Portuguese crew, who killed some and threw the rest overboard. After the *Felicidade* briefly chased the *Echo* (and her prize crew), the ships again separated. But soon HMS *Star* came up with the *Felicidade*. The latter ship was searched, and bloodstains were found on the deck. The crew confessed what had happened; Lieutenant Wilson and six men were put on the *Felicidade* to go to St Helena, recently established as the seat of a prize court. But a storm caused Wilson to abandon ship. He and his men took to a raft and were eventually rescued, after many hardships, by Commander Layton, in the *Cygnet*. Meantime, the prisoners had reached England. The judges had to decide about the 'pirates'. Did an English court of law have jurisdiction over a vessel owned by a Brazilian who had murdered an English prize crew? The assize judge found the pirates guilty of murder. There was an appeal. In the event, the men were freed and sent back to Brazil, at British cost. There was uproar in *The Times*. 'Remember the *Felicidade*' was a cry heard for many years in British naval circles.[28]

The seizure of a slaver was, of course, the occasion for a celebration: 'When you take a slaver', Captain Broadhead explained in 1843, 'you will find lashed on deck puncheons of rum and puncheons of wine, and great quantities of ham and cheeses; and you cannot expect that those men [sailors from an English naval ship] who have been cooped up for such a length of time will not break out when they get on board that vessel. . . .' (Broadhead's crew, on one voyage, included eleven men who had 'never put their foot out of the vessel in three years and a half'.)[29]

The crews of captured slave ships suffered diverse fates. They were rarely treated as fellow seamen by British naval officers, though there were some instances of their officers being admitted to mess with those who captured them. If the seizure was close to the American coast, whether Cuba or Brazil, the seamen would be handed over to the authorities there, and their punishment would be at worst a token spell – of days, not months – in a local prison: 'In the case of one prize which we took in the *Racer*', reported Dr Thomson in 1848, 'I saw the crew after they were supposed to have been put in prison; I saw several of them walking about [in Rio] and conversed with them.'[30] In 1836 Lieutenant Mercer, in the *Charybdis*, on the other hand, told a legitimate United States merchant that his orders were to 'put all [such] crews on shore and starve them'. Sometimes the crews were left for months in Sierra Leone, where they exercised 'a decidedly bad influence', it was generally agreed. On one such occasion, a group of such men – eleven slave captains and seventy-six crew – bought a vessel, the *Augusta*, which the Governor of Sierra Leone supplied with six weeks' worth of provisions, to take them to Havana. But their intention surely was to buy slaves, as another captain in a similar plight, Francisco Campo, had done, obtaining 357 slaves on the River Gallinas only nine days after leaving Sierra Leone with the *Dulcinea*, which he had bought for only £150.[31]

Sometimes these crews were left in disagreeable circumstances in the Bight of Benin or Lagos, where they had difficulty in surviving; but 'most of them no doubt very soon find a passage ... to a place where slave trading exists'. A Liverpool merchant, Robert Dawson – a kinsman of John Dawson, of Baker and Dawson, the shipbuilding firm of the 1790s – wrote with respect to this practice in May 1842: 'The natives laugh at our philanthropy, when they allude to the system of our cruisers of landing poor Spaniards on the beach without food or clothing to a certain but lingering death.'[32] Captain Bosanquet recalled that when he captured the *Marineto* in 1831 he put the crew onshore: 'Nine of them attempted to escape in three small canoes; two of the canoes were never heard of again; one of them was picked up by us after it had been fourteen days at sea; one of the men had died and, almost in a dying state, they were [all] landed at Fernando Po.' Asked whether if captains were hanged by the yardarm for trading in slaves it would be one of the 'modes of suppressing slavery', another naval officer, Captain Thompson, replied that would indeed have this effect. Most British officers thought that to treat Spanish or Portuguese crews as if they were pirates would bring the trade to an end very soon.[33]

In 1850 Captain Denman captured his first slaver off the coast of South America. He took her to Rio, but the Court of Mixed Commission there declared itself incapable of judging her, and Denman was ordered to take his prize back across the ocean to Sierra Leone. That he did, though every rope was rotten on board this 'mere wreck upon the waters', every mast was sprung, and the 500 slaves on board had already once made the Middle Passage. At Sierra Leone, Denman again failed to get the ship judged, because she was a Portuguese vessel captured south of the equator. The slaves were caused to make a third voyage across the Atlantic, back to Brazil, where the survivors were disposed of as usual.

Arrival in Brazil or Cuba was often painful. José Cliffe described how many slaves who reached Rio or Bahia were so emaciated that they could hardly walk, and had to be lifted off the ship.

Usually in the Americas the slaves were kept after their arrival in barracoons similar to those whence they had been shipped, and there fed, fattened, and treated well prior to sale. Sometimes they were held up to six months in these encampments before being sold. In Brazil these places might be remote. But in Havana the most important camps were in the city, next to the Captain-General's residence.

It was frequently necessary, off both Cuba and Brazil, for slave captains to try to confuse the British navy about where slaves would be landed. Thus catamarans might take the slaves from their ship and deliver them in small harbours along the coast. Canot reported that so far as Cuba was concerned, 'a wild, uninhabited portion of the coast, where some little bay or sheltering nook exists, is commonly selected by the captain and his confederates. As soon as the vessel is driven close to the beach and anchored, her boats are packed with slaves, while the craft is quickly dismantled to avoid detection from sea or land. The busy skiffs are hurried to and fro incessantly till the cargo is entirely ashore, when the secured gang [of slaves], led by the captain, and escorted by armed sailors, is rapidly marched to the nearest plantation. There it is safe from the rapacity of local magistrates who, if they have a chance, imitate their superiors by exacting gratifications.'[34]

A messenger would be sent to Havana or Matanzas or Santiago, where the owners would send clothes for the slaves and money for the crew. Preparations would be made through the brokers for the sale. The ship, if small, would be sent under a coasting flag to a port of clearance. If the craft was large, she might well be sunk or burned where she lay at anchor. But sometimes no concealment was necessary.

Then began the new life for the slaves, and it is fair to say that there is not much evidence that slaves wanted thereafter, in Brazil or in Cuba, to return to Africa 'and again to be made slaves and sold to someone else'. Perhaps, as William Ewart Gladstone suggested to José Cliffe in 1848, at one of the meetings of the Hutt Committee, that was 'from fear of another middle passage'.[35]

Theodore Canot argued that after the rigours of the journey the reception of the slave at the plantation in Cuba must have seemed as if it were an arrival at paradise. The slave was often 'amazed', he thought, 'by the generosity with which he is fed with fruit and fresh provisions. His new clothes, red cap, and roasting blanket ... strike him dumb with delight. . . . The climax of wonder is reached when that paragon of oddities, a Cuban postillion [a slave, of course], dressed in his sky-blue coat, silver-laced hat, white breeches, polished jackboots and ringing spurs, leaps from his prancing quadruped and bids them welcome in their mother tongue.'[36] All the same, the expectation of life of a slave as a picker of coffee or a cutter of sugar cane in Brazil in the 1840s would not have been more than eight years.

*

Profits in the nineteenth century were greater than they had been in the eighteenth. Rossel and Boudet's the *Cultivateur* of Nantes in 1815 cost just under 600,000 francs to fit out, and the sale of about 500 slaves brought 1,236,200 colonial livres: say, 1,100,000 francs, a profit of 83 per cent. José Cliffe, a North American who had a long experience of the Brazilian trade, told a committee in London that his transactions in the slave trade in the 1830s or 1840s, 'were very profitable'. It was, he said, 'the most lucrative trade now under the sun'. Lord John Russell, Prime Minister in London in the late 1840s, looking at the figures presented to a House of Commons select committee, said that a cargo of slaves which cost 5,000 dollars on the coast of Africa might sell in Brazil for 25,000: a profit of 400 per cent. Canot gave a figure of costs which showed that his vessel, the *Fortuna*, carrying to Matanzas 217 slaves which he bought for 200,000 cigars and 50 ounces of Mexican gold (costing about 11,000 dollars), made a profit in 1827 of over $40,000.

To examine the matter in greater detail: in 1848, a United States built slave ship of, say, 180–200 tons, a reasonable average, plying between Brazil and Africa and bringing back slaves, might cost £1,500. The owner would have to pay about twenty seamen one hundred Spanish dollars a trip – say, £416. Food for those men for ninety days would cost £90. The captain would be paid 400 Spanish dollars: another £83. Food (and medicine) for 450 slaves might cost three pence a day per slave if the food were 'flour', which it usually was: another £169. Luxuries for the captain and other contingencies (water casks, wood for the slave deck, etc.) might cost another £300. Slaves would cost about an average of £4-10s in Africa – whether paid for in specie or in trade goods – £2,025 in all. The outlay, therefore, might be a little more than £4,500. Perhaps fifty slaves would die en route. But the sale of 410 slaves at £45 each would bring the merchant £18,450, or a profit for the voyage, therefore, of just under £14,000. Even if every other ship were captured by the British, there would still be a 100 per cent profit. These figures were, of course, considerably higher than those in the era of legitimate trade.[37]

Another estimate was worked out by Edward Cardwell, the future reformer of the British army (himself the son of a merchant of Liverpool), in conversation with Admiral Hotham in 1849: 'An adventure of this kind' would yield 'upon the average profit of £45-10s upon an outlay of £14-10s.'[38] Captain Drake said that on one voyage – on the *Napoleon*, a Baltimore clipper of ninety tons, carrying 350 slaves in 1835 – the profits were about $100,000 (the price of the slaves being $16 a head, the costs totalling $20,000, and the sales in Havana yielding $360 a head).[39] Consul Crawford thought in Havana that one successful slave voyage would pay the costs of the loss of ten empty or five laden slavers. He thought that a ship whose costs were $150,000 could expect to make nearly $400,000 if the slaves could be sold for $1,200 each, a profit of 166%. Another estimate, using Crawford's figures but reducing the average price of slaves in Havana to $500, would have, all the same, produced a profit of 53 per cent.[40]

Still, many of the biggest merchants carrying slaves in the illegal era, either to Cuba or to Brazil, seem, unless they invested in sugar or coffee plantations, to have gone bankrupt. The British Commissary Judge in Havana commented in 1849: 'The profits of the trade are much over-stated. All persons are apt to boast much of their gains, but the slave traders more especially, as a triumph over the cruisers, and even the Government of England, as well as to console themselves for the discredit they could not but feel attached to their trade. Thus we hear of a few fortunate individuals who . . . formerly amassed fortunes in it, but of the many who have lost fortunes and life in it we hear but little. . . . the trade has not recently been a productive one. One proof of this is that the insurance offices lost so much on the policies of slave trade vessels that it is nearly ten years since they resolved to take none of them on any terms. . . .'[41]

The profits above-mentioned might have to be abbreviated a little, because they do not take into account the necessary bribes to local police and other officials at the point of landing: even to the Governor of the province and, in Cuba, the Captain-General.

The benefits to the seamen explain their interest. Most seamen in those days were able to buy a slave of their own. The sailor would have to contribute to that slave's cost while crossing the Atlantic. But, assuming that the slave lived, every seaman might be able in, say, 1848 to make a clear profit of £30 or £35: a good sum for a Brazilian sailor.

34

CAN WE RESIST THE TORRENT?
I THINK NOT

The Brazilian Foreign Minister Soares de Souza proposing the end
of the slave trade in the Brazilian Chamber of Deputies, 1850

THE 1840S SAW THE RETURN of the United States as an international combatant against the slave trade. For President Van Buren's decision to revive the United States naval patrol led to the reappearance of Matthew Perry on the African coast (where he had been in the 1820s), with the sloop-of-war *Saratoga* and four other vessels. Perry was a bad choice as commander. He was a native of Rhode Island, connected to the de Wolfs by marriage, and so inclined to be favourable to the commerce in slaves on which his state's prosperity had been partly built. He had turned a blind eye to the evidence of slave trading on his previous tour of duty in Africa; and he was almost as keen to prevent ships with United States flags from being inspected by the British as he was to abolish the slave trade. Moreover, he established his base in the Cape Verde Islands which, though healthy, and full of men experienced in the slave trade, were far indeed from the then centres of the traffic in the Bight of Benin and the Congo. Occasionally his frigates were even further away, at Madeira. Perry's enthusiasm for putting down the slave traffic was modest: he even wrote on 5 September 1843 to the Virginian Secretary of the Navy Abel Parker Upshur (he supported slavery and disliked England): 'I cannot hear of any American vessels being engaged in the transportation of slaves; nor do I believe there has been one so engaged for several years.'[1] These United States naval vessels were not concerned with any equipment clauses with respect to the slave traffic, and indeed their main task was to protect trade – as was made clear by an order of Secretary of the Navy John Mason to Perry's successor, Admiral Charles Skinner: 'The rights of our citizens engaged in lawful commerce are under the protection of our flag. And it is the chief purpose, as well as the chief duty of our naval power, to see that those rights are not improperly abridged.'[2]

Still, after a while, slave ships began to be seized by United States naval vessels. One such was the 350-ton barque *Pons*, with 896 slaves on board, which in 1845 the *Yorktown* took from Cabinda to Liberia. In 1846 Lieutenant Bisham, in the *Boxer*, seized the Boston ship *Málaga* (under Captain Charles Lovett, owned by Josiah Lovett, Elliot Woodbury, and Seward Lee), also in Cabinda Bay, as an auxiliary to the slave trade. The *Málaga* was sent home to Boston. But the criminal case against it was abandoned, since there was no proof of slaving; indeed, auxiliaries never carried slaves. Bisham also seized the *Senator* but released her. She went on to take on board 900 slaves, of which 300 died. Bisham was later sued by the owners of the *Málaga* for false arrest.

The naval officers were upset. What incentive was there for the energetic pursuit of justice if at the end of a dangerous journey and a slave trader was finally seized, they were, if the case faltered, to be faced with the possibility of damage for false arrest? That anxiety continued. When, as late as 1860, Lieutenant William Le Roy, in the USS *Mystic*, seized a suspicious New York brig, he declared as a preliminary that should his 'expectations not be realized, I most earnestly hope the court will find the cause of supposition sufficiently strong to relieve me of all claims of damage etc. . . . '

Despite these impediments, the patrolling continued. Thus in 1848 Lieutenant O. H. Berryman, in the *Onkahye*, seized the US whaler *Laurens* as a slaver, just outside Brazilian waters, on the evidence of her first mate. Lieutenant Commander William W. Hunter, in the US steamer *Allegheny*, seized the *Louisa*, of Philadelphia, Captain Joseph Souder, but could not prove that she was a slaver. Then he seized the *Juliet*, 138 tons, from Portland, Maine, Captain Nathaniel Gordon, son of a respectable seagoing family, but again Hunter could find no 'equipment'. But subsequently she sailed across the Atlantic, and there were rumours, almost certainly true in view of the later history of Captain Gordon,* that she carried slaves back, though not to Rio. In all, twenty-eight slave ships were seized by the United States Navy between 1844 and 1854.

Perry was succeeded by Admiral Skinner in 1844, and he by Captain Andrew Hull Foote in 1849. As a Temperance captain, Foote was responsible for abolishing the liquor ration in the United States Navy, not the slave trade.† He sought good relations with Britain, but the inferior size of his squadron prevented joint cruising, and he no doubt agreed with a subordinate who wrote: 'It is the policy of the English ship-masters to represent the Americans as engaged in the slave trade; . . . if, by such accusations, they can induce British or American men of war to detain and examine the fair trader, they thus rid themselves of troublesome rivals.'[3]

As for British cooperation with France, in 1845 the latter country at last agreed to establish twenty-six cruisers between the Cape Verde

---

* See page 774.
† He was known as a rigid disciplinarian and once delivered a sermon in a church in Cairo on the text 'Ye believe in God; believe also in me'.

Islands and 16°30′S (approximately the Bay of Dos Tigres, in southern Angola), provided that Britain did the same. British ships were still not permitted to search ships flying the French flag even if their captains' suspicions about the real identity of a vessel were aroused. The French too would continue to limit themselves, insofar as power of capture was concerned, to ships flying their own flag and ships with no flag, and they would not seek any authority to interfere with Spanish, Portuguese, and Brazilian ships: 'The effect of the French squadron', Palmerston said, 'is more to prevent than to capture; they effectively prevent any slave trade under the French flag.'[4]

Still, it seemed in 1845 that at last an international force against the slave trade was in being. Britain had over thirty ships engaged in the naval patrol, and France had twenty-eight. North American ships numbered three to eight, and even the Portuguese had nine. Neither Brazil nor Spain were making any contribution to the naval patrol. But there were in the late 1840s some sixty ships of other nationalities off Africa: a formidable challenge to the traffic in slaves.

Nevertheless, imaginative slave captains continued to make fun of this parade of an international police. One who did so was a United States shipbuilder, Joshua Clapp, from New York, who first came to public notice in 1845 when he was tried in his home city but acquitted for taking a ship of his own, the *Panther*, to buy slaves in Africa. He then removed to Rio, where he bought two full-rigged ships, three barques, three brigs, and two schooners, several of which he had himself built. In reality these ships belonged to Brazilians, but Clapp was the formal proprietor. About half the vessels bringing slaves to Brazil were in the 1840s thus owned by citizens of the United States. George Profitt, United States Minister in Rio, reported in 1844 that the trade 'is almost entirely carried out under our flag, in American-built vessels'.[5] In 1850 Congress demanded a report from the executive about illegal searches; the report, signed by President Fillmore, stated that of ten United States vessels recently (illegally) inspected by the British nine were in fact slavers.

In 1842 Britain arranged that a new equipment clause should be introduced into yet another anti-slave-trade act in respect of Portugal. Echoing the earlier convention made between Britain and Spain on the same subject, it permitted search on the high seas, 'provided it was carried out in the mildest manner'. The Brazilian Parliament debated the matter. That chamber was against all recent British anti-slave measures. A fine speech was, however, made by Antônio Carlos de Andrada, a younger brother of that José Bonifácio who, as Prime Minister, had opposed the slave trade in the 1820s: 'I am an enemy of the traffic in slaves. I see in this commerce all possible evils, an attack on Christianity, on humanity, and on the true interests of Brazil. . . . This commerce is carried on for the benefit of one race, is anti-Christian, and I do not believe that man was born for slavery. I believe that the blacks, the mulattos, the greens, if there are any, are quite as good as we are.'[6] But even Andrada disliked the high-handed way in which Britain had imposed her laws on Brazil, and abhorred the idea of British action off the Brazilian coast.

Aberdeen's new Brazil (Slave Trade) Bill only received the royal assent in England after long debates in Parliament. It seemed necessary to the government, since the Anglo-Portuguese Treaty of 1817 abolishing the trade in 1831 fell into desuetude in 1845: unless something were done, Britain would have no legal basis on which to arrest any Brazilian ships. But Brazil would not allow a new treaty. So Aberdeen's bill declared unilaterally that the British navy now had the right to seize pirates, on the ground that Brazil herself had once accepted that the trade constituted piracy. Any vessel which was apprehended would be tried by British Admiralty courts, not the Mixed Commissions set up under the treaty of 1826. It was a harsher document than any which Britain had passed, or would pass, in relation to Spain, even if it had more respect for the façade of legality than Palmerston's act had had. Even Joaquim Nabuco, the statesman who was becoming leader of the Brazilian anti-slavery movement, described Aberdeen's new bill as 'an insult to our dignity as an independent people'.

Aberdeen received an official protest ten pages long from his counterpart, Limpo d'Abreu: was it not a principle of international law that ships of one state could not in peacetime search the ships of another? Unless, of course, the right were specifically conceded by both sides. The treaty of 1817 might have given Britain such a right, but that convention had by then expired. The treaty of 1826 obliged Brazil, but only Brazil, to treat her slave traders as pirates. Britain had nothing to do with the matter. That treaty to had anyway lapsed, and no one in Brazil would make any effort to renew it. The court at Rio was also wound up in 1845. It seemed, therefore, in the middle of the 1840s, that all Britain's efforts were being made to seem pointless.[7]

Abreu soon fell, but his successor, Cavalcanti, an aristocrat from one of Brazil's oldest families, told the British Chargé: 'You cannot expect us to assist England or consent to stop the trade while you are seizing Brazilian vessels, insulting our flag, and illegally condemning them.' So Brazil refused to negotiate while Aberdeen's act remained law and rejected British terms for a new treaty.

In the meantime, the trade in these years to Brazil exceeded previous records, most of the slaves being disposed of to the coffee and sugar plantations now stretching along the 200 miles south of Rio. 'All the appliances of this trade were brought to a peak of perfection which is astonishing and which nothing but the immense profit can explain', Lord Howden, the British Minister in Rio, wrote in the late 1840s. The slave merchants now made careful studies of manoeuvres of the British fleet in Africa, they devised decoys, and they brought fast new steamers into use (including, apparently, some of 'the best that England could manufacture', as 'Hurry'

Hudson observed when he was British Minister in Rio). The British government's records suggested that there were over 3,000 slave voyages to
Brazil between 1821 and 1843.[8] A British merchant living in Brazil reflected
in 1846 that Brazil was comparable to the British West Indies a generation
before: 'Scarcely an individual exists', he wrote, 'who either directly or indirectly is not personally interested in the support of the slave system, and
who would not look with the utmost distrust upon any change. . . .'[9]

There was some United States navy activity off Brazil. A small force
had been stationed there to deal with the matter of slaving under the
United States flag. But it was inadequate. The cruisers were too large to
surprise Brazilians landing slaves in small ships. The volatile United
States Minister, the Virginian Henry Wise, discovered a United States
vessel, the *Porpoise*, in the harbour of Rio. A man 'far gone in chivalry',
Wise had been defender of slavery when a member of the House of
Representatives; and he would, in 1859, as the Governor of his state, both
praise and hang John Brown, after the attack on Harpers Ferry. Now,
despising Brazilians more than he hated abolitionists, he was an improbable but effective ally of the British in the campaign against the trade in
slaves. The *Porpoise* had not actually been a slaver but had been an auxiliary to the trade, carrying to Africa cargoes needed for the purchase of
slaves but not bringing back captives herself. Wise asked the Brazilian
authorities to arrest four United States citizens on the ship so that they
could be sent to North America for trial. While waiting for a reply, he
went on board himself and instituted a United States guard at the
gangway. No one could land, not even Brazilians. There was outrage in
the city, the Brazilian naval authorities threatened to seize the *Porpoise*,
and Wise abandoned the prize. He sent home a dispatch: 'I beseech – I
implore the President . . . to take a decided stand on this subject. You have
no idea of the effrontery and the flagrant outrages of the African slave
trade and of the shameless manner in which its worst crimes are licensed
here. . . . Every patriot . . . would blush for our country did he know and
see how our citizens sail and sell our flag to the uses and abuses of that
accursed traffic. . . . We are a byword among nations . . . the only people
who can fetch and carry . . . everything for the slave trade.' But all he
received was a reprimand for exceeding his instructions.[10]

The fact was, as the Minister in Rio told Palmerston (Foreign Secretary in London again, after the fall of the Tory government in June 1846):
'Brazil [still] lives upon slave labour. The government is carried on by the
daily receipts of the Customs Houses. Foreign trade depends upon
exports, and they cannot be obtained at present, unless by that most
expensive of all systems of production, the labour of the slave.'[11] The
United States Consul in Rio, for his part, wrote in 1847: 'The slave power
in this country is extremely great, and a consul doing his duty needs to be
kindly and effectually supported at home. In the case of the *Fame*, where
the vessel was diverted from the business intended by her owners, and

employed in the slave trade . . . I sent home two mates . . . for trial, the first mate to Norfolk [Virginia], the second mate to Philadelphia. What was done with the first mate I know not. In the case of the man sent to Philadelphia, Mr Commissioner Kane states that a clear *prima facie* case is made out, and then holds him in bail in the sum of $1,000 which would be paid by any slave trader in Rio . . . !'[12]

Most Brazilians, their ancestors having used African slaves for 300 years, still thought of slavery as part of the natural order of things. In this they were in agreement with the slave owners of the South of the United States. Brazilian entrepreneurs, however, also believed that people of Portuguese stock were the European colonizers who had 'best succeeded in fraternising with the so-called inferior races', through manumission and sexual liberty. 'Slothful but filled to overflowing with sexual concerns', the greatest of Brazilian historians, Gilberto Freyre, wrote, 'the life of the sugar-planter tended to become a life which was lived in a hammock: a stationary hammock, with the master taking his ease, sleeping, dozing. Or a hammock on the move with the master on a journey . . . or, a squeaking hammock, with the master copulating in it. The master did not have to leave his hammock to give orders to his negroes.'[13]

Slave traders continued to seem the 'nabobs of the Brazils. . . . They form the dazzling class of the *parvenu* millionaires', declared a British naval surgeon. In 1846 Henry Wise wrote to James Buchanan, then Secretary of State, a 'northern man with southern principles': 'There are only three ways of making a fortune in Brazil, either by the slave trade, or by planting, or by a coffee commission house. . . . The slave traders then are either the men in power, or those who lend to the men in power and so hold them by the purse strings. Thus the government is itself in fact a slave trading government, against its own laws. . . .'[14] Immensely rich merchants, such as Manuel Pinto da Fonseca or José Bernardino da Sá, whose main concerns were slaving, dominated Brazilian society. They were the chief capitalists of the country as well as the chief providers of labour. They alone could easily provide loans and mortgages. The Foreign Minister, Barão de Cairu, told the British Minister in January 1847, with astonishing frankness, that he could not see how any government of Brazil could enforce the law of 1831, or indeed any other such law: 'I know of none who could do it or attempt it and, when ninety-nine men in every hundred are engaged in it [the trade in slaves], how is it [abolition] to be done? . . . The vice [of trading slaves] has eaten into the very core of society. Who is so sought after, so feasted in this city as Manuel Pinto [da Fonseca]? You know him to be the great slave trader par excellence of Rio. Yet he and scores of minor slave dealers go to court – sit at the tables of the wealthiest and most respectable citizens – have seats in the Chamber as our representatives, and have a voice even in the Council of State. They are increasing in vigilance, perseverance, audacity. . . .

What they touch turns to gold. . . . You know my individual abhorrence of this cursed traffic – but . . . what am I to do? . . . I cannot be *the* man in Brazil from whom all his countrymen would turn away in contempt and aversion. I will not bell the cat. . . .'[15]

Given that the slave trade to Cuba was no less prosperous than that to Brazil, questions began to be asked again in Britain as to how long Palmerston's 'benevolent crotchet for patrolling the coasts of Africa and Brazil' (John Bright's expression) was to last. Though the arguments of Joseph Sturge and Thomas Fowell Buxton against naval patrolling had not made much headway, a new, original, more powerful opposition was now taking shape. This was the Free Trade group in Parliament, led by William Hutt, Member for Gateshead, supported by Richard Cobden, John Bright, and Gladstone; the first two had close connections with Manchester, the latter had been brought up in Liverpool.˙ These Free Traders had allies in the Whig Cabinet in the shape of the third Earl Grey, Colonial Secretary in the late 1840s and a critic of Palmerston.

Hutt and his friends disliked the threat of force implicit in Britain's anti-slavery policy. They thought that Palmerston's menaces to Brazil over the slave trade were ruining Britain's long-term trading interests: no good cause was worth the trouble if it damaged trade. They also thought the naval patrol too expensive. Hutt called the West Africa Squadron 'buccaneers', and denounced Britain's 'blundering and ignorant humanity'. Not only, he declared, had Britain failed to suppress the slave traffic, but it was growing (180,000 slaves were being exported a year, in his opinion, rather than the Foreign Office's figure of 36,758: a discrepancy characteristic of such estimates in that era of illegal trade). Nor, he thought, could the country afford the cost of the naval detachment off Africa; that expense was serious, since 'England is annually weeded of her best and bravest in order to carry on this idle and mischievous project of stopping the slave trade'. Hutt argued that quarrelling with such good commercial partners as France and the United States over the right of search was threatening the peace of the world; and that 'our unavailing attempts to suppress the traffic worsened the lot of the slaves by making the misery of the Middle Passage worse than ever'. He also pointed out that merely during the previous five years the cost in wages of the naval operations against slavery had totalled £655,000, that of the Mixed Courts had mounted up to £103,000, while 385 sailors had died on the coast or had been killed in action.[16]

Cobden, the great Free Trader, who lived in Cottonopolis – Manchester – put the matter even more brutally: what moral right had

---

˙ *Gladstone's father, John Gladstone, had bought sugar estates in the West Indies after 1815, principally in Guiana, but owned also two plantations, Holland and Lacovia, in Jamaica. He had over half his fortune invested in the West Indies in the 1830s and had 1,000 slaves at the time of emancipation in 1833.*

the English, the largest sellers of textiles to Brazil, made from slave-grown cotton, to refuse to take slave-grown sugar in return? The government, he and his friends thought, was merely advocating 'lucrative humanity'. Did not British firms sell three-eighths of the sugar, half the coffee, and as much as five-eighths of the cotton exported from Brazil?[17] In 1845 another voice was heard: that of Macaulay, the Whig historian, who had distanced himself from his father Zachary's concerns, and who believed that his obligations 'in respect to negro slavery had ceased when slavery itself ceased in that part of the world for the welfare of which I, as a member of this House, am accountable'. He insisted on the hypocrisy of importing, for refining and re-exporting, Brazilian sugar: 'We import the accursed thing; we bond it; we employ our skill and machinery to render it more alluring to the eye and to the palate; we export it to Leghorn and to Hamburg; we send it to all the coffee houses of Italy and Germany; we pocket a profit on all this; and then, we put on a pharisaical air, and thank God that we are not like those sinful Italians and Germans, who have no scruple about swallowing slave-grown sugar. . . .'[18]

The complexity of these matters was seen in 1846, when the British government followed its repeal of the Corn Laws by a similar revision of the law imposing duties on foreign-grown sugar. This was, of course, an encouragement to the sugar producers of both Brazil and Cuba: Captain Matson, the determined naval officer who had destroyed the barracoons in Cabinda, was by chance in Havana Bay on patrol at that time. He observed sharply how the price of slaves rose in consequence by 15 per cent.

Free Trade created difficulties for British abolitionists. The Sugar Duty Act, passed in 1846, seemed to *The Anti-Slavery Reporter*, the journal of Buxton and Sturge's British and Foreign Anti-Slavery Society, to be causing the House of Commons to vote for the entry of the 'blood stained sugars of Brazil and Cuba'. Year after year these idealists, such as Sir Edward Noël Buxton, would introduce motions in Parliament to reinstate the sugar duties at least against Brazil and Cuba. Year after year, they would be defeated; and the cause evaporated. The affair was the occasion for eloquence, if not action.* Disraeli's hero in the debates against the Corn Laws in 1846, Lord George Bentinck, thought that it would cost far less to seize Cuba than to maintain the naval squadron, 'paying ourselves thereby . . . a just debt.'[19] (This speech may have had an influence on the United States Secretary of State Buchanan when a little later he made an offer to Spain to buy Cuba.)

The late 1840s were thus a conflicting time: questions were being raised about a major item of British government policy which had been supported by both parties since 1808. Palmerston and the Whigs had always supported abolition. But now they were helping slave-grown

---

* It was after a successful oration on sugar duties, in July 1845, that Peel remarked to the orator: 'A wonderful speech, Gladstone.'

sugar. At the same time, Quakers, who had done so much to inspire the Anti-Slavery Society, were, with pacifist arguments, deploring the use of force, such as that used by Captain Denman on the River Gallinas, and Captain Matson in Cabinda. Another difficulty was seen in the divisions of opinion within the British navy: was close blockade or distant cruising more effective?

In March 1845 the first of the apostles of abolition, Clarkson, then aged eighty-five, with the great prize of the international abolition of the slave trade still beyond his grasp, presented Lord Aberdeen with a memorandum arguing that Britain would never have the resources adequate to patrol all the potential areas of slaving. Nor was there hope of negotiating anti-slave-trade treaties with all the powers concerned; were it to be done, some countries would have bad faith, and 'the cunning, fraud and audacity of slave dealers', with their fast ships, would always outmanoeuvre the navy. So why did not the government turn its attention to slavery itself?[20]

Aberdeen was unconvinced: he, as well as Peel, Palmerston, and Lord John Russell, Foreign Secretary and Prime Minister after 1846, still believed that the trade should be dealt with first. Palmerston, indeed, had always considered that slavery raised an issue of property which was more difficult to resolve than the trade, which he saw as iniquitous.* Russell told the radical Free Traders that Britain 'would have no right to further blessings from God' if 'this high and holy work', the naval patrol, were to be abandoned without success. Yet Gladstone, still a Conservative, said that 'it was not an ordinance of providence that the government of one nation should correct the morals of another and that it was impracticable to try and put down a great branch of commerce'.[21] Others pessimistically asked: how could the British navy hope to intercept such fast ships as the *Dois Amigos*, which carried 1,350 slaves to Bahia in 1846, or the *Audorinha*, a yacht of eighty tons belonging to Joaquim Pereira Marinho, which made a brilliant series of eight voyages between October 1846 and September 1848, bringing nearly 4,000 slaves, and earning £40,000? Was Britain ready to go to war with her oldest ally, Portugal, as well as with her newest protégé, Brazil, over the issue of the slave trade, as it was argued might be necessary by John Hook (Commissary Judge in Freetown), by James Bandinel of the Foreign Office's Slavery Department (he talked of 'redress by force of arms'), and even by Sir Charles Hotham, the new commander of the West Africa Squadron, who spoke of the existing slave-trade patrols as 'perfectly futile'? James Hudson, the Minister to Brazil, suggested that there should be a general blockade of Rio ('No port in the world is so capable of being blockaded as Rio'). Palmerston and Russell also toyed with blockade. But the British Cabinet

---

* In 1843, it had been, however, forbidden for a British subject to own slaves anywhere in the world.

was against the heavy deployment of force, even in favour of what Palmerston amiably described as 'the common principles of humanity and the fundamental precepts of the Christian religion'. (That statesman had recently told the British Consul in Zanzibar to 'take every opportunity of impressing on the Arabs that the nations of Europe are destined to put an end to the African slave trade and that Great Britain is the main instrument of Providence for the accomplishment of this purpose.')[22]

Palmerston himself was more hostile than ever to the slave trade. When out of office he had told the House of Commons in 1844, with some hyperbole: 'If all the crimes which the human race has committed from the creation down to the present day were added together in one vast aggregate, they would scarcely equal . . . the amount of guilt which has been incurred by mankind in connection with this diabolical slave trade. . . .' One of his biographers looked on this speech as the greatest of his life, though most of the details which he recounted had figured in speeches by Wilberforce and others in the 1790s.[23]

In 1847, when again Foreign Secretary, Palmerston returned to his most bellicose stance and told the Admiralty that the commander of the West Africa Squadron, Sir Charles Hotham, 'ought to be instructed to compel king Pepple and the chiefs of Bonny by force, if necessary, to respect the lives and property of Her Majesty's subjects, and that the Commodore will be justified in enforcing the payment of debts due to British subjects'. This was not at first sight a matter of slave-trade politics but it undoubtedly was under the surface. For Hotham instructed one of his captains, Commander Birch, to overthrow the Chief Priest, Awanta. Regardless of King Pepple, Birch did as asked, and imprisoned Awanta on a man-of-war. Lord Grey, in the Colonial Office, suggested that the priest should be set onshore as far as possible from Bonny, 'leaving him to take his chance'. That Whig policy of extreme laissez-faire was carried out, Awanta was landed alone in a remote part of Angola, and no more was heard of him. Soon after, Birch imposed a new treaty on Pepple, by which that king guaranteed to afford protection to British subjects in Bonny, and to accept a new version of the slave treaty concluded in 1839.[24]

The Foreign Secretary was heartened by the long-delayed decision in February 1848 in a trial before the High Court in favour of Captain Denman against the Spanish slave merchant José Antonio Burón, who was convicted of being a criminal by the terms of his own country's laws. (Burón had been one of those who had lost property, slaves, and trade goods during Denman's attack on the barracoons on the River Gallinas. He had sued Denman for £180,000. Not without difficulty, Denman arranged to be defended by the government.)

But Palmerston was still under attack from the Free Traders: William Hutt returned in February 1848 to denounce again 'our darling and hopeless project' (that is, the naval squadron) by moving in the House of Commons that a new select committee should consider the best means

Above: Slaves in a mine in Hispaniola, in the sixteenth century. The pursuit of gold on this Spanish island led to the traffic in slaves

Right: A black slave in sixteenth-century Spain depicted by Christopher Weiditz

Slaves as servants: with a lady of quality in Brazil

1. Negre qui gjambe le tabac.
2. Negre qui torque le tabac.
3. Negre qui le met en rolle.
4. Tabac a la pente.

Slaves at work on a tobacco farm in Virginia

Above: Slaves on
a sugar plantation
in Antigua

Right: Slaves in
a diamond mine
in Brazil

Shipping sugar from Antigua *c.* 1823

Profits from sugar and slaves allowed successful merchants, such as
Richard Oswald, to commission houses such as Auchincruive, Ayr,
built by the Adam brothers

Thomas Clarkson of Cambridge, who devoted his life to gathering material about the slave trade (*c.* 1785)

Montesquieu, who
mocked the slave trade
in his *L'Esprit des Lois* and
inspired two generations
of abolitionists (*c.* 1748)

William Wilberforce,
who led the parliamentary
fight for the abolition
of the slave trade by
Britain from 1789 to 1807

Right: Lord Palmerston, who devoted his zeal to seeking the international abolition of the traffic in slaves

Below: The meeting in Exeter Hall, London, 1840, where 'the great and the good' of Britain show themselves converted to abolition. The Prince Consort in the chair

Left: Cánovas del Castillo, who introduced a bill into the Spanish Cortes (1867) abolishing the Spanish slave trade

Right: This picture designed by Josiah Wedgwood, *c*. 1790, was the symbol of the abolitionists

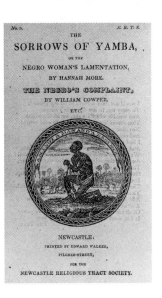

ENDPIECE

Equiano: a slave who lived to tell the tale *c*. 1793

of suppressing the trade. The motion was carried, and Hutt himself was the Chairman. Gladstone, the Free Trader Cobden, and Monckton Milnes were members.

Many witnesses were interviewed. Sir Charles Hotham, for instance, admitted that if the trade were stopped in one place it would be likely to break out again, like an epidemic, in another. There was also Thomas Tobin, the main Liverpool trader in palm oil, who had happy memories of his old days in the slave trade. The committee listened to an ex-slave merchant, José Cliffe. They heard the dynamic Macgregor Laird insist that the solution for Africa was to arrange voluntary emigration of Africans to the British West Indies, with free return passages available. James Bandinel, by then in retirement but for so long head of the Foreign Office's Slavery Department, admitted that the naval patrol had in no way diminished the traffic. The committee heard how the naval patrol had, in the opinion of several witnesses, interrupted legitimate trade, by wrongly accusing certain ships of preparing to slave (for example, the brig *Guiana*, wrongly held in 1840; or the *Lady Sale*, in 1845). They heard Commander O'Bryen Hoare explain that the Consul in Bahia had told him in 1844 on no account to land at that port, since $3,000 had been offered to anyone who would murder him, as a member of the naval patrol; he went on to suggest that, in the interests of the slaves, the slave trade should be legalized to Cuba and to Brazil, and the patrol withdrawn! Above all, they heard reports of naval officers who had spent months on the West African coast, watching for slavers, risking their lives, through ill health more than enemy action; and they familiarized themselves quickly, as politicians can, with the names of a hundred inlets, sandbars, creeks, and slaving islands. The committee also received a great quantity of papers, of the greatest interest to historians even if they exhausted the members. For example, there was the Foreign Office's remarkable list of slavers which apparently delivered slaves between 1817 (the legal abolition of the Spanish slave trade) and 1845: and the committee even heard the evidence of one-time slaves, such as James Frazer, who brought the reality of enslavement home to the legislators as they sat calmly in the new Palace of Westminster.[25]

Ultimately, in 1849, the committee produced a negative report: it insisted that the navy had no hope of stopping the trade, that the sufferings of the slaves were indeed increased by the navy's activities, that the price of slaves was lower than ever in Africa, and that the size of the African slave trade was still determined by the European desire for sugar.

In consequence of this, Hutt urged the House of Commons in March 1850 to demand the withdrawal of the West Africa Squadron. One member, Mr Baillie, argued that it was hypocritical to claim a moral purpose in British policy. Gladstone thought: 'If we really felt it our duty to cut down the slave trade at all costs, we should repeal the Sugar Duties Act, persuade America and France to allow us to search their ships, double the strength of our naval squadron, and be ruthless in using force against Spain and Brazil.'[26]

This heated debate in the House of Commons would probably have been lost by the supporters of the West Africa Squadron had it not been for the eloquent advocacy of the Prime Minister, Lord John Russell, who said: 'It appears . . . to me . . . that if we give up this high and holy work, and proclaim ourselves to be no longer fitted to lead in the championship against the curse and the crime of slavery, we have no longer a right to expect a continuance of those blessings which, by God's favour, we have so long enjoyed. I think . . . that the high, the moral and the Christian character of this nation is the main source and secret of its strength.' It was no doubt the right line to take in reply to Gladstone, who had spoken just before. The motion was defeated by 232 to 154.[27] Still, an internal report by the Admiralty of later the same year was as pessimistic as the Hutt Committee's had been, even though the navy had intercepted 625 vessels on suspicion of being engaged in the slave trade between 1840 and 1848: nearly 70 a year on average. Of these, 578 had been condemned, and over 38,000 slaves had been freed.

Sir Charles Hotham had, meantime, returned to the River Gallinas. Once again a British force, this time led by Captain Hugh Dunlop, entered the murderous estuary and established itself on an island there, just as Captain Denman had done ten years before. Hotham was determined to finish with the slave traders of this waterway. He believed that he could do that by ensuring that the Africans supported him more firmly than they had Denman. He would ensure this, or so he persuaded himself, by a mixture of threats and promises of a subsidy. He knew that Palmerston would support him. So a British force destroyed barracoons (including those of a Spaniard, Víctor de Bareda), liberated slaves, and browbeat the local African leaders to admit the error of their ways. Hotham accompanied this by declaring a blockade of the whole stretch of land. He acted, he reported to the Admiralty in London, with the backing of both the United States and French patrol commanders. Neither Hotham nor the navy received instructions to desist. The Spanish or Portuguese-Brazilian merchants were, on the contrary, ordered to leave by the local kings, bowing at last to this indication of British resolve. The merchants concerned were found requesting permission to leave for Brazil. Indeed, they chartered a boat for that purpose and set off for Rio. Captain Dunlop described how he received fifty-five slave merchants and their assistants on his ship – four Spaniards, the rest Portuguese – 'in a miserable plight, exhausted from bad living. . . . Many of them came on board with nothing but their shirts. . . .'[28]

Thus the curious effect of the agitation of Hutt and his friends was to strengthen the naval position. Supported by Palmerston, Hotham had achieved results. Most of the African coast north of the equator was now covered by anti-slaving treaties, and slavers preferred to beach their ships rather than face a British cruiser. Both legitimate trade (in palm oil, ivory, and gold) and British territorial influence were growing. In 1850, for example, the British bought the Danish castles on the Gold Coast, above all Christiansborg at Accra. In 1851, after interminable negotiations and unsuccessful intrigues, Commodore Bruce, with a small force, attacked and captured Lagos, since its King, Kosoko, refused to sign a treaty obliging him to end the slave trade. A puppet, Akitoye, was put on the throne, and on New Year's Day 1852 an anti-slavery treaty was duly signed. A small number of Portuguese slave traders were expelled in March, though several returned within a year. This was a triumph for 'gunboat diplomacy'.

Victory in Africa was followed by another, greater one in Brazil. There, despite the strenuous efforts of the naval patrol, the prospects for abolition did not at first look promising in the late 1840s. Indeed, the merchants were still bringing in substantial numbers of slaves: nearly 23,000 in 1844, 16,000 in 1845, 50,000 in 1846, and nearly 60,000 in 1847, probably the same in 1848, perhaps 50,000 the following year. British naval reports were full of stories of powerful new steamers, 200–300 horsepower strong, such as the *Providencia*, commanded by a Genoese captain and crewed by Spaniards, which brought 1,400 slaves from Angola. The British Consul in Rio sent home a list of suspected slave vessels which landed slaves in 1849. The slave merchants residing at Rio, he added, included two Frenchmen, one Italian, one Spaniard, two Americans, and one 'Anglo-Saxon' – a certain Russell. The Consul in Bahia concluded a similar report with a comment that the people concerned in the trade in that city included five Brazilians, seventeen Portuguese, three Italians, a Belgian, a Frenchman, and one Englishman (Marback). Their ships were of all sorts, ranging from the *Antipático*, which carried over 1,000 slaves, to the *Leteo*, which carried only 105. It was true that half the slavers sent out from Bahia in 1848 seemed to have been captured. But that scarcely mattered, provided that at least a quarter of the vessels completed their journeys and brought their shining 'lumps of coal' into Rio or Bahia to work on the coffee plantations, the splendid old sugar estates, and the rich gold mines of this great 'country of the future', as Brazil then, as ever, seemed. In 1848 a steamship was for the first time used in the Brazilian slave trade: Tomás da Costa Ramos, a one-armed Portuguese ('Maneta'), sent his *Teresa* to Angola and carried back 1,200 slaves in a space intended only for 400.

The attraction of Brazil for investment was so great that a small trade in slaves thence from the United States even began. Hall Pringle, a British stipendiary magistrate, for example, saw the barque *Roanoke* leaving the Chesapeake Bay in 1849 with 'six carriage loads of slaves' bound for Rio. He heard of several other ships with the same purpose. Pringle mentioned these occurrences to the British Consul in Baltimore; but 'he did not wish to know of them'. Many North Americans also continued in the traffic:

between 1840 and 1845, sixty-four ships built in the United States were bought or sold in Rio alone and, in the same time, fifty-six ships left or entered that harbour for or from Africa. Profitt, the United States Minister in Rio in 1844, had baldly told the State Department that year that the slave trade could not be carried on to any extent to Brazil 'were it not for the use made by our flag and the facilities given by the chartering of American vessels to carry to the coast of Africa the outfit for the trade'.* Much the same was reported by David Tod, who succeeded Henry Wise as United States Minister. He told his Secretary of State in January 1850: 'Citizens of the United States are constantly in this capital, whose only occupation is the buying of American vessels with which to supply the slave trade. These men obtain sea-letters which entitle them to continue to use the United States flag and it is this privilege which enables them to sell their ships to slave traders', who continued to use that emblem 'until the Africans are landed on the coast of Brazil'. One example of the international complexity of the traffic was the case of the *Agnes*, Captain Hiram Gray, a vessel which traded regularly between Rio and Philadelphia. In 1843 the captain rented the ship to the most active slave trader, Manuel Pinto da Fonseca, an arrangement made, incidentally, by Weetman and Nobkirk of London. The *Agnes* went to Liverpool, bought muskets, bars of iron, and other British 'coast goods', and then set off via Rio for Cabinda (clearing for Montevideo). At Cabinda, Gray sold the vessel to Cunha, Pinto's representative in that port, and 500 slaves were immediately put on board and taken to Brazil, where they were sold at Cape Frio. (Gray was later tried and acquitted at Baltimore for slave trading.) This was a typical event, as the masters of about sixty United States ships sold in Rio between 1840 and 1845 could have testified.

Yet January 1850 turned out to be the British navy's best-ever month against the Brazilian slave trade – thanks largely to the activities of an informant, Joaquin Paula Suedes Alcoforado, an ex-slave-trader who gave the British details of many journeys. Another British agent was the captain of the port of Rio, Leopoldo da Câmara, who organized the mulatto dockers to give the British information about movements of ships on a regular basis. At least one newspaper, the *Correio Mercantil*, seems to have been in those days in receipt of a subsidy from the British secret fund, as was the editor of *O Brasil*, the most important newspaper. The new anti-slavery societies in Brazil probably also received financial support from their mother country's oldest ally.[29]

---

* *This was made possible by the practice of giving sea letters to vessels sold in foreign ports by one United States citizen to another. The rule was introduced in 1792 to encourage shipbuilding. United States citizens living in Brazil could buy ships from fellow countrymen and then ask the Consul for permission to trade on the African coast. The ships would be chartered by Brazilians who would take 'passengers' aboard. In Africa the 'passengers' would take over the ship.*

The explanation for this change seems to be that Palmerston, disturbed by the threat to his policy offered by the debate on the Hutt Committee's report, determined to use secret funds lavishly to assist a Brazilian surrender.ˑ Palmerston's resolve was the greater since he had received in June 1850 the enthusiastic support of the House of Commons, and the country, after his famous if inappropriate speech in favour of 'Don Pacifico'; and he had been given a subscription dinner by 250 members of the Reform Club.

In consequence, also in June 1850, Admiral Barrington Reynolds, an experienced Napoleonic War veteran who was now commander of the West Africa Squadron, rightly assuming that he had the support of his government, and able to take any resonable action without consulting them (the transatlantic telegraph was fortunately still over ten years away), ordered his captains to enter Brazilian ports to 'flush out' all ships which they found to be fitted out for the slave trade. They did this first at Macaé, about 150 miles to the north of Rio. HMS *Sharpshooter* covered the small boats and captured the brig *Polka*. Then Commander Herbert Schomberg, member of a distinguished naval family of Jewish origin, in HMS *Cormorant*, captured four slave ships, 'very fine vessels of 300 and 350 tons ... American bottoms', off Cape Frio and on the Paranaguá River, south of Santos. (One vessel scuttled herself; Schomberg burned two, in sight of the shore, and sent the last to St Helena.) There was some fighting, and one British seaman was killed, before Schomberg sailed up to Rio, looking for other slavers in the creeks to the north.

The difference between these actions and what had gone before is that the Foreign Secretary, Lord Palmerston, and the Foreign Office (not always the same thing), openly approved. Palmerston told the Admiralty that his predecessor Aberdeen's Act of 1846 contained no restrictions on 'the limits within which the search, detention and capture of slave traders ... are to take place ... in Brazilian waters as well as on the high seas'.[30] This was an interpretation which Palmerston decided for himself. No more important statement was made in the history of abolition. In so deciding, Palmerston must have taken into account the large stake that Britain had in the Brazilian economy, in the mines as in the mercantile houses, in insurance and in shipping. He knew that he could take action in Brazil in the interests of philanthropy, because so much of the wealth of the country was owned by British investors. Oddly enough, he was not at that time especially supported by the abolitionists, who were every day more critical of the use of force.

What may have weighed most with Palmerston was the sense that he had had in the debate in the House of Commons in March that

---

ˑ *This was a special triumph, since the Under-secretary in the Foreign Office who disbursed Secret Service money was Henry Unwin Addington, a reactionary whom Palmerston disliked.*

parliamentary and popular patience was running out. Despite Gladstone's opposition, he and Russell had won the debate on that occasion. They might not do so again.

The uproar in Rio was considerable. 'A great sensation ensued and it was dangerous for English officers to land', Captain Schomberg reported. Several newspapers, and in the Chamber angry deputies, demanded war. At that time, there were probably about 80,000 slaves in the city of Rio alone (a little less than 40 per cent of the total population), and the place seemed to depend on them absolutely for its survival. Ownership of slaves was still widespread, and craftsmen and even many people accounted poor owned slaves. Some lived from the hiring out of slaves. But in contrast with the slaves of the North American South, the majority of these had been born in Africa, having come in recent ships: 66 per cent, according to a census. In these circumstances, the Foreign Minister, the astute Conservative Paulino José Soares de Souza, wisely delayed a decision. The Council of Ministers, with the Emperor Pedro in the chair, privately decided in July that, though threatened by possible insurgency in both Rio Grande do Sul and Pernambuco, given Britain's commercial eminence Brazil had no choice but to suppress the illegal slave trade. The influence of Britain in Brazil in those days extended far beyond commercial matters. Dress, taste, houses, language, and food in Rio were all influenced by what was done in London. The Emperor had always opposed the slave trade, and his voice counted for much.

Soares de Souza gave an account of the Cabinet's attitude to the British Minister, Hudson, but demanded that in order to assist Brazilian abolitionists he and Reynolds first call off the search-and-burn policies. They agreed. Soares de Souza then persuaded the Brazilian Chamber to accept genuine abolition, in a remarkable speech, which admitted the fact of British pressure. He pointed out that all countries except Cuba had abolished the trade: 'Can we resist the torrent? I think not.' Brazil could no longer resist 'the pressure of the ideas of the age in which we live. . . . And ought we indolently to sleep on and not take steps to find a substitute for African labour?'[31] Inaction might lead to war with Britain, an eventuality which would damage Brazil more than the abolition of the trade. The Foreign Minister reminded the deputies that thanks to the nomination in Paris of the persistent Victor Schoelcher, the most prominent abolitionist in France, to the post of Under-secretary of State for the Colonies after the Revolution of 1848, even Britain's hereditary enemy had abolished the institution of slavery.* (That was on 27 March 1848: one of the few events of lasting significance of that year.)

The quarrels in the Chamber of Deputies in Rio continued: an ex-Minister of the Navy, Joaquim Antão, called on the government to

---

* All slaves in French territories were freed. As with Britain, protectorates still accepted slaves.

'destroy the ladders by which you have risen to power!' 'What ladders?' 'Can it be that noble ministers did not require the support of friends in the slave traffic in order to come to power?' Soares de Souza later admitted: 'During the period when fifty to sixty thousand Africans entered the country annually, when speculation concerning Africa was at its peak, there were many people more or less directly engaged in the trade. Who amongst us did not have relations with someone engaged in the traffic when it was not condemned by public opinion?'[32]

The resolute Captain Schomberg was in Bahia, where he delayed 'five most beautiful ships evidently intended for the trade'. He persuaded the Brazilian government to buy three of these ships for its own navy, while the other two were turned over to legitimate trade. To those seeking to establish the role of Jews in the slave trade, Captain Schomberg should be cited as an important actor in achieving abolition in Brazil.

For a bill abolishing the slave trade was now adopted in the Chamber of Deputies in Rio de Janeiro on 17 July 1850. It was accepted by the Senate, and Dom Pedro, the Emperor, signed it. He did so with great satisfaction.* On 4 September the bill became law. Henceforth, Brazilian slave ships were liable to seizure, the import of slaves into Brazil was declared piracy, all captured vessels were to be sold, and the proceeds were to be divided between captors and informers (if any). For the first time, this legislation led to a real transformation.

Manuel Pinto da Fonseca (who was said by Captain Schomberg to have lost sixty ships as a result of recent British naval action) and his brother Antonio were expelled from the country, along with the trader who was by now probably their chief competitor, the Italian Paretti. (He had landed thousands of slaves in Bahia the same year.) The President of the state of São Paulo even brought himself to denounce the insolent foreigners (that is, the Portuguese!) who had provoked the British attacks.

Cynics would argue that the change in mood derived from an outbreak of yellow fever brought from Africa in a slave ship (apparently of French nationality) which swept off 16,000 people and 'set a great many people very much against the slave trade; they were frightened out of their wits'. Palmerston thought that this revolution in attitudes was the result of British naval action: 'These half-civilised governments', he breezily commented, 'all require a dressing down every eight or ten years to keep them in order.' He demanded that Hudson and Admiral Reynolds press further. Hudson, busily buying more support among newspapermen and harbour-masters, threatened new attacks. Soares de Souza, astonished, pointed out that abolition was an immense task for

---

* The greatest of Brazilian historians, Gilberto Freyre, described Dom Pedro as 'a chaste man and a pure' one, and 'the ideal type of husband for a Queen Victoria.' At twenty, dressed in a frock coat and wearing a silk hat, he already seemed a European, and a middle-aged European at that.

Brazil: for example, an intelligence service had to be established, and public opinion had to be won round. For the change to be lasting, Brazil had to carry through the work of control herself.

Many other arguments followed. There were some further forceful maritime acts by Britain (including the seizure of a few slave ships on the high seas), as well as new protests by Brazil, and renewed threats of war. But in 1851 only about 3,000 slaves were imported into Brazil. One captain, bringing the *Tentativa* into the harbour of Rio, found that there were no buyers for his cargo of 400 slaves, even when he dropped the price to $10 a head. The schooner *Relampago*, built in Baltimore, 295' long, 23' 8" broad, two masts, 229 English tons, and owned by Marcos Borges Ferras, 'Senhor Marcos', was among the few ships to manage a landing of slaves that year. It had sailed to Bahia from Lagos, where it had been sold to Borges Ferras by an Italian, Jeronimo Carlos Salvi.˙ Most of those involved in this shipment were captured, some tried, fined, and even imprisoned.

Borges Ferras for a long time denied his real identity, but was eventually tried in 1858 and imprisoned for three years. When he had served his term in Rio, he returned to Whydah, where he lived out the rest of his days. He was not bitter: talking to the Abbé Pierre Bouché, who met him in the late 1860s, he said, 'I was admitted to the academy; and I came out with my diploma.'[33]

In July 1851 Palmerston, with understandable pride, announced in the House of Commons that the Brazilian slave trade had concluded. The next year, Admiral Henderson, who had succeeded Reynolds, reported that the Brazilian trade really did seem at an end. One hundred and forty slave traders were supposed to have left the country hurriedly in these months for Portugal. They brought back to Europe perhaps 100,000,000 cruzados. In 1856 the British Consul in Lisbon even estimated that these ex-slavers from Brazil were the biggest capitalists of the country.

It is true that most Brazilian slave owners were glutted as a result of the big imports of the late 1840s. Many middle-class Brazilians also came to support Soares de Souza, not because of philanthropy but because they had come to fear 'Africanization' and revolt. Others expected an increase in the value of their slaves, as prices rose. (They doubled between 1852 and 1854.) Some landowners may have thought that abolition of the trade was a temporary matter, or that they would get all the slaves which they needed from intra-Brazilian trade. (The early 1850s certainly saw an increase of that commerce in Bahia and the north-east: over 26,000 slaves were imported into Rio City and Province during 1852–9.) Nor did the laws on the trade seem to pose any threat to slavery itself. (A bill in 1850

˙ *Pursued by the Brazilian naval police, the* Relampago *disembarked its cargo fast. The slaves were forced to swim to shore; those who did not drown were received by men from the sugar plantation of Hygenio Piris Gomes.*

for the liberation of children born to slave mothers was defeated without discussion.)

Some further slaves did slip in. In December 1852, for example, the North American brig *Camargo* put into the bay of Ilha Grande a few hours to the west of Rio, carrying 5–600 Africans from Mozambique. They were disposed of so quickly that when the Chief of Police arrived from Rio he could find nothing. He challenged Joaquim José de Sousa Breves, the landowner who had bought them. In the end, however, only thirty-eight of *Camargo*'s slaves were recovered. Planters assumed that that might dictate the pattern of the future. But the last attempt to land slaves in Brazil seems to have been in January 1856, when the *Mary E. Smith*, 122 tons, of New Orleans but sailing from Boston, Massachusetts, was arrested by the Brazilian authorities off São Mateus, halfway between Rio and Bahia, carrying about 400 slaves. She had been sent to Brazil by a party of Brazilian slavers at that time in New York, who were primarily concerned with the Cuban trade. The *Mary E. Smith*'s captain had difficulty in disposing of his cargo. Water began to give out, the slaves started to die. The principal Brazilian-North American concerned died in prison. Evidence also later reached the British legation in Rio of the arrival of over 200 slaves at Serinhaém, near Recife. Palmerston made his usual threats, but by then the Brazilians had already punished those concerned. All the slaves involved were freed.

Abolitionists, of course, claimed a famous victory. All the same, at least 500,000 slaves had been imported into Brazil in the putatively illegal days of 1831–55. Perhaps 6,000,000 slaves were living in Brazil in 1851: twice as many as had been there in 1793! Slavery was still very well established throughout the economy, mostly in large-scale plantations, above all in farms producing coffee, now responsible for 50 per cent of Brazil's exports. In Rio, half the population were slaves.

In the long term, abolition of the trade stimulated immigration from Europe. Concurrent Brazilian efforts to obtain free African labour were, however, opposed by Britain, whose representatives argued, recalling the fate of the *emancipados*, that free Africans would be treated much as slaves on arrival. This attitude may perhaps seem hypocritical when it is recalled that after 1841 many African contract workers had been hired for the British West Indies.[*]

In fact, in contrast with what obtained in the United States, abolition of the trade did mark the slow beginning of the end of slavery in Brazil:

---

[*] *Some of these, though, were Krus, real volunteers from the coast of Liberia, and all were in theory free not to go: 10,000 went to Jamaica, 13,970 to British Guiana, 8,390 to Trinidad, 1,540 to Grenada, other, lesser, numbers to St Vincent, St Lucia, and St Kitts. In 1852, France adopted a scheme whereby a slave might be bought in Africa, liberated on board the ship, and carried to the Antilles as a worker under contract. Fifteen thousand or so were carried in that way until 1867.*

the institution there, as in the Spanish empire, had always depended on large imports, for, as has been often stated, the birthrate of slaves was low, mortality was high, and there was much manumission.

Lord Palmerston in 1864, the year before his death, said that 'the achievement which I look back on with the greatest and purest pleasure was forcing the Brazilians to give up their slave trade'.[34] He was deceiving himself only a little. Though Brazilian fears and, to give Brazilian statesmen their due, some brave Brazilian speeches played an essential part, the trade in slavery would not have ended when it did had it not been for Britain's moral crusade. That was one of Britain's most remarkable achievements, which partly atones for that country's unquestionable, and largely unquestioning, enthusiasm for the slave trade in the seventeenth and eighteenth centuries.

Domingos Martins, the last of the great slave merchants of Africa and Brazil, died in Lagos the same year as Palmerston made this remark. The Brazilian government, in its new mood of morality, had refused him permission to retire to Bahia. Richard Burton saw Martins in January 1864, a few days before he died, and admired his house, though he could see that the end of the trade in slaves had damaged him. Five of Martins's daughters, all rich heiresses, nevertheless married well in Brazil, and he left a family in Africa too. His living descendants are the heirs of the Brazilian slave trade, the largest forced emigration in history.[35]

35

THEY ALL EAGERLY DESIRE IT,
PROTECT IT
AND ALMOST SANCTIFY IT

*Comment by Captain-General Cañedo on the attitude to the
slave trade of Cuban planters c. 1853*

THE BRAZILIAN SLAVE TRADE, one of the longest-lasting businesses in the
history of commerce, was now at an end; but an even older one, that to
Cuba, was still prospering. Between 1840 and 1860 about 200,000 slaves
were probably carried to Cuba (and perhaps 7,200 to Puerto Rico). But
beneath such an austere statement of figures, the diplomatic, maritime,
economic, and social life of the island of Cuba went through an
astounding series of upheavals.

In one respect, this era represented an unusual triumph for Spanish
foreign policy. Through dissimulation, procrastination, and evasion, the
weak governments of Queen Isabella in Madrid continually resisted
the demands of the British at their most bombastic. Had the matter not
been the continuation of the slave trade, the diplomacy of Spain would
have received accolades, and avenues might have been named after those
responsible.

But this success for diplomacy in Madrid began in a curious way.
Though the census of 1841 indicated that slaves constituted a majority of
the population of the island, the slave trade itself seemed to be coming to
an end. The reason had nothing to do with England, nor with philanthropy. The fact was that, as in Brazil, there were several slave revolts.
The new thirty-four-year-old Captain-General, whose responsibility was
to suppress these challenges, was Leopoldo O'Donnell, one of the many
Spanish officers of distinction with Irish antecedents. Like most captains-
general of Cuba, he had spent his youth fighting in the civil wars of
Spain. Whereas his predecessor Valdés owed his lucrative place in Cuba
to his friendship with General Espartero, a friend of Britain, O'Donnell
owed his own appointment to his support for General Narváez in

overthrowing Espartero. He would afterwards have a long career in politics surely financed by his five years' stay in Cuba, where he was an assiduous friend of both slavery and, even more, of the slave trade. He was said to have taken £100,000 back to Spain with him. He was always backed in Madrid by his patron Narváez and by the Queen Regent. O'Donnell's own view was that a sudden end of the slave trade would result in a catastrophe, and he advised that the government in Madrid ought to do all it could to avoid all discussions of the matter in the Cortes.

The facts of the 'Escalera Conspiracy' (so called because suspects were tied to a wooden staircase in a ruined coffee plantation near Matanzas and whipped till they confessed), which faced O'Donnell in Cuba, are unclear. Broadly, though, a group of free blacks and mulattos seem to have discussed a scheme to proclaim the independence of Cuba, and the manumission of all slaves who supported the idea. An assistant of the late British Consul Turnbull, Francis Ross Cocking, was implicated, but the lead was taken by a group of free blacks headed by a certain José Rodríguez. Cocking apparently encouraged these men to suppose, inaccurately, that he, and they, had the approval of the British government. He himself imagined that he had the backing of certain enlightened *criollos*. But the scheme was betrayed by the writer Domingo del Monte, who Cocking foolishly supposed to have been in support of him, but who described the matter, in an exaggerated form, in a letter to Alexander Everett, sometime Minister of the United States in Madrid, once the President of that country's special representative in Havana, and a keen supporter of the idea of annexation of Cuba to the North American Union. Everett came then to believe, with his friends among the Cuban planters, that Britain might be planning an armed intervention in Cuba in order to establish an 'Ethiopico-Cuban republic' (del Monte's expression) and 'to form round our southern shores a cordon of free negroes'. He sought, unsuccessfully, to awaken his masters in Washington to the iniquity of the matter. Daniel Webster, Secretary of State under President Tyler, was sceptical, but concerned enough to inform the Spaniards of the alleged conspiracy.[1]

Apparently independent of this plot, there were a number of slave revolts in late 1843 and 1844, similar in character to rebellions which had often occurred before: a rising of twenty-five slaves at the Alcancia sugar mill in Cárdenas; a protest of slaves on the Cárdenas–Júcaro railway; and other minor outbursts, which were all suppressed by O'Donnell with considerable brutality. Perhaps 3,000 slaves and free blacks were tried summarily, and about eighty were shot or died under a panicky interrogation, either in the stocks or in overcrowded cells. No evidence was forthcoming of a large-scale revolutionary conspiracy, but that did not prevent many free blacks who had been born outside Cuba from being deported, along with a number of *criollo* leaders, such as José de la Luz y Caballero and even the inadvertent informer, Domingo del Monte. Those who were executed included Cuba's best-known poet, Diego Gabriel de la Concepción Valdés, 'Plácido', a free mulatto, who was accused of being an English agent but who seems to have been innocent of all participation in any plot.

> *The black is born and tomorrow*
> *For lack of training his mind*
> *In a chaos of sorrow,*
> *He seems sad and blind.*ˑ

O'Donnell made no secret of his view that Cocking, Turnbull, and the might of the English Crown had been the inspiration of these rebellions. Indeed, his hostility to England was remorseless. It was as if he was determined to avenge the defeat of Red Hugh O'Donnell, his ancestor, by the English in Ireland in 1600.

If O'Donnell hated England, the sentiment was cordially returned. After the repression of 1844 even the serene Aberdeen was roused to anger, and he exerted himself to secure his withdrawal. 'Unless they remove him, I do not see what we can do but recall you', Aberdeen wrote to the Minister in Madrid, the languid but effective Henry Bulwer, 'Unless they make reparation for his monstrous cruelties and acts of gross injustice . . . we shall be obliged to order reprisals.'[2] But Bulwer knew that such a thing would be far from easy, because of that general's friends in Madrid. Palmerston summed up the position when he returned to the Foreign Office in another letter to Bulwer: 'It appears that the practice of re-selling *emancipados* which has been going on for some time past, under the sanction of the captain-general of Cuba was the public topic of conversation [in Havana]. . . . It is also stated that upwards of 5,000 of these unfortunate persons have been re-sold at rates varying from 5 to 9 ounces of gold – for example, 50 *emancipados* were sold to the Gas Company of Havana for a period of five years to serve as lamplighters, by which means a profit of upwards of $600,000 has been made by persons in Government house [*sic*]. . . . 400 *emancipados* have been transferred to the Marquis of las Delicias, chief judge of the mixed court, to be held by him for the benefit of the Countess of Guerega, wife of General O'Donnell . . . [so] You will express the confident hope that the Government of Spain will give positive and peremptory orders to General O'Donnell to obtain . . . liberty for these nominally emancipated negroes.'[3] . . . But these efforts were unsuccessful.

O'Donnell busied himself with inquiries, commissions, and recommendations much as Valdés had, but always with the aim of enabling

---

ˑ 'Nace el negro, y desde luego / Por falta de cultura / En un caos de amargura / Se ve atribulado y ciego.' *Plácido was son of a dancer from Burgos and a mulatto hairdresser.*

those engaged in the slave trade to continue it. But he was every year encountering further difficulties, less because of a sudden fit of philanthropy among the *criollos* than from their fear, comparable to what had transpired in Brazil, that one day the presence of a large black slave population might bring to them the same kind of revolution which had destroyed Saint-Domingue. For an identical reason, ironically, O'Donnell abandoned Valdés's scheme for the liberation of *emancipados* after five years: he was convinced, he said, that 'free men of colour were compromised en masse in the vast plot'. *Emancipados* after 1845 remained, indeed, slaves de facto if not de jure, though now, as a rule, they worked for the government – Roman emperors would instantly have recognized them as 'state slaves'. They must then have numbered about 2,000 in Cuba (alongside another 2,000 who had been freed, 1,000 who had gone to British colonies, and about 6,000 who were listed as 'dead, lunatic or disappeared').

In 1844, meantime, the veteran Spanish liberal Martínez de la Rosa – the playwright-statesman of the Cortes of 1820, friend of Canning and Chateaubriand, who had signed on Spain's behalf the Anglo-Spanish Treaty of 1835, with its famous equipment clause – returned to power, as Foreign Minister. In keeping with the wishes of his English friends, he introduced a law into the Cortes in Madrid naming penalties for those convicted of being concerned in the slave trade. Owners and investors in slave voyages, as well as captains and other senior officers, would be imprisoned for six years, or eight if they resisted arrest, as well as being subject to exile and fines; crews would suffer half those fines; and there were other punishments if slaves were maltreated.

The bill caused trouble in Spain. Even liberal politicians were hostile to it, and the opponents of the measure sought to ruin it by introducing wrecking amendments. The bill became law only because it seemed not to damage the institution of slavery. Indeed, one of the amendments which the government did accept allowed that once slaves had reached a plantation in Cuba they could not be touched.[4]

If the bill inspired difficulties in Madrid, it provoked something close to panic among planters in Cuba. Though the then State Prosecutor in Havana, Vicente Vázquez Queipo de Llano, privately thought that an end of the slave trade was the only way to ensure indefinite white supremacy, Captain-General O'Donnell believed that the law, if carried out, would ruin the colony. He prevented any mention of it from appearing in the newspapers in Havana – one more remarkable treatment by a colonial governor of a law proclaimed by the imperial power. The Council of the Indies in Madrid, however, merely commented that Britain, presumably jealous of the success of Cuban sugar, must be seeking to destroy the island's prosperity by making demands on Spain which it did not dare to make on the United States. That Council now seems to have thought that the slave trade should be slowly run down and the deliberate propagation of slaves (in keeping with what was believed to be practised in the United States) should be encouraged to offset the shortage of labour.

The panic took some time in Cuba to be assuaged. There was, though, for several years an almost complete end to the import of slaves into the island: the only people able to continue, thought the British Commissary Judge in Havana, 'were persons like Don Julián Zulueta' who were simply 'desirous of obtaining slaves at a low price, not for sale'. It would seem that no more than 1,500 slaves were imported in 1848. Cholera also killed many slaves already in Cuba. Some sugar planters sold up and went to Texas. Most coffee farms were ruined by hurricanes.

The economics of slavery were in these years discussed ad infinitum in the Cuban periodical press. Thus in 1845 Vázquez Queipo de Llano estimated in a public report that slave labour cost 70 pesos per person a year and free labour 140, and that the rising price of slaves would soon make free labour competitive.

In 1845 it was hard to see that twenty years of efforts by the British governments, with occasional sporadic support by liberal Spanish governments, had had the slightest effect on the Cuban slave-powered economy. The Spanish governments in these days were not malign. Bruised by civil war, or the fear of it, with the political consequences of having a child queen and a strong-minded but self-indulgent queen regent in a semi-absolutist regime, they still did not have the strength to carry out policies which seemed against the interests of their richest colony. The administration was quick to take offence. Thus in 1848 Bulwer was asked by General Narváez to leave Madrid after (false) accusations that he had been concerned to support a rebellion against the Spanish government. There was outrage in London, and Palmerston even considered asking the navy to blockade Seville.

But in 1849 and 1850 imports of slaves rose again in Cuba, and after 1851, with prices in Africa very low because of the end of the traffic to Brazil, the trade returned to its old high levels. The profits in the business were too high to ignore. Washington Irving, the inspired author who had become, so curiously, yet so appropriately, the United States Minister in Madrid, reported to Washington: 'It seems beyond a doubt that, under . . . captain-general O'Donnell, slaves are again admitted in great numbers' to Cuba.[5] A slave in the 1840s could be bought for half what he would have cost in 1780, but he could be sold for at least twice as much. As we have seen, the cost of maufacturing goods, the main items used to barter slaves, had also fallen dramatically. Even when all costs were paid, a slaver capable of carrying 500 slaves might make $100,000 a journey: a profit of 200 per cent.

The renaissance of the trade in the late 1840s in Cuba was largely the work of a clever native of Cádiz, Manuel Pastor, a retired colonel who had been a friend of Tacón, who had used him as an adviser on public works, then given him control over the new markets which he had built in

Havana. This made Pastor's fortune. Unlike Tacón, he believed in railways, and he helped to finance several. In the late 1840s he was the brain behind a new sugar company in which the Queen Mother, María Cristina, still in effect the Regent of Spain, participated, along with such well-known merchants as Pedro (once Pierre) Forcade of Bordeaux, Antonio Font, and Antonio Parejo, a close friend of the Queen Regent's second husband, General Muñoz (the Duke of Riañasares) and generally held to be the agent of the Queen Mother herself. This company's biggest plantation, Susana, received its regular 'sacks of coal' (that is, new Africans) thanks to Parejo – as well as courtesy of the new Captain-General, Federico Roncali (Count of Alcoy). Roncali, like his predecessor, O'Donnell, feigned ignorance of the slave trade. But he was engaged in protecting it, all the same: 'The CG [captain-general] pockets 51 pesos a head', wrote a merchant to his New York partner in 1849.[*] (The Spanish Queen Regent was, meantime, as a result thought to be the 'richest individual in Europe'. The intelligent British Minister in Madrid in the 1830s, George Villiers, had reported, 'All her money is secured in foreign funds.')[6]

Parejo, looked on in 1850 as the 'person now considered the most extensively engaged in slave trading', died in Cuba, leaving debts to the Queen Mother which she apparently never recovered. That financier's widow, Susana Benítez (it was after her that the big plantation had been named), all the same provided him a funeral which cost 10,000 pesos. In these years, the small Cuban port of Cabañas, in the western province of Pinar del Río, became the most important of the slave harbours, where could be seen 'the cream [la flor y nata] of the slave ships', commented Captain Impiel, in Baroja's Los Pilotos de Altura.[7]

Still, there was one critical change in the late 1840s and 1850s in Cuba: though slaves were cheap in Africa, they were becoming too expensive in Cuba for all but the large proprietors. This confirmed a trend whereby small farmers gave up grinding their own cane, and increasingly took their product to a larger establishment where there were modern facilities, a steam engine, and a Derosne or Rilleux centrifugal mechanism, introduced from France. These modern haciendas were the origin of the modern centrales afterwards found throughout the island, and though the biggest and newest of them (Zulueta's Alava, Parejo's Susana, the Queen Mother's San Martín, the last two of which joined to found a new company, La Perseverencia) adapted to the new conditions, many, more modest, abandoned slave society.

Rich and internationally aware criollos had begun in these years to think in terms of annexation to the United States as a way of preserving their slaves and their position. This 'annexationism' in Cuba merged with

---

[*] On leaving the island in 1850, Roncali is said to have received a present of 50,000 pesos so that he could continue to protect the interests of the merchants when he got back to Madrid.

the expansionist movement in the United States known as Manifest Destiny. The United States was, just at that time, in the wake of the Mexican War, acquiring Utah, Wyoming, California, Arizona, and New Mexico, as well as parts of Colorado and Nevada. Why should the rainbow of Union ever end? Southern politicians in the United States began to see annexation of Cuba as the next step, both as a way of helping to guarantee slavery in their own country, and as marking the beginning of a new Caribbean empire. Further, the Spanish Minister in Washington, Ardáiz, received private warnings from Southern members of the United States Congress that they would support the Cuban planters if after Spanish abolition of the slave trade in Madrid they were to rebel against the *madre patria*.

Two societies were formed to agitate for annexation to the United States. First of these was a secret society, La Rosa Cubana, headed by Narciso López, a Venezuelan adventurer who had lost his father in the wars of independence and who, after taking part in the Carlist Wars in Spain on the liberal side, had briefly been Governor of the elegant city of Trinidad. Second, there was the more restrained Club de la Habana, directed by Miguel de Aldama, a planter of imagination who hoped for annexation to the United States as a means of preserving slavery if not the slave trade. López made several attempts to inspire rebellions in Cuba, with help from volunteers from Hungary as well as Louisiana. He was eventually arrested by the Cuban authorities and garrotted, his last words being a ringing appeal: 'Don't be frightened, Cubans, of the scarecrow of the African race that has served so often the tyranny of our oppressors. Slavery is not a social phenomenon exclusive to Cuba or incompatible with the liberty of citizens. . . . Nearby you have the example of the United States, where three million slaves do not prevent the flourishing of the most liberal institutions in the world. . . .'[8] Thus did Cuban nationalism start its melancholy history on a flawed premiss.

It also had a curious enemy, in the mother country. In addition to her requirement to treat Britain as a great economic power with which it was unwise to quarrel, Spain was beginning also to see Britain as an ally to help her thwart the annexation of Cuba to the United States; and it was true that British governments wanted to prevent the United States' capture of the ever-faithful isle, not only because of her own commercial relations with her, but because such a consummation might cut her off from Mexican and other promising markets. All the same, Britain could not assist Spain until the latter had put into practice the treaties on the slave trade. But the unhappy rebellion of López changed that attitude. In September 1851, after the execution of that patriot, Palmerston gave the unusual order to British naval forces in the West Indies to help Spain in any way necessary to defeat North American filibustering expeditions. Even more remarkable, the French associated themselves with this. It was an indication of solidarity against what was seen by the European powers as a United States threat to their interests.

Despite his help to Spain against the United States, Palmerston had not abandoned his passionate mission to end the slave trade internationally. In 1851, the year of his success in Brazil, he wrote to Lord Howden (who, having been in Rio, had become Minister to Madrid) to say that Britain was 'desirous of coming to a plain understanding with the government in Madrid, and to make that Government comprehend that Great Britain will no longer consent to be baffled in regard to the Spanish slave trade . . . by unsatisfactory excuses and by unperformed assurances . . . while the Spanish authorities in Cuba have continued systematically and notoriously to set at nought the stipulations of the treaty. . . . It is high time that this system of evasion should cease.' Palmerston suspected that the government in Madrid had two purposes: 'first, to afford income to a number of ill-paid public officers or to appointed favourites, by means of the bribes given by slave traders upon the importation of negroes; and, secondly, [to retain] a hold on the island, because it is thought at Madrid that, as long as there is in Cuba a large number of negroes, the white population will cling to the mother country for protection. . . .'[9]

The next Spanish Captain-General in Cuba, in the long series of corrupt and patriotic officials in that place, was General José (Gutiérrez) de la Concha, son of a hero of the wars against Argentina, and yet one more veteran of civil conflicts in Spain. He came to Havana as Captain-General in 1850 with a name as a strong governor who would be capable, on the one hand, of dealing with filibustering from the United States and, on the other, of ensuring that Cuba comply with the slave treaties. His instructions told him that he was, of course, to remember that Cuba was an island of two races, either one of which might, if unwisely treated, threaten continuing Spanish possession. He was told, too, to seek a solution to the long-standing problem of the *emancipados* which would both satisfy Britain yet not lose the services of the people concerned. After all, the mere sale of these virtual state slaves brought into the government $40,000 a year.

La Concha started well. Thus he dismissed the Governor of the province of Matanzas, Brigadier Pavia, on the accusation of conniving at the landing of 840 slaves at Camarioca, on the northern coast of Cuba, in the *Emperatriz*, belonging to a Catalan company; but the government in Madrid found that promising officer innocent and reinstated him. La Concha had also a scheme for the *emancipados*: to allow them to remain a supplementary labour force for sugar plantations, to be employed on public works and to be available to serve retired officers or their widows. Some of the income available from their sale ('reassignment' was the euphemism) would go to assist a fund for the children of Spaniards who had served in the empire before independence.

The British were now almost as interested in the problems of the *emancipados* as in the slave trade itself. Lord Stanley, a youthful Under-secretary of Foreign Affairs in the nine-month government of his father,

Lord Derby, had been to Cuba, and so had direct knowledge of the condition of these Africans. Both he and the new Foreign Secretary, Lord Malmesbury, tried to be, if anything, more rigorous than Palmerston had been, and to insist that the Captain-General in Cuba give an account every six months of the fate of the *emancipados*. At that time, reports from Havana showed that of over 7,000 Africans liberated under the treaty of 1817, only half had really been freed.

Malmesbury's successor, Lord Clarendon (who as George Villiers had been the successful Minister in Madrid in the 1830s), then promoted a plan for a tripartite guarantee of Spanish interests in Cuba by France, Britain, and the United States. But both Daniel Webster, briefly back as Secretary of State under Millard Fillmore, and his successor and disciple, the splendid orator Edward Everett, rejected any such idea of European involvement in Cuba. Everett explained, 'There was no hope of a complete remedy [for the slave trade] while Cuba remained a Spanish colony.'[10] The phrase was, not surprisingly, greeted as an explicit approval of the idea of annexation.

The election of Franklin Pierce as president of the United States in 1852 seemed to make that point only too clear: Pierce, the famous 'dark horse' in the electoral race, was, like Buchanan, a 'northern man with southern principles', and considered the idea of acquisition of Cuba by the United States as nothing less than a 'fundamental principle'. The British Minister in Washington, John Crampton, thought that the administration had decided that the United States 'will and must take' Cuba.

Ministers in Britain racked their brains as to what to do. Some of them wanted a more forward policy – acting against Cuba, say, as Palmerston had against Brazil – for example, sending the fleet to blockade Havana in order to bring the slave trade to a violent conclusion. Lord Malmesbury tried to leave the impression with Spain that if that country were to refuse to act much more strongly against 'the ST', Britain would not help against United States annexationism. But that threat was not carried through. Lord John Russell would tell Howden in Madrid: 'Your lordship may rest assured that, however friendly the Councils of her Majesty may be to Spain; whatever may be the interest of this country not to see Cuba in the hands of any other power . . . ; yet . . . the destruction of a trade which conveys the natives of Africa to become slaves in Cuba will furnish a large compensation for such [a] transfer.'[11] But such protestations could always be made to seem insincere when Britain was each year taking more and more Cuban sugar: from under 200,000 hundredweight in 1845, the figure had risen to over 800,000 by 1851 and would be nearly 1,600,000 in 1854.

La Concha, meantime, had been abruptly succeeded in Havana in 1852 by General Valentín Cañedo. A man of neither wealth nor significance, he was if anything on even worse terms with the British Consul-General, Crawford, and so with Britain, than O'Donnell had been.

Yet that enmity derived from a misapprehension: Cañedo authorized governors of provinces to send officials to enter plantations to seek slaves newly introduced from Africa (*bozales*) and, if necessary, seize them. It was Cañedo who took the brave step of having Julián Zulueta arrested in 1853, and held in La Cabaña, overlooking Havana Bay, for receiving a large consignment of slaves on the *Lady Suffolk*, though the charges against that millionaire were dropped for 'lack of evidence'. This new Captain-General accurately reported to his government that the planters, great and small, all defended the slave trade: 'Without exception', he wrote, 'they all eagerly desire it, protect it and almost sanctify it.'[12] Despite these indications of seriousness, Spain demanded Consul Crawford's recall, and Britain asked for that of Cañedo. The latter adopted the curious ruse of sending a friend, the mercurial Aragonese writer Mariano Torrente, author of a history of the Latin American wars of independence and editor of various journals in Havana, to London to defend him, but to no avail: Cañedo was sacrificed and withdrawn after only a year in Cuba, and General Juan de la Pezuela, a well-known and hitherto effective liberal, was transferred from Puerto Rico, where he had been Governor, to Cuba.*

Pezuela was a new kind of captain-general for Cuba. He was experienced, being the son of the ill-starred penultimate Viceroy of Spain in Lima, where he was born. He was also a poet and playwright, though his lifeless translation of the *Divine Comedy* had given him the nickname of 'El Danticida'. In Havana, he began his time in office by refusing to be bribed into complicity with the traffic – the first captain-general to do so since Valdés. He ordered all slaves illegally introduced to be seized, and sought to detain owners of slave ships and organizers of slave expeditions. He made common cause with Monsignor Antonio Claret, the enlightened Archbishop of Santiago, who had long been asking that slaves be better treated. Pezuela encouraged marriage between white and black, and planned a militia in which he hoped to welcome free blacks. He issued a decree freeing the *emancipados*, and then introduced a plan whereby those of them who had already been given masters would be reassigned to them for annual periods. He personally inspired articles in Havana's main daily newspaper, the *Diario de la Marina*, calling for Cuba to fulfil Spain's treaty obligations with Britain, and discussing the merits of free labour. He dismissed the Governors of Trinidad and Sancti Spíritus for allowing slaves from Africa to land in their zone of authority, and his ruling was upheld in Madrid. Like La Concha, he decreed that officials could enter plantations if they knew of any rumour of clandestine slaves there. That decree, of May 1854, also provided for the compilation of a register of slaves to be

---

* *Pezuela had prevented the re-emergence of a slave trade in Puerto Rico, though that island had in 1846 for the first time a majority of black or mulatto persons: 216,000 whites and 226,500 slaves and free blacks.*

made after the next harvest, which in theory would free all illegally imported slaves thereby discovered. Officials would lose their jobs if they failed to act on hearing tales of improper landing. Pezuela told his government that these measures were essential in order to ensure British support against the United States. In February 1854 Pezuela even confiscated, in the harbour of Havana, the United States ship *Black Warrior* and placed her captain, James Bulloch, under arrest on the ground that the ship's manifest misrepresented what was on board.

These high-minded policies of Pezuela were denounced as 'Africanization' by the planters. All the old hatreds of *criollos* for *peninsulares* which had characterized Spanish imperial rule in all her dominions were revived. The planters thought it certain that Pezuela was going to abolish slavery itself. One Cuban planter, Cristóbal Madán, wrote to President Pierce to ask him to intervene and save the island from the British-inspired emancipation which, it was thought, the Captain-General was planning to introduce. (Madán had been educated in the United States and was a friend of Pierce's clever but autocratic Attorney-General, Caleb Cushing.) The mood of anxiety seemed to inspire the United States Consul, W. H. Robertson, to seek to precipitate a crisis which would enable immediate United States annexation. He assured the planters that Spain had accepted the British policies, and that Britain would soon use her influence to have Cuba filled with Africans, so that the island would become an 'African colony given over to barbarism', as Secretary of State William Marcy put the matter in a letter to James Buchanan, then United States Minister in London: 'an act which, in its consequences, must be injurious to the United States'. A special agent of the United States in Cuba, Charles Davis, told Marcy that if all slaves imported since 1820 were freed there would be 'a disastrous bloody war of the races. . . . Should the United States remain passive spectators of the consummation of the plans of the British ministry, the time is not distant when they will be obliged to rise and destroy such dangerous and pernicious neighbours.'[13] A certain George Francis Train declared that Cuba should be seen as a deposit of aluminium from the Mississippi: 'What God has joined together let no man put asunder', he curiously proclaimed.[14]

These obsessed declarations explain why Marcy, on 3 April 1854, instructed his Minister in Madrid, the tempestuous Louisianian Pierre Soulé, to try to buy Cuba from Spain for $120,000,000. If that was impossible, Marcy went on, 'you will then direct your efforts to . . . detach that island from the Spanish dominion and from all dependence on any European power'. He was the right man to whom to send such a dispatch, for the night before he left New York for Madrid he had heard with emotion exiled Cubans beg him to bring back a 'new star' to 'shine in the sky of Young America'.

Meantime, General John Quitman, twice Governor of Mississippi, a hero of the Mexican War, a man with friends in the Cabinet of the

United States who tacitly backed him, began to organize at New Orleans an expedition of Southern gentlemen to liberate Cuba from Spain and the fearful threat of 'Africanization'; while friends of his such as Senators Stephen Mallory of Florida and John Slidell of Louisiana sought to repeal the Neutrality Laws to enable the legal departure of the amateur force.

'El Danticida', busy in Havana with a new translation of Tasso's *Gerusalemme Liberata*, hesitated on hearing of all these plans and, as has happened to many other good-natured intellectuals in politics, was forced into retreat before being dismissed (after the Spanish revolution in July 1854), since in Madrid it was supposed that the planters in Cuba would welcome filibusters from the United States with open arms if the Captain-General's policies continued.

That there was then a genuine United States threat was demonstrated by the Ostend Manifesto of October 1854, in which the United States Ministers to Britain (James Buchanan), France (John Mason), and Spain (Pierre Soulé) jointly declared that if Spain were to persist in refusing to sell Cuba the United States ought to take it by force. For, if Spain were to refuse the offer of $120,000,000, then 'by every law, human and divine, we shall be justified in wresting it from Spain if we possess the power'.[15]

This declaration, and the enthusiastic terms in which the proposal was couched, caused much emotion: in Spain and Cuba, for obvious reasons; in the slave states of the United States, too; but also in the free ones, whose political leaders saw Cuba as a likely, and dangerous, addition to the slave community.

After Pezuela, his predecessor but one, La Concha, returned to Havana with an instruction to do everything necessary to prevent the annexation of Cuba to the United States. He also came with orders to suppress the traffic in slaves, though that was a lesser consideration; but if annexationism could only be fought by making concessions to the planters that would have to be accepted. La Concha would remain in Havana for five years, almost a record for these captains-general.

La Concha had learned from Pezuela's disquieting experience, and decided that his approach to the slave trade would be to demand that personal identification cards, '*cédulas personales*', be put on the neck of every slave, and obtainable for a fee – that is, essentially, a tax. Slaves without such identification would be assumed to have been illegally imported, and so be liable to be freed. That scheme was started, eventually, in July 1855, but it failed, because neither planters nor officials would cooperate, except in case of Yucatecs and 'coolies' from Mexico and China. Identification cards could, of course, be forged, and they were. La Concha was made a fool of.

On the other hand, La Concha opposed the inspection of estates by officials looking for illegally imported slaves, and he repealed Pezuela's decrees on the matter. He also abandoned Pezuela's scheme to declare the trade piracy. Instead, he placed faith in the idea of offering bribes to informers, and prize money to officials who denounced slave ships. None of these arrangements was effective. So the slave trade continued 'to be carried on ... almost with impunity'.[16] Between 9,000 and 12,000 slaves were landed in 1853, between 8,000 and 11,000 in 1854; Zulueta, Pastor, and Parejo were the biggest traders. The traffic in *emancipados* also continued, even if these were now to receive wages after their five years' apprenticeship. They were never able to choose their masters, being assigned to them by the officials.

The pattern of the recent past was thus repeated: Captain Baillie Hamilton testified in London that in 1853 he stopped the slave ship *Arrogante Emilio* outside Havana and found, as he expected, 'an immense quantity of stone ballast, [and] the beams and planks for a complete slave deck; that, on examining the captain's trunk [he found that it] was ingeniously contrived with false sides.... They found concealed ... 419 Mexican ounces [of gold], and a track chart with tracks in pencil to the Bight of Benin.'[17]

Spanish warships were now asked to control the slave trade off Havana – two heavy sailing frigates, three steam frigates, four steam sloops, and nine sailing brigs. But the arrangement was somewhat schizophrenic since officials seemed to continue to receive payments by the leading slave traders for every slave landed. Minor bureaucrats had come to find bribes as necessary to their survival as slaves were to the planters.

A new Prime Minister in Madrid, the Count of San Luis (the businessman José Luis Sartorius) told Queen Isabella in 1854 that he wanted to stop the slave trade, but maintain the institution of slavery, and provide for adequate labour on sugar estates by forcing domestic slaves into plantations with a further tax on slaves used merely as house servants. He would encourage slave marriages, and immigration (from Mexico and China). His ideas included immediate liberty for all *emancipados* and a slave register. These arrangements would both please Britain and prevent the loss of Cuba to America. But the pious hopes of San Luis in Madrid continued to be the bad jokes in Havana.

Havana was now not only the main destination of the slave ships but the best starting point, and by 1858 most outfitting was done there, even if the ships were, as was still often the case, North American built.

Despite the continuing despotism of the captains-general, some ideas for the future were now being aired publicly. There had been a plan to import Spanish and also some non-Spanish European workers to make tropical labour more attractive to white men, who were to be employed in tobacco and coffee cultivation. But nothing came of this scheme, nor of others like it. White workers could not be persuaded of the charms of working in cane fields in the tropics. On the other hand, 200,000 Chinese were imported into Cuba, between 1847 and 1867, in conditions similar to, though legally different from, slavery. Well-known slaving firms (including that of Zulueta) organized these arrangements. Contracts were made with companies which brought the 'volunteers' from Hong Kong and Macao. Each 'coolie' would be paid 125 pesos, sometimes up to 200, for which he would have to work for four years. During that period, the Chinese could be bought, sold, and transferred just as slaves were (slaves cost 600 pesos at this time). But they would be fed and kept, after a fashion. In the mid-1850s, a few planters even preferred 'coolies' to slaves. One enlightened sugar king, Juan Poëy, had, on his three planta- tions, Las Cañas, San Martín, and Pontifex, 44, 358, and 379 Chinese respectively, alongside 480, 436, and 89 slaves.

The Chinese were satisfactory as workers if well looked after. But as a rule they were not. Suicides were frequent. Many ran away. These 'Mongols', as they were often absurdly known, gained a reputation for being thieves, homosexuals, and rebels, as well as being denounced as both lazy and impulsive: every imaginable accusation was thrown against them. But those who treated Chinese workers intelligently (for example, Antonio Fernández Criado) met with excellent service. Some of these workers, after their years of labour were over, eventually set up small businesses in Havana.

Another innovation was the import of 2,000 Yucatec labourers from Mexico, contracted by none other than Charles Tolmé, the British Consul before Turnbull. The first Yucatecs came from prisons to which they had been condemned after the Mexican Caste War, which ended in 1848. These were bought at twenty-five pesos each and sold at a hundred. They had left home on the understanding that their removal would improve their condition, while the Mexican government would be relieved of dangerous enemies. But they did not work well, were badly treated, and most died very soon.

Other schemes included one for importing African free labour with contracts lasting eight years like the Chinese. But the British opposed 'free African labour' as they had done in Brazil, and that factor weighed a good deal. The Cuban proprietors, meantime, were still reluctant to increase the population of slaves by encouraging the import of women: a female slave, above all a pregnant slave, continued to seem a waste of money.

The end of the Brazilian trade also led several Portuguese merchants who had done well in Rio or Bahia to move up to New York with the intention of using their expertise, often gained in Africa as well as in Brazil, to develop the Cuban commerce. The most interesting of these men was Manoel Basilio da Cunha Reis, an agent in Africa of a Brazilian slaving firm, before founding his own, in 1852, the 'Portuguese Company', in New York, in partnership with the Portuguese Consul,

César de la Figanière. They specialized in obtaining large cargoes of slaves from Mozambique for Cuba.* Though everything to do with this body is confused (including whether the enterprise was as important as it seemed), it was apparently soon absorbed by a Spanish company, also established in New York, and directed by Inocencio Abrantes of Havana. Both these clandestine companies had many tentacles, in all parts of the Caribbean, and several of the ships were often involved in legitimate trade. Then, suddenly, these vessels would change to slaving, after refitting in, say, Mexico. There was believed to be some collaboration with a similar, and even more shadowy, company concerned to sell slaves in the United States.

The Portuguese Company apparently chose New York as its headquarters because, unlike Havana, that city had a genuine legal African trade. The Company's ships were mostly American-built, inquisitive British officials were few and far between, and so many vessels changed hands in New York that the Portuguese Company's activities attracted little attention. The company had at least twelve ships and may have had more. Their first, the *Advance*, left New York for Africa on 18 September 1852.

This trading from New York was, of course, intended to serve the Cuban market. There was little trading to the United States itself. Even the Texan gate of entry had declined after the entry of that state into the Union in 1845. Captain Denman testified in a British inquiry in 1843, 'I have no reason to believe that any slave trade whatever exists there, except the slave trade from one part of the coast to another. I believe that no new slaves are introduced.'[18]

Yet in the late 1850s some transatlantic trade to North America seems to have revived. As has been noticed, Richard Drake, in his untrustworthy memoir, talked of a slave depot being established in one of the Bay Islands off Honduras for the purpose of receiving slaves from Africa for gradual infiltration into the United States through Texas, Louisiana, or Florida. The Savannah letter book of Charles Lamar suggests how some trade may have been managed in the mid-1850s. Lamar, from a well-known Georgian Huguenot family of Savannah, a nephew of Mirabeau Lamar, second President of Texas, was said, by *The North American Review*, to have been 'a Southern gentleman of the most approved type'; but, the anonymous author added ironically, he 'possessed just enough of the Yankee spirit of enterprise and thrift to render him human'. Lamar apparently entered the slave trade in 1857, buying slaves first from Cuba, then direct from Africa. One of his ships was the *E. A. Rawlins*, said to have landed slaves in 1857 in numerous places. Lamar, like so many

---

Others involved were William Manuel Basilio da Cunha, and another Portuguese, José da Costa Lima Viana. Other partners included a Cuban, John Alberto Machado, and two North Americans, Benjamin Weinberg and John P. Weeks.

before him, was attracted by the idea of making a profit of well over 100 per cent on the voyage. He estimated that the figures might be:

Cost of the expedition	$300,000
Say we bring 1200 negroes @ $650	$780,000
Deduct 1st cost	$300,000
Leaves nett profit and steamer on hand	$480,000 [19]

Yet though Lamar plainly liked profits he also seems to have had an ideological obsession with the need to revive the international carriage of slaves.*

The United States naval patrol was easily circumvented. The British diplomat John Crampton reported from Washington in 1853: 'The United States naval officers are zealous enough in capturing slavers, but the force is so small, particularly now that they have sent the greater part to Japan [with Matthew Perry], that little is done.' He sensibly added: 'The difficulty of getting slavers condemned by Admiralty courts when captured and brought into American ports is another encouragement to the slave traders.' Crampton also pointed to another weakness: that difficulty of ensuring conviction was, it seemed, 'much greater in the northern states, which profess abolitionism, than in the south, where slavery exists'. Shipbuilders of the North were interested in the prosperity of the trade, for which, the diplomat reported, they still furnished 'by far the greatest part of the vessels under whatever flag they afterwards sail'.[20]

There were other reasons for inaction in the United States, apart from the anxiety about damages and the continuing disinclination of the United States to accept the naval leadership of Britain. Consider the case of the *Martha*. The US naval patrol ship *Perry* (a ship called after the hero of Lake Erie, Matthew Perry's brother), reached Ambriz, Angola, on 5 June 1850, in search of her commodore's ship, the *John Adams*. She found that this ship had gone to Luanda. En route to that port, the *Perry* saw a large ship, the *Martha* of New York, standing off the coast, and brought her to. Up till then, the *Perry* had not shown her flag, but she then did so. The master of the *Martha* then observed that the *Perry* was a US cruiser, at which he hoisted a Brazilian flag and threw overboard his writing desk, with his instructions in it. Lieutenant Rush of the *Perry* boarded the *Martha*, but a Portuguese captain insisted that he was the master. The real master's writing desk was, however, retrieved and a North American, dressed as a sailor, was identified as the captain. This man later admitted that had it not been for the interruption he would have taken on board 1,800 slaves that night. The *Martha* was escorted to New York. A farce followed. The captain was released on $3,000 bail, which he immediately abandoned.

---

* *It has been suggested that Lamar's account was forged in order to discredit a cousin of his, Lucius Lamar, Secretary of the Interior under President Cleveland.*

Still, during the 1850s, the United States Navy began to have some success in relation to the trade to Cuba. In 1853–4 Commander Isaac Mayo, in the *Constitution*, captured the schooner *Gambrill* when about to load slaves, but Mayo released all the crew except for two because he did not wish to be sued. Then in 1854, again off Ambriz, Lieutenant Richard Page, in the *Perry*, seized the slaver *Glamorgan*, whose captain, Charles Kehrman, sought to escape by hoisting a British flag. Page sent Kehrman home to be tried in Boston, but allowed the Portuguese super-cargo to go free – for which act of generosity he was himself arraigned. In November of that year New York District Attorney John McKeon brought to trial James Smith, sometime master of the *Julia Moulton*, a New York ship owned by a certain Lamos, a Cuban, which had carried 645 slaves from Ambriz to Trinidad, Cuba. Smith claimed that he was in reality a German, Julius Schmidt of Bederkesa, Hanover, and that he had never been naturalized as a citizen of the United States. He was, however, found guilty of trading slaves, the first man to be so convicted under the law. But a mistrial was proclaimed, on a question of technicalities, and after many legal complications Smith-Schmidt served only thirty-two months.

'Joint-cruising' off Africa between the United States Navy and the British was decided upon in the 1850s. But the policy was 'from the first and in spirit dead. . . . The flagships of the American and British squadrons on the coast in the years 1855, 1856, and part of 1857 met only once and that at sea. They were two miles apart; they recognized each other by signal and, by the same means, held the following exchange: "Anything to communicate?" to receive the inaccurate answer, "Nothing to communicate." '[21]

The year 1857 was a good one generally for the interception of slave ships: HMS *Prometheus* overtook the US brig *Adams Gray*, a fully equipped slaver, with $20,000 in cash aboard. Between then and January 1858 the British seized twenty-one slavers, while the United States, Spanish, and even Portuguese naval patrols captured six more. From that time the British had the services of an effective spy, a Cuban shipbroker, Manuel Fortunat, a Cuban equivalent of the agents whom Palmerston had inspired in Rio. He passed much information to the British consulate in New York. It was this which probably led the British commander on the coast of Africa, Commodore Wise, to believe that, despite everything, the trade to Cuba was still growing: 'Slaves are procurable in thousands; the natives are selling their children, and the traffic in slaves is rapidly destroying legal trade. These ill effects', he added, 'are produced by the shameful prostitution of the American flag for, under that ensign alone, is the slave trade now conducted. . . . Out of 23 vessels said to have escaped, eleven were repeatedly visited by Her Majesty's cruisers but, though known to be slavers, they were necessarily left unmolested, through being *bona fide* American vessels. Had we a treaty with the United States, every one of these vessels would have been captured. . . . Last year, slavers were (in the majority of cases) captured through their captains forgoing the protection of the American flag; but now American slavers are arriving and sailing with almost as much impunity as if they were engaged in legal trade.'[22]

At much the same time, Commander Moresby of the British West Africa Squadron seized the *Panchita* off Africa and sent her to New York. The United States Minister in London protested and stated firmly that the 'question whether the *Panchita*'s journey [was] with the slave trade could have no bearing on the violation of sovereign right'.[23] The British Foreign Secretary, Lord Palmerston, admitted that Moresby had made a mistake, but pointed out the difficulties under which that captain had been labouring.

Palmerston had other difficulties. The Crimean War was now over, and British public opinion was turning its attention again to the matter which had defeated two generations of politicians. *The Times*, on 25 May 1857, argued in favour of a blockade of Cuban ports. Two months later the House of Commons urged the government to do all in its power to end the slave traffic, Spain being pressed by many members of Parliament to declare the trade to be piracy. Charles Buxton repeated all the old arguments, with an urgency which would have suggested the subject was a new one for that legislature; the prospects for peaceful trade with Africa were as never before; cotton could be grown there on a large scale; and why not ask the navy to do in Cuban waters, as *The Times* suggested, what she had done so successfully in Brazilian? Palmerston replied with a defence of his policy of inactivity which might have surprised his own personality of twenty years before: Spain, he rather feebly said, had a different kind of treaty with Britain from that which Brazil had had.[24]

In these circumstances, when nothing serious seemed to be happening to affect the traffic in slaves to Cuba, in April 1858 a British gunboat seized the United States vessel *Cortez* just after she had sailed out of Havana Bay, and begun to harass other ships in Cuban waters. British officers boarded 116 ships by the end of May, of which sixty-one were owned in the United States. One naval captain boarded no fewer than eleven merchant ships in the tiny Cuban port of Sagua la Grande alone. These actions seemed more of an insult to the United States than the sporadic seizures off Africa. On this matter, the states of the North and South of the United States were for once at one, and not only Lewis Cass (in his seventies, that veteran Anglophobe had agreed to serve President Buchanan as Secretary of State) but the Senate itself demanded a firm stand. Senator James Henry Hammond of South Carolina said, 'We had just and ample cause for war, for we had received a flagrant insult.'[25] Even Senator Stephen Douglas of Illinois suggested that a British ship should be seized and her crew held responsible. The mood was so violent in the United States that the British Minister in Washington, Lord Napier, prudently (if unheroically) advised the Commander-in-Chief of Britain's North America station, Sir Houston Stewart, to suspend further action.

In the continuing fortunate absence of the international telegraph, it was some time before this capitulation was communicated to British captains in Cuban waters, and several more incidents occurred. Sir Houston Stewart had begun his naval career under the command of the brilliant Lord Cochrane and knew, therefore, very well the importance in naval matters of audacity, courage, and imagination. Even when the naval captains knew that they could not board and search United States vessels, they still believed that they could board ships which showed American colours to which they had no right. The question when a vessel might or might not be visited remained, therefore, as the historian of the right of visit says, neither 'more nor less a matter of guesswork'.[26]

The activity of United States vessels in carrying slaves to Cuba in these years suggested to many in the increasingly vociferous South that the slave trade to the Union should itself be officially revived. The idea was not new, for it had been proposed as long ago as 1839, by the *Courier* of New Orleans; but it was not till 1853 that Leonidas Spratt, the editor of the *Standard* of Charleston, began a systematic advocacy of this revival, a cry taken up by Robert Barnwell Rhett, in the *Mercury* of the same city. The action of Charles Lamar has been noticed. In 1856 the Governor of South Carolina, James Hopkins Adams, also demanded a legal revival of the African slave trade. In March 1858 the Louisiana House of Representatives called for the import of 2,500 free Africans as apprentices; but the Senate of that state absented itself from the discussion. The same year, William Lowndes Yancey, the secessionist leader of the League of United Southerners, in Montgomery, Alabama, and once a United States senator, asked, with a certain logic, 'If it is right to buy slaves in Virginia and carry them to New Orleans, why is it not right to buy them in Cuba, Brazil and Africa?' Jefferson Davis, on this occasion, stated that he was against reopening the African slave trade because he thought that the consequences would be to swamp Mississippi: 'The interests of Mississippi, not Africa, dictate my conclusion.' He strongly denied that he himself had any connection with those who 'prate of the inhumanity and sinfulness of the trade'. In 1859 similar things were said at the Southern Commercial Convention in Vicksburg, Mississippi: 'A brilliant speech on the resumption of the importation of slaves', wrote Henry Stuart Foote, a liberal ex-Governor of the state,* 'was listened to with breathless attention and applauded vociferously. Those of us who rose in opposition were looked upon as traitors to the best interests of the south.' There was now much support in the Southern press for the idea. Thus the *New Orleans Delta* thought that those who voted for the slave trade in Congress were men

---

* He would resign from the Confederate Congress when Jefferson Davis refused to accept Lincoln's peace proposals. He afterwards crossed the lines and became a Unionist.

whose names 'will be honoured hereafter for the unflinching manner in which they stood up for principle, for truth, and for consistency, as well as for the vital interests of the South'.[27]

Had the South won the Civil War, the African trade would indeed have been reopened. The demands of cotton plantations might have been endless: the crop of 5,000,000 bales in 1860 was nearly double what it had been ten years before, and five times what it had been in 1830.

The most famous slaving case in these years just before the Civil War was that of the *Wanderer*, a fast ship which sailed to Africa in November 1858. It was said of this vessel, 'You'd think she could fly instead of sailing.' Samuel Eliot Morison wrote of this kind of clipper in lyrical terms: 'These . . . ships were built of wood in shipyards from Rockland in Maine to Baltimore. Their architects, like poets who transmute nature's message into song, obeyed what wind and wave had taught them, to create the noblest of all sailing vessels and the most beautiful creations of man in America. . . . They were our Gothic cathedrals, our Parthenon.'[28] Yet many of these jewels were used in the Cuban slave trade; and one at least in that of the United States.

There were many rumours in the South of the United States during the 1850s that slaves had been brought in. There was the instance of Charles Lamar's vessel, the *E. A. Rawlins*, of which mention has been made. Many people knew people whose friends claimed that in Georgia or South Carolina they had seen a coffle of slaves direct from Africa. But the only attested case of the late 1850s was that of the schooner *Wanderer*. Ninety feet long on her keel, 108' overall, with a beam of 26', this fine vessel had been built in Brookhaven, New York, during the winter of 1856–7 for Colonel John Johnson, who had made money in sugar on a plantation near New Orleans. He sold the boat to a number of Southern gentlemen, prominent among whom were Captain William Corrie, a member of the New York Yacht Club, and Charles Lamar, who, as has been mentioned earlier, was a member of a well-known family of Savannah, with investments in cotton, shipping, and banking.

The *Wanderer* was fitted out at Port Jefferson on Long Island, where a number of alterations were set in train: including the provision of those extra-large water tanks which would suggest to all informed yachtsmen that the purpose of the vessel was to bring slaves from Africa. But the boat retained the luxurious fittings which enabled her to be called 'a yacht': there were mirrors, damask, satinwood cupboards, a library, prints, and 'Brussels carpets'.

The *Wanderer* set off for Charleston, then went to Trinidad, with Corrie on board, the master being a certain Captain Semmes. The vessel reached Port-of-Spain, pleasantries were exchanged with the Governor and the other British authorities, and then the ship set off, theoretically for St Helena, in fact for the Congo River. The British warship *Medusa* found her in the latter estuary, flying both the flag of the New York Yacht Club and that of the United States. The captain of the *Medusa* dined, with some of his officers, aboard the *Wanderer*. Captain Egbert Farnham, who had joined the vessel as supercargo, and had once been one of the filibusterers of William Walker, the 'grey eyed man of destiny', ˙ jokingly asked the British if they would like to inspect the *Wanderer* in order to see if she were equipped to carry slaves. The British officers laughed: the idea that such a sumptuous boat sailed by such gentlemen could descend to such a thing seemed preposterous. The British officers left after dinner; and the *Wanderer*, for her part, made for a prearranged rendezvous and picked up 409 slaves aged between thirteen and eighteen.

This United States ship encountered no naval intervention, for, 'notwithstanding that . . . the river Congo is the great slave mart to which America vessels resort', the British Commissioner in Luanda reported in 1859, 'no cruiser of the United States has entered that river for six months'.

The *Wanderer* returned to Georgia about 1 December, losing about seventy or eighty dead slaves en route, and landing her cargo of about 325 slaves at Jekyll Island, off Brunswick, Georgia, in small boats. A local sailor reported that 'a few of them appeared sick, but the majority appeared lively'. Most were then taken up the River Saltilla, in a steamer of Lamar's (the *Lamar*), to his Duigbonon plantation; a few others passed by Savannah itself. Over the next few months, numerous reports occurred all over the South of these slaves being seen. Some were taken to New Orleans by train. But the true story came out; the ship was confiscated at Brunswick in December; several of the owners, including Corrie, were arrested. Lamar raged: 'I distributed the negroes', he wrote, 'as best I could; but I tell you things are in a hell of a fix; no certainty about anything. . . . The yacht has been seized. They have all the pilots and men who took the yacht . . . to testify. She will be lost certain and sure, if not the negroes. Dr. Hazelhurst [has] testified that he attended the negroes and swore that they were Africans of recent importation. . . . All of these men must be bribed. [And] I must be paid for my time, trouble, and advances. . . .'[29]

Lamar was soon charged with slave trading and other offences. But in the summer of 1860 it was easy enough for a Lamar to be acquitted by a court in Savannah. Egbert Farnham also escaped condemnation because his jury was deadlocked. The ship was publicly sold, but it was bought back by Lamar for a quarter of its value. Most of the slaves seem to have been sold at $600 or $700 a head, or even $1,000, and some, in Alabama, were reported to have been sold at $1,600–$1,700. Captain Semmes set off in no time for a run to China for 'coolies . . . worth from $340 to $350 each in Cuba and cost but $12 and their passage'. The British Embassy was

---

˙ *Walker, an adventurer in Nicaragua, had recently been executed.*

naturally informed. The Minister, Lord Napier, reported, a trifle optimistically, that the event had 'had the effect of waking up the American
cabinet to a sense of their disgraceful position in regard to the abuse of
the American flag on the coast of Africa'.* [30]

* *The* **Wanderer** *undertook another journey, perhaps with Charles Lamar's connivance, under Captain D. S. Martin, to Dahomey. But the crew rebelled, and left the captain in a rowing boat off the Canary Islands. Corrie was briefly imprisoned and expelled from the New York Yacht Club, but that seems to have been the only loss of standing encountered by Lamar's gang of imaginative lawbreakers.*

36

CUBA, THE FORWARD SENTINEL

'Cuba ... the forward sentinel of our interests in the New World.'

Captain-General Dulce, 1859

THE PLANTERS OF CUBA were conscious in 1860 that they served a major international enterprise, for the island was by then producing over a quarter of the world's sugar. The Spanish Antilles supplied a fifth of the British market, and three-quarters of that of the United States. It is, therefore, comprehensible that Spanish governments should still not wish to act in a way which might lose the revenue which this saccharine eminence brought, or drive the planters of sugar to rebellion.

But others were unprepared to accept that serene indifference to the cruelty which reliance on slavery entailed. Thus in 1860 the persistent English Liberal Lord John Russell (now Foreign Secretary again, in a government headed by Palmerston) proposed a conference of the main powers (Spain, Britain, France, the United States, Portugal, and Brazil) to put an end to 'an increasing traffic [in slaves] and finally to assure its complete abolition'. Eighty-five ships, Russell understood, presumably from his secret agent's reports, had been fitted out in the previous eighteen months, and a mere twenty-six of these had landed from 12,000 to 15,000 slaves in Cuba.[1]

Russell was probably influenced by the evidence of growing support in the British West Indies for the idea of the annexation of Cuba to the United States. Planters there were disillusioned by Britain's apparent double-headed attitude to slavery, buying Cuban-grown sugar with one hand and seeking to end the slave trade with the other. Robert Baird, writing in 1849, had even said he thought that 'Cuba would be a much better customer of England in the hands of our enterprising brethren of the New World than she is at present in the hands of Spain'. Others said the same in Jamaica.

Secretary of State Lewis Cass discussed Russell's idea of a conference with Tassara, the Spanish Minister in Washington. Conferences did not then have the automatic charm for diplomats that they have in the twentieth century. Cass was certain that at such an occasion the British would assert their claim to inspect foreign ships. Neither he nor Tassara accepted that the trade was on the increase: 'In this policy of the English', he agreed, 'there is something of fanatic self-interest.'[2] Spain, too, rejected the proposal of Russell, arguing, with tacit support from the United States, that other powers should not discuss purely Anglo-Spanish matters.

Cass knew that the efforts to prevent the slave trade adopted after the Webster–Ashburton Treaty had failed. But he considered that American captains destroyed their papers only because of the wanton threats of British captains. He sought every argument to defend the United States, and even in September 1860 was ready to announce that his country had reached 'the happy condition of having no objects of concern to engage the philanthropic care and sympathies of the government and people, so that their benevolent energies, having no employment in their own country, must necessarily seek it in other countries less blessed. . . .'[3]

Cuba was on everyone's mind in the United States during those last months before the Civil War. In 1860, for example, Secretary of the Navy Isaac Toucey, insisting that his department was active in the pursuit of slavers (a boast which in the late 1850s was beginning to have a basis of truth), added, in his report to Congress, that 'Cuba is the only [legal] mart in the world open to this [international] trade. . . . If Cuba were to pass under the constitution of the United States by annexation, the trade would then be effectively suppressed.'[4] That was true, though if Cuba had become a state of the Union it would presumably have ceased to be illegal to sell there slaves born in the United States; and the Cubans could have sold their slaves to the Southern Confederacy.

Meantime, the slave trade was still being undertaken illegally in New York, though it is improbable that any slaves followed those on the *Wanderer* into the Union: all had Cuba as their destination. In 1856 the New York Deputy Marshal declared that the business of fitting out slavers 'has never been prosecuted with greater energy than at present. The occasional interposition of the legal authorities exercises no apparent influence for its suppression. It is seldom that one or more vessels cannot be designated at the wharves, respecting which there is evidence that she is either in or has been concerned in the traffic [to Cuba].'[5] The British Consul in New York reported that out of 170 slave-trading expeditions, presumably to Cuba, fitted out in the three years preceding 1862, 74 were known or believed to have sailed from New York. For example, in the summer of 1859, the barque *Emily* set off from New York with all the equipment necessary for a slaver: 15,000 feet of lumber, 103 casks of fresh water, 100 barrels of rice, 25 barrels of codfish, 20 barrels of pork, 50 barrels of bread, 150 boxes of herring, two boilers, 10 dozen pails, and two cases of medicines. Commander John Calhoun in the USS *Portsmouth* sent her home under guard. But the case was dismissed. Then there was the case of the *Orion*, under Captain John E. Hanna, 450 tons, owned by Harrison S.

Vining, a merchant who seems to have only dabbled in the slave trade. HMS *Pluto* caught her, bound for Havana, with 888 captives. She was sent home, under escort, from Africa, and some of the traditional difficulties followed between Britain and the US. But on this occasion the ship was condemned by Judge Nathan Hall, an honest if austere magistrate the climax to whose parochial life had been his service as Postmaster-General under Millard Fillmore. Then, while Secretary of the Navy Isaac Toucey urged the rather lazy United States commander of the Africa squadron, Commodore Inman, to 'renew his exertions', United States Special Agent Benjamin Slocomb found what he described as evidence of a slave company directed by 'Colonel' John Newman of Tuckpaw River, Louisiana, with agencies in Mobile, Nashville, and New Orleans. Its purpose was to dispose of African slaves from a diversity of sources, including some brought by the *Wanderer*, some bought in Cuba, and some kidnapped in the Bahamas. But Newman turned out to be a liar, and eventually Slocomb would assure Secretary of the Interior Jacob Thompson that despite the endless rumours the only real expedition to Africa from the United States during these years had been that of the *Wanderer*. Stories continued, however, of slave dealing, and there were frequent tales of large secret companies, with headquarters in New York. The case of the *Clotilde*, under Captain Meagher, alleged to have landed 116 slaves in South Carolina in July 1859, may have been a hoax, despite accusations to the contrary by many historians, including the great Bancroft.[6]

All the same, Senator Stephen Douglas, the Democratic leader, said he thought that 15,000 slaves had been landed that year in the United States by North Americans. He himself claimed to have seen 300 in a pen at Vicksburg, Mississippi, and also some in Memphis, Tennessee. It seems possible that in 1859 eighty-five slavers, capable together of carrying between 30,000 and 60,000 slaves, were fitted out in New York alone, intending to serve the markets of Cuba. However many were carried, they sold at high prices, well over $1,000 a head (a few extra qualifications, such as some agricultural training or fluency in Spanish, raised further the price). The profit was such that the captain of the New York ship *Sultana* thought it economical to destroy his ship after landing nearly 1,000 Africans in northern Cuba rather than risk capture; the crew could claim that they were castaways. The difficulties seemed merely to stimulate the slave traders to efforts every day more international. By 1857 the British had concluded no fewer than forty-five treaties against slaving on the West Coast of Africa, yet the trade continued. In the late 1850s yet one more new company was founded in Cuba, whose agents were to be found in Mozambique as well as in New York. The crews were mixed Spanish and Portuguese, and the ships included steamboats made in Hartlepool in England.

The *Continental Monthly* reported, imaginatively: 'The number of persons engaged in the slave trade and the amount of capital embarked in it exceed our powers of calculation. The city of New York has been, until of late, the principal port in the world for this infamous commerce; although the cities of Boston and Portland [Maine] are only second to her. . . . Slave dealers . . . contributed largely to the wealth of our commercial metropolis; they contributed liberally to the treasuries of political organization, and their bank accounts were largely depleted to carry elections in New Jersey, Pennsylvania and Connecticut.'[7] But after several seizures, the centre of the traffic moved elsewhere; some ships in these years even set off, it was said, from Liverpool, England, and Wilmington, Delaware (where the Cuban John A. Machado's *Mary Francis* was certainly fitted out) – as well as, of course, from Havana. (The accusation against Liverpool derived from the appearance of the brig *Lily*, which sailed from that city in 1852 with a cargo of rum and gunpowder. Some ships from Cardiff were said to jettison their coal as soon as they were out of sight of Wales, and head south for the profitable harbours of tropical Africa.)

Late in 1859 President James Buchanan (well disposed to England, having had a happy time leading the United States legation in London during the Crimean War) took two decisive steps in the United States' campaign against the slave traffic. First, he allowed four private steamships (which had been brought together by the US Navy for an ultimately unnecessary naval action against Paraguay) to be added to the Africa Squadron. That squadron itself was also at last moved from its twenty-year headquarters in the remote Cape Verde Islands to the centre of the slave trade in Angola. Second, four American steamers were stationed for the first time off Cuba. The significance of the latter departure was shown by the fact that in July 1860 Lieutenant Stanley, in the *Wyandotte*, off Havana, reported that three separate individuals had offered him $25,000 not to cruise off various ports in Cuba at certain times.

These assignments of ships were important. Between 1841 and 1859, only two ships laden with slaves had been detained by the US Navy, though many suspicious vessels had been boarded. But in 1860 alone the United States naval squadron captured eight slave ships, carrying over 4,000 slaves. Off Angola, the naval vessel *San Jacinto* captured the *Storm King* of New York, bound for Cuba with 619 slaves, and also the New York slaver *Bonito*, with 750 slaves, with the same destination. (The captain of the *Storm King* outmanoeuvred the US Marshal's officers, and later the Deputy Marshal of New York, Thomas Rynders, who admitted accepting a bribe of $1,500 for allowing the ship to leave.) Off Cuba the steamer *Mohawk*, under Lieutenant T. A. Craven, arrested the *Wildfire*. Craven also detained the barque *Mary J. Kimball* and the brig *Toccoa*, the latter owned by Anthony Horta, but leased to Galdis and Nenniger of Havana, both bound for Africa. Craven took these vessels to Key West, where Judge William Marvin declared the *Toccoa* indeed to be a slaver, on circumstantial evidence. He challenged Horta to prove that she was not so. Horta secured the liberty of his boat; she immediately sailed across the Atlantic, to be captured later by the Spanish naval ship *Neptuno*, with 627 slaves on board. The future Confederate raider Lieutenant John Maffitt, in the *Crusader*, seized the *Bogotá*, in the old Bahama channel, with 400 Africans on board. (Maffitt always recalled how the slaves broke their hatches with a shout and much singing.) Later, Maffitt seized the brig *Joven Antonio*, on which he found everything ready for slaves. He took the ship into Key West, where José Colón of Cárdenas claimed it. Finally, Commodore Inman, the commander of the United States squadron, in the *Constellation*, captured the *Cora* two days out of Sagua la Grande with 705 slaves.

Yet despite these minor triumphs of the US Navy the Cuban slave trade still prospered. In 1859 more slave-trading expeditions set out from Cuba or the United States for Africa than at any time since 1820. Perhaps as many as 170 slave voyages for the benefit of Cuba were arranged in New York in 1859–61; and the Consul of the United States in Havana, Robert Shufeldt, a veteran of the African and Brazilian naval squadrons and a man of gigantic frame and great diplomatic skills, would report in 1863 that: 'However humiliating may be the confession . . . nine tenths of the vessels engaged in the slave trade are American.'[8] The British thought that in 1859–61 nearly 80,000 slaves were imported. These cost $1,000 each, so only the rich could buy them, but there were an increasingly large number of rich men on the island. There seemed no reason to suppose that the state of affairs would change. The size of Julián Zulueta's new steam-powered ships grew and grew: one such brought in 1,500 slaves in 1860. Thomas Wilson, a British merchant in Havana, thought that 'the only remedy is to back the Americans to acquire the island'.[9] Joseph Crawford, in his twentieth year as British Consul-General in Havana, wrote in February 1861 to Palmerston that there was still no will on the part of the Spanish government, or its officers, to carry out any of the provisions of the treaty banning the slave trade. He thought, therefore, that 'we have to abandon our efforts of persuasion with Spain to put an end to the traffic . . . and proceed to the immediate adoption of the most energetic measures to compel its observance'.[10] Palmerston, in a fine speech in the House of Commons that same month, said that over the slave trade, 'the conduct of Spain might have given us just cause for war if we had thought proper to avail ourselves of it'. (The origin of this debate was a motion by Stephen Cave, whose interest in the subject may derive from his Bristol origins, to the effect that the means chosen by the government for suppressing the slave trade had failed. Cave made one of the strongest anti-Spanish speeches that the House of Commons had heard: Spain, he said, 'enjoyed a pre-eminence for barbarity in the dark annals of the New World. . . .')[11]

The British and Foreign Anti-Slavery Society seemed willing, at a conference in Lord Brougham's house in London in June 1861, to abandon its long-held pacifism in support of Palmerston's position. But surely war could not be the answer.

Part of the solution lay in securing effective legal action in North America; and now, for the first time, that seemed to be forthcoming. In August 1860 Commander Sylvester Gordon of the US Navy, in the *San Jacinto*, detained the slave ship *Erie*, captained by his namesake Nathaniel Gordon, to the west of Cabinda, with 900 slaves on board. Nathaniel Gordon, who was said to have carried out at least three slave journeys before (when the *Erie* had been called the *Juliet*), had fitted out his ship in Cuba and sailed forty-five miles up the Congo to fetch this consignment of Africans. He was already at sea, preparing to sail back to Cuba, when he was detained. His slaves were taken to Liberia, and he was himself sent to New York. The ship was sold, and Gordon was tried with his mates, William Warren and David Hale, before Judge William Shipman, who was hearing his first slavery case.

Gordon's defence was that he had sold the *Erie* to a Spaniard before the slaves were loaded, and that he was just a passenger at the time of arrest. But several seamen testified that they had been offered a dollar a head by Gordon for every slave landed peacefully in Cuba. After one mistrial, Gordon was, to the general surprise, condemned to be hanged. Judge Shipman said: 'Do not imagine that because others shared in the guilt of this enterprise, yours is thereby diminished. But remember the awful admonition of your Bible: "Though hand join in hand, the wicked shall not go unpunished."'

This sentence must have astonished Gordon. Many slave captains had been captured, but none had been severely punished, much less hanged, even though the offence of slave trading had been a capital one since 1820. Between 1837 and 1860 seventy-four cases had been brought in the United States on charges related to slaving, but few captains had been convicted, and those had received trifling sentences, which they had usually been able to avoid.

Gordon took strychnine, but the prison doctor saved him for the gallows. He was hanged in public on 21 February 1862: the first, and only, North American to be executed for slave trading.[12]

This was a landmark in the history of the slave trade, though it was not quite a turning point, for old ways survived, even in the North of the United States. In 1861, for example, Commander John Taylor, in the sloop-of-war *Saratoga*, arrested the *Nightingale* (Captain Francis Bowen), off Cabinda, just after loading 961 slaves, bound for Cuba. But all concerned were treated leniently, including Samuel Haynes, the first mate, who suffered two retrials. On 30 October 1862 Erastus Booth, captain of the *Buckeye*, was also tried – before Judge Shipman, indeed – for trading slaves. After he was released on bail, the evidence was dismissed, and Booth acquitted. In the same month, Albert Horn, owner of the slaver the *City of Norfolk*, was convicted at New York City but was, inexplicably, pardoned by President Lincoln on grounds of ill health. In the spring of 1863 Appleton Oaksmith, owner of the supposed whaler *Margaret Scott*, was convicted in Boston of slaving, but he escaped from jail while awaiting sentence, with the connivance of a guard. In 1862 the Dutch instigated their first case against a slave trader when an English naval captain reported that the mate of the slaver *Jane* had lived in Rotterdam. But this man claimed that he had not realized that the ship on which he was serving was a slaver, and the case was dismissed.

The administration of President Lincoln desired to end the slave trade, but it required its ships for war duties, and called home both the Africa and the new Cuba squadrons. This action appeared likely to stimulate the slave trade again. The hanging of Captain Nathaniel Gordon of the *Erie* did not seem to be a determining deterrence. Diplomacy was still necessary.

So Charles Francis Adams – United States Minister in London, and son of John Quincy Adams – was asked by Secretary of State Seward (Cass's benign successor) to request Lord John Russell to send a force into Cuban waters to intercept slavers. An amazed Russell replied that sending cruisers was pointless unless British warships were allowed to search and, if necessary, seize United States ships. Lincoln and Seward 'capitulated', as Howard, of the British legation in Washington, put it – partly because the administration hoped to gain British support for the Federal side. On 5 October 1861, the Admiralty in London received an astonishing memorandum from the Foreign Office: 'The American Secretary of State, in speaking of the jealousy of the United States respecting the Right of Search, has expressed to Lord Lyons [the tactful British Minister in Washington] the willingness of the Washington cabinet that British cruisers should overhaul any vessels which gave reasonable grounds of suspicion. ... Mr Adams, the United States Minister ... has apprised Lord John Russell that the fitting out of vessels designed for the Slave Trade will no longer be permitted at New York.'[13] Lord Lyons, who had as a boy served as a midshipman on his father's HMS *Blonde* in the Mediterranean in the 1820s, drafted a ten-year treaty to allow such inspection. By then, the Federal Navy had blockaded the Confederate coastline and put paid to any chance of a revival of the slave trade to the North American mainland.

The subsequent treaty allowed warships of both nations the right to search each other's merchant vessels in the Atlantic. A later protocol also permitted search off the East African coast. If any slaving equipment, or any slaves, were found, the ships could be taken to a mixed court at New York, Cape Town, or Sierra Leone. Decisions in those cities had to be made by both a British and an American judge, and if they could not agree a US or a British arbitrator would be called in. There would be no damage for false arrest: a great relief to United States naval officers.

Thus in a single document Lincoln abandoned the principles of United States foreign policy which John Quincy Adams had enunciated, and which every United States President and Secretary of State, not to speak of every Minister to London, had referred to as if they had been Holy Writ. The establishment of a mixed court was also a great concession, since it had always been maintained that no foreign judge could ever play any part in deciding United States law. Secretary of State Seward remarkably wrote to his protégé, Charles Francis Adams, John Quincy's son, in London: 'Had such a treaty been made in 1808, there would have been no sedition here.'[14]

The Senate considered, and approved, this extraordinary treaty behind closed doors, in executive session, and there was no report in the newspapers.

The treaty with the United States should have been a great satisfaction to the ageing Lord Palmerston, who, for all his intolerable pride, bombast, and condescension towards those peoples whom he considered inferior, had done almost as much as Wilberforce and Clarkson to secure the end of the international slave trade. But his own and his Cabinet's attitude to Lincoln and the North in the Civil War had been lukewarm (if not actually hostile) until this moment and he and Russell had already recognized the Confederates in the United States as belligerents. Palmerston believed for a time that the North was planning to invade Canada, and his hostility to slavery as such, as opposed to the trade, had never been strong. He was also exercised by the thought of the slaves of the cotton-producing and aristocratic South being freed by democratic generals from the North. Adams, whose work in London was made much easier by the fact that he had gone to school in England, reached the conclusion that though the matter of slavery had previously been the main question dividing the United States and Britain, 'the sentiment of anti-slavery had disappeared'.[15]

The detention of the two Southern envoys in the British ship *Trent*, en route from Havana to England, by Admiral Charles Wilkes (a great-nephew of John Wilkes) returning from his time in the United States anti-slave naval patrol on the coast of Africa, in that same USS *San Jacinto* which had captured Nathaniel Gordon, brought Britain and the federalists near to conflict. (Had the Atlantic cable been in operation in December 1861, wrote Charles Adams's son, Henry, 'the two countries would certainly have gone to war'.)

Lincoln's government, meantime, after its well-known hesitation on the matter, in the interest of maintaining the integrity of the Union introduced the Thirteenth Amendment to the Constitution and so abolished slavery in the United States. The death of Charles Lamar, the protagonist of the affair of the *Wanderer*, acting as an aide to General Howell Cobb (Buchanan's Secretary of the Treasury, who had married a Lamar) in the Battle of Columbus, Georgia, in April 1865, marked the end of an era.

Two other developments, a hardening of the British position and internal changes in Cuba, need to be taken into account. As to the first, Captain Wilmot of the Africa Squadron had suggested at the end of July 1861 a two-pronged attack on the chief African sellers: first, a special visit to the King of Dahomey to persuade him to abandon trading slaves, and, second, a close naval blockade of about 300 miles of the African coast to prevent the shipment of slaves. Palmerston, however, agreed with Charles Buxton (Fowell Buxton's son) who, in the House of Commons, had suggested an attack on Whydah ('he could not see why they should not use violent means'), and thought that with the United States preoccupied by the Civil War, 'we ought to . . . begin by taking possession of Whydah and either tell him [the King of Dahomey] why, or wait until he asks us why. . . . It is only the strong arm which can prevail with these barbarians.' But the Admiralty opposed this and, in the end, Palmerston merely sent Wilmot, and subsequently the explorer Richard Burton (at that time Her Majesty's Consul in Fernando Po), on a peaceful mission to the King. Wilmot explained to King Gelele: 'England has been doing her utmost to stop the slave trade in this country. Much money has been spent, and many lives sacrificed to obtain this desirable end, but hitherto without success. I have come to ask you to put an end to this traffic and to enter into some treaty with me.'

Gelele refused: if white men came to buy, why should he not sell? Wilmot asked how much money he needed. 'No money will not induce me . . . I am not like the kings of Lagos and Benin. There are only two kings in Africa, Ashanti and Dahomey: I am the King of all the Blacks. Nothing will compensate me for the [loss of the] slave trade.' Gelele also told Burton, 'If I cannot sell my captives taken in war, I must kill them, and surely the English would not like that?'[16]

It was an argument for which abolitionists were unprepared. The slavers were not; and many new ships were fitted out for the Cuban trade in the early 1860s: some in France (Fécamp, Marseilles), and Spain (Cádiz).

The only way in which the British intervened in Africa at this time was, with some reluctance, to accede to a suggestion of Consul Beechcroft in Lagos and agree to the occupation of that city in order to complete the abolition of the slave trade in the Bight of Benin. That at least was the explanation offered by Lord John Russell, then Foreign Secretary, in June 1861: the government 'are convinced that the permanent occupation of this important point in the Bight of Benin is indispensable to the complete suppression of the slave trade in the Bight'. King Docemo was dismissed by Acting Consul William McCoskry, a legitimate trader of long experience on the coast, and subsequently allowed an annual income of £1,000, to be paid in cowries.[17]

The British had scarcely patrolled the coasts of Cuba between 1858 and 1861. The risk of a serious naval clash with Spain seemed too great.

But with the new situation in the United States, they changed their policies. Russell, still Foreign Secretary, sought, like the United States before 1860, to organize a blockade by four steam cruisers in Cuban waters. Spain refused to allow those ships to anchor off any Cuban port. The idea seemed a renunciation of their sovereignty. All the same, in 1863, the British navy did have six ships cruising off Cuba. Despite the Civil War, the United States also maintained a sporadic patrol, and Admiral Charles Wilkes, the controversial officer who had captured the *Trent*, seized the *Noc Daqui*, one of Julián Zulueta's large steamers, in 1863.

In these critical moments, Cuba had the benefit at last of a succession of genuinely liberal captains-general. Thus in 1859, in the face of accusations that the international trade in slaves was doing better than ever – perhaps 23,000 were carried into Cuba that year – and with the British continuing to send to Madrid all the evidence which they had gained from their Consul in Havana,˙ Captain-General de la Concha proposed to exile from Cuba anyone even *suspected* of being involved in a slave expedition. The Spanish government thought that idea far too arbitrary. Concha, to begin with suspected of being too tolerant to the planters, then resigned, apparently in disgust at the planters' disloyalty.

The eclipse of La Concha was providential, for the next Captain-General was the enlightened General Francisco Serrano, a competent and tolerant ex-Minister of War and ex-lover of Queen Isabella, the 'handsome general' whom the Queen had desired always to retain at the palace. He, like his predecessor, had a solution to the problems of Cuba: an organic law, in which numerous political freedoms would be granted. Slavery would be preserved, he told the British Consul, Joseph Crawford, but on the other hand the slave trade would be declared piracy, and any offenders would be punished by martial law. It is true that the government in Madrid dismissed the plan as being against 'the principles of morality and justice'. But by now there was a real abolitionist group in Spain, not just a few isolated writers such as the botanist Ramón de la Sagra. A radical group in the new Cortes of 1855 (including Emilio Castelar and Laurent Figuerola) talked of the matter. These were still minority voices, but they were eloquent: the first-named was among the finest orators in Europe, the second an intelligent economist who would one day introduce Spain's first free-trade budget. General Serrano, in June 1862, suggested that the Civil War in North America should cause Spain to talk genuinely of abolition – before events precipitated the matter. He thought that unless the slave trade were abolished, slavery

---

˙ *The British First Lord of the Admiralty, then the Duke of Somerset, circulated a paper to his Cabinet in January 1860: 'The slave trade,' he wrote, 'is rapidly increasing, and . . . in the present year it has grown more extensively and more successfully than for many years past. . . . There is now no effective check on the slave trade and but little risk of capture to those who conduct it.'*

itself would be destroyed. Serrano had already tried to infuse the Spanish navy with a serious capacity for preventing the slave traffic, by using a few shallow-draught steamers. But though the government agreed with him in principle, in practice it was still resolved to be ineffective.

Next as Captain-General was General Domingo Dulce. He had first come to the public notice when he defended Queen Isabella and her sister against an insurrection faction of officers on the staircase of the royal palace in Madrid in 1841. He sought to govern with generosity but strength, although he had no sympathy for Africans.* When he took office in Havana in December 1862, he announced that he had been sent to fulfil the treaties which the Queen had made with other countries for the suppression of the trade in slaves. He said that he had all the names of those concerned in such activities and he would not hesitate to use his powers to destroy them. For the first time, a British judge of the Mixed Court (Robert Bunch) reported favourably of a captain-general: 'It is impossible that anyone should express himself more strongly against this infamous traffic than General Dulce did.' Bunch said he believed that he was often deceived by false reports. Dulce admitted that that was often the case, and said: 'Send in all the information you can get, be it true or false, and we will do our best to sift it.' He began by expelling two minor slave traders, Antonio Tuero and Francisco Duraboña, and followed that by sending home eight more important Portuguese ones in the spring of 1863. He also suspended the Governor of Havana, Pedro Navascues, for complicity in a slaving expedition. By this time, the British Consul-General had begun to trust Dulce and even to collaborate with him, as he had suggested. In 1864 José Agustín Argüelles, Governor of Colón in central Cuba, despite his famous name in anti-slaving circles, fled to the United States when accused of selling 141 slaves whom he had freed after intercepting a ship of Zulueta's (the two were probably in collaboration). He was sent back to Cuba, to be tried and sentenced to life in the galleys (which sentence, admittedly, he did not serve).[18]

Though as Captain-General Dulce continued to enjoy emergency powers, as all his predecessors had done since 1825, he allowed the Cubans to publish newspapers; and one of these, El Siglo, became the centre of liberal Cuban opinion which, led by the progressive agronomist the Count of Pozos Dulces (Francisco Frías y Jacott) and José Morales Lemus (both of whom had been in favour of Cuba's annexation to the United States in the 1840s),† was prepared to argue in favour of an immediate abolition of the slave trade, including an end to the brutal Yucatec and Chinese immigration. El Siglo also suggested trying again to

---

* He said, for instance, 'By his very nature the African is indolent and lazy and to give him liberty, something which he has not known even in his own country, will make him into a vagabond.'
† Pozos Dulces was a brother-in-law of the nationalist Narciso López.

find incentives to attract white colonists. Though hoping to maintain slavery, at least for the time being, these enlightened planters feared a Southern victory in the North American Civil War, for they believed that a triumphant Confederacy would be sure to impose high tariffs on Cuba in order to protect their own increasingly important sugar in Louisiana.

The reasons for these changes in mood were various: first, there was the continuing high cost of slaves which the merchants thought that they could obtain (in 1864, prices of slaves in Havana reached $1,250–$1,500); second, manumission had depleted the slave labour available; thirdly, despite the relative political failure of most of the new independent Latin American states there was an increasing sense of national destiny among Cubans; and finally, the Civil War in North America stimulated abolitionist sentiment on the island.

All the same, 1863, the second year of that conflict, saw the entry into Cuba of nearly 25,000 slaves, according to Spanish archives. A leading merchant of Havana summed things up as they still seemed to him: 'For many reasons Spain would gain with the abolition of the slave trade . . . but the government recognizes, as does everyone here, that the economic problem is connected with the existence of slavery, since the island's wealth depends on slave labour. Hence the benign tolerance and leniency that is employed in dealing with such an infamous trade.'[19] Slavery itself still seemed to be firmly established: there were over 350,000 slaves on the island, of whom two-thirds were male; almost half lived on sugar mills, about 25,000 on coffee plantations, and under 18,000 on tobacco farms.

Yet the trade in slaves in Cuba seemed at last to be in decline. The Captain-General insisted, indeed, that no slaves landed in 1865, and the Foreign Office admitted that Consul Joseph Crawford had exaggerated the figures for 1859. As for Africa, the British Commodore A. P. E. Williams found the fifteen old factories at Punta da Lehna, on the Congo, on the point of collapse, though the traders themselves were still living well.

Francisco Martí y Torres, once a friend of Tacón, with two José Ricardo O'Farrills, uncle and nephew, descendants of the South Sea factor of 1713, sought ways round the obstinately philanthropic approach of Dulce, and planned an expedition to bring slaves from Africa to the plantations which he owned in Malas Aguas and Pan de Azúcar. The expedition was betrayed, and the Captain-General ordered the commander of the navy to pursue their ships. Several other incidents (the seizure of slaves on board the schooner *Matilde*; and the discovery of 278 slaves who had been disembarked from a brigantine which had been burned after delivery of the cargo) caused Dulce to begin legal proceedings against Martí, which would have been a cause célèbre had the by then aged slaver not died, in his own house in Havana, in the spring of 1866.

Even Julián Zulueta was soon thwarted. He had bought a fast steamer in Liverpool, named it the *Cicerón*, and in it carried over 1,100 slaves from Dahomey to Panama. On the latter beach, Zulueta in person marched the slaves along the Central American coast to a point where he planned to transport them to Cuba. But the local Governor betrayed him and the slaves were lost. When the *Cicerón* returned to Africa for another cargo she was prevented from trading by a cordon of boats which the British had flung round her destination. Several other slavers were similarly apprehended. But some stories often had less satisfactory endings. For example, in 1864, HMS *Dart* seized what was assumed to be a United States slaving brig, but the crew destroyed the papers and the vessel was let go.

That same year the Spanish abolitionist movement acquired a new leader: the Puerto Rican planter Julio Vizcarrando. He held the first meeting of the Sociedad Abolicionista Española in Madrid in that year, with two other Puertoriqueños (José Acosta, Joaquín Sanromá). But he had the support of liberal Spanish politicians such as Emilio Castelar, Juan Valera (a fine novelist), Segismundo Moret (grandson of an English general and an Anglophile), Manuel Becerra (later a reforming Colonial Minister), and Nicolás Salmerón (a philosopher and federalist). Vizcarrando was the outstanding guide whom the Spanish abolitionists needed, and he had the advantage not only of knowing the United States well, but of being married to a formidable agitator, Harriet Brewster of Philadelphia. He had liberated his own slaves in Puerto Rico, publicly denounced the injustices practised on them and others, and founded a house of charity for the poor of San Juan; in Madrid, he used the same emblem for his movement as that which had been employed in Britain: a chained Negro on bended knee. He soon established branches of his movement in Seville, León, Barcelona, and Saragossa. He inspired a journal, the *Revista Hispana-Americana*, whose first editorial demanded an end to the Cuban slave trade as a precursor of other colonial reforms. Many committees in Spain asked many old questions ('What are the means for promoting matrimony among slaves?'), which lost none of their urgency for having been put by others a hundred years before.

There were defenders of slavery in Spain, as there had been in England, France, and the United States: for example, the popular journalist José Ferrer de Couto, in his *Los negros en sus diversos estados y condiciones*, argued that 'the so-called slave trade is . . . the redemption of slaves and prisoners', who, he thought, were far better off under Spain than they were in vile Africa. But Vizcarrando had a decisive effect.

It was in consequence of Vizcarrando's activity that on 6 May 1865 Antonio María Fabié, a *sevillano*, could rise in the Cortes to second a motion on abolition: 'The war in the United States is finished,' he declaimed, 'and, it being finished, slavery on the whole American continent can be taken as finished. Is it possible to keep . . . this institution in the dominions [of Spain]? I don't think so. . . . The Government must comply with its great obligations. . . .' Fabié admittedly had preceded this with the by then customary, even obligatory, eulogy of Spanish slavery in comparison with that of the Anglo-Saxons: 'In all the history of slavery', he said, 'no country has known how to organize it as Spain has, no country has made the situation of the Negro race more elevated, more tolerable or, at times, more sweet.... This explains why we have preserved the institution longer than in other countries.'[20]

A few days later the liberal Cuban planters associated with the news-paper *El Siglo* sent a memorandum to the still influential Captain-General Serrano in Madrid (12,000 Cuban *criollos* signed), requesting his support for Cuban representation in the Cortes, a reform of tariffs to allow the import of flour from the US, and, astonishingly, an end to the traffic in slaves, which they spoke of as 'a repugnant and dangerous cancer of immorality.... Private interests have shown themselves more powerful than the honour and conscience of the nation.' Here was a remarkable transformation![21]

It is true that a pro-Spanish party (headed by Julián Zulueta) made their own protest in reply, in a letter to the Queen: whose signatories were, they said, not against changes in tariffs, but they were against polit-ical reform, including any idea of representation of Cubans in the Cortes in Madrid. But the reformers were now dominant in Spain; and, in August 1865 Dulce was permitted to exile all persons 'who had repeat-edly endangered the peace of the island', and to include slave merchants in this category. Those exiled to Spain included the astonished multi-millionaire Zulueta: a brave and unforeseeable act.

The following February the Conservative Antonio de Cánovas, then Minister for the Colonies, finally introduced into the Cortes in Madrid a bill for the suppression and punishment of the slave trade. Cánovas would become the great Spanish statesman of the later part of the nine-teenth century, but if he had not been that he would have been recognized as a historian. He was a statesman in the mould of Edmund Burke, but a Burke who exercised power. The preamble of his bill included the remarkable reminder that the ancient laws of Castile 'punished the stealing of freemen by death' and also accepted that Africans were freemen.

The bill was debated over several weeks, Generals Gutiérrez de la Concha, Pezuela, and O'Donnell, all sometime captains-general in Cuba, being among those to speak. A commission set up by Cánovas described the traffic as 'infamous and inexplicable in the eyes of Christian civiliza-tion'. But slave interests continued to be well represented in Madrid – for example, by José Luis Riquelme, who had property and slaves in Cuba. He deplored the idea in the proposed new law that officials could enter plantations looking for newly imported slaves. That would revive all the troubles of 1854. 'On my own plantation', said Riquelme, 'I have given liberty to those slaves who asked for it, and they have remained to work on the plantation. That is the way.'

Cánovas replied that the belief that the prosperity of the island demanded the slave trade was out of date. The government would accept slavery for the time being 'as it now exists'. But 'I am obliged to suppress the slave trade ... and I will stop at nothing in order to achieve this result.' His bill passed the Senate in April 1866, but because of further procedural complexities associated with the fall of the Spanish government it did not become law till May 1867, and was only promulgated in Cuba in September 1867. Its article 38 provided at last for the registration of all slaves. Black men and women not included in the registration would be deemed free. Anyone connected with the trade in slaves was to be liable to heavy punishments. As had by then occurred in most other European countries, any slave who reached Spain was also to be declared automatically free.[22]

Spanish abolitionists complained that the law was less rigorous than laws in other countries, for it did not denounce slave traders as pirates. Colonial officials still found it very difficult to carry out inspections within plantations; and many believed that 'while slavery exists, all efforts to suppress the traffic will prove futile'. Even General Dulce thought the law inadequate: he favoured the arbitrary exiling of all slave merchants, men who 'are very well known in the island, those who prepare slave ships; [for] in the secretariat of the civil government, information can be found concerning the most prominent people engaged in this odious speculation'.[23]

By that time the institution of slavery itself seemed to be endangered. On 3 April 1866 the *New York Times* published an extraordinary report: 'The negroes of the *haciendas* of Zulueta, Aldama and the other big owners of slaves, in the jurisdiction of Matanzas, have declared themselves on strike in the last days, demanding that they be paid for their work. ... Some troops have been sent to the *haciendas* to oblige them to start working again. If the mania of not wanting to work without payment extends to other *haciendas*, it would be difficult for their proprietors to accustom themselves to such a revolutionary state of affairs.'[24]

There were few slave landings in the late 1860s. In 1867 Captain-General Joaquín del Manzano talked of just such an event, and the Admiralty in Britain confirmed the tale. About the same time, the British Consul-General reported that he had seen 275 Africans brought into Havana by a Spanish naval ship, the *Neptuno*. Some newspapers recorded what they claimed to be landings. *L'Opinion nationale* reported in Paris in August 1866 that the slave traffic had reached even greater proportions, and declared that one dealer had paid $50,000 as a bribe to introduce 700 Africans. The *New York Herald* also claimed that 1,000 Africans were landed near Jaruco that summer. Three hundred were said to have been taken by schooner to Marianao, a residence 'where the [new] Captain General is living [probably Francisco Lersundi, not Manzano] ... [and] afterwards, to the farm of a wealthy Spaniard. They were duly provided with the necessary passes. . . .' The abolitionist lawyer in Madrid, Rafael Labra, said that a Havana paper had advertised blacks from Africa for sale (though without specifying the paper). In December 1867 the captain of the British cruiser *Speedwell* discovered ninety-six Africans on board a slave ship off Africa, and reported that he had been told of another 700 being maintained in a barracoon nearby; and Cuba of course was their destination. A German traveller observed a slave ship leaving the Loango coast in 1868, but there is no evidence of when and where it arrived. The last verified landing of slaves in Cuba appears to have been in January 1870, when 900 captives seem to have been disembarked near Jibacoa, in the province of Havana. The Cuban historian José Luciano Franco remembered meeting in Havana in 1907 an African known as María la Conguita who said that she had been carried as a slave with others to Cuba as late as 1878. But she may have had a poor memory for dates.[25]

There is really no evidence for any landing of slaves in Cuba after 1870. In 1871 the head of the Slavery Department of the Foreign Office in London told a select committee of the House of Commons that he had heard stories that some slaves had found their way from Zanzibar to Cuba, but, he commented, 'I do not think there is any foundation for such a statement.' Even the always sceptical British Consul thought that no landings of slaves were made between 1865 and 1872.

Meanwhile, the cause of the *emancipados* was also resolved. In September 1869 the Captaincy-General in Havana began the task of distributing certificates of liberty to all who had survived the years of ignominy, brutality, and indifference. But most of them remained to all intents and purposes slaves till their dying days. Twenty-six thousand *emancipados* had been liberated in Cuba since 1825: the number of really free men could not have been more than a few thousand.

So now at last the British and other nations' West Africa and South America squadrons, not to speak of their North America stations, could be brought to an end; about 200,000 slaves had been freed from slave ships in consequences of their efforts, even if not far short of 2,000,000 had been carried. The British West Africa Squadron, which had done so much for the cause of abolition, was merged with the Cape Squadron in 1870. Its captains had over sixty years freed about 160,000 slaves, probably about 8 per cent of the slaves shipped from Africa, mostly (85 per cent) off Africa. They or their French, North American, Portuguese, and Spanish colleagues captured about 1,635 ships altogether: about a fifth of the 7,750 or so ships which set off for the trade in that time. Perhaps another 800,000 additional slaves would have been shipped if there had been no Africa squadron. Many British seamen died (1,338 in all between 1825 and 1845) as a result of skirmishes at sea or, even worse, yellow fever and malaria contracted on land or in the rivers of the slave coast still in an age of ignorance of the causes of those diseases.[26]

The Mixed Court at Sierra Leone was closed in 1871, but, though it was never used again, its sister judiciary court in Havana survived till 1892. The judges appointed under the United States–British treaty of 1861 never had to hear a case.

So it was that the 350 years of the slave trade from Africa to Cuba came to an end without special celebration, without fanfare, and without a victory procession. But it was a triumph, all the same, for reason and humanity.

EPILOGUE

IN 1840 TURNER EXHIBITED his painting *Slave Ship*, depicting slavers throwing overboard dead and dying slaves. There is a typhoon coming on; the seamen seem to be in almost as bad a condition as the slaves. The picture, recalling the fate in 1781 of the *Zong*,* was intended to commemorate the doom of slavery.

The exhibition of *Slave Ship* coincided with a grand meeting in Exeter Hall, in London, summoned to inaugurate the Africa Civilisation Society, inspired by Thomas Fowell Buxton. The meeting marked the final conversion of 'the great and the good' in Britain to abolitionism, for it was inaugurated by the President of the new body, the Prince Consort, in his first public address in England. The Duke of Norfolk, the Earl Marshal, was present, as was the Leader of the Opposition, Sir Robert Peel. If the Prince Consort knew how the recently dead monarch, William IV, had spoken so often against abolition in the House of Lords while his father was still King, he kept quiet. Perhaps the Duke remembered his ancestors' investments in the South Sea Company. If so, he did not allude to the matter. If Peel recalled how his father had opposed abolition in the House of Commons earlier in the century, he too kept his thoughts to himself. Another age had begun – at least in England.

But though the Atlantic slave trade was in 1840 within sight of its end, the end of slavery itself in the Americas took longer than Turner had imagined. Britain had already just abolished the institution, France would do so in eight years, and the United States in twenty-five. To own a slave became an offence in British India in 1862. In both Cuba and Brazil, however, the main concern of the last chapters of this book, slavery itself survived till nearly the end of the nineteenth century, with controversies raging there (as in Spain) as if the matters concerned had never been discussed in other countries. Advertisements were still placed in Brazil in the 1870s for the sale of slaves; the wording sometimes left it uncertain whether it was a human or an animal that could be bought: a *cabra* might be a goat, but it could also mean a female 'quadroon'.

The Ten Years War in Cuba, in 1868–78 (which failed to secure Cuban independence), hastened emancipation in that colony: though the Cuban rebels, representing small planters rather than great industrial sugar monarchs, did not commit themselves to immediate abolition,

* *See page 488.*

they did proclaim freedom, as Bolivar had done, to slaves who fought for
them.

A new law of 1870 in Madrid of Segismundo Moret provided, in a
qualified fashion, for the liberty of children born to slave families; and
it also conceded liberty to all slaves over the age of sixty-five (later
amended to sixty). Slaves who fought for Spain in the war against the
Cuban nationalists were also proclaimed free, but there were still nearly
200,000 Cuban slaves at the end of the war.

The passage of Moret's law was the occasion for the great liberal
orator Emilio Castelar to make one of his finest speeches, and one of the
noblest of many fine orations on the matter in European legislatures.
Rising from the front bench, shaking with the nerves which usually characterize the great speaker, he declaimed: 'I no longer see the walls of this
room, I behold distant peoples and countries where I have never been. . . .
I will say that we have had nineteen centuries of Christianity, and still
there are slaves. They only exist in the Catholic countries of Brazil and
Spain. . . . We have experienced barely a century of revolution, and the
revolutionary peoples, France, England, and the United States, have
abolished slavery. Nineteen centuries of Christianity, and there are still
slaves among Catholic peoples! One century of revolution, and there are
no slaves among revolutionary peoples. . . . Arise, Spanish legislators,
and make this nineteenth century the century of the complete and total
redemption of slaves . . .!'

Castelar's part in the abolition of slavery is commemorated in the
statue to him in the Castellana in Madrid. All the same, slavery was not
abolished in Puerto Rico until 1873, in Cuba only in 1886.

In 1869 Portugal finally abolished slavery: later than any other
European country. Since Portugal had led Europe into the slave trade
from Africa, and for 200 years (1440–1640) had managed it, it is perhaps
unsurprising that it should have taken so long for the institution to be
abolished at home. Portugal still held much of Angola and Mozambique, and was busy converting those territories into something like
conventional European colonies. Between 1876 and 1900, she behaved
much as France was doing in Sénégal: she liberated her slaves, but put
them to work for fixed periods, so that they were slaves in all but name.
Portugal only formally abolished slavery throughout her empire in
1875; and whether that change meant as much to the populations of
Angola and Mozambique as abolitionists would have desired is an open
question.

In 1870 there were still 1,500,000 slaves in Brazil – many more than
there had been in 1800. Two-thirds of this population of slaves lived in
Rio de Janeiro, Minas Gerais, and São Paulo – above all, on coffee plantations, whose *fazendeiros* continued, whatever Adam Smith might have
thought, to find slavery profitable. In 1871 the Emperor Dom Pedro, who
knew, through his many European connections as well as from his

conscience, that slavery in Brazil could no longer be justified, took the initiative in pressing *'o lei do ventre livre'*, by which children born to slave mothers would be declared free. State-owned slaves would be freed immediately, and the right of slaves to buy freedom was codified. A public fund would assist manumission, and a register of slaves was announced. This law passed 65 to 45 in the Chamber, 33 to 7 in the Senate, after long, entirely worthy, and important debates. But as late as 1884 a bill introduced by a Liberal Prime Minister to emancipate without compensation slaves who reached the age of sixty was lost, and the government indeed fell on the issue. The following year, thanks to the efforts of the Brazilian Anti-slavery Society led by Joaquim Nabuco, a new bill on the same subject did pass, though even then slaves over sixty were obliged to work without payment for another three years for old owners – a form of compensation.

Only during the late 1880s did Brazilian slavery collapse. Three-quarters of a million slaves were still left in March 1887, but by then many were fleeing their farms, in acts of mass desertion. It is not altogether fanciful to see these unpunished escapes as a repetition of the flight from servitude which occurred at the beginning of the eleventh century in Europe, and which signalled the end of the institution there. The army in Brazil was now no longer willing to round up runaways, as it had done for so many generations, and prices collapsed. Planters began to free slaves on the condition that they signed labour contracts for three or four years. The Church, for the first time, overtly backed abolition, probably from fear that revolutionary blacks would sweep the country in an *onda negra*, in the style of Haiti. *Fazendeiros* began to find in Italians a cheap alternative to slavery on coffee plantations: and 750,000 European immigrants arrived on subsidized passages in the 1890s.

In March 1888 the Conservative government of Correia de Oliveira proposed the *lei áurea*, which provided for the immediate abolition of slavery in Brazil. No indemnification would be available for slave owners. The bill became law in May, just eighteen months before the army deposed the Emperor Dom Pedro, whose kind and cultivated personality had done so much for the black people of his country – one reason, it is to be feared, why he had become unpopular with the oligarchy which ran the economy. To conclude the era of slavery in Brazil, and in America, the abolitionist Minister Rui Barbosa in 1890 issued his famous order which commanded papers in the Ministry of the Treasury relating to slavery and the slave trade to be burned. But it remains a matter of controversy what was, and was not, thereafter consigned to flames. Among those, all the same, who watched the burning was a black worker in the customs house, aged 108, determined to see for himself 'the complete destruction' of the documents which bore witness to the 'martyrdom' of his race.

*

Yet in Africa the trade in slaves continued; eunuchs were still in demand for northern harems; and as late as the 1880s slaves were still being exchanged for horses, as they had been by the Arabs and the Portuguese in the 1450s. The differentials in price in the nineteenth century were remarkable, for, the explorer Captain Binger remembered, a horse valued at two or three slaves by the Moors in the north could be sold for fifteen to twenty slaves at Ouassoulou. The cowrie also continued to play its part. The German explorer Heinrich Barth in the 1850s saw a slave 'of very indifferent appearance' being exchanged for 33,000 of them. (By 1870 a new unit of the old currency of cowries had been added in Bambara: a captif, a 'slave', meaning 20,000 shells.) David Livingstone would tell audiences in London in 1857 that though the European slave trade might be dying, that of the Arabs in East Africa was growing. In the 1870s de Brazza in the interior of the Congo found that slaves were still being exchanged there for salt, guns, and cloth from Mayumba. In the 1880s in Senegambia, at the beginning of the era of direct French rule, slaves accounted for two-thirds of the goods traded at markets. Slaves may have constituted nearly a fifth of the population of Haut-Sénégal–Niger in the first quarter of the twentieth century, a quarter of that in the Sokoto caliphate. Muslim scholars still had their slaves in that region, as their predecessors had had in the fifteenth century, and so did noble-men. In 1883, Commandant Joseph-Simon Gallieni, the future proconsul of Mada-gascar, who spent some time at Ségou on the upper Niger, an ancient slaving city 350 miles south-west of Timbuktu, described how 'nothing equals the horror of the scenes of carnage and desolation to which the incessant war gives rise in regions renowned for their unexampled fertility and their wealth of minerals. The villages are burned, the old of both sexes put to death, while the young are carried into captivity and shared out among the conquerors.' In the now wholly British Gold Coast, slave labour was outlawed. Sir Bartle Frere forbade any governor to recognize the institution in 1874. But a generation later it was still winked at, and probably used in the palm-oil industry, including by the mulatto descendants of Danes who had experimented with cotton in Akuapem. British civil servants sometimes returned escaped slaves to their masters. If St Paul had done so, why should not an English ex-public-schoolboy do likewise? Perhaps 750,000 slaves were carried into the Anglo-Egyptian Sudan in the nineteenth century, many in the last half of it. The volume of the Ottoman slave trade was also probably about 11,000 a year in the second half of that era.

The General Act of Brussels of 1890 committed the European powers interested in Africa to act against slavery: not precisely to end it, but at least to place the pursuit of liberty in Africa on the agenda of Europe's civilizing mission. In the end, the European empires did abolish slavery in the territories for which they became directly responsible. But they did not so act in protectorates: and the European will to rule Africa lasted barely two generations. Awkward new states have taken the place of old polities; but ancient systems of labour survived the changes and, at the time of writing, newspaper reports are frequent of the incidence of slavery in Mauritania where, despite the abolition of the institution at least three times, most recently in 1980, 90,000 black Africans are said to live as full-time slaves to Arab masters: precisely whence the Portuguese, in 1441, first carried black slaves away to a remote northern destination.

THE SLAVE TRADE:
A REFLECTION

THE ATLANTIC SLAVE TRADE took the shape that it did in consequence of
the survival of slavery, both black and white, in the Mediterranean world
during the Middle Ages. Black slaves had been carried to all the principalities in North Africa and the eastern Mediterranean for hundreds of
years, beginning in ancient Egypt. Those slaves in antiquity derived principally from Ethiopia, with the consequence that, as late as the fifteenth
century, black slaves were often known as 'Ethiops', whencesoever they
really derived. The expansion of Muslim power in West Africa during the
Middle Ages made possible an expansion of a trade in black slaves northwards across the Sahara from West Africa: the traveller Ibn-Battuta
recorded meeting them at almost every stage of his journey there in the
fourteenth century; and he left with 600 women slaves. Black Africans
worked as servants, soldiers, and in fields in the Arab Mediterranean.
Throughout modern history, blacks were especially sought after as
eunuchs in the Muslim world, for use both as civil servants and in
harems: the well-known picture by the painter Rassam Levnî in Istanbul
entitled *The Chief Black Eunuch Conducts the Young Prince to the Circumci-
sion Ceremony* is dated *c.* 1720–32; but it could have represented a scene at
any time between AD 1000 and 1900. There were many slaves in Renaissance Italy, some of them black.

Some black slaves reached Muslim Spain and Portugal from Africa in
the late Middle Ages, and some went to the Christian territories: indeed,
the religious brotherhood still known as 'Los Negritos' was founded in
Seville in the late fourteenth century by a benign archbishop.* Not long
afterwards, the Portuguese began first to kidnap, and then to barter for,
slaves as they made their way down the West Coast of Africa in the
second half of the fifteenth century. They were looking for gold but,
finding little of it, made do with men and women. These slaves were
brought back to Lisbon and sold either there or in Spain or Italy; the
Lisbon Florentine Bartolommeo Marchionni, a Renaissance man in every
sense of the word, became the first modern European slave merchant on
the grand scale.

King Ferdinand the Catholic of Aragon and the King-Emperor
Charles V did not realize that they were initiating a great change when, in

---

* *The brotherhood seems now to be entirely white, but it was black until the eighteenth
century.*

the early sixteenth century, they gave permission, first for 200, then for 4,000, slaves to be carried to the New World. Yet they were nonetheless the pioneers of the slave trade as we know it: when the admirable North American novelist Louis Auchincloss caused his character Winthrop Ward, in the story 'The Beauty of the Lilies', to ask himself, walking down to his office in Wall Street in 1857, why had 'the first blithering idiot to bring a black man in irons to the New World not been hanged?' he was unwittingly referring to those monarchs.

The reason why the Atlantic slave trade lasted so long is that in the Americas the Africans proved to be admirable workers, strong enough to survive the heat and hard work on sugar, coffee, or cotton plantations or in mines, in building fortresses or merely acting as servants; and, at the same time, they were good-natured and usually docile. Many black slaves had experience of agriculture and cattle. Both indigenous Indians and Europeans seemed feeble compared with them. That was why European slaves, of whom there had been some in Spain, especially from Greece or the Balkans, in the fifteenth century, were never tried out in the Americas. African Muslim slaves were more difficult to control, for, as the Brazilians found in the 1830s in particular, some of them were at least as cultivated as their masters, and were capable of mounting formidable rebellions.

This large labour force would not have been available to the Europeans in the Americas without the cooperation of African kings, merchants, and noblemen. Those African leaders were, as a rule, neither bullied nor threatened into making these sales (for sales they were, even if the bills were settled in textiles, guns, brandy, cowrie shells, beads, horses, and so on). When in 1842 the Sultan of Morocco told the British Consul that he thought that 'the traffic in slaves is a matter on which all sects and nations have agreed from the time of the sons of Adam', he could have been speaking for all African rulers; or indeed all European ones fifty years before. There were few instances of Africans' opposing the nature of the traffic desired by the Europeans.

Some slaves were stolen by Europeans – 'panyared', as the English word was – and some, as occurred often in Angola, were the victims of military campaigns mounted specifically by Portuguese proconsuls in order to capture slaves. But most slaves carried from Africa between 1440 and 1870 were procured as a result of the Africans' interest in selling their neighbours, usually distant but sometimes close, and, more rarely, their own people. 'Man-stealing' accounted for the majority of slaves taken to the New World, and it was usually the responsibility of Africans. Voltaire's sharp comment that while it was difficult to defend the conduct of Europeans in the slave trade, that of Africans in bartering each other was even more reprehensible, deserves to be better remembered. But then there was no sense of Africa: a Dahomeyan did not feel that he had anything in common even with an Oyo.

The slave trade was a disgraceful business even if considered in relation to the other brutalities of the time: the ill treatment of workers generally in Europe (as well as of sailors and of soldiers), and the harsh way in which indentured English labourers, for example, or their French (the *engagés*) and other European equivalents were looked after. The traveller William Baikie was right when he pointed out, after a journey to Africa in the 1850s, 'There is no captain who has carried slaves who has not been, either directly or indirectly, guilty of murder, [for] a certain number of deaths are always allowed for.' For captains, read also merchants; for, though some of those traders were insulated from knowing what the slave trade was, and looked upon it as just one more business, a high proportion of them had once been captains or mates in the traffic, and in their calm houses in Liverpool or Nantes could easily imagine the crowding, the smell, the savagery, and the fears normal on every voyage which they financed.

The consequence for the Americas was remarkable. In the first three and a quarter centuries of European activity in the Americas, between 1492 and 1820, five times as many Africans went to the New World as did white Europeans; and, even in the next fifty years, until 1870, probably as many blacks were taken to Brazil and Cuba as there were white men arriving in the continent. Most of the great enterprises of the first 400 years of colonization owed much to African slaves: sugar in Brazil and later the Caribbean; rice and indigo in South Carolina and Virginia; gold in Brazil and, to a lesser extent, silver in Mexico; cotton in the Guianas and later in North America; cocoa in what is now Venezuela; and, above all, in clearing of land ready for agriculture. The only great American enterprise which did not use black labour extensively was the silver mining at Potosí in Peru, and that was only because it was at too high an altitude for Africans to be able to work there with their usual energy. The servants of the Americas between Buenos Aires and Maryland were for four centuries usually black slaves.

Henri Wallon, the moralistic French nineteenth-century historian of slavery in antiquity, argued that the discovery of the Americas was an accidental development which led to retrogression in Europe: the settlement of America offered, he said, to a small group of selfish merchants and planters the chance to upset, through the development of large-scale slavery, the course of progress. But slavery had continued throughout the Middle Ages in Europe, and it was not only merchants but kings and noblemen who inspired much of the early slave trading. Yet there is a sense in which Wallon was right: most of Northern Europe had said goodbye to slavery by the early twelfth century. Most countries there which allowed themselves to become implicated in the slave trade to the Americas had some hesitations at first. Richard Jobson in England, Brederoo in the Netherlands, Mercado and Albornoz in Spain, Fernão de Oliveira in Portugal, not to speak of King Louis XIII in France, were exponents of a different attitude at the end of the sixteenth century or at the beginning of the seventeenth. The reason why these humane doubts or even open hostility had no effect is surely to be accounted for by the memory of antiquity which dominated culture and education for the next three centuries. If Athens had slaves with which to build the Parthenon, and Rome to maintain the aqueducts, why should modern Europe hesitate to have slaves to build its new world in America? Busbecq's regret should be remembered.*

The effect of this traffic on Europe and on the Americas was considerable. The slave trade should not be seen as the main, much less the sole, inspiration of any particular development in industry or manufacture in Europe or North America. The memory of Dr Eric Williams may haunt the modern study of the Atlantic slave trade, but his shocking argument that the capital which the trade made possible financed the industrial revolution now appears no more than a brilliant *jeu d'esprit*. After all, the slave-trading entrepreneurs of Lisbon and Rio, or Seville and Cádiz, did not finance innovations in manufacture. Yet those who became rich as a result of trading slaves often did put their profits to interesting uses: Marchionni, for instance, invested in Portuguese journeys of discovery, as did Prince Henry the Navigator; John Ashton of Liverpool helped to finance the Sankey Brook Canal, between his own city and Manchester; René Montaudoin was a pioneer of cotton manufacture in Nantes, and so was James de Wolf in Bristol, Rhode Island. Such investments aside, the slave trade had a great effect on shipbuilding, on marine insurance, on the rope industry, on ships' carpenters in all interested ports, as also on textile manufacture (such as linen in Rouen), the production of guns in Birmingham and Amsterdam, and iron bars in Sweden, of brandy in France and rum in Newport, not to speak of beads from Venice and Holland, and on the sugar refineries near important European and North American ports.

The effect of this emigration on Africa is extraordinarily difficult to estimate, for it is unclear what the population of Africa was at any stage before 1850. Still, most of the millions of slaves shipped from Africa were not members of an established slave population but ordinary farmers or members of their families, suddenly deprived of their liberty by fellow Africans in response to what a modern economist might call 'growing external demand'. Professor W. M. Macmillan, in *Africa Emergent*, argued that Africa was, for many centuries, underpopulated. He attributed the continent's backwardness to the 'lack of human resources' adequate to tame an inhospitable environment. Then Dr Kenneth Dike, most eminent of a new generation of African historians in the 1960s, insisted that, whatever might be the position in Central Africa, that could not be true of Iboland, in what is now south-eastern Nigeria, where land hunger has been the most important 'conditioning factor' in history.

* See page 113.

The truth is that though a drop in population must have been caused by the sustained trade in slaves, a fertile population would have added as many as, or more than, it lost in the slave trade as a result of normal reproduction. Most statistics suggest that females, after all, constituted only a third of the slaves transported, even if most of those probably were of childbearing age. A fast-growing population might even have found relief from the inevitable pressure on resources through the export of some of its members. If, as seems possible, the population of West Africa in the early eighteenth century was about 25,000,000, enjoying a rate of growth of, say, seventeen per thousand every ten years, the effect of the export slave trade (say, 0.2 per cent of the population a year) would have been to check the growth in population, since the rate of slave exports and that of natural increase would have been much the same. The introduction of those two wonderful American crops, maize and manioc, also did something to compensate Africa for whatever loss it suffered in population by being implicated in the Atlantic slave trade.

There were some obvious political effects. One was to strengthen those monarchies or other entities which collaborated with the Europeans, above all, naturally, the coastal kings; and the riches obtained from the sale of slaves enabled some rulers to extend their political, as well as their commercial, activities into the interior. The growth of the slave trade clearly helped some states, such as Dahomey, to expand and consolidate themselves. But Benin avoided the trade and also matured as a state. The slave trade must have encouraged African monarchies not just to go to war (they had always done that) but to capture more prisoners than before, and also to substitute capture for killing in battle. Dispersed coastal communities often experienced, as a result of the slave trade, territorial growth, political centralization, and commercial specialization. That may have been a consequence of European traders' desire to gather an entire cargo from a single port. Thus the city of New Calabar vigorously developed its own version of monarchy. By 1750 the Efik had excluded all other Africans from contacts with the Europeans, and their political leader (Duke Ephraim, of Duke Town, in the nineteenth century) had political control over all the local slave trade, dominating his city without being formally a ruler, much as the Medici had done in Florence. But Calabar was a tiny city state considered against the powerful internal empires, even if it was important in the coastal slave trade; and those empires, from the Songhai to the Oyo, not forgetting the Vili kings in Loango or those in the Congo and the various monarchies in what is now Angola, seem to have risen and declined without being decisively affected by the Atlantic commerce.

The effects on the African economy, apart from the matter of population, were also diverse. One was to stimulate the idea of a new currency: thus cowries became a general trading money in the Niger delta, displacing old iron currencies there, while European-made iron bars, copper rods, and brass manillas also played a part. Yet cowries were increasing in circulation in 'Guinea' before the doom-laden Portuguese caravels first drew inshore.

One effect on coastal African agriculture was to stimulate the growth of rice, yams, and later manioc and maize, and even the development of cattle, to provide the slave ships or the slave prisons – the *'captiveries'*, as the French customarily described them – with at least a modicum of food while the captives were awaiting embarkment. The success of slaving as a commercial proposition also implied that many older businesses – such as the trade in palm oil, gum, cattle, cola nuts, even ivory – diminished. Only gold remained an effective competitor to the slave trade. But all those other things survived, especially the first, to be revived in the nineteenth century.

The entrepreneurial spirit of Africa must have been stimulated by the Atlantic slave trade. Most European captains came to realize that their negotiating partners knew as much about European practices as the Europeans knew of them. The era of the trade also saw a great expansion of fairs, and an expansion too of the overall level of trade, in which the traffic in slaves formed only a part. Africans involved in the trade, however, benefited greatly. Some of that wealth was creatively used locally. The prosperity of the entrepôts stimulated employment; and the trade necessitated large numbers of porters, canoemen, and guards at every port along the West African coast.

It is also interesting to speculate on the effects of the imports deriving from the sale of slaves. The slave-trading peoples chose carefully the goods which they exchanged for slaves, and so slave ships had often to be floating emporia, for a European trader would look foolish if he arrived off Loango, say, with a supply of brandy when a previous ship had sold all that the ruler or the merchants concerned needed at that time.

As has been repeatedly noticed, the item most commonly exchanged for slaves was cloth. The import of woollens and cottons did not inspire a tailoring industry, because most Africans liked to wear those European goods untailored, wrapping the cloths round them. But local spinning, weaving, and dyeing did not as a rule suffer. The production of African woollen cloth even appears to have expanded in many places. Despite the apparent abundance of imports, foreign cloth remained rare enough in the hinterland of, say, south-eastern Nigeria not to compete with traditional local products either in price or quality.

The most interesting aspect of the slave trade is that during the 500 years of constant contact between the Africans and the Europeans the former did not develop further in imitation of the latter. The reluctance of Africans to Europeanize themselves is often presented as a weakness. But it is more likely to be explained by some innate strength of the African personality which, however close the political or commercial relation with the foreigner, remains impervious to external influence.

*

Some priests or monks from the sixteenth century onwards were always critical of the revival of slavery by Europeans and there was also some unease among Protestants. The saintly conduct of Fray Pedro Claver on the quays of Cartagena de Indias deserves more extended recognition. But his and other denunciations were voices crying in the wilderness, and once countries such as England had begun to trade Africans there was little effective opposition until the late eighteenth century. The abolition movement which arose then was the consequence, first, of the diffusion of ideas made possible by the pamphlet and the book operating in conditions free of censorship, as was possible in Britain and North America, and to a lesser extent in France; and second, the conversion to abolition of one Protestant sect, the Quakers, who had participated in the trade, and so knew exactly what it was they were up against. It must be doubtful whether abolition would have carried the day when it did had it not been for the Quaker movement's capacity for organizing first their members and then others.

The determined efforts of philanthropists, in France, North America, and Britain, and later in Spain, Brazil, and elsewhere, working through the press, parliaments, and diplomacy, eventually achieved the abolition of the Atlantic slave trade and of slavery in the Americas, so paving the way for the beginning at least of the abolition of slavery and the traffic in Africa. Experience of what occurred between 1808 and 1860 suggests that the end of the slave trade came not because, as the French historian Claude Meillassoux put it, 'slavery as a means of production hindered agrarian and industrial growth', but because of the work of individuals, with writers such as Montesquieu playing an essential part. Thomas Clarkson and Wilberforce in England, Benezet and Moses Brown in the United States, and Benjamin Constant and other friends and relations of Madame de Staël in France, were the heroes. The effectiveness of Louis Philippe's first government, in particular of the Minister of the Navy, Count Argout, showed that a determined leader could do much. Isidoro Antillón, who first spoke against the slave trade in Spain in 1802 and who may have been murdered for repeating his views in Cádiz in 1811, should not be forgotten. Other Spanish abolitionists such as Labra and Vizcarrando should have their places in the Pantheon. Nelson Mandela, during his visit to the British Parliament in 1995, recalled the name of Wilberforce. He might have mentioned others, not to speak of the British West Africa Squadron. In Brazil, Dom Pedro's opposition to the slave trade was continuous and the role of several statesmen there (culminating in Soares de Souza) should be remembered, not least in Angola.

No French, North American, or Spanish abolitionist would have accepted the famous judgement of the nineteenth-century Irish historian Lecky when he remarked: 'The unweary, unostentatious and inglorious crusade of England against slavery may probably be regarded as among the three or four perfectly virtuous pages comprised in the history of nations.' British arrogance and aggressive pleasure in intervening in the commerce of other countries made the British navy's conduct hard to forgive, as Richard Cobden, John Bright, and even Gladstone pointed out. All the same, the British led the way to abolition, in a way which surely compensates for the high-handedness.

Any historian of the slave trade is conscious of a large gap in his picture. The slave himself is a silent participant in the account. One may pick out the slave from of a seventeenth-century engraving of Benin, let us say, in one of the many handsome illustrations to the famous travelogue of Jean Barbot. One learns a little of a few slaves in the reports of Eustache de Fosse in the fifteenth century or de Marees in the sixteenth; the Sieur de la Courbe or Bosman in the seventeenth, or, let us say, Alexander Falcon-bridge or Captain Landolphe, among innumerable memoirs, in the eighteenth. Pío Baroja, a great Spanish writer, has vividly depicted the life of nineteenth-century slave captains in fiction. In the nineteenth century there are the splendid designs of Maurice Rugendas, some of them repro-duced in this book. One may find a few direct testimonies of slaves from the late eighteenth or the nineteenth century. Several of these are mentioned in Appendix 1. The best of these is probably the memorable work of Equiano, several times cited. But how pitifully small is the mate-rial! Nor has the historian any means of knowing whether those few spokesmen adequately speak for the captives whose fate he has followed as best he can over five centuries. For the slave remains an unknown warrior, invoked by moralists on both sides of the Atlantic, recalled now in museums in one-time slave ports from Liverpool to Elmina, but all the same unspeaking, and therefore remote and elusive. Like slaves in antiq-uity, African slaves suffered, but the character of their distress may be more easily conveyed by novelists such as Mérimée than by a historian. No doubts, though, the dignity, patience, and gaiety of the African in the New World is the best of all memorials.

Appendix One

Some Who Lived to Tell the Tale

A TINY MINORITY of the captives consigned to slave ships can be identified, and most of those who can were slaves of the late eighteenth or the nineteenth century: men (there seem to have been no women) who gave evidence in inquiries in London, or who were talked to by missionaries, or proto-anthropologists, in Sierra Leone. There were men who, like the hero of Mérimée's *Tamango*, or the resolute Tambo, directed rebellions severe or successful enough to remain in the mind of the *négriers*. There were African kings or queens whose adaptation to life as a slave in Jamaica has been chronicled or, at least, as in the case of the mother of King Gezo of Dahomey, not forgotten. With respect to the vast slave market of Brazil, there are few accounts, and nearly all from the nineteenth century: for example, that of Mahommah G. Baquaqua, sold in Pernambuco and taken to Rio, who, after numerous attempts to escape in Brazil, found freedom by jumping ship in New York.

Few slave journeys had happy endings. But there were some. The extraordinary case of Equiano has been mentioned several times in this book. But there was also the curious instance of Ayuba Suleiman Diallo, a Fulbe, known to Europeans as Job Ben Solomon, son of a mullah of Bondu, a town high up a tributary of the River Sénégal. In 1730 he set out to sell some slaves on the River Gambia. He was robbed, captured, and himself sold by non-Muslims at Joar, a city lower down that waterway, to Captain Pike of the *Arabella*, an English slave ship, which carried him to Maryland. There he lived as a slave for a year with Vachell Denton of Annapolis, an amiable master, who sold him to a Mr Tolsey, who had a tobacco plantation on Kent Island, in the Potomac River. Ben Solomon eventually sent a letter in Arabic to his father in Africa via London, where James Oglethorpe, then a director of the Royal African Company, and about to embark on the establishment of Georgia as a penal colony, sent that letter to Oxford to be translated. He also sent to Maryland for Job. Once in England, Job was employed by Sir Hans Sloane, the benign botanist and co-founder of the British Museum, who had spent his youth in Jamaica (hence his catalogue of Jamaica plants) and who was, at that time, President of the Royal Society. (He was also, like Oglethorpe, a promoter of Georgia.) Sloane found not only that Job was a master of Arabic but that he knew much of the Koran by heart. Either Sir Hans or the Duke of Montagu, a noted Afrophile and practical joker, introduced him at Court. After living in London for fourteen months, Job returned to Africa, taking with him presents from Queen Caroline and the Duke of Cumberland. In a subsequent letter to Mr Smith, writing master at St Paul's School, Job described how he returned to Bondu and 'how elevated and amazed they [his old friends] were at my arrival, I must leave you to guess at, as being inexpressible, as is likewise the raptures and pleasures I enjoyed. Floods of tears burst their way and some little time afterwards, we recovered so as to have some discourse and in time I acquainted them and all the country how I had been redeemed and conducted by the Company from such distant parts as are beyond their capacity to conceive, from Maryland to England and from thence to Gambia first. . . . The favours done to me by the queen, the duke of Montagu and other generous persons I likewise acquainted them of.'

One day, some years after his homecoming, Job was sitting under a tree at Damasensa, not far from Elephants Island, on the River Gambia, with the English slave captain Francis Moore (whose acute memories have often been quoted), when he saw several of the men who had captured him so many years before. Moore persuaded him not to kill them, but instead to ask questions. They said that the King, their master, had killed himself by mistake by letting off one of the pistols which Captain Pike had given him in return for Job. Job then gave thanks (to Allah, of course), for causing that king to die by means of the very goods in return for which he had been sold into slavery. He later admitted, though, that had the King lived he would have forgiven him, 'because, had I not been sold, I should neither have known . . . the English tongue, nor had any of the fine useful and valuable things I now carry over, nor have known that there is in the world such a place as England, nor such noble, generous people as Queen Caroline, Prince William [the Duke of Cumberland], the Duke of Montagu, the Earl of Pembroke, Mr Holden, Mr Oglethorpe, and the Royal African Company.'

Job was not the only slave to return from captivity in the Americas. In 1695, for example, a Dutch interloper, Captain Frans van Goethem, captured a Sonyo prince. The African traders in the Sonyo region (Angola) thereafter made trade impossible until that captive was returned. The Dutch West India Company found the slave, and sent him back from Suriname, via Holland.

Then Jean Barbot described how a certain Emanuel, governor of a large town, explained that his king had once sold him 'for a slave to a Dutch captain who, finding me a good servant in his passage to the West Indies, . . . carried me with him into Holland, where I soon learnt to speak good Dutch and, after some years, he set me free. I went from Holland into France, where I soon got as much of that language as you hear by me. Thence I proceeded to Portugal, which language I made myself master of with more ease than either the French or Dutch. Having spent several years in travelling through Europe, I resolved to return to my native country, and laid hold of the first opportunity which offered. When I arrived here, I immediately waited on the King ... and, having related my travels ..., added I was come back to him, to put himself into his hands, as his slave again, if he thought fit. The King was so far from reducing me to that low condition that he gave me one of his own sisters in marriage and constituted me Alcaide or governor of this town. ...'

'Jack Rodney', a cousin of King Naimbanna of Sierra Leone, should also be remembered. He was asked by an English slave captain to pilot a slave ship down the River Sierra Leone from Bence Island. He agreed, on condition that he be put on shore at the small port of Robanna. But the captain said that he would land him further downriver at its mouth. Instead, however, he took him to Jamaica. Rodney talked to the governor there and succeeded eventually in returning. Mungo Park encountered an African servant, Johnson, who had been taken to Jamaica as a slave, had been freed, and then found his way home.

Perhaps the most curious story of all was that of Thomas Joiner, who began life as a minstrel slave, on the Gambia. He was sold in Jamaica as a slave, gained his freedom, learned to read and write English, and made enough money to return to Africa, where he set up as a trader at Gorée (not in slaves) about 1810. He moved back to the River Gambia, where, by 1830, he was the most important shipowner. His brigantine, the *General Turner*, sixty-seven tons, was then the biggest ship on the upper river.

In the nineteenth century there were several accounts of slaves returning to Africa from Brazil. In 1832 four freed women of Benguela came back; and sometimes slaves were punished by being deported to Africa. In 1830 thirty-five prominent citizens of Cabinda were sent home from Rio because they had been criminally seized in Africa by slave traders who had asked them to dinner on a ship. Nearly sixty Africans from 'Mina' bought their passage back from Rio to the Gold Coast in 1835. In 1852 about sixty 'Muslims' from the same part of Africa were returned to Africa on an English ship (the *Robert*, George Duck master) for £800, having first assured themselves that the coast whence they had originally come was then free of slave dealers. In the 1850s and 1860s there were numerous saving societies in Brazil designed to collect enough money to return their members to Africa. All along the West African coast, from Dahomey to Angola, little settlements of returned slaves from the Americas were soon to be found, sometimes giving such names as Pernambuco, Puerto Rico, or Martinique to their new African homes.

Appendix Two

The Trial of Pedro José de Zulueta in London for Trading in Slaves

Pedro José de Zulueta, son of a successful London merchant, a first cousin (and frequent partner) of the planter and slave merchant Julián Zulueta in Cuba, and an associate of the slave trader Pedro Blanco, was in 1841 charged in London with trading slaves. The accusation was that the previous year Zulueta had fitted out and used a ship, the *Augusta*, for the purpose of trading in slaves. He was tried with Thomas Jennings, who had captained the ship when it was detained off the notorious River Gallinas, in what is now Liberia. The cargo shipped seemed suspicious – 29 hogsheads of tobacco, 60 cases of arms, 1 case of looking-glasses, 10 casks of copperware, 134 bales of unidentified merchandise (probably cloths) 1,600 iron pots and 2,370 kegs of gunpowder – just the sort of cargo used in the slave trade. The prosecution established that the *Augusta* had in 1839 been known as the *Gollupchick*, and was sailing under a Russian flag, with Thomas Bernardos as the captain, commanding a crew that was mostly Spanish. Detained by a British naval officer, Captain Hill, the court in Sierra Leone declared that they could not act against a Russian ship – though there was plainly slave equipment aboard; in the judgement of Captain Hill, there were 'more water casks than are necessary for an ordinary trading vessel . . . a caboose [kitchen] to hold a very large copper, gratings covered with temporary planks. . . .'

The ship was then sold to Zulueta and Co., at Portsmouth, for £650, and according to the prosecution dispatched as the *Augusta* to the River Gallinas, as part of an arrangement with the well-known firm of slave merchants of Cádiz and Havana, Pedro Martínez. The agreement was that payments should be made by the firm of Pedro Blanco with his associate Carballo, dealing from Cádiz, in Havana. There was no written specification that the ship was to take on slaves on the River Gallinas, but, the prosecution argued, it could have no other purpose than that in that place: the only buildings there were slave barracoons.

The *Augusta* picked up part of her cargo at Liverpool and part of it at Cádiz. She was detained again by Captain Hill on the high seas off the River Gallinas; he was surprised to see his old prize, the *Gollupchick*, back on the West African coast in new colours.

The weakness of the prosecution's case was that there was no sign of 'slave equipment' by Canning's definition on the *Augusta* when she was detained under that name. But Captain Hill testified that any ship could be turned into a slave ship in a short time. Numerous witnesses were called to prove that the River Gallinas had no other business than slaves, so that, if the *Augusta* were bound for there, the purpose must have been the slave trade. But did Zulueta know that? The prosecution could not prove that he did; and the jury returned a verdict of not guilty.

In the light of the realization that on the one hand, there was no trade other than the slave trade on the Gallinas, and on the other that both Pedro Blanco and Pedro Martínez were major slave merchants (the former was called the largest slave trader in the world by Judge H. W. Macaulay), the verdict must seem rather generous. Zulueta formally told a House of Lords select committee that neither he, his father, nor his grandfather had ever had 'any kind of interest of any sort, or derived any emolument or connexion from the slave trade'; and he was believed. Yet Pedro Blanco usually had all his bills in London drawn on Zulueta and Co.; and later evidence (not found in time for the trial) showed that the cargo of the *Augusta* was destined for three well-known slave merchants on the river: José Pérez Rola, Angel Ximénez, and José Alvarez.

APPENDIX THREE

ESTIMATED STATISTICS

I. CARRIERS

COUNTRY	VOYAGES	SLAVES TRANSPORTED
Portugal (including Brazil)	30,000	4,650,000
Spain (including Cuba)	4,000	1,600,000
France (including French West Indies)	4,200	1,250,000
Holland	2,000	500,000
Britain	12,000	2,600,000
British North America & US	1,500	300,000
Denmark	250	50,000
Other	250	50,000
TOTAL	54,200	11,000,000

II. SLAVES DELIVERED TO

Brazil	4,000,000
Spanish empire (including Cuba)	2,500,000
British West Indies	2,000,000
French West Indies (including Cayenne)	1,600,000
British North America & US	500,000
Dutch West Indies (including Suriname)	500,000
Danish West Indies	28,000
Europe (including Portugal, Canary Islands, Madeira, Azores, etc.)	200,000
TOTAL	11,328,000

III. ORIGINS

Senegambia (in Argiun), Sierra Leone	2,000,000
Windward Coast	250,000
Ivory Coast	250,000
Gold Coast (Ashanti)	1,500,000
Slave Coast (Dahomey, Adra, Oyo)	2,000,000
Benin to Calabar	2,000,000
Cameroons/Gabon	250,000
Loango	750,000
Congo/Angola	3,000,000
Mozambique/Madagascar	1,000,000
TOTAL LEAVING AFRICAN PORTS	13,000,000

IV. LABOUR

(First employment in the Americas)	
Sugar plantations	5,000,000
Coffee plantations	2,000,000
Mines	1,000,000
Domestic labour	2,000,000
Cotton fields	500,000
Cocoa fields	250,000
Building	250,000
TOTAL	11,000,000

Note: the discrepancy between all the estimates and the overall figure of 'ten million or more' estimated on the cover of this book is, of course, marginal and is due to rounding up. No final figure can be expected.

For sources see Notes.

Appendix Four

Selected Prices of Slaves
1440–1870

THESE PRICES ARE mere indications. In general, one can say that prices rose slowly throughout the period of the trade, but at the end of the eighteenth century the price of slaves in Africa was too close to that in the Americas for the comfort of the slave traders. In the nineteenth century, prices rose in the Americas (Cuba, Brazil) and fell in Africa, so some great fortunes were made.

1440s   in Senegambia, one horse for 25 or 30 slaves

1500   12 to 15 manillas on the coast of Guinea

1500–1510   average price in Seville, 20 ducats

1500–1510   in Senegambia, 8, 7, or 6 slaves exchanged for a horse, or 20 to 25 manillas in Benin

1504   Lisbon price 5,300 réis (hereinafter rs.)

1550   80–90 ducats

1552   Lisbon price as high as 50,000 rs.

1556   in America, 100 ducados fixed by cédula in Caribbean, 110 on northern coast of South America and most of Central America, 120 in New Spain and Nicaragua, 140 in New Granada, 150 in Peru and River Plate, and 180 in Chile

1593   average price 20,000–30,000 rs.

1594–95   price reaches average of 75–80 pesos per Angolan slave

1595   average for *ladino* slave in Lima is 727 pesos, because of extra transport costs

1612   in Brazil, prime slaves from Angola sold at 28,000 reals each

1615   a male slave with much sugar experience is sold in Mexico for 800 pesos

1620   270–315 pesos for a Guinea slave, 200 for an Angolan

1650 or so   one slave valued at 10 cabess (40,000 cowries)

1654   Dutch charging 2,000 pounds of sugar per slave

1657   in Brazil, a *pieza* sold at 22,000 reals, various others at lower prices, down to 12,000

1657   Spaniards offering the Dutch to pay 200 reals (pieces of eight) per slave plus heavy taxes – 113 pieces of eight

1698   in Madagascar, slaves can be bought for 10 shillings in English goods; in Guinea, price rising from £3 to £4

Late seventeenth century   prices in Lima never below 600 pesos de plata

1700   Grazilier in the *Albion* buys 2,900 slaves at 24 and 26 bars a man, but a year later the price falls to 12 bars a man and 9 for a woman at Calabar

1700   £44 for a man, £23 for a boy, £16 for a girl in Barbados

1700–1704   slaves imported into Barbados vary between £23 and £16 a head

1700–1750   slave prices in Virginia £28–£35

1702   André Brüe reported that one might buy slaves from natives south of Gambia River for 10–15 bars a head, and from the Portuguese for 30

1750   cost of slave is 500 livres in Africa

1750–1800   slave prices in Virginia perhaps averaged £40

1750s   £12–16s at mouth of the Gambia

1753   Gold Coast slaves cost £16 each, Windward Coast ones £12–£14; in the West Indies, the cost was £35

1800   in Cuba, slaves at $90, according to Humboldt

1801–10   price per slave in Senegambia is £29-5s-2¼d.

1802   prices at Buenos Aires, 300 pesos if slave came direct

1807   slaves from Costa da Mina sell at Bahia at $100 each, as opposed to $80 for the less favoured slaves from Angola

1810   new slaves each in Brazil $150 to $200

1811–15   'the price of a good slave' in Bahia is 150,000 reis (£45 sterling), according to the British Consul in Bahia, Lindemann, who also estimated slaves cost £130–£150 sterling in Chile

1848   slaves in Brazil selling at 400 milreis or £45–£50

1850   slaves at $360 in the US

1850   Saint-Louis, Sénégal, prices at £28

1851   prices of slaves in Mozambique about $3–$5; in Pongas, about $12; in Luanda about $14–$16

1852   slaves in Cuba at £75

1859 Cuban slaves at $700, old slaves and young ones at $300; slaves sold in the US after the *Wanderer* affair at $1,151 for a girl of ten, $1,705 for a girl with a child, and $500 for an old man

1860 slaves at $500 in the US

1864 slaves in Cuba at $1,250–$1,500

Appendix Five

The Voyage of the *Enterprize*

I HAVE SELECTED this voyage as being one for which the papers are complete, the profits considerable, the family of the owner (that of Thomas Leyland) interesting, and there are heirs.

The voyage to Bonny (modern Nigeria) and then to Havana of the Liverpool ship *Enterprize*, captain Cesar Lawson, owned by Thomas Leyland, in 1803.

I. Letter of Instruction to Cesar Lawson

Liverpool 18 July 1803

Sir,

Our ship, *Enterprize*, to the command of which you are appointed, being now ready for sea, you are immediately to proceed to in her and make the best of your way to Bonny on the coast of Africa. You will receive herewith an invoice of the cargo on board her which you are to barter for prime negroes, ivory and palm oil. By law this vessel is allowed to carry 400 negroes and we request that they may be all males if it is possible to get them anyway buy as few females in your power, because we look to a Spanish market for the disposal of your cargo, where females are a very tedious sale. In the choice of the Negroes, be very particular, select those that are well formed and strong; and do not buy any above 24 years of age, as it may happen that you will have to go to Jamaica, where you know any exceeding that age would be liable to a Duty of £10 per head. While the slaves are on board the ship, allow them every indulgence consistent with your own safety, and do not suffer any of your officers or crew to abuse or insult them in any respect. Perhaps you may be able to procure some Palm Oil on reasonable terms, which is likely to bear a great price here, we therefore wish you to purchase as much as you can with any spare cargo that you may have. We have taken out letters of marque against the French and Batavian republic, and if you are fortunate enough as to fall in with and capture any of their vessels, send the same to this port, under the care of an active prize master, and a sufficient number of men out of your ship; and also put a copy of commission on board her, but do not molest any neutral ship, as it would involve us in expensive lawsuits and subject us to heavy damages. A considerable part of our property under your care will not be insured and we earnestly desire you to look out to avoid the Enemy's cruisers, which are numerous and you may hourly expect to be attacked by some of them. We request you will keep strict and regular discipline on board the ship; do not suffer any drunkenness among any of your officers or crew, for it is sure to be attended with some misfortune, such as insurrection, mutiny, or fire. Allow to the ship's company their regular portion of provisions etc., and take every care of such as may get sick. You must keep the ship very clean and see that no part of her stores are embezzled, neglected or idly wasted. As soon as you have finished your trade and laid in a sufficient quantity of yams, wood, water, and every other necessary for the Middle Passage, proceed with a press of sail for Barbadoes and on your arrival there call on Messrs Barton, Higginson and Co., with whom you will find letters from us by which you are to be governed in prosecuting the remainder of the voyage. Do not fail to write to us by every opportunity and always enclose a copy of your preceding letter.

You are to receive from the House in the West Indies, who may sell your cargo, your coast commission of £2 in £102 on the gross sales, and when this sum with your Chief Mate's privilege and your Surgeon's privilege, gratuity and head money are deducted, you are then to draw your commission of £4 in £104 on the remaining account. Your chief mate, Mr James Cowill, is to receive two slaves on an average with the cargo, less the island and any other duty which may be due or payable thereon at the place where you may sell your cargo; and your surgeon Mr Gilb't Sinclair is to receive two slaves on an average with the cargo less the duty beforementioned, and one shilling s'tg head money on every slave sold. And in consideration of the aforementioned emoluments, neither you nor your crew, nor any of them, are directly or indirectly to carry on any private trade on your or their accounts under a forfeiture to us of the whole of your commissions arising on this voyage. In case of your death, your chief mate, Mr Cowill, is to succeed to the command of the ship, and diligently follow these and all our further orders. Any prize that you may capture, direct the prize master to hoist a white flag at the fore and one on the main top gallant mast-heads, on his approach to this port, which will be answered by a signal at the light house.

We hope you will have a happy and prosperous voyage and remain your obedient servants

THOMAS LEYLAND, ½ share
R BULLIN, ¼ share
THOMAS MOLYNEUX, ¼ share

P.S. Should you capture any vessel from the Eastward of cape Good Hope, send her to Falmouth and there wait for our orders. In case of your capturing a Guineaman with slaves on board, send her to Messrs Bogle, Jopp and Co., of Kingston, Jamaica.

I acknowledge to have received from Messrs Thomas Leyland and Co the orders of which the aforegoing is a true copy, and I engage to execute them as well as all their further orders, the dangers of the sea only excepted, as witness my hand this 18 July 1803.

CESAR LAWSON

II. Report

Sailed from Liverpool 20 July 1803
26 August detained the Spanish brig *St Augustin*. . . .
10 September recaptured the *John*, of Liverpool . . . with 261 slaves on board. . . .
23 September The *Enterprize* arrived at Bonny, and sailed from thence on December 6th. . . .
(In January 1804, the *Enterprize* arrived at Havana and there sold 392 slaves.
On 28 March she sailed from Havana and arrived at Liverpool on 26 April 1804.)

III. Outfitting of the Ship

The outfitting cost £8,018 9s 7d, of which the most important items were the cost of the ship (£2,100 0s 0d), and the carpenter's fees (£1,340 9s 11d). Advance on wages to the ship's company, which numbered sixty-five, including the captain, was £727 14s 0d.

IV. Cargo

The cargo loaded cost £9,050 8s 8d, of which the most important item was India goods (£3,197 0s 8d). Other important items were powder and neptunes (£942 19s 3d), callicoes and bandanas (£918 14s 0d), brandy (£620 0s 0d), arms (£484 14s 6d), Manchester goods (£446 17s 0d), beads (£414 11s 4d), and iron (£357 17s 0d). There were also articles of cooperage, manillas, ironmongers' goods, lead bars and shot, split beans, red ells, earthenware, wine (from Thomas Leyland and Co.), worsted caps, hats, chairs, sticks and umbrellas, and, very low on the list (£22 13s 6d), medicine.

BIBLIOGRAPHICAL NOTE

THE MOST IMPORTANT collections of documents are J. W. Blake, *Europeans in West Africa 1466–1559*, Hakluyt Society, 2 vols. (London, 1942); V. Magalhães-Godinho, *Documentos sobre a expansão portuguesa*, 3 vols. (Lisbon, 1943–6); and above all Elizabeth Donnan, *Documents Illustrative of the Slave Trade to America* (Washington, 1930), a superb work even if it does largely neglect the Portuguese trade and the nineteenth century, and is fairly skimpy on the Spanish empire. For antiquity there is Thomas Wiedemann, *Greek and Roman Slavery* (London, 1981). For the Arab Middle Ages there is J. M. Cuoq, *Recueil des sources arabes concernant l'Afrique occidentale du VIIIe au XVIe siècle* (Paris, 1985). Jean Cuvelier and Jadin, *L'Ancien Congo d'après les archives de la Vaticane* (Brussels, 1954), has some interesting material, as does Frédéric Mauro, *Le Brésil au XVIIème siècle, documents inédits* (Coimbra, 1963). Useful documents for the North American trade in the nineteenth century can be found in Norman Bennett and George E. Brooks Jr., *New England Merchants in Africa* (Boston, 1965). One day let us hope a historian will publish selected documents from that wonderful source FO/84 on British policy to the slave trade in the nineteenth century, as well as from some Spanish sources such as the division Estado in the Archivo Histórico Nacional also for the nineteenth century.

First-hand accounts can be found in the works of many travellers and traders. But no slave trader seems to have written his memoirs, with the possible exception of Nicholas Owen's *Journal of a Slave Dealer*, ed. E. C. Martin (London, 1930); Owen was an Irishman established in West Africa. Forty-four letters from a London trader, Edward Grace, were published as *Letters of a West African Trader*, ed. T. S. Ashton, London 1950. Captains did write, for example Jean Barbot's *A Description of the Coasts of North and South Guinea*, 2 vols., ed. P. E. H. Hair, Hakluyt Society (London, 1992), Thomas Phillips's *A Journal of a Voyage Made in the* Hannibal *of London 1693–1694* in Churchill's collection of voyages, 1732, VI, 173–239, Francis Moore's *Travels into the Inland Parts of Africa* (London, 1738), Captain William Snelgrave's *A New Account of Some Parts of Guinea* (London, 1734), and John Newton's 'Thoughts on the African Slave Trade', in *Letters and Sermons*, 3 vols. (Edinburgh, 1780). Others who wrote of the trade from personal observation or participation included Olfert Dapper, *Nouvelle description des pays africains* (Amsterdam, 1670), Willem Bosman (*A New and Accurate Description of the Coast of Guinea* (Eng. tr. London, 1705), and Père Labat (*Voyages aux îles* (new ed. Paris, 1993)). Later there were a number of fascinating travellers' tales, especially by French officials or other visitors (Antoine Biet, Ducasse, Pruneau de Pommegorge, Pierre du Caillu). In the illegal age, the unreliable but interesting works of Theodore Canot (*Memoirs of a Slave Trader* (New York, 1854)) and Richard Drake (or was his name Philip?), *Revelations of a Slave Smuggler* (New York, 1860), are useful.

A good introduction to the study of slavery in antiquity is Moses Finlay, *Ancient Slavery and Modern Ideology* (London, 1981), but see also Joseph Vogt, *Ancient Slavery and the Ideal of Man* (Eng. tr. London, 1974). For Greece there is Yves Garlan, *Les Esclaves dans la Grèce ancienne* (Paris, 1982; Eng. tr. Ithaca, 1988). There is also M. L. Bush, ed., *Serfdom and Slavery* (London, 1996). For the position of Africans, see J. R. Snowden, *Blacks in Antiquity* (Cambridge, Mass., 1970), and Mary Lefkovitz, *Not Out of Africa* (New York, 1996).

The sources for the study of slavery in the Middle Ages are for Europe, Charles Verlinden, *L'esclavage dans l'Europe médiévale*, vol. I (Bruges, 1955), a marvellous book. In addition there is Marc Bloch, *Land and Work in Mediaeval Europe* (Eng. tr. London, 1966); Pierre Dockés, *Mediaeval Slavery and Abolition* (Eng tr. London, 1982); Georges Duby and R. Mandrou, *L'Histoire de la civilisation française*, vol. I (Paris, 1958); and Pierre Bonnassie's excellent *From Slavery to Feudalism in South-western Europe* (Cambridge, 1991).

For Islam, see Bernard Lewis, *Race and Slavery in the Middle East* (Oxford, 1990), and also Raymond Mauny, *Tableau géographique de l'ouest africain au moyen age* (Dakar, 1961); Paul E. Lovejoy, *Transformations in Slavery* (Cambridge, 1982); and Mervyn Hiskett, *The Development of Islam in West Africa* (London, 1984). There is also a collection of essays and texts, *Slaves and Slavery in Muslim Africa*, ed. John Ralph Willis, 2 vols. (London, 1985), which discusses the entire modern history till the present day.

For the Portuguese penetration of West Africa, the best work in English is Bailey Diffie and George Winius, *The Foundations of the Portuguese Empire* (Minneapolis, 1977). Guillermo Céspedes del Castillo, *La exploración del Atlántico* (Madrid, 1992), is, however, a most distinguished work. There are excellent essays in G. Winius, ed., *Portugal the Pathfinder* (Madison, 1992). V. Magalhães-Godinho, *Os Descobrimentos e a economia Mundial* (Lisbon, 1963) is the best Portuguese introduction, but also see his *L'economie de l'empire portugais au XVe et XVIe siècles* (Paris, 1969), and *A economia dos descobrimentos henriquinos* (Lisbon, 1962). See too the first chapters of C. R. Boxer, *The Portuguese Seaborne Empire* (New York, 1969). Alberto Vieira's *O comerciante interinsular* (Funchal, 1986) and *Portugal y las Islas del Atlántico* (Madrid, 1992) deal with the islands, as does, very well, Manuel Lobo Cabrera, *La Esclavitud en las Canarias Orientales en el siglo XVI* (Santa Cruz de Tenerife, 1982). For Portugal see A. C. de M. Saunders's admirable *A Social History of Black Slaves in Portugal* (Cambridge, 1982). The best description of the building of Elmina is now P. E. H. Hair's *The Founding of the Castelo de San Jorge da Mina* (Madison, 1994), but it is still worthwhile to read the relevant chapter in A. W. Lawrence's *Trade Castles and Forts of West Africa* (London, 1963).

The first generations of the Portuguese slave trade can be pursued in V. Magalhães-Godinho, *Os Descobrimentos,* especially chapter 9, but see too José Gonçalvez Salvador, *Os Magnatos do Trafico Negro* (São Paulo, 1981), and the same author's *Os Cristãos Novos e o comercio no Atlântico meridional* (São Paulo, 1978). Edmundo Lopes Correia's *Escravatura: subsidios para a su historia* (Lisbon, 1944) is a general study of the Portuguese slave trade. See too Mauricio Goulart's *Escravido africano no Brasil* (São Paulo, 1950).

Virginia Rau, 'Notes sur la traite à la fin du XVe siècle et le florentin Bartolommeo di Domenico Marchionni', *Bulletin de l'Institute Historique Belge de Rome* XLIV, 1974, 535–43, touches tantalizingly on the life of that great entrepreneur. The early days of Brazil are masterfully considered in the early chapters of John Hemming's admirable *Red Gold* (London, 1978), and in Stuart Schwartz's excellent *Sugar Plantations in the Formation of Brazilian Society, Bahia 1550–1835* (Cambridge, 1985). For the trade from São Tomé see John Vogt, 'The Early São Tomé Trade with Mina', *International Journal of African Historical Studies* 6, 1973; and the same author's book, *Portuguese Rule in the Gold Coast* (Athens, 1979). Fr. Dieudonné Rinchon, *La Traite et l'esclavage des congolais par les européens* (Brussels, 1929), is still useful.

Other works of value for the Portuguese empire and slavery are by C. L. R. Boxer, *Race Relations in the Portuguese Colonial Empire* (Oxford, 1963), and *Portuguese Society in the Tropics* (Madison, 1965). For Portuguese trade in the seventeenth century, there is Frédéric Mauro, *Le Portugal et l'Atlantique au XVIIème siècle, 1570–1670* (Paris, 1960), and two other works by the same author: 'L'Atlantique Portugais et les esclaves, 1570–1670', in *Revista da Faculdade de Letras* xxii (Lisbon, 1956), and *Le Brésil du XVème siècle à la fin du XVIIIème siècle* (Paris, 1977).

Gilberto Freyre's *The Mansions and the Slaves,* tr. Harriet de Onis (New York, 1970), remains an immensely rewarding work. See too two other important books of C. L. R. Boxer, *The Golden Age of Brazil* (Berkeley, 1962), and *The Dutch in Brazil* (Oxford, 1957). For the Cacheu Company there is Cândido da Silva Texeira, 'Companhia de Cacheu', *Boletim do Archivo Historico Colonial* (Lisbon, 1950). There is a fine study of Pombal's new monopoly companies of Brazil by Carreira, *As companhias pombalinas de navegaçao . . .* (Bissau, 1969). Joseph Miller, *Way of Death* (Madison, 1988), is a pathbreaking work of distinction about the trade in the late eighteenth and early nineteenth century in Angola. José Honorio Rodrigues, *Brazil and Africa* (Eng tr. Berkeley, 1964), is one of the best works on the whole subject of the trade to Brazil.

The early Spanish slave trade can be followed in Vicenta Cortés Alonso, *La Esclavitud de Valencia durante el reino de los reyes católicos* (Valencia, 1964), and in Antonio Rumeu de Armas, *España en la Africa Atlántica*, 2 vols. (Madrid, 1956). Georges Scelle's *La traite negrière aux Indes de Castille*, 2 vols. (Paris, 1906), continues to be essential, and even José Antonio Saco's *Historia de la Esclavitud*, 5 vols. (Paris, 1875–1893), is still useful too. Volumes 2 and 3 refer to African slavery and were separately republished in 1938 in Havana with an introduction by Fernando Ortiz. There is much useful information in Consuelo Varela, *Colón y los florentinos* (Madrid, 1988). For Seville in the sixteenth century see Enriqueta Vila Vilar, *Los Corzos and los Mañara* (Seville, 1991); and Ruth Pike's two admirable volumes, *Enterprise and Adventure* (Ithaca, 1966), and *Aristocrats and Traders* (Ithaca, 1972). A valuable recent work is José Luis Cortés López's *La esclavitud negra en la España Peninsular der Siglo XVI* (Salamanca, 1989). For Spain's intellectual life, see Bernice Hamilton, *Political Thought in Sixteenth Century Spain* (Oxford, 1963); and for Spanish mercantile life generally, Eufemio Lorenzo Sanz, *Comercio en España con América, en la época de Felipe II*, 2 vols. (Valladolid, 1979).

The early days of the Caribbean can be examined in Carl Sauer's pessimistic study, *The Early Spanish Main* (Berkeley, 1966), and several works of Luis Arranz (*El Repartimiento de Albuquerque en 1512* (Santo Domingo, 1992), and *Diego Colón I* (Santo Domingo, 1993). Spanish relations with the Indians are followed in Lewis Hanke's *The Spanish Struggle for Justice in the New World* (Philadelphia, 1949). Frederic Bowser's *The African Slave in Colonial Peru* (Stanford, 1972) is far the best introduction to that theme. The best study of Las Casas is the remarkable work of Manuel Giménez Fernández, *Bartolomé de las Casas*, 2 vols. (Seville, 1953–1960), but see also Benjamin Keen and Juan Friede, eds. *Bartolomé de Las Casas in History* (De Kalb, 1971). There is as yet no good life of Bishop Fonseca. For pre-Conquest slavery there is Carlos Bosch García, *La esclavitud prehispánica entre los Aztecas* (Mexico, 1944).

For the late sixteenth and early seventeenth centuries see Pierre and Huguette Chaunu, *Séville et l'Atlantique*, 12 vols. (Paris, 1957), of which vol. 3, pp. 35–163 lists ships approved for slave voyages; Eufemio Lorenz Sanz, *Comercio en España con América, en la época de Felipe II*, 2 vols. (Valladolid, 1979); and Ruis Rivera et al., *Los Cargardores de Indias* (Madrid, 1992). The *asientos* of the late sixteenth and early sevententh centuries are magisterially analysed by Enriqueta Vila Vilar, *Hispanoamerica y el comercio de esclavos* (Seville, 1977). For the diplomacy, see Jonathan Israel, *Empires and Entrepôts* (London, 1990).

For the Spanish empire generally see Leslie B. Rout, *The African Experience in Spanish America* (Cambridge, 1976). For Mexico there is

Gonzalo Aguirre Beltrán, *La población negra de México* (Mexico, 1972), and Jonathan Israel's *Race, Class and Politics in Colonial Mexico* (London, 1975). See also Eleanor Melville, *A Plague of Sheep* (Cambridge, 1994), and D. M. Davidson, 'Negro Slave Control in Colonial Mexico', *HAHR* xlvi, 1966. For Chile see Rolando Mellafe, *La introducción de la esclavitud negra en Chile* (Santiago, 1959). For New Granada see Nicolás del Castillo Mathieu, *Esclavos Negros en Cartagena* (Bogotá, 1982). See too two works of Jorge Palacios Preciados, *La Trata de Negros por Cartagena* (Tunja, 1973) and *Cartagena de Indias, gran factoria de obra esclava* (Tunja, 1975). For the trade to Buenos Aires there is Elena Scheuss de Studer, *La Trata de Negros en el Rio de la Plata* (Buenos Aires, 1958).

For the Spanish trade in the late seventeenth century see Marisa Vega Blanco, *El Tráfico de Esclavos* (Seville, 1984), and Irene Wright, 'The Coymans *asiento*', in *Bijdragen voor de Vaderlandse Geschiedenis en Oudheidkunde*, reeks vi, deel I, afleverung 1–2 (Arnhem, 1924). For Spain in the eighteenth century there is Bibiano Torres Ramírez on the Cádiz company, *La Compañía Gaditana de Negros* (Seville, 1973).

The opening up of Africa can be studied in Philip Curtin, *Economic Change in Precolonial Africa: Senegambia in the Era of the Slave Trade* (Madison, 1975); and Walter Rodney, *A History of the Upper Guinea Coast* (Oxford, 1970), though the latter underestimates the number of slaves in Africa. Benin can be studied in A. J. C. Ryder, *Benin and the Europeans* (London, 1969), and Dahomey in I. A. Akinjogbin's *Dahomey and Its Neighbours* (Cambridge, 1966). See also Robin Law's excellent books, *The Oyo Empire* (Oxford, 1977), *The Slave Coast of West Africa* (Oxford, 1991), and *The Horse in African History* (Oxford, 1980). For the region of the delta of the Niger, see Kenneth Onwuka Dike, *Trade and Politics in the Niger Valley* (Oxford, 1956), which illuminates the whole period (even if it concentrates on the nineteenth century); and David Northrup's *Trade without Rulers* (Oxford, 1978). The best work on the Congo seems to me to be Anne Hilton, *The Kingdom of Congo* (Oxford, 1985). Trade with Central Africa can be studied in David Birmingham, *Trade and Conflict in Angola* (Oxford, 1966); and J. Vansina, *Kingdoms of the Savanna* (Madison, 1966). See too Phyllis Martin's excellent *The External Trade of the Loango Coast* (Oxford, 1972). There is also John Thornton's very interesting *Africa and the Africans in the Making of the Atlantic World* (New York, 1992), which illuminates the whole region. Evelyn Martin, *The British West Africa Settlements* (London, 1927), has much to commend it. For a general introduction, see *The Cambridge History of Africa*, vol. 3, ed. Roland Oliver (Cambridge, 1977), and vol. 4, ed. Richard Gray (Cambridge, 1973). See too J. D. Fage, *A History of West Africa* (Cambridge, 1969), and A. G. Hoskins, *An Economic History of West Africa* (London, 1973).

For the beginnings of the French slave trade there is J.-M. Deveau's *France au temps des Négriers* (Paris, 1994) and *La Traite Rochelaise* (Paris, 1990). Robert Louis Stein, *The French Slave Trade* (Madison, 1979), is still useful. See also Gaston Martin's pioneering *Nantes au XVIIIe siècle* (Paris, 1931), and his *L'Histoire de l'Esclavage dans les colonies françaises* (Paris, 1948). For the late seventeenth century see E. F. Berlioux's *André Brüe* (Paris, 1874), Jean-Baptiste Ducasse, *Rélation du voyage du Guinée*, ed. P. Roussier (Paris, 1935), and Marcel Trudel, *L'esclavage au Canada français* (Quebec, 1960). See too Abdoulaye Ly's *La Compagnie du Sénégal* (Paris, 1958).

For the eighteenth century there is also Éric Saugera, *Bordeaux Port Négrier* (Paris, 1995). For the French trade generally there is also Jean Mettas's remarkable *Répertoire des expéditions françaises au XVIIIe siècle* (Paris, 1978–1984). The study is completed by Serge Daget's no less remarkable similar work on the nineteenth century, *Répertoire des expéditions négriers françaises à la traite illégale* (Nantes, 1988). See also Jean Meyer, *L'armement nantais* (Paris, 1967) and Pierre Dardel, *Navires et marchandises dans les ports de Rouen et du Havre au XVIIIe siècle* (Paris, 1963), Maurice Bégouen-Demaux, *Une famille de marchands de la Havre*, 2 vols., 1948–51; for Honfleur, there is J. C. Benard, 'L'armament honfleur-ais et le commerce des esclaves à la fin du XVIIIe siècle', *Annales de Normandie* 10, 1960, 249–64; and Jean Mettas, 'Honfleur et la traite des noirs au XVIIIe siècle', *Revue française d'histoire d'outremer* lx, 1973.

For the Dutch trade there is the formidable book of Johannes Postma, *The Dutch in the Atlantic Slave Trade* (Cambridge, 1990). See also Cornelius Ch. Goslinga, *The Dutch in the Caribbean* (Assen, 1971), J. F. Jameson, *Willem Usselincx*, Papers of the American Historical Association, 1887, and Jonathan Israel's fine general work *The Dutch Republic* (Oxford, 1995). For the Dutch in Brazil there is C. L. R. Boxer's work of that title mentioned above (Oxford, 1957), and H. Wätjen, *Das Hollandische Kolonial Reich in Brasilien* (Berlin, 1921), of which there is a Portuguese translation. For the Dutch in New York there is Oliver Rink, *Holland on the Hudson* (New York, 1986). For sugar see Sidney Mintz, *Sweetness and Power* (New York, 1985).

For the English trade there is G. F. Zook, *The Company of Royal Adventurers* (Lancaster, Penn., 1919), and K. G. Davies, *The Royal African Company* (New York, 1970). For Hawkins's voyage, apart from the account in the Hakluyt volume, there is Antonio Rumeu de Armas' accomplished *Viajes de Hawkins a América* (Seville, 1946), and J. A. Williamson, *Sir John Hawkins* (Oxford, 1927). Nigel Tattersfield, *The Forgotten Trade* (London, 1991), is an outstanding work on the slave trade from smaller English ports. For the slave trade aspect of the South Sea Company there is Colin Palmer's excellent *Human Cargoes* (Urbana, 1981). For Liverpool there are many works, such as C. N. Parkinson's *The Rise of the Port of Liverpool* (Liverpool, 1952), and, still interesting, Agnes Mackenzie-Grieve's *The Last Years of the Liverpool Slave Trade* (London, 1941). For Bristol there is the great work of David Richardson, *Bristol, Africa and the Eighteenth Century Slave Trade*, 3 vols. (Bristol, 1986–1990).

There is nothing satisfactory on London, though much can be found in David Hancock's splendid *Citizens of the World* (New York, 1995), a study of Richard Oswald and his partners. Roger Anstey's *The Atlantic Slave Trade and British Abolition* (London, 1975), covers a lot of ground. For the eighteenth-century Caribbean Eric Williams, *Capitalism and Slavery* (London, 1964), is still good to read, but his economics about the decline of Jamaica are corrected by, for example, B. W. Higman, *Jamaica Surveyed* (Kingston, 1988).

The best work on the slave trade to North America is Jay Coughtry's *The Notorious Triangle* (Philadelphia, 1981), but he concentrates on Rhode Island, and J. A. Rawley's *The Transatlantic Slave Trade* (New York, 1981), corrects this emphasis especially chapters 10 to 25. See also Roger Anstey, 'The North American Slave Trade 1761–1810', *Revue française d'histoire d'outremer* lxii, 1975, 226–7. For the slave trading of individual territories in the United States there is James G. Lydon on New York ('New York and the Slave Trade', in *William and Mary Quarterly* 35, 1978), Darold Wax on Pennsylvania ('Quaker Merchants and the Slave Trade in Colonial Pennsylvania', *Pennsylvania Magazine of History and Biography* lxxxvii, 1962) and Maryland ('Black Immigrants', *Maryland Historical Magazine* 73, no. 1, March 1978). For Maryland see, too, the letters of Mary and Henry Tilghman in *Maryland Historical Magazine* xxi, 20–39, 123–49, and 219–40, and Elizabeth Donnan on New England ('The New England Slave Trade', *New England Quarterly* III, 1930). Philip Hamer's wonderful collection of Henry Laurens's papers (Columbia, SC, 1968 onwards), are a constant pleasure and source of information for South Carolina. For Aaron Lopez, there is a poor biography by Stanley Chyet, *Lopez of Newport* (Detroit, 1970), and B. M. Bigelow, 'Aaron Lopes, Merchant of Newport', in *New England Quarterly* IV, 757, as well as Virginia Platt, 'And Don't Forget the Guinea Voyage', *William and Mary Quarterly*, 3rd series, xxxii (1975). The de Wolfs are considered rather lightly in George Howe's *Mount Hope* (New York, 1959).

The history of the British Caribbean is rich, and many excellent works have been written about it, though the treatment of the slave trade is less complete, and the introductions to Donnan's splendid volumes of documents are probably the most instructive, especially Volume II.

For the Danish entry into the trade see Georg Norregård, *Danish Settlements in West Africa* (Boston, 1966). For the Brandenburgers, see Adam Jones, *Brandenburg-Prussia and the Slave Trade* in Daget's *Colloque*, cited below. For the Swedes, see Ernst Ekman, 'Sweden, the Slave Trade and Slavery', in *Revue française d'histoire d'outremer* LXII, 1975, 13.

Book V: Abolition

Far the best introduction is David Davies's *Slavery in Western Culture* (Ithaca, 1966) and *Slavery in the Age of Revolution* (London, 1975). Thomas Clarkson's admirable history of abolition, *The History of the Rise, Progress and Accomplishment of the Abolition of the African Slave Trade*, 2 vols. (London, 1808), repays reading even now. John Francis Maxwell's *Slavery and the Catholic Church* (London, 1975), reminds us of innumerable statements which the churchmen made against slavery. The works of Benezet, Granville Sharp, Jonathan Woolman, and all the Scottish philosophers, Hutcheson, Ferguson, Smith, and Wallace, are all still very interesting. The great writer on the subject of slavery seems to me to be Montesquieu, though Diderot, Voltaire, and Rousseau of course repay examination. Raynal is still remarkable. (See references in chapters 23 and 24.)

For England there is Roger Anstey's book cited above (*The Atlantic Slave Trade and British Abolition* (London, 1975)), and Seymour Drescher's excellent *Econocide: British Slavery in the Era of Abolition* (Pittsburgh, 1977) and *Capitalism and Antislavery* (London, 1986). The study of Wilberforce, Clarkson, and Pitt is best approached by means of biographies (R. I. and S. Wilberforce, but also Robin Furneaux for the first, and now John Ehrman for the last), though Clarkson's life by Earle Leslie Griggs (*Thomas Clarkson, The Friend of Slaves* (London, 1936)) now seems old fashioned. The various reports for the Privy Council (1789) and for the House of Commons (1790) are invaluable, as are the debates in the Houses of Commons and Lords, 1788–1807. See also Moses D. E. Nwulia, *The History of Slavery in Mauritius and the Seychelles 1810–1875* (London, 1985).

The best book on United States abolition remains, astonishingly, W. E. B. Dubois's *The Suppression of the Atlantic Slave Trade to the United States* (New York, 1896). The debates on the Constitution in 1787 have now been conveniently published in the Library of America, 1993. The subject of the French Revolution and abolition has to be approached by a host of specialist monographs about the main characters, though the beginning of Serge Daget's thesis on abolition in France is penetrating.

Book VI: The Illegal Era

The most important general secondary work is David Eltis's excellent *Economic Growth and the Ending of the Transatlantic Slave Trade* (New York, 1987). He knows that mine of information, FO/84 in the Public Record Office, better than anyone. For Spain (and Cuba) there is David Murray's masterly *Odious Commerce* (Cambridge, 1983), which led me to me several interesting discoveries in the Spanish archives. The financial side of Spanish slaving is well considered in Angel Bahamonde and José Cayuela's *Hacer las Americas* (Madrid, 1992), and a Cuban angle is to be seen in José Luciano Franco's *Comercio clandestino de esclavos* (Havana, 1980): the author has used several interesting Havana archives, such as the papers of Joaquín Gómez. Rolando Ely's *Cuando reinaba el rey de azúcar* (Buenos Aires, 1963), is a good study of social life in nineteenth-century Cuba. Pío Baroja's novel *Los Pilotos de Altura* (new ed. Madrid, 1995) gives a vivid impression of the reality of sailing on slave ships from Cuba. Arthur Corwin's *Spain and the Abolition of Slavery in Cuba* (Austin, 1967), is still much the best picture of the complicated Spanish political impact of abolition, but H. S. Aimes's *A History of Slavery in Cuba* (New York, 1907), cannot be overlooked. Rebecca Scott's *Slave Emancipation in Cuba* (Princeton, 1985), argues interestingly how slavery and modern technology can be compatible.

The end of the Brazilian slave trade is admirably treated in Leslie Bethell's *The Abolition of the Brazilian Slave Trade* (Cambridge, 1970), which directed me to many interesting sources. It may be supplemented by Joseph Miller's *Way of Death* mentioned above (Madison, 1988), Mary Karasch's *Slave Life in Rio de Janeiro* (Princeton, 1987), and Peter Conrad's *World of Sorrow* (Baton Rouge, 1986); Conrad's *The Destruction of Brazilian Slavery* (Berkeley, 1972), is also excellent. José Honorio Rodrigues's *Brazil and Africa* (English tr. Berkeley, 1965), is the best study by a Brazilian, its chapter 6 being a good study of abolition from a Brazilian angle.

The French slave trade in the nineteenth century is now possible to study thanks to the Homeric work of Serge Daget, both his admirable *Répertoire* of ships cited above (Nantes, 1988), and his unpublished thesis, *La France et L'abolition de la traite des noirs* (Paris, 1969), on which I drew extensively.

The British naval patrol is still best considered in Christopher Lloyd's *The Navy and the Slave Trade* (London, 1949), but there is also W. E. F. Ward's *The Royal Navy and the Slavers* (London, 1969), not to speak of E. Philip Leveen, *British Slave Trade Suppression Policies* (New York, 1977), and Raymond Howell's *The Royal Navy and the Slave Trade* (London, 1987). A United States study on the same theme is Warren Howard's. Many naval officers (for example Andrew H. Foote, *Africa and the American Flag* (New York, 1862) also wrote memoirs.

For Africa in the nineteenth century there is Suzanne Miers's *Britain and the Ending of the Slave Trade* (London, 1975), and there are also innumerable travellers (James Tuckey, *Narrative of an Expedition to Explore the River Zaire* (London, 1818); John Adams, *Sketches Taken During the Ten Years' Voyage to Africa Between the Years 1786–1800* (London, 1827); Pierre du Chaillu, *Voyage en Afrique Équatoriale* (Paris, 1863)). Ehud R. Toledano's *The Ottoman Slave Trade and its Suppression: 1840–1890* (Princeton, 1982), is an excellent introduction to the subject. The evidence to Hutt's committee of the House of Commons (London 1849–1850) is the best of many British inquiries, for which there remains no equivalent in any other country. There is no adequate study of the United States illegal slave trade after 1808.

General works on the slave trade are headed by Philip Curtin's *The Atlantic Slave Trade, A Census* (Madison, 1969). There is also James Rawley, *The Transatlantic Slave Trade* (New York, 1981), which has many virtues, but it concentrates on the North American trade and omits the post-1807 era. Herbert Klein's *The Middle Passage* (Princeton, 1978), illuminates the whole field. Robin Blackburn's volumes on slavery unfortunately appeared too late for me to take them into account.

A number of collections of essays are useful; for example, Serge Daget's *Actes du colloque internationale sur la traite des noirs*, 2 vols. (Nantes, 1985); Henry Gemery and Jan Hogedorn's *The Uncommon Market* (New York, 1979); Roger Anstey and P. E. H. Hair's *Liverpool, the African Trade and Abolition* (Liverpool, 1976); the UNESCO publication *The African Trade from the Fifteenth to the Nineteeth Century* (Paris, 1979); David Eltis and James Walvin, *The Abolition of the Atlantic Slave Trade* (Madison, 1981); and Suzanne Miers and Richard Roberts, *The End of Slavery in Africa* (Madison, 1988). A modern study is Jonathan Derrick's *African Slaves To-day* (London, 1974).

NOTES

IN THESE NOTES I have tried to give the sources for all important direct quotations. I have abbreviated many names of books. Thus David Birmingham's *Trade and Conflict in Angola* is so rendered without the explanatory subtitle, 'The Mbundi and their neighbours under the influence of the Portuguese 1483–1790'.

The first time that a reference is given the full title of the source is given; the second time the title is not given, but a reference is made to the first time it was mentioned, with chapter and footnote named. For example, Ca'da Mosto [1, 2] means that the first mention and full reference is given in chapter 1, note 2.

ABBREVIATIONS

AGI: Archivo General de Indias, Seville

AHN: Archivo Histórico Nacional, Madrid

BFSP: British and Foreign State papers

C: Philip Curtin, *The Atlantic Slave Trade, A Census* (Madison, 1969)

CDI: Colección de Documentos Inéditos por la Historia de España Ultramar, 42 vols., Madrid, 1864 onwards

CO: Colonial Office

D: Elizabeth Donnan, *Documents Illustrative of the Slave Trade to America*, 4 vols. (Washington, 1930)

DNB: Dictionary of National Biography

FO: Foreign Office

FRUS: Foreign Relations of the United States

HAHR: Hispanic American Historical Review

Hutt Committee: Four reports of the Parliamentary Select Committee on the Slave Trade, November 1847 to September 1848, chaired by Sir William Hutt MP

JAH: Journal of African History
JNH: Journal of Negro History
Muñoz: the collection of papers of Muñoz in the library of the Real Academia de la Historia, Madrid
PD: Parliamentary Debates
PH: Parliamentary History
PRO: Public Record Office
Qu: Quoted in
R & P: reports and papers, that is, British parliamentary series
RFHO: Revue française d'histoire d'outremer
WMQ: William and Mary Quarterly

Introduction

1. H. R. Trevor-Roper, *The Past and the Present – History and Sociology* (London, 1969).
2. Richard Jobson, *The Golden Trade* (London, 1623), 89.

Book One: GREEN SEA OF DARKNESS

1. What Heart Could Be So Hard?

1. Zurara (Azurara)'s *Chronicle of the Discovery of Guinea*, Eng. tr. ed. C. R. Beazley and Edgar Prestage, Hakluyt Society, 1st ser., vols. 95 and 100 (London, 1896 and 1899). Vol. 95, 81–3.
2. *Alvise Ca'da Mosto (Cadamosto)*, ed. by G. B. Ramusio as vol. I of *Naviggationni et Viaggi* (Venice, 1551), Eng. tr. ed. G. R. Crone, Hakluyt Society, 2nd ser., vol. 80 (London, 1937), 18.
3. Qu. Mervyn Hisketts, *The Development of Islam in Africa* (London, 1984), 6–7.
4. Zurara [1, 1], 114.
5. Ibid., 62.
6. Egidio Colonna, *Li livri du Gouvernment des rois*, facs. ed., Samuel Paul Molenauer (New York, 1899); Bernard Lewis, *Race and Slavery in the Middle East* (Oxford, 1990).

2. Humanity Is Divided into Two

1. André Piganiol, *L'Empire chrétien*, A.D. *325–395*, in vol. iv (2), 404, of *L'Histoire générale de G. Glotz*, Hist. Rom. (Paris, 1947).

2. Edward Gibbon, *The Decline and Fall of the Roman Empire*, vol. vii (New York, 1907), 244.
3. Seneca, *Letters to Lucilius*, 3 vols. (London, 1920), vol. 1, 220.
4. Martial, *Epigrams*, 2 vols. (London, 1919), vol. 1, 103.
5. Song of Solomon I: 5–6.
6. Herodotus, Everyman's Library ed., 2 vols. (London, 1924), vol. 1, 220.
7. Aristotle, *Politics*, ed. Ernest Barker (Oxford, 1946), 91253 b.
8. Plato, *Republic*, ed. Francis Cornford (Oxford, 1941), 168.
9. Matthew 7: 12; Acts of the Apostles 17: 26.
10. Ephesians 6: 5; I Corinthians 7: 20–21.
11. All these matters are discussed at length in Charles Verlinden, *L'Esclavage dans l'Europe médiévale*, I (Bruges, 1955), chapters 1 and 2.
12. St Augustine, *The City of God*, Everyman ed. (London, 1945), xix, 15.
13. PH, vol. VII, 581, 19 June 1806.

3. The Slaves Who Find the Gold Are All Black

1. Pierre Bonnassie, *From Slavery to Feudalism in South-western Europe* (Cambridge, 1991), 35.
2. St Isidore, qu. Bonnassie [3, 1], 57.
3. Austin Lane Poole, *From Doomsday Book to Magna Carta* (Oxford, 1935), 40.
4. Bonnassie [3, 1], 341.
5. PH, 28, 60–61, 12 May 1789.
6. Qu. Richard Fletcher, *Muslim Spain* (London, 1996), 75.
7. Lewis [1, 6], 65.
8. Verlinden [2, 11], 253.
9. Los Códigos Españoles, Los Siete Partidas, part 4, tit. 21, ley 1.
10. Verlinden [2, 11], I, 320, 337, 349, 352. For slaves in Genoa, see Domenico Gioffré's *Il mercato degli Schiani a Genova nel secolo XV* (Genoa, 1971), where it is shown that 1,132 'oriental slaves were sold in that port between 1400 and 1499, along with 187 Moors, eight blacks and nineteen Canary Islanders'. Most were female.
11. Ibid., 358–62; see M. Gual Camarena, 'Una cofradía de negros libertos en el siglo XV', *Estudios de edad media en la Corona de Aragón* XV, 1952; and also for Seville, Isidoro Moreno's *La Antigua Hermandad de los Negros de Sevilla* (Seville, 1997).
12. Alfonso Zuazo, in a letter to Charles V in CDI, I, 292.
13. Leo Africanus, *Description of Africa*, ed. R. Brown, Hakluyt Society, ser. I, vol. 93 (London, 1890), 309.
14. Qu. Ralph Austen, 'The Trans-Saharan Trade', in Henry Gemery and Jan Hogendorn, *The Uncommon Market* (New York, 1979).
15. Qu. Lewis [1, 6], 57.
16. Leo Africanus [3, 13], 145.

17. Ibn Hawkal, qu. J. W. Bovill, *The Golden Trade of the Moors* (London, 1958), 97.
18. Ibn Battuta, *The Travels of Ibn Battuta*, ed. H. A. R. Gibb, Hakluyt Society, 4 vols. (London, 1958–94), III, 321.
19. Valentim Fernandes, *Description de la côte occidentale d'Afrique, 1506–1510*, ed. Theodore Monod and Raymond Mauny (Bissau, 1951).
20. Ca'da Mosto [1, 2], 36, 49.

4. The Portuguese Served for Setting Dogs to Spring the Game

1. Bailey W. Diffie and George Winius, *Foundations of the Portuguese Empire* (Minneapolis, 1977), 34.
2. Felipe Fernández-Armesto, in G. Winius, ed. *Portugal the Pathfinder* (Madison, 1992).
3. Diogo Gomes, *De Primea Inventione Guinee*, in Raymond Mauny's edition of his chronicle, as told to Martin Behaim (Bissau, 1959).
4. Ca'da Mosto [1, 2], 2.
5. Duarte Pacheco Pereira, *Esmeraldo de situ orbis*, ed. Raymond Mauny (Bissau, 1956), 27.
6. Zurara [1, 1], 40.
7. Ibid., 85.
8. Ibid., 59.
9. Ca'da Mosto [1, 2], 18.
10. Zurara [1, 1], 121.
11. Ca'da Mosto [1, 2], 28.
12. Zurara [1, 1], 107 ff.
13. Ca'da Mosto [1, 2], 41.
14. Es-Sadi, qu. Bovill [3, 17], 102.
15. Al-Bekri, in Philip Curtin, *Economic Change in Precolonial Africa* (Madison, 1975).
16. Willem Bosman, *A New and Accurate Description of the Coast of Guinea*, Eng. tr. (London, 1705), 82.
17. Fernandes [3, 19], 41.
18. Filippo Sassetti, *Lettere edite e inedite* (Florence, 1855), qu. A. C. de M. Saunders, *A Social History of Black Slaves in Portugal* (Cambridge, 1982), 168.
19. Florencio Pérez Embid, *Los descubrimentos en el Atlántico* (Seville, 1948), 163.
20. Gomes [4, 3], 52.

5. I Herded Them As If They Had Been Cattle

1. Gomes [4, 3], 22–3.
2. Fr. Martín de Córdoba, *Un jardin de las doncellas* (Valladolid, 1500), qu. Peggy Liss, *Isabel the Queen* (Oxford, 1992), 304.
3. Qu. A. W. Lawrence, *Trade Castles and Forts of West Africa* (London, 1963), 32.
4. Gabriel Tetzel and Václav Sasek, *Travels of Leo of Rozmital*, tr. by Malcolm Letts, Hakluyt Society (London, 1957).
5. Hernando de Pulgar, *Crónica de las Reyes Católicos*, 2 vols. (Madrid, 1943).
6. Antonio Rumeu de Armas, *España en la Africa Atlántica*, 2 vols. (Madrid, 1956), I, 103.
7. Eustache de la Fosse, 'Voyage a la cóte occidentale de'Afrique', *Revue Hispanique* 3 (Paris, 1896).
8. Diffie and Winius [4, 1], 317.
9. Anthony Luttrell, 'Slavery and slaving in the Portuguese Atlantic', Edinburgh conference on the Transatlantic slave trade, Edinburgh, 1965, Mss.
10. Ruy de Pina, *Crónica del Rey João II* (Coimbra, 1950), 74; Pacheco [4, 5], 134.
11. *Documentos sobre relaciones internacionales de los reyes católicos*, ed. Antonio de la Torre (Barcelona, 1968), IV, 46–8.
12. Thomas Münzer in *Boletín de la Real Academia de la Historia* (Madrid, 1924), 63.
13. For Bartolommeo Marchionni see Virginia Rau, 'Notes sur la traite à la fin du XVe siècle et le florentin Bartolommeo di Domenico Marchionni', *Bulletin de l'Institute Historique Belge de Rome* XLIV (1974), 535–43. Two letters from Marchionni in the Ricardiana Library in Florence (MS 1910), which I have myself examined, were printed in the Hakluyt ed. of Cabral's voyage, ed. W. B. Greenlee (London, 1938), 147–50.

6. The Best and Strongest Slaves Available

1. Alice B. Gould, *Nueva Lista documentada de los tripulantes de Colón en 1492* (Madrid, 1984), 304ff.
2. Qu. Carl Sauer, *The Early Spanish Main* (Berkeley, 1966), 88.
3. Bartolomé de las Casas, *Historia de las Indias* (Mexico, 1966), II, 173.
4. Vespucci to Lorenzo Pierfranceso de' Medici, in Frederick Pohl, *Amerigo Vespucci* (New York, 1944), 77.
5. CDI, XXXI, 104.
6. Ovando's instructions are in Juan Pérez de Tudela, *Las Armadas de Indias, y los origenes de la política de colonización* (Madrid, 1956).

7. Georges Scelle, *La traite negrière aux Indes de Castille*, 2 vols. (Paris, 1906), I, 124. There is much useful information in Consuelo Varela, *Colón y los florentinos* (Madrid, 1988).
8. Casas [6, 3], III, 273.
9. AGI, Indif. gen., leg., 418.
10. CDI, XXXI, 453.
11. AGI, Indif. gen., leg. 418, 1.2., f. 98 and f. 104 v.
12. Niccoló Macchiavelli, *The Prince*, ed. George Bull (London, 1961); Víctor Pradera, *El Estado Nuevo* (Madrid, 1941), 276.
13. Ferdinand to Lizarazo and Miguel Pasamonte, in Muñoz, I, 1695, item 605.
14. José Antonio Saco, *Historia de la Esclavitud Africana en el Nuevo Mundo*, 3 vols. (Paris, 1879), I, 67.
15. CDI, IV, no. 3; Bernardino de Sahagún, *Florentine Codex*, ed. Charles Dibble and Arthur Anderson, 12 vols. (Salt Lake City, 1953 onwards), XII, 19; Fernando Alva Ixtlilxochitl, *Historia de la Nación Chichimeca*, ed. (Madrid, 1988), 270.
16. Judge Zuazo to the King, in CDI, V, 292.
17. Manuel Giménez Fernández, *Bartolomé de las Casas*, 2 vols. (Seville, 1953 and 1960), II, 434.
18. Giménez Fernández [6, 17], II, 552.
19. Casas [6, 3], III, 129.
20. The grant in AGI, Indif. gen. 1.7, old style, of 21 October 1518, is published as an appendix to Scelle [6, 7], I, 755.
21. Qu. Scelle [6, 7], I, 174.
22. AGI, Justicia leg. 7, no. 3. Braudel in his *La Mediterranée au temps du Philip II* mistakenly gave this date as 1526. The lawsuit is no. 4 of that legajo.
23. Frederic Bowser, *The African Slave in Colonial Peru* (Stanford, 1972), 4.
24. AGI, Indif. gen., leg. 422, no. 16, f. 99 (I am grateful to Doña Enriqueta Vila Vilar for directing me to this legajo); and Ruth Pike, *Enterprise and Adventure* (Ithaca, 1966), 89.
25. Manuel Fernández de Oviedo, *Historia General y Natural de Indias*, ed. Juan Pérez de Tudela (Madrid, 1959), bk. 4, ch. 8.
26. Saco [6, 14], I, 158.
27. In Greenlee's *Cabral* [5, 13].
28. Antonio Rumeu de Armas [5, 6], I, 418.
29. Qu. A. J. C. Ryder, *Benin and the Europeans* (London, 1969), 47.
30. Ibid., 52.
31. Letter of 6 July 1526, in the Vizconde de Paiva Manso, *Historia do Congo* (Lisbon, 1877), 54.
32. C, 99–101, gives a larger figure.
33. Diego Angulo Iñigues, *Alejo Fernández* (Seville, 1906), 110.
34. Antonio Moreno Ollero, *Historia de Sanlúcar de Barrameda a fines del la Edad Media* (Cádiz, 1983), and Loic Mananteau et al., *Los Pueblos de*

la Provincia de Cádiz, 32, Sanlúcar de Barrameda (Cádiz, 1991).

35. Qu. John Hale, *The Italian Renaissance* (London, 1993), 359.
36. Antonio Cánovas del Castillo, *Historia de la decadencia en España* (Madrid, 1910), 19.
37. Nicolas Clenard, *Correspondence*, 3 vols., ed. A. Roersch (Brussels, 1940).

7. For the Love of God, Give Us a Pair of Slave Women

1. These figures derive from C, 18, 101, but corrected by reference to, for example, Colin Palmer's *Slaves of the White God* (Cambridge, Mass., 1976), 70, 112, and Enriqueta Vila Vilar, *Hispanoamerica y el comercio de esclavos* (Seville, 1977).
2. Cortés' will is in Antonio Muro Orejón, *Hernando Cortés, Exequías, . . .* (Seville, 1967); Peruvian figures derive from Bowser [6, 23].
3. Clenard [6, 37], III, 32.
4. Veturino in *Herculano Opusculos*, vi, 64, qu. Saunders [4, 18].
5. Enriqueta Vila Vilar, *Los Corzos y los Mañara* (Seville, 1991).
6. Clenard [6, 37], III, 36.
7. John Hemming, *The Conquest of the Incas* (London, 1970), 150.
8. Alonso de Castillo Solórzano, *La Niña de los Embustes* (Madrid, 1929), 126, cit. Pike [6, 24], 190–91.
9. Alonso de Zorita, *Brief Relation of the Lords of New Spain*, Eng. tr. Benjamin Keene (London, 1965), 205.
10. Qu. Palmer [7, 1], 70.
11. Francisco Paso y Troncoso, *Epistolario de Nueva España* (Mexico, 1939–42), iv, 96.
12. Mariano Cuevas, *Documentos inéditos del siglo xvi para la Historia de México* (Mexico, 1914), 115.
13. John Hemming, *Red Gold* (London, 1978), 37.
14. Sir Thomas More, *Utopia* (New Haven, 1964), 108.
15. Lewis Pastor, *History of the Papacy*, 40 vols. (London, 1891), viii, 447.
16. Lewis Hanke, *Spain's Struggle for Justice in the New World* (Philadelphia, 1949), 72–3.
17. Moses Finlay, *Ancient Slavery and Modern Ideology* (London, 1981), 23.
18. Giles of Rome, *De Regimine Principium*, ed. H. Samaritani (Rome, 1607), qu. Quentin Skinner and Eckhard Kessler, *Cambridge History of Philosophy* (Cambridge, 1988), 407.
19. Luther, qu. David Brion Davis, *The Problem of Slavery in Western Culture* (Ithaca, 1966), 106.
20. Domingo de Soto, *Tratado de la justicia y el derecho*, tr. into Spanish by Jaime Torrubiano, 2 vols. (Madrid, 1922).
21. Silvio Zavala, *La Filosofia política en la conquista de América* (Mexico, 1947), 98.
22. Scelle [6, 7], I, 205; F. Cercada in 'Asiento de Esclavos para América

en el año 1553', in *Missionalia Hispanalia*, Madrid, III, 580–97.

23. F. de Oliveira, *Arte de Guerra no mar* (Coimbra, 1555).

24. Martín de Ledesma, *Commentaria in Quartum Sententiarum* (Coimbra, 1560).

8. The White Men Arrived in Ships with Wings

1. Letter of Father Gouveia, qu. David Birmingham, *Trade and Conflict in Angola* (Oxford, 1966).

2. Letter of Father García Simães of 7 November 1576, qu. Fr. Dieudonné Rinchon, *La Traite et l'esclavage des congolais par les européens* (Brussels, 1929), 59.

3. Andrew Battell, Hakluyt Society, series II, vol. vi, ed. E. G. Ravenstein (London, 1901).

4. Willy Bal, ed., *Description du royaume de Congo et les contrées environnantes, par Filippo Pigafetta et Duarte Lopes, 1591* (Louvain, 1963).

5. Samuel Purchas (Hakluytos Posthumus), *Pilgrimes*, 20 vols. (Glasgow, 1905–7), vi, 444.

6. Cit. C. L. R. Boxer, *Portuguese Society in the Tropics* (Madison, 1965), 2.

7. João Lúcio de Azevedo, *Os Jesuitas no Grão Para . . .* (Coimbra, 1930), 65.

8. Qu. Gilberto Freyre, *The Mansions and the Slaves*, Eng. tr. (New York, 1970), 178.

9. R & P, Commons Select Committee report, 1790, vol. 1, 211.

10. P. Hentzer, *A Journey into England, 1598*, tr. Horace Walpole, ed. (London, 1757), 109.

11. R & P, 1790, vol. 67, 316.

12. C. J. Abbey and J. H. Overton, *The English Church in the Eighteenth Century* (London, 1878), II, 106.

13. Higgins in Hutt Committee, 535.

14. AGI, Mexico. leg. 258, qu. Palmer [7, 1], 81.

15. Freyre [8, 8], xxiii.

16. Ambrosio Fernandes Branão, *Diálogos das grandezas do Brasil*, ed. José António Gonçalves de Mello (Recife, 1968), 44.

17. Letter 6 April 1570, in Coll y Toste, *Boletín Histórico de Puerto Rico* XI, 199f.

18. Emilio A. Coni, *Agricultura, comercio e industria coloniales* (Buenos Aires, 1941), 15.

19. Here the figures of C, 166–77, have been again corrected by the estimates imaginatively suggested by Doña Enriqueta Vila Vilar.

20. Hugh Crow, *Memoirs* (London, 1830), 21.

21. Tomás de Mercado, *Suma de tratos y contratos* (Salamanca, 1569), lib. 2, cap. 20.

22. Bartolomé Frías de Albornoz, *Arte de los contratos* (Valencia, 1573), cit. Saco [6, 14], I, 237.

23. Discussed in Marcel Bataillon, *Bulletin Hispanique* 54, 368.

24. Juan Suárez de Peralta, *Noticias Históricas de la Nueva España* (Madrid, 1878), 50. ('No hay otra diferencia más de ser más subidos de color y mas prietos.')

25. Letter of 24 July 1604, qu. in Francisco Rodrigues, *Historia da companhia de Jesus na assistência da Portugal*, vol.iii (Porto, 1944), 458.

26. Alonso de Sandoval, S.J., *De Instauranda Aethiopium Salute, Historia de Aethiopia* . . . , ed. Enriqueta Vila Vilar (Madrid, 1987).

27. J. Gabriel de Lurbe, *Chronique bordelaise* (Bordeaux, 1619), 42, qu. Gabriel Hanotaux and Alfred Martineau, *Histoire des colonies françaises* . . . , 6 vols. (Paris, 1920–34), iv, 7.

28. Jean Bodin, *The Six Books of a Commonweal*, facsimile ed. of Eng. tr. of 1606, ed. Kenneth Mc Rae (Cambridge, Mass., 1962), 42.

29. Qu. in UNESCO, *The Atlantic Slave Trade from the Fifteenth to the Nineteenth Century* (Paris, 1979), 165.

Book Two: The Internationalization of the Trade

9. A Good Correspondence with the Blacks

1. Jean-Michel Deveau, *La Traite Rochelaise* (Paris, 1990).

2. Lawrence [5, 3], 35 and 280fn.

3. *The Hawkins Voyages*, ed. Clements Markham, Hakluyt Society, vol. LVII (London, 1878), 5. See also Antonio Rumeu de Armas' *Viajes de Hawkins a América* (Seville, 1947). See too J. A. Williamson, *Sir John Hawkins* (Oxford, 1927).

4. Jean Barbot, *A Description of the Coasts of Guinea*, 2 vols., ed. P. E. H. Hair (London, 1992), I, 194.

5. *De Werken van G. A. Bredero*, II (Amsterdam, 1890), qu. Johannes Postma's *The Dutch in the Atlantic Slave Trade* (Cambridge, 1990). I failed to find an English translation of *The Little Moor*.

6. Vila Vilar [7, 1], 214.

7. Loc. cit.

8. Johann Gregor Aldenburg, *Reise nach Brasilien, 1623–1626* (The Hague, 1930).

9. J. F. Jameson, ed., *Narratives of New Netherland* (New York, 1909), 129; also Broadhead and E. B. O'Callaghan, *Colonial History of the State of New York* (New York, 1858), vol. 2, 759–76.

10. C. L. R. Boxer, *The Dutch in Brazil* (London, 1957), 83; Manuel Calado, *O balersoso Lucideno e triumphe da libertade* (Lisbon, 1648), 30, qu. C. L. R. Boxer, *Golden Age of Brazil* (London, 1962), 16.

11. Phyllis Martin, *External trade of the Loango coast* (Oxford, 1972), 58; Ralph Delgado, *Historia do Angola*, 4 vols. (Benguela and Lobito, 1948

onwards), II, 281, n. 62, qu. J. Vansina, *Kingdoms of the Savana* (Madison, 1966), 142.
12. D, I, 97.
13. D, IV, 2.
14. Jobson [Introduction, 2].
15. D, IV, 49.
16. Qu. K. G. Davies, *The Royal African Company* (New York, 1970), 41.
17. J. T. Scharf, *History of Maryland* (Baltimore, 1878), I, 66.
18. John Winthrop's journal, qu. D, III, 6.
19. *Cambridge History of the British Empire* (Cambridge, 1920), I, 69.
20. Cadereita, qu. Vila Vilar [7, 1].
21. Diary of Guijo, qu. Solange Alberro, *Inquisition et société au Méxique* (Mexico, 1988), 295.
22. William Atkins, *A Relation of the Journey from St Omer to Seville* (London, 1652), ed. Martin Murphy in Camden Fifth Series (London, 1994), 245.

10. The Black Slave Is the Basis of the Hacienda

1. AGI, Indif. gen. leg. 2796.
2. See Vila Vilar [7, 1] for further discussion.
3. H. Wätjen, *Das Hollandische Kolonial Reich in Brasilien* (Berlin, 1921), 487.
4. Alberto Vieira, *Cartas*, ed. J. Lúcio d'Azevedo, 3 vols. (Coimbra, 1925–8), I, 243.
5. C, 106–107, corrected by Vila Vilar [7, 1].
6. E. B. O'Callaghan, ed., *Documents Relative to the Colonial History of the State of New York* (New York, 1856), I, 162.
7. Qu. D, I, 125 fn. 2.
8. Loc. cit.
9. *Trends and Forces of World Sugar Consumption* (Rome, 1961), 11.
10. Fr. Antoine Biet, *Voyage de la France équinoxiale* (Paris, 1664).
11. Jean Clodoré, *Rélation de ce qui s'est passé dans les Isles et Terre Ferme de l'Amérique* (Paris, 1671).

11. Lawful to Set to Sea

1. D, I, 125.
2. D, I, 128–31.
3. *Samuel Pepys' Diary*, ed. Robert Latham and William Matthews (London, 1971), IV, 152.
4. D, I, 88.
5. Pepys [11, 3], V, 352–3.
6. Charles Davenant, *Reflections on the Constitution and Management of the Trade to Africa* (London, 1709).

7. Davies [9, 16],179–80; Curtin [4, 15], 7, 119, 122; David Galenson, ed., *Markets in History* (Cambridge, 1986); Richard Dunn, *Sugar and Slaves* (Williamsburg, 1972), 155.

8. Jacob Judd, 'Frederick Philipse and the Madagascar Trade', *New York Historical Society Quarterly* LV, 1971.

9. D, I, 271.

10. David Richardson, *Bristol, Africa and the Eighteenth Century Slave Trade to America*, 3 vols. (Bristol, 1986–90).

11. For the lesser ports see Nigel Tattersfield, *The Forgotten Trade* (London, 1991), 202–349.

12. Qu. E. D. Ellis, *An Introduction to Sugar as a Commodity* (Philadelphia, 1905), 82.

13. Calendar of state papers, col. 17080–17090, cit. D, III, 2.

14. N. B. Shurtless, *Topographical and Historical Description of Boston* (Boston, 1871), I, 48.

15. D, III, 1.

16. D, IV, 6.

17. D, IV, 1–2.

18. D, II, 241; Maurice Cranston, *John Locke* (London, 1985), 178.

19. D, I, 124.

20. D, IV, 243, 250–56.

21. *The Writings and Speeches of Oliver Cromwell* (Oxford, 1988), IV, 521.

12. He Who Knows How to Supply the Slaves Will Share This Wealth

1. Cit. Roberto Arrazola, *Palenque, primer pueblo libre de América* (Cartagena, 1970), 68–70.

2. Memorial of Captain Fernando de Silva Solís 1642 in AGI, Indif. gen. leg. 2796 published by Enriqueta Vila Vilar in 'La Sublevación de Portugal y la Trata de Negros', *Iberoamerikanisches Archiv*, ns. 2,3 (Berlin, 1976), 175.

3. I. A. Wright, 'The Coymans Asiento', *Bijdragen voor de Vaderlandse Geschiedenis en Oudheidkunde*, reeks vi, deel I, afleverung 1–2 (Arnhem, 1924).

4. Enriqueta Vila Vilar [12, 2]; also Jonathan Israel, *Empires and Entrepôts* (London, 1990), 439.

5. Davies [9, 16], 329.

6. D, I, 329, 341.

7. AGI, Indif. gen. 153–7–10 (old categorization), qu. D, I, 50.

8. D, I, 280, 350, 370.

9. Barbot [9, 4], I, 273.

10. Scelle [6, 7], 125.

11. Mauricio Goulart, *Escravido Africano no Brasil* (São Paolo, 1950).

12. Boxer [9, 10], 47.

13. Goulart [12, 11], 203. See too C, 209.

14. Daniel Defoe, *Robinson Crusoe* (London, 1891), 38–9: 'they desired to make but one voyage, to bring the negroes on shore privately and divide them among their own plantations and, in a word, the question was whether I would go their super-cargo in the ship to manage the trading on the coast of Guinea . . .'
15. *Le Gentil de la Barbinais, Nouveau Voyage autour du monde* (Paris, 1728–9), qu. Freyre [8, 8], 445.
16. Adam Jones in Serge Daget, ed., *Actes du colloque internationale sur la traite des noirs* (Nantes, 1985), I, 285.
17. Qu. H. A. Wyndham, *The Atlantic and Slavery* (1935), 59.
18. E. W. Martin, *The British West Africa Settlements* (London, 1927), 48–9.
19. C, 119.
20. Jean Bazin and Emanuel Terry, 'Guerres des lignages et guerres d'état en Afrique', *Archives Contemporaines* (Paris, 1992), 9–32.
21. Qu. Postma [9, 5], 96, 85.
22. Saint-Simon on Ducasse in Pléiade ed. (Paris, 1988), vol. V, 211, also II, 403.
23. The grant is in AGI, Santo Domingo leg. 2515.
24. Calendar of state papers, qu. D, I, 3 fn.
25. D, II, 4.
26. D, II, 82.

Book Three: APOGEE

13. No Nation Has Plunged So Deeply into This Guilt As Great Britain

1. Elizabeth Donnan, 'Early Days of the South Sea Company', *Journal of Economic and Business History* II (3), May 1930. See Victoria G. Sorsby, *British Trade with Spanish America Under the Asiento, 1713–1740*, Ph.D. thesis, University of London, 1975.
2. Daniel Defoe, 'An Essay on the South Sea Trade' (London, 1711).
3. As recalled by the Duke of Clarence in PH, 34 1094.
4. Colin Palmer, *Human Cargoes* (Urbana, 1981), 10.
5. D, II, 295, 159.
6. D, II, 171–3.
7. Qu. Lord Erleigh, *The South Sea Bubble* (London, 1935), 36.
8. Far the best work on the Bubble is that of John Carswell (London, 1993), on which I leaned heavily for these paragraphs.
9. Palmer [13, 4], 75–6, 85–6.
10. D, II, 195.
11. Lady Mary Wortley Montagu, *Complete Letters*, ed. R. Robert Halsband (Oxford, 1965), I, 232.
12. Qu. Leslie Stephen, essay on Chandos in *DNB*.
13. D, II, 256.

14. J. A. Rawley, 'Humphrey Morice', in Daget [12, 16], I, 269.
15. David Richardson, *Bristol, Africa and the Eighteenth Century Slave Trade to America*, 3 vols., Bristol Record Society, nos. 38, 39, 42, 1986–90.
16. C, 140, 215–16.
17. Daniel Defoe, *A Tour Through the Whole Island of England*, 3 vols., 1724–7.
18. *A General and Descriptive History of Liverpool*, 1798, qu. D, II, 49.
19. James Picton, *Memorials of Liverpool*, 2 vols. (London, 1873), I, 182, 185–6.
20. David Richardson, *The Bristol Slave Traders, A Collective Portrait* (Bristol, 1985).
21. Folarin Shyllon, *Black People in England* (London, 1977), 6–7.
22. Jean-Joseph Expilly, in his *Dictionnaire Géographique* (Paris, 1762), V, 17.
23. A. Perret, 'René Montaudoin', in *Bulletin de la société d'Archeologie d'Histoire de Nantes*, t. lxxxviii, 1949, 78–94.
24. Expilly [13, 22], V, 80.
25. George Collas, *René-Auguste de Chateaubriand* (Paris, 1949), 39.
26. L. Peytraud, *L'Esclavage aux Antilles Françaises avant 1789* (Paris, 1897), 380.
27. C, 170; Gaston Martin, *Nantes au xviiième siècle* (Paris, 1931).
28. Goulart [12, 11] 203; Pierre Verger, *Flux et reflux de la traite des nègres entre le Golfe de Benin et Bahia de todos los santos* (Paris, 1968), 100.
29. D, IV, 235 fn.
30. D, IV, 263, 273.
31. D, IV, 236.
32. *Boston Gazette*, 22 May 1721.
33. D, IV, 236.
34. *Boston Gazette*, 1721.
35. D, IV, 238.
36. Hedges, *The Browns of Providence Plantation* (Providence, 1968).
37. James G. Lydon, ' New York and the Slave Trade', *WMQ* 35 (1978).

14. By the Grace of God

1. Malachy Postlethwayt, *The African Trade, the Great Pillar* (London, 1745), 4.
2. D, II, 474–84.
3. Philip Hamer et al., *The Letters and Papers of Henry Laurens* (Columbia, SC, 1964), I, 202, 313.
4. D, III, 320, IV 313, 321.
5. D, IV, 321.
6. Hamer [14, 3], II, 123.
7. Ibid., II, 177.

8. Francisco de Arango, *Obras completas* (Havana, 1952), I, 117.
9. Hamer [14, 3], III, 412.
10. D, II, 514–15.
11. Gaston Martin [13, 27].
12. Ibid.
13. Collas [13, 25], 128.
14. E. Saugera, *Bordeaux, port négrier* (Bordeaux, 1995), 69.
15. Letter of Silva, 18 October 1781, cit. José Honorio Rodrigues, *Brazil and Africa* (Berkeley, 1964).
16. Kenneth Maxwell, *Pombal* (New York, 1996), 54.
17. Louis-Antoine de Bougainville, *Voyage autour du monde* (Paris, 1958).
18. AGI, Indif. gen. leg. 2819.
19. Bibiano Torres Ramírez, *La Compañía Gaditana de Negros* (Seville, 1973), 35.
20. Loc. cit.
21. D, IV, 245.
22. D, IV, 471.
23. For Oswald see David Hancock, *Citizens of the World* (New York, 1995).
24. For Clement Noble, see Sir Andrew Noble, *The Nobles of Ardmore* (privately printed *c.* 1973).
25. Richard Brooke, *Liverpool as It Was During the Last Quarter of the Eighteenth Century* (Liverpool, 1853), 328.
26. House of Lords MSS 14–19 February 1778.
27. Richard Miles in D, II, 522.
28. B. W. Higman, *Jamaica Surveyed* (Kingston, 1988), *passim*.
29. George Howe, *Mount Hope* (New York, 1959), 87.
30. Robert Louis Stein, *The French Slave Trade* (Madison, 1979), 180.
31. Jean-Philippe de Garran-Coulon, *Rapport sur les troubles de Saint-Domingue* (Paris, Year V–VII, that is, by the revolutionary calendar), iv, 18.
32. J.-F. Landolphe, *Mémoires du capitaine Landolphe*, 2 vols. (Paris, 1823).

Book Four: THE CROSSING

15. *A Filthy Voyage*

1. W. E. Minchinton, 'The Virginia Letters of Isaac Hobhouse', *Virginia Magazine of History and Biography* 66 (1958), 279.
2. D, III, 195.
3. Hancock [14, 23], 1995, 432–45; I. A Wright [12, 3], 50.
4. For Isaac Norris, see Darold Wax, 'Quaker Merchants and the Slave Trade', *Pennsylvania Magazine of History and Biography* LXXXVII (1962) and the same author's 'Negro Imports into Pennsylvania',

Pennsylvania History XXXII (1965).

5. For the Galtons, see B. M. D. Smith, *The Galtons of Birmingham, Business History*, 138.

6. Qu. C. L. R. Boxer, *The Portuguese Seaborne Empire* (London, 1963), 271.

7. Minchinton [15, 1], 278.

8. Jean Mettas, *Répertoire des expéditions négriers françaises au XVIIIe siècle*, vol. 1, *Nantes* (1978); vol. 2, *Ports autres que Nantes* (1984).

9. Cit. Palmer [13, 4], 21.

10. Pierre Boule, 'L'origine du racisme en Europe', in Daget [12, 16], I, 535.

11. Darold Wax, 'A Philadelphia Surgeon on the Coast of Africa', *Pennsylvania Magazine of History and Biography* XC (I) (1968).

12. Maurice Bégouen-Démeaux, *Une famille de marchands de la Havre*, 2 vols. (Le Havre, 1951–71), I, 20.

13. Hamer [14, 3], VI.

14. D, II, 82.

15. Collas [13, 25], 177.

16. Crow [8, 20], 176–7.

17. D, IV, 496.

18. Thomas Phillips, *A Journal of a Voyage Made in the* Hannibal, *1694* (London, 1746), 233.

19. John Newton, 'Thoughts on the African Slave Trade', *Letters and Sermons*, 3 vols. (Edinburgh, 1780), 103.

20. J.-M. Deveaux, *France au temps des négriers* (Paris, 1994).

21. Barbot [9, 4], xcviii

22. R & P, 1790, vol. 82, 27.

23. R & P, 1790, vol. 73, 163.

24. R & P, 1790, vol. 82, 29.

25. Edouard Corbière, *Le Négrier* (Paris, 1832).

26. D, III, 229.

27. D, II, 327.

16. Great Pleasure from Our Wine

1. D, III, 269–70.

2. D, II, 274.

3. For Malemba see Rinchon [8, 2], 32.

4. For Loango Bay see Rinchon [8, 2], 71, 74.

5. Barbot [9, 4], II, 493.

6. Captain William Snelgrave, *A New Account of Some Parts of Guinea* (London, 1734), 88.

7. Bosman [4, 16], 174.

8. Lord Edward Fitmaurice, *Life of William, Earl of Shelburne*, 3 vols. (London, 1875), I, 400, 404.

9. Fernandes [3, 19], 17.
10. Francis Moore, *Travels into the Inland Parts of Africa* (London, 1738), 87.
11. Barbot [9, 4], I, 172.
12. As put by Eric Williams, *Capitalism and Slavery* (London, 1942), 81.
13. Qu. Verger [13, 28], 30.
14. D, II, 541.

17. Slave Harbours I

1. Fernandes [3, 19], 7.
2. N. Bennet and G. Brooks, *New England Merchants in Africa* (Boston, 1965), 15.
3. R & P, 1790, vol. 72, 39.
4. Sir George Collier's Report, in Parliamentary Papers 1821, vol. xxiii.
5. Qu. John Thornton, *Africa and the Africans in the Making of the Atlantic World* (New York, 1992), 66.
6. Olfert Dapper, *Nouvelle description des pays africains* (Amsterdam, 1670), 471.
7. C. L. R. Boxer, *Race Relations in the Portuguese Colonial Empire* (Oxford, 1963), 11.
8. Barbot [9, 4].
9. Barbot [9, 4], II, 404.
10. D, II, 520.
11. Davies [9, 16], 178–9.
12. See Saugera [14, 14].
13. Albert van Dantzig, *Les Hollandais sur la côte de Guinée* (Paris, 1980).

18. Slave Harbours II

1. I. A. Akinjogbin, *Dahomey and Its Neighbours* (Cambridge, 1966), 134.
2. Pieter de Marees, *Description and historical account of the Gold Kingdom of Guinea*, 1602, tr. and ed. Albert van Dantzig and Adam Jones (Oxford, 1987), 224.
3. Antoine-François Prévost, *Histoire générale des voyages* (Paris, 1746 onwards). For an interesting study of Prévost see Shirley Jones, 'Les esclaves sont des hommes', in R. J. Howells, *Voltaire & His World, Studies Presented to W. H. Barber* (Oxford, 1985).
4. D, I, 399.
5. Antoine-Edmé Pruneau de Pommegorge, *Description de la Nigritie* (Amsterdam, 1789).
6. Qu. Robin Law, *The Slave Coast of West Africa* (Oxford, 1991), 262–3.
7. Lambe's letter in William Smith, *A New Voyage to Guinea* (London, 1744), 169–81.
8. Qu. Akinjogbin [18, 1], 164.

9. Macgregor Laird, qu. in Howard Temperley, *White Dreams, Black Africa* (New Haven, 1991).
10. D. Forde, ed., *Efik Traders of Old Calabar* (London, 1956), 81.
11. John Adams, *Remarks on the Country Extending...* (London, 1823), 129.
12. Abridgement of the minutes of evidence taken before the whole House [of Commons], III, 1790, 53–4.
13. Cit. Vansina [9, 11], 181.
14. Louis-Marie-Joseph Count Grandpré, *Voyage à la côte occidentale d'Afrique*, 2 vols. (Paris, 1801), I, 223.
15. William Beckford in the House of Commons, 1752, cit. John Latimer, *Annals of Bristol* (Bristol, 1893), 128.

19. A Great Strait for Slaves

1. D, II, 255.
2. Barbot [9, 4], I, 106.
3. Bosman [4, 16], 363.
4. Moore [16, 10], 41.
5. R & P, House of Commons Reports of 1790, vol. 73, 207.
6. R & P, House of Commons Reports of 1790, vol. 73, 213.
7. Palmer [13, 4], 20.
8. D, II, 527.
9. Qu. D, II, 570.
10. C. B. Wadström, *Observations on the Slave Trade* (London, 1789), 1.
11. Alexander Falconbridge, *An Account of the Slave Trade* (London, 1788), 16.
12. Vansina [9, 11], 248.
13. Qu. Postma [9, 5], 90.
14. John Atkins, *A Voyage to Guinea, Brasil and the West-Indies* (London, 1735), 71–2.
15. Wadström's evidence to the Privy Council inquiry.
16. Olaudah Equiano, *Equiano's Travels*, 2 vols., ed. Paul Edwards (New York, 1967), I, 47.
17. Wadström [19, 10], 16–20.
18. Bosman [4, 16], 364.
19. Moore [16, 10], 20.
20. Phillips [15, 18], 217.
21. Wadström [19, 10], 18.
22. William Towerson, *Hakluyt's Principal Navigations 1598–1600*, II, part II, 23–52.
23. Bosman [4, 16], 475.
24. Palmer [13, 4], 39.
25. Richard Drake, *Revelations of a Slave Smuggler* (New York, 1860), 3.
26. D, IV, 148.

27. Mungo Park, *The Travels of Mungo Park*, Everyman ed. (London, 1907), 221, 244.
28. Barbot [9, 4].
29. Bosman [4, 16], 364.
30. Xavier Golbéry, *Fragments d'un voyage en Afrique fait pendant les années 1785–1787* (Paris, Year X [1802]) in D, II, 567.
31. Wadström [19, 10], 16.
32. Park [19, 27], 149.
33. Ibid., 249.
34. Luiz Antonio de Oliveira, *Memoria a respeito dos escravos e tráfico da escravatura . . .* (Porto, 1977), 48.
35. The historian was Joseph Miller, whose *Way of Death* (Madison, 1988) is far the best introduction to the Anglo-Brazilian trade *c*. 1800.

20. *The Blackest Sort with Short Curled Hair*

1. Bosman [4, 16], I, 441.
2. Phillips [15, 18], 216.
3. Ibid., 218–19.
4. Snelgrave [16, 6], 39.
5. Postma [9, 5], 87; Phillips [15, 18], 219; Barbot [9, 4], I, 374.
6. Gaston Martin [13, 27], 91–2; Mettas [15, 8], I, 206–7.
7. D, II, 567.
8. Phillips [15, 18], 220.
9. D, II, 265.
10. D, II, 186.
11. D, I, 399; Drake [19, 25], 43.
12. Rinchon [8, 2], 162.
13. Phillips [15, 18].
14. Palmer [13, 4], 69.
15. Gaston Martin [12, 18], 112.
16. Adam Jones, in Daget [12, 16], I, 289.
17. Letter from Pedro de Espinosa, SJ, to Fr. Diego Ruiz, 1622, in Pablo Pastells, SJ, *Historia de la Compania de Jesús en la provincia de Paraguay* (Madrid, 1912–49), I, 300–301.
18. Prévost's voyage cit. Jones [18, 3], 225.
19. Grandpré [18, 15], II, 25.
20. Qu. Palmer [13, 4], 61.
21. Ibid., 63.
22. Mary Karasch, *Slave Life in Rio de Janeiro* (Princeton, 1987), 22.
23. Qu. James Rawley, *The Transatlantic Slave Trade* (New York, 1981), 272.
24. Phillips [15, 18], 212.
25. Postma [9, 5], 107–8.
26. 'Considerations on the Present Peace', London, 1763, in D, II, 515–16.

27. Ryder [6, 29], 169.
28. Smith [18, 7].
29. Hutt Committee, 421.
30. Martin [13, 26], 104.
31. D, IV, 372.
32. Qu. Palmer [13, 4], 35.
33. Thomas Clarkson, *The History of the rise, progress and accomplishment of the abolition of the African Slave Trade by the British parliament*, 2 vols. (London, 1808), I, 307–8.
34. Qu. Dantzig in Daget, ed. [12, 16], I, 591.
35. Phillips, [15, 18], 219.
36. Bosman [4, 16].
37. Phillips [15, 18], 219.
38. Snelgrave [16, 6], 162.
39. D, IV, 498.
40. Martin [13, 26], 117; John Newton, *Letters and Sermons*, 3 vols. (Edinburgh, 1780), I, 75.

21. If You Want to Learn How to Pray, Go to Sea

1. Equiano [19, 16], I, 76.
2. Jacques Savary, *Le Parfait Négociant* (Paris, 1757), cit. Gaston Martin [13, 27], 111.
3. Phillips [15, 18], 230.
4. R & P 1790, vol. 83, 35.
5. Bosman [4, 16], 364.
6. Dionigio Carli de Piacenza, *A Voyage to Congo, etc. . . . in 1666 and 1667*, with Michael Angelo Guattini, in Churchill's collections of voyages (London, 1732).
7. Report of the House of Commons inquiry, 1792.
8. Barbot [9, 4].
9. Wadström evidence to the Privy Council.
10. Ibid.
11. Equiano [19, 16], I, 78.
12. Lady Knutsford, *Life and Letters of Zachary Macaulay* (London, 1908), 87–9.
13. R & P 1790, vol. 72, 84.
14. Thomas Clarkson, *Essay on the Comparative Efficiency of Regulation or Abolition as Applied to the Slave Trade* (London, 1789), in D, II, 573.
15. D, I, 272.
16. See for example H. S. Klein, *The Middle Passage* (Princeton, 1978).
17. Barbot [9, 4], II, 779.
18. Phillips [15, 18], 229; Hutt Committee, II, 7.
19. Postma [9, 5], 308.
20. Barbot [9, 4], I, xcvii.

21. *London Magazine*, XXVIII, 162.
22. Mettas [15, 8], 123.
23. Hutt Committee I, 472.
24. Phillips [15, 18], 221.
25. Ibid., 232.
26. Barbot [9, 4], II, 790.
27. Speech by Wilberforce in PH, vol. 28, col. 258.
28. D, I, 462.
29. Barbot [9, 4], II, 791; Phillips [15, 18], 233.
30. Mercado [8, 21].
31. Barbot [9, 4].
32. Phillips [15, 18].
33. Bosman [4, 16], 365.
34. This was in John Atkins's *A Voyage to Guinea* . . . (London, 1753), qu. D, II, 266.
35. Smith [18, 7], 19.
36. D, III, 321.
37. D, III, 213
38. Georg Nørregård, *Danish Settlements in West Africa* (Boston, 1966), 89.
39. Gaston Martin [13, 27], 120.
40. Newton [15, 19], 104.
41. Park [19, 27], 271.
42. Marcel Delafosse, *L'Histoire de la Rochelle* (Paris, 1991), 169.
43. D, II, 494.
44. D, IV, 118.
45. *Boston News* letter, 9 May 1723, in D, IV, 186 fn. 6.

22. *God Knows What We Shall Do with Those That Remain*

1. Amadée-François Frézier, *Voyage to the South Sea*, Eng. tr. (London, 1717), 301.
2. Qu. Boxer [9, 10], 7.
3. Qu. Robert Edgar Conrad, *World of Sorrow* (Baton Rouge, 1986), 49.
4. Nicolás del Castillo Mathieu, *Esclavos negros en Cartagena* (Bogotá, 1982), 95.
5. Sandoval [8, 26], 109.
6. Drake [19, 25], 44.
7. Jean-Baptiste Labat, *Voyages aux îles* (Paris, 1993), 228.
8. Gaston Martin [13, 27], 130.
9. Loc. cit., 125.
10. W. R. Gardner, *History of Jamaica* (London, 1909), 165.
11. D, III, 273.
12. Equiano [19, 16], 63.

13. Barbot [9, 4], 550.
14. R & P, 1790, vol. 72, 160.
15. D, II, 460.
16. Hamer [14, 3], I, 255.
17. Ibid. Bostock later became a successful slave merchant.
18. Ibid.
19. Qu. Darold Wax, 'Black Immigrants, the Slave Trade', *Colonial Maryland* 73, no. 1, March 1978, 43.
20. Newton [20, 40] I, 81.
21. Roger Anstey, *The Atlantic Slave Trade and British Abolition* (London, 1975), 47.

Book Five: ABOLITION

23. Above All a Good Soul

1. D, II, 627.
2. PH, 34 1798–1800, col. 1092 (5 July 1792).
3. Arthur Young, *Travels in France* (London, 1929), 116.
4. Francis Lefeuvre, *Souvenirs nantais et vendéens* (Paris, 1913).
5. PH, 19, col. 305 (23 May, 2 June 1777): 'Mr Burke was against revising the state of the trade to Africa in general.'
6. Milton, *Paradise Lost*, vii, 64.
7. John Locke, *Two Treatises on Government*, ed. Peter Laslett (Cambridge, 1960), 302. Laslett's note 24 explains that Locke seemed to suppose that the RAC's slave raiding forays were just wars and that the slaves captured had previously forfeited their lives by 'some act that deserves death'.
8. Philip had in 1601 prohibited the use of Indian labour in any capacity on plantations, which had the effect of forcing planters to buy African slaves.
9. John Francis Maxwell, *Slavery in the Catholic Church* (London, 1975), 71.
10. Deveaux [15, 20].
11. Davis [7, 19], 201.
12. D, III, 4.
13. D, III, 108.
14. D, III, 7.
15. Lawrence Towner, 'A Fondness for Freedom', *WMQ*, 2nd ser., xix, April 1962.
16. D, III, 36.
17. Aphra Benn, *Oroonoko, or the History of the Royal Slave* (London, 1688).
18. Qu. Tattersfield [11, 11], 18.
19. Thomas Aubrey, *The Sea Surgeon, or the Guinea Man's Vademecum*

(London, 1729).

20. James Thomson, *Summer, Complete Works* (Edinburgh, 1853), 67.
21. William Shenstone, *Complete Works* (Edinburgh, 1852), 233; Pope, 'Essay on Man', 1, 107.
22. Fr. Jerome Merollo da Sorrento, *A Voyage to Congo*, tr. into English, in John Pinkerton, *A General Collection of the Best and Most Interesting Voyages* (London, 1814), qu. Donnan, I, 319.
23. Qu. Walter Rodney, *A History of the Upper Guinea Coast* (Oxford, 1970), 120–21.
24. D, I, 319.
25. Labat [22, 7], 219.
26. Clarkson [20, 33], I, 112, 134.
27. Darold Wax, 'Quaker Merchants and the Slave Trade in Colonial Pennsylvania', *Pennsylvania Magazine of History and Biography* LXXXVII, 1962, 143–59.
28. Qu. Tattersfield [11, 11] , 119.
29. Albert Matthews, 'Protests Against Slavery in Massachusetts', *Publications of the Colonial Society of Massachusetts* VIII, Transactions (Boston, 1906), 288.
30. Clarkson [20, 33], I, 148.
31. Ibid., 140.
32. *John Woolman's Journal*, ed. Philips Marlton (New York, 1971), and Clarkson [20, 33], I, 162.
33. Clarkson [20, 33], I, 114.
34. D, IV, 132.
35. D, IV, 131.
36. Clarkson [20, 33], I, 184.
37. D, IV, 289.
38. D, IV, 294.
39. D, IV, 321.
40. D, III, 291.
41. André João Antonil, *Cultura e Opulencia do Brasil* (Lisbon, 1711); Manuel Ribeiro da Rocha, *Ethiope Resgatado* (Lisbon, 1758).
42. Jorge Palacio Preciados, *La trata de esclavos por Cartagena de Indias* (Tunja, 1973), 349.
43. Pierre Marivaux, *L'Île des esclaves* (Paris, 1753).
44. Voltaire, *Romans et Contes*, in Pléiade ed. (Paris, 1954), 104–5.
45. Voltaire, *Dictionnaire philosophique* 1764 ('we are superior to the Africans because they sell each other').
46. Voltaire, *Complete Works of Voltaire*, ed. Theodore Besterman (Banbury, 1974), vol. 117, 374.
47. Montesquieu, *Oeuvres complètes*, ed. Edouard Laboulaye (Paris, 1877), vol. iv, I, 330.
48. Rousseau, 'Du Contrat social', in *Oeuvres complètes*, Pléiade ed., vol. I, iv.

49. *Encyclopédie*, vol. xvi (Neuchatel, 1765), 532.
50. Brief *Immensa Pastorum* of 20 December 1741, addressed to the Bishops of Brazil and other Portuguese dominions; Pastor [7, 15], 36, 10.

24. The Loudest Yelps for Liberty

1. Horace Walpole, *Letters* II, Cunninghame ed., 149.
2. *Gentleman's Magazine* X, 341.
3. *London Magazine* VII, March 1738, 129.
4. Horace Walpole, *Correspondence*, Yale ed., 20, 126.
5. Francis Hutcheson, *A System of Moral Philosophy* (London, 1755), II, 213.
6. Adam Smith, *The Theory of Moral Sentiments* (London, 1759), 402.
7. *Gentleman's Magazine* XXXIV, 493.
8. George Wallace, *The System of the Principles of the Laws of Scotland* (London, 1761), I, 91.
9. Adam Ferguson, *Institutes of Moral Philosophy* (Edinburgh, 1769), 223.
10. William Blackstone, *Commentaries on the Laws of England*, 1765, I, 411–12.
11. As discussed in Shyllon [13, 21], 55ff.
12. 'The London Stage', no date, *The Padlock*, 3.
13. *An Account of Giants Lately Discovered* (London, 1766), 15. I am grateful to Gina Thomas for drawing my attention to this work.
14. Anthony Benezet, *A Caution to Great Britain and Her Colonies . . .* (London, 1767), 11.
15. R & P, 1788, vol. 67, 308, 316.
16. Granville Sharp, *A Representation of the Injustice and Dangerous Tendency of Tolerating Slavery* (London, 1769), 9.
17. Peter Hutchinson, *The Diaries and Letters of Thomas Hutchinson Esq.* (Boston, 1884), II, 277.
18. Richard Pares, *A West-India Fortune* (London, 1950), 121.
19. Benezet qu. David Brion Davis, *The Problem of Slavery in the Age of Revolution* (Ithaca, 1975), 406.
20. John Wesley, *Thoughts Upon Slavery* (London, 1774), 10–14.
21. Boswell's *Life of Johnson*, ed. Augustine Birrell (Boston, 1904), IV, 202.
22. Op. cit., IV, 207.
23. Samuel Johnson, *Taxation No Tyranny, an Answer to the Resolutions and Addresses of the American Congress* (London, 1774), 89.
24. Adam Smith, *The Wealth of Nations* (New York, 1994), 415.
25. *History of Parliament 1754–1790*, ed. Sir Lewis Namier and John Brooke (London, 1964), II, 593.
26. Qu. Latimer [18, 16], 412.
27. Massachusetts Archives CCXV, 96. I am grateful to David Hancock of the University of Michigan for this reference.

28. Frederick Law Olmsted, *A Journey in the Southern Slave States* (New York, 1856), 125.

29. W. E. B. Dubois, *The Suppression of the African Trade to the United States of America* (Cambridge, Mass., 1899), 48; Jefferson, *Works*, ed. H. A. Washington, 1853–4, I, 23–4.

30. PH, vol. 18, col. 486 (22 March 1775).

31. David Cooper ('A farmer'), *A Serious Address to the Rulers of America* (London, 1783).

32. Louis-Sebastien Mercier, *L'An 2440* (Paris, 1977).

33. Abbé Guillaume Raynal, *Histoire philosophique et politique des Indes*, ed. Yves Benot (Paris, 1981), 193–211.

34. *Recueil des pièces présentées à l'Academie de Marseilles 1777*, qu. Charles Carrière, *Négociants marseillais au XVIIIe siècle*, 2 vols. (Marseilles, 1973), I, 349.

35. Peytraud [13, 26], 390.

25. The Gauntlet Had Been Thrown Down

1. Esmond Wright, *Franklin of Philadelphia* (Cambridge, Mass., 1986), 344, suggests that Franklin inspired the idea that Britain had imposed slavery on the colonies.

2. Fr. Dieudonné Rinchon, *Les armements négriers au XVIIIe siècle* (Brussels, 1955), 360.

3. D, III, 335; L. V. Briggs, *History and Genealogy of the Cabot Family* (Boston, 1927), II, 478.

4. D, II, 555.

5. Thomas Day, *A Fragment of a Letter on the Slavery of the Negroes* (London, 1785).

6. Cit. in Clarkson [20, 33], I, 120; PH, XXIII, 1026–7.

7. Jacques Necker, *De l'administration des finances de la France*, 3 vols. (Paris, 1784), qu. Clarkson [20, 33], I, 104.

8. William Paley, *The Principles of Moral and Political Philosophy* (Dublin, 1785).

9. Clarkson [20, 33], I, 284.

10. PH, vol. vii, 580 (10 June 1806).

11. Clarkson [20, 33], I, 332.

12. R & P 1788–9, 6 March 1788.

13. *Boston Gazette*, 26 March 1788.

14. Sharp, 4 September 1788, in P. Hoare, *Memoirs of Granville Sharp* (London, 1820), 329.

15. Martin [12, 18], 126.

16. *Congressional Debates on the Constitution*, Library of America, 2 vols. (New York, 1993), I, 645–6.

17. Ibid., 395.

18. P. L. Ford, *Pamphlets on the Constitution of the United States* 367

(Brooklyn, 1887).

19. *Congressional Debates* [25, 16], II, 65.
20. Ibid., 21, 117.
21. Loc. cit.
22. D, IV, 480 ff.
23. Dubois [24, 29], 198.
24. Add. MSS. 38416, ff.24–7, 216 in D, II, 577.
25. Picton [13, 19], I, 219.
26. Robin Furneaux pointed out (*Wilberforce*, London, 1974, 238) that this must be the explanation of the comment of Clarkson ([20, 33], II, 506). See too G. R. Mellor's evidence, *British Imperial Trusteeship* (London, 1950), 69–70; Wilberforce's life by his sons, R. I. and S. Wilberforce, *The Life of William Wilberforce* (London, 1838), vol. I, 165; and Anstey [22, 21], 300–302. Fuller's comment is in his papers at Duke University.
27. Williams [16, 12], 148.
28. Clarkson [20, 33], II, 504.
29. Qu. ibid., I, 536.
30. The Dolben debate is in PH vol. 27, col. 495ff. and 573ff. (21 May 1788).
31. Jeremy Bentham to Jeremiah Bentham, 9 November 1785, in *Collected Works of Jeremy Bentham*, ed. Ian R. Christie, III (London, 1971), 386.

26. Men in Africa of as Fine Feeling as Ourselves

1. Clarkson [20, 33] II, 26.
2. PH, vol. 28, May 12, 1789.
3. Latimer [18, 16], 477.
4. D, II, 49.
5. Qu. Davis [24, 19], 33.
6. D, II, 601–10.
7. Loc. cit.
8. Smith's failure to discuss the trade should be examined.
9. R & P 1790, vol. 72, 224.
10. Ibid., 35.
11. Ibid., 138.
12. R & P 1791–2, vol. 83 125–6.
13. Annals of Congress, I Congress, 1 session, 336–41, 903.
14. See Marcel Chatillon, *La diffusion de la gravure du* Brookes, in Daget [12, 16], 141. The diagram appeared in a pamphlet issued by the Societé des amis des noirs, 1789.
15. Saugera [14, 14], 331.
16. Chatillon [26, 14], 145; Honoré-Gabriel, Count Mirabeau, *Mémoires*, Bruxelles (1836), vol. 10, 146–9.
17. Saugera [14, 14], 340.

18. Saugera [14, 14], 116.
19. Clarkson [20, 33], II, 141.
20. Qu. Furneaux [25, 26], 98.
21. PH, vol. 28, col. 359; Peter Fryer, *Staying Power, The History of Black People in Britain* (London, 1984), 64.
22. Horace Walpole, *Letters*, IX, 306 (to Mary Berry).
23. AGI, Santo Domingo, leg. 2207. This Captain Courtauld may have been that individual listed in Burke's *Landed Gentry* as of Delaware, merchant 1752–1821. The second captain's name was given in Havana as Hugo Tomás. Compare seven ships only in 1790.
24. Hans Christian Johansen, in David Eltis and James Malvin, ed., *The Abolition of the Atlantic Slave Trade* (Madison, 1981), 221ff.
25. PH, vol. 29, cols. 1055–7.
26. PH, vol. 29, col. 1349.
27. Philip Ziegler, *King William IV* (London, 1971), 98.
28. B. W. Higman, *Jamaica Surveyed* (Kingston, 1988), 37.
29. Maria, Lady Nugent, *Journal of a Residence in Jamaica*, ed. Philip Wright (Kingston, 1966), 26.
30. Postma [9, 5], 118.
31. I. B. Richman, *Rhode Island*, 2 vols. (New York, 1902), I, 261; Samuel Hopkins, *Works*, 3 vols. (Boston, 1852), I, 122.
32. Condesa de Merlin, *La Havane*, 3 vols. (Paris, 1844), II, 88.
33. José Pablo Valiente and Diego de Gandóqui to the Council of the Indies, 5 September 1792, AGI, Indif. gen. leg. 2827, f. 1315; for the second voyage, see f. 1318.
34. Briggs [25, 3].
35. Essex Institute MSS letters, in Elizabeth Donnan, 'The New England Slave Trade', *The New England Quarterly* III (1930), 266.
36. Howe [14, 29], 107–9; also Jay Coughtry, *The Notorious Triangle* (Philadelphia, 1981), 47.
37. Federico Brito Figueroa, *Estructura ecónomica de la Venezuela colonial* (Caracas 1963), 128; see for Barry, AGI, Indif. gen. leg. 2827 ff.1–199.
38. James Beattie, *Elements of Moral Science*, 2 vols., London 1790.
39. Hopkins [26, 31], I, 152.
40. PH, 30, 1439.
41. Shelburne's autobiography in Lord Edward Fitzmaurice's *Life* (London, 1875–6).

27. *Why Should We See Great Britain Getting All the Slave Trade?*

1. PH, 31, 1321.
2. *The Letter Journal of George Canning 1793–1795*, ed. Peter Jupp, Royal Historical Society (1991), 215–16.
3. PH, 32, 737, 866.
4. Clarkson [20, 33], II, 469.

5. Furneaux [25, 26], 180.
6. PH 33, 563–79.
7. James Stephen, *The Crisis in the Sugar Colonies* (London, 1802), 137.
8. Seymour Dreschler, *Econocide: British Slavery in the Era of Abolition* (Pittsburgh, 1977), 27.
9. Qu. Stuart Schwartz, *Sugar Plantations in the Formation of Brazilian Society* (Cambridge, 1985), 341.
10. James Stephen's annotation on a copy of the Foreign Slave Bill, cit. Dreschler [27, 8], 73.
11. AGI, Indif. gen. leg. 2827, 15 April 1803.
12. Annals of Congress, 26 April 1800, X, 686.
13. Ibid.
14. Qu. George Brooks, *Yankee Traders, Old Coasters, and African Middlemen* (Boston, 1970).
15. R. I. and S. Wilberforce [25, 26], I, 343.
16. Knutsford [21, 12], 258.
17. Pierre Labarthe, *Voyage à la côte de Guinée* (Paris, 1802).
18. Saugera [14, 14], 128.
19. Ibid., 134.
20. D, IV, 248.
21. D, IV, 249.
22. Isidoro Antillón, *Fragmentos de la conferencia pronunciada en la Real Academia matritense, de derecho Español y público el día 2 de abril de 1802* (Mallorca, 1811). There is a copy in the British Library.
23. Bernardino de Andrade, *Planta da Praça e Bissau*, 50, cit. Rodney [23, 23], 257.
24. PD, vol. 2, 1803–4, 439.
25. R. I. and S. Wilberforce [25, 26], III, 180.
26. Annual message of President Jefferson, 1806, in *The Writings of Thomas Jefferson*, ed. H. A. Washington (New York, 1853–4).
27. Thomas Jefferson, *Notes on the State of Virginia* (Chapel Hill, 1955), 162–3.
28. Dubois [24, 29], 103–4.
29. Annals of Congress, 21 Congress, 1 session, III, 348. See *The Life of William Harris Crawford*, by Philip Green (Charlotte, 1965).
30. Clarkson [20, 33], II, 352.
31. A. Aspinall, *The Later Correspondence of George III* (London, 1962), vol. 4., 517–18.
32. PD, vol.7, 19 June 1806.
33. PD, vol. 9, 23 March 1807.
34. Loc. cit.
35. Loc. cit.
36. Loc. cit.
37. Crow [8, 20], 137.
38. Clarence to Sir Samuel Hawker, qu. Ziegler [26, 27], 99.

39. PD, vol. 7, col. 31–4.
40. Henry Brougham, *An Inquiry into the Colonial Policy of the European Powers*, 2 vols. (Edinburgh, 1803), vol. 2, 490–91.

Book Six: THE ILLEGAL ERA

28. I See . . . We Have Not Yet Begun the Golden Age

1. Park [19, 27], 9.
2. Lords Select Committee, 1843, 199.
3. Ibid., 226.
4. Béraud, *Note sur le Dahomé* (1866), cit. Law [18, 6], 67.
5. René Caillé, *Journal d'un voyage à Temboteu et à Jenne*, 3 vols. (Paris, 1830), I, 460.
6. Al-Nasiri, qu. Lewis [1, 6].
7. Nicholas Owen, *Journal of a Slave Dealer*, ed. E. C. Martin (London, 1930), 153.
8. See James Tuckey, *Narrative of an Expedition to Explore the River Zaire* (London, 1818).
9. J. Adams, *Sketches Taken During the Ten Years Voyage to Africa Between the Years 1786–1800* (London, 1822).
10. Crow [8, 20], 137; Verger [13, 28], 274–5.
11. In his 'Analysis', qu. Rev. R. Walsh, *Notices of Brazil* (London, 1830), 318.
12. H. M. Brackenridge, *Voyage to South America . . .* , 2 vols. (London, 1819), I, 139.
13. Alexander von Humboldt, *Viaje a los regiones equinoctiales . . .* (Caracas, 1966), I, 63.
14. D, III, 101, and Briggs [25, 3], II, 517.
15. 'The Rhode Island Slave Trade in 1816', *Proceedings of the Rhode Island Historical Society* VI (Jan. 1899), 226.
16. Howe [14, 29], 191.
17. John L. Spears, *The American Slave Trade* (New York, 1900), 123.
18. House Journal, 11 Cong., 3d session, VII, 435.
19. D, IV, 249.
20. Spears [28, 17], 122.
21. Drake [19, 25], 52. 'Piccanninny' is of course a word deriving from the Spanish *pequeño niño*.
22. R & P 1790, vol. 73, 16.
23. R & P 1790, vol. 83, 43.
24. R & P 1790, vol. 82, 53.
25. Hutt Committee, I, 422.
26. PD, 1st series, vol. 19, 233.
27. James Prior, *Voyage Along the Eastern Coast of Africa [etc.] . . .* (London, 1819), 99.

28. James F. King, 'The Latin American Republics and the Suppression of the Slave Trade', *HAHR* XXIV (1944), 391.

29. John Lynch, *The Spanish American Revolutions* (London, 1986), 85.

30. Archivo Nacional de Cuba real consulado, leg. 74, no. 2836, qu. José Luciano Franco, *Comercio clandetino de esclavos* (Havana, 1985), 121.

31. AGI, Indif., gen. leg. 2827, ff. 1303–27. Aguilar said that he approached '*al principal socio de la mencionada compañia don Pedro de la Cuesta y Manzanal intersandolo para que me ayudase a llevar adelante el . . . commercio directo de Negros a la costa de Africa desde nos puertos con buques capitaines y tripulación española.*'

32. Speech printed in Enriqueta Vila Vilar, *Los abolicionistas españoles, siglo XIX* (Madrid, 1996), 106.

33. '*Se trata de nuestras vidas, de toda nuestra fortuna, y de nuestros descendientes*'). In Cuba, there was not a hacienda which had '*los negros que deba tener*' (AGI, Indif., gen. leg. 2827, ff. 1436–84).

34. Ramirez, *Instrucciones a Power*, in Luis Díaz Soler, *Historia de la esclavitux md negra en Puerto Rico* (Madrid, 1953), 126.

35. See commentary in H. G. Soulsby, *The Right of Search and the Slave Trade in Anglo-American Relations* (Baltimore, 1933), 17.

36. Davis [24, 18], II, 69.

37. Duke of Wellington, *Supplementary Despatches*, 15 vols., ed. the 2nd Duke (London, 1858–72), vol. 9, 165 (July 29, 1814); see also Betty Fladeland, 'Abolitionist Pressures on the Concert of Europe', *Journal of Modern History* xxxviii (1966), 361.

38. Castlereagh to Henry Wellesley, 1 August 1814, in *Memoir and Correspondence of Castelereagh*, 3rd series, ed. the Marquess of Londonderry, 12 vols. (1848–53), vol. 2, 73.

39. Francis Dorothy Cartwright, ed. *The Life and Correspondence of Major Cartwright*, 2 vols. (London, 1826), 2, 84.

40. Earl Leslie Griggs, *Clarkson, the Friend of Slaves* (London, 1936), 116.

41. General Treaty signed in Congress at Vienna (London, 1816), 132.

42. Serge Daget, *Répertoire des expéditions françaises a la traite illégale* (Nantes, 1988), 4.

43. Ibid., 10; also Charles Cunat, *Pierre Surcouf* (Paris, 1847).

44. J. Dodson, *Report of Cases Argued Before the High Court of Admiralty* (London, 1828), ii, 263–4; see also Daget [28, 41], 21–2.

45. Archivo Nacional de Cuba, Asuntos Políticos, leg. 110, no. 73 qu. Franco [28, 29], 261.

46. PD, 1st ser., vol. 31, 172.

29. The Slaver Is More Criminal Than the Assassin

1. *Table Talk of Samuel Rogers* (London, 1903), 198.

2. *The Diary of John Quincy Adams*, ed. Allan Nevins (New York, 1928), 177–8.

3. *Memoir . . . of Castlereagh* [28, 37], 1853, xi, 309.
4. Ibid., xii, 361.
5. Stern, *Gesichtes Europas*, 1, 474, qu. Sir Charles Webster, *The Foreign Policy of Castlereagh* (London, 1925), 168.
6. W. E. F. Ward, *The Royal Navy and the Slavers* (London, 1969), 44.
7. Ibid., 84–6.
8. Ibid., 98.
9. Qu. Deveaux [15, 20], 290.
10. Canning to Stratford Canning in Washington, *BFSP* X, 254.
11. Goethe, in *Conversations with Eckermann* (London, 1930), 329 (1 September 1829).
12. PD, 1st ser., vol. 37, col. 251.
13. Frances Calderón de la Barca, *Life in Mexico*, ed. Howard T. and Marion Hall Fisher (New York, 1966), 26.
14. David Murray, *Odious Commerce* (Cambridge, 1983), 56.
15. Tacón to the Ministers of Foreign Affairs and the Navy, in AHN Estado, Leg. 8035, 27 June 1844. The paragraph is one of the most important in the history of the slave trade: '*al efecto creé deber observar que al concluirse el tratado de 1817 se comunicó una Rl. Orden reservada á los capitanes generales de las Islas de Cuba y Puerto Rico, y al Intendente, superintendente delegado de ellas, para que se disimilase le importación de negros procedentes de Africa, fundandose en que se consideraban necesarios para la conservación y fomento de la agriculture.*' I found this document thanks to David Murray's reference in *Odious Commerce*.
16. Howe [14, 29], 210.
17. Ibid., 208.
18. Saco [6, 14], III, 141.
19. Memoria presented by Fr. Varela in ibid., 1–17.
20. Juan Bernardo O'Gabán, *Observaciones sobre la suerte de los negros . . .* (Madrid, 1821), 7.
21. Kilbee to Canning, 25 February 1825, published in PP, 1825.
22. Foreign Slave Trade: abstract of the information, 36–7, qu. Conrad [22, 3], 63.
23. Leslie Bethell, *The Abolition of the Brazilian Slave Trade* (Cambridge, 1970), 32–47.
24. Qu. Rodrigues [14, 15], 148.
25. Walsh [28, 11], I, 465; II, 328, 322.
26. Conrad [22, 3] 80–81, for commentary.
27. Nina Rodrigues, *Os Africanos no Brazil* (São Paulo, 1933).
28. Larry Yarak, *Asante and the Dutch* (Oxford, 1990), 123; for Dubois see Daget [28, 41], 291 ff.
29. Ward [29, 6], 82.
30. Foreign Relations of the United States, vol. V, 72.
31. William Wetmore Story, *Life and Letters of Joseph Story*, 2 vols. (Boston, 1851), I, 336–47.

32. House Docs., 16 Cong., 1 sess., III, no. 42, 7.
33. Drake [19, 25].
34. C, 232 ff.
35. For the relationship, see Howe [14, 29], 213; see also Samuel Eliot Morison, *Old Bruin* (Boston, 1967).
36. Ward [29, 6], 77.
37. BFSP, 1820–21, 397–400.
38. *Memoirs of John Q. Adams Comprising Portions of His Diary* . . . , 12 vols., ed. C. F. Adams (Philadelphia, 1874–7), V, 416.
39. Daget [28, 41], 37ff.
40. Ibid., 43.
41. Serge Daget, 'L'abolition de la traite des noirs en France', *Cahiers d'Études Africaines* 11 (1971), 14–58. The speech of Broglie is in his 'Discours prononcé le 28 mars 1822'.
42. Duchesse de Duras, *Ourika* (Paris, 1825).
43. Victor Hugo, *Bug-Jargal* (Paris, 1833).
44. Daget [28, 41], 126–7.
45. Ibid., passim.
46. Serge Daget in *La France et L'abolition de la traite des noirs* (Thesis) (Paris, 1969), 304.
47. C. Lloyd, *The Navy and the Slave Trade* (London, 1949), 50; an excellent account which inspired this one.

30. Only the Poor Speak Ill of the Slave Trade

1. *A lavoura da Bahia* . . . (Bahia, 1874), qu. Conrad [22, 3], 68.
2. George Gardner, *Travels in the Interior of Brazil, 1836–1841* (London, 1846), 1.
3. Thomas Ewbank, *Life In Brazil* (New York, 1856), 282.
4. Cit. Conrad [22, 3], 86.
5. Freyre [8, 8], 49.
6. Qu. Bethell [29, 23], 84.
7. Freyre [8, 8], 346.
8. Humboldt [28, 13], 212.
9. Rafael Labra, *La abolición de la esclavitud en el orden económico* (Madrid, 1873).
10. Select Committee of the House of Commons, 1850, 80.
11. Select Committee of the House of Commons, 1853, 96.
12. Kilbee and Macleay to Canning, 1 January 1827, in PP, 1827.
13. Palmerston's comments in 1849, Hutt Committee, II, 19.
14. Archivo Nacional (Havana) Reales Ordenes y Cédulas, leg. 178, no. 40, qu. Franco [28, 29], 325; Vives to Minister of Foreign Affairs, 6 January 1825, qu. Murray [29, 14], 85.
15. PRO Commisioners in Havana (Kilbee and Maclean) to Canning, 19 March 1827, FO 84/68, item 10. The letter included a translation

of one from Vives which said that from the examination of the logbook of the ship concerned it could not be suspected that the vessel had touched at any port in Africa, much less had carried slaves to Cuba.

16. George Villiers to the Foreign Minister, in AHN, Estado, leg. 5034\4.
17. L. M. Sears, 'Nicholas P. Trist, A Diplomat with Ideals', *Missouri Valley Historical Review*, June 1924.
18. Evidence of Judge Macaulay, in *The Trial of Pedro de Zulueta* (London, 1844), 11.
19. Merlin [26, 32], I, 310.
20. Corbière [15, 25], 192.
21. All these references in Calderón de la Barca [29, 13], 9–29.
22. Loc. cit.
23. Merlin [26, 32], I, 302.
24. Edward F. Atkins, *Sixty Years in Cuba* (Cambridge, Mass., 1926), 12.
25. Carlos Martí, *Los Catalanes en América (Cuba)* (Havana, 1921), 26.
26. Angel Bahamonde and José Cayuela, *Hacia las Américas* (Madrid, 1992), 201–22.
27. See the will of Don Tiburcio in Angel Mari Arrieta, *La emigración alavesa a América en el siglo XIX* (Vitoria, 1992), 461, kindly shown me by Don Julián de Zulueta of Ronda. Also see Murray [29, 15], 313; Franklin Knight, 'Origins of Wealth and the Sugar Revolution in Cuba', *HAHR* 57 (1977); A. N. Gallenga, *The Pearl of the Antilles* (London, 1873); and also Franco [28, 29], 251.
28. Ward [29, 6], 144.
29. Bahamonde and Cayuela [30, 26].
30. For the trial of Pedro de Zulueta, see Appendix 2.
31. Herbert Maxwell, *Life and Letters of George, Fourth Earl of Clarendon* (London, 1913), I, 94.

31. Active Exertions

1. A. E. M. Ashley, *Life of Palmerston* (London, 1846–65), II, 227.
2. Joseph Denman, *West India Interests, African Emigration and the Slave Trade* (London, 1848), 12.
3. PP, 1842, XI, pt. 1, Appendix and Index, No. 7, 29.
4. CO 82/6 1143 FP Nicolls to Hay, 10 December 1833, in Kenneth Onwuka Dike, *Trade and Politics in the Niger Valley* (Oxford, 1956), 65.
5. Spears [28, 26], 145.
6. Denman evidence in Lords Select Committee on West Africa 1842, 405.
7. Murray [29, 14], 93ff., and also W. L. Mathieson, *Great Britain and the Slave Trade* (London, 1929), 13–17.
8. AHN, Estado leg. 8035/4. A typical letter from George Villiers in

Madrid included statements such as 'I deeply regret to have . . . to communicate to your Excellency that certain authorities of Her Catholic Majesty in the Havannah instead of zealously endeavouring to carry into effect the Treaty of 1835 . . . appear to countenance the means which are resorted to for its evasion.'

9. Sir Charles Webster, *The Foreign Policy of Lord Palmerston, 1830–1841*, 492.
10. PD, 3d series, vol. 50, col. 309, 383. The Duke's protest is in col. 386.
11. Commander Riley in Hutt Committee, II, 25.
12. Francis Swanzy in Lords Select Committee, 1843, 67.
13. Webster [31, 9].
14. Miller [19, 35], 366.
15. Palmerston to Stevenson, 27 August 1841, in Soulsby [28, 34], 54.
16. Ibid., 60.
17. Kenneth Bourne, *Palmerston* (London, 1982), 596; Jasper Ridley, *Lord Palmerston* (London, 1970), 281–2.
18. Qu. Bethell [29, 23], 207.
19. David Turnbull, *Travels in the West Indies* (London, 1840), 60.
20. Arthur P. Corwin, *Spain and the Abolition of Slavery in Cuba* (Austin, 1967), 70.
21. Mariano Torrente, *La cuestión importante sobre la esclavitud* (Madrid, 1841), 4–7.
22. AHN, Estado leg. 8035, 27 June 1844.
23. *Centón epistolario*, vol. v, 14, 24, 31.
24. Murray [29, 14] 177.
25. Hutt Committee, I, 109.
26. Ibid., I, 88.
27. Soulsby [28, 34], 100ff.
28. The letter is published in Commons Select Committee 1850, 130.
29. Hutt Committee, I, 88.

32. Slave Harbours of the Nineteenth Century

1. Daget [12, 16], 419.
2. J. C. Furnas, 'Patrolling the Middle Passage', *American Heritage* IX, 6 (October 1958).
3. Hutt Committee, I, 170.
4. Tacón's comment is in a report by him in AHN, Estado.
5. PRO 84/95, f. 82, where Lord Ponsonby is shown to have reported that British capital was indirectly concerned in the Brazilian slave trade on a vast scale: there were few merchants in Rio 'who do not annually receive large shipments of goods for the carrying on' the trade in slaves (27 June 1829). This is qu. by David Eltis, *Economic Growth and the Ending of the Transatlantic Slave Trade* (New York, 1987), 83 and 326. He discusses these links with perspicacity. 'It is

calculated', Lord Ponsonby continued, 'that one third of all British manufactures imported into this harbour [Rio] consists in articles eventually used in the commerce with the coast of Africa.'

6. Lords Select Committee, 1843, 210.
7. Ibid., 767.
8. Hutt Committee, II, 212.
9. Wise to Buchanan, 6 March 1846, Dispatches XV, qu. L .F. Hill, in *Diplomatic Relations between the United States and Brazil* (Durham, NC, 1932), 141.
10. Lords Select Committee, 1843, 767.
11. Hutt Committee, II, 21.
12. Theodore Canot, *Memoirs of a Slave Trader* (New York, 1850), 50. For this interesting figure see also the following: L. G. Bouge, 'Théophile Conneau, alias Theodore Canot', *Revue d'Histoire des colonies* XL (1953), 1, no. 138, 249–63; Roger Pasquier, *RFHR*, LV (1968), no. 200, 352–4; and, S. Daget, 'Encore Théodore Canot . . . ,' *Annales Université d'Abidjan* ser. I (histoire) V (1977), 39–53; and, Svend E. Holsoe, 'Théodore Canot at Cape Mount', *Liberian Studies Journal* 44 (1972), 263–81.
13. George Coggeshall, *Second Series of Voyages to Various Parts of the World* (New York, 1857), 123.
14. Temperley [18, 9], 74.
15. Loc. cit.
16. Lords Select Committee, 1843, 523.
17. Brooks [27, 14], 186.
18. Hutt Committee, II, 4.
19. Captain Blount evidence in Lords Select Committee, 1843, 408–9.
20. Ward [29, 6], 48–9.
21. Lords Select Committee, 1843, 527.
22. O. George in Daget [12, 16], 565.
23. See Carol McCormack in Claire C. Robertson and Martin A. Klein, *Women and Slavery in Africa* (Madison, 1983), 278. His death is described in Canot [32, 12] 226; C. Fyfe, *A History of Sierra Leone* (1962), 66, 185.
24. Hutt Committee, II, 8.
25. Lloyd [29, 47], gives a vivid picture, on which I have drawn freely, 132.
26. Hutt Committee, I, 402.
27. Brooks [27, 14], 61.
28. Hutt Committee, II, 184.
29. Canot [32, 12], 326.
30. Ward [29, 6], 73–5.
31. Archivo Nacional de Cuba, Misc de Libros no. 11408, Franco [28, 29], 242.
32. Bennet and Brooks [17, 2], 87.

33. Select Committee House of Commons 1843, 466.
34. Bennet and Brooks [17, 2], 35, 38.
35. Van Dantzig in Daget [12, 16], II, 601.
36. Edward Reynolds in Daget [12, 16], I, 576.
37. Brooks [27, 14], 235.
38. Reynolds in Daget [12, 16], I, 576.
39. Hutt Committee, II, 57.
40. Prince de Joinville, *Vieux Souvenirs*, new ed. (Paris, 1986), 230.
41. Andrew H. Foote, *Africa and the American Flag* (New York, 1862), 82.
42. Hutt Committee, II, 70–71.
43. See Verger [13, 28], 467–74; David Ross, 'Diego Martínez in the Bight of Benin', *JAH* VI (1965), 79–90.
44. Ward [29, 6], 109.
45. Joseph Wright, *c.* 1825, in Philip Curtin, *Africa Remembered* (Madison, 1967), 320.
46. PRO CO 82/6 Fernando Po 67, Nicholls to Hay, 28 October 1833, qu. Dike [31, 4], 53.
47. PRO FO 84/383 HMS *Viper* at sea, Burslem to Tucker 10 September 1840, qu. Dike [31, 4], 83.
48. Papers relating to this treaty can be seen in FO 84/383, 87ff.; also PP 1842, XI, 551.
49. Lords Select Committee 1843, 430.
50. The treaty was enclosed in a letter from Captain William Tucker in PRO FO 84/385, 22 August 1841.
51. Evidence in Lords Select Committee, 43, 340.
52. Hope Masterton Waddell, *Twenty-nine Years in the West Indies* (London, 1863), 429.
53. Sir C. Hotham to the Admiralty, 7 April 1847, in RC 16, XXII (1847–8), 2.
54. Paul du Chaillu, *Voyages et aventures dans l'Afrique Équatoriale* (Paris, 1863), 45.
55. Surgeon Peters in Lords Select Committee 1843, 355.
56. Brooks [27, 14], 145.
57. Peter Knickerbocker, *Sketches in South Africa* (1850–51), vol. 37, 38, 39.
58. Parker in Knickerbocker [32, 57], 39, 134.
59. Georg Tams, *A Visit to the Portuguese Possessions in South West Africa*, tr. from German (Hamburg, 1845), vol. I, 116.
60. Captain A. Murray in Select Committee 1850, 38.
61. Bennet and Brooks [17, 2], 192.
62. Ibid., 262.
63. Ibid., 427.
64. José Capela, *O escravismo colonial em Moçambique* (Porto, 1993), 180.
65. Lords Select Committee 1850, 239.
66. Canot [32, 12], 252.
67. Admiral Dacres in Commons Select Committee 1850, 14.

68. Bennet and Brooks [17, 2], 9; see too George Francis Dow, *Diary and Letters of . . . Benjamin Pickman* (Newport, 1928).

33. Sharks Are the Invariable Outriders of All Slave Ships

1. PD, 3d ser., vol. 109,. col. 1093–5.
2. Hutt Committee, I, 322.
3. Qu. Temperley [18, 9], 4.
4. Hutt Committee, I, 2.
5. Ibid., 401.
6. Warren Howard, *American slavers and the Federal law* (Berkeley, 1963).
7. Hutt Committee, I, 82.
8. Ibid., 623.
9. Ibid., 655.
10. Narrative of Joseph Wright, in Curtin [32, 45], 330–31.
11. Hutt Committee, I, 211.
12. Captain Bailey in Lords Select Committee, 1843, 138.
13. Evidence of Macgregror Laird in Lords Select Committee, 1843, 363.
14. Hutt Committee, II, 257.
15. PP, 1822, 561, 633.
16. PP, 1824, 261.
17. Hutt Committee, I, 106.
18. G. F. Dow, *Slave Ships and Slaving* (Salem, 1927), xxviiii ff., and PD 2nd ser. 5 1288 1821; also Daget [28, 41], 88.
19. Richard Madden, *The Island of Cuba* (London, 1849), 228–41; Dubois [24, 29], 142; William A. Owens, *Slave Mutiny* (London, 1953).
20. Jas. Badinel in Hutt Committee, I, 256.
21. PP 1865, vol. v, 165, 171.
22. T. R. H. Thomson to Hutt Committee, I, 397.
23. Log of *Fantome* in PRO Adm 51/3718, nos. 7–10, 31 October 1839 to 20 October 1842; *Memoirs of Sir W. Symonds*, ed. J. A. Sharp (London, 1858), 651.
24. Hudson cit. Mathieson [31, 7], 199.
25. Ward [29, 6], 122.
26. *Nautical Magazine* 1834 , 649, qu. Lloyd [29, 47], 77–8.
27. Ward [29, 6], 116.
28. Summarized in Lloyd [29, 47], 87–88.
29. Hutt Committee, I, 168.
30. Commons Select Committee, 1850, 108.
31. Lords Select Committee, 1843, 168.
32. Lords Select Committee, 1843, 770.
33. Ibid., 283.
34. Canot [32, 12], 107.
35. Gladstone in Hutt Committee, I, 212.
36. Canot [32, 12], 107.

37. These figures derive from Howard [33, 6] but the most interesting calculations of cost and profit in the trade in the nineteenth century are those of Eltis [32, 5], appendix E, but see also E. Philip Le Veen, *British Slave Trade Suppression Policies* (New York, 1977).
38. Hutt Committee, II, 57.
39. Drake [19, 25], 92.
40. Crawford to Russell, 5 February 1861, in FO 84/1135, 20 v. The last estimate here is that of Howard [33, 6].
41. Hutt Committee, II, 13.

34. Can We Resist the Torrent? I Think Not

1. Spears [28, 16], 155.
2. Mason to Skinner, in Warren Howard, *American Involvement South of the Sahara* (Garland, 1989), 118.
3. Horatio Bridge, *Journal of an African Cruiser*, ed. Nathaniel Hawthorne (Boston, 1845), 53.
4. See Palmerston's evidence in Hutt Committee II, 6–7.
5. Foote [32, 41], 218.
6. Qu. Bethell [29, 23], 245.
7. Ibid., 270.
8. PP, vol. 49 (1845) 593–633, gave a list of 2,185 slave voyages. David Eltis, in Henry Gemery and Jan Hogedorn, ed., *The Uncommon Market* (New York, 1979), pointed out that the Foreign Office had record of another 914 probable expeditions.
9. T. Nelson, *Remarks on Slavery and the Slave Trade* (London, 1846).
10. Wise dispatch, 18 February 1845, XIII, qu. Hill, [32, 9], 114.
11. Qu. Bethell [29, 23], 289.
12. House Exec. Doc., 30 Cong., 2 sess., VII, no. 61, 18.
13. Freyre [8, 8], 429.
14. Rodrigues [14, 15], 186.
15. Qu. Bethell [29, 23], 290.
16. PD, 3rd ser., vol. 93, col. 1000 (24 June 1845); PP, 1847–8, xxii, appendix.
17. PD, 3d ser., vol. 96, col. 1096 (22 February 1848): the figures are for 1843. Cf. A. K. Manchester, *British Pre-eminence in Brazil* (Chapel Hill, 1933), 315.
18. PD, 3d ser., vol. 77, col. 1290.
19. PD, 3d ser., vol. 96, col. 41.
20. Bethell [29, 23], 297.
21. PD, 3d ser., vol. 109, 1160–70.
22. David Brion Davis, *Slavery and Human Progress* (New York, 1984), xviii.
23. PD, 3rd. ser., vol 93, col. 1076, 16 July 1844.
24. Hutt Committee, II, 123.

25. House of Commons, Accounts and papers, Slave Trade, 22, session 4 February to 9 August 1845, vol. xlix.
26. PD, 3d series, vol. 109, 1850, col. 1093.
27. Ibid., col. 1185.
28. Dunlop evidence in Lords Select Committee, 1850, 135ff.
29. A partial list of British agents, which included at least one foreign minister, Caetano Mario Lopes Gama, and one vice-president of the parliament, Leopoldo Muniz Barreto, can be seen in Eltis [32, 5], 115. Alcofarado was still being paid an allowance by the British in 1860: see his letter of 9 March 1860 (Fo/84, 1130, f. 79) to Lord Palmerston requesting the continuance of this stipend, where he says that he had by then worked for Britain for twenty years. He says the proof of this is not only in the archives of the Foreign Office, but also in 'the personal knowledge which your lordship possesses of such services'. In Palmerston's papers now in the University of Southampton there are receipts for secret service payments though they do not indicate what the services were.
30. Schomberg's evidence in Lords Select Committee, 1853, 58ff.; letter from Under-secretary of the Foreign Office to Admiralty, 22 April 1850, published in Commons Select Committee, 1853, 60.
31. Qu. Rodrigues [14, 15], 170.
32. Ibid., 190–92.
33. Verger [13, 28], 437.
34. Ashley [31, 1], II, 263–4.
35. David A. Ross, 'The Career of Domingo Martinez', *JAH*, vi, 1965, 1.

35. They All Eagerly Desire It, Protect It and Almost Sanctify It

1. Murray [29, 14], 167.
2. Aberdeen to Bulwer in BM Add. Mss. 43146 f. 343.
3. Qu. Corwin [31, 20], 82.
4. Murray [29, 14], 202.
5. Irving to Calhoun, 23 April 1844, in William Ray Manning, *Diplomatic Correspondence* (Washington, DC, 1925), vol. XI, 339.
6. Webster [31, 9], 462.
7. Pío Baroja, *Los Pilotos de Altura* (Madrid, 1995), 247.
8. H. Vidal Morales, *Iniciadores y primeros martires* (Havana, 1916), I, 165.
9. Qu. Murray [29, 14], 227.
10. Qu. Murray [29, 14], 230.
11. PRO Russell to Howden in FO 84/871, 31 January 1853.
12. Qu. Murray [29, 14], 250.
13. Manning [35, 5], 789.
14. Qu. David Potter, *The Impending Crisis* (New York, 1976), 182, fn.15.
15. Amos Ettinger, *The Mission to Spain of Pierre Soulé* (London, 1932), 390–412.

16. Murray [29, 14], 244.
17. Consul Crawford in Havana in evidence of Captain Hamilton in Lords Select Committee, 1853, 19.
18. Lords Select Committee, 1843, 457.
19. *North American Review*, November 1886, 447 ff.
20. James and Patience Barnes, *Private and Confidential* (Selinsgrove, 1992), 165.
21. Ward [29, 6], 318.
22. Wise to the Secretary of the Admiralty, 28 October 1858, in BFSP 1859–60, 763–5.
23. Ward [29, 6].
24. PD, 3d ser., vol. 186, col. 1492–1501 (1857).
25. Ward [29, 6].
26. Soulsby [28, 34], 168.
27. Ronald Takaki, *A Pro-slavery Crusade: The Agitation to Reopen the African Slave Trade* (New York, 1971).
28. Samuel Eliot Morison, *The Oxford History of the American People* (New York, 1966).
29. Letter of Charles Lamar to Trowbridge in *North American Review*, November 1886, 456.
30. Barnes [35, 20], 209.

36. Cuba, the Forward Sentinel

1. Corwin [31, 20], 127; Soulsby [28, 34], 159.
2. Corwin [31, 20] 67.
3. Cass to Dallas in London qu. Soulsby [28, 34], 155.
4. Report of the Secretary of the Navy, 1860, 9.
5. Friends' appeal on behalf of the coloured races, 1858.
6. Howard [33, 6], 302.
7. *Continental Monthly*, January 1862, 87.
8. Frederick C. Blake, ed., *Secret History of the Slave Trade to Cuba... JNH*, LV, no. 3, 1970, 229.
9. Wilson letter to Lord John Russell, 12 September 1860 in PRO, FO 84/1130, f. 85. Wilson, who had spent twenty-seven years in Havana, thought Spaniards were 'similar to Moors'.
10. PRO, Crawford to Palmerston in FO 84/1135 of 5 February 1861 (f. 14). Crawford complained that some slave merchants had even been ennobled. The calculation in chapter 33, footnote 40, appears in this letter.
11. PD 3rd ser., 1861, vol. 161, cols. 950–89.
12. Lloyd [29, 47], 69.
13. FO 84/1150, 5 October 1861.
14. C. F. Adams Jr., *Life of C. F. Adams* (Boston, 1900), 241

15. Henry Adams, *The Education of Henry Adams* (New York, 1918), 56.
16. Sir Richard Burton, ed., *A Mission to Gelele King of Dahomey* (London, 1966).
17. FO 84/1135, 21. An official wrote on 20 April 1860: 'if it should be considered advisable to take possession of the place, no consideration founded on the insalubrity of the climate should be allowed to have any weight.'
18. Murray [29, 14], 311.
19. Antonio Barras y Prado, *La Habana a mediados del siglo xix* (Madrid, 1925), 52.
20. Diario del Congreso, 1864–5, 6 May 1865.
21. Corwin [31, 20].
22. Diario del Congreso, 1865–6, 20 April 1866.
23. Ibid.
24. *New York Times*, 3 April 1866.
25. Franco [28, 29], 256.
26. These calculations derive from Eltis [32, 5], 97–101.

Appendix Three: Statistics

For many years, it was supposed that the Atlantic slave trade was of the order of 15,000,000 persons shipped between the fifteenth and the nineteenth centuries. Historians, journalists, even demographers (such as Kuczynski) based their theories on this statistic. In one of the most brilliant chapters of recent historical writing, Philip Curtin, in his admirable work *The Atlantic Slave Trade, A Census* (Madison, 1969) showed that that estimate was based on a nineteenth-century guess. Curtin made a more modest extimate. A serious, though neglected, estimate of the dimension of the African slave trade had been made in 1950 by Noël Deerr, in his *History of Sugar*, 2 vols. (London, 1950): on the basis of an analysis country by country, Deerr suggested a figure of about 11,970,000 might be right (vol. II, 284). Curtin also looked meticulously at estimates for different countries and suggested that the total might be lower: about 10,000,000, certainly not less than 8,000,000, probably not more than 10,500,000: say, 9,566,100 (*The Atlantic Slave Trade*, 268).

But Joseph Inikori in 1975 suggested that the old guess of 15,00,000– 15,400,000 was his estimate – might be nearer the truth than Curtin's figure: he repeated his suggestion in 1982 (*Forced Migration* [London, 1982], 13–60; also, Inkori, D. C. Ohadikhe, and A. C. Unomah, *The Chaining of a Continent* [UNESCO, Paris, 1986]). But a year earlier, in 1981, James Rawley, in a general survey, put the figure at 11,345,000 (*The Transatlantic Slave Trade* [New York, 1981], 428). After a careful new look at the evidence (for after 1700 only, however), Paul Lovejoy suggested in 1982 that 11,698,000 slaves might have been sent from Africa, of whom perhaps 9,778,500 may have arrived ('The Volume of the Atlantic Slave

Trade: A Synthesis', *JAH* 23). Then, Catherine Coquery-Vidrovitch talked in terms of 11,700,000, between 1450 and 1900 (in Daget's *Actes du colloque internationale sur la traite des noirs*, vol. 2 [Nantes, 1985], 58). In 1989 a further revision was suggested by David Richardson, the historian of the Bristol trade ('Slave Exports from West and West-central Africa', *JAH* 30) and, later that same year, Paul Lovejoy provided yet another figure, of 11,863,000 ('The Impact of the Slave Trade on Africa . . . ', *JAH* 30 [1989]). David Henige ('Measuring the Unmeasurable,' *JAH* 27 [1986]), and Charles Becker ('Notes sur les chiffres de la traite atlantique française au dixhuitième siecle', *Cahiers d'études africaines* 26, 633–79) have also made overall estimates. The historian of La Rochelle Jean-Marie Déveaux gave his total in 1994 as 11,500,000 (*France au temps des négrier* [Paris, 1994]).

The diversity of these estimates is explained by the fact that some of Curtin's detailed country-by-country estimates, especially by his own admission those in the Spanish empire, were full of uncertainties. Even on something so apparently important as the number of slaves imported illegally into the United States after the abolition of the trade in 1808 he was rather general; and he would, I think, now question his own sugges- tion that evidence that 54,000 slaves were imported illegally into the United States after abolition: 5,000 might now seem to him a good guess. Curtin, like most of his successors in seeking a grand total, had been understandably baffled as to how to face the vast Portuguese-Brazilian slave traffic.

Inikori's criticisms of Curtin were based on the judgement, echoing Leslie Rout (*The African Experience in Spanish America* [Cambridge, 1976], 65), that Curtin underestimated both the illegal Cuban and Brazilian trades in the nineteenth century; and these figures are certainly difficult to decide upon. Similar corrections have been made by Enriqueta Vila Vilar in respect of the contraband Spanish deliveries in the early seven- teenth century (*Hispanoamerica y el comercio de esclavos* [Seville, 1977]). Magalhães-Godinho (*Os Descobrimientos e a economia Mundial* [Lisbon, 1963]), like C. L. R. Boxer (*The Portuguese Seaborne Empire* [London, 1963]), would double Curtin's figures for 1440 to 1500. There are other such revisions to be considered, especially in relation to the hard-to-estimate Cuban figures of the 1850s.

The attempt by many meticulous historians to decide figures to the last digit in a number is a vain one. I am not even sure that it is necessary. I prefer to think that the approximate figure would seem to be something like 11,000,000, give or take 500,000.

INDEX